ANY GUN CAN PLAY
THE ESSENTIAL GUIDE TO EURO-WESTERNS

First published by FAB Press Ltd, May 2011

FAB Press Ltd.
2 Farleigh
Ramsden Road
Godalming
Surrey
GU7 1QE
England, U.K.

www.fabpress.com

Text copyright © 2011 Kevin Grant.
Foreword copyright © 2011 Franco Nero.
The moral rights of the authors have been asserted.

Edited and Designed by Harvey Fenton,
with thanks to Francis Brewster for production assistance.

Front cover created by John Coulthart.

This Volume copyright © FAB Press Ltd, 2011.

World Rights Reserved.

No part of this book may be reproduced or transmitted in any form or by any means, electronic or mechanical, including photocopying, recording, or by any information storage and retrieval system, without the prior written permission of the Publisher.

Copyright of illustrations reproduced in these pages is the property of the production or distribution companies concerned. These illustrations are reproduced here in the spirit of publicity, and whilst every effort has been made to trace the copyright owners, the author and publishers apologise for any omissions and will undertake to make any appropriate changes in future editions of this book if necessary. Acknowledgements are due to the following companies:

Abkco Films, Aitor Films, Albatros, Alcifrance, American International Pictures, Artistes Associés, Atlantida Film, Avco Embassy Pictures, Brepi Films, CAM, Capitol International, C/A/U Productions, C.B. Films, C.C. Astro, C.C. Champion, Cecchi Gori, Centauro Films, C.I.C. Films S.A., Cine España, Cinefilms Zodiaco, Cinema International, Cinemaster International, Cinerama Releasing, Cineriz Distribuzione, CIO-Film, Circus Film-Fono, CIRE Films, Cobelciné, Columbia Pictures, Compton, Compton-Cameo, Concordia Films, Constantin-Film, Copacabana Filmes, Copercines, Cosmopolis Films, C.R.C. Produzione, Dischi Ricordi, Discobolo, EKO, Embassy Pictures, Euro International, Excelsior Films, Explorer Films '58, FIDA, Film Ventures International, Filmax, Filmways Pictures, Flora Film, Fono Roma S.p.A., Fox-Rank Distributors, Gala, GGP, Golden Era, GSF Productions, G.V. Roma, Harlequin International Pictures, Hispamex Films, iFiSA, I.F.C., Inex Film, Intercontinental, Interfilm, Inter-Ocean, Italcid, JF Films, Kinekor, Le Film Trianon, Lea Films, Leone Film, Les Films Jacques Leitienne, Lutecia Films, Lux Cinematographique, Magna S.p.A., Marco Film, Mediaset, Medusa Distribuzione, Mercurio Films, Mercury Films, Metheus Films, Metropolitan Films, MGM, Midega Film, Miracle Films, Mundial Films, National General Pictures, N.C. Roma, Nora, Orbita Films, Orphee Productions, PAC, Panta Cinematografica Distribuzione, Paramount, Parnass Film, PEA, Poli Films Mundiales, Procines, Prodimex, Produzione Europee Associate, Producciones Cinematograficas Balcazar, Promofilm, Protor Film, Rafran Films, Rank, Regal Film, Rizzoli Films, R.M. Films, Sanchez Ramade, Scotia-Barber Distributors, Selenia Cinematografica, Seven Seas, Stellar IV Film Corp., Tecisca, The Pisces Group, Titanus, Tobis Filmkunst, Toho, Towa, Transvue Pictures, Tritone, 20th Century Fox, UGC, UIP, Ulyses Films, UMC Pictures, United Artists, United International Pictures, United Producers, Universal Pictures, Universel Exportation Films, Uranos Cinematografica, Variety Film, Vis Radio, Warner Bros., Warner-Pathe Distributors.

Front cover illustration
Montage adapted from the Italian poster for Lucio Fulci's **Massacre Time** (Franco Nero, foreground), and the German poster for Sergio Leone's **For a Few Dollars More** (Klaus Kinski, background, and Clint Eastwood, right).

Back cover illustration
Gunfighter or grim reaper? Gianni Garko stars in Gianfranco Parolini's **If You Meet Sartana, Pray for Your Death**.

Frontispiece illustration
Mean, moody, mysterious: Franco Nero playing the lead role in Sergio Corbucci's Euro-western classic **Django**.

Title page illustration:
Detail from an ad-mat for the Spanish/Italian co-production **A Few Dollars for Django**.

Dedication page illustration:
Reluctant heroes Rod Steiger (*right*) and James Coburn (*left*) in Sergio Leone's **A Fistful of Dynamite**.

A CIP catalogue record for this book is available from the British Library.

hardback:
ISBN 978 1 903254 60 8

paperback:
ISBN 978 1 903254 61 5

ANY GUN CAN PLAY

The Essential Guide to Euro-Westerns

Kevin Grant

A FAB PRESS PUBLICATION

Dedication

For Lucy and Melody, my leading ladies, and Elliott, beloved son of a gun.

Contents

FOREWORD 7
By Euro-western legend Franco Nero, star of *Django*, *A Professional Gun* and *Keoma*, among others.

PREFACE 8
Including author acknowledgements

INTRODUCTION 11
An overview of Euro-westerns, their origins and characteristics, plus the major professionals whose careers they launched, prolonged or transformed.

TARGET PRACTICE 37
Early Euro-westerns were hit-and-miss affairs, but *A Fistful of Dollars* is not the only film worthy of recognition from the genre's formative period.

A BULLET SPENT, A DOLLAR EARNED 67
In the wake of *For a Few Dollars More*, the genre matured and broadened its horizons, presenting a misanthropic world-view, leavened with irony, that perfectly matched the tenor of the times.

RELATIVES AND RELIGION 129
Many Italian westerns skewed their content towards the home market, serving up stereotypical stories of troublesome females and feuding families often seasoned with a satirical or critical treatment of religion.

"GOD FORGIVES… I DON'T!" 163
Euro-westerns posit a world where betrayal is rife and violence ever-present, taking the theme of revenge to extraordinary extremes.

"DON'T BUY BREAD, BUY DYNAMITE" 185
Euro-westerns were unashamedly populist, and many of them adopted a left-wing stance in the late Sixties, reflecting the influence of radical filmmakers and the political atmosphere of the times.

BEWARE OF FAKE GUNS 235
While American westerns had Jesse James, Wyatt Earp and Billy the Kid, European filmmakers invented a pantheon of their own, populated by the likes of Django, Ringo, Sabata, Sartana and Trinity.

HYBRID WESTERNS 281
Many Euro-westerns were hybrids of cultural traditions and film-making styles, but also tones, subjects and settings, with elements such as mystery, comedy, horror and martial arts not uncommon.

DESOLATION AND DECONSTRUCTION 325
The genre burned brightly but briefly, and by the early Seventies it was in decline. This chapter examines what these latecomers have to offer, and whether they have been dismissed too lightly.

WHO'S WHO IN EURO-WESTERNS 385
A biographical A-Z of the most important and prolific actors, directors, composers, etc.

EURO-WESTERN FILMOGRAPHY 433
A chronological listing of European westerns.

BIBLIOGRAPHY 471

INDEX 472

Foreword by Franco Nero

Django Speaks First

Everyone has a first love in his life and mine was the western, as a spectator first and then as an actor. The 'spaghetti and *speroni* [spurs]' genre was launched in 1964 by the unexpected success of a little film called *A Fistful of Dollars*, directed by Sergio Leone. It earned over 3 billion lire, which is equivalent to about 80 million euros today! And so the whole of the Italian film industry began making hundreds and hundreds of westerns, giving rise to an extraordinary period of internationally successful Leone-style productions, from Duccio Tessari's 'Ringo' films to Sergio Corbucci's *Django*, an international box-office hit that marked my western debut.

Italian westerns were successful because they represented American myths in a distorted and exaggerated way: they featured blood, violence, greed and dozens of killings. Little of the heroic John Wayne model remained: our protagonists were mostly bounty hunters, people who killed for a living. The hero of the spaghetti western was a silent loner, almost an alienated gunslinger. Although he killed people worse than himself this was not out of altruism, but simply in order to take all the money; if he happened to be on the side of good, it was by chance.

Although we lacked Hollywood's budgets and were forced to reinvent the west in Spain and Italy, we were nevertheless highly competitive. On *Django*, shooting was frequently stopped for a few days when money ran out, yet the film went on to earn over a billion lire. They were entertaining and inventive times and we filled our films with genial ideas, like the coffin that Django drags behind him and which, it turns out, actually contains a machine gun!

Every now and then I like to return to the western. In recent years I starred in Enzo Castellari's *Jonathan of the Bears* and I hope to return to the western again soon with a project that I have been pursuing with great persistence, just like our gunslingers pursued their spoils. Although we never won an Oscar, the fact that an entire generation of Hollywood directors, beginning with Quentin Tarantino, grew up with these films is, in itself, a sort of honorary Oscar.

I'd like to finish by remembering a piece of advice that the greatest of all western actors, John Wayne himself, gave me: "Never choose a horse that is too big, otherwise the audience will end up watching him, not you."

~ Franco Nero

Franco Nero as the conflicted Tom Corbett in Lucio Fulci's **Massacre Time** (*above*), and (*opposite*) as a treasure-seeker-cum-freedom-fighter in Sergio Corbucci's **Compañeros**.

Any Gun Can Play

Preface

European westerns captured my imagination from the moment I first saw the animated credits of *A Fistful of Dollars* cantering across the television screen when I was eight years old, and they have never relinquished their grip. This book is distilled from many years spent seeking and viewing as many of *Fistful*'s stablemates as possible, as well as countless hours of research and interviews. It will be obvious that mine is an enthusiast's perspective, although a certain degree of objectivity is obligatory in this kind of undertaking. From the outset there seemed a number of possible avenues of approach. Euro-westerns can easily be appreciated – or dismissed – as nothing more than rugged adventures or escapist exploitation flicks. Like other popular forms, however, they also reward closer examination. They can be treated as violent, liberating fantasies or Mediterranean amorality tales; a mishmash of ancient myths and contemporary mores; as vehicles for cult actors or diversions for writers and directors of subsequent renown. They can be considered as pastiches of American westerns, or in relation to their own domestic film traditions. They can be regarded as part of the Sixties vogue for deconstruction and stylisation, viewed as socio-political commentaries or simply, en masse, as the correlative to some great music. All these interpretations are valid – and these are just the most common ones – but only in combination can they convey a sense of the genre's development from something imitative to something inspiring in its own right.

This evolution is the subject of this survey. The focus is not on Sergio Leone's accomplishments, which have been extensively studied elsewhere, although as the prime mover behind most of the Euro-western's finest qualities, he remains a source of reference throughout. To fully appreciate the genre's diversity and strength in depth, one must follow a parallel path, meeting the many other filmmakers who were drawn into its orbit and either adapted Leone's themes and ideas, expanded on them or steered this exciting new vehicle into previously uncharted terrain. While mapping this journey I inevitably acquired a great deal of baggage, much of which was jettisoned along the way. This isn't intended as a comprehensive, all-inclusive guide; indeed, there can be no 'last word' on a subject that invites such a range of readings and emotional responses. Considerations of space and time have prohibited separate chapters on aesthetic ingredients such as locations (excellent work on which has been, and continues to be, done by Internet-based researchers), cinematography and soundtracks, while biographical material is largely restricted to the *Who's Who*. Nor have I run each interview *in toto*, preferring to season the book with anecdotes and comments wherever relevant. Instead, what follows is a round-up of the genre's recurring motifs, assembled from a mixture of research and opinion, contextualisation and extrapolation. The purpose is to paint what is, from my point of view, as complete a picture of the Euro-western's core characteristics as practicable. I hope this will prompt a reconsideration of established works as well as stimulate interest in the neglected majority, to dispel the lingering notion that the genre has little to offer beyond the Leone films and a fistful of others.

Unlike a typical Euro-western gunslinger, the author could not have achieved his ends alone. On the contrary, assistance has been essential over the course of this project. Firstly, my gratitude goes out to all those who consented to interviews: Alessandro Alessandroni, Debra Berger, Giuliano Carnimeo, Enzo G. Castellari, Sergio Donati, Gianni Garko, Ernesto Gastaldi, Giuliano Gemma, Brett Halsey and Nancy Parke-Taylor, Brad Harris, Richard Harrison, George Hilton, Leonard Mann, Robert Mark, Franco Nero (who also contributed the foreword), Aldo Sambrell and Anne Twomey, Claudio Undari, and Robert Woods. I am greatly indebted to Kit Gavin, who put me in contact with several of the above, and to Prof. Mario Marsili, who spoke to three filmmakers on my behalf, tirelessly translated the results and permitted me to quote from his own interviews with Sergio Sollima, Tonino Delli Colli, Giulio Petroni and Benito Stefanelli. Carlos Aguilar kindly supplied me with copies of his books and provided a Spanish perspective on the subject, as did 'Nzoog Wahrlfhehen', whose additional help with translations and titbits of Spanish film history was invaluable. Tom Betts, editor of the trail-blazing magazine *Westerns all'italiana*, and Laurence Staig, co-author of *Italian Western: The Opera of Violence*, the first English-language book on the subject, offered advice and encouragement in the early stages, as did Simon Gelten towards the end. Tom also supplied pictures, while Matt Blake, Julian Braithwaite and Ian Caunce also generously allowed access to their collections of illustrations. Nils Markvardsen and Daniel Meier put several rare and hard-to-find movies my way, while Yoshifumi Yasuda was both a trading partner and a source of images. Special thanks are also due to director Gianfranco Parolini, who kindly furnished me with material from his personal archives.

Preface

Finally, I am especially grateful to all those who found the time to proof the book as it was progressing. My father-in-law, Donald Hawes, did his best to instil in me his grammatical good sense (any remaining errors are entirely my fault). Clark Hodgkiss (who also supplied illustrative material) and Mike Hodgkinson were full of enthusiasm and sound suggestions. James Cheney was a crucial ally, reading assiduously and bringing his staggering knowledge of Italian cinema and pop culture to the table. Julian Grainger and Alex Marlow-Mann, two of the friendliest film fanatics you could hope to meet, balanced guidance with insight and inspiration. They also took time out on a trip to Rome to put my questions to Giuliano Gemma. Last but not least, Harvey Fenton and Francis Brewster steered the whole thing home in style. To all of you – and to anyone else I might have forgotten to include – my appreciation knows no bounds.

A note on the text: films are referred to by their most familiar English-language title where available, or else the closest translation is provided, with the year of release supplied on the first reference per chapter. Where discrepancies exist between UK and US release titles, I have generally favoured the former, except where this would complicate matters or contradicts my personal preference – *God Forgives... I Don't!* is far more evocative than the generic *Blood River*, for example, and I have borrowed the US title of Enzo Castellari's *Vado... l'ammazzo e torno* for this book's title. (For more details of alternative titles, consult the filmography.) Films are dated according to when they were first domestically released – in the case of co-productions, the date refers to first release in the country that supplied the lion's share of financing and/or personnel. (The Italian ANICA and Spanish Ministerio de Cultura online databases proved particularly valuable references.) When introducing actors, directors and other artists I have given both real names and aliases, where these were used, and referred to them thereafter by their real names unless this would cause confusion (Karl Hirenbach is more familiar as Peter Lee Lawrence) or seems pedantic (Antonio de Teffé remains Anthony Steffen throughout).

above: George Hilton as the Stranger in a French lobby card for **Any Gun Can Play**.

above: Stark Japanese poster for **A Fistful of Dollars** emphasising Sergio Leone's bleak, blackly humorous vision.

Any Gun Can Play

Introduction

By any standard, the Sixties was an exciting time for Italian cinema. A mixture of recently established artists and bright young upstarts on both sides of the camera delivered films that were bursting with vitality and imagination, securing simultaneously an unprecedented level of international exposure and acclaim. At a time when the industry deified the director, such distinguished figures as Michelangelo Antonioni, Federico Fellini, Pier Paolo Pasolini, Francesco Rosi, Bernardo Bertolucci, Elio Petri, Luchino Visconti and Pietro Germi were all either at the summit of their powers or nearing their peak. Together with like-minded filmmakers elsewhere in the world, they refused to be bound by traditional cinematic practice. Like their neorealist predecessors, they eschewed safe subject matter and conventional casting, breaking taboos and confronting issues of immediate importance. They also exhibited a strong sense of self-awareness, with the artificiality and responsibility of cinema itself – in the context of a global upsurge in political understanding and upheaval – becoming an increasingly common mutual concern.

The situation was equally buoyant where popular films were concerned, even if the resulting titles – and the names behind them – don't have quite the same cachet. While most critics today would grudgingly add Sergio Leone to the list above, few outside the field of genre studies would consider Sergio Corbucci, Sergio Sollima, Duccio Tessari, Giulio Petroni, Giuseppe Colizzi, Gianfranco Parolini, Franco Giraldi, Giuliano Carnimeo or Enzo Castellari as worthy of inclusion. Yet directors such as these – artisans rather than auteurs – were as much a part of the golden age as their more illustrious peers. In collaboration with an array of similarly unsung actors, writers, composers and cinematographers, they were among the *maestri* of the Euro-western, the most unexpectedly successful of the many popular *filoni* ('formulas') that appeared during this period. These films managed to capture not just domestic audiences, gaining ground at the box office on Hollywood imports, but to establish a foothold in the global market as well, helping to offset the costs of more prestigious enterprises. The juxtaposition of award-winning masterpieces with 'lowbrow' potboilers – a "felicitous conjunction between artistic and commercial success" in Peter Bondanella's words – elevated Italy to the front rank of film producers.[1] And her closest neighbours and partners in these projects, notably France, Germany and Spain, shared in the success at the same time as their own auteur movements were thriving.

Westerns and other prosperous genres were just the tonic the industry required. The acknowledged classics of the era accrued plenty of awards but they weren't necessarily profitable (major exceptions being Fellini's *La Dolce Vita* and Visconti's *Rocco and His Brothers*, both big hits in 1960). "Directors like Antonioni, Rosi, Petri ought to be grateful to the western," argued Sergio Corbucci. "Having made their heaps of money (from us), the producers could then redistribute a bit of the cash to the more 'serious' directors. At that time, producers knew that they could produce a couple of westerns and make a killing overseas, something that wouldn't be easily done with, say, Italian comedies, which didn't travel well, nor even the Italian political films, because their concerns were too peculiarly our own."[2] More seriously, as in other nations, consumer goods, television and other pastimes were seducing people away from cinemas: between 1954 and 1964, the year of *A Fistful of Dollars*, annual ticket sales in Italy fell from 800 million to 683 million, having peaked at 819 million in 1955.[3] The result was a scaling down of

above: Spanish promotional artwork for **A Fistful of Dollars**.

theatre numbers. In this climate, producers and filmmakers tried various formulas and tactics to entice audiences back, notably by seizing on popular fads, assimilating 'foreign' (particularly American) genres, and slathering on the sleaze and violence. Co-production accords between different countries were vital to the success of this system, splitting the financial burden and widening the potential audience base. In the case of westerns, for example, especially in the early days, "Producers were forced to bend over backwards and plan little stratagems, whether technical, bureaucratic or administrative, each making the film pass as [if it were] their nationality," remembers director Mario Caiano, one of the *filone*'s unsung trailblazers.[4] These dealings also contributed to the films' cosmopolitan, multicultural complexion, with the casting of local stars often a crucial condition in the arrangement.[5]

While the majority of titles in any given *filone* were merely slavish, others were rich in new ideas, their creators training a fresh, irreverent eye on long-established conventions while merging their own cultural traditions with those embedded in the material. The Euro-western achieved this difficult synthesis more successfully and more consistently than any of its rivals. The term itself needs narrowing down. There have been European westerns made since the dawn of cinema, and countries as far and wide as Finland, Denmark, the former Soviet Union and Turkey have dabbled in the genre at one time or another. While these are no doubt worthy of analysis in themselves, the term truly denotes the groundbreaking Italian, Spanish, French and German productions that were made individually or in collaboration from the early Sixties onwards. Italians were the dominant force, responsible for the largest number as well as the most innovative of titles, hence the once-derogatory, now-affectionate 'spaghetti' soubriquet. It was Sergio Leone's vision in the 'Dollars' trilogy, shaped with the help of astute writers, iconic actors, inventive cameramen and, not least, the magnificent music of Ennio Morricone, that dictated the style and tone of the vast majority of films that followed. It wasn't long before the genre had taken on a life of its own, its stylised design, hard-edged humour, unapologetic violence and nimble-witted anti-heroes having put the traditional cowboy picture out to pasture.

Considering the volume of titles produced between the early Sixties and late Seventies – in the busiest year of 1967, 79 of 247 Italian films were westerns[6] – quality control was not all it might have been, to say the least. Yet even allowing for the many mediocrities, mannered examples and outright failures, we are still left with a substantial number of audacious works that not only revitalised a fundamental aspect of American folklore but have also been much imitated themselves – not least by Americans.

Rome and the rise of 'runaway' productions

With its conflation of mythic and historical archetypes and its ambivalent attitude towards America, the Euro-western was, in a way, a logical progression for the industry after years of Italian-American co-operation on a series of star-studded, pseudo-historical spectaculars. MGM's *Quo Vadis* (1951) was shot at Cinecittà; Dino De Laurentiis and Paramount financed Mario Camerini's *Ulysses* (1954), with Kirk Douglas in the title role; while *Helen of Troy* (1956), *Ben-Hur* (1959), *Sodom and Gomorrah* (1962) and *Cleopatra* (1963) were among the other major so-called 'runaway' productions (i.e. American movies made outside America in order to cut down production costs) with classical themes. These largely leaden dramas profited both parties – Hollywood studios took advantage of Italy's cheap labour and location costs and Cinecittà's excellent facilities, and were able to finance the films with prior earnings that were frozen in Italian banks. This was an effect of the 'dubbing tax' introduced in 1949, one of several protectionist measures passed by Italy's new Christian Democrat government to limit the access of foreign films to the home market. At the same time, there were subsidies and tax breaks available to stimulate national production, while a quota system required all cinemas to show Italian films for at least 80 days a year, rising to 100 days in 1956. Other European countries enacted a range of near-identical provisions. For the Italians, meanwhile, the epics bolstered their profile and bank balance, and provided valuable experience for numerous aspiring filmmakers and technicians. A young and eager assistant director named Sergio Leone, for example, was employed on four of the above titles in various capacities and was thrilled to work with veteran American western directors such as *Ben-Hur*'s William Wyler and *Sodom*'s Robert Aldrich.[7]

A parallel situation developed in Spain, where numerous Euro-westerns would later be filmed and where maverick American independent producer Samuel Bronston arrived in the late Fifties with ambitions to challenge Hollywood's hegemony. In a five-year period he assembled vast budgets for a series of starry historical blockbusters, most of them shot in 70mm Super-Technirama: *John Paul Jones* (1959); *King of Kings* (1961); *El Cid* (1961); *55 Days at Peking* (1963); and, the most ambitious of all, *The Fall of the Roman Empire* (1964), furnished with a then-astonishing budget in the region of $20m. (*Circus World*, made in 1964, was the only one of Bronston's films without a defined historical setting.) Bronston eventually overreached himself and his company collapsed, but, as was the case in Italy, his hosts reaped enormous benefits from his operations: "The films he made… helped to train and influence a

Introduction

whole generation of Spanish technicians, who for the first time had the opportunity to work on a continuous basis in the style of films made in Hollywood."*8*

As discussed below, the epic phase inspired cut-price Italian versions of the same 'classical' material – the sword-and-sandal film or 'peplum', a term referring to the short tunics worn by many of the heroes – and encouraged commercial producers to increasingly consider the export potential of their films, how they might satisfy audience tastes beyond their own borders as well as those within. *Pepla* and westerns sold particularly well in places such as the Far East, South America, Africa, the Middle East and the Caribbean. "Although Italian national cinema has always been tied to international production and dependent on international modes of dissemination," writes Marcia Landy, "the 1960s can be characterized as a moment when cinema broke loose of its national moorings, financially and culturally, participating in what is now described as globalisation."*9*

The effect of all this frenetic filmmaking, combined with the feel-good factor generated at the time by Italy's 'economic miracle' and the hedonistic vision of Rome projected by *La Dolce Vita*, was to transform the country's image – or at least the capital's – from the poverty-stricken shell painted by neorealism into a glamorous utopia. Rome was indeed an open city, but not in the Rossellinian sense; now an army of foreign actors (plus their agents, lovers and entourages) was the occupying force. As well as big stars such as Heston, Douglas, Burton and Taylor, there were less fêted actors, particularly from America, a mixture of young television performers, B-movie leads, contract players, muscular hunks and veteran character actors all eager for the

above: Before spaghetti, beefcake was on the menu at the Italian box office: this 1964 peplum, starring American Dan Vadis, was typical for the period.

kind of steady employment and golden opportunities that had become elusive in Hollywood. For a blissful, heady period, Rome seemed like the centre of the cinematic universe, with actors and artists of all statures caught up in its gravitational pull. Robert Woods, one of the first Americans after Clint Eastwood to break into Euro-westerns, remembers the egalitarian spirit among the filmmaking community: "The wonderful thing about Italy in those days was that you could meet people like Henry Fonda, or sit on the Via Veneto with Robert Mitchum and have a coffee. It was a good time – every star you'd ever want to know was out there… You wouldn't meet them in America – there's a class system here. Over there everybody hung together."[10] It helped if, like Woods, you spoke the local lingo and could translate for your iconic peers. Italian-American Leonard Mann, who arrived in Europe from his native New York at the tender age of 21 in 1968 and starred in three westerns, found the atmosphere similarly exhilarating. "Italy was magical in those days. I actually was able to sit down and speak one on one with the likes of De Sica, Fellini, Pasolini, Antonioni, Visconti, Zeffirelli, Carné and many others, besides playing out my childhood fantasy of being a cowboy. My only regret is that I wasn't quite able to really appreciate what was happening to me at the time. It was like a fairy tale."[11]

A fistful of *filoni*

The stampede of westerns in the mid-Sixties conformed to a pattern of (mostly) short-lived crazes that had characterised Italian popular cinema since the Second World War. Although neorealism had elevated the industry's international prestige to its highest level since the teens, the films grouped under this label were few in number and failed to secure a significant audience within the peninsula itself. (Among the exceptions were *Open City* [1945], *Bicycle Thieves* [1948] and *Bitter Rice* [1949], the last-named seducing audiences with a melodramatic narrative and the sensual presence of Silvana Mangano.) Domestic audiences preferred dubbed Hollywood films, actor-driven comedies (two of their biggest heroes at this time were Erminio Macario and the Neapolitan Totò, star of more than 100 movies) and, especially, home-grown melodramas of the calibre of *Chains* (1949), *Torment* (1950) and *Nobody's Children* (1951), all directed by Raffaello Matarazzo. Emotionally wrenching stories such as these were the biggest money-spinners in the Fifties, coinciding with the dilution of neorealism in the shape of the so-called 'rose-tinted' or 'pink' form, popularised by films in a lighter, more optimistic vein like Renato Castellani's *Two Pennyworth of Hope* (1952). These in turn segued into a new style of comic film, distinctively Italian in attitude, which treated the same kind of social issues as neorealism but in a blackly humorous manner. Controversial at the time, titles such as Mario Monicelli's *The Great War* (1959) and Luigi Comencini's *Everybody Go Home* (1960), both of which looked back in anger, with an ironic edge, at Italy's performance in the First and Second World Wars respectively, and Pietro Germi's scathing portraits of Sicilian sexual mores, *Divorce Italian Style* (1961) and *Seduced and Abandoned* (1964), are today regarded, quite rightly, as classic works. Other examples, such as Dino Risi's *The Easy Life* (1962) and *The Monsters* (1963), were preoccupied with the impact on Italian society of consumerism and the economic upswing – the unscrupulousness and self-centredness of their protagonists were very much signs of the times. Quite apart from their biting wit, many examples of *commedia all'italiana*, as it came to be known, helped to cement the star status of such legends of Italian cinema as Marcello Mastroianni, Sophia Loren, Vittorio Gassman and Alberto Sordi. In addition, the caustic nature of these comedies is similar to that found in the most representative Italian westerns – most famously, *The Great War*, for example, with its picaresque narrative and tragicomic view of warfare, was a precursor to *The Good, the Bad and the Ugly* (1966), with the same team of writers – Luciano Vincenzoni, Agenore Incrocci and Furio Scarpelli – contributing to both films.

above: Italian poster for one of the many re-releases of **The Good, the Bad and the Ugly**.

Introduction

Money-spinning melodramas and comedies, with their caricatures of everyday Italians, topical themes and increasingly sophisticated storytelling, posed a challenge to the box-office supremacy of American imports. Although many of the aforementioned import restrictions were lifted in 1962, Hollywood was experiencing a lull in production activity, and simply wasn't making, and therefore exporting, enough mass-market fare to meet demand in a country – Italy – where cinema attendance was among the highest in Europe. (Although ticket sales there declined steadily from the mid-Fifties and throughout the Sixties, they were consistently higher than in the UK, France, Germany, Spain or any other comparable country.) This is where comedies and other *filoni* filled the gap. Encouraged by state support, they came in cycles during the late Fifties and Sixties, fuelling Rome's rising status as the Hollywood of Europe – something that had first been established, ironically enough, at Hollywood's expense, with all those grandiose super-productions contributing to Cinecittà's coffers.

The oft-used 'assembly-line' metaphor for commercial cinema is especially apt when considering the popular genres that thrived at this time. They were the perfect counterparts to consumerism, which was then as rampant in Italy as it was elsewhere. They were made quickly and cheaply with the principal aim of relieving consumers from their everyday cares; it was left to 'auteur' films to stimulate a more intellectual reaction. The plotting, especially in the different adventure formats outlined below, was by rote, as was the casting. They were eye-catchingly packaged, brazenly advertising their fashionable ingredients, their shelf life lasting only as long as the public's interest. Opera films, for example, flourished from the Forties to the early Fifties, typified by Carmine Gallone's *Rigoletto* (1947) and *Il trovatore* (1949), which both employed Sergio Leone as assistant director, and the Sophia Loren vehicle *Aida* (1952). Later there was a brief vogue for portmanteau dramas, often directed by and starring some of the biggest names in Italian cinema. A good example, *Boccaccio '70* (1962), was assembled by Vittorio De Sica, Fellini, Visconti and Monicelli, and starred Sophia Loren and *La dolce vita* icon Anita Ekberg among others. Gualtiero Jacopetti and Paolo Cavara's *Mondo cane* (1962) ushered in a new kind of sensationalistic cod-documentary, its affected objectivity undermined by the relish in its (often staged) reporting. Jacopetti teamed with another director, Franco Prosperi, to make several further films in the 'mondo' sub-genre, which continued on and off for the next two decades, casting a prurient eye over everything from Western decadence to Third World primitivism. Closely related was the 'Sexy' series, launched by the bizarre *Sexy proibito* (1963), a collage of striptease sketches set at different points in history.

Sex is also a fundamental aspect of the modern Italian horror film, which has existed in various permutations since 1957, when Riccardo Freda and his cameraman, Mario Bava, jointly helmed *The Devil's Commandment*. The genre reached its erotic, oneiric peak in the early and mid-Sixties, when Freda, Bava and Antonio Margheriti made the best of several Gothic chillers with period settings, usually shot in black and white and mostly disguised as Anglo-Saxon productions. The use of pseudonyms points to an inferiority complex: in what would become a familiar ruse, directors, actors and crews assumed English-sounding aliases in the fear that audiences – both in Italy and beyond – wouldn't accept Italian attempts at traditionally 'foreign' genres. The films themselves became progressively sleazier, wilder and bloodier as the Sixties progressed, dovetailing with the *giallo* – a type of slick, twisted murder-thriller named after a series of yellow-jacketed crime novels, mostly translated from English and American originals, in the same way that French *Serie Noire* publications christened *film noir*. Mario Bava was once again at the forefront of this craze, with his films *The Girl Who Knew Too Much* (1963) and *Blood and Black Lace* (1964) establishing the main narrative and stylistic trademarks. This gifted and versatile filmmaker was also involved in Italy's short-lived science-fiction cycle (his *Planet of the Vampires* [1965] skilfully blends horror with futuristic fantasy), while his deliriously entertaining *Diabolik* (1967) was, and remains, the best attempt to translate an Italian *fumetto* or comic book to the big screen. (Bava was much less successful when tackling the western, contributing three forgettable examples: *The Road to Fort Alamo* [1964] and *Savage Gringo* [1966 – his direction of this is disputed], both starring arboreal Ohian Ken Clark, and the comedy *Roy Colt and Winchester Jack* [1970].) *Fumetti* films were the camp, colourful cousins of Bond-esque spy flicks, which were churned out by countries across the continent, along with like-minded caper films and contrastingly downbeat detective stories. Together with low-budget war films, all these action-oriented genres overlapped with westerns, sharing their insouciant anti-heroes, a glib, hip attitude to brutality, and a pop-art visual style, not to mention many of the same directors, writers, actors and so on.

The *filone* with the strongest bearing on the western was the peplum. Following on from the epic craze, the success of Pietro Francisci's *Hercules* (1958), revived a tradition dating back to the silent era, when sumptuous historical dramas like *Cabiria* (1914) had taken the fledgling film world by storm. *Hercules* was rather less grand, more like a live-action cartoon with American bodybuilder Steve Reeves in the title role battling nefarious villains, mighty beasts, script inconsistencies and shaky special effects. The film was successful enough in Italy to spawn a sequel the following year, by which time Joseph E. Levine had made a small fortune by distributing the first *Hercules* in an English-dubbed version. Immune to critical ridicule and, like westerns, a major export earner, close to 200 *pepla* were produced between 1958 and 1964, many of them starring American or pseudonymous Italian musclemen as an assortment of legendary heroes. Hercules's chief rival was an Italian 'national', Maciste, who first appeared in *Cabiria* and saw service in a number of propaganda features in the late teens (he fought the Austrian army in *Maciste alpino* [1916]), while Ursus, Samson (another 'star' of Italian silent films), Atlas and Goliath all had their turn, as did mortals of lesser proportions including centurions, gladiators and, at the furthest edges of the *filone*, Vikings, pirates and other swashbucklers. The stories unfolded in all manner of historical or mythical epochs, from ancient Greece and Atlantis to Roman times and the Middle Ages, with predictably scant regard for accurate period detail.

The similarities with Euro-westerns are many. Both genres appropriated historical archetypes without aspiring to historical authenticity. Both glorified masculinity in stark contrast to two of the major formulas that preceded them: melodramas, with

above: One of the elaborate sets from Giovanni Pastrone's 1914 proto-peplum **Cabiria**.
bottom left: German film programme for **Hercules Unchained** (with Steve Reeves and Sylvia Lopez).

their female points of view; and new-wave comedies, many of which satirised Italian males and machismo in general. The peplum hero's superhuman strength paralleled the gunfighter's miraculous pistol skills; the plots in both cases were rarely original, frequently involving a quest and providing the protagonists with one trial of strength after another, and a certain degree of populism (the villains are predominantly tyrannical types) was more-or-less obligatory. The production design and costuming, on usually low budgets, was often inventive, with picturesque parts of Spain popular as locations. The direction emphasised action over all other considerations, the array of tortures was exhaustive and imaginative, and a tongue-in-cheek attitude was prominent. Both *pepla* and westerns were also subject to the vagaries of distribution, being re-edited, retitled and, of course, dubbed, to suit the needs of individual territories. Most of all, the sword-and-sandal saga was an important proving ground for new talent. Many of the western's leading lights honed their skills on *pepla* and related films, from writers and directors such as Leone, Corbucci, Tessari, Sollima, Parolini and Ferdinando Baldi, to actors such as Giuliano Gemma, Gianni Garko and Anthony Steffen [Antonio de Teffè] of Italy, and Richard Harrison and Gordon Mitchell of America, not to mention a legion of supporting players and stunt performers.

Introduction

"The Italian soul in western garments"

Despite their overlapping properties, the peplum remains of marginal interest while the Euro-western occupies a more prominent position in film history, testament to the greater range of its ambitions and achievements and the hardier, more enduring nature of the western in general. Equal parts homage, parody and critique, the genre thrives on paradox and contradiction, proffering superhuman protagonists while skewering heroic clichés; pitting comic-strip mayhem and baroque stylisation against gritty physical detail; absurdity and escapism against anti-imperialism and other fashionable socio-political currents. This mixture of modes, of "irony… with a sense of reality", as prolific writer Ernesto Gastaldi defines it, succeeded in making westerns relevant again to Sixties filmgoers who had grown tired of conservative, simplistic cinema.[12] "Euro-westerns showed the real side of the human soul, which is not clear cut, but shady, double-faced. People liked that," said actor Claudio Undari, who, as Robert Hundar, fittingly played both good and bad characters in the genre.[13]

The *filone*'s support among Italian spectators – measured in blockbuster box-office takings for the 'Dollars' films and other key early works – was the springboard to global success. Clearly, in addition to their action-packed narratives, the piquant flavour of these films, their irreverent attitude towards the lore of the west and their modish celebration of economic individualism, were much to Italians' liking. As Giuliano Carnimeo, director of a dozen offbeat westerns, puts it: "American westerns were a representation of the popular culture and history of the US frontier. The Italian audience was, in the end, much more attracted to our non-historical characters; this allowed for greater identification of the viewer with the 'hero' on the silver screen. It was even stronger, this identification, when irony and comedy elements came into play. Indian warfare was not as interesting for us as a clever double agent who gets money from here and from there, like Clint in *A Fistful of Dollars*, for example. This is like Arlecchino [Harlequin], a traditional figure from Italian theatre. The Italian western, in short, revealed the Italian soul in western garments."[14]

above: Tomas Milian, the archetypal peasant bandit, under pressure in the gun-in-cheek **Compañeros**.

The popularity of westerns was a shock and an affront to those left-wing Italian critics for whom neorealism represented the ultimate in cinematic integrity. Carlo Lizzani, an important figure in the development of neorealism and the director of two Italian westerns, remarks, "Perhaps to the left the western appeared like an escape, a fantasy, a compromise."[15] Fantastic they were, but, at the same time as they allowed audiences to "escape" from everyday reality (the opposite of neorealism's intention), they displayed a tangible anti-establishment quality as well. The central character tends to be an outsider or outcast, corresponding with the way many young people saw themselves in the Sixties and pointing to a rejection of societal strictures and a criticism of its values. (This is especially the case where the outsider is a 'foreigner' or racial 'alien'.) Communities are usually portrayed as weak or bigoted, the foundations of society being so unstable that they are forced to look to mercenaries for their salvation and survival. The law is generally depicted as corrupt, the middle classes as grasping and hypocritical, while landowners and other capitalists are almost invariably tyrants, a viewpoint that reflects, indeed exploits, a traditionally anti-authoritarian attitude among the core audience for spaghettis – working-class Italians, for example, and spectators in the Third World, where these films were particularly big sellers. As Franco Nero, for whom the genre helped paved the way to international stardom, states: "Westerns make people dream of another life – especially the Italian westerns. They were made mainly for the workers, who dream of one day going into the office and saying, 'Hey boss, today everything has changed'. Westerns are like the revenge of the workers against the bosses."[16]

This populism – familiar from Hollywood westerns – expanded into political pamphleteering in a series of revolutionary fables set in Mexico. As explained in *"Don't Buy Bread, Buy Dynamite"*, these works flourished alongside all manner of political films, from modernist tracts to agit-prop adventures (the writer Franco Solinas unites all these 'fronts'), combining historical reconstruction with contemporary allusions. They spoke to a generation radicalised by social inequality at home and 'imperialist' misadventures abroad – it's not unreasonable to ascribe at least some of the appeal of films like *A Bullet for the General* (1966) to their subversion of American mythology at a time when millions were protesting against the country's involvement in Vietnam. Nero, who played cynical profiteers in Sergio Corbucci's self-styled 'Zapata' westerns, says: "While the Americans used to do westerns where the Indians were the bad guys, in a way we did the contrary – in *A Professional Gun* (1968), *Compañeros* (1970) and other political westerns, the Mexican peons were the real heroes."[17]

As well as this sharp turn to the left, the genre branched out in several other directions. A number of variants emerged, some reworking Hollywood western tropes, others inspired by Leone's films or reflecting the popular mood or latest box-office trend. A legion of 'superheroes' enjoyed mini-series of their own. They bore mysterious names and were often supplied with distinctive costumes and weaponry – Django is the most famous, but there were also Sartana, Sabata, Ringo (a name rooted in American frontier folklore), and the self-mocking Trinity and Hallelujah. There were vehicles for pop stars, Gothic and psychedelic westerns, treasure hunts, tragic dramas and family feuds *alla Siciliana*. Towards the end of the cycle, filmmakers fell back on farcical humour – accentuating the ironic undertones that had always been present – to bolster its ailing fortunes. This was also the motivation behind a string of early Seventies martial arts westerns, which attempted to capitalise on the kung-fu craze. Above all, there was revenge – a key western theme that permeated almost all sub-categories.

All the while that public interest was strong enough to sustain these separate strands, filmmakers had little reason to worry about the inevitably negative critical response. Giuliano Carnimeo states: "We made commercial movies, so really never expected positive judgements from the critics… [they] were not very relevant at that time."[18] In addition, Peter Bondanella notes, "In Italy, critics tend to punish a director for commercial success, admitting only American films to the category of popular entertainment that may also embody great art."[19] The best westerns began to collapse this distinction – who would now deny that Leone's *The Good, the Bad and the Ugly* and *Once Upon a Time in the West* (1968), at the very least, are not just classic westerns but exemplary films? The leading examples also displayed the potential of the western that had yet to be tapped, despite six decades' worth of intensive exploitation in Hollywood and despite the widely shared critical opinion at the time, and the evidence of then-recent American productions, that the genre had been mined to exhaustion.

A central factor in the films' success was their stylised design – few westerns had ever deployed such bold visuals and brash music to such consistently intoxicating effect. Many of the sets and locations – from realistically ramshackle studio-built towns to the whitewashed, weather-beaten villages of southern Spain and the dry *ramblas* and rolling hills of Almería's Tabernas desert – became as iconic in their way as Monument Valley, Lone Pine and the Sierra Nevadas had been for American audiences. Director Mario Caiano says of Almería: "It was the perfect place

above: German lobby card for **The Price of Power** showcasing the western town at La Calahorra-Ferreira (also the site of 'Flagstone' in **Once Upon a Time in the West**), one of several full-scale sets constructed in southern Spain during the spaghetti boom.
bottom right: Almería's arid, majestic Tabernas desert – seen here in **Sabata** – became the Euro-western equivalent of Monument Valley.

for shooting westerns that had to seem American because it has an arid, bleak landscape made of canyons, in tones of grey, green and red, with hardly any vegetation, with a few villages here and there that look like Mexican villages. And, on top of this, a population of Spanish gypsies that ride horseback very well and look like Mexican Indians… there were these infinite stretches of canyon where you could do what you wanted."[20] "In Cinecittà you had to keep the camera always at a certain angle, or you would shoot into TV antennas on the roofs of surrounding buildings", added Giulio Petroni. "In Almería you could make *campi lunghi* [wide angles] encompassing the whole landscape."[21] These desolate landscapes were perfectly in keeping with the tone of the films. The typical Euro-western backdrop "has no mercy for a man", observes director Mario Lanfranchi, whose only western, *Death Sentence* (1967), makes particularly effective use of exteriors. "In a place like that you can only die."[22] In the right hands, set design and interior decoration played an equally important role in shaping the genre's worldview. The central figure in this regard was architect-turned-art director Carlo Simi, who worked with all the leading directors and almost single-handedly advanced western iconography beyond its hackneyed limits. He styled sets, and costumes for that matter, for classic works

like the 'Dollars' films (he was rewarded for his labours on *For a Few Dollars More* [1965] with a cameo as the manager of his own 'El Paso' bank), *Django* (1966), *The Big Gundown*, *Face to Face* (both 1967) and *Once Upon a Time in the West*, and his designs salvaged a number of mediocre productions as well.

The characteristically oppressive atmosphere of heat, sweat, dust and violence was enhanced by innovative photography – from Massimo Dallamano's use of hard-edged lighting for a parched, sun-baked effect in *A Fistful of Dollars* and *For a Few Dollars More*, to the grittier, hyper-realistic style perfected by Tonino Delli Colli in *The Good, the Bad and the Ugly* and *Once Upon a Time in the West*. (Delli Colli, winner of an American Society of Cinematographers Outstanding Achievement Award in 2005, was one of the first in his profession to fully master Techniscope,

Whither the placket shirt? Terence Hill (*above*) dresses down (and out) as the laid-back protagonist of **They Call Me Trinity**, while (*top right*) Clint Eastwood's mix-and-match ensemble in the 'Dollars' films made the poncho a popular accessory.

a cost-effective wide-screen process developed by Technicolor's Rome lab in the early Sixties that gave countless Euro-westerns a detailed and deceptively opulent appearance.[23]) At the opposite end of the spectrum was the lurid, comic-strip look associated with cinematographers such as Sandro Mancori – Gianfranco Parolini's right-hand man – and two future directors, Stelvio Massi, who shot *The Moment to Kill* (1968) and several other Giuliano Carnimeo movies, and Enzo Barboni, who filmed *Django* in a mixture of muddy gloom and surrealistic hues.

Even more striking were the soundtracks. Starting with Ennio Morricone's groundbreaking compositions for the 'Dollars' trilogy, music assumed unprecedented importance in terms of narrative function and sheer emotive power. Such was its significance for Sergio Leone that he famously had Morricone's pre-recorded score played during the filming of *Once Upon a Time in the West*, much to Delli Colli's chagrin: "The music kept going and going; sometimes I had to tell Sergio to turn it down or cut if off, because I couldn't be heard by my crewmen during a take."[24] The scoring did more than merely establish mood in the conventional sense; music provided dramatic or ironic punctuation, 'announced' individual characters, and was even an aid to (or substitute for) character development, as in the case of Harmonica in *Once Upon a Time in the West* – neither the first nor the last time that a character would be *seen* to play his own theme. The integration of music and visuals was at its most masterly during set pieces and climactic events, with such famous examples as the protracted, suspenseful accompaniments to Leone's final showdowns and the trumpet-heavy duel themes in *The Big Gundown* and *A Professional Gun*, which bestow an almost transcendental quality on the action. Morricone's experiments with offbeat instrumentation, onomatopoeic effects and haunting vocals, from soprano solos and whistling to choral grunting and chanting, filtered through to most of his contemporaries, although few were quite so adept at combining a collage of different styles into a coherent whole. Other typical elements included catchy melodies carried by twanging electric guitars, often played over colourful rotoscoped credits,[25] ballads sung by popular crooners of the day (many of these were released as singles), and a strong emphasis on the trumpet, which combined with Spanish guitars, boleros, mariachi music and folk songs to impart a stereotypically hot-blooded Mexican/Mediterranean flavour that bore little relation to the heroic, romantic grandeur of Hollywood's old west. Even the gunshots and ricochets were louder, more varied and more distinctive than in American films, hence Blondie's observation that "every gun makes its own tune" in *The Good, the Bad and the Ugly*.

Magnificent strangers

Euro-westerns have often been criticised for the woodenness of their lead performances (not always without justification), yet their ineffably cool, poker-faced protagonists are one of the films' most original and influential features, embodying a number of key themes. Men of ambiguous motivations, dubious morality and, in many cases, obscure origins, they retain and even exaggerate the strong, silent mien of the classical cowboy – offsetting the ebullience of sidekicks and other secondary characters – while outstripping his murderous abilities (indeed, he is almost as brutal as his adversaries) and downgrading his chivalrousness and civic spirit. Unlike the typical Hollywood hero, who generally served a higher moral purpose, the Euro-western anti-hero, very much a child of the Sixties, is usually self-seeking and unscrupulous, his goals typically cash-based or vengeful. He will often provoke a crisis in an existing tense situation not primarily for the common good but for his own profit. If third parties do happen to benefit from his actions, it is often incidental or only because they have paid for the privilege. (In an amusing incident in the otherwise mundane *A Bounty Killer for Trinity* [1972], the protagonist [Jeff Cameron] demands money from an old man for seeing off his assailants. Similarly, Craig Hill's gang in *Fifteen Scaffolds for a Killer* [1967] make a widow pay for returning her recently deceased husband's horse. So much for virtue being its own reward.) This accounts for the elevation of scurrilous, slippery characters such as bounty hunters, gun-runners and other mercenaries – largely marginal figures in American westerns – to leading status.

Although there are different types of protagonist – from sardonic or sinister adventurers of the Eastwood/Sartana variety to surly, embittered avengers in the Django/Steffen mould – what unites the bulk of them is their proclivity for gambling, a mastery of brinkmanship in the riskiest situations. They approach physical confrontations with the same composure they bring to the poker table; money – and survival – may be at stake, but danger seems to be an end in itself. Certainly, something other than courage drives them on. Do they beckon danger out of fatalism – chiming with the numerous chance encounters and twists of fate in these films – or, like many of their peplum progenitors, are they truly superhuman? One can only wonder as their combination of self-possession and superior skills continually overcomes outlandish odds. Not since Bret Harte's prototypical gambler-gunfighters has 'dicing with death' been such an appropriate metaphor in a western setting. Consider 'Joe' staking everything that Ramon will "aim for the heart" as always in *A Fistful of Dollars*; Colonel Mortimer pitting his composure and marksmanship against an outlaw's recklessness at the beginning of *For a Few Dollars More*; the cat-and-mouse motif that weaves its way through countless entries (notably *Yankee* [1966], whose dialogue resonates with references to risk and the deadly pleasure of playing – its director, Tinto Brass, envisioned its villain and anti-hero as bull and bullfighter, respectively); the simmering tension of the games played in *Death Rides a Horse* (1967), *Death Sentence*, *God Forgives... I Don't!* (1967), *Ace High* (1968), *A Man Called Sledge* (1970) and others; and not forgetting frock-coated conjurors-cum-cardsharps such as Sartana and Sabata. The Euro-western protagonist proves time and again that he can out-bluff, outwit and out-cheat even the most nefarious of villains.

Adding to the anti-hero's slick demeanour was his idiosyncratic attire, typically a mixture of functionality and flamboyance. Clint Eastwood's get-up in the 'Dollars' films – designed, like so much else that caught the eye in this genre, by Carlo Simi – was unlike anything seen on a 'cowboy' before, the ambiguousness of his Anglo-Mexican ensemble facilitating his shifts of allegiance at the same time as throwing his opponents off their guard.²⁶ He doesn't look like a threat – quite the opposite in fact – whereas gunfighters in American westerns had tended to advertise themselves with fancy rigs and ostentatious clothing. (*My Name Is Nobody* [1973], a knowingly nostalgic epitaph for westerns of all complexions, takes us full circle when the protagonist declares, "I like folks to see me.") As well as establishing disguise and deception as vital to survival in the cut-throat Leonean West, and therefore as key thematic tropes, Eastwood's distinctive garb quickly set a trend for distressed yet stylish outfits complete with offbeat accoutrements (the poncho, a particularly apposite item considering the Anglo-Mexican milieu, caught on particularly quickly) and an ever-present layer of trail dust. Other Euro-western characters, heroes and villains alike, were more extravagant, the flattering cut of their clothes making them resemble contemporary rock stars, complete with confident strut and designer stubble, or they aligned themselves with styles of the times by adopting 'hippie' traits – look at the bad guys in *Matalo!* and *More Dollars for the McGregors* (both 1970) for example, or Franco Nero's hirsute half-breed in *Keoma* (1976), another film that benefits from Carlo Simi's magic touch. (Marijuana – indulged in by more than a few genre villains – was

above: For many Euro-western protagonists, gambling was more than a casual pursuit – it governed their very existence, none more so than Sartana, here played by Gianni Garko in **Have a Nice Funeral, Sartana Will Pay**.

Introduction

another tellingly contemporary accessory.) Others mixed and matched Civil War-era military gear with civvies or Native American with Mexican attire, diluting the traditional Westerner's all-American image and underlining the difficulty of safely identifying the loyalties and identities of characters. Also popular were dusters and other long coats – historically accurate items that briefly became fashionable among late-Sixties hipsters, especially in the wake of *Once Upon a Time in the West* – and the sinister, funereal silhouettes of Colonel Mortimer in *For a Few Dollars More*, Django, Sartana and Sabata. Their snappy black costumes, with their deliberate connotations of villainy, made them look like a combination of gambler, undertaker and clergyman and became uniforms in their own right. Each of the last-named characters accessorised with unusual or customised weaponry, as did numerous others in the genre. Modified derringers and palm pistols, sawn-off shotguns, extendable pistols and portable machine guns became increasingly common sidearms (it didn't seem to matter to audiences that many of the weapons were either inauthentic – fruits of the production designers' imaginations – or anachronistic) and were carried in a variety of ways, whether holstered at the hip in the traditional manner, slung over the shoulder Mexican-style, or secreted up the sleeve or inside props in yet another example of the deception motif. By the time of *They Call Me Trinity* (1970), with Terence Hill's shabby tramp clothed in filthy rags and shooting enemies without even needing to look in their direction, the deconstruction – and demythologisation – of the western hero was just about complete.

The Euro-western was a boon for both up-and-coming actors and others past their prime. The same could be said of most *filoni* – many an actor enjoyed parallel careers in the Sixties playing secret agents, cops, soldiers and the like – but it was the western that transformed and sustained individual careers most successfully. (Since we're dealing with an overwhelmingly macho genre, it's not surprising that actresses failed to benefit in the same way as actors – many talented women gave strong performances in westerns, but were consigned almost exclusively to stereotypical roles as vamps or victims.)

The genre was especially fertile ground for American expats. Clint Eastwood swiftly succeeded Steve Reeves as the most influential American leading man in Europe, just as the new-wave western initiated by *A Fistful of Dollars* eclipsed the peplum formula that made Reeves's name. (Reeves belatedly jumped aboard the western bandwagon in his final film, the efficient revenge tale *A Long Ride from Hell* [1968], directed by Camillo Bazzoni.) The 'Dollars' films also made a star out of Lee Van Cleef, whose Hollywood career had

above: A clean-cut Clint Eastwood – "a block of marble" ready for sculpting, as Sergio Leone is alleged to have said – in a publicity portrait from his **Rawhide** days.

never progressed beyond villainous featured roles, and elevated method actor Eli Wallach into something of an icon for bringing the genre's most empathetic character type – known as the 'ugly' after Wallach's designation in *The Good, the Bad and the Ugly* – so vividly to life. Both Wallach and Van Cleef top-lined several further Euro-westerns, while their compatriot Charles Bronson's appearance in *Once Upon a Time in the West* made him one of the biggest box-office draws on the Continent. He starred in several further features there, including the westerns *Red Sun* (1971), *Chato's Land* (1972) and *The Valdez Horses* (1973), prior to a triumphant return to Hollywood.

More marginal performers from American film and television also made their mark in the genre: the aforementioned Richard Harrison and Robert Woods were among Eastwood's earliest box-office rivals; Hunt Powers, Mark Damon, now a leading film producer, Edd Byrnes of *77 Sunset Strip*, and Craig Hill, who would eventually settle in Spain, all alternated hard-bitten roles with lighter parts; the singular Tony Anthony, who

Starring roles in high-profile Euro-westerns like **Day of Anger** (*above*) were just reward for Lee Van Cleef following a long lean spell in Hollywood, where he spent much of the Fifties in thankless walk-on, get-shot roles; (*opposite*) this early publicity shot displays his trademark glower.

co-produced and wrote some of his films, may have dressed like 'No Name' but had a street-punk style of his own; Brett Halsey and Leonard Mann made memorably brooding and, in Mann's case, angst-ridden avengers; and William Berger, Gordon Mitchell and Frank Wolff each excelled as villains and double-dealers. Other supporting parts, meanwhile, were filled by a crowd of grizzled veterans, including Lionel Stander (one of a number of Americans who sought to bypass the Hollywood blacklist by working in Europe), Jack Palance, Woody Strode, Guy Madison, John Ireland, Gilbert Roland, Van Heflin and Walter Barnes. We will encounter these and several others over the course of this survey. Finally, more illustrious figures also made contributions to the cause: Henry Fonda's aura of integrity was crucial, in contrasting ways, to the impact of two of Sergio Leone's most ambitious projects, *Once Upon a Time in the West* and *My Name Is Nobody*; James Coburn, Jason Robards and Rod Steiger also answered Leone's call; and the increasingly erratic Orson Welles, his Mercury Theatre alumnus Joseph Cotten, and former Oscar winners Yul Brynner and Anne Baxter all dabbled in Euro-westerns at one point or another.

Unless you were a proven star of Brynner's calibre (he had his luxuriously appointed personal trailer shipped to every out-of-the-way location he was called to), the production process could be an arduous one, certainly nothing like American actors had experienced back home. Richard Harrison, who made 17 westerns in Europe, found dealing with the delays and long hours on a typical shoot frustrating: "It was much more casual in Europe... In America you feel the pressure always on you, although you don't consume as much time – you don't spend 12-14 hours on set. In America, they tell you to come at seven and you'll finish in maybe three hours. In Europe, they'll call you at five [in the morning] and you'll go the whole day. At 10pm that night they'll shoot one scene. I spent my whole life on the set – sometimes even slept there... There was always a lot of time wasted sitting around doing nothing."[27] Actor and dubbing artist Robert Mark, real name Roger Francke, concurs: "I was never on a Sixties film [in Italy]

that had even a degree of organisation... We played a lot of cards, smoked a lot of cigarettes, and read a lot of books while we sat around waiting for these thespian neurotics to try to decide on something that at least two or more of them could agree on."[28]

Native Italian Franco Nero offers one explanation for this 'casualness': "Most of the Italian directors have very low blood pressure in the morning. They hate to start shooting very early, so they come to the set quite late. For example, I was making a western in a village outside of Rome and every day the director, I won't tell you his name, was late on the set in the morning. One day he had a phone call, another day he had a flat tyre; always there were excuses. One day he turned to me and said, 'Franco, you see all these guys' – meaning the crew – 'they're waiting for me to have an idea so we can start shooting. And you know what: I don't have any idea how to start. Let's go to the bar.' So we went to the bar and, little by little, the idea came and we started to shoot. And strangely enough, late in the afternoon, Italian directors rush like you have no idea to get things finished."[29]

Another potential source of irritation for pampered actors were the basic facilities, especially in the early days when the rugged locations, particularly those in southern Spain, had barely been developed. "Usually [the set] was quite a way outside the city, and there would be no decent place to wash your hands or shower," recalls Richard Harrison. Robert Woods remembers having to change behind rocks on more than one occasion. Brett Halsey seems to have fared better in terms of facilities, but still had to rough it from time to time: "Location accommodations were always the best available, and were generally pretty good. As remote as they seemed, the locations were never more than an hour's drive from adequate lodgings. By Hollywood standards the working conditions were a bit primitive, but we got the work done."[30]

Nor were the sets especially well ordered – the Italian practice of shooting without direct sound meant that actors had to adapt to what could be a noisy and distracting atmosphere. Many Euro-western veterans tell colourful anecdotes about the problems of communicating on a multi-lingual set, of interacting with

performers of different nationalities; the most common solution seems to have been to memorise all of the dialogue for all of the characters in your scenes, and simply respond to your counterpart's expressions. That way, remembers Robert Woods, "If I didn't know what they were saying, I at least knew the *intent* of what they were saying, so I was able to react – acting is close to 90 per cent reacting, or overreacting in the case of Italian westerns." Adds Richard Harrison: "An Italian western script was usually in English and Italian, though sometimes the English was so bad I would rewrite it and try to work it out from the Italian." At any rate, scripts were often changed many times during shooting.

Films at the cheaper end of the scale were often bedevilled by money shortages, another potential source of concern and frustration for the actors, although Woods pays tribute to his employers' enterprise amid adversity: "The thing I'll give to the Italians and Europeans in general is that there's order in chaos. They find a creative way to do it no matter what. With Americans it's like, 'There's a drop of rain, let's go'. With the Italians it's innovative things like, they might not have a boom for a shot so they'll pile tyres up to 8-10 feet, then put a board on it and have somebody turn the board. It's bizarre, but it creates the same effect you would get from expensive equipment. Creative innovation – spur of the moment stuff."[31]

It was in the same spirit that filmmakers set about cutting costs and keeping to schedules, from reusing sets, props and costumes to utilising music and action footage from different films. Brett Halsey made two westerns with director Alberto Cardone: "Once while we were shooting on a hill in Almería, a very large group of riders from a high-budget film shooting nearby suddenly appeared galloping across the valley below. Cardone immediately ordered the cameraman to get them on film! Needless to say, the shot was included in the final version of the movie."[32] Hunt Powers was bemused to discover that prolific director Demofilo Fidani had taken scenes from one film they'd made and used them to pad out another, while Richard Harrison remembers Spaniard Ignacio Iquino as being particularly clever at compensating for his meagre resources: "Sometimes we would shoot three scenes in the same corner of a house – we could never understand how some people chose big sets and went miles away to do another scene when you could do different scenes on the same spot. All you have to do is change a couple of things."[33] Economising measures such as these were nothing new. As Brad Harris, an Idaho native who arrived in Europe at the turn of the Sixties, recalls, they had been integral to the production of *pepla* as well: "In Yugoslavia [c.1961] we shot *The Fury of Hercules* and *Samson* simultaneously; then we shot *79 A.D.* and *The Old Testament* simultaneously. [All four films

above: Spanish lobby card for **Tequila** showing the brooding Brazilian-Italian leading man Anthony Steffen, star of almost 30 westerns.
opposite: Craig Hill – hamming it up à la Terry-Thomas in **Run, Men! Eldorado Is Coming to Trinity** – was one of many American expats who revived their flagging careers by decamping to Europe.

were directed by Gianfranco Parolini.] Sometimes we'd shoot two or three parts of one film and two or three of another in the same day, because we had to make use of the sets. It got a little confusing! Change costumes, put on a beard, take off a beard..."[34]

At the same time as the Americans were adjusting to their new working conditions, a host of Italian, European and Latin leading men came to the fore, often working under English aliases. Some, such as the athletic Giuliano Gemma ('Montgomery Wood'), versatile Gianni Garko ('John Garko' or 'Gary Hudson') and the dour Anthony Steffen, already had a profile from *pepla*, while others found fame as a result of their stint in the saddle. These three, along with blue-eyed matinee idols Franco Nero (the only one to achieve true international fame) and Terence Hill [Mario Girotti], Hill's frequent partner Bud Spencer [Carlo Pedersoli] and swarthy Uruguayan George Hilton [Jorge Hill], became the most prolific and popular Euro-western leads, amassing 120 titles between them. They quickly overtook the likes of Wayne and Widmark as audience favourites in the western's new heartlands. George Hilton, for example, was greeted as a hero whenever he returned home from his base in Italy: "Euro-westerns were enormously successful in South America. I was recognised on the streets everywhere. We had a villa in Montevideo, where paparazzi were constantly lingering... I couldn't go anywhere without being 'harassed' by fans and photographers."[35] Robert Hundar [Claudio Undari] was surprised by how far his fame had spread: "One time I was in Morocco with my ex-wife... and met this group of Arabs, who started screaming: 'Robert Hundar'!"[36] While all these actors, with the exception of the bearish Spencer, were blessed with classical good looks, and each in his way adhered

Irascible, egocentric, hedonistic and a mesmerising screen presence, Klaus Kinski helped fund his lavish lifestyle with well-paid cameos in numerous Euro-westerns. He had a more substantial role in the marvellous **The Ruthless Four**.

broadly to macho motifs – albeit inflected with irony, especially where Hill and Hilton were concerned – the genre was flexible enough to accommodate more idiosyncratic stars as well. Blond, slender Peter Lee Lawrence (the assumed name of Germany's Karl Hirenbach, glimpsed briefly in the flashback scenes in *For a Few Dollars More*) played unusually youthful, clean-cut heroes and, occasionally, mentally fragile villains, while the political western provided a platform for some of the genre's most powerful performers: Tomas Milian came to Italy from Cuba via New York and built up a strong worldwide following as a kind of revolutionary ragamuffin; 'Dollars' villain Gian Maria Volonté, a fervent Communist, shared the lead in both *A Bullet for the General* and *Face to Face*; and a man of similar ideological beliefs, the deceptively cherubic Colombian/Swedish actor Lou Castel [Ulv Quarzéll], co-star of *Bullet*, followed his searing debut in Marco Bellocchio's *Fists in the Pocket* (1965) with unconventional leading roles in some equally offbeat westerns.

For many of these actors, whatever their original aspirations or inclinations, the western was almost a rite of passage. Gianni Garko remembers: "In Italy in this period it was not easy for an actor to work, and sometimes you accepted an offer because you didn't have another… They were producing mostly western films, so in one way an actor was forced to do them." At the same time, Garko, who counts *My Darling Clementine* (1946), *High Noon* (1952) and *Gunfight at the O.K. Corral* (1957) among his favourite films, admits that, "To shoot an Italian western, for me, was also a way to realise a teenager's dream."**37** Giuliano Gemma adds, "Almost all children were fans of westerns. Among the actors that I followed I can remember James Stewart in *Winchester '73* [1950], Glenn Ford in *The Sheepman* [1958], and many films with Burt Lancaster, from *Vera Cruz* [1954] to *Apache* [1954]."**38** Leonard Mann, born into an Italian family in America, has already spoken in this chapter of the "childhood fantasy" the genre helped him to fulfil but, although he enjoyed his tenure, he quickly realised the dangers of being typecast: "Italian westerns were fun to watch and to make. Unfortunately they were not all made that well. It became a money thing: churn them out as fast as you can. I remember being looked at as a second-rate actor who just did westerns. There was actually a stigma attached to doing westerns back then, unless you were working with good productions like Sergio Leone and company, who I feel made westerns as good as have ever been made."**39** Claudio Undari, who was making westerns before any of these actors, recalled: "I was so much in love with the idea of becoming a silver-screen cowboy that it all started from a big lie. I told both the producer and Joaquín Romero Marchent, the director of my first western in Spain, that I was a skilled horseman. It was the biggest lie. I had never been on a horse in my life, and one week before we started shooting I went to the Roman Villa Borghese public park, where they rented 'zombie' horses, which were plodding along with kids on their back. I shut my eyes and 'rode'. In Spain, luckily, the horses were excellent, and I left totally to the horse the responsibility for what had to be done… [Laughs] There was I sitting on a horse, knowing that he knows more than me!"**40**

The leading men may have drawn the crowds, but, just as in American westerns, a roster of first-rate character actors provided much of the genre's vitality. Between them they represented almost as many different physical types and acting styles as they did nationalities. "My God, what faces!" the great American western director Anthony Mann had exclaimed after seeing *For a Few Dollars More*, a film boasting a particularly vivid assortment of weird and weather-beaten features.**42** Mann's (culture) shock was understandable: in his and other Hollywood films, the bad guys were generally the only characters with fearsome looks; in many Euro-westerns, almost the entire supporting cast has a battle-scarred, bestial complexion (closer to how the west's historical inhabitants appeared in archive photos), complemented by cunning, savagery and other feral traits. There are too many colourful characters and full-blooded performances to mention here (more information can be found in the *Who's Who*), but it would be remiss to move on without honouring the seemingly ubiquitous Spanish contingent, which includes brawny, imposing brutes such as Aldo Sambrell, Frank Braña, Antonio Molino Rojo, José Canalejas and Luis Barboo; sly, weaselly types such as Eduardo Fajardo and José Manuel Martín; and bullish eccentrics such as Roberto Camardiel, Cris Huerta and the irreplaceable Fernando Sancho, the ultimate blustery *bandido*. Many of them reside in the genre's rogues' gallery, where they rub shoulders with several Italians worthy of singling out, among them Gian Maria Volonté, the lupine Piero Lulli, shifty Luigi Pistilli, towering Claudio Undari, hulking Mario Brega and the anxious, eccentric Luciano Rossi and Rick Boyd [Federico Boido]. There was also Gérard Herter, a self-deprecating German actor who perfected an arrogant air and mock-Teutonic mannerisms, while also from Germany came the suavely sinister Horst Frank and the incomparable, uncontrollable Klaus Kinski, whose griping about his workload of westerns – "they get shittier and shittier, and the so-called directors get lousier and lousier" – didn't stop him from willingly twitching, grimacing and raging his way through no fewer than 22 of them.**42** By his own admission, money was the most important thing to Kinski, and westerns paid well even if (as was usually the case) he had no more than a specially billed cameo role.

"We were absolutely fascinated by westerns"

Having proved to be the most lucrative of all *filoni*, thanks in no small measure to its cool, callous anti-heroes, the Euro-western proceeded to saturate the market during the Sixties and early Seventies – estimates vary, but it is safe to say that upwards of 600 of them were made, with supply rapidly outgrowing demand.[43] Yet the genre wouldn't have exhibited such durability if, in addition to proving its worth to the moneymen, it hadn't also captured the imaginations of enough talented artists to keep freshening up the formula. Nor would it have seeped into popular culture to such an extent, or launched and supported as many careers as it did, had mockery and mimicry been the sum of its authors' ambitions. On the contrary, the finest Euro-westerns were put together with considerable care and creativity, while even lesser examples often boast striking photography, unusual settings or a memorable music score.

The initial appeal of the genre for Italian commercial filmmakers is not hard to fathom. Most were rabid cineastes with a particular fondness for the westerns of Ford, Hawks, Boetticher, Mann et al. Their hunger for Hollywood product had been fired further by a wartime Fascist embargo on American films, which left a backlog of hundreds of titles to catch up with. Leading screenwriter Sergio Donati remembers: "After 10-15 years of cultural blackout, we received ten years of American movies and culture… in literature it was Steinbeck, Hemingway, Faulkner and so on. In movies for us young people it was mainly adventure, and adventure meant westerns. Think of the effect of seeing ten John Ford movies in a row. Obviously, we were absolutely fascinated by westerns."[44] This fascination with Hollywood and the western marked a handful of films in the neorealist vein, most famously Pietro Germi's *In the Name of the Law* (1949), a tense and sobering drama set in rural Sicily where a magistrate (Massimo Girotti in Gary Cooper mode) tries, and fails, to curb the influence of the Mafia, who usually appear in the film like outlaws on horseback. Regarding the first wave of Italian westerns proper (pre-*A Fistful of Dollars*), they showed little appetite for anything beyond aping the American style, but it wasn't long before filmmakers began to impose their own personalities and cultural perspective on the material. "The quality came out of directors such as Leone, Sollima and others," Donati continues. "The approach was a typically Italian approach – ironic, sarcastic, cynical maybe, like *commedia dell'arte*, neorealism, from De Sica to Risi, Monicelli, Germi. It was natural to us."[45]

For obvious reasons, European artists had less emotional investment in 'the west' – with everything it represents for Americans in historical/ideological terms – than they had in 'the western' as a vehicle for what Jim Kitses termed "displaced myths". Few westerns, whatever their provenance, have ever been faithful to the facts of frontier life, elaborating instead on the apocryphal adventures of legendary heroes. As such, they offer considerable freedom for personal interpretation, and this artistic liberty was even greater for 'outsiders', who could strip the stories down to their constituent parts and substitute American themes – westward expansion, Manifest Destiny and so on – with domestic and universal subjects. This is how Sergio Leone and the brightest of his colleagues set about deconstructing the western, not because they wanted to trample on American history or because they were plagiarists, but to revive "a noble kind of cinema", as Leone put it, that was in disrepair.[46] Theirs was an elemental vision of a mythical era, and what they appreciated above all else about the western was its flexibility, and that provided the sets, locations and costumes looked the part, you were free to make the allusions and develop the themes of your choice. "Westerns… can contain any number of things, from Greek tragedy to Shakespearean drama, psychology, everything," commented Franco Giraldi. "There are so many different ways of interpreting the horizons, the solitary heroes, the various conflicts.[47] There was a certain amount of historical revisionism involved in all this – Leone talked a great deal about correcting the myopic vision of the traditional western, especially where violence and characterisation were concerned – but the principal aim and achievement of European artists was to update and expand upon the form, evincing a combination of fascination and effrontery, a desire to simultaneously celebrate and subvert western conventions.

Maintaining a level of objectivity not available to American filmmakers, the genre's leading exponents overhauled the outmoded moral values and righteousness that had gradually worn down the Hollywood western. This is not to say that there was no moral viewpoint expressed in the European version, despite what its harshest critics may have contended, just that the divisions between opposing characters are clouded rather than clear, something that proved more plausible to Sixties audiences. Judging from the success of these films on the domestic market, it was also much closer to the everyday Italian's way of thinking. "Our cultural roots are not American, but European. For us the distinction between good and evil, black and white, doesn't exist," was Duccio Tessari's summary.[48] While this mind-set united the vast majority of films, there was almost unlimited space for individual expression and for the pursuit of personal agendas. Sergio Leone's protagonists are a mixture of rogues and demigods, the tone of his movies ranging from bleak to nostalgic, with a strong emphasis on treachery – seen as inevitable, even admirable in the circumstances – and, by contrast,

above: Sergio Leone's success rested on disrespecting the western's outdated moral codes; in **A Fistful of Dollars**, Clint Eastwood's man with no name character disrespects even the dead.

on male interdependency, the main positive force in his films. Sergio Corbucci's westerns comment on a range of issues – social exclusion, political oppression (a favourite theme of frequent Corbucci co-writer Adriano Bolzoni), First World-Third World relations, religious hypocrisy, counter-culture and racism – while pushing irony and violence to the furthest extremes. One of his most subversive notions was to handicap his heroes – quite literally – by disabling them in some way, and on more than one occasion he was bold enough to let them die. Like Corbucci, Sergio Sollima did much to popularise political topics (both benefited from the incisive writing of Franco Solinas), similarly pairing professional gunmen, whose integrity is constantly under question, with underprivileged outcasts. Sollima also showed an unusual interest in the social and psychological conditions that engender violence: "I try to shed some light on *why* people use guns," he has said.

Tonino Valerii was a Leone acolyte who shared his mentor's earnest admiration for the genre, reflected in his films *Day of Anger* (1967) and *My Name Is Nobody* – both written by Ernesto Gastaldi, the latter made with Leone – which are essentially westerns *about* westerns. (Valerii and Gastaldi also put together an audacious critique of American history with *The Price of Power* [1969], conflating the assassinations of President Garfield in 1881 and JFK in 1963 and setting the story in the unsettled Reconstruction era.**49**) Looking at the subject from a different angle, Duccio Tessari and Franco Giraldi fondly but sharply satirised western clichés, working in tandem on *Seven Guns for the MacGregors* (1966), written by Tessari under Giraldi's direction, while Giuseppe Colizzi and Enzo Barboni successfully anticipated the public's desire for light relief after hundreds of corpse-strewn kill-fests, separately developing the comic partnership of Terence Hill and Bud Spencer. For Enzo

Castellari, another director closely associated with the western's breezier side, the genre's cathartic power was the main draw: "In real life you have to suffer a lot of arrogance... in the western, your hero redeems you and also takes revenge."[51] Although many of Castellari's films are quite frivolous, he directed one of the last truly significant examples, *Keoma*, in 1976, and still yearns to make another.

Giulio Petroni, who touched upon revenge, political topics and slapstick comedy in five disparate but equally handsome westerns, looked back on the experience of making them with heartfelt pride: "I found them good for the soul. Those characters, their moods, the open spaces, the basic feelings of friendship and justice, good and evil. I believed in what I was representing."[51] Not that belief was a prerequisite – many solid, reliable artisans made westerns merely out of a desire to entertain, displaying the professionalism they applied to whatever *filone* happened to be in fashion; indeed, this applies to many of the 'specialists' I have introduced above. Writers and directors of higher critical standing crossed the western's path as well – from Vincenzoni, Solinas and Bertolucci to Pasolini, Lizzani and Fellini, who alluded to its popularity in his episode of the Poe compendium *Spirits of the Dead* (1968) – while others ventured in from leftfield, pushing demythologisation as far as it would go. The most interesting and (in)famous example is Giulio Questi, co-writer and director of *Django, Kill!* (1967), a withering critique of both American *and* Italian westerns.

Although it is not my purpose to deflect all the criticism that has come the Euro-western's way over the years, it is as well to confront the main issues before commencing the study in earnest. To view just a few scenes from a Leone, Corbucci or Sollima western, or hear a few bars from Morricone or Bruno Nicolai at their best, is enough to rebut the accusation that all Italian/European westerns are pseudo-American forgeries. It doesn't take long, in other words, to see beneath the surface similarities and discern the fundamental differences of form, style, tone, concept of character and, above all, intent, that set the two schools apart. Only the earliest Italian/Spanish efforts, and a smattering of others in later years, had *intended* to replicate Hollywood films, almost all of them without a shred of conviction. The overlooked Joaquín Romero Marchent was one of the few pathfinders who did manage to capture the flavour of classical westerns. He has always resented the American charge that Europeans have no understanding of westerns, that their efforts are inherently inauthentic, insincere. In his view, European productions, at least those he was involved in, are no more factually inaccurate than classic Hollywood oaters. "Real cowboys had nothing to do with Gary Cooper or John Wayne. They were like our shepherds, like the farmers of Las Hurdes [a rugged region of Extremadura visited by Luis Buñuel for a 1932 documentary]... they wore a handkerchief beneath their hats so that sweat wouldn't damage them, because they didn't have money to buy another one. And the last thing they could dream about owning was a pistol or a cartridge holder, because they didn't even have a belt to keep their trousers, which were worn and baggy, in place." Americans, he continues, have made "ridiculous films" on all kinds of subjects, including Spain. "I still remember that audiences were falling about laughing in the cinema where I saw *Blood and Sand* [Rouben Mamoulian, 1941], with all those phoney Andalucían settings. What's more, I would actually go as far as saying that a cowboy from any of my films is closer to the real thing than Tyrone Power is to a Sevillian bullfighter."[52]

Many Euro-western writers and directors reacted in the same way as Marchent when the 'rootlessness' or artificiality of their films was raised, pointing to Hollywood's appropriation of Old World legends for many of its blockbusters, for example, to show that copyright has no hold over myths, or even to the superficial presentation of Native Americans in most westerns as evidence of a similarly cavalier treatment of history. Sergio Corbucci bridled at critical barbs that Europeans were "trespassing on American territory – as if they hadn't done their fake papier-maché version of Ancient Rome with their various *Ben-Hurs*... Our westerns don't resemble theirs at all; we subverted the rules to such a point that the Americans started imitating us, with dusters and stubbly beards, the violence, guts dribbling out..."[53] Ultimately, the question of verisimilitude is a red herring. The fact that Europeans were detached from the 'code' of the west, and from the conservatism of conventional westerns, worked in their favour, providing them with the latitude to reinterpret overly familiar motifs from a different cultural vantage point.

In an article published in the *Saturday Evening Post* of 6 April 1968, Maurizio Lucidi, a journeyman director, spoke to reporter William Price Fox on the set of his latest western, *The Greatest Robbery in the West*, in an attempt to clarify the European approach: "Americans are wrong, thinking we're just copying their westerns. It isn't so. We're adding the Italian concept of realism to an old American myth, and it's working... Europeans today are too sophisticated to believe in the honest-gunman movie any more. They want the truth, and that's what we're giving them." This points to another bone of contention – not only were foreigners 'duplicating' the western (a nonsensical charge), they were 'debasing' it with ugly, squalid details and characters lacking moral accountability.

'Realism', in the sense that Lucidi means, translates into a dystopian vision of the west and a depiction of violence that ripped through Hollywood's habitual

Introduction

reticence. The juxtaposition of this coarse texture with heady stylisation – quite the opposite of realism – was perhaps the Euro-western's most distinguishing feature, although it wasn't long before American and British studios tried to emulate the blend, producing a string of Spanish-shot, spaghetti-style bloodbaths in the late Sixties and early Seventies. While violent conflict has always been central to the western, most critics felt that the Europeans went too far, especially since they rarely dealt with the 'positive' ends – the settlement of the land paving the way for civilisation – that were deemed to 'justify' the means. Bosley Crowther and Judith Crist led a moral crusade in the *New York Times* against the 'Dollars' films, while a *Variety* pundit's quip concerning *Day of Anger* sums up the general reaction: "It's shooting and killing all the way and the bloodbank runneth over." While Sergio Leone excused the brutality in his films as an accurate reflection of mid-19th Century frontier life, as opposed to the sanitised sheen of orthodox westerns, Sergio Corbucci saw the *filone*'s ferocity as a barometer of modern times: "We assume or re-create the atmosphere of our time, a time of violence. A violence without reason and often just for the sake of violence."

These arguments make sense – the turbulence of the Sixties fuelled an aggressive, antagonistic spirit across all the arts and in all manner of movies. But for every filmmaker who deployed violence to say "violence is wrong", there were ten more simply following what had become a fashionable, lucrative formula.

Along with Hammer horror films, Hitchcock's *Psycho* (1960), the Bond series, *Bonnie and Clyde* (1967) and *The Wild Bunch* (1969), Euro-westerns were prominent in the aestheticisation of screen violence that caused such controversy during the decade. While this was a spontaneous, international development, other 'explanations' can be advanced that set spaghetti westerns and related *filoni* apart. It's tempting to link them to a hypothetical Mediterranean mind-set, tracing their bloody trail back via Renaissance drama to the gruesome tragedies of ancient Greek and Roman times, sating the blood-lust of a spectator type that likes to gets wholly involved in the action and, it is banked upon, has a predilection for the grotesque, the brutal and the bizarre. While all this is so much speculation, it is strongly supported by post-war Italian, and wider European, box-office trends.

above: The early films of Spanish director Joaquín Romero Marchent – epitomised by this excellent vehicle for Richard Harrison – accommodated both Hollywood clichés and European sensibilities.

above: Sadistic scenes like this one from **Django**, involving Loredana Nusciak, identified Euro-westerns with a rising tide of cinematic savagery in the Sixties, and provoked a brutal response from the critics.

Surveying Italy's popular films of the Fifties in the defunct British weekly *The Movie*, Barry Edson noted a "disturbing mixture of juvenile plot development and blatant sadism [that] was exemplary of a recurrent theme in Italian popular culture".[54] He was commenting, in a rather superior way, on pirate films and *pepla*, but his observations are apposite for westerns as well. Charles Bronson, who rebuffed Sergio Leone on two occasions before accepting the role of Harmonica in *Once Upon a Time in the West*, understood where the Euro-western's priorities lay: "It was never a question of showing Americans how to make a western. [Italian] films are destined for a strictly European audience, and particularly an Italian one… Italians love violence and can laugh at it."[55] Another actor, Brett Halsey, who made everything from swashbucklers and westerns to spy flicks and splatter films in Europe, gained an identical impression of his audience: "They [Italians and Europeans] would often rate a picture's popularity by how many bloody bodies were piled up… the story in most spaghetti westerns was primarily a thread between scenes of bloody killing."[56] Of course, this doesn't account for the success of many of these films on the export market, a reminder that audiences of all backgrounds and nationalities shared a taste for taboo-breaking cinematic savagery. More compellingly, the genre's excesses, like its emotionalism, have been entwined with its Italian-Spanish roots, its transgressions treated as a revolt-cum-provocation against strict censorship and the suppressive teachings of Catholicism. This theory applies equally – if not more so – to the sexy comedies and gory horror films that erupted from Italian and Spanish studios in the Sixties and successive decades.

In fact, comparatively few Euro-westerns are as visceral as their reputation suggests, even in their uncut forms. They are not generally as graphic, for example, as the American westerns they immediately influenced, which attempted to trump their rivals in terms of gore. What critics originally found hard to stomach, and hard to fathom, about Euro-westerns is the ferocity of the beatings and the preposterously high body counts (a case of overkill if ever there was one), which, true to the films' collectively paradoxical nature, cried 'authenticity' at the same time as being blatantly absurd. (One *Variety* scribe estimated that Parolini's tongue-in-cheek *Sabata* [1969] contained "a body count that would be a record campaign for a Marine regiment".) Ultimately, only a combination of these factors can 'explain' the films' sadistic streak, if such an explanation is sought. If the cultural conditioning of artists and audiences predisposed a taste for carnage, the critical intent of certain exponents must also be acknowledged, with violence employed topically or as an unflinchingly honest riposte to conventional Western restraint. The bottom line is that bloodshed was big business – it was an established feature of Italian genre cinema and an increasingly popular trend worldwide. Speaking for his colleagues, Giuliano Carnimeo is unapologetic: "We made westerns, not Snow White movies, and the Italian spicing was, as everybody knows, violence. Certainly, at the end it became nonsensical and overabundant, to blunt the edge." Giuliano Gemma, whose westerns made him a superstar in Italy, sees the over-the-top brutality as a form of authorial self-awareness: "In many cases it was so excessive that it was almost like winking at the audience… there was almost a hint of deliberate irony in this excessive violence." There was also, no doubt, a fear on the filmmakers' part that fickle spectators might lose interest if there wasn't a steady stream of thrashings and killings, although if anything it was the numbing predictability of second-rate films padded out with punch-ups and shoot-outs that eventually wore out their welcome. "At first, the Italian westerns were revolutionary because they gave a more realistic picture of the west than some American films normally do," commented Giuseppe Colizzi. "But then we began to overdo it – too much cynicism, too much blood and gore."[57] Claudio Undari concurred: "Violence becomes useless when minor directors show it just because it is trendy. This is futile… Many Italowesterns [sic] had redundant violence and contributed to the decadence of the genre."[58]

During its peak years, however, the genre was nothing short of a phenomenon. "We gave Italy a seam of gold," said Undari. "It was truly a stupendous adventure."[59] Over the course of four or five years of intensive experimentation in the mid-Sixties, and more than a decade of production in general, it successfully revived interest in the western – albeit a very different kind of western from those that had been made before – by using the familiar trappings as a template rather than a covenant, setting amoral adventurers, not outright heroes, against larger-than-life villains in a bleak environment where survival of the fittest, fastest and most ruthless was the natural order. Avarice and treachery were commonplace, with only a depleted sense of personal honour, often manifested in a remorseless vindictiveness, separating the antagonists.

Just as the tone of the films was fashionably nihilistic, the style was modishly narcissistic, with expressionistic sets and photography and bombastic, neo-operatic music making the restrained style of conventional westerns seem redundant. As the following chapter explains, there was little at first to inspire confidence that the Euro-western would be anything other than another flash in the pan. Instead of fizzling out like most previous *filoni*, however, it quickly outgrew its influences, building on the advances of Leone and his partners and achieving a momentum of its own that continues to resonate.

footnotes

[1] *Italian Cinema: From Neorealism to the Present*, p.142. The high turnover of both 'artistic' and 'popular' films – and the impression of an industry in the rudest of financial health – masks a few surprising facts. Cinecittà, for example, which had invested heavily in 'runaway' productions with American companies, suffered grave debts for many years from the late Fifties onwards, and Titanus, one of the biggest independent production houses, was crippled by huge cost overruns on *Sodom and Gomorrah* (1962) and the dismal box-office performance of Luchino Visconti's stately *The Leopard* (1963). (For details of all books/articles referenced in the text, see bibliography.)
[2] Quoted in *Spaghetti Cinema* (translation by James Cheney).
[3] Source for figures: *Encyclopedia of European Cinema*.
[4] Quoted in 'Conversation with Mario Caiano' on the Italian DVD release of *Bullets Don't Argue*.
[5] Co-productions began to assume an important place in the Italian industry as it sought to recover its position in the post-war years. Although the numbers were small to begin with – two out of eighty three features in 1946, five out of seventy in 1947 – there were some landmark films among them. Alessandro Blasetti's deluxe historical drama *Fabiola* (1949), for example, was made with partial French financing and French stars. Numbers rocketed in the following decades; in 1960, the figure was 66, peaking at 155 in 1964. From 1965 a new law, the Legge Corona, offered Italian partners in co-productions even greater protection against the risk of financial failure, and therefore greater incentive to pursue such deals, through higher state subsidies and tax rebates. (Figures from *Encyclopedia of European Cinema*.)
[6] The figure of 247 titles, sourced from *Encyclopedia of European Cinema*, includes co-productions as well.
[7] For Leone's disillusionment following these encounters, see Sir Christopher Frayling, *Something to Do with Death*, pp.110-117.
[8] Peter Besas, *Behind the Spanish Lens: Spanish Cinema Under Fascism and Democracy*.
[9] Marcia Landy, *Italian Film*, p.181.
[10] Author's interview with Robert Woods.
[11] Author's interview with Leonard Mann.
[12] Author's interview with Ernesto Gastaldi.
[13] Interview with Claudio Undari conducted for this book by Mario Marsili.

14 Interview with Giuliano Carnimeo conducted for this book by Mario Marsili.
15 Interview with Carlo Lizzani by Luca Beatrice in *Al cuore, Ramon, al cuore*, p.195.
16 Author's interview with Franco Nero.
17 Ibid.
18 Interview with Giuliano Carnimeo conducted for this book by Mario Marsili.
19 Peter Bondanella, *Italian Cinema: From Neorealism to the Present*, p.354.
20 Quoted in 'Conversation with Mario Caiano' on the Italian DVD release of *Bullets Don't Argue*.
21 Interview with Giulio Petroni by Mario Marsili, used with kind permission.
22 Interview with Mario Lanfranchi on the Koch Media DVD of his film *Death Sentence*.
23 A long-overdue analysis of Techniscope's contribution to the Euro-western was provided by Barbara Grespi in a recent Italian journal. She states: "Its main application was in 'spaghetti westerns', whose characteristic style, still imitated today, would have been inconceivable without the advantages of this technology. For Techniscope is in fact the only technique allowing not just the use of close-ups, but also the use of the zoom as well as wide-angle shots through which great depth of field can be obtained, a feature that was impossible for American Cinemascope motion pictures… It is shown in the article that during the 1960s the frame became the focal point in directing the film: it was experienced as a picture or a fresco, and its internal composition henceforth became fundamental, not merely for the authors." Barbara Grespi, 'Sergio Leone e il wide screen all'italiana' in *Comunicazioni sociali*, XXVI n.1, Jan-April 2004, pp. 87-99 (thanks to Alex Marlow-Mann for the translation).
24 Interview with Tonino Delli Colli by Mario Marsili, used with kind permission.
25 The rotoscope is a gadget that allows animators to trace live-action movement. Developed by legendary animator Max Fleischer in the teens, it was put to good use by the likes of Disney and Ralph Bakshi, gave the light sabre duels a dynamic dimension in the original *Star Wars* trilogy and has recently been adapted for such big-screen fantasies as *A Scanner Darkly*, *Sin City* and *300*. Numerous Euro-westerns used the process to liven up their credits sequences, usually featuring silhouettes of riders, gunfights and tumbling bodies against bright backgrounds – *A Fistful of Dollars* is the classic example.
26 Just who devised Eastwood's iconic 'Dollars' look has always been a subject of dispute. Both the star and Sergio Leone have claimed at least part of the credit over the years, but Carlo Simi's surviving sketches show clearly the outline of 'Joe's' outfit, including the poncho. One item that Eastwood definitely contributed was his character's snake-motif pistol grips – these were old *Rawhide* props first seen in the second episode, *Incident at Alabaster Plain*, in which Eastwood's young ramrod, Rowdy Yates, takes a revolver – along with a tan leather gun belt – from stricken bad guy Peter Mark Richman.
27 Author's interview with Richard Harrison.
28 Author's interview with Robert Mark.
29 Author's interview with Franco Nero.
30 Author's interview with Brett Halsey.
31 Author's interview with Robert Woods.
32 Author's interview with Brett Halsey.
33 Author's interview with Richard Harrison.
34 Author's interview with Brad Harris.
35 Interview with George Hilton conducted for this book by Mario Marsili.
36 Interview with Claudio Undari by Roger A. Fratter in *Dieci ricercati dello spaghetti Western* (Nocturno Dossier, October 2007).
37 Author's interview with Gianni Garko.
38 Interview with Giuliano Gemma conducted for this book by Alex Marlow-Mann and Julian Grainger.
39 Author's interview with Leonard Mann.
40 Interview with Claudio Undari conducted for this book by Mario Marsili.
41 Quoted in Fenin and Everson, *The Western: From Silents to the Seventies*, p.347.
42 Kinski records his thoughts in no uncertain terms in his autobiography, *Kinski Uncut*.
43 There is no definitive figure because 'Euro-western' means different things to different people. Some sources include only Italian or Italo-Spanish productions, excluding French and German films, to arrive at a lower total; others include semi-westerns, such as European Zorro adventures, as well as American productions shot on Spanish soil and employing local talent. There are also likely to be a number of titles that never saw distribution – especially in the peak years – and have subsequently disappeared.
44 Author's interview with Sergio Donati.
45 Ibid.
46 Quoted from an interview conducted in 1971 between Leone and Franco Ferrini (a screenwriter who later contributed to Leone's *Once Upon a Time in America*).
47 Quoted in *Westerns all'Italiana Volume One: The Specialists*.
48 Interview with Duccio Tessari by Lorenzo De Luca in *C'era una volta il western Italiano*, 1986.
49 Massimo Patrizi is the credited writer of *The Price of Power*, but, as Gastaldi told me, it was "an enormous script, 400 pages long. Valerii tipped [the producer] to call me… I accepted the request to rewrite it, even if I couldn't sign it, to help Tonino. And for money, of course…". (Author's interview with Ernesto Gastaldi).
50 Author's interview with Enzo Castellari.
51 Interview with Giulio Petroni by Mario Marsili, used with kind permission.
52 Carlos Aguilar, *Joaquín Romero Marchent: La firmeza del profesional*, p. 40.
53 Quoted in *Spaghetti Cinema* (translation by James Cheney).
54 'Sweat, lust and dreams' in chapter 51 of *The Movie* (Orbis Publishing).
55 Quoted in *Charles Bronson: Superstar* by Steven Whitney, p.168.
56 Author's interview with Brett Halsey. Halsey courted controversy when he collated his own and others' experiences into a salacious novel, *The Magnificent Strangers*, written in the mid-Seventies after he had returned from Italy to the US. The book paints an unflattering portrait of expat actors, agents, entrepreneurs, wives and girlfriends as arrogant, uncultured, oversexed and self-absorbed, gorging on the fruits of Italy's economic boom before *la dolce vita* turns decidedly sour.
57 Quoted in *Westerns all'italiana*, vol 1 no 2.
58 Interview with Claudio Undari conducted for this book by Mario Marsili.
59 Interview with Claudio Undari by Roger A. Fratter in *Dieci ricercati dello spaghetti western* (Nocturno Dossier, Oct 2007).

Introduction

above: French ad for **A Fistful of Dollars**, with Clint Eastwood modelling the iconic outfit – complete with pistol grips and gun belt plundered from the **Rawhide** prop department – that defied the traditional western hero's dress sense.

above: Yvonne Bastien imperilled by Piero Lulli, one of the Euro-western's most colourful villains, in Mario Bava's **Savage Gringo**.

below: An early example of the genre's crucifixion fixation from Bava's **The Road to Fort Alamo**. Like **Savage Gringo**, this rudimentary effort lacks the dash and vigour of the director's finest work.

Chapter 1

Target Practice

The continental western takes shape

As interest in the European western has grown, so too has the attention it has received from sympathetic critics and film historians keen to study its origins. Thanks to their efforts it is no longer necessary to point out that, contrary to its American advertising slogan, *A Fistful of Dollars* (1964) was not strictly speaking "the first motion picture of its kind". Certain precursors are now commonly if cursorily acknowledged, most famously the West German Karl May adaptations, and research has established that westerns have been produced in Europe for as long as they have in Hollywood. Yet it remains the case that so much attention has been paid to the spectacular *arrival* of the modern Euro-western – more or less fully formed in *Fistful*'s case – that its *evolution* has been generally overlooked, the films made just prior to Leone's breakthrough, like those that immediately followed, broadly dismissed. This chapter is concerned with this hidden history, the unheralded films and filmmakers that undertook the groundwork for the Leonean revolution. I shall also trace developments, or the lack of them in films produced around the same time that *Fistful* and its sublime sequel, *For a Few Dollars More* (1965), were transforming the genre. What themes and ideas did these lesser-known titles contribute to the canon? Are they deserving of their sub-Hollywoodian reputation, or have they and their participants been unfairly neglected?

The answer to the latter question is an admittedly unsatisfactory 'yes and no'. Before the lessons of the first two 'Dollars' films had been fully absorbed, the European western in its formative years was in thrall to its American source of inspiration. Although the number of imported Hollywood productions available to the Italian market was dwindling, with American studios turning out just 28 westerns in 1960, compared with 130 in 1950, the demand for them by certain sectors of the film-going public remained strong.[1] To meet this need, low-cost imitations rolled on Italian studio sets, with Cinecittà, still state-owned at the time, and its commercial rival Elios (built in 1964) being particularly busy sites. Exteriors, meanwhile, were shot around Rome, Madrid and Andalucía, with the occasional foray into central and Eastern Europe. The financing was predominantly Italian, French, Spanish and German, the countries already having several years' worth of joint ventures behind them, with US companies chipping in at the tail end of the Euro-Hollywood epic cycle.[2] There was a similar situation in Germany, where the Karl May films, responding to the same kind of commercial imperative and similarly multi-national in their make-up, generated a different kind of western revival and proved a boon for bucolic Yugoslavian and Czechoslovakian locations.

At this stage, the main consideration was to make these films resemble their Hollywood antecedents as much as possible – most replicated the visual style, narrative patterns, stock characters and situations of second-rate US westerns with scant discrimination. Leading roles were often filled by low-ranking American actors, their presence meant to aid 'authenticity', while most of the supporting players and technical staff were Europeans disguised behind pseudonyms. Then there were the "stolen titles", as Sergio Leone put it, to go with the purloined plots, cowboy colloquialisms and cloned characters, with a disproportionately large number of films made between 1963 and 1965 making reference to American locations – Arizona, Dallas, Fort Worth, the Grand Canyon, Kansas, Minnesota, the Mississippi, Oklahoma, Rio Bravo, Sacramento, Santa Fe, Texas, Tucson...

The American western itself had become increasingly fatigued. Despite demonstrating a new level of confidence and sophistication for much of the Fifties, it lost its way towards the end of that decade as studios tried to reclaim audience attention from the simple-minded horse operas clogging up television schedules. (Jostling those 28 big-screen westerns released in 1960 were no fewer than 46 TV series spread across various networks.) As a result, the much-lauded 'adult' western went into decline. A lengthy sequence of intelligent, revisionist titles – including the likes of *Broken Arrow* (1950), *The Gunfighter* (1950), *High Noon* (1952), *Shane* (1953), *Vera Cruz* (1954), *The Man from Laramie* (1955), *The Searchers* (1956) and *The Left Handed Gun* (1958), plus oddities like *Johnny Guitar* (1954) and *Forty Guns* (1957) – had sheared away much of the genre's sentimentalism about how the west was won and the type of men, and in some cases women, that were required to win it. There was a new honesty afoot – violence was more realistic, heroes harder to take for granted – as the genre's idealistic underpinning crumbled from within. Yet by the turn of the Sixties this brand of western, which had always been outnumbered by routine programmers, had been all but killed off by the major studios' decision to concentrate resources into big-budget, self-satisfied star vehicles like *Gunfight at the O.K. Corral* (1957) and *Rio Bravo* (1959). For all their entertaining interplay, films like these signalled an artistic retreat from the high ground

so recently secured. (Another expensive ensemble piece, *The Magnificent Seven* [1960], though made with the same motives as the last-named films, retained some of the moral ambiguity and anti-heroic leanings of earlier proto-spaghetti westerns like *Vera Cruz*.) These were desperate times for a genre that had once been the backbone of Hollywood. What few westerns that were made in the early Sixties tried either to overcompensate through sheer scale (*How the West Was Won* [1962], shot in Cinerama, hitched itself to the epic trend – top *that*, television) or effectively accepted that the game was up, that knights of the plains were out of time (the eloquent lament of *Ride the High Country* [1962]) and out of space (Kirk Douglas's fenced-in contemporary cowboy in *Lonely Are the Brave* [1962]). With his elegiac *The Man Who Shot Liberty Valance* (1962) and apologetic *Cheyenne Autumn* (1964), even John Ford, Sergio Leone's bastion of optimism, succumbed to pessimism, questioning, if not actually quashing, many of the concepts that he more than any other American director had enshrined down the years.

Something radical was required to spearhead a revival, but there was no sign of this in Europe's meagre early efforts, which wouldn't have looked out of place alongside the tamest TV shows of the Fifties. That most of these films fail to convince has less to do with the filmmakers' grasp of the 'syntax' of the western – in that sense they are idiomatically fairly accurate – than with an inability to tap into the intangible meanings behind the myths, the reasons why stories of this kind not only gripped the soul of America but also, and more importantly, why they fuelled the fantasies of audiences worldwide. They lack any sense of the *universality* of western lore, how the characters and conventions are not specific to one chapter in American history, but have their roots in ancient legends belonging to all mankind, and are therefore open to many different interpretations and applicable to other cultural traditions. This was the principal lesson of the 'Dollars' trilogy – if these films with their incongruous details and allusions struck audiences as 'alien' in relation to conventional westerns, well, that was the whole point. And yet, even among the majority of stale productions whose character make-up, moral lines and cultural references are based squarely on the defunct B-western, one can see here and there the kernel of ideas and motifs that would be fully explored and exploited in the following years. These include the beginnings of a fascination with violence, venality and individual tragedy; recurring themes like obsessive revenge; sympathy for the underdog and the outcast; and the calling into question of traditional heroic virtues. Equally, some of the directors, technical staff and actors involved in this early stage – besides Leone one thinks of Joaquín Romero Marchent, Sergio Corbucci, Ennio Morricone, Carlo Simi, Massimo Dallamano and Giuliano Gemma, to name just a few – showed flashes of the ingenuity that later helped the European western to exceed all expectations.

Counterfeit cowboys

The first major advances in modern Euro-western filmmaking were made when Sergio Leone was still learning his craft as an assistant director. Although they are of tangential interest as westerns – or rather, as films in the western vein – *El Coyote* and *La justicia del Coyote*, filmed simultaneously in 1954 but released in 1955, are of considerable historical significance as the first efforts in this direction by Spanish director Joaquín Romero Marchent, the genre's elder statesman. They were made with Spanish and Mexican funding and starred Mexican idols Abel Salazar – in the lead role – and Gloria Marín (the pair would later marry). Adapted by, among others, future cult filmmaker Jesús Franco from stories by prolific pulp novelist and screenwriter José Mallorquí,[3] the films chart the daring adventures of César de Echagüe, foppish dandy by day, masked hero by night, in mid-19th-Century California. The parallels with Johnston McCulley's Zorro are obvious, although El Coyote prefers revolvers to a sword, except for a duel involving sabres at the end of the second adaptation. Designed principally for Spanish and Mexican consumption, the 'Coyote' films performed adequately but gave little indication that Romero Marchent was a man to watch. The director wouldn't display his considerable abilities as a western filmmaker until the early Sixties.

We will take up Romero Marchent's story at a later point. Suffice to say here that by the time he reached his creative peak, the European-made western was floundering in much the same way as its beleaguered Hollywood equivalent. Too many early productions lack the strength of Romero Marchent's best films, to say nothing of Leone's, in two crucial areas – imagination and conviction. The choice of subject matter and settings, the bland photographic style and stereotypical characterisations all conform to what audiences would have grown accustomed to from average Hollywood fare – exactly the kind of stories, with their clean moral lines, straight-shooting heroes, sluggish romantic passages and predictable denouements, that Leone and later directors realised filmgoers had grown weary of.

In the period 1964-66, for example, there appeared a rash of westerns with cavalry heroes and Indian villains. While these are clichéd figures in American movies and mythology, neither group has much of a presence in the European western as a whole. When soldiers appear it's generally in the context of the American Civil War or the Mexican Revolution, while Indians and their typical narrative functions are replaced by Mexicans.[4] That the likes of *The Fury of the Apaches*, *Massacre at Fort Grant*, *Heroes of Fort Worth* and the Canada-based *Cavalry Charge* (all 1964), *The Secret of Captain O'Hara* (1965), and *Mutiny at Fort Sharp* and *Mestizo* (both 1966) trespass on such well-travelled territory indicates the timid thinking

above: Cavalry heroes, court martials, Indian attacks… Stale ingredients in the outmoded Spanish western **The Secret of Captain O'Hara**.
opposite: Gary Cooper and Burt Lancaster – the former embodying nobility, the latter contemptuous of it – in Robert Aldrich's **Vera Cruz** (1954), a key reference point for Italian western directors.

and lack of adventure behind this first wave of films. All repeat the stock situations – Indian attacks against military outposts or some other fortified structure – and reflect the traditional bias of narratives of this kind. Unlike the Indian-friendly 'Winnetou' series and contrary to the ideological perspective of East Germany's anti-imperialist *Indianerfilme* – a chain of slickly made socialist westerns produced by the state-run DEFA studios – the aforementioned films show little interest in Native Americans as people.[5] There were partial exceptions, however, one being Marino Girolami's *Bullets and the Flesh* (1964), which picks up where America's liberal pro-Indian westerns of the Fifties had left off. Although romanticised, it is staunchly sympathetic towards a Cherokee tribe whose woodland idyll is under threat from a bigoted white logging family.

Other titles set about re-creating the exploits of individual American myths and legends. Many of these films are fun to watch, if only for their enthusiastic abandon. Mario Costa's *Buffalo Bill, Hero of the Far West* (1964),[6] one of the most popular pre-Leone Italian westerns on home soil and one of the first to receive widespread international distribution, is sheer

comic-book fantasy along the same lines as Joaquín Romero Marchent's subsequent *Seven Hours of Gunfire* (1965). Erstwhile Tarzan and peplum star Gordon Scott played the lead in swashbuckling style and, at a time when Anglicised aliases were the norm, director Costa chose one of the cheekiest, signing the film as 'John W. Fordson'. There were films produced about Pat Garrett (*Bullets Don't Argue* – see below) and a pseudo William Bonney (*Billy the Kid* [1964], with Francisco Martínez Celeiro, soon to become a fixture in the genre as George Martin), about Wyatt Earp (*Gunmen of the Rio Grande*, with Guy Madison), and about the legacy of Jesse James (*Son of Jesse James* [1965]), all showing a cavalier attitude towards the 'facts' in each case that is even more eccentric than in most Hollywood renditions. As enjoyable as some of these films are, however, it's doubtful whether the European western would have survived the mid-Sixties had it continued to trade on plots and characters that had already been overworked on American cinema and television screens.[7]

In the same way that the genre was awaiting a director of vision to inject it with new life, so too it was lacking a charismatic leading actor willing to play against type, to break or at least bend the laws that continued to govern heroic characterisations. Some of the peplum stars who drifted into westerns in the early Sixties fared reasonably well in their new roles: Brad Harris made a virile hero in three all-action West German westerns and went on to become a cult figure in that country; and hard-working Richard Harrison starred in the first significant Euro-western, Joaquín Romero Marchent's *Gunfight at High Noon* (1963), following it with *Gunfight at Red Sands* (1963), a routine revenge story tinged with anti-racism. (It was after *Red Sands* had wrapped that its producers,

top: Gordon Scott starred as another stalwart of dime novels and B-movie hagiographies in Mario Costa's **Buffalo Bill, Hero of the Far West**.

Giorgio Papi and Arrigo Colombo, approached Harrison with an offer to star in their next film, *A Fistful of Dollars*. Unimpressed with the script, and sharing a widespread lack of faith in the relatively inexperienced Sergio Leone, Harrison opted for another peplum, Antonio Margheriti's *The Giants of Rome* [1964], instead. "That was the biggest screw-up of my career," he concedes. "The one time my agent actually insisted on something. I asked everybody and they all said Margheriti was the better director. Leone was following me around – I thought he was a weirdo. He was following me on sets, looking at me and hiding."[8]) But too many other Hollywood imports failed to make an impression. Whither Alex Nicol, Fred Beir, James Philbrook or Briton Edmund Purdom? All these actors took leading roles in early Italian and Spanish westerns but, generally, they are unassuming on screen to the point of anonymity. This is not to say they were bad actors – Nicol had been superb as the unbalanced Dave Waggoman in *The Man from Laramie*, Purdom proved a versatile player in all manner of exploitation films – but they abided by outmoded rules in which a hero was a hero, a longstanding tradition, briefly interrupted by those neurotic westerns of the Fifties, whereby leading men avoided any suggestion of psychological complexity or moral ambiguity. One has to consider, however, that their characters and dialogue were recycled from exactly the same tradition, allowing the actors little flexibility. Given this, and the fact that most of the directors involved were content to emulate American western motifs, it seems almost churlish to criticise Nicol et al. They were simply doing what was asked of them.

Canadian Rod Cameron, a rugged cowboy in the Randolph Scott mould, remains more relevant in Euro-western history than many of his peers by virtue of the 1964 Mario Caiano film *Bullets Don't Argue*. This streamlined western was, famously, the senior production in a two-picture deal prepared by Jolly Film, the other being *A Fistful of Dollars*. Leone's pet project was seen as the makeweight in the deal, the producers allowing him to utilise the same sets and locations (and, according to legend, leftover film stock, although Caiano denies this) that *Bullets* was using, as well as many of the same personnel, while the budget for Caiano's film dwarfed that of Leone's – Cameron's salary alone was reputedly more than the cast of *Fistful* was paid. (There may also have been a discrepancy between the films in terms of distribution and publicity, although Leone's assertion that *Fistful* was consigned to a small cinema in Florence for its initial release, achieving its success through word of mouth, has been exposed as a myth.[9])

The producers' faith in *Bullets* as opposed to *Fistful* appeared well-founded: they had an experienced, if not exactly top-of-the-range, American western actor on board, a crew of proven proficiency and an agreeable young writer-director who already had a handful of

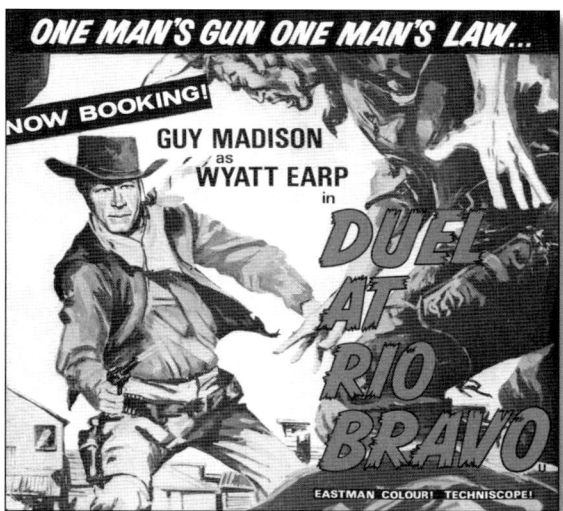

above and opposite bottom left: British and Italian artwork for **Gunmen of the Rio Grande** aka **Duel at Rio Bravo**. With its American leading man (Guy Madison) playing a legendary American lawman (Wyatt Earp), plus allusions to American locations, its Hollywood leanings could not be more plain.

costume adventures to his name and was keen to further his career. (The director landed this assignment partly because of his distributor father's business relations with producer Arrigo Colombo, and partly on the strength of action scenes he had shot for an earlier Papi-Colombo western, *Gunfight at Red Sands*.) Caiano delivered what his employers wanted. "It was intended to be a traditional film that followed all of the classic schemes of the American western," he says.[10] Indeed, *Bullets* – in which Cameron plays none other than Pat Garrett, who interrupts his own wedding to pursue bank robbers Billy and George Clayton into Mexico – could easily pass for an above-average Hollywood B-western. It has a polished look and clear-cut, broadly Anglo-Protestant moral values but, in a way, its efficiency is its undoing. Almost every aspect conforms to the same rigid stereotypes that Leone was in the process

above: 1964's **Ride and Kill** is paired with the peplum **With Fire and Sword** on a typically swashbuckling double bill.

of demolishing. *Bullets* is affirmative, *Fistful* nihilistic. The cinematography, credited to Massimo Dallamano but actually the work of Enzo Barboni and Julio Ortas,[11] while crisp, doesn't offer the density of Dallamano's images in *Fistful* with its scuffed-up, sweaty texture; while Ennio Morricone's mid-paced symphonic score is almost pastiche Americana, complete with a saccharine ballad that, strangely, commemorates the villain rather than the hero. Carlo Simi's set design and costumes are attractive but, with the exception of an impressive ghost town, they lack the realistically weather-beaten quality he gave to *Fistful*'s San Miguel and its denizens. Rod Cameron's Garrett, weighed down by mythical baggage, is a throwback to the uncomplicated, upstanding heroes of pre-Fifties American westerns, the kind of man who would see it his duty to throw Clint Eastwood's troublemaker from the 'Dollars' films in prison. The conventions – including talk of "notches" on pistols and the cavalry riding to the rescue – are cosily familiar. And where Garrett and Angel Aranda's sympathetic George stress the basic decency in man (Horst Frank's malicious, Bible-quoting Billy is killed off halfway through), Leone's puppet-show grotesques are venal and violent. The irony is obvious – while *Bullets* pulled in a respectable figure of just under 1.7 million lire at the Italian box office, *Fistful* scored close to a staggering 3.2 billion, making it the most successful film that year. And while the latter remains a landmark in popular cinema history, *Bullets Don't Argue* has been largely forgotten. As, by all but die-hard western fans, has Rod Cameron.

Joaquín Romero Marchent: a taste for the western

But for *A Fistful of Dollars*, the European western might well have faded into obscurity. We will return to that film in due course but, before Leone's brainchild broke new ground, there was one man mining the same old seam with more distinction and assurance than any other filmmaker on the continent, demonstrating, in a different way from the contemporaneous 'Winnetou' series, how a sentimentalised strain of western might be sustained. Born in Madrid in 1921, Joaquín Luis Romero Hernández Marchent was the son of journalist, author, critic and film producer Joaquín Romero Marchent Gomez de Avellaneda, founder of one of the first film periodicals in Spain, *Radio Cinema*, and partner in the successful production company Intercontinental Films with the actor Rafael Durán. Joaquín junior's achievements, coming as they did before the Euro-western was recognised on its own terms, have been overshadowed by those of other directors, including his own younger brother Rafael, whose westerns generally have a grittier texture than his sibling's and a stronger standing among enthusiasts. Yet Joaquín's importance in the development of the genre cannot be overstated. Although his initial desire was to become a professional footballer, Romero Marchent dedicated himself to cinema from the late Forties, working assiduously as an assistant director before helming his first film, the crime drama *Juzgado permanente* ('standing court')

above: "When a man with a .45 meets a man with a rifle, the man with a pistol will be a dead man": Gian Maria Volonté is made to eat his words at the end of **A Fistful of Dollars**.

in 1953. In the aforementioned 'El Coyote' series he demonstrated a passion for classical (i.e. Hollywood) techniques – fast cutting, film noir-style chiaroscuro – and a fluent understanding of the dynamics of action-and-adventure filmmaking. The showdowns and shoot-outs are choreographed along established western lines, although, unusually, many of these take place at night, enhanced by the high-contrast lighting of cinematographer Ricardo Torres. The 'El Coyote' films also betray the dramatic weaknesses of the B-movies Romero Marchent was emulating, as well as the haste with which they were assembled (he had assumed the director's chores quite suddenly, following the acrimonious departure of the first choice, Mexican Fernando Soler); that said, his use of montage to establish context, especially in *El Coyote*, shows the value of economy in skilful hands. These problems persist in Romero Marchent's other early westerns, which all broadly adhere to the Hollywood method, but the vigour and fluidity of his direction, his attention to detail and the intelligence and purity of his narratives are ample compensation.

In the late Fifties, Romero Marchent dabbled in such staple genres as comedies and historical stories before segueing into 'Zorro' adventures with the lively *Zorro the Avenger* and its José Mallorquí-authored sequel, *The Shadow of Zorro* (both 1962). Frank Latimore, a former Twentieth Century Fox contract player who had relocated to Rome at the beginning of the Fifties, plays the title character with a light touch, and both films demonise their Yankee military villains; in *Zorro the Avenger*, US soldiers are often shown drunk and disorderly, and three of them even desecrate a church and kill the priest – you couldn't get much more nefarious than that in the eyes of conservative Catholic Spaniards. *Shadow* is of particular interest since it was for this film that Spanish producer Eduardo Manzanos's Copercines cooperative oversaw the construction of a western town at Hojo de Manzanares, near La Pedriza di Colmenar Viejo in the San Pedro region of Spain, north of Madrid. This fabled site would be used in several other Euro-westerns, notably doubling for the main street of San Miguel in *A Fistful of Dollars*. In addition, *Shadow* was one of the earliest Spanish co-productions with Alberto Grimaldi's Produzioni Europee Associates (PEA). Grimaldi, originally an attorney, had already made a tidy profit by distributing *Zorro the Avenger* in Italy, and his company would part-finance all but three of Romero Marchent's subsequent westerns before working with the likes of Leone, Corbucci, Sollima and, outside the genre, Pasolini, Fellini, Bertolucci and, more recently, Martin Scorsese. This film shows Romero Marchent edging ever closer to traditional western terrain in terms of costuming, plot elements and the staging of ballistic action scenes – the kind of material that had enraptured him since boyhood in Zane Grey novels and American films. There was another important reason for his change

above: Shoot-outs are as significant as swordfights in Joaquín Romero Marchent's western-flavoured **The Shadow of Zorro**, with Frank Latimore in the title role.

of direction – he realised that neutral adventure stories like these would allow him the kind of artistic freedom otherwise unavailable in Spain at that time. As modest as they are, his westerns express *his* beliefs and ideas, not government propaganda. "The European western", he told his biographer, Carlos Aguilar, "was born as an indirect consequence of Franco's censorship." (The director was right to be concerned. Even something as seemingly inoffensive as *The Shadow of Zorro* displeased the censors, whose report on the film states: "Change what Zorro tells his girlfriend: 'I've got to avenge him until all his murderers are dead' for 'I'll have to do justice' or anything that will avoid the idea of revenge.")**12**

For his first western proper, Romero Marchent again turned to José Mallorquí for inspiration. *The Magnificent Three* (1963) was based on Mallorquí's series *Tres hombres buenos*, written between 1942 and 1947. Although the stories are formulaic, the author strove to distinguish them from American western sagas – and inject them with a degree of historical realism – by inventing protagonists from different ethnic backgrounds – César Guzmán is of Spanish parentage, Diego is a Mexican, Joao Silveira from Portugal – and furnishing them with a brand of gallantry typical of Spanish literary figures. Not much of

above: Robert Hundar – hulking star of a number of early Euro-westerns – menaces an opponent in Romero Marchent's **The Magnificent Three**.

above: Geoffrey Horne – an Actors Studio alumnus – as the aggrieved César Guzmán, with Turia Nelson as the catalyst of his revenge quest in **The Magnificent Three**.
opposite top: Fernando Sancho (with rifle) and Carlos Romero Marchent (the director's younger brother) in Romero Marchent's **Gunfight at High Noon**, a significant advance on all preceding Euro-westerns.

this survives the transition from page to screen, however. Mallorquí's attempt to capture the ethnic diversity of the west – an implicit challenge, perhaps, to the dominance of the Yankee in American frontier folklore, and a nod towards the Europeans' preference for outcasts and anti-heroes – is lost in the film version, even though the author himself wrote the script. Guzmán's background is never remarked upon and the presence of a Portuguese gunfighter merely seems anomalous; in all other respects he is a conventional figure. While The Magnificent Three plays rather like a substandard Hollywood B-western, hampered further by stiff line reading and atrocious English dubbing, certain aspects would become European genre staples: a pronounced distrust and disliking of authority figures (another B-western cliché, although dignitaries in American films rarely suffered as the crooked mayor does here); deglamourised set design; a gunfight staged in a darkened cellar; and Guzmán, tracking down the killers of his wife, decorating the corpses with pin badges identical to one he found at the scene of the crime. In addition, several of the actors would work repeatedly with the same director and/or become regular genre players: from Spain, Paul Piaget (Silveira), a lanky, versatile performer who was in both of Romero Marchent's 'Zorro' films; Fernando Sancho (Diego), portraying a good-natured rogue before pantomime villainy became his trademark (so struck was Alberto Grimaldi by Sancho's performance that he insisted a part be created for him in Romero Marchent's next western); and perennial supporting actors Lorenzo Robledo and Aldo Sambrell. Italy, meanwhile, was represented by the giant figure of Claudio Undari and by Raf Baldassarre, a specialist in volatile characters, while the obligatory Anglo/American import was British actor Geoffrey Horne (Guzmán), prolific on US TV in the Fifties and among the cast of The Bridge on the River Kwai (1957).

After these hesitant first steps, Romero Marchent hit his stride with El sabor de la venganza (1963) – 'the taste of vengeance' – released in the UK as Gunfight at High Noon. The director's command of the well-worn material is much more confident than in his previous film, partly, perhaps, because here he was acting as his own producer for the first time. It was a surprise critical hit both at home – Film Ideal magazine voted it one of the year's ten best films – and abroad, where even Britain's Monthly Film Bulletin, which generally gave Euro-westerns a rough ride, was impressed, noting that "Marchent's direction shows signs of a considerable talent at work". Indeed, this is the most satisfying pre-Fistful European western. It works well as a straightforward genre film: the moral component of the story is strong without seeming forced, it boasts decent production values and period detail (save the usual carelessness in the armaments department, with everybody using fake-looking double-action pistols), and there's a fittingly strident score by Riz Ortolani. But it also pays closer attention to the corrosive psychological effects of revenge, a prominent theme in Fifties 'adult' westerns and later dominant in Italian/Spanish productions. Gunfight straddles both traditions assuredly, underlining its director's belief that the western was open to all: "I believe that the western is a frame more than a genre. It reflects universal problems… Only the reactions change – the motivations are always the same."[13] We can see the film evolving beyond its roots in the character of Chet Walker (Undari), one of three brothers avenging their father's murder. In Undari's career-defining portrayal – a sympathetic spin on his furiously vengeful villain in The Shadow of Zorro – Chet is consumed by hatred to the extent that he drifts into crime and violence, obsessed with finding the killers even as he becomes more like them himself. (At one point he comes perilously close to re-enacting his family tragedy, threatening the homesteaders on an isolated farmhouse until the woman's cries remind him of how his mother had pleaded with her husband's murderers all those years before.) Although, like many of his contemporaries, he later came to resent being typecast as a cruel killer, Undari, a model of professionalism, immersed himself in the role to maintain the required intensity: "I transformed myself into Chet, I was bad both on and off the set. I merged with this character in order to avoid mechanical acting. I carried the role with me wherever I went; I did not want to leave it in case I might not be able to find it again the next day."[14]

The strong bond between matriarch (played by Cagliari-born Gloria Milland, another member of the director's repertory company) and sons, and the friction between the brothers themselves, is early evidence of the centrality of family in the genre and the contradictory emotions that result. (*Gunfight* was a family affair in more ways than one: Joaquín's younger brothers, Rafael [b.1926] and Carlos [b.1944], were both involved, the former as writer, the latter as actor.) The film's main problem, at least from a traditional critical (and moral) standpoint, is that Chet completely eclipses his brothers: the bland Jeff (Richard Harrison in his first western) is Chet's moral counterpoint, a clean-cut Hollywood hero who keeps faith in the legal system; while the eldest, Brad (Spanish actor Miguel Palenzuela, aka 'Billy Hayden'), has to mediate between his siblings. Chet's hot-blooded pursuit of personal retribution engages our attention to a far greater degree, and seems like a more satisfying option, than Jeff's law-abiding approach. Very little is made of Jeff's ethical dilemma – his duties as a lawman versus his fraternal ties, frayed though they are, with Chet – even though he is nominally the hero. None of his scenes have the emotional impact of Chet's, whose tragic qualities are underlined by his death at the climax, which is inevitable given the trajectory both he and the plot have been following. ("I would say in some ways he was the lead," Harrison concedes of Undari. "His character is certainly more flamboyant [than mine]."[15]) As well as being a variation on the good-badman of popular fiction and western lore, it's not difficult to see the violently inclined and morally ambiguous Chet as the prototypical Euro-western avenger.

Adding to the attraction of *Gunfight at High Noon* are its gritty action scenes and its Almerían exteriors. Romero Marchent was keen to give his film a convincingly rough edge, something that supporting actor Aldo Sambrell

Lobbies for **Gunfight at High Noon** that show Robert Hundar *(with pistol)* and Gloria Milland with Richard Harrison *(above)*.

appreciated in later life but came close to regretting at the time. "Joaquín liked very hard, realistic things. If he [staged] a fight in a tavern, he would leave real glasses and bottles on set, and there were even people who cut themselves with the glass. In… *El sabor de la venganza*, my death scene almost cost me my life for real. At one point, there's a challenge, I escape and then turn round to shoot. At this point I was meant to nudge a post so the roof, made of wood and cane, would fall down. It all fell right on the bit of post there was left on the floor, some 20 centimetres away from my head."[16] As for Almería, while it was not quite virgin territory for filmmakers (portions of *Lawrence of Arabia* [1962] had already been shot there, for example), neither was this sun-baked province of Andalucía the mecca it would become. Romero Marchent calculates (and most researchers corroborate) that only one genre film, the British-Spanish *The Savage Guns* (1962), had been shot in Almería before *Gunfight*.[17] It was certainly this director, with his cinematographer Rafael Pacheco, who first fully realised the hypnotic appeal and cruel majesty of the place, having been alerted to its potential by Alfredo Fraile, director of photography on *The Savage Guns*. Inspired by the surroundings, Romero Marchent – in *Gunfight* and *Seven from Texas* (1964) in particular – synthesised character, emotions and landscape in a manner reminiscent of the best American westerns. Pacheco, meanwhile, showed a keen eye for the varied shapes and textures and the shifting colour patterns of the area. Furthermore, Romero Marchent, together with some of his compatriots, set in motion the wheels of the Euro-western industry in Almería, turning around the fortunes of what was then the poorest province of Spain. "There was nothing of anything. It not only lacked a cinematographic infrastructure, it did not have an airport, or hotels, nothing. Almería in 1963 was like it appeared in the films… the end of the world."[18] As westerns began to roll there with increasing frequency, taking advantage of 12 hours of sunlight on average per day, this desolate, inhospitable environment was transformed into a movie-making hub and the centre of a mythical universe. Its cinematic heritage is still celebrated today in the form of both tourist attractions and an annual short-film festival.

Romero Marchent's evident affection for the visual style, characters and narrative rhythms of American westerns, not to mention their epic potential, is reflected in his other films of the period. *Seven from Texas* follows the classic 'wagon train' format, throwing together a disparate set of characters for a cross-country trek pitted with stock situations and dangerous encounters including infighting, hold-ups, Indian attacks and shoot-outs. The drama unfolds against a range of imposing backdrops – in addition to Almería and the desertscape of Cabo de Gata in the south of Spain there are the Sierra Morena hills in the centre and the Picos de Europa mountains and Colmenar Viejo in the north – stressing in true western (and mythical) fashion the pettiness of human power struggles compared with the magnificence of nature. Epic in structure but intimate in scope, the film concerns a journey of compassion rather than discovery, its characters locked in a personal drama that has nothing to do with pioneering or prospecting. Wisely, considering his 'foreign' background and the slender budget at his disposal, Romero Marchent avoids drawing the kind of nation-building parallels that have underpinned American epic westerns from *The Covered Wagon* (1923) onwards.

Involving but uneven, *Seven from Texas* alternates between heart-tugging melodrama and romance on the one hand – a love triangle involving gunfighter Paul Piaget, his old flame Gloria Milland, whose character, based on Romero Marchent's mother, has a malignant brain tumour, and her reliable husband, Jesús Puente – and hard-heartedness on the other. Piaget's hero is killed off, as are several of the film's more genial characters, and Milland's fate remains unresolved. The mixture of ruggedness and romanticism is quintessential Romero Marchent, while the characters' physical hardships were shared, up to a point, by the actors and crew, as Claudio Undari remembered: "We were making this film where [our characters] were exhausted and thirsty, in the middle of the desert… If you look closely at the film, look at the actors – you can see that our lips were so dry they were cracked. Because what was supposed to happen was this tanker full of water would arrive on the set, but it never turned up. So the only water that we had was in these tiny bottles."[19]

In a much lighter vein, the fanciful *Seven Hours of Gunfire* (1965), a co-production with Germany's Constantin Film, co-backers of *A Fistful of Dollars*, is a factually dubious but rip-roaring conflation of western legends that features Buffalo Bill Cody, Wild Bill Hickok, Calamity Jane and the great Oglala Sioux chief Red Cloud, a grouping that recalls such multi-heroic peplums as *Ulysses Against Hercules* (1962) and *Hercules, Samson and Ulysses* (1963). The script plays just as fast and loose with frontier history as the Hollywood westerns the film resembles, although, to be fair, many of its assertions are historically sound: Cody (played by Rik Van Nutter under the name 'Clyde Rogers') did ride for the Pony Express as a young teenager; there was a gold rush by white prospectors to the Sioux's hallowed Black Hills in Dakota in 1874; and Hickok (Adrian Hoven) and Calamity Jane (Milland) were, reputedly at any rate, on-off lovers. However, the film's focus is firmly on action rather than accuracy and, by painting the Indians as victims of white manipulation and aggression, it is broadly in line with its European contemporaries.

With *$100,000 for Lassiter* (1966), made after Sergio Leone had begun to overhaul generic conventions, Romero Marchent veered towards a more Leone-like

above: The stars of **Seven Hours of Gunfire**, from left: Raf Baldassarre, Paco Sanz, Helga Sommerfeld, Gloria Milland, Rik Van Nutter and Adrian Hoven.

approach. Aside from a reduced emphasis on exteriors, there is nothing visually about this land baron/revenge western to distinguish it from the director's previous works (he continues to avoid rhetorical effects), nor is it especially violent; but the mood established by Claudio Undari's protagonist is much more ironic. Lassiter is a sardonic opportunist, seemingly amoral and unscrupulous but, as it transpires, not quite as self-centred as he appears. The welcome injection of irony can be attributed to writer Sergio Donati. Having previously turned down Sergio Leone's invitation to work on *A Fistful of Dollars*, Donati was persuaded to give the nascent Euro-western genre the benefit of the doubt by Romero Marchent and his producer, Alberto Grimaldi. "Romero Marchent came to Milan to work with me," remembers the writer. "He was a very nice Spanish gentleman. We talked a lot about *corridas* and bull runs. He knew absolutely everything about matadors, and we spent many nice hours together."[20] Besides the happy-go-lucky title character, who resembles Giuliano Gemma's 'Ringo' persona, the Donati touch results in blackly humorous asides (the saloon cleaner keeps a trunk full of dead men's clothes, removed from corpses after shoot-outs and repaired for further use) that anticipate his work on his next western, a rather better-known Grimaldi production entitled *For a Few Dollars More*.

By now there was another Romero Marchent on the scene. Joaquín's younger brother Rafael made his first directorial venture in 1965 and, although he did his best work in the genre towards the end of the decade, he made a strong opening statement of intent. This is despite the fact that *Hands of a Gunfighter* – written with Joaquín, who initially 'supervised' his brother at the request of co-producer Alberto Grimaldi – seems on the surface like just another ersatz B-western, with plot elements, character types, visual detail and sharp moral contrasts struck from the Hollywood template. As the film progresses, however, the mood darkens considerably. The clichéd story of a retired gunman, Dan Murphy (Craig Hill, making his European debut), striving for a peaceful life with his wife (Gloria Milland) and young son, is treated with all the pessimism that has come to be associated with continental productions. The family ideal, sacred to many American westerns and revered in Mediterranean societies, is undermined with almost cynical contempt. The Murphys' seemingly idyllic relationship is revealed to be a sham. Unable to accept the death of their young son, who was killed by a sheriff's stray bullet, his parents kidnapped the lawman's baby boy and have brought him up as their own. When they eventually have to hand the youngster back, shattering the illusion of harmony, Dan's violent nature resurfaces; it's clear that only the presence of his 'son' was helping him suppress his murderous instincts.

Using this melodramatic back-story as a basis, the Romero Marchents fashion a bleak variation on a common western theme – ex-pistolero haunted by the past – that has its origins in Greek tragedy. They are strongly aided by a commendable performance from Hill. His character has a long western lineage – Gregory Peck perfected the role in *The Gunfighter*, while in Europe Cameron Mitchell played a similar part in Sergio Bergonzelli's melodramatic *The Last Gun* (1964), as did the veteran French actor Jacques Berthier in Roberto Mauri's *Colorado Charlie* (1965). Hill, whose US career peaked with the TV series *Whirlybirds*, scores by stripping all sentimentality from the role; Murphy's descent into violence and mean-spiritedness reminds us that, at heart, he is a ruthless killer. Rafael's direction is, understandably, rough around the edges, but he demonstrates a fascination with the cruelty and tragic ironies of fate, and with the psychological instability of his central character, that would mark his finest films: *Garringo* (1969), with Peter Lee Lawrence as a pathological killer and Anthony Steffen his ruthless pursuer; and *Clumsy Hands* (1970), in which Lawrence plays a young pacifist drawn inexorably towards violence.

The Romero Marchents' films are among the better of the Hollywood-derived 'first wave' of Sixties European westerns. Joaquín in particular demonstrated a genuine affinity with the material, a respect for its traditions, faith in its hard-bitten heroes and suffering heroines, and a firm command of classical storytelling. His earnest intentions as a western director were diametrically opposed to those of Sergio Leone, his fellow pioneer whose immediate impact will be considered next. Romero Marchent laments Leone's influence on the genre even as he admires his technique and perspicacity. "I think people kill for greed, hatred or revenge," he explained to Carlos Aguilar. "Therefore, I think that the hand that holds the weapon must be guided by some motive born either from the head or the heart. This motive may be premeditated, or instinctive, if one feels cornered, or emotional if it is the result of an obsession. So obviously, if someone kills out of mere sadism, the point of view involved is different from all those I have mentioned. For that reason, if a commercial exhibition is made of death for the sake of appealing to the tastes of the audience, you only prevail if you are perfectly in tune with the public and with current society. Leone's films appeared at a time [when] violence had taken over society to such a point that it was only possible to surprise viewers with a particular perspective on death, and that was irony. [Leone] guessed right there and hit the commercial jackpot."[21] This 'ironisation' of violence was anathema to Romero Marchent, whose own films are comparatively mild (the uncharacteristically grim *Cut-Throats Nine*, made in 1971, being an obvious exception), and accounts for the limited role, chiefly that of scriptwriter, that he played in the genre after this point.

"There's money to be made in a place like this"

A Fistful of Dollars, which proved to be the shock to the system the western had been waiting for, has been debated, imitated and admired for more than 40 years. So much so that all I intend here is to summarise the reasons why. Although almost 30 predominantly Italian-made productions had preceded it, Leone's was the first *Italianate* western. The distinction arises from the way that the director and his collaborators chipped away at the canons of the American western to reduce it to its mythical essence, using irony and imagination as their tools and their own cultural heritage as a reference point.[22]

Where earlier European examples, inscribed with a fascination with Americanism, replicated western codes, *Fistful*, sceptical of the values prescribed by its parent genre, was the first to *translate* those codes into an international form. (As highly as he regarded Joaquín Romero Marchent, Claudio Undari made a clear distinction between the Spaniard's place in the genre's history and that of Leone: "Even if [Romero Marchent] anticipated Leone in time [by making westerns earlier], he did not introduce the *style* of the Italowestern [sic] at all. This merit goes to Leone only. Therefore, if we talk about European production, then Marchent is there at the beginning; but if we talk about the strictly Italian interpretation of the western subject, then Leone sets the point of origin."[23]) Leone and his writers – who included an uncredited Duccio Tessari and Fernando Di Leo, efficient directors in their own right – eliminated conventional heroes and heroines (and the love that usually blossoms between them – this is a film in which the 'hero' punches his leading lady, albeit inadvertently, rather than kisses her). Cow towns, prairies, rustlers, Indians and other western clichés were also excised from their plans and replaced with archetypes and imagery of much greater relevance to European and, especially, Italian audiences. The filmmakers combined their primary influences – a hard-boiled Dashiell Hammett novel (*Red Harvest*) and a Japanese samurai film (*Yojimbo*) – with elements of Sicilian puppet shows, the *commedia dell'arte* (specifically Carlo Goldoni's *The Servant of Two Masters*), religious symbolism, Greek mythology and Roman street smarts. The setting – the US-Mexico border – not only made a lot more sense of the Spanish filming locations but also removed the action from the industrialising western frontier to a more primitive, undeveloped environment, a netherworld scorched by the sun, blighted by physical decay and populated by scavengers, oddballs, tyrants and cut-throats.

Leone brought considerations of cinematic style to the forefront. His own approach, following the example of Homer (in Leone's view, the first and best writer of 'western' narratives), was "a fusion of

above: No way to treat a lady: Sergio Leone, second from left, directs Clint Eastwood and Margarita Lozano on the set of **A Fistful of Dollars**.

reality and fantasy" founded on extravagance and exaggeration – in visual, aural and emotional terms.**24** This meant obsessive attention to detail, particularly physical quirks and imperfections magnified in close-up, baroque sets, enhanced use of colour and lighting, ostentatious camera angles and contrived framing, and a portrayal of violence that was both realistic (showing its effects) and absurd (the speed and accuracy of the characters' gunplay, the protagonist's superhuman endurance, the mountain of corpses). The soundtrack was equally innovative, Ennio Morricone's idiosyncratic score amplifying emotions, provoking a sense of solitude through the use of whistling and a jew's harp, 'commenting' on characters, and creating and shattering tension; an interaction of sound and vision that became increasingly sophisticated as Leone's films and Morricone's range developed. And the hyperactive supporting cast – from the bell-ringer who bounds like a marionette, to the swaggeringly sadistic villains – combine with the visuals and music to create an atmosphere of energy and passion. Leone's world is both recognisably Mediterranean and purely fantastical, just as the characters are simultaneously vital – in all their grubby, sweating, twitching, bleeding glory – and mythical.

The most paradoxical of all is Clint Eastwood's 'hero'. He almost makes a mockery of the term, from his offbeat appearance and his anonymity (he offers no name, prompting the hugely effective United Artists marketing campaign; the coffin-maker calls him 'Joe', but probably refers to all gringos that way) to his Machiavellian mentality and mercenary nature. He isn't chivalrous like the majority of American western leads, nor is he possessed of the tragic nobility of Romero Marchent's heroes. Instead, he is what *Fistful*'s second-unit director Franco Giraldi (responsible for filming the massacre at the river, among other key scenes) called a kind of "Roman rogue" in (stylised) western garb, a man seeking selfish advantage over all other concerns, who makes the same sort of cynical assumptions and has the same get-rich-quick attitude as the tarnished but immensely popular heroes of contemporaneous Italian comedies. (As has frequently been noted before, 'Joe', like the film he stars in, also connects with a much older Italian comedy tradition in the way that he manipulates other parties like a latter-day Harlequin.) Little wonder that Italian audiences flattered this opportunist with their admiration – they could recognise him as one of their own, or at least as one they aspired to be like – or that so many subsequent Euro-western protagonists were based on Eastwood's interpretation. At the same time, however, Leone exaggerates the allegorical link between the hero-figure of popular myth and fiction with that of the Christian Saviour. Eastwood's interloper arrives in San Miguel atop a mule, and before the end has experienced a mock crucifixion, martyrdom and resurrection, as well as delivering the 'Holy Family' of Marisol, Julio and little Jesus from evil. He has the vestiges of a creed, then, but otherwise breaks completely with the tradition of the benevolent western stranger, exemplified by Alan Ladd's Shane and upheld in other European films of the time such as *$5,000 on the Ace* and *Minnesota Clay* (both 1964).

The foregrounding of religious imagery, bound up with an ambivalent attitude towards the church, would henceforth be an important aspect of many major Italian westerns. So too Leone's dark brand of humour, manifest in his casually disrespectful attitude towards death: the cadaver on horseback that Eastwood passes as he enters San Miguel; the "useful" corpses he utilises for the shoot-out in the cemetery; and the numerous references to death in the dialogue. The director's fascination with rituals – the way he expands set pieces into grand, solemn, symbolic occasions – is another of *Fistful*'s much-imitated innovations. The sheer boldness of the film, the audacity and inventiveness of its design, the manner of the storytelling and the richness of Leone's cinematic technique place it obviously and openly in a different cultural tradition from the genre it was immediately accused of undermining.

Enter Corbucci

Besides *A Fistful of Dollars*, the other major Italian westerns of 1964, at least in retrospect, were those that introduced another of the genre's great innovators to the scene. Sergio Corbucci had followed a similar career path to many of his peers – as film critic, screenwriter for hire and assistant director (he had worked alongside Leone and Tessari on *The Last Days of Pompeii* in 1959) – and was an expert in the workings of commercial cinema. Barring a few uncharacteristic social dramas, his own early films were adolescent musicals and freewheeling parodies, many of these starring Totò. He also showed a command of action and spectacle with three of the better *pepla* – the Steve Reeves/Gordon Scott double-header, *Romulus and Remus* (1961), the Scott-starring horror hybrid *Goliath and the Vampires* (1961), co-directed with Giacomo Gentilomo, and *The Son of Spartacus* (1962), again with Reeves.

Like so many of his contemporaries, Corbucci had been a fan of westerns for as long as he could remember. It was during his peplum phase that he first realised how the atmosphere of the west could be re-created, in a purely visual sense, in any number of locations. Seeing for himself the deserts of Spain (*The Last Days of Pompeii*) and Egypt (where chunks of *The Son of Spartacus* were filmed), he could easily imagine cowboys and stagecoaches careering across the dunes, and this convinced him that westerns could be staged effectively in Europe. His first

above: "Aim for the heart, Ramon": Gian Maria Volonté's characteristically neurotic performance as Clint Eastwood's principal antagonist in **A Fistful of Dollars** gained the actor international recognition, although he was later dismissive of the 'Dollars' films and westerns in general.

efforts, *Massacre at Grand Canyon* and *Minnesota Clay*, are both conventional affairs. They have superficially similar plots and themes – two rival clans/gangs, one hero in the middle, along the same lines as *A Fistful of Dollars* – but where *Massacre* is rigidly Americanised, albeit with some Sicilian-vendetta seasoning, *Minnesota Clay* is a good deal more 'European' in outlook and treatment.

Shot in what was then Yugoslavia, *Massacre at Grand Canyon* is, like *Bullets Don't Argue*, a near-perfect imitation of the American style. This extends to having the look-alike son of a famous Hollywood actor – Jim Mitchum, whose father, Robert, played in more than 20 westerns – in the lead role. The crises and climaxes are staged and resolved according to well-established conventions (and expectations), and Mitchum junior's protagonist, despite initially seeming like a lone avenger, is swiftly reintegrated into the (favourably depicted) community. Corbucci directs from a distance, metaphorically speaking, confessing in later years to having little faith in either the script or the filming locations and conditions. (It seems that Corbucci actually took over the direction from co-producer Albert Band, after second-unit director Franco Giraldi had declined the opportunity; that might explain Corbucci's detachment from the project.) There is no evidence of the agility and inventiveness of the camera movements, distinctive cutting, over-the-top violence or black humour that characterise the director's classic westerns, while the themes of revenge and unyielding enmity fail to register with the force of later films.

above: Sergio Corbucci's first western, **Massacre at Grand Canyon**, displayed few of the director's idiosyncrasies. Routinely scripted, shot and edited, and stolidly acted by Jim (son of Robert) Mitchum, it is a far cry from the delights of **Django**.

Minnesota Clay, a grittier variation on its predecessor, has greater resonance. Filmed against the rugged, rocky backdrop of Spain's La Pedriza di Colmenar Viejo and Manzanares el Real, it benefits from Carlo Simi's vivid designing, the storytelling skills of Adriano Bolzoni – who became a key Corbucci collaborator – and a stirring, dramatic score by Piero Piccioni. Again, it relies on an American leading man, Cameron Mitchell, and many elements akin to B-westerns, including a romantic subplot, family-related sentimentality and some buffoonish humour. The difference here is the downbeat, almost tragic tone, the air of doom and desperation hanging over

above: With **Minnesota Clay**, Corbucci, like Cameron Mitchell in this still, began to find his range. Mitchell plays the first of Corbucci's impaired heroes, afflicted by encroaching blindness and the need to protect his daughter (Diana Martin) from a **Fistful of Dollars**-style gang feud.

above: Fernando Sancho as Ortiz, the Mexican bandit chieftain in **Minnesota Clay**. It was a role he was born to play, and he would continue to do so, with scant variation and always the same scenery-chewing relish, for much of his western career.

Mitchell's sombre hero. The plot foreshadows a number of later Euro-westerns such as *The Hills Run Red* (1966) and *Hate for Hate* (1967), with Clay (Mitchell), a legendary gunfighter, escaping from a forced labour camp intent on clearing his name. Fox (Georges Riviere), the man who betrayed Clay to the authorities, is now terrorising the latter's hometown (dubbed "terror town" by the locals), which is also subject to attacks by Mexican bandits led by Ortiz (Fernando Sancho). As in Corbucci's previous film, the townsfolk see Clay as their saviour; his revenge and their deliverance are thus one and the same thing. Mitchell's character is customarily tough and taciturn, well versed in terse, macho ripostes; but, as with subsequent Corbucci protagonists (and even some of his villains), Clay has handicaps. He's plagued by the onset of blindness – a disability first suffered by a Corbucci hero in the 1954 drama *Acque amare* and by an American western hero in *The Proud Ones* (1956) – and has an emotional Achilles heel in the form of his adult daughter (Diana Martin), who remains unaware of his identity until the conclusion.

Undermining the hero like this, hinting at his essential powerlessness against the fates, is typical of Corbucci. In particular, burdening his protagonists with physical disabilities was an extra way of challenging them – and of firing his own imagination: "I always wanted [my lead characters] impaired," he said, "because the idea of a disabled hero intrigued me, made certain solutions more difficult, required more thinking and study, allowed for some *coups de théâtre* and striking initial premises that made the hero more interesting than the usual stereotype."[25] Ironically, his intentions have their strongest expression in the slightly abridged international cut rather than the complete Italian release. The former ends, abruptly but appropriately, with Clay, now almost entirely sightless, apparently dying in his daughter's arms, preserving the integrity of the story and maintaining its downbeat direction. The Italian version, on the other hand, has an unnecessary coda in which Clay has survived his wounds and finds his vision improving, to the extent that he discards and shoots the spectacles he has been supplied with. (This situation was reversed later in Corbucci's career when his preferred conclusion to *The Great Silence* – the death of his protagonist – was replaced for particularly sensitive markets with an absurd, optimistic alternative ending. See note 11 in *A Bullet Spent, A Dollar Earned*.) Other aspects of *Minnesota Clay* give notice of Corbucci and his fellow European filmmakers' intentions (the pessimism, the stylisation of violence – including a man having his earlobe shot off in anticipation of *Django* [1966]), and show soon-to-be-familiar themes and character traits taking shape. As well as the sophistication and relatively high social standing of the chief villain – an early example of spaghetti-style social commentary – there is Fernando Sancho's prototypical bandit leader. The first shot of Ortiz shows him lounging on a throne, bandoleer and medals strewn across his chest, gnawed chicken leg poised between hand and grease-smeared, bearded face. Sancho's unfettered acting style – consider a live-action Yosemite Sam – would sustain him in countless westerns as the genre developed, influencing several other players of a similar stripe.[26]

"Love everything that is good and hate everything that is evil"

This simplistic philosophy would seem to have no place in a survey of European westerns, yet no such undertaking is complete without reference to the source of this statement. It comes from the film *Desperado Trail*, aka *Winnetou III* (1965), and is spoken by Old Shatterhand, the buckskin-clad Teutonic-American hero played by former Tarzan Lex Barker. Barker's character is summarising the guiding principles he shares with his Mescalero Apache blood-brother, chief Winnetou, immortalised by French actor Pierre Brice. Brice was a mainstay in 11 predominantly West German productions between 1962 and 1968 that transferred the wildly popular western novels of 19th Century romanticist Karl May to the screen. Barker played Shatterhand (named for his thunderous punch) in all but four of these films, with Stewart Granger (as Old Surehand) stepping in for three adventures and Rod Cameron (Old Firehand) for one.

May is a controversial figure in German literary and cultural history. This is not the place for a detailed description of his life and legacy – facts and opinions concerning both of which are hotly disputed by academics and admirers alike – but the most pertinent points ought to be addressed. Born into poverty in 1842, May quickly revealed a talent for deception and fraud (he spent between seven and eight years in prison in his 20s) before he turned his fertile imagination towards the writing of exotic so-called 'travel narratives'. From the early 1870s onwards he wrote more than 70 books, the majority of them adventure stories set in far-flung places and centred on superhuman heroes.

May's books are estimated to have sold more than 100 million copies in several different languages. By far the most popular of his creations were Winnetou the warrior and his friend Old Shatterhand, representing between them what May, and his millions of readers in Germany and across Europe, perceived to be the finest qualities of their respective cultures. Winnetou is the archetypal 'noble savage' of European romanticism, harmonious with nature, a seeker of peace and justice, while Shatterhand is an equally idealised German emigrant, embodying strength, vitality and incorruptibility. Not surprisingly, May did little to dissuade those readers who imagined Shatterhand to be the writer's alter ego – he always claimed to have travelled in the American west (he almost certainly didn't; scholars say he conducted much of his research in prison libraries), and the character's birth name just happens to be Karl.

The film versions of this fantasist's adventures dispense with many of their more nationalistic and sentimental qualities – Shatterhand's German origins are barely acknowledged, while he and Winnetou don't express quite the same *intense* mutual admiration as they do in May's novels, except at the end of *Desperado Trail*, when Winnetou lies dying in his comrade's arms – along with the Christian values May was so enamoured of. (These elisions and omissions were no doubt intended to broaden the films' international appeal.) Even so, they are a far cry from the modern conception of a European western. Stranded between May's Manichaean worldview and the mechanical melodramatics of B-westerns at their most banal, the adaptations seem almost childishly naïve today, filled with the kind of dime-novel morality, saddle-sore plot conventions, stilted dialogue and trite characterisations that filmmakers such as Sergio Leone were rebelling against. Leone and his followers set about challenging and transforming the by-now staid and ideologically outmoded tenets of the classical western, constantly probing its boundaries, updating and assailing it with a wide variety of satirical, political and social criticisms. Despite sharing a sense of generic self-awareness, the May series is retrograde in comparison, scrubbing the format clean of all moral complications. As Tassilo Schneider observes in one of the few serious discussions of the May-film phenomenon in the English language: "The ironic or even parodic quality that this generic self-consciousness (or self-reflexivity) takes on in many Italian westerns is missing from the May adaptations. While the spaghetti western might be said to 'deconstruct' the genre, the German films may be said to *reconstruct* it. If the Italian films might be said to be interested in 'demythologisation', the May adaptations seem to pursue the opposite objective: to construct, or recontruct, a viable generic mythology."[27] Yet it was the stunning box-office performance of the initial instalments that convinced Italian directors and producers that there was a substantial European market for westerns.

Maverick Berlin producer Horst Wendlandt launched the series in 1962, against a background of fading cinema attendances and changing audience demographics that was familiar right across Europe. In a bid to reverse the tide, Wendlandt, one of the top producers of *krimis* – lurid, lucrative pulp crime thrillers – turned to the perennially popular May and secured what was then, at DM3.5m, the highest ever budget for a West German movie.[28] Three studios – Wendlandt's Rialto, another West German company, Preben-Philipsen, and Yugoslavia's Jadran – split the cost and *The Treasure of Silver Lake* was the spectacularly successful result, grossing more than any other domestic film since the end of the Second World War and setting a highly profitable series in motion. The director chosen was Harald Reinl, a one-time skiing champion, master of *Heimatfilme* ('homeland' films – sentimental rural dramas), dab hand at Edgar Wallace and Dr Mabuse potboilers (Lex Barker had starred in two of the latter) and husband of one of the country's top starlets, Karin Dor, who has a role in *Silver Lake* and three further May adaptations. Reinl did a professional job, splashing the *pfennigs* at his disposal on several impressive large-scale action scenes, while the sets and costumes, questions of authenticity notwithstanding, were clearly prepared with great care. He helmed four other titles in the series, including the emotionally charged *Desperado Trail*, in which Winnetou's death sparked public outrage and prompted his 'resurrection' for the next chapter, while *krimi* specialist Alfred Vohrer (three films), Harald Philipp (two) and Argentinian Hugo Fregonese (one) were the other directors involved. In truth, there is little discernible variation in directorial style or technique; all the films profit from decent production values and a high level of technical proficiency. They are also characterised by exquisite photography and gorgeous locations – mostly in the former Yugoslavia, although *Winnetou and Shatterhand in the Valley of Death* (1968) includes random inserts of the Grand Canyon – plus the lush, romantic, soporific music of Martin Böttcher, who scored nine out of the 11 titles.

All the films stick to a fairly inflexible format. Almost without exception, the drama centres on a breach in the fragile relations between Indian tribes and white settlers. Scaremongering Yankee villains are always to blame, exploiting the mutual distrust of the races for their own financial gain. This breach must then be mended by the universally respected Winnetou and/or Shatterhand or Surehand. (The 'Old Firehand' entry, *Thunder at the Border* [1966], directed by Alfred Vohrer, is the only one that doesn't focus on interracial conflict). Although many of May's concerns are watered down, and not every film is sourced directly from one of his books, the plots and themes reflect the author's belief in the inherent moral superiority of Native Americans over Yankee bigots, gold hunters and industrialists. Up to a point, this inverts the traditional ideological bias of most American westerns – a bias that had been replicated in several of the early Italian/Spanish-made imitations – to the extent that the almost compulsory siege scenarios usually have *white* besiegers and *Indians* riding to the rescue. The standoff in a fort that concludes Fregonese's *Apaches' Last Battle* (1964), for example, could have been the first one where audiences were invited to cheer for the Indian attackers rather than the military defenders. Not that May's fascination for tribal customs and rituals is replicated faithfully on screen – all the various villages are furnished with totem poles and tepees as a matter of course; it was left to

above: Pierre Brice as Winnetou, the archetypal Noble Savage, with Lex Barker as Old Shatterhand, his implausibly earnest companion, in **Apaches' Last Battle**, third film in a lucrative franchise that revived writer Karl May's popularity in the Sixties.

above: Before becoming a star in Italian westerns, Mario Girotti, aka Terence Hill, earned his living in German ones. Here, he's in a tight spot with one-time Bond girl Karin Dor in the Karl May adaptation **Last of the Renegades**.

DEFA's *Indianerfilme* to dig deeper into anthropological detail. Unlike the *Indianerfilme*, the May adaptations are not disguised anti-colonial tracts or displaced political commentaries; their moral lessons are more transparent than that. The Yankee villains, who are usually a rogue element in white society rather than representative of society itself – desert-dwelling bandit gangs, crooked army officers or, like Forrester (Anthony Steel) in Reinl's *Last of the Renegades* (1964), a land-grabber who can say with arrogant conviction "I make my own laws" – are brought low by greed, whether for territory or for gold. The various conflicts and oppositions spell out the need for tolerance and understanding among different races and cultures – a theme most obviously apparent in *Halfbreed* (1966) by Harald Philipp – and for good neighbourliness in general. Perhaps there *was* a subliminal message in these films after all, a plea for rapprochement directed at a nation, and a world at large, physically and ideologically divided by the Cold War's Iron Curtain.

On both sides of the May films' cultural divide, characters are either good (albeit sometimes misguided – stubborn army officers, bereaved and blinkered tribes and/or settlers) or bad; there is no grey area. Winnetou and Shatterhand are the purest of all. (Surehand/Granger and Firehand/Cameron take themselves much less seriously.) As the Apache chief, the graceful Brice radiates a calm, measured authority, effortlessly capturing the character's mythic essence. His chemistry with Barker is convincing enough, although Shatterhand comes across as overbearing rather than endearing, partly because of the blandly heroic Hollywood baggage that Barker brings with him. His interpretation of the role is almost *too* virtuous – robust, brave, compassionate and unfailingly honest ("I've never lied in my life," he assures dubious Ute warriors in *The Treasure of Silver Lake*) but also stolid, stiff and humourless. Perhaps Barker felt his responsibility as a role model too keenly. Also, one must bear in mind that he, like other American actors in early European westerns, was schooled in a set style of one-dimensional leading portrayals. Brice connected even more closely with his character. "What Winnetou believes is what I believe," he has said. "His message is that we have to live in harmony with each other and with nature. That's a message for all time."[29] But Brice's words underscore the fact that Winnetou is a *symbol*, not a protagonist in the strictest sense; he's not supposed to draw in the audience in the same way that Shatterhand is (although the latter, of course, has symbolic properties of his own).

For this reason, the adaptations that play the best today are those featuring the far less formal Stewart Granger, who maintains an ironic distance from his role as Surehand and from the material. In *Among Vultures* (Vohrer, 1964), *Rampage at Apache Wells* (Philipp, 1965)

above: For **Among Vultures**, fifth title in the 'Winnetou' series, Stewart Granger took the place of Lex Barker as Pierre Brice's right-hand man, his suave, self-deprecating manner providing a welcome injection of irony.

and *Flaming Frontier* (Vohrer, 1965), Granger, who shared the same agent as Barker, imports a self-effacing sense of humour, gently sending up both himself and the trappings of the genre. His wit can be good-natured (ribbing a hapless comrade in *Among Vultures* that "You'd get captured by ants if I wasn't around") or barbed (the sarcastic comments he spits at the odious Harald Leipnitz in *Rampage at Apache Wells*), but is never less than welcome. When Britain's *Films and Filming* visited the multilingual set of *Rampage at Apache Wells* based at Split on Croatia's Adriatic coast, Granger explained how he tried to loosen up his character from the way he had originally been written. "They had me as the usual stereotype Lex Barker, I am dramatic, I am heroic. I thought that isn't what goes with the public. What they want is a sympathetic character who doesn't take himself too serious [sic]." By that time a veteran of more than 70 movies, including several westerns, Granger was under no illusions about the clichéd nature of his latest venture, but added, without condescension, "What western *is* original?"**30**

Indeed, part of the series' appeal to audiences at the time, and one of the reasons they seem so oddly affected when viewed today, is their eager fulfilment of every generic expectation, which goes hand-in-hand with their return to a romanticised, unadulterated vision of frontier life. There are pulp-fiction clichés – fabled treasures, secret passages – and bands of brigands with colourful monikers like the Tramps, the Vultures and the Fingers Gang. There are feisty heroines, whether Indian (Winnetou's sister crops up a few times) or white (typified by Elke Sommer in *Among Vultures*) or of mixed race (*Apaches' Last Battle*, *Halfbreed*). There are figures of fun, from bumbling trapper Sam Hawkens, regularly played by Ralf Wolter (his function fulfilled by Wabble [Milan Srdoc] in the Granger/Surehand titles), to pompous, interchangeable 'foreigners', whose values and manners are comically contrasted with those of the 'westerners'. And one can tick off the stock situations that recur throughout. The chases, battles and confrontations are often grand, complex and efficiently filmed – there are impressive crane shots in Reinl's *Winnetou the Warrior*

(1963) and in the opening scenes of *Thunder at the Border* – although a static camera is common elsewhere. The notion that personal honour can be proved by physical valour underpins the ritualistic challenges that either Winnetou or Shatterhand/Surehand are set by Native tribes in almost every film; these range from individual duels to tests of their athletic prowess – Shatterhand must row to a sacred statue in the middle of a lake in *Winnetou the Warrior*, evading flying arrows all the way, if he is to win the chief's confidence – or, as in *Among Vultures*, their marksmanship. Similarly, there is often an occasion for Winnetou to perform a self-sacrificial act of some kind, staking his integrity and reputation, and sometimes his life, to save the lives of others, epitomised when he takes a bullet meant for Shatterhand towards the end of *Desperado Trail*, thus meeting the noblest of deaths.

No matter how implausibly wholesome the films may be or how quaint their interpretation of western regulations, they represent a landmark for a number of reasons. For transcribing for the first time the most popular works of a man who, for good or ill, had largely shaped generations of Germans' perception of the American west and of what 'America' entails. For moving Native American characters and their predicament from the margins of the western to the centre (or thereabouts – it remains the case that a white hero is the fulcrum). For practically relaunching West Germany's commercial film industry and reclaiming it for a family audience, putting the relative financial success of then-prevalent *krimis*, horror films and sex comedies into perspective. For showcasing a varied group of actors, many of whom graduated afterwards to Italian/Spanish productions: these included up-and-coming European stars such as the muscular Götz George and a pre-'Terence Hill' Mario Girotti, who were both generally cast as headstrong or naïve youngsters involved in romantic subplots; seasoned Hollywood and British veterans (Guy Madison, Walter Barnes, Herbert Lom); and versatile character actors (Mario Adorf, Klaus Kinski). Above all, the May films were a catalyst in the European western renaissance, their commercial success across mainland Europe partly the springboard for Leone and *A Fistful of Dollars*. (Tellingly, they weren't so popular in the USA, where their ingenuousness was too much even for audiences reared on clear-cut frontier morality. Columbia picked up several for distribution, but few people noticed.) And while the series as a whole seems decidedly sedate when compared with the hot-blooded Italian westerns it helped to initiate, the later entries do perhaps betray a little of those films' influence – *Thunder at the Border*, in particular, exchanges the usual picture-postcard settings for the kind of dusty, parched, pseudo-Texas/Mexican border town favoured by Leone and company.

The big-screen success of the 'Winnetou' films in Germany instigated a May revival. A handful of his non-western stories were adapted, with Lex Barker starring in five of these, and May merchandise spilled from shop shelves. The cult continues to this day – Brice played Winnetou in a seven-part French-German television series in 1980, with Ralf Wolter returning as Hawkens and Siegfried Rauch playing Shatterhand, and saddled up again for the German TV film *Winnetou Returns* in 1998. For many years he also played the character in annual festivals, the Karl May Spiele, which are still staged each summer in the Kalkberg Open Air Theatre at Bad Segeberg, near Hamburg. In 1992, Gojko Mitic, the iconic star of DEFA's *Indianerfilme* and a supporting actor in five of the original May films, took over the part when Brice retired, and later starred in new adaptations made for German television. (Mitic himself handed over the reins to Erol Sander in 2006.) The Apache chief has also been the subject of the *Winnetoons* children's cartoon series, plus a big-screen spin-off, and May's characters were heartily parodied in two vehicles for popular TV entertainers: Thomas Gottschalk, a madcap game-show host, includes an impersonation of Old Shatterhand among his repertoire in *Three Crazy Jerks* (1987), which features a cameo by Pierre Brice; while the uproarious *Manitou's Shoe*, produced, directed by and starring comedian Michael Herbig, amplifies the camp aspects of the Winnetou legend and was one of the most successful German films of 2001. (Germany's romantic attachment to May's mythology was a motivating factor in the opening of a wild-west theme park, Silver Lake City, near Berlin in 2004.)

The May films inevitably faced competition from other German westerns, though none came close in terms of popularity. Brice and Barker took a break from their most famous roles to play amicable rival gunfighters in *A Place Called Glory* (1965), a West German/Spanish co-production directed by American Sheldon Reynolds. (It was distributed in America before *A Fistful of Dollars* and shares several of that film's cast members, including Marianne Koch, Wolfgang Lukschy, Aldo Sambrell and Antonio Molino Rojo.) This methodical tribute to Hollywood B-westerns is two films in one: a pair of professional gunmen become embroiled in a land dispute between ranchers and homesteaders, then find themselves drawn against each other in the annual Glory City duel, the highlight of the town's Founder's Day festivities. Although the ending is fudged – German audiences would presumably have been outraged had either Barker or Brice killed the other on screen – this is an interesting twist on generic expectations. The reduction of the time-honoured western showdown to a gladiatorial contest staged for the benefit of bloodthirsty spectators anticipates Lamont Johnson's more pointedly cynical *A Gunfight* (1971), in which Kirk Douglas and

Johnny Cash fulfil essentially the same roles as Barker and Brice, as well as Sam Raimi's Sergio Leone tribute *The Quick and the Dead* (1995).

Harald Reinl attempted to replicate the success of his 'Winnetou' titles with the pallid *The Last Tomahawk* (1965), a bastardised version of James Fenimore Cooper's *The Last of the Mohicans* with Spaniard Daniel Martín and Euro-western star-in-the-making Anthony Steffen filling the roles of valiant Native American and white accomplice respectively. Just as imitative but far more enjoyable are a trio of films produced by Wolf C. Hartwig's Rapid Film with French and Italian partners and mainly Eastern European locations: *Pirates of the Mississippi* (1963), *Massacre at Marble City* (1964) and *The Black Eagles of Santa Fe* (1965). All were contrived largely as vehicles for American bodybuilder and peplum star Brad Harris, alongside local favourites including Horst Frank, unusually but plausibly cast in heroic roles in two of the films; Hansjörg Felmy, who became a major German television star; Sabine Sinjen; Tony Kendall [Luciano Stella], who would be Harris's partner in the long-running 'Kommissar' X spy series; Mario Adorf and Serge Marquand. Although they echo the pro-Indian sentiments of the 'Winnetou' series – Natives are peaceable, driven to violence by the machinations of double-dealing white men – they are nowhere near as self-conscious or sentimental. Instead, and despite having lower budgets and arguably even greater disregard for historical verisimilitude, they attempt to outdo their rivals in terms of unbridled escapism and sheer spectacle, such as *Mississippi*'s impressively reconstructed riverboat chugging down the Lonja river in Croatia, battle sequences teeming with extras and, as one would expect, handsome location photography.

Harris, who'd done TV work in Germany while stationed there as a soldier at the end of the Fifties, sheds some light on the ad hoc nature of the films' production. "The 'Winnetou' series was going on and Wolfgang Hartwig wanted to make his own westerns. I suppose it was competitive in a way. I remember one time we got a telegram from the distributor saying that in the latest 'Shatterhand' or something they killed 27 Indians and we had to kill more Indians. That was the absurdity of it... There was hardly any research done – the only research was to try to have the clothes, the saddles, the guns and the horses look like they did in American westerns. Because all those films were fantasies based upon what they saw in American westerns. And I don't know how close to the truth the American movies were – they make ten Jesse James pictures and all of them are a bit different."[31]

above: There's *pfennigs* in them thar hills: Sundry German production companies sought to capitalise on the success of the Karl May films in the early Sixties. **Massacre at Marble City**, with Horst Frank cast against type in a positive light, was one of the more vigorous examples.

A watershed year

As we look further, into 1965, we notice more divergence between the narrative patterns and characteristics of the Hollywood western and those of its European counterpart. The unexpected success of *A Fistful of Dollars* suddenly made the Euro-western a box-office proposition of *Hercules*-style proportions. The rate of production accelerated – more than 40 Italian/Spanish westerns were made that year, almost twice as many as the previous year, including a few that each scored well over a billion lire in Italy's prestigious *prima visione* cinemas; indeed, six of the seven top money-makers that year were westerns.**32** As Christopher Wagstaff has observed, this explosion of westerns was clearly "a consumer-led phenomenon", since nobody in the industry had anticipated the success of *Fistful*. And yet, at the same time, "In a period of falling attendances, producers and distributors saw the spaghetti western as a salvation, and proceeded to impose it on the Italian cinema-going public."**33** And although most films continued to abide by Hollywood rules, there were also signs of a new sensibility emerging, a realisation that those same rules were there to be broken – *Fistful*'s box-office receipts had proved that. Specifically, 1965 yielded three enduring classics: the two 'Ringo' films by Duccio

above and top: In **$5,000 on the Ace**, Fernando Sancho upstaged angular American leading man Robert Woods as his slippery Mexican sidekick.

above: Gritty films like **A Coffin for the Sheriff**, starring Anthony Steffen, helped Euro-westerns, and their stars, to assert their own identities.

Tessari (covered in *Beware Of Fake Guns...*) and, right at the end of the year, *For a Few Dollars More* (see next chapter), while several other titles were infused with a similarly ironic/iconoclastic spirit.

There is evidence of this new direction in the treatment of revenge, for example, which assumes a level of unprecedented intensity in a film like *Why Go On Killing?*, jointly credited to Italian director Edoardo Mulargia and Spaniard José Antonio de la Loma. None of the characters involved in a suicidal feud between two neighbouring clans can answer the titular question, but their motivation is rooted in the fanatical loyalty to one's family widely perceived as fundamental in Mediterranean cultures. The sombre mood of the film is well matched to its star, the dour Anthony Steffen, who played another downcast avenger – his speciality – in the same year's *A Coffin for the Sheriff*, smartly directed by Mario Caiano. Elsewhere, Alfonso Balcázar's little-seen *Viva Carrancho* anticipates the genre's ideological shift towards Mexico with its Adriano Bolzoni-penned story of a loveable ragamuffin, Carrancho (Fernando Sancho), who inspires exploited miners to overthrow their brutal employer (Robert Woods). The garrulous, wily Carrancho is a forerunner of Tuco and other 'ugly' characters, especially picaresque rebels such as Chuncho in *A Bullet for the General* (1966) and Cuchillo in *The Big Gundown* (1967). He has a sense of purpose that was missing from Sancho's first turn in the role in the less stimulating but highly profitable *$5,000 on the Ace*, which

above: Franco Lantieri and Helga Liné share a moment of intimate violence in Giovanni Grimaldi's **In a Colt's Shadow**, one of several transitional films poised awkwardly between traditionalism and baroque stylisation, not to mention a more graphic depiction of brutality.

above: Anthony Steffen broke through as a bankable leading man in the period 1965-66, when he appeared in seven mid-budget westerns. Slim and solemn, he was usually cast as an avenger or, as in **A Few Dollars for Django**, pictured here, a bounty hunter.

above: Stunt co-ordinator and supporting actor Benito Stefanelli mid-fight scene in **One Silver Dollar**.

earned more than any western apart from *A Fistful of Dollars* and comic duo Franco and Ciccio's *Two Gangsters in the Wild West* at the Italian box office in 1964. The populist tone of *Viva Carrancho* is one of Bolzoni's trademarks – he later co-wrote the political westerns *Requiescant*, aka *Kill and Pray* (1967) and *A Professional Gun* (1968), and adapted a book on Che Guevara for an Italian-made biopic in 1968.

Sergio Leone's fascination with moral ambiguity is reflected in various Euro-western characters whose make-up, in turn, reflects the clash of cultures – Hollywood versus Europe – inherent in films of this period. Certain protagonists, although outwardly similar to their American western brethren, do not share their counterparts' noble bearing. Consider Craig Hill's doomed Murphy in *Hands of a Gunfighter*, the rival hired killers in the romantic/violent *In a Colt's Shadow*, and Ringo, the cheery, charming mercenary of *A Pistol for Ringo*. A number of mediocre films were made more colourful by the addition of devious or unscrupulous secondary characters, often played with vigour and wit, a good example being Aldo Berti's cynical gunman in *A Stranger in Sacramento*, who repeatedly has to rescue Mickey Hargitay's unprepossessing hero. As for the villains, they begin to take cruelty to such exuberant extremes that it can be difficult to take them seriously, as demonstrated by Livio Lorenzon as *Colorado Charlie* and Fernando Sancho in *A Pistol for Ringo*, although there is nothing amusing about Indio's atrocities in *For a Few Dollars More*.

The other main development in this year took place in front of the camera, where several notable leading men made their breakthrough, including Americans Craig Hill, Robert Woods and Brett Halsey; and Italians Anthony Steffen and Franco Nero, who had a supporting role in 1965 under Joseph Cotten and Gordon Scott in *The Tramplers*. Most significantly, Giuliano Gemma, not yet 30 at the time, emerged as the top Italian-born western lead. His swashbuckling style – modelled, in part, on Burt Lancaster – was honed in his childhood and adolescence, when he was fanatical about sport and physical exercise, everything from gymnastics to swimming and boxing. (It was during his childhood, in wartime Reggia-Emilia, that Gemma sustained the facial scar that is visible to this day, when a discarded hand grenade exploded while he was playing with it.) He later enjoyed a spell as a trapeze artist and worked as a military fireman until, at the end of the Fifties, he answered the demand for stunt performers in the mythological films that were to catapult him, almost literally, to stardom. Working on Vittorio Cottafavi's *Messalina* (1960), Gemma made the acquaintance of Duccio Tessari, Cottafavi's assistant, who was preparing a peplum of his own. Gemma's physical skills and geniality persuaded Tessari that here was his leading man, and the resulting collaboration, *Sons of Thunder* (1962), was a great success. Where most of the mythological heroes had taken themselves and their increasingly preposterous *above:* Giuliano Gemma almost single-handedly bridged the gulf between Americanised westerns and the bold new style initiated by Sergio Leone. **Adios Gringo**, one of the most successful Italian films of 1965, was cut from the same cloth as numerous Hollywood B-movies, but the trimmings – sadistic violence, a loathing of nepotism and localised corruption – were clearly tailored to a different audience and for a different cultural climate.

adventures seriously, Gemma's bleached-blond Crios bounds through Tessari's impudent film like a carefree, cocksure teenager, defeating his foes with wit and cunning as much as with brawn. A string of lesser films followed in this historical-mythological vein ("[I was] living in a constant fiction", says Gemma), until swords and sandals gave way to six-guns and spurs. This was when Gemma's popularity soared, his combination of wholeheartedness and humour, his way of "winking" at the audience, as he puts it, providing an alternative to the ruthlessness and amorality of Clint Eastwood and co. "No matter how much violence there was in my films, the spectator never lost sight that this was a game, an entertainment," he says.[34]

Gemma entertained more spectators than most: of the 20 most successful westerns at the Italian box office between 1964 and 1967, he starred in no fewer than nine of them.[35] His first four all came in 1965, each one tailored to his dynamic personality and athletic abilities. While the 'Ringo' films displayed the actor in contrasting moods – light-hearted in the first, doleful in the second – the other westerns he made that year, *One Silver Dollar* and *Adios Gringo*, both fairly traditional in nature, established him as a more chivalrous protagonist than many of his peers. Using violence in self-defence rather than as a form of self-expression, his characters are driven by a strong sense of injustice: in *Adios Gringo*, directed by Giorgio Stegani, he must defend himself against a cattle-rustling charge and unmask a conspiracy; while Giorgio Ferroni's *One Silver Dollar*, Gemma's own favourite among his westerns, requires him to seek revenge and uphold the disputed

above: Thai poster for **Fort Yuma Gold**, with Gemma playing another of his unbowed Confederate veterans.

Publicity portrait of Giuliano Gemma flashing his trademark smile in place of the scowls and sneers favoured by many of his peers, taken at the peak of his – and the Italian western's – popularity.

honour of the recently defeated Confederacy, a theme that Gemma would return to in *Fort Yuma Gold* (1966) and *California* (1977). Although they are neither radical in style nor revolutionary in content, these are well-balanced films. The directors pay partial homage to Hollywood – both ensnare their heroes in love affairs, for example, while *Adios Gringo* (based on a novel by legendary American pulp writer Harry Whittington) develops into a Hawksian siege western – but seething beneath the surface are the enthusiastic brutality and baroque characterisations, coupled with a dim view of society, that were beginning to distinguish European-made westerns from their predecessors. It was a distinction that became all the more pronounced the following year, when Sergio Leone managed to surpass what he had achieved in *A Fistful of Dollars* – while also raising the bar for his directorial rivals – with the spectacular success of *For a Few Dollars More*.

footnotes

1   The source for these figures is *The BFI Companion to the Western* (see bibliography).

2   Lacklustre US-Spanish westerns such as *Gunfighters of Casa Grande* (1964), *Finger on the Trigger*, *Son of a Gunfighter* (both 1965), *Kid Rodelo* and the Audie Murphy vehicle *The Texican* (both 1966) emphasise how monotonous Hollywood's staple genre had become. Only Sid Pink's *The Christmas Kid* (1967), a parable with Jeffrey Hunter reprising his *King of Kings* persona in cowboy gear, tried something different.

3   Although ignored by Spain's own literary historians, far keener to promote Calderón and Cervantes, Mallorquí is one of the country's most widely translated, widely read authors. Working within the confines of the fast-turnaround pulp fiction market, Mallorquí, who began his literary career as a translator, treated his material seriously and his characters and readers with respect. While his stories are adventurous and escapist in nature, they contain a certain degree of realism – characters develop, age naturally and die during the series' lifetimes – that is unexpected in the medium. They also occasionally coalesce. Two of his *Tres hombres buenos*, for example, César Guzman and Joao Silveira, guest-starred in El Coyote adventures. The last-named character, undoubtedly the writer's most popular creation, was also the subject of a 1963 Mario Caiano film, while a new version was made for Spanish television in 1998. Called *The Return of El Coyote*, it was directed by the respected Mario Camus with a screenplay written by Mallorquí's son, fittingly named César.

4   This does not take account of a small number of 'revisionist' Italian westerns made in the early to mid-Seventies in response to allegorical American films such as *Soldier Blue* and *Little Big Man* (both 1970). For more on the likes of *Vengeance Trail* (1971) and *Apache Woman* (1976), see *Desolation and Deconstruction*.

5   The dozen *Indianerfilme* made by Deutsche Film AG (DEFA) between 1965 and 1983 were among the most successful films produced in the former GDR. Very different in style and tone from the 'socialist realist' pictures that preceded them, they were intended partly as a criticism of Hollywood westerns and partly as a historically more accurate riposte to the West German 'Winnetou' series. (The two sets of films were photographed in many of the same central European locations.) Although they deliver all the thrills and spills associated with conventional westerns, the point of view of *Indianerfilme* is Native American rather than white American, with muscular Yugoslavian Gojko Mitic usually employed as the embodiment of Indian resistance and resolve. (Some of his characters, such as Tecumseh and Osceola, were drawn directly from history.) DEFA made a few other westerns as well, including a couple starring Dean Reed, the left-wing Colorado singer/actor who lived for much of his life in eastern Europe, but its pro-Native American, revisionist accounts of the settling of the frontier were by far the most popular.

6   Although it doesn't give him a screen credit, *Buffalo Bill* was the first feature-length western written by pulp-fiction specialist Ernesto Gastaldi, who later authored some of the genre's key works. In 1953, Gastaldi had collaborated on a short amateur western called *Cowboy Story*, directed by Peppo Sacchi, which won an award at a festival in Montecatini. Gastaldi remembers: "It was filmed without sound in black and white. When we showed it at the festival there were 10 of us behind the screen and we did a live dubbing. I think that was something almost unique in film history." (Author's interview with Ernesto Gastaldi.) Sadly, the film is now lost.

7   One area of American history that Euro-westerns returned to with more rewarding results was the Civil War, especially after its prominent role in *The Good, the Bad and the Ugly* (1966). Although they mostly avoid famous names and battles from the conflict itself (these would have been very expensive to restage and required a greater amount of research than was typically undertaken for these films, with their quick turnaround), a number of titles feature the war as a backdrop, *GBU* style, or take place in the immediate post-war period, soaking up the lingering atmosphere of tension and hatred and following the further adventures of decommissioned soldiers or unyielding rebels. Writing on www.fistfulofpasta.com, Euro-western enthusiast Simon Gelten thinks there was more than just expediency behind the use of this setting: "Italian directors often use the American Civil War as a substitute for the Second World War… Most Italians felt humiliated [after their country's ignominious role in WWII]", and audiences may have recognised themselves, to an extent, in the despised, disgruntled Confederates who typically populate these films. Gelten also sees the legacy of the Risorgimento – which profited the industrial north of Italy much more than the predominantly rural south – reflected in a number of Civil War films that focus explicitly on defeated and/or downtrodden southerners. See the Giuliano Gemma vehicles *One Silver Dollar* (1965), *Fort Yuma Gold* (1966), *The Price of Power* (1969) and *California* (1977), for example. Other notable entries include Franco Giraldi's *Sugar Colt* (1966) and Sergio Corbucci's *The Hellbenders* (1967), Peter Lee Lawrence in *Days of Violence* (1967), Nando Cicero's *Red Blood, Yellow Gold* (1967), Enzo Castellari's *Seven Winchesters for a Massacre* (1967) and *Kill Them All and Come Back Alone* (1968), Paolo Bianchini's *Gatling Gun* (1968) and *I Want Him Dead* (1968), Julio Buchs's *Vengeance Is Mine* (1969) and Edoardo Mulargia's *Shango* (1970).

8   *Gunfight at Red Sands*, though a minor work, has a number of connections to *A Fistful of Dollars*. It was the first western worked on by both cinematographer Massimo Dallamano and composer Ennio Morricone (whose score is worlds apart from the one he created for Leone's film), and the first to be co-produced by *Fistful*'s Jolly Film.

9   Marco Giusti, *Dizionario del western all'Italiana*, p368.
10 Quoted in 'Conversation with Mario Caiano' on the Italian DVD release of *Bullets Don't Argue*.
11 Marco Giusti, *Dizionario del western all'Italiana*.
12 The director is quoted in Carlos Aguilar, *Joaquín Romero Marchent: La firmeza del profesional*, p.32. Censors' quote taken from *Aspectos jurídicos de la censura cinematográfica en españa. Con especial referencia al periodo 1936-1977* by Teodoro González Ballesteros.
13 Carlos Aguilar, *Joaquín Romero Marchent: La firmeza del profesional*, p. 39.
14 Interview with Claudio Undari conducted for this book by Mario Marsili.
15 Author's interview with Richard Harrison.
16 José Manuel Serrano Cueto, *Aldo Sambrell, la mirada más despiadada*.
17 *Savage Guns*, originally *Tierra brutal*, was a co-production between Hammer alumni Michael Carreras (also the director) and Jimmy Sangster, and Spain's José Gutierrez Maesso. It is believed that Maesso made the suggestion to shoot exteriors in Almería.
18 Carlos Aguilar, *Joaquín Romero Marchent: La firmeza del profesional*, p.42. Romero Marchent credits a knowledgeable taxi driver named Diego for first showing him Almería and its environs; this man subsequently became a sought-after scout during the western boom. "Diego was one of the most important individuals in the history of the cinema in Almería," says the director. Gracias, Diego.
19 Interview with Claudio Undari by Roger A. Fratter in *Dieci ricercati dello spaghetti western* (Nocturno Dossier, October 2007).
20 Author's interview with Sergio Donati.
21 Carlos Aguilar, *Joaquín Romero Marchent: La firmeza del profesional*, p.49.
22 Not everybody appreciated Leone and company's intentions. While the more straightforward *Bullets Don't Argue* – produced, like this film, by Giorgio Papi and Arrigo Colombo – received its producers' enthusiastic backing, *Fistful* was far more difficult to get off the ground, as the late Benito Stefanelli, who was stunt co-ordinator and supporting actor in all of Leone's westerns, remembered: "The producer reads about a guy riding into town on a mule, with a poncho, with a cigar stump. Eh? We were linked to an old-fashioned mentality, Hopalong Cassidy, the clean, shining hero. But Clint goes left and right, collects money from everyone, does what in reality we would do in a similar situation. The audience recognised themselves in Clint. The era of Tom Mix was gone for good." Interview with Benito Stefanelli by Mario Marsili, used with kind permission.
23 Interview with Claudio Undari conducted for this book by Mario Marsili.
24 Leone is quoted in Frayling, *Something to Do with Death*, p.143.
25 Quoted in *Spaghetti Cinema*.
26 Sancho had already made more than 100 films by that point in his career and had developed an inflated opinion of himself, as American actor Richard Harrison, who worked with Sancho on a handful of occasions, witnessed. "I liked Fernando but he had the biggest ego of any actor I've ever known. People wouldn't even ask him but he'd go and give them his autograph. I remember one time outside Barcelona, he was driving [*too fast*] and a policeman was going to put him in jail. Fernando said, 'I'm Fernando Sancho!' The policeman didn't know who the hell he was – I had to go and talk to him in Spanish by myself and explain to him. After we left Fernando said, 'You see, we don't get a ticket!' Fernando was Fernando – he loved being an actor, loved the fame". Author's interview with Richard Harrison.
27 'Building a new *Heimat* in the Wild West: Karl May and the German western of the 60s', in Buscombe and Pearson, *Back in the Saddle Again: New Essays on the Western*.
28 Although this was the first time May's westerns had been adapted for the screen, several of his other tales had previously been made into films in Germany, some dating back as far as the silent era. Nor were these the first German-made westerns – several were produced in the Thirties, most significantly Luis Trenker's nationalistic *The Emperor of California* (1936).
29 From Stephen Kinzer, 'Oh no! Noble Apache bites the German dust' in *The New York Times*, 6 September 1990.
30 From Robin Bean, 'Way out West in Yugoslavia' in *Films and Filming*, September 1965.
31 Author's interview with Brad Harris.
32 *For a Few Dollars More* led the way, making just under 3.5 billion lire, with *A Pistol for Ringo* earning 2 billion and Franco and Ciccio's *For a Fist in the Eye*, a satirical response to Sergio Leone, taking almost 1.3 billion.
33 Christopher Wagstaff, 'A Forkful of Westerns', in Dyer and Vincendreu, *Popular European Cinema*, p. 247.
34 Carlos Aguilar, *Giuliano Gemma: El factor romano*, p.55.
35 For the record, *One Silver Dollar* places fourth, followed by *Adios Gringo* (five), *A Pistol for Ringo* (six), *The Return of Ringo* (seven), *Day of Anger* (10), *Fort Yuma Gold* (11), *Arizona Colt* (12), *Long Days of Vengeance* (16) and *Wanted* (20). To no great surprise, the top three films on the list are *For a Few Dollars More*, *A Fistful of Dollars* and *The Good, the Bad and the Ugly*. Source: *Cine Spettacolo* magazine, February 1968.

above: Japanese promo for **The Return of Ringo**, which was a blockbuster hit in 1965.

Target Practice

above: Spanish poster for Florestano Vancini's **Long Days of Vengeance**, yet another box-office triumph for Giuliano Gemma.

Chapter 2

A Bullet Spent, A Dollar Earned

The Euro-western makes a killing

If *A Fistful of Dollars* was a revolutionary assault upon the crumbling edifice the western had become, then *For a Few Dollars More* established a new order for the genre. Released at the end of 1965, the sequel is, in many ways, the *locus classicus* of its kind, defining the tone and direction the Euro-western would take in its middle phase. It not only bettered its predecessor at the box office (it was the top-grossing film in Italy that season) but saw Sergio Leone refining and enlarging upon both the terms of his discourse and his technique as a filmmaker. Benefiting from a bigger budget (roughly three times that of *Fistful*)[1], and with Luciano Vincenzoni and an uncredited Sergio Donati assisting on the script, Leone's vision of an infernal west and its ruthless, eccentric inhabitants broke out of the confines of *Fistful*'s one-mule town and into broader thematic terrain.

Clint Eastwood's mythic protagonist, referred to here as Monco (a colloquialism for 'maimed' or one-handed) now has a vocation – bounty hunter; a fearsome enemy in the psychologically unstable Indio (Gian Maria Volonté); and a rival/partner in the form of Lee Van Cleef's redoubtable Colonel Mortimer. While Eastwood/Monco relaxes into his role, the secondary characters expand the scope of the story in diverse ways. Indio is a truly unforgettable antagonist: volatile, morbid and sadistic, mock-minister to a trigger-happy flock of cut-throats. Hooked on marijuana and violence, Indio is also cowardly and manipulative, ordering the deaths of women and children and sacrificing his own followers so that he might escape. The men competing for Indio's prize, meanwhile, are cut from different cloth. While Monco is driven by greed, plus the attraction of danger, Mortimer's motivation centres on revenge and family loyalty – once his account is settled with Indio, the Colonel gives up the bounty and gives the impression he may be quitting the business altogether. This, combined with the intelligence and sensitivity that Van Cleef – cast against type in the first substantial role of his career – brings to the part, ultimately ennobles him at the expense of his materialistic accomplice. Moreover, Mortimer's meticulousness and sinister bearing, combined with his sophisticated armoury, identify him as the forerunner of such mysterious figures as Sartana and Sabata, the latter also played by Van Cleef.

Bounty hunters would become a staple of the genre, the cynical nature of their business underlining the devaluation of life and the degradation of social order in the west of the European imagination. It also points to Leone's fascination with the murkier aspects of frontier history, his contempt for conventional moral judgements – the weakness, in his view, of most American westerns and early European imitations – and his pessimism regarding human nature. Equally unconventional at the time, and just as influential on the remainder of the genre, was the mutual duplicity that characterises the anti-heroes' relationship. Equal parts *commedia dell'arte* trickery and streetwise one-upmanship, their sparring is also reminiscent of that between Burt Lancaster and Gary Cooper in Robert Aldrich's *Vera Cruz* (1954), a watershed western, which, as many commentators have pointed out, numerous European directors dipped into for inspiration. Monco and Mortimer also represent duelling generational values (teacher versus pupil/father versus son) and conflicting cultural traditions (Italian versus American), anticipating Lee Van Cleef's best westerns as well as the Leone-produced *My Name Is Nobody* (1973).

above and opposite: More dollars, bigger stars, grander themes… Sergio Leone's second western was better value all round.

above: Clint Eastwood hauls a cargo of corpses (value: $27,000) in this Italian poster for a re-release of **For a Few Dollars More**.
opposite: A necessary evil: Eugenio Martín's **The Bounty Killer** attempted a more nuanced view of the title character's profession. Initially viewed with suspicion, the protagonist, played by Richard Wyler (*top*), earns the cooperation of a small community in his fight against Tomas Milian (*bottom*) and his gang.

At a formal level, *For a Few Dollars More* peaks at the point where many preceding westerns had so often fallen flat – the climactic showdown. The duel between Mortimer and Indio, overseen by Monco, demonstrates Leone's developing confidence, if not yet mastery, of *mise-en-scène*, as well as his veneration of this most sacred western set piece. Instead of the moribund stand-off at ten paces, Leone confines his characters in a threshing circle – effectively an arena – magnifying their every twitch and choreographing the confrontation to Ennio Morricone's 'La resa dei conti', one of the composer's most powerful themes. Leone made the showdown the summit of a character's existence, a timeless ritual for which time itself must be interrupted, the tension building via a series of close-ups until it is shattered by gunfire. One senses that, for Leone, his combatants could as well be Hector and Achilles, gladiators of the Roman age or knights of the Middle Ages. He removed the duel from the temporal to the mythological, becoming increasingly adventurous with his staging (his style, like his subject matter, was inevitably much imitated), while other directors, notably Sergio Sollima, experimented with this motif in different ways.

"Where life had no value, death, sometimes, had its price. That is why the bounty killers appeared"

Unless he wears a star or a uniform (and sometimes even then), the hero in westerns occupies a difficult position. Poised between savagery and civilisation, he doesn't quite belong in either sphere. And at no time is this ambiguity so pronounced as when said 'hero' is a bounty hunter, whose business may benefit society but, in the eyes of the moral majority, is work of the dirtiest kind. This controversial figure is comparatively rare in mainstream American westerns, reflecting his position on the fringes of frontier history. What scant references there are in standard texts on the period suggest that he was considered at best a necessary evil, at worst little more than a scavenger. As Sergio Leone put it, "The bounty killer is a very ambiguous character in the old west, perhaps the most ambiguous of them all, for he demonstrates a law of the west and of America itself: that in order to live, one must be inclined to kill."[2] In real terms his was an inglorious role; he was as likely to find employment in rounding up escaped slaves or other relatively harmless absconders, as he was in tracking down dangerous outlaws. He certainly can't compete for sympathy with more prominent historic/folkloric archetypes such as the chivalrous cowboy or the heroic, town-taming peace officer. Instead, he is closer in stature to the professional gunfighter, a morally dubious character trading in violence and killing for profit.[3]

In Hollywood terms, the bounty hunter is usually depicted as a pariah or outcast, viewed with deep suspicion and not a little loathing by society. (Television generally skirted moral scrutiny of this kind, hence Steve McQueen's character in the series *Wanted: Dead or Alive* [1958-1961] was never afflicted by public disapproval in the same way as his counterparts on the big screen.) In rare westerns where he is the protagonist, and thus expected to engage his audience more closely, there has to be a solid reason why the man in question has taken up this despicable trade. Usually it is out of bitterness or desperation: in Anthony Mann's *The Naked Spur* (1952), James Stewart needs money to reclaim land lost after the Civil War, while Randolph Scott (in André de Toth's *The Bounty Hunter* [1954]), Henry Fonda (in Mann's *The Tin Star* [1957]) and Glenn Ford (in Gary Nelson's *Santee* [1973]) are vicariously avenging the murder of loved ones by outlaws. In these cases, the casting of sympathetic actors in uncharacteristic roles suggests a (temporary) falling from grace, commensurate with the low social status of their profession. Redemption comes with the renunciation of the role (*The Naked Spur*) or through caring for others (*The Tin Star*, *Santee*). There's a similar premise in *The Bounty Killer* (1965) – a showcase for a host of veteran screen cowboys including Johnny

Mack Brown, Broncho Billy Anderson and Bob Steele – in which Dan Duryea stars in the title role as a formerly peaceable man corrupted by the demands of the job. The most contemptuous bounty hunters in an American western are the railroad lackeys in Sam Peckinpah's *The Wild Bunch* (1969), in which Strother Martin, L.Q. Jones and the rest of Robert Ryan's "gutter trash" make up what Paul Seydor calls "a spectacle of human avarice and opportunism at its most carnal".[4] Peckinpah compares them with insects and vultures, and further shows his disdain by having them killed off-screen.

As Jim Kitses observes of Henry Fonda's fundamentally good-natured Morg Hickman in *The Tin Star*, "The role of bounty hunter [sits] uneasily on one so warmly committed to human worth".[5] For such a man as this, whose moral fibre is frayed but still intact, whose self-respect and faith in humanity are shaken but not quite shattered, tracking outlaws for money is a means to an end. In the Euro-western, on the other hand, where faith in human nature is a dangerous misconception, bounty hunting is a genuine calling. The promotion of bounty hunter to protagonist on such a regular basis offers a telling distinction between American and European productions – the former shaping a myth from history, the latter a fantasy from the myth; the optimism and myth-reinforcement of the former clashing with the nihilism and myth-deflation of the latter. Indeed, to a great extent, this amoral adventurer embodies the essence of the post-Leone European western. He stands for its radical reinterpretation of heroism, in which traditionally admirable virtues such as selfless nobility are replaced with a self-centred survivalist ethic; this particular differential implicitly and ironically acknowledges changes in popular attitudes and aspirations wrought by capitalism and consumerism. He likewise personifies the genre's cynical vision of society as a free-market for killers, thieves and swindlers, where the political and legal establishment is awash with corruption, as well as its then shockingly flippant attitude towards the taking of life, which, in the bounty hunter's case, becomes something of an art form.

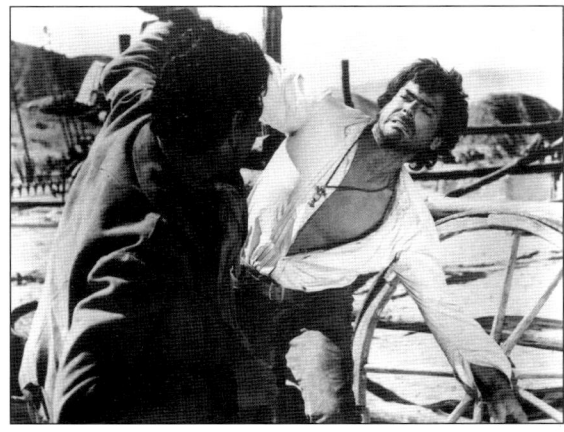

above: Locandina for Rafael Romero Marchent's **Dead Men Don't Count!**, in which Anthony Steffen and Mark Damon, as the avaricious anti-heroes, personify a fashionably derisive attitude towards conventional morality.

Not all bounty hunter films offer him equal acclaim. While plenty of titles blithely celebrate his activities, others are more considered, delving into the character's background and motivation, or even sharply critical, condemning the practice and the socio-economic conditions that support it. In virtually all cases there are traces of *For a Few Dollars More*: some bounty hunters are of Monco's variety, cool, callous and carefree; others are more like Mortimer, menacing or melancholy; while some are grouped into prickly, unstable partnerships. And just as Monco and Mortimer are characterised as overgrown children, there's a feeling that, for many protagonists, the whole business of hunting, double-crossing and killing is no more morally taxing than a game or a sporting pastime. They crave the challenge and relish the thrill of the chase. These characters and their escapades far exceeded American westerns' sense of moderation; instead, as Oreste De Fornari notes of Leone's films in particular, "[they] resembled the way one reinvented [such adventures] in one's childhood games: a series of gunfights where the *pistoleros* never stop conceding encores".[6] The fact that these men act with such abandon and élan, without the ethical or logical constraints imposed upon conventional genre heroes, was both a slap in the face to puritanical critics and a refreshing surprise for receptive audiences bored with the classical formula and its staid heroes. At last, they had 'cowboys' that thought and acted in a 'realistic', contemporary manner far removed from the romanticism previously prescribed.

In pro-bounty hunter films, he is lauded as both tactician and technician. Based in an unstable environment governed by treachery and deceit, these titles glorify the central character's ability to outsmart his opponents just as much as his ability to outgun them. The atmosphere of mistrust in *For a Few Dollars More* comes to a head in the robbery sequence, in which Mortimer surprises Monco in Agua Caliente, having anticipated that the younger man would ride in the opposite direction from the one they had previously agreed upon. "I just reasoned it out," he explains, knowing full well that Indio, being of the same mind-set, wouldn't trust Monco's suggestion to ride south and instead would lead them east. As spectators, we are invited to admire both Monco's underhandedness, resulting as it usually does in the acquisition of wealth, and Mortimer's powers of rationalisation. Either way, deception – the ability to practise it and to discern it in others – is seen as key to survival.

As demonstrated by their unapologetic choice of profession, these protagonists are abiding by different rules from the majority of their American western counterparts, a much looser set of regulations that allow for more spontaneous action irrespective of either moral considerations or society's displeasure. The irreverence of the bounty hunter, the crafty way he manipulates the law to his advantage, probably accounts to a large extent for his popularity as a character, especially in a period – the Sixties – when authority in all its guises – state, church, family, education – was facing unprecedented popular opposition. More conjecturally, his ruthless, reckless, money-grabbing mentality may well have fed into aspirational audience fantasies of wealth and upward mobility. In *Ringo and His Golden Pistol* (1966), Mark Damon's impertinent, restlessly acquisitive anti-hero mocks noble Sheriff Norton (Ettore Manni) for his adherence to a code of honour that could lead to the destruction of his town. It is only when the sheriff allows the more imaginative, less scrupulous Ringo a free hand against the Mexican/Indian besiegers that the situation is resolved. Hank Fellows (Craig Hill), the protagonist of Tonino Valerii's directorial debut, *A Taste for Killing* (1966), is another stranger to probity. Hank, whose motto is "you can never have too much money", favours a long-range rifle fitted with telescopic sight for maximum advantage and, as the film opens, he watches from afar as bandits attack an army escort, only tracking the felons *after* they have slaughtered the soldiers so he can 'earn' a higher reward. Despite the introduction of a revenge motive (the film's villain, played by George Martin, murdered Hank's brother), Hank remains a rather shallow mercenary but, again, he is slick, quick-witted and successful on his own terms. In another entertaining but uneven western, *Dead Men Don't Count!* (1968), wisecracking bounty hunters Fred (Anthony Steffen) and Johnny (Mark Damon) are horrified when a judge refers to them as "men of honour" after they intervene in a land dispute. This is clearly not how they would like to think of themselves. They also find it hilarious that a woman (María Martín playing one of the genre's 'black widows' with a murderous past) has mistaken Johnny for her long-lost son, mocking her misplaced maternal feelings even as she kills a man on Johnny's behalf.

Sincerity, sentimentalism, emotional attachments, civic duty – all factors that entrapped heroes in traditional American and early European westerns – were rejected and scorned by this new breed of bounty hunter. He is a professional cynic, the anti-hero of choice for an ignominious era. He shuns responsibilities and respects only money; even human beings are reduced to the status of merchandise, their worth measured purely in monetary terms. Whereas this line of thinking develops like an ailment in James Stewart's Howard Kemp in *The Naked Spur*, triggering a moral crisis for him, in Euro-westerns it is more often the source of cruel humour. Monco tallies up the corpses of Indio's gang at the end of *For a Few Dollars More* as if he was counting stacks of money rather than bodies. (This was one of Sergio Donati's key contributions to the script: "[In the original screenplay] Clint Eastwood looks at the corpses and names them, realises that one is missing and he shoots him. I thought it was more in the Leone spirit – and in the spirit of the movie – to have him count, '$2,000, $3,000, $4,000' and so on."[7]) The catch-and-release game played by Blondie and Tuco in *The Good, the Bad and the Ugly* (1966) – alluded to or copied in a number of other westerns – is cold-blooded comedy at its most acute. After disposing of the bounty hunter who has just killed his outlaw father in *Django Shoots First* (1966), the title figure (Glenn Saxson) decides to collect the reward himself, reasoning that, "It's a shame to let that money go to waste." And perennial sidekick Pedro Sanchez [Ignazio Spalla] lends comic relief to the violent revenge western *May God Forgive You – I Won't* (1968), as a scurrilous scavenger who doesn't even kill or capture his own prey; he simply bribes undertakers to release the bodies of outlaws, which he then turns in for the reward.

above: Dutch actor Roel Bos (*left*) changed his name to Glenn Saxson and joined the ranks of the Euro-western's amoral adventurers in films like **Django Shoots First**, a light-hearted bounty hunter story studded with fight scenes.

above: British front-of-house still displaying an alternative title for **Django Shoots First**.

below: Blood brothers: many westerns suggest that bounty hunters and bandits are merely two sides of the same coin. Romolo Guerrieri's **$10,000 Blood Money** develops the theme more thoroughly than most, as Gianni Garko (*right*) and Claudio Camaso (*left*) complement each other's rapacity, cunning and ruthless flair.

gunfighter played by Hunt Powers cites "honour and revenge" as his motivations, fitting director Demofilo Fidani's quaintly colour-coded world view. (Fidani was a big fan of bounty killers; they feature in two of his other 'Django' films, *Django and Sartana Are Coming... It's the End* and *One Damned Day at Dawn... Django Meets Sartana!*, as well as in *Dead Men Don't Make Shadows*, all 1970.) For Guy Madison's ex-bounty hunter in Marino Girolami's *Reverend Colt* (1970), vengeance for his assassinated father had been his driving force until he accidentally shot and killed an innocent child and turned to religion in expiation. He still carries a gun, but uses it to warn off or wound opponents rather than to kill, and piously preaches tolerance and non-violence for the duration of the film.

Two of the finest studies of bounty hunting are Romolo Guerrieri's *$10,000 Blood Money* and its companion piece, Giovanni Fago's *For $100,000 Per Killing* (both 1967). Our first impressions of the central figure – played with able conviction in both cases by Gianni Garko – are that he epitomises the laid-back, carefree, cold-blooded killer for money, with a mordant wit and a flair for the theatrical. (Garko is literally at repose as both films begin: in *$10,000*, his character is relaxing on a beach, conversing with the corpse of his latest victim; in the second film, he lies in wait in a coffin to surprise a bandit gang.) Yet the scripts, written largely by Ernesto Gastaldi, have more substance than others in this category, verging on tragic drama, and quickly curtail the moral freedom the bounty hunters seem to enjoy. Their emotional detachment crumbles as a conflict of interest arises – love versus avarice in the first film, hatred against blood ties in the second. Both films employ a doubling device, a common motif in male-centred action narratives, to voice criticism of the protagonists and the nature of their business. In *$10,000 Blood Money*, Django is twinned with bandit Manuel Vasquez (Claudio Camaso), who asserts that both are "like merchants, dealing in blood". His point is proved early on when Django, having belittled Manuel as a "three-bill bandit" and challenged him to increase his 'value', provokes him into killing a poker cheat, even taking a share of the dead man's money, and later when he agrees to help the outlaw hijack a gold shipment. The distinction between hunter and hunted is even more ambiguous in the second film, since Garko's John Forest and Camaso's outlaw, Clint, are half-brothers, jostling with contradictory emotions that culminate in a showdown of pathological intensity that resembles, without quite rivalling, the famous conclusion of Anthony Mann's *Winchester '73* (1950). In Gastaldi's melodramatic scenario, John had been imprisoned in Clint's stead for the killing of the latter's father, but has to balance his vengeful desire against their mother's dying wish that he bring Clint to justice rather than kill him. His efforts to do so result, as in the previous film, in the death of his lover, and prove ultimately futile. The complementary nature of

The most bizarre examples of this satirical treatment of the theme are the two 'Providence' movies, in which Tomas Milian's protagonist follows price fluctuations on the bounty-hunting equivalent of the stock market.

This ironic reverence for the bounty hunter's dark arts is not universally shared. Certain films explore the root cause of his cynicism in an attempt to engage with the moral issues he provokes and to provide more complex, or at least more rounded, characters. We learn in *For a Few Dollars More*, for example, that Mortimer, like Kemp in *The Naked Spur*, was reduced to this ignoble profession by economic difficulties in the aftermath of the Civil War. (Presumably, the killing of his sister by Indio had something to do with it, but Mortimer never states as much.) In *The Ballad of Django* (1971), the eponymous

the characters, casts and themes extends to the morbid, haunting mood and style of the films, with elegiac scores by the underrated Nora Orlandi and landscapes marked by death and decrepitude. The bounty hunter's way of living and killing is shown to have both cause and effect. For both protagonists, triumph equates with defeat and leaves each man contemplating an empty future.

This equivocation towards the central character extends to Enzo Castellari's modest first western, *A Few Dollars for Django* (1966), in which Anthony Steffen's bounty hunter is almost lynched when, after posing as a town's sheriff, his true vocation is discovered. The residents' anger is not due to his deception but because of their contempt for his kind.[8] More interesting is *The Bounty Killer* (1966), Eugenio Martín's compelling siege western adapted from a novel by Marvin H. Albert, whose works had previously formed the basis of several impressive American westerns, among them *The Law and Jake Wade* (1958) and *Duel at Diablo* (1966). Here, British actor Richard Wyler's hard-hearted Luke Chilson encounters the hostility of a small, isolated township when he seeks the reward for outlaw José Gomez (Tomas Milian in his first western). José is a local hero, considered a victim of circumstance by his friends, and, at first, the townsfolk aid him in restraining Chilson. Eventually, the depredations of José and his men give the lie to the locals' naïve assumptions and they transfer their support to the bounty killer. Wyler/Chilson makes a solid, flawed hero (comparable to the actor's roles in *Rattler Kid* and *Turn... I'll Kill You*, both 1967), but he never elicits our sympathy or that of the townsfolk except at the most basic level – that is, in opposition to José and his associates. The film's focus shifts swiftly and decisively to Milian, giving a multi-faceted performance that debunks the romantic myth of the social bandit, the same character-type Milian went on to portray so vigorously in his political westerns. (Martín's film, incidentally, is held in unusually high regard in Spain, where critics have generally tended to overlook the European western. According to Spanish film historian Carlos Aguilar, "*The Bounty Killer* was one of the few westerns directed by a Spaniard that was commercially and critically successful. It won several official prizes, and today is considered a classic of Spanish cinema, beyond any particular genre.")

Elsewhere, Sergio Garrone's lively *No Room to Die* (1969) and José Luis Merino's offbeat *More Dollars for the McGregors* (1970) also view this trade with a deal of displeasure.[9] The former tells a common story of two rival bounty hunters who enter into an unsteady alliance – in this case to smash a slave-labour market – but there's a distinction drawn between them. Whereas Brandon (Anthony Steffen) possesses a modicum of decency, his counterpart, Murdock (William Berger), is irredeemably venal and corrupt. As is so often the case, the bad guy is the more flamboyant figure – a false preacher, modelled,

above: **No Room to Die** teamed Anthony Steffen (*right*) as a straight-shooting bounty hunter and William Berger (*left*) as his mendacious, Bible-bashing rival.

outwardly at least, on Colonel Mortimer, complete with customised weapon (a multi-barrelled shotgun) and a personal file of wanted posters – but this is chiefly because Berger, who excelled in morally unsavoury roles of this nature, plays the part with tongue-in-cheek relish, in sharp contrast to the dry and monosyllabic Steffen. Just as reprehensible but in a different manner is George Forsyte (Carlos Quiney) in *More Dollars*, who owes much

above: Giovanni Fago's **For $100,000 Per Killing**, like many other Euro-westerns in Germany, was advertised as a follow-up to **Django**.

above: Anthony Steffen finds that scruples rarely pay off in Euro-westerns, as he bids to thwart a people-trafficking racket in **No Room to Die**.
bottom right: A bounty hunter's ruthlessness rebounds on his wife in José Luis Merino's gloomy western, sold abroad as an extension of the 'MacGregors' franchise under the title **More Dollars for the McGregors**.

Seven Guns for the MacGregors and *Sugar Colt* (both 1966) – was abbreviated in some versions of the film, but is entirely apposite. It is precisely the kind of disconcerting conclusion reached by many of the most defining films of the Sixties and Seventies: from *Bonnie and Clyde* (1967), *Easy Rider* (1969) and *Zabriskie Point* (1970) to *The Wild Bunch* (1969) and *Pat Garrett and Billy the Kid* (1973), rebels and romantics cannot be accommodated in the type of society that shackles and subordinates its subjects.

Still more pessimistic is the justly celebrated *The Great Silence*, which posits bounty hunting as a form of social cleansing. If Corbucci's *Django* (1966) can be classed as an anti-western – and the director said as much himself – then this film is an *anti-European* western, in that it either inverts or inquires into many of the genre's well-established clichés, conventions and characterisations. In Corbucci's allegorical terms, the bounty hunters led by Loco (a masterly interpretation of insidious evil by Klaus Kinski) are not laconic, ironic anti-heroes but agents of oppression, assassins hired by the rich to kill the poor. And where most Euro-westerns are content to portray banditry as an end in itself, a source of pleasure and fulfilment for the perpetrators, here crime is put into its socio-economic context. Corbucci's 'criminals' are just ordinary men unable to find work – largely the fault of wealthy Policutt (Luigi Pistilli), the man who pays the bounties – and forced to

of his success at bounty hunting to his wife, who acts as a decoy to trap bandits. Inevitably, one such trap fails and the woman is killed, leaving George a shattered man who will eventually submit to death at the hands of his vengeful brother-in-law (Peter Lee Lawrence).

In virtually all cases, whether the bounty hunter is viewed in an ironic-positive light or with greater circumspection, he is portrayed as a symptom of society's ills. No matter how distasteful his methods, his function is still broadly beneficial given the virulence of his quarry. This is not the case, however, in the final two films I wish to discuss. In Franco Giraldi's *A Minute to Pray, a Second to Die* (1968), released in the UK as *Dead or Alive*, and Sergio Corbucci's *The Great Silence* (1968), the usual order is upturned. Here, the hunters are unequivocally the villains, while outlaws and outcasts are the victims; the former are also intimately associated with political corruption and social injustice, the long arm of a short-sighted and narrow-minded legal system that persecutes the most vulnerable members of society. In Giraldi's film they play a relatively minor role, but are so vile as to be almost self-parodic. Shortly before killing a priest whom they suspect of harbouring a wanted man, two bounty hunters (Antonio Molino Rojo and Aldo Sambrell) reveal that they decapitate their victims – why lug heavy corpses around with them when the heads will serve as proof? In the complete version of the film, the ending also has the ring of bitter irony, not so much because it involves the death of Alex Cord's outlaw hero, who has been marked for doom throughout, but because bounty hunters shoot him down *after* he has been pardoned, the governor's newly imposed amnesty having taken them by surprise. This wretched outcome – quite a mood swing for a director best known for two highly successful comic westerns,

eke out a precarious existence in the white-blanketed mountains surrounding fictitious Snow Hill, looting and robbing when the opportunity arises. (Their pathetic plight is reminiscent of the misfits who inhabit Escondido, a lawless enclave run by profiteers in *A Minute to Pray, a Second to Die*, as well as the flotsam of Puerto de Fuego, a similarly self-contained commune in Sergio Sollima's *Face to Face* [1967]. In each case the unwanted element is physically excluded from society – voluntarily in Sollima's film – but not quite beyond its reach.) Furthermore, they have all suffered from persecution of one kind or another. Since the film is set in Utah (doubled by the Dolomite Mountains in Cortina d'Ampezzo), it seems reasonable to suppose that at least some among the outcasts are Mormons. Viewed sympathetically in a number of Euro-westerns, most famously *They Call Me Trinity* (1970), the Mormons in reality experienced plenty of travails, territorial disputes and violent episodes in their trek westward across America in the mid-19th Century. In *The Great Silence*, the outcasts' leader, anticipating an amnesty, pointedly assures his followers that "we'll soon be able to *think* as we want" (my emphasis). At any rate, they are a long way from being "enemies of God and man", as Loco would have it, justifying his bloody campaign on the grounds of patriotism and in the name of authority – "all according to the law" is his cynical refrain.

Ranged against the inequity that Loco and Policutt keep in place are the mute gunfighter, Silence (Jean-Louis Trintignant), scourge of bounty hunters and whose own 'trade' is to kill them (in an unacknowledged irony he, too, profits from the poor, who pay him for each hit), and Burnett (Frank Wolff), the bumbling but altruistic sheriff of Snow Hill. These men are similar in style and action to Loco – again we have the notion of symmetry between characters – but very different in manner and thinking. They express, in their own ways, the film's ideological arguments. Wolff's portrayal is uncustomary on two counts, in that it's an unusually sympathetic role for him and a surprisingly generous depiction of a Euro-western lawman. (Gastone Moschin enacts a similar character in Corbucci's subsequent *The Specialists* [1969], released in the UK as *Drop Them or I'll Shoot*.) Burnett finds himself in a difficult position, a champion of the same laws that Loco, who irritates the sheriff with his sarcastic complaisance, professes to be upholding. Both men are legally sanctioned to kill transgressors, and so we are left with an ethical conundrum that is as relevant today as it was in 1968 and, indeed, in 1898, when the film is set – what is justice and whom does it serve? There is no answer here, only opinions. Neither Burnett's ("When the law kills it's not murder but punishment") nor Loco's is convincing, while Corbucci's is as bleak as the freezing conditions.

above: Outlaw blues: hounded by bounty hunters and plagued by muscle spasms and anxieties, Alex Cord cuts a lonely figure in Franco Giraldi's **A Minute to Pray, a Second to Die**.

above: Spanish poster for Sergio Corbucci's **The Great Silence**.
top right: Jean-Louis Trintignant, as the tragic Silence, meets Pauline (Vonetta McGee), the widow who hires him and later becomes his lover
opposite top: Trintignant effortlessly expressed emotions without the encumbrance of clichéd dialogue.
opposite bottom: Trintignant tussles with Mario Brega, cast as usual as a daunting brute, in one of the genre's most vicious fight scenes.

For this left-wing director, as for so many socially conscious filmmakers in the Sixties, justice as defined by the state has very little meaning for those that society discriminates against, represented here by the freethinkers and by Pauline (a dignified first performance by American actress Vonetta McGee), widow of a black man murdered by Loco, with some amusement that his 'value' is equal to a white's. The only law that governs these people's existence is that of survival. For the outlaws and their families this is attained by petty crime, menial labour and personal sacrifice, but to prosper in this kind of environment rather than merely exist, characters must surrender their principles, their beliefs, their compassion and their pride – the bounty hunters, with their complete lack of scruples, are simply better acclimatised to these conditions than those who oppose them.

Silence, who delivers justice of a different kind, is another of Corbucci's patented maimed protagonists, bearing the physical and psychological scars of a tragic and traumatic past. (The director's penchant for dismemberment is illustrated by Silence's habit of shooting off the thumbs of his enemies, ensuring they can never fire a gun again.) For Trintignant, appearing in his only western, the absence of throwaway dialogue

was key to his acceptance of the role: "In most westerns they talk too much and say nothing," he commented.[10] (It is no coincidence that many non-Italian actors starring in Euro-westerns insisted on shearing away or adjusting much of their dialogue to improve their performances – it is one of Clint Eastwood's most famous contributions to the success of the 'Dollars' films, and every American actor I interviewed for this book stressed how they did the same thing.) This makes his characterisation that much more stoical, although Silence's enslavement to his code of never-shoot-first, which leads ultimately to his doom, is difficult to comprehend unless one accepts that Corbucci felt the need to compromise his character to make the film's sobering political message register all the more forcefully. Silence is also a living testament to injustice: years previously, his father was cold-bloodedly killed by bounty hunters (working for Policutt) who then slashed the young boy's throat. In one sense, then, Silence is fighting 'the system' – the target of so much popular anger and opposition around the time this film was made – and *The Great Silence* is all the more radical and remarkable compared with its contemporaries in that the system wins. Policutt is killed, but his death only serves to close the circle of Silence's revenge, which isn't the main thrust of the film; while the exploitation, corruption and complicity Policutt represents lives on. The numbing

above: Klaus Kinski, subdued to chilling effect, as the cynical Loco.

effect of this downbeat denouement – regarded as too shocking and not commercially viable for some markets – is exacerbated by the unusual care and sensitivity with which the central characters are portrayed and directed.[11]

For Corbucci, *The Great Silence* was, in some ways, his own *Django, Kill!* (1967) – a critical commentary on the escapism and perceived vacuity of Italian westerns made up to that point. It's instructive to compare the famous climax of this film with that of *Django*: in both cases, the title characters have crippled hands and other injuries and must confront a far greater number of adversaries. But whereas Django triumphs and survives, Silence loses and dies. One ending sustains heroic myth; the other shatters it. This seems to indicate profound disillusionment on the director's part, recognition of the fallibility even of heroes in increasingly violent times, a comment, in part, on developments in the world around him. And yet, in the same year, he made the first of his rousing, idealistic political parables, *A Professional Gun*, with the more ambiguous *Compañeros* following in 1970. In those films, Corbucci – influenced by and perhaps genuinely imbued with the exuberance of the global mood for change, the vaunted 'spirit of '68' – celebrates the power of popular pressure in the fight against oppression in the Third World. But closer to home, in so-called democracies, he tells us that resistance is futile, whether it be the platitudes of politicians, the earnest efforts of Burnett (whose advice to the outlaws leads inadvertently to their capture and deaths), the defiance of Pauline, the endurance of the outlaws or the obstinate, almost suicidal heroism of Silence. In that sense, *The Great Silence* anticipates, to an extent, the ultimate failure of the May uprisings (a failure that would inform *Compañeros* in a different way). With this bleak and powerful social statement, the director, whose career encapsulates perhaps more than any of his contemporaries' the contradictions and conflicting demands of commercial cinema, set aside fantasy in favour of cold reality. (There is even an element of neorealism, in Corbucci's heroisation of the suffering classes.)

His reworking of the bounty-hunter motif is a case in point. Like all such figures in the genre, Loco and his acolytes are victorious by slyly exploiting loopholes in the law and the fears and prejudices of society; they know how to play the system, not so much making up the rules as interpreting them to their advantage. But their success is not something we can cheer or share, nor are their victims the usual psychopaths and reprobates. It is a triumph that crushes not just attractive individuals – Silence, Pauline, Burnett – but the dream of freedom embodied by the captive outlaws, who are mercilessly slaughtered "all according to the law". Despite the epitaph that precedes the closing credits, promising that ameliorative action was taken to curb the bounty hunters' cruelty, no other film in the genre concludes on such a dispiriting, bravely, brutally honest note.[12]

"Isn't a sheriff supposed to be courageous, loyal and above all honest?"

Corbucci's subtext in *The Great Silence* expresses the view, widely held in the genre, that officialdom is self-seeking and corrupt. Any voices of protest are silenced – literally, in the hero's case. This aspect of the films has tended to be overlooked or dismissed by mainstream critics as little more than fashionable anti-authoritarianism, just as the majority of political westerns were derided as radical chic – this was the Sixties, after all, and the kind of audience that would have flocked to films of this nature would, it is assumed, have been predisposed to this kind of thinking. There is, no doubt, some truth in this. The new-wave Euro-western, like any commercial film trend, was largely driven by the demands and tastes of its spectators, and it was common practice for writers to slip facile social statements into the most routine of screenplays. But this only partially accounts for the genre's derogation of public figures. While American westerns have often portrayed individual lawmen, business leaders, landowners and politicians as rotten apples, in Italian examples the problem is endemic. Sir Christopher Frayling notes that in Sergio Leone's conception of the west, which chimed with or was followed by the majority of his peers, "corruption [among officials] was a structural problem", the director giving his fantasies what he called a "documentary basis" and countering the myth of the incorruptible marshal with a representation he felt was more likely to be closer to the truth.[13] Monco's exposing of the complicity of White Rocks's sheriff in *For a Few Dollars More* (see the quote that opens this section) is an early indication of a satirical/critical attitude towards authority that quickly lost its bite through overuse. In innumerable Italian westerns, the lawman is not an upright figure but a criminal hiding behind a badge. Very often, he is in league with bandits and/or a cartel of 'respectable' citizens – bankers, judges, mayors, etc. – who are shown to have abused their positions and the public trust to acquire wealth and power.[14] This type of scenario is almost as widespread in the genre as the town-tyrant and revenge plots, with both of which it often overlaps. As Luigi Barzini tells us, Italians are notoriously mistrustful of anyone in authority (and, by extension, social climbers and the moneyed elite), suspecting their positions are owed to anything from nepotism to blackmail, on which the recurrence of plots like these, with their far from surprising twists and revelations, may well have been intended to capitalise.[15]

Running alongside this populist plot-type is a stream of titles that may be labelled 'anti-populist'. Here, it is not only the head but also the body of the community that is infected. Such scepticism, which sometimes escalates into outright antipathy, contrasts sharply with the romantic view of small communities and their

above: Giuliano Gemma as the principled pistolero in **Day of Anger**, here attracting the attention of the judge's daughter (Anna Orso).
right: Kill or be killed: Gemma's misplaced compassion proves too little, too late for the stricken Al Mulock in **Day of Anger**.

inhabitants in typical American westerns. We are closer here to what Will Wright, in *Sixguns and Society*, called the 'transition theme', at its peak in the Fifties, in which the values and virtues of the social group, previously upheld to be the very fount of civilisation, are called into question. In Wright's 'transition' westerns, which included *Broken Arrow* (1950), *High Noon* (1952) and *Johnny Guitar* (1954), there was a clear correlation between the fictional social group and contemporary American society – criticism of one implicitly referred to the other. Although removed from this cultural context, the aims of the 'anti-populist' Euro-westerns are broadly similar. In part, they were challenging what was still, 'transition' films notwithstanding, a prominent western convention – the bland and/or benign depiction of small communities, giving the latter more of an active part in the drama: that of a negative force to be overcome. Again, this can be read as a displaced comment on the dissatisfaction and alienation of modern man, and supplies evidence of the popularity of parable and metaphor in popular Italian culture, where the moral of the story, whatever form the story takes and however colourfully it is told, is the primary consideration. Portraying society as seething with hypocrisy, corruption and prejudice is consistent with the genre's predominantly bleak view of humanity, as well as its preference for outcasts and cynical observers over conventional western heroes. The trend reached its apex in the early- and mid-Seventies, typified by a rather synthetic series of pro-Native-American westerns, as well as by powerful films such as *The Four of the Apocalypse* (1975) and *Keoma* (1976). This was when the genre was at its most nakedly, self-consciously contemporary in terms of its allusions and concerns – its heroes began to resemble political crusaders and civil-rights campaigners, while themes such as racism, reactionism, ethnicity and oppression were dominant. (For more on this period in the genre's history, see *Desolation and Deconstruction*.)

In the best-known and most extreme of the genre's 'social critiques', Giulio Questi's *Django, Kill!*, civilisation is virtually indistinguishable from savagery: strangers are greeted in town with suspicion and violence; gold fever mutates into mass, murderous hysteria; and perversion lurks behind every door. The bulk of the townsfolk bend easily to stronger wills, which has alarming implications in a film that alludes, among other things, to fascism. *Day of Anger* (1967) by Tonino Valerii offers a subtler subversion of traditional western mores, challenging and demystifying genre tropes – in particular the venerated 'lore of the West' as embodied by the gunfighter – at the same time as lambasting power-figures. The high-minded notables of Clifton despise Scott Mary (Giuliano Gemma) for being a bastard, fit only to clean out the toilets and

above: An example of the superior stunt work (arranged by Benito Stefanelli, one of the film's supporting players) in **Day of Anger**.

sewers. Yet four of its leading citizens – the same "clean hands" that consider Scott untouchable – once concocted a robbery scheme over which they are being blackmailed by unscrupulous gunfighter Frank Talby (Lee Van Cleef). Scott regains his pride, and a measure of revenge, by helping Talby effectively take over the town ("He was born a wolf – you made him rabid, not me", Talby responds to charges that he has corrupted the youth), but ultimately he asserts his moral superiority over both Talby and his late tormentors by renouncing his reign. Sergio Corbucci's predilection for social commentary recurs in *The Specialists*, a deceptively innocuous vehicle for French rock star Johnny Hallyday. (It had first been announced as a project for Lee Van Cleef.) Having discovered the collective guilt of Blackstone's residents in the death of his brother, Hallyday's *pistolero* spitefully burns the town's money, which his sibling was lynched for 'stealing' and is clearly all the locals care about. Corbucci underlines his contempt for the citizens – stand-ins for the bourgeoisie and cold-hearted capitalism – by having them stripped by hippies, who are arguably even lower in the director's estimation, and forced to slither along the street.

Parochialism can also equate with puritanism, with 'immoral' characters made scapegoats for the community's repressive tendencies and repressed desires. This is the premise of *Tails, You Lose...* (1969), the penultimate film by peplum specialist Piero Pierotti, who died a year after making it. Here, fanatical female moralists (a nod in the direction of Mercedes McCambridge's Emma Small in *Johnny Guitar*) instigate a witch-hunt against Shanda (Sheyla Rosin) and her saloon girls to "expiate" the town's sins. Inevitably, there is hypocrisy here – the leader of the moralists has ordered the murder of her husband, pinning the blame on Shanda, and derives undisguised sado-erotic pleasure from seeing the "harlots" whipped. (The maenadic fury of the puritans anticipates a similar scene in Pasquale Squitieri's *Vengeance Trail* [1971], the most potent of Italy's responses to *Soldier Blue*. In Squitieri's film, a young Indian girl, considered a 'savage', is stripped and brutalised by an angry crowd of 'civilised' white townsfolk, an action that aids the enlightenment of the film's Indian-hating anti-hero.) The theme of injustice is undermined, however, along with any liberal intent, by the film's flagrant misogyny – the female villain is turned on by violence, while Shanda, marginalised for much of the running time, has to rely on a man (John Ericson) to clear her name and avenge her punishment. Similar ideas are put across more successfully in *The Price of Death* (1971), in which the killing of a prostitute brings to light the murky secrets and double standards of a sanctimonious town, director Enzo Gicca Palli using this platform to satirise rough justice, religion and provincial propriety. The film also makes wonderful use of the scapegoat motif, with a belligerent Klaus Kinski cleared of one killing only to be justly condemned for another.

An especially damning portrait of a social group (read society) is found in Sergio Corbucci's unfairly maligned *Navajo Joe* (1966). Unusually for a European-made western, the focus here is on the animosity between whites and Native Americans, or, to give a more accurate reflection of the film's ideological position, the oppression of the latter by the former. Not that Corbucci and his writers, Ugo Pirro and Fernando Di Leo, show much concern for historical veracity where the titular tribe is concerned; then again, the tribes are interchangeable in most 'Indian' westerns – the only reason for singling out this one is because it proffers a Native American hero. *Navajo Joe* was packaged like a straightforward action/revenge flick – an attempt to do for Burt Reynolds (whose disparaging comments over the years have contributed to the film's poor reputation) what the 'Dollars' trilogy had done for Clint Eastwood – and it can be enjoyed or dismissed on that basis. The filmmakers' antagonistic approach to genre conventions, however, makes it more rewarding. The town of Esperanza seems, on the surface, like a classic Fordian settlement: the people are God-fearing and hard working, newly awarded a $500,000 grant from the state to build for the future; but they're also small-minded, bigoted and weak-willed. Threatened by a band of renegade scalphunters, they are forced to accept the help of Reynolds's Joe, a lone Navajo warrior whose motivation has less to do with saving the town than with settling a personal score with the villains. Besides contrasting the citizens' collective impotence and helplessness with Joe's virility and self-assurance, the irony of the arrangement is twofold: the townsfolk neither trust nor like Indians, while Joe's qualified offer of assistance underlines his contempt for their weakness and hypocrisy, as well as their enslavement to the dollar – he knows that charging them for his services is hitting them where it hurts. He mocks white law by demanding to be appointed sheriff for the duration of his campaign. Told that the position is reserved for 'Americans' only, he points out to the incredulous incumbent that while the latter is the son of immigrants, Joe's own ancestors have always been natives: "Now which of us is American?" To Joe, the star is, therefore, a symbol of the continuing discrimination against his people; his point made, he never actually wears it. It is not integration into this prejudicial society that he desires – that would signal the acceptance of defeat and the second-class status that goes with it, something suffered by Nicoletta Machiavelli's Estella, an Indian girl who works in Esperanza as a white woman's maid. Joe prefers the isolation of the mountains and the ghostly surroundings of his ancestral burial ground, a poignant reminder that the land hereabouts was home to another civilisation long before it was forcibly cleared to make way for Esperanza.

The culpability of the community is revealed by its relationship to the film's other principal character. In psychoanalytical readings of the western, Native Americans are traditionally interpreted as white society's id, but here it is not Joe but the scalphunters' vociferous leader, Duncan (Aldo Sambrell), who manifests the deepest urges of Esperanza. In one sense he is their creation: in times past they would pay him a dollar per scalp (the same price that Joe charges, from each man in the community, hence the film's Italian title, *Un dollaro a testa*), but now that the Indian threat has been contained, Duncan and his men are both an embarrassment and a danger to them. "That was the best character that anybody offered me," remembered Sambrell – unsurprisingly, since he was more often cast as henchman than head honcho – and he didn't waste the opportunity. Given considerable licence by Corbucci, Sambrell creates one of the most malevolent and spiteful of genre villains, a half-breed who turns a lifetime of rage and resentment against both whites and Native Americans. "Nobody ever had mercy on me", he snarls when Esperanza's priest begs

above, opposite top and below: The only good Indians… Native American protagonists were a rarity in Euro-westerns. In **Navajo Joe**, Sergio Corbucci cast Burt Reynolds – partly of Cherokee descent – and Nicoletta Machiavelli as symbols of racial oppression.

him to spare the town, illustrating his ruthlessness in the next instant by needlessly killing his beseecher. While he and Joe separately express the 'anti-populist' aspect of the film, demonstrating once more the kinship common among western antagonists, this diminishes as the characters' personal conflict escalates. Joe systematically wipes out Duncan's band in a series of violent skirmishes, culminating in a showdown between anti-hero and villain at the burial ground where each man eliminates the other. Corbucci once again sacrifices his protagonist, the better to contrast his fortitude and conviction with the callousness and self-interest of Esperanza, the town he indirectly liberates, whose residents don't even care to investigate their saviour's fate once they have their money back in their hands.**16**

"If trust gets you a penny, distrust will get you millions"

With its double-dealing dual protagonists, *For a Few Dollars More* codified the rules of survival and advancement that were followed by a vast number of subsequent films. The theme of friction between two or more adventurers sharing the same goal or chasing the same prize is widespread in the genre and occurs in all manner of plots – everything from treasure hunts and revenge scenarios to mentor-pupil rivalries and the slapstick comedies of the Seventies. Characters are guided through these stories by suspiciousness, duplicity and ruthlessness. Motives are rarely what they seem, alliances are only ever temporary, allegiances shift with the sand. The characters' cynical assumptions are based on experience – the world mapped out in Euro-westerns is an ugly and pitiless place, in which betrayal is to be expected and compassion a sign of weakness, from which the unholy glow of gold promises escape or at least the opportunity to make the best of a bad deal. It is a world of characteristically pessimistic Italian imagining, conforming to deep-rooted cultural preconceptions and deriving from a centuries-old dramatic and literary tradition that assumes the worst in humanity, and celebrates the strong and the quick-witted over the meek and the noble.

The most vivid rendition of this environment and its opportunistic inhabitants is undoubtedly *The Good, the Bad and the Ugly*, in which Sergio Leone, Luciano Vincenzoni and Sergio Donati expanded upon the format of *For a Few Dollars More* and firmly established the picaresque plot type, inspiring a slew of similarly themed, seriocomic treasure-hunt westerns. Celebrated critic Raymond Durgnat astutely summarised this masterly work as "the code of the west as it might have been interpreted by Machiavelli", a reference to the much-misunderstood political philosopher, statesman and playwright who insisted that principles had no place in politics or the pursuit of power. The irony of Leone's title reflects Machiavellian thinking in that clean moral divisions between the protagonists cannot be drawn. This idea is central to the construction and meaning of the European western. As in life and as in the old west itself, there are only subtle degrees of separation between characters. Angel Eyes is that much more ruthless than the others (one can't imagine Blondie or Tuco slaughtering whole families with such apparent relish); Blondie is a smarter strategist than the emotional Tuco; the Mexican – tactile, excitable – is

above: Clint Eastwood, Eli Wallach and Lee Van Cleef aim for iconic status on the set of **The Good, the Bad and the Ugly**, one of the most influential westerns of its era.

the most sympathetic of the trio. All three demonstrate great cruelty, although, just as their movements are juxtaposed with the manoeuvres of the armies, so their savagery is diminished by the immense, fratricidal violence of the Civil War. Every action is calculated according to the characters' convenience – identities assumed and discarded, armies temporarily joined and abandoned, partnerships formed and dissolved. The business arrangement of Blondie and Tuco is severed by selfishness and mutual suspicion; Angel Eyes proposes an alliance with Blondie, who breaks it off to take up with Tuco again. Ultimately, everyone is on his own side.

Attempts to condense the spirit and themes so brilliantly realised in Leone's epic were manifold. Setting the shenanigans within the context of a quest for gold or a wider conflict proved especially popular, providing the opportunity for all manner of vicissitudes, contrasts and violent or comic encounters. Enzo Castellari's *Any Gun Can Play* (1967) was a response to the success of *The Good, the Bad and the Ugly* (even the Italian title was based on a line spoken by Tuco in that film), following the squabble for $300,000 in stolen army gold between a bounty hunter (George Hilton, in a role Castellari wanted Charles Bronson for), a swindler (Edd Byrnes) and a bandit (Gilbert Roland). Again, they make and break alliances at will, reacting to each double-cross with ironic resignation. Castellari followed this with *Kill Them All and Come Back Alone* (1968), in which an excellent cast (including Chuck Connors, Frank Wolff, Leo Anchóriz and Franco Citti) band together for a dangerous robbery scheme during the Civil War. Although the plot is basically pilfered from *The Dirty Dozen* (1967), there are also explicit references to *The Good, the Bad and the Ugly*. There are many false trails laid and tricks enacted, and Frank Wolff's 'Confederate' officer later turns out to be running a Union prison camp, *à la* Angel Eyes, and confesses to having worn "many uniforms" to acquire cash from different sources. (A later film by Tonino Valerii, *A Reason to Live, a Reason to Die* [1972], runs over similar ground in more muted fashion, with disgraced Union officer James Coburn trying to marshal seven reprobates plucked from the gallows to seize a strategic fort.) Another Civil War adventure with Leone leanings, Nando Cicero's *Red Blood, Yellow Gold* (1967), follows three rogues on a mission to steal back a shipment of Union gold that changes hands several times over the course of the film (traitorous soldiers are involved, as well as the obligatory Mexican bandits). What's noteworthy here is that in a plot where treachery is a major theme, the three protagonists remain doggedly loyal to each other, maintaining a sense of duty that is sufficiently rare in this class of film to be significant. (Other 'ensemble westerns' boasting camaraderie of this kind include *Five Giants from Texas* [1966], *Death Walks in Laredo* [1967], *No Graves on Boot Hill* [1968], *Today It's Me... Tomorrow You!* [1968], *The Five Man Army* [1969] and *Chuck*

above: A fortune in army gold, a trio of roguish protagonists, double-crosses galore… Enzo Castellari's **Any Gun Can Play** cribs from **The Good, the Bad and the Ugly**. George Hilton (pictured), who specialised in tongue-in-cheek treasure hunters, starred alongside Edd Byrnes and Gilbert Roland.

above: For **Kill Them All and Come Back Alone**, Castellari plundered not just Leone's westerns but also **The Dirty Dozen**, as Chuck Connors leads a scratch squad of misfits on a mission for the Confederate army. Frank Wolff, as Connors's foil, excels in this unsubtle but satisfying action film.

above, left to right: Edd Byrnes, George Hilton and George Martin in **Red Blood, Yellow Gold**.

above: German poster for **Three Silver Dollars**, a cat-and-mouse treasure-hunt western with a sting in the tail, directed by prolific screen-writer Mario Amendola.
below: Hollywood veterans (Van Heflin and Gilbert Roland) spar with Euro-western upstarts (George Hilton and Klaus Kinski) in a narrative resembling *The Treasure of the Sierra Madre* – **The Ruthless Four** successfully infused a traditional structure with contemporary motifs.

Mool [1970].) They are no less frivolous as characters, however, nor do they take much interest in the issues or causes of the conflict around them. The same is true for most of the adventurers trawling for profits in the boisterous caper westerns set in war-torn Mexico that were made at the tail end of the political cycle. In the best of these – *Adios, Sabata* (1970), *They Call Me Hallelujah* (1971) and *His Name Was Holy Ghost* (1972) – the anti-heroes are recruited by revolutionary forces to retrieve or acquire money/gold for the cause, but the cause itself is secondary to the inventive ruses and individual styles of the protagonists. (We might also note how often that money earmarked for a particular cause is diverted into somebody's personal coffers. The revolution and the American Confederacy in particular – the latter in such films as *Johnny Hamlet* and *The Moment to Kill* [both 1968] – are frequently short-changed and betrayed by dubious activists, crusaders or philanthropists.) Only in *Adios, Sabata* does the lead have the semblance of a social conscience, a consequence, perhaps, of an established international actor with a persona of sturdy reliability, Yul Brynner, being cast in the role. The other two, Holy Ghost and Hallelujah, are archetypal Italian western rogues – money-motivated individualists cocking a snook at nobility.

There were several sobering variations on the treasure-hunt format that function like morality plays, in which stress is laid on the noxious effects of greed on individuals or the group dynamic. Characters may be consumed, deformed and destroyed by avarice and suspicion, or cut down to size by ironic reverses. The fruits of the protagonists' unsavoury labours may be contaminated with innocent blood. In Giuseppe Vari's *A Hole Between the Eyes* (1968), Anthony Ghidra donates most of his profits to a monastery to salve his conscience – or withheld entirely – the treasure is never found in Mario Amendola's *Three Silver Dollars* (1968), burned in Tulio Demicheli's *Viva Sabata!* (1970) and forcibly handed over to Mexican revolutionaries in Tonino Ricci's *The Great Treasure Hunt* (1972), while so-called partners eliminate each other in Roberto Bianchi Montero's *Two Faces of the Dollar* (1967) and León Klimovsky's *Quinto* (1969), among others. The fragile unity and collective rapacity of criminal confederacies frequently result in mutual destruction. A band of fugitives is promised the contents of a gold mine if they assist a stricken woman in Giuliano Carnimeo's *Find a Place to Die* (1968), but all bar lapsed hero Jeffrey Hunter are wiped out by their uncontrollable greed and savagery. (Greed-delirium is a constant feature of Carnimeo's westerns – it is the source of the drama in *The Moment to Kill* and defines most of the characters in his 'Sartana' films.) And grim allegorical stories such as *Kill the Wicked* (1967), *Black Jack* and *Vengeance* (both 1968), *A Man Called Sledge* (1970) and *The Boldest Job in the West* (1971) display an almost anthropological fascination for man's savage potential that conveys a moral message almost by default.

An atmosphere of desperate greed and paranoia is evoked superbly in *The Ruthless Four* (1968), the closest the genre came to emulating *The Treasure of the Sierra Madre* (1948). Directed with commendable understatement by Giorgio Capitani, better known at the time for comedies and later a prolific TV director, its power rests on a quartet of excellent characterisations and a taut script by Augusto Caminito and the ever-dependable Fernando Di Leo. (Di Leo allegedly wrote it with Lucio Fulci in mind, the duo having previous collaborated on *Massacre Time*.) As in *Sierra Madre*, the story is simple: grizzled prospector Sam Cooper (Van Heflin) makes a long-awaited gold strike and is forced to team up with three other men to dig it out and transport it. This nucleus expands into a gripping character study, not something the genre is usually renowned for, as mutual mistrust, simmering animosity and the lure of gold expose the cracks in an already tenuous alliance. Group loyalties, such as they are, are divided in various ways. Cooper believes he can trust his adopted son, the seemingly insouciant Manolo (George Hilton), but the latter is 'controlled' by the sinister Blond (Klaus Kinski), hinting at an oppressive homosexual relationship involving coercion and manipulation. To counter the threat of Blond and the unreliable Manolo, Cooper turns to an old associate, the malaria-stricken Mason (Gilbert Roland), a man of the old school like himself. Yet Mason has long harboured a suspicion that Cooper ran out on him years before when they both deserted the army, meaning neither can rely on the other man's support. (Late in the film it's revealed that Mason has an 'insurance policy', having paid a couple of gunmen to shadow the group to and from Cooper's mine. Ironically, Mason's prudence eventually leads to his death at their hands.)

The body of the narrative is familiar, even classic – various physical hardships, suspicious 'accidents' and attacks from outside turn up the tension in the group – and it provides a useful opportunity to compare and contrast the concept of character in the American and European approaches to the western. Kinski's Blond, for example, shifty and sadistic by nature, represents the European version; Cooper and Mason, like the actors that play them, are of Hollywood provenance, cagey by dint of bitter experience but at least recognising the value and meaning of honour and loyalty, even in a world as wicked as that depicted here. Each performance in this engrossing ensemble piece is impressive, but the under-rated Heflin's is the finest. His portrayal of the stubborn prospector recalls the battered dignity of his characters in *Shane* (1953) and *3.10 to Yuma* (1957). Cooper's years of toil have yielded nothing but disappointment, yet he clings to his dreams with a tenacity that's as admirable as it is pathetic. Only at the end, when he alone has survived the disintegration of the group with all the cursed gold in his possession, do despair and disillusionment take hold.

Of the many films predicated on partnerships that either borrowed or built upon Leone's ideas, by far the most popular in Italy and most influential on its own merits was *God Forgives... I Don't!* (1967), which set box-office registers ringing to the tune of almost 3 billion lire. (It was the fourth biggest moneymaker in Italy that season, just behind *The Dirty Dozen* and just ahead of *Day of Anger*.) By the same token, one of the most interesting and talented of Leone's acolytes was this film's director, Giuseppe Colizzi, academic, novelist and nephew of Luigi Zampa, a noted director of street-smart comedies such as *To Live in Peace* (1946), a humorous take on neorealist subject matter, and *The Art of Getting Along* (1955), one of several Zampa films to star Alberto Sordi. Colizzi died in 1978 at just 52, having completed only six films. Three of those were westerns structured around the pairing of Terence Hill, a relative newcomer to Italian westerns at the time (although he had made a batch of German ones), and former swimming champion Bud Spencer, and together they became arguably the most successful and certainly the most enduring double act in Italian film history. *God Forgives... I Don't!* was not the first film in which Hill and Spencer had both appeared – they had previously acted in Carlo Ludovico Bragaglia's *Hannibal* (1959), a peplum starring Victor Mature – but it was under Colizzi's direction that the relationship blossomed. Originally entitled *The Cat, the Dog and the Wolf*, the film was conceived by the writer-director like an Aesop fable: Hill's character has feline stealth and agility (and happens to be called Cat); Spencer's Hutch is like a mastiff, thick-set, hirsute and quick-tempered; and the aptly named Frank Wolff plays their antagonist, who, like Aesop's wolves, is intelligent and cunning but ultimately overreaches himself. Hill's ex-outlaw and Spencer's insurance agent establish a spiky rapport as they unite to track down Wolff's artful, arrogant Bill San Antonio, who has faked his own death and masterminded a murderous train robbery. Colizzi thrusts the trio into a battle of wits that ranges from the one-upmanship of Hill and Spencer, which is good-humoured rather than broadly comedic as in the 'Trinity' films and their many derivatives, to the tension and violence that characterises their sparring with Bill and his gang. A great example of the latter occurs in a flashback scene, one of several that fragment the narrative, that establishes how Bill tricked Cat, his one-time protégé, into thinking he had killed him, subsequently framing his charge, whom he derisively refers to as "pretty face", for the disappearance of the gang's loot. Although he sometimes allows the pace to slacken, an excusable sign of inexperience, the first-time director demonstrates remarkable control of his material, from the cut and thrust of the characters and the keenly judged irony, to the tempo of the violence. He also shows a confident grasp of genre aesthetics as established by the 'Dollars' films, alternating dramatic editing (a horrific montage of dead faces aboard the train in the opening scene) with serene wide shots and judicious close-ups, cinematographer Alfio Contini capturing the arid, barren exteriors and smoky, sweaty interiors with equal clarity. In the sequels, *Ace High* (1968) and *Boot Hill* (1969), the emphasis on grimy physiognomies and grubby morality is sustained, but the tension between Cat and Hutch is dissipated by the addition of other sympathetic characters. In *Ace High*, the duo are augmented and upstaged by Eli Wallach's vengeful, shifty, over-emotional Cacopoulos – a Greek-American version of Tuco – while the supporting cast of *Boot Hill* includes Woody Strode and Lionel Stander as members of a travelling circus troupe. While both films show a taste for the burlesque that was not apparent in *God Forgives*, Colizzi doesn't neglect the loyalty theme, which is memorably articulated by Wallach at the close of *Ace High* when his aggrieved, tearful reaction to a stream of invective from former partner Kevin McCarthy is as unexpected as it is affecting.

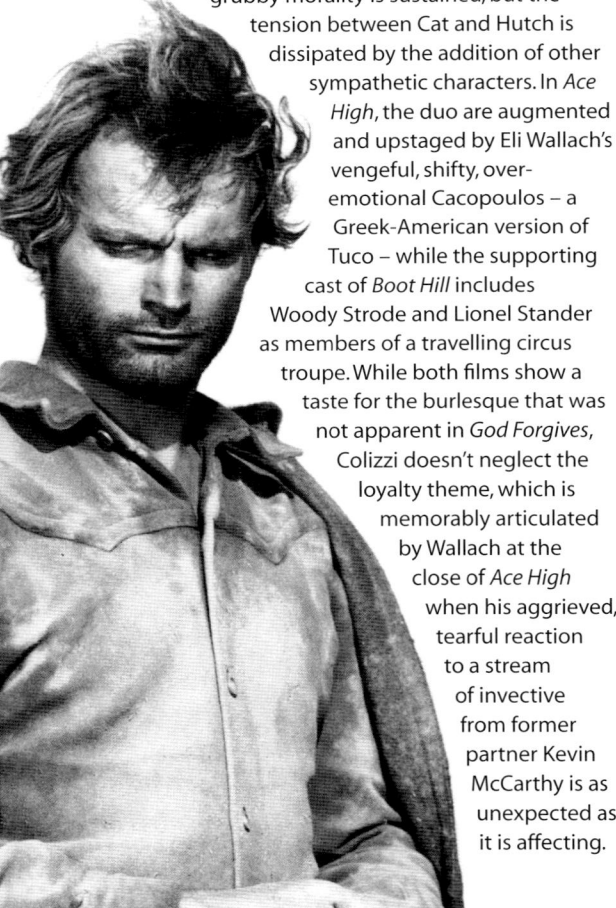

Apprenticeships and rivalries

The path through the genre from the 'Dollars' trilogy leads also to a series of films that expanded upon the rivalry between Monco and Mortimer, exploiting the dramatic potential of a quasi-paternal relationship between a mature gunfighter and a younger man or the exchange of values between a 'mentor' and 'pupil'. This type of plot has several permutations. Many of the political westerns, for example, contrast the materialism of a mercenary with the idealism of a revolutionary: the gringo figures in *A Bullet for the General* (1966), *A Professional Gun* and *Compañeros* pass on their technical know how for a price as our sympathies are directed towards their uncouth disciples, who all at one point or another turn the tables on their tutors, decisively so in the case of the first of these films. The situation is more complicated in *Face to Face* (1967), in which an intellectual absorbs the influence of an outlaw and vice versa, each character simultaneously teacher and subject, culminating in a clash of alter egos. And in *A Fistful of Dynamite* (1971), James Coburn's world-weary insurgent trades life lessons with Rod Steiger's peasant, an experience that dampens Coburn's faith in revolution and affirms for Steiger the precedence of family over politics and patriotism, something he forgets only briefly but with tragic consequences.

Three of Lee Van Cleef's post-'Dollars' westerns made particularly rewarding use of the motif: Giulio Petroni's *Death Rides a Horse*, Tonino Valerii's *Day of Anger* and Giancarlo Santi's *The Grand Duel* (1972). (Santi, like Valerii, was another former Leone assistant, having worked on both *The Good, the Bad and the Ugly* and *Once Upon a Time in the West*. He was briefly in the running to direct *A Fistful of Dynamite* before Leone took the reins.) Each of these builds upon the ambiguity and authoritativeness of Colonel Mortimer. They also continue to display the dexterity of an actor grossly underused by Hollywood. The resuscitation of Van Cleef's career in Europe was delayed justice for a man who'd put in plenty of hard work back home for little artistic reward. The former farmer, soldier and office administrator had come to film and television via a stage role in a highly rated touring version of *Mister Roberts* (supporting Henry Fonda), which earned him the attention of *High Noon* producer Stanley Kramer. His noteworthy cameo as one of Gary Cooper's antagonists in that film was the first of many undemanding but eye-catching appearances in westerns and thrillers, most of which exploited his hawk-like looks and imposing physique. Pigeonholed as a hired gun or psychopath, he found genuine acting opportunities hard to come by – his affecting death scene in *The Bravados* (1958) showed that menace was not the extent of his range – until the advent of the Italian westerns and their relaxation of moral guidelines allowed performers to move beyond simplistic definitions of good and evil.

above: Eli Wallach stole his co-stars' thunder again in Giuseppe Colizzi's **Ace High**, first sequel to the blockbusting **God Forgives... I Don't!**
centre: US poster for Colizzi's **Boot Hill**, flagging up the post-**Trinity** popularity of Hill and Spencer.

Van Cleef's anti-heroes are magisterial figures, both intimidating to their enemies and inspirational to their apprentices. As well as the threat implicit in that sinister smile and a stare that could freeze fire, his characters in the three titles cited above convey maturity and experience, which they pass on, with mixed motives, to their younger allies. Jailbird Ryan in *Death Rides a Horse* and ex-sheriff Clayton in *The Grand Duel* are both partly motivated by guilt: Ryan rode with the gang that murdered the family of Bill (John Phillip Law) when the latter was a boy, while Clayton carried out the killing for which Philip Vermeer (Peter O'Brien) is currently blamed. There's a more devious reason for ageing gunman Frank Talby's schooling of Scott Mary (Giuliano Gemma) in *Day of Anger*. Realising his powers are fading, he attempts to mould Scott in his image, but can no more control the latter's spirit than the town that has rejected him can. (Talby is like a ripened version of the short-lived henchmen Van Cleef had played in Hollywood. One particular role of note is that of Clanton, who executes the murderous will of 'respectable' banker Raymond Burr and other crooked burghers in *A Man Alone* [1955], a taut 'anti-populist' western directed by and starring Ray Milland.)

Van Cleef's characters are father figures, mentors and rivals, nurturing their protégés even as they keep them at arm's length, guiding them towards their goals but allowing themselves space and time to pursue their own agendas. Viewed from the youngsters' point of view, each film plays like a *Bildungsroman*, with the characters afflicted by loss and motivated partly by bitterness against a social order that has driven them astray while accommodating their enemies. They learn to channel their anger under the influence of an older man who has seen it all before, but their development is only complete when they take a stand on their own terms, even if it means challenging their 'father'. (The difference in ages between Van Cleef and his co-stars adds bite to the drama – he was 12 years older than Law and 13 years Gemma's senior. The birth date of O'Brien, real name Alberto Dentice, is not known, but he looks well over a decade younger than Van Cleef.)

The cat-and-mouse games are at times reminiscent of the 'Dollars' trilogy and *The Big Gundown* (1967), in which Van Cleef sparred so effectively with Tomas Milian, and, as in those films, the interaction of the characters takes alternately humorous and dramatic turns. In *Death Rides a Horse* and *Day of Anger*, in particular, the threat of discord is never far from the surface: Bill eventually discovers Ryan's secret but opts to let him live, accepting that Ryan had no part in the killing – indeed, has been a kind of guardian angel for him – and proving he has absorbed some of the older man's wisdom; while Scott breaks with Talby when the latter cold-bloodedly kills Murph (Walter Rilla), an upstanding former lawman and Scott's other surrogate father in the film. The resultant confrontation sees the various lessons Talby has taught Scott during the film – a digest of western 'commandments' compiled by writer Ernesto Gastaldi – turned against him.[17] If this ending doesn't quite have the resonance of *My Name Is Nobody* (see below), Scott's act of 'patricide', signifying that he has dominated his own inner demons, remains one of the most satisfying conclusions to an individual character's story within the

Bud Spencer (*above*) and Terence Hill (*opposite bottom left*) in **God Forgives... I Don't!**, the film that established their partnership.

above: John Phillip Law can shoot, but needs Lee Van Cleef to keep him alive in **Death Rides a Horse**, one of the biggest hits of 1967.

genre, comparable with Chuncho's cathartic shooting of Tate in *A Bullet for the General*. And the subtlety of Van Cleef's acting at this point – the strong, self-assured gunfighter stricken and begging for mercy from the boy he has moulded into a man – provokes a complicated emotional response that testifies to his too-often untapped potential as a performer.

The most ambitious use of the Monco/Mortimer set-up was made in *My Name Is Nobody*, the best of the two-handed comedy westerns that were rife in the early Seventies. This was itself a collaboration of sorts between mentor – producer Sergio Leone – and student – director Tonino Valerii, who had been Leone's assistant on *For a Few Dollars More* and was acutely aware that he owed the *Nobody* job to the perception that he would direct in a Leone-like fashion. (Of course, Valerii was no mere cipher, having already completed six features of his own before *Nobody*. At any rate, Leone wound up directing certain scenes personally.**18**) Fittingly, in a film replete with signs, symbols, references and reflections, the central characters have a range of functions beyond the scope of the narrative. Nobody and Jack Beauregard are indivisible from the actors that play them and from the different styles of western they represent. Nobody is Terence Hill, the second-generation Italian western hero, one step further removed from the American ideal than his cynical predecessors and subscribing anew to the heroic myth of the west, which had been distorted almost beyond recognition over the course of the preceding decade by Leone and his contemporaries. Nobody's counterpart here embodies that myth – the regal Henry Fonda even refers to himself as a "national monument", his

above: Never come between a gun and its target: Giuliano Gemma absorbs another of Lee Van Cleef's lessons in **Day of Anger**.
opposite bottom right: The stars pose for a publicity shot on the set of the same film.

one remaining ambition to live out his days in Europe, an obvious reference to the influx of ageing American actors since the beginning of the Sixties. Hill/Nobody also stands for the European western itself, hyperactive and ostentatious, its characters equipped with the quick wits and tricks necessary for survival in the corrupt and cluttered modern era of "organised" violence – an era in which Fonda/Jack, as the stately, reserved face of the classical American western, feels he has no place. The protagonists' relationship bears traces of that between Fonda's Frank and another anonymous mystery man, Charles Bronson's Harmonica, in *Once Upon a Time in the West* (1968), one of this film's major points of reference: Nobody similarly reels off a list of Jack's victories in gunfights, but this time in admiration rather than admonishment: "'82 was one of your best years…".

Jack regards his persistent young admirer with a mixture of bemusement and irritation, which gradually mellows into affection and gratitude. Unusually for a continental production in which two different interpretations of the same mythological material collide, it is the more traditional character, the American, who debunks the Italian's romantic notions of heroism and honour (it's significant that Beauregard declines to avenge his murdered brother, feeling him not worth the trouble), and the younger man who reminds the older of his responsibilities as a role model. In Marcia Landy's description, "Beauregard, as the French indicates, is the fine-looking, the ideal appearance that must be maintained to keep the tradition of the western alive." Nobody's mission is to preserve and embellish this tradition, this idealised past, for the benefit of present and future generations. To this end, he 'directs' the unwilling Beauregard towards a spectacular shoot-out with 150 outlaws, ensuring his 'star' will leave a

above: Seasoned gunfighter tutors hot-headed youngster… Giancarlo Santi's **The Grand Duel** found Lee Van Cleef (here with his charge, Peter O'Brien) on familiar ground.

glorious legacy. All that remains is to engineer Jack's 'death' at Nobody's hands, the culmination of a series of seriocomic encounters reminiscent of *For a Few Dollars More* (including a hat-shooting contest). The showdown – which, inevitably, evokes the final duel in *Once Upon a Time in the West*, as well as, musically at least, *The Good, the Bad and the Ugly* – underlines one of the major themes of the film, the unreliability of appearances. Even though Hill's happy-go-lucky adventurer is seen to win the duel – the shadow eclipsing its subject – the history books will still record that where Jack Beauregard is concerned, "Nobody was faster on the draw". If Nobody's triumph is a surrogate for the achievements of the Italian western, which had deposed its own Hollywood 'mentor', then both character and film have the good grace to acknowledge their indebtedness to those, like Jack/Fonda, who came before, an acknowledgement the latter reciprocates in his poignant farewell address.

above: in **My Name Is Nobody**, master gunfighter Henry Fonda is 'trained' to fulfil his destiny by his mischievous disciple, Terence Hill.

"When the chimes end, pick up your gun"

Another point at which the Euro-western diverged from its parent form – and frequently surpassed it – is the climactic settling of accounts. From being something of a formality in most Hollywood films, this timeworn convention gained greater thematic significance in European hands – particularly if, as in the political westerns, the result has implications beyond the survival of the individuals involved – and is often the aesthetic highpoint of the film. In most cases it is sufficient that the 'coolest' character, which covers anything from his temperament and technique to his fashion sense, is triumphant. His moral justification, if he has one, is generally redundant. Yet even if the outcome of the showdown is rarely in doubt, the direction frequently places an accent on surprise and suspense, with cheating and trickery practised by all parties. The gentlemanly civility of the historical duel of honour has no place here. Nor, indeed, does the formal simplicity of most American westerns. With characteristic self-indulgence, many European directors inject visual interest and vitality into their duel scenes with adventurous framing and unusual camera angles and/or the use of symbolic locations or conditions, while the rhythm of the action is determined by dynamic editing and use of music.

As with most of the genre's aesthetic/thematic advances, the foremost figure in the renovation of the western showdown was Sergio Leone. In his work the duel is like an apotheosis, a clash of demi-gods on a mythic plain. His hermetic, circular settings define a space for the combatants like a *corrida* or a gladiatorial arena, a place where "nothing matters", as Frank says in *Once Upon a Time in the West*, but the business at hand. The co-ordination of music and visuals to operatic effect; the picturesque/symmetrical arrangement of figures in the frame; the variety and greatly differing length of shots; the shifts in character perspective; the rapid intercutting of details (eyes, hands, pistols, holsters); the famously oppressive facial close-ups that scrutinise the duellists' emotions… all these stylistic traits amounted to an exaggeration of abiding western clichés, with an undercurrent of irreverence, that proved enormously influential in the genre. Variations, parodies and mannered imitations of Leone's style abound. The final, three-way face-off in *Any Gun Can Play* plays on the anticipation of violence in Leone's duels and apes the editing format, but is ultimately a joke at the audience's expense – when the characters finally draw their guns, they turn them not on each other but on the pipes of an ornate church organ, repository of a coveted horde of coins. (This recalls, of course, the famous opening of *The Good, the Bad and the Ugly*, in which three gunmen approach each other with menace, only to turn their attentions towards Tuco.)[19] In *A Professional Gun*, Sergio Corbucci and screenwriter Luciano Vincenzoni manage to send up the painstaking formalism of *For a Few Dollars More* and *The Good, the Bad and the Ugly*, both co-written

above: The settling of accounts was Sergio Leone's forté. At the conclusion of **For a Few Dollars More**, Colonel Mortimer (Lee Van Cleef) and Indio (Gian Maria Volonté) met in a makeshift arena as if they were combatants of the classical era. Ennio Morricone provided epic accompaniment.

by Vincenzoni, at the same time as styling a powerful confrontation of their own. Franco Nero referees a duel à la Monco between Tony Musante, in full clown get-up, and black-suited Jack Palance in a genuine *corrida*; the deep-focus shots, alternating between medium and close-ups, cut to the tempo of Ennio Morricone's searing trumpet theme. The influence of Morricone's music cannot be overstated. The genre resounds with echoes of his gundown motifs: the composer quotes his own *For a Few Dollars More* watch melody, for example, during the duels in *The Good, the Bad and the Ugly* and *My Name Is Nobody*. And Giuseppe Colizzi makes imaginative use of music in the witty finale of *Ace High*, which also picks up on the notion of the combatants as partners in a deadly dance first suggested by the rhythmical movements of the characters in the triello sequence of *The Good, the Bad and the Ugly*. The scene takes place in a gambling saloon, where the four heroes – Terence Hill, Bud Spencer, Eli Wallach and Brock Peters – line up against Kevin McCarthy and his associates. Wallach's character calls for music and a waltz strikes up, composed by Carlo Rustichelli and played on-screen by an orchestra, the two parties backing away from each other in unison as if dancing. Colizzi cuts from faces and figures to a spinning roulette wheel, which, when it stops, is the signal to shoot.

The observance or non-observance of signals heightens the ritualistic nature of many of these duel scenes, particularly in Leone's films, and connects them, however tenuously, with a centuries-old tradition of nobly settling disputes that spread from Europe to the New World. So prevalent was the custom that a 26-point list of commandments, the *Code Duello*, was drawn up in Ireland in 1777. Of course, rules are there to be broken and, in new-wave Euro-westerns, cheating is not the preserve of the bad man. As previously established, the majority of characters obey their own sense of survival rather than arbitrary regulations such as waiting for a signal before firing, much less the restrictions of 'fair play'. Even so, the subtlest of distinctions is preserved between the superior wits and sang-froid of the heroes, who only cheat when they have to, and the rash desperation or plain bad faith of the villains. The protagonists of *Ringo and His Golden Pistol* and *A Taste for Killing* overcome unfavourable odds by distracting their cowardly enemies before dispatching them. Cuchillo (Tomas Milian) uses a hidden knife to kill an opponent who had tried to gain an unfair advantage in *Run, Man, Run* (1968). And Sartana (Gianni Garko) has a trick in reserve when the devious Lasky (William Berger) attempts to dupe him at the end of Gianfranco Parolini's *If You Meet Sartana, Pray for Your Death* (1968). Even in the most formalised of duels – as fought in Parolini's *Sabata* (1969) and *Adios, Sabata*, complete with vintage pistols and life-size artificial targets – the aim is not to resolve a point of honour but to establish supremacy. In both films, the title character is challenged by an elitist opponent to determine which of them is the greater marksman and, implicitly, the better man. Inevitably, there is artifice

above: "We're going to have to earn it": The protagonists' tortuous quest in **The Good, the Bad and the Ugly** deserved a fittingly intense finale. Again, the setting is circular, the tempo set by a Morricone composition, the tension stretched until the final snap of gunfire.

above: Nobody (Terence Hill) assures his place in history, and that of his hero (Henry Fonda), with a cleverly staged showdown (filmed in New Orleans) towards the end of **My Name Is Nobody**.

involved on both sides: both Stengel (Franco Ressel), in the first film, and Skimmel (Gérard Herter) in the sequel, think they have Sabata at a disadvantage, only for the last named – a skilled conjuror in the Sartana mould – to trump them with quick thinking and sharp reflexes. The pleasure for men like this is in the competition itself; the pride at stake is professional rather than personal.

This explains why characters undertake such contrived tests of their skill and senses as duels in darkened rooms, as staged in *The Magnificent Three* (1963), *The Wrath of God* (1968), *Cowards Don't Pray* (1968), *I Am Sartana, Your Angel of Death* (1969) and *The Price of Power* (1969), usually involving the deceptive use of targets such as fluorescent paint and lit cigars. Pride permeates the clash between 'Joe' and Ramon, *pistolero* versus rifleman, at the end of *A Fistful of Dollars*, and that between Corbett (Lee Van Cleef), a down-to-earth, seasoned man hunter, and the meticulous, aristocratic Baron von Schulemberg (Gérard Herter) in *The Big Gundown*, with Corbett's emphasis on accuracy compensating for the Baron's greater speed. And it is the reason why Owen (Benito Stefanelli), hired to kill Frank Talby in *Day of Anger*, arranges the equivalent of a horseback joust between them. Armed with antiquated, front-loading rifles, which they load as they ride, the two men charge at each other across an open plain, Talby proving the most dextrous and the most accurate shot. In this kind of environment, superiority is not gauged by orthodox skills on their own, much less by moral virtues. Rather, it is less salubrious qualities such as gamesmanship, cunning, ingenuity and resourcefulness that are the true measures of a man.

The location of the final reckoning can have a significant effect on the dramatic impact of the scene. Leone's circular spaces, with their connotations of ritual combat, are a famous example – they transmit a sense of timelessness, the circle "a physical symbol of cosmological action".[20] Other highly suggestive settings include cemeteries (*The Good, the Bad and the Ugly*, *Django*, *Django Shoots First*, *Viva Django* [1967], *Death Sentence* [1967], *A Gun for a Hundred Graves* [1968]) and an undertaker's workshop (*Arizona Colt* [1966], *If You Meet Sartana...*), the immanence of death hardly needing to be remarked upon. These sites impart a Gothic flavour to events that also marks the ghost-town showdown of *For $100,000 Per Killing*; the eerie, forest-based finale of *Today It's Me... Tomorrow You!* (1968); the claustrophobic climax of *Vengeance*, with its camera-compressed spaces; and the infernal ending of *And God Said to Cain* (1970), all shattered mirrors, baroque decor and flickering flames. In other cases, natural backdrops and conditions work with *mise-en-scène* to create an atmosphere of primordial tension, emphasising what Jim Kitses, speaking of Anthony Mann's brutally rugged westerns, called the "metaphysical conflict" of the characters. In several films with a familial theme – typically but not exclusively pitting brother against brother – the characters' emotional turbulence is externalised in the elements. Siblings confront each other amid swirling dust clouds in *Blood at Sundown* (1966) and *For $100,000 Per Killing*, while rain lashes father and son as they fight in *Seven Dollars to Kill* (1966). The Gothic trappings of these scenes and stories are crossed with tragic themes, the protagonist cursed at the very point of his tarnished triumph. (This type of film will be considered in more detail in the next chapter.)

Landscape plays an intimate role in the duels in Leone's second and third 'Dollars' films and *Once Upon a Time in the West*, in which the combatants are secluded from civilisation and, in a figurative sense, from time itself. Open-air settings were also favoured by Sergio Sollima, who, like Leone, used the opportunity to explore spatial relationships between man and environment, his use of the 'Scope frame consistently imaginative. The duels involving Tomas Milian in *The Big Gundown* and *Run, Man, Run* have the same triangular composition associated with Leone – two combatants and a referee – although

above: Sabata (Yul Brynner) proves that cheats can prosper after his duel with the equally deceitful Skimmel (Gérard Herter) in **Adios, Sabata**.

Sollima favours wide shots and medium distances over close-ups. Finally, in the same way that these contests achieve a mythical connection (Leone) or convey a veiled political message (Sollima) by taking place well away from society – thus nobody can witness the murderous plans of Milian's powerful enemies, for example – it is vital that the showdown between Nobody and Jack Beauregard in *My Name Is Nobody* be seen by as large a crowd as possible. The choice of a town street lined with spectators not only locates the duel in the tradition of the Hollywood western – a point of reference throughout – it also grants Nobody the attention he constantly craves and enables the unlikely pairing to seal Jack's escape from the west.

Nobody's victory, which takes place on the eve of the 20th Century, is a thinly disguised metaphor for the succession of one generation, one set of cultural values and traditions, over another. With allegory such a familiar feature of the genre, the result of many showdowns carries a symbolic meaning above and beyond mere narrative closure. In the mentor-pupil plot type, for example, the novice almost invariably prevails over the more experienced character, a victory that indicates psychological growth and maturity, the subduing of whatever negative tendencies the mentor figure represents. We have already seen this at work in *Day of Anger*, while variations include *Django, the Last Killer* (1967), the plot of which manoeuvres world-weary Anthony Ghidra and his young apprentice, George Eastman [Luigi Montefiori], into an inevitable shoot-out ("Guess I was a pretty good teacher" acknowledges Ghidra upon defeat), and the more pessimistic *Clumsy Hands* (1970), in which Peter Lee Lawrence's troubled avenger, schooled in killing by a merciless bounty hunter, defeats the latter in a duel while being fatally wounded himself, destiny thus claiming its due. The political westerns work a potent variation on this trope: the confrontation between rebel and master, regardless of whether it involves a formal showdown, signifies the insurgent's enlightenment and declaims the pertinacity of the revolutionary spirit. *The Big Gundown* sounds out just such a clarion call, echoed in its sequel, *Run, Man, Run*. Their shared hero, Cuchillo, the victimised Mexican peon, fights foreign oppressors in the manner of an impoverished David against an imperialist Goliath. Armed with only a crude weapon and feral cunning, Milian's ragamuffin strikes a blow for his class, his race and, by extension, the causes of Third World guerrillas. "Cuchillo uses a knife because he is a proletarian," explains Sollima. "He is too poor to buy a gun and ammo. So the knife and Cuchillo bring a whole new view of the western myth into play, the one of the really poor, the forsaken, the people with no choice. In reality, he traces an image of those who did not sustain the myth of the wild west; on the contrary, Cuchillo abates the myth itself."[21] Sollima's fairy-tale finale has its counterpoint in *The Great Silence*, where the protagonist's ultimate defeat reinforces the domination and persecution of the same "forsaken" classes that Cuchillo represents.

From the sublime of Leone and Sollima we come to the ridiculous of the parodists and the mannerists. All traces of myth and momentousness disappeared from the duel scene, along with all sense of restraint, as the genre's undercurrent of self-mocking absurdity swelled to a torrent in the Seventies. The fetishisation of armaments associated with Euro-westerns from *A Fistful of Dollars* onwards reached new peaks. The most elaborate of the gadget-laden 'Sartana' series, Giuliano Carnimeo's *Gunman in Town* (1970), has the stylish pistolero facing his foes with a church organ-cum-cannon-cum-machine gun, while the last of the 'Stranger' films, Ferdinando Baldi's *Get Mean* (1975), pits Tony Anthony and outsized shotgun against a manic Lloyd Battista and cannon. Not since Sterling Hayden turned up for a showdown armed with a harpoon in *Terror in a Texas Town* (1958) had there been such an absurd display of weaponry in a western. And in the midst of the genre's slapstick phase, Carnimeo's anarchic *A Man Called Invincible* (1973) and *The Crazy Bunch* (1974) reduced the duel to a mating ritual for repressed homosexuals, the director doing the work of the Freudians and the feminist critics for them. Before then, however, the showdown, as both an examination of character and as a spectacle, flourished alongside the revival of bounty hunters and treasure quests as indispensable narrative components. Each of these conventions, conjoined with such finesse in *For a Few Dollars More*, allowed for a fresh examination of standard western themes such as honour and courage, the kind of values that could no longer be taken for granted as the genre, in tune with developments in the modern world, entered a radical and, for all its excesses, arguably more realistic new phase. With most European directors, and an increasing number of American films, following Leone's lead, the anti-hero's place in the body of western myths was assured.

above: Mocking convention – and confounding expectations – the end of **Any Gun Can Play** sees animosity give way to the common cause of greed.

footnotes

1. *For a Few Dollar More* was, of course, the first Leone film to be co-produced by Alberto Grimaldi's PEA. Grimaldi soon negotiated a production/distribution deal with Hollywood studio United Artists, which would subsequently put money into *The Good, the Bad and the Ugly* and reap huge dividends from distributing the 'Dollars' trilogy in the US.
2. Quoted in *Spaghetti Cinema*.
3. In several Euro-westerns, these two character-types – bounty hunter and *pistolero* – are fused into one personage. See, for example: Peter Lee Lawrence as a sharp-dressed, cynical gunman in *32 Caliber Killer* (1967) and a good-natured nomad in *God in Heaven, Arizona on Earth* (1972); Gianni Garko at his most suave in *The Price of Death* (1971); and Garko and William Berger as friendly rivals in *They Call Him Cemetery* (1971).
4. Paul Seydor, *Peckinpah: The Western Films: A Reconsideration*, p.195.
5. Jim Kitses, *Horizons West*, p.39.
6. Oreste de Fornari, *Sergio Leone: The Great Dream of Legendary America*, p.45.
7. Author's interview with Sergio Donati.
8. *A Few Dollars for Django* is another film, like the aforementioned *Reverend Colt* by Castellari's father, that was signed by Spanish director León Klimovsky, even though, according to Marco Giusti, Klimovsky did little actual directing before Castellari took over. Castellari explains the reasons for this then-common practice: "To realise a minority co-production in Spain [Italy was the junior partner in this case] it was necessary to credit a Spanish director. I perfectly understood the situation, but the Italian co-producer was my father and I directed the movie to protect the family interests" (author's interview with Enzo Castellari).
9. The title of Merino's film is misleading – it has nothing whatsoever in common with the two 'MacGregor' comedy westerns (note the different spelling) directed by Franco Giraldi in 1966 and 1967.
10. The star, along with director Corbucci, is interviewed on the set of *The Great Silence* in the 1968 documentary *Westerns Italian Style*, which is included as an extra feature on the Region 1 DVD release of Sergio Sollima's *Run, Man, Run*. Narrated by Frank Wolff, the 38-minute film also includes interviews with Sollima, Enzo Castellari and Chuck Connors (on the set of Castellari's *Kill Them All and Come Back Alone*), as well as behind-the-scenes footage and 'evidence' of the western phenomenon sweeping Italy – from cowboy-themed weddings to country-music club nights.
11. The alternative ending, prepared for Asian and North African countries, is so preposterous that Corbucci and company clearly never intended for anyone to take it seriously. Just as he is about to be killed by Loco, Silence is rescued by the miraculous reappearance of Burnett, who had earlier been sent crashing into freezing waters by Loco. The duo kill all the bounty hunters and free the captive outlaws, and Silence is revealed to be wearing a metal gauntlet beneath the bandage on his 'wounded' right hand.
12. The grim tidings of *The Great Silence* doubtless contributed to its lacklustre box-office performance in Italy – it made considerably less than the upbeat *A Professional Gun*, although it may well have been hindered by a more limited distribution. Despite being held in high critical esteem these days, the film achieved, in fact, one of the lowest domestic grosses of any Corbucci western.
13. Frayling, *Spaghetti Westerns: Cowboys and Europeans*, p.128.
14. See the 'Sartana' series (1968-70) and the first *Sabata* (1969), for instance, which contain elaborate networks of well-heeled schemers manipulating, and being manipulated by, criminal underlings. And in two historically contorted westerns, corruption is seen to reach into the highest echelons of the establishment – the vice-secretary of defence, in Paolo Bianchini's *Gatling Gun* (1968), and even the vice president, in Tonino Valerii's *The Price of Power* (1969), are both involved in traitorous conspiracies with embittered Southern aristocrats.
15. Luigi Barzini, *The Italians*, p.157.
16. As is the case with other Corbucci westerns such as *Minnesota Clay* and *The Great Silence*, an alternative 'happy' ending is reputed to exist for *Navajo Joe* in which he survives his wounds, riding off on his horse when it returns to him from town.
17. Although Talby's teachings assume greater significance in the denouement of *Day of Anger*, they echo the lessons received by Peter Lee Lawrence's callow protagonist in *Fury of Johnny Kid*, released earlier in the same year, in which grizzled gunfighter Andrés Mejuto tells his charge that "the Holy Colt has six commandments", including – as in *Day of Anger* – shoot to kill, finish off the wounded and never turn your back on another man's gun.
18. See *Hybrid Westerns* and, in particular, Sir Christopher Frayling's *Something to Do with Death*, for a detailed discussion of Leone's involvement.
19. Duels deferred or faked are further evidence of the genre's obsession with trickery and artifice, as well as its restless reconsideration of western conventions. Two men advance on each other at the beginning of the playful *A Pistol for Ringo* (1965), only to exchange pleasantries rather than gunfire; Monco and Mortimer test each other's mettle with the famous hat-shooting duel in *For a Few Dollars More*; the tension in *A Place Called Glory* (1965) centres on the build-up to a gunfight that never occurs; in *Face to Face* (1967), Tomas Milian tests the will of Gian Maria Volonté by inviting him to draw on him with, as it turns out, an empty gun; John Phillip Law and Lee Van Cleef reach a final reckoning in *Death Rides a Horse*, but their mutual respect proves to be greater than any recrimination; Anthony Steffen and Mark Damon face off at the end of *A Train for Durango* (1968) with, it turns out, empty pistols, and mutually surrender; in both *Sartana's Here... Trade Your Pistol for a Coffin* (1970) and *They Call Me Hallelujah* (1971), one partner 'kills' another in order to fool a third; the standoff between Franco Nero and Tomas Milian in *Compañeros* (1970) is interrupted by the need to eliminate bad guy Jack Palance; two famous gunmen prefer to maintain parity rather than shoot it out in *They Call Him Cemetery* (1971); and Terence Hill's 'defeat' of Henry Fonda in *My Name Is Nobody* is staged for two different cameras – one belonging to a photographer in the narrative, the other capturing the images for cinema-goers.
20. Staig and Williams, *Italian Western: The Opera of Violence*, p165.
21. Interview with Sergio Sollima by Mario Marsili, used with kind permission.

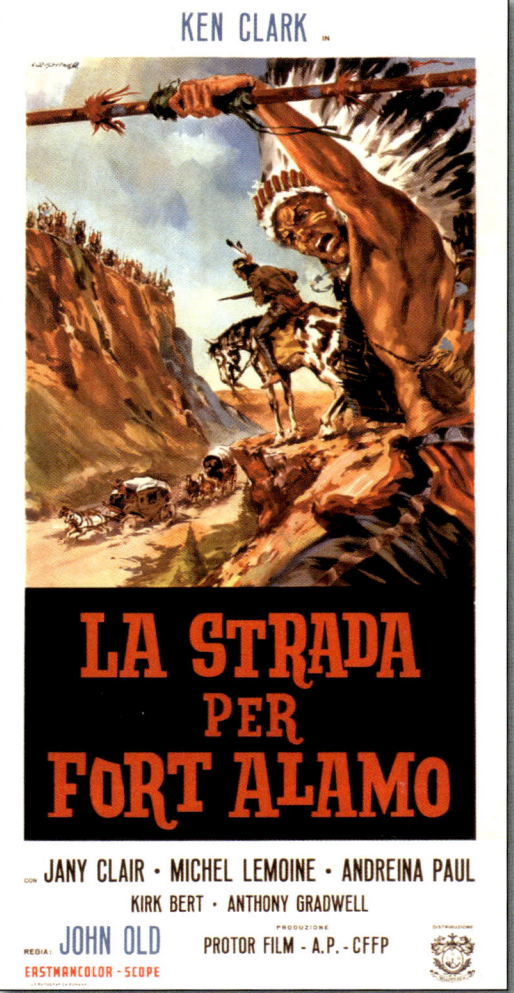

Director Mario Bava earned his spurs for his witty and stylish *gialli* and horror films, not for his westerns: **Savage Gringo** (*top left*, for which Bava is uncredited) and **The Road to Fort Alamo** (*top right and bottom* – this French poster promises more vigorous action than the film delivers), both starring lumbering American leading man Ken Clark, display little of Bava's customary flair.

Social activism, Shakespearian demagoguery and shaggy hair – Enzo Castellari's **Keoma**, arguably the last great Italian western, has a busy agenda. Franco Nero (*left, below*) plays the dynamic protagonist, antithesis of the impassive avengers of old, with Orso Maria Guerrini (*above*) as one of his bigoted half-brothers.

You say you want a revolution? "Tortilla westerns" incorporated the radical spirit of the Sixties into stories set in the Mexico of Villa and Zapata – but with one eye on riot-torn student campuses, Vietnam and the Congo. Fashionably anti-imperialist films such as **A Bullet for the General** (*below*) and **Companeros** (*above*) established the party line.

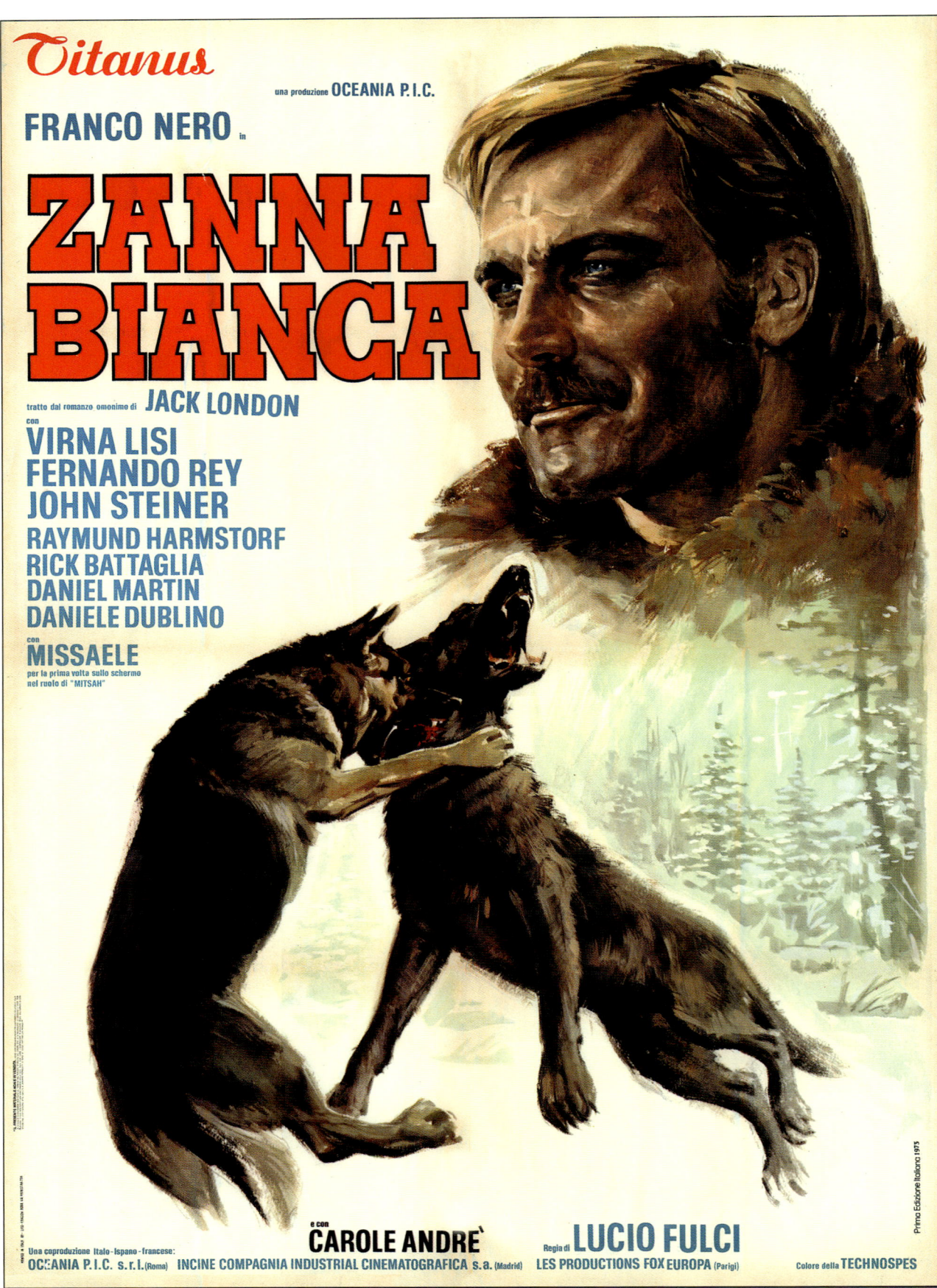

Horror specialist Lucio Fulci also proved adept at the western. **Massacre Time** (advertised by a typically lurid Thai poster, *top left*, and French artwork proffering an Antonio das Mortes-like figure, *top right*) and **The Four of the Apocalypse** (*bottom*) revel in sadism, while **White Fang** (*opposite*), one of several Italian 'tributes' to **The Call of the Wild**, was more family-friendly.

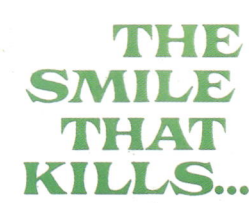

left: Lightweight westerns like Enzo Castellari's **Any Gun Can Play** signalled a change in the climate during the genre's peak production period.
above: Giuseppe Colizzi's **God Forgives... I Don't!** was similarly leavened with humour, mainly the result of Terence Hill's partnership with Bud Spencer.
below: In Colizzi's first follow-up, **Ace High**, Hill and Spencer were augmented – and upstaged – by Eli Wallach.

opposite: Whatever Clint can do… Stranded in TV series like **Gun Law** and **Hawk** (in which, as here, he played a Native American), Burt Reynolds followed in his friend's boot-steps in 1966 to star in **Navajo Joe** for Sergio Corbucci. Neither revolutionary like the 'Dollars' films nor as invigorating for Reynolds's career, it is nevertheless a better film than his subsequent negative comments suggest.

left: With **They Call Me Trinity**, Enzo Barboni turned his nose up at the violence and mean-spiritedness of most mainstream European westerns.
top right: Among many films in Barboni's debt was the Leone-produced **My Name Is Nobody**, alternately classy and crude, which paired **Trinity** star Terence Hill with Henry Fonda.
below: Film-noir style shadow play in the *giallo*-esque **The Moment to Kill**, starring George Hilton – prime suspect in a number of *gialli* in his post-western career.

above: Enzo Castellari wielded slapstick just as readily as Enzo Barboni, and with an even heavier hand: **Tedeum**, aka **Father Jack-Leg**, encouraged an over-the-top performance from Jack Palance in a tiresome tale of scamming that lacks the charm of the **Trinity** films.

Protests and profit margins: For a time in the Sixties, films with socialist ideals cleaned up at the box office. The likes of **The Big Gundown** (*above* – this fallacious US admat does Lee Van Cleef a disservice; he was of course the bad, not the ugly – *and below*), **A Professional Gun** (*opposite top left*) and **Compañeros** (*opposite bottom*), with Tomas Milian in Che Guevara mode, channelled popular dissent and disgruntlement while making a fortune for their capitalist investors. Duccio Tessari's **Long Live Your Death** (*opposite top right*), meanwhile, poked fun in the idealists' direction.

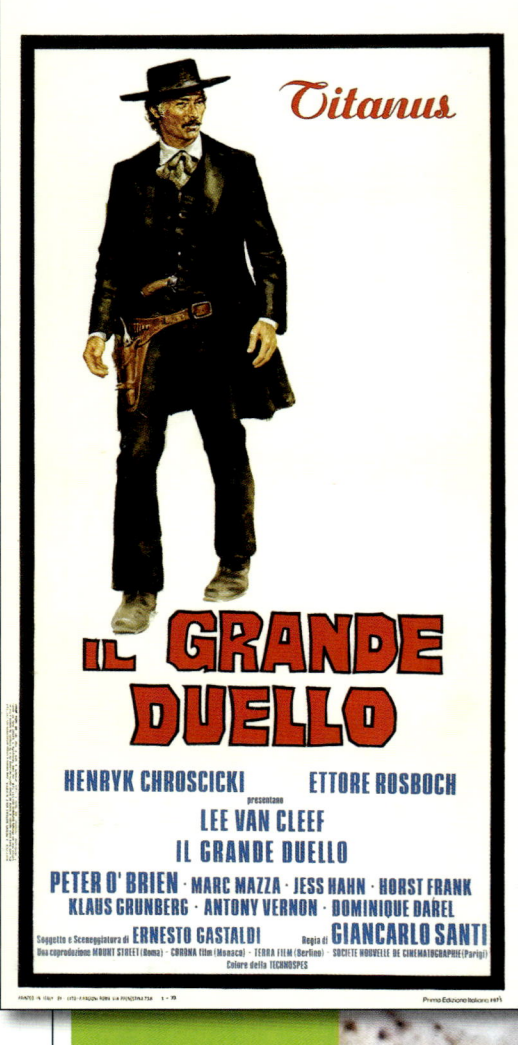

above: Terence Hill in a tussle from **Ace High**.
left and below: Lee Van Cleef was frequently cast as the mentor to a younger, more impetuous man, as in **The Grand Duel** and **Death Rides a Horse**, with John Phillip Law.
opposite: The bleak side of bounty hunting was emphasised in José Luis Merino's acid-tinged revenge film **More Dollars for the McGregors** (*top left*) and Romolo Guerrieri's **$10,000 Blood Money** (*top right*), a pseudo-sequel to **Django** with tragic leanings.
opposite bottom: Gold fever, treachery, an arduous trek – **The Treasure of the Sierra Madre** is revisited in Giorgio Capitani's **The Ruthless Four**.

above: The long-suffering Tony Anthony at the mercy of En Plein's gang in **Shoot First, Laugh Last**.
opposite: Sergio Corbucci liked to cripple his protagonists – Franco Nero, his hands crushed by horses' hooves, sampled the director's cruel streak in **Django**.
right: Locandina for Gianfranco Baldanello's **This Man Can't Die**, a routine vehicle for Guy Madison, veteran of many American westerns.
below: The finale of **Viva Django**, with Terence Hill exhuming a machine gun for a showdown in a cemetery, underlines the debt owed by the film to **Django**.

above: Terence Hill and Bud Spencer ponder their options in **Boot Hill**, Giuseppe Colizzi's western swansong.
right: Tomas Milian made his debut in the genre in **The Bounty Killer** and gave a finely judged performance as an outlaw protected – to their subsequent regret – by his neighbours.
below: Lee Van Cleef lines up a shot in **The Grand Duel**, the best of the westerns he made in the Seventies
opposite: Hectic Spanish poster for **Day of Anger**, another of Van Cleef's master-apprentice westerns, co-starring Giuliano Gemma as a fledgling gunfighter.

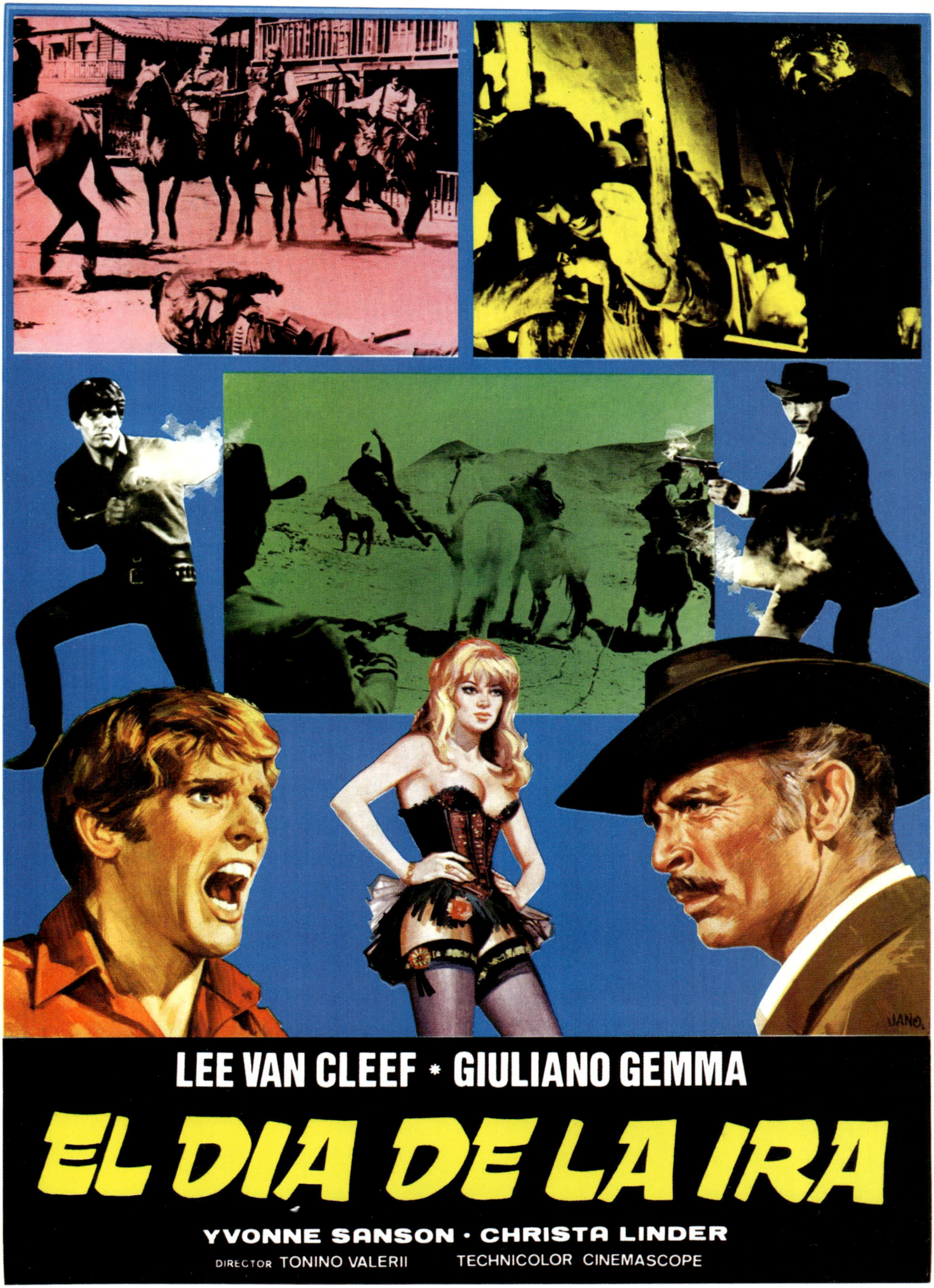
LEE VAN CLEEF • GIULIANO GEMMA
EL DIA DE LA IRA
YVONNE SANSON • CHRISTA LINDER
DIRECTOR TONINO VALERII
TECHNICOLOR CINEMASCOPE

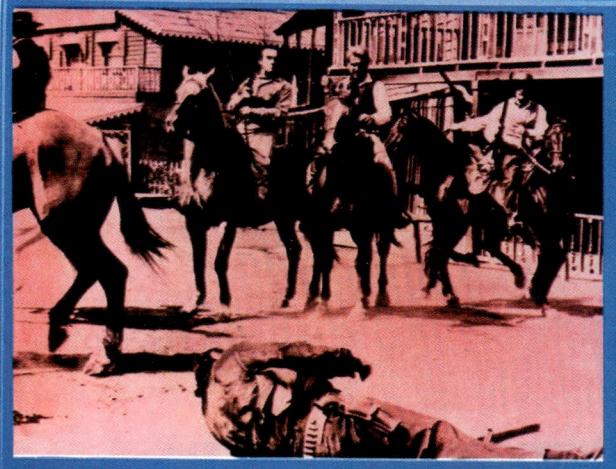

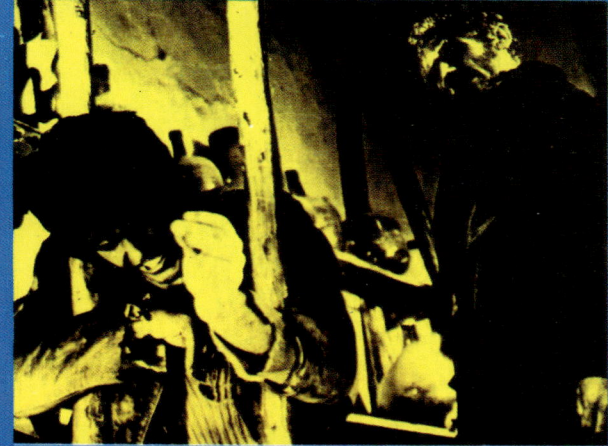

KILLER-KID

IM ADRIA-FILM-VERLEIH

above: Yul Brynner plays it straight – camp costume notwithstanding – in Gianfranco Parolini's hectic **Adios, Sabata**.

opposite top: Rod Steiger unwittingly becomes a revolutionary hero in **A Fistful of Dynamite**.

opposite bottom, and right: Anthony Steffen – in a plot not predicated on revenge, for a change – infiltrates a Mexican rebel outfit in **Killer Kid**, an earnest, exciting 'tortilla western'.

below: Psychedelic front-of-house still featuring Klaus Kinski in **A Bullet for the General**.

above and right: Promotional material for **The Big Gundown**, with Tomas Milian joining Lee Van Cleef for another of the latter's cat-and-mouse westerns.
below: Franco Nero and Tony Musante enacted a similar setup in **A Professional Gun**, based, like **The Big Gundown**, on a story by renowned Marxist writer Franco Solinas.

opposite: 'Trinity' producer Italo Zingarelli's **The Five Man Army** was an adventure in the mould of **The Magnificent Seven**, **The Professionals** and **The Wild Bunch** that paid lip service to fashionable political themes.

this page: In-your-face theatrical poster and stills for Tony Anthony and Ferdinando Baldi's **Comin' at Ya!**, a variation on **Blindman** that spearheaded a brief 3-D revival in the early Eighties. Ever the opportunist, Anthony has thrown his support behind a plan to re-release the film during the 21st Century 3-D craze.
opposite top: Complementary posters for the Stateside releases of Gianfranco Parolini's **Adios, Sabata** and **Return of Sabata**.
opposite bottom: Sergio Leone is reported to have nominated Homer as the greatest writer of westerns. Duccio Tessari evidently agreed, patterning **The Return of Ringo** after 'The Odyssey', with Giuliano Gemma as the war hero usurped in his absence by George Martin (far left in the fotobusta, with dagger).

An ALBERTO GRIMALDI Production
YUL BRYNNER
in
"ADIÓS, SABATA"
SABATA AIMS TO KILL ...and his gun does the rest!
with
DEAN REED
PEDRO SANCHEZ
JOSEPH PERSAUD
SUSAN SCOTT and with GIANNI RIZZO
Story and Screenplay by RENATO IZZO and GIANFRANCO PAROLINI
Produced by ALBERTO GRIMALDI · A Film by FRANK KRAMER
COLOR
GP
United Artists
71/120

HE'S JUDGE... JURY... EXECUTIONER!
THE MAN WITH THE GUNSIGHT EYES IS BACK!
An ALBERTO GRIMALDI Production
LEE VAN CLEEF
in
"RETURN of SABATA"
with REINER SCHONE
and ANNABELLA INCONTRERA GIANPIERO ALBERTINI JACQUELINE ALEXANDRE PEDRO SANCHEZ NICK JORDAN VASSILLI KARIS
and with GIANNI RIZZO
Story and Screenplay by RENATO IZZO and GIANFRANCO PAROLINI
A Film by FRANK KRAMER
A COPRODUCTION PEA/ROME - LES PRODUCTIONS ARTISTES ASSOCIES/PARIS - ARTEMIS FILM/BERLIN
TECHNICOLOR® TECHNISCOPE®
United Artists
PG
72/291

GIULIANO GEMMA (MONTGOMERY WOOD) in
IL Ritorno di Ringo
un EASTMANCOLOR della Tecnostampa
CINERIZ
FERNANDO SANCHO
HALLY HAMMOND
NIEVES NAVARRO
ANTONIO CASAS
PAJARITO
GEORGE MARTIN
Regia di
DUCCIO TESSARI
Prodotto da
ALBERTO PUGLIESE
LUCIANO ERCOLI
P.C.M. PRODUZIONI
CINEMATOGRAFICHEMEDITERRANEE, Roma
ZZOLI FILM S.p.A. Roma

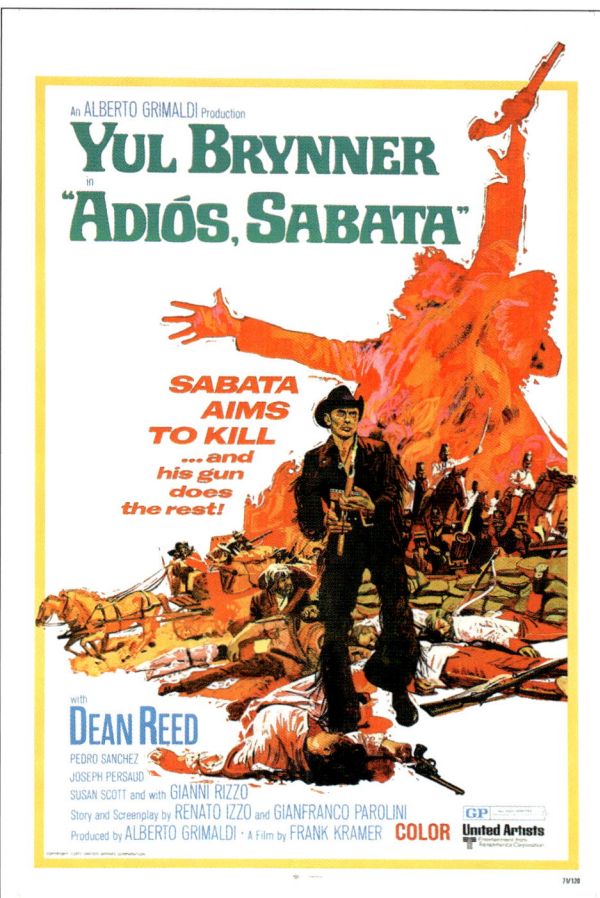

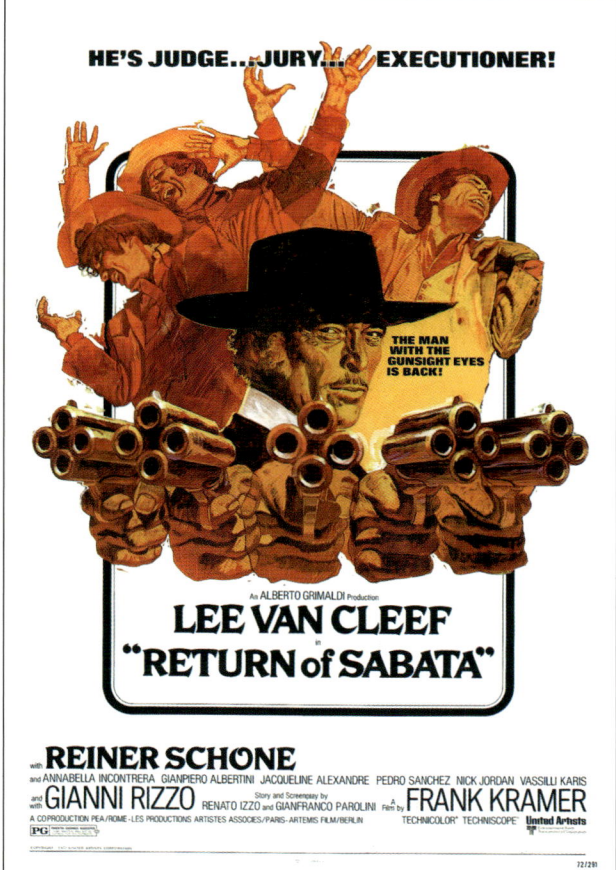

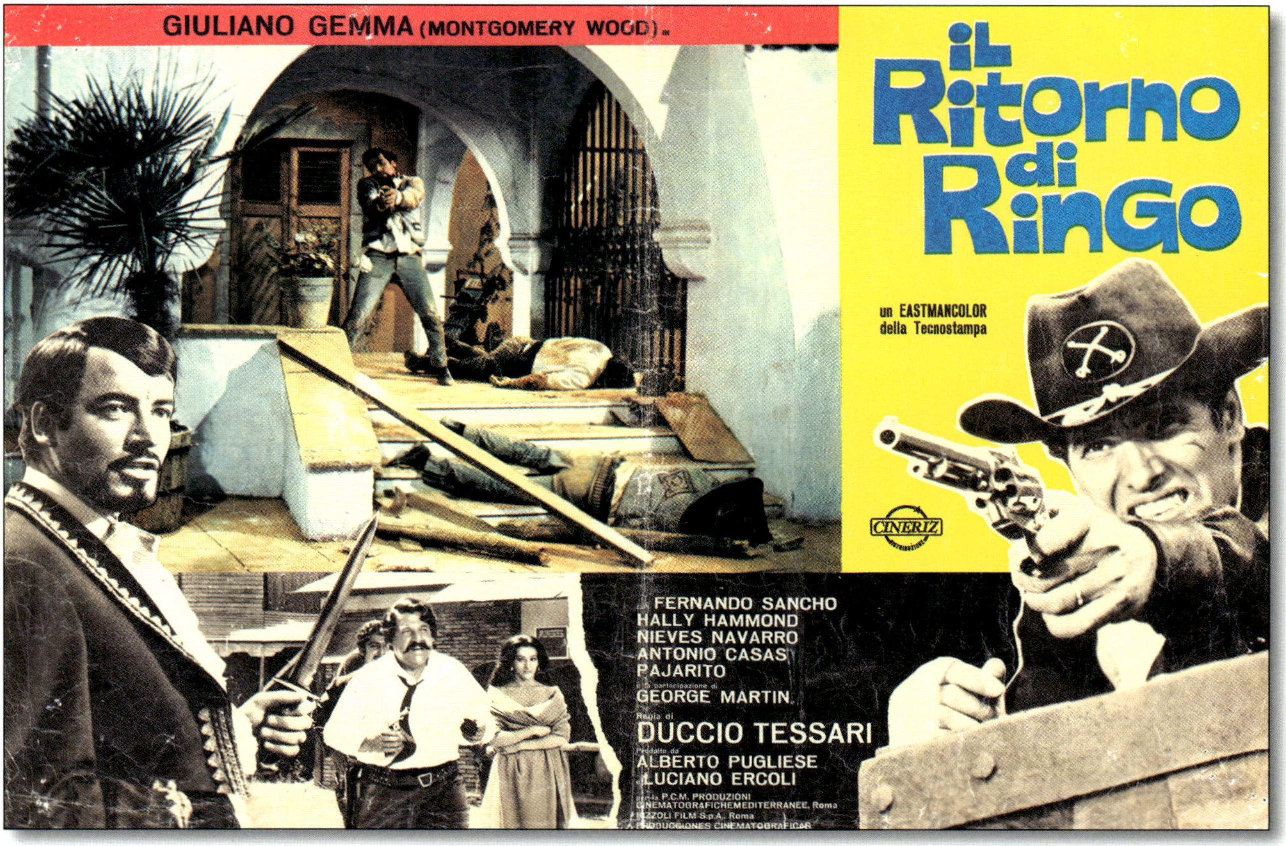

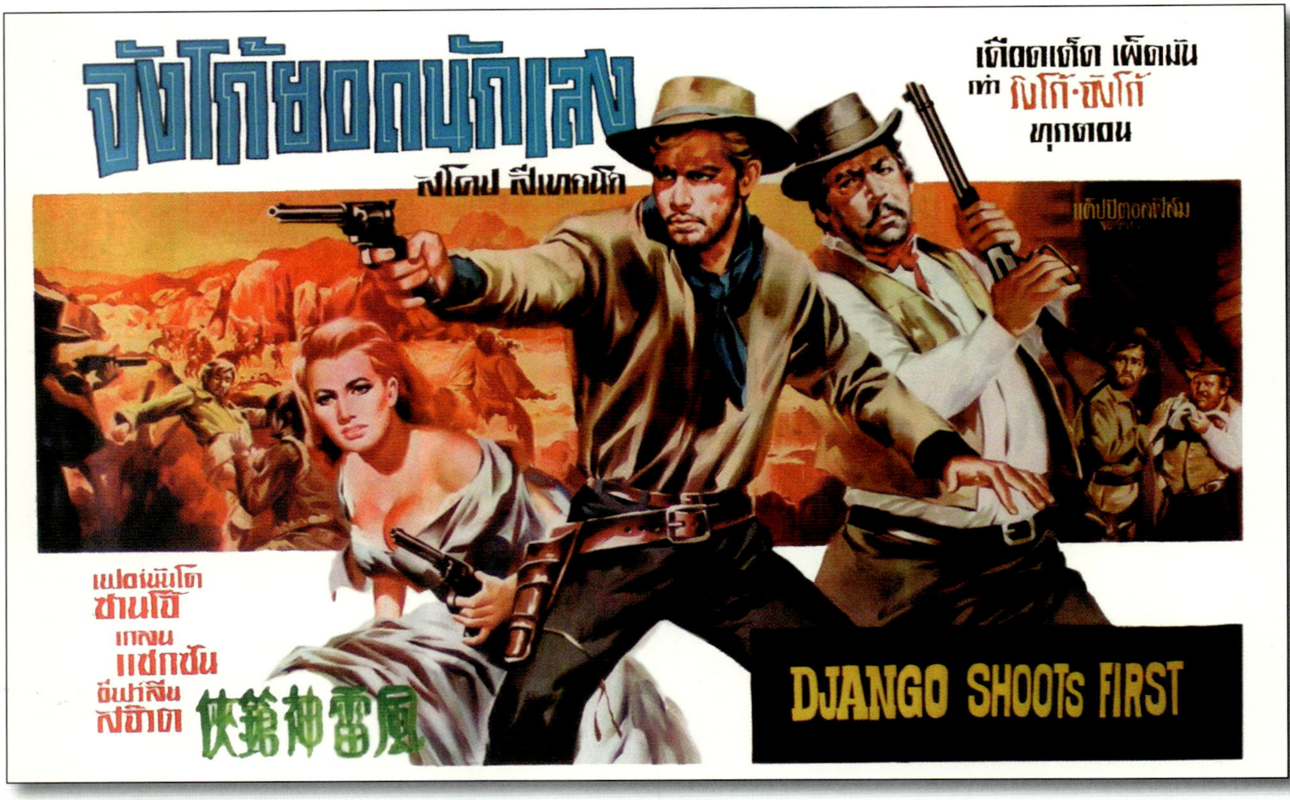
DJANGO SHOOTs FIRST

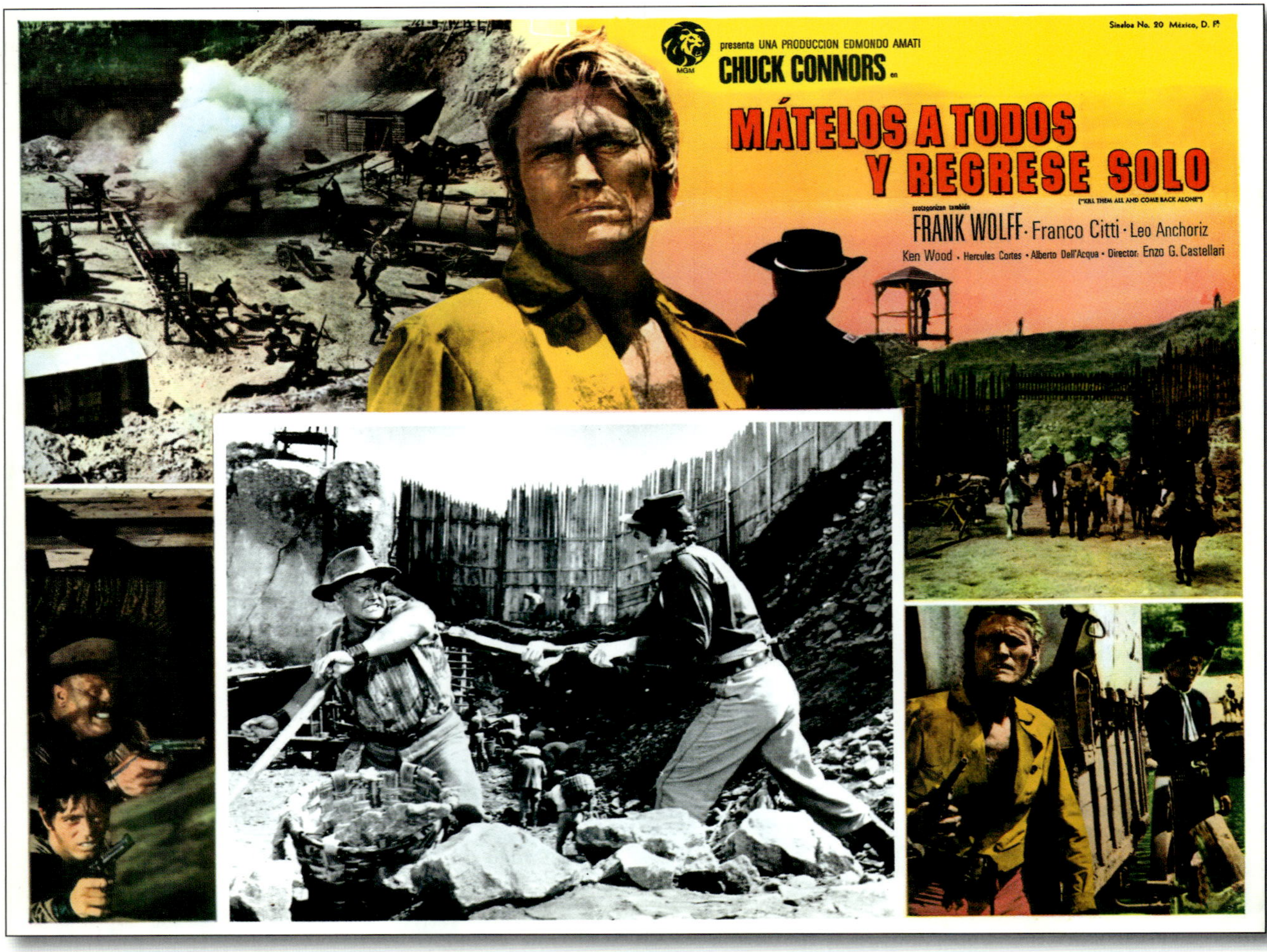
Sinaloa No. 20 México, D. F.
presenta UNA PRODUCCION EDMONDO AMATI
CHUCK CONNORS en
MÁTELOS A TODOS Y REGRESE SOLO
("KILL THEM ALL AND COME BACK ALONE")
protagonizan también
FRANK WOLFF · Franco Citti · Leo Anchoriz
Ken Wood · Hercules Cortes · Alberto Dell'Acqua · Director: Enzo G. Castellari

above: Mexican lobby card for **I Am Sartana, Your Angel of Death**, the second film in the series, which benefits from Klaus Kinski's presence as a surprisingly good-natured bounty hunter.
left and below: Twenty years on, Franco Nero returned to his most iconic role in **Django Strikes Again**, the only sequel supposedly endorsed by Sergio Corbucci.

opposite top: Alberto De Martino's light-hearted **Django Shoots First** wrong-foots those expecting the brooding tone of **Django** itself; it's also unusual to see Fernando Sancho as a good guy, without a sombrero or bandoleer in sight.
opposite bottom: Mexican lobby card for **Kill Them All and Come Back Alone**.

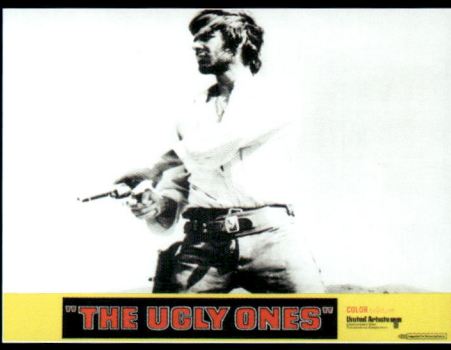

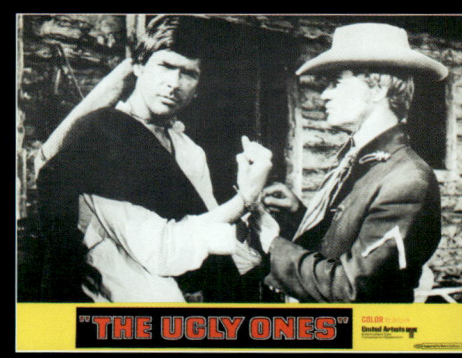

top: Fotobusta for **The Ruthless Four** spotlighting an especially sinister Klaus Kinski.
above: Two lobby cards for **The Bounty Killer**, retitled in the US to cash in on all things Sergio Leone.
left: Crude American ad for **Day of Anger** that trumpets Lee Van Cleef's credentials.
opposite: Action-packed Spanish poster for **A Bullet for the General**, first and arguably foremost of the 'tortilla westerns'.

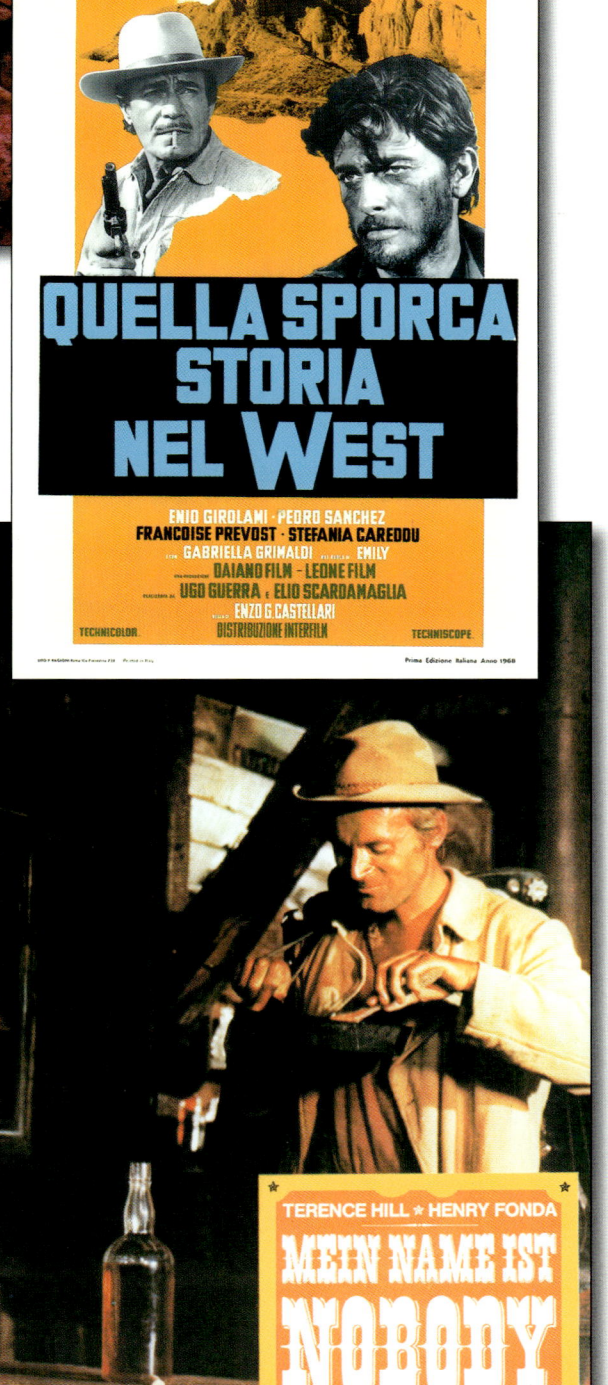

above: Norma Jordán – later a minor star of sexploitation movies – in a German lobby card for Tonino Valerii's **The Price of Power**.
right: Locandina for **Johnny Hamlet** showing Andrea Giordana and Gilbert Roland.
below: Terence Hill's anonymous trickster pesters his idol, Jack Beauregard (Henry Fonda), in **My Name Is Nobody**.
opposite: This Italian poster for **Once Upon a Time in the West** grants Claudia Cardinale a Leone-esque close-up. The inset image shows Leone acolyte Claudio Mancini as Harmonica's murdered brother.

top left: Japanese poster comprising a tableau of arresting images from **The Return of Ringo**.

top right: Franco Nero in two scenes from Ferdinando Baldi's **Texas Adios**, one of the star's more traditional, American-style westerns.

left: Giovanni Grimaldi's **In a Colt's Shadow**, one of those early Italian productions suspended between Hollywoodian romanticism and European iconoclasm.

opposite:
Lady killer: Raquel Welch strikes a disarming pose as the aggrieved heroine of **Hannie Caulder**, a surprisingly gritty rape-and-revenge tale shot in Spain by American director Burt Kennedy. It was quite a departure for Kennedy, for whom jokey buddy westerns were the norm.

By the time of **God's Gun**, a late vehicle for Lee Van Cleef, sacrilegious imagery was par for the course.

Chapter 3

Relatives And Religion

Brotherly feuds, troublesome priests and other recurrent themes

Although the post-Leone Euro-western was geared towards international acclaim – hence the use of universal themes and archetypal antagonists – it maintained strong links with the popular culture and cinematic traditions of Italy.[1] Commercialisation played its part in sustaining at least a general awareness of the genre. In its heyday, western imagery was used to sell Italians everything from canned meat ('Ringo' was a notable brand) to clothing, much of it via the popular nightly *Caroselli* – advertising segments consisting of commercials starring the likes of Giuliano Gemma, George Hilton, Peter Lee Lawrence and Terence Hill, directed by such luminaries as Duccio Tessari, Franco Giraldi, Giulio Questi and Giulio Petroni, photographed by Massimo Dallamano and Tonino Delli Colli, among others, and scored by such leading composers as Ennio Morricone and Francesco De Masi – while *fumetti* (comics), *cineromanzi* (photo-storybooks) and pop music were all part of the phenomenon.[2] But filmmakers remained at the forefront and looked to engage domestic viewers on an emotional level by repeatedly exploring such fundamental areas of national interest as family relations and honour, religion and revenge. It's not that Italian westerns were 'Italian' in the sense of *Rocco and His Brothers* (1960) or *The Leopard* (1963), to take two famous films that interrogated familial themes in the context of the social reality and political history of the peninsula. But neither are they all as detached from national considerations as their usual dismissal as ersatz-Americana or abstract, mythic fantasies would suggest. Protagonists were often a mixture of individualistic loner and Italianate everyman, especially in the stark revenge stories that cluttered up the *seconda visione* circuit. Accompanying characters, particularly bandits and rogues like Eli Wallach's Tuco, displayed exaggeratedly Latin/Mediterranean emotionalism, while the prominence of churches, cemeteries, crosses and clergymen, not to mention tolling bells and organ chords on the soundtracks, is a constant reminder of the Catholic background shared by the filmmakers and their immediate audience. There is also an argument, proposed by Marcia Landy among others, that the backdrop of crumbling, sweltering border towns encountered in Leone's films, for example, substitutes in a metaphorical sense for the clichéd image of southern rural Italy. Both regions, like the wild west of yore, are usually portrayed as lawless and plagued by official corruption, and we shall see in the next chapter how these conditions engendered what is perceived to be a cynical, self-defensive sensibility among the inhabitants.

This kind of dramatic material and typology is not, of course, restricted to the Italian film industry alone, nor can we know to what extent domestic audiences truly participated, vicariously, in the characters' travails. The fact remains, however, that themes like these have always bisected the often paper-thin divide between 'high' and 'low' cinema in Italy, running through everything from genre pieces (the *commedia all'italiana* cycle of the Fifties/Sixties,

above: Sergio Leone's westerns are distinctly Italianate. Eli Wallach's Tuco, for example, was almost a caricature of Latin hyper-emotionalism.

Raffaello Matarazzo melodramas) to more 'respectable' fare (neorealist dramas, historical reconstructions and literary adaptations like *The Leopard*). The westerns that trade on these themes can thus be examined in two ways: firstly, at face value, as variations on a mythological pattern that was never 'set' in the first place; and secondly, despite their pseudo-American historical context, as part of an ongoing inquiry into the nature of 'Italianness' and the function and value of Italy's dominant social institutions.

With this in mind, the films' provenance seems particularly significant in their ambivalent treatment of the family, the role of women, and the Church. Taken as a whole, the genre reveals a range of emotional responses to these traditionally sanctified structures, from sentimentality to, more characteristically, suspicion and hostility, with the harmony of the family seen as an illusion, the benevolence of the Church a facade. From comedic in tone to tragic, the films featured in this chapter exemplify the kind of subversive sensibilities – or at least a healthy scepticism towards prevailing conventions and values – that fuelled the Euro-western in general and have been ever-present in Italian popular cinema almost since its inception.

Family feuds and *femmes fatales*

"The family extracts everybody's first loyalty. It must be defended, enriched, made powerful, respected, and feared by the use of whatever means are necessary, legitimate if at all possible, or illegitimate. Nobody should defy it with impunity. Its honour must not be tarnished. All wrongs done to it must be avenged."[3]

Luigi Barzini's approximation of (chiefly southern) Italy as more like a network of families than a centrally governed nation, each clan united against the outside world and its laws, obedient only to their own codes and honour-bound to defend them, may, as Sir Christopher Frayling has pointed out and Barzini himself acknowledged, have more to do with stereotyping than serious sociology, but it does provide a key to the emotional tone and narrative trajectory of many Italian westerns. After all, westerns, like all forms of popular cinema, deal largely in stereotypes. Time and again, allegiance to the family, whether as an ideal or as a physical entity, conflicts with conventional morality and legal requirements, propelling protagonists into a vengeful quest or some other contravention of social order. Dramatic tension is also wrung from the ancient theme of brotherly

above: Marianne Koch and Nino Del Arco – Leone's alternative Madonna and child, respectively – in a shot from **A Fistful of Dollars** that not only apes the Renaissance masters but also taps into Italian/Catholic sensibilities.

rivalry, often connected with questions of illegitimacy and paternity, strength and supremacy, belonging and identity – issues that evidently had enormous resonance for Italian filmmakers and spectators. This is not to say that family traditions were necessarily weak in other countries where the films were co-financed or distributed, nor that audiences there could not have identified with the central figures in their loss and fury. The acknowledged pre-eminence of *la famiglia* in the Italian consciousness, however, aligned with a tendency towards unilateral action in matters of honour, is surely a significant factor in the shaping and longevity of the genre on home turf. And, for that matter, in the shaping of other Italian *filoni* that have flourished and faded in the intervening years – from urban cop thrillers and vigilante dramas in the early Seventies, which often involved the rape or murder of the hero's loved ones, to tear-jerkers towards the end of that decade. The trend has continued in recent years, with numerous comedies and dramas exploiting domestic and community themes, from Alessandro D'Alatri's *Casomai* (2002) and Carlo Vanzina's *Sunday Lunch* (2003), to Gabriele Muccino's *Remember Me, My Love* (2003) and Stefano Mordini's *Smalltown, Italy* (2004), the last three all receiving several nominations each at the David di Donatello Awards, Italy's equivalent of the Oscars.

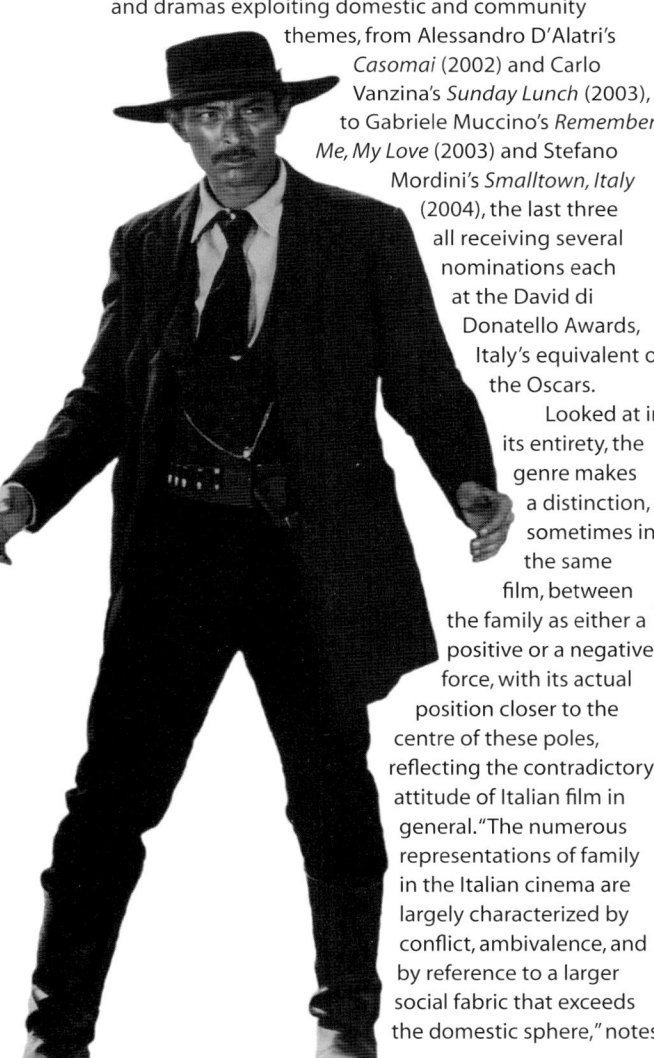

above: Putting the family first: Rod Steiger (*above*) as Juan Miranda – doting father, dutiful son – in **A Fistful of Dynamite**, and Lee Van Cleef (*bottom left*) as Colonel Mortimer, whose preoccupation with avenging his sister's death in **For a Few Dollars More** defines his existence.

Looked at in its entirety, the genre makes a distinction, sometimes in the same film, between the family as either a positive or a negative force, with its actual position closer to the centre of these poles, reflecting the contradictory attitude of Italian film in general. "The numerous representations of family in the Italian cinema are largely characterized by conflict, ambivalence, and by reference to a larger social fabric that exceeds the domestic sphere," notes Marcia Landy.[4] In Sergio Leone's works, family is a rare object of compassion, unsullied by cynicism, although the obduracy of the director's overall vision still applies. 'Joe' takes pity on the substitute Holy Family in *A Fistful of Dollars* (1964) and receives a savage beating for his pains from the Rojos, with the latter, like the Baxters, contrasted with the wholesomeness of Marisol and her husband and child. Both Mortimer in *For a Few Dollars More* (1965) and Harmonica in *Once Upon a Time in the West* (1968) are obsessed with avenging a sibling's death, their lives effectively in stasis until this objective is attained, while elsewhere in these films entire families are needlessly massacred. Tuco and his brother Pablo dispute the meaning of family loyalty in *The Good, the Bad and the Ugly* (1966) in a sequence that greatly boosts our understanding of the outlaw's mentality, while Juan, Tuco's counterpart in *A Fistful of Dynamite* (1971), is the genre's clearest example of what sociologist Edward Banfield famously termed an 'amoral familist', his efforts and affections reserved almost exclusively for his kinfolk. (Students of the genre will be familiar with Banfield via Sir Christopher Frayling's classic *Spaghetti Westerns*.) In the first part of the film Juan is rarely seen apart from his many sons ("Each of them from a different mother") and his aged father. The family travels, steals and kills as a unit, and it is when Juan is distracted away from his responsibilities by John and the revolution that his loved ones are killed.

There are comparatively few films where families *en masse* – as opposed to avenging husbands or feuding brothers, for example – play an active part in the drama. Like women, the clan is usually there for the sole purpose of suffering and providing the central character with his motivation. (There is another intriguing parallel here between the western, unequivocally a male-oriented genre, and melodrama, which is traditionally directed at, and often centred on, women, although the nature of female suffering and the crises that arise are, of course, of a different nature.) Even fewer films convey an upbeat impression of families as interdependent and steadfastly loyal, and of family life as comforting and attractive – in other words, as being worthy of the reverence they have traditionally been accorded. Among these exceptions are a number of titles from the genre's formative years, when a conventional attitude towards the family prevailed and the shadow of Hollywood and its moral imperatives still loomed large. Here we find the revenge western *Gunfight at Red Sands* (1963) by Ricardo Blasco, in which three siblings fight side by side to punish their father's killer. (In the same year, Joaquín Romero Marchent's ostensibly similar *Gunfight at High Noon* dwelt more on the fraught relationship and contrasting dispositions of vengeful brothers than on their common cause.) A later, better-known example is the comedic *Seven Guns for the MacGregors* (1966), which lionises a doughty Scottish clan that eliminates a band of marauding Mexicans, with the seven virile brothers of the title joined by their elders for the final confrontation. The majority of familial revenge films, meanwhile, of which there are a great many, uphold unquestioningly Barzini's 'laws': the avenger has a near-sacred duty to right his family's wrongs and is rarely troubled by doubts or anything resembling a conscience. (The next chapter looks at the revenge motif and its many derivations in greater depth.) The genre also produced several variations on *Shane* (1953), the classic expression of the nomadic hero's dilemma when the comforts of hearth and home are opened up to him. Most of these efforts prove that sentimentalism – one of the perceived

above: **Shane**, Italian-style: Ivan Rassimov as the titular hero of **Cjamango**, part phlegmatic gunfighter, part surrogate father to Giusva Fioravanti.

weaknesses of the Hollywood western that Leone, Corbucci etc. were reacting against – was not completely eradicated in Europe but survived, even flourished, in more 'parochial', less imaginative productions. For example, *Clint the Stranger* (1967), *Cjamango* (1967), *I'll Sell My Skin Dearly* (1968), in which the hero is even named Shane, and *If You Want to Live... Then Shoot!* (1968) are concerned with their protagonists' potential as husbands and fathers as much as their pistol skills. These films preserve, more

above: Sibling loyalty, rather than the more prevalent sibling rivalry, is one of the themes of **Gunfight at Red Sands**, aka **Gringo**, with Richard Harrison (in his first western) in the kind of steadfast, square-jawed role that suited him best.

above: Sergio Garrone's **If You Want to Live... Then Shoot!** (featuring the director's brother, Riccardo, *centre*) has the sour tone of a typical Euro-western, cut through with a dash of Hollywood romanticism.

or less intact, the romantic qualities that their bolder contemporaries mostly dispensed with. At the same time, they lack *Shane*'s mythic potency, its grasp of the gunfighter's existential dilemma. Their central figures are docile rather than conflicted, seemingly only too willing to be 'tamed'. The endings of *Clint the Stranger* and *I'll Sell My Skin Dearly* epitomise the soft-heartedness of these films: their respective heroes, played by George Martin and Mike Marshall, accede to the pleas of an adoring young boy to stay – despite Marshall insisting for much of the film that hate has rendered him emotionally impotent – where before them Alan Ladd's Shane had kept on riding.

Echoes of these cloying strains can be heard in the genre's autumn years, with Gianfranco Parolini's *God's Gun* (1976) and Lucio Fulci's maudlin *Silver Saddle* (1978), which team Lee Van Cleef and Giuliano Gemma respectively with surrogate sons, as conspicuous examples. This doesn't necessarily imply that the genre had returned to its ingenuous, inoffensive beginnings. Made in the same era, *California* (1977) veers towards romanticism only to jolt us back into reality, as Gemma's hard-bitten soldier finds a warm welcome in the home of a fallen army comrade only for tragedy to intervene. Michele Lupo's film provides a timely reminder that

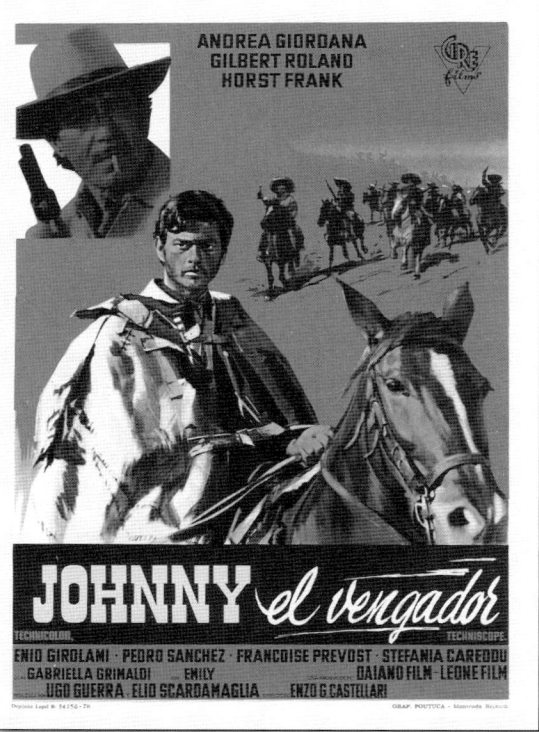

above: Spanish poster for **Johnny Hamlet**. Shakespeare's heady mixture of tragedy, bloodshed and dysfunctional relationships was tailor-made for the Italian western.
bottom left: Spanish admat for Alberto Cardone's **Blood at Sundown**, a film steeped in Italian cultural stereotypes, not least a powerful matriarch with two squabbling sons under her thumb.

domestic bliss is not inscribed in the true Euro-western protagonist's destiny.

In stories like these, as in most westerns where a pastoral image of family life is set forth, the threats to its survival are external, emanating from the lawless wasteland around it. More representative of the genre's provocative and pessimistic line of thinking are those films in which the foundations of the family are threatened from within, its fabric rent by destructive passions, individual weaknesses and the rebellious instincts of those who, for one reason or another, don't conform. Classical tragedy proved a useful vehicle for opposing the veneration of the family. In *Fedra West* (1968), *Johnny Hamlet* (1968), *The Forgotten Pistolero* (1969) and *In the Dust of the Sun* (1971), families are torn asunder by greed, incestuous desires and mutual animosity. The various influences on the films – Shakespeare, Greek tragedy, melodrama, Mediterranean customs – coalesce around the themes of revenge and the troublesome nature of female characters. In each case, a woman is the principal agent of tragic developments and the prime threat to family stability, corresponding to an underlying ambiguity concerning women in popular cinema, where sentimentality often collides with a latent misogyny; this is certainly evident

above: Rosalba Neri's character in **Johnny Yuma**, a hard-hearted temptress who engineers a murderous plot, was straight out of the school of film noir. She also epitomised a jaundiced (male) vision of malicious, conniving femininity widespread in Italian popular cinema.

in Italy's output.[5] Considering the dearth of strong roles for actresses in the Euro-western, however – most filmmakers being in agreement with Sergio Leone that "usually, the woman [in a western] just holds up the story"[6] – it is at least appreciable to see female characters in positions of power and influence, providing the scope for commanding performances such as Luciana Paluzzi's tormented wife and mother in *The Forgotten Pistolero*, Carroll Brown [Carla Calò] as the brooding matriarch in *Blood at Sundown* (1966), and Rosalba Neri's wicked aunt in *Johnny Yuma* (1966). The 'normal' order of gender relations is upturned as these women dominate the men in their lives: Paluzzi's power in both hacienda and the bedroom intimidates and frustrates her lover (Alberto de Mendoza), who channels his feelings of inadequacy into brutality against his workers; Brown's feuding sons become meek before her, each desperate for her approval in sharp contrast to their assertiveness with others; and the smouldering Neri wields her sexuality like a weapon, controlling both her brother, with whom it's implied she has an incestuous relationship, and her old flame, a renowned gunfighter who becomes embroiled in her schemes. Imposing women like these, who turn up in all manner of Italian films, from neorealism to *pepla*, comedies and *gialli*, are a world away from the passive heroines one encounters in more prosaic examples of the genre, represented at one extreme by Cameron Mitchell's wife in *The Last Gun* (1964), who proclaims that "a woman wants to feel protected"; and at the other by the infuriatingly meek Susan George in *Bandits* (1972), who tolerates all manner of abuse from Tomas Milian's sexist *bandido*. Yet, while they provide a breath of fresh air in terms of typology, in most cases these 'black widows' or *malafemmine* ('bad women') are condemned as deviants, two-faced *femmes fatales* who, by attempting to rise above their allotted positions, inevitably crash back down again. Order is thus restored.

This punitive posture towards independent women, especially those involved in traditionally male undertakings, persists elsewhere in the genre, betraying a combination of male fear, loathing and misunderstanding where the fairer sex is concerned. In *The Big Gundown* (1967), a widowed rancher, played by Nieves Navarro [Susan Scott], revels in the part of "queen bee" with a retinue of macho men at her bidding. This unusual set-up is shattered when first Tomas Milian and then his pursuer, Lee Van Cleef, show her defiance, and when Van Cleef kills her retainers she is reduced in stature to a pitiful, lonely woman whose assertion of sexual power ("It must be at my orders") masks a willing submissiveness and a desperate need for companionship. Feistier females often court even greater humiliation, illustrated by Magda Konopka's fate as Sweet Mama, sister of the principal villain in *Blindman* (1971). Her aggressive personality is sharply contrasted with that of docile heroine Agneta Eckemyr and her dissipation with the pathetic plight of the captive women at the centre of the plot. By assisting in their torment she's more like one of the boys than one of the girls, which makes her fair game, in terms of the film's archaic sexual politics, for being ignominiously stripped and tied to a pole and, later, having her neck broken in a vicious fight with anti-hero Tony Anthony.

Konopka's is an extreme case, but the genre shows a similarly hard-hearted attitude towards any woman bold and unscrupulous enough to take on the men at their own cynical, greedy games. It's as if their spirit and ingenuity are tolerated, even celebrated, up to a point, but they must be reined in eventually – a meeting of conventional western conservatism and entrenched

above: The return of Ringo: Agneta Eckemyr is menaced by a Beatle in Ferdinando Baldi's **Blindman**.

Italian chauvinism. Striking blonde Linda Veras played strong-willed, seductive and surreptitious characters in *Run, Man, Run* (1968), *Sabata* (1969) and *Chapagua's Gold* (1970), grasping after gold in each case but losing out to male rivals in the end. (Caterina Trentini fares slightly better at the conclusion of *A Golden Sheriff* [1966]; she doesn't get to keep any of the gold that she and her male accomplices, Luigi Giuliani and Jacques Berthier, have spent much of the film squabbling over, but then neither do they.) Nieves Navarro outwits most of the characters vying for a treasure chest in *Gunman in Town* (1970), although she fails to outsmart the omniscient Sartana and is eventually killed by her (male) accomplice, while Evelyn Stewart in *Django Shoots First* (1966) and Françoise Fabian in *The Specialists* (1969) shine as calculating vixens who are eventually knifed and shot to death respectively. This type of duplicitous female had become a stock figure by the time of the comic-western phase, but the opportunity remained for a charismatic actress to make the most of the part. Gina Lollobrigida grasps the nettle in *Bad Man's River* (1971), managing to be both charming and devious as she entices and discards a chain of gullible men (including Lee Van Cleef and an ill-at-ease James Mason) to suit her purpose. The film's indulgence of this scheming character results from

above: The legendary Gina Lollobrigida eclipsed a strong male cast – led by James Mason (*left*) and Lee Van Cleef (*right*), with Gianni Garko in the background – in the comedic **Bad Man's River**.

the genial tone it shares with other comedies of the time and, of course, the affection that *La Lollo* engendered in her collaborators and the public.

Clearly, the majority of European productions shared the reductive view of womanhood found in traditional American westerns, exacerbated by the 'Madonna-whore' complex prevalent in Latin cultures,

above: Striving for equality (of a sort): Linda Veras, here with William Berger, dreams of a better life away from the saloon halls in **Sabata** but, like other female schemers in the genre, she ends up duped by a man and empty handed.

and did little to liberate female characters from their stereotypical categorisations. Nevertheless, as we have seen, certain performers were able to give a spark of individuality to even the most clichéd of roles, testifying to the untapped talent of many of the actresses who, like their male counterparts, found themselves typecast during this period. Gloria Milland brings genuine pathos to her suffering heroine roles in Joaquín Romero Marchent's *Gunfight at High Noon* (1963) and *Seven from Texas* (1964). María Cuadra ably conveys the ambiguities of spurned lover Roselyn – based on the hero's former flame in *Romeo and Juliet* – in *Fury of Johnny Kid* (1967). Corinne Marchand's bereaved saloon owner gives a good account of herself against Giuliano Gemma's characteristically smart-mouthed gunfighter in *Arizona Colt* (1966), even throwing his own catchphrase back at him at one point. The characters played by Nieves Navarro in Duccio Tessari's 'Ringo' films fulfil a familiar function – she is the dark-haired and sexually alluring counterpart to the fair-haired, prim and proper Lorella De Luca – but they are more proactive than their nominally decorative purpose might suggest. In both cases, Navarro uses her charms benignly to undermine the worst excesses of the villains (with whom she is allied), even assisting in their rout in the sequel. Female freedom fighters make a strong impression in several of the political westerns, with Martine Beswick's fiery Adelita in *A Bullet for the General* (1966) especially outstanding. It's equally noteworthy when female victims display unexpected dignity and defiance, even though their actions often herald a tragic outcome. Michèle Mercier in *Cemetery Without Crosses* (1969) and Vonetta McGee in *The Great Silence* (1968) give understated and affecting performances as recently widowed women who engage avengers to pursue the guilty, setting in motion a chain of events that can only end in their own destruction. Pilar Velázquez pursues a similarly vindictive campaign against her mother and the latter's lover in *The Forgotten Pistolero*, utilising her youth and beauty to create jealous tension between them. While Velázquez survives the resulting cataclysm, it is only at the cost of significant emotional scarring.

Certain films rang the changes by way of gender confusion. In *Gunman of 100 Crosses* (1971), the requisite 'mysterious' gang boss is revealed to be a woman (Monica Miguel), albeit one who dresses like a *caballero* complete with an elaborately embroidered sombrero. This sexual role-reversal adds a kinky *frisson* to the film's only memorable scene, when Miguel uses her ever-present whip to strip the clothes from beleaguered heroine Marina Malfatti (real name Marina Rabbissi, director Carlo Croccolo's wife) until she is completely naked, all for the delectation of Miguel's leering male underlings and, of course, for the film's male spectators,

above: Vonetta McGee as the downtrodden yet dignified Pauline in **The Great Silence** – widowed and seemingly powerless, she refuses to accept her lot.
inset: Poster for **The Tall Women** positing the film as a distaff **Magnificent Seven**, although its actual model was the lesser-known **Westward the Women**.

although this scene – unusually revealing in a genre curiously coy when it comes to female flesh – is trimmed in most versions. (Not least in the domestic print, since Italian censors – obliged to appease the ruling Christian Democrats and, by extension, the Catholic Church – took a much dimmer view of nudity than they did of violence.) Elsewhere, Patty Shepard, an eye-catching American actress in the Barbara Steele mould who was prominent in Seventies Spanish horror movies, reworks another stock figure in *The Man Called Noon* (1973). As Peg Cullane, Shepard first appears as a seemingly sweet, shy girl in mourning garb, transforming later into a ruthless, black-clad gunslinger, a woman capable of killing her own brother in her pursuit of riches and who takes on Rosanna Schiaffino in a *Johnny Guitar*-style shoot-out. Equality thus arrives in the Euro-western at last, such monstrous crimes as fratricide having previously been the preserve of male characters.

As effective and well acted as they are, these gold-diggers, victims and villainesses are essentially supporting characters. It is rare to see female *protagonists* in European productions, which makes it important to credit the exceptions. The Italian-Spanish-Austrian *The Tall Women* (1966), directed by American Sidney Pink, trumps all others by centring on no fewer than *seven* females, most of whom prove to be resilient and capable – more so than the men they encounter – on a dangerous trek through Indian country. Although obviously indebted to *Westward the Women* (1951), it doesn't rely as that film did on a strong male presence to galvanise the women into action. An army scout is introduced late on but promptly gets himself wounded – "A man finally shows up and he's too sick to help us," complains one of the heroines. Instead, there is a commanding turn from Hollywood veteran Anne Baxter, who balances compassion and tough-minded common sense as the group's natural leader.

Other 'women's westerns' include a string of disposable star vehicles that shoehorn their heroines into the kind of roles traditionally played by actors – more examples of gender confusion – at the same time as relentlessly exploiting their stars' most marketable assets. Pint-sized pop singer Rita Pavone played a singing gunfighter in *Rita of the West* (1967), for example, while Cuban-American singer/dancer Lola Falana, the so-called 'First Lady of Las Vegas', capitalised on her popularity in Italy with the title role in *Lola Colt* (1967), playing a showgirl who rouses a cowed town against a land-grabbing tyrant. (Falana was a regular on the weekly Italian variety show *Sabato sera* ['Saturday night'] alongside domestic pop goddess Mina.) Siro Marcellini's film is a traditional B-western in every sense but one – the hero happens to be a leggy black *chanteuse*, and the narrative is broken up regularly by raunchy song routines more suited to the glitzy casinos of contemporary Vegas than the saloons of the old west.

above: Rosanna Schiaffino, with Stephen Boyd in the foreground, joins in the gunplay at the end of **The Man Called Noon** – she is even granted a showdown with bad girl Patty Shepard.

Even stranger is *Garter Colt* (1968), Italian starlet Nicoletta Machiavelli's attempt to rise above supporting status. She plays an adventuress named Lulu (purportedly the niece of Dumas' Marguerite Gautier), who becomes involved in the Mexican insurrection against Maximilian. Lulu is a distaff version of the Euro-western's then fashionable gambler-cum-gunfighter: free-spirited, an expert in armaments and seemingly indestructible. Incongruously, considering the ideological bent of most genre films and, indeed, of much Italian cinema at the time, Lulu intervenes on the side of the colonialist French, represented by dashing young heroes, against the indigenous rebels led by bungling, brutal Walter Barnes and mentally unstable Claudio Camaso as 'the Red' – a none-too-subtle dig at the far left. In between changing in and out of a series of cleavage-revealing dresses designed for her by the esteemed Piero Gherardi, a favourite of Fellini's, Machiavelli finds time to fall in love with a French double agent.

This peculiar project was initiated by Machiavelli, her brother Brandino, who produced and co-stars as a Frenchman, and her boyfriend at the time, who was co-producer. The mixture of action, romance and titillation centred on a sexy, super-confident heroine may have looked promising on paper as a kind of Modesty Blaise out west, but its realisation by director Gian Andrea Rocco, an obscure figure with only three titles to his name, leaves much to be desired. As a character, Lulu is as scantily developed as she is often clad, Machiavelli's uncertainty as an actress at this young stage of her career further undermining the protagonist's credibility. *Garter Colt* is ultimately more interesting for its odd details and amusing implausibilities, such as Lulu's personalised

Continental westerns were very much *à la mode* in the mid-Sixties; even Brigitte Bardot, the era's hippest sex symbol, graced its presence, injecting glamour into **Shalako** (*above*) and – alongside the equally bewitching Claudia Cardinale – **The Legend of Frenchie King** (*right*).

pistol with its heart-shaped barrel, and for Rocco's stabs at surrealistic humour: Lulu's helper is a gun-toting dwarf she transports in a carry-cot, for example, while her lover is aided by a resourceful parrot. Rocco's visuals, too, are occasionally arresting, making imaginative use of the frame and the unusual landscapes, with exteriors shot around the salt flats of Sardinia's Oristano province.

Machiavelli's gambit was an interesting failure in artistic and commercial terms, achieving only limited distribution. Wider exposure was granted to Louis Malle's atypically screwball semi-western *Viva Maria!* (1965), which paired fashionable French stars Jeanne Moreau and Brigitte Bardot as good-time girls involved in insurrectionary activities in an unnamed South American country. Via a supporting role in the multicultural western *Shalako* (1968), Bardot later teamed with another great screen siren, Claudia Cardinale, in the comic *The Legend of Frenchie King* (1971), where they play feuding outlaws who at one point have a sensationally sexy scrap to settle their differences. Elsa Martinelli, meanwhile, who had a brief flirtation with Hollywood in the late Fifties /early Sixties, portrayed the title character in *The Belle Starr Story* (1968), the only Italian western to be directed by a woman, Lina Wertmüller.**7** Although it posits its infamous heroine as a feminist role model, with Martinelli interpreting her as a tough-talking, cigar-chomping tomboy spurred into action by male aggression, Belle's attraction and submission to rival outlaw George Eastman compromises her espousal of independence, just as her adoption of masculine traits compromises her femininity. Equally uneven is the Raquel Welch vehicle *Hannie Caulder* (1971), a British production, from Tigon, in which a feminist-friendly vision of female empowerment – the star punishing three brothers who violated her and killed her husband – is undermined by the use of Welch as an erotic object. The notion of merging a female archetype – rape victim – with the role of avenger normally occupied by a man has great potential in a western milieu, but is not fully realised here. This is mostly because co-writer and director Burt Kennedy, then a prolific source of light-hearted American westerns, can't decide between a serious tone and a crudely comedic one. (He joked about the premise of the film, with its sexy, serape-wearing heroine, in his production diary – reprinted in his memoirs, *Hollywood Trail Boss* – saying that, "Sergio

above: Raquel Welch, here with Robert Culp, sets out to avenge her own rape, and the killing of her husband, in Burt Kennedy's **Hannie Caulder**.

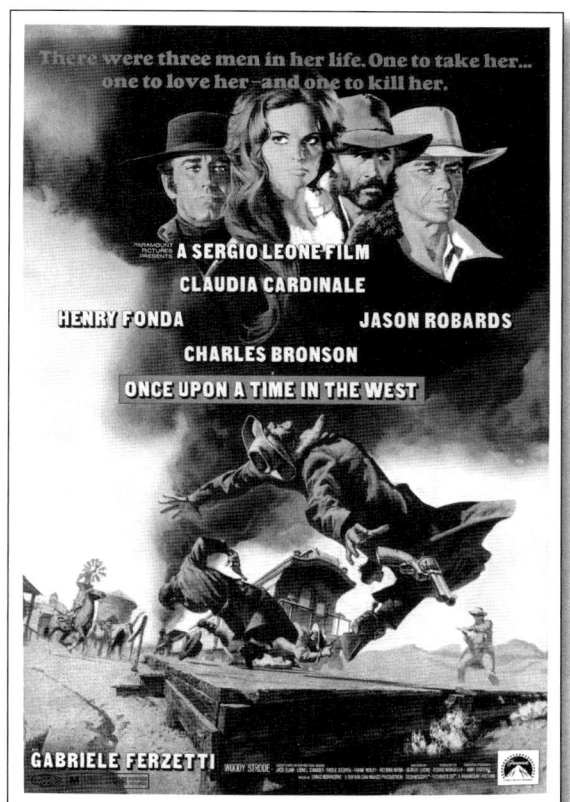

above and left: For Sergio Leone's most expansive western, **Once Upon a Time in the West**, Claudia Cardinale was cast centrally in a story that celebrates those aspects of femininity that appealed to the filmmakers while mourning the passing of an era dominated by male endeavours.

[Leone] would probably call it *A Titful of Dollars*.") Nevertheless, Welch's character possesses a gritty resolve that's both admirable and unusual. And even though for part of the movie she has a male mentor – a bounty hunter (Robert Culp) whom she persuades to teach her to shoot – her determination to succeed in the face of sexist oppression is very much her own.

Sergio Leone exemplifies the genre's ambiguous approach to womankind. For all his argument that women characters interrupt the rhythm of a western (he famously remarked how Rhonda Fleming's part should have been cut from *Gunfight at the O.K. Corral*[8]), and for all that he marginalised them in his own films, women make a profound impression in two of his key works. In *A Fistful of Dollars*, the film that announced a definitive break with American western traditions, nominal heroine Marisol's influence on the action greatly outweighs the time she spends on screen. Ramon's obsession with her, which intensifies when she is 'kidnapped', exacerbates his feud with the Baxters, destroying the *détente* he had earlier insisted was best for business. And as we have already noted, the uncharacteristically altruistic intervention by 'Joe' on her behalf earns him a great deal of pain and scythes into his profits. *Fistful*'s other female is the formidable Consuelo Baxter (Margarita Lozano, Fernando Rey's accomplice in the entrapment of the heroine in Buñuel's *Viridiana* [1961]). Indisputably the head of the family, she is both businesslike – she handles negotiations with the Rojos – and a demanding but devoted wife and mother. Indeed, as with the Rojos, family affairs and business matters are intertwined. For *Once Upon a Time in the West*, partly a hymn to the American tradition, Leone finally placed a woman at the centre of events, albeit one who doesn't become truly proactive until the end. Claudia Cardinale's enchanting performance as Jill adds a warm, romantic quality previously absent from Leone's work. (Co-writer Bernardo Bertolucci has laid claim to Jill's central role in the narrative but, as with other aspects of this most prestigious of Italian westerns, who contributed what is a subject of some dispute. Sergio Donati, who co-wrote the screenplay, stresses *his* influence in focusing Leone's attention on the woman as much as on the men in the narrative.) Jill, like Marisol, causes all the male characters to alter their behaviour, sometimes, as with Frank, against their better judgement. Quickly bereaved upon her arrival in Sweetwater (although she is the antithesis of the poisonous black widows encountered elsewhere in the genre), she also seems bereft of purpose until Harmonica intervenes. Slowly, with his help and that of Cheyenne, she realises her true role. It has been argued that the film is patronising and chauvinistic in its treatment of Cardinale's character. The way she is manipulated by the film's three male protagonists supports this view but, equally, *Once Upon a Time…* is a celebration of what, from a southern Italian male perspective, is an idealised woman, one who combines sexual attractiveness with maternal qualities in one voluptuous frame. Jill is called upon to exercise all her talents in the course of the story: as a whore, she sleeps with Frank in 'self-defence', forestalling his murderous designs; and finally, she evolves into the metaphorical 'mother' to the railroad workers at the hub of a nascent community. She thus achieves the ambition of every western tart with a heart who hopes to leave her shady past behind and become respectable, or at least accepted, elsewhere. More than this, Jill embodies the triumph of civilisation and modernity over the savage but in many respects simpler age when men settled their differences at gunpoint. She represents a world more inclined towards 'feminised', family values – "a world without balls" was Leone's typically rustic and ambivalent assessment – and in this respect she is arguably the most significant and successful character in any Leone film.

An assertive woman has a vital narrative function in the post-Civil War 'trek' western, *The Hellbenders* (1967), where the corrosion of family values is made synonymous with the decline of the Confederate cause, which the clan at the centre of the story claims to represent. Made by Sergio Corbucci in one of his busiest spells as a director, this under-rated film was produced and co-written by Albert Band, a former assistant to John Huston who had helmed a few low-budget features in Hollywood before relocating to Europe in the early Sixties.**9** *The Hellbenders* was a reinterpretation of *The Tramplers*, an American-style western produced, co-written and directed by Band in 1965, although the mood and style of the films are very different.**10** In *The Tramplers*, Joseph Cotten played a fanatical Southern patriarch, Temple Cordeen, who adheres to a debased code of honour that permits him to kill to protect his family heritage and the traditions of the South, which in both cases means the right to keep slaves, and refuses to accept the result of the war. Cotten is opposed by two of his five sons, played by Gordon Scott and a quietly impressive Jim Mitchum, and his daughters, who all break free from the family home (where women are restricted to the first floor) until the rival factions meet for a traumatic showdown. Although *The Tramplers* falls short of its potential – Mitchum's anguish over his true nature, whether he is more like his fair-minded brother or narrow-minded old man, is given insufficient attention – it should not be dismissed as merely a dry run for a more dynamic treatment of the same themes. Band observes the disintegration of the dynasty and the mental collapse of its leader with compassion, and holds out the promise of renewal in the person of Scott, who resists the urge to burn down the Cordeen ranch and instead decides to rehabilitate the family brand in his own noble image.

There is no hope of restitution and very little occasion for compassion in *The Hellbenders*, in which a delusional hypocrite, his three squabbling sons and a hired saloon girl make up a sham Southern family. The title refers to Jonas (Cotten in baroque mode) and his sons Ben (Julián Mateos), Nat (Angel Aranda) and Jeff (a superbly viperous Gino Pernice), remnants of an obsolete Confederate regiment who rob and massacre a Union convoy. They pay first Kitty (María Martín), a boozy harlot with designs on Jonas, to act as widow on their trek homewards, and then Claire (Brazilian expat Norma Bengell), a gambler, who becomes Kitty's replacement when the latter is murdered by Jeff. Jonas, disgusted by General Lee's recent surrender, intends to use the money to fund a guerrilla campaign against the North, but his vision is not shared by his sons – Nat and Jeff are in it for the money, and Ben, although he acts out of filial duty, knows that the cause his father is fighting for is a lost one. This is emphasised by the fact that the money is hidden in a coffin, purportedly containing the corpse of an officer killed at Nashville. The metaphor is apt – it signifies the futility of Jonas's obsession and also the death of the noble Southern creed he and his sons repeatedly violate throughout the film.

Corbucci had already derided Southern values in *Django* (1966), in the form of Major Jackson, and here the characters make a mockery of everything from religious observance and hospitality to family solidarity and honour in general. Jonas leads his sons in prayer before they cold-bloodedly shoot down the soldiers, following this by killing two hired helpers. "They're no kin", says Jonas dismissively, "they died for the cause". Later, in a stunningly photographed nocturnal scene, the boys desecrate a cemetery after Claire, who becomes progressively more proactive, arranges for her 'husband' to have an army burial. And Jonas, belying his espousal of traditional values, shoots at a bandit (Aldo Sambrell) even though he's bearing a white flag, an incident that has ironic repercussions at the end of the film. All these offences illustrate the Hellbenders' moral decay and contribute to the (self-) destruction of the group, but above all it's the absence of common purpose and feeling among them that heralds their defeat. Jonas seems oblivious not only to the absurdity of his dream but also to his sons' lack of faith ("Maybe I believe enough for us all"), and is blind to Nat and Jeff's rapacity. Ben has a good heart but exerts little influence on the others; he was born to a different mother and tells Claire, the only other rational character, that he has always felt like an outsider among his siblings, a common theme in the genre. Not that Nat and Jeff display any fraternal loyalty towards each other. When Jeff's savagery incurs the wrath of an Indian tribe, Nat refuses to allow any of the money to be used to buy his brother's life. "I ain't got no brothers, not since we took that convoy," he spits, and the two of them kill each other in an exchange of fire that also catches Ben.

Where *The Tramplers* was akin to a dynastic power struggle in the mould of *Broken Lance* (1954) or *The Halliday Brand* (1957), which also starred Cotten, *The Hellbenders* is a confluence of influences. Echoes of westerns past, including Corbucci's previous works, mingle with Greek tragedy in the way that happenstance conspires with arrogance in the ruination of the characters. As in *Django*, there is a highly unconventional tragic 'hero' whose hopes for the future are carried in a coffin, although Jonas has fewer empathetic qualities than Franco Nero's gunfighter in the earlier film. Jonas's strength – his sense of purpose – is outweighed by his weakness – the intransigence that has distorted his moral vision – and Corbucci seals the character's downfall with a cruelly ironic reminder of one of his earlier ignoble actions. Dying of wounds, Jonas realises that the coffin contains not the money but the bandit's corpse, the boys having mistakenly unearthed the wrong box. In the light of the bandit's curse, uttered just before his death, this adds an almost supernatural sheen to the outcome – as in classical tragedy, the dead assert a kind of destructive power over the living.

In historical terms, *The Hellbenders* marks something of a halfway point in the development of the genre. Band's story forms a solid basis for Corbucci and co-scenarists Ugo Liberatore (who also worked on *The Tramplers*) and José Gutiérrez Maesso (*Minnesota Clay*, *Django*, *The Bounty Killer*), with Band's acolyte, American writer and producer Louis Garfinkle, working on the dialogue, to darken the waters.[11] While not as immediately radical as *Django* or the 'Dollars' trilogy in form or content, *The Hellbenders* breaks with western traditions in other ways – there is no individual protagonist as such, not even of the ironic Italian variety – while regular motifs and metaphors are utilised in imaginative ways. The explicit association of money with death recalls *Django*, *The Good, the Bad and the Ugly* and others, and the Hellbenders collectively perform the familiar roles of dysfunctional family, Confederate renegades and social outcasts. While the last-named are often favourably contrasted with society in the genre, this can't be said of Jonas, who embodies redundant values, or of his fractious, murderous brood. Their invariably tense encounters with other groups only emphasise how desperate and dishonourable the Hellbenders have become, even in relation to Sambrell's bandit gang. There is no clearer example of how loyalty to the clan and its codes, however questionable, is incompatible with the moral standards of civilisation.

above: Spanish admat for **Seven Dollars to Kill**, another Alberto Cardone western with a strong Italian focus.

"We've too much in common brother – there's no room for both of us in this world"

The typical effect of blood-bonds on seemingly invulnerable Italian western anti-heroes is to humanise them. Instead of the freedom to kill and go as they please, they are forced into moral quagmires and tragic choices, their itinerary and emotional detachment compromised by the urge to rediscover their roots and resolve outstanding family business. At the same time, the theme of brotherly strife expands upon the genre's preoccupation with treachery and avarice, its insistence on the baseness of human motives. If most Euro-western protagonists are cynical to some extent, then as we saw in the previous chapter this is not always without cause. When a man's own kin conspire against him, he has every reason to rage against his fate. Alberto Cardone's *Seven Dollars to Kill* (1966) and *Blood at Sundown* are apposite introductions to this idea. Tragedies masquerading as melodramas masquerading as westerns, they are at once the most self-consciously 'classical' thematically and the most stereotypically Italian emotionally. Cardone was an experienced second-unit director – this was probably his function on the trailblazing German westerns *Massacre at Marble City* (1964) and *The Black Eagles of Santa Fe* (1965), for which he is often wrongly assigned sole directorial credit – and was also among William Wyler's assistants on *Ben-Hur* (1959). This wasn't the springboard to greater things, however, and among the scant dozen or so titles Cardone has directed, it is only his westerns that have garnered any interest. Even in that category his work is erratic – many scenes seem rushed or ill considered, the editing is often ragged, the low budgets prohibitive. Yet if we discard the banal *$20,000 on Number Seven* (1967), a failed attempt at a star vehicle for Cardone regular Jerry Wilson [Roberto Miali], who also co-wrote the script, and *The Long Day of the Massacre* (1968), a formulaic Peter

above: The family that slays together… The first part of the maxim holds true, at least, in **The Hellbenders**.

Martell film with many *longueurs*, there is a unifying rawness about the emotional tone and a boldness in the visual design that makes this director's output at least intermittently exhilarating. His sparse vendetta story *The Wrath of God* (1968) is rich in inventive set pieces, while *$20,000 Stained in Blood*, aka *Kidnapping* (1969), as we shall see later in this chapter, was one of the key 'redemption' westerns.

Seven Dollars to Kill and *Blood at Sundown*, made in tandem with producer Mario Siciliano, later to turn director himself,**12** are brooding, biblically inspired parables of revenge and remorse in which a perfectly cast Anthony Steffen wrestles with ambivalent emotions relating to fatherhood, brotherhood and filial duty. A family man-turned-outlaw killer's vengeful odyssey leads to a fateful showdown with his own son, kidnapped as an infant and raised by bandits; two brothers fight for supremacy under the eyes of their formidable mother… this is vengeance at its most complicated, killing at its most consequential. The air is thick with tragic ironies and overlapping motivations. *Seven Dollars* taps the Oedipus myth for its tempestuous conclusion – Steffen's Johnny Ashley refuses to fire on his progeny, although it's unclear whether the latter (Jerry Wilson) is aware of his opponent's true identity, or whether, with his 'father' (Fernando Sancho) dead at Steffen's hands, the facts would sway his mind in any case. (Considering the enraged Wilson has already gunned down his adoptive mother, it seems unlikely.) The pride and profound affection of fathers for their sons extends even to the rough and ruthless Sancho, a bloodthirsty killer who treats his woman like dirt ("Womenfolk are worse than rattlesnakes") and his 'son' like a prince. The more polished *Blood at Sundown* – infused with emotional punch by scriptwriters Ernesto Gastaldi and Vittorio Salerno, and burnished further by an emphatic Michele Lacerenza trumpet theme – was one of the earliest examples of the 'Cain and Abel' motif. Johnny Liston (Steffen) was imprisoned for murder in place of his power-crazed brother, Sartana (Gianni Garko), and returns home to challenge him. (For an explanation of how Garko transformed Sartana from villain to the genre's most original anti-hero, see *Beware Of Fake Guns…*) What makes this so quintessentially Italian is the coordination of the brothers' enmity with their competitiveness regarding their mother's affections. The contest between good and evil son is in turn spurred by their mother and mirrors her own moral turmoil. Rhonda (Carroll Brown) lives like a queen in the house where once she was a servant, enthroned by Sartana, who has inherited her bitterness towards society as well as her confusion of fear – Sartana having subjugated all the local towns – with respect. This is something she only genuinely receives from her boys, in a series of telling scenes in which they humbly seek her counsel or her favour. As the momentum swings Johnny's way, Rhonda, responding to the townswomen's pleas, takes a hand against Sartana's gang and is mortally wounded. The scene where granite-faced gunfighter Johnny sobs over her body only seems absurd if one ignores the production's cultural background – Luigi Barzini's description of Italy as a "crypto-matriarchy" makes a lot of sense in this context. The finale is equally charged, Sartana embracing his brother in what amounts to a chilling farewell gesture before they duel; their faces, which are hidden from each other, bear thunderous expressions to match the darkening skies, with Johnny reduced to tears for a second time after shooting Sartana down. There is a strong sense in both films of the gravity of Steffen's actions. Although the guilt he bears is psychological rather than criminal – Ashley's son falls on his own knife during a struggle, Sartana is finished off by a secondary character – Steffen ends up a broken man bearing a lonely and terrible burden. Cardone's cheerless western-tragedies will be too bombastic for many tastes – specifically, those attuned to the more restrained, optimistically inclined Hollywood output – but they are indispensable to an understanding of how Italians reformulated ancient themes and western tropes to reflect their own customs, beliefs, experiences and expectations.

above: Life imitated art, up to a point, with Claudio Camaso's casting in **For $100,000 Per Killing** as a man outshone by a high-achieving sibling, since Camaso's brother was the more esteemed Gian Maria Volonté.
opposite: Spanish admats for Alberto Cardone's doom-laden diptych, **Blood at Sundown** (*top left*) and **Seven Dollars to Kill** (*bottom left*), linked by biblical themes and melodramatic denouements.

In other examples, strained fraternal relationships reach breaking point when one brother is discovered to be illegitimate, clouding his own sense of identity and impugning his honour. It also fuels the resentment of his invariably lesser sibling, who has always felt insecure given the other man's superior abilities and higher place in their parents' affections. Flashbacks in *For $100,000 Per Killing* (1967), for instance, reveal that the unstable Clint Forest (Claudio Camaso) was driven to kill his own father in a jealous rage when the latter refused to expel his illegitimate son John (Gianni Garko). Compounding John's anguish, he is then blamed for the murder, suffering the same fate as Johnny Liston in *Blood at Sundown*. The plot becomes an intimate, intense variation on the theme of brothers/friends on opposite sides of the law, with John a bounty hunter and Clint an outlaw, director Giovanni Fago capitalising on the ambiguity of John's position *vis-à-vis* the law and conventional morality and forcing the characters into a neurotic showdown in a ghost town. (It's possible that Camaso empathised with his role particularly closely since his own brother was Gian Maria Volonté, already a well-established actor by the time that Camaso broke into the business. Gianni Garko remembers: "[Claudio] felt the shadow of his big brother – he was very similar in his way of acting – but he had the courage to change his name, so he had a strong sense of autonomy."[13]

Equally pessimistic is Lucio Fulci's first western, *Massacre Time* (1966), which shows that home, far from being a haven for the hero, can be as hazardous as the viperous towns and deserts outside. It also

above: Franco Nero confers with a Confucius-quoting Chinese caricature in **Massacre Time**.

above: Brothers in (fire)arms: George Hilton (*right*) stops sniping at Franco Nero (*left*) as the two find common cause in Lucio Fulci's **Massacre Time**.

adheres to the pattern of return and revenge implicit in the homecoming motif, a popular dramatic device for reawakening dormant tensions among characters, particularly families, which has its origins in Homer and Greek tragedy.¹⁴ (We have already seen this at work in *Blood at Sundown* and will encounter it again in *Chuck Mool* [1970], *Keoma* [1976] and the extraordinary *John the Bastard* [1967], below). Nero's prospector Tom Corbett answers a mysterious summons to his hometown, where the climate is heavy with suspicion, secrecy and fear. Eventually, his cynical, unwelcoming, alcoholic brother Jeff (George Hilton) informs him they are only half brothers – they share the same mother, but Tom's father is actually the town tyrant, Scott (Giuseppe Addobbati), who had Jeff's father murdered years earlier and the Corbett property sequestered to cover his tracks. It transpires that Scott, rather a tame tyrant in truth, beckoned Nero in the hope that he could rein in the old man's acknowledged son, Junior (Nino Castelnuovo), a pathological sadist. (*Massacre Time* bears a resemblance to another of Franco Nero's westerns, *Texas Adios*, directed by Ferdinando Baldi in the same year. In that film, Nero's character, Burt Sullivan, undertakes a quest to avenge his father's murder that is complicated by the revelation that the culprit sired Burt's coltish younger brother. Burt is therefore in the same position as Jeff in *Massacre Time*, although his anger is reserved solely for the killer, not the son.)

Nero's prince-in-waiting is thus opposed on two fronts for different reasons, but Tom is too foursquare to really engage our attention. While he resembles Django and Nero's avenger in *Texas Adios* superficially, with his single-minded efforts to unlock the secrets of the past causing the deaths of friends and loved ones, Tom is less captivating hero than intruder, disrupting Junior's private

above: Nino Castelnuovo (in the white outfit) gives Nero a hot reception in this Mexican poster for **Massacre Time**.

above: Strife for Leonard Mann (*close-up, left*) and his friends Woody Strode (*top left*) and George Eastman (*main image*) in Enzo Barboni's **Chuck Mool**.

family-fantasy and butting into what should rightly be Jeff's revenge story. As Junior, Castelnuovo – a hot property at the time having starred opposite Catherine Deneuve in Jacques Demy's melodic romance *The Umbrellas of Cherbourg* in 1964 – impresses as a young man who's both mentally and physically unbalanced. His displays of filial affection are loaded with menace. "Don't let anyone come between us", he simultaneously implores and warns his father, reminding him they used to be like "one person" and coming across like a spiteful child who has been spoiled with a share of papa's power and wants to keep the old man – and his legacy – all to himself. As for Jeff, his hostility towards Tom is justified on a number of levels. The latter has been shielded from the suffering that Jeff has both witnessed and endured: the death of his father at Scott's hands and the loss of his heritage; the lies that have obliterated his own identity in an alcoholic haze. He'd (almost) be within his rights, as established by the genre, to kill Tom, the latter paying for the sins of his father, the same sins that Tom's real brother, Junior, continues to commit. But this is not the tale of a drunkard's redemption in the vein of *Tequila Joe* (1968) or *Night of the Serpents* (1969). Indeed, Jeff functions admirably in his sozzled state (it certainly doesn't affect his marksmanship), his bitterness only occasionally interrupting his boozy, sardonic bravado. (Hilton recycled parts of his performance here – which impressed no less a director than Michelangelo Antonioni – to play a well-oiled rogue in the caper western *The Greatest Robbery in the West* [1967].[15]) His role remains that of comic buffoon/hero's helper familiar from classical and Shakespearean comedy, drip-feeding Tom cryptic clues as to why Scott's men refuse to fire on him. Whatever vengeful intentions Jeff may harbour towards Scott dissipate when the old man is killed at Junior's command, conveniently shifting the onus onto the more conventional figure of Tom for the spectacular finale.

Like Tom Corbett, the title characters in *Chuck Mool* and *Keoma* are of mixed blood, with Keoma of mixed race, and the favoured sons of strong fathers. The enmity of jealous half-brothers guarantees each man a distinctly frosty reception when they return home, one to restore his identity, one to confront his destiny and his demons. *Keoma* has been analysed at length over the years (I discuss it in *Deconstruction And Desolation*), so I shall focus here on the minor but intriguing *Chuck Mool*. This was the downbeat directorial debut of Enzo Barboni (though it had been intended for Ferdinando Baldi), who went on to give sibling rivalry a hugely successful comedic twist in the 'Trinity' films. The script, by Mario Di Nardo

above: Armando Crispino's **John the Bastard** recasts the legend of Don Juan for the cynical Sixties and unites a number of prominent Euro-western motifs. John Richardson's eponymous Lothario (*top left*) denigrates family values – those of his own kin, as well as others – in a relentless campaign of seduction that ultimately incurs the wrath of a sinister assassin, played by the redoubtable Gordon Mitchell (*right*).

and the influential Franco Rossetti, with an uncredited contribution by one of the lead actors, George Eastman, is an Italianate take on the Raoul Walsh/Robert Mitchum classic *Pursued* (1947), Hollywood's first 'Freudian' western, although Barboni renders into melodrama what Walsh had shaped into *noir*. (He also manages to incorporate a messy eating scene and a lengthy bar fight in anticipation of his most famous films.) Leonard Mann exercises the anxious persona he had affected so well in *The Forgotten Pistolero*, playing a young gunfighter whose mind has blanked out his traumatic past and who yearns to retrace his origins, in contrast to the typical spaghetti western anti-hero who courts anonymity and often hides behind a meaningless appellation. Lacking any sense of self, Chuck resides in Dodge City asylum until some opportunistic bank robbers set it alight as a distraction, freeing some of the inmates while others succumb to the flames. (This unusual opening recalls a bizarre episode in Umberto Lenzi's diverting revenge tale, *A Gun for a Hundred Graves* [1968], in which a band of homicidal psychopaths break out from custody during a fire and terrorise a town.) With only fragmented memories and some tantalising clues to go on, Chuck teams up with three fellow escapees (played by Eastman, Peter Martell and Woody Strode) to try to piece together the puzzle.

Cruelly but inevitably, Chuck's discoveries destroy his chance of resuming his former family existence. Like his counterparts in the films above – and like Mitchum in *Pursued* – he is compelled to kill his half-brother, whose vindictive attack three years previously resulted in Chuck's amnesia and whose death drives a wedge between Chuck and his once-adoring father. There is an almost sadistic relish in the script's relentless manipulation and tormenting of its befuddled hero – besides his half-brother's betrayal, Chuck's memory loss and longing for family are exploited by his father's rivals, who pretend to be his relatives in order to turn him against his own kin. Even his former sweetheart is forced to become his 'sister', her lingering kisses triggering flashbacks in his mind and offsetting the incestuous advances of her true brother. Against this jaundiced view of home and family there is at least a healthier depiction of friendship, with Chuck's comrades all losing their lives in his cause, but the inescapable conclusion is that Chuck and his friends were all better off in the "crazy house" where they began.

The demythologisation of family is at its most determined in Armando Crispino's *John the Bastard* (1967), a fascinating conflation of the Don Juan legend with Italian western motifs. The equation of family identity with honour informs every dastardly or desperate action the misbegotten anti-hero (John Richardson) undertakes in his obsessive efforts to acquire prestige. His amorous adventures, some of which we are privy to in the opening credits, shot from John's point of view, reflect a deep-rooted hatred of women, combined with a scorn for family values, stemming from his mother's longstanding refusal to reveal his father's identity. When John learns that he is descended from the wealthy Mexican Tenorio clan, he determines to reclaim his birthright – against the wishes of his half-brother, Francisco (Claudio Camaso) – and avenge his sense of abandonment by precipitating a tragedy that rocks his new-found family to its core.

Writer-director Crispino's second feature has a noble lineage of its own. This classic morality tale appeared in story form as early as 1630 in Tirso de Molina's play *El burlado de Sevilla y convidado de piedra* (*The Libertine of Seville and the Stone Guest*). It was later immortalised in Mozart's opera *Don Giovanni*, composed in 1787, José Zorrilla's 19th Century drama *Don Juan Tenorio*, and Byron's similarly titled satirical poem (1818-23). Crispino skilfully synthesises the ironic and tragic aspects of the story while smoothly integrating Euro-western tropes such as the lot of the outcast, the corruption of family values, social inequality and revenge. Richardson's cruel, charismatic playboy is a worthy successor to Mozart's caddish libertine, with all the bitterness of one who believes he was born for greatness but, stigmatised by illegitimacy, has lived much of his life in shame. (His actions in the final act recall another possible antecedent, Shakespeare's black-hearted Don John the bastard, who spitefully sows discord in *Much Ado About Nothing*.) And where Don Giovanni had Leporello, John has his own retainer, Morenillo (Glauco Onorato), a cross between conscience, servant and Sancho Panza-style sidekick. He is also the vehicle for John's exploits: the circular structure of the narrative – it begins and ends with a mortally wounded Morenillo imagining the spectre of his late, lamented master – allows the entire plot to be read as his mindscreen.

John mocks the sanctity of family and the honour it bestows even as he seeks it. We first see him being pressured into marriage by the father and brothers of one of his romantic conquests. He has no intention of obliging, however, and escapes from them by sweet-talking the younger sister of his fiancée, later seducing and abandoning her with the same ease. At one point he *does* cynically swear a marital oath, but only so that he can have his way with two Mormon women – a betrayal of religious faith that will ultimately lead to his downfall at the hands of a fearsome Danite assassin (an intensely menacing Gordon Mitchell cameo).[16] He tricks his estranged mother into thinking he's a changed man, exploiting the filial bond in order to sniff for clues about his paternity. He seeks out his father, Don Diego (Claudio Gora), who has effectively been overthrown by the power-hungry Francisco, not to establish a relationship but to grasp "the keys to the kingdom", as well as the wealth and esteem that go with it. (Francisco, in the requisite role of selfish half-brother, correctly interprets John's manoeuvre as a power play against him.) John presents himself as the saviour of the dynasty when his real intention is to dishonour it by sleeping with his sister-in-law, Antonia (Martine Beswick, then Richardson's lover in real life), out of spite as much as desire, provoking her suicide and a showdown with Francisco.

Besides its pleasingly bizarre diversions – notably a delirious battle scene in which John and Morenillo help Mormon women to defeat a group of persecutory Klansmen – *John the Bastard* captures the attention on two main counts, firstly by virtue of Crispino's shrewd direction. He recounts even the most unusual events with a minimum of authorial intervention, raising major themes and suggesting parallels between characters and situations without unnecessary explication. John's affinity with the Mormons, for example, goes further than his cynical admiration for their polygamous ways and hints at their shared status as outcasts from society. The brotherhood motif is represented not just by John and Francisco but also by Hilario, Francisco's foreman; he acquiesces in his own sibling's punishment on the estate – thereby betraying his class as well as his blood – only to apparently seek vengeance later on. As with other characters, however, there is insufficient psychological insight to make a precise judgement about his motivation, which remains rather fuzzy. John and Francisco, meanwhile, are both exploiters in their own way: John's hypnotic power over weaker personalities compares with Francisco's reliance on brute force to keep his workers in check. The workers in turn embody, together with Morenillo, the theme of masters and servants, rebellion and subservience. There is something disturbing about Morenillo's self-abnegation. He believes he was "born a servant", is "just another arm", and bears John's insults with a level of humility that contrasts with the disaffection of the "slaves", as Francisco defiantly calls them, on the Tenorio estate.

The film's other strong suit is John Richardson's authoritative performance. This rangy, handsome British actor spent most of his career in Italian genre cinema after failing to make the grade in England, although he was, allegedly, in the running to play Bond in *On Her Majesty's Secret Service* (1969). With his penetrating gaze and aura of self-assurance, he conveys all sides of John's character with equal conviction, from the rakish charm that sets women swooning to the domineering, brutish aspect he assumes in Mexico. He and Crispino craft a character who's neither hero nor villain, both the author of his own misfortune and the victim of social stigmatisation. Having endured an unhappy and ignominious earthly existence, he finally welcomes his symbolically divine punishment – being crushed to death beneath a religious statue in a final homage to *Don Giovanni* – with a sigh of relief.

As with all the genre's most popular refrains, the theme of brotherly rivalry was eventually played out. Its

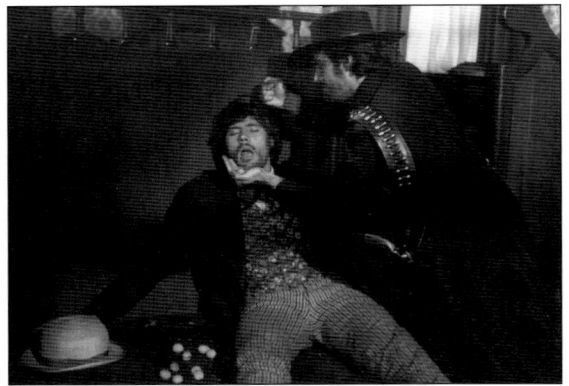

above: Knockabout humour in **The Return of Hallelujah**.
bottom left: Detail from an admat for **Alive or Preferably Dead**.

dramatic possibilities were exhausted in too many low-impact revenge stories, even before films such as *Alive or Preferably Dead* (1969), *They Call Me Trinity* (1970) and its offshoots and *The Return of Hallelujah* (1972), with its slapstick, Bible-bashing brothers Cain and Abel, turned the same situations to comedic advantage. By this stage, bickering brothers and other family members no longer tried to engineer one another's destruction but merely got on each other's nerves, dispensing a few bruises along the way, representing a thawing of relations if not a complete reconciliation between individual endeavour and familial responsibility. A more pessimistic conclusion prevailed overall, however, evident in the jaded irony and broken-hearted bitterness of the films we have been discussing. Their portrayals of families seething with jealousy or splintered by sectional strife are far removed from the ideal image of close-knit clans projected by Italian state propaganda and the Catholic Church, conflicting too with the wholesome stereotypes featured in classical American westerns. They are entirely fitting, however, in a fictional environment and in historical circumstances – the Sixties – in which individualism, self-preservation and self-gratification expanded at the expense of more utilitarian, family-centric values. They also parallel some of the most corrosive Italian modernist movies, the likes of *Fists in the Pocket* (1965) and *Theorem* (1968), which probe relentlessly the fissures in bourgeois domesticity, while the hierarchical structure of family life was one of the pressure points for rebellious Italian youngsters. Indirectly, these narratives advocate the slipping of familial bonds where they exist, and the avoidance of emotional entanglements in a wider sense, not with the gusto with which the genre assailed other cherished conventions but with resignation.

Not for the first time in the genre, the appeal to the individual of the wilderness, the arena of adventure, over civilisation – specifically the hypothetical 'security' of hearth and home – is self-evident.

"Didn't you know better than to trust the words of a minister?"

The recurrence and irreverent treatment of Christian symbolism and imagery in Italian westerns identifies them as products of a culture, and a filmmaking tradition, where religion – specifically Catholicism – is a dominant and deeply divisive issue. Italian cinema reflects what has always been an "uneasy cohabitation" in the country between the Church and lay society, with the former's authoritarian aspect and political influence – especially in the years of Christian Democrat supremacy, which included the period in question – provoking as much resentment among sceptics as its spiritual and charitable work inspired respect and devotion among the faithful.[17] Italian westerns and other popular genres, made predominantly by left-wing artists voicing and prompting the opinions of their audience, have typically depicted churchmen in the same unflattering light as they have portrayed politicians, lawmakers and other members of the ruling elite. On the other hand, numerous westerns correlated their violent protagonists with Christ; witness the many instances of crucifixion (*A Fistful of Dollars*, *Navajo Joe* [1966], *Django, Kill!* [1967], *Johnny Hamlet* and *Keoma* contain the most explicit examples), 'resurrection' (again, *Fistful* and *Django, Kill!* most notably) and stigmatisation (see in particular *Django*, *Arizona Colt* [1966] and *The Great Silence* [1968]). This is not blasphemy; it merely affirms the filmmakers' awareness of the powerful emotions these allusions are capable of provoking. The intent is not to mock the Saviour but to bring him down to earth (at the same time, of course, as elevating the anti-hero). We are still dealing with a mythical figure, but he's become a militant as much as a martyr – as Giuliano Gemma cynically retorts in *A Pistol for Ringo* (1965) when a young lady exalts Christ's 'weapons' of compassion and mercy, "A good six-shooter, that's what he should have had." Given this ambivalent attitude towards religion and its representatives on the part of cinema, it's little wonder that the Church has historically shared the wariness of politicians of all stripes where this particular medium is concerned.

In the years following the Second World War, as Italian film entered what is today regarded as its second golden age (the first being the early silent period, the era of *Cabiria* [1914]), the clergy's monitoring body, the Catholic Centre for Cinema (CCC) established in 1934, displayed what Pierre Sorlin has called "a pathological phobia of the cinema". These fears didn't stop, indeed partly prompted, the Church's efforts to harness the power of the medium to increase its agency. As Sorlin recounts, in keeping with the Catholic slogan "un cinema per ogni campanile" (a cinema for every town), the clergy "opened some three thousand parish cinemas during the period of the Reconstruction [post-WWII to Sixties], and managed to show the most popular films, westerns [presumably this means predominantly or exclusively American imports] and comedies, whose success was certain."[18] Equally, the Church had the power to restrict or ban outright whatever films it deemed unsuitable, and regional bodies may well have added further titles to the pyre. Considering that parish cinemas were often the only ones available in many rural areas and city outskirts, the Church thus had a major influence on viewing habits. (This is nicely illustrated in *Divorce Italian Style* [1961], where the parish priest, having already urged his flock to vote Christian Democrat, admonishes them, fruitlessly in this case, to boycott the licentious *La Dolce Vita*; and in *Cinema Paradiso* [1988], the prelate previews films before screening, scrutinising them in particular for illicit screen kisses.) The CCC's publications readily denounced 'immoral' content and negative visions of society or, indeed, of the clergy itself; its evaluations would also be printed on the cinema listings pages of newspapers. It took umbrage with neorealism, for example, which exposed not only Italy's social problems but also too much female flesh for the CCC's liking, and was, moreover, generally ill disposed towards the Church. The CCC even attacked *Open City* (1945) on this subject, despite the inclusion by director Roberto Rossellini of a heroic priest (Aldo Fabrizi's Don Pietro) who strives for the liberty of the people. Perhaps the authorities simply couldn't stomach the sight of a clergyman and a Communist working together. The government, meanwhile, "whose survival was largely dependant on the support of the church" (Sorlin), sought to placate the latter by setting up, in 1947, a system of unofficial "pre-production control" that scrutinised voluntarily submitted scripts and discouraged controversial subject matter by the implicit threat of a ban on exhibition. This could even stretch to a veto on the export of films that government censors (at this point under the direction of future Prime Minister Giulio Andreotti) feared would malign Italy's image abroad. Tax incentives were also on offer to films of "artistic quality", this to be defined by a board of officials. Only the stronger, wealthier production houses were in a position to resist this financial pressure.[19]

With their anti-authoritarian populist instincts, not to mention sadistic bent, new-wave Euro-westerns were the targets of Church censure as often as pastoral figures themselves were either criticised or ridiculed by genre writers and directors. To take five random examples, *A Dollar of Fire* (1966) was lambasted by the CCC for its "sadistic brutality"; *Johnny Yuma* condemned as "utterly violent"; *For a Dollar in the Teeth* (1967) as an "orgy of sadism"; *Navajo Joe* deemed "disgusting"; and *The Magnificent Bandits* (1969) attacked for its anticlericalism. Good Catholics were therefore urged to avoid such monstrosities at all costs.[20] The majority of films share, or reflect, the suspicion-cum-contempt of the common man for the pious and the high-minded. In numerous cases, churchmen or religious zealots, whatever their denomination, are tarred with the brush of hypocrisy, corruption or intolerance, or otherwise abuse their position of trust and their duty of care. Self-righteous bigots beset the towns in *Django*, *Django, Kill!* and *Tails, You Lose...* (all 1969) and *A Man Called Blade* (1977), while their brethren in *Death Sentence* (1967), *The Price of Death* (1971) and *The Stranger and the Gunfighter* (1974) take religious conservatism to murderous extremes.[21] In *Find a Place to Die* (1968), softly spoken "wandering

In the line of fire: **Johnny Yuma** (*left*) and **Navajo Joe** (*above*) were among many westerns subjected to broadsides from Italy's Catholic Centre for Cinema.
top right: Catholic imagery in this admat for **Johnny Hamlet**.

above: The cloak of religion: in **Compañeros**, Franco Nero's unprincipled mercenary demonstrates the efficacy of clerical disguise, both as a cover for sundry misdemeanours and as a useful device for satirising piety and sanctimoniousness.
opposite: William Berger (*bottom*, holding a pistol on Riccardo Garrone) revelled in the role of a two-faced, evangelical bounty hunter – one of the genre's most extreme examples of religious hypocrisy, or at least affectation – in Sergio Garrone's **No Room to Die**.

missionary" Reverend Riley (played by sharp-featured character actor Adolfo Lastretti) is revealed to be a sexual pervert and convicted murderer; "the poor creature is now an angel" he says, with impeccable self-possession, after torturing a captive to death. Among the assorted thieves, rapists and killers corralled by James Coburn for a deadly mission in A Reason to Live, a Reason to Die (1972) is a religious agitator who is singled out as "the worst of the bunch". The comedy Can Be Done... Amigo (1972) invents a novel solution to the political wrangling between priests and lay officials in small communities – which Italian viewers would have recognised from Giovanni Guareschi's 'Don Camillo' novels – by having its town clergyman (Francisco Rabal) simultaneously holding the positions of sheriff, judge and mayor. (He's also the land-grabbing villain of the piece.) It may also obliquely allude to the popular perception of ecclesiastical/political collusion on a wider scale by wrapping up so many authority figures in one parcel. Similarly, in A Fistful of Dynamite (1971), a priest is lumped together with other gluttonous enemies of the people – the filthy rich, the bourgeoisie and a foreign capitalist – when their coach is intercepted and appropriated by the Miranda gang.

Elsewhere, continuing a tradition in Italian film that dates back at least as far as the Aldo Fabrizi vehicle Welcome Reverend (1950), clerical dress provides a convenient, respectable cloak for the ribald or nefarious activities of rogues, rebels and cut-throats. Proceeding from the premise that the clergy is, or ought to be, unfailingly trustworthy, countless Italian westerns gleefully insinuate otherwise. Con artists take up the cloth to further their scams in Long Live Your Death (1971), Pistol Packin' Preacher (1972), Hallelujah & Sartana Strike Again! (1972), and Enzo Castellari's One Dollar Too Many (1968) and Tedeum (1972). Sergio Corbucci has his revolutionaries dress up as angels in A Professional Gun (1968) and as monks in Compañeros (1970), which adds to the carnivalesque flavour of the films and continues Corbucci's personal crusade against religious hypocrisy. He also pokes merciless fun at the clergy in What Am I Doing in the Middle of a Revolution? (1972). Not only is Don Albino (Paolo Villaggio) characterised as a cowardly

bumbler, and the Church in general as little more than a nest of crooks, there is also a scene where Guido (Vittorio Gassman), an atheistic Italian actor, is butted by a bull while dressed in the glaring red robes of a cardinal. Furthermore, visual innuendoes in which bandits or other devious characters adopt clerical disguises abound. Frank Wolff's gang are thus introduced at the beginning of *For a Dollar in the Teeth* before massacring some soldiers; bank robber Hunt Powers poses as a preacher in *The Greatest Robbery in the West* and devises the ruse of hiding the loot in the (figuratively and literally) hollow statue of a saint; and in *No Room to Die* (1969), devout bounty hunter Everett Murdock (a wonderful turn by William Berger), cynically quotes from the Bible to justify his murderous methods while railing hypocritically against whatever harm is done unto him. The trend extended to other popular genres as well. In Stelvio Massi's *poliziesco Emergency Squad* (1974), Gastone Moschin and gang wear priests' clothes to aid their flight, reasoning that since "every Catholic has a guilty conscience", nobody will interfere in their business.

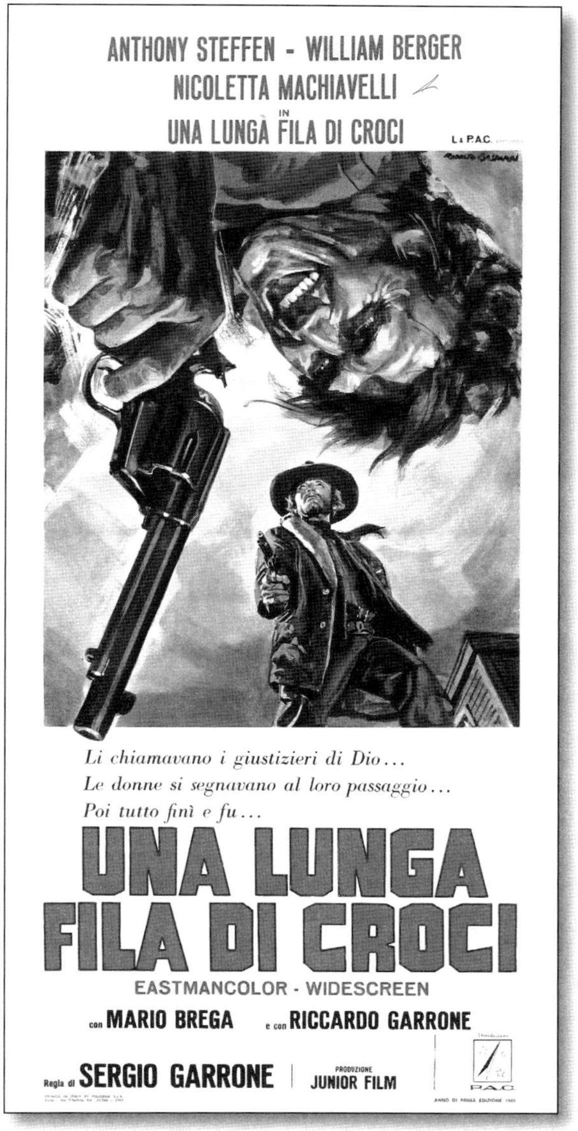

Religion is deemed to be powerless in a world ruled by greed and ruthlessness, where men think in temporal rather than spiritual terms and seek satisfaction in the here and now rather than the hereafter. We see this with Klaus Kinski's avenger disputing the Lord's authority before an astonished reverend in *And God Said to Cain* (1970),

above: George Hilton (*centre*) tosses out biblical quotations as regularly as he does explosives in **Red Blood, Yellow Gold**.

above: Profanation and impersonation: Julián Mateos (*left*) and Charles Southwood (*right*) in **Three Silver Dollars**.
bottom left: No, vengeance is *mine*: George Hilton played a character who rejects his religious background in **Full House for the Devil**.

Rod Steiger's broken-hearted bandit in *A Fistful of Dynamite* discarding his rosary after discovering the bodies of his murdered family, as well as the disillusioned monk (Leo Anchóriz) who throws in his lot with George Hilton's brigands in *Vengeance Is Mine* (1969). Hilton himself plays the part of a defrocked priest-turned-adventurer in *Red Blood, Yellow Gold* (1967), while in *Full House for the Devil* (1968), his impious Johnny King favours earthly pleasures (chiefly "other men's women") over the spiritual rewards his preacher uncle anticipates in the afterlife. (The film backtracks on Johnny's joke that he gave up studying for the priesthood because he didn't look good in black by having the character adopt funereal attire in the story's angrier latter stages.) For others, religious observance has more to do with superstition or hypocrisy than genuine belief, the rituals being akin to a performance: Tuco habitually crosses himself, erroneously, in *The Good, the Bad and the Ugly*, but his lengthy catalogue of crimes – including "theft of sacred objects" – rather outweighs such external displays of faith. In *Three Silver Dollars* (1968), a ruthless gang boss (Mirko Ellis) seeks to assuage his Catholic guilt in church, crying sacrilege when the film's anti-heroes drag him out for interrogation, while numerous bandit chieftains juxtapose crucifixes with the bandoleers and meaningless medals strung across their chests.**22**

The proliferation and, more importantly, profanation of churches, missions, monasteries, cemeteries and other religious institutions and 'props', as well as regular (mis)use of the resurrection motif, signals both an acknowledgement of an important part of the genre's cultural heritage and something of a rebellion against it. In keeping with the inversion of another type of sanctuary, the family home, these holy spaces are regularly defiled by evildoers. Indio delivering his 'parable' from the pulpit of an abandoned mission in *For a Few Dollars More* is the most notorious mockery of religious rites in a genre that was quickly overflowing with such acts, often with far less narrative or thematic relevance than Leone brought to this scene. Come the slapstick era, in *A Man Called Invincible* (1973), for example, the depiction of Aureola Joe and gang living in a mission, wearing habits and gambling with playing cards illustrated with saints and other religious figures, was far from unusual. There was a similar flavour to other *filoni* as well: *gialli* often posited priests as sex maniacs and murderers (see note 21); the sleazy 'nunsploitation' sub-genre was in full flight, inspired by *The Devils* (1971) and typified by films such as *Story of a Cloistered Nun* (1973) and *Flavia the Heretic* (1974); while the many *Decameron* rip-offs based much of their humour on anticlericalism. Equally common in westerns was the shedding of blood on holy ground and the brutal treatment of clerical characters, which further emphasises the feebleness of the clergy in practical terms. Jason Robards's Cheyenne may have foresworn the killing of (Catholic) priests, but few of his contemporaries shared his scruples. Duncan (Aldo Sambrell) shoots dead the pastor in *Navajo Joe*, as do bounty hunters in *A Minute to Pray, a Second to Die* (1968) – even though "it's bad luck to kill padres" – with the villains in *And God Said to Cain* and *Comin' at Ya!* (1981)

following suit. *Django*'s reprehensible Brother Jonathan (Gino Pernice) is memorably mutilated and murdered by Mexican rebels, and in *Sabata* (1969), the title character's killing of the false 'Father Brown' (Luciano Pigozzi) in church is accompanied by Banjo (William Berger) playing a mock-solemn requiem on the organ. (The identical gag turns up in the same year's *I Am Sartana, Your Angel of Death*.) Duels and shoot-outs are also regularly staged in hallowed locations, if only for baroque effect. Cemeteries, as we noted in the previous chapter, were popular settings for showdowns, with *The Good, the Bad and the Ugly* and *Django* sharing first prize for originality. Churches, too, often echo to the sound of gunfire and the cries of the dying and distressed: Gianni Garko ambushes Fernando Sancho and his men at the beginning of *For $100,000 Per Killing*; Ettore Manni outdraws an opponent in *I Am Sartana, Your Angel of Death*; villains are strung up from a bell rope in both *Sartana Does Not Forgive* (1968) and *Django the Bastard* (1969); James Garner's girlfriend (Laura Antonelli) is violated in the ruins of a once-grand church in *A Man Called Sledge* (1970); Robert Shaw conducts a massacre of churchgoers in the British-Spanish *A Town Called Bastard* (1971); the town church has become a gun store in *A Man Called Django* (1971); and Lee Van Cleef – as a false priest with relatively benign intentions for a change – punishes some of Jack Palance's gang before the altar in *God's Gun* (1976).

Sympathetic images of religious orders are comparatively rare. Monks, Mormons and missionaries fare better than most, perhaps because they live separately from society and have no stake in power games or politics. Mormons, furthermore, as previously noted in *John the Bastard*, are generally portrayed as victims of persecution or associated with outcasts. In *The Good, the Bad and the Ugly*, Blondie and Tuco seek respite with monks who have converted their quarters

above: Monk-ey business: Terence Hill and Bud Spencer mocked up for the knockdown, drag-out finale of **Trinity Is Still My Name**.

into a hospital for wounded Civil War soldiers, while other monks (and Mormons) show hospitality to the central characters in *The Big Gundown* and *A Hole Between the Eyes* (1968), paying with their lives in the latter for their unwitting involvement in Anthony Ghidra's affairs. In the 'Trinity' films, these groups even become proactive: the brothers firstly convince the harassed Mormon settlers to fight as well as pray for their rights, while in the sequel, monks help Trinity and Bambino to rout a power-hungry rancher and his associates, who have been misusing the mission as a combination of trading post and illicit bank. In *The Four of the Apocalypse* (1975), meanwhile, a religious commune and a kindly missionary (Adolfo Lastretti atoning for his vile Reverend Riley in *Find a Place to Die*) prove to be both generous and non-judgemental, providing shafts of light in an otherwise gloomy scenario. Even then, the people of the Joyful Church of the Living Christ fall foul of the predatory Chaco (Tomas Milian), learning the hard way the limitations of the so-called "land of freedom" they have been exploring.

Lee Van Cleef urges repentance at the point of a revolver – seeking, at the same time, to atone for his own sins – in Gianfranco Parolini's **God's Gun**.

True respect, however, is reserved for those holy figures who, like Rossellini's Don Pietro, combine their spirituality with militancy in the service of the people or the pursuance of a noble cause. Exemplified by Klaus Kinski in *A Bullet for the General*, these are men who carry a cross in one hand and a weapon in the other, identifying the will of God with social reform and revolutionary zeal. (Their mindset, if not their hands-on methods, was consonant with the socio-political awakening of large sections of the Catholic clergy in Sixties Latin America, where the Church, which for so long had appeased and even supported the dictators, began actively campaigning for democratic reform. Pope Paul VI's *Populorum Progressio* of 1967 provided further impetus with its emphasis on social justice, and in 1968 a congress of Latin American bishops in the Colombian city of Medellin denounced the continent's various afflictions, from the poverty gap to foreign imperialism, with unprecedented boldness.) Kinski's dynamic Santo has the same stridency as Enrique Irazoqui's Christ in Pier Paolo Pasolini's *The Gospel According to St. Matthew* (1964), but words are not his only weapons – he throws dynamite at government troops in the name of the Father, Son and Holy Ghost, justifying his violence to a wounded opponent by saying "Christ was always for the poor and downtrodden". Even though he is portrayed as a fanatic, with the derangement common to most of Kinski's characters, Santo's commitment to the impoverished and the insurrectionist cause is unwavering and inspirational. He is even prepared to execute his own brother for leaving a vulnerable town at the mercy of the enemy. (Although cast in a different ideological mould, Santo can be considered a relative of the legendary 19th Century Spanish warrior-priest Santa Cruz, a member of the ultra-conservative Catholic Carlist movement. Santa Cruz's spiritual descendants fought on the side of the Nationalists in the Spanish Civil War of 1936-39, and a film was made of his story in 1991.) Religion is also a force for social change in *Kill and Pray* (1967). Lou Castel, who had previously enacted a radicalised version of Francis of Assisi in Liliana Cavani's debut film of the same name, plays the angelic Requiescant. Raised by a preacher but with the soul of a fighter, he is inducted into revolutionary activity by an agitator-priest, played by Pasolini himself. Although reluctant to recruit a gunfighter, even one with such an unusually caring disposition who prays for those he kills, the priest nevertheless shares Requiescant's belief that "God provides forces for good as well as evil." (He may be right – at one point, the hero seems to benefit from divine intervention when his Bible stops a bullet from penetrating his flesh.) And while Requiescant's involvement springs initially from his twin desire to free his half-sister from effective slavery at the hands of Mark Damon's arrogant aristocrat and to avenge the killing of his father by the same man, he adapts to his calling with enthusiasm – his late father, after all, was a rebel himself.

In search of salvation

Some of these 'holy warriors' are explicitly seeking redemption, which leads us to another of the genre's most intriguing, if underdeveloped, themes. The gun-toting clerics in *The Big Gundown* (in which the character is nicknamed 'Brother Smith & Wesson'), *Wanted* (1967) and *Reverend Colt* (1970) have all turned to religion to atone for their violent pasts. (*God's Gun* works a variation on this: Lee Van Cleef's reformed gunfighter dons his late brother's sacerdotal outfit to smite the latter's murderers, managing to scare most of them into killing each other.) Their old ways are not forgotten, however: *Wanted*'s Brother Carmelo (a nice change of pace for habitual villain Nello Pazzafini) and the eponymous Reverend Colt (Guy Madison) still carry a gun to bolster their moral authority – in an amusing coda, Colt fires at the church bell to summon his reluctant parishioners to Sunday service. William Berger, departing from cynical supporting roles, played the lead in the wretched *God's Executioner* (1973), as a gunman-turned-priest who hung up his guns following the tragic death of his son, a plotline similar to that of *Night of the Serpents* (see below). The most remarkable transformation of all occurs in *Django Strikes Again* (1987), where Franco Nero, returning to his most iconic western role 20 years on, is introduced as Brother Ignacius, a penitent monk who claims never to want to hold a weapon again, but quickly has to resurrect his Django persona – symbolised by the exhumation of his famous machine gun – to combat slave traders.

above: Spanish poster for the Giuliano Gemma vehicle **Wanted**, which features a pistol-wielding padre among its dramatis personae.

above: Lee Van Cleef displayed his versatility by playing an amiable outlaw who becomes a sheriff in **Beyond the Law**, only to find himself torn between loyalty to his old confederates (and the lure of a fortune in silver) and his new responsibilities.
opposite bottom: Robert Woods in the title role of **El Puro** as an alcoholic gunfighter who longs to dry out and go straight. While he manages to overcome his demons, as well as a gang of ruthless killers, fate proves to be a more formidable opponent.

What works against these films, and the uplifting message they try to deliver, is that these born-again characters are often pedagogic or moralistic – just as priests on screen often function as agents of ideological/humanist doctrines – which can render them staid or sanctimonious and therefore uninspiring, especially if they are contrasted with more flamboyant figures. In *Son of Django* (1967), Father Fleming (Guy Madison) tries to turn the title character from the path of vengeance, having trodden it himself in years gone by. Despite being a stolid character, he eventually succeeds, unlike Richard Harrison in a similar role in Marino Girolami's trek western *Between God, the Devil and a Winchester* (1968). Harrison's dull padre vies with the wily, charismatic Chasquido (Gilbert Roland) for the affections of an impressionable young boy, who ultimately chooses the guide over the man of God, a life of adventure over one of peace, platitudes and contemplation. One can hardly blame him in the circumstances.

There is also a 'secular' school of redemption films that are not so much concerned with spiritual renewal as with an individual's psychological, physical or moral rehabilitation. While some of these stories plot the uncharacteristically decent deeds of picaresque types (Lee Van Cleef's grubby outlaw hitting the straight and narrow in *Beyond the Law* [1968], three rascals saving an innocent man from the gallows in *No Graves on Boot Hill* [1968]), they are more often framed around a stock character – a drunkard with an unhappy past, living with guilt and shame, who accepts a task or challenge in the hope of recovering his self-respect and soothing painful memories. The pursuit of positive, humanitarian or philanthropic ends, albeit with the usual mixed motivations, provides a counterweight to the nihilism and strict self-interest that drives most genre protagonists. In early, American-influenced films such as José Luis Borau's *Ride and Kill* (1964) and Alfonso Balcázar's *The Man Who Came to Kill* (1965), there is never any doubt that their wayward protagonists will emerge from their experiences freshly purged. These are sentimental stories of decent men overcoming unfavourable odds: Alex Nicol, in the first film, plays a town drunk who routs his tormentors and becomes a hero; Carl Möhner, in the second, a wanted man who helps save a village from the attentions of a bandit gang, convincing a bounty hunter to let him go free.

In later years, this figure took on a darker cast and bore greater tragic weight. Anthony Steffen's characters in *A Stranger in Paso Bravo* and *Two Pistols and a Coward* (both 1968) are implicated in the deaths of family members, as is Brett Halsey's dishevelled ex-sheriff in Alberto Cardone's *$20,000 Stained in Blood*. In *Tequila Joe* (1968), Anthony Ghidra's unkempt lawman seeks comfort in the bottle after the murder of his brother, while Luke Askew, in Giulio Petroni's pitch-black *Night of the Serpents*, has accidentally shot his own son in drunken emulation of William Tell. These personal tragedies have guided and limited their activities ever since, dragging them to the depths of indignity and degradation. An unusually greater onus is placed on the actors in these films to communicate the mental and physical effort required to lift themselves out of their torpor. Steffen, ordinarily the epitome of steely resolve, is a nervous wreck for much of *Two Pistols*, while Halsey, who was rarely required to do anything more than scowl or glower in his westerns, exudes a plausible air of desperation in *$20,000 Stained in Blood* while foraging thirstily for dregs and gradually recovering his sense of purpose. Ghidra's typically vivid portrayal in *Tequila Joe* lifts an otherwise mediocre film, his character's decrepit office mirroring his shattered integrity and sour cynicism, while Askew in *Serpents* keeps it low key as a gringo gunfighter who has become a bandits' lackey in Mexico. Such is the extent of his dipsomania that at one point he is fooled into drinking urine from a canteen.

Each man is given an opportunity to make partial amends for past misdemeanours by performing heroic endeavours in the present. The two Steffen vehicles are resolved fairly cleanly, his investigations erasing the stains on his character, while Ghidra is pestered by his new deputy – in reality the son he had abandoned years before – to take his duties as both a sheriff and a family man seriously again. Halsey and Askew, true to their characterisations, remain besmirched even though they rescue endangered children who, inevitably, they identify as surrogates for their own late offspring. Askew, indeed, had been offered his ticket out of Mexico – treated here, as in many American westerns, as a gringo purgatory – if he had killed the boy in question to help settle an inheritance dispute. It is no accident, incidentally, that these slow, *noirish* character studies are among Cardone and Petroni's rarest films: they may as well be thrillers as westerns, action is sparse and the mood – intimate interiors, lots of solo scenes, spare, haunting music – subdued. In Petroni's case in particular, the introspective *Night of the Serpents* proved to be a commercial wrong turn after the hugely successful and relatively starry *Death Rides a Horse* (1967) and the modish *Tepepa* (1968). The choice of an icy-eyed, understated and largely unknown American character actor for the lead was another marginalising factor. Despite Askew's fleeting appearance as a hippie in *Easy Rider* (1969), the success of which may have influenced his casting here, he has never transcended supporting status and has been restricted to minor roles as villains and other violent types.

Once removed from these comparatively upbeat stories, and the last word in 'drunk gunman' westerns, is Edoardo Mulargia's *El Puro* (1969). In this gloomy, slow-moving variation on *The Gunfighter* (1950), Robert Woods plays a notorious outlaw who yearns for redemption and a quiet life without any hope of achieving it. Tired of killing but unable to avoid it, he languishes in weary anonymity, preserved in an alcoholic limbo. (Woods, who had a hand in shaping the film's story along with co-star Marco Fiorini, had a different conception of the character in mind, although it didn't work out as they had planned. "We wanted to write a 'Buddhist' western [in which] a gunfighter dies and another guy takes his place. It was almost like the reincarnation of a gunfighter… We even took the director out one night and got him loaded to try to convince him."[23] There is barely a trace of this idea in the finished film but, at the very least, it makes a change from the overtly Christian resurrection metaphor employed in so many other Euro-westerns.) While Puro ruminates, monologue-style, on fate and fortune, a trio of glory-hunting gunmen closes in, led by the demented Gypsy (Fiorini overacting wildly as 'Ashborn Hamilton Jr'), forcing Puro to dry out and meet this latest challenge to his reputation. The signal that he is ready is his shooting of a whisky bottle, a symbolic act (and hardy cliché) that reoccurs in *Night of the Serpents*. Even though Gypsy's band viciously murders Puro's girlfriend (Rosalba Neri) to provoke him, the protagonist's enforced recovery speaks more of primal instinct than a thirst for revenge, an acceptance that if he doesn't kill them, they'll kill him. He's not acting to save his soul or salvage his honour, having recognised despairingly what the more sardonic genre protagonists seem to have grasped with insouciance – that while there is plenty of sin and damnation in the world they inhabit, redemption is almost certainly beyond their reach. In this respect, the uncompromising pessimism of *El Puro* is more consistent with genre thinking than the open-ended optimism of the films above, especially when its protagonist rides away from a hollow victory over the villains only to suffer an ignominious death.

In his book *Italian National Cinema*, Pierre Sorlin pondered whether Italian westerns, like other popular co-productions of the Sixties, should be classed as international because of external participation – the financial involvement of foreign companies – or genuinely Italian because they assimilated

above: **The Man Who Came to Kill**, with Carl Möhner, was more optimistic than most redemption westerns.

and 'domesticated' Hollywood material. For Sorlin, the question was ultimately meaningless since these were "hybrid, heterogeneous" productions, essentially devoid of nationality. Yet, as I have suggested, there was a deep vein of Italianism running through the genre, a distinctive Mediterranean sensibility that accounts to a large extent for its hot-blooded, hyperbolic temperament and the recurrence of specific themes. Certain films even made allusions to Italian history: consider *Django, Kill!*'s Blackshirts and *Face to Face*'s (1967) proto-fascist dictator;

above: **A Taste of Death** would have reminded its Italian audience of their nation's traumatic experiences in the Second World War.

A Taste of Death (1968), widely viewed as an allegory of Italy's wartime occupation by the Nazis and their Fascist allies and the rise of the Partisan resistance movement; and references to the Second World War massacre in the Fosse Ardeatine and the death of Mussolini in *A Fistful of Dynamite*. Italian nationals, too, occasionally turn up in these Americanised settings, if only to be roundly ridiculed for their mannerisms and mentalities. Ever since Erminio Macario was thus humiliated in the comedy *Come scopersi l'America* (1950), this has been a recurring motif in Italian cinema, and was also the fate of Gassman and Villaggio in *What Am I Doing in the Middle of a Revolution?*, Pietro Ceccarelli's pizza maker in *Pistol Packin' Preacher* (1972), and the stereotypically macho Sicilian avengers in *Gunmen and the Holy Ghost* (1972) and *A Man Called Invincible*.

If few of the films in this chapter reveal anything meaningful about what it means to be Italian (just like any form of mass culture, they deal in generalisations rather than specifics), the widespread preoccupation with themes and imagery relating to family and religion – cornerstones of Italian life – is a telling insight in itself. As is the despondent spirit in which these stories are told, whether their tone is mocking and cynical or melodramatic and tragic. What it ultimately reflects is the iconoclasm of the genre in general, which began with the deconstruction and transformation of the American western by Leone and his acolytes and continues here with attacks – partly reflexive and partly, as in the political sub-genre, idealistic – on the integrity of any form of authority, specifically home/family and the Church. Home, in the distraught imagination of writers and directors, is often not where the heart is but where jealousy and hatred are nurtured, while religion is either a retreat from reality or a front for venal, violent or deviant desires, correlative with the worst aspects of officialdom. Only in its idealised social-reformist/militant form – seen in *A Bullet for the General* and *Kill and Pray* in particular – or when functioning independently of the (Catholic) Church hierarchy does religion have true value in the Italian western.

Whether the filmmakers involved were merely feeding, and feasting on, the prejudices of their public, a common accusation where commercial cinema is concerned, or proceeding from personal beliefs – we must remember that the Italian industry was a bastion of socialism and communism, both avowedly anticlerical, for example – we can't be sure. The results are, as always, extremely varied, and the dearth of individual testimonies from writers or directors on questions like these precludes a reliable conclusion being reached. The most interesting films flourish on the tension between the demands of a popular genre (and its audience) on the one hand, and the points of view and individual interests of writers, actors and directors, who were generally part of the same culture they were addressing, on the other. This forms an intriguing counterpart to the stress between the conventions of the American western and the deviations of the Italian version. Most of the titles I have covered in this chapter were majority-Italian productions, so it is natural that they reflect their own cultural background and incorporate national stereotypes at the same time as they assimilate/transform aspects of Americana. "Obviously, there's a culture behind me that I can't just wish away. I can't just negate it," said Sergio Leone. "For example, we live and breathe Roman Catholicism, even if we don't believe all of it. So perhaps that comes through in aspects of my films."[24] At times this seems to have been a conscious process – Leone's strategic use of Marisol as substitute Holy Mother in *A Fistful of Dollars*, to cite one famous example, acknowledges, and exploits, the exalted place of *la madonna* in Italian culture – but in a general sense it was more likely subliminal or incidental, resulting from the mere fact of filmmakers being Italian. "Is there a strong Catholic influence on my westerns?" Enzo Castellari throws my question back at me. "Yes, because I am a Catholic. To have 'Christ' represented in these films [viz. the crucifixions of Castellari's western heroes]… has been a dream for me."[25] His comments remind us yet again that the primary appeal of the western to Italian (and European) filmmakers was that its recurring characters, plots and themes were timeless and universal – not specifically 19th Century American – in their nature and narrative functions.

above: Japanese poster for **The Man Who Came to Kill**.

footnotes

[1] Of course, the genre was largely, though not entirely, made up of co-productions, and this statement applies principally to films where Italians were in the ascendancy. These, in turn, make up the bulk of the genre's better works. Certain predominantly French films (*Cemetery Without Crosses* and *In the Dust of the Sun*, for example) and majority German entries (the 'Winnetou' series) also reflect their national filmmaking traditions and cultures to a certain extent, the former showing a certain sensuality and fatalism, the latter a romantic view of man and nature. It is harder, in general, to discern Spanish sensibilities informing films where Spaniards had greater creative input, although earlier examples follow Spanish dramatic traditions more closely than later ones.

[2] Italian comic strips were quick to capitalise on the fashionableness of the western *filone*, with titles such as *El Gringo* (1965-68), *El Desperado* (1968-69) and *Mortimer, cacciatore di taglie* ('Mortimer, bounty hunter', 1973-74), mimicking the movies' dynamic style and violent action. *Cineromanzi*, which had their equivalents in other European countries, were 'novelisations' of popular films in splash-photo style. They tied in with all the main genres, including the western. The French *Star-Ciné* series re-created the plots of numerous Euro-westerns from 1966 onwards. A good list is printed in *Western all'italiana: The Wild, the Sadist and the Outsiders*. As far as music is concerned, many western themes and title songs were released as singles, with vocals recorded by popular artists of the day, from Bobby Solo [Roberto Satti] to Sergio Endrigo, to boost the films' appeal to the youth market.

[3] Luigi Barzini, *The Italians*, p.193.

[4] Marcia Landy, *Italian Film*, p.207.

[5] See Landy, *Italian Film*, pp.205.

[6] Quoted in Frayling, *Spaghetti Westerns*, p.129-30.

[7] According to co-star Robert Woods, Martinelli had personal problems with the film's original director and co-writer, the virtually unknown Piero Cristofani, and had him replaced with her friend Wertmüller, then at the beginning of her career. The pseudonymous 'Nathan Wich' was credited with direction in their stead.

[8] Quoted in Massimo Moscati, *Western all'italiana*, 1978.

[9] Band's son Charles later founded the fleetingly successful Empire production house in the Eighties, specialising in low-budget science fiction and horror movies.

[10] Italian sources credit the direction of *The Tramplers* jointly to Band and Mario Sequi, although this seems to be another instance of a domestic director's name being applied for the purpose of tax breaks. Franco Nero, who plays an aspiring young rancher in the film, insists that Band alone was at the helm.

[11] *The Hellbenders* is broadly similar to a number of American westerns made around the same time that featured malformed western clans, such as the 'rawhiders' led by Donald Pleasence and son Bruce Dern in *Will Penny* (1968), and a film that seems to owe more than a little to Band and Corbucci, *The Desperados* (1969), in which Jack Palance plays a deranged Southern guerrilla leader whose band includes his three sons. The army of recalcitrant rebels in European westerns may also have influenced the low-budget Lee Frost picture *The Scavengers* (1969), which begins with a Hellbenders-style attack by renegades on a Union monetary convoy.

12   Siciliano's directorial debut was inevitably a western, 1968's *Cowards Don't Pray*. Co-written, like *Blood at Sundown*, by Ernesto Gastaldi, it stars that film's Gianni Garko as a decent man turned into an unhinged, compulsive killer by cruel fate. He aligns with brothers Jerry Wilson and Ivan Rassimov before Garko's murderous urges force a rift between them. Siciliano's direction, allied to a melodramatic plot concerned with moral dilemmas and divided loyalties, is very much in the style of Cardone, suggesting he either absorbed the latter's influence or, perhaps, played a more creative role himself in the production of *Blood at Sundown* and *Seven Dollars to Kill*.

13   Author's interview with Gianni Garko.

14   The 'homecoming' westerns with the clearest debt to classical drama are the *Odyssey*-derived *The Return of Ringo* (1965) and the Aeschylus-based *The Forgotten Pistolero*, which both require their heroes to return home in disguise while they work out a plan to recover their identities and carry out their revenge. *Massacre Time* is also one of a number of westerns in which parental authority, invested in a strong patriarchal figure, is usurped without the father's full awareness by his scion. The classic Hollywood example of this kind of story is Anthony Mann's *The Man from Laramie* (1955), in which James Stewart's obsessive pursuit of a gun-runner leads to a cattle baron realising his son and stepson are unworthy of their inheritance – they have all of his ambition but none of his ideals. Among European westerns, Giuliano Carnimeo's *The Moment to Kill* (1968) has Arturo Dominici and Horst Frank as father and son with very different designs on $500,000 in missing Confederate gold, with Frank eventually engineering the other's death. And in *John the Bastard* (1967), Don Diego Tenorio (Claudio Gora) has fled to a monastery in fear of his jumped-up son Francisco (Claudio Camaso), who rules the family estate with a rod of iron.

15   "[*Massacre Time*] did so well that I actually received a phone call from none other than Michelangelo Antonioni. He said to me… 'I love westerns. I arrived in Rome yesterday, went to the Adriano Cinema and I saw an actor I didn't recognise but who surprised me a lot – you!' Antonioni then proposed a film to me that I never ended up doing. And this interest from Antonioni is the thing that's pleased me the most in my career." Interview with George Hilton by Roger A. Fratter in *Dieci ricercati dello spaghetti western* (Nocturno Cinema, October 2007).

16   The Danites were a Mormon faction renowned for their zeal in defending the movement against its many enemies in the American west. Mitchell's character may have been based on the notorious and much mythologised Orrin 'Porter' Rockwell, known as the 'Destroying Angel', who acted as bodyguard to Mormon leaders Joseph Smith and Brigham Young and was implicated in several killings and violent incidents, including the attempted assassination of former Missouri Governor Lilburn Boggs in 1842.

17   The quote is from Martin Clark, *Modern Italy*, p.82.

18   Later in the Sixties, the Church, by now fighting a rearguard action against its dwindling influence, was active in the proliferation of 'cine-forums', where young audiences would debate what they watched. For more on this subject, see Sorlin.

19   Censorship operated in a similarly prescriptive fashion in Catholic Spain, where so many Euro-westerns were shot, before liberalisation set in at the end of the Sixties. Daniel Kowalsky writes: "The Church's heavy influence cast a long shadow over the arts and popular culture, not least in the cinema. The Franco regime took film censorship very seriously, and from early 1937 until 1978, approximately sixty thousand films were scrutinised by state censors [pre- and post-production] for images or dialogue that mocked or challenged Catholic sensibilities." ('Rated S: Softcore pornography and the Spanish transition to democracy, 1977-82', in *Spanish Popular Cinema*, p.189).

20   Quoted in *Western all'italiana: The Wild, the Sadist and the Outsider*.

21   *The Price of Death*'s Reverend Tiller – "God's avenger" – was one of many clerical serial killers on Italian screens in the Seventies. Priests became the quintessential culprits, or else made convenient red herrings, in *gialli*, whether 'exorcising' or punishing sinners in *Don't Torture A Duckling* (1972) and *Seven Blood-Stained Orchids* (1972), or crushing the objects of their own desires in *Who Saw Her Die?* (1972) and *The Bloodstained Shadow* (1978). *Bread and Chocolate* (1974), Franco Brusati's bittersweet comedy of displacement, seems to allude to this trend by working a homicidal cleric into its plot. Even these characters seem charitable, however, compared with the suicidal priest of Lucio Fulci's *City of the Living Dead* (1980), who returns from the grave commanding an army of the undead.

22   When Spanish censors checked the script of *Three Silver Dollars* prior to location shooting, they objected to an "element of deliberate religious irreverence" concerning Mirko Ellis's character, "a bandit of the most brutal instincts and actions, yet at the same time a devoutly religious man given to prayer and the observance of the Christian sacraments". Filming permission was granted but it would be interesting to know whether this "religious irreverence" was toned down in the version prepared for Spanish release. (Quote from Rafael Heredero García, *La censura de guión en España*).

23   Author's interview with Robert Woods.

24   Quoted in Sir Christopher Frayling, *Once Upon a Time in Italy*, p.75.

25   Author's interview with Enzo Castellari.

above: Franco Nero goes to ground in this German lobby card for **Massacre Time**.

above: Marino Girolami's variation on *Treasure Island* pits a platitudinous priest (Richard Harrison) against a worldly adventurer (Gilbert Roland).

Chapter 4

"God Forgives... I Don't"

Films of Hate and Retribution

"I don't have any feelings – except maybe hate." When Bill Kiowa (Brett Halsey) is released from prison at the beginning of Tonino Cervi's *Today It's Me... Tomorrow You!* (1968), he has only one thing on his mind – to find the man who murdered his wife, framing Kiowa for the crime, and to kill him. His first action is to visit a gunsmith, having spent most of his time in prison practising quick draw with a pistol painstakingly carved from wood. He then recruits four gunmen to help him and sets out for revenge.

Kiowa's single-mindedness typifies the Euro-western avenger, just as revenge has always been fundamental to the western itself, emphasising the need for individual action in an untamed environment where perfidy is rife and the rule of law is either weighted towards evildoers or has yet to be established. The classic Hollywood western, governed by stricter moral codes than its European counterpart, places greater stress on the tension between the protagonist's pursuit of revenge and the values of society, however imperfect, from which he (and it is almost invariably a male character) has strayed. There is usually more time taken to establish motivation, and at the end of the film a way is usually found to reintegrate the temporarily unbalanced individual into civilisation. John Wayne's love for Claire Trevor helps absolve him at the close of *Stagecoach* (1939); Henry King's *The Bravados* (1958) ends with a crisis of conscience but the promise of redemption for Gregory Peck; Budd Boetticher's *Ride Lonesome* (1959) sees Randolph Scott achieve psychological release by burning the hanging tree that symbolises his revenge; Steve McQueen lets Karl Malden off at the point of his gun in an unconvincing volte-face at the climax of *Nevada Smith* (1966); and Clint Eastwood reins in his savage urges, much more plausibly, in *Hang 'Em High* (1968) and *The Outlaw Josey Wales* (1976). In all these cases the central characters retain, or regain, their humanity (even if, as in *Nevada Smith*, it is forced upon them by a contrivance). The hate that has possessed them begins to subside once they have settled their accounts – they may even be persuaded to partially or completely abandon their quest – and by the end of the film they have achieved a kind of emotional and moral equilibrium, albeit at a significant cost.

above: Brett Halsey (*right*) with one of the "scum of the earth" he tracks down in **Today It's Me... Tomorrow You!**, an exemplary revenge western.
opposite: Devious outlaw Frank Wolff swears to pursue his own ends in **God Forgives... I Don't!** The pithy title perfectly captures the tone of the genre.

European revenge westerns tend to reach bleaker conclusions. They have more in common with angrier examples from the American school, films mired in a moral grey area like Anthony Mann's *Winchester '73* (1950) and *The Man from Laramie* (1955), which both end with James Stewart burnt out through bitterness; Fritz Lang's outré *Rancho Notorious* (1952), with Arthur Kennedy transformed from mild-mannered to murderous; and John Ford's *The Searchers* (1956), with John Wayne left to "wander forever between the winds". (The European approach also anticipates Clint Eastwood's *High Plains Drifter* [1973], his oneiric, ironic homage to Leone, in which – if one chooses to interpret it this way – the avenger may be acting from beyond the grave and is therefore beyond redemption. In a further twist, his revenge is partially directed against the very society from which he has 'strayed'.) In Euro-westerns, vengeance is so corrosive that it erodes almost every other emotion. Nothing much exists for the hunter except the pursuit of his prey – just as little time is wasted by writers and directors in getting the revenge plot under way – and whatever modifying factors or conflicting considerations there may be are nearly always overridden. Where they are not outsiders in the first place, it is difficult, if not impossible, to imagine these recalcitrant figures slotting back into society, especially since the latter is almost exclusively portrayed in a distinctly unflattering light, if indeed it features at all. As will be seen, the treatment of revenge in Italian and certain Spanish westerns reaches back to the roots of tragic drama, which are, significantly, European in origin. It also adheres to the concepts of machismo, honour, 'amoral familism' and independence embedded in the vendetta tradition so closely associated with the hot-blooded cultures of southern Italy and other parts of the Mediterranean, extending out to the quasi-Mexican milieu in which the stories so often take place.

Vengeance has been a popular dramatic motif since the advent of Greek tragedy, which exerted a strong influence on the genre. (A particularly fine Italian revenge western, *The Forgotten Pistolero* [1969], is a reworking of Aeschylus's trilogy, *The Oresteia*.) The theme was taken up by the Roman playwright Seneca, whose works inspired Elizabethan and Jacobean authors to write the greatest, most violent revenge dramas in history. The most famous of these of course is *Hamlet*, template for one of Enzo Castellari's most ambitious westerns (and, as Euro-western stalwart Gianni Garko would have it, for around half of the films in the genre[1]), while Thomas Kyd's *The Spanish Tragedy* and John Webster's *The Duchess of Malfi* are among the other classics of the form. Interestingly, most Jacobean dramas of this type were set in the Italy of the Borgias and the Medici or, occasionally, in Spain, which allowed their authors to 'Latinise' their 'noble' characters and involve them in the kind of debauchery and carnage popularised by Boccaccio and his ilk – and much later recounted by Thomas V. Cohen in *Love and Death in Renaissance Italy* – without appearing to criticise the English establishment. Just like European westerns, many of these plays were vilified in their time for being salacious and sensationalistic, while their broadly 'realistic' nature and purgative properties were either overlooked or dismissed. Another variety of revenge drama, referred to by literary historians as the 'French-Spanish' school, is also preoccupied with themes later exploited by the Euro-western. In the works of 17th Century Spaniard Pedro Calderón de la Barca, for example, vengeance is intimately entwined with notions of love and honour in a manner adopted by countless genre films.

While European westerns can hardly be considered on the same level as these august achievements, they are clearly offshoots of the same cultural tradition. They pursue the revenge motif with similarly full-blooded fervour, unashamedly targeting their spectators' basest emotions and embracing many of the same timeless themes in the process. All are preoccupied with human weakness – corruption, treachery, cruelty and ambition devour their characters, leading to a great deal of bloodshed, inevitably some of it being innocent. In this type of film, the avenger is closer in spirit to the nihilistic Jacobean malcontent than to the Hollywood cowboy, whose own anti-societal impulses are generally seen to be reversible. The dividing line between protagonist and antagonist, always thinner in European than American westerns, is here barely discernible, with embittered, broken-hearted 'heroes' ranging from dogged to frenzied in nature. Many have been contorted by hatred, their sanity – and in some cases their souls – hanging in the balance, and either blindly or willingly manipulate events and other people to their own vengeful ends. (We will see in this chapter how these extreme emotional states are often expressed in a baroque filmic style, with heavy-handed use of symbolism and Gothic imagery more reminiscent of horror movies than westerns.) The ethical questions associated with individual retribution are pushed aside, perhaps relegated to a line or two of perfunctory dialogue from a supporting character. This might seem like negligence – or even advocacy – on the filmmakers' part, but it also provides another intriguing point of comparison with past works. In Robert Ornstein's study, *The Moral Vision of Jacobean Tragedy* (1960), he writes: "There is not one great tragedy of the period [the Jacobean era] in which the ethical attitude towards blood vengeance is a central moral issue. In *Hamlet*, the greatest revenge play of the age, the question is quite simply ignored." Euro-westerns are more concerned with methodology than moralising, with actions than motivation; although the brutalising effect of his deeds on the central character, combined with the collateral damage he inflicts along the way, functions as a perfunctory denunciation of revenge if so desired. The admonition may only be implied, but it is usually present nonetheless.

It is no exaggeration to say that most genre films involve revenge at some point in their narratives; it's often thrown in almost as an afterthought at a very late stage. It plays a secondary but significant role in such major works as *The Return of Ringo* (1965), *Django* (1966), *Navajo Joe* (1966), *Day of Anger* (1967), *The Great Silence* (1968) and *The Price of Power* (1969), but is more often than not the central pivot around which the action revolves. The prevalence of this motif, part of the genre's inheritance from past forms of popular drama, can also be explained by the socio-historical and cultural significance of the vendetta, at least for southern Italian and Mediterranean audiences. (One European critic, writing in 1974, noted of the vengeance-themed *Massacre at Grand Canyon* [1964]: "Here is a story that recalls Sicily or Corsica more than the far west.") It shows an instinctive mistrust of authority, coupled with a tradition of self-reliance, which is reflected in other Italian *filoni* as well, from the peplum to the *poliziesco*. It is no coincidence that revenge plots in all these categories (though they're not all that common in *pepla*) reek with disillusionment, nor that they are frequently bound up with attacks on the political order and the impotence or culpability of the law. This chimes not only with the Euro-western's status as working-class revenge fantasy, but also with the time-honoured preconception in most types of popular drama that public figures are inherently corrupt. ("Italians don't kid themselves about power – they know its corrosive, and recognise their society has defects," comments director Damiano Damiani.[2]) The protagonist commonly discovers that his prey has become a town boss or a crooked banker, judge, politician or lawman, usually augmented by an army of hired guns. This effectively lets the avenger off the hook, ethically speaking, firstly because he has no recourse to the law, which his enemy controls, and secondly because his private retribution simultaneously has a wider liberatory effect. Whether the people he frees deserve their deliverance is another matter. In *Navajo Joe* and *Day of Anger*, the petty-minded, prejudiced citizens of small, endangered communities are partly the *source* of the avengers' ire. In the former, Joe goes into battle at least partially on the town's behalf, but they show no interest in his fate, only in their own financial security and survival.

Of course, the Euro-western is as sceptical about individuals as it is about society and, in tune with its fundamentally negative view of human nature, a great many of these revenge sagas trace the consequences of betrayals among thieves, professional gunmen and other undesirables. The more restrained of these films

above: There's no justice, there's just us: Brett Halsey (*right*) enlists Bud Spencer, among others, to his cause in **Today It's Me... Tomorrow You!** The straightforward script – co-written by Dario Argento and director Tonino Cervi – follows a more direct path than many of its peers.

above: Denizens of Clifton, including José Calvo (*standing, second from left*) and Lukas Ammann (*kneeling, centre*), count the cost of the vindictive campaign waged against their town by Lee Van Cleef and Giuliano Gemma – who both have a score to settle against them – in **Day of Anger**.

above: Nicoletta Machiavelli, outcast and avenger's helpmate, in **Navajo Joe**.

above: Brett Halsey and the pseudonymous Diana Madigan are right to look wary in this flashback scene from **Today It's Me... Tomorrow You!**
opposite: Genial James Garner toughened up as a hard-bitten outlaw in **A Man Called Sledge**.

maintain a subtle distinction in the moral shading between characters. The central figures in *Minnesota Clay* (1964), *The Hills Run Red* (1966), *Bandidos* (1967), *Hate for Hate* (1967), *Long Days of Vengeance* (1967), *A Long Ride from Hell* and *Today It's Me... Tomorrow You!* (both 1968) are all either romantic or old-fashioned types; honour still has some meaning for them even though most of them are criminals. In all except *Bandidos*, the protagonist has been either framed or imprisoned, usually as a result of a scheming partner – who, as well as keeping all the loot for himself, may also have seduced or killed the hero's woman – and seeks retribution upon release or escape. *One-Eyed Jacks* (1961) seems to have been the principal model here; the opening of *The Hills Run Red* certainly brings Brando's film to mind.

The finest film on the list, *Bandidos*, takes a more measured view of revenge than is usually the case. It was the only western directed by Massimo Dallamano, the influential cinematographer of *A Fistful of Dollars* (1964) and *For a Few Dollars More* (1965), and is anchored by Enrico Maria Salerno's persuasive interpretation of a man shaped and destroyed by his vengeful desire. Salerno's character, Richard Martin, is an upstanding travelling marksman with several prizes to his name. One day he encounters his old partner, the feared outlaw Billy Kane (Venantino Venantini), on a train the latter is robbing. Instead of killing him, Kane sadistically puts a bullet through each of Martin's hands, ensuring the latter will never be able to draw a gun on him. The once elegant Martin becomes a bitter, bedraggled shadow of himself; his livelihood, his reputation and his pride are blown away in the blaze of Billy's gun. Unable to exhibit his own pistol skills, he roams the west as a showman passing off various apprentices as the fictitious sharpshooter 'Ricky Shot'. His fourth such sidekick (Terry Jenkins) proves more promising than the others, and we quickly realise that Martin's true purpose is to mould his protégé into his personal instrument of vengeance.

Salerno was an A-list talent who bolstered many B-movies with his presence. (He also put his voice to good use, dubbing Clint Eastwood in the 'Dollars' trilogy for the Italian market.) His other western roles had a villainous edge – the cardsharp Montero in *Death Sentence* (1967), delusional 'Caesar' Fuller in *Death Walks in Laredo* (1967) and double-crossing Luca in *A Train for Durango* (1968) – but outside the genre he often portrayed weary, ageing authority figures not unlike Martin. Salerno was only 41 when he played the part, the prime of life for an actor but a ripe age for a Westerner who made his living with a gun, and Martin's advancing years add pathos to his plight. He's a sympathetic character but not exactly a likeable one, which makes him more believable. He can be cantankerous and demanding, especially during his lessons with Ricky, but the way that he clings to his dignity, the memory of the commanding man he once was, gives him a tragic quality. Eventually, Martin's desperation gets the better of him and, as Ricky, who has been implicated in the opening train robbery, gets waylaid trying to clear his name, Martin takes a sawn-off

above: Venantino Venantini as the malicious Billy Kane in **Bandidos**.

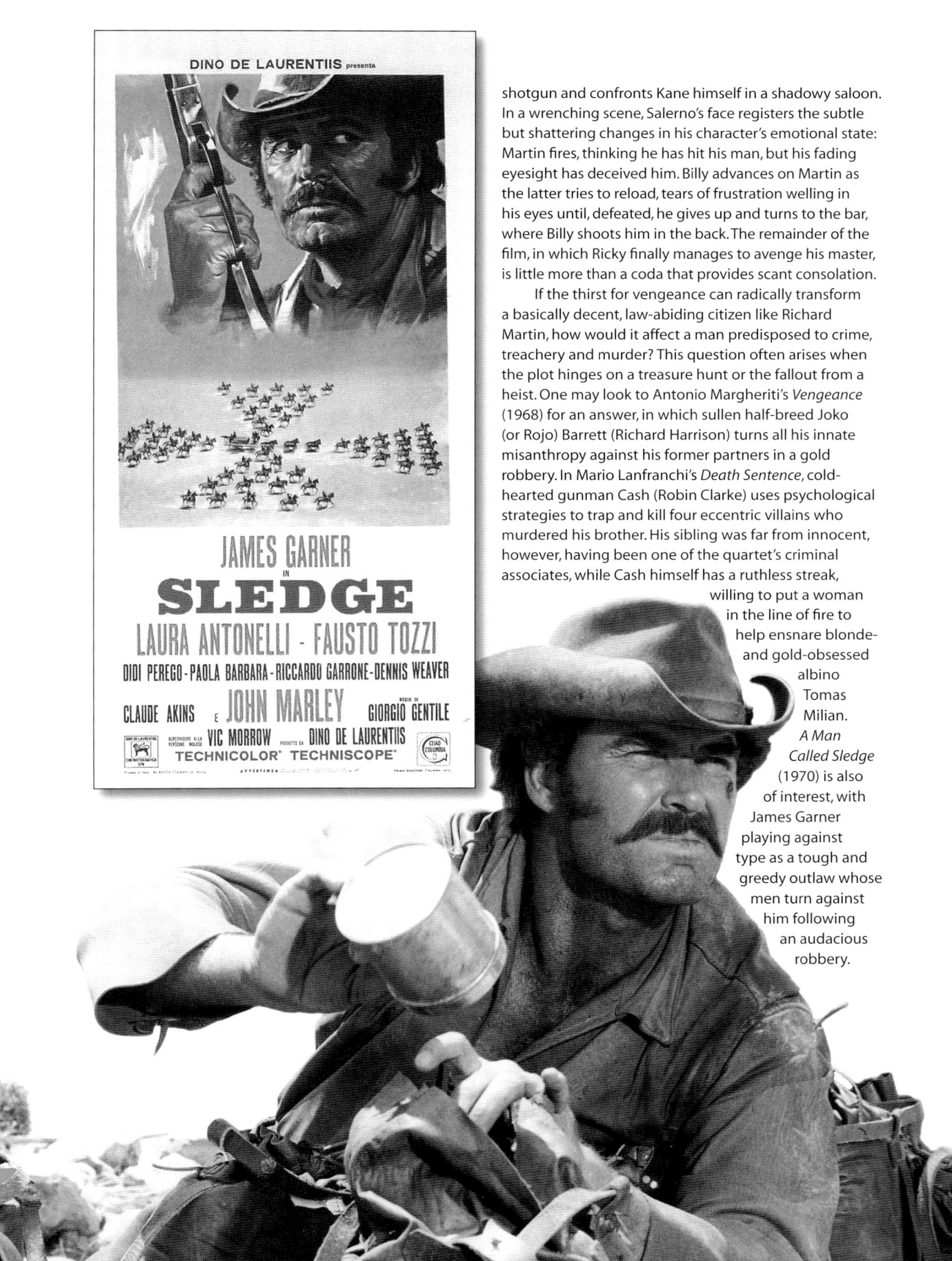

shotgun and confronts Kane himself in a shadowy saloon. In a wrenching scene, Salerno's face registers the subtle but shattering changes in his character's emotional state: Martin fires, thinking he has hit his man, but his fading eyesight has deceived him. Billy advances on Martin as the latter tries to reload, tears of frustration welling in his eyes until, defeated, he gives up and turns to the bar, where Billy shoots him in the back. The remainder of the film, in which Ricky finally manages to avenge his master, is little more than a coda that provides scant consolation.

If the thirst for vengeance can radically transform a basically decent, law-abiding citizen like Richard Martin, how would it affect a man predisposed to crime, treachery and murder? This question often arises when the plot hinges on a treasure hunt or the fallout from a heist. One may look to Antonio Margheriti's *Vengeance* (1968) for an answer, in which sullen half-breed Joko (or Rojo) Barrett (Richard Harrison) turns all his innate misanthropy against his former partners in a gold robbery. In Mario Lanfranchi's *Death Sentence*, cold-hearted gunman Cash (Robin Clarke) uses psychological strategies to trap and kill four eccentric villains who murdered his brother. His sibling was far from innocent, however, having been one of the quartet's criminal associates, while Cash himself has a ruthless streak, willing to put a woman in the line of fire to help ensnare blonde- and gold-obsessed albino Tomas Milian. *A Man Called Sledge* (1970) is also of interest, with James Garner playing against type as a tough and greedy outlaw whose men turn against him following an audacious robbery.

Any Gun Can Play

above: Director Gianfranco Baldanello rose about mediocrity with **Black Jack**, a bleak portrait of a bank robber – played with wild-eyed relish by Robert Woods – consumed and contorted by hatred and revenge.
below: Traditional imagery for the irreverent **Johnny Yuma**.

The most ferocious example, however, is the lesser-known *Black Jack* (1968), directed by Gianfranco Baldanello largely on location in Eilat in Israel (it was part-financed by Alexander Hakohen, a former brewery owner who bought his way into the film business during the co-production boom). Bank robber 'Black' Jack Murphy (an uncharacteristically manic Robert Woods[3]), double-crossed by his own gang, becomes a demented, sadistic monster, every bit as cruel as the men he is pursuing. In fact, it was Jack's attempt to cheat his gang that caused them to attack him, in a staggeringly nasty sequence in which he is tied, beaten, stabbed in the hand, his shins riddled with bullets and his sister – the only wholesome character in the film – raped, scalped and murdered.

The plot of Baldanello's film is little more than a framework recycled from, and in, countless other westerns. Yet in its misanthropic tone, Gothic production design and, above all, its crazed hero-villain, who wouldn't have looked out of place at the Theatre du Grand Guignol, *Black Jack* distils just about every distinctive aspect of the second-tier Italian revenge western into 90 savage minutes. Not for Jack the formality of simply shooting his prey or even necessarily killing them himself. In a film where betrayal is for sale (the malevolent Indian Joe, played by Mimmo Palmara, is paid separately by both Jack and the gang for his complicity in their dealings), he cynically offers the poor peons of a Mexican pueblo $10,000 to kill one of their own – one of Jack's former associates. He also exploits his enemies' weaknesses, tricking the trigger-happy Gordon (Federico Chentrens, who was also the film's assistant director) into shooting his own brother (Goffredo Unger), and applies the *lex talionis* – shooting one of his assailants in the legs, stabbing another in the hand and kidnapping the daughter of Sanchez (Rik Battaglia), another gang member, and luring him into a showdown in the ghost town where Jack fully intends the girl to suffer the same fate as his own late sister. Ironically, the downfall of this deranged character is the result of somebody else's momentary delusion.

Black Jack's catalogue of Jacobean sadism exemplifies the intensification of violence in the revenge film. Given that the genre as a whole is traditionally labelled as gratuitous in this regard, it may seem strange to single out one strain from the others; in the vengeance plot, however, violence is unquestionably more deeply felt, characters more emotionally charged than elsewhere. Of all the genre's variations, this is the one most fascinated by man's capacity for cruelty and, as a consequence, it often takes a particularly vicious form and is depicted in unflinching detail. Stuntman and supporting actor Benito Stefanelli, a specialist in the choreography of carnage, puts it simply: "When you hate the bad guy for the whole movie, then you expect him to die in a certain manner. He has to pay for his evil deeds, so the act of death has to be portrayed as we do, the Italian way, from the guts."[4] This helps explain why the avengers frequently prolong the death of their prey, savouring the moment for which they have waited so long and maximising the other's suffering, which, in the usual way of revenge narratives, is for the audience to vicariously 'enjoy' as well. There is a formal pattern to many of the climactic confrontations: the protagonists of *The Return of Ringo*, *Texas Adios* (1966), *Today It's Me... Tomorrow You!* and *The Forgotten Pistolero*, among others, cripple their opponents with bullets before firing the fatal shot. The comparatively tame Anthony Steffen vehicle *A Stranger in Paso Bravo* (1968) concludes with a variation on this pattern, when his character ignites a fire with rifle shots and watches his enemy burn to death. In other cases, the only outlet for the characters' frustrations is raw physical force: Pecos (Robert Woods) throttles the racist Joe Klein (Pier Paolo Capponi) in an ugly close-up at the end of *My Name Is Pecos*; Navajo Joe (Burt Reynolds) carves a tribal symbol in the forehead of a scalp hunter before dispatching him with a rock; Johnny Ashley (Anthony Steffen) engages in a savage fistfight with Sancho (Fernando Sancho) in *Seven Dollars to Kill* (1966), which ends with them attacking each other with baling hooks; and Mark Damon in *Johnny Yuma* (1966) pummels the cowardly Pedro (Luigi Vannucchi), snapping his arm in the process, as payback for the deaths of Johnny's father and an innocent young Mexican boy.

"God Forgives... I Don't!"

Clearly, from a conventional critical/moral standpoint the Euro-western goes further than necessary in its depiction of retributive violence, certainly further than its Hollywood counterpart had until that time. Yet it remains a mistake to judge these films according to standards that belonged not only to a different cultural tradition but also, effectively, to a different era. These are neither conventional westerns nor straightforward revenge dramas, but a hybrid of the two. They adapt elements of both traditions to suit their purposes – the hyperbolism and emotional torment of revenge tragedies, the iconography of westerns – striving simultaneously for greater relevance in the context of increasingly tense and violent times and to secure an advantage in the competitive and progressively more bloodthirsty exploitation market. Lest we forget, these were very much films of and for their time. No matter how shocking Euro-westerns may have seemed compared with most previous American productions, however, they were nowhere near as gruesome as the Elizabethan and Jacobean tragedies whose spirit they evoke. Nor were they quite so transgressive as their reputation suggests in other regards. Most, if not all, of the individual reprisals are morally justifiable if one looks closely enough. The Euro-western avenger may be predominantly self-serving but, as previously suggested, he also acts in the interests of society as well, albeit unconsciously or inadvertently, and his savagery is generally awakened by, and seen in contrast to, the calculated cruelty of his enemies. The protagonist thus maintains the *reactive* quality of the classical western hero, even if in most other respects he goes against the grain – he is quicker to resort to violence, for example, and is less prone to doubts or hesitation in the course of his pursuit. Many of his attributes were subsequently adopted by the frustrated policemen and vigilantes who outgunned cowboys at the box office – in Italy and elsewhere – in the Seventies.

The most common type of revenge story involves a hero inflicting punishment for the murder of family members or a loved one. Euro-westerns can hardly be said to have introduced this scenario to the screen, but the repetition of this particular plotline, and the sheer intensity with which it is so often enacted, emphasises many stereotypical aspects of Latin culture and temperament, chiefly the duty to defend/avenge the honour of the family. (In several of the more subversive entries, vengeance is an inter-family affair, in which all manner of destructive neuroses come to the surface.) As in the archetypal American revenge western, *The Searchers*, these stories often involve the avenger in a long and lonely quest, which may take many years to complete. The three most famous examples come from the genre's A-list – the Harmonica/Frank strand in *Once Upon a Time in the West* (1968); Colonel Mortimer's patient pursuit of Indio in *For a Few Dollars More*; and Bill (John Phillip Law) tracking his family's killers in *Death Rides a Horse* (1967), which was written, like the preceding film, by Luciano Vincenzoni. The most interesting of the remaining quest westerns are those, like *Death Rides a Horse*, that are rooted in childhood trauma. In each case, the loss of parents and/or other family members determines the youngsters' bullet-riddled destinies. Whether they would have grown into killers without these early violent experiences, which in a way have arrested their development, is a moot point, on film as in life. What's clear, however, is that the craving for revenge has moulded them into the men they have become.

above: In **Death Rides a Horse**, John Phillip Law (*kneeling*) plays a young man whose life has been mapped out by the requirements of revenge.
below: Indio's (Gian Maria Volonté) time is almost up as he prepares to face the Colonel (Lee Van Cleef) in **For a Few Dollars More** – the watch symbolises the traumatic event that binds the combatants together.

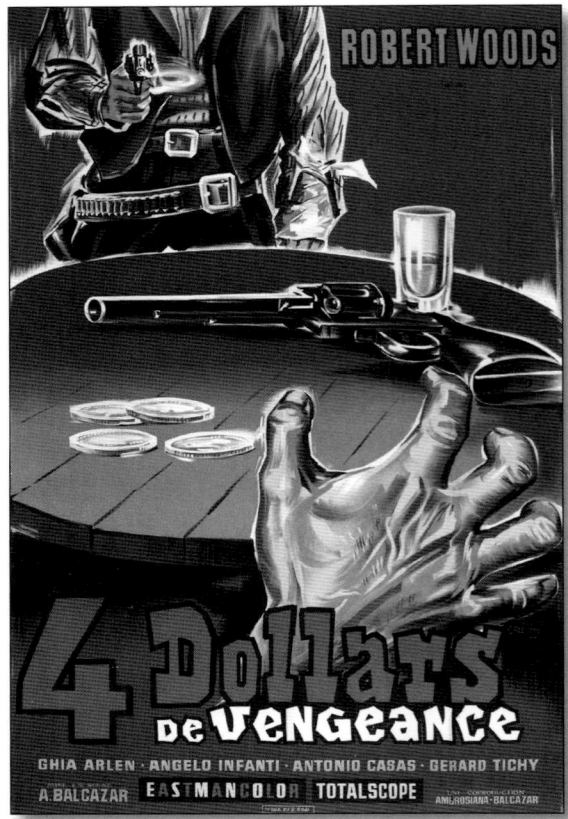

The notion of a child or children nurturing vengeful intent into adulthood features in a number of other titles. *Texas Adios*, *Day of Anger*, *Two Crosses at Danger Pass* (1967), *The Great Silence*, *Hate Is My God* (1969), *The Forgotten Pistolero*, *Vengeance Trail* (1971) and *A Man Called Blade* (1977) all play up, to one degree or another, the psychological and/or tragic side-effects of the pursuit. *Texas Adios* fades on a familiar romantic image – Franco Nero riding into the sunset – with the twist that Nero has his younger brother's corpse in tow, while death, despair and isolation are common fates elsewhere. Genre pioneer Joaquín Romero Marchent was the first to use this device effectively in *Gunfight at High Noon* (1963), having rehearsed the quest narrative in *The Magnificent Three* earlier the same year. In *Gunfight*, Richard Harrison, Claudio Undari and Billy Hayden [Miguel Palenzuela] play three brothers who get the opportunity to punish their father's murderers after 20 years, having witnessed the killing as young boys. Harrison takes up a marshal's badge for the purpose while the violent, scowling Undari steps outside the law. Undari was adept at these 'good-badman' characters; he played another who waits 20 years to settle a score in *Son of Jesse James* (1965), in which he finds that 'uncle' Bob Ford (Luis Induni, who had played Undari's chief antagonist in the Romero Marchent film) has prospered into a wealthy rancher, presumably on the back of his ill-gotten reward money. Osvaldo Civirani's *Son of Django* (1967) tells a similar tale in a similar manner, only this time the famous gunfighter betrayed by a friend is of Italian invention rather than historical extraction.

In the majority of these films the avengers have grown up to become bitter and withdrawn. They are loners tormented by the past, which usually presents itself in the form of stock stylistic/dramatic clichés such as flashbacks and trigger images that relate to the scene of the crime. Giulio Petroni's *Death Rides a Horse* makes use of both these devices in the course of one of the leanest of all revenge narratives. In the dark and stormy opening sequence, young Bill notices distinguishing details about his family's assailants – a face, a scar, a tattooed chest, an earring, a skull-shaped pendant – which help him to identify them later in the film. Each confrontation is accompanied by a flashback to that terrible night. (The red tint to these brief inserts is a reminder of Leone's influence, bringing to mind Indio's drug-hazed recollections in *For a Few Dollars More*.[5]) The skull pendant comes into play at the conclusion, where it is revealed that Ryan (Lee Van Cleef), Bill's accomplice, an ex-con with a grudge against the same men, was the fifth member of the gang but took no part in the killing, even lifting Bill away from the flames. Bill grants Ryan a reprieve, the latter having taken the headstrong younger man under his wing, although this kind of last-minute twist usually has a more cynical edge, stressing the deviousness and venality of so-called friends who are ultimately revealed to be anything but. *Four Dollars of Revenge* (1966), *The Wrath of God* (1968), *A Name That Cried Revenge* (1968) and *A Man Called Django* (1971) are among many films that conclude this way.

Flashbacks prove a particularly useful tool when the plot includes subdued memories and unknown traitors – as in *A Name That Cried Revenge*, *Chuck Mool* (1970), *Twice a Judas* (1969) and *The Man Called Noon* (1973), which all feature amnesiac gunslingers – even if the identities and motivations in question are usually obvious from the outset.

Haunted by the past: Richard Crenna (*above and, inset, striking an assailant*) seeks to reclaim his identity in **The Man Called Noon**.

"God Forgives... I Don't!"

above: The devil is in the details: the killers' physical idiosyncrasies later prove to be their undoing in Giulio Petroni's **Death Rides a Horse**.
opposite top left: Coins become the avenger's trademark in **Four Dollars of Revenge**. There were variations on this trope throughout the genre.

Befitting his reputation, Sergio Leone employs flashbacks with more flair and imagination, in a "Freudian" fashion, as he put it, in *For a Few Dollars More* and *Once Upon a Time in the West*. British director Peter Collinson may well have had Leone's approach in mind when scattering fragments of flashbacks throughout *The Man Called Noon*. There is also a wide role for trigger images, *mementos mori* and the like. The physical details burned on to Bill's memory in *Death Rides a Horse*, the twin musical watches held by Mortimer and Indio in *For a Few Dollars More* and Harmonica's mouth organ in *Once Upon a Time in the West* are loaded with psychological significance, emblematic of the pain, anger and remorse that dominate each character. Rafael Romero Marchent's *Prey of Vultures* (1972) steals from *Death Rides a Horse* in its story of a young artist (Peter Lee Lawrence) who sketches the physical quirks and distinctive accessories of the masked men who killed his father. In *The Forgotten Pistolero* it is a sound – the tolling of a bell – rather than an image that signals the protagonist's trauma, but the idea is the same. In other instances the item may be a red herring – a necklace that ends up in Antonio Sabato's possession in *Hate for Hate* (1967) and leads John Ireland to mistakenly believe the former has killed his daughter – or perhaps a lucky charm, such as the titular coin that repeatedly saves Giuliano Gemma's life in *One Silver Dollar* (1965).

above: Treachery and misunderstandings lead to tragedy in Domenico Paolella's **Hate for Hate**.

Then there are many episodic westerns where a fetish object of some kind not only symbolises revenge but also keeps a tally of the killings, like notches on a pistol butt, as the films move from one set-piece showdown to another. In *Vengeance*, Richard Harrison leaves a bloodied piece of rope, which had earlier been used to kill his friend, on the corpse of each enemy he eliminates. In *The Magnificent Three* the item is a pin badge, in *I'll Sell My Skin Dearly* (1968) the links from a chain, while coins perform the same function in *Four Dollars of Revenge*, *Seven Dollars to Kill* and *The Wrath of God*. On the one hand these devices can be dismissed as little more than gimmicks, confining these films within the boundaries of pulp fiction, but on the other they help to characterise Euro-western avengers as neurotic compulsives obsessed by the past, of which these morbid keepsakes are a constant and painful reminder.

The most impassioned revenge films are those that centre on jealousy, rivalry and resentment between or within families. Invariably pessimistic in tone, they are closely patterned after classical tragedy. Shakespeare's *Hamlet*, for example, is the inspiration for both Enzo Castellari's audacious *Johnny Hamlet* (1968), via a story by Sergio Corbucci, and *In the Dust of the Sun* (1971) by Parisian director Richard Balducci. Both follow the plot of the play fairly faithfully (the former is even bold enough to feature a theatrical troupe rehearsing *Hamlet* itself), although they omit or downplay notable characters and subplots – in particular Laertes – and add their own embellishments: Gothic frills, Catholic symbolism (and ubiquitous Mexican bandits) in the former; psychedelic and erotic frissons in the latter. In Castellari's film, returning soldier Johnny (a suitably brooding Andrea Giordana), having 'seen' his father's ghost in a Mario Bava-style dream sequence, unmasks evil 'uncle' Claude (the always reliable Horst Frank) as the murderer, fighting off his henchmen Ross (Rosencrantz, played by Enio Girolami, the director's brother) and Gill (Guildenstern, Pedro Sanchez) with the aid of Horace (Horatio, Gilbert Roland). (Johnny's mother, played by Françoise Prévost, has the fitting name of Gertie.) Castellari's film is light on philosophising but strong on striking visuals: a candlelit grotto-cum-graveyard; a rather anomalous crucifixion (almost obligatory for a Castellari film); and the haunting image of Emily (Gabriella Grimaldi), who takes the place of Ophelia, lying dead beneath a stream in a direct reference to the play. Balducci's effort has a very different mood and alters the balance between the characters. His Claudius, in the personage of Joe Bradford (Bob Cunningham), dominates the film. Despotic and egotistical, he overshadows the tragic queen, also named Gertie, played in a minor key by Maria Schell. Balducci's highly unconventional 'Hamlet', meanwhile, played by willowy blond actor-singer Daniel Beretta, who once essayed the lead in a stage production of *Jesus Christ Superstar*, is more like a contemporary hippie than the

above: "It is not, nor it cannot come to good": Andrea Giordana (*centre*) in the clutches of pernicious villains in Enzo Castellari's **Johnny Hamlet**.

brooding figure of the Bard's imagination. He barely speaks, and most of his screen time is spent gazing into the middle distance, cradling a pistol or playing with children, until the arrival of the travelling players (here led by a certain Goldoni, in a nod to the *Servant of Two Masters* author) sets his revenge plan in motion. There is an unusual degree of nudity and some incestuous innuendo when Beretta 'comforts' his mother a little too passionately, with Balducci's direction stressing a distinctly 'modern' sensibility.

Another pseudo-Shakespearean western, the intelligent *Fury of Johnny Kid* (1967), adopts the idea of star-crossed lovers and feuding families from *Romeo and Juliet* – only here it's *Johnny* and Juliet, played by real-life husband and wife Peter Lee Lawrence and Cristina Galbo. Directed by Gianni Puccini, a well-known critic and filmmaker who once wrote scripts for Giuseppe De Santis, and written by Bruno Baratti and Maria del Carmen Martínez Román (*Django Kill!*, *Requiem for a Gringo*), this is the most self-conscious of adaptations. At one point, Johnny's jealous lover, Roselyn (Maria Cuadra), interpreted here as a saloon floozy, even refers to the Bard and *Romeo and Juliet* directly, as she spitefully sets the psychotic Rodrigo (Peter Martell), Juliet's brother, against her former beau. The ending here is adjusted, however, in a more positive direction, although it's a perverse display of optimism in the circumstances as the love-struck young couple escape while their kinfolk resolve their bitter feud – rooted in the historical territorial disputes of Mexicans and Americans in early California – by wiping each other out with suicidal zeal in a frenetic firefight. The tragedy here is not so much centred on the lovers, then, as on the inexorable fate of their families – "There couldn't be another way," as Johnny laments.

Greek tragedy, meanwhile, is the basis for Joaquín Romero Marchent's *Fedra West* (1968), derived in turn from Jean Racine's 17th Century play *Phèdre* and Euripides's *Hippolytus*; and Ferdinando Baldi's *The Forgotten Pistolero*, a reworking of the first two plays in the *Oresteia* trilogy by way of a late 19th Century Mexican melodrama.**6** The former is a sterile rendering of a tempestuous story, involving an incestuous affair between a rancher's wife, Norma Bengell (Phaedra), and her stepson, Simón Andreu (Hippolytus), that results in their deaths at the rancher's hands. By his own admission, the director undertook the assignment without much enthusiasm, and this is reflected in the development of the plot, which has an air of predictability rather than tragic inevitability. The performances are similarly uninspired. Although Bengell transmits at least a degree of the heroine's ambiguity, Andreu makes it hard to understand why his character would inspire such dangerous passion, while James Philbrook as 'Theseus' is less the proud victim of deception than a bullying, selfish autocrat, whose pursuit of the couple seems more like a way of saving face than avenging his honour.

Revenger's tragedies: Locandina posters for **The Forgotten Pistolero** (*above*) and **Fedra West** (*bottom*), along with a Spanish poster for **Fury of Johnny Kid** (*left*).

Baldi's film is a far more accomplished transposition, replacing the rulers of ancient Mycenae with an aristocratic family of Oaxaca destroyed by betrayal and murderous greed. By greatly condensing the material – reducing the return from war and subsequent murder of Agamemnon to a flashback sequence and omitting entirely *The Eumenides*, the concluding part of the trilogy – Baldi and his team of writers (led by Vincenzo Cerami, who according to Baldi was the driving force behind the project), circumvent many of the play's most problematic issues – matricide, natural versus legal justice – to focus more strongly on the core themes of revenge, remorse and their destabilising effects on the characters. (In one respect the film enlarges on the text, transforming one of Aeschylus's minor characters, Pylades, Orestes's companion in *The Libation Bearers*, into a former family servant, played by Peter Martell, who has his own score to settle. His emasculation at the hands of Piero Lulli's hacienda foreman parallels, in a metaphorical sense, that of Alberto de Mendoza's powerless 'Aegisthus'.) The performances are as acutely observed as the Mexican setting. Playing the equivalent of Clytemnestra, Luciana Paluzzi captures the complexity of this most troublesome of female tragic characters: traitorous wife, murderess, decorous socialite, guilt-stricken mother. The genre has an abundance of 'Clytemnestras' – manipulative, murderous, power-crazed women – but Paluzzi's interpretation invites scrutiny and sympathy more than outright condemnation. As her children, Leonard Mann/Orestes and Pilar Velázquez/Electra are almost as impressive, carefully measuring rage and sorrow as they contemplate revenge against their mother and her lover for the killing of their father. ("It wasn't necessary to research the play to interpret the part," recalls Mann of only his second film role. "I grew up in an Italian family that had daily tragedies. That part was easy. The hard part was trying to pretend I knew what I was doing."*7*) Unlike in the *Oresteia*, the avengers' actions are not submitted to objective judgement, partly because the debate about the degree of man's responsibility for his actions – the crux of the drama – takes place mainly in the missing *The Eumenides*, and partly because the film's (male) villains are so obviously deserving of their fate. It can be argued, however, that Baldi's characters' volition is just as restricted as that of Aeschylus's. Orestes was commanded to seek vengeance by the god Apollo; Italian western heroes are bound by an unwritten obligation, almost a pathological compulsion, to defend the honour of the family. This creates tensions and conflicts that undermine the very structure of family itself. Even so, there are boundaries. In *The Forgotten Pistolero*, for example, the siblings are spared the horrific task of actually killing their mother, an act that would almost certainly have lost them the support of Italian spectators – she is shot in the final reckoning by her co-conspirator, de Mendoza, who also reveals that she was infertile and not their natural mother after all, a fact that only compounds Paluzzi's personal tragedy. The denouement thus allows Mann the untainted satisfaction of avenging his father by killing de Mendoza in a fair fight, while his mother's death serves as both punishment for her crimes and as merciful release from the torments of remorse. This is hardly an upbeat conclusion for the avengers, however, who stagger distraught from the flaming remains of the hacienda with not a chink of *The Eumenides*'s regenerative light to guide them.

As discussed in the previous chapter, these films often question, albeit obliquely, the very meaning and value of blood ties, and concern themselves, if only superficially, with the complicated relationship between family and individual identity. Many revenge titles make use of the ever-popular 'Cain and Abel' motif: the protagonists of *Blood at Sundown* (1966), *Massacre Time* (1966), *For $100,000 Per Killing* (1967), *Twice a Judas* and *Chuck Mool* are the victims of selfish plots by their half-brothers that inevitably lead to an emotionally charged final reckoning. This fascination with family rivalry extends beyond siblings. In *Johnny Yuma*, the title character is conspired against by his aunt and her brother, who have already murdered Johnny's uncle in a bid for the family estate; the eponymous *John the Bastard* (1967) nurses a collective grievance against all his relatives, his mother included; while wicked paternal figures, the most primeval of dramatic villains from Cronus down, must be eliminated in *Texas Adios*, *Johnny Hamlet*, *The Forgotten Pistolero* and by the masked hero of *Starblack* (1966). One of the most tragic conflicts of all occurs in *Seven Dollars to Kill* when a father (Anthony Steffen) and his son (Jerry Wilson) meet at the intersection of their respective revenge trails. As with so many of the more overwrought Italian westerns, the setting for the story is incidental, the symbolism spread thickly and the themes – irony, hubris, cruel fate – timeless and universal.

above: Erstwhile rivals Mark Damon (*foreground*) and Lawrence Dobkin (*background*) join forces to foil a family plot in **Johnny Yuma**.

Death in the afternoon: having baited fate – and the Mexican army – one too many times, the outlaw heroes of **Vengeance Is Mine** meet their end in a corrida (*above*). The film lost its biblical title for its US release (*right, from left:* Alberto de Mendoza, Leo Anchóriz, George Hilton and Antonio Pica).

It's become accepted critical wisdom that the genre is not only guilty of exalting vengeance as the only form of viable justice in a wicked world where the law is weak, but also that it skirts around the consequences. A number of films are more broad-minded than this, however, with certain characters belying the Euro-western's ruthless reputation by turning away from revenge, whether because they have become sickened by the escalation of violence – as in Sergio Garrone's grim *The Last Day*, aka *Vendetta at Dawn* (1971), with George Eastman sparing the last of the sociopaths who have slaughtered his family[8] – or because they realise that the man they have hated for so long is unworthy of killing, such as the old, crippled McGowan (Philippe Leroy) in *A Man Called Blade*. In that film, Blade (Maurizio Merli) finds the evil Voller (John Steiner) a much more satisfying opponent. Some protagonists are shown to have matured through their experiences, such as John Phillip Law in *Death Rides a Horse*, Peter Martell in *Two Crosses at Danger Pass* and Leonard Mann in *Vengeance Trail*. Sometimes, as in traditional revenge westerns, the avenger's change of heart comes about after listening to the wise words, or following the example, of others – typically an experienced gunfighter (*May God Forgive You – I Won't* [1968]), a *pistolero*-turned-priest (as in *Son of Django*) or a woman (*Hate Your Neighbour* [1968]). In other examples, revenge is portrayed explicitly as both a corrupting ambition and a futile endeavour. In *Cowards Don't Pray* (1968) and *Garringo* (1969), previously innocent and peaceful characters become homicidal outlaws as a direct result of their vengeful cravings, one for the death of his wife, the other his father. When Confederate soldier John Warner follows the same trail in Julio Buchs's exceptional *Vengeance Is Mine* (1969), his transformation is made more dramatic by the casting of George Hilton in the role. Generally associated with lighter characters, Hilton – who describes himself as "a sunny kind of person" and appreciates how unusually "serious and dramatic" this undertaking was for him[9] – here affects a terse, mean-spirited disposition in response to his character's tribulations – the deaths

above, from left: Frank Wolff, Klaus Kinski – still in control of the scene, despite being behind bars – and Luigi Pistilli in Sergio Corbucci's **The Great Silence**.
opposite main: Robert Hossein as the lugubrious gunfighter Manuel in **Cemetery Without Crosses**. For all its dramatic crescendos, Hossein's film, which co-starred his regular screen partner Michèle Mercier (*see locandina, inset*) as an unusually proactive female avenger, is the most sobering of revenge westerns.

from cholera of his Mexican lover and their infant son – for which he blames the stubborn pride and prejudice of his lover's gringo-hating father, the rich, ruthless Don Pedro Sandoval (Ernest Borgnine). Further embittered at his treatment by society and the authorities, Warner gathers together a band of cut-throats and becomes the scourge of the Texas-Mexico border, while Sandoval leads the campaign to have him stopped. The roots of Warner's moral degradation may lie in a combination of factors – personal trauma, the rigours of war, social injustice – but as far as the film is concerned, it is his deadly hatred for Sandoval, an entirely mutual enmity, that drives him – and pretty much anyone he comes into contact with – towards destruction.

The self-perpetuating nature of revenge is pressed home with the greatest force in the French-Italian co-production *Cemetery Without Crosses* (1969). Directed, co-written by and starring Robert Hossein, *Cemetery* is the tragic tale of a widow's vengeance that whips up a whirlwind of emotions. It is marked equally by its director's experience in fatalistic French *policiers* (one of his breakthrough roles was in the classic *Rififi* [1955]) and his obvious enthusiasm for the western. Certain camera shots and plot points seem inspired by Leone (Hossein's friend, to whom the film is dedicated and with whose *Once Upon a Time in the West* it has certain similarities), but the film's key elements – story, production design and main characters – share a faded romantic lustre that is Gallic rather than Italian in inspiration. Hossein's earlier *The Taste of Violence* (1961), for example, a rugged monochrome drama set in a revolution-torn South American country, had a similarly pensive mood and leisurely pace.

Cemetery is additionally unusual in that it reminds us that revenge is not a male prerogative – although men commit the majority of the film's violent deeds – nor can it be cleanly undertaken or controlled, whether by physical strength or moral resolution.[10] Shattered by grief and anger at the injustice of her husband's death, and frustrated at her precarious position as a woman out west, Maria (Michèle Mercier) concocts a plan whereby those responsible – the Rogers family, another of those outwardly respectable, land-grabbing western clans – will have to publicly account for the killing at a specially staged funeral. To force them to attend she employs her former lover, the gunfighter Manuel (Hossein), to kidnap old man Rogers's daughter. The extent to which revenge has cast a cloud over Maria's judgement and her conscience is shown when she allows her husband's brothers to violate the girl; her signal to them can be read as either tacit permission or an instruction, but either way it indicates how desensitised she has become. This is the most powerful scene in a film where a subtle glance or a significant gesture, combined with expressionistic use of music, achieve more dramatic impact than words or violent action. We don't see the assault itself, only Manuel and Maria, framed separately outside, unable to look at each other as they try to ignore the girl's screams.

The film's motto is a simple one: "revenge never ends", and the story – created by Hossein and his regular collaborator Claude Desailly, with Dario Argento credited in some versions[11] – is resolved mercilessly, with all the major players paying with their lives. Hossein and Mercier, already a popular screen couple in France due to the 'Angelique' adventures, give sincere performances as weary, lonely people scarred by the violence and solitude of frontier life. Mercier in particular epitomises the understatement that characterises the whole, investing Maria with a kind of heroic resolve, a determination born of desperation. The film's atmosphere of *mal du pays* is reminiscent of another great Italian-French joint venture, *The Great Silence*; both titles demonstrate compassion for their stoical protagonists but are just too honest to let them survive.

Vengeance is at its most paradoxical when it is placed in a specific historical context, when there is what Jim Kitses in *Horizons West* refers to as "a *social* extension to the personal drama". In Paolo Bianchini's *I Want Him Dead* (1968) and Tonino Valerii's *The Price of Power* (1969), an individual's quest for revenge is at once trivial and imperative since, by coincidence, the fate of a nation rests on its outcome. Exercising considerable artistic licence, both films reinterpret epochal events in American history to serve their narrative and thematic purposes. *I Want Him Dead* is set in January 1865, when peace moves are being undertaken to end the Civil War. Clayton (Craig Hill), a non-combatant, is on the trail of the men who raped and killed his sister. In one sense his pursuit is

above: **The Price of Power** places a heavy burden on Giuliano Gemma's shoulders. His father is murdered, his best friend (Ray Saunders, *right*) unjustly incarcerated and a seditious plot erupts around him.

irrelevant in the chaotic context of the war ("People die all the time"), yet it is also a matter of great urgency considering that his prey are involved in a plot to prolong the conflict by fostering mistrust among the peace parties. Corrupt entrepreneur Mallek (Andrea Bosic) is the ringleader, having invested heavily in munitions, and employs deserters and brigands, led by the fittingly named Jack Blood (a welcome feature-length role for José Manuel Martín), to assassinate a general from each side when they meet to discuss a treaty. Clayton is not an idealist and is seemingly indifferent to the turmoil around him, but his personal vendetta, which is tinged with guilt at having left his sister alone in a rough town long enough for Jack to attack her, does the country a great service.

The Price of Power offers an even more distorted view of history, displacing the assassinations of James Garfield from Washington DC in 1881 and John F. Kennedy from Dallas in 1963 to the latter city in the aftermath of the Civil War. In a tense and vividly realised atmosphere of political intrigue, Bill Willer (Giuliano Gemma) has to avenge both his father and his best friend, victims of the plotters, and simultaneously defeat a conspiracy to destabilise the country by secessionist interests. Bill was no supporter of the naive late president (Van Johnson); indeed, he had a personal grudge against him. Nevertheless, it happens that the men on his hit list – a crooked sheriff and a fanatical ex-Confederate guerrilla – are working with a cadre of Southern politicians who want to wreck the president's race reforms and return the country to a divisive state of war. As in *I Want Him Dead*, the revenge angle is skilfully incorporated into a suspenseful, politically charged story where it is ultimately overshadowed by matters of immeasurably greater historical significance.

In *Once Upon a Time in the West* there is a more complex interplay between personal vendetta and historical forces that touches upon the juxtaposition of wilderness and civilisation fundamental to the western tradition. In Leone's most lauded film, avenger and prey are mythic figures, members of "an ancient race" that will shortly become extinct in a modernising world. Harmonica and Frank occupy what Sir Christopher Frayling calls a "fictional, rhetorical domain" that is eventually subsumed into history. This is why Leone stages their duel close by, but just out of sight of, the Sweetwater construction site, where the tracks of civilisation are being laid and the future is taking shape. In Leone's mythical vision, the two men are primeval figures; they are identified with the dust and rocks that make up their arena in the same way that Jill is associated with progress and community. And just as progress will eventually blast and bulldoze the rocks to make way for civilisation, so it will overwhelm obsolete warriors like Harmonica and Frank. Before that, however, they have an account to settle, and Leone treats the showdown with all the reverence due an elemental occasion. Here, it's not history being distorted but time itself, which Leone stretches and interrupts with flashbacks. The duel is a ritual – contained, as in his two previous westerns, in a circular space, its circumference described in this case by the movement of the camera rather than a physical boundary – to mark the passing of one era, which fades into myth, and the arrival of another, in which people like Jill and "other Mortons" will flourish where Frank and Harmonica (and the fatally wounded Cheyenne) no longer have a place.

above: The executioner's song: Charles Bronson's imperturbable Harmonica sets the tempo in **Once Upon a Time in the West**.

Since so many Euro-western protagonists have retribution as their goal, they tend to blend into one all-purpose archetype – they could just as well be aggrieved heroes of antiquity in *pepla* or hard-bitten cops with a score to settle in *polizieschi*. Nevertheless, certain performers distinguished themselves in roles of this kind, usually because they projected the ideal blend of brooding self-absorption, simmering rage and obsessive determination. Charles Bronson's Harmonica is the paradigmatic Euro-western avenger. Bronson's features couldn't fail to attract a connoisseur of physiognomies like Sergio Leone, who had tried for years to interest the actor in a western. "Bronson was most important for me because that face of his could stop a train. He was the executioner who even if you went to Greenland would follow you there and find you."**12** In *Once Upon a Time...* those famous craggy features are inscribed almost imperceptibly with anger and sorrow, accumulated over untold years spent shadowing his prey like the tireless, implacable Furies of myth. Harmonica's uncommon patience is unnerving; he has waited not just for the ideal opportunity for revenge – being so well acquainted with Frank's movements over the years, he must have had many of those – but for the optimum moment in history.

Looking further, we can note that the role of avenger proved well suited to a wide range of performers, not all of them as physically imposing as Bronson. Notable here is Leonard Mann, née Manzella, one of the youngest and slightest of all the genre's leading men, whose career was beginning just as Euro-westerns started their decline. An Italian-American born in upstate New York, Mann's career in Italian films began with a trip to Europe in 1968: "I remember being bored in college and decided to go to Europe for the summer. I ended up staying for about 15 years." A number of Mann's early roles typecast him as a troubled youngster struggling with ethical, moral or existential dilemmas, typified by his performance as Antonio, an anti-Fascist student in love with an older woman with government connections in Florestano Vancini's historical drama *Bitter Love* (1974). "Preparing for the 'angry young man' roles was easy because I had a lot of anger inside of me, even though it was well under the surface," he remembers. "Like all young people who are angry, it's because they've been hurt. I knew hurt, and that was the source I turned to for my characters." He introduced an unusual degree of youthful angst to his western roles as well. In both *The Forgotten Pistolero* (his second film, made when was just 22) and *Chuck Mool*, he plays a confused character uncertain of his origins, whose return to the family fold resolves the mystery at the cost of the family itself, happy homecomings in the genre being exceedingly rare. In his remaining western, *Vengeance Trail*, Mann is more fiery and self-righteous (qualities that would mark his performances in *polizieschi*) as the lone survivor of a faked Indian attack that killed the rest of his family. Mann offers some well-qualified insight into the popularity of the revenge motif. "I think [vengeance] is a big part of Italian life. Being a psychotherapist now, I have a much better understanding about the subject than when I was living in Italy. Italians appear to be much more passive-aggressive because they have a hard time saying 'no' and confronting others. They also seem to hold grudges and still be able to carry on relations with each other. It's a dance that I never quite got used to."**13**

Also noteworthy is American expat Brett Halsey, one-time husband of Luciana Paluzzi and author of the trashy but fascinating semi-autobiographical novel *The Magnificent Strangers*. (Coincidentally, Halsey

above: Brett Halsey's resolute demeanour served him well in revenge westerns such as **The Wrath of God**.
below: Halsey and his co-stars in **Today It's Me... Tomorrow You!** (*from left:* Franco Borelli, Wayde Preston, Halsey, Bud Spencer, William Berger.)

was the man who first put Leonard Mann in contact with an agent while the latter was staying in Rome.) Having arrived in Europe in the early Sixties to star in swashbucklers such as Riccardo Freda's *The Seventh Sword* (1962), he played a Texas Ranger in Gianfranco Baldanello's forgettable *Kill Johnny Ringo!* (1966) before finding his niche as a glowering avenger in two terse, episodic westerns: *Today It's Me... Tomorrow You!* and *The Wrath of God*. Garbed in both films in a black broad-brimmed hat and cape, looking not unlike Franco Nero's Django, Halsey – acting under the alias 'Montgomery Ford' so that his 'real name' (itself a pseudonym) wouldn't be solely associated with westerns – convinces as a hunter wholly absorbed in the pursuit of his prey, grim-faced and focused, yet with a hint of dejection in his eyes. That spark of humanity establishes a connection, however slight, between actor and audience that makes all the difference in films of this kind.

The true embodiment of nemesis, however, was the monolithic Anthony Steffen. The son of a Brazilian noble and diplomat, Steffen was born Antonio Luis de Teffé von Hoonholtz in Rome in 1932. After playing in a few youth-oriented films he drifted, inevitably, into *pepla* (he was among the cast of the ill-fated Robert Aldrich film *Sodom and Gomorrah* [1962], for which Sergio Leone directed the second unit). It was the western, however, that proved his calling, his tall, rangy physique marking him out, physically at least, as the Italian answer to Clint Eastwood. Yet there was more to Steffen than this, even though the range he displayed in his western career was, admittedly, rather narrow. With his melancholic air, slow, imperious gait, downcast mouth and haunted expression, he was regularly cast in the role of avenger. It is as common to see Steffen cradling a dead or dying loved one, pain radiating from his features, as it is to see him using his gun, and his films frequently have a tragic denouement, reinforcing the futility-of-revenge message. We have already seen how, in the rigorously downbeat *Seven Dollars to Kill*, he is forced into a showdown with his estranged son, and in another of his early westerns, *Why Go on Killing?* (1965), his former girlfriend is caught in the crossfire of a feud between Steffen's family and a Mexican clan. The classic *Blood at Sundown*, while not a pure revenge western, pits his character against his power-mad brother, with all the emotional seesawing to be expected, while in Salvatore Rosso's *A Stranger in Paso Bravo*, Steffen's pursuit of the tyrant responsible for the death of his wife and child is coloured by the guilt he feels for being drunk at the time the incident took place.**14**

Steffen's other revenge westerns ease off on the tragedy in favour of a more formulaic, action-oriented approach. In *Gentleman Killer* (1967), *A Name That Cried Revenge*, *A Man Called Joe Clifford* (1970) and *A Man Called Django*, Steffen isn't given the opportunity to do much more than go through the (barely discernible) motions. (*Joe Clifford*, helmed by Leopoldo Savona, misses a trick by not making the most of Steffen's character's calling, that of a Shakespearean actor. There can be few more intriguing prospects for an audience accustomed to Steffen's minimalist, some would say nonexistent, acting style than to see him performing Shakespeare.) Mario Caiano's *A Name That Cried Revenge* is the most interesting of these, both in the way that it asks more of Steffen as an actor – his character, suffering from memory loss, is required to piece together the elliptical plot – and because it points towards Steffen's finest hour and one of the ultimate revenge westerns, *Django the Bastard*. In Caiano's post-Civil War film, former soldier Davy Flanagan (Steffen) must avenge his own 'death', or at least the attempt on his life by a treacherous officer that has rendered him amnesiac and effectively dead as far as his wife and the wider world are concerned. This basic premise – a variation on the oft-used resurrection/

Death becomes him: Anthony Steffen, dourest of Euro-western leading men, was also the genre's avenger nonpareil, an irresistible force of unyielding retribution. Shot and styled like a horror film, **Django the Bastard** (*above and below*) exaggerated his protagonist's inhumanity.

reincarnation motif, closely reminiscent of *The Return of Ringo* – is carried over into *Django the Bastard*, which Steffen co-wrote with director Sergio Garrone. Here, however, we are in Gothic horror territory, and it's feasible, in the context of the film, that Django is avenging himself from beyond the grave. (It is easy to see – though impossible to substantiate – how this film is often cited as an influence on Clint Eastwood's *High Plains Drifter*.) Steffen's performance is suitably ambiguous and, perhaps because he had a hand in crafting the story, the part is tailor-made for him. His lack of emotion is entirely fitting given the doubts over his character's very humanity.

The genre often explores the notion of the avenger as an incarnation of death, as "something metaphysical", in Garrone's words, exaggerating his implacability and symbolising his emotional and spiritual dissolution.[15] Harmonica is the classic example, while in *Death Sentence*, Robin Clarke's Cash feels "like one of those rocks out there" in the desert, obdurate and unfeeling. *Django the Bastard* takes this idea a step further. With its strong supernatural allusions it is reminiscent of Italian horror films of the Sixties such as *The Ghost* (1963), the 'Drop of Water' episode in *Black Sabbath* (1963), *The Night of the Doomed* (1965) and *The Long Hair of Death* (1964), all of which centre on posthumous retribution. Garrone's film represents the revenge western at its fantastical extreme. It is joined on the outer limits by two films of Antonio Margheriti, director of *The Long Hair of Death*. Margheriti demonstrated his mastery of the mood and visual texture of Italian Gothic in the cavernous climax of the self-explanatory *Vengeance*, where Richard Harrison and comic-strip supervillain Claudio Camaso battle it out. The director then crafted the extraordinary *And God Said to Cain* (1970), an intoxicating combination of western and horror motifs that fully exploits the inherent menace of Klaus Kinski. The remorseless way in which Kinski's Gary Hamilton stalks and terrorises his enemies

above: Pale rider: Klaus Kinski's spectral complexion dominates **And God Said to Cain**, a Gothic companion piece to **Django the Bastard**.

is almost identical to Steffen's methods in *Django the Bastard*, while Kinski's pallor and hypnotising glare give him the appearance of a vengeful wraith. These are the most fearsome avengers of all – they seem to exist solely for this purpose. A bit like Sartana at his most magical, but without his impartiality, it's almost as if they are merely visiting the terrestrial sphere before returning to another plane. (For a fuller discussion of the connection between *Django the Bastard*, *And God Said to Cain* and the horror genre, see *Hybrid Westerns*.) And while he's not quite on the level of Django and Hamilton, Lang Jeffries's gunman/astronomer in José Luis Merino's singular *Requiem for a Gringo* (1968), a variation on the revisionist Japanese samurai drama *Harakiri* (1962) still manages to unnerve his opponents. With his predictive abilities and portentous manner, Jeffries's character, Ross Logan, is believed to possess "magical powers". (Somebody in the wardrobe department conjured up what is presumably supposed to be a jaguar-print poncho for Jeffries to wear – jaguars having been considered sacred by the Mayans – to give him a terrifying aura, although it looks more like the kind of costume the actor would have worn in one of his earlier *pepla*.) Logan exploits this advantage to avenge the murder of his younger brother by a band of oddly affected sadists, among them a treacherous Lothario (Ruben Rojo), a preening gunfighter (Carlo Gaddi) and a childlike, superstitious half-breed (Aldo Sambrell). Using his awareness of an impending solar eclipse, Logan then exacts an apocalyptic revenge on their boss, Carranza (Fernando Sancho at his finest), in a finale made frenzied by Merino's hyperactive zoom lens. (The film's astronomy gimmick was later used in the disastrous Leopoldo Savona comedy *Pistol Packin' Preacher* [1972].) Jeffries, a well-built Canadian, is suitably deadpan as the ominous, slow-moving Logan, but, in the established western tradition, his protagonist is eclipsed, as it were, by the villains of the piece.

In this chapter we have looked at a relatively small percentage of European revenge westerns. Inevitably, the production system spewed out a great many films that all more or less adhered to the same crowd-pleasing formula. Most are of little interest and simply regurgitate the clichés and conventions of earlier influential westerns, both European and American, but I have outlined some that strive for and achieve greater originality and resonance. The best examples bear a distinctive cultural imprint, transposing (chiefly southern) Italian cultural values, along with aspects of classic revenge tragedies, into a bastardised western setting, taking the genre's inherent every-man-for-himself ethos to misanthropic extremes. Many titles stress the traumatic repercussions of vengeance and catalogue the moral and emotional transformation of the avenger, not necessarily through monologues or expressions of remorse, but through the escalating brutality of his actions. They demonstrate a complex and contradictory attitude towards the family – its honour must be upheld, but at the same time it is a source of estrangement. They also emphasise the tension between individualism and authority, with the legal system deemed unreliable at best and crooked at worst. (In *Death Rides a Horse*, there is a rare example of a well-intentioned sheriff who knowingly aids a character's quest for revenge. Having made a half-hearted attempt to dissuade Bill from his plan, the lawman implicitly accepts the helplessness of his own position by passing on a crucial piece of evidence that points the avenger in the right direction.) This characteristically cynical assertion acknowledges the superior justice of personal retribution, but at the same time the films don't blithely celebrate the taking of one life for another. The act itself may appear to release the hero from the shackles of hate but, as with Elizabethan and Jacobean revenge tales, the films' denouements are generally tragic or, at best, ambiguous. In most cases there is nothing for the avenger to move on to. Whatever accomplices or loved ones he may have had are likely to have been destroyed in his wake, or else he is so emotionally bereft that, like Charles Bronson at the end of *Once Upon a Time in the West*, he simply rides on, facing an uncertain or empty future. Rarely is there a comforting coda, with little hope of redemption or relationships. While not an outright condemnation of revenge, nor is it an endorsement, and is the closest the genre comes to delivering a conventional moral message on the subject.

footnotes

1   'Gianni Garko: Gli fumavano le Colt… lo chiamavano Sartana' in *Wanted: dieci ricercati dello spaghetti western* (*Nocturno Dossier*, October 2007).
2   Quoted in a documentary about Italian political cinema, entitled *The Camera Is a Molotov Cocktail*, which was shown, without credits, on the UK's Channel 4 in the early Eighties.
3   The actor's biggest complaint about his European movies, especially the westerns, was their insistence on histrionic performances. "Westerns are always bigger than life but the acting within isn't really acting at all. When I was just an awestruck kid, Henry Fonda told me to just be real – get in touch with what's real inside you when you deliver the lines. It's easy to do if you have a director supporting that, but you can't do it in an Italian western in general, because they want it so freaking big. I'm already big anyway – I'm 6ft 4in – and in those days I weighed 179 pounds soaking wet; I was a bean among men. If you're that big and have my bone structure you're already expressive, so what the hell do you need to grimace for? That always bothered me – everybody wanted you to overblow what was real." In *Black Jack* he seems to have reasoned "if you can't beat them, join them". Author's interview with Robert Woods.
4   Interview with Benito Stefanelli by Mario Marsili, reproduced with kind permission.
5   Luciano Vincenzoni has claimed that he 'supervised' western novice Giulio Petroni on behalf of United Artists, which distributed the 'Dollars' trilogy and wanted another Leone-style western to follow. That may have been understandable from their viewpoint, but would Petroni – a perfectly capable director then making his seventh feature – have put up with such interference? We'll probably never know for certain.
6   A precedent for setting the *Oresteia* in 'western' dress had been set by Eugene O'Neill in his ambitious and complex play *Mourning Becomes Electra* (1931), set in post-Civil War New England. *Phaedra*, meanwhile, had been adapted for the screen five years before Romero Marchent's film by Jules Dassin, who updated the story to contemporary Greece and focused the tensions on a shipping magnate and his family.
7   Author's interview with Leonard Mann.
8   Eastman has claimed that this film was actually directed by Gino Mangini, who had already worked with the star on *Bastard, Go and Kill* (1971), released in Italy a few months before *The Last Day* and written by Sergio Garrone.
9   Interview with George Hilton by Roger A. Fratter in *Dieci ricercati dello spaghetti western* (*Nocturno Dossier*, October 2007).
10   The role of women in revenge sagas is traditionally to be the catalyst, the voice of reason or, by contrast, a scheming vixen. Very few European westerns challenge this position. A widow (Mónica Randall) seeks justice on a cruel Mexican family in *Five Giants from Texas* (1966), but the focus is firmly on the eponymous gunmen who help her. (This is reminiscent of a similar situation in the earlier *Gunfight at High Noon* [1963].) Jill shows no interest in avenging the McBains in *Once Upon a Time in the West*; at any rate, whatever hatred she may harbour for Frank is deemed insignificant compared with that felt by Harmonica. The only female avenger worthy of the name is Raquel Welch as the title character in the gritty Tigon production *Hannie Caulder* (1971), who is determined to punish the three louts who raped her and killed her husband.
11   Hossein firmly denies Argento's contribution in a supplementary feature on the film's Anolis/Buio Omega DVD release. He also talks about his friendship with Sergio Leone, which almost resulted in a role for Hossein in *Once upon a Time in the West* and led to Leone allegedly directing a dinner scene in *Cemetery*.
12   Quoted in Massimo Moscati, *Western all'Italiana*.
13   Author's interview with Leonard Mann.
14   Curiously, several of the character names in *A Stranger in Paso Bravo* are identical to those in the later *And God Said to Cain*, even though they have no scriptwriters in common – the protagonist is called Gary Hamilton, the villain, at least in the Italian version, is named Acombar, and among his henchmen are the Santa Maria brothers.
15   Sergio Garrone quoted in issue seven of the Italian magazine *Nocturno Cinema*, June 1998.

above: Henry Fonda, almost at the point of dying, in **Once Upon a Time in the West**.

Chapter 5

"Don't Buy Bread, Buy Dynamite!"

The Political Western in Context

During 1966, Che Guevara was in Bolivia on the fatal last leg of his revolutionary journey, Vietnam was ablaze, the Congo was simmering and protest was in the air worldwide. At the same time, Damiano Damiani and a clutch of left-wing firebrands were in southern Spain forming the political wing of the Italian western. *A Bullet for the General* (aka *Quien Sabe?*) brought the genre into its most ambitious, topical and controversial phase. While Che's dream of global rebellion was destined to die with him in a schoolhouse in a grubby Bolivian hamlet, his ideals lived on. Governments around the world were shaken out of their post-war complacency as students, workers and activists – many flying Che's banner and championing his anti-imperialist beliefs – began expressing their disaffection in the form of mass demonstrations. Film, like all forms of popular culture, felt the reverberations: a new politicised brand of indigenous cinema exploded in Third World countries; counterculture films sewed dissent in America; and in Europe an unofficial cinematic 'revolutionary cell' – comprised of assorted Marxists, propagandists and noncommittal fellow travellers – challenged orthodoxy on many levels.

This radical spirit was not the preserve of auteurs and the avant-garde. Among commercial films, the instinctively anti-authoritarian European western, blessed as it was with widespread appeal, proved an ideal outlet for artists attracted to historical and political themes. Along with Damiani there was avowed Communist Carlo Lizzani, the writers Franco Solinas and Sergio Donati, actors Gian Maria Volonté, Lou Castel and Tomas Milian ("The symbol of rebellious youth", as one director called him[1]), and populist directors such as Sergio Sollima and Sergio Corbucci. Even Pier Paolo Pasolini, a member of Italian cinema's intellectual elite, was sufficiently intrigued by the spaghettis' potential to take the part of a revolutionary priest in Lizzani's *Kill and Pray* (1967). The genre also acquired a new type of figurehead: out went the self-serving avenger and the bounty hunter; in came the ragged bandit-rebel.

above: A new breed of hero for a new brand of western: rough-hewn rebels like Chuncho (Gian Maria Volonté, *centre*) in **A Bullet for the General** replaced cynical gunfighters as the central figures during the genre's ideological phase.
opposite: Five years later, **A Fistful of Dynamite** painted a picture of the Mexican Revolution (any revolution, in fact) in far murkier tones.

Let's first define our terms. If we accept Volonté's argument that "*every* film, in a general manner, is political", it follows that some films will be left wing or liberal in their outlook, others conservative or reactionary. The type of 'political cinema' we are talking about here clearly belongs in the former camp. Films like these seek to raise awareness and stimulate opposition to social and economic inequality, promoting alternative or 'subversive' views in the process. But can a film, however oppositional its attitude, be truly political if it is a commercial venture – a product of the capitalist money-making machine it seeks to undermine? This contradiction ruled out the revolutionary westerns in the opinions of most idealistic critics and commentators, who championed instead the interrogative dramas by the likes of Francesco Rosi, Gillo Pontecorvo and, to a lesser extent, Costa-Gavras. Where hard-line Marxist critics were concerned, even these directors made too many concessions to mainstream tastes. There is a school of thought that says commercial films made by bourgeois liberals cannot succeed in raising political consciousness because they are made – with 'dirty' money – within a recognised, i.e. Hollywoodian, frame of reference; they engage their audiences on an emotional level without stimulating their analytical abilities. (This is clearly not the case with Rosi and Pontecorvo, whose films consistently invite, indeed demand, an analytical response.[2]) I counter this blanket criticism, but mine is a qualified position. It is not only possible but can also be highly effective to combine anti-oppressive sentiments with entertainment. This avoids the risk run by more elitist/experimental political works that circulate among a minority audience of predisposed intellectuals. In addition, 'entertainment' can provide a useful smokescreen for political content in territories where distribution is tightly controlled and where seditious works encounter politically motivated censorship and prohibition. At the same time as defending one form of political cinema in particular, however, it is unwise to overstate the politicising capacity of cinema in general. Films can provide stimulation – and the larger the scale of this stimulation, i.e. the wider the distribution they achieve, the better – but they do not equal action. All strands of political cinema, from commercial through avant-garde to Third Cinema (see below), have their validity, though equally all fall short of their potential for different reasons.

The radicalisation of cinema in the Sixties was a global phenomenon. In certain Third World countries, dedicated filmmakers responded to the upsurge in liberation struggles and took advantage of technological developments such as more affordable film stock and lightweight equipment – ideal for shooting in difficult conditions – to make raw, powerful statements of revolutionary intent. This belligerent cinematic practice, which came to be called Third Cinema (with First Cinema denoting mainstream productions and Second Cinema 'auteur' films), targeted not only the producing countries' political and cinematographic institutions, but also the complacency of the masses. Around this time in Europe, a parallel debate was raging in cultural and cinematic circles about how to channel the disillusionment and growing militancy of the post-war generation. European film industries had always afforded their artists considerable scope to experiment and express themselves (a more conservative climate prevailed in America), and this is reflected in the strength and diversity of political films produced on the continent in the Sixties. Leading the way was Jean-Luc Godard, who experimented with narrative structure in a bid to "make political films politically". (As we shall see, he was also to make a singular 'western' of his own.) Godard's efforts represented a radical attempt to shatter the safe, stable relationship between viewer and cinema. This was taken to be a political act in itself, forcing the audience to draw their own conclusions about the meaning of images, denying them the false assurances of conventional cinematic technique and thereby shutting out what Robert Kolker – in his excellent study of international cinema, *The Altering Eye* – called "the subliminal whisperings of the dominant ideology". Other filmmakers chose different tactics: the sly surrealist satire of Luis Buñuel; the influential non-fiction films of Frenchman Chris Marker; Britain's hard-edged 'kitchen sink' school and experimental features such as *Praise Marx and Pass the Ammunition* (1970); the docu-dramas initiated in Italy by Rosi's *Salvatore Giuliano* (1962) and Pontecorvo's *The Battle of Algiers* (1966), which gave rise to the kind of political thriller popularised by Costa-Gavras's *Z* (1969); the art-commercial hybrids from intellectual socialists such as Pasolini, Elio Petri and Marco Bellocchio; and, still in Italy but some way down the league table of critical respectability, the 'revolutionary' westerns that began with *A Bullet for the General*.

The political western is a curious beast. On one level it represents escapist entertainment and can be appreciated and/or dismissed as nothing more than that. But the sub-genre also invites another reading, with most examples using Mexico and its revolution as a metaphor for contemporary convulsions. The question, of course, is whether pulling in such different directions makes the films inherently unstable, insubstantial? Or is that really where they demonstrate what Third Cinema advocate Mike Wayne has termed a (vital) "porous" quality?[3] For Mexico read Bolivia or Vietnam, for Zapata read Guevara. (Italy even ventured a Guevara biopic in 1968, titled *Rebel with a Cause* for the English-language market, directed by Paolo Heusch and with the swarthy Spaniard Francisco Rabal in the title role. Rabal, a Communist, took the project to heart, but left-wing friends and critics denounced the results as 'reactionary'. I have not seen the film to comment.) This apparent discrepancy has and will always be at the centre of debate about political westerns, and is something we shall consider throughout this chapter.

Many of the films are thinly veiled allegorical attacks upon imperialist/colonial aggression, specifically America's perceived paternalistic/exploitative attitude towards the Third World, and on the ruling classes in underdeveloped nations – and, for that matter, in Christian Democrat-dominated Italy – that submit to America's whims. This contrasts with the majority of Hollywood's Mexico-based westerns, the likes of *Vera Cruz* (1954), *The Magnificent Seven* (1960) and *Villa Rides* (1968), in which the country is merely a picturesque proving ground for Yankee heroes' firepower and finesse. Using the Mexican Revolution as a context afforded left-leaning filmmakers ample scope to comment upon a range of socio-political topics that all retained contemporary relevance: the class struggle and the suppression of minorities, represented by the gross inequality of Mexican society at the outset of the uprising, with Porfirio Diaz and his cronies luxuriating in power while peasants were trapped in debt peonage; the urgent need for land redistribution (Emiliano Zapata was the talismanic figure in this regard); militarism and the arms race; the unhealthy alliance of church and state (anti-clericalism was a characteristic of many Mexican revolutionary forces, particularly Venustiano Carranza's Constitutionalist Army); and political corruption, mirrored by the inequity of the Porfiriato and the ease with which the successive liberal administrations of Francisco Madero and Carranza slipped into Porfirian practices, heightening the peasant fighters' sense of injustice and hardening their resolve to fight on. This last theme plainly relates not just to the myriad conflicts sweeping the Third World in the Sixties, but also to the disillusionment felt by students, workers, idealists and activists in the west, frustrated at the slow pace and/or complete absence of promised political reforms.

Westerns were a fading force in Hollywood in the mid-Sixties but they still commanded a healthy worldwide market, providing a solid platform for left-wingers like Damiani, Sollima and Solinas to project their ideological beliefs. These were far removed from the relative conservatism of the classical Hollywood western, and directly opposed to its arguably imperialist subtext. Only belatedly, in the Cold War-dominated Fifties and the turbulent Sixties, had US westerns begun to review their mythic foundations and to consider with clarity for the first time their implications in terms of burning issues such as race relations and minority rights.[4] There was no thoroughgoing re-examination, however, as certain preconceptions seemed impossible to shift. Although aggressive capitalism, for example, is usually depicted

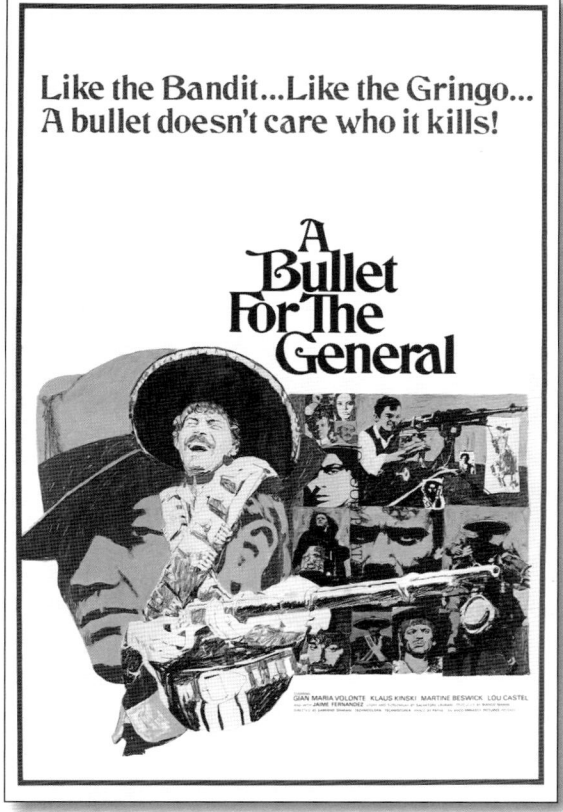

above: This American poster for **A Bullet for the General** has a misleading slogan – neither the bandit in Damiano Damiani's film (Gian Maria Volonté) nor the gringo (Lou Castel) kills indiscriminately.

as a negative force in the classical western – as in the common plot that pits hard-working settlers against greedy land barons – it is not the villains who are shown to represent the values inherent in the Constitution. In that case, the Constitution itself might appear corrupt and oppressive, something that no American film of a certain vintage – with or without the coded criticism of socio-economic inequality that the previous sentence implies – would have dared to suggest. Rather, it is the settlers and their heroic champions, the gunfighters who deliver them from evil, who embody the spirit of the nation, stressing the importance of individual moral and physical virtues such as perseverance, courage and controlled, punitive violence. While this emphasis doesn't dismiss the case for reform along socialist lines – the redistribution of land and wealth – it does push it firmly to the margins.[5] In Europe, the genre had no such cultural heritage to embellish and, once it had captured a significant share of the market and gained sufficient self-confidence, it could address a broader range of issues, from a variety of different ideological perspectives, with greater commercial freedom.

above and opposite top: Robert Woods as the "greaser" who takes on the gringos in Maurizio Lucidi's **My Name Is Pecos** and **Pecos Cleans Up**. Woods/Pecos became a minor icon in certain Third World countries for his efforts.

'Imperialist' or not, Hollywood westerns had always been a staple form of global mass-market entertainment, packing out flea-pits around the world with their cathartic violence and stylised gunslinging fantasy figures. When the irreverent European version came along, it met with even greater success in developing countries. Laurie Gunst provides anecdotal evidence for this in *Born Fi' Dead*, her study of the Jamaican posse underworld. "The island desperados... are a Caribbean cultural hybrid: tropical bad guys acting out fantasies from the spaghetti westerns, kung-fu kill flicks, Rambo sequels, and *Godfather* spin-offs that play nightly in Kingston's funky movie palaces." Gunst's observations are supported by posse members themselves ("Jamaicans... want to be tough like outlaws"), while even the police are susceptible. In the course of her investigations, Gunst meets legendary 'killer cop' Keith Gordon, who earned the nickname 'Trinity' for his prowess with a pistol. This crossover between fiction and violent reality, a staple of the reggae sub-culture, is memorably stressed in the Jamaican classic *The Harder They Come* (1972), in which director Perry Henzell cuts between the ecstatic faces of young male filmgoers in a shantytown cinema and the film they are watching – *Django* (1966), in which Franco Nero is shown gunning down Klansmen. The hero of Henzell's film, renegade reggae star Jimmy Cliff, identifies with Django as he brazenly confronts the police at the climax.[6]

In a wider sense, the ethnic diversity and outcast status of many European western protagonists helps to explain their elevated standing among poor and Third World audiences, who were accustomed to watching, perhaps unquestioningly, as white Hollywood cowboys forged a colonial form of 'civilisation' while cleansing the plains of savages. It had taken a long time for Native American concerns to be addressed in Hollywood – progressive works such as *Broken Arrow*, *Devil's Doorway*, *Apache* and *Run of the Arrow* were all produced in the Fifties – but, right from the start, a large number of Euro-westerns, beginning with but not restricted to the pro-Indian Karl May adaptations, took the side of the oppressed. This has nothing to do with political correctness – the genre as a whole merrily propagates

"Don't Buy Bread, Buy Dynamite!"

an image of Mexicans as giggling, sadistic *bandidos*, for example; and the underdog theme often provided little more than a fashionable gloss. For the first time, however, Third World filmgoers had 'western' heroes of their own, albeit played for the most part by Anglo actors, who were subjected to the same kind of abuse and intimidation as their impoverished constituencies but blessed with the ability to strike back.[7] It was as if Third World audiences' long-suppressed urge to turn the tables on Yankee imperialism had erupted on to the screen. Robert Woods, who played the gringo-baiting Mexican anti-hero of *My Name Is Pecos* (1966), supplies further evidence of the way in which Third World filmgoers took this type of 'ethnic' warrior, in stories about "the sense of injustice and the little guy winning", to their hearts. Woods was surprised to discover the extent of Pecos's popularity when, some ten years later, he and a girlfriend took a holiday in Senegal. "We got off the plane and I was stopped by customs. The guy said, 'Can you step this way?' I thought I was going to get strip-searched or something. He took me to a room and asked, 'Can I have a picture of you? My son's name is Pecos!' I had no idea it was even released there! But it was about the little guy rising up and winning, and in those Third World countries they live for that. There were three or four tailor shops called the Pecos Tailor Shops. One guy came in from the beach and asked to be my guide, the usual stuff, and I said, 'Sure, what's your name?' and he said, 'My name is Pecos!' [laughs]. I gave him a cowboy hat and belt. No matter where I went in that country I was mobbed. I wanted to kick back, have some privacy... If I knew I was going to be mobbed I would have chosen a different vacation spot."[8]

As Sergio Donati explains, the Italian westerns' left-wing leanings ruffled few feathers in his homeland. "The Communist elite was the dominant one in Italian cinema since 1944-45. It was the heart of neorealism."[9] This movement was a conscious attempt to break away from the studio-bound fluff Italian audiences had been force-fed in the war years and to address the nation's political and social problems honestly, with poverty and inequality paramount. This flew in the face of political pressure on the industry to paint a more 'positive' picture of the country.[10] While neorealist filmmakers presented unvarnished images of poverty and suffering, their followers, exemplified by Francesco Rosi, assumed the voice of investigators or documentarists on controversial and painful subject matter such as the Mafia, political corruption and the legacy of Fascism. Rosi's strategy was to give Italian cinema what Peter Bondanella terms a "civic function" as a forum for debating important topics. This proved very successful with audiences, especially in a climate of rapidly collapsing public faith in politicians,

and, as Bondanella says, "It was perhaps inevitable that the spaghetti western would also be made to carry the burden of ideological arguments, produced, as they were, in a country where political debate is so important an element in the popular culture of the audience."[11] Many Italian westerns squeezed in social issues amid the gunplay, from political skulduggery (*Death Rides a Horse* [1967], *The Price of Power* [1969]) to the blind intolerance and/or criminal collusion of the law (*A Minute to Pray, a Second to Die* [1968], *The Great Silence* [1968]). These films are not for consideration here, however, nor do I intend to pry open each western that merely uses Mexico's domestic upheavals as a backdrop for rambunctious action.[12] Instead, this chapter will focus on the most important anti-imperialist westerns, plus some borderline cases, as well as the artists who looked to this most enduring and malleable of genres to tap into a rumbling mood of militancy that was sweeping the world.

It will be useful before progressing to list the films I will feature in a roughly chronological order. This shows how the themes and the spirit of the relatively big-budget, prestige productions that set the trend – *A Bullet for the General* and *The Big Gundown* – quickly filtered down to more modest fare on the *seconda* and *terza visione* circuits. *Killer Kid* and, to a lesser extent, *A Man and a Colt* and *Say Your Prayers and Dig Your Grave*, all released in 1967/early 1968, were sold as minor 'star' vehicles, and yet they are much more 'radical' in terms of content than their formulaic packaging and recapitulated plots would

above: Lee Van Cleef – stylishly attired as ever – in **The Big Gundown**, one of the most popular political westerns of the era.

above: Heroes' welcome: the members of **The Five Man Army** are acclaimed by the peons they have protected.

have led their audiences to expect. This supports Peter Bondanella's point that political dissemination was not the preserve of cinema's socialist-intellectual elite, and even 'ordinary' westerns, marketed without any fanfare, were considered suitable vehicles for ideological issues. By 1967, the scope of the burgeoning sub-genre was broad enough to encompass works that were more oblique in their approach to political themes (*Kill and Pray*, *Face to Face*), before the peak period of 1968 to 1970 produced a sequence of full-scale revolutionary westerns, most of which, like *A Bullet for the General*, are colourful, well-drawn allegories about contemporary upheavals: *Run, Man, Run*, *A Professional Gun*, *Tepepa* (all made in 1968), *The Five Man Army*, *The Magnificent Bandits* (both 1969) and *Compañeros* (1970). While these are generally bullish, boisterous affairs, the final films in the cycle reflect the waning enthusiasm and optimism of the political movement as a whole.
The Anger of the Wind (1970), an honorary western set in turn-of-the-20th-Century Spain, and *A Fistful of Dynamite* (1971) deal with reactionism, counter-revolution and the crushing of ideals, while *Long Live Your Death* (1971) and *What Am I Doing in the Middle of a Revolution?* (1972) are satirical 'commentaries' on their predecessors.

above: Franco Nero (*left*) and Eli Wallach (*right*) in **Long Live Your Death**, a send-up of Sixties idealism.

"What do we want? Everything!"

The immediate causes of the political stirrings of the late Sixties have been well documented and debated, from the uprisings in Cuba and Algeria to the Chinese Cultural Revolution and the Vietnam War, the assassinations of Malcolm X and Martin Luther King to the martyrdom of Che Guevara. Not that the architects of the political western were restricted to events overseas for inspiration. By 1968, Italy itself – under the latest in a series of inefficient centre-left coalition governments dominated by Aldo Moro's Christian Democrats – was experiencing unprecedented levels of social unrest. Indeed, Italian students had launched their protest movement before the more headline-grabbing disturbances in France, and while they never reached the revolutionary intensity of their Gallic counterparts, they managed to sustain their challenge for longer. Educational reforms of the Sixties had made access to universities much easier so that, by the end of the decade, student numbers had swollen, overwhelming the institutions themselves. By 1968, for example, the universities of Rome, Naples and Bari were running, or rather stumbling, at something like ten times their capacities. Compounding the students' frustration was a shortage of lecturers for those who did manage to squeeze into the universities, and a lack of jobs after graduation.

The inevitable rebellion attacked authority in all its guises, from the shambolic education system to the nuclear family. An increasing number of students eschewed the consumerist values of society and embraced new Catholic and Marxist ideas on collectivism and social justice. Direct action soon followed. The university of Trento was the first to be occupied, in the autumn of 1967, and the movement reached a peak the following year with a pitched battle between students and riot police in Rome's Valle Giulia. While the middle classes and the media may have feared an Italian version of the Cultural Revolution, it was significant that there was no central authority directing events; rather, much like the partisan movement of the Second World War and, indeed, the Mexican Revolution, it was a spontaneous combustion. Ironically, the very quality that gives such movements their romantic appeal – the lack of any effective guiding structure – meant that the students were never likely to achieve their aims, and their protest fizzled out. Nevertheless, the authorities could not relax. Echoing the situation in France, worker militancy grew in intensity, partly inspired by the students, and reached its own Valle Giulia in July 1969, when a strike involving several thousand workers set out from the Fiat factory in Turin and clashed with riot police, events that came to be known as 'Fiatnam'. The strikers' slogan summed up not just their own self-confidence, but also the spirit within Italy at the time: "Che cosa vogliamo? Tutto!" ("What do we want? Everything!")[13]

One other feature of the Italian political landscape of the time is worth noting. While the official left, in the form of the Communist Party, was caught off-guard at this critical juncture, and was loathed by the students in any case, there was a proliferation of Italian revolutionary groups from the autumn of 1968 hoping to fill the void. In terms of numbers these groups represented "the largest new left in Europe", but there were so many different factions and ideologies jostling for supremacy that genuine collective action was never very likely.[14] Sneering at bargains struck in the factories by trade unions, they strove for, and naively anticipated, a working class revolution, and were not interested in piecemeal reform. The same internal ideological divisions that had prolonged the civil war in Mexico reappeared with gnawing inevitability – thankfully without the commensurate loss of life – in the political and social upheavals of the late Sixties, paralysing the popular movements in France, Italy and elsewhere. It was the old schism between extremists and moderates, one group determined to smash the system, the other to repair it, to effect change from within. The more extreme Italian revolutionary groups continued to snipe at the state throughout the first half of the Seventies, with fictitious versions often appearing in the ferocious urban thrillers that came to supplant spaghetti westerns at the domestic box office.

Many of the Italians who worked in westerns, from the Communist contingent to less outspoken figures such as Gianni Garko and Franco Nero, talk of a symbiotic relationship between the development of the genre and the simmering tensions in society. "In this period in Italy it was very difficult for the working man," says Garko. "There was a lot of social injustice... we had no divorce, no abortion law – many civil rights and human rights were not respected. Also, you were fighting for your life in politics. After 1968 Italian society exploded, with the Red Brigades, many bombs, many killings, many terrorist attacks. Society expressed itself in the Sixties and Seventies with strong violence. When westerns started, many directors felt that underground in our society the tension was very strong, and the western film was a metaphor for this underground tension. And so the Italian western is not just superficial, not only a commercial type of film; it's something more."[15] Contemporaneous Italian comedies and crime thrillers distilled this tension in much the same way. Even in Hollywood, where dissenting political voices were muted for much of the Sixties, cinema was forced to acknowledge the concerns of the counterculture and made several attempts to turn them to profitable advantage. Responding to independent hits such as *Wild in the Streets* (1968) and *Easy Rider* (1969), Twentieth Century Fox produced the anodyne *Che!* (1969), with Omar Sharif as the romanticised rebel poster boy; MGM financed Michelangelo Antonioni's ambitious *Zabriskie Point* and Stuart Hagmann's campus drama *The Strawberry Statement* (both 1970); while Paramount distributed *Medium Cool* (1969), Haskell Wexler's masterly dissection of contemporary disaffection. And the close of the decade saw production of a raft of allegorical and/or revisionist westerns – including *The Wild Bunch* and *Tell Them Willie Boy Is Here* (both 1969), *Soldier Blue* and *Little Big Man* (both 1970) and *Ulzana's Raid* (1972) – that either questioned or condemned both Manifest Destiny and America's presence in Vietnam.

As far as artists in developing countries were concerned, it would take more than a few new brooms to sweep Hollywood clean of what they saw as its neo-colonial agenda. Nor did they have much time for progressive or populist filmmakers from Europe, feeling the latter displayed a lack of faith in their audience's intelligence by proffering political themes in a conventionally entertaining manner. For the young standard bearers of "guerrilla cinema", as the documentary-makers Fernando Solanas and Octavio Getino of Argentina's Grupo Cine-Liberación put it, radicalism and anti-imperialism were not just fashionable, temporary concerns; they were impulses – the lifeblood of their films. They aimed to achieve "the decolonization of culture" through a new form of cinema, Third Cinema, which challenged the hegemony of Hollywood, scorned pseudo-Hollywood movies and aimed to liberate brainwashed Third World peoples from cultural enslavement by showing them the reality of their situation.[16] This would be a vital step on the road to economic liberation. Solanas and Getino documented the history and processes of cultural enslavement in Latin America in their powerful film manifesto, *The Hour of the Furnaces* (1968), portions of which were assembled and screened in secret, at different stages during production, to various militant groups up and down Argentina. (The film was eventually smuggled out of the country and assembled into a whole in Italy. It played the European festival circuit to great acclaim.) This seminal work indicts colonial and neo-colonial powers and fully endorses Che Guevara's call for armed insurrection as the only cure for the subcontinent's ills. Indeed, as theorist and critic Teshome H. Gabriel terms it, in war-torn regions film should operate like "a soldier of liberation", a key weapon in the revolutionary struggle.[17]

Similar sentiments are expressed by the best of the revolutionary westerns, with the obvious difference being that the latter, regardless of the intentions of individual actors, writers and directors, were made for the profit of producers and investors. Haile Gerima, an Ethiopian filmmaker resident in the USA, takes particular umbrage at the representation of the Third World by filmmakers from developed nations. He objects to the stereotypical characterisations that litter Hollywood films, for example, when they venture into 'exotic' locales, and is even more offended when western stars are cast as Third World figures. To his mind, even the well-meaning political spaghettis we are discussing would be an abomination, despite their unequivocal support for liberation causes. "We are told again and again that in order to make the world understand our cause it must be endorsed by the stars of the west playing our experiences for us... Personally, if it has to take the stars and the toys of cultural domination to depict my grandmothers, my fathers and mothers, I call this dictatorship, obscene and unacceptable."[18] The problem for audiences residing in the developed world, accustomed to the star system and a straightforward aesthetic/narrative tradition and generally resistant to alternative techniques, is that it's difficult to identify with Gerima's viewpoint. This means that even in the unlikely event that Third World filmmakers achieve a breakthrough in terms of distribution – and it's hard enough for them to find an outlet in their own countries, let alone get their films on to screens in significant numbers (i.e., beyond the art-house circuit) in wealthier nations – there remains a formidable cultural barrier to overcome. The political spaghettis, which pushed Third World protagonists (albeit played in the main by western actors) to the forefront of the action, were at least seen by a great many people, and not just in the west. And while the impact they made, politically and educationally, was limited, at least they were visible, whereas too many Third Cinema films, through no fault of their own, are not.

Perhaps the most prominent Third World filmmaker of the era in question, and the one most relevant in a study of westerns, was Brazil's Glauber Rocha, who took a slightly different tack from those mentioned above. While Rocha, ideological figurehead of his country's underground Cinema Novo movement, dutifully insisted that "commercial cinematography... as an industry, is committed to untruth and exploitation", and castigated the "imitative, colonized films" made by many of his contemporaries, he refused to label his own political films as "propagandist".[19] He was also aiming for greater exposure; not just striving for a new system of distribution (though this was certainly one of Cinema Novo's objectives) but making his films

A massacre (*above*) and post-Cannes festival marketing (*top right*) from **Antonio das Mortes**, Glauber Rocha's exuberant western *brasiliana*.

with an international audience in mind. Speaking of his most famous work, *Antonio das Mortes* (1969) – an anti-capitalist mythological adventure in which a bounty hunter switches allegiance from a landowner to the peasants he has helped to oppress – Rocha said: "I make films about the Third World because I am from the Third World. If *Antonio das Mortes* were an American film, it would probably be a western, or if Japanese, a Samurai film." (One of the key inspirations for *Antonio* was Sam Peckinpah's *Ride the High Country* [1962], with its world-weary gunfighters seeking redemption serving as models for Rocha's own anti-hero; another, closer to home, was an Argentine film by Leopoldo Torre Nilsson, *Martín Fierro* [1968], celebrating the life of the legendary gaucho.) He might have added Euro-western had the film been Italian – Rocha's associates assert that he was a major influence on European western directors.[20] (In Italy, *Antonio* was promoted as a genre film, complete with posters – designed by the prolific Rodolfo Gasparri – depicting Antonio in the manner of a typical spaghetti gunfighter. Brazilians, meanwhile, had ample opportunity to see genuine Euro-westerns – no less than 23 of them were released there in the year of *Antonio* alone[21].) But while there are generic patterns in this film and its ferocious predecessor, *Black God, White Devil* (1964) – both of them take place in the *sertão*, a barren, desolate region of north-eastern Brazil that superficially resembles both the American southwest and Almería, and feature bandits (*cangaceiros*), hired gunmen (*jaguncos*) and shoot-outs – their method of storytelling is defiantly and dramatically different. Rocha incorporates elements from Brazilian folklore, popular culture and mythology to articulate the struggle of the rural poor and, while he takes a predictably socialistic stance on the need for land reform, he is also critical of populism (represented by the messianic figure of Sebastião in *Black God*) and of the passivity of the people. There is a raw energy and anger about these films that is absent from most mainstream political cinema of the period. Characters seem trapped as much by their emotional states – frustration, despair, bitterness and delusion – as they are by deprivation and the unforgiving landscape. The expository scenes in *Black God, White Devil* have an almost neorealist quality but, by the time of *Antonio das Mortes*, Rocha's technique is much more operatic and theatrical – he called it a "tropicalist" style, an attempt to portray the "real" Brazil. The scenes of violence have a delirious, almost orgiastic intensity, and the climactic shoot-out between Antonio and the landowner's hired guns could almost be a mockery of Leone and Peckinpah. Rocha's films were well received at festivals and art cinemas abroad – *Antonio* won him a share of the Best Director prize at Cannes – but in his own country they encountered opposition from the government and the national press. Indeed, shortly after completing *Antonio*, Rocha opted to go into voluntary exile, eventually returning several years later.

above and bottom left: Provocative imagery from Rocha's **Black God, White Devil**, featuring Othon Bastos as Corisco, *cangaceiro* and would-be liberator.

The only western filmmaker regarded as a kindred spirit in Third Cinema circles was Jean-Luc Godard, who made the one political 'western' that meets Solanas and Getino head-on. (It even includes a cameo by Glauber Rocha.) Around 1969, Godard, together with Jean-Pierre Gorin, formed the Dziga Vertov group, named after the radical Soviet documentary-maker who chronicled life in the post-revolutionary Soviet Union. For Godard it was not enough for a film's content to be radical; the form itself had to subvert 'bourgeois' cinematic conventions and confound audience expectations. The director even dismissed his own previous films as being too conventional, and now felt impelled to contest the imperialistic bureaucracy that oversaw film financing and distribution. The most pertinent of the Dziga Vertov experiments from our point of view, *Wind from the East* (1970), reassesses all forms of political cinema and implicitly attacks the ideological bearing of commercial westerns, including those made by Corbucci *et al*. Here, the images the audience must comprehend comprised stock (mock) western situations, used to illustrate the theme of class struggle and interpreted by a small cast that includes Gian Maria Volonté – employed, presumably, as a direct link to a more polished and, in Godard's view, ideologically suspect form of political cinema. (According to some sources, Godard had previously approached another actor-activist, Lou Castel, who preferred to make the fantastical *Matalo!* instead.) As was their practice, Godard and Gorin ('directing', for want of a better word, with Gérard Martin) expose the guts of the filming – there is no artifice or illusion – and the 'action' is signposted by crude, hand-written intertitles. (*The Hour of the Furnaces* was similarly broken down into titled chapters.) The point, underlined repeatedly in the stern Marxist-Leninist commentary that accompanies the images, is that conventional Hollywood-style political discourse merely helps to reinforce the oppressive equilibrium, a heinous construct here termed "Nixon-Paramount". What is called for is an analytical approach, without the diversions of spectacle or sympathetic characters, and an independent system of production and distribution. In fact, all forms of political representation are found wanting, from Eisenstein to Third Cinema, the latter personified by Rocha, who stands like a signpost at the intersection between "aesthetic adventure" and "dangerous cinema". This being Godard, there is a fair amount of self-examination as well, something that rankled with Volonté: "[Godard] is too preoccupied with only one type of problem – *his* problems – which make him forget the essential: the function of the cinema as a means of communication with the masses."[22]

In theory, *Wind from the East* would be far more "dangerous" – in Rocha's terms – and debilitating to the system than a Corbucci western, but this could never be tested in practice. As is so often the case with avant-garde political cinema, the artists have made a film they think their intended audience *ought* to see. But this was a miscalculation. *Wind from the East* is essentially a Brechtian theatre workshop on film, similar in effect, if not in tone, to Marco Ferreri's wilfully absurd Vietnam allegory, *Don't Touch the White Woman* (1974), and devoid of wider appeal beyond its own narrow ideological base. Godard believed, as did Third Cinema theorists, that the commercial film industry underestimated the "critical intelligence" of filmgoers, deliberately distracting their attention from the problems that mainstream political films, for example, purported to address. But surely his own increasingly insular experiments would prove much more stimulating to film students and far-left critical theorists than to the average filmgoer, even if they could have gained wide enough distribution to challenge the populist political adventures of the era. Perhaps we would have been able to compare like with like had Godard and Gorin not steered *Wind from the East* so far from its original direction. Daniel Cohn-Bendit, a student leader at Nanterre University and a prime mover in the May 1968 movement in France, conceived a story about a miners' strike, a left-wing western he hoped to have produced in Rome in collaboration with Godard. Cohn-Bendit put the divergence between his outline and the finished film down to a "misunderstanding" between Godard and himself.[23]

In *The Altering Eye*, Robert Kolker argues that, like the May 1968 events that inspired them, "Godard's films of the period are also an outpouring of emotions and ideas, but they are detached and raw, too cold and abstract to effect a change in attitude or understanding… he forgot briefly that stories are the best way film has to communicate ideas." The key word is communicate, and Kolker's view, like that of Volonté above, was certainly shared by the leading members of our 'revolutionary cell'. Franco Solinas, despite his misgivings about the western genre and the enlightening potential of cinema in general, recognised its value as a tool of *mass* communication, and other political filmmakers such as Pontecorvo, Damiani and Costa-Gavras expressed similar opinions. Pontecorvo rounded on the hard-left critics of his brand of narrative political cinema in an interview with the American journal *Cineaste*, accusing his detractors of failing to see the bigger picture: "They criticise *Battle* [*of Algiers*] and *Burn!* [*Queimada*] always saying the same thing – they are of little use. But in the countries where the problems of colonialism and neo-colonialism are still being confronted, the authorities – who know very well whether something is really useful or not – have prevented the exhibition of this kind of film – in the Dominican Republic, for instance, and several countries of Latin America. And revolutionary people – like the Black Panthers and the Cuban people – they like these films and are glad they are being shown."[24] Indeed, the Black Panthers are reputed to have used *The Battle of Algiers* as a kind of training manual in guerrilla tactics. (It is not just insurgents who have found Pontecorvo's film instructive: the US Department of Defense screened *Algiers* in the Pentagon in September 2003 to study the applicability of French tactics against the FLN to America's ongoing operations in Iraq.)

Clearly, these artists, especially those involved in westerns, felt they could achieve a lot more by injecting their ideas into an established formula with proven widespread appeal. Damiani was particularly bullish about "the kind of political film we make in Italy": "Can we change consumer society using the medium of film, which is in itself a consumer product? I think we can. I think that to promote political awareness among cinema-goers you have to use a medium that is easily accessible to them."[25] In this way, Damiani and his contemporaries were the moderates to Godard's radical, nudging their audience – a *guaranteed* audience, it's worth repeating – rather than lecturing, working within the confines of commercial cinema but subverting it by promoting an alternative ideology. As I have already argued, it is pointless to promote one brand of political cinema over another; all options should be kept open. As Pontecorvo said, "I think to renounce these films is an under-evaluation of what I consider the greatest problem at this time in the approach to radical change: the problem of the alliance of different parts of the population, the alliance of the working class with other classes, such as the petit-bourgeoisie which is its potential ally… it's important to make films for the normal channels. This doesn't mean that a new, alternative cinema must not be born. The two things must go together."[26]

"Do you like Mexico señor?"
"No, not very much"

At their most basic level, the political westerns attempt a dialectical examination of the relationship between the Third World and the west, although this is usually reduced to a black and white contrast between idealism and materialism. This relationship is symbolised by two opposing stock characters – one a naïve insurgent, the other an American or European who may be an urbane mercenary, detached intellectual or misguided law enforcer. All the major Euro-westerns in which Mexico plays a central role have the theme of political/moral awakening at their core, whereby one or sometimes both of the protagonists learn the true meaning of social justice and surrender their personal goals and desires to the common cause, or at least come to respect a different viewpoint. In Damiano Damiani's *A Bullet for the General*, the first and most impassioned of the large-scale political spaghettis, an unusual friendship forms between compassionate, gregarious revolutionary El Chuncho (Gian Maria Volonté) and a cold, nonchalant American, Bill Tate (Lou Castel), who cons his way into Chuncho's band with the aim of getting close enough to assassinate the local *cabecilla*, General Elias (Jaime Fernandez). For this he will collect a hefty fee from the Mexican army in Juarez.27 The bond between these unlikely associates is eventually broken when Chuncho discovers the other's duplicity and witnesses his arrogant attitude towards the poor. Chuncho shoots Tate, though he is unable to explain why ("Quien sabe?"), throws off the expensive suit his friend had bought for him and returns to his rags and revolution. As we shall see, this conclusion is typical of the film's co-writer, the prolific Franco Solinas, in that instinct triumphs over intellect; the alluring charms of capitalism are resisted in favour of violent resistance. By killing Tate, Chuncho has liberated himself. "Don't buy bread, buy dynamite" is his, and the film's, exhortation to the Third World's poor and oppressed.

Later films in the cycle suggest that not all 'imperialists' are bad, and that some are even capable of developing political and/or emotional empathy with the wretched of the earth. A further set of oppositions

above: Belgian poster for **A Man and a Colt**, a straightforward star vehicle with an ideological undertow.
bottom left: Spanish admat for the rousing **Killer Kid**, which diverts Anthony Steffen from his usual solitary path.

comes into play – lone (American/European) hero versus Mexican, Mexican versus oppressors and, finally, lone hero (now enlightened) and Mexican against the oppressors. In *The Big Gundown*, Texan lawman Lee Van Cleef eventually turns his guns on his capitalist paymasters and saves the life of Cuchillo Sanchez (Tomas Milian), a Mexican peon who has been falsely accused of raping and killing a 12-year-old girl. The sequel, *Run, Man, Run*, has Cuchillo aided by another American specialist, played this time by Donal O'Brien. In *Killer Kid*, an American army officer (Anthony Steffen), impressed by the courage of the revolutionary fighters he has infiltrated, opts to desert his post and join their ranks. Wandering gunman Dakota Joe (Robert Hundar), hired to kill a Zapatista doctor for a Mexican overlord, instead throws in his lot with the rebels in *A Man and a Colt*. A Dutch adventurer (Ugo Pagliai) reneges on his deal with a corrupt regional governor to the benefit of bandit Tomas Milian in Giovanni Fago's Glauber Rocha-inspired *The Magnificent Bandits*. And while Franco Nero's gesture of solidarity in the frozen final frame of Sergio Corbucci's *Compañeros* cannot be taken for granted (he doesn't have much choice but to turn back to aid the rebels he has just left behind, given that he is riding right towards the *federales*), his full-blooded

above: The clergy, foreigners and the bourgeoisie are grouped together as enemies of the people in *A Fistful of Dynamite*.
left: **The Anger of the Wind** showed a more serious side to Terence Hill, although this Italian poster tries to have it both ways.
opposite: Hot-tempered Martine Beswick (*right*) gives cold-blooded Lou Castel (*left*) a dressing down in the desert in **A Bullet for the General**.

participation in the preceding battle, which pits 'good' revolutionaries against bad ones – yet another bifurcation – and compels Nero to pick up a machine gun yet again in a Corbucci western, suggests he may have at least temporarily put his pecuniary interests to one side. (If we overlook his attempted theft of a valuable statue from the local church, that is.) One film was bold enough to cap its protagonist's change of heart with a realistically downbeat conclusion – in Mario Camus's *The Anger of the Wind*, Terence Hill's hired gun pays the ultimate price for siding with striking workers against the landowners who first employed him.

Anchored by the political beliefs of Damiani, Solinas, Volonté and Castel, *A Bullet for the General* is more uncompromising than most of these films, and makes no attempt to humanise its Yankee outsider. Within the film's carefully crafted allegorical structure, Tate personifies a critical vision of America – both its capitalist values and, in particular, its self-serving, bullying, paranoid Third World policy. (Tate's attempt to distance himself politically from his country by stating "I don't associate with the president of the United States" anticipates William Holden's words in *The Wild Bunch*, when he tells Mapache's military adviser that he and his men are "not associated with anybody", let alone the US government. In both films, the declared neutrality of the Americans is not quite what it seems.) With this switch to a 'Mexican' perspective, America is depicted not as a friendly giant among nations but as both overseer and parasite. For Tate, money is God. The suffering of the peons never affects him emotionally – he repeatedly states and demonstrates his contempt for the country – but is just another lucrative opportunity for him, and he's not interested in women unless he pays – "that way you don't risk complications". The casting is ironic in that Castel, a committed leftist who had excelled as the murderous Alessandro in Marco Bellocchio's *Fists in the Pocket* (1965), plays against his political beliefs. "For motivation, I told myself that I was interpreting the enemy," he has explained.**28** While Chuncho (Communist Volonté on safer ground) argues that the people of San Miguel, a newly liberated town visited by the rebels, are still human beings despite their poverty and tatty clothes, Tate is a materialist and, by extension, a racist. It's notable

"Don't Buy Bread, Buy Dynamite!"

that he only returns the admiring glances of Adelita, a fiery revolutionary (a terrific performance from future Hammer star Martine Beswick), when she slips into an expensive stolen gown. It's as if previously she had been invisible to him. Similarly, late in the film Tate attempts to mould Chuncho in his own image, dressing him up like an American in fine tailored clothing. Chuncho, to his credit, prefers his humble rags.

If the core of the film is the improbable alliance between Tate and Chuncho, its most significant sequence is the sojourn in San Miguel. It is here that the Mexican reveals his leadership qualities and his compassion, and here that poverty clashes with privilege most explicitly. The peasants lynch wealthy landowner Don Felipe not because he is a rich man, but because they are poor and he has done his best to keep them that way. The sequence also highlights the ideological gulf between Tate and his nominal comrades in arms. Tate tries to prevent Chuncho's men from molesting Don Felipe's wife but Adelita interjects – she was raped by a soldier when she was a girl, so why should a rich woman be spared the same treatment? What we know of Tate's character suggests that his protestations have little to do with chivalry and more with class bias. In his mind, the honour of a refined lady is worth much more than that of a rough *soldadera*.

This key section has several equivalents elsewhere in the sub-genre. Local reprisals of this nature were very common in the revolution, and most political westerns let their ragged heroes lord it over wealthy victims at one point or another. Some incidents are treated relatively light-heartedly: the coach sequence that opens *A Fistful of Dynamite*, in which Rod Steiger and his brood show up polite society as a mess of prejudices, hypocrisy and insecurities (even Steiger's rape of Maria Monti isn't treated seriously – quite the opposite in fact); or the sedate, swanky dinner party in *The Magnificent Bandits* that is gradually transformed by Tomas Milian and his garishly outfitted gang into a hedonistic carnival. In *A Professional Gun*, mine worker and fledgling revolutionary Paco Roman (Tony Musante) forces the owner of the local silver mine to eat a lizard; Paco had previously discovered the delicacy in his own plate of swill, commenting sardonically, "Look amigos, they have given us the meat." Later, as a self-proclaimed general, Paco orders the mayor of a captured city to wash the rebels' dirty underwear. While this exultant, populist tone is perhaps to be expected, considering the core audience these films were pitched at, there are similar instances that demonstrate a surprising degree of pathos – in one of several macabre tableaux in Corbucci's otherwise farcical *What Am I Doing in the Middle of a Revolution?*, the heroes arrive at an isolated hacienda to discover the corpses of a wealthy elderly couple, sitting at the dinner table in their best clothes with a note explaining how they'd poisoned themselves, too scared of the changes to come.

above: **Queimada!** – released in the US as **Burn!** – blended incendiary politics with acute characterisations by Marlon Brando, as an agent provocateur, and Evaristo Marquez, as the slave he prompts to rebel against Portuguese rule.

By having us experience the film through the eyes of Chuncho rather than Tate, *A Bullet for the General*, like most of the films that follow, represents a dramatic departure from Hollywood's Mexican-westerns, in which the focal point is always the 'neutral' American outsider and which surreptitiously justify, or at least rarely question, the US's intervention in the affairs of its southern neighbour. At the level of cinema, Tate can also be seen to symbolise the American western itself, all surface sophistication and hidden agendas, compared with the rough, direct European version embodied by Chuncho. Damiani would probably resist such an interpretation. Speaking to critic Luca Beatrice, Damiani, caught on the defensive, sought to distance his film from the western genre on both ideological and geographical grounds: "*Quien sabe?* is not a western, but a film about the Mexican revolution, just as [the Brazilian drama] *O Cangaceiro* by Lima Barreto [is not a western but] a film about Brazilian bandits. In fact, the west is north of the Rio Grande, whereas in the south there are stories of peons, of Pancho Villa and Emiliano Zapata. Italian cinema of the Sixties took an interest in these heroes... because they were symbols of the Third World. In the Sixties, there was a widespread sub-proletarian revolt and this had nothing in common with the Anglo-Saxon, puritan roots of the western."[29]

Franco Solinas, who embellished the dialogue for Damiani's film and was reportedly very active on the set, conducting discussions and suggesting changes, was one of the most important writers in Italian political cinema and a key creative influence on the revolutionary westerns. He wrote or co-wrote stories or scripts for four of the most debated examples, and provides a bridge between such major figures as Sollima, Corbucci and Donati. Born in Cagliari in 1927, Solinas moved to Rome during the Second World War and became a partisan at the age of 16. After the war he joined the Communist Party and began writing for the Party daily *L'Unità* before branching out into fiction. In the mid-Fifties, he wrote his first scripts for director Gillo Pontecorvo, another former partisan, including *The Wide Blue Road* (1957), adapted from Solinas's novel *Squarciò*. This was followed by *Kapò* (1960), a powerful drama set in a Nazi concentration camp that includes a shocking act of violence perpetrated by a young Gianni 'Sartana' Garko; and the famous *The Battle of Algiers*, for which the writer was nominated for an Oscar.

In the opinions of many, the latter remains *the* benchmark of political filmmaking. Solinas's scrupulous, unemotional depiction of the conflict as a vicious circle, combined with Pontecorvo's pseudo-documentary direction, creates a film of raw, compelling urgency that has gained greatly in potency in the intervening years.

Solinas worked with other mainstream political directors, including Francesco Rosi (*Salvatore Giuliano*) and Costa-Gavras (*Stage of Siege* [1973]), but his relationship with Pontecorvo was the most productive. Their last film together was the underrated *Queimada!* (1969), a kind of western once-removed, with Marlon Brando playing a coldly pragmatic British agent who foments a slave revolt on a Caribbean island, ending Portuguese rule so that the British sugar industry can move in. Another vicious circle is formed, and Walker is called back to the island ten years later to quash the very rebels he inspired. As in *The Battle of Algiers*, the villain is colonialism, and there is no attempt on the part of the filmmakers to demonise individuals – events speak for themselves. While the story is basically the same as the one Solinas wrote for *A Professional Gun*, which Pontecorvo was originally slated to direct (see note 49), the climax of *Queimada!* is reminiscent of *Tepepa* and, to a lesser extent, *A Bullet for the General*, in the way that revolutionary ideals are seen to have taken root in a given culture, not died with a particular individual. In general, Solinas's scripts focus on opposing forces, often within a tense historical context, and seek to find their way through the ideological mire to the truth. Of course, as a dedicated Marxist, Solinas always found the truth in the evils of colonialism and oppression. Another defining feature of his work is the detailed depiction of insurgency/counter-insurgency techniques and the cruel logic behind them, such as the French army's use of torture in Algeria, the bombing of civilians by the Algerian resistance, or Walker's scorched-earth policy to flush the rebels from the cane fields in *Queimada!*

Given Solinas's pedigree, it would be intriguing to know the shape of his original stories for westerns, and how accurately the finished films convey his ideas. I asked Sergio Donati, who adapted a story written by Solinas and Fernando Morandi (Pontecorvo's assistant director on *Algiers*) called *La resa dei conti* (roughly, 'the settling of accounts') for the screenplay to *The Big Gundown*, for his impressions. "Solinas was a gentleman, a man of great integrity… He was a man apart. He never wanted to make commercial movies; he despised them and was very surprised to see that *La resa dei conti* could also be a western. [His story] was originally a story of our days – between a *carabiniere* and a bandit in Sardinia – and he [Solinas] was in a sense amused by the adaptation. Until his last days he always refused to work in commercial movies. I have great memories of Solinas – I repeat, a man of great moral and intellectual integrity."**30**

Sergio Sollima – the politics of the knife

Solinas may have despised commercialism, but there's no lack of integrity in the film version of *La resa dei conti* as realised by Donati and Sergio Sollima, even though it reverses the writer's far more cynical conclusion. As Sollima's first western, *The Big Gundown* is remarkably assured and perfectly weighted between action and ideology, a pulsating chase film that doubles as a political critique.**31** It was the second of three collaborations between the director and Donati, following the Stewart Granger spy film *Requiem for a Secret Agent* (1966) – produced, like his first two westerns, by Alberto Grimaldi, whom Sollima met through Sergio Leone – and preceding the extraordinary *Face to Face*, and the first between Sollima and Cuban actor Tomas Milian, who created one of the genre's most appealing and iconic characters in Cuchillo Sanchez.

The son of a successful lawyer, Sollima, born in Rome in 1921, dutifully studied law for a brief period before his artistic impulses steered him towards theatre and cinema. He began courses at the Centro Sperimentale di Cinematografica in 1939 and was commissioned to direct wartime documentaries – his ticket out of the draft – before gravitating to film criticism on the magazine *Cinema*.**32** Although his early film work was relatively lightweight – he co-directed the portmanteau film *L'amore difficile* (1962), released in the UK as *Sex Can Be Difficult*, and helmed three successful spy thrillers – Sollima's political viewpoint and philosophising tendencies are significant factors in his westerns: the 'Third World' titles, *The Big Gundown* and *Run, Man, Run*, condemn exploitation, injustice, class bias and racism, while *Face to Face* looks over its shoulder at recent European history to offer a parallel with the rise of Fascism. All his westerns invite careful scrutiny of the characters and their motivations, which can rarely be taken at face value, and how they relate to the rules set down by society. "I was interested in the conflict between human moral codes and the distortions that society brings to morality," he says. "The malignant effect of a so-called 'civilised' society, of a system that defines itself as 'law and order'… all my characters struggle desperately to find a little island where some form of *justice* prevails. This justice is not found in canonical social rules, in written moral codes, but uniquely in the inter-relationship between men."**33**

Like his contemporaries, Sollima likes to put seemingly incompatible characters in opposition and observe the effects. His protagonists seem discordant in every way, from their cultural backgrounds to their personalities and mentalities, but the director's chief interest lies in their unexpected similarities and the lessons each can learn from the other. This theme is brilliantly worked out in *The Big Gundown* – in which the wily Cuchillo is pitted against freelance lawman Jonathan Corbett (Lee Van Cleef) – and in *Face to Face*, which pairs Milian as mixed-race outlaw Beau Bennett with Gian Maria Volonté as Brad Fletcher, an eastern academic who adopts Beau's savage ways. Sergio Donati, who also co-wrote *Face to Face* but was a notable absentee from *Run, Man, Run*, has mixed feelings about his former collaborator. "Sollima was very much a politicised kind of director. He was a Communist, and the ideology was very important to him. I was on the left too, but I was more on the creative side. It was always a fight with Sollima because he liked to explain the ideas with words. Leone was very funny to work with – we were on the same wavelength. With Sollima it was work – lots of discussion – but the results were really excellent, because I love *The Big Gundown*, I love *Face to Face*."**34** In previous interviews, Donati has been less complimentary. In Oreste De Fornari's biography of Leone, Donati criticises *Face to Face* (to which Sollima contributed the lion's share of the writing) as "too verbose", and accuses Sollima of "sloganeering", a fault he might have identified in any number of Sollima's politically engaged contemporaries.

Whatever one's view of Sollima and his politics, one has to recognise his skill in creating sympathetic/empathetic characters and charting their development. He envisaged Cuchillo as a Mexican version of Toshiro Mifune's character in *Seven Samurai* (1954), and Milian responded with a raw, earthy blend of braggadocio and defiance that made him a talismanic figure for Italian student radicals. Cuchillo was a new type of 'hero' for the Italian western, a lowlife in many ways but also a victim of political and racial persecution who manages to hold his own against overwhelming odds. In *The Big Gundown* he is numerically, materially and intellectually disadvantaged but, while he doesn't triumph, he endures, shielded by his local community and aided, eventually, by the reawakened Corbett. Cuchillo's vigorous free spirit

The hunt is on: Sergio Sollima's **The Big Gundown** hits just about all its targets. Its transposition of a Franco Solinas story is inspired, the casting of Lee Van Cleef and Tomas Milian (*bottom left, left to right*) spot on, and the ratio of action (*opposite*) to ideological stimulation expertly judged.

clashes with, and complements, Corbett's blinkered sense of justice. Both men kill when they have to, but neither does so in a cold-blooded manner. The Mexican is ruled by his emotions – his feelings are his guide – whereas Corbett is the epitome of rigidity and control. Their characteristics reflect their respective backgrounds and social status, as well as the acting styles of Milian and Van Cleef. Cuchillo is a peon and a thief, a convenient scapegoat for American rail baron Brokston (Walter Barnes), who has him blamed for a sex crime that was actually committed by Brokston's son-in-law. (Sollima teases the audience in an early scene in which Cuchillo plays with a young Mormon girl in a manner either childishly innocent or threateningly guilty.) Brokston then offers to foster Corbett's political ambitions if he'll bring Cuchillo to 'justice'. Cuchillo is also regarded as a troublemaker at home, where he had fought for Juarez.**35** Hunted and harried all his life, quick thinking has become a means of survival, with Milian basing his mannerisms

"Don't Buy Bread, Buy Dynamite!"

on wild rabbits and other alert, endangered animals. Fast reflexes and reactions are also important to Corbett, but for him these are skills, the tools of his trade. He has made his name by hunting and killing bandits but he meets his match in Cuchillo. Their encounters are sparky, full of engaging trickery and barbed humour – "By yourself you couldn't catch a limping snail", scorns the Mexican. Eventually Corbett discovers that both he and his prey are pawns in a rich man's game, and he has unwittingly perpetuated the kind of prejudice that assumes a poor peon is more likely to be guilty than a man of 'higher' birth.

Much is made of Corbett's honour and integrity – he agrees to help Brokston because he believes in progress, not the rail baron's profit – but Sollima and Donati refuse to pander to heroic/generic stereotypes, constantly undercutting Van Cleef's aura of infallible authority. Corbett's introduction is a wonderfully choreographed showdown with a trio of outlaws, which he wins with aplomb, but elsewhere he struggles to exert control, despite his confident bearing and undoubted skills. (This subversive element is missing from the more conventional *Run, Man, Run*, in which Donal O'Brien's Cassidy, like most of the characters, is little more than a cipher.) In Van Cleef's fine, measured performance, Corbett is the classic man in the middle. His experiences have given him a firm belief in the inviolability of the law, but to Sollima, Donati and Solinas, and even more so to Cuchillo, the law goes hand in hand with class bias and racial stereotyping, and has little to do with real justice. Corbett's conviction renders him vulnerable to Cuchillo's charge that he is unconcerned with the Mexican's guilt or innocence. Ultimately, like Charley Siringo, the Pinkerton agent who acts as a kind of moral arbiter at the end of *Face to Face*, Corbett must make a choice: accept Brokston's money and political patronage and follow the job through in the name of the law; or, with the real culprit unmasked, follow his heart in the name of justice.

Solinas's typically pugnacious story targets capitalism, racism and the abuse of law by the moneyed elite. Brokston and his allies are portrayed as manipulative and corrupt, with all the contempt that goes with unscrupulous wealth. Corbett is clearly disturbed by his employer (or 'owner' as Brokston puts it), especially in the film's magnificent closing stages, when the businessman reveals a passion for hunting and the full extent of his arrogance and ruthlessness. Brokston yearns to complete his experiences by taking part in a manhunt. He envies Corbett, who has pursued a career as a hunter of men under the (albeit threadbare) cloak of the law and with a sense of honour.

above: Lee Van Cleef arbitrates during Tomas Milian's duel scene in **The Big Gundown**.

However misguided he may be, Corbett doesn't *indulge* in violence; for him, killing is neither a sport nor an art form, and this is where his rivalry with Brokston's bodyguard, Baron von Schulemberg, rests. The Baron is a chilling creation, played with relish by Gérard Herter, one of those wonderful character actors who flourished in the genre but about whom information is scarce. Aristocrat, sharpshooter and veteran of 23 successful duels, the Baron is a connoisseur of killing, the most clinical and cold-blooded of all the genre's European mercenaries. With his stiff bearing and precise, mechanical movements, not to mention an Erich von Stroheim monocle, Herter is almost a caricature of Teutonic arrogance. His penchant for bombastic observations results in some memorable dialogue: "The sun is rising – it looks like a big ball of blood. I say that for those who believe in foresight." Herter, who first came to note as the Austrian officer who condemns the heroes to death in *The Great War* (1959), later recycled many of the Baron's mannerisms, plus his love of hunting, for his performance in Giovanni Fago's *Full House for the Devil* (1968), while the monocle reappeared when he portrayed another sadistic Austrian martinet in *Adios, Sabata* (1970).

It is when the chase descends into Mexico that the characters and themes come sharply into focus. Brokston and his entourage symbolise the exploitation of developing countries by wealthy nations. This is particularly evident in the scene where Brokston orders his hunting party to "turn this country upside down" to find Cuchillo. Money and power have no respect for borders. Furthermore, the racism that has plagued Cuchillo across the border is intensified in his homeland, reinforcing the vagabond's resolve to keep on running, an urge underlined in the film's rousing theme song, the title of which was borrowed for the sequel. Brokston's ally in Mexico is Don Serrano, a powerful landowner who dismisses Cuchillo as a peon, not a 'real' Mexican. To a man like Serrano, the issue is not merely one of class distinction but *caste* distinction. And when the victims of injustice have no voice and no perceived value, the law – represented by inefficient

above: Gérard Herter, tongue in cheek (and often monocle in eye), was the genre's keenest interpreter of cold-blooded, ruthless militarism, as here in Gianfranco Parolini's **Adios, Sabata**.

police captain Fernando Sancho, who had earlier expressed his hatred for "dogs of Juarez" like Cuchillo – turns a blind eye.

The filmmakers' disgust at this brand of inter-racial prejudice is channelled through Milian's passionate portrayal. The actor's attitude towards the ideological westerns that made his name has swayed over the years. At times, he has recognised their value as allegories: "In my view, so many 'Third World Westerns' were huge hits because, even though the hero was always American, the Third Worlder could be in a certain sense the Italian underclass. I'm not saying that Italy is a Third World country, not at all, but honestly you must admit there is much underdevelopment. So, as in many other countries where my films did and do well – Spain, Turkey, Arabia [sic], Africa, South America – the people needed superheroes: the bounty killer – Anglo-Saxon, hard, inexpressive, made of steel… went on the hunt for a poor little guy, with whom the audience identified."[36] Despite this, and despite acknowledging his own symbolic status at the time – which rested, in part, upon his Cuban provenance, with the island considered a revolutionary Utopia by European activists – Milian has also stated that politics and his profession should not be mixed. This didn't prevent the causes addressed in the films from sinking in – up to a point. "I bought a huge piece of land in Almería," he remembers, "and I was doing one of those revolutionary westerns. And I was sitting on a rock there, looking at the horizon, but I was thinking not as Tomas; I was thinking as my character. And I said, 'I really stink.' Me, a landowner! Making money out of the message for the poor… I didn't give it [*the land*] to the poor though – I sold it!"[37] Sergio Donati doubts whether Milian ever held strong ideological beliefs. "Milian was neurotic, very insecure, but very good, very distinctive. I don't think he was politically very involved… I don't think he was even very conscious that he was doing a political manifesto with Sollima."[38]

The success of *The Big Gundown* inevitably dictated that there would be a sequel and, equally inevitably, *Run, Man, Run* is something of a disappointment. It's by no means a bad film – it is humorous and exciting, skilfully composed and well paced – but fails to match the epic stride of its predecessor. With Donati opting out ("I found an excuse because it was very tiring to work with Sergio"), Sollima wrote the story and drafted Pompeo De Angelis to help with the script. (Sollima also lost his first-choice financier – with Alberto Grimaldi busy, A.M. Chretien and Alvaro Mancori stepped in.) This time, Cuchillo is entrusted with recovering $3m in Juarista gold earmarked for the forthcoming revolution. After a series of skirmishes with sundry greedy characters he secures the booty, though he is still on the run when we leave him. There is a satisfying, fluid sense of continuity in the frequent exhortations to Cuchillo to keep one step ahead. But whereas in *The Big Gundown* this theme

above: **Run, Man, Run** – Sollima's sequel to **The Big Gundown** – brought back Tomas Milian for a gambol through a hand-me-down hunt-the-gold plot.

was expressed with great urgency, here the gravity of Cuchillo's mission is lessened by a combination of a hazy script – a variation on the well-worn hunt-for-the-gold plot that was a firm favourite of spaghetti scriptwriters – and a lighter overall tone. Unlike *The Big Gundown*, where scenes involving subsidiary characters like Nieves Navarro's 'vulnerable' widow were neat little sketches that contributed to the theme of false impressions and hasty judgements, the various chancers and opportunists that Cuchillo comes across are scarcely developed beyond their obvious symbolic functions: Donal O'Brien as a former lawman and Juarista turned gunfighter, a character borrowed from Sergio Donati's school of lapsed idealists; José Torres on fine form as the embodiment of revolution; Linda Veras as a bogus Salvation Army officer; the imposing Nello Pazzafini as Reza, a brutal bandit; Marco Guglielmi and Luciano Rossi as French hired killers working for the Mexican government; and Chelo Alonso as Cuchillo's feisty intended. (All these characters, or sets of characters, have their own themes on the soundtrack – credited to Bruno Nicolai but sometimes attributed, without much conviction, to Ennio Morricone – just as they have their own obvious purpose in the plot.) Milian/Cuchillo is at the centre of everything, a consistent source of comedy and compassion, if not exactly revolutionary inspiration, in an inconsistent film.

Far more stimulating is Sollima's second western with Donati. In the director's terms, *Face to Face* is about "how people change when they find themselves in exceptional circumstances". It expands upon *The Big Gundown*'s ideas about the unreliability of first impressions, the will to power of society's elite and the role of moral choices in shaping identities and altering destinies. The central theme of personality transference looks ahead to *Performance* (1970), and there are also strains of *Lord of the Flies* in the way that a civilised man – bronchial history professor Brad Fletcher (Gian Maria Volonté), who has retired to the clean air of the southwest for health reasons – reverts to savagery in an undeveloped environment. Brad's descent is more frightening, however, because he has none of the innocence of the children in …*Flies*. He is a well-educated man, a professor of history who will be well acquainted with tyranny. He leaves his pupils with a moral lesson – that the answers to both just and unjust truths will be found within themselves – and this is the key to Brad's own psychological transformation. He begins the film with his principles intact, convinced that human rights should apply even in the untamed southwest; when circumstances throw him together with halfbreed outlaw Beau Bennett (Tomas Milian), however, Brad finds himself drawn to Beau's primitive, violent lifestyle, which awakens in him a dormant desire to command and control. Having been "civilised among civilised people", as one character astutely observes, Brad becomes "violent among the violent". Given a gun for the first time, he states, "There's no doubt that holding it gives one a curious sense of power – it seems so natural." He's thrilled when he fires and hits a tree, yet recoils when Beau shoots a rabbit for their dinner: "In the west it's difficult to distinguish between the instinct for survival and the lust to acquire power." As the film progresses, it becomes easier to make such a distinction between the two men.

Volonté's performance is crucial to the film's success. He charts Brad's decline – from smug and condescending in the early stages, to cruel and callous in the latter – with consummate skill, prefiguring his portrayals in other films of the era, particularly his egotistical bank robber in Carlo Lizzani's docu-drama *Bandits in Milan* (1968) and pathetic, neo-fascist police inspector in Elio Petri's *Investigation of a Citizen Above Suspicion* (1970). Eventually, Brad, who kills his first man to save Beau's life, accuses the latter of weakness and treachery when Beau is unable, or rather unwilling, to kill a Mexican child during a bank robbery (masterminded by Brad) and is captured by Charley Siringo (William Berger), a lawman who has infiltrated his gang.[39] With his superior intelligence, Brad discovers how easy it is to attain power. Observing and to some extent imitating his new acquaintances, he succeeds Beau as leader of Bennett's Raiders and imposes a harsh regime on Puerto de Fuego, the community of

"Don't Buy Bread, Buy Dynamite!"

outcasts ("dregs of the old frontier") that Beau calls home. Ironically, when he first arrived at the commune, Brad had been struck by how happy and alive the inhabitants seemed, but not only does he trample on their freedoms, he is also indirectly responsible for the deaths of many of them at the hands of vigilantes hired by the local ranchers to wipe out Brad's gang.

For his part, Beau begins to develop a conscience for the first time in his life, partly as a result of Brad's teaching but more because he sees the latter as a reflection of himself, and is sickened at how violence has corrupted his soul. It's one of Milian's most restrained performances, making his passionate outbursts register all the more forcefully. Beau's "instinct for survival" has always been his guide – in that sense he is consistent with the actor's other major genre characters – but he has never been a cold-blooded killer. Brad's intellectual application of power, the use of violence as a tool rather than a means of survival, is something that his counterpart will never understand. By the end of the film, the protagonists' roles have been almost completely reversed, with Beau becoming 'civilised' and Brad the aggressor. It throws up the question, quintessential to Sollima, of just what constitutes civility and morality, and sets up a powerful and moving climax. Beau, having escaped from jail, confronts his friend in the desert, where he has led the survivors from Puerto de Fuego. When Siringo arrives and convinces the vigilantes to turn tail, Beau prepares to give himself up – he *feels* it is right, whereas Brad tries to convince him to follow his head, not his heart. When Brad goes to finish off the wounded Siringo, Beau kills him – "It was what I had to do" is all he can say, echoing Chuncho's words at the end of *A Bullet for the General*, only this time with Volonté the victim. Beau thus achieves moral and physical liberation (Siringo lets him go, realising that the real Bennett no longer exists), while Brad dies alone, his "great plans" of raising an army of outlaws dying with him.

Although it functions adequately as existential adventure, *Face to Face* has added potency considering its European context. Fascism was still very much an open wound on the continent, not least for Italians, and learning the lessons of history is one of the film's principal themes. Beau could be an analogue for Italy, inviting Brad – Nazi Germany – into his gang and swiftly being superseded, with the character, like the nation, eventually overthrowing the interloper with outside help. This interpretation underestimates Beau, however, who, while sympathetic to Brad, is never taken in by the latter's demagoguery, just as the free-spirited majority of Puerto de Fuego is repelled by Brad's ruthless methods. Throughout the film we are invited to question the traditional definitions of strength and weakness, both physical and mental. Brad's initial timidity is measured against Beau's bravado; Beau is accused of weakness for not killing an innocent child who happens to recognise him during the bank robbery; and Brad surrounds himself with weak minds – cut-throats

above: "Torture is important, Wallace, because it lifts the morale of the torturer": Gian Maria Volonté educates Lorenzo Robledo in **Face to Face**.
opposite: William Berger (*centre*) is the agent who infiltrates emotionally divided desperado Beau Bennett's (Tomas Milian) gang in **Face to Face**.

who brutally maintain his regime, eager for the riches he promises them. Sollima drew the central characters from memory: "They are children of my own personal experience during the Second World War, when I saw people changing from cowards to heroes and heroes becoming cowards."**40** Brad's perception of power is horribly twisted, rooted in the sickness, repression and dissatisfaction of his former existence (his superior at the school had expressed disappointment at Brad never fulfilling his potential – perhaps Brad takes this a challenge), while Beau comes to realise that the kind of compassion he may once have scorned in the kill-or-be-killed atmosphere of the southwest can be just as potent as a quick draw and a keen eye.

There is much greater discipline in *The Big Gundown* and *Face to Face* than in most competing productions. Their political themes are skilfully interwoven rather than imposed on the action; rarely does one aspect detract from the other, which is frequently the case with the humour in Sergio Corbucci's 'Zapata' westerns, for example. Sollima has proved himself to be an expert at navigating the difficult waters of 'ideology' and 'entertainment' – his judgement is equally sound in his downbeat crime thrillers, *Violent City* (1970) and *Revolver* (1973), the latter an urban updating of *The Big Gundown* with elements of *Face to Face* – but much of the credit belongs to Sergio Donati. Regarding *The Big Gundown*, Donati says that the finished movie is almost identical to his script. The main deviation from Franco Solinas's original story comes at the end. Solinas had his lawman execute the scapegoat *despite* discovering his innocence, to secure his own advancement. This profoundly pessimistic conclusion was rejected (partly, it seems, at Sergio Leone's suggestion) because it represents not just the death of a hero (something the genre had not entirely shied away from – Corbucci had already killed off his leads in both *Minnesota Clay* [1964] and *Navajo Joe* [1966]**41**), but also the shattering of ideals. For Donati, Sollima and the other left-wing artists working in Italian westerns at this time, ideals were as integral to the action as gunfights, dust and boots. So their more optimistic ending should not be seen as a commercial cop-out. They wanted to inspire their audience, to encourage opposition, to suggest that the system could be outfoxed if not actually beaten (they weren't *that* optimistic). "It was a time when a certain level of dissent meant something," the director has said.**42** To this end, the symbolic value of the peasant bandit-rebel is of crucial importance. Both *The Big Gundown* and *Run, Man, Run* conclude with duels between the knife and the pistol; of course, the more primitive weapon wins, and the significance of Cuchillo's victories is transparent.

Cuchillo and his cousins – disenfranchised and victimised, but full of cunning and defiance – personify the anti-establishment attitude of the political westerns and belong to a long-standing folkloric tradition in which the bandit is indelibly associated with the oppressed. Glauber Rocha emphasises this connection in *Black God, White Devil* and *Antonio das Mortes*, and the strength of the relationship is underlined at various points and in different ways in *A Bullet for the General*, *The Big Gundown*, *Tepepa* and *The Magnificent Bandits*. As well as representing the racial/social/political underdog – who had previously been largely excluded from heroic leading status in the western, whether American or European – these characters are related to the 'social bandit' of revolutionary-historical lineage, typified by Pancho Villa, and to the romantic outlaw of traditional western narratives. They can also be considered as cinematic substitutes for contemporary guerrilla fighters in Latin America, Africa and so on. Symbols of spiritual and physical freedom, they are always on the run, away from the establishment and the encroaching forces of imperialism and capitalism. For these figures the legal system is a tool of oppression, the strong arm of the state. For Cuchillo in *The Big Gundown*, the law is there to keep the bosses in comfort and the peons in their place. In *Face to Face*, big business and law enforcement unite to suppress nonconformism, as when vigilantes, acting with the tacit approval of the local authorities, set upon the assorted social misfits who live in the mountain commune of Puerto de Fuego. As far as the title character in *Tepepa* is concerned, in Mexico at the time of the revolution "the law is only for people who can read". This profound distrust of lawmakers, politicians, demagogic liberals and intellectuals permeates the whole sub-genre. Like Tuco in *The Good, the Bad and the Ugly* (1966), a closely related character, the bandit-rebel is celebrated for his wits, not his wisdom. Franco Nero's hired guns in *A Professional Gun* and *Compañeros* frequently mock the ignorance of their peasant pupils, and Juan Miranda is the subject of condescension in *A Fistful of Dynamite*, but in these populist adventures qualities such as refinement and intellectualism are synonymous with aloofness, arrogance and indifference to suffering. They may also be masks for exploitative, oppressive or even fascistic urges – see the Baron in *The Big Gundown*, Brad Fletcher in *Face to Face*, and George Bello Ferguson (Mark Damon) in *Kill and Pray*.

above: The wrong arm of the law: Lee Van Cleef follows a false trail in **The Big Gundown**.

"Don't Buy Bread, Buy Dynamite!"

What price heroism?

Whereas most of the political westerns' downtrodden anti-heroes are depicted as picaresque rogues, the title character in *Tepepa*, co-written by Franco Solinas, casts a darker shadow, and the film as a whole is more problematic than its contemporaries. As played by Tomas Milian, here at the height of his symbolic stature, Tepepa is a more-than-usually flawed hero, a genuine man of the people with an unwavering commitment to the freedom of Mexico who also happens to be a rapist.**43** His lack of conscience and accountability consigns this crime to the back of his mind and it is only the audience that sees the aftermath – the suicide of his victim. Other aspects of Tepepa's character invite an equally complex moral response, as when he tearfully shoots Pedro (José Torres), a lifelong friend, for betraying the cause. (Though nothing in this film is that straightforward: Pedro, his hands having been crippled, had taken money from the government to improve conditions for his son.) Speaking many years later, Milian recalled: "When *Tepepa* came out in Mexico (and they are very difficult when foreigners touch their story) I heard that they stood up and applauded at the premiere. They were very proud of that movie."**44** (Note how Milian's assertion conflicts with the view of Haile Gerima from earlier in this chapter.) But it's the anecdotal way in which the details of the rape emerge, and the discoloration of our eponymous hero, that leaves a bitter taste in the mouth at the film's ambiguous climax.

At first glance it may seem surprising to find Solinas rubbing shoulders with director Giulio Petroni, who had scored a major hit the previous year with the big-budget revenge western *Death Rides a Horse*, his first foray into the field. Yet before he began making films, Petroni had been a member of the Communist Party, and before that a partisan in the Second World War who had undertaken missions for the OSS. So the political themes of *Tepepa* would have been all too familiar to him. So too the sense of disillusionment and anger directed in the film towards the revolutionary government; Petroni must have felt similarly betrayed by his own government's rejection of the left in the years following the war, and eventually turned his back on the Party itself in disgust at the Soviet suppression of Hungary and Czechoslovakia. In his later years, however, he resisted the categorisation of *Tepepa* as a 'political' film, stressing instead the story's universal applications: "Where there are people oppressed by some government, and where there is a hero, there by default one assumes that the whole matter has to be defined as *di sinistra*, leftist. I don't want to stick to this limiting definition... I say that these movies are about *libertadores*, and nothing else. It is better not to colour them with too much political content."**45**

Although the story originated with Ivan Della Mea, a popular Italian protest singer/songwriter,**46** his friend Solinas reputedly did more than a little restructuring and rewriting of the material. The end result is a typically thorough and complex meditation on rebellion and counter-insurgency. By concentrating on the period immediately after the first phase of the Mexican

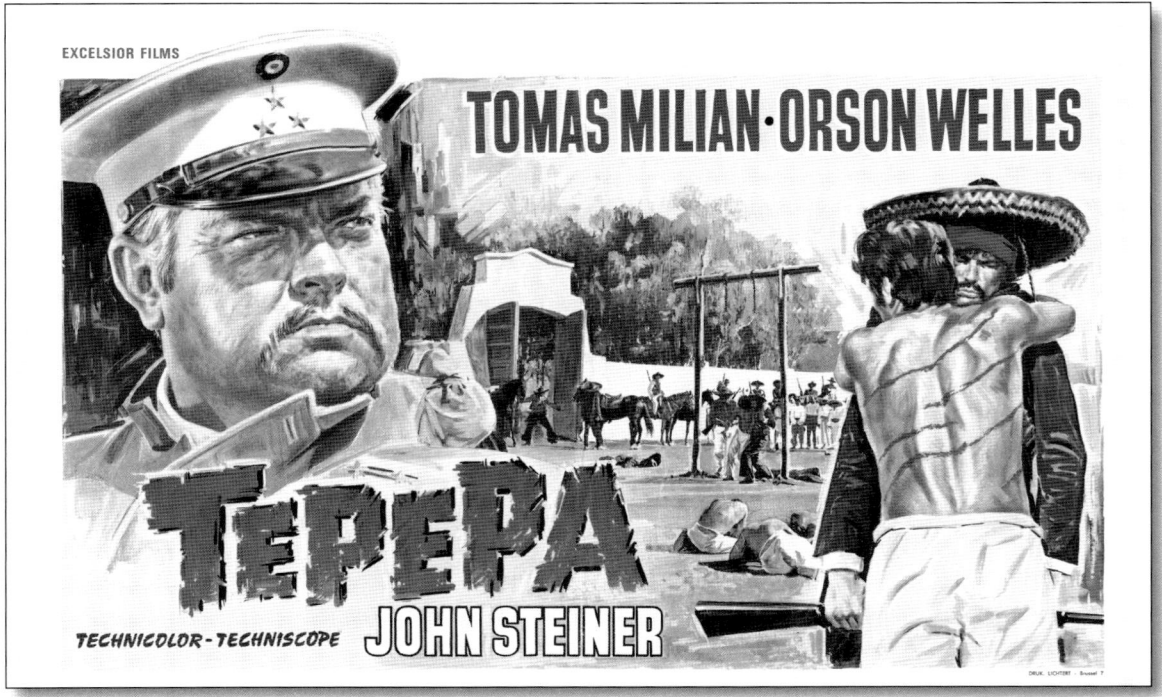

above: Giulio Petroni's **Tepepa** was one of the most problematic political westerns, with Tomas Milian at his most talismanic and Orson Welles typically enigmatic.

revolution, *Tepepa* spotlights the betrayal by liberal technocrats of the freedoms won by the bloodshed and heroism of the poor. Solinas and Della Mea are equally concerned with betrayal among individuals, juggling their political themes with a character study, a revenge quest and a mystery. English doctor Henry Price (a commendably understated John Steiner) arrives in Mexico seeking revenge on Tepepa for the violation of his fiancée during a revolutionary raid. The third major figure in the tale is Cascorro, the local military commander (played by a somnolent Orson Welles), who tries to foster Price's enmity towards Tepepa for his own ends.[47] Like other voluminous villains in the genre – Gianni Rizzo's crooked fat cats, Fernando Sancho's ubiquitous *bandidos* – Cascorro embodies corporeal consumption in true Eisensteinian fashion. Additionally, he symbolises the bloated arrogance and indifference to poverty of Mexico's military establishment – in one scene, he cavorts at a food-laden table with a gaggle of prostitutes, provoking a young shoeblack to foolishly attack him.

In common with other political westerns, this is a film of shifting moods, ranging from anger and irony to defiant idealism, but it accommodates them more comfortably than is often the case elsewhere. It has a non-linear narrative, with flashbacks frequently interrupting the flow of the story to stitch the threads together. Thus, when Tepepa dictates a letter to Madero, reminding him of the first time they met and of the latter's obligations as president, we see his memories and experience his bitterness. Similarly, Price's reveries are often intercut with 'live' action, as when he imagines Tepepa dancing with his late fiancée while watching the rebel cavorting with a wench, and we are invited to share the horror when Cascorro reads Price various eyewitness accounts from the time of the rape, finally convincing the doctor of Tepepa's guilt. (The film's literary structure and leisurely pacing – it is not an action-fest like its contemporaries – condemned it to some drastic cutting for international release, with around 30 minutes excised in the version released in the US and on UK video under the ludicrously reductive title of *Blood and Guns*.)

To reflect their own stance on Sixties world politics, Solinas and Della Mea give us a potted version of a crucial stage in the revolution, just after Madero had taken power. Having won victories in rural states such as Morelos (Zapata's theatre of operations), the insurgents were persuaded to turn in their arms. The script concentrates on the bitter twists that followed, demonstrating how the fledgling revolutionary government exercised no effective control, and certainly no moral authority, over the loose-knit, semi-autonomous rebel factions spread across the country. Nor was it in full command of the army. Given the increasing militarisation of Mexico in those years, which in itself highlights the instability of the state, it's no great surprise that where dialogue failed to encourage disarmament, troops went in. Madero is seen as unable, or unwilling, to deliver the land reforms he had been promising, and too weak to escape the army's embrace. This is implied in a key flashback scene where the president tries to reassure Tepepa that the army is at the service of the state, which he promises will represent both rich *and* poor. The rebel is sceptical but, in a symbolic gesture of trust, he places his rifle in Madero's hands. Significantly, tall army officers flank the diminutive Madero, their proximity suggesting the true balance of power. Subsequently, Tepepa and his fellow *agraristas* find themselves outlawed by the same regime they helped to install – it's the betrayal theme writ large. (The script mistakenly proclaims that Madero was Mexico's president at the beginning of 1911, whereas in fact he was still in exile in Texas at that time and didn't take up the post until October. Such laxity is forgivable – atmosphere being more important than accuracy in this brand of cinema – but it's irritating since this film is otherwise well researched. In defending himself from Price's charge of rape, the title character claims there are "many Tepepas" all over Mexico. Professor Alan Knight, in his exhaustive two-volume history of the revolution, mentions one "Gabriel Tepepa, a hacienda foreman... with a great local reputation, [who] rose in revolt, occupied Tepotzlán, ransacked the houses of the village *caciques* [political bosses], burned the municipal archive, and then made for the hills, safe from government reprisals". He was one of many southern rebel leaders to submit to the authority of Zapata in the Revolution's early stages, but was captured and executed by the planters of Morelos in 1911. Could this have been the source for Milian's character?)

There is a twist in the gringo-bandit relationship that is central to the political westerns. Steiner's Dr Price is not another mercenary, although he does share Tate's dislike of Mexico from *A Bullet for the General*. He also exhibits an inherent class bias, demonstrated in an early scene when, imprisoned by Cascorro, he perceives a non-existent threat from friendly fellow prisoners who happen to be peons. (The scene has an amusing coda in which Price is given a bed to share elsewhere with the guard's overweight wife.) Price never really overcomes

above: Tomas Milian in the title role of the tarnished hero in **Tepepa**.
opposite: Franco Nero as the cynical profiteer in **A Professional Gun**.

his distaste for the country, despite forming a fleeting bond with Pedro's orphaned son, Paquito, whom he tries to disguise in fine clothes (echoing Tate's treatment of Chuncho in *Bullet*). Nor does he manage to reach a consensus with Tepepa; as well as trying to convince Price to lend his medical skills to the revolution, the rebel has to deny his guilt and, ultimately, when at the mercy of the doctor on the operating table, mitigate his crime. This is where the plot takes a distressing turn. The doctor, whose aloofness has already distanced him from us, shelves the Hippocratic oath and takes his revenge, creating a moral dilemma for the audience. The hero is dead but has also been revealed as a rapist, one who even dismisses his offence – and women – as an irrelevance in the context of the conflict: "What is a girl compared to a revolution?" Where does – where should – this leave our sympathies? Tepepa's attitude was broadly in line with the macho culture of revolutionary Mexico, and the film was made before feminist politics made a breakthrough in Italy. Even so, it goes well beyond the genre's casual misogyny. Is it self-defeating to reduce this character, who has been built up as a paradigm of revolutionary zeal, to the level of a common criminal? Does this risk alienating impressionable viewers from him as well as from Price? Or is it a bold attempt to demythologise the '*libertador*', even to argue that any crime perpetrated against the exploiting classes is a revolutionary act – even rape? (This might 'excuse' Rod Steiger's violation of Maria Monti in *A Fistful of Dynamite*, in which, in sharp contrast to *Tepepa*, Steiger's character is practically applauded for what he does.) Perhaps Solinas, Della Mea and Petroni mean to challenge the viewer's own attitude and expectations, arguing that heroes and heroism, especially in the chaotic context of a class-based revolution, cannot be taken for granted. (In keeping with the realistic tone, none of the characters – save, perhaps, for young Paquito – is conventionally sympathetic.) It certainly forms a counterpoint to *The Big Gundown*, in which Milian's character also stands accused of rape but is ultimately revealed to be innocent.

In this case, Solinas shows his faith in the perpetuity of revolutionary ideals through the character of Paquito, who sheds the suit bought for him by his late father and spends the latter's blood-money on arms for the rebels, later shooting the departing Price because "he didn't like Mexico". The film closes with a series of rousing shots: the rebels ride on, Mexican flag borne proudly aloft, with Paquito at the centre of the frame and Tepepa's face superimposed over the action. The final image is a romantic one, with Tepepa on horseback silhouetted against a setting sun, suggesting not only that his rebellious spirit lives on but also that we *are* to cherish the memory of this tainted warrior after all, provided we can put his crime into context and accept that his priorities have been determined by poverty and warfare.

"Keep dreaming – but with your eyes open"

With *A Professional Gun* (the last of the political westerns adapted from a Franco Solinas story) and *Compañeros*, Sergio Corbucci tries even harder than Damiani, Sollima and Petroni to appeal to the widest possible audience. Both of these complementary "proletarian fables", very similar in tone, story and structure, faithfully replicate the relationship between a calculating, cultured mercenary (played in both instances by Franco Nero), who's in Mexico solely to line his pockets, and a naïve, instinctive Mexican rebel. Unlike the superficially similar situations in the films we have covered thus far, however, the contrast is played largely for laughs, muting the political message. Where Solinas strove for analytical lucidity, Corbucci's films project a kind of gut-level anti-authoritarianism – military aggression, industrial exploitation and parasitic foreign business interests all come under fire – that scored sensationally at the box office, even if they missed the mark for the majority of critics at the time. Even more so than most other revolutionary westerns, they veer schizophrenically between spectacle and sermonising, optimism and despondency – reacting to, or at least indicative of, the fluctuations in the political and social situation of the moment, both in Italy and abroad – and epitomise the ambiguities inherent in mainstream political cinema.

above and opposite top: Franco Nero tutors Tony Musante in the finer points of firepower in **A Professional Gun** – the first of Sergio Corbucci's 'Zapata' westerns.
opposite bottom: Tomas Milian – styled à la Che Guevara – spends a little time with Iris Berben as a student agitator – class of 1968 – in Corbucci's **Compañeros**.

Taking his long and varied career as a whole, it is difficult to determine to what extent Corbucci actually shared his colleagues' ideals. The films from his pre-western period – mostly comedies, including several pastiches of international blockbusters – are the work of a man with a sharp populist instinct and the kind of earthy irreverence common among Cinecittà craftsmen in those days. Friends and collaborators such as Franco Nero confirm that Corbucci, like most of his contemporaries, leaned to the left, and his finest western, *The Great Silence*, plays like an outcry from an angry socialist. Even his outwardly lightweight Johnny Hallyday vehicle, *The Specialists* (1969), contains stinging criticism of both the bourgeoisie, represented by the greedy, grasping citizens of Blackstone, and of hippies, portrayed by the director as indolent, apolitical wasters more likely to hinder social change than help drive it forward. So what are we to make of the frenetic, comedic nature of his 'Zapata' westerns, as he called them – qualities that became even more pronounced in the subsequent *What Am I Doing in the Middle of a Revolution?* Displaying all his customary showmanship and bolstered by larger-than-average budgets, he creates a form of politicised pantomime, full of chaotic action, visual puns, satirical barbs and hissable villains. (Step forward Jack Palance, who hams it up outrageously in both *A Professional Gun* and *Compañeros*.) This style was partly a return to Corbucci's roots after an unusually serious sequence of films – *Minnesota Clay* (1964), *Django* and *Navajo Joe* (both 1966), *The Hellbenders* (1967) and *The Great Silence* – and, as already stated, was not entirely out of step with prevailing trends in popular political cinema. Yet the onslaught of punch lines and visual exclamations that punctuate the polemics in his films suggests there was some uncertainty in Corbucci's mind about what type of film was expected from him. It's a very small step from these titles to the 'Hallelujah' films and other mock-political adventures that proliferated in the early Seventies.

Corbucci's statements point to a different motivation: "I was drawn to Mexico for two reasons: first of all because I've always liked the history of the Revolution, and then because of the fact that our films were called 'spaghetti westerns'. That bothered me, as well as Leone, Tessari, Sollima... This label came from abroad... And because here our critics regularly referred to them as imitations of the American westerns. All these aspects, and the fact that Spain, where we shot, was much closer to Mexico than to Texas, led me to embark on the 'Revolutionary Mexican' genre, a truly inexhaustible source."[48]

A Professional Gun – which endured a tortuous journey to the screen[49] – charts the unequal business arrangement between brash peon Paco Roman (Tony Musante) and smooth Polish mercenary Sergei Kowalski (Franco Nero), who agrees to educate Paco in the art of war in return for a handsome share of his gang's liberated money. In *Compañeros*, the sparring partners are Vasco (Tomas Milian), a boorish young rebel dressed to resemble Che Guevara, and Yod Peterson (Nero), a Swedish arms dealer. Yod is in league with bogus 'revolutionary general' Mongo (José Bódalo), whose methods are opposed by Professor Xantos (Fernando Rey), a pacifist agitator adored by a group of bratty, sanctimonious students – a depiction that reveals, perhaps, the director's opinion of contemporary youth, although the students don't incur Corbucci's displeasure quite as much as hippies had in *The Specialists*. (The setting of one revolutionary faction against another is an attempt to distinguish between genuine rebels and the numerous bandit gangs who used the conflict as a cloak for their own nefarious activities. Sergio Sollima presents a similar situation in *Run, Man, Run*.) True to form, the characters all have transparent symbolic functions. Paco and Vasco are the lumpen proletariat, which must be awakened politically and moulded physically into an effective fighting force.

above: Vittorio Gassman and Paolo Villaggio ask **What Am I Doing in the Middle of a Revolution?** in Corbucci's anarchic would-be tragicomedy.

"Don't Buy Bread, Buy Dynamite!"

Meddling in Mexico: Jack Palance's American hired killer (*above*) competes with Franco Nero's Swedish freebooter (*opposite*) for the spoils of war in Sergio Corbucci's **Compañeros**.

Both start out as little more than callow bandits, but gradually they learn from the negative example set by their avaricious accomplices and are steered along the path to revolutionary consciousness by the women they love. For Paco there is Columba (Giovanna Ralli), who joins up with his gang as his notoriety spreads, and for Vasco there is Lola (Iris Berben), Xantos's most fervent disciple.

As far as Paco is concerned, the revolution means one thing: "To kill the bosses and take their money." He enjoys robbing banks, and soaks up the adulation when he liberates a town (Columba sarcastically compares him to Simón Bolívar). Eventually, with Columba's prodding, he realises the revolution is neither a game nor a matter of individual gratification, and that the money he pays Sergei rightfully belongs to the Mexican people. "Paco, you've become an idealist – the shortest way to the cemetery," muses Sergei. Vasco, meanwhile, starts out as a bit of an idiot, gullible and gauche. In the opening sequence of *Compañeros* we see him polishing the boots of a bullying Porfirian officer, only to kill him after one insult too many. Shortly after, when Mongo's gang arrives, Vasco takes to shining Mongo's boots instead, thus switching allegiance from one form of petty tyranny to another. He has a patriotic streak bordering on nationalism that he only learns to moderate under the influence of Xantos and Lola; to his credit, Milian reins in his mannerisms to render Vasco as a more responsible, respectable character by the end of the film. He also seems to have attained independence from his partner, ready to fight Yod to the death rather than allow him to abscond with a sacred statue. At the equivalent stage in *A Professional Gun*, by contrast, Paco's competence is still being called into question. When he spurns Sergei's offer to form a partnership and milk whatever revolution they choose, it suggests that the Mexican has, like Vasco, emerged from under his mentor's wing, but the Polack still has to save him from assassination one last time. Sergei's final piece of advice to the fledgling revolutionary sums up the message of Corbucci's fables to idealists everywhere: "Keep dreaming – but with your eyes open!" (The suggestion that Third World revolutionaries will always be reliant on the assistance of more sophisticated outsiders would doubtless incense

above: Foreign adventurers in Mexico-based westerns were often depicted as parasites – symbolising filmmakers' coded criticism of imperialist exploitation. Franco Nero specialised in parts of this nature, though his suave 'Pinguino' in **Compañeros** is more charming than offensive.

Franco Nero (*above*) and Vittorio Gassman (*opposite*) find themselves up to their necks in trouble in **Compañeros** and **What Am I Doing in the Middle of a Revolution?** respectively. Sergio Corbucci (who was never afraid to repeat a gag) based these punishments on atrocities documented by Sergei Eisenstein for **Que viva Mexico!**, his aborted history of the country's upheavals.

above: Vittorio Gassman as an actor out of his depth in **What Am I Doing in the Middle of a Revolution?**

the Third Cinema lobby, but is in keeping with a tenet of European liberalism that only a tactical alliance between middle and working classes, a diplomatic accord between progressive forces in the First and Third Worlds, can deliver change.)

Both films decry the capitalist exploitation of underdeveloped nations, with Franco Nero's 'heroes' almost as culpable as the villains and their industrial paymasters. In *A Professional Gun*, Sergei bleeds his comrades dry – they must give up their food so that he may eat, and surrender their water so he can have a refreshing makeshift shower during a hot desert march. In *Compañeros*, Yod chooses his partners according to how much they can pay him – first Mongo and then, when their plan to crack the town safe falls apart, he turns to Xantos. "I can be very useful to you", he tells the professor, "with my complete lack of scruples." Xantos promises Yod the contents of the safe but the latter is disappointed to discover it contains not money or jewels but yet another symbol – an ear of corn that represents Mexico's true wealth, says Xantos, "our labour, our soil, our grain". Nero's machinations are presented very humorously, and this, combined with the actor's natural charm and tongue-in-cheek performances, paradoxically weakens the anti-exploitation theme, deflecting much of the ire his characters' selfish and duplicitous behaviour is designed to provoke. Compare this with the superficially similar *Queimada!*, in which Marlon Brando's Sir William Walker begins as a strong and likeable accomplice of the native revolution but transforms into its adversary, a slave to the colonial system he doesn't have the moral courage to oppose.

At least there is nothing equivocal about Jack Palance's interloping villains. In both cases, Corbucci can't resist furnishing Palance's characters with 'deviant' traits – Curly (*A Professional Gun*) is a stereotypical gay baddie oozing equal parts sophistication and cruelty; while in *Compañeros*, John accepts advance payment for a hit in reefers – but it is their alignment with the forces of oppression that truly invites our condemnation. Curly lines up with Garcia's (Eduardo Fajardo) soldiers, chiefly to get a clear shot at Paco and Sergei, an old adversary of his, but also to make some cash out of the conflict; while John is associated with the American oil executives who hope their dollars will buy them a favourable outcome to the revolution. The most explicit symbolic link between John and the predatory Americans is represented by his beloved pet falcon (an eagle would have been more appropriate), which he likes to feed with downtrodden Mexican meat.

Like all the sub-genre's would-be revolutionaries, Paco and Vasco require guidance and encouragement to complete their transformation. Parables and fables often contain a didactic figure whose function is to spell out the moral of the story and ensure that the protagonist gets the point. In the political westerns, this character is usually a wise paternal/professorial type or religious man, or a young, feisty *señorita*. Their complementary qualities – foresight, compassion, fervour, integrity – help to channel the hero's energy and aggression into positive action. Sometimes their names imply the sanctity of the revolutionary cause they represent. Consider Santo/El Santo/Xantos (from *A Bullet for the General*, *Killer Kid* and *Compañeros*), who instruct, berate and inspire Chuncho, Morrison (Anthony Steffen) and Vasco respectively. Of these, Santo, played by Klaus Kinski, is by far the most strident, his religious regalia juxtaposed with bandoleers as he equates the rebels' cause with that of Christ and their treasured machine gun with the power of God. In *Kill and Pray*, Pier Paolo Pasolini's Don Juan is a priest who, like Santo (and like Enrique Irazoqui's Christ in Pasolini's own *The Gospel According to St. Matthew* [1964]), imparts a kind of militant spirituality to the action as he 'directs' the eponymous hero. These crusading figures are accorded an unusual degree of respect in a genre that usually criticises or satirises the church. As a representative of the intelligentsia, Xantos receives notably harsher treatment. While he states his pacifist, humanist beliefs with impeccable piety, it's clear that Corbucci shares Vasco's distrust of "big words" and distaste for those who preach revolution without wishing to dirty their hands (the same message delivered by Leone's subsequent *A Fistful of Dynamite*). He demonstrates the futility of Xantos's beliefs at every opportunity with a verve bordering on ridicule, until, come the closing stages, Xantos, like his students, is forced to betray his principles and take up arms. Characteristically, however, it transpires that the gun he was wielding to ward off an enemy was empty.

The political western also boasts some of the genre's most proactive and resilient female characters, who use a mixture of feminine wiles and positive example to coax the men in their midst. In *A Professional Gun*, Columba chides Paco for letting a foreigner like Kowalski walk all over him, and even gives herself to the Polack to stir up the Mexican's blood. Later, she steers him back onto the correct ideological path when it seems that Paco will settle for being a bandit rather than a rebel. *Compañeros*'s Lola and *Killer Kid*'s Mercedes (Luisa Baratto) have similar roles to play (somehow, Lola falls for the 'charms' of the

oafish Vasco and agrees to marry him), while Adelita, in *A Bullet for the General*, is the strongest of all. A redoubtable fighter and passionate personality, Adelita – named in honour of the famous revolutionary ballad – more than holds her own when the rebels launch their raids. Far from being a mere camp follower or revolutionary plaything, she refuses to surrender to the dictates of men and is the only character, aside from Chuncho, to exit the film with dignity.[50]

Corbucci was making farces almost exclusively by the time he shot *What Am I Doing in the Middle of a Revolution?* in 1972. This film, a revision of sorts of Corbucci's *The Two Marshals* (1961), features another diametrically opposed double act: two bickering, misplaced Italians, ham actor Guido Guidi (Vittorio Gassman) and hapless priest Don Albino (Paolo Villaggio), who find themselves caught between the rebel forces of Carrasco (Leo Anchóriz) and the *federales* of Colonel Herrero (a walk-on part for Eduardo Fajardo). Stumbling from one chaotic situation to the next, the actor and the priest eventually stop their squabbling and discover the true meaning of revolution. While the episodic structure recalls *A Professional Gun* and *Compañeros*, the tone veers even more wildly between slapstick and sloganeering, with Corbucci trying in vain to have the best of both worlds. This unevenness failed to deter Italian spectators, however, whose loyalty to Gassman and Villaggio was underlined by the film's 1.2 billion lire box-office receipts – the third-highest taking for a Corbucci western, behind only *Compañeros* and *The White, the Yellow and the Black* (1975), which, like the former film, pairs Tomas Milian with an Italian superstar, in this case Giuliano Gemma.[51]

The result is a sporadically entertaining mess, in which the political subtext is almost imperceptible. Gassman's furious mugging – the actor sending up, not for the first time on screen, his own stature as a grand theatrical actor – is exasperating rather than amusing. Guido's 'skill' as a thespian proves useful to both Carrasco and Herrero – at various stages Gassman is called upon to impersonate a cardinal, complete with vivid red cassock, Garibaldi (one of whose descendants, it turns out, is helping Carrasco's cause[52]), and, finally, Emiliano Zapata. In addition, Guido and Albino adopt various uniforms in their bid to pass unscathed between one faction and another, firmly situating the film in the farcical tradition and forcing comparisons with Mario Monicelli's influential tragicomedy *The Great War*, in which Gassman, teamed with Alberto Sordi, had blundered through the First World War. All this role-playing sums up the theme of Corbucci's film, expressed rather awkwardly by one character as "the curious and bizarre vicissitudes of guerrilla warfare", but is basically just another excuse for a series of comic interludes.

Corbucci's anti-clericalism is more flagrant than ever. In *A Professional Gun*, the rebels had disguised themselves as carnival angels in order to mount an attack, while in *Compañeros*, Yod and Vasco wore cassocks to cross the US-Mexican border, eliminating a few sentries along the way. If these conceits satirised the sanctity of religious figures, in *What Am I Doing...* Corbucci reverts to base ridicule. Don Albino is portrayed as a blinkered bumbler, indifferent to the revolution, and throughout the film he is furiously harangued by the acerbic Guido. As Albino prepares to face Herrero's firing squad, a young revolutionary, posing as a soldier, assures him he will be rescued: "We help perverts and bandits, we might as well help priests." The director also ensures that Albino is regularly physically humiliated (at one point a bull butts him from behind), no doubt to the delight of blue-collar audiences.

Despite all the horseplay, there are still a few gruesome reminders of both the horrors of war and Corbucci's flair for the grotesque, from the haunting spectacle of the suicidal aristocrats already mentioned, to the sadistic Herrero collecting hands severed from rebel sympathisers. Later on, Guido and Albino fall into the clutches of the bizarre gang responsible for the amputations. This scene typifies the inconsistency of the entire film – and, for that matter, of Corbucci's political westerns in general – turning from crudely comedic, as when Albino, to save Guido's life, has to submit to sex with the hideous crone who leads the gang, to unsettling, with Indian peasants in death masks, each with one bloody stump, scaling the walls of the compound and massacring the perpetrators in retribution.

However seriously one takes Corbucci as a political commentator, the director voiced pride in what he felt he had achieved: "In my westerns there was always a bit of political reference, there were always revolutionary subtexts, a theme never really fathomed or truly appreciated by the Italian critics, in contrast to those elsewhere. Especially in Germany, where they've discovered me to be the head of a school of moviemaking, and famous intellectuals have dedicated incredible words to me."[53]

above: Corbucci's political westerns were anything but dry and didactic. Franco Nero and Tomas Milian – who sparred on-set and off – made a commendable comedic double act in **Compañeros**.
opposite: Locandina for Leopoldo Savona's **Killer Kid**, in which Anthony Steffen eventually allies with the freedom fighters he has been investigating.

Rebels, ribaldry and Requiescant

Despite the inconsistency of his work, Corbucci has joined Damiani and Sollima in becoming synonymous with the political western. This is due to the quality, integrity (in varying degrees) and financial success of their films and, crucially, the rewarding creative partnerships they formed with other prominent left-wing artists. But the greater importance attached to these directors' works, and their wider availability, has tended to obscure the contributions of others in this field, from the intriguing *Kill and Pray* by veteran Communist Carlo Lizzani, to *Long Live Your Death*, in which Duccio Tessari mounts an ironic attack upon the self-righteous radicalism he detected among his peers. These films are covered below, along with an unusual entry by the Spaniard Mario Camus, who used the sub-genre as camouflage for an attack on his country's authoritarian system of government, plus the Brazil-based *The Magnificent Bandits* and, finally, Sergio Leone's *A Fistful of Dynamite*, which effectively ended the cycle. First, however, I would like to look at some lesser known and borderline westerns that echo, even if they don't fully express, the radical spirit that permeated Sixties cinema and society.

Whereas most of the political westerns take place when the Mexican Revolution was in full swing, *Say Your Prayers and Dig Your Grave* (1968), produced by Demofilo Fidani's Mila Cinematografica, looks at the peasants' lot under Porfirio Diaz prior to the upheavals.54 Set in 1889 and opening with a condemnation of Diaz's "tyranny", the film shows little interest in the roots of the uprising, and quickly gets bogged down in a turgid plot that attempts to mix social issues with standard themes such as loyalty and revenge. Director Edoardo Mulargia, who would go on to make much better westerns (this was his fourth), fails to make this jigsaw fit together, and he also failed to inspire the leads, Robert Woods and Jeff Cameron, who do little with their roles as a reluctant rebel and cynical bandit respectively. The best one can say about the enterprise is that it avoids a romantic resolution – Woods's character, for all his sound and fury, rides off at the end having achieved nothing whatsoever. His tactical superiority and martial prowess, which would be enough to win the day in a more conventional western, don't even loosen the grip of the film's token patrician villain.

Leopoldo Savona's *Killer Kid* is another Mexican-western that is usually overlooked in discussions of the sub-genre, yet in its own modest way it is a particularly effective example of 'disguised' political cinema. The reasons why it is often ignored are also the reasons why its message registers with such clarity: firstly, it is packaged as just another solo vehicle for Anthony Steffen, the paradigmatic lone hero of numerous Italian B-westerns; and secondly, while its scope is considerably wider than is customary for a Steffen film, it doesn't subscribe to the kind of snarling socialism that was in vogue at the time. This is more of a liberal-humanist work, with an unusually romantic disposition, which treats the revolutionaries' plight as a matter of simple social justice; "They deserve a better life", as one character puts it. The absence of low-rent comic relief is a relief in itself: Savona's film is a serious, technically accomplished action picture that interprets the revolution as a straight-up fight between the rebels and their peasant sympathisers on the one hand, and the forces of tyranny, embodied by the oligarchic Mexican government and its brutal military machine, on the other. (A subplot about unscrupulous American arms dealers exploiting the revolutionaries complicates but does not compromise the film's simple binary structure.)

With Steffen in the lead, it is understandable that the script depicts his character's conversion to revolutionary ideals as an individual decision (it is also symptomatic of his love for a female rebel) rather than a genuine political awakening. His character, Morrison, is an American army captain who masquerades as a feared gunman to stem the flow of illegal US arms into Mexico. He is not the usual greedy, duplicitous gringo, but more of an old-fashioned brooding hero – Steffen's speciality – whose neutral stance crumbles as he gets increasingly emotionally involved with the fighters' cause. To the film's credit, however, the revolution is not merely a backdrop to Morrison's duty-versus-conscience dilemma. Indeed, a title card makes it plain that the rebels are the true heroes of the piece, although only one of them captures the imagination – a blustery but ultimately noble lieutenant played by the ubiquitous Fernando Sancho – and Savona steers a steady course between Morrison's actions and the story's wider issues with all the steadfastness of one of Steffen's own characters.

There are echoes of *Killer Kid*'s moderate political principles, as well as its sentimentalism, in the better-known *The Five Man Army* (1969), but the sincerity of Savona's film doesn't register here. Enterprising Italian producer Italo Zingarelli, well aware of the financial success of preceding political spaghettis, perhaps hoped that a sprinkling of liberalism would make his inconsequential adventure a little more fashionable. The script (by Dario Argento and Marc Richards) toys with popular themes – contrasting the avarice of the eponymous mercenaries, who rob a fortune in gold destined for Huerta, with the generosity of the peasants and rebels they gradually come to respect – but the main aim is to imitate big-budget sagas of collective endeavour such as *The Magnificent Seven*, *The Professionals* (1966), *The Dirty Dozen* (1967) and *The Wild Bunch*. It suffers in this respect from a lack of commensurate star power, Zingarelli drafting in American TV stars Peter Graves and James Daly, Italians Bud Spencer (then on the cusp of domestic superstardom) and Nino Castelnuovo, and popular Japanese actor Tetsuro Tamba, who had co-starred in the James Bond film *You Only Live Twice* two years earlier. There is an equal lack of directorial guidance – veteran American director Don Taylor was originally in charge, though it seems that he quickly deserted the project and that Zingarelli himself took over.**55** The plentiful action is competently staged (though the central train-robbery sequence, clearly modelled on the equivalent but much more suspenseful event in *The Wild Bunch*, takes up an inordinate amount of time), but when the film does eventually try to score a few polemical points through the philanthropic figure of the Dutchman, the mercenaries' leader played by Peter Graves, it smacks of last-minute desperation. Worse still, considering Graves's lack of authority as an actor, it completely fails in dramatic terms. In what should be the film's pivotal moment, the Dutchman explains why he's giving the gold to the rebels, but the star's oration lacks passion and conviction, robbing the scene of integrity. In the end, only Ennio Morricone's magnificent score has any genuine distinction.

In **The Five Man Army**, Peter Graves (*above, far right*), marshals an uncommonly altruistic squad – comprising (*from left*) Nino Castelnuovo, James Daly, Bud Spencer and Tetsuro Temba – to fight off Federales led by Carlo Alighiero (*top*).

To Zingarelli, temporary membership of the 'revolutionary cell' made good business sense; he was clearly more of an entrepreneur than an idealist – after making a fortune from the 'Trinity' films, Zingarelli diversified and bought a vineyard in Tuscany in 1973, going on to become a successful producer of top level Chianti Classico. Not all Italian commercial filmmakers, however, regarded entry to the political club as desirable. Like Sergio Leone, Duccio Tessari evidently saw little value in popular political cinema, and *Long Live Your Death* was his disparaging commentary on the pious tone and unrealistic aspirations of rival revolutionary westerns. But whereas Leone's *A Fistful of Dynamite* is a (mostly) serious work that jointly expresses the director's cynicism and the profound disillusionment of his more politically engaged co-author, Sergio Donati, Tessari's film is an out-and-out satire. A freewheeling combination of *The Good, the Bad and the Ugly* – a treasure hunt is the lynchpin of the plot, and Eli Wallach shines as another of his picaresque *bandidos* – with elements from Sergio Corbucci's 'Zapata' westerns, *Long Live Your Death* ridicules the notion of revolutionary idealism, not on the part of the fighters themselves, who are the only sincere characters in the film, but the do-gooders and interlopers who, in the eyes of Tessari and his co-writers, aim to boost their sense of self-worth by taking part in uprisings that have nothing to do with them. Having encouraged, and enjoyed, the mayhem that sees a lot of soldiers and peasant fighters slaughtered, Irish journalist Mary O'Donnell (Lynn Redgrave) tries to convince her unwilling comrades-in-arms – Russian mercenary/con

above: and top Duccio Tessari's satirical instincts hit the mark in **Long Live Your Death**. It fuses comedic/Euro-western stand-bys – uneasy alliances (embodied by Franco Nero and Eli Wallach), anti-clericalism – with a firm rejection of radical chic.

above: Eli Wallach immerses himself in another Tuco-esque role in **Long Live Your Death**.

man Orlowsky (Franco Nero, revisiting his Corbucci characters) and bandit Lozoya (Wallach) – to travel to Guatemala, where another revolution is in the offing. When Orlowsky tells her to shove it up her ass, he's not just talking for Lozoya and himself but for the filmmakers as well, whose attitude towards Mary is evident by the way she is regularly humiliated throughout the film.

The executive producer of *Long Live Your Death* was Mickey Knox, the actor, dialogue director, writer and translator best known for penning the pithy English dialogue for *The Good, the Bad and the Ugly* and *Once Upon a Time in the West*. Knox was a victim of the Hollywood blacklist who had decamped to Europe in the Fifties, and was assured of a warm welcome in Italy, where the film industry was overwhelmingly left of centre. (His fellow refugees included Lionel Stander, who also found gainful employment in Italian westerns, notably *Once Upon a Time in the West*.) A dedicated leftist, though never a Communist, Knox put together a package based on a Lewis B. Patten western novel, *The Killer from Yuma*, and brought on board his great friend Eli Wallach and the red-hot Franco Nero. Whatever contributions Knox hoped to make in terms of the script or the picture's political dimension, he found himself effectively sidelined as fellow producer Salvatore Alabiso had a script written cheaply, pre-sold the film and hired Tessari in place of Knox's choice, Sergio Corbucci.[56] Franco Nero had

top: German lobby card for **A Fistful of Dynamite**.
above: Japanese promo for **The Hills Run Red**.

vetoed that idea following a bust-up with Corbucci on the set of *Compañeros*. "Some of the footage [from *Compañeros*] that we shot in Spain got lost on its way back to Rome to be developed, and it included some of my scenes," the actor told me. "Maybe I was too young and showed a little resentment towards Corbucci over this." There are also rumours that Nero was none-too-happy with the attention his *Compañeros* co-star Tomas Milian was receiving.

Despite the scatter-shot nature of the plot and the ribald overall tone of the piece, Tessari and his colleagues are not merely soulless cynics. In juxtaposing the playful activism of Mary and the guilty stirrings of Lozoya with the real suffering of Lozoya's sister and the simple dedication of the rebels, the film calls into question the virtue and value of outside interference in Third World conflicts. There is also a hint of *A Fistful of Dynamite*, in the way that the bandit character unwittingly assumes the mantle of figurehead for the rebels. For the bulk of the action, Lozoya, prompted, for different reasons, by both Orlowsky and Mary, passes himself off as El Salvador, a legendary revolutionary. Like Juan in *A Fistful of Dynamite*, Lozoya's role-playing – instigated, in both cases, by other characters with no emotional investment in the conflict – results in a personal tragedy. But whereas Juan is transformed by the loss of his family, racked by grief, rage and guilt, Lozoya moves on far too easily when he discovers that soldiers have murdered his sister and nephew. (Played differently, this scene could have offered us a fascinating comparison between the respective acting styles of Wallach and Rod Steiger, his fellow Actors' Studio alumnus, who brilliantly conveys Juan's emotional collapse at the equivalent point in *A Fistful of Dynamite*. Had Sergios Donati and Leone had their way, Wallach himself would have played Juan in that film.) In Tessari's scathing vision, his protagonists, like those of other revolutionary westerns, are selfish and shallow; perhaps he doesn't allow Lozoya to dwell on his loss because that would grant the character a degree of dignity the director feels that he (Lozoya) doesn't deserve. Indeed, when the charade is over, thanks to Orlowsky's machinations, and El Salvador is 'killed', Lozoya is relieved that he can return to banditry; the people have their martyr, he and the Russian have a small fortune in gold. It was left to Leone and Donati to fully explore the emotional and ethical impact of revolution on those who take part. Tessari is primarily an ironist, and the film's concluding statement can be read as his unequivocal refutation of political cinema, its pretensions and ambitions.

The most offbeat of the political westerns, *Kill and Pray*, is a minor masterpiece – albeit misshapen by its typically mixed agenda – that examines how the spirit of revolution is transferred from one generation to another. Director Carlo Lizzani, forever dipping his toes in and out of commercial waters, was a Communist who had

above: Locandina for Carlo Lizzani's **Kill and Pray** that juxtaposes two of the film's principal themes – violence and religion. The addition of politics makes for a potent cocktail of prominent motifs.

graduated from the school of neorealism. An esteemed film historian (his book *Il cinema italiano*, published in 1953, was particularly well received), Lizzani began his big-screen career writing for such giants of the neorealist movement as Giuseppe De Santis, Alberto Lattuada and Roberto Rossellini, with whom he collaborated on *Germany, Year Zero* in 1948. His own early work as a director often centred on class struggle, and he believed that *Kill and Pray*, of all the political westerns, "most clearly registers the social tensions of the Sixties".[57] (Lizzani's only other western, *The Hills Run Red* [1966], was much more conventional. Its revenge plot pays partial homage to Hollywood while relying, like a great many Italian westerns, on coincidence and contrivance to keep going. Nevertheless, it is peppered with vigorous action scenes and, although American veteran Dan Duryea is wasted in a minor role, there are full-blooded performances from Henry Silva – making, regrettably, his only sortie into the genre – as the villain's exuberant henchman, and Thomas Hunter as the hate-ridden, borderline hysterical hero. Lizzani directs efficiently but with little enthusiasm, claiming to have made the film as a favour to his friend and producer Dino De Laurentiis.)

Kill and Pray's main themes of liberty, racial prejudice and social inequality are developed alongside the emotional and political awakening of its unusual hero. (This being an Italian western, there's a revenge angle shoehorned in there as well.) Lou Castel is ideally cast as the orphaned man-child name-checked in the film's Italian title. His religious convictions and garb and sweet, kindly nature – all absorbed, theoretically, from the pastor who brought him up – belie an instinctive talent for killing. As the film progresses, Requiescant learns that he has inherited his belligerence from his biological father, a Mexican agrarian rebel who was tricked and murdered, along with the rest of his people, by the wicked American capitalist George Bello Ferguson (Mark Damon). Requiescant, then a young boy, was the sole survivor, a scar on his head the only visible connection with his past. (This massacre opens the film, and is later seen again, in the form of a colour-tinted mindscreen, when Requiescant, in a delirious scene – "Like in some Living Theatre happening", says Castel[58] – realises the truth.) Ferguson owns the town of San Antonio, where Requiescant's half-sister, Princy (Barbara Frey, real-life girlfriend and later wife of Mark Damon), has fallen into a life of prostitution. Her predicament offers another reminder that in an unjust society, individual liberty is at the behest of those in power; it is not just the Mexicans in this scenario who are forced into servitude. Eventually, the girl is killed and the hero, spurred on by Juan (Pier Paolo Pasolini), a militant priest who leads a small group of rebels, kills Ferguson and inherits his father's mantle as a champion of the poor.

To develop his socialist themes, Lizzani wisely avoids putting his rebels on soapboxes (Pasolini's speeches are more effective for being succinct, although they are dubbed without conviction in the English version), relying instead on an old psychological ploy to expose the iniquities of capitalism – give 'em enough rope and they'll hang themselves. Ferguson is the embodiment of Confederate reactionism, a close relation of Joseph Cotten's characters in *The Tramplers* (1965) and *The Hellbenders* (1967), Major Jackson in *Django* and the slave-owning De Winton family of *Face to Face*. He makes the case for land reform almost by default. Lizzani provides his villain with ample opportunity to rail against liberal ideas like the abolition of slavery – just like his historical antecedents, Ferguson views emancipation as an act of suppression against the south by the north, whose own economy, he remarks with unconcealed irony, depends on keeping a low-paid workforce in a perpetual state of poverty and insecurity. So much for freedom, he implies.

Ferguson embodies the worst of both worlds. Racist and ruthless, he scorns the peasants who populate his ill-appropriated land as "monkeys", undeserving of liberty because they have no idea what to do with it except till a pathetic piece of ground. Ferguson's belief in his own superiority is due in part to the fact that here, as with the landowners in so many westerns, he has the law in his pocket: San Antonio's 'sheriff' is a stuffed dummy, and the judge owes his position to Ferguson's largesse. The character's callous disregard for the lower classes is chillingly illustrated in the film's stand-out scene, a shooting-and-drinking game set in his wine cellar, in which he and Requiescant – too inebriated to be fully aware of the irony of his participation – take increasingly drunken pot-shots at a terrified Mexican serving girl. The low-key lighting combines with Lizzani's judicious use of close-ups to heighten the oppressive (and almost Gothic) atmosphere, and the scene concludes with Ferguson beating his wife – who is as much a prisoner as Princy – when she berates him for his sadism.

Damon's colourful display of charismatic cruelty, which stops just short of eyeball-rolling exaggeration, is easily his best work in the genre, eclipsing the flippant gunslingers he usually portrayed. To puncture the character's self-righteousness and his rigid concept of honour, Lizzani and co. furnish him with all the signs of suppressed homosexuality, from the (unrequited) affection he feels for his chief gunman to his rabid misogyny – "Forget about women, they don't let a man think... women are... inferior beings." This is one of several instances in the genre where a member of the ruling classes or an oppressor of some kind is 'tainted' with homosexual traits (see also Jack Palance's Curly in *A Professional Gun*), pandering to popular prejudices if not actually revealing the filmmakers' own views on the subject. Either way, this suggestion

above: Accidental hero: Lou Castel, benign yet deadly, in **Kill and Pray**.

of Ferguson's 'aberrance' also fits comfortably within the film's melange of kinks and quirks – drug-taking, sado-masochism – which can be ascribed to a combination of cultural factors – this being the late Sixties, after all – and, perhaps, to the presence of arch-transgressive (and prominent homosexual) Pier Paolo Pasolini. (Two Pasolini regulars, Franco Citti and Ninetto Davoli, also appear, playing one of Ferguson's gunmen and an enthusiastic follower of Pasolini's priest, respectively.)

Pasolini himself, a close friend of Lizzani's (he had performed a substantial role in the latter's wartime drama *Il gobbo* [1960]), is fairly muted. His presence is more noteworthy than his performance, his character having little to do beyond halting the narrative at various points to pontificate about political responsibilities. To this end, he helps Requiescant to see the bigger picture – that justice will not be served by merely killing Ferguson, which would essentially be an act of individual revenge, an indulgence, something to be frowned upon in this context – and waiting for the next land baron to take his place. "Ideas have to be changed", Juan tells him in suitably dry, dispassionate tones, adding that, "Unfortunately, we [the disenfranchised] need men like you". There is some substance to this sound bite, which underlines one of the many dilemmas that peace-espousing activists faced in the tumultuous Sixties – how far must principles be compromised to enforce, and maintain, change? (Lizzani must have asked himself the same question when trying to reconcile the conflicting aims – entertainment and elucidation – of this and a number of his other films from the period.) It takes force to defeat the villains in the film, but the Mexicans have also shown the wherewithal and courage to organise – they're not cowed by Ferguson's threats or his insistence that they'll die as servants, and this offers long-term hope for the future.

It would be intriguing to know what ideas Pasolini put forward during writing and filming (Marco Giusti reports that Pasolini helped to revise the script, and also that the renowned anti-capitalist took no money for his involvement – just a Ferrari!); it seems unlikely that such a forthright personality would be content with being merely a radical figurehead for Lizzani's project. (In a parallel to the casting of Pasolini, Lizzani himself had earlier played a militant priest, this time a member of the wartime Resistance, in 1946's *Outcry*, directed by one of his neorealist mentors, Aldo Vergano. Another director of a similar stripe, Gillo Pontecorvo, performed one of the leading roles in the same film.) Whatever the sum of his collaborators' contributions, and despite *Kill and Pray*'s shortcomings – shared, in any case, by just about every other piece of agit-prop then produced – Lizzani clearly deserves his place in our 'revolutionary cell', both for his well-known political convictions and for this highly individual, provocative picture.

Redefining the western

The political sub-genre stretched the geographical confines of the western, and therefore the definition of 'western' itself, well beyond its traditional boundaries – even beyond Mexico, which had long been considered an acceptable setting for westerns by filmmakers and audiences alike. Giovanni Fago's *The Magnificent Bandits* and Mario Camus's *The Anger of the Wind* illustrate the flexibility and adaptability of the form. Fago transposes the style and many of the themes of the political spaghettis to a different Third World setting, Twenties Brazil, while Camus dramatises events in his native Spain.

Despite sharing its original title with former documentary-maker Lima Barreto's celebrated Brazilian drama *O Cangaceiro* (1952), one of the first features from that country to gain international recognition, Fago's film is not a remake but rather a simplified variant of the strident political parables of Glauber Rocha. Like Rocha's *Black God, White Devil* and *Antonio das Mortes*, Fago's film is set in the Brazilian state of Bahia, where exteriors were shot, and the script has a factual basis, focusing on rural banditry in the early 20th Century, one of many thorns in the side of the nascent Brazilian republic. In addition, Fago and his writers – José Luis Jerez Aloza, Antonio Troiso, genre filmmaker Rafael Romero Marchent and Fellini acolyte Bernardino Zapponi – give Tomas Milian's central character a quasi-mystical aura, again borrowing from Rocha, and make clear the connection between the feral *cangaceiros*, the land and the rural poor.

The story unfolds in a place called Agua Branca and concerns a young vaquero named Espedito (Milian), lone survivor of an army attack that, as well as wiping out a group of bandits, also accounts for some innocent farmers. After his recovery, aided by a mysterious, hermitic old man, Espedito undergoes a transformation – part spiritual, part political – into an ineffectual messiah-cum-militant, armed with a machete in one hand and a cross in the other. In due course he blossoms into a lordly liberator at the head of a band of brigands. As well as tangling with the army and crossing the path of the film's obligatory outsider, Helfen (Italian TV star Ugo Pagliai), a Dutch adventurer who has found oil in the region, Milian and his men violently oppose the self-seeking trade policies of governor Branco, played with unctuous relish by Eduardo Fajardo. Branco and Helfen conspire to capitalise on the region's oil reserves and manage to embroil Espedito in their plans. Promising him arms and aid, they trick him into killing off rival *cangaceiros* on their behalf – his machete duel with the menacing 'El Diablo Negro' recalls the ritualistic centrepiece of *Antonio das Mortes* – but Branco won't be content until Espedito himself is eliminated.

Beginning in the late Fifties, Fago apprenticed under a variety of directors and worked on a number of

Director Giovanni Fago segued from standard westerns – like the George Hilton revenge film **Full House for the Devil** (*above*) – to the political sub-genre with **The Magnificent Bandits** (*opposite*). Tomas Milian played a flamboyant Brazilian brigand modelled on the *cangaceiros* in Glauber Rocha's rural dramas.

Franco and Ciccio comedies. Having then directed two superior Italian westerns, *For $100,000 Per Killing* (1967) and *Full House for the Devil*, he was considered a safe enough pair of hands to take on this potentially risky assignment. Taking his cue from Rocha, Fago incorporates elements from two traditions: the characters have their roots in Brazilian history and folklore, which are evoked with a tourist's eye for surface detail, but they also fit snugly into the mould of a political spaghetti western. While this mixing and matching gives a fairly superficial overview of the social situation in Agua Branca, Fago's disciplined direction keeps everything in proportion, and despite its many parallels with 'official' genre outings, *The Magnificent Bandits* has genuine vitality and a beguiling exoticism. Milian's exuberance is infectious without being overwhelming, Riz Ortolani contributes a flamboyant Brazilian-flavoured score, and the familiar diet of betrayals, ambushes and confrontations benefits greatly from an unfamiliar backdrop of palm trees and shantytowns.

The filmmakers' political sympathies are, predictably, much more clear-cut than Rocha's, and the film as a whole is more schematic. The writers abide by the revolutionary westerns' doctrine: that social inequality is the root of all suffering. Images of poverty abound – from poor villagers swarming over Helfen's automobile in fevered curiosity, to Milian dispensing looted gifts to black townsfolk. Despite Espedito's dalliance with the governor, Fago doesn't invite the audience to judge the former or his actions. The character is learning and evolving constantly, and this is merely another stage in his development. Nor is there any sense that his error of judgement has dented his popularity with the poor, demonstrated earlier by Helfen's fruitless efforts to elicit information about his erstwhile partner from suspicious locals. The resolution is reminiscent of *The Big Gundown*: the Dutchman, given an inscrutable veneer by Pagliai, becomes sympathetic to the *cangaceiro* cause and alerts Espedito to Branco's betrayal. The warlord traps the governor in an oil plant and shoots him into a vat of black gold – an obvious example of poetic justice and another instance of a genre character consumed, literally, by his own greed, recalling Hagerman's demise at the end of *Django, Kill!* (1967) and the death of Claude in *Johnny Hamlet* (1968).

In terms of what our second displaced western strives to achieve, *The Anger of the Wind*, aka *Revenge of Trinity*, is a failure, albeit an honourable one. Director Mario Camus was considered one of the rising stars of Spanish cinema at the time. Along with contemporaries such as Carlos Saura, Miguel Picazo and Víctor Erice, Camus benefited from the progressive policies of José María García Escudero, Minister of Film from 1962-67, and from a slackening of the country's notoriously strict censorship laws. As in all areas of political, social and cultural life in Franco's Spain, the cinema was closely monitored for any sign of dissension or subversion. As the historians Raymond Carr and Juan Pablo Fusi recount, just as the regime manipulated the mass media, controlling the flow of information, "[it] was fully conscious of the potential propaganda value of the cinema and its dangers in a country where the cinema was extremely popular...[It] met the challenge by rigid censorship: a prior censorship of scripts until 1976, then of the final version. In addition, the ecclesiastical censors classified films 'morally'."[59] As in Italy, films were categorised according to their artistic (read nationalistic/conservative) qualities, with rebates against production costs available to the highest-ranking titles; in 1944, a special category of 'National Interest' was created as a way of recognising particularly 'positive', i.e. ideologically conformist, works. Even when directors did manage to circumvent the regulations, they could reach only a minority of filmgoers. As Carr and Fusi explain, "the mass of Spaniards were immersed in what we call the 'culture of evasion'... an escape from immediate reality... the role of the 'culture of evasion' was particularly important in a Spain of poverty and political repression". The regime didn't encourage this process, but "allowed private interests to exploit a consumer culture, devoid of political or intellectual content, and therefore innocuous".[60]

above: **The Anger of the Wind** was a story of political unrest set in Spain but styled like a western to bypass Franco's censorship board. Terence Hill (*right*) and Mario Pardo (*left*) played hired gunmen embroiled in a dispute between aristocratic landowners and impoverished labourers.
opposite top left: Klaus Kinski's bellicose character in **A Bullet for the General** upset the Spanish authorities.

The rules began to be relaxed in the late Fifties as part of the government's cautious effort to improve Spain's illiberal image abroad. Thanks in large part to García Escudero's enlightened thinking, popular films became racier (Juan Bosch's comedy *Bahía de Palma* [1962] is credited as the first Spanish film to show a woman [Elke Sommer] clad only in a bikini) and a new wave of officially sanctioned and subsidised 'quality' films appeared, giving the opportunity for directors such as Camus to show their worth. Making his feature debut in 1963, he tried his hand at a number of genres, from musicals to comedies, all intended principally for domestic consumption.**61** Co-financed by Italian Mario Cecchi Gori and dressed up – reportedly at Cecchi Gori's insistence – like a western, with correspondingly greater export potential, *The Anger of the Wind* was a case apart. Although the co-production arrangement forced him to compromise his vision somewhat, Camus nevertheless used the film as an attempt to focus international attention on the political oppression still plaguing his country in the twilight years of Franco's reign.

Many of the left-wing westerns mentioned in this chapter were partially filmed and widely distributed in fascist-era Spain, so it was inevitable that they should incur political pressure; it's only surprising that this wasn't more severe. Judging from their published reports, the censors simply didn't take the genre seriously, no matter what themes were being advanced, approving scripts and granting filming permission almost as a matter of course; despite its ideological bent, *Run, Man, Run*, for instance, was dismissed as just another "run-of-the-mill western with Mexicans". Veteran Spanish character actor Aldo Sambrell said, "The westerns were rarely, if ever, touched by the censors, as they were seen as pure entertainment."**62** Where cuts *were* ordered to finished films, they focused mainly on sacrilegious and 'immoral' content, from nudity and swearing to 'excessive' violence. (Before approving *A Bullet for the General* for distribution, the Spanish censors demanded the suppression of "*all*

above: Most revolutionary westerns, such as **Run, Man, Run**, escaped the censors' attention.

rude, tasteless colloquial expressions" and the removal of the shot "in which 'Santo' kills the 'priest' and the subsequent execution of kneeling soldiers".**63**) However, subject matter and political stance *were* targeted in a minority of cases. The inflammatory, Spanish-language lyrics to the title song of *Compañeros* – lines such as "Students, rebels, bandoleros/Let's go and kill, compañeros" – were submerged beneath sound effects, while scenes of soldiers and civilians killing each other in *A Bullet for the General* were edited, perhaps to subdue any possible associations with the Spanish Civil War. Therefore, despite the general laxity where westerns were concerned, Camus and his co-writers, who included the left-wing critics Manolo Marinero and Miguel Rubio, were still taking a calculated risk by pressing ahead with their project. As Spaniards, they would have been subject to much closer official scrutiny than foreign filmmakers.

The Anger of the Wind is set at the turn of the 20th Century in Spain's rural south, a region beset by agricultural labour strikes and anarchist unrest. Terence Hill, soon to metamorphose into the genial, beaming superstar of *They Call Me Trinity*, plays a hired assassin, Marco, assigned by the local Dons (led by Fernando Rey, Buñuel's bourgeois of choice) to kill a political agitator. He carries out his task but eventually switches sides, incites a rebellion against the landowners and is killed for his troubles. (An abridged version, in which Hill is not seen to die, circulated in some markets after the phenomenal success of the 'Trinity' films.**64**) It's obvious from which end of the political spectrum the filmmakers are approaching: the theme song, *Free*, is a paean to liberty; the director delights in scenes of collective debate and organisation; the justice of the workers' cause is self-evident; and the Dons are depicted as selfish, brutal overlords. (The film's left-wing sympathies were emphasised by one of its alternative titles, *Trinity Sees Red*.) Camus also works in a confrontation between the town's teacher and blacksmith, who represent the old schism between intellectualism and direct action. The structure of the film is similar to that of the revolutionary westerns but, even as he refuses to 'distract' his audience with the action and comedy that characterise those films, Camus's ponderous direction fails to communicate the urgency of his appeals. There's a lack of variety in the composition, the dialogue is didactic and dry, and Marco's *volte-face* towards the end – which seems motivated more by the affections of hotel owner Soledad (Maria Grazia Buccella) than by a sudden burst of revolutionary zeal – is rendered lazily. Long shots of Hill looking pensive against the landscape are hardly sufficient substitutes for convincing psychological motivation. Once again, we find a director apparently in two minds about the tone his film should take.

Even though the producers cut the film before it was submitted for approval, which may account for the rather jerky rhythm, *The Anger of the Wind* still represented a bold act of defiance in a country where open dissent, let alone political plurality, was anathema to the ruling authorities. Although Franco's regime was showing signs of liberalisation by 1970, the year this was made, Spain was still subject to severe repression and plagued by social and political discontent. Censorship tightened up again following a change in cabinet at the end of 1969. Martial law had been declared as recently as 1962, strikes were commonplace as the decade wore on, and heavy-handed military justice cracked down on the Basque separatist organisation ETA. Considering this context, the most striking feature of *The Anger of the Wind* is that the agitator, Marco's target, is not the gunfighter the townsfolk – and the audience – were expecting, but an idealist who tries to rebuild the workers' self-respect and preaches an end to the culture of slaves and masters. His incendiary speech, which is the crux of the film, has been attributed to the famed Spanish anarchist Buenaventura Durruti, who fought for workers' rights all his adult life and was killed during the fascist uprising of 1936. (Co-writer Miguel Rubio attributes the anarchist angle to Camus, with Rubio himself the source of the film's socialist perspective.**65**) If the Spanish censors were successfully duped into treating this cryptic, seditious film as a mere genre piece, as it seems they were, then the worth of the western as a vehicle for alternative ideologies is clear to see.

above: The theme song to **Compañeros** was modified in Spain to suppress its insurrectionary lyrics.

After the explosion

With one or two exceptions, the films we have looked at so far conclude on optimistic or at least open-ended notes. When we leave them, most of the rebels and their ragged armies are poised to carry on the fight against tyranny, having seen off their immediate enemies and resisted the overtures of their charismatic capitalist accomplices, most of whom have themselves come to respect, perhaps even absorb, an opposing set of values. Above all else, the revolutionary cause has been upheld and enshrined. *A Fistful of Dynamite* was Sergio Leone's characteristically pessimistic response to all this positivism. Here the 'cause' is not a romantic, abstract ideal that can be realised through solidarity, perseverance and heroic sacrifice. In Leone's view, previous depictions of the Mexican Revolution, whether from Hollywood or from Europe, amounted to little more than dangerously complacent fantasies, overlooking the enormous cost in human lives and ignoring the historical denouement – the betrayal of the poor by the timid reformers and hard-hearted technocrats who came to power at the end of the teens. (He evidently never saw *Tepepa*, which dramatises exactly this situation.) Instead, Leone, using the character of Juan Miranda (Rod Steiger) as his alter ego, expresses a more fatalistic viewpoint, which some left-wing critics at the time found reactionary: that revolutions achieve/change nothing for the poor. Rather than political ideology, the director's faith resides, as always, in male camaraderie and family unity; significantly, both friendships and families are shattered in the film by the violent events unleashed by the intellectual warmongers whom Leone finds at fault.

As Leone saw it, and as the film makes clear, peasants such as Juan are pawns in a game overseen, usually from way behind the battle lines, by blinkered idealists. Hence, whereas Damiani, Sollima and Corbucci shaped their humble protagonists into committed fighters, drawing on historical and contemporary revolutionaries for inspiration, Leone's advice to the poor is summed up in the film's Italian title: *giu' la testa* – keep your head down, and tell bourgeois revolutionaries like Mallory (James Coburn) and Villega (Romolo Valli) where they can stick their upheavals. (Not that either of those characters gets off lightly in the course of events – far from it.) Considered something of an iconoclast when his 'Dollars' trilogy first appeared, the director was now accused, in some quarters at least, of undermining the efforts of those in cinema and society who were pressing for social and political reform, both in his native Italy and throughout the world. While so many commercial and avant-garde filmmakers were trying to persuade their audiences to become actively engaged in political activity, Leone was advocating divorce. While this provides evidence of disillusionment on his part – at this stage in his life the director considered himself an anarchist, fed up with socialism and politics in general – it was not a reactionary attitude. Given that so little had been achieved since revolutionary fervour had first wafted into the air – the European left had failed to capitalise on the widespread disaffection that had erupted in 1968 and had miscalculated the mood among the industrialised masses, while left-wing terrorist groups like the Red Brigades had rubbed the sheen off the popular protest movement – and since, most significantly of all, power had been consolidated in the same old hands, the film's overriding aim was to bring the idealists and propagandists back down to earth by portraying the turbulence and tragedy of revolution in a more realistic manner. If this was 'reactionism', it was consistent with the widely misunderstood 'cynicism' that had marked the 'Dollars' films. (It has also been suggested that Leone may have been piqued by the success of rival directors in taking 'his' genre, something he had been quick to disavow, in a – literally – radical new direction.)

This is why it is important to put some distance between this film and the other major revolutionary westerns. It cannot be considered on the same terms because it was made during the death throes of the global radical upsurge, and looks back, with the comfort and relative clarity of hindsight, upon many of the arguments that emerged during that brief, heady period. Of course, *A Fistful of Dynamite* reflects upon a lot more than that – from the rise of Fascism in Italy and the atrocities carried out in its name, to the Troubles in Northern Ireland (where Leone was concerned, one revolution was essentially the same as the next). For our purposes, however, the film plays like a crestfallen coda to one of the most vibrant chapters in popular cinema history. This is why *Dynamite* places a much greater emphasis than preceding political westerns on the counter-revolution of 1913, when the military and the Porfirian old guard – with the support of the well-to-do, grotesquely caricatured in the film's opening sequence – brought to a violent end Madero's 'liberal experiment' and ushered in the despotic reign of General Victoriano Huerta. Whereas earlier films had made use of small-scale military reprisals to provoke the ire of their heroes and audiences, leading to scenes of triumphant resistance, here the army's crackdown embroils the protagonists in tragedy, treachery and overwhelming guilt, forcing both Juan, who loses his family in the film's most powerful and moving scene, and Mallory, whose idealism becomes increasingly unstable, to reappraise everything they have ever believed in.

A Fistful of Dynamite brings two opposing worldviews into opposition: that of Leone, who played no part and saw little value in the western's radical phase; and that of Donati, whose involvement was intimate. "[This film] is a creative meeting between Leone and me", the writer told me. "The world of Leone meets my little world, and the result is *A Fistful of Dynamite*. Leone was not interested in politics... the political side of it is my thing." That these distinctive artists, with their divergent beliefs and temperaments, failed to find common ground on more than a few points is at once inevitable and frustrating. It makes this Leone's most inconsistent western, an attempt to blend political theory with pathos that never really gels. The director's well-documented reluctance to helm the project, and his aversion to 'militant cinema' in general, leaves the film short of the emotional commitment and extensive preparation he had lavished on his previous westerns. And even though his unparalleled technical acumen – coupled with a substantial budget – resulted in the sub-genre's most convincingly chaotic depiction of a society torn asunder by warfare, the socio-political issues are not realised with the same conviction and success as the interpersonal relationships. These, by contrast, are rendered with a sensitivity that might surprise Leone's detractors, with the bond between Juan and Mallory in particular radiating more warmth, despite the characters' glaring differences, than any other pairing in the director's canon.

Not that Leone's initial ambivalence hindered his volubility once the film was released. His readiness to discuss his work, combined with his tendency to downplay the contributions of others (he was also, perhaps, flattered by the attention he had begun to receive from auteurist critics, although most reviews of *Dynamite* were lukewarm at best), have ensured that, in general terms, *Dynamite* is still perceived as *his* film. Yet while it is full of Leonean concerns, chiefly the central role in life of family and friendship, reflected in Juan's devotion to clan rather than nation ("My country is me and my family") and his pursuit of a partnership with Mallory, there is an obvious distinction to make between *Dynamite* and the director's previous works. In his other westerns, Leone was the maestro, conducting an orchestra of outstanding individual talents whose brilliant work helped bring his personal vision to mesmerising reality. It's important to reiterate, however, that here there are two viewpoints – the simple man, betrayed by false promises, his dreams of a better life for himself and his family swallowed up by the revolution; and the disillusioned intellectual, the radical who has been forced to reappraise his faith in the light of personal tragedy. The first voice is clearly Leone's, the second Donati's. (We can discount Luciano Vincenzoni, author of the principal draft and the source of much of the film's irreverent humour, since he has pointedly distanced himself from the political aspects of the script.)

Donati, whose labours on *Once Upon a Time in the West* (1968) have never received their due, brought a Marxist perspective to bear on Leone's last two westerns. In *Once Upon a Time...*, he explicitly criticised the callousness of big business personified by Morton and symbolised by his inexorably advancing engines. "The [Gabriele] Ferzetti character was a metaphor for the contemporary history of America", he says,[66] the power of Morton's dollars crushing "small obstacles" with as little consideration for the consequences as the bulldozers or wrecking balls of heavy industry, with Morton's physical decay signifying the corruption of his methods. The writer's emphasis on the human cost of momentous events, his attention to the personal tragedies swept into history's slipstream, is something that carries over into *A Fistful of Dynamite*, and he continues to stress his great emotional and professional investment in the film. "In *A Fistful of Dynamite* there is more of me – Mallory is my character. If you read my first mystery novels, this kind of hero is my particular hero. If you see my other movies, you would realise he's a character from my repertory – the unlucky hero, the disenchanted hero."[67] By 1971, Donati, like many left-wing thinkers, felt the same disenchantment, and his final draft of the screenplay for *Dynamite* illustrates, in his words, "the end of the illusions we had at the time of *The Big Gundown*".[68] Hence his almost fraternal bond with Mallory, the melancholy IRA bomber who has lost loved ones to the 'cause' before (and even sacrificed them himself, as in the poignant, powerful flashbacks to his time in Ireland) and for whom dynamite has become the only reliable instrument of change. We have already seen how the Irishman's rough-and-ready ally is as much Leone's character as Mallory is Donati's, and the interaction and trading of influences between the two is the film's strongest suit. His experiences with Juan are a catalyst for Mallory's moral subsidence, with the idea of the peasant educating his mentor being one of Leone's key contributions to the script as well as *Dynamite*'s strongest link with other political westerns. And while the argument that this can be considered the middle film in Leone's theoretical 'American' trilogy isn't entirely convincing, the devastating effect on the characters of past mistakes, painful memories, betrayals and shattered dreams does at least anticipate the third 'chapter', *Once Upon a Time in America* (1984).

above: Rod Steiger's dreams are shattered, and the fatally injured James Coburn's ideals go up in flames, at the end of **A Fistful of Dynamite**.

An unfinished revolution

Now that the dust has settled, it's plain that there were no victors in the cultural-ideological battle between those in Europe who saw anti-cinema as the most useful way of opposing the system, and mainstream left-wingers – from Damiani, Sollima and Donati to Rosi, Pontecorvo and Costa-Gavras – who used generic forms to attack entrenched values from within. Cinematic works certainly have a powerful ability to influence opinion but, on their own, the allegorical adventures turned out by Damiani et al were no more capable of altering policies or voting patterns – where these would make a difference – or, at the furthest extreme, inciting an uprising, than Godard's experimental diatribes were. What both *could* do was stimulate debate, and there has since been plenty of that – much of it, ironically, concerning the nature of the films themselves rather than the socio-political issues they were raising. Ultimately, however, where censorship and political oppression hampered the filmmaking endeavours of Third Cinema artists, in the developed world a combination of factors effectively extinguished the flames of cinematic revolution. We must consider global economic forces, changing popular tastes, the failure of radical groups to inflict serious damage on bourgeois rule, the rise of terrorist groups on both the left and right wings, the consolidation of consumerism and, more recently, the co-option of political/global themes by the filmmaking establishment, which makes increasing numbers of oppositional films and showers them with accolades.

The dampening of expectations on the left, combined with the demoralisation of both the working class and idealistic youth movements in the face of harsh political and economic reality, could not have failed to filter through to the artists we have been discussing in this chapter. Like any commercial filmmakers worth their salt, Italy's exponents have always been renowned for how receptive they are to their audiences' tastes and moods, and never more so than during the Euro-western's radical phase. When they moved on from the genre at the turn of the Seventies, three prominent left-wing directors, Damiani, Sollima and Lizzani, continued to probe the murkier aspects of domestic politics in journalistic dramas and crime stories, all of which were pointedly more pessimistic than their westerns had been. Sergio Corbucci segued into increasingly silly slapstick comedies that pandered to blue-collar workers' baser instincts without attempting to stir their political consciences. Many other filmmakers, meanwhile, switched from the western to the *poliziesco*, which absorbed and exploited the anxiety of everyday Italians at this particularly turbulent point in the peninsula's history and replaced the former genre's broadly left-wing outlook with an arguably reactionary, crush-all-criminals philosophy.**69** At the same time, in front of the lens, strident leftist standard-bearers Gian Maria Volonté and Lou Castel sought out scripts that cohered with their beliefs, the former with far greater success than the latter, while Tomas Milian consolidated his position in Italy as a counterculture superstar by playing rebellious cops and underworld scavengers in his 'Nico Giraldi' and 'Monnezza' films.

They might not be especially reliable as re-creations of revolutionary Mexico – with some being more convincing than others – but, as historical artefacts of a different sort, the political westerns remain valuable for the way they preserve the excitement and confusion of what has become an almost mythological age of protest and provocation, expressing the idealism and, in the case of *A Fistful of Dynamite* (and *Tepepa*, to a lesser extent) the subsequent disenchantment, of a generation. They succeeded in propagating the same kind of political ideas as more 'serious' cine-tracts on a scale that the latter, scorning entertainment and prone to didacticism, could never hope to match. What's more, with their period settings and fable-like qualities, these agitprop adventures remain useful as allegories, whereas other films of the period that portrayed the undisguised political reality of the Sixties themselves have become as dated as the popular slogans and fashions of the era. Even if one chooses to take their political content with a pinch of salt, the westerns' other achievements deserve recognition, including their challenging of genre stereotypes and the elevation of dispossessed Third World characters to heroic status, while their passion, energy and – in the best of them – progressive thinking makes many of the mainstream westerns, and even the revisionist ones, produced in Hollywood during that decade look leaden by comparison.

At the same time, despite their attempts to inflame opinion and despite the heartfelt belief of Damiani and some of his colleagues in cinema's politicising potential, films like these evidently had little or no direct influence on people's actions outside the cinema, underscoring the limitations of the medium itself and misjudging, in the same way as left-wing agitators in general, the popular momentum for change. Historian Paul Ginsborg surmises that at this time, "Vast sections of Italian society were impervious not only to revolutionary ideology, but even to a modest political awareness".**70** Sergio Donati, one of the principal figures in the sub-genre, acknowledges an honourable defeat: "Today I look with nostalgia, tenderness and a bit of irony at our enthusiastic illusions of those years. I don't think the political movies influenced real life any more than real life influenced the stories we told. This is true also for westerns: [there was a] big political influence on my Sollima scripts and the two Leones I signed [*Once Upon a Time in the West* and *A Fistful of Dynamite*], no particular proof of influence on the audience's ideology."**71**

"Don't Buy Bread, Buy Dynamite!"

footnotes

1 The quote about Milian is taken from an interview with Giulio Questi on the Blue Underground DVD release of *Django, Kill!*. Another performer worth mentioning is American singer/actor-turned-Soviet defector Dean Reed, who appeared in some East German-produced 'socialist' westerns (including one he wrote and directed himself, the semi-autobiographical *Sing, Cowboy, Sing* [1981]) but is much better known for a set of largely anodyne Italian entries such as *God Forgive... His Life Is Mine* (1968) and *Twenty Steps to Death* (1970).

2 For specific examples of the criticism levelled at commercial political cinema, see Frayling, *Spaghetti Westerns*, pp. 228-244.

3 *Political Film*, p. 138.

4 See, for example, the *Broken Arrow* school of Fifties pro-Native American westerns, the (arguably) anti-McCarthyite *High Noon* (1952), and the partial deconstruction of the hero in films like *The Gunfighter* (1950), the Anthony Mann series, *The Searchers* (1956) and *The Left Handed Gun* (1958).

5 For a (mostly) persuasive analysis of the American western's socio-economic implications and as a vehicle for raising class consciousness, see Patrick McGee's *From Shane to Kill Bill: Rethinking the Western*.

6 Several reggae producers and artists released records inspired by spaghetti westerns. They named their songs after genre films, stars and characters, and often adopted gun-slinging alter egos of their own invention. Many of these tracks begin with tongue-in-cheek spoken intros in which the artists issue threats and challenges to their rivals; the mock-menacing dialogue, often culled from the films themselves, jars with the jaunty, infectious rhythms. The legendary Lee 'Scratch' Perry instigated the trend with 'Django Shoots First', recorded with his band the Upsetters, and a familiar pattern of tit-for-tat releases, sequels, spin-offs and parodies soon took shape. Among the most interesting titles are Perry's 'Clint Eastwood' ("Clint Eastwood tougher than Lee Van Cleef!"), 'Sipreano' and 'Return of Django', a major international hit that reached number five in the UK singles chart in 1969, while Franco Nero and Lee Van Cleef both had tracks named in their honour. The Rudies' misleadingly titled 'Guns of Navarone' invites Clint Eastwood to a showdown, while Perry's rival Derrick Harriott let fly with 'Golden Chickens', an amusing riposte to Perry's posturing in 'Sipreano'.

7 The list of embittered, racially motivated avengers includes Gringo Martinez (Richard Harrison), half-breed hero of *Gunfight at Red Sands* (1963); the title characters in *Navajo Joe* (1966) and *My Name Is Pecos* (1966); Requiescant (Lou Castel), the son of a murdered Mexican rebel in Lizzani's film of the same name; Joko/Rojo Barrett (Harrison again) in *Vengeance* (1968); and Franco Nero in *Keoma* (1976). This is even before we consider the small army of peasant revolutionaries marshalled by Gian Maria Volonté and Tomas Milian.

8 Author's interview with Robert Woods.

9 Author's interview with Sergio Donati.

10 Peter Bondanella reports the efforts of the post-war Christian Democrat government to control the content of cinematic productions. See *Italian Cinema: From Neorealism to the Present*, p. 86-87.

11 Bondanella, p. 268.

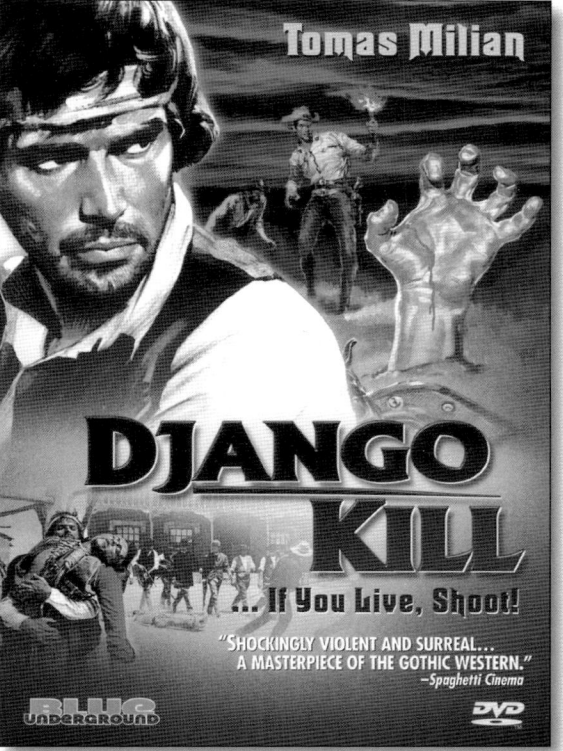

above: "The symbol of rebellious youth" – that was Tomas Milian according to Giulio Questi, who directed him in **Django, Kill!**

12 Many titles involve their protagonists in popular uprisings in Mexico, often incidentally and/or unwittingly, but the fighters' cause is always secondary to the heroes' personal concerns: in *Texas Adios* (1966), the vengeful Franco Nero and Alberto Dell'Acqua are waylaid by a popular uprising against the despotic José Suárez, coincidentally the same man they seek; Eugenio Martín's risible *Pancho Villa* (1972) has Telly Savalas playing the title role opposite Clint Walker and Chuck Connors; and *In the Name of the Father* (1969), *Bad Man's River* (1971), *The Great Treasure Hunt* (1972) and *Halleluja to Vera Cruz* (1973) are knockabout comedies that tell of greedy or idiotic adventurers who become entangled with Mexican revolutionaries. The era of Maximilian and the Juaristas,

above: The revolution was a vehicle for comic escapades, rather than consciousness-raising, in films like **Bad Man's River**.

meanwhile, is the background for *Garter Colt* (1968), a vehicle for the sultry Nicoletta Machiavelli in which, unusually, the rebels are the bad guys, as well as Giuliano Carnimeo's chaotic 'Hallelujah' films and *His Name Was Holy Ghost* (1972), and Gianfranco Parolini's *Adios, Sabata* (1970), all variations on the treasure-hunt format laden with corpses, sight gags and perfunctory populist sentiments.

13 Director Ettore Scola commemorated the conditions for workers and the tense atmosphere of these times in a 1973 drama, *Trevico-Turin: Voyage in Fiatnam*, produced in collaboration with the Italian Communist Party.

14 Paul Ginsborg, *A History of Contemporary Italy*, p. 313.

15 Author's interview with Gianni Garko.

16 Fernando Solanas and Octavio Getino, "Toward a Third Cinema" in *Cinéaste* vol. IV, no. 3, winter 1970-71.

17 Ibid, p. 55.

18 Haile Gerima, "Triangular Cinema, Breaking Toys, and Dinknesh vs Lucy", *Questions of Third Cinema*, p. 75.

19 I have taken Rocha's comments from an interview published in the summer 1970 issue of the American film journal *Cinéaste*.

20 See comments by film critic Ismail Xavier and actor Hugo Carvana in the documentary on the Brazilian DVD release of *Antonio das Mortes*.

21 The source for this figure is the *Guia de Filmes*, Brazil's equivalent of Britain's *Monthly Film Bulletin*.

22 Interview with Gian Maria Volonté by Guy Bracourt, reprinted in *Cinéaste*, Vol 7 No 1.

23 Quoted in Frayling, *Spaghetti Westerns*, p.229.

24 Interview with Gillo Pontecorvo, *Cinéaste* vol. l0, no. 4, autumn 1980.

25 Quoted in a documentary on political cinema entitled *The Camera Is a Molotov Cocktail*.

26 Ibid.

27 'Chuncho' is how Volonté's character is addressed in English-language prints of the film, although on screen in the film's full title the name is given as 'Chucho' – the latter seems more accurate when applied to Volonté's character, being the Spanish word for mongrel.

28 Interview with Lou Castel by David Pellecuer for a 2002 edition of the online film journal *Senses of Cinema*. Castel's enthusiasm for the project was clouded by his doubts over the viability of popular political cinema. "The Manichaean side of those westerns, their escapism and identification – this annihilates the reality of class conflict. And at the same time, it's a reflection of this conflict, in the sense that tensions really existed; this may be the reason why the western genre came into being. Still, the ideas remain hidden. Somebody wrote in *Cinéthique* [magazine] that the western was a 'hypostasis of the class struggle'. Yes, but it's like the Bible: invent a popular language in order to screw the masses even more, meanwhile obscuring the real conflicts of alienated work".

29 Luca Beatrice, *Al cuore, Ramon, al cuore*, p. 130.

30 Author's interview with Sergio Donati.

31 *The Big Gundown* was the first Sollima western to be released but not the first he had written. That was tentatively titled *Pistola da Vendere* ('a gun for sale') and was penned even before *A Fistful of Dollars* had been conceived. Sollima claims that approaches had been made to James Coburn to star. Unfortunately, the project was never resurrected, the director tiring of the genre after seeing so many released during the crowded year of 1968.

32 Although it was overseen by Vittorio Mussolini, the son of Benito, *Cinema* was, according to the left-wing Sollima, a hotbed of antifascism; among his colleagues was Pietro Ingrao, later to become the first Communist President of the Italian Chamber of Deputies, from 1976 to 1979.

33 Interview with Sergio Sollima by Mario Marsili, reproduced by kind permission.

34 Ibid.

35 The scourge of colonial France, and of Mexico's oligarchs, Benito Juarez's interrupted stint as Mexico's first civilian president came to an end in 1872, when he died in office. Many of the revolution's leading lights cited Juarez as an influence, with Madero naming a political club after him.

36 Quoted in *Spaghetti Cinema*.

37 Interview with Tomas Milian on the Blue Underground DVD of *Run, Man, Run*, 2002.

38 Ibid.

39 Sollima undertook detailed research for his westerns and his efforts for *Face to Face* yielded the character of Siringo, based on a Pinkerton agent of the same name who compiled his adventures in a memoir called *A Cowboy Detective*. Among Siringo's assignments was to infiltrate miners' unions on behalf of big business interests – hardly the sort of escapade to endear him to the left-wing Sollima, one would have thought.

40 Interview with Sergio Sollima by Mario Marsili, reproduced by kind permission.

41 For differences between the Italian and international cuts of *Minnesota Clay*, see *Target Practice*.

42 Interview with Sergio Sollima on the Blue Underground DVD of *Run, Man, Run*, 2002.

43 A parallel can be drawn between Tepepa and a later Milian character, Jed Trigado, in Sergio Corbucci's misjudged 'comedy' *Bandits* (1972). Although Jed is a despicable boor, especially in his relations with women, he is also something of a Robin Hood figure, shown distributing stolen goods in a rundown pueblo. Populism was a consistent feature of Milian's quirky anti-heroes, whatever the genre.

44 Interview with Tomas Milian by Eric Maché, *Westerns all'Italiana* no. 25, spring 1990.

45 Interview with Giulio Petroni by Mario Marsili, used with kind permission.

46 Born in Lucca in 1940, Della Mea was a leading figure in the socialist Nuovo Canzionere Italia, or New Italian Singers. He began writing songs in 1959 and was a prolific champion of individual liberty and workers' rights. It should be noted that Giulio Petroni stated that Della Mea had no hand in the script.

47 Petroni had only fond memories of working with the legendary Welles, who was attached to the project even before the director was and whose presence was, understandably, intimidating at first: "He followed my acting instructions without one comment or criticism, not one. What a man, what a professional." (Interview with Giulio Petroni by Mario Marsili, used by kind permission.)

48 Quoted in *Spaghetti Cinema*.

49 As Marco Giusti explains in *Dizionario del western all'Italiana*, the original script by Solinas and Giorgio Arlorio had been influenced by one of Bertolt Brecht's famous 'teaching plays', *The Exception and the Rule* (*Die Ausnahme und die Regel*), about the class differences that emerge between a rich merchant and his working-class porter when they have to cross the desert to close an oil deal. Tensions eventually lead to the merchant, perceiving a threat, accidentally killing the

porter when both are lost in the desert. The bitter conclusion has the merchant acquitted in court, even though it is established that the porter didn't threaten his employer but merely wanted to give him his last water. Reviewing the film for www.spaghetti-western.net, Simon Gelten adds: "Solinas and Arlorio's script was intended as a kind of three-act drama, about an American mercenary and a Third World revolutionary, set shortly after the turn of the century. In the first act, those representatives of two different worlds would meet and decide to cooperate. In the second act, they would slowly become aware that the cultural gap between them was too large, and the final act would describe their inevitable downfall and violent death." The director was to have been Solinas's friend and colleague Gillo Pontecorvo, with Peter O'Toole or Burt Lancaster mooted as the mercenary and Sidney Poitier suggested for the part of the revolutionary. According to Franco Nero, star of *A Professional Gun*, Pontecorvo decided that he didn't want to make a western and, together with Solinas and Arlorio, he simply reworked the story, altering the historical setting and clarifying the political message; *Queimada!* (produced, like *A Professional Gun*, by Alberto Grimaldi) was the result, with Marlon Brando cast in lieu of Lancaster and O'Toole and an unknown cast in place of Poitier. The original script, meanwhile, had been rewritten by Luciano Vincenzoni and Corbucci, among others, into a much more commercial property. (Some elements of the Brecht/Solinas story remain in the film, such as the rebels' arduous march through the desert in which they have to surrender their water for Nero's ablutions.) There remained casting dilemmas to be resolved. Nero remembers that originally he was to have played the part of Paco and that James Coburn had been lined up to play the mercenary: "I think that there must have been a problem over the billing or something like that, because I was very popular in westerns at the time and the Italian producer wanted my name first. Perhaps the Americans couldn't agree to that, but anyway something happened [and Coburn dropped out]." (Coburn, of course, eventually performed a similar role for Sergio Leone in *A Fistful of Dynamite*.) Subsequently, a chance viewing of Tony Musante in American drama *The Incident* (1967) convinced the producers that he was the man to play Paco, with Nero switching characters (author's interview with Franco Nero).

50   When *Blood, Money and Vengeance* editor Clark Hodgkiss and I spoke to Beswick in March 2000, she fondly recalled making *A Bullet for the General* and expressed a high regard for her character and fellow actors. When asked whether her socialist co-stars, Lou Castel and Gian Maria Volonté, made an issue of the working conditions for extras and crew, she claimed it was in fact Klaus Kinski who showed the greater concern. She and Kinski were like brother and sister on the set, the actress remembered, and would spend the nights dancing and drinking with local gypsies.

51   Source: Associazione Generale dello Spettacolo (AGIS).

52   The great Italian hero Garibaldi's grandson, Giuseppe, did actually work with Mexican Revolution architect Francisco Madero, and was the latter's first choice as commander-in-chief in the vanguard state of Chihuahua.

53   Quoted in *Spaghetti Cinema*.

54   According to Robert Woods, *Say Your Prayers…* may have been directed by Fidani, not Edoardo Mulargia, though he admits he can't be sure. And Fidani himself, according to Marco Giusti, did claim the credit. While it's possible that Fidani did shoot some material, however, the film as a whole bears none of the director's peculiar hallmarks, being much more down-to-earth, serious and coherent in content and style.

55   Mystery surrounds the true parentage of this film. Taylor is widely alleged to have quit the production almost as soon as he arrived in Spain, unhappy with the location and working conditions, and lured back to the US by the promise of a less arduous domestic assignment. What happened next is more contentious – one story has producer Zingarelli taking the helm, another that scriptwriter Dario Argento directed the remainder of the film, assisted by Enzo Castellari, and that none of the (minimal) footage shot by Taylor ended up in the finished picture. Actress Daniela Giordano, who has a thankless role in the film as Tetsuro Tamba's love interest, has stated unequivocally in an interview that Taylor did indeed leave – after just one day – and that Zingarelli finished the film, not Argento.

56   Knox recounts his unhappy experience on *Long Live Your Death* in his autobiography, *The Good, the Bad and the Dolce Vita*, and in *Tender Comrades: A Backstory of the Hollywood Blacklist*, by Patrick McGilligan and Paul Buhle, which also contains an entertaining interview with Lionel Stander.

57   Quoted in Beatrice, *Al cuore, Ramon, al cuore*, p. 159.

58   Interview with Lou Castel by David Pellecuer for a 2002 edition of the online film journal *Senses of Cinema*.

59   Raymond Carr and Juan Pablo Fusi, *Spain: Dictatorship to Democracy*, p. 119.

60   Ibid, p. 118.

61   One of Camus's lesser-known projects was an instalment of the award-winning Seventies television series *Los camioneros* ('the truck drivers') in which the hero, played by Sancho Gracia, takes part in a spaghetti western. Genre regular Ricardo Palacios played the role of the director and based his character on Sergio Leone, with whom he had worked a number of times.

62   Author's interview with Aldo Sambrell.

63   Censors' quotes taken from *Aspectos jurídicos de la censura cinematoráfica en españa. Con especial referencia al periodo 1936-1977* by Teodoro González Ballesteros and *La censura de guión en España* by Rafael Heredero García.

64   In Italy, *They Call Me Trinity* was released one week after *The Anger of the Wind* in December 1970.

65   Rubio speaks about the film in the book *Crítica cinematográfica española* by Iván Tubau.

66   Author's interview with Sergio Donati.

67   Ibid.

68   Interview with Sergio Donati by Clark Hodgkiss, *Blood, Money and Vengeance* no. 6.

69   Actor Gianni Garko turned down the chance to further his career in the *poliziesco* on ideological grounds, much to his later regret. "I refused a very important film in this series, *Roma violenta*… The critics were always writing against us in the western film, but they were more severe with the *poliziesco* because they thought it was a kind of fascist film. And because I was on the left, politically, I didn't want to do this kind of film. I also did some political campaigning for divorce with the Communist Party, and I was sympathetic to radical parties. For all these reasons I refused. Today, I have changed my mind, and I think that it was not a fascist film, it was only a film. I think this idea that a film can be fascist or not is a stupid idea – a film is a film." Author's interview with Gianni Garko.

70   Ginsborg, *A History of Contemporary Italy*, p. 341.

71   Author's interview with Sergio Donati.

above: Belgian poster for **A Pistol for Ringo** that captures Giuliano Gemma's title character in a typically surreptitious action.

Chapter 6

Beware Of Fake Guns

Spaghetti Superheroes, Alter Egos and Impostors

As heir to the dime-novel tradition, the Hollywood western has been disseminating the exaggerated exploits of legendary lawmen, pioneers and outlaws since its earliest days. These tales have been told from a multitude of perspectives, just as myriad actors have played the characters themselves. The numbers are impressive: Billy the Kid has been the subject of some 45 films, Wild Bill Hickok has graced around 40 and Wyatt Earp in the region of 25. Jesse James, often with his brother Frank by his side, has plundered trains and banks in more than 30 westerns, while that great showman and master of self-promotion, Buffalo Bill, has notched up almost 40 vehicles. This is before we even consider these characters' TV careers: Guy Madison, who later migrated to European westerns, starred on the small screen in *The Adventures of Wild Bill Hickok* (1951-8), for example, while Hugh O'Brian played Wyatt Earp in a long-running series in the mid-Fifties. Then there was the seemingly endless array of B-western films and serials centred on fictitious heroes like Hopalong Cassidy and The Cisco Kid. When the western was a Hollywood staple, the filmgoer's appetite for pseudo-biopics appeared to be insatiable, and was well fed by a filmmaking system that dutifully regurgitated the same old life stories of the same old legends, albeit with a slightly different spin to suit the particular climate of the time.

With a handful of exceptions, the European western wisely avoided these historical characters and make-believe Hollywood heroes, developing instead its own legends, a pantheon of mythical gunfighters whose exploits were that much more violent and outlandish for not being constrained by history. A precedent for serial heroes in the European western had been set as long ago as 1911, when Joë Hamman, a young Parisian who had worked as a cowboy in America and toured with Buffalo Bill's Wild West Show, mounted up as 'Arizona Bill' for a number of French films that ran concurrently with those of Broncho Billy Anderson, Hollywood's first screen western idol. Europeans had long produced their own cowboy comic strips as well. One of the first featured in Jean Renoir's *The Crime of Monsieur Lange* (1935), in which the hero's outlet from daily drudgery is the imagined endeavours of 'Arizona Jim' (so named, perhaps, as a tribute to Hamman), while square-jawed lawman Tex Willer, created in 1948 by writer Giovanni Luigi Bonelli and artist Aurelio Galleppini, is a mainstay of Italian *fumetti* even today.

There were satirical characters such as *Lucky Luke* (1946-), created by the Belgian-French pairing of 'Morris' [Maurice de Bevere] and René Goscinny, and Benito Jacovitti's *Cocco Bill* (1957) and *Zorry* [sic] *Kid* (1968), a zany take on Zorro, while later titles such as *El Gringo* (1965) and *El Desperado* (1968) betrayed the influence of Leone, Corbucci et al. Back on the big screen, the recurring adventures of 'Winnetou' and friends, the numerous Italian and Spanish 'Zorro' adventures that appeared from the Fifties onwards and, more obliquely, the impact of James Bond and *pepla*, all suggested the efficacy of centring a series of films on a strong single character.[1]

While the majority of Euro-western gunmen were indistinguishable from one another (and, indeed, undistinguished), several fictitious figures caught audiences' imaginations and quickly became successful franchises. Sometimes it was the quality of the original film, sometimes the personality of the actor involved or the character's individual style that elevated him above his peers. Frequently, it was a mixture of all these factors. The peplum cycle had already demonstrated the Italian production system's propensity to recycle its heroes, but the spaghetti western took this regenerative tendency to a higher level. The indiscriminate use of snappy, mysterious-sounding appellations in film titles was an easy, cost-effective way for filmmakers or distributors to associate their product with a money-spinning predecessor, at the same time creating a cult of personality within the genre reflected in the vast number of films beginning *My Name Is...* or *They Call Him...* (That's when the titles weren't proffering various amounts of dollars, though inevitably these buzz words were sometimes combined, as in *A Few Dollars for Django* [1966].) In many cases, these titles were misleading – just because a character with a catchy name and a healthy box-office record is referred to in the credits or pictured on a poster, that doesn't necessarily mean that he appears in the film, even though the dubbed dialogue may indicate otherwise. Indeed, most spaghetti western 'series' are conspicuously lacking in continuity or consistency.

For that reason, however convenient it may be, there is nothing to be gained by lumping each and every 'Ringo' or 'Django' film together, to take two of the most prolific examples, and expect them all to present a coherent personality or unifying thematic thread. Following the success of Duccio Tessari's 'Ringo' films, more than 20 unrelated European westerns used the name in their scripts or titles, some for their Italian release, others for foreign distribution. (In acknowledgement of this burgeoning trend, Tessari's *The Return of Ringo* [1965] was advertised with the slogan, "Beware of fake guns...") Ringo was not alone. With each successive superhero, be it Django, Sartana or Sabata, a familiar pattern of hurriedly assembled imitations and retitled re-releases took shape. The aim was similar to that of television serials and series westerns – to create the illusion of continuity, provoking certain expectations in the audience to keep them coming back for more, and engendering in them a false feeling of familiarity with the characters on the screen. Yet the various incarnations of Ringo or Django have nothing substantial in common with each other: they can be drifting loners in one film, lawmen, bounty killers or other 'professionals' in another. They may act alone or with a sidekick; it may be money they're seeking or revenge. Deceptive marketing was the only thing that firmly linked these figures and their films together. Not that this practice was specific to Italians or, indeed, unique to this particular genre; it was, and remains, the lifeblood of a certain type of commercial cinema the world over. Yet the European western is a particularly apposite example of the lengths to which studios, producers and distributors would go in their readiness to milk another's invention and gamble on filmgoers' gullibility for their own benefit.

Analysing the superhero sub-genre is like attending an elaborate masquerade. Franco Nero remains the definitive Django, for example, but the role has also been played, as scripted or otherwise, by Anthony Steffen, Robert Woods, Hunt Powers, Leonard Mann, Terence Hill, the future Trinity, and Gianni Garko, the quintessential Sartana. Indeed, if we were to include all the westerns that were repackaged as Django adventures in an 'official' filmography for the character, we would encounter just about every prominent leading man working in European westerns at the time. Clearly, with all the idiosyncrasies of the commercial film industry to take into consideration, we cannot make all the fraudulent sequels, spoofs and spin-offs 'fit' together. Obviously there will be familiar motifs – unusual weaponry and black humour, for instance – but these are inherent to Euro-westerns in general (and sometimes filched from other genres), and not the preserve of individual characters. (Having said that, any western made after *Django* [1966] featuring graveyard shoot-outs and a machine gun-wielding protagonist is clearly indebted to Corbucci's classic.) What *is* instructive is to examine the 'genuine' adventures of Ringo, Django, Sartana, Sabata, the Stranger et al, to see what it was about these figures that sustained so many sequels and inspired such a flurry of imitations.

Angel face

A Pistol for Ringo (1965)[2] and *The Return of Ringo* share the respect for Hollywood traditions of the first wave of European westerns with the revisionism associated with post-'Dollars' productions. The name Ringo alone signals an affectionate attitude towards the old west. Unlike most recurring monikers in the genre, it has a firm historical basis – notorious gunfighter Johnny Ringo was involved in a long-running dispute with the Earp family and may have taken part in the O.K. Corral confrontation. He has been played on screen by, among others, John Ireland in *Gunfight at the O.K. Corral* (1957) and Michael Biehn in *Tombstone* (1993), while famous fictitious Ringos include John Wayne's good-badman in *Stagecoach* (1939) and Gregory Peck's world-weary title character in *The Gunfighter* (1950). ('Ringo' had added currency in the mid-Sixties due to *Bonanza* star Lorne Greene's song of the same name, which reached the top of the American singles chart in December 1964. *A Pistol for Ringo*'s theme song, 'Angel Face', was also successfully released as a single in Italy, while in the same year other 'Ringo' songs to reach the Italian top 30 were recorded by singer/actor Adriano Celentano – it featured in the musical western *A Fistful of Songs* [1966] – and crooner Bobby Solo, whose 'Ringo dove vai?' was the theme to Alberto De Martino's *$100,000 for Ringo* [1965].) Director Duccio Tessari's evident admiration for his Hollywood forebears is further reflected in the style and content of the films themselves, which contain more than their share of dime-novel dialogue, stock situations and characterisations, from a square-jawed sheriff and Indian medicine man to virtuous blondes and wicked brunettes. More importantly, Tessari's largely successful integration of seemingly incompatible ingredients established him as one of the leading lights of the Italian western, and proved that there were more than just Leone imitators waiting in the wings. Tessari's approach to the genre was quite different from that of his close associate. As Tessari was quoted at the time, "Leone... really believes in what he does and I don't." (Leone, who

Poetic licence: **The Return of Ringo** channels Homer, as Giuliano Gemma's surrogate Oedipus wrecks the plans of stricken 'suitor' George Martin (*above*). With Gemma are (*from left*) Lorella De Luca, Mónica Sugranes and Pajarito. The film's star is rendered dynamically on this Italian locandina (*right*).
opposite top: Duccio Tessari's **A Pistol for Ringo** subjected aspects of classic American westerns to sardonic Italian scrutiny, refining the idea of the trickster hero – already seen in **A Fistful of Dollars** – in the process.

was generally dismissive of Italian westerns other than his own, underlined Tessari's assertion, belittling *A Pistol for Ringo* for its "sophomoric tone; it was all a joke announced and delivered in the very first frame".) This despite the fact that they had served similar apprenticeships and had worked on some of the same projects: Tessari had been one of Leone's writing partners in the peplum days (they had collaborated on *The Last Days of Pompeii* [1959] and Sergio Corbucci's *Romulus and Remus* [1961]), and assisted him on the treatment of *A Fistful of Dollars* (1964).

As he had already demonstrated with his first film, the playful peplum *Sons of Thunder* (1962), Tessari was both a parodist *par excellence* and a gifted filmmaker. This combination yielded two outstanding westerns with contrasting qualities, shot either back-to-back or within a year of each other (see note) on Italian and Spanish locations (many of the exteriors were lensed at co-producer Alfonso Balcázar's 'Esplugas City' site near Barcelona) with practically identical casts and crews.[3] (The same company went on to make a jaunty spy spoof, *Kiss Kiss... Bang Bang*, released in 1966.) Tessari provided taut, well-constructed screenplays for both films, aided in the sequel by prolific western screenwriter and future noir/poliziesco specialist Fernando Di Leo. Tessari, like Leone, successfully incorporates a range of 'classical' influences within his schema, from the westerns of Ford and Hawks to Homer's *Odyssey*, and shifts skilfully between comic and dramatic modes. *A Pistol for Ringo* – inspired, in part, by Tessari's desire to transpose William Wyler's siege thriller *The Desperate Hours* (1955) to the West – presents a beautifully poised encounter between the old codes and characters of the American western and the cynical, hard-hearted rogues of the European variety.[4] *The Return of Ringo*, on the other hand, is a much darker film, preoccupied with notions of identity, betrayal, courage and retribution. The films' different moods are immediately established by their respective ballads, both crooned by Italian pop star Maurizio Graf. The first one, accompanied by a wistful Ennio Morricone guitar piece, speaks of "springtime" and "green fields", while the second depicts Ringo as a plaintive figure "with downcast eyes and ragged clothes", Morricone's music alternately gloomy and melodramatic.

Giuliano Gemma, the athletic young star of *Sons of Thunder*, gladly seized the chance to work with Tessari again, although American actor Robert Woods says that *he* was the first choice for the role of Ringo, not Gemma. Woods turned it down owing to a prior falling-out with Alfonso Balcázar, with whom he'd previously made the popular *$5,000 on the Ace* (1964). "Duccio Tessari came and asked me if I would do it, but it was with Alfonso and I said 'no way'. So they got Giuliano Gemma and changed his name to 'Montgomery Wood', because of me... [Giuliano] admits freely that if Tessari could have taken me he probably would have, but he [Gemma] had a huge success after that."**5** Gemma's character may be called Ringo in both films (although he's referred to by a different name in the second), but otherwise the roles are dissimilar. In *A Pistol for Ringo*, the title character is a flippant, carefree mercenary, nicknamed Angel Face, who acts out of self-interest. In line with Tessari's satirical take on western conventions, Ringo mark one is an amiable, unusually talkative, amoral counterpoint to the noble, tight-lipped Hollywood hero of yore, embodied here by the character of the sheriff. In *The Return of Ringo*, on the other hand, the protagonist is a man in crisis, an Odysseus of the plains who has to fight not only against tyranny but also to recover his own identity – as does Gemma himself, his performance and shabby appearance in the first part of the film contrasting with his usual upbeat, clean-shaven persona. Ringo mark two is much more vulnerable than his predecessor: late in the film he admits that he needs help to defeat his enemies, a rare confession of weakness from a western protagonist whatever his cultural origins.

A Pistol for Ringo shows the genre still in the process of developing its own personality. The plot has Ringo agreeing to infiltrate a bandit gang that has invaded the home of a local notable, at Christmas time no less, in return for a share of the criminals' loot. In many ways

above: Giuliano Gemma, bloodied but cheerfully unbowed, in a scene from **A Pistol for Ringo**, with Nazzareno Zamperla (*left*) and Fernando Sancho (*right*) as the desperado manipulated and ultimately defeated by Gemma's machinations.

he's like a child: we first see him playing hopscotch with a group of children, pausing only to gun down the Benson gang who have tracked him down to settle a score; he has a casual disregard for danger, drinks milk at the bar (the preferred tipple of ironic western heroes ever since *Destry Rides Again* [1939]), and has an insolent streak a mile wide. His opportunism is evident early on, when he exploits both the urgency of the hostage situation and the authorities' need of his services to secure a speedy self-defence verdict over the Benson killings. He is another of the genre's Harlequins, treating life and all its dangers and distractions in the manner of a game.

The film is contrived as a series of oppositions that highlight the differences between conventional western morality and the casual amorality that would come to define the Italian version. The most obvious contrast is between Fernando Sancho's gruff, brutal bandits and their unwilling hosts, the aristocratic Major Clyde (Antonio Casas) and his daughter, Ruby (Lorella De Luca, Tessari's wife, acting as 'Hally Hammond'), who treat the affair like a slightly distasteful social gathering. Even the random violence of the villains, which includes a macabre sweepstake in which the hacienda workers' lives are at stake, fails to dampen the Major's Christmas spirit. Nor does it deflect him from his infatuation with Sancho's girl, Dolores (Nieves Navarro, wife of producer Luciano Ercoli), who is swept away by his gentlemanly charm. Their unlikely mutual attraction is the source of some affecting comedic business, as when Dolores is momentarily taken aback when the Major presumes she'll want hot water for a bath, then remembers the occasion: "Oh yes, tomorrow's Christmas." Tessari has further fun observing the clash between Dolores and Ruby, who is appalled at the latter's indulgence of Major Clyde's affections. But the most interesting skirmishes involve Ringo. While his relationship with Sancho is played mainly for laughs, with the bandit driven to distraction by Ringo's brazen, impudent manner, and his seemingly callous opinions offend the prim and proper Ruby, he and the sheriff, Dan (George Martin), are incompatible on a more fundamental level. Dan belongs to an outmoded class of upstanding, straight-talking Hollywood heroes. He deplores Ringo's self-centred attitude. "Words like honour and justice don't have any meaning for men like him," he chides, a criticism that could apply to any number of spaghetti western gunslingers, but his words ricochet off Ringo's armour of cynicism and self-confidence.

Ringo's philosophy, which he expresses with a series of witty aphorisms, is centred on self-preservation and the accumulation of wealth. He won't risk his neck unless there's money to be made – "it's a matter of principle" is his ironic explanation – and is always willing to abandon a lost cause, a trait inherited from his father who, he informs us with pride, switched allegiance in the Civil War when the odds favoured the north. When the sheriff

above: Back from the dead: Giuliano Gemma's 'rebirth', directed with a flourish by Duccio Tessari, is the highpoint of **The Return of Ringo** and one of the genre's most stirring examples of the resurrection motif.

advocates another old-fashioned virtue, compassion, Ringo brands him "as sentimental as a schoolgirl"; of course, Ringo is proved right, as the only way to defeat villains of the order of Sancho is with guile, cunning and, ultimately, brute force. "God created men equal," he observes, "the six gun made 'em different," a variation on a mid-19th-Century proverb that marked the popularity of the west's most famous firearm: "God created man, but it was Sam Colt's revolver that made him equal." Compassion has a restricted role in Tessari's vision of the west, though the film is nowhere near as bleak or cynical as the 'Dollars' trilogy. Tessari's treatment is at once impious and affectionate; he toys with tradition where Leone tore it down. As Gemma summarises the distinction between the directors, "Both combined violence with irony, but Leone accentuated the violence and Tessari accentuated the irony."[6]

The affable Gemma was clearly on the same wavelength as his director, sacrificing none of his natural charm even as he revels in his character's moral shortcomings. Ringo is very much an anti-hero, yet he maintains an aura of innocence, unencumbered by emotional or ethical dilemmas. To him, everything is a game – even the way he kills Sancho is frivolous, using an antique pistol and deflecting his shot off a bell. (Gemma, an aficionado of vintage weaponry, must have especially enjoyed this scene.) The role was a welcome deviation from the more straightforward figures Gemma portrayed in two other westerns from

above: Giuliano Gemma gets the drop on Fernando Sancho in Michele Lupo's **Arizona Colt**, in which the stars practically reprise their roles from **A Pistol for Ringo** – Gemma as another cocksure gunman with a catchphrase, Sancho as another gruff bandido.

the same year, Giorgio Ferroni's *One Silver Dollar* and Giorgio Stegani's *Adios Gringo*, which both focus on victims of injustice who strive to prove their innocence. Although he went on to play a similar crusading type in several subsequent westerns, Gemma mimicked Ringo's effrontery in a film written especially for him, Michele Lupo's irreverent *Arizona Colt* (1966). Here, Gemma plays another sardonic, milk-drinking gunslinger who once again outfoxes a gang led by a flustered Fernando Sancho. Ernesto Gastaldi's script apes many aspects of *A Pistol for Ringo*. The hero-as-Harlequin motif is once again pronounced, with the flamboyant Arizona (who has a catchphrase of his own – "I'll have to think about it") toying with his opponents, literally and figuratively disarming other characters with his pistol skills, sharp wits and trickery – wearing fake arms for the final shootout, for example, fooling Sancho and his lieutenants into lowering their guard. Not the least of the film's pleasures is the confrontation between Gemma and beefy bad guy Giovanni 'Nello' Pazzafini, who plays Sancho's right-hand man. Pazzafini, an athlete and stunt performer as well as an actor, proved the perfect foil for his limber co-star in a number of films, and here their typically testy relationship culminates in a mighty punch-up. Gemma recalls his friend with great affection. "Whenever we fought together in a film, he always had to lose, although he was much bigger than I was. The concierge in the apartment block where he lived always said, 'Oh no, not again! Why does he always win?' So Pazzafini said to me, 'You have to do me a favour: one day, come to lunch at my house and when we pass the concierge I'll box your ears and tell you to get a move on.' And so we did this and then he turned to the concierge and said, 'See? I can hit him whenever I want!'"[7]

The Return of Ringo gave Gemma the chance to prove there was more to him than mischievousness, and showed that Tessari was capable of more than just gentle mockery. The star was immediately struck by the differences between this script and its predecessor. "I said to [Tessari], 'This is a different film. We're using the name Ringo but the character has nothing to do with the Ringo from the first film. And he answered that it depended on the market; we had to exploit the success of the first film even though he now wanted to recount an entirely different, much more serious story."[8] The protagonist of this Homeric saga – whose proper name, Montgomery Brown, echoes Gemma's 'Montgomery Wood' alias – is still a wanderer but, unlike his counterpart in the first film, far from a happy one. Having spent time away from home fighting a war (like Odysseus, only in this case it's the American Civil War), Brown comes back to find his hometown of Mimbres in the grip of the cruel Mexican

above: Crowded Belgian poster for **Arizona Colt**, one of two Gemma westerns among the twenty most successful films at the Italian box office in the 1966-67 season (the other was **Fort Yuma Gold**).

above: Director Duccio Tessari's wife, Lorella De Luca (aka Hally Hammond), has pride of place on this fotobusta for **A Pistol for Ringo**.

Fuentes brothers. Brown is believed to have died in the conflict, his home and even his wife taken over by Paco Fuentes (George Martin). His first 'return' is a false dawn, however, and he sinks into a mire of self-pity, rage and sorrow. Adopting the disguise of a Mexican peon, just as Odysseus had worn beggars' rags on his return to Ithaca, bearded and drinking heavily to soothe his torment, Ringo must somehow find himself again. (It's faintly ridiculous that nobody recognises Brown, even beneath the beard and dyed hair, considering what a prominent citizen we're told he had been just a few years before.) At the same time, this tormented figure must galvanise the citizens to overthrow their oppressors. Eventually, with some assistance (Tessari again creates worthy roles for subordinate characters), he pulls himself together for his brilliantly staged second coming, a metaphorical return from a state of living death.

Gemma's performance, like his character, has more depth than the genre usually allows. As a result, *The Return of Ringo* is one of the most emotionally involving Italian westerns, giving its dramatic crescendos and the climactic pitched battle extra potency. Brown's feelings of loss and betrayal reach a near-homicidal peak when he prepares to assassinate his wife, Hally (De Luca), unaware that she is a virtual prisoner of the Fuentes; the only reason he stops is because he sees she has a child with her – their daughter. It is a highly charged moment, with Ennio Morricone's melodramatic score evoking Brown's inner turmoil as the character, under the camera's unyielding gaze, absorbs this latest twist. The film's further revelations are equally powerful, as when Brown confronts his wife directly for the first time in a darkened bedroom, the light of an oil lamp suddenly revealing his face to her. Again the music swells, there are no words spoken, and Tessari times their brief reunion perfectly. The high point of the film, however, is also one of the most impressive individual images in the genre. As Paco Fuentes prepares to marry Hally, the church doors open behind them to reveal Brown, back in his army uniform, dust billowing around him as he defiantly announces his return, just like Odysseus with his wife's suitors or the sacred king of myth when he refuses to surrender his crown and provokes a violent confrontation. Besides its striking visual qualities (reminiscent of the reappearance of 'Joe' for the final reckoning in *A Fistful of Dollars*), this scene has an important thematic function, signifying Brown's moral and physical recovery and the resumption of his true identity.

The atmosphere Tessari creates is very different from that of *A Pistol for Ringo*. In place of that film's bright, busy aspect there is an air of oppression. While the town in *Pistol* was a thriving community bathed in sunshine, Mimbres is under constant assault by a dust storm, its citizens – "killed by fear" as Brown puts it – rarely seen in the streets unless it's to attend another funeral. As in other spaghettis, the only business that really seems to be booming is that of the undertaker, who shrewdly doubles as a florist and is known in different versions of the film as Forget-me-not, Myosotis or Morning Glory (played by 'Pajarito' [Murriz Brandariz], another cast member returning from *Pistol*). The film's morbid undertone is a continuation of Sergio Leone's fascination with the symbolism of death, and anticipates the better 'Django' films and the 'Sartana' series. Brown watches with a wry smile as his own funeral procession passes by, a grand affair staged by Paco Fuentes to expedite his marriage to Hally. Later, the wedding ceremony itself is grotesquely distorted when Brown arranges a group of coffins inside the church, supposedly containing the bodies of an innocent family but actually housing some of Paco's men. Hally even dresses in mourning black for the occasion.

Despite the bleakness, Tessari retains his lightness of touch. Brown's interplay with his perpetually cheerful daughter during the latter stages, while too cutesy at times, is one example, and there are subtly humorous interludes involving Forget-me-not, who fulfils the familiar function of hero's helper, and Nieves Navarro as a sympathetic, fortune-telling saloon girl who is awarded the film's comedic closing shot. Tessari's main achievement, however, is to seamlessly weave together Italian Gothic with Homeric grandeur and Hollywood romanticism – the lone hero/cowardly town theme recalls *High Noon* (1952), the siege scenario is reminiscent of Howard Hawks's *Rio Bravo* series and, as in *Pistol*, there are subtle references to other, lesser westerns as well. The director also presents his audience with fallible, believable characters rather than the usual one-dimensional ciphers, from Gemma's protagonist with his hang-ups and cry for help – a nod towards the tormented heroes of Fifties psychological westerns – to Antonio Casas's cowed but ultimately courageous sheriff, his nerves shattered by old wounds and bitter experience. Tessari generously grants him some of the film's most poignant scenes.

With the exception of Sergio Corbucci's *Ringo and His Golden Pistol* (1966), covered below, the many subsequent 'Ringo' productions are of little relevance here. The lead characters are diverse but nondescript; many of them are not even called Ringo, while those that *are* probably had their identities changed during the dubbing, more than likely at the distributors' behest, in response to Tessari and Gemma's success. (One of the most absurd examples was the rechristening of one of the 'Winnetou' films, *Rampage at Apache Wells*, which played in Italy as *Danza di Guerra per Ringo*.) The 'Ringo' marque continued to be applied to Gemma's own westerns as well – *Long Days of Vengeance* (1967), a slick, suspenseful variation on *The Count of Monte Cristo* (and another film, like *The Return of Ringo*, that requires Gemma to conceal his identity, as he spends the early part of the story with a shabby beard and shaggy hair), was distributed in Italy with the suffix 'Angel Face', while *The Price of Power* (1969) played some South American circuits under the title *Ringo y el precio del poder*.

While nowhere near as accomplished as *A Pistol for Ringo*, *Ringo and His Golden Pistol*, retitled from the Italian *Johnny Oro*, nevertheless shares several traits with Tessari's film. Mark Damon plays a bounty hunter very similar to Angel Face – boastful and cynical, as fast with a quip as he is with his glittering sidearm. As in the earlier film, established western conventions are pitted against a newfangled ruthlessness, although Corbucci can't match Tessari's skill in meshing the various elements together. (Evidently Corbucci wasn't too enamoured by the project, turning in a cut that was barely feature length; Manolo Bolognini, subsequently to produce *Django*, reportedly shot additional footage to bulk it up.[9]) The clash of values between noble sheriff Ettore Manni and Damon's gunman is lifted directly from *Pistol*. The lawman refuses to surrender Ringo to the bad guys encircling his town, despite the violence that results. "You do crazy things for gold," he explains to a dumbfounded Ringo, "I do crazy things for my principles." "That's a word you see on tombstones," is Ringo's cynical retort. Again, like Tessari, Corbucci restages several situations from classic American westerns – the sheriff's son torn between his solid, dependable father and the dashing young gunslinger recalls *Shane* (1953), while the lawman's stubborn resistance and the subsequent siege remind one again of *Rio Bravo* (1959) and also *3.10 to Yuma* (1957). Elsewhere, matinee western clichés, such as the hero's habit of whistling for his dutiful horse, jostle with sadistic violence, as when the saloonkeeper receives an axe-blow to his head, a shot that would reappear in Corbucci's *Navajo Joe* (1966). One other notable point is the twist on the revenge motif – here it is the villain seeking to even the score against the protagonist for the deaths of his outlaw brothers, all victims of Ringo's golden gun.

above: Sergio Corbucci's **Ringo and His Golden Pistol**, shot as **Johnny Oro**, was Mark Damon's first Italian western, a canny response – in part, at least – to the success of Duccio Tessari's films. Damon's irreverent performance, all quips and gun tricks, was typical for the era and he stuck to his guns, golden or otherwise, in his subsequent westerns.

above: The rigged gundown: although Corbucci's film is conventional in many respects (it was filmed in 1965, when Euro-westerns were still at the formative stage), the climactic duel rewrites the rulebook. Instead of a Hollywood-style showdown, it becomes a showcase for the protagonist's quick wits – not to mention his willingness to cheat.

above: Mark Damon went to Italy to become a film star. In later years, he made a killing as one of America's leading independent film producers.

"A mysterious name for a pitiless man…"

More influential than Ringo and even, arguably, Clint Eastwood's 'Dollars' persona in terms of his impact upon the Italian western, was the man with one name but many faces – Django. Created by the Corbucci brothers and a combination of other writers (including an uncredited Fernando Di Leo) and portrayed by nascent Italian superstar Franco Nero, this character and his attributes set a miniature industry in motion. He towers over the Italian western from such a height that he has become just as emblematic in his way, and of his type, as other enduring Italian pulp heroes and *fumetti* icons such as Maciste, the master-criminal Diabolik and Texas Ranger Tex Willer. He easily holds the record for the highest number of dubious or wholly illegitimate sequels and spin-offs. At a conservative estimation, more than 60 titles capitalised on the marquee value of the Django name, especially when they were released in France and Germany, where the character proved particularly popular. (In Germany, the majority of Nero's subsequent westerns, and even some of his non-genre films, were retitled in this way.[10]) There were even a number of protagonists whose names closely resembled or even *rhymed* with Django – consider Shango and Cjamango, for example. The cult continues to this day, with Japanese provocateur Takashi Miike crafting his own homage in the form of *Sukiyaki Western Django* (2007).

This is quite an achievement for a film that is, in plot terms, little more than a revamping of *A Fistful of Dollars*. In place of the Rojos and the Baxters, Django must deal with the tyrannical Major Jackson (a never-better Eduardo Fajardo), who leads the bigoted, red-hooded Klansmen; and the brutal Mexican bandits under General Hugo Rodrigues (José Bódalo). The main difference is that Django sides with only one of these factions – the Mexicans – rather than both in succession.[11] At the same time, however, *Django* is a work of bold, striking individuality. Corbucci explained his motivation in a well-known quote: "I wanted to create, somewhat influenced by Kurosawa, a picaresque western, a bit black, an anti-western *par excellence*, with the hero on foot instead of on horseback, moving in the cold rather than the heat, fighting with mud and snow instead of with sweat and dust."[12] As if challenged by his friend Sergio

above: Cashing in: The 'Django' phenomenon became a licence to print money. Sergio Corbucci's original (*main image*), with Franco Nero (*left*) and José Bódalo (*centre*), was aped or alluded to in the plots, themes, visual style or even just the titles of numerous others, such as **Cjamango** (*inset*).

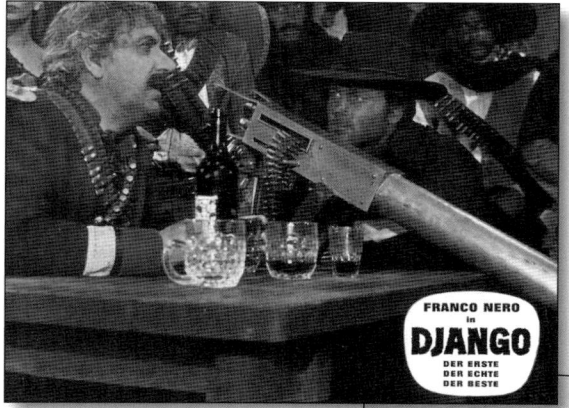

above: German lobby card for **Django** showing José Bódalo, Franco Nero and his trusty machine gun (almost indispensable in a Corbucci western).
inset right: Nero's pensive profile, as drawn by Rodolfo Gasparri, dominates this famous Italian locandina.

Corbucci's film paints as grim and nihilistic a portrait of frontier life as the genre had yet produced. Building upon the sense of desperation that envelops Tessari's *The Return of Ringo*, *Django* emits an atmosphere of torment and inescapable tragedy – consistent with its Gothic inflections – that would reverberate through many other entries. Django himself has the trappings one would expect from an Italian western anti-hero, being taciturn, mysterious and deadly, with a bastardised costume that hints at his itinerant nature and his way of life – an ex-army man (the film is set a few years after the end of the Civil War), well acquainted with death, who now resembles a vagabond or gravedigger. And yet, unlike the magnificent stranger of *A Fistful of Dollars*, Django is a haunted man. Scratch away at his implacable veneer and there are traces of recognisably human emotions – self-doubt, regret and a yearning, however suppressed, for the peace and security of a 'normal' lifestyle. This is denied him when his lust for gold – his fatal flaw, in tragic terms – leads to the wounding of his would-be lover, the prostitute Maria (Loredana Nusciak), forcing him into another bloody showdown.

Leone's achievement, Corbucci heightened and intensified his film in almost every department: the stoical hero could almost have strayed in from Greek tragedy; not content with a sidearm, he totes a machine gun as well (probably the same one wielded by Ramon Rojo in *Fistful*); the violence reaches Grand Guignol proportions (*Django* was the first western to be prohibited to under-18s in Italy, and was refused a certificate in the UK[13]); the setting is chillingly austere; the production design and costumes – the work of Leone's fellow visionary, Carlo Simi – are grittier, tattier and more realistic than almost anything previously seen, yet at the same time Simi freely indulges his artistic licence; and Enzo Barboni's photography is stylised to an almost surrealistic degree. There is a pop-cultural sensibility at play here that is more reminiscent of the era's comic strips and horror films than it is of westerns. It is often reported that Corbucci was partly inspired by a coffin-dragging character he saw in an unidentified Italian *fumetto*, while Barboni's palette recalls the lush, lurid colour schemes of Corman and Bava. In addition, Corbucci pumps up the populist sentiments, including a villain defined in terms of his class bias and a scathing view of religious hypocrisy (coupled with a strikingly provocative misuse of Catholic iconography) that quickly became a standard feature of the genre. It's not difficult to see why so many small-scale Italian westerns, with little else to offer the international market, were subsequently stamped with the Django brand.

What really sets Django apart from his peers is that despite his cool, collected demeanour, he seems as much cursed as blessed by his affinity with violence. The essence of the character is encapsulated in the famous title sequence – a dark-garbed figure struggles on foot (the absence of a horse not only underlines Corbucci's iconoclastic attitude towards conventional westerns, it also allies his anti-hero firmly with the wandering samurais of Kurosawa *et al*) through a muddy, rain-lashed wasteland (Tor Caldara, Anzio), dragging a coffin behind him, the camera cutting from medium

directly above and inset: Django's trademark coffin was another of Corbucci's regular props, manifesting the director's macabre wit.

above: Django's machine gun was modelled on a French Mitrailleuse, and was probably the same prop wielded by Ramon (Gian Maria Volonté) in the riverside massacre sequence of **A Fistful of Dollars** and seen again in later films made by **Django**'s producers, such as **Rita of the West** and **A Long Ride from Hell**.

above: The appearance of the Klansmen in their first confrontation with Django is as unexpected as it is visually arresting. It not only highlights Corbucci's irreverence, but also the vital contribution made by Carlo Simi, as production and costume designer, and Enzo Barboni, who picks out the red of the Klansmen's hoods against the brown, wintry drabness of the Elios town set.

above: A religious hypocrite (Gino Pernice) mixes with mud-wrestling whores; Corbucci relished the role of provocateur.

to long shot to emphasise his solitude as Luis Enríquez Bacalov's bluesy theme song urges him onwards. Franco Nero remembers this as a particularly arduous scene to shoot. "[*Django*] was shot in winter – we filmed in December [1965] in Rome for a few days, then we went to Spain in January [1966], just outside of Madrid, and it was very cold, and then we got back to Rome at the end of January and it was freezing there as well. When we did the title sequence, it was pouring with rain and Corbucci said, 'Keep going, keep going.' The coffin was very heavy and he was saying, 'Go on until you disappear.' He played a joke on me – when I disappeared from view he never told me to stop, so I kept going all that way in the mud. When I really got exhausted and walked back to see where the crew was, they had all left."[14]

Corbucci frequently employed symbolism in his westerns, but never with quite the same visual and thematic acuity. Or, it should be noted, with such keenly judged irony; the director's singular sense of humour could often be an unwelcome distraction. It is clear from these opening shots that wherever he roams, Django literally brings death with him, and his physical struggle with the coffin suggests the burden of his bleak, violent existence. (A coffin serves a more ambitious symbolic purpose in another Corbucci western with tragic leanings, *The Hellbenders*, shot the same year, and the director would reuse the prop in *The Specialists* and *Compañeros*.) The casket also demonstrates Django's sense of self-awareness – when asked who's lying inside, he cryptically gives his own name, implying that, inwardly at least, he feels dead already, and identifying the machine gun, which he first uses to devastating effect against assembled Klansmen in the town's boggy main street, as his lethal alter ego. He also uses his coffin to store a fortune in gold dust, which, ironically, he hopes will enable him to bury his past for ever but is actually the catalyst for much of the film's bloodshed.

From *A Fistful of Dollars* onwards the genre frequently represented the precariousness of life on the American-Mexican border, and this is strongly evoked in *Django*. The anonymous town where most of the action takes place is a particularly dank and desolate place; its few desperate inhabitants – a bedraggled bartender, a few tubercular whores and some hard-pressed peons, all slaves together – are ravaged by nature and terrorised by two distinct but equally sadistic forces. Fajardo's Major Jackson is perhaps the genre's most despicable southern 'gentleman'; like Jonas (Joseph Cotten) in *The Hellbenders*, Ferguson (Mark Damon) in *Kill and Pray* (1967), Blake (Guy Madison) in *Seven Winchesters for a Massacre* (1967) and Fajardo's Major Droster in *Shango* (1970), Jackson is a Confederate renegade who refuses to accept the outcome of the Civil War. His warped concept of honour calls for the total dominance of one, superior class – and race – over another. (Here we can see, in a

Beware Of Fake Guns

above: Stark, haunting Japanese poster for **Django**.

nascent form, the theme of political/racial oppression that would play a central role in all of Corbucci's major westerns, most of which feature Fajardo as a loathsome, supercilious villain.) Jackson is introduced enjoying a little sport – shooting unarmed peasants thrust into his range by his enthusiastic Klansmen. (Long before Mel Brooks gave it the slapstick treatment in the Louis XVI segment of *History of the World Part 1* (1981), this 'game' became a genre classic, played by Gérard Herter in *Full House for the Devil* (1968) and *Adios, Sabata* (1970). It also cropped up in the Italian-inspired American western *Villa Rides* (1968), in which Charles Bronson's targets are army officers rather than peasants for a change.[15]) Ranged against Jackson's men are the ebullient Mexicans led by José Bódalo's Hugo Rodrigues, who claims to be planning a popular uprising in his native land but, like the almost identical figure played by the same actor in Corbucci's later *Compañeros*, he seems more interested in lining his own pockets than in political causes. He and his men have a penchant for torture – evinced in the whipping of Maria, the mutilation of Jackson's odious priest, Brother Jonathan (Gino Pernice, a Corbucci regular), in a scene that inspired the (comparatively less graphic) ear-slicing centrepiece of *Reservoir Dogs* (1992), and the staggering brutality of Django's punishment when he tries to steal their (stolen) gold. Strange behaviour indeed for 'freedom fighters'. As with the Klansmen, the Mexicans' cruelty stems from repressive urges. Corbucci hammers home the point that in the borderlands of the European western, law, order and human rights are in short supply, allowing brigands and tyrants a free hand.

Django is not quite the champion of lost causes who rides to the rescue; that would be too much to expect in a post-*Fistful of Dollars* Italian western, especially one with such an iconoclastic director at the helm. Yet while he is no humanitarian, neither is Django the callous, calculating killing machine one might expect him to be. His intimate moments with Maria – awkward though they are, and marked by insipid dialogue in the English dub – are important in furnishing Django with a human dimension, a weakness, in other words, which the filmmakers exploit further as the film progresses. Django's flight from Hugo's men is hindered by twin encumbrances: his greed, represented by the coffin full of gold; and Maria, who has insisted on accompanying him. Avarice thus plays a large part in Django's downfall, along with his feelings for a woman. These are emotions he has tried to keep in check throughout the film, until perhaps

realising that he and Maria are kindred spirits; they both recognise that the relationship they have forged is little more than an "illusion", yet neither of them can entirely give up hope. Adopting a central theme of Greek's tragic poets, fate overrides human actions and constrains will, a fact that Django ruefully acknowledges when explaining to Hugo how the gold has ended up in quicksand – "a horse stumbles, the casket slips..."[16] Corbucci then stacks the odds even higher against his hero when Hugo's men crush and trample Django's hands – five years on from *One-Eyed Jacks* (1961), this makes Karl Malden's smashing of Marlon Brando's gun hand seem like a playful slap. (The maiming of Django is an explicit reference to his namesake, Django Reinhardt, the great Belgian-born gypsy jazz guitarist who played for most of his career with a damaged hand. He effectively lost the use of the fourth and fifth digits of his left hand in a fire when he was 18.) For all the critical attention devoted to the sadism in *Django* and the amorality of the Italian western in general, the film's moral dimension, which is surprisingly strong, especially where the protagonist's suffering is concerned, has been largely overlooked.

above: Django's mangled hands somehow – absurdly, exhilaratingly – manage to function as he faces his enemies in the concluding scene. In the process he attains the aura of a demigod or even, juxtaposed with the cross, a triumphant martyr.

As well as establishing a kinship with other afflicted Corbucci protagonists such as Minnesota Clay and Silence, Django's debilitating injuries – his gunfighter's stigmata – set the scene for the finale and his near-miraculous victory against Jackson and his remaining Klansmen in the local cemetery. Django's excruciating efforts to control his pistol, using a combination of bloody, bandaged hands, forearms and teeth while leaning on a cross for stability, build up a fair amount of suspense as Jackson and his men take up their positions. Audaciously, Corbucci's staging of the confrontation gives it a sacramental flavour, with Django like a supplicant before the cross while, in the Italian version at least, the sanctimonious Jackson torments him with shots "in the name of the Father, the Son and the Holy Ghost", until the anti-hero answers with "Cosi sia!" ("it will be done" or "amen") and a volley of bullets. Corbucci crowns the denouement with one of the finest closing images in the genre – in the foreground, Django's blood-stained pistol rests on the cross he had used to steady his aim, while the character himself staggers towards the top of the frame, away from the graveyard and into exploitation film history.

As well as evoking Christian imagery, Django's last stand – undertaken on his knees, such is his weakness by this stage – epitomises the kind of superhuman resilience that connects many Italian western protagonists with their counterparts in comic books and the demigods of Greek and Roman mythology, earning character and actor iconographic status for a time all around the world. "When I stayed in hotels in many different countries," says the star, "they didn't put 'Franco Nero' in the registers, they put 'Django'."[17] (Corbucci heard about the stir his film was creating in far-flung places from none other than Pier Paolo Pasolini: "[He] once told me that when he'd visit an African village, or some other godforsaken place, as soon as he was recognised as an Italian, he'd hear murmurs of 'Django', because it was one of a mere handful of films at the time that reached all the movie theatres worldwide." It was notably popular in Jamaica, where its influence can be gauged from the *Django* excerpts used in Jimmy Cliff's *The Harder They Come* [1972] and the many reggae songs written in the character's honour.[18])

Django's journey after that epic cemetery showdown was long and eventful, involving many changes of terrain, personality, costume, profession and objective. Indeed, a film-by-film assessment of the 'Django' phenomenon would require a book in itself.[19] It would also necessitate wading through a large number of spurious films that tell us little about the character apart from how fashionable he quickly became. So popular, in fact, that towards the end of the cycle, Demofilo Fidani, one of the genre's quirkiest directors, constructed a *Little Big Man*-style mock-biopic around his quaint conception of the character. *The Ballad of Django* (1971) is a cut-price collage comprising excerpts from the director's previous westerns – including his two-for-the-price-of-one quickies *Django and Sartana Are Coming... It's the End* and *One Damned Day at Dawn... Django Meets Sartana!* (both 1970) – interspersed with new footage showing the elderly Django (an artificially aged Hunt Powers) regaling a star-struck Wild Bill Hickok with stories from his bounty hunting days.

The true measure of *Django*'s impact is neither the quantity of sham sequels it inspired, nor the way in which its populist themes took root. (Similar themes had in any case been present in earlier films.) For a more accurate reflection of the qualities this landmark film introduced to the genre, we need to look elsewhere. Firstly, to the director himself. "I think Corbucci deserves all the credit because he had the idea to do this movie as a kind of cold comedy, in a similar way to the Japanese samurai films," says Franco Nero.[20] Corbucci's manipulation of sets, landscape and the elements creates a highly expressionistic environment that influenced the texture of many of the more hyper-realistic spaghettis that followed, including the 'sequels' spoken of below. (He couldn't have achieved this without the invaluable assistance of Enzo Barboni, whose juxtaposition of vivid colours with murky browns and cloudy greys is especially

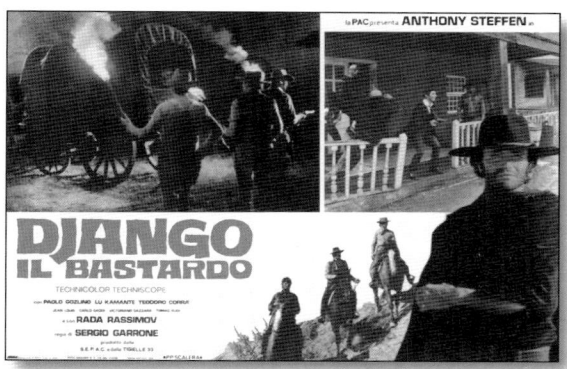

striking; Carlo Simi; and the editors Nino Baragli and Sergio Montanari, who helped realise Corbucci's trademark dynamic shoot-outs, with their rapidly intercut images of blazing guns and tumbling corpses.) Just as inspirational was the greater emphasis on leering violence and graphic bloodshed (although only a handful of subsequent Euro-westerns 'outgrossed' this one, so to speak), something that Sergio Leone – with no little irony, considering the moral indignation his own films had stirred – was critical of: "[Corbucci's] sort of film has contributed to the decline of all the commercial product out there. He may not have understood [that] behind the illustration of violence must reside something more than shock for its own sake; some depth."[21] The correlation of the title character with death, meanwhile, combined with Corbucci's ghoulish imagery and the Gothic trappings of setting and scenery, left an equally lasting impression. Successive films in the cycle, as well as other, non-affiliated westerns, appropriated these elements with varying degrees of blatancy. In *Preparati la bara!* (1967), released as *Viva Django*, Terence Hill's protagonist finds fitting employment as a travelling executioner, and the film's climactic showdown, complete with machine gun, takes place in a cemetery. Tomas Milian's character climbs out of his own grave at the beginning of *Django, Kill!* (1967), while *Django the Bastard* (1969), that most sepulchral of westerns, takes the death metaphor to (il)logical extremes. Besides the eponymous

above: German lobby card and, *top right*, Italian fotobusta for Sergio Garrone's **Django the Bastard**.

above: Abductee Adriana Ambesi develops a case of Stockholm syndrome in **$10,000 Blood Money**, mourning her kidnapper, Claudio Camaso, after his ultimate defeat by Django (Gianni Garko).
bottom left: Spanish admat for **A Few Dollars for Django**, credited to León Klimovsky but substantially the work of second-unit director (and son of the producer) Enzo Castellari.

ghostly gunman, Sergio Garrone's film is replete with coffins, crosses and yawning graves. Elsewhere, Sartana is at least a close relative of Nero's character, if not a direct descendant, while echoes of *Django*'s eerie ambience can be found in Enzo Castellari's *Johnny Hamlet* (1968), repackaged as a 'Django' film in France and Germany; the Gothic-tinged westerns of Antonio Margheriti, *Vengeance* (1968) and *And God Said to Cain* (1970); and two titles from the twilight years, *Keoma* (1976), produced by *Django*'s Manolo Bolognini, and *A Man Called Blade* (1977).

Finally, we return to the character himself. If he doesn't quite display psychological depth, there is at least a certain introspectiveness added to Django's impassivity, and this sense of a man in the grip of an existential dilemma supplements his enigmatic appeal. Nero's low-key performance perfectly conveys the world-weariness of this dishevelled drifter; he seems condemned to wander, imprisoned in the wasteland, the harbinger of destruction for anyone who strays too close, whether potential friends, lovers or enemies. (His mournful demeanour probably has something to do with the violent death of a loved one. Such a loss is briefly mentioned in the film, along with Jackson's culpability, and is a further reference to *A Fistful of Dollars*.) Django's

inability to control his greed, which represents a desire to alter his destiny, forces fate to punish him. He even reaches his own metaphorical crossroads – a bridge over a pool of quicksand. While few of the film's follow-ups picked up on the character's quasi-tragic bearing, it became a firm feature elsewhere in the genre, with the effect varying according to the quality of the individual performance and the realisation of the tragic situation.

Only a handful of 'sequels' are truly worthy of their offhand association with Corbucci's film. *$10,000 Blood Money*, with Gianni Garko (using the pseudonym 'Gary Hudson', a tribute both to his favourite actor, Gary Cooper, and to Rock Hudson, much admired by producer Luciano Martino) in the role, sustains a similar fatalistic atmosphere and takes the trouble to ponder the consequences of the anti-hero's violent lifestyle. Django is again trapped in a spiral of killing from which he seems unable, perhaps unwilling, to extricate himself. Central to the film is the sense of bounty hunter and hunted as clashing alter egos. Django is strongly implicated in the killing of his lover, Mijanou (Loredana Nusciak), who dies during a robbery carried out by unhinged bandit Manuel Vasquez (Claudio Camaso) with Django's assistance. As in Greek tragedy, Django errs when faced with a crucial choice – he opts for danger and financial gain (Manuel) over love and stability (Mijanou) – and his subsequent feelings of guilt and remorse at Mijanou's death are in some way his punishment. Garko breaks with tradition by shedding tears in the scene where Django discovers Mijanou's corpse. As the actor explains, "Usually, an Italian actor in westerns didn't draw attention to sentiments; they tried to be very strong. In this film I tried to be more human. I was always nostalgic when I was doing these films for the American way of shooting westerns, in which they also show human values and sentiments."[22] Garko and director Romolo Guerrieri deserve credit for daring to dwell on the character's distress, although some versions of the film contain only a shortened, dry-eyed version of this scene. The emphasis on Django's hubris is especially strong, and the sense that divine, retributive forces are controlling events extends even to the other characters – Mijanou's prediction of disaster proves all too accurate, while one member of Manuel's gang repeatedly anticipates their fate – and is heightened further by Nora Orlandi's solemn ballad 'Basta cosi', which warns that God will punish any mortal who deigns to seek justice for himself. Django takes his revenge on Manuel in a windswept, Corbucci-esque ghost town, but cuts a forlorn, lost and lonely figure at the end.

While there's no doubt that the 'Django' brand conveyed a certain cachet on many films otherwise lacking in lustre (viz. *A Few Dollars for Django* [1966], *Son of Django* [1967], *Don't Wait, Django, Shoot!* [1967] etc.), it also obscured the identity of more distinctive works. Hence Giulio Questi's phantasmagorical *Se sei vivo spara* –

above: Terence Hill's travelling executioner concocts a cunning revenge plot in Ferdinando Baldi's **Viva Django** (the German title translates loosely as 'Django and the band of hanged men'). Hill's marked resemblance to Franco Nero helped secure him the lead in this 'prequel' to **Django**.

arguably the most idiosyncratic of all European westerns – has always been known abroad as *Django, Kill!*, although the exhortation in the original title – 'if you live, shoot' – gives a clearer indication of the central character's fraught, perilous predicament. The controversy generated by Questi's film, and its corresponding cult appeal as a hybrid of horror and western motifs, has made it, alongside *Django the Bastard*, the best-known 'sequel' in the series. I will examine both on their own merits in the next chapter, but it's worth briefly outlining here their relationship to *Django* itself. Despite its singularity, there are aspects of *Django, Kill!* that Questi may have patterned after Corbucci's original, especially since part of his intention seems to have been to comment on the excesses of the Italian western itself. (Even if Questi hadn't actually seen *Django* before shooting, the hue and cry that Corbucci's film was raising in Italy could well have caught the director's attention.) The most obvious connection is the abundance of gruesome imagery, with torture, scalping, mutilation and viscera all on the menu. Then there is the heady, suffocating atmosphere, the Gothic trappings (the parallels with the Corman/Poe cycle are even more apparent), and the portrait of the town – traditionally the bedrock of civilisation in westerns – as a purgatorial abyss.

The main difference is that in Questi's film the anti-hero doesn't propel the action but is deliberately marginalised, unlike in *Django the Bastard*, with Anthony Steffen in the title role, where he is again centre stage, manipulating the mood and the movements of others as he relentlessly pursues an unearthly vendetta. Steffen's Django is also supplied with a prospective female partner, played this time by Rada Rassimov, but, whereas Franco Nero and Gianni Garko had earlier been tempted to take the path of peace and domesticity, Steffen remains aloof, coldly rejecting Rassimov's advances once his campaign of killing has been concluded.

Of all the purported *Django* sequels, two have a greater claim to legitimacy than the others – one by virtue of its authorship, the other by endorsement. Ferdinando Baldi's *Viva Django* was written by Franco Rossetti, who co-wrote *Django*, and finds the character, here played by Terence Hill, on the vengeance trail after his wife is killed and he is left for dead by bandits. Five years after the attack, Django has become a travelling hangman who assembles a small band made up of "phantoms" – persecuted farmers he has rescued from the gallows – to help him seek retribution. The film consciously emulates *Django*'s visual style, revisits similar

above: Belgian poster for **Viva Django** depicting Hill as Frano Nero's doppelgänger and, *opposite top right*, German lobby card showing the eerily similar cemetery setting for the big showdown.

themes and restages certain set pieces. Terence Hill, not yet a superstar, was cast primarily for his distinct resemblance to Franco Nero (his costume is also modelled on Nero's attire), while cinematographer Enzo Barboni employs colours to baroque effect just as he had done in *Django*. While Barboni's tableaux aren't quite as vivid as those in the earlier film, *Viva Django* still exudes a rich, rarefied atmosphere. It also has a whiff of the earlier film's populism, with chief villain David Barry (Horst Frank) portrayed as an ambitious, ruthless politician who uses cut-throats to enforce his will. In addition, Rossetti peppers the script with references to *Django*, notably when Hill has his hands stamped on during a savage punishment beating and, in an outrageous example of *deus ex machina*, disinters a machine gun during the Corbucci-esque final firefight.

If we were to judge authenticity on looks alone, then Baldi's film, shot by *Django*'s cinematographer in the genre's golden era, has a clear advantage over 1987's *Django Strikes Again*, directed by Nello Rossati under the alias 'Ted Archer'. Yet despite the 20-year time lag, the latter was the only follow-up supposedly 'approved' by Corbucci, and the only one with Franco Nero back in his most iconic role. Nero's presence is a huge bonus, but certain technical shortcomings, combined with the unfamiliar Colombian locations that stand in for Mexico, give the film an artificial feel. (Franco Nero: "I was making movies in Colombia at the time and the director also had business in the country. He said, 'I've an idea for a Django movie, why don't we shoot it in Cartagena?' So, in a way, he set the movie there because it was convenient for both of us, but you can't really have a western where there are rivers and an ocean."[23]) Scriptwriters Rossati and Franco Reggiani, however, are faithful to the legend. The prologue (removed from original export prints) features two veteran gunmen, one of them played by William Berger, wondering whatever happened to the famous Django. Although brief, the scene forms a bridge with the past. The script replays the burial-resurrection motif from earlier entries – at the beginning of the film we find Nero secreted away in a monastery, telling a former lover who comes seeking his help that Django is dead. (In common with earlier ecclesiastical characters in the genre – one thinks especially of 'Brother Smith & Wesson' in *The Big Gundown* [1967] – Django views his religious servitude as a form of atonement for all the lives he has taken.) Once again, Django's violent side is directly associated with his weapon of choice – his machine gun is buried beneath a headstone bearing his name and, when he digs it up, his killer instinct is reborn. And he needs it instantly, since a gang of bandits is conveniently in the process of molesting a mourning widow nearby. But in the unspecified period between Django's original outing and his adventures here – clues in the narrative suggest a gap of anything from 10 to 15 years – the character

has evolved beyond the nihilistic, funereal figure of yore. Django is a wiser and more compassionate man, although his athleticism (as was customary for Nero, he seems to have performed most of his own stunts) and his unerring accuracy remain undimmed by his years in cloisters.

The populist undercurrents of the original *Django* are pushed to the foreground. The villain is the fascistic Count Orlowsky (Christopher Connelly), supposedly Hungarian but whose minions spout Nazi phraseology, who roams the Mexican coast in a fortified steam ship, kidnapping peasants to use as slave labour. (We also see him using them for target practice in a tribute to the original film's Major Jackson.) One of the captives is the daughter Django never knew he had, destined for a local brothel. Django thus assumes the mantle of an ideologically and spiritually righteous crusader, driven additionally by latent parental outrage. Director Rossati provides further vindication with emotionally manipulative imagery to illustrate Orlowsky's tyranny, juxtaposing shots of the ship's luxurious interior with slaves toiling and dead bodies hanging. Rossati does his best to furnish the film with an atmosphere appropriate to the genre – as contradictory as it might sound, the cemeteries look splendid, and for much of the film

above: Back with a bang: **Django Strikes Again** supplemented the character's arsenal with dynamite and a newly altruistic agenda.

Django's mode of transport is a horse-drawn hearse (copying Frank Wolff's character in Nando Cicero's offbeat 1967 western, *Last of the Badmen*), which he converts into a battlewagon – but in most respects *Django Strikes Again* resembles less a western than it does a mid-Eighties Italian action film, right down to the exotic, tropical backdrop, incongruous in this context, and an over-reliance on explosive special effects.

Despite the distancing effect that results, the film provides a unique opportunity – Fidani's *The Ballad of Django* notwithstanding – to see how a spaghetti western superhero might have developed in his middle years. The mature Django may not meet everyone's expectations, but the path to monastic anonymity is a plausible one for the character to have chosen after wandering from the graveyard at the end of the original film, especially since he seemed to have been seeking some form of sanctuary throughout – why not spiritual solace? (It is no less absurd a proposition than having Rambo, the Eighties most talismanic killing machine, holed up with Buddhist monks at the beginning of *Rambo III*.) Having said that, the ease with which Django resumes his destructive ways clearly indicates the aspect of his character that the film is more concerned with. Nero regards the enterprise as a missed opportunity: "The film was not what I really wanted. The idea at the beginning was not bad – two old gunfighters decide to have their last showdown and, before they die, they wonder what happened to all the great heroes. There is only one left alive and that is Django. But I've never been very happy about the movie. It could have been much better."[24] Nevertheless, Nero brings a compelling moral and physical authority to the role, bestowing a welcome measure of integrity upon an otherwise unconvincing film.

above and top left: **Django Strikes Again** proposes Franco Nero as a paternalistic figure – the saviour of children and liberator of slaves. He resembles another of Nero's western characters, Keoma, more than he does the original Django.

A first-class pall-bearer

Of all the spaghetti western superheroes, Sartana is the most consistent. His personality and individual traits were sustained and developed over several films and, while the stories do not follow on from one another, there is a thematic consistency and tonal harmony about the 'Sartana' films that makes them a unified whole. It also helps that the character was played – in four of the five films in the 'official' series – by the same man, Gianni Garko. And of those five, four were helmed by one director, Giuliano Carnimeo, who succeeded Gianfranco Parolini after the initial entry. Garko took a strong interest in Sartana and consulted with the writers of each film to preserve the character's integrity. This consistency of vision, combined with the fact that there is not a dud in the set, makes the series particularly satisfying.

The evolution of Sartana illustrates both the inventiveness and the opportunism of Italian popular filmmakers. In 1966, writers Ernesto Gastaldi and Vittorio Salerno collaborated on the script of *Blood at Sundown*, a tale of brotherly enmity to be directed by Alberto Cardone. In the process, they created a diabolical villain named Sartana, the name being a corruption of Santa Anna, the famed general of the Mexican-American war. Cast in the role (his first in a western) was Gianni Garko, a theatre-trained actor of Venetian/Slav extraction. Playing opposite the brooding Anthony Steffen, Garko, inspired partly by Richard Widmark's performance in *Kiss of Death* (1947) and partly by Klaus Kinski, runs away with the film. Indeed, his character proved so popular with German audiences that *Blood at Sundown* was retitled *Sartana* in that country. A German producer wanted Garko to play Sartana again, but as a more heroic figure, not a villain. He proposed two or three scripts in which the protagonists were indistinguishable from countless other spaghetti western avengers clogging up screens at the time. Garko, disappointed by the lukewarm public response to his bounty-hunter films, *$10,000 Blood Money* and *For $100,000 Per Killing* (1967), was seeking something different, and eventually convinced Italian producer Aldo Addobbati, who was putting together his own Sartana adventure, that audiences were tiring of American cowboy surrogates and wanted more Leone-style anti-heroes. Garko had in mind a "more ironic" character, "not involved with sentiments. He tries to put one gang against another, as in *A Fistful of Dollars*. There is a proverb – 'Tra i due litiganti, il terzo gode'. That means, between two parties that are fighting, the third that is watching is the one who wins."[25] Enter an appropriately maverick director, Gianfranco Parolini – who maintains that "[*Pray for Your Death* is] the film I love the most and gave me the most satisfaction"[26] – and so it was that the megalomaniac fiend Garko played in *Blood at Sundown* gave way to the inscrutable, sardonic

angel of death in Parolini's *If You Meet Sartana, Pray for Your Death* (1968) and its sequels.[27]

Sartana's make-up is different from that of his peers, most of whom were derivations of Hollywood archetypes or facsimiles of Clint Eastwood's 'Dollars' persona or Django. As with Django, Sartana was less like an American western hero and more like a comic-strip character, specifically *Mandrake the Magician*, Lee Falk's black-caped illusionist whose spooky skills and natty apparel directly inspired Garko's interpretation.[28] As the actor told Eric Maché in a 1990 interview, "Cartoon strips, like film, are part of the *arte d'imagine*, and therein lie [Sartana's] cultural roots."[29] He is a multi-faceted character, a gambler, gunman and master of *trompe-l'oeil* trickery who employs these techniques to foil nefarious schemes, amassing a fortune in the process. Besides these tangible qualities, there is a mystique about Sartana that suggests the supernatural; he has a sinister aura that strikes fear into both innocents and enemies. It's this spectral aspect, combined with a nice line in gallows humour, which sets him apart from other spaghetti western protagonists. Says Giuliano Carnimeo: "Django [for example] is a prolongation of Leone's violent anti-hero, into a realm of hyper-violence. Sartana diverges from that drastically. Even if he battles his way seemingly in cold blood, he is nevertheless always on the ironic side of the street – he uses his hands to do magic tricks, has funny weapons, and introduces the first hints of what later would bloom into full parody with Trinity."[30]

Whereas most of Sartana's fellow superheroes are furnished with some kind of background or trade – Gemma's Ringo is a playful *pistolero* in his first film, an army officer in the second, while both Django and Sabata served in the Civil War – Sartana's origins remain a mystery. He is a harbinger of death, constantly associated with funerals, graves and the hereafter. His sidekick in both *Pray for Your Death* and *Have a Nice Funeral, Sartana Will Pay* (1970) is the town undertaker, played in both cases by Franco Pesce, a former silent-era cameraman with a wonderfully flexible face. (The mortician's workshop in the former film is poetically

The 'Sartana' saga boasts a persistence of vision that makes it particularly rewarding. This image from **I Am Sartana, Pray for Your Death** (*above*, with Gianni Garko, *left*, and William Berger) and the artwork for **Have a Nice Funeral, Sartana Will Pay** (*right*) and **Gunman in Town** (*opposite top right*) all show Sartana (Garko) in essentially the same pose, with the same aura of menace and Grim Reaper glare.

described as "the vestibule of the beyond". Sartana seems at home there.) With his first words in *Pray for Your Death*, Sartana declares to a group of gunmen "I am your pall-bearer" before killing them. He makes similarly grim pronouncements throughout the series – "I am your gravedigger", "I'll pray for your souls" – and the connection is picked up by subsidiary characters. As Sartana rides behind a buggy at the beginning of *Pray for Your Death*, an elderly female passenger remarks, "I feel as if a ghost were following me." In *I Am Sartana, Your Angel of Death* (1969), an associate comments, "You must have the devil on your side", while in *Gunman in Town* (1970), arguably the high point of the series, he's referred to as a body-snatcher and "not human" on separate occasions.

The character's otherworldly nature is also suggested by the way in which he is filmed. At certain points in *Pray for Your Death* his appearance is 'announced' by an eerie breeze. He often turns up suddenly and unexpectedly in the foreground immediately after a long shot has placed him in the distance, or steps into the frame as if from another dimension. (Sergio Leone used this technique to similar effect with Charles Bronson in *Once Upon a Time in the West* [1968], as did Sergio Garrone with Anthony Steffen in *Django the Bastard*, in which the supernatural angle is even more pronounced.) These materializations occur most effectively just after an act of murder, such as the massacres that open *Pray for Your Death*, *Have a Nice Funeral* and *Gunman in Town*, whereupon Sartana, his rifle balanced on one shoulder like the Grim Reaper's scythe, proceeds to punish the killers. The fact that he specialises in retribution rather than prevention or protection is significant. In Sartana's milieu, there is rarely anybody worth saving, but many who deserve a bullet for their sins.

Indeed, it could be argued that the 'Sartana' films represent the epitome of the spaghetti western's nihilistic worldview. The moral equilibrium of the classic Hollywood western, dispensed with in *A Fistful of Dollars*, is turned on its head here. A line from *Pray for Your Death*, "Nobody is ever content with what they have", sums up the motivation of most of the greedy, duplicitous souls who cross Sartana's path.

above: The best of enemies: William Berger (*left*) and Fernando Sancho (*right*) excelled themselves as Sartana's principal adversaries in Gianfranco Parolini's **Pray for Your Death**, the film that opened the series.

above: Behold a pale horse: Sartana makes another of his almost inexplicable appearances in Giuliano Carnimeo's **Have a Nice Funeral**. *opposite inset:* Italian and Belgian posters for Carnimeo's **Sartana's Here... Trade Your Pistol for a Coffin**, the final film in the sequence and the only one to star George Hilton in Gianni Garko's stead.

Crooked bankers, businessmen and sheriffs, black widows, outlaws, cheats and bounty hunters all become enmeshed in murderous, convoluted schemes, with the invariable intention of securing a fortune that is not their due. In each film, Sartana proves to be the master of deception, playing one faction off against another, sifting through the suspects, exploiting their greed and paranoia until, ultimately, he has eliminated the competition and 'earned' the money for himself. The fact that Sartana always ends up with the loot, which has invariably been stolen or swindled from anonymous innocent parties, somewhat muddies any message that may have been intended about the wages of sin and the rewards of virtue.

The scripts are diabolically complicated (reviewing *Gunman in Town* when it was belatedly released in the UK in 1975, the *Monthly Film Bulletin* was aghast at the "super-abundance of plot"), combining western action and backdrops with the red herrings, brutal murders and guilty secrets of pulp mysteries. Despite the occasional loose end and needless diversion, these sinuous narratives abound in ingenious twists and turns that serve to highlight Sartana's superior intelligence, his powers of deduction and intuition. "The character entered into popular language," claims Garko. "'You are like Sartana' means you are a very strong, very clever, very quick person." While the various schemers he encounters attempt to cover their tracks with a trail of deception and dead bodies, Sartana weaves a web of his own. There is an added urgency to his investigations in *Angel of Death* and *Gunman in Town*, in which he has to clear his name of bank-robbing and murder charges respectively. Throughout the series, tenuous alliances are formed, inevitably ending in betrayal, while blackmail and bribery are rife. When they can't buy Sartana off, the villains send their hired guns after him, which proves equally fruitless.

Whereas the majority of spaghetti western protagonists suffer horrendous beatings at one point or another – think of Clint Eastwood bloodied and blistered in the 'Dollars' films, and Franco Nero's cruel punishment in *Django* – Sartana barely receives a scratch in any of his films. (An exception occurs at the beginning of *Gunman in Town*, when he is given "a sample of our hospitality" from the sadistic guards at Everglades jail.) His uncanny ability with a pistol, as well as the makeshift weaponry he often employs, is matched by his powers of evasion. "I don't let myself get killed," he announces matter-of-factly in *Have a Nice Funeral*. He seems to have a sixth sense, and is simply too elusive for most of the clods sent to kill him, while the self-styled criminal 'masterminds' further up the hierarchy are generally undone by their own egotistical errors, which Sartana shrewdly exploits. The same gags reoccur throughout the series, showcasing the character's resourcefulness, his mastery of subterfuge and sleight of hand, and typifying the films' sly self-awareness. Whenever he appears to be outgunned, it's a fair bet that he will have a trick in reserve or another weapon hidden somewhere. This is the excuse for some oddball humour in *Sartana's Here... Trade Your Pistol for a Coffin* (1970). Confronted by bandits as he sits in a cantina, Sartana, played in this instance by George Hilton, sees them off with a gun concealed in a loaf of bread. In an identical set-up later on, a different set of bandits, evidently wiser than the first, warn him in all seriousness to "keep your hands away from that loaf of bread"! He dispenses with them nonetheless.

On a number of occasions he feigns death: in *Pray for Your Death*, he secretes a metal plaque inside his hat, knowing that Lasky (William Berger) always aims for the forehead, unnerving his opponent by appearing to have survived the fatal shot. (Parolini borrowed this ploy from *A Fistful of Dollars*.) His favourite trick, however, involves the use of decoys. Time and time again, Sartana drapes a corpse or a captive gunman in his hat and cape, or

above: Apt publicity shot from **Have a Nice Funeral** illustrating Sartana's status as gunfighter-cum-gambler.

rigs up broom handles and other props in the same fashion. He does this so often that it becomes difficult, even for the audience, to tell when it really is him, especially in medium or long shots and when his back is towards the camera. The cleverest example occurs in *Gunman in Town*, when Sartana puts his clothes on backwards to surprise a villain who thinks he is facing the other way, while in *Angel of Death* the trick is turned against him when an impostor robs a bank, putting Sartana in the frame. Deceptive tactics like these had been tried and tested in countless previous westerns, and their repeated use in the Sartana films amounts to a running in-joke. (The series as a whole compares favourably with the final chapter of Parolini's 'Sabata' trilogy, which desperately calls attention to every gag, piling self-parody onto self-awareness and exhausting the formula.)

Parolini, responsible for kick-starting several other outlandish franchises such as the 'Kommissar X' spy films and the juvenile, acrobatic 'Three Fantastic Supermen' cycle, also had a passion for James Bond, and furnished Sartana with an array of gadgets and gimmicks that became more extravagant as the series wore on. (As we shall see, Parolini – once described by Gianni Garko as "an Archimedes of the cinema" because of his directorial ingenuity – would put his taste for peculiar devices and novelty armaments to further use in the 'Sabata' films.) Sartana's armoury includes his trademark four-barrelled derringer, its cylinder decorated with card suits, which he supplements with, among other objects, a set of throwing knives, his watch, a blowpipe and, fittingly for a gambler, a wickedly sharp set of playing cards. This tongue-in-cheek gimmickry peaks in *Gunman in Town*, where Sartana is equipped with a mechanised miniature doll named Alfie, which doubles as cigarette lighter and bomb, and a full-scale church organ with pipes that fire both cannon balls and bullets. (Weird contraptions followed Garko throughout the genre – he wields a prototype sub-machine-gun in *His Name Was Holy Ghost* [1972] and an 'umbrella-gun' in *Those Dirty Dogs* [1973].)

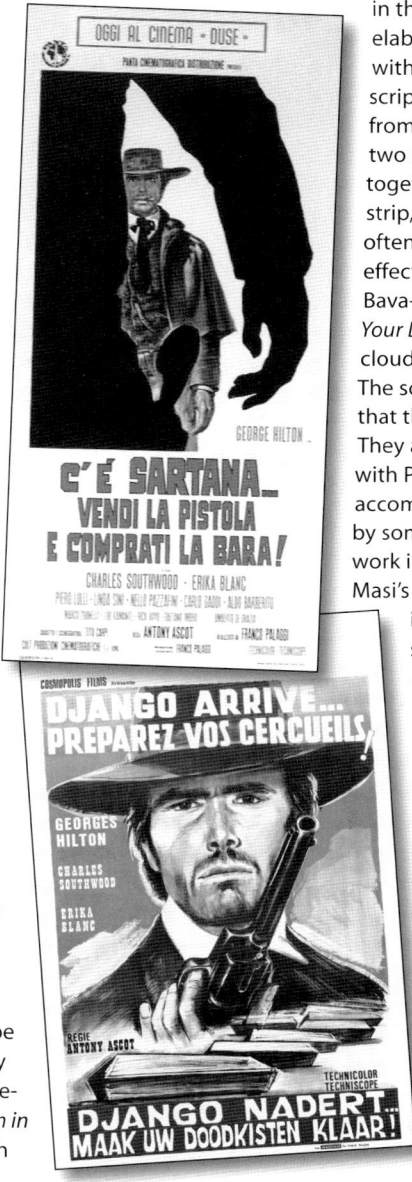

What makes the 'Sartana' formula so successful is the deft balancing of serious action with mordant humour and comic-strip escapism. Parolini's hyperactive directorial style – of which *The New York Times* stated "he seems sometimes to be mounting grand opera, sometimes to be interpreting Kafka and sometimes to be decorating a Christmas tree" – segues neatly into Carnimeo's less frenetic but still kinetic approach in the sequels. The films' increasingly elaborate set pieces are put together with the same infectious abandon as the scripts, the action frequently captured from unusual camera angles so that no two shoot-outs look the same, and cut together almost like panels in a comic strip, with hallucinatory colour schemes often contributing to the out-of-kilter effect – notably Sandro Mancori's use of Bava-esque greens and reds in *Pray for Your Death* and the coloured smoke that clouds the bank robbers in *Angel of Death*. The scores, moreover, reinforce the notion that the devil knows all the best tunes. They are of a consistently high calibre, with Piero Piccioni's jazzy, tongue-in-cheek accompaniment to the first film succeeded by some of Bruno Nicolai's most rousing work in the next two. Only Francesco De Masi's music for *Trade Your Pistol* fails to fully impress. As Sartana, meanwhile, Garko subtly combines self-confidence with self-parody, maintaining a deadly serious countenance broken now and then by a Mephistophelian grin. To achieve maximum impact, Garko obeys the first rule of spaghetti western leading men – let your co-stars do the emoting. To this end he is exceptionally well-served by his supporting casts, exemplified by the wily William Berger and oafish Fernando Sancho in *Pray for Your Death*, while regular co-stars include wizened character actor Franco Pesce, the inimitable Klaus Kinski, who plays a stylish killer in the first film and an amicable, luckless bounty hunter in *Angel of Death*, and eager villains such as Piero Lulli, 'Rick Boyd' [Federico Boido], Sal Borgese and Spaniard Luis Induni, none of whom could be accused of understatement.

With Garko committed to the Enzo Castellari thriller *The Cold Eyes of Fear* (1971), George Hilton took over the role for *Sartana's Here... Trade Your Pistol for a Coffin*, resulting in a more light-hearted adventure that reflects the actor's laidback persona. (Carnimeo, who considers this to be perhaps his best film, found Hilton a better fit for his increasingly "absurd" gags than Garko.[31]) Hilton's Sartana is more down-to-earth, an out-an-out bounty hunter who travels with a portfolio of wanted posters. As well as the usual subterfuge, he winds up with a partner, the dapper, parasol-sporting Sabbath (Charles Southwood), who seems to have strayed in from a series of his own. (Indeed, some Italian film guides credit Southwood as 'Sabata', suggesting an original intention to team up both of Parolini's superheroes in the same film. This is unlikely, however, not only because Southwood's urbane character is nothing like the Lee Van Cleef figure, but also because 'Sabbath' in Italian is *sabato* – note the 'o' at the end.) As a footnote, Sartana's costume, while still pitch black, is different here than in the other four films. Perhaps Garko had been allowed to retain his wardrobe; he had definitely earned his spurs – not to mention the suit, hat and cape – during his tenure in the role.

In the rush to cash in on Sartana, nobody paid much attention to Gastaldi and Salerno's intellectual property rights. Despite inventing the name for *Blood at Sundown*, the writers didn't use it in a film title and consequently couldn't copyright it. Hence, they would not have been entitled to receive any royalties from the many bogus Sartana films that appeared after *Pray for Your Death*. Gastaldi, who, despite his excellent western credits, specialised in thrillers, was reacquainted

with the character in *Gunman in Town*, adding *giallo* elements to the mix. Many years later, he and Salerno finally got the opportunity to resolve the rights issue. "I never saw the other 'Sartana' films," he says, "but [c. 1995] two producers fought to have the right to use the name. Vittorio [Salerno] and I had to go to court to say that neither of them had the right, because it was ours! We said they could both use Sartana without paying us, but they could not pretend it was theirs. The judge laughed."[32] It seems that while the spaghetti western was a going concern, the authors had to tolerate the proliferation of pseudo-Sartanas – none of whom, with the possible exception of George Ardisson in *Django Against Sartana* (1970), bore much resemblance to Garko's incarnation – but found it a bit rich when other parties tried to assert a legal claim to their creation.

above and top right: Belgian and Thai posters – distinguished chiefly by the quality of their artwork – for **I Am Sartana, Your Angel of Death**, which marked Giuliano Carnimeo's debut as a 'Sartana' director.

The man with gunsight eyes

Parolini was quick to capitalise on the success of Sartana, albeit indirectly. Together with writing partner Renato Izzo, who had co-scripted *Pray for Your Death* and Parolini's manic war movie, *Five for Hell* (1969), the director created *Sabata* in 1969. Alberto Grimaldi, the most successful producer of westerns at the time, provided financial backing via his production/distribution deal with United Artists, and Grimaldi's client Lee Van Cleef was signed to star, partly (as Parolini remembers it) on the strength of a rowdy screening of *Five for Hell* he'd attended with the director. (For his part, Parolini was largely motivated to abandon the 'Sartana' series by the chance to work with Van Cleef – at least, that's how Gianni Garko sees it.[33] The larger budget ensured by the Grimaldi/UA partnership can't have been insignificant in his decision either.) Van Cleef's recent record was exceptional, with *Day of Anger* (1967) having taken just under 3 billion lire at the box office, *Death Rides a Horse* (1967) close to 2 billion, and the light-hearted *Beyond the Law* (1968) almost 1 billion. All this gave Parolini the freedom to indulge his tastes for the baroque and the acrobatic on the grandest scale yet. The combination clearly delighted Italian audiences – *Sabata* was one of relatively few Italian westerns to score significantly at the domestic box office in 1969, when returns were generally on the wane. The presence of a superstar clearly made a difference, since other big hits that year starred such crowd-pleasing actors as Giuliano Gemma (*The Price of Power, Alive or Preferably Dead*), Tomas Milian (*Tepepa*) and Hill and Spencer (*Boot Hill*).

Parolini was well qualified to launch another franchise. Having apprenticed with various directors, including Roberto Rossellini and Jean Negulesco, and tried his hand at editing, production design and writing, he spent the first half of the Sixties toiling in that most mythopoeic of genres, the peplum. He made several of these with American bodybuilder Brad Harris, including *Samson* (1961) and *The Fury of Hercules* (1962). (Parolini's connection with Harris scored him some second-unit work on the German-produced *Pirates of the Mississippi* in 1963, the director's first taste of the western.) Despite the occasional flourish, however, Parolini's *pepla* are hard to distinguish from those of many other jobbing Italian directors of the era. It wasn't until 1965 that he really developed a personal style. That was the year he initiated the 'Kommissar X' spy series with *Kiss Kiss... Kill Kill*, a quintessentially Sixties confection financed by, among other countries, Italy, Austria and France. Spun off from a series of paperback adventures that were very popular in their native Germany (though Parolini was distinctly unimpressed: "I couldn't understand why the Germans loved them so much", he has said[34]), the film starred genial Italian leading man Tony Kendall [Luciano Stella] as suave, globetrotting private eye Joe Walker, and

above: **Sabata** refined Gianfranco Parolini's idiosyncratic vision of the West as a circus-cum-fairground, and gave him a more substantial budget – and a much bigger star, Lee Van Cleef – to play with. As in the 'Sartana' series, greed is the major motivator, as shown in this shot in which Van Cleef, guarding a bag full of swag, is flanked by his grasping associates, William Berger (*left*) and Pedro Sanchez (*right*).

above: William Berger enjoyed one of his finest supporting roles in **Sabata**, as the inscrutable Banjo, prototype for a string of fickle 'friends' who challenge the protagonist throughout the series. Here, he bides his time, as ever, in the company of a saloon girl, while a gunman (Gilberto Galimberti) gets the drop – or thinks he does – on Carrincha (Pedro Sanchez, the poor man's Fernando Sancho).

above: Van Cleef and Sanchez prepare for the film's spectacular finale.

above: Italian poster for **Kiss Kiss... Kill Kill**, first of the 'Kommissar X' adaptations and a perfect example of the Parolini aesthetic – cool, collected heroes, pop-art visuals, a perplexing plot and gadgets galore.

Considering his abilities as a showman, Parolini's opening gambit in the spaghetti western stakes, *Johnny West* (1965), is a disappointingly half-hearted affair. This film starring 'Dick Palmer' (Mimmo Palmara in a rare leading role) rarely rises above its standard revenge plot, and cries out for the inventiveness and enthusiasm that characterise Parolini's better works. It is hampered by non-sequiturs – Johnny's feared left hand, which is alluded to in the full Italian title, is crushed, but he proves equally adept with his right – and lurches between farce and drama. The script, partly crafted by Parolini, who claims to have made the film mainly as a favour for his friend Palmara and also wrote its theme song, is padded out with slapstick comedy that detracts from the stone-faced hero, whose potential as another of the genre's embittered half-breeds (he's part Cherokee) is never developed. The film does have pluses and quirky distinctions, however, including Johnny's peculiarly close relationship with his dog, Gypsy, his faithful confidante, whose death moves the otherwise stoical hero to tears, while the final shoot-out, executed with some verve, contains an early example of Parolinian skulduggery: a trick coffin from which the villain emerges, guns blazing.[36]

With *Pray for Your Death* and the 'Sabata' films, Parolini successfully fused the frenzied style of his espionage adventures – all quick cutting, lurid colours, elaborate gadgetry and acrobatic action – with the more down-to-earth demands of the western, creating a bizarre hybrid form in the process. Strictly speaking, the 'Sabata' trilogy is no such thing. While Van Cleef starred in the original and a sequel, *Return of Sabata* (1971), sandwiched in between was *Adios, Sabata* (1970), a vehicle for Yul Brynner that started life as *Indio Black, sai che te dico? Sei un gran figlio di...* (*Indio Black, You Know What They Say About You? You're a Great Big Son of a...*).[37] The filmmakers

Parolini's talisman, Brad Harris, as the long-suffering Tom Rowland, a cop who always gets caught up in Walker's cases.[35] Parolini's screen adaptation was inspired partly by the Bond films and partly by a series of German-made adventures featuring another secret agent, Jerry Cotton (played by American George Nader), whose own fictional progenitor enjoyed a healthy rivalry with the 'Kommissar X' characters at German bookstalls. Six sequels followed in six years, with Parolini directing two of them, all featuring the double act of Kendall and Harris. Harris was also a central figure in the director's *The Three Fantastic Supermen* (1967), a comic-strip caper that owes more to the camp, proto-psychedelic qualities of the *Batman* TV series than it does to Italy's *fumetti*. Inevitably, there were several spin-offs, though Parolini's involvement ended with the original.

above: For **Adios, Sabata**, the star (Yul Brynner) and setting changed, but the style (and sidekick Pedro Sanchez) remained the same.

no doubt hoped it would spawn a sequel or two of its own but, at some point during or after shooting, with *Sabata* doing excellent business, Brynner's character was renamed for the international market, where this film was distributed, like the first one, by United Artists. As we shall see, despite differences in costume and historical setting – it takes place in Mexico during the Juarez uprising against Maximilian in 1867 – *Adios, Sabata* can justifiably be considered an 'official' entry in the series, rather than one of the half-dozen or so misleadingly titled impostors.

Van Cleef's Sabata is a close relation of Sartana. They share a penchant for miniaturised, customised firearms, a similarly sinister ingenuity – Sabata, like Sartana, is called a "pall-bearer" in the first film and told "the devil rides with you" – and the same taste in pitch-black humour and clothing, although Sartana's ghostly quality is replaced by an imposing, martial bearing. (As we learn in *Return of Sabata*, he was a major in the American Civil War.) One other relative aspect is their motivation. On the surface, both men seem to be taking on the villains merely to line their pockets but, while money is a major factor – Van Cleef's Sabata, while he professes to be on the side of the law, has no qualms about blackmailing the criminal triumvirate in his first outing – the key is in their predilection for gambling. They are drawn to danger like

above: Lee Van Cleef was back for **Return of Sabata**, but the last part of the trilogy is also the least, with the in-jokes overstepping the mark.

they are drawn to dice, and relish pitting their wits and skills against self-styled master criminals. For Sabata and Sartana, such contests pose an irresistible test of their mental powers, as well as their physical resilience and technical expertise.

At first glance, Van Cleef could have stepped off the set of *For a Few Dollars More* (1965), draped in a frock coat

above: Lee Van Cleef in **Sabata** calls the shots against the villainous trio of (*from far left*) Antonio Gradoli, Franco Ressel and Gianni Rizzo.

almost identical to that worn by Sabata's fellow old soldier Colonel Mortimer. Sabata even has a Mortimer-esque rifle with an extendable barrel for long-range shooting, and he has the same ambiguous nobility as well. Despite such superficial similarities, *Sabata* was something of a departure for Van Cleef. While the character fits the actor's recast (anti-) heroic mould, there's little of the intensity or potential for growth that marked his other post-'Dollars' starring roles – Jonathan Corbett in *The Big Gundown*, Ryan in *Death Rides a Horse* and Frank Talby, the gunfighting Svengali, in *Day of Anger*. Sabata is a more abstract creation. Despite being in the thick of the action he seems removed from it at the same time, remaining unruffled and mildly amused by all the chaos he unleashes. As with *Pray for Your Death*, Parolini and his leading man perfectly judge the serious and comedic aspects of the enterprise, a feat they unfortunately failed to repeat in *Return of Sabata*. Like Gianni Garko in the 'Sartana' series, Van Cleef is clearly in on the joke, and it adds immensely to the enjoyment of the film. Speaking in 1982, the actor stressed the importance he placed on humour in his spaghetti westerns. "What we're trying to do is more or less right on the borderline of tongue-in-cheek. Sometimes we went a little bit *more* than tongue-in-cheek, but it was on the borderline at least."**38**

Van Cleef's easygoing approach contrasts with that of the dour Yul Brynner, a more self-conscious performer. In *Adios, Sabata*, Brynner practically replays his role as Chris from *The Magnificent Seven* (1960), maintaining his inscrutable composure while around him Parolini's stock

above: Lee Van Cleef and Pedro Sanchez in a shot from **Sabata** that sums up the avaricious nature of most of Parolini's western characters.

company of carnivalesque eccentrics act their hearts out. Sabata is the straight man in this good-humoured romp through revolutionary Mexico, in which the causes of the conflict are swiftly forgotten as Brynner's soldier of fortune and his rebel allies chase after a hoard of gold. It's never clear whether Sabata – armed, like Charles Southwood's Sabbath in *Sartana's Here... Trade Your Pistol for a Coffin*, with a sawn-off repeating rifle – wants the treasure for himself, for his partners or for the revolution, but, ultimately, even the rebels put profit before patriotism, with Sabata staying aloof. With his slight stature and stolid nature, Brynner looks uncomfortable in his elaborate outfit, a tight-fitting black number complete with tassels, medallion and a serape slung lazily over one shoulder, but his authoritative manner and aura of reptilian menace carry him through.

Whether played by Van Cleef or Brynner, Sabata is a stylish, purposeful figure, who carries out his killing with considerable panache and no little enthusiasm. (Brynner's habit of lighting up a cigar after a massacre is like an expression of displaced post-coital satisfaction.) Throughout the trilogy he is supplied with the requisite contrasting supporting characters: a gregarious, grubby sidekick (played in each case by Pedro Sanchez); one or two acrobats who either help or hinder his cause, such as the mute, enigmatic Alley Cat (Aldo Canti) in *Sabata*, who perches on the rooftops above the main street and bounds down when summoned, and Settiembre (Sal Borgese) in *Adios, Sabata*, who fells foes with metal balls flung by his feet; and some comically sadistic villains, in particular Stengel (Franco Ressel) in *Sabata* and Skimmel (Gérard Herter) in *Adios, Sabata*, both of whom strut through the action with a kind of fascistic pomp. Stengel, who is introduced reading a book called *Inequality Is the Basis of Society*, purportedly written by 19th Century slavery enthusiast Thomas Dew, is fond of making Nietzschean pronouncements such as, "Those men with

above: **Adios, Sabata**, with Yul Brynner (*right*) and Pedro Sanchez (*left*), was conceived as the vehicle for a new protagonist, Indio Black.

superior talents, and consequently with superior powers, always have one last card to play," a statement that rebounds on him in his final duel with Sabata. And when we first see Skimmel, an officer in Emperor Maximilian's regime, he is shooting peons for fun *à la* Major Jackson in *Django*. Herter's self-parodic performance is very similar to those he gives in *The Big Gundown*, complete with monocle, and *Full House for the Devil*.

The 'Sabata' series contains a further archetype, a slick, shifty friend-cum-foe whose amiable exterior, all superficial charm and insincere smiles, barely conceals an avaricious, treacherous core. This type of character flourished in the Machiavellian universe of the Italian western. William Berger played the first and most colourful of these untrustworthy rogues – Banjo, a flamboyant, romantic figure bedecked with tassels and bells who keeps a rifle hidden inside the instrument that provides his name. (Since many spaghetti directors were enthusiastic students of the American western, perhaps Parolini picked up this gag from the Roy Orbison vehicle *The Fastest Guitar Alive* [1967]. *Return of Sabata* extends the idea – the protagonist's sidekick possesses a bass drum that is rigged up with pistols for the final shoot-out.) Like his successors, Ballantine (Dean Reed)

Return of Sabata sidekicks, Bronco, played by Pedro Sanchez (*top*), and Clyde, given a smarmy sheen by German actor Reiner Schöne (*above*).

265

above: Japanese pressbook cover for **Adios, Sabata**.

in *Adios, Sabata* and Clyde (Reiner Schöne) in *Return*, Banjo has sparred with Sabata before, and tries on numerous occasions to double-cross him, proposing a new partnership each time his plan is defeated. Banjo and Clyde are particularly unscrupulous when it comes to women, stringing along their respective paramours for as long as they are of some use – Banjo even has a nightmare in which he agrees to settle down with his girl; as a typical western drifter, the idea of commitment leaves him in a cold sweat – while Ballantine is chiefly employed as a cynical counterpoint to the Mexican rebels led by Escudo (Sanchez). In each case, Sabata has "one last card to play", and ensures that his so-called partners finish up with, at most, a pittance of the disputed gold or cash. As with Sartana, Sabata is not only a faster draw and better marksman than his supposed allies, but also a more accomplished cheat.

Clearly, *Sabata* and its sequels are not to be taken seriously. Like the 'Sartana' films, they are steeped in cynicism and populated by ignoble, eccentric scavengers, while Parolini stages action scenes more like a ringmaster than a director, packing them with tumbling and trickery. (Sabata is like Parolini's alter ego in this respect – at one point in *Return of Sabata*, the protagonist is compared to a stage manager for his arranging and controlling of events.) He conjures them at the slightest opportunity, sacrificing narrative development for thrills and spills, but they are skilfully and imaginatively conceived and often brilliantly realised by cinematographer Sandro Mancori, who shot all the director's genre films. As *Films and Filming* observed, in a Parolini western "any whiff of a relationship to real life – or death – is completely eliminated". While the first two films are equally divided between the sublime and the ridiculous, *Return of Sabata* inclines more to the latter. Overrun by base humour, the script also demeans the title character by giving him a 'steady' girlfriend, an inane pop ditty in lieu of a theme, and suggesting he's a kind of ageing Lothario who seduces girls from town to town. All of this hampers Van Cleef's efforts to give Sabata the stature he enjoyed in his first adventure, and also conflicts with the star's persona, hinting at his wretched misuse in such ill-conceived westerns as *Captain Apache* (1971) and Parolini's *God's Gun* (1976). Even the villain, a paranoid Irish brute played by Giampiero Albertini, is bland. Yet despite being an unsatisfying conclusion to the series in general, in at least one respect *Return of Sabata* cleverly summarises Parolini's approach to the genre and to cinema in general. The highly stylised opening sequence, in which Sabata eliminates a group of white-shirted gunmen in what turns out to be a travelling circus sideshow, is brilliantly realised. Lit like a Mario Bava film and dressed with Gothic accessories, with Sabata's name hissed sinisterly on the soundtrack, it has a surreal, macabre quality broken only by the sudden appearance of clowns and the realisation that this, like so much else in Parolini's canon, is an exercise in the power of illusion, a theatrical conceit. It plays like a commentary on the artificiality and style-consciousness of the spaghetti western, especially as practised by showmen like Parolini and Giuliano Carnimeo. The sequence is grandiose, specious, but carried off with such aplomb that, like the audience in the film, one can only applaud the effect. It is Parolini's own brand of post-modernism, with the director running wild with in-jokes and allusions just as he does in his other westerns, particularly *God's Gun*. Furthermore, the opening captures the essence of Sabata and gunfighters like him, presenting him as a kind of fairground attraction, a mixture of trick shooter and illusionist who exists in a fantasy world where only he is indestructible.

above: Giampiero Albertini (*far right*) as the villain of **Return of Sabata**.
opposite: Tony Anthony fires a salvo in **For a Dollar in the Teeth**.

"I like places that smell of trouble – something good might turn up"

The established impression of the spaghetti western superhero is of a tight-lipped, self-sufficient, hyper-efficient killing machine, a deity of death. Even when his tongue is in his cheek, he still has an imposing, all-conquering aura. Which is what makes Tony Anthony's Stranger, who is usually dismissed as a mere Clint Eastwood clone, such an anomaly. First appearing in Luigi Vanzi's *Un dollaro tra i denti* (1967), released in America as *For a Dollar in the Teeth*, the Stranger is a much more down-to-earth, even down-at-heel creation. Although dressed like Eastwood, he resembles a streetwise scavenger more than a self-possessed gunfighter, relying on low cunning and resourcefulness rather than skill and technique. Whereas his peers have a kind of mythical stature, albeit tainted by contemporary cynicism, greed and ruthlessness, the Stranger avoids face-to-face confrontations wherever possible, preferring to engineer situations where there is minimal personal risk. To load the odds in his favour, he opts for close-range killing, often utilising a shotgun (the more barrels the better), shooting opponents from behind, from the shadows or even from beneath floorboards. He's mercenary, conniving, sometimes clumsy, but has a doggedness that continually wrong-foots his opponents. Anthony credits Vanzi, who directed under the name Vance Lewis, with the Stranger's core characteristics: "He used to talk to me about the old west, that everybody was a coward. He used to talk about trying to get that 'street' thing."[39] But the star, who wrote the stories for the last two films in the series, deserves the lion's share of the credit for the way he fleshes out the character as the series progresses, developing a deadpan sense of humour and a contradictory blend of world-weary resignation and bloody-minded determination designed to appeal to anybody who ever felt themselves hard done by. When he was sold to American filmgoers on the strength of his proto-punk mentality, the Stranger became, for a short time at least, the dog-eared darling of the drive-in circuit.

Of all the genre's American leading men, Anthony invested the most in his films – by the end of his stint in Italy he was producing as well as writing and starring in them. A West Virginian of Italian-Hungarian parentage, he began realising his artistic ambitions while still a student by establishing a theatre group, and in his early 20s he enrolled in New York's Actors' Studio. The Method style influenced his first film role as a misunderstood working-class kid in Saul Swimmer's *Force of Impulse* (1961), which Anthony also co-wrote, but his aspirations stretched further. He wrote and directed a Cannes prize-winning short, *The Boy Who Owned a Melephant* (1959), narrated by Tallulah Bankhead, while *Without Each Other* (1962), his second feature with Swimmer, had pretensions as an allegorical social drama (Anthony plays 'Boy', other characters include 'Mother', 'Girl' and 'Father'). Deciding to further his career in Italy's buoyant film industry, Anthony gained a few supporting roles – appearing in the Rossano Brazzi vehicle *Engagement Italiano* (1964) and Lina Wertmüller's *Let's Talk About Men* (1965), a portmanteau comedy starring Nino Manfredi – before venturing into westerns with Vanzi.

Critics were almost united in condemning the 'Stranger' films, taking predictable umbrage at their violence, which does have a conspicuously nasty edge to it in places, and disapproving of the way in which Anthony mocked heroic virtues to an even greater degree than most of his contemporaries. They made almost no effort to understand his revisionist approach, finding in his films only the same bad faith they had been deploring since the new wave Euro-western first emerged. Critical attacks on Vanzi's direction are easier to understand, if rather excessive, with *The New York Times* reckoning his work "could set westerns back a generation".

Any Gun Can Play

He shot the first film quickly and cheaply, the economic limitations evident in his sparse compositions and the relative lack of action and incident ("[it] comes as close as a film can to a still picture", reckoned *Time*), although results improve as the series goes on. Anthony told the fanzine *Spaghetti Cinema* that the director initially seemed to feel the project was beneath him. "He's one of those artistic type guys... he was a Roman snob and he did this for money." Given his background, it would be understandable if Vanzi looked on the western with condescension. He had begun his film career as assistant director to the likes of Fellini, Antonioni and Alessandro Blasetti, with whom he collaborated on the hit documentary *European Nights* (1959), co-written by Gualtiero Jacopetti of *Mondo cane* fame. Vanzi's first film as director was a follow-up to Blasetti's work entitled *World By Night* (1960), with Jacopetti again co-writing, but despite its commercial success – it was the fifth most popular film at the Italian box office in the 1959-60 season – he made just seven further films, including another documentary, *So This Is God's Country?* (1966), an outsider's view of the States narrated by novelist Italo Calvino. His 'Stranger' films have garnered cult popularity, but the limitations of the Vanzi-Anthony partnership were exposed when they tackled a straight-up gangster revenge story (written by Anthony) in *Pete, Pearl and the Pole* (1973). With its stereotypical mobsters and hackneyed dialogue, the film is mundane in all departments, and loses further points by wasting Richard Conte and Lionel Stander in pointless cameos. It is notable only for some nasty torture meted out to Anthony's small-time hood by liquor boss Adolfo Celi, a bloodstained climax and a few characteristically misogynistic one-liners from the star. It remains Vanzi's last feature to date.

We can split the four 'Stranger' films into two halves. The first two belong to the second phase of European western initiated by *A Fistful of Dollars*, while the last two transplant the character to 'foreign' shores, spicing up the action with ingredients from other genres. The plot of *For a Dollar in the Teeth* is basically a low-grade version of *Fistful*, with only one gang for the Stranger to exploit and a villainous turn by Frank Wolff that blatantly apes Gian Maria Volonté's performance as Ramon Rojo. (It's rumoured that Wolff had been offered the role of Ramon before Volonté came on the scene.) While Vanzi's direction is lethargic overall, his voyeuristic camerawork successfully transmits the threat of seemingly vacant places, especially in the opening sequence, and the outbursts of violence and other surprises – Anthony disturbed by a fluttering dove while exploring a darkened cellar, for example, leading to his discovery by the bandits – are well timed. The raw, grubby texture is enhanced by sexual innuendo, including a hint of lesbianism, and by Benedetto Ghiglia's cut-price guitar- and piano-based score, parts of which sound like they were recorded in a *taverna*. The film's prurient elements, combined with its offbeat, approachable protagonist, ensured a healthy box-office return (MGM made a decent profit when they distributed it in the States), prompting Roberto Infascelli's Primex Italiana, which produced *For a Dollar in the Teeth* in association with New York's Taka Productions, to team up with another NY production house, Reverse, and Berlin's Juventus Film, for a sequel, *Shoot First, Laugh Last*, aka *The Stranger Returns* (1967). While the plot is no more substantial than it was in the first film, Vanzi's direction

above, right and opposite: Where **For a Dollar in the Teeth** was an impertinent variation on **A Fistful of Dollars**, its first sequel, **Shoot First, Laugh Last**, brought Tony Anthony back for a concerted assault on western conventions, beginning with the make-up of the 'hero' himself.

is more assured and the satirical treatment of western machismo is even more pronounced – Anthony, shielding himself from the sun with a pink parasol, rides around on a horse called Pussy, and, in a recurring gag, he can't even manage to roll a cigarette successfully, spitting each one out in disgust after barely one drag. Giuseppe Mangione's script rings a few changes by introducing a couple of shady supporting characters, but essentially the formula is the same as in the first film, with Anthony, after numerous setbacks and beatings, eventually overcoming a bandit gang, this time with the aid of a four-barrelled shotgun. Besides Anthony, the acting plaudits belong to Marco Guglielmi as an eccentric preacher with a penchant for fireworks, who helps the Stranger, and himself, in the scramble for a gold-plated stagecoach, and to peplum graduate and future Clint Eastwood associate Dan Vadis, who gives an intimidating performance as bandit chief En Plein (his name, we're told, means "dead centre, never misses"). The scene where Vadis disrobes a sultry Mexican woman with rifle shots before killing her helpless, irate husband, is supremely sadistic.

With the third title in the series, *The Silent Stranger* (1968), the filmmakers made a commendable effort to stretch the boundaries of the genre.**40** The plot once again reworks the format of *A Fistful of Dollars* but, intriguingly, ships it back to Japan, from where Sergio Leone had borrowed it from Akira Kurosawa in the first place. The Stranger has travelled here hoping to be rewarded for delivering what he believes is a sacred scroll, only to land in the centre of a clan war. As in *Fistful*, the Stranger hopes to profit from both sides in the dispute, but here he never manages to exert control, his characteristic impotence exacerbated by the impassable cultural divide. Anthony's wandering vagabond is eventually told that the scroll is basically a promissory note; had he known, he could have exchanged it for a fortune held in a bank in San Francisco. "I never made an easy buck in my life," he sighs, as the realisation sinks in that his long, bruising trip has been in vain.

In many ways *The Silent Stranger* is the best film in the series. There are several well-choreographed battle scenes that make good use of the alien terrain (and its

above: Italian album sleeve art for Stelvio Cipriani's soundtrack to **Shoot First, Laugh Last**.

above and below: Stranger in a strange land: In **The Silent Stranger**, Tony Anthony and director Luigi Vanzi shipped their anti-hero off to Japan, paying homage in the process to Kurosawa, who inspired the film's rain-lashed battle scenes. Although its creators' ambitions were thwarted by a five-year hold-up between shooting and release, along with a number of studio-mandated cuts, this remains the most satisfying entry in the series.

changeable weather – the scenes in Japan were shot during typhoon season, giving the action sequences a hint of Kurosawa), involving traditional samurai weaponry and contemporary gunplay, while Anthony captures all the confusion of an outsider imperilled in a hostile foreign land with his customary fatalistic sense of humour. It also anticipates the meeting of orientals and gunslingers in several Seventies westerns, notably Terence Young's *Red Sun* (1971). The film's effect is lessened, however, by re-editing undertaken in America, presumably while it was sitting on the shelves at MGM for more than five years awaiting release. (It didn't see the light of day in Italy until even later, in 1977.) As with Anthony's previous westerns, and the subsequent *Blindman* (1971), the American rights were held by the Beatles' producer, Allen Klein, whose ABKCO entered into a distribution deal with MGM. According to Anthony, the five-year hiatus between production and release was a side effect of musical chairs among the top brass at MGM, combined with a reassessment of the commercial value of westerns. Studio chiefs were also unsure how to market a genre film that owed as much to Kurosawa, if only in a superficial sense, as it did to Leone. It still seems odd how nobody took the opportunity to capitalise sooner on the success of the previous 'Stranger' films, or at least the brief vogue for East-meets-Westerns. At any rate, the fate of *The Silent Stranger* continues to rankle with Anthony, who rated the original version his best work.

The Stranger's final adventure, *Get Mean* (1975), takes Anthony even further outside the realms of reality, following the offbeat trail he and director Ferdinando Baldi had taken in *Blindman*. This is laudable enough – the best European westerns set out to explore new frontiers, and Anthony's eccentric personality would hardly suit neorealism – but *Get Mean* is so haphazardly plotted that it lacks even the internal logic essential in any successful fantasy. This time, Anthony, as well as starring and writing the story, took on the production chores (under the appropriate banner of Strange Films), and must have hoped that he and Baldi could conjure up the same magic as they had in *Blindman*. (There was apparently talk of extending the series even further had this entry been a success.) The end result, while containing its fair share of magic, plays like an elongated episode of *The Twilight Zone* – a mishmash of spaghetti western styling, second-rate surrealism, slapstick and a dash of kinky eroticism. After a bizarre opening sequence in which he is dragged behind a riderless horse into a ghost town, the Stranger travels to Spain in the company of an exiled princess, whose Moorish allies are striving to oust the barbarian hordes that have overrun the country. The plot is basically the same as in *The Silent Stranger*, with Anthony caught between two feuding forces in a foreign land, but here it's laced with wilfully weird incidents, inane comedy and mismatched characters thrown together in the forlorn hope they might mesh. A mysterious silver orb appears at the beginning and the end, presumably intended to represent a portal through which the Stranger crosses not merely oceans but time and space as well. This 'explains' the presence in 19th Century Spain of Moors, Vikings, Goths and other disparate marauders. The end result is as contrived and disposable as it sounds, but at least it's never dull, unlike many other Euro-westerns from the mid-Seventies, and Anthony's face registers reversals with fine comic timing. *Get Mean* also contains the long-suffering Stranger's key philosophical statement: "When things are even up, a man really should fight fair, but when they just keep puttin' it to ya buddy, and when they're stompin' on your ass, there's only one way to fight – get mean!"

What the 'Stranger' films lack in substance they make up for in irreverence, largely as a result of Anthony's oblique approach to the genre. It's this quality that makes the Stranger unique among his fellow franchisees. Whereas Django, Sartana et al rework the classic western hero's commanding demeanour into a menacing aura of invincibility, Anthony's response to adversity is a curious combination of obstinacy and fatalism. He and Vanzi's original intention – to strip away the reverence, honour and dignity accrued by fictional western heroes over the years – is underscored by the

above: Tony Anthony's hard-pressed Stranger was perhaps the genre's ultimate martyr, suffering numerous beatings and embarrassing predicaments over the course of four films. In **The Silent Stranger**, besides being strung up like a scarecrow, he is confronted by a malevolent dwarf, knife-wielding women and thrown into a pigsty.

way the Stranger suffers constant affronts, which vary from beatings and trussings to being thrown in with chickens and pigs. He reaches perhaps his lowest point in *Get Mean*, in which his Spanish hosts roast him on a spit. To heap further degradation upon the character he is frequently attacked by women, to which he responds with misogynistic quips and violence when necessary, most starkly in *For a Dollar in the Teeth* (aka *A Stranger in Town*) when he brutally bashes the head of Gia Sandri's fashionably attired dominatrix against the floor. Hardly a sympathetic figure, then, yet Anthony manages to endow this scurrilous louse with a ragged charm, while his deadpan humour never flags. He also shows traces of magnanimity and generosity, as when he aids a woman and child in *For a Dollar in the Teeth* (another aspect stolen from *A Fistful of Dollars*) and shares his reward with the preacher at the end of *Shoot First, Laugh Last*. If only for these flecks of humanity, perhaps the Stranger deserves the scraps he ends up with more than most genre mercenaries – he's certainly made to sweat blood for them.

Forgotten pistoleros

Looking beyond the five figures whose careers I have chronicled, the European western landscape is crowded with characters that seemed destined or designed for series of their own. However, for one reason or another, chiefly for lack of a sufficient spark at the box office, they never quite caught fire. It would have been fun to see more of *Starblack* (1966), for example, a black-masked bastardisation of Zorro, the Lone Ranger and Euro-western avenger. As played by Robert Woods, Starblack combines old-fashioned heroism with new-fangled Italian western ruthlessness, but the film's domestic takings were insufficient to take his escapades any further. (To add insult to injury, *Starblack* was promoted in Germany as a 'Django' film.) Another Woods character, Pecos Martinez, made a much stronger impression in Maurizio Lucidi's *My Name Is Pecos* (1966). The star's cool, laconic performance effectively displaces characteristics usually associated with American gunfighters onto a traditionally racially abused and marginalised figure – the Mexican half-breed.

Despite his obvious appeal as a champion of the oppressed (as we saw in *Don't Buy Bread – Buy Dynamite*, Woods was feted in certain Third World countries on the strength of his performance), the filmmakers chose to take Pecos in a different direction in the follow-up, *Pecos Cleans Up* (1967), again directed by Lucidi, which plays more like an exotic adventure in the vein of H. Rider Haggard or Emilio Salgari than it does a western. Woods, not a fan of sequels, agreed to reprise the role because he liked the character, but felt that Pecos was out of place in the new film. "They wanted to cash in on what the first one made. As long as the cast was there it didn't matter. So they wrote this pedestrian script. It was amusing in places, but wasn't really a western."[41] Producers Franco Palombi and Gabriele Silvestri made their point, however, since *Pecos Cleans Up* did just that at the Italian box office, making almost as much money as the first film.

Another obvious candidate for commercialisation was Tony Anthony and Ferdinando Baldi's *Blindman* (1971), their answer to Japan's Zatoichi, the hugely popular blind masseur/swordsman immortalised by Shintarô Katsu. Whereas Zatoichi's celluloid adventures at present number 27, including the 2003 instalment by

above: Have fun with your gun: In **Blindman**, Tony Anthony's deconstruction of the western hero reached a self-parodic peak almost unparalleled in a 'straight' production

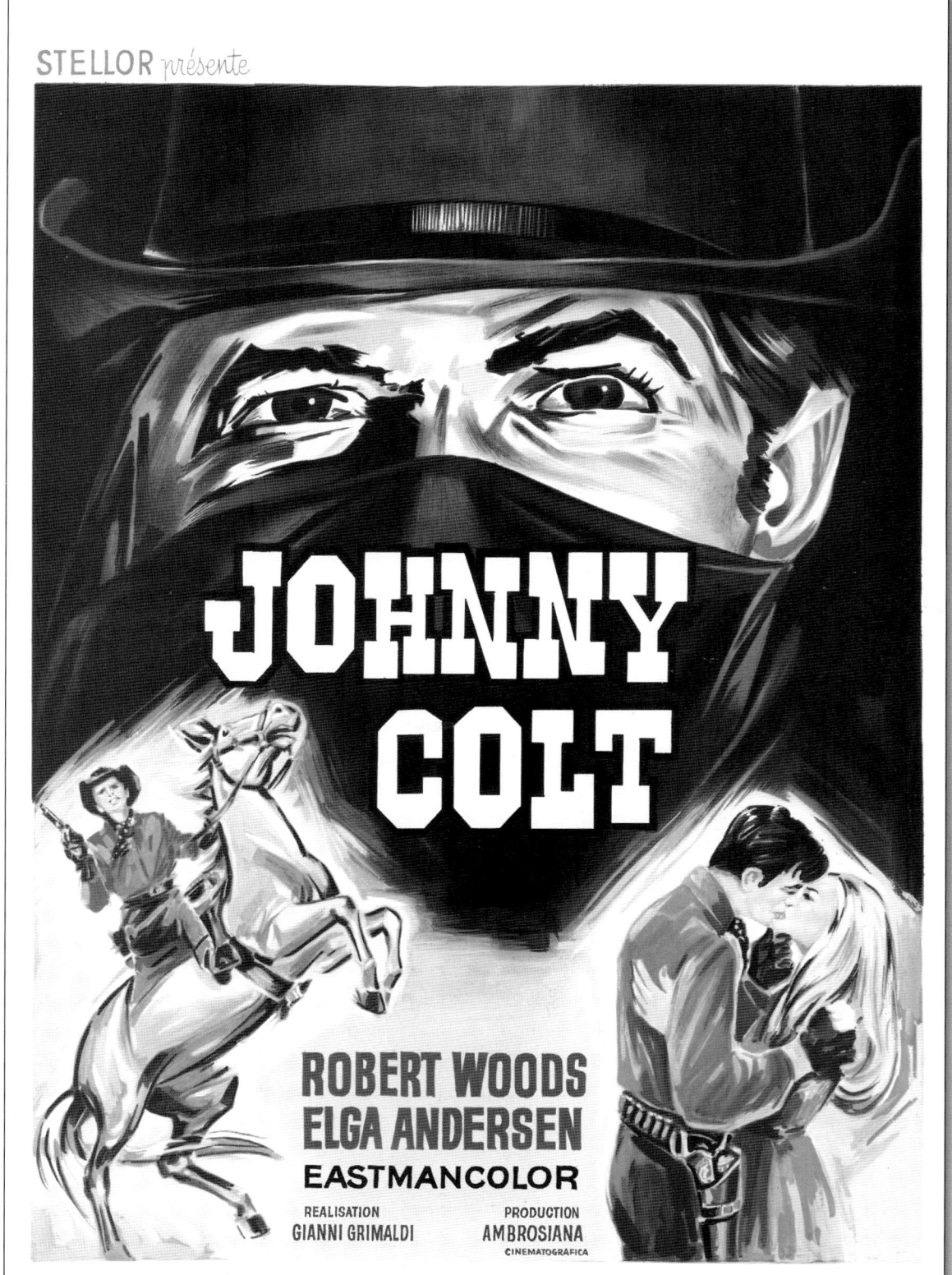

above and opposite top: French and Italian posters for **Starblack**, the story of a masked avenger whose violent methods often seem out of place in a largely juvenile adventure.

Takeshi Kitano, plus more than 100 television episodes, this was Blindman's sole outing. One of the main reasons for this was Anthony's physical discomfort in the role as a result of the special contact lenses he was obliged to wear. As well as acting, he wrote the story and co-signed the script (with Piero Anchisi and Vincenzo Cerami, the latter a future Oscar-nominee for *Life Is Beautiful* [1997]), and co-produced with long-time creative partner Saul Swimmer and Allen Klein's ABKCO. Their investment paid off: *Blindman* made substantial profits around the world, though it lagged behind the 'Stranger' series in America, and Anthony claims he received offers from, among others, Universal, Fox and Paramount, to take the character further. He was beginning to concentrate more on producing than acting, however, and this, combined with his suffering during filming, prompted him to turn them down, much to his regret in later years. "It was probably one of the biggest mistakes that I made in my career."[42]

For most mainstream critics, habitually hostile to Anthony's output, this one outlandish adventure was more than enough. Besides taking exception to its mixture of sadism and salaciousness, the inevitably negative reviews focused on the film's efforts to enlarge upon the genre's essential ingredients while sending them up at the same time – "Everything is exaggerated, but played straight," was how Anthony expressed it. As a pastiche – and that's the only reasonable way to view it – *Blindman* has no equal in the canon. The star offers his most offbeat interpretation of 'heroism' to date: he's a sightless, shabby adventurer whose impairment, rather than being treated in the usual way as a tragic flaw, is the excuse for a lot of tasteless jokes at his expense. The plot, for instance, provides him with 50 beautiful mail-order brides to deliver to some sex-starved Texan miners; of course, our hero is the only one who can't appreciate their looks, and at one point they are stolen from him and replaced with a number of crones.

above and top left: Inspired by the Japanese 'Zatoichi' films, **Blindman** varied the overused treasure-hunt format by converting the treasure at stake into a consignment of mail-order brides.

Nor is he necessarily wiser for his disability, which is often the way with blind characters in films, although his other senses and intuitive powers are sharp enough, like the bayonet affixed to his rifle, to enable him to make a living as a mercenary. He also leans heavily on his 'seeing eye' horse, parodying the cowboy's traditional telepathic relationship with his trusty steed.

The character shares many traits with the Stranger: deviousness, tenacity and the same laconic, self-deprecating wit, expressed here in the form of cod-philosophical observations on fate and misfortune."To have no eyes is to be half a man. To have no eyes and no money, now that's a bitch," is just one such nugget of motivational wisdom. When Anthony describes Blindman, he could easily be talking about his earlier role."He's not your typical gunslinger. He's more of an existential hero… I never wanted to be a superhero; I felt audiences could relate to me as someone in the street."[43] Indeed, aside from the Stranger, no other Euro-western protagonist was quite so attuned to the counterculture vibe; Blindman even uses summer-of-love phraseology at one point.

This unorthodox protagonist spars with supporting characters that are eccentric even by Italian western standards. These include ex-Beatle Ringo Starr as a lovesick Mexican bandit; Lloyd Battista (in a role at one stage earmarked for *Thunderball*'s Adolfo Celi) as Starr's increasingly exasperated brother; and Raf Baldassarre as a crazed army officer. Baldi fashions some bizarre set pieces, like the absurd funeral/wedding of Starr's character, all to the accompaniment of a cacophonous, mock-Morricone score by Stelvio Cipriani. As well as echoing previous Italian westerns, the story combines elements of *Westward the Women* (1951) with Japanese *chambara eiga*, minus the feminist undertones of the former (consider the dehumanisation of the 50 brides, condensed into one precious cargo disputed between men, and the indignities suffered by leading ladies Agneta Eckemyr and Magda Konopka) and lacking the ethical preoccupations of *chambara*. The budget, meanwhile, which increased considerably when Starr's involvement was secured, allows for an unusually lavish treatment – there are scores of extras and several spectacular action sequences, including a number of massacres and large-scale chases photographed with almost hallucinatory intensity by Riccardo Pallottini, notably when the captive women in their white robes flee from Battista's bandits across the white-hot desert dunes. The exuberance and enthusiasm of all involved is especially striking considering that most Euro-westerns of the time, certain comedies excepted, were listlessly going through the motions. 'Exaggerated', to use Tony Anthony's adjective, is only partially adequate to describe this most extravagant and outrageous of films.

The casting of Ringo Starr is one more reason for *Blindman*'s continuing cult appeal. Starr's far-from-illustrious film career had begun in 1968, when he played another Mexican in the sloppy all-star sex farce *Candy*. Not by chance, Candy is the name of his character in *Blindman* and, while he's no Olivier, Starr attacks the role with gusto. "I took the part because it was so far apart from anything I had ever done before. I start every scene fairly straight, and end up as an out-and-out madman, and the energy you have to use for that! It was the first time I ever saw what actors could get off on. It was the first time, as an actor, that I felt, 'Well, that's why they keep on doing it. It was one of those things that you can't really describe. The whole thing takes over your body, and you just get elated with it. In that film I play another Mexican. I raped the girl, stabbed her father and beat up everybody, because I was a paranoiac brother of the bandit chief. That was funny, but the only drag was that they kept putting me on horses. I don't particularly like horses, but they found Mount Olympus for me to ride so they had to keep cutting because I couldn't get on this horse. The stirrup was eye level. Every time I went to get up on the horse, they had to cut and lift me up on to the horse because it was so big."[44]

A few more superheroes rode into town in the early Seventies, when the genre was beginning its decisive shift towards self-parody, but they appeared too late in the day to make a lasting impression. Apart, that is, from Trinity and Bambino, who set the tone for all the most successful westerns of the period. Characters such as Hallelujah, the Holy Ghost and Tresette – all brought to the screen by Giuliano Carnimeo – have their tongues wedged firmly in their cheeks, and the majority of screen time in their films is given over to slapstick brawling, very fashionable at the time. Accordingly, their exploits are chronicled in the context of comedy westerns in the next chapter.

In the same way that different mythological characters had been shoehorned into shared stories towards the end of the peplum cycle in the hope that their combined personalities might overcome audience ennui – recalling in turn the matches served up in series westerns of the Forties, DC and Marvel comics,

above: Director Demofilo Fidani – perhaps the closest thing to a true auteur the genre possessed – sadly squandered the potential inherent in the 'Django' and 'Sartana' brands. His **One Damned Day at Dawn… Django Meets Sartana!** – featuring Benito Pacifico, a member of Fidani's stock company – was particularly anticlimactic: the day in question is not especially tempestuous, and the protagonists' encounter elicits little more than a shrug.

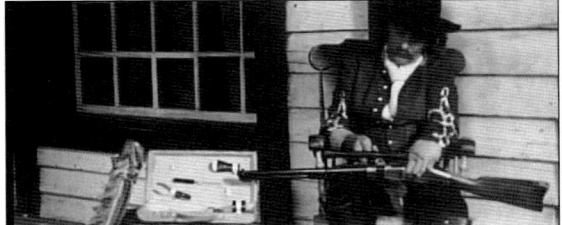

above: William Berger as Duke, a character who deserved a spin-off or sequel of his own, in Giuliano Carnimeo's **They Call Him Cemetery**.

and Universal horror films – so their gun-slinging descendents were paired off in the early Seventies.[45] Hallelujah and Trinity, Hallelujah and Sartana and, inevitably, Django and Sartana, were all brought together in a number of superfluous double-headers. Pasquale Squitieri helmed the disappointing *Django Against Sartana*, with Tony Kendall and George Ardisson in the title roles, while Demofilo Fidani made *Django and Sartana Are Coming… It's the End* and *One Damned Day at Dawn… Django Meets Sartana!* Squitieri's film promises a titanic struggle but compromises with a single, albeit lengthy, punch-up between the lacklustre leads before they strike up a partnership. Fidani's efforts exhibit his strange brand of camp machismo but, again, the potential of pairing two pulp icons is not fulfilled. *One Damned Day* in particular is a missed opportunity. Although more competently made than most films by this particular director, it is virtually over by the time that Fabio Testi's previously anonymous, ineffective character reveals that he is actually Sartana. Hunt Powers's Django looks suitably unimpressed by the revelation. Once again, somebody – whether writer-director Fidani or the distributor – has pulled off a confidence trick in time-honoured B-movie tradition, promoting the film on a false basis and offering the slightest of justifications for its misleading title. If ever there was a case of taking a great character's name in vain, this was it.

It seems fitting to round off this chapter with another of those films that seemed preconceived with a series in mind. *They Call Him Cemetery*, aka *Bullet for a Stranger* (1971), was a late entrant in the superhero stakes from Giuliano Carnimeo, a man who specialised in comic-strip style characters. This most prolific of western directors (he made 12 in all) had abandoned a budding law career in favour of the cinema, where he began by assisting Giorgio Simonelli on a number of Franco and Ciccio comedies. In 1968, his first solo features, directed under the alias 'Anthony Ascott', were both westerns: the witty, *giallo*-esque *The Moment to Kill*; and *Find a Place to Die*, a loose remake of Henry Hathaway's *Garden of Evil* (1954), and the following year he succeeded Parolini as director of the 'Sartana' series. *They Call Him Cemetery*, his eighth western, incorporates both the dual-protagonist format outlined above (and used already by Carnimeo in *The Moment to Kill*) and an abundance of comedy, both of which were symptoms of fatigue in the genre. Even so, it succeeds against the odds. This is due largely to the charismatic central partnership of Gianni Garko and William Berger, who play two notorious gunfighters who take different sides in a land dispute. The stars draw on their own screen personas to give their performances added resonance, resulting in the pleasing spectacle of two experienced genre campaigners sizing each other up, a mutual professional respect that is woven into the fabric of the film. Both men go by lofty nicknames – the Ace of Hearts (Garko) is moody and mysterious, haunted by the death of his wife years beforehand, while Duke (Berger) is more loquacious and laid-back. Despite being on opposite sides, and even though there's money at stake, the characters engage in brinkmanship, using delaying tactics or deceit to avoid an unpleasant confrontation. Their macho taunts are reminiscent of Monco and Mortimer in *For a Few Dollars More* (at one point they shoot each others' spurs off), and ultimately they seem relieved to have skirted the issue of superiority. For once, the lack of a definitive showdown is not a disappointment, such is the expertise of the characterisations.

They Call Him Cemetery is a frustrating film. Its strong centre is undermined by ill-fitting slapstick humour – the signature of its writer, Enzo Barboni – and erratic direction from Carnimeo, who can't quite make the film's serious and comedic aspects or its distinct 'sets' of characters gel (besides the two gunfighters there are twin brothers and two servants). Despite these flaws, it's a pleasure to watch two excellent actors together at their peak. In Garko's estimation, the Ace of Hearts is second only to Sartana, and he speaks highly of the film itself: "Carnimeo directed people with a very fine, intelligent hand – he had a light touch. The film had a good rhythm, a good sense of humour and a good sense of adventure... [And] there was a very good relationship between the two gunslingers. We [he and William Berger] were very mature in our western experience, we were at the top of our profession."**46** He says there was never a sequel proposed, which is a shame considering the chemistry of the co-stars. Carnimeo remarks: "The Italowestern [sic] in 1971, in all its perspectives and interpretations, was fading away. One could not plan on sequels any more." (Despite what he says, Carnimeo was able to make two 'Hallelujah' films and two 'Holy Ghost' films over the following few years.) Then again, it's likely that any second outing for Ace and Duke would have focused more on the comedy than the characters, which would have been a travesty.

footnotes

1 For more on the 'Winnetou' series, see *Target Practice*. Zorro (the Spanish word for 'fox') first appeared in 1919 in Johnston McCulley's serialised novel *The Curse of Capistrano*. A dashing romantic hero in the Scarlet Pimpernel mould, he has featured in countless books, comic strips, films and television series. His appeal stretched across the Atlantic and yielded several European-made adventures, some of which played very much like westerns. The cycle began with Mario Soldati's parody *The Dream of Zorro* (1952), starring the genial Walter Chiari, with subsequent entries involving the talents of several prominent genre filmmakers, including the brothers Joaquín and Rafael Romero Marchent, Mario Caiano and Duccio Tessari, whose raucous 1975 version with Alain Delon is the best known of the European Zorro films. Other notable titles include Caiano's *The Sign of Zorro* (1963), which saw Sean Flynn, son of famed swashbuckler Errol, in the title role, and the inevitable Franco and Ciccio spoof, *The Nephews of Zorro* (1968), with Dean Reed behind the black mask. Europe also spawned a number of Zorro imitators, including Joaquín Romero Marchent's *El Coyote* (1955), which had several follow-ups of its own.
2 The title was imposed on Tessari by his producers, displacing the director's choice of 'Troppi morti per un uomo solo' – roughly, 'Too many victims for a single man'. Tessari's affection for the name 'Ringo' cannot be doubted, however: as revealed in Marco Giusti's *Dizionario del western all'Italiana*, Tessari had given Clint Eastwood's character that name in his treatment for *A Fistful of Dollars*, only to have it vetoed by Sergio Leone.
3 Although most accounts state that the two 'Ringo' films were shot almost simultaneously (they were released in Italy within seven months of each other), Giuliano Gemma remembers it differently: "They were shot a year apart and in between I made another western, *One Silver Dollar*, which was a great success... It was shot in just over 30 days and broke box-office records. Then we shot the second 'Ringo' film with Tessari." Interview with Giuliano Gemma conducted for this book by Alex Marlow-Mann and Julian Grainger.
4 Other westerns with a similar 'siege mentality' include: *A Taste of Death* (1968), an admirable though little-seen snowbound saga that borrows from André de Toth's *Day of the Outlaw* (1959) while constructing an allegory of totalitarianism; the slow-burning *Shoot the Living and Pray for the Dead* (1971), with Klaus Kinski; and, off at a tangent, the Gothic, claustrophobic *Kill the Wicked* (1967) and its psychedelic pseudo-remake, *Matalo!* (1970).
5 Author's interview with Robert Woods. Gemma's pseudonym 'Montgomery Wood' also may be a conflation of American actors' names – Montgomery Clift and Clint Eastwood.
6 Carlos Aguilar, *Giuliano Gemma: El factor romano*, p.52.
7 Interview with Giuliano Gemma conducted for this book by Alex Marlow-Mann and Julian Grainger.
8 Ibid.
9 Marco Giusti, *Dizionario del western all'Italiana*, p248.
10 Pointed examples include *Texas Adios* (*Django der Rächer/ Django the Avenger*), *Massacre Time* (*Django, Sein Gesangsbuch war der Colt/His Prayer Book Was His Colt*) and the Enzo Castellari *Jaws* knock-off *The Shark Hunter* (1979), which was resold in Germany as *Dschungel – Django/Jungle Django*.
11 Frayling supplies further structural similarities between *Django* and *A Fistful of Dollars* in *Spaghetti Westerns: Cowboys and Europeans from Karl May to Sergio Leone*, p.79.

above: European 'Zorro' films – with Piero Pierotti's **Zorro the Rebel** among their number – dovetailed with westerns in the Sixties.

above: Italian locandina for **Mestizo**, an unassuming Spanish western re-branded to entice fans of **Django**.

war, challenged ten at a time by Fierro to see if they could run 100 yards and climb a wall to freedom before he could shoot them. Apparently, only one man could manage it.

16   It seems appropriate that chance, which plays a decisive role in Django's adventures, also played a part in the casting of the role, as Nero recalls. "Originally there was another actor, Mark Damon, who was supposed to play Django. He was busy and they would have had to wait for him for three or four weeks. Corbucci didn't want to wait... There was also another actor involved – I think it was Peter Martell – so the producers had a discussion and Manolo Bolognini said, 'None of these people are well known so we'll go to the distributor, Fulvio Frizzi of Euro International Films, and show him their photos and let him choose the face for the film.' Frizzi put his finger on my face and that's the reason that they chose me." Author's interview with Franco Nero.

17   Ibid.

18   Corbucci is quoted in *Spaghetti Cinema*. For more on *Django*'s influence on reggae culture, see '*Don't Buy Bread, Buy Dynamite*', note 6.

19   Sir Christopher Frayling provides plot summaries for the major follow-ups in *Spaghetti Westerns*, revealing a set of recurring motifs in which, as with the 'Ringo' cycle, the identity of the protagonist is almost a moot point. Given the sheer volume of spin-offs, it is useful to divide them into three categories. First are those films that incorporated certain aspects of the original – whether it was merely the name of the character or something more substantial – but are in most respects indistinguishable from a hundred other westerns. These include Alberto De Martino's *Django Shoots First* (1966), Enzo Castellari's *A Few Dollars for Django* (1966) and Osvaldo Civirani's *Son of Django* (1967). (It's worth giving a brief mention to the musical western *Rita of the West* [1967], which contains an amusing *Django* skit.) Then there are many extrinsic or previously unsuccessful westerns that underwent a change of title, or some drastic dubbing, for a second bite at the box office. Here we find the likes of *Mestizo* (1966), a Canada-based Mountie film re-released in 1967 as *Django Does Not Forgive*, and *Django the Honourable Killer/Django the Condemned*, a retitling of the 1965 Spanish production *Outlaw of Red River*, directed by American Maury Dexter. The final category contains many westerns, distinctive in their own right and with their own well-drawn personalities, which were nevertheless transformed into 'Django' films, principally for the German and French markets. *God Forgives... I Don't!* (1967), for example, became *Gott vergibt – Django nie!* (*God Forgives – Django Doesn't!*); and even Sartana wasn't immune, with *Sartana's Here... Trade Your Pistol for a Coffin* (1970) released in France as *Django arrive... préparez vos cerceuils* (*Django is Here...Prepare Your Coffins*) and in Germany as *Django – Die Gier nach Gold* (*Django – The Greed for Gold*).

20   Author's interview with Franco Nero.

21   Quoted in *Spaghetti Cinema*.

22   Author's interview with Gianni Garko.

23   Author's interview with Franco Nero.

24   Ibid.

25   Author's interview with Gianni Garko.

26   Interview with Gianfranco Parolini by Matteo Norcini and Stefano Ippoliti in *Cine 70* magazine.

27   For an alternative version of Sartana's origins, see Marco Giusti, *Dizionario del western all'Italiana*, in which scriptwriter

12   Quoted in Bruschini & Tentori, *Western all'Italiana Volume One: The Specialists*, p.54-55.

13   *Django* was rejected outright by the BBFC on 6 April 1969 when submitted there by a small distributor, Butchers Film Service Ltd. Although there was a UK video version in circulation before that industry was regulated, the film didn't receive a certificate until 16 February 1993, when Arthouse Productions revived it for a theatrical run and video release.

14   Author's interview with Franco Nero.

15   This incident is based on fact (or possibly folklore): Bronson's character, Rodolfo Fierro, was one of Villa's most feared and brutal associates. Among his documented exploits was the single-handed slaughter of almost 200 prisoners of

above, from left: Glenn Saxson, Fernando Sancho and Alberto Lupo in **Django Shoots First**, which was quick off the mark in the race to profit from the worldwide popularity of **Django**.

Fabio Piccioni claims that he and his colleagues took the name from a dialectal term for frying pan (!), and it's revealed that before Parolini was assigned, Guido Zurli was scheduled to direct.

28   The dapper, unflappable illusionist Mandrake predates even Superman as a costumed comic-book hero. First published in 1934 – four years before the Man of Steel's debut – Mandrake learnt his skills in Tibet; one of his teachers later embraced evil and became a recurrent villain in the strips. As well as print media, Mandrake starred in a Thirties cinema serial, a 1979 TV movie and an Eighties cartoon show called *Defenders of the Earth*, where he was teamed with Flash Gordon and Lee Falk's best-known creation, The Phantom.

29   Interview published in the autumn 1992 issue of *Westerns all'Italiana*.

30   Interview with Giuliano Carnimeo conducted for this book by Mario Marsili.

31   Quoted in Marco Giusti, *Dizionario del western all'Italiana*.

32   Author's interview with Ernesto Gastaldi.

33   Author's interview with Gianni Garko.

34   Interview with Gianfranco Parolini by Matteo Norcini and Stefano Ippoliti in *Cine 70* magazine.

35   The 'Kommissar X' characters were created in 1959 by Karl Heinz Guenther, a staff writer for the Erich Pabel publishing house. Guenther wrote more than 100 'Kommissar X' titles up to 1964, while a stable of writers, sometimes working under the collective alias Bert F. Island, contributed hundreds of others. 'Island' receives script credit on most of the 'Kommissar X' films. Guenther later introduced the secret agent Bob Urban, aka Mister Dynamite, as a German counterpart to James Bond. Urban was subsequently interpreted by an American, Lex Barker of Old Shatterhand fame, in the big screen spin-off *Spy Today, Die Tomorrow* (1967).

36   Parolini is credited as director by some sources of another transcontinental western, *The Tall Women* (1966), a revamping of *Westward the Women* starring Anne Baxter, of all people. Parolini's involvement is presumed by the directorial alias that appears on some versions of the film, Cehett Grooper, but this was really a *nom de plume* of Austrian director Rudolf Zehetgruber and, in any case, Parolini has stated that he had nothing to do with the film. It seems most likely that it was actually the work of American veteran Sidney Pink.

37   The film's UK release title was the generic *The Bounty Hunters*.

38   Interview with Lee Van Cleef by Max Alan Collins, *European Trash Cinema* vol.2, no.7.

39   Interview with Tony Anthony by William Connolly, *Spaghetti Cinema* no.40.

40   Although *The Silent Stranger* is credited solely to Luigi Vanzi, co-writer Vincenzo Cerami reportedly filled in for the director for a few weeks while the latter was incapacitated (Marco Giusti, *Dizionario del western all'Italiana*).

41   Author's interview with Robert Woods.

42   Quoted in issue 65 of *Spaghetti Cinema*, August 1995.

43   Quoted in issue 20 of *Westerns all'Italiana*, winter 1989.

44   Quoted in Keith Badman, *The Beatles Off the Record: The Dream Is Over* (Omnibus Press, 2001).

45   See Frayling, *Spaghetti Westerns*, p71-73.

46   Author's interview with Gianni Garko.

above: A Shaw-fire success? Euro-westerns and martial arts movies seemed like a perfect match in the early Seventies, but most – even this vehicle for two of the genres' heaviest hitters – lacked punching power at the box office.

Chapter 7

Hybrid Westerns

The Influence of Horror, Humour and the Martial Arts

The adulteration of the European western in the Seventies is traditionally perceived as a sign of its decline. The preponderance of all-out comedy westerns beginning with the 'Trinity' films and the introduction of newly fashionable martial artists into the schema looked, on the surface at least, like last-ditch gambits to re-engage jaded audiences. Yet this is a simplistic reading that overlooks the fact that Euro-westerns were anything but 'pure' in the first place. These films had always displayed magpie tendencies. Irony, in both subtle and intemperate doses, had been present almost from the genre's inception, while shades of melodrama, Gothic horror and fantasy mark many of its most distinctive examples. It can't be argued, however, that the greater emphasis on slapstick comedy in the early Seventies signalled a change of course, away from the misanthropic world view that had previously underpinned the genre and towards a more easy-going, though still cynical, perspective. And the kung-fu westerns made at this time were obviously attempts to siphon off some of the popular support for martial arts movies, which, abroad if not so much in Italy, shared the same sort of audience base as the Euro-western at its peak. Yet even during this desperate period, when such experimentation was essentially a countermeasure dictated by dwindling box-office returns, one could still detect flashes of artistry and inventiveness, evidence of the continuing commitment by individual filmmakers to expanding the western's parameters.

This process had begun several years earlier. One of the defining traits of the post-Leone Euro-western was the way in which its leading filmmakers gave themselves carte blanche to redefine Hollywood's version of the old west (which was hardly a faithful re-creation in the first place) according to their imaginations. Once the commercial potential for a radical reinterpretation of western motifs had been tapped, there were no further restrictions for irreverent artists who wanted to confound audience expectations at the same time as they appeared to be meeting them, their films engaging and disengaging with the genre at will. In this way they acknowledged the cultural gulf between themselves and their mythic material, accepting that they could never make a 'western' in the traditional sense, but choosing to treat this as an opportunity rather than an obstacle. Historical veracity, if it had any meaning at all by this stage in the western's existence, was seen by many as almost an irrelevance. "Maybe we were a bit irresponsible, a little devil-may-care, and we had the idea that few would have seen [our films], so we could go ahead and invent, it made no difference. This was the sort of spirit that reigned," says director Mario Caiano, who made the best of the kung-fu crossovers.*1* In the words of scenarist Sergio Donati, who tried his hand at comedy hybrids, "For Americans, westerns were a part of their history; for us they were just a part of our imagination, our mythology, so we could be a little less respectful."*2* This 'irresponsibility', this disregard for the rules, was intrinsic to the adventurous spirit of so much Sixties cinema and is the driving force behind the offbeat westerns featured in this chapter.

To a large extent, the genre itself was a hybrid, a celluloid melting pot with a wider range of references than has generally been acknowledged. As Marcia Landy puts it, "The Italian western can be characterised by its eclecticism, drawing on different genres, national film traditions, international casts, a combination of comedy and melodrama, and an innovative approach to the cinematic medium."*3* Even so, there are extreme examples – hyper-stylised films with multiple personalities that could only have been conceived in the cultural and creative tumult of the Sixties. With less pressure to 'respect', as Donati puts it, a prevailing set of ideals, writers and directors had a licence to roam. Euro-westerns constantly evolved and regenerated, absorbing influences from cinema, society and other cultures – from Gothic imagery, goofy comedy and martial arts (all covered in this chapter) to the abstract style of avant-garde film, demonstrated by discordant westerns such as *Django, Kill!, Kill the Wicked* (both 1967), *Matalo!* (1970), a psychedelic reimagining, rather than a straight remake, of the previous film, the elliptical *Death Sentence* (1967) and the obscure revenge film *Hate Is My God* (1969), with its allegorical characters and Godardian jump cuts. Popular culture and the protest movement also had a considerable impact, from the visual style of Tinto Brass's lurid, pop-art-inflected *Yankee* (1966) – heavily inspired, as the director has acknowledged, by Dalí and De Chirico and the semi-surreal comic strips of Guido Crepax – and the fashionable cut of many characters' clothes (style over substance is a charge frequently levelled at the protagonists, as well as the films themselves), to the strident sloganeering of the political westerns.

As with so many aspects of the European western, the presence of schizophrenic films like these provokes diametrically opposed responses. A pedantic view, prevalent at the time of production and persistent in some quarters, points to the absence of realism, even the qualified form that applies to westerns, the obsession with style and the reliance on characteristics from other types of film, as further evidence of the *filone*'s inherent illegitimacy, of the filmmakers' inability and/or unwillingness to comprehend the codes of the west and, indeed, of the western itself. But to many minds those very codes were either obsolete or, if not totally outmoded, they imposed too narrow an artistic vision and were therefore something to be opposed. And while this kind of experimentation was undertaken primarily to woo straying spectators with the promise of something new – proving at the same time that Cinecittà and its production partners, like other studios with a populist instinct such as America's AIP, were up to speed with the tides of fashion – the most offbeat Euro-westerns also represent the transgressive spirit that was coursing through the medium at the time. Just as elsewhere radical upstarts and high-minded 'auteurs' were forcing audiences and critics to readjust their perceptions of cinema in general, so commercially oriented craftsmen invited filmgoers to consider anew what constitutes a western.

Horror on horseback

As they set about remodelling the western, European writers and directors drew inspiration from their own cultural and cinematic heritage. Having rediscovered the Gothic horror film in the late Fifties and early Sixties with titles such as Riccardo Freda and Mario Bava's *The Devil's Commandment* (1957) and Bava's *The Mask of Satan* (1960), Italian filmmakers and, less frequently, their Spanish counterparts, began applying its crepuscular ambience to the western. This may seem like cultural vandalism to some – the contamination of one genre with another – but it was not such a revolutionary concept. There are two reasons for this. Firstly, American filmmakers, to whom the western 'belongs', had made sporadic attempts to spice up the genre with fantastic material themselves. As early as the Thirties, the American western crossed over into the realms of mystery, horror and even science fiction. The bizarre Gene Autry serial *The Phantom Empire* (1935), later re-edited into a feature, was partly set in a subterranean

above: Antonio Margheriti revisited his Gothic roots for **And God Said to Cain**, as demonstrated in this shot of Luciano Pigozzi by the combination of a high angle with low-key lighting.

city where robots roamed, while the atmospheric *The Riders of the Whistling Skull* (1937), featuring the popular Three Mesquiteers, introduced supernatural elements into a *Raiders of the Lost Ark*-style cliffhanger plot. In the Fifties and Sixties, schlock tactics were employed to entice drive-in crowds with such oddities as *Curse of the Undead* (1959), the first vampire western, and William Beaudine's campy spoofs *Billy the Kid vs. Dracula* (1965) and *Jesse James Meets Frankenstein's Daughter* (1966). The occasional horror-western hybrid has surfaced in more recent times as well, with the likes of *Ghost Town* (1988), *From Dusk Till Dawn 3: The Hangman's Daughter* (2000), *The Burrowers* (2008) and, give or take their modern-day settings, *Near Dark* (1986), *Sundown: The Vampire in Retreat* (1990) and *John Carpenter's Vampires* (1998) keeping the old drive-in spirit alive.

Secondly, in Europe, just prior to the western's reign, similar exercises had already been undertaken in the peplum. It might not seem so noteworthy given the essentially fantastical, ahistorical nature of *pepla* (of course, the same qualities might be ascribed to Euro-westerns) but, even so, a number of these films were decidedly more outré than their contemporaries. The resurgence of the horror film in Italy coincided with the peplum at its prime, and a mini-genre of Gothic-mythological adventures provided their muscular heroes with supernatural and diabolical obstacles. Giacomo Gentilomo and Sergio Corbucci's *Goliath and the Vampires* (1961), Mario Bava's *Hercules in the Centre of the Earth* (1961) and Riccardo Freda's *Maciste in Hell* (1962) are the best known, and, with the exception of Freda's disappointing effort, they stitch their ingredients together fairly seamlessly. The protagonists of many other *pepla* also faced challenges of an uncanny or otherworldly nature: a shape-shifting deity (*Hercules Conquers Atlantis* [1961]); a death ray (*The Giant of Metropolis* [1961]); prehistoric beasts (*Colossus of the Stone Age* [1962]); an army of undead soldiers (*Rome Against Rome* [1964], a prototype of the Italian zombie film); and extraterrestrial forces (*Hercules Against the Moon Men* [1964]). Equally peculiar was Umberto Lenzi's *Zorro contro Maciste* (1963), whose overseas title, *Samson and the Slave Queen*, gives no hint of the script's eccentric notion of pairing the 19th Century swashbuckler (called El Toro in the English language version) with the fabled Italian muscleman Maciste. Pierre Brice, taking a break from playing Winnetou, and Italian peplum star Alan Steel [Sergio Ciani] filled the title roles. Perhaps inevitably, given the crossover between the peplum's decline and the blossoming of the western, at least one attempt was made to splice them together: the preposterous, kitchen-sink plotted *Hercules and the Treasure of the Incas* (1964).**4**

The influence of horror and fantasy on the European western was far subtler, partly as a result of the tighter restrictions the western imposes on filmmakers in terms of setting, timeframe and so forth, and partly because an unsettling atmosphere can be achieved in many different ways. Eschewing traditional manifestations of the Gothic (there are no death rays or demons) but embracing its tone and imagery, this particular strain of European western is macabre in a broader sense. *Django* (1966) and the 'Sartana' films (covered in the previous chapter), *Django, Kill!*, *Django the Bastard* (1969) and *And God Said to Cain* (1970) show this manipulation of seemingly incompatible modes at its most masterful, and comprise a subset of their own. The central figures in most of these films appear like death incarnate, their terrifying aspect accentuated by framing, shot selection (plenty of low angles), lighting, soundtrack motifs and other technical tricks. These are not the only examples where the most sinister characters are the protagonists rather than the villains. Another example might be Lang Jeffries as Ross Logan, the anti-hero of José Luis Merino's beguiling *Requiem for a Gringo* (1968), who uses his knowledge of astronomy and meteorology to unnerve his opponents by seemingly summoning up storms and, in the climax, a solar eclipse. One western went further than any other by having Death himself put in an appearance, surveying the carnage after the massacre that concludes Gianni Puccini's Shakespeare homage *Fury of Johnny Kid* (1967). Dressed *a la* Mortimer, Sabata et al in a black suit and broad-brimmed hat, and played by an actor in a skull mask, Death even finishes off the wounded with shots from his pistol, announcing in suitably Shakespearean language, "This is the day of a black peace. Whoever calls Death will be answered by Death. And he has only one answer for all of them. The rest is silence." This astonishing conclusion was evidently *too* literal for some markets, where it was edited out in favour of a more conventional ending. (One other cameo for horror fans to appreciate in this film is that of Spanish genre icon Paul Naschy [Jacinto Molina], who plays an arm wrestler in a bar scene whose hand gets impaled on spikes.)

above: Lang Jeffries looms large as the portentous protagonist of **Requiem for a Gringo**.

above: Belgian poster for **And God Said to Cain** that conveys none of its funereal atmosphere. (Focusing on Klaus Kinski's unflattering attire does neither the costumer department not the actor any favours. This wouldn't have happened on Carlo Simi's watch.)

Another way in which these offbeat westerns wander off the trail is through allusion and symbolism, good examples being the link between the protagonist and the elements in both *Requiem for a Gringo* and *And God Said to Cain*, the association of the crazed Mendoza (Claudio Camaso) with diabolical sulphur in *Vengeance* (1968), and the eerie, incongruous red mists that signal danger in Alberto Cardone's *The Wrath of God* (1968) and *$20,000 Stained in Blood* (1969). A group of zombie-like plague victims make a startling appearance in Rafael Romero Marchent's coming-of-age-cum-revenge tale *Clumsy Hands* (1970), shuffling forth from a ghost town to unsettle a trio of outlaws, one of whom ends up tied face to face with a suppurating corpse. Equally confounding is the inclusion of baroque or Gothic backdrops, whether overdressed interiors stuffed with esoteric objects, or cemeteries and caves – from the desecrated graveyard in *Django, Kill!* to the subterranean settings in *Vengeance* and *And God Said to Cain*. Enzo Castellari's *Johnny Hamlet* (1968) combines both these locales, featuring a number of scenes set within a cavernous sepulchre, an inspired design by Enzo Bulgarelli (fresh from achieving similar results with his sets for *Kill and Pray* [1967]) and lit by numerous candles. (The disconcerting effect of these interiors is enhanced by their supposed location among the bizarre natural rock sculptures of the 'Enchanted City' national park in Cuenca, central Spain.) Production and set design are also notable features of another Alberto Cardone western, *Blood at Sundown* (1966), in which Gianni Garko's power-crazed despot dwells in the remains of a pre-Christian temple, set against a matte shot of a desert backdrop and decorated with statues of ancient deities that look suitably fearsome in close-up.

above: Spanish promo for the anomalous **Clumsy Hands**, which plunges Peter Lee Lawrence into a plot top-heavy with foreboding.

above: Brett Halsey in a publicity shot for **The Wrath of God**, an otherwise standard revenge film kitted out with Gothic frills.

above: Giallo fever: with its tortuous plot, red herrings and claustrophobic settings, **The Moment to Kill** – with George Hilton and Loni von Friedel – absorbed elements from another popular Italian *filone* of the day.

A number of other titles play like pulp thrillers, complete with serial murders and master-villains who remain anonymous until the final reel, with a handful of directors attempting to incorporate the mood, pace and style of *gialli*, those quintessentially Italian murder mysteries, into a western setting. Primo Zeglio's *Killer Adios* (1968) and Giuliano Carnimeo's debut, *The Moment to Kill* (1968) demonstrate this hybrid style in embryonic form. The former provides a neat twist on the 'town-tyrant' plot type, with Peter Lee Lawrence investigating a chain of killings that seems to point towards rancher Eduardo Fajardo and surly foreman Nello Pazzafini. Zeglio successfully creates an atmosphere of malevolence and mistrust, and the revelation of the murderer's identity has genuine surprise value, even though the actor in question has played more than his share of creepy parts. *The Moment to Kill* centres on a pair of engagingly brutal private investigators (George Hilton and Walter Barnes, who were good friends in real life as well) who scythe their way through a shortlist of suspects – and a long list of hired guns – in the hunt for $500,000 in pilfered Confederate gold. The plot, devised by Tito Carpi and Enzo Castellari, describes wheels within wheels, while the anti-heroes' artful antics are cleverly realised by cinematographer Stelvio Massi, Carnimeo's right-hand man on a number of further films.

Not every director got the balance right. Mario Pinzauti rung a few changes on the vengeance motif with *The Revenge of Ringo*, a film so plagued by budgetary problems that it wasn't released until 1971, five years after its inception. In that respect it partly anticipates the mystery-western trend, even if the results are rather laughable: a grade-Z hotchpotch of hocus pocus, serial poisonings, cackling 'witches' and a disappearing leading man (Mickey Hargitay filmed only a few scenes before quitting the production, forcing Pinzauti to hastily draft in another actor, Jean Louis, to play Hargitay's avenging brother). Mario Bianchi, the son of prolific exploitation director Roberto Bianchi Montero, fails to bridge the gap between genres in *Kill the Poker Player* (1972) and *In the Name of the Father, of the Son and of the Colt* (1971, released 1975). With infrequent action and lacking of Personville culminates in the jarring, slow-motion stabbing of a female character, a scene that could have been lifted from any contemporaneous murder-thriller. (The film's Italian title, *La notte rosso del falco* – 'red night of the hawk' – certainly connotes more with *gialli* than with westerns.)

The ace in the pack is Vincenzo Gicca Palli's *The Price of Death* (1971). Gianni Garko, in one of his favourite films, gives another finely judged performance as a Sartana-style private detective named Silver – "a kind of Sherlock Holmes in cowboy dress", in Garko's words – who sets out from his luxurious hacienda to investigate a series of killings linked to a bank robbery. There is also the small matter of a sex murder, filmed subjectively in the claustrophobic opening scene, and the film contains several other *giallo* tropes: 'respectable' people with guilty secrets, multiple assassins and so on. Gicca Palli is better known as a scriptwriter (he wrote this film based on a character he had created for Peter Lee Lawrence in 1967's *32 Caliber Killer*), but his direction is assured, even though his satirical asides are occasionally overstated, and the mood established by Franco Villa's excellent photography and Mario Migliardi's ominous musical score, particularly when the camera is prowling the set at night, is suitably menacing and mysterious.

above and right: Taking a break from playing callow or hot-headed youths, Peter Lee Lawrence turned detective for Primo Zeglio's **Killer Adios**, another western-cum-thriller. The plot combines blackmail, embezzlement and mysterious assassinations with the expected ambushes and shoot-outs.

the gore and nudity to attract *giallo* fans, these desultory films offer only convoluted narratives and poorly shot nocturnal skulking in a concession to 'thriller' dynamics, although, to be fair, the cowl-wearing maniac of *In the Name of the Father...* does have a quirky flamboyance. More diverting is *Prey of Vultures* (1972), a vehicle for Peter Lee Lawrence that combines revenge western clichés (stolen mostly from *Death Rides a Horse*) with serial killing, spoiled somewhat by Rafael Romero Marchent's over-reliance on rhetorical effects. Later in the decade, Romero Marchent's compatriot, Juan Bosch, delivered his best effort in the western genre – though that's not saying much – with *La ciudad maldita* ('damned town', 1978), a more-or-less straightforward transposition of Dashiell Hammett's influential crime novel *Red Harvest*. Its story of a dour detective (the pseudonymous 'Chet Bakon') investigating a chain of killings in the small town

above: Garko and Kinski, investigator and suspect respectively, in **The Price of Death**.

"You've come back from hell!"

As already intimated, the most successful hybrid westerns work by distorting an already warped 'reality', and nowhere is this more apparent than in Giulio Questi's *Django, Kill!*, arguably the most extraordinary and disquieting film in the genre. It is the touchstone for all spaghetti western hybrids, moving beyond distortion for its own sake and dissecting the western, both the Hollywood and emergent European variety, for a close inspection of its moral, narrative and aesthetic traditions. Despite the gruesome violence and nihilistic tone, there is no formal connection between *Django, Kill!* and *Django* itself other than the inclusion of that iconic name in the export title. Indeed, as groundbreaking as Corbucci's film was, Questi's interpretation of a western is even more jaundiced, his vision far more provocative. His approach can be seen as both an extension and a questioning of the thematic and stylistic developments of the new-wave European western. Whereas the likes of Leone and Corbucci aimed to recast the mould of the western, Questi, in tandem with scriptwriting partner and outstanding editor Franco Arcalli, brutally shatters it. He inverts many given features of the genre – the pre-eminence of the hero, for example – while the trajectory of the plot involves considerable narrative turbulence. Questi brings to the project an artistic sensibility quite distinct from that of his contemporaries. One detects no underlying cineaste revisionism, no hint of compromise in his depiction of the western milieu as a violent, desolate world peopled by sadists, scavengers and perverts motivated by spite, greed, hatred or dementia.

Like many of his contemporaries, Questi came to cinema from journalism. In the Fifties he directed several well-regarded documentaries before becoming a scriptwriter and working as an assistant director in feature films. (He also played a small role in Fellini's *La Dolce Vita*.) His first fictional directorial work coincided with the vogue for anthology films, which became worthwhile ventures after the success of *Boccaccio '70* (1962). During the Sixties, some of Italy's most prestigious directors dabbled in this field, Visconti, De Sica, Pasolini and Fellini among them. Questi directed the episode 'Viaggio di nozze' in *Le italiane e l'amore*, aka *Latin Lovers* (1961), 'Il passo' in *Amori pericolosi* (1964), and was one of three directors behind the pseudo-documentary *Nudi per vivere* (1963), alongside Elio Petri and Giuliano Montaldo. (The trio were given a collective pseudonym for the film, Elio Montesti, a combination of their names.) Fashionable though the anthology was for a time, it was far removed in box-office terms, not to mention subject matter and mood, from the populist parodies and *pepla* on which most architects of the spaghetti western cut their teeth. Questi seemed an unusual choice, in other words, to direct a western – indeed, he and Arcalli had been working on a more avant-garde project until they were cajoled by a typically opportunistic producer into concocting a genre piece instead – but his unique perspective and idiosyncratic style did his unlikely feature debut the power of good.

Tomas Milian takes the leading role as an anonymous Mexican-American bandit, the victim of a double cross who crawls out of his desert grave – filmed through a green filter, horror-movie style – and is nursed by two wandering Indian mystics keen to know what he has witnessed "on the other side of the river of life."[5] Milian has revenge on his mind, only to find that his treacherous ex-partners, led by Oaks (Piero Lulli), have been butchered and strung up by the inhabitants of a nearby settlement known as "the unhappy place" by the Indians. Soon, Milian also has the ebullient villain Zorro (or Sorro, played by prolific Spaniard Roberto Camardiel) and his black-clad *muchachos* to contend with, as a squabble for the bandits' hoard of stolen gold brings an undercurrent of greed and hostility bubbling to the surface.

The subplots in this sordid tale amount to an excoriating attack upon parochial hypocrisy. In many classic westerns an endangered town is symptomatic of the weakness of society, but it is generally a mere backdrop for the action, a stage for the hero to display his skills, its citizens either passive or persecuted. At the core of these nascent communities there is a basic decency that is seen as worth defending. The more forthright Italian westerns had already begun stripping away this facade, and what Questi reveals beneath is a seething morass of sin, perversity and self-righteousness, where a paranoid mob mentality replaces the rule of law. This is an insular, unwelcoming place ("We don't like folks we don't know"), alternately fearful and hostile towards Milian's mysterious stranger who, unlike them, has the stamp of self-sufficiency. Questi introduces the town with squalid, disconcerting images and details – a scrawny, naked little boy watching the procession of Lulli and his gang down the main street; an old man retching; another using his niece's head as a foot-rest; a woman fighting off her husband in a domestic dispute. This sequence cleverly alters our focus from the murderous outlaws to the community, which, in more traditional fare, Lulli and co. would be expected to terrorise. "It's kind of black in here; sure don't seem natural," comments one of the outlaws in an ominous inkling of the events to unfold.

The town's most representative character is the storekeeper, Hagerman (Paco Sanz), a religious fanatic who keeps his demented wife, Lizabeth (Patrizia Valturri), imprisoned in his house. Hagerman leads the sheep-like locals in a mock-religious persecution of his rival, Tembler (Milo Quesada), who runs the town saloon, condemning the latter for living openly with a woman, Flory (Marilù

above: Expect the unexpected: the nominal hero (Tomas Milian) and his adversary (Piero Lulli) are quickly pushed to the margins as Giulio Questi's macabre, mischievous **Django, Kill!** departs from the customary course.

Tolo), out of wedlock. Hagerman's self-imposed moral authority, combined with all-consuming avarice, later compels him to cold-bloodedly murder Tembler and steal his share of the gold, telling the townsfolk the killing was a crime of passion perpetrated by Flory and her new lover – Milian's stranger.

Tembler's household may appear more stable than Hagerman's – he and Flory plan to use the gold to start a new life in a big city – but there is a spectre in the form of Tembler's fragile son, Evan (the screen debut of 17-year-old Roman Ray Lovelock, later a popular leading man), who shreds his prospective stepmother's dresses in frenzied disgust and begs the stranger to take him away. The boy's personal tragedy is complete when he is taken hostage by Zorro, who uses him as a bargaining tool in his own bid to secure the disputed gold. Evan is subjected to leering pseudo-homosexual games at Zorro's hacienda during a night of debauchery, after which he shoots himself. (The implication is that Evan has been gang-raped. Questi had originally planned for the boy to be buggered to death, but changed his mind during shooting.) Tembler's grief is tempered by the convenience of having a place to stash his share of the gold – Evan's coffin. The coffin thus becomes a symbol of greed much as it had in *Django*, and *Django, Kill!* reaches another of its baroque crescendos shortly after when Zorro's *muchachos* dig up Evan's casket in the cemetery to recover the gold. Discovering it is empty – save for Evan's corpse, of course – they proceed to tear open all the other graves as well. Eventually, the stranger, a largely peripheral figure, manages to destroy Zorro and his men, while Hagerman meets an appropriate demise in an intensely Gothic climax in which he is confronted by his insane spouse and dies smothered by molten gold, his house burning around him. The infernal atmosphere bears a strong similarity to Roger Corman's similarly overwrought screen adaptations of Poe, in particular *The Fall of the House of Usher* (1960) and *The Tomb of Ligeia* (1964).

This horrific set piece is one of many in a film that combines the nightmarish with the grotesque in a manner both shocking and savagely comic. Taking a cue from his contemporaries' endeavours, Questi portrays death, violence, mutilation and desecration in unflinching detail – Oaks's body is torn into when it's discovered he was shot with gold bullets, hardened bandits scream in fear, there are close-ups and inserts of bloodied corpses, viscera and contorted faces. (Questi has stated that his intention was, in part, to draw parallels with the atrocities of the Second World War, in which he fought as a young partisan. He also had the *muchachos* dressed in black to recall Fascist attire.[6]) The almost gloating sadism reaches a peak with the graphic on-screen scalping of one of Milian's Indian sidekicks by townsmen, one of whom rubs his own bald pate in contemplation. Questi is not being sensationalistic in the manner of Sixties schlock merchants such as H.G. Lewis. Rather, his purpose is twofold: to explore the outer reaches of the genre's new permissiveness – peeling away the veneer of comic-strip escapism that had to some extent shielded sensibilities before that point – and to underline his contempt for the barbaric behaviour of his characters.[7] The violence is gleefully cruel like that of children, and Questi's closing images implicitly acknowledge the connection: two youngsters play among the corpses, distorting their faces in imitation of the death masks surrounding them.[8]

The director's use of extreme violence is not the only way in which he confounds audience expectations. Tomas Milian's protagonist is almost tangential to the increasingly deranged action. Milian displays a nicely weighted mixture of bravado and bewilderment as his character finds that the reactionary townsfolk have denied him his revenge. He consistently fails to impose himself on the proceedings, being manipulated by Hagerman and tortured by Zorro, and finds himself powerless to prevent Evan from killing himself. He also shows scant interest in rescuing Lizabeth, the film's highly original damsel-in-distress, but is perfectly willing to sleep with her. Such moral ambiguity is to be expected in a spaghetti western, but the way in which the stranger is reduced to the status of bystander for much of the time illustrates Questi and Arcalli's disdain for genre conventions. (The next film the pair made together, *A Curious Way to Love*, aka *Death Laid an Egg* [1968], is an equally unorthodox psychological thriller that is, if anything, even more hallucinatory than *Django, Kill!*)

Django, Kill! is the genre's closest approximation to a truly surreal experience, operating on a subconscious level as well as a conscious one. (One way to read the film is as the fevered imagining of the injured stranger or perhaps his dying nightmare, with the town as either Purgatory or hell itself.) If some of its bizarre incidents and details seem gratuitous when considered alone or in the context of what one would expect from a more conventional western (Zorro's antagonistic relationship with his abusive parrot, for example), they seem entirely 'natural' within the film's dreamlike milieu. (Its closest equivalent in the wider, wilder world of westerns is perhaps Alejandro Jodorowsky's mystifying *El Topo* [1971], the prototype 'midnight movie', which owes a sizeable debt to the excesses and stylistic extravagance of Euro-westerns.) Arcalli's jagged, staccato editing creates a feeling of disorientation at key moments, abetted by the urgent camerawork of Franco Delli Colli and the jarring incidental music of Ivan Vandor; it's a

above: Roberto Camardiel (*right*), more often cast as a bumbling or drunken sidekick, played a convivial sadist with an argumentative parrot and a taste for refinement and male rape in **Django, Kill!**

successful ploy, as the spectator is made party to the confusion generated by the often-nightmarish events on screen. The best illustrations of this technique are the maddening montage of rapidly edited shots that introduces the opening flashback and establishes, against a blisteringly bright desert background, how Oaks's men betrayed Milian and his fellow Mexicans; and, later in the film, when Questi intercuts shots of an explosion with gory evidence of the resultant carnage.

The film's singularity derives almost entirely from the insolent attitude of its creators. Questi and Arcalli use the European western as a vehicle to probe the confines of commercial cinema and analyse the human condition, defined here as an innate propensity for greed and desensitised violence. Their efforts have polarised opinion since *Django, Kill!*'s initial release, with judgements varying from 'masterpiece' to 'travesty'. It manages both to define and disdain the excesses and eccentricities of the European western, but neither of its authors made any further contribution to the genre. Questi, one of Italy's most elusive directors, made only a handful of features after this one, mainly for national television. Arcalli was much more prolific and soon entered the orbit of Bernardo Bertolucci, performing the unusual dual roles of editor and writer on several of Bertolucci's films. He also collaborated on the celebrated editing of Antonioni's *Zabriskie Point* (1970), cut the same director's *The Passenger* (1975), and was one of the many hands involved in the crafting of Sergio Leone's *Once Upon a Time in America* (1984).

In *Django, Kill!*, the initial resurrection scene hints at a supernatural subtext, although the stranger's corporeal status never really becomes an issue, underlining the authors' lack of interest in their nominal protagonist. By contrast, the same metaphysical question dominates *Django the Bastard*, which explores the intersection between fantasy and reality with ghoulish enthusiasm, transforming a stripped-raw revenge saga into a compelling Gothic conundrum. Suffused with illusion and subterfuge, Sergio Garrone's film – easily his best, as the director himself has affirmed – is the genre's most fanciful and far-reaching exploration of the anti-hero as ethereal being. Indeed, this "devil from hell", as he describes himself, may be the *reductio ad absurdum* of the spaghetti western protagonist. The script, co-written by Garrone and his star, Anthony Steffen, complies with literary critic Tzvetan Todorov's famous definition of the 'fantastic' in fiction, never conclusively revealing whether Django is spirit or flesh. While the denouement is strongly inclined towards the supernatural (like Sartana, Steffen's Django seems able to materialise at will), there is enough contradictory evidence – even more than there is in *Django, Kill!* or Clint Eastwood's *High Plains Drifter* (1973), a film with strong parallels to this one – to plant doubt in the viewer's mind.

above: Crazed and confused: Luciano Rossi specialised in creating psychopaths and losers – his role as the volatile Luke Murdock in **Django the Bastard** was a mixture of both.

The opening scene sets the tone with wit and ingenuity. The camera adopts a bird's-eye-view to introduce a mysterious stranger walking along a deserted street. Successive shots reveal further details of his lean frame and black attire, his poncho ragged like bats' wings, before he suddenly stops and slams a crude cross into frame, carved with a name and that day's date. His prey, Sam Hawkins, emerges from the cantina and in a blur he and his henchmen are wiped out. Sepia-tinted images showing Confederate soldiers under fire flicker across the screen as Django confronts his victim, the camera alternately adopting his viewpoint and showing him from an extreme low angle, the first of many instances in which he assumes imposing proportions on the screen.

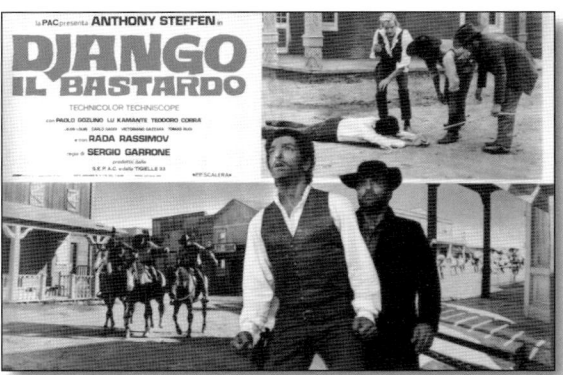

above: Fotobusta for **Django the Bastard** featuring Paolo Gozlino (*centre left*) and Carlo Gaddi (*centre right*).

above: Rada Rassimov's down-to-earth materialist tries, without success, to tempt Anthony Steffen's otherworldly avenger with riches and the promise of romance at the conclusion of **Django the Bastard**.

Django's motivation – that during the Civil War, he and the rest of his platoon were sold out to the enemy by three officers – is the stuff of basic revenge scenarios, but the imaginative execution, combined with the supernatural frissons, reinvigorate tired material. Django's principal target, Rod Murdock (Paolo Gozlino), is now a powerful landowner whose hired gunmen have taken over Desert City to prepare for Django's arrival. Most of the action takes place here during one long night of escalating mayhem. As Django methodically eliminates the gunmen, Garrone exploits every opportunity to build up the character's fantastic, fearsome qualities, using a range of stylistic devices familiar from innumerable horror films. The director's use of cinematic deception mirrors Django's diabolical subterfuge. The character frequently turns up where he shouldn't logically be – revealed in the background of a scene, for example, moments after we've seen him leave via the foreground, or, vice versa, he seems to disappear before his victims' eyes. Not before ours, however, since Garrone generally favours well-executed cutaways over optical effects to keep us continually off-balance where Django's true nature is concerned. There are other simple, time-honoured techniques – Django emerging from, or suddenly illuminated in, the pitch-blackness – that are highly effective in context. In addition, Django deceives the hapless gunslingers in a number of underhanded ways, similar to those found in the Sartana films. Some of these situations display a grim sense of humour, such as one incident in which Django poses as a corpse, improbably clutching a set of bank notes in one hand. When another gunman approaches the cash, the 'corpse' comes alive and shoots him, deadpanning the admonishment "greed is a sin". Cinematographer Gino Santini's shadowy, softly lit tableaux provide an appropriate backdrop for Garrone's carefully composed images.

The source of Django's power is the terror his seemingly supernatural abilities inspires in most of those he comes across. Not everyone reacts in the same way, however. Murdock's unhinged brother, Luke (genre favourite Luciano Rossi, sporting a deathly pallor), and his trophy wife, Alida (Rada Rassimov), are the only ones who don't, or can't, believe that a phantom is in their midst.

The film suggests that their contradictory personalities – one is psychotic, the other rational – may be protecting them from Django's aura, whereas most of the other characters are susceptible because of their superstitious natures. Luke is a volatile, childlike figure who yearns for the respect of his big brother and is prone to hysterical fits of rage and violence. He is the only one who manages to wound Django, but while this incident would seem to prove that the gunfighter is human after all – and gives Luke the flattering, if temporary, glow of the limelight – there is always the possibility that Django's bloodshed is just another devilish trick, that he is manipulating the weaker man's emotions. At any rate, in narrative terms his wound is all but forgotten when he meets Luke again in the town church and kills him. Alida, meanwhile, is a self-confessed gold-digger who agreed to marry Luke in exchange for Murdock's money. Rassimov plays her as a smart, down-to-earth hustler, completely immune to the fear that creeps through the town like a malaise, and, while Alida is not exactly a positive representation of womanhood, she is still a far cry from the weak, one-dimensional female characters one usually encounters in the genre.**9** Django's attitude towards her is icily indifferent – she is merely a fleeting distraction in his ruthless pursuit of revenge. At the end of the film, Alida helps herself to Murdock's fortune and implores Django to share it with her."We'll be rich for ever," she claims, but Django's response is characteristically cold:"We won't live for ever." With this, he sets off down the corpse-strewn main street, the camera cutting back and forth between his departing figure and that of Alida as she gathers up bank notes and calls after him. The final shot, which suggests that Django has disappeared into the ether, reasserts the air of mystery.

Garrone's skilful manipulation of mood and imagery conceals the surprising fact that he had no prior experience in the horror genre. (The three films he directed before this had all been westerns, although the ending of *No Graves on Boot Hill* [1968], an otherwise run-of-the-mill conspiracy western, suggests that its trio of heroes may have returned from the dead – as in *Django the Bastard*, Garrone lets us wonder.) The same could not be said of Antonio Margheriti, another director whose best westerns are steeped in a Gothic atmosphere. Margheriti was one of Italy's most prolific commercial filmmakers, but his most significant achievements date back to the golden years of Italian horror. Along with Mario Bava and Riccardo Freda, Margheriti spearheaded the country's Gothic renaissance; like his peers, he found a muse in the form of Barbara Steele, who starred for him in both *Castle of Blood* (1963) and *The Long Hair of Death* (1964). Margheriti segued from horror to science fiction (he was considered one of the few Italian specialists in this field), and then moved on to westerns with the middling *Dynamite Joe* (1967), a vehicle for Rick Van

above: Richard Harrison (*centre, at the bar*) as the sullen, mixed-race protagonist of Antonio Margheriti's **Vengeance**.

Nutter (*Thunderball*'s Felix Leiter). Far superior was the Richard Harrison vehicle *Vengeance* (1968), which reveals Margheriti's passion for the *fantastique* in a number of ways, from the imaginative cruelty that sets the plot in motion (a man torn apart, off-screen, by fleeing horses), to the brilliantly mounted climax in a cave system where Claudio Camaso's villain, Mendoza, has established his base. Cinematographer Riccardo Pallottini's use of enhanced colours in the closing stages, combined with the dank setting and the use of a wide-angle lens, creates a disorienting effect reminiscent of Mario Bava. Above all there is the demonic Mendoza, whose unpredictability, malign genius and flamboyant costume mark him out from his nefarious peers. (The character is similar to Frank Wolff's egomaniacal Bill St. Antonio from the previous year's *God Forgives... I Don't!*, and also resembles the same actor's black-cloaked, hearse-driving sociopath in 1967's *Last of the Badmen*.) These offbeat inflections make the film's final reckoning in particular linger in the memory, but don't inform *Vengeance* as a whole. It was with his next western, *And God Said to Cain*, that Margheriti gave the same revenge theme a full-blown Gothic treatment. Indeed, despite focusing on a vengeful gunfighter, Gary Hamilton (Klaus Kinski), who intends to pay back those whose lies consigned him to ten years in a sweltering prison camp, *Cain* could almost be bracketed with the director's official horror films. Margheriti attributed its "different, disquieting quality" to his fascination for macabre and fantastic subjects.**10** The film never suggests that Hamilton is a ghost, but the intense atmosphere of fear, guilt and hatred engendered by his return to society is typical of Gothic melodrama *all'italiana*, as are the alternately ornate and gloomy interiors.

In simple narrative terms, *Cain* is little more than a rerun of *Django the Bastard* – during the course of one tornado-stricken night, an implacable avenger picks off

above: Typefaces run riot on this Mexican promo for **Vengeance**. The torturing of Richard Harrison's anti-hero harks back to director Margheriti's often ingeniously cruel Gothic horror films.

an army of gunmen, who likewise refer to the "ghost" or "monster" in their midst, before exacting revenge on their boss, Acombar (Peter Carsten), whose betrayal led to his incarceration. There are even the same familial complications, with Acombar's son, Dick (Antonio Cantafora), and lover, Mary (Marcella Michelangeli), once Gary's woman, being the rogue elements here, as Murdock's brother had been in Garrone's film. Yet in this case the plot is even thinner – virtually the entire running time is given over to scenes of nocturnal slaughter – while Margheriti ladles on the Biblical allusions, Gothic themes, symbolism and stylisation. This is not a film for those who favour a subtle build-up, but then subtlety has never been a signature of the Gothic – nor of spaghetti westerns, of course. The furious storm seems generated as much by Hamilton's wrath as by atmospheric instability, evoking the "terrible nature" of Gothic parlance, while the portentous tolling of the church bell, set in motion by Hamilton, proclaims the presence of death. The double-edged dialogue is frequently punctuated by natural sounds or occurrences, as if the inanimate world is asserting its power over man. Acombar's brazen claim that his house is impregnable is immediately contradicted by a gust of wind that blows open the window next to him, underlining the metaphorical connection between the encroaching Hamilton and the elements. As might be expected from such a visually oriented director, his priorities are the camera placements, lighting, settings and scenery (Hamilton makes use of a network of caves running beneath the town, recalling the subterranean climax of *Vengeance*, and his confrontation with Acombar takes place in a flaming room of mirrors), but Margheriti also emphasises the emotional consequences of Hamilton's vendetta. In doing so he revisits a timeless Gothic device, the ancestral curse, which was a fixture of Sixties Italian horror films. (Margheriti had previously employed it in *The Long Hair of Death*.) In the near-hysterical final act, Dick becomes the innocent victim of his father's misdeeds when the latter accidentally shoots him dead; in a fury, Acombar then turns his gun on Mary and prepares to face his tormentor.

The choice of title may seem arbitrary, but is more intriguing on closer inspection. Italian westerns frequently invoke the Almighty in their titles – consider *God Forgives... I Don't!*; *God Forgive... His Life Is Mine*, *God Will Forgive My Gun*, *ad nauseam* – or make use of biblical archetypes in their narratives, in particular the story of Cain and Abel. Yet in most instances these allusions are purely superficial, contrived as a provocative marketing ploy or to set an apocalyptic tone, whether appropriate to the action or not; to aggrandize the protagonist and consecrate his (usually vindictive) campaign; or to signify an ambivalent attitude towards religion and the Church. *And God Said to Cain* is more specific, however, and while the Biblical passage it refers to is full of life lessons, the film itself is more nihilistic than didactic. When God speaks to Cain in Genesis, chapter four, he rebukes him for his pride and challenges him to abjure sin and follow the path of righteousness. Cain rejects God's counsel, slays his own brother and is cursed to wander the world branded as an outcast, unrepentant and embittered. Gary Hamilton feels himself to be similarly afflicted; he has a life sentence "ingrained in his skin" – his very own mark of Cain – and, after ten long years of unjust imprisonment, he has come to share that character's hard-hearted arrogance. Echoing Cain, his attitude suggests that the Lord should supplicate before *him*, and not the other way around. Who else but Kinski, the master of disdain, could pull this off?

Hamilton is one of the most avowedly atheistic figures in a genre notorious for its sceptical and often contemptuous attitude towards religious doctrine. His faithlessness stems from the injustice he has suffered and the stain of dishonour it has left on his character. (We are told that he was an upstanding Confederate war hero prior to his betrayal.) When he confronts the town priest, a predictably weak and ineffectual figure, Hamilton could be speaking for all his fellow avengers when he asserts that vengeance is a wronged man's prerogative and not the Lord's preserve. "If innocence is repaid with prison," he sneers, "I've earned the right to kill, even if God chooses to punish me for it." Such is the power of his hatred and the depth of his bitterness that Hamilton makes a conscious choice to embrace eternal damnation. (This reiterates his connection to Cain – "So Cain went out from the Lord's presence", and echoes Laertes's furious resolve in *Hamlet*, the greatest of all revenge dramas – "I dare damnation... Let come what comes, only I'll be revenged most thoroughly for my father".) This short but pivotal scene tenuously ties together the Biblical and Gothic threads in Margheriti's film. Shut out from salvation, Hamilton resembles not only Cain but also the Wandering Jew of Gothic lore. This blighted figure, also known as Ahasuerus, Cartaphilus, Malchus or John Buttadeus, arose from a legend about a Jew who may have mocked or ignored Jesus on his way to the cross. His punishment was to roam the world until Judgement Day, and some variations on the legend have linked this character to that of Cain. Hamilton is a more recalcitrant, malevolent version of the Jew. He has the unshakeable conviction of one who knows and has accepted his fate, which makes him a truly terrifying adversary.

Cut-throats and carnage

Despite the bloodthirsty reputations of both Euro-westerns and horror films, the hybrids covered thus far, with the obvious exception of *Django, Kill!*, were surprisingly restrained in what they showed, especially considering the increasingly permissive climate of the times. Although no less violent than conventional westerns, most rely on dynamic quick cutting rather than graphic gore for effect (saving on the special effects budget, for a start). In examples from the mid-Seventies onwards, however, after censorship laws had relaxed further in line with cultural attitudes (and not forgetting that forthright films from the Sixties, including Euro-westerns, had also forced the pace of change), we see make-up effects employed to a much greater degree, doubtless with the aim of enticing back audiences who now preferred blood-splattered action films and gruesome horror flicks to westerns. The kung-fu crossover *The Fighting Fists of Shanghai Joe* (1973) is replete with the kind of bloody mayhem common to the martial arts genre, including eye gouging and dismemberment, with the addition of explicit bullet wounds and even a flesh-eating hired killer. Lucio Fulci, whose name has become synonymous with celluloid gore, shows a man being flayed and having a sheriff's

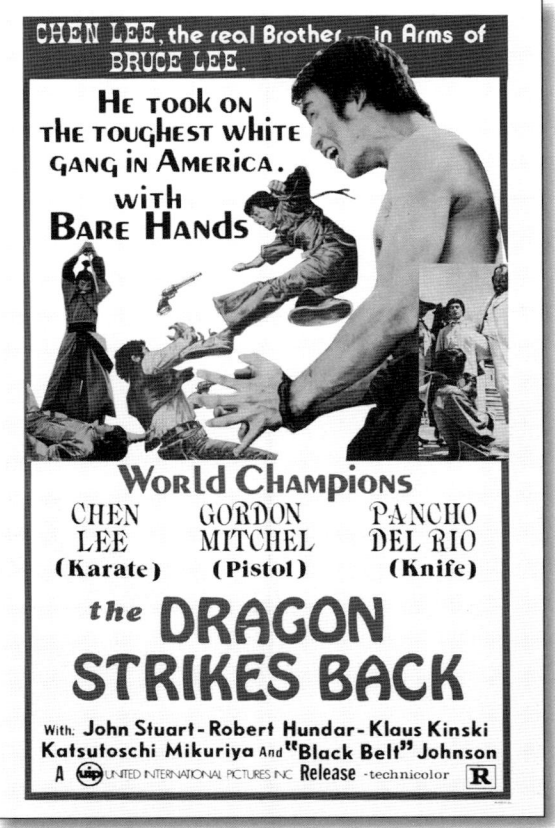

above: US poster for **The Fighting Fists of Shanghai Joe** that trumpets its grindhouse credentials.

above: When director Lucio Fulci called "cut", he often meant it literally. Here, Tomas Milian leaves his mark on Lorenzo Robledo in a gruelling scene from **The Four of the Apocalypse**.

badge embedded in his bare chest in *The Four of the Apocalypse* (1975). Fulci also plays a devastatingly cruel joke on the film's travelling companions in one sequence, which ties together the death of the most sympathetic character with an act of (inadvertent) cannibalism. Another director better known for his work in horror and fantasy, Sergio Martino, deploys blood squibs aplenty in the semi-Gothic *A Man Called Blade* (1977), which also includes brief shots of the damage caused by Blade's trusty throwing axe, a weapon more closely identified with the modern horror film. The pattern continues in titles from the Eighties: grisly close-ups of the mummified corpses in *Tex and the Lord of the Deep* (1985), in most respects a family-friendly film, complement its fantastical leanings, while the uncut versions of Bruno Mattei's *Scalps* and *White Apache* (both 1986) contain scalping, dismemberment and similar carnage.

While all the aforementioned films blur the distinction between western and horror to one degree or another, one title obliterates the boundary all together. Joaquín Romero Marchent's *Cut-Throats Nine*, released in 1971, was the director's second 'trek' western after *Seven from Texas* (1964), but the two films couldn't be more different in content and tone. *Cut-Throats Nine*, whose Spanish title translates as 'condemned to live', was produced (by Romero Marchent) and marketed with the burgeoning audience for splatter movies in mind (in America, distributor United International Pictures even offered prospective viewers 'terror masks' to shield their eyes from the gore), but it also expands upon the thematic obsessions of the European western. The genre's nihilistic undertone bursts to the surface, expressed with a visceral, uncompromising ferocity made all the more severe by the harshness of the environment – all ice, snow and rock – and the unbridled venality of the characters, who consist mostly of violent criminals en route to prison. Brilliantly shot by Luis Cuadrado (responsible for the amber-hued, dreamy haze of Victor Erice's magical-realist *The Spirit of the Beehive* [1973]) in freezing conditions in the Picos de Europa mountains and scored in stark, repetitive style by Carmelo Bersaola, Romero Marchent's harrowing film zeroes in on one of the genre's chief preoccupations – man's capacity for, and tendency towards, violence – with a relentlessness bordering on misanthropy. The tensions among the prisoners are resolved in the only way they know how, and their inability to resist their savage impulses points to a profoundly pessimistic view of human nature.

"There's a little story tied up with that film," revealed its lead actor, Claudio Undari. "After it was done, several scenes were inserted to make it more violent, according to the wishes of its American producer [it's unclear exactly who he was referring to]. When, for example, I cut off the foot, you didn't see any details, only the gesture. But they added a lot of stuff that made it more cruel." The various stabbings, slashings and eviscerations – often crudely inserted – not only provide splatter-movie style punctuation points to satisfy the blood-lust of horror fanatics, but also comprise a typically heavy-handed Euro-western metaphor for the bestiality of the title characters, their willingness to do whatever it takes to survive, just as the leg chains made (improbably) from gold bind the prisoners together and represent their enslavement by greed.

Besides the grotesque violence, *Cut-Throats Nine* deviates from the western rulebook in a number of other ways. Halfway through, the nominal hero, army officer Brown (played by Undari, making his sixth film with the director), is tortured and killed, a far cry from the mutual respect that usually develops between convicts and captor in the oft-used *Dirty Dozen* scenario. This leaves the audience, as well as Brown's daughter, Kathy (Emma Cohen), in the hands of the desperadoes, one of whom, as yet unidentified, murdered Brown's wife. Robbed of an identification figure, we are disturbed further when the film veers into the supernatural – one of the prisoners makes a break on his own and becomes delusional; birds and other creatures seem to threaten him, and he 'sees' Brown's disfigured ghost following him. And the hint of a romance between Kathy and Dean, the one vaguely sympathetic prisoner, is obliterated when it turns out that he was the one who mutilated her mother. The film's exceedingly dim view of humanity is unlikely to have originated with Romero Marchent, even though on paper he was its main creative force, having co-written and produced it as well as directing. He seems to have approached it with some hesitation, running the idea by Claudio Undari in Rome before production: "He asked me for my opinion: 'Can it be done?' It was outside of all schemes and rules... strange episodes, strange things."[11] None of the director's earlier works even approach the bitterness of this film, which, if anything, resembles the genre titles of his brother, Rafael. However, the bleak tone does fit the output of screenwriter Santiago Moncada, author of Rafael's *Clumsy Hands* and two cruelly cynical psychological horror films, *The Corruption of Chris Miller* (1973) and *The Bell of Hell* (1973), as well as a few Italian *gialli*.[12] The despairing spirit of the piece is summed up in an exchange between Dean and Kathy: "Life is all we have," he says to her at one point. "It's not much, is it?" she responds. And whereas the use of dynamite to resolve matters often indicates that the filmmakers have run out of ideas (the costliness and complexity of staging a more satisfying solution – such as a free-for-all gunfight, for example – was perhaps another consideration), here it acts like a purgative, and it's fitting that Kathy be the one to set it off.

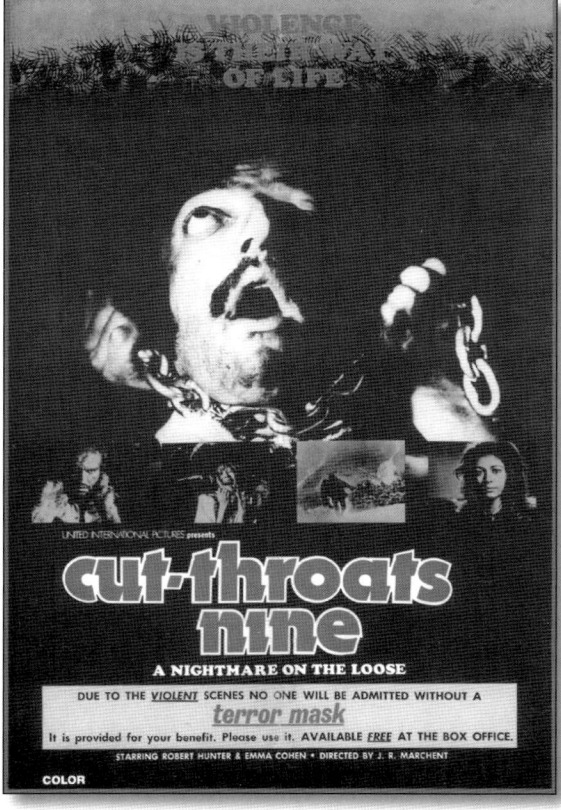

above: Sensational US artwork for the notoriously gory **Cut-Throats Nine**.

"Ridicule is the most powerful weapon there is"

Throughout the long and distinguished history of the Italian film industry, comedy has consistently drawn the largest crowds, permeating all genres and transforming many performers into household names. From the silent era, comic stars, often possessing an anarchic bent, have endeared themselves to Italian audiences by stumbling wholeheartedly through any given social situation, frequently puncturing bourgeois pretensions in the process. Supplementing this unwavering mass appeal – which springs from the films' carefully weighted mixture of empathetic heroes, escapism and anti-establishment effrontery – is a relatively recent critical respectability, although this applies chiefly to a cycle of films directed by the likes of Pietro Germi, Mario Monicelli and Dino Risi in the Fifties and Sixties. These works – sometimes banded together into the catch-all category of *commedia all'italiana* – succeeded in dispensing ironic treatment to all manner of troubling and controversial subjects, from war, crime and poverty to murder and divorce. They portrayed Italian society as riddled with cynicism and unscrupulousness, and established the country's comedic cinema as one of the most sophisticated and daring in the world. Latterly, critics have also embraced such idiosyncratic, diverse comic talents as Nanni Moretti and Roberto Benigni, whose *Life Is Beautiful* (1997) was a rare instance of a quintessentially Italian blend of irony, tragedy and sentimentality achieving global success.

As well as original comic stories, Italy's popular filmmakers have a longstanding tradition of rapidly following a commercial or critical success with a scabrous spoof of their own. The early Sixties was arguably the golden age of such quick-fire satire, with a range of talented actors, writers and directors at their creative peak. There were numerous parodies produced of both highbrow hits – viz. *The Shortest Day* (1963) as opposed to *The Longest Day*, *Totò of Arabia*, a showcase for the eponymous comedian, *Walter e i suoi cugini* ('Walter and his cousins', 1961), a take-off of Visconti's *Rocco and His Brothers* – and genre films, including several wholehearted comic variations on the western that both anticipated and complemented the early works of Leone, Tessari et al.

While those early films were mainly amiable affairs, the slapstick westerns of the Seventies are a different proposition, and are viewed by an overwhelming majority of the genre's aficionados with antipathy. The relative quality of individual films is almost a moot point; to those nurtured on the hard-bitten anti-heroes and heady stylisation of yore, the relentlessly idiotic, scatological comedies that cut the genre down to size in its later years are considered an abomination. Although it is simplistic to hold the post-'Trinity' westerns solely responsible for the genre's decline – it had run out of steam by that point in any case – there is little to say in defence of most of these raucous latecomers. This is not merely a question of taste. Almost all the best Euro-westerns possessed an ironic undercurrent, their protagonists exhibiting a dry, devilish wit as they went about their brutal business, with the general tone not dissimilar to that of the '*commedia all'italiana*'. It's for this reason that so many of the later comedy westerns, which forsook irony for all-out farce, seem not merely overblown but superfluous, even before one considers their shortcomings in terms of scripts, direction and performances.

This does not tell the whole story, however. As indicated above, irony and comedy played an important part in the development of the genre as well as contributing to its downfall, and worthwhile comedic westerns continued to be made even while the worthless ones were doing the rounds. Giuliano Carnimeo, whose films ranged from slyly humorous in tone to decidedly funny-peculiar, views the ascent of comedy in the Euro-western, like the exaggeration of violence, as a key stage in its evolution: "Our westerns have no explicit link with American history. Even the Leone masterpieces are not to be considered in relation to historical facts, they represent just *events*. Personal events, if you like. Leone utilised the American western as a platform to introduce, in a groundbreaking way, irony, a typical Italian feature, as well as violence in an unprecedented form. However, Leone's movies were very costly. The Italians tried to find alternative approaches requiring smaller budgets. One way was to augment violence, the other was to augment the ironic side, the comical side, which would make up for the missing grandiosity of landscapes, large-scale battles etc... I started to like the comedy aspect because this is closer to our theatrical culture. So, the parody became an important element in the overall panorama of Euro-westerns. I just felt much more comfortable working with elements of the all-Italian *commedia dell'arte*, deeply rooted in Italian tradition, than to emulate stories that had to do with American history."[13]

Send-ups were made both prior to and alongside the first wave of serious Euro-westerns and, as the latter developed during the decade, the country's resident clowns continued to enjoy themselves at the genre's expense. In 1959, two of Italy's most popular humorists, Ugo Tognazzi and Tina Pica teamed up for *La sceriffa*, largely an exhibition for Pica's comic abilities, and Giorgio Simonelli, a veteran director of 30 years' standing, paired Tognazzi with another talented light leading man, Walter Chiari (of *Walter e i suoi cugini*) for the following year's *Un dollaro di fifa*, about a pair of bungling swindlers.[14] Chiari and Tognazzi headed west again for Simonelli's *The Magnificent Three* (1961), which enjoyed great success at the box office and also featured Raimondo Vianello, Tognazzi's partner in many films as well as in the much-loved television review *Un, due, tre*. In a typically farcical development, the hapless trio are mistaken for tough gunslingers and put in opposition to a band of outlaws. Chiari and Vianello reunited as the good-natured Bullivan brothers in *Two Against All* (1962), in which they pose as lawmen to expose the crooked town mayor, gaining strength along the way by eating a local farmer's fortified chickens, and in two films for Steno [Stefano Vanzina]: *Heroes of the West* (1963) and, playing double roles, the following year's *Twins from Texas*.

Comedians of other nationalities got in on the act as well. Fernand Raynaud, one of France's comic superstars, played in *Fernand Cowboy* for Guy Lefranc in 1956, while the erstwhile Don Camillo, Fernandel of the lugubrious features, starred in a western spoof in 1961, the Jean Bastia-directed *Dynamite Jack*, in which his innocent abroad discovers he's a dangerous gunman's *doppelgänger*. Meanwhile, *madrileño* Tony Leblanc, later a respected producer/director, headlined one of the earliest Spanish westerns, *Torrejón City* (1962), in which he's involved in a mistaken identity plot very similar to those outlined already.

These are generally good-natured, affectionate parodies, playing around with cowboy clichés and poking fun at the western's macho mentality without challenging the conventions themselves. *Two Against All*, for instance, opens with Chiari and Vianello approaching each other slowly, apparently for a shootout, but at the command of "fire", one obligingly lights the other's cigarette. (This anticipates the jokey opening of Duccio Tessari's *A Pistol for Ringo* [1965].) They are examples of what Marcia Landy calls "comedian comedy", geared to the strengths of their stars in much the same way that American cinema fashioned western vehicles for its most popular jesters – Laurel and Hardy, the Three Stooges, the Marx Brothers, Abbott and Costello and Bob Hope all found themselves donning chaps and ten-gallon hats at some point during their careers. These early Italian parodies, like their Hollywood predecessors, also contain romantic asides and vaudevillian qualities, with song and dance routines not uncommon. (*Two Against All* contains one such sequence with the stars in black-face.)

We now reach an intermediate stage in the blending of western and comedy, where send-ups of the *European* western come to the fore. Just as the success of the 'Dollars' films initiated a slew of straight-faced imitations, so it marked a golden opportunity for Italy's popular comedians. Among the titles of note are two starring Lando Buzzanca, who would go on to become a major star in bawdy comedies in the Seventies. *Rebels on the Loose* (1966), directed by Bruno Corbucci (with whom Buzzanca had created the spoof spy James Tont the previous year), and Mario Mattoli's *For a Few Dollars Less* (1966), which was written by Corbucci and his brother Sergio, both consist of various slapstick scenarios in which Buzzanca and co-star Raimondo Vianello adopt a range of disguises. The former is a tale of two moronic Confederate soldiers who aid a pair of beautiful Southern belles in their campaign of sabotage against the recently unified government. This generic western spoof veers into Leone territory in one sequence when the stars dress up like Clint Eastwood and Lee Van Cleef and stage a mock showdown to the accompaniment of Vianello's musical watch, which blares out an incongruous oompah tune in lieu of Morricone's trumpet theme. There's a lot more of the same in *For a Few Dollars Less*, a full-blown parody of Leone's second western that satirises the director's fascination with violence and is also, arguably, a comment on the feminisation of modern Italian man. Buzzanca affects a camp, cowardly disposition as a bank cashier who needs to make up a shortfall and, on the advice of his cousin (Vianello), becomes an outlaw. At one point, Buzzanca's criminal ineptitude sees his reward value slashed from $500 to $75, but ultimately the duo make good by accidentally capturing a coca-leaf addicted Mexican bandit (Elio Pandolfi doing a fair Gian Maria Volonté impression). Among the more obvious Leone references is a surreal flashback revealing the root of Vianello's grudge against the Mexican – it seems the latter once stole Vianello's prized pig!

The front line in this new comedic assault was led by the indomitable Franco Franchi and Ciccio Ingrassia, the bumbling Sicilian buffoons whose films together were as determinedly silly as they were numerous, totalling more than 100 titles. The duo's persistent tomfoolery – basically an updated version of medieval farce – was honed in the open-air variety shows where they first worked together in the early Fifties. (Oddly, before linking up, Franco, real name Francesco Benenato, had used the stage name Ciccio, while Ciccio's pseudonym had been Franco.) Discovered for the cinema by singer/actor Domenico Modugno of 'Volare' fame, over the course of their long career they played spies, historical or literary characters such as Don Quixote and Sancho Panza, politicians, journalists, soldiers, gangsters and, of course, cowboys – a wide range of internationally recognisable archetypes. "The context [of the story]," Franco once said, "had little importance." Their simple-minded shenanigans earned them the title of the "two cine-idiots most cine-watched in the country", despite the scathing reaction of the critics, who seemed to feel it their duty to disparage the duo. "When you saw them [as a spectator]… you couldn't but laugh," says critic Tullio Kezich. "Then, in the article, you'd say: 'Another one of those bad films.'"[15] Yet despite their popularity in the peninsula, Franco and Ciccio remain little-known abroad.

Of course, it is extremely rare for comedy to break down cultural barriers, especially when it is tightly moored to domestic concerns and characteristics. Very few comic performers have managed to develop a personality and a style of humour that has proved palatable worldwide; Chaplin and Keaton remain the most influential, along with a few of their contemporaries. Furthermore, comedy in Italy has always been regionally biased – few comedians have ever really been considered as *national* favourites – and Franco and Ciccio's fan base was restricted mainly to the provinces and the cheap and plentiful *seconda* and *terza visione* cinemas. Although much of their output consisted of basic physical humour, which crosses all cultural and national boundaries, their routines also involved local gestures and linguistic gags that are largely lost in translation. They often played up their southern roots as well (in the westerns *For a Fist in the Eye*, *Two Gangsters in the Wild West*, *Two Sergeants of General Custer* and *Franco and Ciccio on the War-Path*, for example), reinforcing the negative impression in mainland Italy of stupid Sicilians. Compounding the difficulty for other cultures is the emphatic manner of Franco and Ciccio's portrayals. Not that they were alone in this. Pierre Sorlin, summarising the travel sickness of post-war Italian comedies in general, puts it diplomatically: these films "depended mostly on personal performances which were not easily appreciated outside the cultural context in which they were produced".[16]

The "cultural context" in the case of Franco and Ciccio was the *commedia dell'arte*, filtered down through silent slapstick and brought up to date with a smattering of topical satire. Much has been written about the influence of the *commedia dell'arte* on Sergio Leone's films, in particular the *zanni* – the duelling clowns from whose antics (*lazzi*) much of the humour is drawn. (Marcia Landy and Sir Christopher Frayling provide especially useful insights.[17]) But this ribald, ritualised form of farce is clearly the template for Franco and Ciccio as well, not to mention the much-maligned comic westerns of the Seventies. All share a reliance on exaggerated performances, physical action, recurring stock characters (who are repeatedly humiliated), humorous wordplay and almost endlessly recyclable comic routines, frequently centring on mistaken identity or deception and involving extensive use of props. (It is significant that *commedia dell'arte* bequeathed the term 'slapstick' to the world, after a wooden bat wielded by Harlequin, one of the central figures.) We will see shortly how this basic set of ingredients sustained numerous titles in the genre's dying days, but first it is necessary to see how Franco and Ciccio put this blend of ancient and modern comedy styles into practice.

As with any commercially oriented artist, the duo's success depended to a large extent on their ability to satisfy audience expectations time and again. While the outcomes of their films were predictable, however, the scripts and direction – at least in the early stages of their screen career – were often inventive and skilful, with much of the action being improvised by the actors.

Working regularly with the same writers and directors, Franco and Ciccio starred in nine westerns altogether, a tiny proportion of their overall output but sufficiently representative of what may be termed the Franco and Ciccio formula, a narrative pattern geared to their distinct personalities and performance styles. A brief overview of their westerns will clearly demonstrate this formula in full effect, as well as the speed with which their writers reacted to the latest genre trends.

The duo made their first appearance in western garb in *Two Gangsters in the Wild West* (1964), one of a dozen or so films they made with director Giorgio Simonelli. It was a big hit in Italy, but their definitive title in this area was their second, *For a Fist in the Eye* (1965), which was also by far their most successful western at the Italian box office. It trounced almost every other Italian western made that year, taking almost 1.3 billion lire; only *For a Few Dollars More* and *A Pistol for Ringo* could better that. As the film's title makes plain, it seized on the unexpected popularity of *A Fistful of Dollars* and was one of the earliest comedies to take advantage of the latter's success, appearing in Italian cinemas in April 1965, just four months after *Fistful*'s nationwide release. Director Michele Lupo wastes no time in mimicking Leone's visual style: after an animated *Fistful*-esque credit sequence (accompanied by pastiche Morricone), Ciccio is seen framed through a noose that's looped over a branch, just as Clint Eastwood had passed beneath a hanging tree on his way into San Miguel and prefiguring a similar shot in *The Good, the Bad and the Ugly*. The film's basic plot, many of its gags and even much of its dialogue rely on *Fistful*'s familiarity: Franco and Ciccio play bungling gun salesmen (whose first prospective customers are a group of children) who become embroiled in a feud between rival families, the Cocos and the Brentons, in a border town whose signpost promises newcomers "terror, terror, terror!!" Where Clint Eastwood had peeked inside the army-escorted stagecoach in Leone's film to be greeted by the barrel of a pistol, here Franco's inquisitiveness is rewarded with an eyeful of cleavage, followed by the eponymous fist in the eye. There are characters named Ramon and Marisol (she of the cleavage) and a garrulous old coffin maker, and, at the end, poncho-clad Franco and Ciccio confront a Winchester-toting villain in Lupo's parody of *Fistful*'s famous climax, urging him to aim for the heart while wearing bullet-proof vests made from tinned tomatoes.

These insolent jibes aside, Lupo reminds us what a capable comic director he could be with some neat visual puns, such as the positioning of a cuckolded army captain beneath a pair of horns that adorn the wall behind him. Ultimately, however, like every other director who worked with Franco and Ciccio, he has to compromise his creativity to accommodate the duo's party pieces. These include chase scenes, a typical impersonation sequence in which they pose as mean, black-clad gunfighters but are quickly exposed as whimpering cowards, and a long and tiresome passage where they stumble around drunk. Throughout, the stars play to type: Franco the gibbering proletarian halfwit, all manic gesticulation and facial contortion (not for nothing was the actor described as the Italian Jerry Lewis), Ciccio the gaunt, wiry straight man, struggling to maintain a semblance of dignity but really only a handful of brain cells better off than his accomplice. It is usually he who decides upon their course of action, but given that his plans depend partly upon Franco for success, one must consistently question his judgement, not to mention his wisdom. According to George Hilton, who made two films with the duo, the role of Ciccio as the 'brains' of the partnership was a reversal of their off-screen arrangement: "Franco Franchi was the one with the wit and inventiveness; Ciccio kind of rode along."[18] Giuliano Carnimeo, who co-directed *The Sons of Ringo* (1966), concurs, but adds that Ciccio was the superior actor of the two.

above and below: Italy's resident clowns, Franco Franchi (*below, left*) and Ciccio Ingrassia (*below, right*), sated their public's appetite for pratfalls and slapstick in more than 100 films. **For a Fist in the Eye**, one of their biggest hits, was a surprisingly astute parody of Leone.

Most of their remaining westerns similarly seek inspiration from a mainstream success. The titles alone are a giveaway: *The Sons of Ringo*; *The Handsome, the Ugly and the Stupid* (1967), in which Mimmo Palmara completes the triumvirate; *Ciccio Forgives... I Don't!* (1968); and, spoofing a spoof, *The Two Sons of Trinity* (1972). They also have many scenes, characters and costumes in common with the films they satirise. Marino Girolami's *Two R-R-Ringos from Texas* (1967), for example, reworks various aspects of *The Good, the Bad and the Ugly*, transforming Sentenza/Angel Eyes into 'Sentenza Jane' (Hélène Chanel) and building towards a comic travesty of the *triello* sequence. (This film looks beyond Leone for inspiration – there are no talking horses in the 'Dollars' trilogy, for example.) *The Two Sons of Trinity* goes further by parading not just Euro-western heroes, including Sartana, Ringo and Django, but also the historical figure of Calamity Jane, who is supposedly the boys' aunt. The best of these subsequent films is probably *The Sons of Ringo*. The title is a bit misleading; the film's target is not Duccio Tessari's 'Ringo' films but *For a Few Dollars More* and the bounty-hunting theme it popularised. Franco and Ciccio operate a scam whereby Ciccio, dressed and armed in the manner of Colonel Mortimer, pretends to kill mock-bandit Franco; they even perform a variation on the Monco-Mortimer boot routine beforehand, which escalates to a bout of shin kicking. Following this preamble, the duo meet a genuine bounty hunter, Joe (George Hilton, complete with poncho), who ropes them into a money-making scheme that involves them posing as the descendants of legendary gunfighter Ringo. Besides the usual pratfalls there are some playful tributes to *For a Few Dollars More*, including a bandit chieftain named El Indio (and yet another Marisol) and a wagon piled high with outlaws' corpses, driven by the heroes, in a scene that plays upon the iconic image at the close of Leone's film. The stars are humiliated throughout; the ending is particularly smarting as they are sent scampering out of town (dressed just in their long johns) by Ringo's genuine offspring – two beautiful sisters – seemingly for no other reason than the amusement this provides.

The distinction between these pathetic figures and the calculating characters that populate the Italian western couldn't be clearer (Joe uses them like stooges because their stupidity and subservience, born of cowardice, make them easy to manipulate), and it is probably this ingenuousness that endeared them to Italian audiences at the time. They also provide a contrast to the brashness and arrogance of other comic stars of the period such as Alberto Sordi and Vittorio Gassman, whose characters brought the foibles and shortcomings of modern Italian men to the surface. Franco and Ciccio performed more like contemporary jesters. Their films occasionally dally with themes prevalent in Fifties/Sixties Italian comedy, such as the shifting values in gender relations, but the humour is painted in such broadly satirical brushstrokes that any social commentary that may have been intended is obscured. The stars themselves felt that their on-screen stupidity provided a kind of catharsis. "We represent those who can't cope with any situation," as Franco once said. "People who are caught up in logic and reasoning all day like our illogic [sic] and carelessness."**19**

above and below: Under Franco Giraldi's deft direction, **Seven Guns for the MacGregors** – starring Robert Woods and Agata Flori – was one of the earliest, and most successful, attempts to lighten the Euro-western's tone without resorting to farce.

Franco and Ciccio's inane antics would reverberate in the surfeit of identikit comedies made after 1970. Before considering those films, however, we need to spotlight several light-hearted transitional titles that illustrate the Italian industry's innate satirical leanings while also acknowledging the influence exerted by *Cat Ballou* (1965), a worldwide commercial and critical success. Here we find such gems as *Seven Guns for the MacGregors* and *Sugar Colt* (both 1966), both directed by Franco Giraldi, which manage to combine the kind of vigorous action that had become a Euro-western trademark (Giraldi himself had helped set the pace, with his thrilling second-unit footage for *A Fistful of Dollars*) with jokes and humorous situations, without sacrificing the dramatic potential of their narratives. Both films incorporate familiar comic ploys: *Seven Guns* (which spawned a boisterous, by-the-numbers sequel, *Up the*

above: Franco Giraldi followed **Seven Guns...** with **Sugar Colt** – Hunt Powers's first western – an equally effective blend of humour and blazing action (as in this still, with prolific Spanish character actor Luís Barboo in the centre, firing a pistol).

MacGregors [1967]), caricatures its Scottish clan but manages not to denigrate them (owing, perhaps, to the delicate touch of Duccio Tessari, one of its co-authors), while *Sugar Colt* boasts a delightful example of multiple role-playing from Hunt Powers, making his genre debut. In the same year, Alberto De Martino made *Django Shoots First* (1966), a flippant fusion of bounty hunting and revenge motifs that concludes with a 'Trinity'-style free-for-all fistfight. The far-out musical western *Rita of the West* (1967), meanwhile, from the unlikely source of Ferdinando Baldi, was a sop to the youth market. One of several vehicles for diminutive pop star Rita Pavone, it parodies Django and Clint Eastwood in between the song routines (including a Native American number in which Gordon Mitchell plays the chief) and features Terence Hill as Rita's beau.

It was also around this time that Enzo Castellari emerged as a leading proponent of comedic themes. Echoing other directors, he explains: "After watching many Italian western films where violence and cruelty were ever-present, I decided to create a new style including comedy. It was like winking an eye at the spectator to tell them that this is all fiction, created for them to enjoy."[20] In 1967, Castellari delivered the breezy *Any Gun Can Play* (released in the UK as *For a Few Bullets More*), which begins with barefaced cheek – George Hilton's character shoots down three menacing riders, dressed identically to Clint Eastwood, Lee Van Cleef and Franco Nero – and proceeds to ape the Machiavellian structure of *The Good, the Bad and the Ugly*. His *One Dollar Too Many* (1968), a poor film by comparison, puts a farcical spin on the same sort of material and points towards the laboured trickery that would come to characterise Euro-western comedies in later years.[21]

above: George Hilton is caught with his trousers down by Edd Byrnes in the jocular **Any Gun Can Play**.

above: **Django Shoots First** – with, *from left*, Alberto Lupo, Evelyn Stewart, Glenn Saxson and Fernando Sancho – treated its hero's vendetta lightly, striking a more serious note for a subplot involving Lupo and Stewart.

There were other, similar films centred on dubious partnerships with a slightly more genial quality than had become the norm, such as *Beyond the Law* (1968), which gave Lee Van Cleef the opportunity to demonstrate his versatility with a lighter role; *The Greatest Robbery in the West* (1967), a superior caper western by Maurizio Lucidi with fine turns by George Hilton and Hunt Powers; and *Red Blood, Yellow Gold* (1967) by Nando Cicero, later to specialise in sex comedies. While all these titles have something of the picaresque about them, it was Giuseppe Colizzi's *God Forgives... I Don't!* (1967), Giulio Petroni's *A Sky Full of Stars for a Roof* (1968) and Duccio Tessari's *Alive or Preferably Dead* (1969) in particular that paved the way for *They Call Me Trinity* (1970) et al. *God Forgives...* was the first film to demonstrate the chemistry between *They Call Me Trinity*'s stars, Venetian Terence Hill and Neapolitan Bud Spencer, although had Peter Martell not broken his foot shortly before the start of filming, having originally been cast in Hill's role, it could have been a different story. *A Sky Full of Stars...*, with Giuliano Gemma and Mario Adorf, prefigured the 'Trinity' films' rambling narratives and use of dual, contrapuntal character types – one smooth, lithe and brainy, the other gruff, broad and brawny.²² *Alive or Preferably Dead*, meanwhile, which teamed Gemma with boxing champion Nino Benvenuti, a former colleague of Gemma's from his fire-fighting days, showed the comic potential of pitting one brother against another and, as in *Sky*, an inordinate amount of time is given over to lengthy physical brawls that entail a great deal of material destruction. (In America in the early Seventies this film played as *Sundance Cassidy and Butch the Kid* – "Don't confuse them with those other guys!" – with ads depicting the male stars in Redford and Newman mode, and co-star Sydne Rome standing in for Katharine Ross.)

above: Cat on a hot adobe roof: Terence Hill's character takes it easy in **God Forgives... I Don't!**

above: Spanish poster for **Alive or Preferably Dead**, a tale of bickering brothers that anticipated the 'Trinity' films.

above and opposite top: Move over Franco and Ciccio… The spectacular box-office receipts of **God Forgives… I Don't!** (*above*) and **They Call Me Trinity** (*opposite top*) transformed Terence Hill and Bud Spencer into Italy's most profitable screen pairing and confirmed that the Euro-western could never take itself entirely seriously again. Their comedy of opposites attracted vast numbers of Italians – between 1967 and 1975 at least one Hill-Spencer film, or one of their respective solo vehicles, featured among each year's top 10 moneymakers.

Of these, *God Forgives* was the biggest box-office hit, with Italian audiences immediately appreciating Hill and Spencer's fractious, quasi-fraternal relationship, though neither the actors nor Colizzi had anticipated the success of this unplanned, instinctive double act. "What we enjoyed together was something unexplainable [sic]," Hill has since commented. "Big-screen couples are rare because it's not, if you ask me, something that's studied or intellectual; it's an emotional thing. It would be simple if you could always just say, 'Let's put him together with somebody and make them a couple.' Producers would love it if they could do that. With us, it did happen like that, and it happened by chance."**23** Their relationship developed in Colizzi's two semi-serious sequels to *God Forgives* – *Ace High* (1968), in which their thunder is stolen by Eli Wallach; and *Boot Hill* (1969), one of a small number of rather camp 'circus' westerns – and would soon establish them as the heirs to Franco and Ciccio. Hill and Spencer's popularity was at least comparable with that of the Sicilian duo, and their influence upon the European western far greater.

They Call Me Trinity and its even more successful sequel, *Trinity Is Still My Name* (1971), are almost as well known internationally as the 'Dollars' films, albeit for different reasons. (They also stand shoulder-to-shoulder with Leone's classics in terms of box office receipts, making Italo Zingarelli and Roberto Palaggi's West Film one of the country's most lucrative production houses at the time.) The undercurrent of humorous absurdity so skilfully reined in by Leone is set loose by cinematographer-turned-writer/director Enzo Barboni, proceeding to run wild in many inferior copycat productions. At the same time, the level of violence is drastically reduced. (Although the first of the 'Trinity' films does include a few killings.) The 'Trinity' franchise was very much Barboni's pet project. He had conceived the original story and written the script (as early as 1966 according to Franco Nero, to whom Barboni first offered the lead) based on a desire to "demystify the [Italian] western". In his words, "As a director of photography, I'd done many westerns, and one thing about them that made me laugh

above: Terence Hill, sunny side up, in **God Forgives… I Don't!**

TERENCE HILL · BUD SPENCER
DIE RECHTE UND DIE LINKE HAND DES TEUFELS
REGIE: E. B. CLUCHER

was their use of violence as an end in itself, which really irked me as a viewer. I believed that westerns ought to be amusing; there's something inherently comic about [them]... in part because they started off from the imitation of a world we'd dreamed about but wasn't our own, one we'd never even seen."[24] Zingarelli accepted the project after many other producers had dismissed its chances, and engaged the services of Hill and Spencer in place of two other actors Barboni had in mind, George Eastman, who was to have played Bambino, and Peter Martell, who lost out on a major role to Hill for the second time in five years. (According to actor Leonard Mann, star of Barboni's directorial debut, *Chuck Mool* [1970], he and co-star Woody Strode had also been approached by the director to play the 'Trinity' leads.)

The 'Trinity' films' success is not hard to fathom: they mock both American and European western clichés; pull the rug from under propriety and authority; and make merry at the expense of supposedly taboo subjects such as religion and the family – actually, two of the most prolific targets for ridicule and irreverence. (Although Barboni's brothers are in constant dispute, they are a far cry from the mutually destructive siblings in films such as *Blood at Sundown* and *Twice a Judas* (1969). You may not be able to choose your relatives, seems to be the message, but you have to stick by them. Not that family enterprises are always likely to succeed, as the duo's faltering outlaw partnership in the second film goes to show.) There is also a much greater concentration on knockabout physical comedy in the style of silent movies and Franco and Ciccio, while food and bodily functions are prime sources of humour – *They Call Me Trinity* and its sequel were labelled '*fagioli* westerns' in the States, a spin-off from the 'spaghetti' tag that refers to the inordinate amount of beans that are consumed in them. There is also a debt owed to the wacky Italian comic strips of Benito Jacovitti, in particular his laid-back, lightning-fast cowboy Cocco Bill, and the laconic Lucky Luke, created by the Belgian/French team of Morris and Goscinny, a character later played on film by Terence Hill. Above and beyond these traits, however, *Trinity* and its sequel boast two wonderful characterisations from Hill and Spencer – both very likeable in their own ways and displaying fine comic timing.

Virtually all the threads that run through Barboni's films (except, notably, their charm) also bind their derivatives. Since these titles are too numerous to cover in detail, and because I share the majority view that most of them contribute little positive to the genre, what follows is a digest of representative examples, using the 'Trinity' films as a point of reference and, where necessary, a point of departure.

In classic buddy-movie fashion, Trinity and Bambino are contrasting yet complementary characters – one a figure of almost feline stealth and flexibility, with a sunny disposition and heart of gold, the other corpulent, bad-tempered and ever so slightly dense. The former has

above: Before Hill and Spencer were assigned the roles of Trinity and Bambino in **They Call Me Trinity**, other actors considered by director Enzo Barboni included Peter Martell and George Eastman and, according to Leonard Mann, he and Woody Strode. It quickly became apparent that Barboni had made the correct choice: **Trinity** was the second most successful film in Italy in 1971 behind Nino Manfredi's wry commentary on Catholicism, **Per grazia ricevuta**.

above: The stars' charisma alone would not account for the 'Trinity' films' success. Like all the comedy westerns that followed in their wake, the switch from gunplay to horseplay was another significant factor, although slapstick brawls rapidly became just as gratuitous as gunfights had.

above: The second 'Trinity' film was for many years Italy's most successful film.

a fondness for hare-brained schemes and a knack for causing trouble that agitate the latter. The humour in many of the 'Trinity' spin-offs is similarly based upon the heroes' tetchy relationship, dwelling on their differences – often reflected in their physical size – and disagreements. As we have seen, humorous westerns featuring bickering protagonists had been released before *They Call Me Trinity*, but it was after the sequel smashed box-office records that the trend really took off.[25] Allusions to Barboni's films abound in plots, jokes and performance styles, as well as in titles. Richard Harrison and Donal O'Brien play squabbling siblings in *Jesse & Lester: Two Brothers in a Place Called Trinity* (1972), while Mario Siciliano offered *Trinity and Sartana Are Coming* (1972), starring Alberto Dell'Acqua and black British actor Harry Baird. (It was a relief when one Spanish comedy arrived called *Ninguno de los tres se llamaba Trinidad* – literally, 'none of the three was called Trinity' – although ironically the English title was *The Fat Brothers of Trinity*.) The most blatant Trinity-Bambino clones were Antonio Cantafora, acting as 'Michael Coby', and American Paul Smith (who later played Bluto in Robert Altman's disastrous *Popeye* [1980]), who were chosen by director Ferdinando Baldi for their physical resemblance to Hill and Spencer when he failed to secure the latter pair for his dire 1974 comedy *Carambola* and its sequel, *The Crazy Adventures of Len and Coby* (1975).

This bleak sequence of witless production-line fodder was broken up by the occasional surprise. Giuliano Gemma returned to the western after a three-year hiatus to team up with George Eastman for Michele Lupo's superior *Ben and Charlie* (1972), based on a story by Eastman and a script co-written with Sergio Donati. This picaresque adventure is not a comedy per se, although it does indulge in rumbustious brawling and copies the episodic structure of *Trinity Is Still My Name*. Lupo, like Franco Giraldi before him, proves adept at blending humour with hard-edged western action; it's like a much-improved version of Gemma's earlier *A Sky Full of Stars for a Roof*. Another highly watchable partnership is that of Tomas Milian and the ursine Gregg Palmer in *Sometimes Life Is Hard, Right Providence?* (1972) and *Here We Go Again, Eh Providence?* (1973). Milian's eccentric, fastidious bounty hunter is a Charlie Chaplin look-alike who travels in a wagon armed with all manner of gadgets (in the sequel, it's equipped with a telegraph machine so that he can follow the ups and downs of outlaws' rewards). In *Here We Go Again*, director Alberto De Martino even makes a cameo in one scene to help Providence explain how the latter pulled off a seemingly impossible trick, breaching the barrier between illusion and reality and nodding towards the wacky world of cartoons. Providence makes most of his money by capturing, releasing and re-capturing Palmer's outlaw Hurricane Kid, acknowledging the debt that most of these double-cross comedies owe to the relationship

"Which way to the costume department?": Giuliano Gemma (*left*) and George Eastman (*right*) as squabbling, ill-starred outlaws in the seriocomic **Ben and Charlie**, yet another response to the 'Trinity' films but not, in this case, a one-note imitation.

above: Enzo Castellari's **Tedeum**, released in the UK as **The Con Men**, typified the worst excesses of the comic-western phase: it is overacted (not least by Jack Palance), overdirected and overlong (some might say by as much as 100 minutes).

between Clint Eastwood and Eli Wallach in *The Good, the Bad and the Ugly*. (Wallach himself got in on the act, playing a very similar role to Tuco in *Long Live Your Death* [1971], Duccio Tessari's raucous send-up of the political westerns that features Franco Nero as another of his patented 'foreigners', a Russian con artist at large in the Mexican Revolution.)

The comedy westerns are rife with Tuco-Blondie style one-upmanship, with professional cheats and swindlers taking the central narrative roles previously occupied by bounty hunters and brooding avengers. This leads to many ironic reversals of fortune, use of false disguises and other forms of subterfuge, lots of chasing to and fro and exasperated expressions. The promotion of shifty characters to the forefront keeps the films in the established cynical mode (the general attitude can be gauged from an aphorism of Gianni Garko's Holy Ghost persona: "If trust gets you a penny, mistrust will get you millions") while also allowing for non-lethal confrontations, befitting the overall lightening of tone and facilitating the kind of time-consuming scraps so

beloved of the era's filmmakers. A typical title in this regard is Enzo Castellari's astonishingly crass *Tedeum* (1972), also known as *Father Jack-Leg*, in which all the primary characters are "jacklegs" – swindlers looking to offload useless mining deeds. Of course, one such deed proves to be genuine and various parties compete to get their hands on it, culminating in a soggy mass brawl in a public bathhouse. While all the principals attack their irksome roles with (too much) relish – Jack Palance, as a sham monk, makes his earlier turn in *Compañeros* (1970) look understated by comparison, and lead Timothy Brent [Giancarlo Prete], who got the role when Tomas Milian, wisely, turned it down, confuses smarmy for charming – Castellari is guilty of over-directing the elongated chase scenes and telegraphing the many visual gags that pad out the action. The same criticism could be levelled at any number of other films.

Certain films rang a few changes on the odd-couple set-up. Some extended the number of partners – to three, for example, in Sergio Corbucci's clumsy interracial parable *The White, the Yellow and the Black* (1975), and four in the misleadingly titled *The Three Musketeers of the West* (1973), directed by Corbucci's brother Bruno – but the pattern of mutual abuse remained the same. Other examples presented the central relationship as a clash of generational, cultural or ethical values. The sentimental *Can Be Done... Amigo* (1972) by Maurizio Lucidi teams a typecast Bud Spencer with a principled young boy (Renato Cestiè), while Michele Lupo gave Spencer another troublesome sidekick, his Native American 'blood brother', in *Buddy Goes West* (1981). *My Name Is Nobody* pits Terence Hill's youthful prankster against Henry Fonda, the ageing face of westerns gone by, and yet another Sergio Corbucci film, his wayward political farce *What Am I Doing in the Middle of a Revolution?* (1972), builds upon the comical sparring of his 'Zapata' westerns with its story of an atheistic actor (Vittorio Gassman) and a cowardly priest (Paolo Villaggio) caught up in the mayhem of war-torn Mexico. (In the same year, Corbucci made the crude, misogynistic 'comedy' *Bandits*, a loose amalgamation of buddy-movie motifs and *Bonnie and Clyde* that has Tomas Milian as an obnoxious outlaw and Susan George as his simple-minded, masochistic love interest and partner in crime.)

The 'Trinity' films' ironic reinterpretation of western conventions begins with Trinity himself, whose manual dexterity takes the speed-on-the-draw motif to absurd extremes; this became Hill's trademark, from the fast-motion shots of him drawing his pistol before a trio of bewildered gunmen in *My Name Is Nobody*, to the bizarre sight of his sidearm leaping from its holster by itself in *A Genius, Two Partners and a Dupe* (1975). Gunmanship aside, Trinity couldn't be further removed from the ruthless, brooding *pistoleros* that preceded him. Indeed, machismo comes in for quite a battering in this style of film. Dressed like a saddle tramp, Hill eagerly sheds the rock-hard persona he had projected in westerns such as *Viva Django* (1967) and *God Forgives... I Don't!*, his character reacting to praise of his legendary pistol skills with a self-effacing, "Gee, is that what they say?" (Giuliano Gemma, Franco Nero, George Hilton and Gianni Garko all had fun with their images in a similar way.) Barboni, meanwhile, pokes fun in Leone's direction in the first film when Trinity single-handedly humiliates two posturing, black-clad hired gunslingers that are obviously modelled on Lee Van Cleef in *For a Few Dollars More*; one of them is even named Mortimer, just in case we don't make the connection. These are the first of many terse, scowling tough guys, invariably clad in black, to be ridiculed in the sub-genre. The most extreme example occurs in Giuliano Carnimeo's surreal 'Tresette' movies, named after a popular card game, in which Antonio Monselesan (pseudonymously credited as Tony Norton) appears as a tough-talking, leather-clothed closet homosexual gunman named Twinkletoes, whose frequent challenges to George Hilton's hero are blatant expressions of unrequited love.

above: Tough customers: Menacing gunmen like those played by Dominic Barto (*left*) and Antonio Monselesan (*right*) in **They Call Me Trinity** would have been dispatched to the graveyard in a serious western; in Enzo Barboni's world they are merely humiliated. Shortly after this shot, they are debagged by Terence Hill.

In addition to mocking machismo, the Seventies comedies take frivolous liberties with the staging of action sequences. The almost invariably frantic, stylised direction pays tribute to the *commedia dell'arte* and the silent era, while the more extreme titles play like live-action cartoons. What violence there is – and there is a lot of it, although deaths are comparatively rare – owes more to Mack Sennett or Tex Avery than to Sergio Leone. Stunt-filled saloon brawls, chases on foot, horseback and in all manner of vehicles, food fights (cheese is used as a weapon in *The Three Musketeers of the West*, while the humble onion makes for an unlikely comic prop in *Cipolla Colt* [1975] – 'cipolla' being the Italian word for onion), devastation of property – the full range of slapstick routines is faithfully represented. The action is often speeded up and accompanied by the flexing of facial muscles, while barely a blow is landed without a clang or some such noise on the soundtrack. Aping the comic dynamics of Hollywood cartoons, characters bloodlessly spit out their teeth when punched, or leave impressions and indentations where they fall. Sprightly anti-heroes grin and quip their way through the mayhem, often presenting a calm, Keaton-esque countenance in contrast to the chaos, while bands of bumbling villains perform like contemporary Keystone Kops, their sheer stupidity contributing to their downfall.

Populism, which was central, in different ways, to both Italy's westerns and its comedies, inevitably ran riot when the two genres were married together. In a further echo of the *commedia dell'arte*, figures of authority, in the form of stock characters such as sheriffs, civic dignitaries and pious types, are regularly brought low. The standard 'evil capitalist' plot is repeatedly reworked: land grabbers and speculators, instead of being merely demonised, are depicted as incompetent eccentrics or out-and-

above: Populism was very much on the menu in Italian westerns, especially the comedies. A stuffy restaurant stands in for high society in **Trinity Is Still My Name**, in which the brothers' provincial manners are contrasted (favourably) with the pretensions of maître d' Franco Ressel and his clientele.
bottom right: Tomas Milian's talent was tested in the screwball 'Providence' movies, in which he plays a whimsical bounty hunter modelled on Charlie Chaplin. His bizarre escapades – which involve a Bambino-like sidekick and a Chinese retainer – are rendered via a series of absurd set-pieces.

out lunatics, from the (literally) barking mad Wolf (Ezio Marano) in *Hallelujah & Sartana Strike Again!* (1972) to Martin Balsam's mechanical-handed oil baron in *Cipolla Colt*. And as noted in the chapter *Relatives And Religion*, most religious figures are given a similarly rough ride. With a few exceptions, such as the sympathetic treatment of Mormons and monks in the 'Trinity' films, the comedy westerns brand holy men and women in the same way as all the other chisellers and schemers that populate these films. While this kind of provocation was nothing new in a country where resentment of the Church's political power had always been rife in the filmmaking community – certainly among the left-leaning majority – its prevalence in westerns and other popular genres of this period seems particularly significant in the context of Catholicism's subsiding influence in Italian society. Deliverance from sin and suffering, meanwhile, became the task not of pure-hearted martyrs but amoral adventurers and outlaws, whose names – Trinity, Hallelujah, Providence, Holy Ghost – mislead one as to their methods.

In a similar vein, the comedies have no time for artifice or pretension, celebrating raw, earthy individualism over arrogance and affectation. Trinity looks like a vagrant, is a stranger to soap, and both he and

his brother eat like scavengers, but at least he doesn't have the stench of corruption clinging to him like Farley Granger's suave, fey villain in the first film, another of the genre's morally bankrupt southern aristocrats. This situation works in reverse in Barboni's later *Man of the East* (1972), in which Terence Hill's title character is gradually taught to relinquish his refined manners by his roughneck associates. Many other comedies set their humble heroes loose on polite society with predictably anarchic results. The central scene in *Trinity Is Still My Name*, for example, has the brothers – dressed, against type, in snappy suits and bowler hats – treating themselves to lunch in a fancy French restaurant, where their rough table manners and ignorance of dining etiquette cause chaos. Reacting with disgust at their minuscule portions, Trinity and Bambino help themselves from the serving dish, and end up by dousing a flambéed dessert, pulling their guns at the sound of a popping cork and knocking out the maitre d' (a perfectly cast Franco Ressel). (The restaurant setting was a popular one, recurring in *Tedeum* and *Buddy Goes West*, among others.) The twist is that the joke is not exclusively on the heroes, which would have been the case had this been a Franco and Ciccio movie, but on their fellow diners as well, who cast haughty, condescending glances in the brothers' direction. Clearly, behind their social graces these people are uptight and insincere, and Barboni delights in their squirming embarrassment. Elsewhere, however, this populist tract – the triumph of the great unwashed – is too often an excuse for the presentation of vulgar detail as a comical end in itself, shrouding whatever satirical intentions that may have been intended in a malodorous cloud of gags about bowel functions and personal hygiene.

While most of the comic westerns produced after the 'Trinity' films blend into one – the plots are usually episodic and cluttered with extraneous characters and diversions, the humour remains resolutely on one low level, and very rarely are the ingredients outlined above mixed with anything amounting to inventiveness or enthusiasm – it would be unfair not to credit the exceptions before we leave this subject behind. The famous *My Name Is Nobody* has been aptly summarised as "a comic counterpart of *Once Upon a Time in the West*".[26] The rueful tone of the latter, the sense of nostalgia for a lost age of heroes and legends, is accentuated in *Nobody* by the turn-of-the-century setting and Ernesto Gastaldi's self-conscious script, and co-exists uneasily with the self-mockery and exuberant clowning then in vogue. According to director Tonino Valerii, the project originated in Sergio Leone's desire to trump the 'Trinity' films. "Barboni's movies [pushed] Leone off his throne as the master of the Italian western... So Leone was planning artistic vengeance. Terence Hill, having ridiculed the Italian western, would have to pay with an eye for an eye by playing straight man to one of the western's most mythical interpreters, Henry Fonda, and so learn to recognise his own insignificance."[27] Leone abandoned his 'vendetta' during pre-production, however, with Hill given licence to extend his Trinity persona rather than renounce it. Leone wanted to set this lovable layabout in "a bigger story", and even proposed that Hill direct it.[28] While this didn't pan out, Leone himself is alleged to have filmed many of Hill's comedy scenes, although exactly how much footage he is responsible for remains in dispute. (Ernesto Gastaldi insists that the famous Street of Pleasure sequence, which he personally resents, was devised by Leone as a way of demonstrating that this was not one of his 'important' westerns.[29]) Valerii, for his part, preferred the wistful aspects of the story associated with Fonda's character, and this conflict is one reason why the film fails to fully achieve its ambitions. (Nor could Leone realise his ambition of toppling Barboni from the top of the box-office chart, if that really was one of his aims, though he came close: *Nobody* registered takings of 3.6 billion lire, making it the second most successful Italian western after *Trinity Is Still my Name*.[30])

The fact that it has ambitions beyond simple entertainment, however, is what differentiates *Nobody* from other comedies and aligns it with the revisionist westerns made, in America and elsewhere, around the same time. Through the iconic casting of Hill and Fonda, not to mention abundant references to earlier works, it examines the relationship and respective merits of Italian and Hollywood westerns.[31] There are also ruminations on the nature of myth – Nobody (Hill) behaves like a folklorist-cum-filmmaker, with Jack Beauregard (Fonda)

above: Terence Hill as the title character in **My Name Is Nobody**, another feast for '*fagioli*' western' fans.

above: The monikers of many Italian comic-western heroes, from Trinity and Providence to the Holy Ghost and George Hilton's Hallelujah (*above*), were emblematic of the genre's casual disdain for Catholicism.

a reluctant legend-in-the-making – and of cinema itself. Prominent motifs such as showmanship and spectatorship, illusion and reflection draw attention to the artificiality of the action, as well as making a connection between the filmmakers of today and the popular historians, dime novelists and pioneering photographers who shaped the legends of the past. (There's also a nod to Homer, one of Leone's great inspirations and the source, of course, of Nobody's 'identity'.) The film's slapstick centrepiece, when Nobody defeats all-comers in the Street of Pleasure, brings many of these ideas into focus, as well as being a bravura demonstration of comic dexterity, timing and visual ingenuity. Much of the sequence relies, like many comedies, upon deception, disguise and distortion for effect: a giant is revealed to be a dwarf on stilts; Nobody displays impossible hand speed (courtesy of some fast-motion photography) as he slaps a bald villain senseless; and a fight in a hall of mirrors is one of several reminders the film provides that in life, as in film, appearances are not to be trusted. Although Nobody's carnivalesque capers – he is the most explicit of the genre's Harlequin figures – threaten to overwhelm the quieter, more elegiac passages centred on Jack, this imbalance is corrected somewhat by the perfectly weighted contrast between the leads, the indefatigable idealist (Hill) and world-weary realist (Fonda). (Ennio Morricone defines these contrary characters with two wonderful themes: a jaunty piece for Nobody featuring flute, acoustic guitar and electronic effects, with a childlike chorus; and the sentimental strains of 'Good Luck, Jack', an ode to Fonda complete with Edda Dell'Orso vocals.) Without wishing to slight Valerii, perhaps a director like Duccio Tessari, or even Leone himself, might have stitched *My Name Is Nobody*'s many excellent qualities together with greater success. (Leone seemed to agree – he felt the film "uncertain" and lacking "equilibrium".**32**)

Finally, we come to the deranged films of Giuliano Carnimeo, although his initial forays into comedy were relatively sedate compared with what he would eventually deliver. Following the Sartana series, he set another franchise in motion with *They Call Me Hallelujah* (1971), which originated, the director says, in George Hilton's wish to have a character of his own – to escape the shadow of Sartana, as it were, having recently stepped in for Garko as that famous character for one film in the series. Here, Hilton stars as a nonchalant, wisecracking mercenary armed with a bullet-spitting sewing machine (made by 'Senger', not Singer – either a careless misspelling or, perhaps, a bid to avoid litigation). The blend of throwaway political sentiments, large-scale action scenes and lavatorial humour ensured broad popular appeal (*His Name Was Holy Ghost*, below, was a very similar cocktail), and Hilton reprised the role in an even zanier sequel, *The Return of Hallelujah* (1972). Here, the title character is even more laid-back – he types up his terms and conditions in the midst of a battle before helping some rebels – and the bizarre imagery includes a sheriff armed with a fish and Hallelujah almost castrating a line of soldiers with a whip.

The director then re-teamed with Gianni Garko for *His Name Was Holy Ghost* (1972), a caper in the "comic-grotesque style", as Garko puts it, with the actor decked out in white suit and cape, matching white dove perched on one shoulder. (His name wasn't Holy Ghost in Spain, incidentally, where in deference to the Church the title was changed to *They Call Him the Hawk*.) A chaotic action film in the mould, if not the mind-set, of the revolutionary westerns, it starts out tongue-in-cheek but takes a slapstick turn with the introduction of chubby Cris Huerta as Garko's comic foil, and concludes with a knockabout fight in which the forces of the Holy Ghost – comprising prostitutes (his "Trojan whores") and various hairy men dressed as women – subdue a fortress full of soldiers.**33**

From here, Carnimeo, in collaboration again with George Hilton, created yet another character, abandoning all restraint in the process, with the fast-moving 'Tresette' movies – *A Man Called Invincible* (1973) and *The Crazy Bunch* (1974). Carnimeo assails the viewer with a plethora of surreal sight gags that are more cartoonish than ever, typified by a scene in the first film set in a jail cell, where Hilton paints over the bars (presumably using Acme paint) to make the sheriff believe he's sawn through them and escaped into the clear blue yonder. The films are a weird mixture of childishness, satire and lewd suggestiveness. There's nothing new in the way that prolific writer Tito Carpi (who also worked on *His Name Was Holy Ghost* and co-wrote *The Return of Hallelujah*) portrays the West as a haven for corruption and conspiracy, drawing crude parallels with the political landscape of the early Seventies (Hilton's devious character is called Tricky Dicky in the English dialogue – this was, after all, smack in the middle of the Watergate scandal). What is notable, however, is that the town at the centre of the first film, Apple Pie City (an innocuous translation from the Italian Melabacata, or 'rotten apple'), is run by a clique of crooked homosexuals, including the equally harmless-sounding Mr. Apple and Mr. McPiedish, and there is a strong homosexual subtext throughout both films. Among the other villains Hilton has to face are the Bent Gang, the Closet Cousins and Fruity Tooty, not to mention the singularly unimposing Twinkletoes – "I am Twinkletoes, and Twinkletoes spells death!" The cheap gags at homosexuality's expense, combined with the numerous double-entendres that pepper the dialogue, were fairly typical of lowbrow Italian comedies of the period; even the seemingly straight Tresette's sexuality is called into question at times, as in his sado-masochistic relationship with the ludicrous Twinkletoes. The obvious inference is that masculinity is a mask for repressed homosexuality, although whether this would have penetrated the intensely macho mentality of the everyday Italian at the time, especially the type of Italian drawn to comedies and westerns, is unlikely to say the least.

The 'Trinity' films and their descendants were as much an acknowledgement of changing public tastes – plus the fact that broad, unsophisticated comedy is a perennial box-office draw – as they were an artistic statement in their own right, although they can also be taken as a deliberate move away from the nihilistic, increasingly politicised and 'meaningful' tone that the most prosperous European westerns had adopted before that point. Statements from Hill and Spencer certainly suggest they had been looking for a project in the 'Trinity' films' more positive vein, which determined the remainder of their careers. As Hill says: "Mothers stopped me in the street to tell me to continue with these films because they could bring their children to the cinema without worrying about nasty surprises. So I felt obliged to continue along the same lines, just as I'm doing today."[34]

However one approaches Barboni's blockbusters, they succeeded in keeping the western alive in Europe for a few more years, even if the results too often portrayed Italian cinema at its basest and most formalised.[35] (We ought to note that Spanish studios also caught the comedy bug, with all the regular directors like Ignacio Iquino and Juan Bosch trying their luck, but their output was limited and just as derivative as the bulk of the Italian 'Trinity' clones.) In real terms, however, the genre was fading fast and had been for a number of years; the comic cycle merely accelerated the process. "It was a natural event," concludes Giuliano Carnimeo. "Think about it – we had years of serious, violent westerns, then the need for self-mockery became apparent; it is a natural evolutionary process, it can't be stopped. And as there were too many violent westerns before, there were too many comedies released after, until the natural vanishing of the genre."[36]

Unwilling to let it die just yet, however, the industry looked to the latest exploitation craze for inspiration.

above: Another Giuliano Carnimeo western, another sardonic George Hilton performance, yet more ridiculous horseplay (literally, in this case) – **A Man Called Invincible** paired self-parody with surreal humour and a dash of contemporary satire.

"The fastest gun in the west meets the most brutal hands in the east"

In 1972, director Cheng Chang-ho's tough, bloody martial arts drama, *King Boxer*, revolutionised the Hong Kong film industry. Not because it was the first film of its kind, nor necessarily the best, but because it was the first to receive a prominent international release. This archetypal story of retribution among rival fighters was financed by Shaw Brothers, Hong Kong's pre-eminent production house, and centred on an aggressive performance by Lo Lieh as a young man who masters the Iron Palm technique in the pursuit of revenge. Picked up for worldwide distribution by Warner Brothers, which was well aware of the popularity of this type of film in Asia, *King Boxer* performed admirably in all the major western markets, including the UK, the US, where Warners changed the title to *Five Fingers of Death* to maximise its marquee value, and Italy, where it was one of the 20 highest-grossing films at the box office in the 1972-73 season and was parodied in the Franco Franchi vehicle *Ku Fu? Dalla Sicilia con furore* (1973). Its success confirmed the latent box-office appeal of martial arts in the west, where these exotic fighting styles had previously featured in a handful of films, from *Bad Day at Black Rock* (1955) and the Derek Flint spy spoofs to *Marlowe* (1969), with its devastating Bruce Lee cameo, as well as television series such as *The Avengers*, *I Spy*, and two more early showcases for Lee's abilities, *The Green Hornet* and the crime series *Longstreet*. Then there was Warners' *Kung Fu*, which had premiered in 1972 and achieved excellent ratings, its success contributing to the studio's decision to gamble on *King Boxer*. The series also proved the viability of injecting Far Eastern spice into an old west setting and, since it was an international hit, this may well have piqued the interest of Italian western producers desperate for a new direction. Bruce Lee, already a cult figure thanks to *The Green Hornet* and at one point considered for the lead in *Kung Fu*, soon made his big-screen breakthrough and a flurry of dubbed, re-edited kung-fu/karate films (the terms became erroneously interchangeable) followed in his wake. Several Hong Kong titles out-performed domestic productions in the US for a magic few months in 1973 while, in the UK, kung-fu films were released at the rate of at least one or two a month until the bubble burst a year or two later, all the while competing for attention with other imports including blaxploitation flicks, *Decameron*-style erotic comedies and, of course, European westerns. Many of these were only now seeing the light of day after spending several years sitting on distributors' shelves.

Despite the vast cultural gulf that separates the popular cinematic traditions of the Orient and the West, there's a symmetry between them that points to their shared thematic obsessions and mythologising tendencies. Hollywood romanticises the legends of the frontier just as Japanese *chambara eiga* (samurai or swordfight films) carve epic adventures from the country's feudal era, and many of the Chinese/Hong Kong armed and unarmed combat films centre on warriors and events from dynasties past. Furthermore, in each of these categories the landscape is imbued with metaphorical significance and often has a symbiotic relationship with the protagonist. Aspects of these distinct cultures cross over and occasionally coalesce, revealing a mutual fascination, at least on the part of individual filmmakers, stemming from both rivalry and respect. Akira Kurosawa is a key figure in this regard, the noir-soaked post-war Tokyo of his *Stray Dog* (1949) reflecting Hollywood's hard-boiled thrillers, while his classic *chambara*, *Seven Samurai* (1954) and *Yojimbo* (1961), proved, arguably, the two most important stimuli in the renaissance of the western in the Sixties. (What goes around comes around – Kurosawa himself talked about learning from the "grammar" of John Ford's films.[37]) Japan has even produced its own 'cowboy' films, set in Japan but borrowing plots, costumes and clichés from Hollywood. Nikkatsu Studios, renowned for hyper-stylish gangster thrillers, produced a string of western-style adventures in the early Sixties, with stars such as Joe Shishido and Akira Kobayashi, Japan's answer to Roy Rogers, gamely giving cowboy impersonations.[38] More recent attempts at genre/cultural fusion include the disappointing *East Meets West* (1995), an ambitious flop made by Japanese and American personnel and filmed on US locations by avowed western buff Kihachi Okamoto, director of *chambara* classics *Samurai Assassin* (1965) and *The Sword of Doom* (1966); and Takashi Miike's characteristically way-out tribute, *Sukiyaki Western Django* (2007), with a plot modelled equally on *A Fistful of Dollars* and *Django* (a Japanese-language cover version of Luis Bacalov's theme song from the latter film plays over the end credits), phonetically spoken English dialogue, *anime*-meets Enzo Barboni colour schemes, eclectic sets and costume design, and a cameo appearance by a poncho-adorned Quentin Tarantino. Meanwhile, the *Kung Fu* format – Asian outsider roaming the rugged west – continues to be adapted, as in two relatively recent vehicles for Bruce Lee's most successful descendants, Jet Li (*Once Upon a Time in China and America* [1997]) and Jackie Chan (*Shanghai Noon* [2000], which features a villain named Van Cleef). Outside the western genre, the clearest example of this trading of influences lies in the new-wave Hong Kong action film, which revitalised film noir and gangster movie motifs and has given directors such as John Woo and Ringo Lam unprecedented opportunities in the US. Tarantino's *Kill Bill* (2003-4) is a post-modern synthesis of all these modes, synchronizing dramatic themes and musical styles from Japanese, Chinese and Italian revenge fantasies.

Hybrid Westerns

It is, of course, the correlation between the western and its Asian counterparts that concerns us here. Each genre shares the same essential features and functions. Themes of justice, honour, heroism, repression, exploitation, betrayal and revenge are common to all, as are formalised narratives that move mechanically from set-piece to set-piece before reaching the final apotheosis – the duel. Their respective protagonists – the cowboy, the samurai and the kung-fu warrior or swordsman – share a near-mythical status and a flair for violence, which is seen as the only viable means of survival or instrument of justice in an unstable environment where law is either absent, impotent or corrupt. These characters' motives are generally either personal or familial (family and fraternity in a wider sense exert a particularly strong pull on heroes in martial arts movies, with their wise, paternal masters and brotherly disciples), although their vendettas are often set within a social context that allows for socio-political criticism or comment, especially in westerns dealing with land rights, samurai sagas detailing the instability of the late Tokugawa period and the inequities of the feudal system, and some of the more overtly nationalistic (read anti-Japanese) Chinese kung-fu films.

If we narrow our focus, the kinship of European western and Asian action film becomes clear. The genres developed to their fullest extent in the same era, the late Sixties. Japanese swordplay pictures, under pressure domestically from a new wave of vicious *yakuza* dramas, had become bloodier and more brooding, while samurai film scholar Alain Silver points out the "manifest alienation" of many *chambara* swordsmen. And just as Leone had earlier absorbed some of Kurosawa's gritty realism, so Japanese productions began to approximate the style and tone of Euro-westerns, which were hugely popular in Japan and continue to be accorded unusual respect there. In Hong Kong, meanwhile, directors such as King Hu and Chang Cheh were reinvigorating the martial arts film with lavish stylisation, dynamic widescreen compositions, exhilarating action choreography, epic scale and grandiose themes (which is partly why Hu has been likened to Sergio Leone) and, in Chang's case, spectacular Corbucci-style bloodletting (his *One-Armed Swordsman* trilogy and later *Crippled Avengers* make perfect companion pieces to Corbucci's tales of disabled pistoleros). The revenge motif in these films is pursued with a feverish intensity. Just as many Italian western narratives follow a Sicilian-style vendetta pattern, so there is an ancient, unwritten Japanese code of vengeance –

above: Akira Kurosawa's **Yojimbo** was one of the most important precursors in terms of the tone the Italian western adopted in its prime – it was the direct inspiration, of course, for **A Fistful of Dollars**.

above: US pre-release poster artwork for **The Silent Stranger**, advertised under its working title.

kataki-uchi – that imposes a duty of revenge on characters in *chambara eiga*. And not for nothing was one of the earliest English-language studies of the Hong Kong kung-fu film entitled *Cinema of Vengeance* (Verina Glaessner, 1974), such is the prevalence of the theme in that genre.

The severity of the violence in each of these strains is matched by the amplified evil of the villains, which in turn justifies the cruelty of the protagonist. This violence is highly stylised and often exaggerated to a fantastic degree. The careful choreography of the carnage offers a telling distinction between the approach to action in these films and that of more mainstream fare. There is an obsession with skill and technique; the martial artist's mastery of esoteric weapons, like the samurai's blade expertise, can be compared with the Euro-western gunman's fast draw and his proficiency in unusual armaments such as palm pistols and multi-barrelled guns. The protagonists have a similarly murky ethical make-up; traditional heroic virtues are muted or corrupted, especially in the case of the *chambara ronin* (masterless samurai) and the Euro-western bounty hunter, who both kill for money, although the former is more likely to ruminate on moral quandaries than the latter. (The kung-fu hero, by contrast, is usually rigorously upstanding.) Western series centred on a distinctive protagonist such as Django and Sartana had their equivalents in Japan, for example the massively popular 'Zatoichi' (who, as earlier noted, was the inspiration for the Italian western *Blindman* [1971]), 'Sleepy Eyes of Death' and 'Lone Wolf and Cub' films. There are structural similarities – the master/apprentice plot, a staple of martial arts movies, is utilised in several notable Euro-westerns, including *Bandidos* (1967), *Day of Anger* (1967) – whose Oedipal connotations are paralleled in numerous kung-fu and swordplay films that feature 'good' and 'bad' father figures – *Fury of Johnny Kid* and *Clumsy Hands*, where the master is, indeed, an elderly Asian man. Sets and locations are similar in nature and narrative function – town streets and taverns/saloons are commonly the sites of violence, besieged ranch houses alternate with temples and martial arts schools. Finally, the central characters in both genres are united by their superhuman powers of recovery and agility, the ability to overcome crippling injuries and defeat an army of opponents – and to do it in style. The vicious hand mangling suffered by Franco Nero's Django translates into the almost identical beating administered to Lo Lieh in *King Boxer*, and similar examples are legion. It is no coincidence that these two genres, equal parts escapism and wish-fulfilment fantasy, were targeted at, and adored by, the same audience demographics.**39**

The best-known precursor of these 'Eurasian' hybrids is Terence Young's Spanish-Italian-French *Red Sun* (1971), which I will come to later, but the potential for an East-meets-Western, European style, had first been tapped by Tony Anthony and Luigi Vanzi in the third film in the 'Stranger' series, *The Silent Stranger* (1968; see *Beware Of Fake Guns*). Though many of the rules of this sub-genre were established there, the conflict between Anthony's shallow, materialistic westerner and the stereotypically intense Japanese is not reduced to one of opposing moral values, as is so often the case when these two great cultures clash in fiction. The Japanese are no nobler than Anthony himself, and the clan intrigue in which he gets involved is centred on a dispute over money, not a point of honour. There is little effort made to resolve the two sides' apparent incompatibility, let alone to explore the reasons behind it, and neither party can be said to have gained from the experience. Then again, any spurious diplomatic resolution would have been out of place in an Anthony western. *The Silent Stranger* is a typically sardonic affair that refuses to patronise the Japanese or to laud one ideology over another; all the characters are treated in the same unsentimental fashion. It scores extra points by shooting on location in Japan, which gives it an air of authenticity that compensates somewhat for the lack of insight.

A few other European westerns took note of the increasing influence of oriental action cinema in the late Sixties with significant casting choices, although the actors involved were rarely given the chance to stretch more than their muscles. Hawaiian-born Asian-American

James Shigeta plays a Japanese karate expert in Enzo Peri's gimmicky *Death Walks in Laredo* (1967), while the compelling Tatsuya Nakadai, an icon of Japanese film and Toshiro Mifune's pistol-packing opponent in *Yojimbo*, brings genuine menace to the role of the pseudo-Mexican villain in Tonino Cervi's *Today It's Me... Tomorrow You!* (1968), a film that consciously evokes the austere visual style of Sixties *chambara eiga*, notably during the climactic gunfight shot in the ancient Etruscan forests near Bracciano, north of Rome. (Nakadai – of whom his antagonist in the film, Brett Halsey, says, "I have never worked with an actor who was more single-mindedly dedicated to his craft"[40] – has only ventured twice more to the west, appearing in the dismal *Return from the River Kwai* [1988] and the aforementioned *East Meets West*.) Nakadai's contemporary, Tetsuro Tamba, was fresh from his role as Tiger Tanaka in the James Bond entry *You Only Live Twice* (1967) when he enlisted as a displaced swordsman in *The Five Man Army* (1969), while George Wang [George Wang Jue], perennial bit-part player in Italian exploitation films, launches a surprise martial arts attack on Gianni Garko at the end of *Have a Nice Funeral, Sartana Will Pay* (1970). This gives Wang's character a belated sense of purpose, having spent the preceding 90 minutes or so as little more than a red herring. Wang virtually disappeared from Western screens in the mid-Seventies, by which time he had become a regular in Hong Kong productions.

above and below: "Where are you from, stranger?" Tatsuya Nakadai (*above right*, with Brett Halsey, and *below, second from left*) played an orientalised Mexican gang boss (at one point he wields a machete in the manner of a samurai sword, a more familiar prop for the actor) in **Today It's Me... Tomorrow You!**

To return to *Red Sun* – a huge hit with Italian audiences[41] – it is a little like *The Silent Stranger* in reverse: here a Japanese is the 'alien' and the backdrop is the American southwest of the 1870s. Toshiro Mifune plays Kuroda, a samurai guarding a priceless sword intended as a gift for the American president; when the sword is stolen (by a miscast Alain Delon), Kuroda is given seven days to retrieve it, and teams up with one of the bandits, Link (Charles Bronson), for that purpose. There is plenty of potential in the story but Terence Young fails to locate it, glossing over the cultural and political issues in favour of exoticism and action, and like so many then-fashionable cosmopolitan co-productions, this one lacks focus. What saves it is the relationship between Mifune and Bronson as noble, obdurate samurai and coarse, cynical gunman respectively. Neither role is taxing, but the stars complement each other nicely, their characters developing a level of understanding and respect that goes beyond their respective fighting skills. Mifune is particularly good at fleshing out his stereotypical role of ascetic warrior, bound by centuries of tradition and a rigid code of honour, which he is forced to compromise. Young doesn't display much understanding of, or interest in, the western, but the scenes involving Kuroda's deadly swordsmanship show some knowledge of *chambara eiga* – blades flash and blood sprays, and it's clear that this was the aspect of Japanese culture the filmmakers were most enthusiastic about.

Italy's efforts at kung-fu filmmaking in the early Seventies are similarly superficial with regard to their source material, betraying the hurried, opportunistic nature of their production. Pairing off its by now barely profitable take on the western with the martial arts movie, pitting guns against fists and feet, would have seemed good business sense in kung fu-crazy 1973, especially considering the Italian film industry's past success in mixing and matching diverse genres and gearing the resultant hybrid towards an international audience – the Euro-western itself being the most obvious example. This time the gamble failed, however, both artistically and commercially. Most of the films, and tellingly there were only a few of them, come across as desperate and shabby, mirroring the motives behind their making. Martial arts on screen can be a dazzling exhibition of human athleticism, grace and power but, when poorly filmed, they make for a clumsy, confusing spectacle – quick edits, inappropriate close-ups and off-putting camera angles do the performers few favours. The Asian characters and their customs are sketched very thinly, suggesting that the filmmakers had no more regard or respect for their protagonists' backgrounds than the casually racist villains in their films do.

The Fighting Fists of Shanghai Joe and *The Stranger and the Gunfighter* (1974), released in the UK as *Blood Money*, are the best of a bad bunch. The former is an assured piece of exploitation filmmaking by the reliable Mario Caiano. Its strongest point is a composed, sympathetic performance by a virtual unknown, Chen Lee, as the eponymous Joe, a wandering Chinaman who arrives in the land of opportunity only to encounter oppression and prejudice. To force the point, the only people who treat him with respect are downtrodden Mexican peasants. Lee, who passed away in 2004, was actually Japanese (his casting as a Chinaman underlines the cavalier approach to cultural sensitivities in these films), born Myoushin Hayakawa in Aichi in 1939, and this was his first screen role. He had taught karate in England in the mid-Sixties before moving to Italy in 1970, where he opened a karate academy and was apparently working in a laundry before passing a screen test and winning the part of Joe. (He later established himself as a successful businessman.) In the film he is a model of dignity and compassion in a clichéd role, while even his pious dialogue is dubbed with some kind of conviction. "They're men," Joe observes of a group of wetbacks he's been hired to help transport, "I just can't think of them as cattle." In the fight scenes he displays the energy and power of an uncoiled snake, although the film's X-rated violence – he plucks out eyeballs, chops off hands and thrusts his fist into a chest cavity – is at odds with Joe's egalitarian philosophy. This was clearly Caiano's mandate, however – to combine the mayhem of two bloodthirsty genres in one picture.

above and opposite bottom left: **Red Sun** set the seal on Charles Bronson's superstar status on the Continent, and was the seventh most popular film in Italy during the 1971-2 box-office season. Bronson's self-effacing performance was the perfect foil for his co-star, the tightly wound Toshiro Mifune.

And such is the vociferousness of the film's anti-racist tract and the savagery of its villains (a "happy bunch of murderers" hired by local landowners to kill Joe) that a more measured degree of punishment would have seemed equally out of place.

Caiano's direction of the martial arts is more intelligent than that of his contemporaries, although he, like most Western directors, relies too much on camera techniques and sound effects to exaggerate the characters' speed of movement and agility, such as low-angle shots of Joe leaping through the air. The final duel between Joe and a rival Chinese fighter is particularly well executed, Caiano framing the combatants against a deserted adobe village backdrop where they use various props to pummel each other. As a late-period Euro-western the film is almost incomparably gritty, shunning the overt comedy of its contemporaries. It is also blessed with a wondrous Bruno Nicolai soundtrack that incorporates subtle oriental motifs (elements of the same score had been used in both *Have a Nice Funeral, Sartana Will Pay* and *God in Heaven... Arizona on Earth* [1972]), plus a clutch of distinctive actors in colourful cameos – Klaus Kinski as the evil Scalper Jack, for instance, and Robert Hundar as the feral Pedro the Cannibal. Yet nobody steals the film from Lee, who has all the physical attributes, and a better grasp of acting, than many of the period's more established screen martial artists.

Apart from Bruce Lee, the most bankable of these actor-athletes at the time was *King Boxer*'s Lo Lieh. Lo's producer, Run Run Shaw, was quick to take advantage of the West's fascination with all things Far Eastern and signed a co-production agreement with foreign investors, including Italian behemoth Carlo Ponti, to make a western. For this, the first such venture Hong Kong had undertaken, Lo was cast alongside one of the Euro-western's greatest stars, Lee Van Cleef, with an Italian veteran, Antonio Margheriti, in the director's chair.**42** The resulting film, *The Stranger and the Gunfighter*, is as contrived as its background suggests, a convergence of comedy, martial arts and straight-up gunplay that doesn't really work on any level. The plot can be summed up by one of the script's many bad puns – "at the bottom of every woman is a fortune". (The film was sold to Italian audiences under the euphemistic title

Là dove non batte il sole – there, where the sun doesn't shine.) Lo plays a young Chinaman who arrives in the West to locate his late uncle's treasure; the clues to its whereabouts are tattooed on the backsides of various ladies the old man had seduced. (Duccio Tessari's *Long Live Your Death* had already utilised this idea, although the bottoms in that case were male.) Van Cleef plays Dakota, "thief by profession, bum by choice", who goes along for the ride and helps Lo see off the attentions of a maniacal religious zealot.

While the script skirts carelessly over issues of import to both genres – family honour, revenge, religious fanaticism – this bawdy, comic variant of *Red Sun* is held together, as that film was, by the genial interplay between the stars, who work together surprisingly well. Van Cleef takes none of it seriously and projects an air of amiability that complements his character's roguish nature. Dakota is by far the most positive, open-minded occidental character in this sub-genre; indeed, at the end of the film, the cowboy follows Lo to China, keen to get to know his new friend's country. Indonesian-born Lo, who went on to specialise in villainous roles, is similarly unaffected, although his athleticism is obscured by Margheriti's uncharacteristically clumsy direction; for a man renowned for crafting impressive action sequences on meagre budgets, this aspect of the film is sorely disappointing. (There isn't much improvement in the Jim Kelly fight sequences in Margheriti's subsequent *Take a Hard Ride* [1975].)

The Stranger and the Gunfighter was hardly a high-minded concept in the first place, but its weakness for crude comedy cheapens it further. The same can be said for *Kung Fu Brothers in the Wild West* (1973) and *Return of Shanghai Joe* (1974), in both of which the comedy is either unintentional or simply ill-judged and overplayed. Since the martial arts vogue coincided with that of comedy westerns, it is no surprise to see Asian stereotypes mixed into these films' batteries of comic caricatures. Japanese karate champion Iwao Yoshioka joined Dean Reed and Cris Huerta in Tonino Ricci's episodic caper *Karate, Fists and Beans* (1973), and there are isolated instances of kung-fu clowning in *Here We Go Again, Eh Providence?*, *The Three Musketeers of the West* and, to a lesser extent, *The White, the Yellow and the Black*, attesting yet again to the fashionable standing of Asian fight films. (Similar slapstick would become commonplace in Hong Kong's kung fu output later in the Seventies, especially after the success of Jackie Chan's *Drunken Master* [1978].)

Kung Fu Brothers, like *The Stranger and the Gunfighter*, was a co-production between Italian and Hong Kong-based interests, but the partners involved were not quite of the same calibre as Run Run Shaw and Carlo Ponti.**43** Novice director Yeo Ban Yee's Yangtze Productions and Italy's Eureka International intended the film to be the first of several such enterprises, but whether any others saw the light of day is unknown. Italian reference sources are equally vague where this film is concerned, suggesting it had a very limited cinematic release. (The most notable point about the Italian version is that it was dubbed as a comedy rather than the – more or less – straight drama its makers apparently intended it to be.) It is significant, at least, as the only Italian western-martial arts hybrid to have been helmed by a Far Eastern native. Not that this would have ensured greater authenticity or integrity, although the fight scenes, at least those between the film's Asian stars, do benefit from the unobtrusive camerawork. Jason Pai Piao, a prolific performer in Hong Kong action films, is especially impressive as the more aggressive of the eponymous brothers. Elsewhere, however, Yeo's inexperience is embarrassingly apparent, as in the way he frequently cuts to needless, idiotic facial reaction shots during the action, and he is clearly ignorant about pacing. The film also possesses one of the most crass, tasteless 'jokes' in film history, when Pai Piao is about to rescue a woman from an attempted rape only to realise that she and her partner are only pretending – she gives Pai Piao a sly wink and they all have a good laugh. The promising plot of *Kung Fu Brothers* offers plenty of scope to explore concepts like fraternity, loyalty, tradition and race relations, but it required greater talent and commitment, not to mention a more generous budget, to make it anything more than a minor curiosity.

The jaunty pop song that opens *Return of Shanghai Joe*, meanwhile, signals a radical shift away from the serious tone of its predecessor. Gone is the likeable Chen Lee, replaced by the multi-talented Ernest Van-Mohr, billed as 'Cheen Lie', and cinematographer-turned-director Bitto Albertini abandons drama in favour of foolish humour. The clichéd 'evil town boss' plot is made more bearable by the presence of Klaus Kinski as the boss in question, but in all other respects the film is abysmal. Even its most original character, a kindly, wandering medicine man (Tommy Polgar), is gradually transformed into a generic buffoon, and Van-Mohr is given few opportunities to demonstrate his fighting abilities.**44**

As bad as they are, *Kung Fu Brothers in the Wild West* and *Return of Shanghai Joe* do not represent the nadir of this short-lived sub-genre. That dubious distinction belongs to *The Tiger from the River Kwai* (1975), which attempts to do for Thai kick boxing what Bruce Lee's films had done for jeet kune do. While the jaw-dropping fight scenes in *Ong-Bak* (2003) and its follow-ups have proved that kick boxing can look as dynamic on screen as any other discipline, Franco Lattanzi's inept direction in *Tiger* does this gritty fighting style a disservice, and the film's token Thai boxer, Krung Srivilai, is an extremely diffident performer. His bouts with workhorse villain

Gordon Mitchell are slow moving and desperately unconvincing, and the whole production reeks of semi-professionalism. Director Lattanzi (responsible for the equally insipid revenge/redemption western *God's Executioner* [1973]) simply turns the camera on and lets the clichés unfold. There is no originality, no momentum to the standard 'alien abroad' plot, no atmosphere and precious little logic. The dialogue is appalling ("That damn yellow face, I'll squeeze him like a lemon"), editing askew, sets and scenery drab, acting and characterisation practically nonexistent, the comic relief Chinese caricatures – a married couple who come to Srivilai's aid – embarrassing. The soundtrack consists of anachronistic electronica, culled perhaps from some early Seventies prog-rock music library, and Srivilai wanders around dressed like a denizen of London's Carnaby Street. The film is a careless, clueless mess, and it's hard to see how it could have found an audience in all but the most undiscerning markets.

It hardly needs stating that Italian filmmakers were much more comfortable working with horror and comic themes – both staples of Italian popular cinema, especially during the period under discussion – than they were with martial arts. Producers evidently hoped that a dose of exoticism would prove just the tonic for the ailing western genre, but this was not to be – times and tastes had changed and no amount of tinkering was going to entice audiences back, certainly not when the results were this clumsy and contrived. The best that can be said about these films is that their Asian leads are proactive, driving the narrative rather than being subsumed within it, which is the usual fate of oriental characters in westerns. Apart from *The Fighting Fists of Shanghai Joe* and, to a lesser extent, *The Stranger and the Gunfighter*, however, these films are shallow, superficial and technically inefficient, offering audiences nothing they hadn't seen many times before in much better productions.

In the interests of symmetry, it is worth highlighting some of the many Far Eastern adventures that were structured and styled in the manner of spaghetti westerns. These generally assimilated their influences more successfully than their Italian counterparts, which merely threw Asians and gunfighters together and hoped for the best. From the Shaw Brothers stable, Yueh Feng's *The Bells of Death* (1968) was an early response to the influx of Euro-westerns, a cut-to-the-chase revenge yarn with an anti-hero whose presence is announced by the ringing of ornamental bells; Chor Yuen's fantasy *The Magic Blade* (1976) is a nod to the 'Dollars' trilogy, with a quick-draw swordsman (Ti Lung), complete with stubble and poncho, standing in for Clint Eastwood; the Taiwanese *The Seven Commandments of Kung Fu* (1979) covers the same ground as *Day of Anger*; and the Wu Ma film *Along Comes a Tiger* (1977) is a variation on *Once Upon a Time in the West*.

Many *chambara eiga* showed signs of the Euro-western's influence, particularly the stylisation of the violence and the unmistakable stench of cynicism. Here we can include Hideo Gosha's *Samurai Wolf* (1966), with its capricious characters and numerous betrayals; the 'Jokichi of Mikogami' trilogy (whose director, Kazuo Ikehiro, has stated, "As the Sixties progressed, I was influenced by the spaghetti westerns", citing in particular *Django*[45]); Eiichi Kudo's *The Fort of Death* (1969), whose Leone leanings saw it included in the 2007 Venice Film Festival's Euro-western retrospective; plus the famous 'Lone Wolf and Cub' series, which even features gunslingers and *Django*-style machine gun massacres (*The Fort of Death* also puts a Gatling gun to murderous use). The short-lived television series *Oshi samurai* (1973-74) bore more than a passing resemblance to *The Great Silence* as it chronicled the vengeful adventures of a bounty-hunting swordsman (portrayed by Tomisaburo 'Lone Wolf' Wakayama) whose throat had been slashed when he was a child. Of more recent vintage is the aforementioned *Sukiyaki Western Django*, a deliriously gaudy homage-cum-deconstruction assembled from a hotchpotch of ingredients by the audacious yet erratic Takashi Miike, whose evident fondness for the genre is matched by his disdain for trifles such as verisimilitude and linear narrative development. Logic is swiftly jettisoned as the obligatory mysterious gunfighter (Hideaki Ito) becomes embroiled in 12th Century clan warfare (the script throws in unexpected allusions to England's medieval Wars of the Roses) and draws two feuding factions – one dressed in red, the other white – towards their destruction. Samurai weaponry clashes with pistols, most explicitly during a bravura showdown in the snow between Ito and swaggering villain Yusuke Iseya, while yet another Gatling-style machine gun makes an appearance (it is transported, inevitably, in a coffin). Elsewhere, a gang leader unrolls a saddlebag of weapons like Lee Van Cleef in *For a Few Dollars More*, the stranger employs a hidden Derringer, and we're told that a young orphan boy, son of a slain female character, later "went to Italy and was known as Django", as Miike and his colleagues, tongues wedged firmly in cheeks, drain their well of references dry.

The martial arts film itself faded as an international phenomenon almost as quickly as it had arrived but, unlike the Italian western, it has continued to develop as an art form at home despite the waning of its appeal abroad, to the extent that acclaimed directors such as Ang Lee and Zhang Yimou elevated the genre to new heights with the likes of *Crouching Tiger, Hidden Dragon* (2000), *Hero* (2002), *House of Flying Daggers* (2004) and *Curse of the Golden Flower* (2006). Yet the older, grittier style retains a fervent cult following overseas and is increasingly well represented on DVD. In this respect, at least, Asian adventures and European westerns still have something in common.

footnotes

1   Quoted in 'Conversation with Mario Caiano' on the Italian DVD release of Caiano's film *Bullets Don't Argue*.
2   Author's interview with Sergio Donati.
3   Marcia Landy, *Italian Film*, p.182.
4   Christopher Wagstaff addresses the hybrid nature of Italian adventure formulas in his article 'A Forkful of Westerns' in *Popular European Cinema*.
5   In the original Italian release Milian was referred to as Hermano, the Spanish word for 'brother', although some Italian sources christen him Barney – fine for cuddly dinosaurs not such much for Euro-westerns. *Barney, Kill!*, anyone? For the film's re-release in the mid-Seventies, at the peak of Milian's popularity, he was addressed as Hondo.
6   Quoted in Luca Beatrice, *Al cuore, Ramon, al cuore*.
7   The film caused such a stir in Italy – where adverts proudly proclaimed its "exceptional cruelty" and "hallucinatory" qualities – that it was withdrawn just over a week after opening and ordered drastically re-edited. (It seems to be the only Italian western to have suffered this ignominious fate.) The golden bullet scene and the scalping were removed, and it wasn't until 1975 that an uncut edition was reassembled for Italian audiences. Rumours persist that even more grisly action was shot (such as the infamous 'bandits on a spit' scene) and excised at some point during the film's complicated release history. Unsurprisingly, it was also heavily censored upon its international release. When it finally reached British screens in 1970, promoted by posters promising "terror from the depths of hell", it was shorn of some 20 minutes of footage. Thankfully, the full-length Italian version is now widely available on DVD.
8   More than one critic has noted the connection between Questi's suggestion of the effects of violence on minors with Sam Peckinpah's *The Wild Bunch*, while Mario Bava's *Bay of Blood* (1971) extends the theme.
9   In a rare interview, Rassimov told Clark Hodgkiss, editor of the fanzine *Blood, Money and Vengeance*, "That role [Alida Murdock] was the most interesting I played in western movies".
10   Quoted in *Bizarre Sinema! Horror all'italiana 1957-1979* by Antonio Bruschini.
11   Interview with Claudio Undari conducted for this book by Mario Marsili.
12   In Carlos Aguilar's book *Joaquín Romero Marchent: la firmeza del profesional*, the director reveals little about his feelings for *Cut-Throats Nine* beyond how challenging it was to shoot a western in snow and ice.
13   Interview with Giuliano Carnimeo conducted for this book by Mario Marsili.
14   Chiari garnered almost as much attention for his romantic affairs as for his comic abilities. His conquests are said to have included Lucia Bosè, Anita Ekberg, Ava Gardner and Elsa Martinelli.
15   Quoted in *How We Got the Italian Movie Business into Trouble – the True Story of Franco and Ciccio*, a documentary co-produced by Rai TV.
16   Pierre Sorlin, *Italian National Cinema 1896-1996*, p.111.
17   See Landy, *Italian Film*, p.189, and Frayling, *Something to Do with Death*, pp 14 & 126.
18   Interview with George Hilton conducted for this book by Mario Marsili.
19   Quoted in *Newsweek*, 21 March 1966.
20   Author's interview with Enzo Castellari.
21   The one noteworthy aspect of *One Dollar Too Many* is the basing of Frank Wolff's frustrated actor and con artist, Edwin Kean, on the legendary English tragedian Edmund Kean (1787-1833), who toured America a few years before his death. The film also borrows the name of Edmund's uncle and mentor, Moses, for the character played by Antonio Sabato.
22   This idea originated with the affection felt by Gemma for *Of Mice and Men*: "I had read and enjoyed Steinbeck's book and these two characters, George and Lenny – one cunning and the other rather simple – seemed like good characters to put in a western." Interview with Gemma conducted for this book by Alex Marlow-Mann and Julian Grainger.
23   Interview with Terence Hill conducted in public by critic Fabio Melelli at Saint Cecilia's auditorium in Perugia, 15 June 2002.
24   Quoted in *Spaghetti Cinema* (translation by James Cheney).
25   Some of Terence Hill's films were re-released to cash in on the brand – *The Anger of the Wind* became *Trinity Sees Red*, for example, and many of Hill and Spencer's joint efforts have been deceivingly packaged as 'Trinity' adventures on video; in Germany, comic dialogue was even dubbed over some of these films' soundtracks.
26   Peter Bondanella, *Italian Cinema*, p.272.
27   Quoted in Sir Christopher Frayling, *Something to Do with Death*. According to the book, the project had its roots in the early Seventies when producer Fulvio Morsella suggested a western be made using *The Odyssey* as a template. (The potential for such a transposition having already been demonstrated by Duccio Tessari and Fernando Di Leo in *The Return of Ringo*.) Leone developed this idea into a story, which Sergio Donati then worked into a treatment set during the American Civil War. Only the 'name' of Terence Hill's character remained as a direct allusion to Homer's epic.
28   Hill speaks about Leone's intentions, and his own fond feelings for the film, in an interview included on the 2003 Nouveaux Pictures DVD release.
29   Marco Giusti includes further information about which director shot which footage in his *Dizionario del western all'Italiana*. One thing that does seem certain is that Leone directed the opening sequence of *A Genius, Two Partners and a Dupe* (1975), the semi-sequel to *My Name Is Nobody*. Credited director Damiano Damiani has admitted as much in the past.
30   Source: AGIS.
31   The film's most famous allusions are to Sam Peckinpah and *The Wild Bunch*, with Leone jokily putting his counterpart's name on a grave marker (some lingering resentment, perhaps, about the collapse of a mooted deal for the American to relieve Leone of the direction of *A Fistful of Dynamite*) and calling his 150-strong army of cut-throats after Peckinpah's best-known film. To cap it all, Jack Beauregard's confrontation with the gang is shot in slow motion. Clint Eastwood inserted a similar in-joke in his first western as a director, *High Plains Drifter*. Although not noticeable in the finished film, stills exist showing grave markers inscribed with the names of three of Eastwood's directorial mentors – Leone, Don Siegel and Brian G. Hutton.
32   Quoted in Marco Giusti, *Dizionario del western all'Italiana*, p.309.
33   Like the majority of Carnimeo's westerns, this one seems as if it was conceived to inspire sequels and spin-offs. None followed, although another company, Cepa, ran an unrelated Holy Ghost franchise of its own, all with Roberto Mauri behind

He Was Called the Holy Ghost (1971), a mediocre B-western, was followed by two dire sequels, *Return of the Holy Ghost* and *Gunmen and the Holy Ghost* (both 1972), with Karis joined by some oafish comedy sidekicks.

34   Interview with Terence Hill conducted in public by critic Fabio Melelli at Saint Cecilia's auditorium in Perugia, 15 June 2002.

35   Barboni attempted to resurrect his world-famous franchise in 1995 with *Sons of Trinity* but, without the participation of Hill and Spencer (American actors Heath Kizzier and Keith Neubert play Trinity and Bambino's respective offspring), the film achieved very limited distribution, despite the best efforts of producers Italo Zingarelli and Horst Wendlandt. A later film, *Trinity Goes East* (1998), stood even less chance of reviving the brand. A low-budget, modern-day martial arts film shot largely in Vietnam and produced by Toby Russell, son of Ken Russell, it has no official connection to the series but has been blessed with a soundtrack by the great Alessandro Alessandroni. Indeed, it's probable that more people will hear the score than see the film. More recently, a documentary was produced for Italian television entitled *Trinità... e fu tempo di fagioli western* (2006), which commemorated Barboni's enduringly popular originals, revisiting locations and speaking to some of the participants.

36   Ibid.

37   *Yojimbo* was also, of course, the source for *A Fistful of Dollars*, while another Kurosawa classic, *Rashomon* (1950), was transposed to the American West with much less success as *The Outrage* (1964). For a more detailed discussion of Kurosawa's relationship to John Ford and the western, see Stephen Prince, *The Warrior's Camera: The Cinema of Akira Kurosawa*, pp.12.

38   For further information, see Fenin & Everson, *The Western: From Silents to the Seventies*, pp.350.

39   The two genres were subject to almost identical distribution and marketing patterns: in the US and UK they were released to the same kind of cheaply priced inner-city cinemas, frequently paired together in double bills, often cut for length as much as content and both encumbered by distracting, often ludicrous English dubbing. Filmgoers would also have noticed the Euro-western's grandiose music scores turning up again, illegitimately, in kung fu films. Elements from Morricone's score for *The Big Gundown* were used in the Godfrey Ho film *Dragon on Fire*, Chan Hung Au's *Revenge of the Patriots* and Ng See Yuen's *The Secret Rivals*; his music for *A Fistful of Dynamite* can be heard in Chan Sin's *Revenge of the Dragon*; *The Return of Ringo* theme is used in some prints of Chang Cheh's *The Savage Five*; and 'Death Rattle', from *Once Upon a Time in the West*, famously graces the Colosseum climax of Bruce Lee's *The Way of the Dragon*. Riz Ortolani's strident theme for *Day of Anger* was another popular piece, featuring in the Ming Dynasty epic *Invincible Armour* among a number of others.

40   Author's interview with Brett Halsey.

41   According to AGIS figures, *Red Sun* took almost 3 billion lire at the Italian box office in 1971, more even than *A Fistful of Dynamite*.

42   Shaw Brothers sought a flying foothold in the Gothic horror genre in the same year by co-producing *The Legend of the Seven Golden Vampires* with Britain's Hammer Studios. This featured another of the Shaws' leading lights, David Chiang, alongside horror icon Peter Cushing. Cushing then co-starred in another Hammer/Shaw joint venture, the action thriller *Shatter* (1974).

43   *Kung Fu Brothers* has been referred to under a variety of titles – which is not uncommon for such a low-budget production that has done the rounds of numerous video distributors over the years – and it is difficult to ascertain which came first. Its original Italian moniker seems to have been ...*Altrimenti vi ammucchiamo*, complete with 'Trinity'-style poster artwork. The authoritative but not infallible Gremese dictionary suggests it was also known in Italy at one time as *Golden City*, while other sources claim the latter was used for the film's American release. Further optional Italian titles include *Kung fu nel pazzo west* and *I fratelli del kung-fu*, but these could, of course, have been used for re-releases. The English-dubbed video print I had the pleasure of watching is called *Kung Fu Brothers in the Wild West*.

44   The real 'Cheen Lie', Ernest Van-Mohr, is actually something of a polymath. Musician, artist, soccer fanatic (and philanthopist – he founded the International Friendship Football League in Tokyo in 1977) and, since 1980, successful architect, he began acting while studying in Rome in the Sixties. (His film career dovetailed with bass-guitar duties in a pop group called the Nations, who had a few minor hits and were also based in Rome.) He had small roles in a number of forgettable films, working with directors Liliana Cavani, Giuseppe Vari, Rolf Olsen and Silvio Amadio, among others, and appearing alongside the likes of Jean Yanne, Curt Jurgens and Silvia Monti. He quit the business after starring in *The Return of Shanghai Joe* to concentrate on his studies in architecture.

45   Quoted in Chris D., *Outlaw Masters of Japanese Cinema* (IB Tauris, 2005).

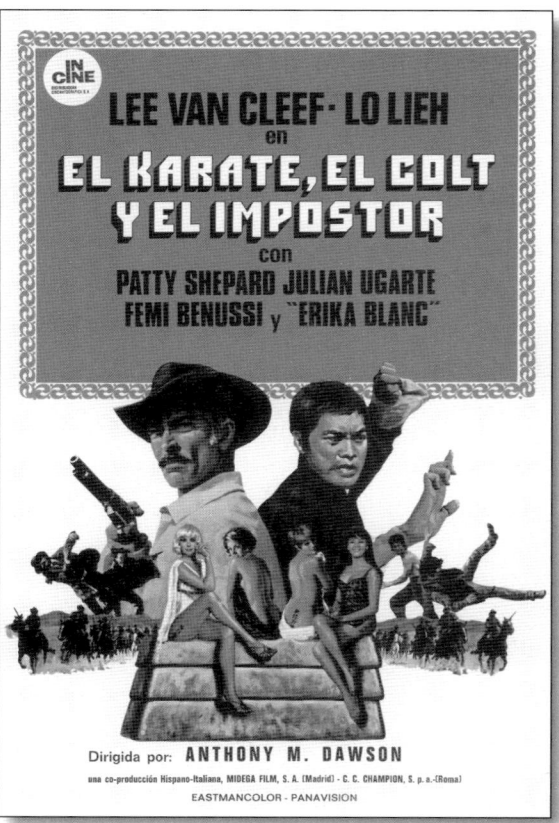

above: Spanish poster for **The Stranger and the Gunfighter**.

Franco Nero stars in **Keoma**.

Chapter 8

Desolation And Deconstruction

The Genre's Twilight Years

When opinions are canvassed and charts compiled of what are the best European westerns of all time, only one title that regularly appears, Enzo Castellari's *Keoma* (1976), was produced well after the genre's heyday. Most of the acknowledged classics, as well as the biggest money-spinners, are clustered around the period from 1964 to 1970, with the years since then generally regarded as something of a creative wasteland. "The westerns of the Seventies", reflected Duccio Tessari in a 1986 interview, "were like the still moving tail of the dying prehistoric animal."[1] He could equally have been talking about the situation in Hollywood, where the western entered another of its periodic declines in the mid-Seventies, a time when neither audiences nor filmmakers themselves – judging from the increasingly bitter tone of the few westerns that were actually produced – could identify with the romantic illusions that had sustained the genre in the past. (The western's cause was not helped by the satirical savaging it received from Mel Brooks's hugely successful *Blazing Saddles* [1974].) Of course, the process of erosion had begun earlier, in the Sixties, when a succession of elegiac westerns had concerned themselves with transition and the 'end of the west', and it's also worth re-emphasising how the Euro-western had already anticipated its parent genre's turn in the next decade towards cynicism, demythologisation and self-criticism.

In European and, specifically, Italian terms, the genre's decline in the same period was also the most spectacular example yet of the boom-and-bust nature of commercial film cycles. To a large degree, this was a consequence of over-production. "In the end", comments George Hilton, one of the most prolific Euro-western stars, "they just made too many films because they wanted an easy win. And at the time, a western was an easy win. And they also made some tremendous rubbish, as a result of which the public became disillusioned with the genre."[2] It also reflected more general pressures on the Italian industry, in particular intense competition from television and from American imports, which began to recover in the mid-Seventies after falling back in the Sixties. After 1973, the number of westerns put into production in Italy declined dramatically, with fewer than 10 majority-Italian titles appearing in 1974 and just a dozen or so in 1975 – and even some of these were 'polluted' with elements from other genres. There were also fewer places for Italians to actually *view* this type of movie, given the reorganisation of the exhibition sector that saw the upmarket *prima visione* circuit expand at the expense of the cheaper *seconda* and *terza visione* cinemas, many of which closed down as high inflation and rising ticket prices took their toll.[3] To make matters worse, other *filoni* had begun to eat away at the once all-conquering western's core support. One in particular, the violent cop thriller or *poliziesco*, transposed many of the western's themes and obsessions into a contemporary urban context, which, in the tense and violent *anni di piombo* or 'years of lead', seemed a lot more relevant to anxious Italians than deserts and dusty plains.

Many of the genre's most influential filmmakers and iconic actors drifted away along with their audience, whether because they had tired of the form, said what they had wanted to say within it, or simply because the work they needed was now to be found elsewhere. Only a handful of Italy's western 'specialists' maintained an interest in the genre once the glory days had passed. Castellari and Franco Nero are the most prominent (as of writing, they still hope to shoot another western in Spain[4]), while Giuliano Gemma, Terence Hill, Lee Van

above: **The Tough Ones** was one of the brutal Italian crime thrillers that muscled in on the Euro-western's thematic terrain in the Seventies.

325

above: Italian poster for **Keoma**, which gave Franco Nero's rootless anti-hero a radical, righteous agenda.

Cleef, Tony Anthony, Ferdinando Baldi, Gianfranco Parolini and Michele Lupo all made the occasional foray into the genre once it had ceased to be a going concern, with decidedly mixed results. There have been westerns produced by Italy, Germany, France and Spain in the past 35 years or so, often in disguised form with modern settings, comedic or fantastic plots or as vehicles for local stars, but none of them have achieved widespread international distribution.

It would be unjust to overlook the period from the mid-Seventies to the present day, however, which, artistically if not commercially, has seen peaks as well as troughs. The end-of-the-west theme, which chimed with the crumbling idealism and disillusionment of the post-1968 era, was addressed with surprising lyricism in *My Name Is Nobody* (1973), a part-celebration, part-deconstruction of western mythology given added poignancy by the casting of ageing icon Henry Fonda. Four more of the genre's most challenging works were produced in quick succession even later than this, just when its lustre seemed to have faded: *The Four of the Apocalypse* (1975), *Keoma* (1976), *California* (1977) and *A Man Called Blade* (1977) all have a common stamp and demonstrate the elasticity and durability of the western format in ambitious and enthusiastic hands. Even in more disparate films it's possible to identify similar themes – some timeless, others topical – in both good works and bad, serious and comedic. There is a certain self-reflexivity evident in the likes of *My Name Is Nobody*, *God's Gun* (1976) and *China 9, Liberty 37* (1978). Though different from each other in tone and effect, each of these 'post-westerns' comments on the artificiality of myths and movies, and displays a more philosophical attitude – if not always a mature one – towards life, death and violence than that of most of the irreverent films of the genre's golden age.

In general, however, Europe's later westerns induce an overall sense of displacement. Many films from the autumnal era struggle to generate a convincing atmosphere and seem oddly removed from their subjects and settings. This is partly because of their increasingly desperate efforts to accommodate changing cultural trends (in line with the truism that films with a historical setting – and futuristic ones, for that matter – tend to reflect the times in which they are made), from characters' anachronistic appearance and hairstyles, which clearly belong to the 1970s rather than the 1870s, to the use of music, which turned in the direction of derivative folk-rock – fashionable when the films were made, but not a style that ages well. There is a tendency towards moralising and sentimentality – areas of weakness the Euro-western had largely avoided since *A Fistful of Dollars* first broke the mould – suggesting a desire for broader appeal. And with the genre deemed unfashionable and therefore unprofitable, at least where the major markets were concerned, filmmakers faced greater economic restraints, often necessitating the use of cheaper film stock and equipment, minor or ill-suited actors and unattractive or unfamiliar locations. In place of the imposing, scenic deserts of southern Spain, more and more productions were forced to settle for drab and indistinct, though cheap and convenient, rural areas near Rome, resulting in a generally blander texture. Others, paradoxically, utilised more exotic climes: as Italians found it necessary to look further afield for production partners, westerns were shot in such alien environments as the Canary Islands (the US-Italian *Take a Hard Ride* [1975]), Israel (site of *God's Gun* and *Kid Vengeance* [1976]), Colombia (*Django Strikes Again* [1987]) and Russia (*Jonathan of the Bears* [1993]).

above: Torch-wielding bigots – fascists by proxy – bear the weight of **Keoma**'s ideological baggage.

Desolation And Deconstruction

Putting a further topical twist on traditional themes, in several late films there is evidence of a wide-ranging liberal agenda. Liberal issues such as race relations and civil rights are enthusiastically if rather solemnly embraced, along with fashionable ideas about conservation and social justice. With no evidence to suggest that these topics had any relevance in the Seventies for everyday Italians, let alone for the country's main political parties, the thrust of the genre at this juncture suggests that filmmakers had almost given up on the domestic market in favour of addressing an international audience (always one of the main considerations for cheaper productions in particular), as well as a younger generation of filmgoers. The Euro-western's new priorities were also commensurate with developments in mainstream American cinema. Luigi Bazzoni's *The Blue Gang* (1973), for instance, was a partially successful attempt to weave counter-cultural concerns into a story of romantic outlawry modelled on such films as *Bonnie and Clyde* (1967), *Butch Cassidy and the Sundance Kid* (1969) and *Bad Company* (1972). Shot by future Oscar-winner Vittorio Storaro (his only western) in a mixture of natural hues and monochrome, Bazzoni's film has a wonderfully nostalgic sense of time and place; there's certainly nothing bland about the visual texture here. Set at the turn of the 20th Century and espousing the same anti-establishment sentiments as Europe's political westerns, it follows a band of free-living young outlaws, male and female, whose leader accuses the banks and the law of having "the blood of the poor" on their hands. The criminals' career is treated as a challenge to authority, which is represented jointly by the banking system that forced the gang leader's father into economic deprivation, and by Jack Palance, in an almost wordless cameo as a sinister Pinkerton agent. The gang's anti-capitalist philosophy clashes, however, with their eager acquisition of loot. A more accurate description of their beliefs might be 'live fast, die young', and they do just that.

These liberal soundings were not surprising in a genre that had always been prone to polemical outbursts, but at this late stage they became especially pronounced. Scratch beneath the surface of *Keoma*, for example, and you encounter urgent pleas for racial and social integration. The title character returns to what passes for his home town to find it racked by racial hatred – his half-brothers give him an ice-cold welcome, having always despised him for being part-Indian, while family friend George (Woody Strode), a once-proud black man, has been worn down by years of abuse. Keoma also discovers that those locals not infected with plague are stricken instead with fear, ignorance and bigotry. Another allegorical work, Lucio Fulci's *The*

above: **Keoma**'s title character (Franco Nero) confronts the pitiless Caldwell (Donal O'Brien, *centre*, on horseback) and his bovine horde amid the ramshackle remains of Elios studios' western town set.

Four of the Apocalypse, is similarly concerned with civil rights and the plight of the outcast. Its brutal opening sequence can be seen as a critique of social cleansing, an attack on the kind of reactionary, vigilante-style justice then being advocated in Italy's popular press and violent crime thrillers. It seems fitting that the gunmen who shoot down the unwanted element in the town of Salt Flat are kitted out like the Ku Klux Klan. And in Michele Lupo's post-Civil War western, *California*, the portrayal of bounty hunters as little more than hired killers cleaning up the dregs of the defeated Confederates – another form of social cleansing – is symptomatic of both Lupo's sober reassessment of (Euro-) western conventions and of the genre's penchant for underdogs, which was now very much to the fore.

In addition, *Keoma* alludes to the increasing interest in environmentalism in the late Sixties and Seventies (again, however, this was more the case outside Italy than within), something seized upon by several Italian westerns that combine this theme with attacks on capitalist exploitation. The villains in this and two further Castellari films, *Cipolla Colt* (1975) and *Jonathan of the Bears*, as well as Sergio Martino's *A Man Called Blade*, are all industrialists, who make convenient contemporary hate figures and whose illicit or unscrupulous operations are seen to have sullied the land and/or caused much death and suffering. (Castellari told the Italian fanzine *Amarcord* that the evil forces in *Jonathan of the Bears* were intended to represent big business magnates such as Silvio Berlusconi and Gianni Agnelli, an ironic statement considering that Berlusconi provided a chunk of the film's financing.[5]) Both *Keoma* and *Blade* are rife with images of disease and decay, much of it man-made – plague-stricken outcasts and dilapidated buildings, clouds of sulphurous fog and filthy open sewers. The films were shot on the hallowed western-town set at Elios Studios, which was in such a state of disrepair by the mid-Seventies that it provided the ideal symbolic backdrop for the drama. Indeed, for *Keoma*, Castellari and production designer Carlo Simi dressed it down further to enhance the effect, while Martino saved money on repairs by shrouding the sets with mist to give his film a 'polluted' effect. While the landscape has always been a significant factor in the appeal of westerns, this streak of eco-consciousness is surprising because neither European nor American productions had previously expressed this veneration in such explicitly ecological terms.[6] Not that it penetrates the films too deeply. It is not allowed to sidetrack the protagonists from more primal pursuits such as revenge, for example, at least not for too long, but it does steer them in a fashionably altruistic direction and suggests that filmmakers were trying to put a new spin on old stories in an attempt to reach beyond their steadily dwindling traditional audience base.

Race and revisionism

The strain of these efforts at conscientiousness and social comment – in a type of film, and a filmmaking industry, that has often sought to mediate between exploitation and populism – is particularly apparent where the twin themes of race and racism are concerned. One of the more over-eager films in this tricky area, Sergio Corbucci's comedy *The White, the Yellow and the Black* (1975), is a spectacularly clumsy integrationist parable. With its credibility hamstrung by a crass, insidious pop ballad by Guido and Maurizio De Angelis, the film uses mixed-race characters – Swiss-Italian Blanc de Blanc (Giuliano Gemma) and Japanese-American Sakura (Tomas Milian) – to suggest that cultural differences are only skin-deep, while the oft-used plot device of crooked whites posing as Indians to commit crimes expresses a modish anti-imperialism. (The 'black' of the title, incidentally, is irrelevant, referring not to a character's skin tone but to the colour of sheriff Eli Wallach's outfit.) No doubt Corbucci and company's collective heart was in the right place, but, as in the later *Jonathan of the Bears*, good intentions are marred by a lack of sophistication; jokes aside, the film – basically a comedic version of *Red Sun* (1971) – plays more like a formulaic pre-Leone western than a true reflection of Corbucci's canon. (Ironically, one character in the Italian version name-checks a trio of Corbucci's previous westerns – *Navajo Joe*, *A Professional Gun* and *Compañeros* – in the course of a diatribe, adding the likes of *The Big Gundown*, *A Fistful of Dynamite*, *My Name Is Nobody* and even the names 'Leone' and 'Barboni' for good measure.) Nor is it helped by poor judgements on the director's part. Preaching respect for all cultures and races is all well and good, but allowing Milian to enact a grating and gratuitous Japanese caricature – typifying, incidentally, the gross insensitivity and cheap stereotyping of most contemporaneous Italian comedies – rather queers the pitch.[7] Nevertheless, with Gemma

above and opposite bottom left: Sergio Corbucci squandered a dream cast (Tomas Milian, in Japanese dress, Eli Wallach and Giuliano Gemma) in his final western, **The White, the Yellow and the Black**, a farcical rip-off of **Red Sun** that nevertheless became a box-office hit.

also 1975, which downplays the race theme even though it stars blaxploitation icons Jim Brown, Fred Williamson and Jim Kelly. (The trio had just made another joint venture, the paranoid action film *Three the Hard Way* [1974], with two of *Hard Ride*'s producers.) There's no sign of the aggressive anti-racism of the stars' American films. One need only compare it with the incendiary westerns that Williamson made back home, in particular the strident 'Nigger Charley' series, tag line: "Somebody warn the west, Nigger Charley ain't running no more". The script acknowledges the problem – there is casual use of racist epithets and fleeting reference to the illusory "freedom" for blacks in the wake of the Civil War – but even the protagonists seem resigned to prejudice rather than enraged by it; Brown reacts to it with stoicism, Williamson with sardonic humour. It becomes just another obstacle in their quest to escort the proceeds of a cattle drive back to the ranch. Despite the novelty of having black performers in traditionally white roles – Brown as a ranch foreman, Williamson a sharp-dressed gambler (Kelly, who gets to show off his martial arts skills in some ham-fisted fight sequences, is passed off as a half-breed Native American) – the protagonists' colour – like the potentially mouth-watering melange of Euro-western, blaxploitation and martial arts motifs – is almost an irrelevance in what is ultimately a peculiarly old-fashioned and anodyne production.

and Milian – two of the most bankable stars in Italy – on board, *The White, the Yellow and the Black* enabled Corbucci to sign off from the genre with domestic takings in excess of any of his earlier westerns.**8**

Much less forthright – surprisingly so, considering the actors involved – is Antonio Margheriti's *Take a Hard Ride*,

above: **Take a Hard Ride** was an equal-opportunities western, of sorts, assigning traditionally white genre roles – ranch foreman, cool gambler – to black performers, in this case two of the leading lights of the blaxploitation boom, Jim Brown and Fred Williamson.

A small number of Italian films followed the lead of the revisionist pro-Indian Hollywood westerns of the Seventies, a sub-genre that Sergio Leone saw as a kind of "*mea culpa*" on the part of Americans. But where titles such as *Tell Them Willie Boy Is Here* (1969), *Soldier Blue* (1970), *Little Big Man* (1970) and *Ulzana's Raid* (1972) ignited impassioned critical debates – mainly about whether they should be interpreted allegorically, substituting Native Americans for other cultures such as Vietnamese or African-Americans, or as apologetic retellings of historical events from an indigenous point of view – the majority of Italy's efforts are flat and redundant. Mired in clichés, they tamely echo the American films' guilt-induced, anti-oppressive sentiments without revealing anything of Italy's own attitude towards race relations beyond a traditional European fascination with, and sympathy for, the 'Noble Savage' way of life. If anything, they underline just how insignificant race was as a socio-political issue in Italian society. The one outstanding film among them was the first of Italy's responses to be released, Pasquale Squitieri's *Vengeance Trail* (1971), which threatens to boil over with indignation on several fronts. During the course of a generic revenge plot, Squitieri, who later made crusading films about organised crime, shows us different sides of racial intolerance and oppression: the blind loathing of Jeremiah (played by Leonard Mann, a contender for Peter Lee Lawrence's crown as the genre's resident angry young man), who kills 'savages' to avenge the slaughter of his family; the ruthless, land-hungry cattle baron Perkins (Ivan Rassimov), a borderline white supremacist who stages 'Indian' raids, like that on Jeremiah's farm, to justify his campaign of extermination and the expansion of his empire; and the hatemongering journalist Prescott (Klaus Kinski), whose poisonous prose whips up public support for Perkins's endeavours. The film's effectiveness derives from strong performances, an unvarnished visual style and, above all, from Squitieri's committed approach (he even cast seven or eight genuine American Indians, who were studying in Italy at the time). "Pasquale Squitieri was a passionate man", remembers Leonard Mann. "He was active in Italian politics and was very sensitive to political issues dealing with the underclass, etc. He was sincere about the film's anti-racist sentiments. That's what drew me to the project. He could be difficult to work with at times because of his unbending vision, but I appreciated his passion and desire to do good things."**9** Although Mann's character eventually simmers down and sees the light, influenced by a young Indian woman, the rest of white society retains its narrow-minded, lynch-mob mentality to the end.

The key reference for these works is *Soldier Blue*, the most outspoken and controversial of the American films mentioned above. The vapid *Apache Woman* (1976), directed by prolific screenwriter Giorgio Mariuzzo, and a brace of films by exploitation specialist Bruno

Mattei, *Scalps* and *White Apache* (both 1986), all engage in the central argument of Ralph Nelson's film – that the savagery of 'redskins' was a justified response to the violence inflicted on them by whites. Despite the serious tone they affect, however, they signal their intentions with an abundance of violence, rape, nudity and negligent characterisations, all excused by pseudo-historical 'honesty' and a purported sensitivity towards Indian issues. (Exactly the same kind of criticism, incidentally, that has always dogged *Soldier Blue*.) Each film, like *Vengeance Trail*, offsets the growing tenderness and mutual understanding of a white man and an Indian girl with the hostility and hatred around them, while the military is dutifully depicted as racist to the core. Significantly, however, they elide the political aspects of *Soldier Blue* and concentrate on the titillation and graphic violence that contributed to that film's notoriety: *Apache Woman*'s Yara Kewa spends much of her screen time semi-naked or fully disrobed, while, in their uncut forms, *Scalps* and *White Apache* contain a fair amount of torture and dismemberment. There is no scope, therefore, for the kind of education or enlightenment that Nelson hoped audiences, like his characters, would gain from the experience. The Indians are presented as peaceable and misunderstood, but we learn nothing about tribal customs or values. There was clearly no effort made to research these areas and, as in 99 per cent of westerns, even revisionist ones, white characters provide the films' moral centre, and it is white society, rather than Native American, that receives most of the films' attention.

Far more sincere, though not without problems of its own, is Castellari's *Jonathan of the Bears*, begun in 1993 but not released until 1995, which ties together the pro-Indian and ecological strands of the director's earlier *Keoma*, but suffers from a sentimental attachment to its subject. The last major European western to date, *Jonathan* was conceived by its star, Franco Nero, who was making a film in Russia at the time and sewed up a deal to finance a western between his Muscovite producer and Silvio Berlusconi's Mediaset. The story picks up on the greater political urgency attached to issues in the Nineties, and belongs to a tradition that portrays Native Americans as bastions of the environment – with which they are, mystically, 'one' – and whites as eco-rapists. As far as Euro-westerns are concerned, the pattern was set in the Sixties, when East Germany's DEFA studios began producing its *Indianerfilme*, which consistently opposed the tenets of Manifest Destiny and what they saw as the imperialist subtext of the Hollywood western. Even the West German 'Winnetou' films, compromised as they are by sentimentalism and stereotyping (the trite good Indian-bad Indian dichotomy), have more in common with 'progressive' American westerns of the *Broken Arrow* type than with more conservative examples. *Jonathan*

above and opposite bottom: Revisionism spread from the American western to the Italian version in the early Seventies, though only **Vengeance Trail**, directed by Pasquale Squitieri, treated the persecution of Native Americans with the seriousness the subject deserves.

also follows on from Damiano Damiani's *A Genius, Two Partners and a Dupe* (1975) and Terence Hill's misjudged Morris-Goscinny adaptation, *Lucky Luke* (1991), both of which depict Indians as an almost abstract, imperilled civilization, the victims of oppression and exploitation by white industrial society.[10] A more immediate influence on Castellari's film would seem to be Kevin Costner's *Dances with Wolves* (1990), although Franco Nero insists that *Jonathan* was in preparation before Costner's Oscar-laden epic gave the western, and ecological considerations, renewed impetus.

A Genius... and *Lucky Luke*, in both of which Terence Hill reprises his Nobody persona in all but name, as it were, dilute their politically correct themes with slapstick comedy and, despite their professed sympathy for Native Americans, the Natives themselves are peripheral figures. Great care was taken by the makers of *Jonathan* to correct this imbalance. Franco Nero, who also contributed to the script, travelled to America to seek the involvement of Floyd Red Crow Westerman, a lauded Dakota Sioux singer, poet and actor who had played the tribal chief in *Dances with Wolves*. (This supports the view that Castellari's film *was* influenced by Costner's.) Nero also brought on board Knifewing Segura, a singer/musician of Chiricahua Apache descent, who sings on the film's soundtrack. The casting of Native Americans, and the valuable insights they provided into tribal customs and attitudes towards

above: Fotobusta for **Jonathan of the Bears** featuring Franco Nero and Melody Robertson. For this film, Nero and director Enzo Castellari revived the former's **Keoma** persona in all but name, with racism and environmentalism – bound together in a plot about an oil baron's designs on sacred Indian land – both on the activist's agenda.

the environment, give the film added verisimilitude. This is *Jonathan*'s strongest asset, along with Castellari's prowess with action scenes and Mikhail Agranovich's rustic cinematography, which lovingly depicts animals, wildlife, sunsets, rivers and mountains. The filmmakers certainly did a convincing job of converting Russian landscape into an effective substitute for Western America.

While the earnestness and technical proficiency of Castellari and his team are never in doubt, the picture's maudlin tone, particularly in the first half, which follows young Jonathan's friendship with an infant bear, robs the straightforward storyline of the power it possesses. The message, although valid in itself, is delivered in a pious, preachy manner that's likely to turn off as many viewers as it engages. Like so many westerns with a revisionist agenda, the film is content simply to reverse the good/evil stereotyping of whites and Indians – no further analysis is offered or deemed necessary. Jonathan, a white man who was adopted by Natives as a boy, makes a solid, magnanimous hero, but he lacks the dynamism that made Keoma such a powerful protagonist. (The connection between these characters, and the films that bear their names, is plain throughout, from Castellari's stylistic touches and the score's use of ballads, to Nero's hirsute physical appearance and his character's philosophy. Jonathan even has to suffer a Keoma-style crucifixion.) Moreover, the clichéd and platitudinous dialogue – Jonathan and the Indians vowing to defend the "sacred skin" of Mother Earth, racist rhetoric from bad guy John Saxon – contributes to the naïveté of the whole. The results were neither sophisticated enough to attract a mainstream audience nor sufficiently gritty to draw in western fans or the exploitation crowd.

Nero blames two factors for the film's commercial failure: "The distributors promised me they would show the movie at Christmas, but they didn't. Because two or three westerns came out that were flops [Costner's *Wyatt Earp*, Walter Hill's *Geronimo: An American Legend*] the distributors didn't believe in our movie any more. So they waited and waited and finally they released it in May.[11] In Italy this is the worst period for opening movies; from May to September, nobody goes to the cinema. The other reason why *Jonathan* was not a financial success was that the first half looks like a movie for children, with the boy and the bear, and then the second part is a proper Italian western. I have always said to Castellari, 'Enzo, you should have cut at least 10 or 15 minutes out of the first part.' And Enzo says now that I'm right, but it's too late."[12]

Gunfighters and guardian angels

Jonathan's soft-heartedness is a feature of many late westerns and, indeed, of other popular Italian genres. As many writers and cultural commentators have attested, Italians are, at heart, a deeply sentimental people, and their filmmakers have never been shy about exploiting this. In the Seventies, for instance, there was a vogue for tear-jerkers in the *Love Story* mould – Raimondo Del Balzo's *The Last Snows of Spring* (1973) and Ruggero Deodato's *Last Feelings* (1978) received the most international exposure, shamelessly manipulating images of dying children and wallowing in stories of sorrow, grief and suffering. The twilight westerns' juxtaposition of sentimentalism with violent action and rugged characterisations is shared by two closely related *filoni*. The success of Ken Annakin's Jack London adaptation, *The Call of the Wild* (1972), was met with a flurry of furry imitations from Italian studios, with Lucio Fulci's *White Fang* (1973) and *Challenge to White Fang* (1974), both starring Franco Nero, the best examples. These and other titles in the series aimed to capture a wider audience demographic by giving prominent roles to children, not to mention faithful canines, while the North American settings and eco-friendly themes provide further parallels with the westerns under discussion. In addition, several of Italy's *polizieschi* blunt their hard edges with melodramatic subplots or sympathetic supporting characters, and pander to the paternal instincts and aspirations of Italian males. Maurizio Merli, who specialised in playing irate, uncompromising policemen, forms a bond with an archetypal Neapolitan street urchin or *scugnizzo* (Massimo Deda) in *Violent Naples* (1976), for example, as does Leonard Mann in *Weapons of Death* (1977), which is also based in Naples and has Deda reprising his role. And Franco Nero's character in *Day of the Cobra* (1980), another of his collaborations with Enzo Castellari, has a young son who meets a predictably tragic end after a series of interminable inter-family 'bonding' scenes.

This father/child dynamic, along with a renewed sensitivity towards familial concerns, is one source of the uncharacteristic, though increasingly common, sentimentalism of these westerns. With many of the stars approaching middle age, it was

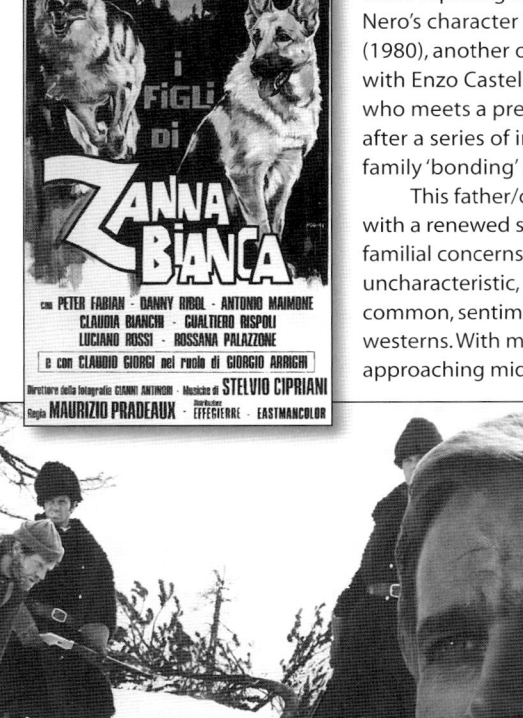

above and inset: **The Call of the Wild** resounded with Italian studios, with several of them producing their own variations, softening the texture of the Euro-western in the process. Lucio Fulci's 'White Fang' films, with Franco Nero, led the pack, chased by the likes of **Sons of White Fang**.

above: The Eighties incarnation of Django presented a more benevolent face – machine-gun notwithstanding – as the 'greed is good' mantra he and his peers had pioneered in the Sixties became the ethos of the era.
inset below: Stills from Lucio Fulci's **Silver Saddle**, part aggressive revenge film, part man-and-boy bonding drama (Giuliano Gemma and Sven Valsecchi, both on horseback, being the man and boy in question).

evidently deemed fitting to broaden their characters' responsibilities: Nero is teamed with children in *Cipolla Colt* (which was targeted squarely at a family audience) and is their heroic champion in *Django Strikes Again*; Lee Van Cleef takes traumatised teen Leif Garrett under his wing in Gianfranco Parolini's *God's Gun*; and Giuliano Gemma becomes the surrogate father of an angelic boy (Sven Valsecchi), really the son of his mortal enemy, in Lucio Fulci's *Silver Saddle* (1978). While the stars generally cope manfully with these extra demands on their abilities, which may have reflected changes in their own lives and a desire to project a more compassionate screen image – and one can hardly blame them for wanting to try something different after so many identikit roles – it must be said that their characters are nowhere near as charismatic as their old callous, carefree selves. Furthermore, few directors have demonstrated the ability to control their films' shifting emotional currents, nor to restrain their young charges' irksome efforts at endearment. As a result, most of these titles are divided against themselves, with cloying passages that jar against the more dramatic or aggressive parts. *Silver Saddle*, for example, is crippled by the tension between its Euro-western traits – the classic revenge plot; the devious character Two Strike Snake (played by perennial Clint Eastwood co-star Geoffrey Lewis) – and the sickly scenes between Gemma and Valsecchi. (Gemma disagrees that the attention devoted to Valsecchi, or to any child co-star, compromises the end product. "Anything that improves the production, that helps arouse the public's sympathy, works in the film's favour. Perhaps a child… can steal the film from you, but this doesn't detract from the film." One begs to differ.[13]) And in the Nineties, the most popular Italian western stars of all, Terence Hill and Bud Spencer, marked their return to 'Trinity' territory with the saccharine *Troublemakers* (1994). Directed by Hill, written by his wife and co-produced by Spencer's son, it's a sanctimonious hymn to family values that's about as far removed from the provocative, ironic, subversive westerns of Europe's golden age as it's possible to conceive. Even the actors' old mentor, Enzo Barboni, hardly a cynic by disposition, judged it "too puritan" for its own good. (Fifteen years on, Hill achieved a finer balance between romanticism and ruggedness with *Doc West* [2009], in which he directs himself – looking remarkably well preserved for a 70-year-old, complete with his trademark duster – as a gunslinger-cum-physician who rescues a town from tyranny.[14]) It is no surprise that these latter-day Italian westerns struggled to find an audience at home, despite their calculated appeal to Italian sensibilities and their stars' renown, while countries and cultures of a more stoical persuasion would no doubt scoff at the films' futile efforts to mix melodrama with violent action.

The continued involvement of established leading men at this juncture suggests a lingering attraction to western roles irrespective of the downturn in the films' fortunes. Says Giuliano Gemma: "I believed in the genre… I couldn't betray a genre that had given me so much satisfaction and which the foreign markets were still calling for."[15] Even so, the presence of stars is no guarantee of quality or box-office success. As we shall see, Nero and Gemma both made excellent westerns late in the day but could not rescue such ill-considered endeavours as *Django Strikes Again*, *Silver Saddle* or the fantasy-crossover *Tex and the Lord of the Deep* (1985), which reunited Gemma with director Duccio Tessari in an attempt to transcribe the long-running Italian comic-book series for the screen. The failure of *Tex* was particularly disappointing. If any Italian western was going to revive public interest, it should have been this one. The hero, Texas Ranger Tex Willer, is an Italian institution. Writer Giovanni Luigi Bonelli and graphic artist Aurelio Galleppini created the character in 1948, part of an explosion of interest in Americana following the

above: Bless you my (surrogate) son: Lee Van Cleef – in a paternal role similar to parts given to Giuliano Gemma and Franco Nero during the Euro-western's decline – offers teen idol Leif Garrett a helping hand in **God's Gun**, simultaneously saving the boy from his real father, bad guy Jack Palance.

cultural strictures, censorship and relentless nationalism of the Fascist years. Gemma, too, was a national icon, and a public poll on who should play the part picked him out as the only domestic western star capable of faithfully interpreting a character of scrupulous honesty and even-handedness, virtues shared by many of his own genre roles. (It was the first time Gemma had donned western garb since enacting a showdown sequence with William Berger for Giuliano Montaldo's giallo/sci-fi curio, *Closed Circuit* [1978], which also utilised scenes from Gemma's 1968 film *A Sky Full of Stars for a Roof*.)

Begun as the pilot for a prospective television series, the production gambled on public nostalgia for the oldest extant Italian western hero, the box-office pulling power of Gemma, and the increasing popularity of special effects-driven fantasy films of the *Raiders of the Lost Ark* variety, with Tessari specifically citing Steven Spielberg as an inspiration. (Indeed, *Tex* was sold, optimistically to say the least, as "*la risposta Italiana a Indiana Jones*".) The impossibly upstanding Tex sets the tone of a film that seems rather artless in the wake of two decades' worth of acrid westerns that had practically rendered this type of arcane adventure obsolete. If the presence of Gemma is a positive (although it's hard to warm to his stolid hero), he is outnumbered by negatives: a fatal lack of self-awareness (*Raiders...*'

secret weapon); Tessari's direction is uncharacteristically humourless; the set pieces fail to generate excitement; the dime-novel dialogue is clunky rather than charming (William Berger, as Tex's companion Kit Carson, bears most of this particular burden); and the special effects needed a lot more money thrown at them. The fantastical nature of the story, with its mummified corpses, Aztec curses and mysterious rituals, is not uncommon in *Tex* terms – many of the strips involve magic and the supernatural – but, as Gemma says, "We had very limited means for a film of this kind and they chose a story that was too expensive." The star, a boyhood fan of the comics, felt an obligation towards the source that clearly wasn't matched by the moneymen, but a higher budget may only have alleviated the film's many artistic failings.

Another of the genre's most venerated actors, Lee Van Cleef, began to look increasingly uncomfortable in his mid-Seventies westerns. He was last cast effectively in Giancarlo Santi's *The Grand Duel* (1972), as an embittered sheriff who strays outside the law in search of justice. The rot set in with *God's Gun*, in which he plays twin brothers, one a saintly priest, the other a reformed gunfighter, with neither character allowing him to display the range that he was capable of. They are both throwbacks to pre-spaghetti western archetypes, men of principle without the moral ambiguity that Van Cleef thrived upon. Even his villainous roles in *Take a Hard Ride* and Joseph Manduke's *Kid Vengeance* – touted as *Take Another Hard Ride* when reissued by opportunistic promoters – are bereft of genuine menace, and Van Cleef looks weary and ill at ease (partly due to years of hard drinking and partly because he was often required to wear unflattering wigs), seemingly unable to summon the enthusiasm to lift a tired script and uninspired direction. He had been down this road too many times before, and this is apparent in the listlessness of his performances.

Tony Anthony fared better by staying true to his screen persona's (lack of) principles. Significantly, he was actively involved in both the creative process and the financing of his films, and this explains why they are all geared towards his singular world-view and sense of humour. His last westerns, *Get Mean* (1975) and *Comin' at Ya!* (1981), both directed by Ferdinando Baldi, rely on outrageous plotting, special effects and over-the-top action for attention (this certainly paid off for *Comin' at Ya!*, which briefly revived the popularity of 3-D technology), but even with all these distractions, Anthony's personality still manages to peep through. He is undaunted by the most ludicrous of situations, even the fantastical leaps in time and space in *Get Mean* (see *Beware Of Fake Guns*), not to mention the sheer scale of the forces arranged against him. In *Comin' at Ya!*, Anthony plays his usual anti-heroic loser, inept outlaw H.H. Hart, who nevertheless prevails in a scenario closely modelled on his and Baldi's earlier *Blindman* (1971), complete with a dungeon full of captive women. Anthony and Baldi's taste for vicious mayhem is undiminished, and their sexual politics have not matured, yet there is something noble about the indefatigable Hart that was missing from his scuzzy Stranger and the whimsical Blindman. The wry humour is largely absent as well, replaced by an unexpected injection of romance in the form of Hart's relationship with his bride-to-be, Abilene, played by a young Victoria Abril. Abilene is kidnapped from Hart's side at the altar by the despicable Thompson brothers, Pike (Gene Quintano) and the particularly obnoxious Polk (Ricardo Palacios), and the film traces Hart's efforts to get her back. (Palacios, a large man in the Fernando Sancho/Cris Huerta mould, recalls the rigours of filming his vile role with self-deprecating good humour: "This film contains one of the craziest memories in my career. Obviously, I played a villain and at one point I was almost naked, wearing a miserable loincloth and crucified. Then in came an assistant and emptied a bucketload of hungry rats all over my body, supposedly so they would eat me. And then the cameras started rolling. Well, such are the drawbacks of not playing romantic leads."[16]) Anthony is thus fighting for something other than self-gratification for once, and this gives the film a solid emotional base, although it's difficult to pick up such nuances while under the constant three-dimensional assault of arrows, spears, rifle barrels, bats, rats and assorted everyday objects. ("Warning", screamed the lurid Filmways poster for the film's American release, "the management is not responsible for where the screen ends, and you begin!")

Desolation And Deconstruction

above: A prison of their own making: Fabio Testi and Jenny Agutter as the lovers torn between desire and a sense of duty in **China 9, Liberty 37**. Their quandary mirrors that of the film's creators, resulting in a curious mixture of romanticism and demythologisation.
opposite: Tony Anthony, as indefatigable as ever, with Victoria Abril as his endangered intended in the only 3-D Euro-western, **Comin' at Ya!**

Comin' at Ya! fully justifies its title, relentlessly exploiting the 'Dimensionscope' 3-D system that was specially developed for this film. Thus, although it does have merits as a western, including a beautiful score by Carlo Savina, Anthony's genre swan-song was more of a marketing triumph than an artistic one. (The critics were unimpressed. "What good is a fancy cereal box with a stale product inside?" complained the *Los Angeles Times*, summing up the general response.) Anthony and Baldi concocted a 3-D follow-up, the *Raiders of the Lost Ark* derivative *Treasure of the Four Crowns* (1982), which is far sillier, while the 3-D craze fizzled out with such terrible films as *Parasite* (1982) and *Amityville 3-D* (1983).**17**

Fabio Testi, one of Italy's most bankable male leads in the Seventies, diversified from action films into some off-the-range westerns. After seeking revenge by proxy in Aldo Florio's *Dead Men Ride* (1971), he starred in Gianfranco Baldanello's *Blood River* (1974), another pro-Indian western heavy on the mysticism, and Aristide Massaccesi's sentimental Mountie-gets-his-man saga, *Red Coat* (1975). Most significantly, Testi appeared in two films with strong revisionist credentials. *The Four of the Apocalypse* is discussed below; the other title, *China 9, Liberty 37* (1978), is famous for the participation of three Americans central to the shaping of the modern American western: director Monte Hellman, who made the pivotal Sixties genre films *Ride in the Whirlwind* and *The Shooting*; Hellman's great friend, the peerless Warren Oates, who acted in both those titles; and their mutual *compadre* Sam Peckinpah, who has a memorable cameo role. (Marco Giusti reports that Hellman had also sought the participation of Sergio Leone and Federico Fellini.) The calibre of the participants notwithstanding, this is a frustrating film, suspended between romanticism and demythologisation. The clichés, pedestrian plotting and ponderous pace are offset by a sense of self-awareness embodied by Peckinpah's dime novelist Wilber Olsen, a maker of myths who's only too aware of the limitations of his art, but this never quite builds up steam. Too much time is lavished on ill-fated outlaw with a heart Clayton Drumm (Testi) and his romance with Jenny Agutter, the wife of Oates's grizzled miner Matthew Sebanek, and too little on Clayton's mental fatigue or his timeworn moral dilemma – he's been paid by the railroad to kill Matthew, a former hired gun, but has too much respect for the older man. While Testi broods, Oates is typically superb, by turns disgruntled, sympathetic and sadistic, eliciting a certain amount of audience sympathy only to snatch it away again. To its credit, the film ends on a relatively realistic note, questioning and finally denying the romantic impulses it has indulged throughout.

Strangers in town

A prominent feature of many twilight titles is the presence of budding actors from other fields. The participation of musicians or sportsmen testifies not only to the western's enduring romantic appeal – especially to wannabe cowboys – but also, more pertinently, to the desperation of producers and distributors, for whom contrived casting of this kind was yet another gimmick designed to bolster their films' box-office appeal and crack new markets. (This continued an existing trend: consider Mick Jagger's starring role as Australian outlaw *Ned Kelly* [1970]; psych-rockers Country Joe & the Fish and the James Gang in *Zachariah* [1971]; Kris Kristofferson, Bob Dylan and other musicians in *Pat Garrett and Billy the Kid* [1973]; and Ringo Starr's wholehearted performance in *Blindman*.) Actor/singer Leif Garrett was at the height of his popularity as a teenage recording star, for example, when he joined the international casts of *God's Gun* and *Kid Vengeance*, but neither film did anything to further his career; nor do they benefit from his presence. When Panama-born Miguel Bosé co-starred in Michele Lupo's *California* at the age of 21, he was already several years into a successful acting and recording career that today encompasses more than 20 albums and 30 films. The son of popular actress Lucia Bosé, he equips himself adequately as a naive youngster teamed with the more experienced Giuliano Gemma, and his appearance in the film may well have garnered extra custom in Spain and South America.

From the sports world, Dick Butkus, a notoriously fierce linebacker for the Chicago Bears, was cast as a heavy in *Cipolla Colt* at the behest of its American co-financer, Zev Braun, who felt that Butkus's name would help sell the picture Stateside. Again, despite the successful precedent set by footballers-turned-film-stars Woody Strode, Fred Williamson and Jim Brown, the effect of Butkus's appearance on takings seems to have been negligible. Elsewhere, Joe Bugner, the Hungarian-born British heavyweight boxer who twice fought Muhammad Ali for the world title, exchanged (simulated) blows with Bud Spencer in Michele Lupo's amiable comedy *Buddy Goes West* (1981). Bugner essays the role of a crooked sheriff, having sparred previously with Spencer in Lupo's *Bulldozer* (1978) and *The Sheriff and the Satellite Kid* (1979), and supported the Hill-Spencer partnership in Italo Zingarelli's *I'm for the Hippopotamus* (1979). He still takes film roles and even made a comeback in the ring in the late Nineties.

A contemporary of Bugner's, Argentina's Carlos Monzón, tried his luck with leading roles rather than supporting turns, befitting his stature in the sport. Regarded as one of the finest fighters in his division, Monzón became World Middleweight Champion in 1970 by defeating Italy's Nino Benvenuti, who had made a western himself the previous year, playing Giuliano Gemma's brother in the comedy *Alive or Preferably Dead* (1969). Monzón defended his title 14 times and was undefeated over a 13-year period. Towards the end of his boxing career he made a few films in his homeland, mainly alongside Susana Giménez, his girlfriend of the time and a major star in Argentina, before heading to Europe, where he enjoyed great popularity with the boxing cognoscenti. His first Italian film, the taut Stelvio Massi crime drama *The Last Round* (1976), is effectively a spaghetti western in modern guise, with Monzón playing a drifter out for revenge on a mob boss. His only official western followed: *El Macho* (1977), which, like *The Last Round*, also featured Giménez, was released a few months before Monzón fought his final bout. Unfortunately, it's a dull and muddled affair, directed with indifference by the little-known Marcello Andrei. Monzón, with his powerful build and passing resemblance to Charles Bronson, has considerable physical presence in the title role, with dark features testifying to his Indian heritage, a boxer's nose and powerful build, but is miscast here as a happy-go-lucky gambler hired to impersonate a bandit's lackey. Monzón convinces in the action scenes, as expected, but the film itself sorely lacks conviction, not least because the plot hinges on an absurd implausibility – that the unusual-looking El Macho bears such a striking resemblance to an unrelated man in the same territory. There is a bonus, however, in that George Hilton, in his first western for three years, provides flamboyant support as the refined, camp villain, the Duke, who wears a flowing white scarf and has champagne served to him wherever he goes. (Hilton, a boxing fan, already knew Monzón, and claims to have approached him about the project in the first place.) *El Macho* was marginally more profitable than *The Last Round*, but not enough to launch a European film career, and Monzón soon went back to Argentina, where, 11 years after retiring from the ring, he was convicted of the murder of his estranged wife, Alicia Muniz. He was sentenced to 11 years in prison and died in a car crash in 1995 while on furlough.

above: Soundtrack cover art for **El Macho**, which was sadly not as hard-hitting as its star, boxing legend Carlos Monzón.

Twilight's last gleaming

Among the many false dawns and disappointments of the last 35 years or so, four Italian westerns stand out for their outstanding individual qualities, distinctive visual design and sense of self-awareness. *The Four of the Apocalypse, Keoma, A Man Called Blade* and *California*, all made between 1975 and 1977, represent, in retrospect, the last hurrah for this style of film, although, with the exception of *Keoma*, none of them made much of an impression at the box office. There are many points of comparison between them – formally, structurally and thematically – but equally each can be appreciated on its own merits. While each adheres to the traditions of the genre – attacking political/social inequality and exploitation; engaging with familiar themes such as vengeance, violence and family relationships – they simultaneously reassess these motifs in the light of contemporaneous political thinking and cultural trends. Each film involves a quest of some form, and collectively they resemble a kindred genre of the western, the road movie, with which they share an episodic narrative structure and a preference for alienated, disconnected characters yearning for freedom. Irony remains important but it has a decidedly bitter aspect, in keeping with the overall downbeat mood. This informs not just the look of the films – harsh terrain shot in muted earth tones; shattered, festering townscapes – but their melancholic protagonists as well. With the exception of Stubby Preston, the male lead of *Apocalypse*, the others are quintessential Euro-western anti-heroes, only more introspective and world-weary than the majority of their forebears. While Blade is a fairly straightforward avenger, Keoma and California, and Stubby to an extent, are men seeking meaning and repose in their hitherto rootless lives. Each finds it temporarily, whether in philanthropic acts or in romantic associations, but the moment is tarnished by tragedy in a reminder of the cruelty and frailty of existence. The subtext of determinism versus free will – especially pronounced in *Keoma* – places the films in the tragic vein of Italian western best represented by *Django* (1966), *$10,000 Blood Money* (1967), *Cemetery Without Crosses* (1969) and *The Forgotten Pistolero* (1969).

Made nine years after *Massacre Time*, *The Four of the Apocalypse* was Lucio Fulci's second western. It is one of the most striking titles from the director's 'middle period', a time when he was dabbling in various genres, from *gialli* (the excellent *A Lizard in a Woman's Skin* [1971] and *Don't Torture a Duckling* [1972]) to farce (*The Eroticist* [1971]) and Boys' Own (two 'White Fang' adventures with Franco Nero). He was also developing his taste for the *fantastique* (evinced by the horror-thriller *The Psychic* [1977]), gearing up for his greatest successes in the Eighties. The latter quality is certainly evident in *Apocalypse*. Slowly paced and very loosely structured, with eruptions of visceral violence, it achieves an oneiric ambience that pre-empts his Gothic horror films. *Keoma* and *A Man Called Blade* have something of the same dream-like state, and Fulci's film anticipates these works, as well as *California*, in other ways as well, not least in the bleakness of its vision. Technically it is outstanding, with stunning ambient cinematography by Sergio Salvati, who would become one of Fulci's key allies in his triumphant horror phase, and careful production design that reflects its despondent world-view, emphasising raw nature, damp, muddy, misty conditions, man-made squalor and decay. More problematic is the score, composed by Franco Bixio, Fabio Frizzi and Vince Tempera and attuned to the folk-rock market. The understated, guitar-driven instrumental pieces are fine, matching Salvati's elegiac imagery and the script's meandering rhythm, but the songs – performed by Greenfield and Cook and the Benjamin Franklin Group – are artless, plaintive and repetitive. Some of the lyrics 'commentate' on the action; as we shall see, *Keoma* and *Blade* would take this kind of vocal accompaniment to another level.

Like much of Italy's popular cinema of the period, *Apocalypse* speaks directly to the post-1968 generation, addressing their concerns about the elusiveness of freedom in a world governed by reactionary and repressive forces. Yet, perversely, the counter-culture's untamed, free-living ethos (embodied here by the film's principal villain) proves equally unpalatable. This was neither the first nor the last time that a commercial Italian production's outwardly liberal sympathies clashed with an innate conservatism; it was a conflict that rumbled throughout Fulci's career. The plot, conceived by B-movie veteran Ennio De Concini and based loosely on stories by pulp western writer Bret Harte, brings together four kindred spirits – narcissistic gambler Stubby (Fabio Testi), young pregnant prostitute Bunny (Lynne Frederick), drunkard

above: In thrall to the demon drink, Michael J. Pollard is humiliated by the demonic Chaco (Tomas Milian) in **The Four of the Apocalypse**.

Clem (Michael J. Pollard) and black spiritualist Buck (Harry Baird) – for a journey across a microcosmic wilderness where good coexists with evil. They encounter the former in the shape of a benign religious commune; a friendly wandering missionary (Adolfo Lastretti); and the isolated, all-male colony of Altaville. But their paths also cross that of the monstrous Chaco (Tomas Milian), a mysterious hunter who insists on joining them and is revealed to be a sadist. For all the film's focus on its likeable quartet of losers – especially the development of Stubby from shallow gambler to responsible group leader and surrogate husband for Bunny – it is the carnage wrought by Chaco that creates the strongest impression. He's arguably the most malevolent character in the annals of the European western, personifying the inexplicability of serial killers and the ritualistic savagery of blood cults – sources of popular shock and fascination since the close of the Sixties and the souring of the 'summer of love'. Elaborating upon a character he had played in Franco Prosperi's crime drama *The Boxer* (1972) and following his psychotic role in the scuzzy *poliziesco The Executioner* (1974), Milian drew also on Charles Manson for inspiration, from Chaco's appearance – long-haired and bearded, draped in charms, and with mystical symbols painted underneath his eyes – to his manipulative mind-set. In one sense, Chaco is the Antichrist to the Messianic Keoma, who shares some of his counter-cultural associations, although Fulci eventually strips his villain of his mythic aura and reduces him to the level of bandit in the film's deliberately anti-climactic resolution.

Betraying a nihilism that is challenged elsewhere in the narrative but never quashed, the film delivers its travellers from the murderous attentions of a restrictive society, represented by the death squad of Salt Flat, into the evil embrace of the nonconformist Chaco. Whereas in Salt Flat, the sheriff (Donal O'Brien) had shielded them from the gunmen, out here in the wild they are cruelly exposed. In the film's most notorious sequence, Chaco humiliates and tortures his non-comprehending companions, plying them with peyote, raping Bunny and wounding the three men. Fulci, as was his wont, spares us few details, particularly when Chaco is discovered flaying a captive lawman (played by the long-suffering Lorenzo Robledo, who was often subjected to drawn-out, nasty demises in his westerns – see also *Face to Face*). The director's fascination with physical destruction hinders any objective statement he and De Concini may have intended to make. The rape scene, in particular, is difficult to watch. With Testi's character a helpless, agonized observer, this episode looks ahead to another outré example of sexual violence in a later Fulci film, *The Naples Connection* (1980), in which the same actor's heroic smuggler is forced to listen while his wife is assaulted on the other end of a telephone line. Stubby, though not a man of violence, swears revenge, his resolve stiffened when the foursome trek on and discover the corpses of the commune, victims of Chaco's bloodlust.

Perhaps the most striking aspect of *Apocalypse*, and of the three films that followed, is the contrast between this despairing outlook and a defiant optimism. Soon after their ordeal, the group seek refuge from a rainstorm in a ghost town. While Salvati renders the elements and gloomy interiors in ethereal hues – here and elsewhere he makes use of diffused lighting to gain a hazy, dreamy effect – Fulci switches to a surprisingly tender tone as Stubby and Bunny's relationship blossoms into love, with Testi and Frederick rekindling their on-screen romance from the earlier *Red Coat*. Once again, however, this positive development is offset by tragedy – the death of Clem, who finally succumbs to the wounds inflicted by Chaco – and by Fulci's predilection for the mysterious and the macabre, as when Stubby discovers the origins of the meat Buck has

above: Chaco (Tomas Milian) rapes Bunny (Lynne Frederick) during one of the cruellest scenes in the genre, in **The Four of the Apocalpyse**.

brought for them. For his part, Buck has now surrendered to his delusions, and Stubby and Bunny leave him in the company of the spirits in the town cemetery, "fine folk", he says, who don't judge a man by his colour. The lovers' departure is traced via a series of subjective camera shots, filmed, illogically, from different vantage points. Buck can't be in all of them at once – perhaps the ghosts are watching, too? The resulting ambiguity is typical of the film's disorienting fluctuations in mood.

The duelling strains of the story are juxtaposed most starkly towards the end, when Stubby and Bunny seek solace in Altaville. The various petty outlaws, outcasts and misfits that live in this mountainous, snowy retreat are not as misanthropic as they initially appear. Despite their voluntary seclusion from civilization and distrust of women (they only value the whores they visit periodically in the valley below), these rough-hewn men are moved by Bunny's plight and even help deliver the baby, awed at the prospect of new life in such a barren environment. To hammer home the point, they ask the missionary to christen the child Lucky. Inevitably, this lengthy sequence is marked by a degree of sentimentalism but, importantly, Fulci suppresses the mawkishness that would sink his subsequent western, *Silver Saddle*, treating the birth with the same kind of dignity and respect, and not a little wonder, as exhibited by the men, who shoot their guns in the air with excitement when they hear the child's first cries. Of course, the pattern of the film dictates that a positive must be balanced by a negative, and Bunny duly dies after giving birth, another delayed reaction to Chaco's assault. Stubby leaves the child in Altaville, whose inhabitants have demonstrated that benevolence and compassion can survive in even the harshest conditions, and rides on to face the demonic Chaco.

The culmination of the revenge scenario is entirely in keeping with the almost antithetical approach to western conventions that Fulci has taken throughout. The settling of accounts is shorn of all its customary cathartic charge; there is no grandeur about the staging, no epic dimension, not even a man-to-man confrontation. Stubby creeps up on the villain and two companions in an abandoned way station, blasting the henchmen where they sit and wounding Chaco in the arm. Enduring Chaco's curses, Stubby, eerily calm, prolongs the other's pain, taking time to shave and slashing Chaco's face when he crawls towards a pistol, the uncharacteristically vicious act of a desensitised man. When Chaco starts to taunt him about the rape, Stubby shoots him repeatedly. Fulci refrains from embellishing the moment. Testi's face registers nothing but blank despair, and in place of the usual sense of satisfaction at the villain's comeuppance there is a sense of emptiness. Stubby is going through the motions and Fulci, his vision of an inglorious west intact unto the end, follows suit, just as vengeance will be deferred and deflected in *Keoma* and *A Man Called Blade*.

above: "I want peace, I want love…": The ballad of Keoma (Franco Nero) chimes with his appearance and some of his statements ("A man who's free never dies"), if not with his propensity for violence.

Released a year after Fulci's anomalous film, *Keoma* is not only a highpoint in the genre's history but also a summation of its major themes and a testament to its aspirations. Born of a love of westerns but deviating dramatically from the form, it conjoins timeless existential and philosophical concerns with a contemporary focus on racial intolerance and environmentalism. Franco Nero seems almost possessed in the title role and creates arguably the genre's most compelling protagonist, a combination of knight errant, Christ-like saviour and western avenger. It is certainly Enzo Castellari's finest achievement, all the more striking considering his previous westerns had been lightweight affairs; only *Johnny Hamlet* (1968) had hinted at a more serious approach and pointed towards *Keoma*'s Gothic atmosphere, while Castellari's urban thrillers of this period, several of which starred Nero, have some of the same stridency.

The film evolved from a story by Italian genre actor George Eastman: "I was commissioned to write it by [producer] Manolo Bolognini, without going through any formal contract procedures… At the time, they were looking for a story to suit Franco Nero, to release as a sequel to *Django*… I set to work and came up with something rather different, a sort of fable in the framework of a western. I based the story on a character I'd loved as a child, 'L'ussaro della morte' from the comic *Il Vittorioso*, then I threw in a bit of Eduardo De Filippo (a male version of *Filumena Marturano*: one of Keoma's stepbrothers is his real brother, but his father refuses to tell him which one so that he won't kill any of them)."[18] Although the broad outline of the story was retained, the subsequent script, credited to Mino Roli, Nico Ducci, Eastman (under his real name of Luigi Montefiori) and Castellari, was deemed insufficient and was abandoned, with the production proceeding on a semi-improvised, collaborative basis that has gone down in genre folklore. Much has also been written of the references Castellari includes to his favourite films and directors: Sam Peckinpah's slow-motion violence and editing patterns inspired many of the action scenes (Castellari had already experimented with these techniques in his crime films and would go on to belabour them in subsequent titles); certain plot points and images bring to mind *Django* (the two films share the same producer, Manolo Bolognini); and, having parodied Sergio Leone in *Any Gun Can Play* (1967), Castellari indulges here in a rich, occasionally over-elaborate visual style that evokes Leone's widescreen *mise-en-scène*. Ingmar Bergman is another recipient of the director's artistic tributes: the plot, along with art director Carlo Simi's vivid, quasi-medieval milieu and the morbid symbolism, owe much to Bergman's *The Seventh Seal* (1957), which also dealt with a wandering knight (Max von Sydow's crusader Antonius Block) and his privations in a plague-ridden environment. Further testifying to the production's grandiose objectives, much of the dialogue has Shakespearean overtones – a decade after directing *Johnny Hamlet*, the Bard was clearly still in Castellari's blood. (The director credits co-star Gianni Loffredo, a Castellari regular who plays the youngest of Franco Nero's brothers and helped shape the film's dialogue, with much of *Keoma*'s lyricism.)

The end result of the filmmakers' ambitions can be pretentious and preposterous in places – there are cumbersome passages and misjudged elements, in particular the Greek chorus-style, ballad-heavy score by the De Angelis brothers – but it is also invigorating. Castellari's intentions may be serious, but his approach is never solemn; he remains true to his populist instincts and wisely keeps the project grounded in the dynamics of the western genre he admired so much. *Keoma* is as kinetic as it is contemplative: Castellari's visual sense has never been as acute, and his mastery of action scenes and fight choreography is at its most complete. Yet while the film possesses all the trappings one would expect of an Italian western, including intricate production design and costuming, skilfully edited showdowns and chases, energetic stunt work and creative camerawork, and while it reworks familiar plot devices such as the evil landowner and brotherly rivalry, Castellari offers a much more substantial experience, one that can be appreciated on different levels.

Notionally set in post-Civil War southern America, *Keoma* transpires entirely on a mythic plane. Its highly charged hero is a ragged, hirsute half-breed, without a place or a people of his own, who has returned to his adoptive home partly to face his demons and partly in search of his true purpose in life, driven, he believes, by destiny. This spurs the dedication with which he sets about liberating the plague-stricken community from the rule of tyrannical mining entrepreneur Caldwell (Donal O'Brien), and heightens the inevitability and intensity of Keoma's confrontation with his hated half-brothers (Loffredo, Orso Maria Guerrini and Antonio Marsina). The film itself is full of portents and symbols – Keoma's first act is to rescue the pregnant Lisa (Olga Karlatos), who symbolises life, and he is haunted by a mysterious, prophetic old woman (Gabriella Giacobbe), who may or may not be a witch and serves as the director's Bergman-esque figure of death. She appears ominously at the most dramatic points in the film – in one of Castellari's most rhetorical effects, she suddenly emerges in an open doorway during a gunfight, silhouetted by strong, supernatural backlighting. In the climax, Castellari extends the idea inherent in the Altaville sequence of *The Four of the Apocalypse* by staging a metaphorical battle between the opposing forces these characters represent, cross-cutting between Lisa's agonized labour, watched over by the old woman, and Keoma's showdown with his half-brothers. As we watch Keoma's struggle, the only sounds on the track are Lisa's screams of pain – the child's fight for life mirrors the hero's fight for freedom, Castellari summing up the principal theme of his film with a poetic final flourish.

Visually and stylistically, *Keoma* is the richest of all its contemporaries. As in *The Four of the Apocalypse* and *A Man Called Blade*, some of the director's formal devices seem contrived merely to revitalise the clichés (not that's there's anything wrong with that) – such as the careful framing of the confrontations, the choice of unusual camera angles and perspectives in the action scenes – while others serve to underline prominent themes, to strengthen the effect of dialogue or enhance the characterisations. When Keoma, in an early exchange with his father, William Shannon (William Berger), speaks of the years he has spent "chasing shadows", roving from one place and one encounter to another, the camera circles around him, seemingly synchronised with his restless nature. The film takes on a surrealistic quality at several points, notably in the celebrated flashback scenes in which the past, source of much of Keoma's unresolved angst and inner turmoil, is integrated with the present in the same shot. There are no fades or dissolves; he watches from the background or the edge of the frame as his memories manifest around him.[19] Veteran cinematographer Aiace Parolin uses unnaturally bright lighting to signal the shift from a narrative to a psychological mode, contrasting with the gloomy, moody tone of the film overall. While most of the film's technical and stylistic aspects add to the potency of the drama, it's unfortunate that the De Angelis brothers' hyberbolic score overwhelms some of the emotional flashpoints. Castellari wanted the same kind of poetic, haunting commentary provided by Leonard Cohen in *McCabe & Mrs. Miller* (1971) and Bob Dylan in *Pat Garrett and Billy the Kid*, but the lyrics and vocals in *Keoma* are frequently obtrusive and distracting. The idea is interesting – a female singer narrates and commentates on the action, while a deep male voice externalises Keoma's thoughts –

but the accompaniment is often unnecessary and reaches such hysterical peaks, especially the lamentations during Keoma's crucifixion and the scene where his father is killed, that it undermines Castellari's evocative imagery.

The main reason why *Keoma* has such resonance is the title character himself. Portrayed with great passion and vitality, he is a paradox of anger and compassion, introspection and dynamism, both a brooding loner and a force for social change. In one sense he is the ultimate Euro-western drifter, but the explosive, feral energy he exerts gives him a momentum that few of the genre's self-absorbed protagonists can match. As an outcast, Keoma is also the focal point of the film's attacks on oppression and racial intolerance. Much of the anger directed at these forms of social injustice flows through him, largely because he suffered racial abuse as a child at the hands of his half-brothers. Since the film is structured as an allegory, Keoma's feud with his siblings is not merely personal, but a battle on behalf of humanity. By the same token, the brothers, and the other villains for that matter, are more interesting for what they represent collectively than as individuals. Always shown together ("three names, one brand"), the Shannon boys are reactionary, surly and manipulative, using the conflict between Caldwell and their sibling to manoeuvre their way into power. Like Keoma, they seem to have been shaped to a large extent by the tangled emotions engendered in their childhood, but the script never gets to grips with their fear of Keoma or their resentment of his place in their father's affections. As a result they're not much more than racist bullies, albeit with a nice line in neo-Shakespearean demagoguery. As for Caldwell, he is also rather bland, notable mainly as a standard-bearer for ruthless capitalism and environmental exploitation.

The hero is not entirely alone in his fight against these forces – his father, played amiably by Berger, just 13 years Nero's senior, eventually joins him, as does the latter's dispirited black ranch hand, George (Woody Strode), who once taught Keoma about racial harmony – but it takes Keoma to galvanize them into action.[20] In the same way that Lisa is sacrificed to bring new life into the world, both Shannon and George become martyrs, losing their lives in a rousing gunfight in the pursuit of principles each had always held dear but that had become suppressed for different reasons. Shannon, a former gunfighter, has proved powerless to prevent his sons from taking up with Caldwell, his paternal feelings overriding his philanthropic instincts, while George has discovered the limitations of emancipation, especially with Caldwell's redneck ex-Confederates controlling the area. "I used to have something to hope for – freedom... I found out what it was worth," he tells Keoma, using the kind of gnomic language that may repel as many viewers as it attracts. While neither of these characters is fully developed, they have considerable symbolic weight, not least because of significant casting. William Berger, better known for devious and villainous roles, confirms his flexibility as the virtuous Shannon (he plays a similar part in *California*), while the film's liberal philosophy would doubtless have accorded with the actor's own freethinking beliefs. And it's a shock to see the imposing Woody Strode, a talismanic figure in John Ford westerns and an icon of physical strength, succumbing to degrading abuse and alcoholism. Strode was a more sensitive performer than many of his credits might suggest, something that Castellari obviously recognised and encouraged. George's inaction adds pathos to the drama, while his rediscovery of his dignity and his heroic death, wailing defiantly under a hail of bullets, conjure memories of the towering Strode of *Sergeant Rutledge* and *Spartacus* (both 1960).

Keoma turned a moderate profit in Italy, raking in more than 500 million lire, performed well elsewhere in Europe and earned respectable notices, albeit tinged with surprise that a genre most critics considered moribund could still produce a work of imagination and originality. Had it been made a decade earlier, this modest success would no doubt have inspired a spate of imitations. As it was, two factors militated against that occurring: *Keoma* has a conclusiveness about it that left other filmmakers with little room for manoeuvre: how to follow something that effectively announced the end of an era? Also significant, of course, was the lack of sufficient public demand for a western revival, and one has to wonder

above: Belgian poster for **Keoma**, Enzo Castellari's defining statement as a director of westerns.

whether *Keoma* would have been so successful on home turf had the hugely popular Nero not been the star.

Undeterred, the irrepressible Sergio Martino, one of Italian cinema's most proficient counterfeiters, delivered *A Man Called Blade* in response. Produced by Devon Film, a company run by Martino and his brother Luciano, this is the story of a roving gunfighter, the bounty hunter Blade (Maurizio Merli), returning to his childhood home and crossing swords, or rather hatchets, with unscrupulous mine owner McGowan (Philippe Leroy), who also happened to have killed Blade's father many years before. Once again, as in *Keoma*, Blade's ire transfers to a more sinister enemy, in this case McGowan's vicious henchman, Voller (John Steiner), who, rather refreshingly in the midst of all this allegorical material, represents nothing except ruthless, unbridled ambition. Much more linear than its predecessor, *Blade* plays down *Keoma*'s psychological and philosophical aspects and inflates its atmospheric and exploitative qualities. While it doesn't have the earlier film's fantastical air, the misty, murky texture of Federico Zanni's photography creates a Gothic aura while simultaneously evoking the sulphurous fumes spewing from the mine. (Martino shot exteriors around Manziana near Rome, a region known for its sulphur deposits.) Blade himself has none of Keoma's spiritual unrest; he's more of an old-fashioned, embittered loner, conditioned by violence and ever willing to mete it out. Guido and Maurizio De Angelis compose another dolorous commentary, this time using animal metaphors: Blade the shaggy hunter, constantly snarling and clad in fur, is likened to a wolf, for example, while his devious sidekick, the verminous outlaw Bert Craven (Donal O'Brien), is compared to a snake. The gore is more graphic, with Blade's axe doing bloody damage, and there is greater use of squibs, Martino efficiently copying the Peckinpah/Castellari slow motion/cross-cutting technique. There are several hallucinatory and horrific sequences: the eerie opening chase that introduces Blade and Craven effectively employs subjective camera shots and establishes mist and mud as prominent visual elements; there's a nasty instance of eyeball torture, Blade's punishment here one of several reminders of Antonio Margheriti's *Vengeance* (1968); and Blade advancing on Voller through a cloud of vapour for the final reckoning recalls *A Fistful of Dollars*. Voller, for his part, with his flowing black cape, clipped Mittel-European accent and attendant hounds, would look equally at home in the cobwebbed corridors of a Transylvanian castle. (*Blade*'s shades of horror show Martino acknowledging one of his early mentors, Mario Bava, whom he assisted on the latter's *The Whip and the Body* [1963].)

Like many of his compatriots, Martino forged a successful career by latching on to current trends and imitating popular hits; he just happened to do it better than most. This is not to damn him with faint praise. The Euro-western's success – like that of the entire Italian film industry at its peak – was due largely to its talented artisans. (The Martino brothers had a cinematic legacy to uphold, being the grandsons of a prolific and well-regarded Italian director, Gennaro Righelli, who made numerous films from the silent era to the Forties, including Italy's first sound film, *La canzone dell'amore* [1930].) Time and again, Martino has demonstrated a priceless ability to disguise derivative material, to repackage it with style and ingenuity. His early Seventies *gialli*, patterned after Dario Argento's thrillers, with a dash of Poe here and a touch of *Rosemary's Baby* there, are put together with panache; his *polizieschi* are brutally efficient; and his fantasy tales – take your pick from cannibals, fish monsters, giant alligators and cyborgs – old-fashioned and engaging.

Considering his abilities, it is unfortunate that Martino made only two westerns, a consequence of his relatively late start as a director (he made his first film when the genre was winding down, in 1969) and of his preference for working in different categories. His first western, very early in his career, was the Anthony Steffen vehicle *Arizona* (1970), a tenuous sequel to Giuliano Gemma's *Arizona Colt* (1966), written, like that film, by Ernesto Gastaldi and produced, as usual, by Martino's brother Luciano (co-writer of *Arizona Colt*), with Roberto Camardiel reprising his role as Double Whisky, the comic-relief character. It has never been widely distributed (an English-language version has only recently surfaced on DVD), but, despite the awkward seriocomic tone affected by many westerns of the time, it does close with a satisfying, well-executed shootout between Steffen and Aldo Sambrell's band of brigands. In *Blade*, Martino simultaneously deconstructs generic tropes (Blade contemptuously sparing the crippled McGowan's life, for example), capturing the downbeat, meditative mood of the time it was made, and confidently wields the clichés that established the Euro-western in the first place. Hence the reassuring presence of a crotchety old eccentric, a bandit gang with a 'surprise' leader, and the evil landowner – who's a puritanical bigot into the bargain – who has subjugated an entire community, while scenes depicting slave-like miners and the heavy-handed oppressive measures of McGowan's gunmen push all the expected emotional buttons. The protagonist goes through the usual painful rite of passage and makes a providential and timely recovery from his wounds. Finally, duplicity is rife – Voller conspires with McGowan's daughter against the old man, while Craven, played by O'Brien with the gusto he normally reserved for his horror films, is a vintage spaghetti western turncoat. Captured and maimed by Blade, then released, he rescues the latter towards the end but then betrays him; in the cut-throat

above: Italian fotobusta for **A Man Called Blade**, regrettably the only western to star Maurizio Merli, king of Italy's urban crime thrillers. He plays a bounty hunter armed with an axe, a social conscience and – Merli's trademark in his *polizieschi* – a fiery self-righteousness.

environment of the European western, one good turn deserves another but, after that, all bets are off.

Like most of Martino's films, *A Man Called Blade* was conceived with popular tastes and international sales in mind. The casting of the late Maurizio Merli as Blade was particularly shrewd. While he never achieved global fame, leading roles in several of the most successful Italian crime thrillers had made Merli a major box-office draw in his homeland, and he displays the same brutish charisma here in his only western. Like Terence Hill before him, Merli first came to prominence because of his facial resemblance to Franco Nero – Tonino Ricci cast him in *White Fang to the Rescue* (1975), a follow-up to Lucio Fulci's Nero vehicle *White Fang*, and, also in 1975, director Marino Girolami responded to the great success of nephew Enzo Castellari's *High Crime* (1973) with the pyrotechnic *Violent Rome*, in which Merli played a pugnacious cop modelled on Nero's inspector in the former film. The Martinos, therefore, knew who would be the ideal man for their *Keoma*-inspired western. Merli's law enforcers are characterised by righteous indignation, spitting dialogue with the same ferocity they deliver body blows, and he's a similarly seething presence in *Blade*, venting Keoma-esque moral outrage against the hypocritical McGowan,

the sadistic Voller and the treacherous Craven. There is more to Blade than anger – his treatment of Craven and his affections for a showgirl suggest a capacity for compassion, his criticism of McGowan a degree of social/environmental consciousness. Yet it's the unyielding intensity that Merli brings to the character, and which he brought to all his signature roles, that is his defining feature, just as the mixing and matching of Euro-western clichés with topical issues tailored to a mid-Seventies audience defines Martino's film as a whole.

The last of the four westerns I have selected is the most traditional in style, eschewing the stylistic and narrative experimentation that mark the three films above. *California*, like *Keoma*, is set at the end of the American Civil War, and has the same broad objectives as that film and *The Four of the Apocalypse* – to puncture Euro-western myths, contaminate its air of escapism and deflate its characterisations – but aims more for gritty realism. The grim tone, which is only partly redeemed towards the end, was a striking departure for Michele Lupo, a director associated with much breezier films, while Giuliano Gemma gives one of his most perceptive performances as an uncharacteristically hostile loner, a worn-down, jaded version of the affable cynics and

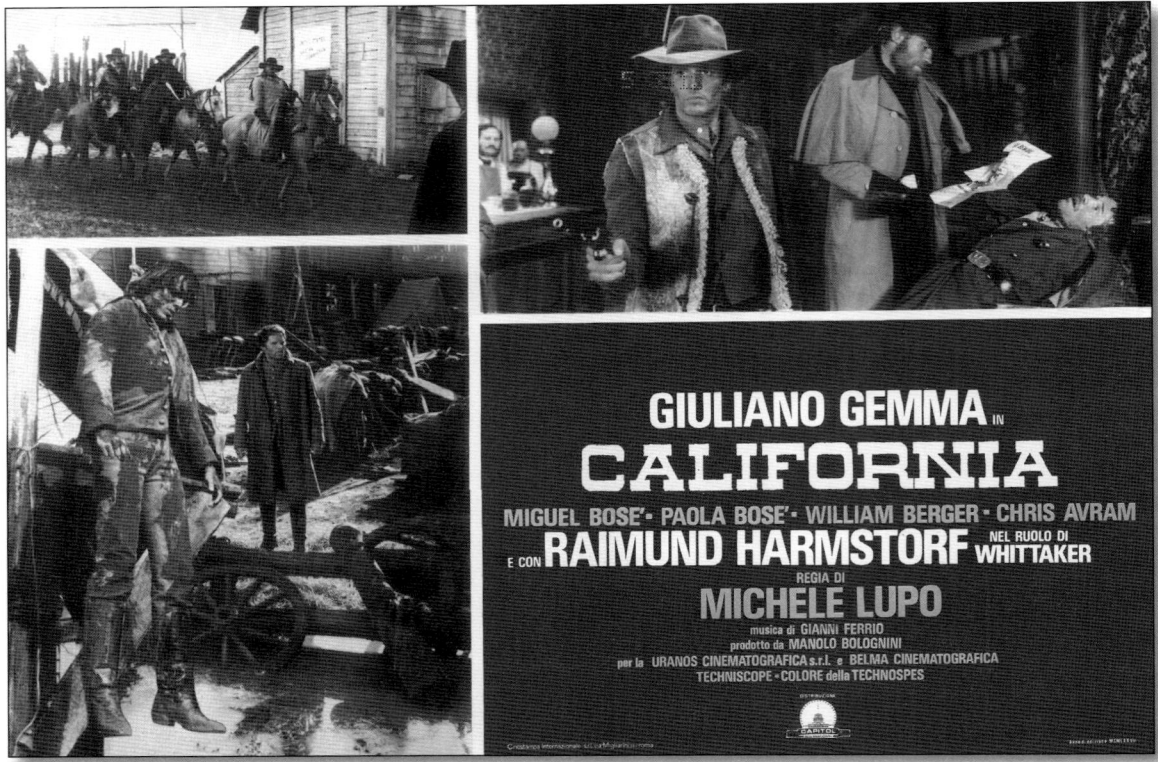

above: An unusually muted performance by Giuliano Gemma (*top right,* holding pistol, next to Raimund Harmstorf) sets the tone of **California**, in which the irreverence associated with his earlier films, representative of the genre at its peak, struggles to assert itself.

defiant Confederates he portrayed in many of his earlier westerns. (The 'Ringo' films, *Arizona Colt* and the post-Civil War stories *One Silver Dollar* [1965] and *Fort Yuma Gold* [1966] are particularly apposite reference points.) Flashes of Gemma's warmer, friendlier side emerge late on, but in general this is a character for whom the cumulative effects of violence and personal loss, not to mention the tragedy of the Civil War, have reinforced his avoidance of meaningful personal relationships and his desire for anonymity. It's notable that both of Gemma's sobriquets in the film are impersonal – in his gunfighting days he was known simply as California in tribute to his state of origin, a nod perhaps to Arizona Colt, and he also uses the name Random, acknowledging the interchangeability of Gemma's protagonists and the meaninglessness of identity in the genre as a whole. For men like these, identity equates with family and friendship, the kind of emotional entanglement it is better to avoid if one is to survive and not endanger others.

Lupo's film (produced, like *Keoma*, by Manolo Bolognini) is a variation on Clint Eastwood's *The Outlaw Josey Wales*, a sizeable success on its release in 1976. Eastwood's motto in that film, "When I get around to likin' someone, they ain't around long", could also explain Gemma's lone-wolf attitude. Like Josey Wales, California/Random undertakes a violent post-Civil War odyssey of redemption and retribution, reluctantly taking a chirpy young soldier, Willy Preston (Miguel Bosé), under his wing. The relationship between the gruff older man and the idealistic youth parallels that between Eastwood and Sam Bottoms in *Josey Wales*, and both youngsters meet violent deaths. Lupo's vision of the Civil War's aftermath is darker, however. The title theme, a sombre chant, leads into an opening sequence that depicts dishevelled, shattered Confederate soldiers shuffling around a squalid prison camp. On the outside, still in 'enemy' territory, they face suspicion and prejudice from society, compounding the ignominy of defeat. They're also easy prey for bounty hunters led by Rope Whittaker, played by the powerful German actor Raimund Harmstorf, who has a contract with the Union to round up Confederate 'outlaws', killing them without mercy and on the merest of pretexts. The film decries this collusion, but its level of social criticism diminishes as California's personal enmity towards Whittaker intensifies. Even the lighter moments in *California* are tainted with bitterness – a scene where a group of Confederates chase after frogs for their supper is both comedic and indicative of how pathetic and desperate these fighting men have become. Not since *The Good, the Bad and the Ugly* (1966) has an

Italian western treated warfare with such seriousness or painted such a tragic picture of its effects.

Where violence in the three previous films is stylised to varying degrees, generally reducing its emotional impact, here it is ugly, jarring and fierce. Traditional gunfights are replaced by execution-style killings, and the hand-to-hand bouts are savage and frenzied. One brief instance of slow motion apart, Lupo films the carnage in a raw, uncompromising style, similar to the *polizieschi* of the era. Allied with cinematographer Alejandro Ulloa and production designer Carlo Simi, Lupo convincingly depicts a war-torn society riven by lawlessness and sectarian hatred, where life has been devalued to such an extent that Willy is callously shot down by a rancher for stealing a horse. California scatters for cover but the rancher is satisfied, declaring with ironic magnanimity "one man's enough for one horse".

Akin to the other twilight westerns, *California* is a film of shifting moods. It divides roughly into three sections, each with a different emotional climate and visual style. The opening third is exceptionally bleak, all dark skies and muddy trails, the browns and greys of Ulloa's palette only brightened by splashes of blood red. After Willy's death, California makes his way to the boy's ranch, where his family has been in stasis while Willy has been at war. In the film's most optimistic passage, California helps them to move on emotionally, telling them Willy died in battle and relaxing enough to form a close bond with Preston senior (William Berger) and Willy's sister, Helen (Paola Bosé, sister of Miguel). Gemma's demeanour changes; he becomes cheerful, less guarded, while Berger is quietly impressive as a man juggling pride and sorrow at his son's 'heroic' death. The gentler tone is emphasised by warmer colours – rustic green and orange – while soft interior lighting complements the nostalgic, wistful mood in the Preston household.

Two thirds of the film thus communicates the physical and emotional fallout of warfare, from the destitution of the vanquished and deep-rooted enmity of the victors, to the mixed emotions of soldiers' relatives. The final section changes to more traditional spaghetti western terrain, both in terms of the scenery and the vengeful thrust of the plot, as California sets out into the dry and dusty desert badlands to rescue Helen from the now outlawed Whittaker. Were this a Gemma western from the Sixties, we could expect him to accomplish his mission with superheroic aplomb and the heroine to emerge unscathed. Befitting the film's more anguished outlook, however, when California does retrieve Helen she is a forlorn figure, having obviously been repeatedly abused by Whittaker's men. The dismantling of western conventions is not as wide-ranging as in *The Four of the Apocalypse* and *Keoma*, but Lupo's film is more rigorously de-romanticised, stripping the glamour and mystique from its characters – good and bad – and grounding their actions in grubby reality.

The last round-up

Since this late flowering of European westerns that shared some kind of thematic unity, the genre has greatly diminished in both scope and scale. Westerns have continued to be made on the continent, but only sporadically; few of these have a common perspective and many have been financed and screened only by television companies. Until very recently the picture was similar in America, where the negative reception and disastrous performance of *Heaven's Gate* (1980) threatened to put an end to the western's A-feature status just when consumer tastes and audience demographics turned – decisively it seems – in favour of high-concept productions, marginalising most forms of low- to mid-budget mass-market cinema, especially those not predicated on big stars or special effects. Factor in the stranglehold on distribution of the major studios, which generally only place (and frequently waste) their money on supposedly safe bets – star-laden remakes and television/comic-strip adaptations, expensive fantasies and historical epics, with many of the lessons of *Heaven's Gate* remaining unheeded – and it looks as if the western's place in the commercial wilderness is assured for some time. (It doesn't help that when major studios *do* take a punt on westerns, the receipts are usually disappointing, as in cases such as *Wyatt Earp* [1994], *Gods and Generals* [2003] and *The Alamo* [2004] – all costly flops. Thankfully, there is still room for exceptions: Clint Eastwood's career-defining *Unforgiven* [1992]; Kevin Costner's *Open Range* [2003]; James Mangold's muscular remake of *3:10 to Yuma* [2007]; Ed Harris's *Appaloosa* [2008]; and the Coen Brothers' take on *True Grit* [2010] all earned respectable returns, demonstrating that traditional westerns still have popular appeal, while Ang Lee's more unorthodox *Brokeback Mountain* [2005] enticed a much broader spectrum of spectators.)

Nostalgia seems to have been the principal motivation behind most latter-day European and, indeed, American, productions. Some have tried to recapture the anarchic spirit and style of Leone's generation (though it's been Asian filmmakers who have achieved this most successfully, with the likes of *Tears of the Black Tiger* [2001], *Sukiyaki Western Django* [2007] and *The Good, the Bad, the Weird* [2008] – see below), while others emphasise traditional western virtues and universal values, particularly nobility and idealism. One of the earliest European western heroes, Winnetou, has returned to the saddle on a number of occasions in the past couple of decades, firstly in 1980, when Pierre Brice picked up the lance again for the French-Swiss TV series *Winnetou the Mescalero*. Brice carried off the role effortlessly, despite not having played the Apache chief on screen for 12 years, but he later starred in a poorly received two-part German TV movie, *Winnetou Returns*

(1998), made when he was 69. The environmental themes of the story are predictable and trite, and Winnetou lacks the solid, reassuring presence of a Shatterhand or Surehand, not to mention the energy he was able to display at his physical peak. (Other actors, notably Gojko Mitic, have subsequently kept Winnetou's name in the public domain, both on stage and screen.)[21]

Aside from the handful of star vehicles previously mentioned in this chapter, Italy has produced a few contemporary westerns such as *Man Hunt* (1984), starring John Ethan Wayne, whose staunchly traditional father reportedly loathed what the Italians had done to his beloved genre, and Enzo Barboni's *Renegade* (1987), a trifling vehicle for the ever-enthusiastic Terence Hill. The highly rated Daniele Luchetti – whose most recent film, *La nostra vita* (2010), competed for the Palme d'Or at Cannes – made his debut with *It's Happening Tomorrow* (1988), a charming "philosophical western" (the director's term) based in 19th Century Tuscany. An episodic, comic fable following the adventures of two low-calibre criminals, it earned Luchetti – a protégé of Nanni Moretti, who produced the film and plays a small role – a prestigious David di Donatello award in his home country as Best New Director. Not the least of its pleasures is a baroque turn from Ciccio Ingrassia as a grizzled bandit, another of the arresting performances the actor gave once he was unshackled from long-time partner Franco Franchi. A decade on came the politically correct *My West* (1998, later released in America under the clichéd and misleading title of *Gunslinger's Revenge*), a reflexive, affectionate showcase for actor/writer Leonardo Pieraccioni, a major star in Italy but unknown overseas. Shot in Tuscany, the film is noteworthy for supporting turns by Harvey Keitel, as Pieraccioni's father, and David Bowie, who takes a big bite at his role as a psychotic gunman. The affable Pieraccioni's character is far removed from Italian western protagonists of the past – he's a doctor, conspicuously avoids trouble, doesn't eat meat and actively cares for the environment, rather than merely espousing eco-friendliness à la Keoma and Blade. Director Giovanni Veronesi, Pieraccioni's regular writing partner, was frank at the time of the film's release about his ambitions to emulate the west of Ford and Hollywood rather than Leone and Cinecittà ("I have never liked the Italian western movies"), and to attract young people with a "modern" take on an old-fashioned morality tale. Despite outgrossing a number of Hollywood productions in Italy, however, it made little impact abroad.

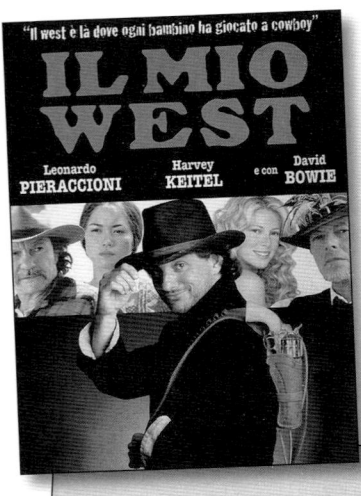

Spain's output since the close of the Seventies has been even less memorable. Rafael Romero Marchent revisited territory he'd not traversed for a decade with a pair of inoffensive Zorro-esque adventures made for Spanish television as vehicles for Mexican actor-singer Fernando Allende. Although technically proficient, *The Black Wolf* and *Revenge of the Black Wolf* (both 1980) are of interest to Euro-western fans mainly for the presence of ageing stalwarts such as Frank Braña and Roberto Camardiel in supporting roles. The same could be said of *Al este del Oeste* ('East of the West' [1984]), a hearty parody by the prolific director-star pairing of Mariano Ozores and comedian Fernando Esteso, which is also flush with craggy, experienced character actors including Fernando Sancho, Víctor Israel and José Manuel Martín. It's a throwback to the send-ups of the Sixties and Seventies, faithfully re-enacting all the expected brawls and comedy routines, referencing Leone along the way and adding plenty of bare-breasted women. In a similar vein, another popular Spanish funny man, Chiquito de la Calzada [Gregorio Sanchez], whose shtick includes flamenco and musical numbers, put his own spin on the bumbling sheriff stereotype in *Here Comes Condemor* (1996), produced solely for the home market. And Mario Camus, who excited critical attention when he broke into features in the Sixties but has never really lived up to expectations, directed *The Return of El Coyote* in 1998. This old-fashioned exercise briefly revived interest in the Zorro-like adventurer created half a century earlier by José Mallorquí, whose son wrote the script for Camus's film; not enough interest, however, to earn it a wide release.

The most significant Spanish film in this 'revival' was Alex de la Iglesia's *800 Bullets* (2002), a vivid, compassionate comedy steeped

above: Italian posters for the revisionist **My West** and the 'traditional' **A Taste for Killing** (look out for Sancho Gracia).

in nostalgia for the genre's golden age that received favourable reviews at international festivals.**22** Its director was, at the time, one of Spain's most precocious talents, whose ferociously original genre pieces – the anarchic sci-fi/horror hybrid *Acción mutante* (1993), diabolical horror story *The Day of the Beast* (1995) and road movie/revenge flick *Perdita Durango* (1997) – have earned him cult status and opened up vital distribution channels abroad. A much warmer work, *800 Bullets* is no less politically incorrect than those films – a 12-year-old boy's first sexual experience involves joyously pawing a prostitute's naked breast while simultaneously talking to his mother on the phone – but in terms of mood and characterisation it is closer to some of de la Iglesia's more 'respectable' works, the bittersweet comedy *Dying of Laughter* (1999) and skilfully judged Hitchcockian thriller *Common Wealth* (2000). Sancho Gracia – popular star of Spanish TV series *Curro Jiménez* (1976-78), in which he played a 19th Century brigand, and veteran of a handful of Euro-westerns including *A Taste for Killing* (1966) and *Django, Kill!*, where he was Roberto Camardiel's principal "muchacho" – plays Julián, an ageing stuntman who boasts of doubling for Clint Eastwood in the 'Dollars' films, driving a tank in *Patton* (1970) and bedding Raquel Welch on the set of *100 Rifles* (1969). (Gracia did actually have a small role in the last-named film.) Estranged from his family and haunted by guilt for the death of his son in a stunt that backfired, his life consists of boozing, whoring and performing for tourists in Texas-Hollywood, one of the few remaining western-town sets in Almería. While the plot juxtaposes Julián's burgeoning relationship with his young grandson (Luis Castro) with his leadership of a rebellion by his fellow misfits against plans to demolish the town and erect a theme park, de la Iglesia pays homage to Almería's cinematic legacy and the stunt fraternity's role within it. The *especialistas*' efforts to cling onto their livelihood is a fight to preserve that legacy and recover some of the dignity they have lost over years of throwing themselves out of windows for the amusement of German and Japanese tour parties. De la Iglesia's film is his own contribution to the cause. As a movie buff with an affection for fantasy and a satirical bent, he is squarely on the stuntmen's side, and frames the final confrontation between Julián's gang, now armed with real bullets, and hordes of militaristic policemen as a glorious last stand of ideals and individualism against economic imperatives.

Formally, the influence of Euro-westerns is immediately apparent. Roque Baños's title theme is a raucous cover of *The Good, the Bad and the Ugly* plucked out on Spanish guitar, played over computer-animated credits in the style of the brightly coloured, rotoscoped openings much loved by genre devotees, and de la Iglesia's 'Scope camera restlessly explores the gaping contours of Texas-Hollywood with Leone-like relish.

But *800 Bullets* is more than just a visual pastiche or quirkily nostalgic romp. The script, co-written by the director and Jorge Guerricaechevarría, engages with some of Leone's most cherished themes, such as loyalty and betrayal, regret and revenge, and, while de la Iglesia clearly admires his anachronistic reprobates and their mock-heroic deeds, he neither sentimentalises them nor romanticises their lifestyle. Gracia's earthy performance anchors the entire film: robust yet faintly ridiculous (we never know for sure, for example, how much of his boasting is booze-addled bravado), Julián comes to believe that "a man with balls", as he styles himself, can still make a difference, even as reality comes crashing into fantasy with tragicomic consequences.

If the Euro-western doesn't appear to have a future, at least its past achievements are slowly gaining wider recognition and appreciation. It is increasingly regarded as an important stage in the development of the western rather than merely a factor in its decline, which was the opinion of many observers in the late Sixties and early Seventies who despaired at the irony of American filmmakers, spurred by the spaghettis' success, dressing their westerns up as European productions where once it had been the other way around.**23** In the genre's heartlands of Italy, Spain, Germany and France, despite popular cinema continuing to get short shrift from mainstream critics, a number of enthusiastic, intelligent books and journals have championed forgotten films and filmmakers in a bid to rehabilitate the Euro-western's image. (For more details, see the bibliography.) No less an institution than the Venice Film Festival organised a retrospective tribute to the genre in 2007, complete with screenings of 40 films, exhibitions and cameos by contributors to the films themselves – as part of its ongoing 'Secret History of Italian Film' initiative. Even scholars of the American western, who have produced an abundance of literature on the subject in recent years, have begun to accord the European version greater respect than was once the case, although this continues to be limited largely to Leone's work. Revised editions of two classic western texts have been especially welcome in this regard: in *Horizons West*, Jim Kitses places Leone among his pantheon of directorial greats; while Philip French in *Westerns: Aspects of a Movie Genre* admits that his earlier blanket dismissal of Euro-westerns was unfair, although he remains uninterested in the films themselves.

Furthermore, in this age of post-modernism, remakes and reappraisals, the *filone* has taken its place as one of the key cult film movements of recent decades, a pop-cultural phenomenon whose characteristics continue to inform all manner of contemporary films. It has inspired countless tributes and parodies, on both big screen (*Straight to Hell* [1987], *Back to the Future Part III* [1990], *Once Upon a Time in the Midlands* [2002]) and small (notably the Comic Strip's *A Fistful of Travellers'*

above: A fairy-tale ending?: An exhibition devoted to Sergio Leone in Los Angeles and, more recently, a guest-laden Euro-western festival in the same city suggest the genre has finally been accepted on its own merits in America.

Cheques [1984]). Along with the James Bond films, the Euro-western is also largely accountable for the rise of the modern action hero, with his carefree destructive bent and ironic disposition.**24** Its legacy of stylistic excess is evident in everything from self-conscious, high-octane Hollywood fare – from *The Matrix* (1999) and *Once Upon a Time in Mexico* (2003) to *Shoot 'Em Up* (2007) and, inevitably, Euro-western fanatic Quentin Tarantino's *Kill Bill* saga (2003-4) and *Inglourious Basterds* (2009) – to Asian action fantasies. John Woo's ballistic thrillers and the 'heroic bloodshed' school led the way, while other examples include the *Once Upon a Time in China* series of the Nineties (with, as we've seen, one episode set in the West); the far-out Thai 'western' *Tears of the Black Tiger*; Zhang Yimou's rapturously received *Hero* (2002), with its nameless, enigmatic protagonist and Leonean grandeur; Johnnie To's thriller *Exiled* (2006), with its close-knit hired killers; and two films previously mentioned, the hyperactive, schizophrenic Korean treasure-hunt adventure, *The Good, the Bad, the Weird*; and Takashi Miike's hyper-stylised *Sukiyaki Western Django*, which is nothing less than a full-blown pastiche.

Sergio Leone, of course, no longer needs apologists. His works have been the subject of academic analysis, been lovingly restored by studio archivists, issued in deluxe DVD editions and screened at prestigious retrospectives. Confirmation of his acceptance into the pantheon of western greats came in 2005, when the Autry National Center's Museum of the American West in Los Angeles ran 'Once Upon a Time in Italy: The Westerns of Sergio Leone', an impressive seven-month exhibition co-curated by Sir Christopher Frayling and featuring costumes, props, posters, scripts and more. (L.A. also hosted a spaghetti western festival in March 2011, a feast of screenings and guest appearances.) Although they continue to suffer in comparison with Leone, other key directors such as Damiani, Sollima, Corbucci and Petroni are now well represented in digital format, finally allowing us to fully appreciate their artistry after years of sub-standard releases. By the same token, the DVD/Blu-ray revolution, along with the advance of the internet, has made the genre's outer reaches more accessible than at any time since the films were first released, permitting the curious to trace the overlapping properties and personalities of these works and contemporaneous productions – whether *pepla* and *polizieschi* or more lauded titles – as these also reach the market.

This increasing ease of access won't necessarily make mainstream critics any more favourable to Euro-westerns as a result but, together with the resurgence of writing on the subject, it may at least apprise a wider audience – and remind existing admirers – of the genre's diversity. Not that scrutiny is necessary or even warranted in many cases – these were essentially formula films, and plenty of them are as perfunctory as that implies. In general, however, European westerns merit closer inspection in much the same way as their Hollywood counterparts do, a process that accentuates the tension on which these films thrive. Juxtapositions abound: dishonourable men are flattered like demigods; stark, naturalistic settings stylised with painterly skill; a welts-and-all attitude to violence – part of a wider drive for 'realism' – swollen to preposterous extremes; an implicit fascination with American mythology conjoined with a desire to subvert the same. Then there is the pressure exerted by competing influences and traditions: the different ways of interpreting themes and judging character inherent in Hollywood and European productions; the clashing cultural perspectives, discordant ideologies and opposing ideas about the form and function of cinema in general. It is contradictions such as these, combined with the *filone*'s sheer multiformity, that make Euro-westerns such a rewarding subject of study. From leaden imitations of American 'oaters' to the 'Dollars' trilogy with its Italianate imprint; from political parables and ruthless revenge tales to farces and parodies; from rogues with no name to a seemingly endless parade of Ringos, Djangos, Sartanas and Sabatas – each phase in the genre's progression illuminates the potential – and the pitfalls – of popular cinema if the timing is right and the aim is true.

above: **Sukiyaki Western Django** translates the cinematic language of Leone and Corbucci for a different culture.

footnotes

1   Interview with Duccio Tessari by Lorenzo De Luca in *C'era una volta il western Italiano*, 1986.

2   Interview with George Hilton by Roger A. Fratter in *Dieci ricercati dello spaghetti western* (Nocturno Dossier, October 2007).

3   See Peter Bondanella, *Italian Cinema*, p.319; Christopher Wagstaff, 'A Forkful of Westerns' in *European Popular Cinema*, p.251.

4   The Leone-inspired working title for this long-rumoured project is *The Angel, the Brute and the Sage*.

5   Interview with Enzo Castellari by Antonio Tentori in *Amarcord*, October 1995.

6   The 'eco' strain has a few antecedents of sorts. In the American canon, Philip French in *Westerns: Aspects of a Movie Genre* identifies the Gene Autry vehicle *Back in the Saddle* (1941) as a precursor, with its polluting mill owner taken to task, while William Wellman's *Across the Wide Missouri* (1951) and *Track of the Cat* (1954) bemoaned man's assault on nature, a mood sustained in 'mountain man' films like *Jeremiah Johnson* (1972). The hippie ideal of getting back to nature, meanwhile, was evoked in George Englund's naïve 'electric' western, *Zachariah* (1971). In Europe, Marino Girolami's Hollywood-style *Bullets and the Flesh* (1964) condemned white industrial expansion and the destruction of Native Americans' natural habitat. Even more prescient was *Man of the East*, Enzo Barboni's wistful 1972 comedy. In between pratfalls, three rough but loveable rural types (played by Americans Gregory Walcott, Dominic Barto and Harry Carey Jr.), friends of Terence Hill's hero, continually bemoan the encroachment of developers and railroad companies on their green and pleasant land. (And the film does boast some of the most verdant and beautiful terrain in the genre, with several scenes shot in Plitvice National Park in Croatia, which had earlier featured in the 'Winnetou' cycle.) Eventually, the trio resolve to ride as far west as possible, only to find, when they reach the ocean, that the trains can still be heard; progress marches inexorably on.

7   Milian was to employ the same mannerisms several years later in *Delitto al ristorante cinese* (1981), one of his 'Nico Giraldi' capers.

8   According to AGIS [Associazione Generale Italiana per lo Spettacolo] figures, the film raked in close to 2 billion lire.

9   Author's interview with Leonard Mann.

10   Hill also played Lucky Luke in an eight-part television series (1990-91), worth seeing for supporting turns by grizzled American veterans such as Jack Elam, John Saxon and John Quade.

11   The Italian film industry's ANICA database records that *Jonathan* was in fact first shown domestically on 20 April 1995.

12   Author's interview with Franco Nero, 3/5 September 2002.

13   Interview with Giuliano Gemma conducted for this book by Alex Marlow-Mann and Julian Grainger.

14   Shot largely in New Mexico, *Doc West* was culled from a TV mini-series; at the time of writing, it is awaiting widespread distribution.

15   Ibid.

16   Quoted in *Ricardo Palacios: Actor, director, observador* by Carlos Aguilar. Thanks to 'Nzoog Wahrlfhehen' for the translation.

17   *Comin' at Ya!* has recently been updated in a new digital format – Noir 3-D – coinciding with a revival of interest in 3-D movies. More details at cominatyanoir3d.com.

18   Interview with Luigi Montefiori by Luca Palmerini and Gaetano Mistretta in *Spaghetti Nightmares*, p.108. Eduardo De Filippo (1900-1984) was a director/actor/screenwriter and one of Italy's most renowned playwrights, specialising in comic works. He wrote *Filumena Marturano*, the story of a resourceful heroine, for the stage in 1946, adapting and directing the film version in 1951.

19   Castellari was inspired by Elia Kazan's innovative use of flashbacks in his 1969 film *The Arrangement*, while a similar approach was employed by Richard Brooks in 1967's *In Cold Blood*.

20   Intriguingly, the part of Keoma's father was first offered to William Holden. Nero was in Germany making the drama *21 Hours in Munich* when Castellari and Manolo Bolognini came to tell him about the western they were planning. Nero immediately suggested his co-star, Holden, for the role of William Shannon. According to Nero, Holden was interested, but his commitments in America clashed with the Italians' shooting schedule.

21   Reports emerged in recent years that Brice was working on a new western with Gojko Mitic to be called *Der Letzte Ritt* ('the last ride'). If there were any solid plans they appear to have fallen through.

22   Unfortunately, *800 Bullets* wasn't picked up for theatrical distribution in English-speaking markets, partly as a consequence of disappointing box-office figures in Spain, where it earned a fraction of the receipts for the director's previous hits *Dying of Laughter* and *Common Wealth*. The only consolation, a meagre one in truth, was a reward for special effects at the Goyas, Spain's equivalent of the Academy Awards. Thankfully, the film is at least available with English subtitles on DVD in both America and Europe. The Spanish release, in particular, boasts a flawless transfer.

23   The 'Europeanisation' of American westerns is discernible as early as 1966, when films like *Return of the Seven*, which was shot in Spain, and *Ride Beyond Vengeance* displayed heightened levels of violence. The exaggerated style, extravagant brutality, characteristic cynicism and settings of Euro-westerns marked both exploitation films (*The Desperados*, *The Scavengers*, *Macho Callahan*) and star-driven studio productions (*Villa Rides*, *100 Rifles*), while their European experiences weighed heavily on the further films of Clint Eastwood (*Hang 'Em High*, *Two Mules for Sister Sara*, *Joe Kidd*, *High Plains Drifter*) and Lee Van Cleef (*Barquero*, *Captain Apache*, *El Condor*). Even John Wayne's *Big Jake* (1971) appeared to jump on the bandwagon, with conspicuously bloody action scenes and a poncho-clad Richard Boone leading perhaps the vilest villains the Duke had ever faced. Some of the most blatant imitations were predominantly British productions, such as *A Town Called Bastard*, *Hannie Caulder*, *The Hunting Party* (all 1971) and *Charley One-Eye* (1972) – "roast beef and Yorkshire pudding" westerns as opposed to spaghetti ones, joked the *Monthly Film Bulletin* – all of which bring together black humour, squalor and stylised brutality with crudely constructed allegories and allusions. As for *The Wild Bunch* (1969), the arguments for and against the Italian influence on the ultimate American western of the Sixties are too finely balanced for a conclusion to be reached, although Peckinpah scholars report the existence of a memo from the film's producer, Phil Feldman, advising the director to view the 'Dollars' trilogy as a benchmark of cinematic savagery. In addition, Sergio Leone claimed, "Peckinpah said – when there was the debate about which of us had influenced the other – that he would never have existed without me… I'm convinced Peckinpah would never have been able to do *The Wild Bunch* without me." Given Leone's tendency to self-aggrandize, however, a pinch of salt is required here.

24   When it first distributed the 'Dollars' films, United Artists explicitly portrayed the Man with No Name – as its marketing department 'christened' Clint Eastwood's character – as "a James Bond of the West".

above: This German promo for **Keoma** plunders the artwork from **Once Upon a Time in the West**'s Italian poster.

opposite:
Wild man Klaus Kinski was disdainful of most of the films he appeared in, but still deigned to appear in more than 20 Euro-westerns. He steals his few scenes in **For a Few Dollars More** as a twitchy, hair-triggered hunchback.

Sergio Leone's **For a Few Dollars More** was the great leap forward for Italian westerns: As bounty hunter Monco, Clint Eastwood models his poncho with panache (*right* and *below*) while Gian Maria Volonté redefines villainy as the unhinged, drug-addled Indio (*top*).

Franco Nero uses religion as a crutch at the audacious conclusion of Sergio Corbucci's **Django** (*below*). Numerous other films were retitled to reflect its success, especially in Germany – see the lobby card (*above*) for the Anthony Steffen vehicle **A Name That Cried Revenge**.

opposite:
Sergio Leone felt that women only cluttered the scenery in westerns, yet in **Once Upon a Time in the West** he placed Claudia Cardinale at the heart of his epic adult fairy tale.

An ALBERTO GRIMALDI Production

LEE VAN CLEEF
WILLIAM BERGER

"sabata"

TECHNICOLOR®
TECHNISCOPE®
United Artists
Entertainment from Transamerica Corporation

GP

above:
A bit-part heavy in Hollywood, Lee Van Cleef built on his roles in the 'Dollars' films to become an Italian western icon. In Gianfranco Parolini's **Sabata**, he used Colonel Mortimer as a model for one of his biggest post-Leone successes.

opposite:
Support for Lee Van Cleef came from Linda Veras (*top*) and William Berger (*bottom*), as the dashing, duplicitous Banjo.

below:
Aldo Canti contributed to the acrobatic action scenes that characterised Parolini's westerns.

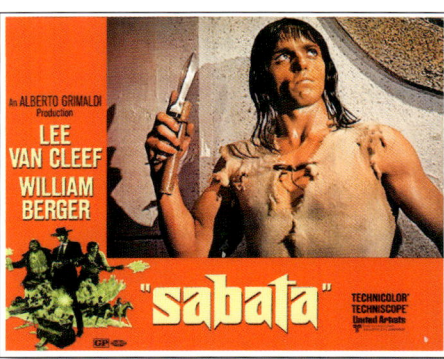

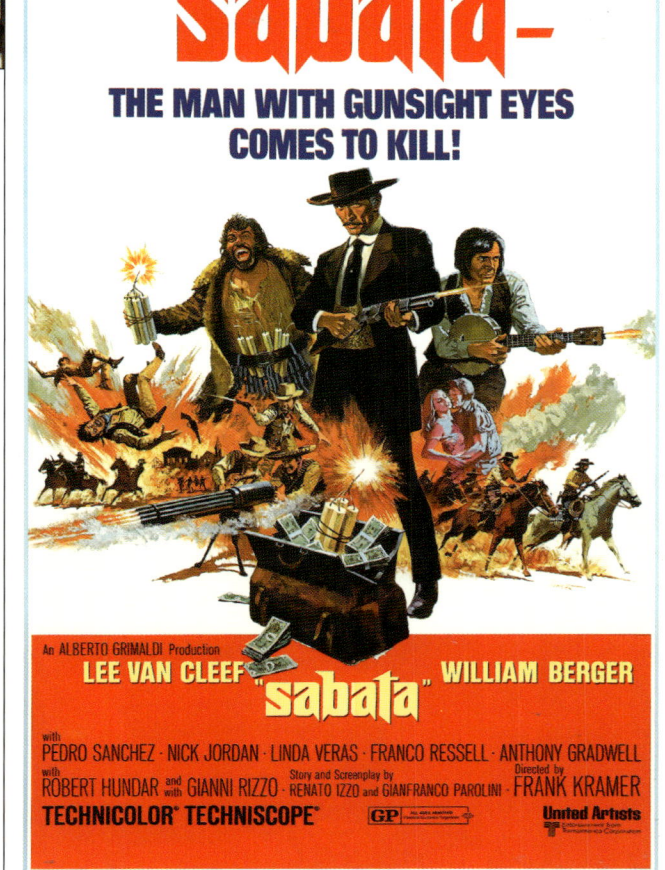

above: Terence Hill, who by the early Seventies was a giant of the genre, prepares to cut an opponent down to size in the playful yet poignant **My Name Is Nobody**.

opposite: Strength in diversity: numerous Euro-westerns veer off the beaten track. **They Call Me Trinity** (*top*) and **Trinity Is Still my Name** (*bottom*) successfully incorporated slapstick, while **Django the Bastard** (*centre*) was the best of a handful of horror hybrids.

above:
How to get ahead in a revolution without really trying: Franco Nero doesn't take setbacks too seriously as a carefree Swedish mercenary in **Compañeros**, one of Sergio Corbucci's self-styled 'Zapata' westerns.

below:
José Bodalo (in the red jacket) co-stars in **Compañeros** as a faux guerrilla general.

Few actresses were given a chance to shine in spaghetti westerns – Linda Veras was among those who grasped their opportunities with gusto, usually playing a blonde with avaricious ambitions.

SABATA

left: Italian locandina for **A Gun for a Hundred Graves**, a vehicle for the boyish Peter Lee Lawrence, who died (by his own hand, by most accounts) aged just 29.

below: US lobby card for **Return of Sabata**.

bottom: Tony Anthony as the sardonic, sightless adventurer on the trail of 50 kidnapped women in **Blindman**.

US and German promotional material for **Day of Anger**, which paired two of the genre's most bankable stars – Lee Van Cleef and Giuliano Gemma – at the height of their popularity; note the baroque design of the town saloon (*bottom*).

East meets western: **Red Sun** (*top*) reflected the vogue for things oriental in the early Seventies, with Toshiro Mifune joining Charles Bronson and a multi-national cast, while Mifune's contemporary Tatsuya Nakadai played the mixed-race villain of **Today It's Me... Tomorrow You!** (*above*).

ght: Lucio Fulci's **Massacre Time** was saddled with an even more exploitative title for its American release.

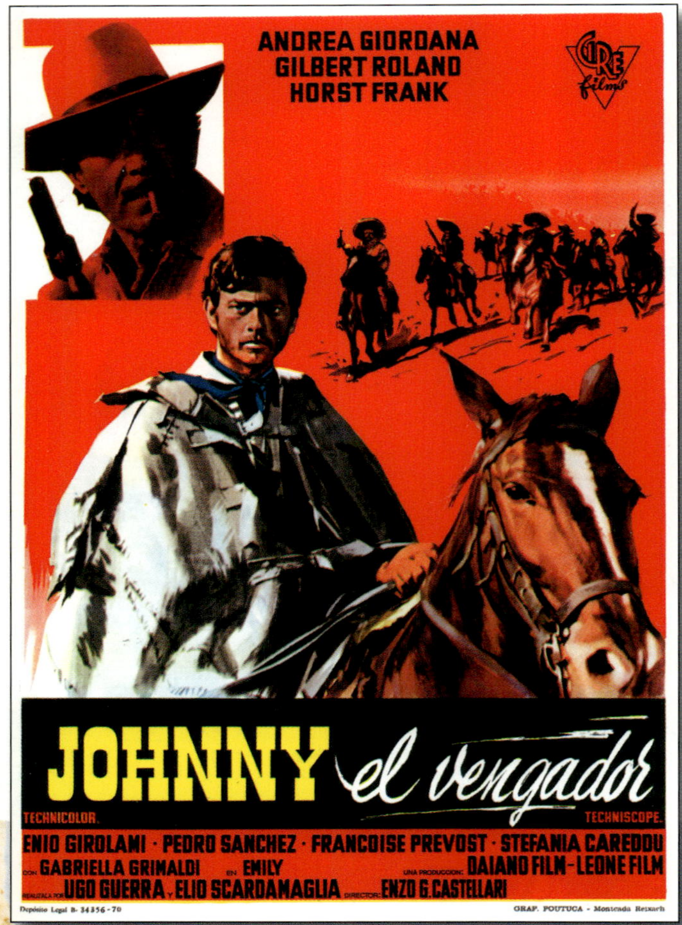
ANDREA GIORDANA
GILBERT ROLAND
HORST FRANK
JOHNNY el vengador
TECHNICOLOR.
TECHNISCOPE.
ENIO GIROLAMI · PEDRO SANCHEZ · FRANCOISE PREVOST · STEFANIA CAREDDU
CON GABRIELLA GRIMALDI EN EMILY
UNA PRODUCCION DAIANO FILM - LEONE FILM
REALIZADA POR UGO GUERRA Y ELIO SCARDAMAGLIA DIRECTOR ENZO G. CASTELLARI

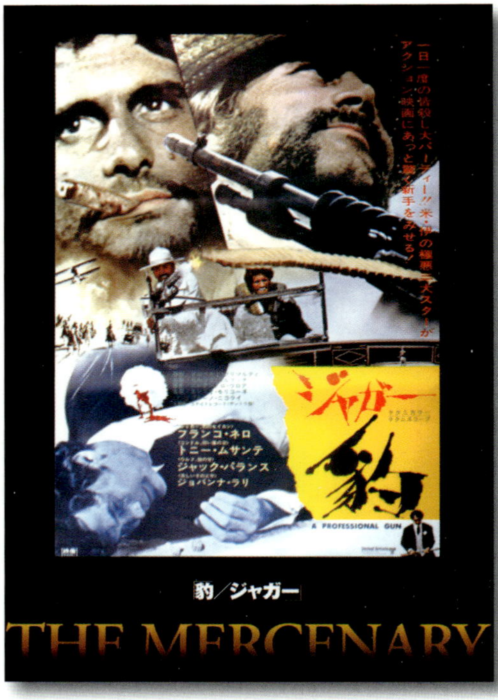
ジャガー
豹
フランコ・ネロ
トニー・ムサンテ
ジャック・パランス
ジョバンナ・ラリ
A PROFESSIONAL GUN
豹／ジャガー
THE MERCENARY

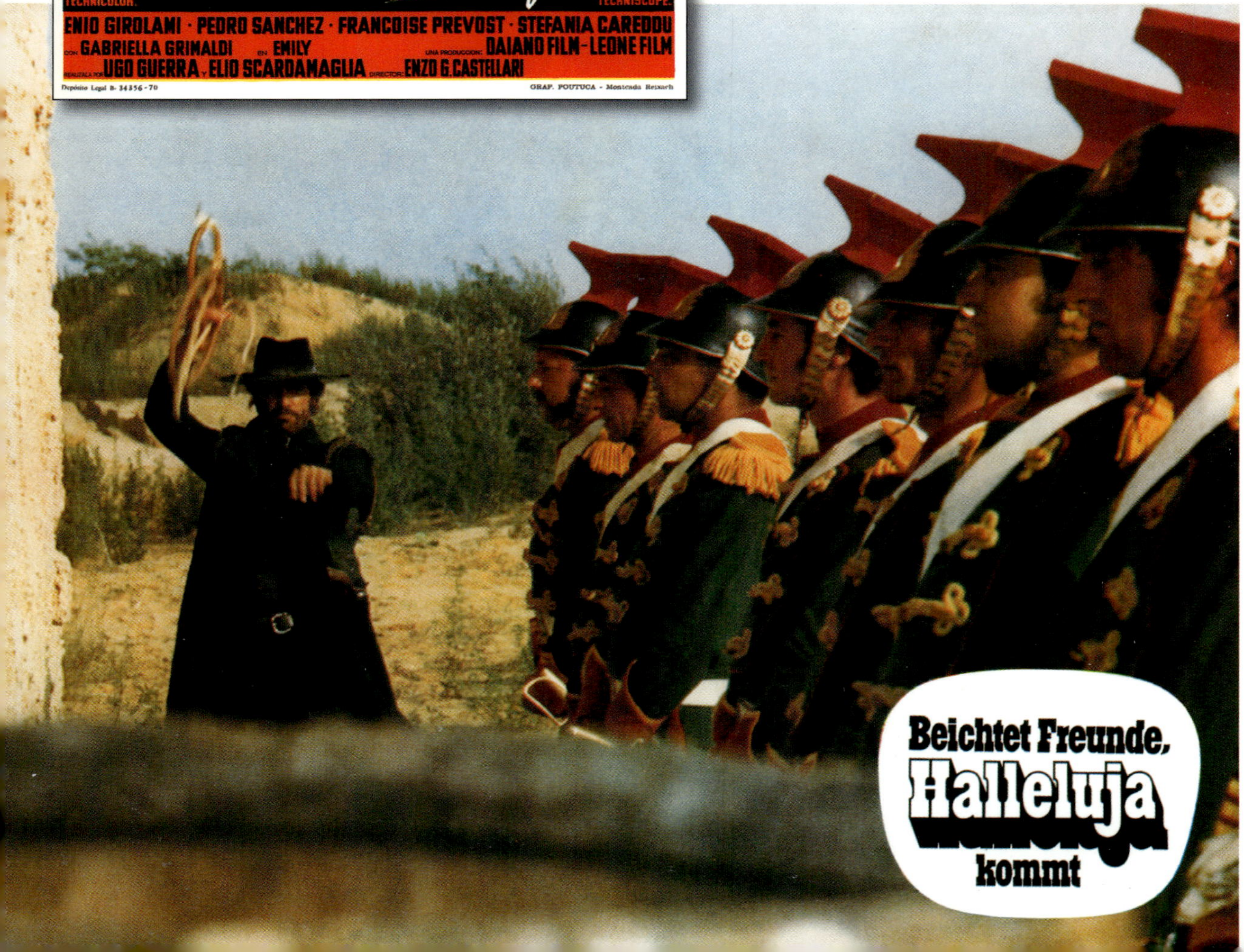
Beichtet Freunde,
Halleluja
kommt

opposite top left:
Spanish poster for **Johnny Hamlet**, Enzo Castellari's stab at transposing Shakespeare to the West.

opposite top right:
Japanese artwork for Sergio Corbucci's **A Professional Gun**.

opposite bottom:
George Hilton – a Uruguayan expat who found his niche in lightweight westerns – whips a contingent of Austrian soldiers into shape in Giuliano Carnimeo's Tex Avery-inspired **The Return of Hallelujah**.

this page:
There are two types of western in the world – those that innovate, like **The Good, the Bad and the Ugly** (*right*), with its perfectly realised Machiavellian protagonists and pitch-black wit, and those that follow the same picaresque pattern, like Enzo Castellari's **Kill Them All and Come Back Alone** (*below*), which borrows from **The Dirty Dozen** to boot.

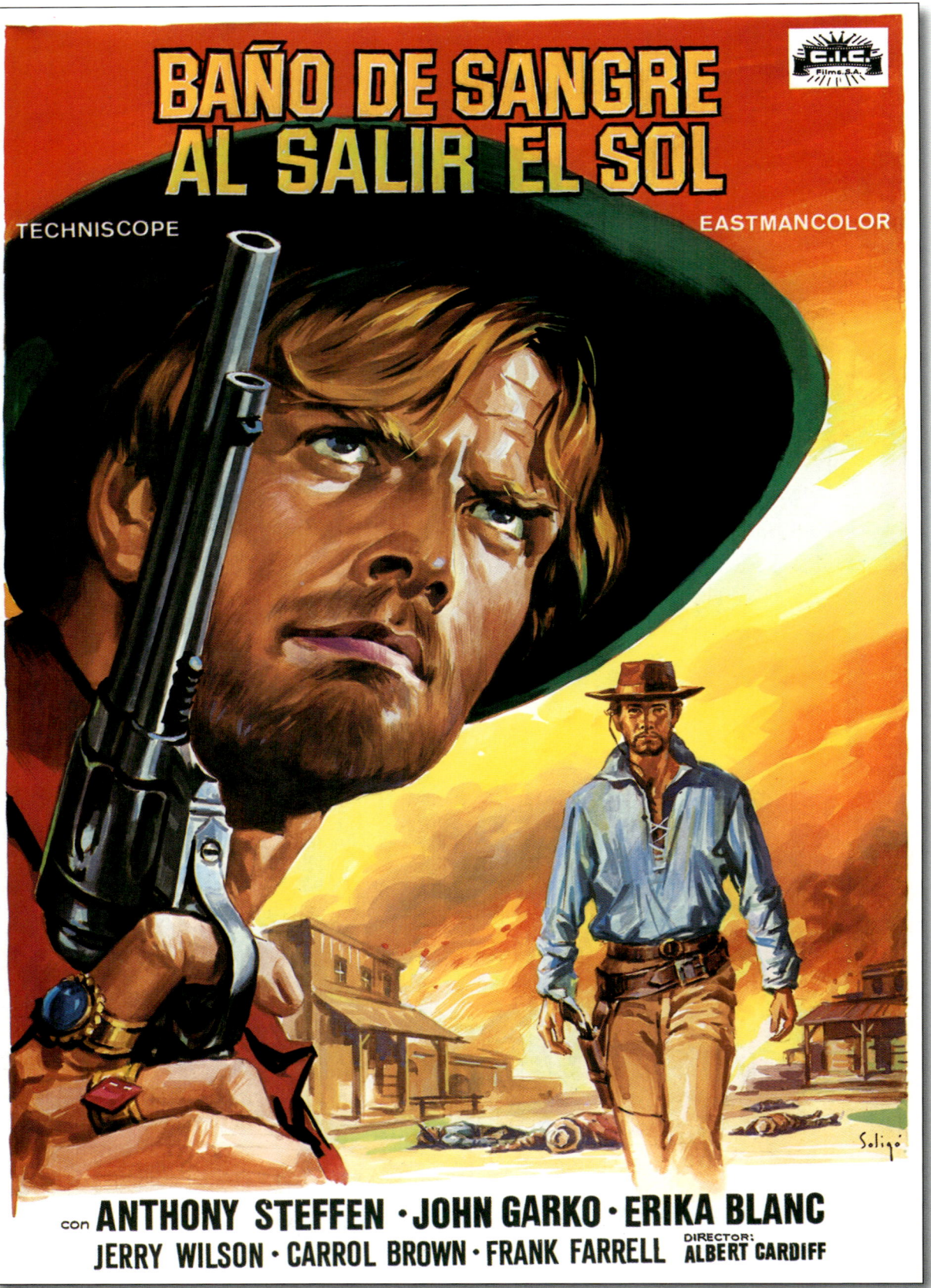

Brothers at war: Alberto Cardone's **Blood at Sundown**, starring Anthony Steffen and Gianni Garko, was one of many Italian westerns to exploit the Cain and Abel motif.

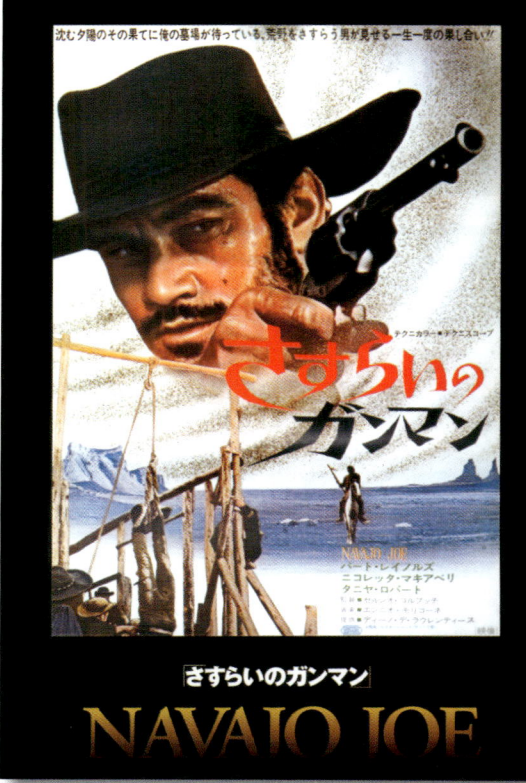

above: Aldo Sambrell, possessor of another of the genre's great faces, as Duncan, the halfbreed antagonist of **Navajo Joe**.

top: Pierre Brice and Lex Barker in **Apaches' Last Battle**, one of the German Karl May adaptations that helped establish Eurowesterns as a viable commercial proposition.

middle right: Gordon Mitchell's fierce features – shown here in **Beyond the Law** – enlivened more than thirty westerns.

bottom right: US poster for **Deaf Smith & Johnny Ears**, Anthony Quinn's only fully fledged Italian western.

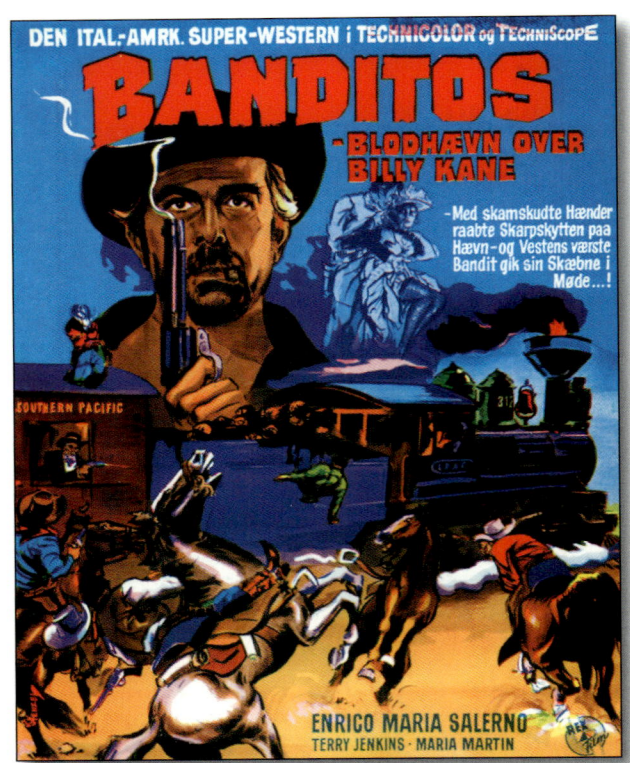

Two exemplary revenge westerns: **Bandidos** (*top left*) and **Black Jack** (*above*).

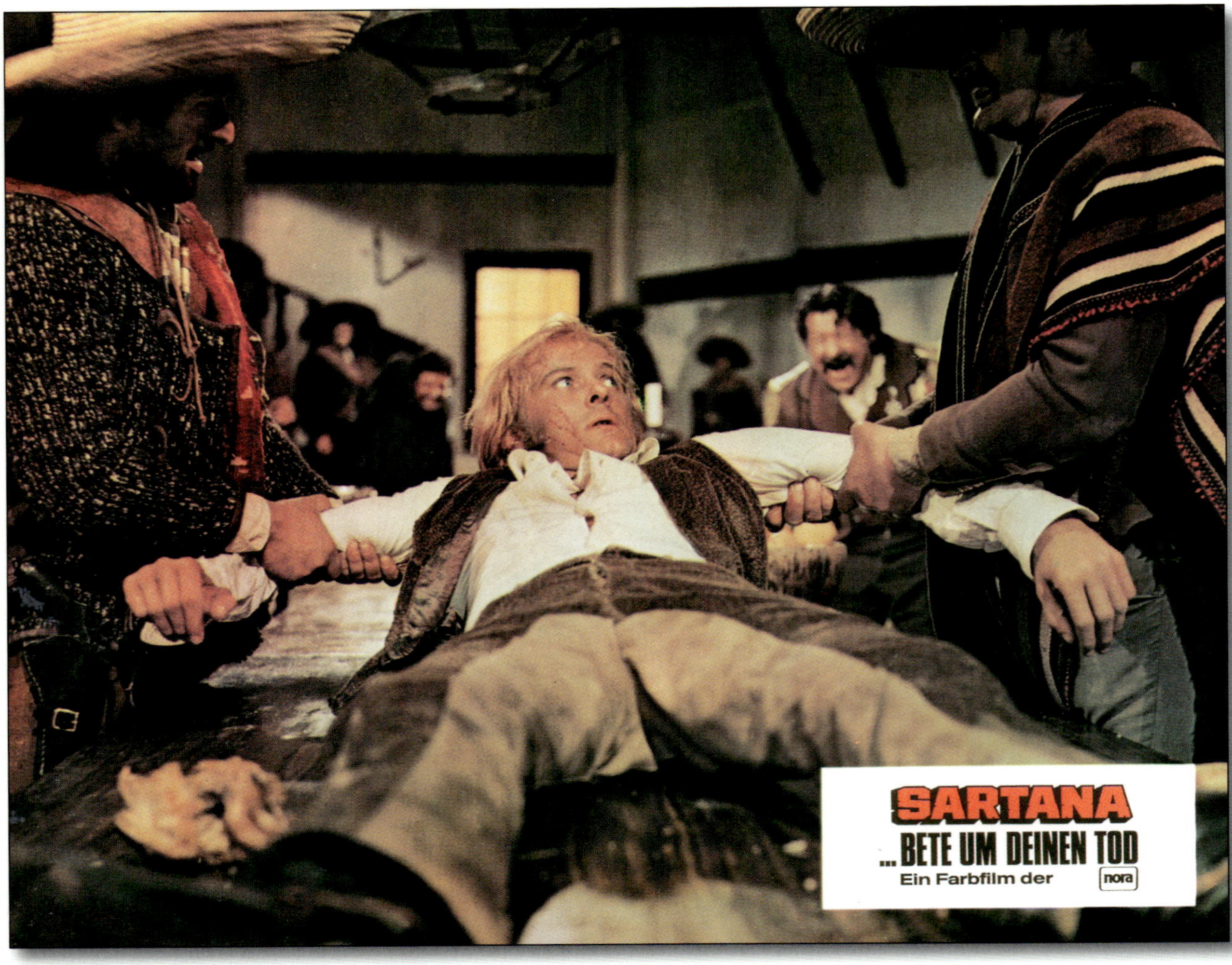

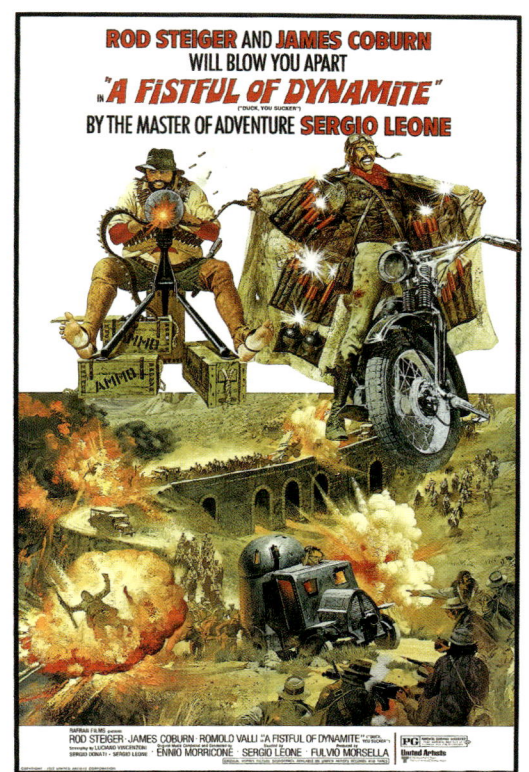

left and below: US artwork for Leone's final western, the undervalued **A Fistful of Dynamite**, which countered the exuberance of other political films.

opposite bottom: The treacherous Lasky – a role tailor-made for William Berger – falls foul of Tampico's gang in Parolini's **If You Meet Sartana, Pray for Your Death** and (*this page bottom*) Gianni Garko, cool, cunning and controlled, as the sinister anti-hero of the same film, which set yet another franchise in motion.

above: Spanish promo reusing early artwork for **A Fistful of Dollars**.

top left: US poster for **A Minute to Pray, a Second to Die** (heavily cut on its American release).

above: Angel face: Spanish artwork for **A Sky Full of Stars for a Roof**, one of many vehicles for Italian idol Giuliano Gemma, although here he looks more like Robert Woods.

opposite bottom: Nieves Navarro, aka Susan Scott, as the widow with burly ranch hands at her bidding in **The Big Gundown**.

The Euro-western was a haven for unsung American actors in search of the sweet life:
Tony Anthony (*top*) may have dressed like Eastwood but, as this shot from **Shoot First, Laugh Last** shows, he was far more self-effacing; while Brett Halsey (*below*) typically played brooding avengers, as in **The Wrath of God** (Halsey later chronicled his exploits as an expat – and those of his contemporaries – in a lurid novel).

above: Lee Van Cleef in an atypical role as a genial outlaw who gradually renounces crime in the tongue-in-cheek **Beyond the Law**. (Bud Spencer, sans beard, is second from the right.)
below: Sending up all the self-serving gringo mercenaries in Sergio Corbucci films, George Hilton (*left*) types up his contract before agreeing to aid embattled revolutionary Roberto Camardiel (*right*) in Giuliano Carnimeo's **The Return of Hallelujah**.

POLI FILMS MUNDIALES, S. A. presenta a

PREPARA TU ATAUD... VUELVE DJANGO

¡ES EL VERDUGO DEL OESTE!

Estrellas:
TERENCE HILL y **HORST FRANK**

¡EL MAS DESALMADO PISTOLERO DEL OESTE EN EXPLOSIVAS AVENTURAS!

¡TRAE EN SU CORAZON EL FUEGO DE LA VENGANZA Y EN SUS OJOS LA FRIALDAD DE LA MUERTE!

EN EASTMANCOLOR

Dirección de **FERDINANDO BALDI**

opposite top:
Spanish artwork for **Viva Django**, one of the many "sequels" to **Django** (at least this one had the same writer and cinematographer – plus Terence Hill trying his damnedest to look like Franco Nero).

opposite bottom:
From left to right: James Daly, Tetsuro Tamba, Peter Graves, Bud Spencer and Nino Castelnuovo enlisted in **The Five Man Army**, a semi-political western co-written by Dario Argento and produced by Italo Zingarelli before he hit the jackpot with the 'Trinity' films.

top left:
Spanish pressbook for **Boot Hill**, the final instalment in Giuseppe Colizzi's carnivalesque Hill/Spencer trilogy.

below:
Carlo Lizzani, a writer/director with roots in neorealism and Resistance dramas, contributed the striking **Requiescant** (aka **Kill and Pray**) a political allegory starring Lou Castel as an unconventional gunfighter and notorious provocateur Pier Paolo Pasolini in a supporting role as a militant priest.

US promotional material for Giuseppe Colizzi's **God Forgives... I Don't!** (*above* and *right*), a blockbuster in Italy due in great part to the chemistry of Terence Hill and Bud Spencer.

below: German lobby card for **The Great Silence**, proof that Sergio Corbucci was at his best when he took the genre seriously.

opposite: The grim countenance of Anthony Steffen, the dour Brazilian-Italian leading man dubbed "the poor man's Clint Eastwood" by some critics, is captured well in this Spanish poster for **A Few Dollars for Django**.

above:
Spanish lobby card for Rafael Romero Marchent's offbeat coming-of-age tale **Clumsy Hands**, which mixes melodrama with motifs from horror and martial arts movies.

left:
The Winnetou films inspired other German ersatz westerns in the early Sixties – **Massacre at Marble City** was one of three to star American bodybuilder Brad Harris (with pistol), here squaring up to Mario Adorf.

opposite:
Belgian poster for the tragic western **Cowards Don't Pray**, sold in some territories as a 'Django' movie. It was directed by Mario Siciliano in the style of an Alberto Cardone film – Siciliano produced all of Cardone's most interesting works.

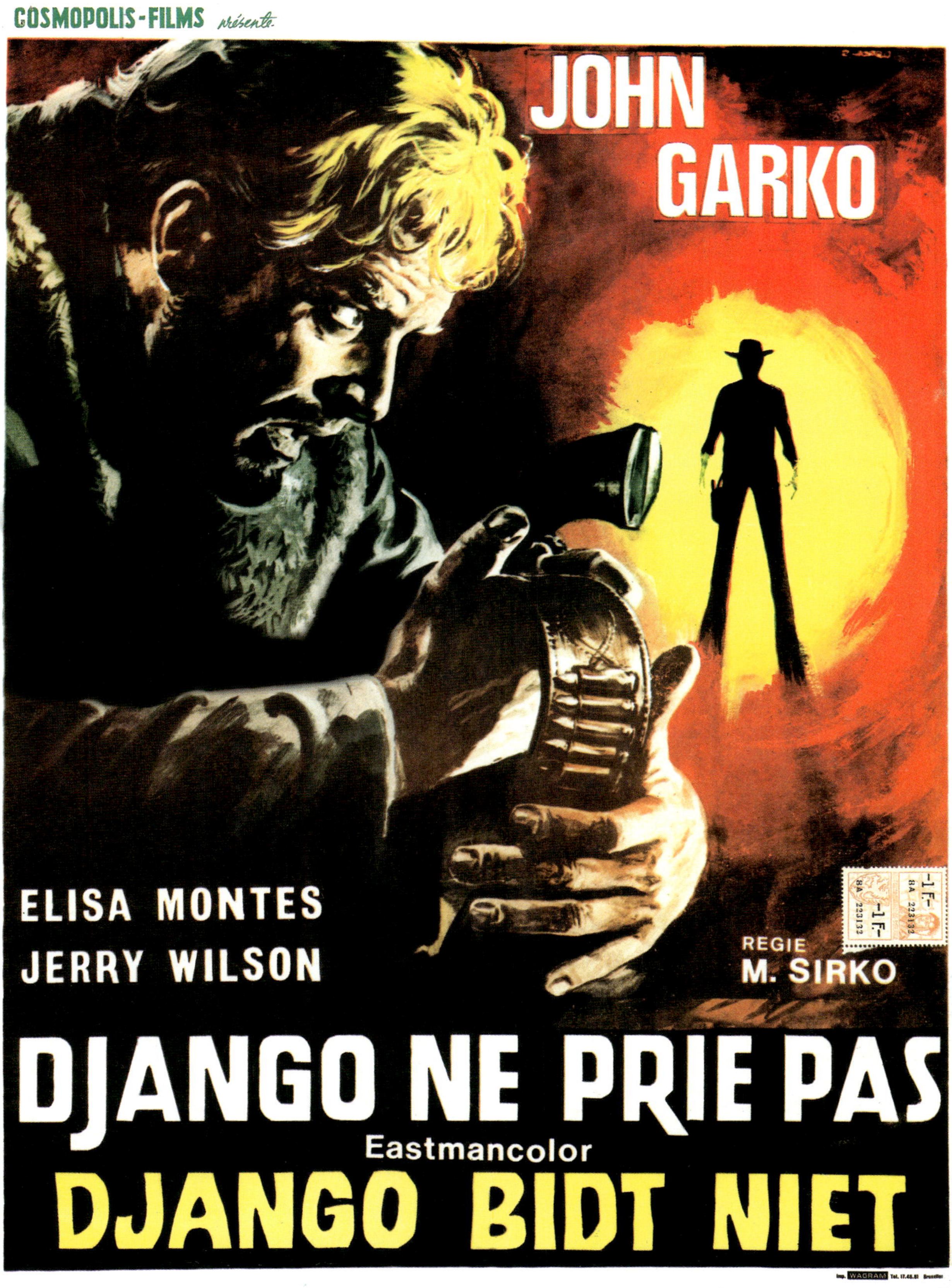
COSMOPOLIS-FILMS présente
JOHN GARKO
ELISA MONTES
JERRY WILSON
REGIE
M. SIRKO
DJANGO NE PRIE PAS
Eastmancolor
DJANGO BIDT NIET
Imp. WAGRAM Tel. 17.48.81 Bruxelles

Incandescent Belgian artwork for **Have a Nice Funeral, Sartana Will Pay** that emphasises the title character's devilish demeanour.

Appendix 1

Who's Who In Euro-Westerns

A Biographical A-Z

The Euro-western cast its net far and wide, employing a dizzying and diverse array of talent on both sides of the camera. This is not a comprehensive list, but all the major players are represented, along with the most significant of the 'second-rank' performers, technicians and other artists who constituted the bedrock of the genre's success. Entries are arranged by most familiar name first, whether this is the person's real name or a pseudonym, with birth names and/or other 'pseudonyms' in square brackets, followed by place and date of birth where known. Entries for on-screen performers are accompanied by illustrations to aid identification.

The vagaries of film credits – especially on low-budget and/or multinational co-productions – are notorious. Quite often, prints for different territories had alternative credits, whether to abide by union rules or justify tax breaks. It was not uncommon with Euro-westerns, for example, for directors, composers and cinematographers from one country to be credited for work undertaken by their counterparts from another. In other cases, credits were minimal to the point of being meaningless, not to say misleading (this is even before one begins the process of deciphering pseudonyms). In addition, each production or distribution company often credited their own prints to suit their needs, making it difficult to state that a certain performer is uncredited for a particular film – they may well be credited on a print that no one has easy access to. We should be grateful, then, for the diligent efforts of enthusiasts who have checked film prints, rather than credits, to confirm actors' presence and identify their roles. Much of this work – which is an ongoing process – is accessible via the Internet.

Key: act=actor; ad=assistant director; d=director; p=producer; w=writer

ADORF, MARIO
(Zurich, Switzerland. 1930-)
Stocky, Swiss-born character actor who began performing in the Fifties. With his fierce scowl and grandstanding tendencies, he thrived in villainous and eccentric supporting roles, snarling his way through a string of early German westerns before landing roles in a variety of Italian *filoni* and, occasionally, Hollywood productions, giving a pugnacious performance in Sam Peckinpah's *Major Dundee* (1965). (According to fellow actor Brad Harris, Adorf's Hollywood jaunt went to his head: "When we were working on a cowboy film in Prague [*Massacre at Marble City*], he had just finished working on *Dundee* and [the producers] sent him a telegram saying, 'Do we still have enough money for you?' They figured that if he had a part in an American film, he was automatically a big star. But he came back and he was like a diva.") Equally content in potboilers and prestige productions, he is immensely popular in Germany (he received a lifetime achievement award at the 2005 Munich Film Festival), and in recent years has alternated features with television work and theatre. His daughter is actress Stella Maria Adorf.
1961: *The Taste of Violence*. 1963: *Winnetou the Warrior*. 1964: *The Last Ride to Santa Cruz; Massacre at Marble City*. 1965: *Sunscorched*. 1968: *A Sky Full of Stars for a Roof*. 1969: *The Specialists*. 1970: *Deadlock*.

ALESSANDRONI, ALESSANDRO
(Rome, Italy. 1925 or 1933-)
One of the key figures in the development of Italian western music, although, remarkably, he had no formal musical training. A multi-instrumentalist, composer and choirmaster, his signature whistling skills, discovered by Nino Rota and first heard (in a western) in *A Fistful of Dollars*, became a hallmark of the genre. He also marshalled the unique vocal talents of the Cantori Moderni, a group of singers who performed on countless Italian soundtracks in the Sixties and Seventies. (Its most distinctive members were sopranos Edda Dell'Orso, whose sublime tones are best represented in *Once Upon a Time in the West*, and Gianna Spagnulo, the spine-tingling voice on the *Navajo Joe* soundtrack, and tenor Ettore 'Raoul' Lovecchio, who sang many theme songs.) Eventually he decided to write his own scores: "I had given [other composers] lots of ideas for many years. They got the same money in one month that I got in one year of working hard. So I changed – better late than never." The first western score he composed by himself, *El Puro*, is an attractive anthology of spaghetti motifs.
(As composer): 1969: *El Puro*. 1971: *Hands Up, Dead Man! You're Under Arrest; Zorro, the Mask of Vengeance*. 1974: *The Crazy Bunch*. 1975: *White Fang and the Gold Diggers; White Fang and the Hunter*.

ÁLVAREZ, ÁNGEL
[Ángel Álvarez Fernández]
(Madrid, Spain. 1906-1983)
Plump character actor and occasional screenwriter with a doleful countenance, one of the most prolific performers in Spanish cinema history. In westerns he played weather-beaten bartenders, bankers, father figures and the like. Best known to genre fans as Nathaniel, the put-upon saloonkeeper in *Django*.
1955: *The Judgement of the Coyote*. 1960: *Juanito*. 1962: *Zorro, the Avenger*. 1964: *The Return of Clay Stone; Three Dollars of Lead*. 1966: *Django; Navajo Joe*. 1967: *Fury of Johnny Kid*. 1968: *A Professional Gun; Requiem for a Gringo*. 1969: *Cemetery Without Crosses; The Price of Power*. 1970: *Adios, Sabata*. 1972: *A Reason to Live, a Reason to Die; Tedeum*. 1973: *Yankee Dudler*.

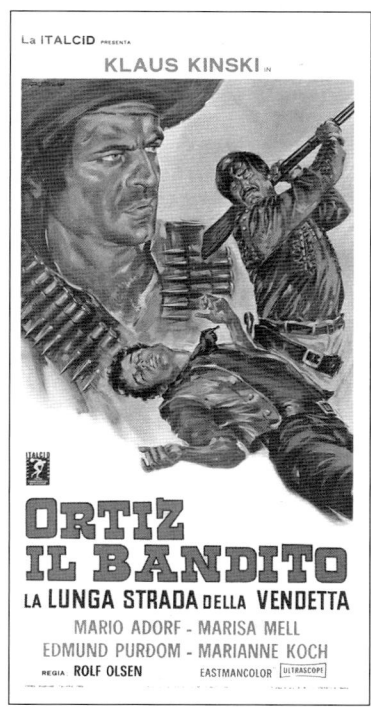

above: Italian poster for **The Last Ride to Santa Cruz**, featuring the likeness of **Mario Adorf** (*top right*).

above: **Ángel Álvarez**.

AMATI, EDMONDO
(Italy. 1920-2002)
Producer. Commercial films were Amati's forte – he had a hand in most popular genres in the Sixties and Seventies, with a special fondness for horror films. His most lucrative westerns were a pair of vehicles for Franco and Ciccio.
1964: *$5,000 on the Ace; Two Gangsters in the Wild West*. 1965: *$100,000 for Ringo; Two Sergeants of General Custer*. 1966: *Django Shoots First; Fort Yuma Gold*. 1967: *Any Gun Can Play*. 1968: *Gatling Gun; Kill Them All and Come Back Alone*. 1973: *The Three Musketeers of the West*. 1975: *White Fang to the Rescue*.

AMENDOLA, MARIO
['Irving Jacobs']
(Genova, Italy. 1910-1993)
Writer/director. Prolific writer of B-movies and a specialist in comedies, he also contributed to a handful of westerns, the best being *The Great Silence*. He was a long-time creative partner of Bruno Corbucci, with whom he created the enormously popular anti-heroic policeman Nico Giraldi, played by Tomas Milian in a series of rough-hewn Seventies comedies. His nephew is actor Ferruccio Amendola.
1959: *The Sheriff* (w); *Terror of Oklahoma* (d). 1963: *The Sword of Zorro* (w). 1964: *Behind the Mask of Zorro* (w). 1966: *A Fistful of Songs* (w); *Kill or Be Killed* (w). 1967: *Days of Violence* (w); *Hate for Hate* (w). 1968: *The Great Silence* (w); *Killer Adios* (w); *Shoot, Gringo, Shoot* (w); *Three Silver Dollars* (w/d). 1972: *Bandits* (w); *Panhandle Calibre 38* (w). 1973: *Bad Kids of the West* (w). 1975: *The White, the Yellow and the Black* (w).

ANCHÓRIZ, LEO
[Leopardo de Anchóriz Fustel]
(Almería, Spain. 1932-1987)

Actor. He studied painting and worked in theatre before entering films in the late Fifties, quickly earning good notices. Broad nosed and tough looking, he was typecast as a villain in westerns (most successfully in *Seven Guns for the MacGregors*), although he showed a humorous side when permitted. He later moved into television and hosted a quiz show, abandoning acting altogether in the late Seventies.
1965: *Finger on the Trigger*. 1966: *Seven Guns for the MacGregors*. 1967: *Up the MacGregors*. 1968: *Kill Them All and Come Back Alone; One Dollar Too Many*. 1969: *The Magnificent Bandits; Vengeance Is Mine*. 1972: *What Am I Doing in the Middle of a Revolution?* 1973: *The Three Musketeers of the West*. 1975: *Cipolla Colt*.

ANTHONY, TONY
[Roger Petitto]
(Clarksburg, USA. 1937-)
Actor. Unconventional American leading man whose anti-heroes in the 'Stranger' films and *Blindman* are as ignoble as they come, but, equally, more vulnerable and approachable than the majority of their peers. The son of

a coal miner, he studied drama and enrolled at the New York Actors' Studio in the Fifties. Stage work was followed by two typical 'youth' dramas of the early Sixties, both of which he co-wrote and starred in. Travelling to Italy, he landed some disparate supporting roles before emerging as one of the genre's most idiosyncratic protagonists. He was involved in the writing and production of most of his films, starred in a semi-autobiographical road movie, *Come Together* (1968), and made a comeback in the early Eighties with the 3-D western *Comin' at Ya!* (he has recently overseen its re-release). He now owns a medical photo-equipment company, although he did co-produce a spaghetti-style TV western in 1998, *Dollar for the Dead*, shot in Spain by his long-time friend and *Comin' at Ya!* co-star Gene Quintano.
1967: *For a Dollar in the Teeth; Shoot First, Laugh Last* (act/w). 1968: *The Silent Stranger* (act/w/p). 1971: *Blindman* (act/w/p). 1975: *Get Mean* (act/w/p). 1981: *Comin' at Ya!* (act/w/p). 1998: *Dollar for the Dead* (p).

ARDISSON, GEORGE
[Giorgio Ardisson]
(Turin, Italy. 1931-)

A former boxer, he played a small role in Fellini's *Juliet of the Spirits* (1965) but made his mark as a tough, taciturn leading man and occasional villain in pepla, Zorro films, espionage adventures and westerns. He was reportedly in the running to play Ramon in *A Fistful of Dollars*, but performed mainly in second-rank productions. He made a sullen Sartana in *Django Against Sartana*.
1962: *Zorro at the Court of Spain*. 1964: *Massacre at Grand Canyon*. 1968: *A Man Called Amen; May God Forgive You – I Won't; Zorro the Fox*. 1970: *Chapagua's Gold; Django Against Sartana*.

ARGENTO, DARIO
(Rome, Italy. 1940-)
Italy's leading director of *giallo*/horror cinema was one of the first Italian critics to champion Sergio Leone and helped draft a story outline for *Once Upon a Time in the West* with Bernardo Bertolucci. "I would write on my own, then Bernardo would write on his own, then we would write together," Argento recalled in an article for the UK's *Guardian* newspaper in May 2009. "Once a week Sergio would come to see how we were getting on, and offer his thoughts. He was incredible at generating ideas. He made me realise the director should always be involved in some way with the screenwriting." He co-wrote two other westerns and is credited on some prints of *Cemetery Without Crosses*, though his involvement is denied by the film's director, Robert Hossein.
1968: *Once Upon a Time in the West; Today It's Me... Tomorrow You!* 1969: *Cemetery Without Crosses; The Five Man Army*.

BACALOV, LUIS ENRÍQUEZ
(San Martín, Argentina. 1933 or 1937-)
Composer/arranger. Classically trained, Bacalov modified his ambitions when he arrived in Italy in the early Sixties, making a living as an arranger of pop songs for the likes of Sergio Endrigo and Rita Pavone. He wrote his first film score for Damiano Damiani's *The Empty Canvas* (1963) and later composed the invigorating 'Mexican' music for the same director's *A Bullet for the General*. His other key westerns include *Sugar Colt, Django* (which contains several pieces also used in *A Bullet...*) and *A Man Called Noon*, for which he created some exceptionally haunting themes. He later earned an Oscar for *Il postino* (1994), which he only scored when Ennio Morricone became unavailable, and pieces by him are scattered throughout the *Kill Bill* films, notably the beautiful theme to *The Grand Duel* used in Vol. 1.
1966: *A Bullet for the General; Django; Sugar Colt*. 1967: *The Greatest Robbery in the West*. 1968: *One for All*. 1969: *Death on a High Hill; In the Name of the Father; The Price of Power*. 1970: *Chapagua's Gold*. 1971: *His Name Was King*. 1972: *Can Be Done... Amigo; The Grand Duel; The Great Treasure Hunt*. 1973: *Halleluja to Vera Cruz; The Man Called Noon*.

BALCÁZAR, ALFONSO
['Al Bagran']
(Barcelona, Spain. 1926-1993)
Producer/writer/director. With a background in the leather trade, Balcázar was a mixture of entrepreneur and artisan. In 1951, he formed a production company, PC Balcázar, specialising in modest commercial films, and later co-financed numerous westerns with

Italian companies. Many films were also shot at his 'Esplugas City' studio, built in 1964 near Barcelona (the set was destroyed deliberately for the fiery climax to one of his Seventies westerns, *Now They Call Him Sacramento*) and he also set up a distribution company, Filmax. In later years he directed low-budget sexploitation films under the name 'Al Bagran'.
1964: $5,000 On the Ace (w/p/d). 1965: The Man from Oklahoma (w/p); The Man Who Came to Kill (w/p/d); $100,000 for Ringo (w); A Pistol for Ringo (p); The Return of Ringo (p); Sunscorched (w/p); Two Sergeants of General Custer (w/p); Viva Carrancho (w/p/d); Why Go On Killing? (p). 1966: Dynamite Jim (w/d); Five Giants from Texas (w); Four Dollars of Revenge (p); Seven Guns for Timothy (w/p); Yankee (w). 1967: Clint the Stranger (w/p/d). 1968: Sartana Does Not Forgive (p/d). 1969: The Law of Violence (w/p). 1972: Now They Call Him Sacramento (w/p/d); The Return of Clint the Stranger (w/p/d); Watch Out Gringo, Sabata Will Return (w/p – credited as director on some versions). 1973: Karate, Fists and Beans (w/p).

BALCÁZAR, JAIME JESÚS
(Barcelona, Spain. 1934-)
Writer/producer/director. Younger brother of Alfonso – the two are frequently confused in credits and filmographies. Among the films he directed for his brother's company was the superior Robert Woods vehicle *Four Dollars of Revenge*. Woods remembers him as "by far the more sympathetic" of the Balcázar brothers, "a nice young guy, willing to take suggestions".
1965: The Man from Oklahoma (d); Sunscorched (d). 1966: Four Dollars of Revenge (d); Thompson 1880 (w). 1967: Gentleman Killer (w); Red Blood, Yellow Gold (w). 1968: Sartana Does Not Forgive (w). 1969: Twice a Judas (w).

BALDANELLO, GIANFRANCO
['Frank G. Carrol(l)']
(Merano, Italy. 1928-)
Director. Son of character actor Emilio, he was assistant director from 1952 on some 70 films and directed second unit on a few *pepla*. From the mid-Sixties he began making B-movies, most of them forgettable save for one exceptionally nihilistic western, *Black Jack*, a revenge tale partially shot in Israel.
1962: Zorro at the Court of Spain (ad). 1963: Zorro and the Three Musketeers (ad). 1964: Buffalo Bill, Hero of the Far West (ad). 1965: Gold Train (w/d). 1966: El Rojo (ad); Kill Johnny Ringo! (d). 1968: Black Jack (w/d); This Man Can't Die (w/d). 1973: A Colt in the Hand of the Devil (w/d); The Son of Zorro (w/d). 1974: Blood River (w/d). 1975: The Cry of the Wolf (d).

BALDASSARRE, RAF
['Ralph/Raf/Rajan Baldwin';
'Ralph Baldassar']
(Rome, Italy. 1932-1995)

Shifty-looking Italian supporting player who often portrayed volatile characters. He was especially exuberant as the devious Mexican army officer in *Blindman*.
1962: The Shadow of Zorro. 1963: The Magnificent Three; The Sign of the Coyote. 1964: A Fistful of Dollars; Seven from Texas. 1965: Hands of a Gunfighter; Outlaw of Red River; The Relentless Four; Seven Hours of Gunfire; Son of Jesse James; The Three from Colorado. 1966: El Rojo; Legacy of the Incas. 1967: For a Dollar in the Teeth; A Man and a Colt; Shoot First, Laugh Last. 1968: Between God, the Devil and a Winchester; Dead Men Don't Count!; The Great Silence; A Gun for a Hundred Graves; A Name That Cried Revenge; One for All; A Professional Gun; The Silent Stranger. 1969: Garringo; Quinto: Fighting Proud. 1970: And Sartana Kills Them All; Arizona. 1971: And the Crows Will Dig Your Grave; Blindman; Dig Your Grave Friend... Sabata's Coming; Doomsday; Four Pistols for Trinity; Hey Amigo! A Toast to Your Death. 1972: Prey of Vultures. 1975: Get Mean.

BALDI, FERDINANDO
['Ferdy/Free Baldwin'; 'Ted Kaplan']
(Cava dei Tirenni, Italy. 1927-2007)
Efficient director of action-oriented *pepla* and westerns, among them the excellent *Viva Django* and *The Forgotten Pistolero*. He teamed up with Tony Anthony for the delirious *Blindman* and equally overt but far less coherent *Get Mean*. They also contributed to a brief 3-D revival with *Comin' at Ya!* Baldi, who migrated to film from an academic milieu (he was a professor of literature), also foisted his own Hill and Spencer clones upon the public with the 'Carambola' films starring 'Smith and Coby' – Paul Smith and Antonio Cantafora.
1966: Texas Adios (w/d). 1967: Rita of the West (w/d); Viva Django (w/d). 1968: Hate Your Neighbour (w/d). 1969: The Forgotten Pistolero (w/d). 1971: Blindman (d). 1974: Carambola (w/d). 1975: The Crazy Adventures of Len and Coby (w/d); Get Mean (w/d). 1981: Comin' at Ya! (d).

BAND, ALBERT
['Alfredo Antonini']
(Paris, France. 1924-2002)
Writer/producer/director. Son of impressionist painter Max Band, who moved the family to America in the Forties. Albert's film career began in the editing suite before he became John Huston's personal production assistant. He directed a few low-budget films in Hollywood before relocating to Rome in 1960. He wrote and produced several westerns and *pepla* and directed *The Tramplers*, a dry run for *The Hellbenders*, co-writing and financing the latter for Sergio Corbucci. Back in America in the Seventies he specialised in exploitation films, and helped his son Charles launch the like-minded Empire Pictures in the early Eighties. Another son, Richard, is a composer.
1963: Gunfight at Red Sands (w/p). 1964: Massacre at Grand Canyon (w/p – Band also directed some footage). 1965: The Tramplers (w/p/d). 1967: The Hellbenders (w/p). 1968: A Minute to Pray, a Second to Die (w/p).

BARAGLI, NINO
(Rome, Italy. 1925-)
Editor. Although he worked repeatedly with Pasolini and also cut films for Fellini, Baragli's talents were truly tested by Leone from *The Good, the Bad and the Ugly* onwards. Like Eugenio Alabiso, with whom he often worked, and Roberto Cinquini, who cut *A Fistful of Dollars*, Baragli made a major if under-appreciated contribution to the Leone style and, consequently, to the Euro-western aesthetic in general.
1966: Django; The Good, the Bad and the Ugly; Seven Guns for the MacGregors. 1967: The Hellbenders; Rita of the West; Up the MacGregors. 1968: Once Upon a Time in the West. 1971: A Fistful of Dynamite; Lucky Johnny: Born in America. 1972: Sometimes Life Is Hard, Right Providence? 1973: My Name Is Nobody. 1975: A Genius, Two Partners and a Dupe.

BARBONI, ENZO
['E.B. Clucher']
(Rome, Italy. 1922-2002)
A war correspondent-turned-cameraman-turned-cinematographer (brother of DP Leonida Barboni), with a bold sense of colour and texture (see *Django* and *The Hellbenders*), Barboni is best known as writer/director of the 'Trinity' films, among the most financially successful Italian westerns – indeed, Italian films – of all time. (He signed these and most of his directed works as 'Clucher' – his mother's maiden name.) He made several further features with 'Trinity' stars Terence Hill and Bud Spencer, all highly popular, although his final film, *Sons of Trinity*, was a misguided and financially disastrous attempt to relaunch the famous franchise with unknown young actors.
1964: Bullets Don't Argue (ph – uncredited); Massacre at Grand Canyon (ph). 1966: The Bounty Killer (ph); Django (ph); Texas Adios (ph). 1967: The Hellbenders (ph); Rita of the West (ph); Viva Django (ph). 1968: A Long Ride from Hell (ph); A Name That Cried Revenge (ph); A Train for Durango (ph). 1969: The Five Man Army (ph). 1970: Chuck Mool (d); They Call Me Trinity (w/d). 1971: They Call Him Cemetery (w); Trinity Is Still My Name (w/d). 1972: Man of the East (w/d). 1987: Renegade (d). 1995: Sons of Trinity (d).

BARBOO, LUÍS
(Vigo, Spain. 1927-2001)

Fearsome-looking, well-built Spanish character actor distinguished by a prominent facial scar. He was a sportsman and circus artist before entering films as a stunt performer. As well as numerous westerns, he was a fixture in the Spanish horror boom of the early Seventies.
1964: Cavalry Charge; A Fistful of Dollars; Heroes of Fort Worth; Massacre at Fort Grant. 1965: A Coffin for the Sheriff; A Place Called Glory. 1966: The Bounty Killer; Kid Rodelo; Sugar Colt. 1967: The Big Gundown; Clint the Stranger; Gentleman Killer; God Forgives... I Don't!; Kitosch, The Man Who Came from the North; The Man Who Killed Billy the Kid; Rattler Kid. 1968: Between God, the Devil and a Winchester; Cowards Don't Pray; Dead Men Don't Count!; Killer Adios; A Name That Cried Revenge; One After the Other; One

Dollar Too Many; One for All; Ringo the Lone Rider. 1969: Alive or Preferably Dead; Vengeance Is Mine. 1970: Arizona; Cannon for Cordoba. 1971: Doc; Hands Up, Dead Man! You're Under Arrest; Hannie Caulder. 1972: The Call of the Wild. 1973: Three Supermen of the West; Yankee Dudler. 1974: Patience Has a Limit, We Don't. 1976: Potato Fritz. 1978: China 9, Liberty 37. 1981: Comin' at Ya!

BARKER, LEX
[Alexander Crichlow Barker Jr]
(Rye, USA. 1919-1973)

Actor. The brawny Tarzan star achieved heroic status in Germany in the Sixties for his rigid portrayal of Karl May's *übermensch*, Old Shatterhand, in several of the 'Winnetou' films, and also brought to life the author's Arabian adventurer, Kara Ben Nemsi. A Princeton alumnus from a well-to-do family, he was a legendary womaniser, his wives including actresses Arlene Dahl, Lana Turner and Carmen Cevera.
1962: The Treasure of Silver Lake. 1963: Winnetou the Warrior. 1964: Apaches' Last Battle; Last of the Renegades. 1965: Desperado Trail; A Place Called Glory; Pyramid of the Sun God; The Treasure of the Aztecs. 1966: Halfbreed; Who Killed Johnny Ringo? 1968: Winnetou and Shatterhand in the Valley of Death.

BARNES, WALTER
(Parkersburg, USA. 1918-1998)

Bulky American supporting player who worked in Europe throughout the Sixties as both actor and dubber. A professional football player before becoming an actor, he played ranchers and wagon-train bosses in 'Winnetou' films (he was especially popular with German audiences) and gave a powerful performance as ambitious bad guy Brokston in *The Big Gundown*.
1963: The Sign of Zorro; Winnetou the Warrior. 1964: Among Vultures. 1965: Duel at Sundown; Rampage at Apache Wells. 1966: Halfbreed. 1967: The Big Gundown; Clint the Stranger; The Greatest Robbery in the West. 1968: Garter Colt; The Moment to Kill.

BARRY, BARTA
[Bernabé Barta Barri]
(Budapest, Hungary. 1911-)

Actor. A former trapeze artist, he was discovered for the cinema by Ignacio Iquino, who appreciated his sinister Mittel-European bearing. A steady stream of roles as gangsters and other villains followed, and he made several westerns during the co-production boom. He was a favourite of Spain's commercial specialists, the likes of Iquino, the Romero Marchent brothers, Ramón Torrado and León Klimovsky.
1963: Gunfight at Red Sands. 1964: Cavalry Charge. 1965: Johnny West; Son of a Gunfighter. 1966: Savage Pampas. 1967: The Big Gundown; Custer of the West; Dynamite Joe; The Man Who Killed Billy the Kid. 1968: Dead Men Don't Count!; White Comanche. 1969: Garringo. 1970: Cannon for Cordoba; A Man Called Sledge. 1971: Bad Man's River; Red Sun. 1972: Pancho Villa. 1973: The Man Called Noon; Three Supermen of the West. 1974: The Stranger and the Gunfighter; Whisky and Ghosts.

BARTHA, JOHN
[János Barta]
(Budapest, Hungary. 1920-)
A flexible, lugubrious-looking actor of Hungarian extraction, Bartha was cast in minor roles in numerous European westerns and other genre pieces, playing lawmen, townsmen and bad guys as required. Arguably best known for having his hat shot off his head by Clint Eastwood just as Bartha is about to hang Eli Wallach in *The Good, the Bad and the Ugly*.

1964: Man of the Cursed Valley; Seven from Texas. 1965: Hands of a Gunfighter; The Relentless Four. 1966: El Cisco; El Rojo; The Good, the Bad and the Ugly; Massacre Time; Ringo and His Golden Pistol. 1967: The Dirty Outlaws; Last of the Badmen; Son of Django; 32 Caliber Killer. 1968: If You Want to Live... Then Shoot!; Johnny Hamlet; Kill Them All and Come Back Alone; Lynching; A Minute to Pray, a Second to Die; A Sky Full of Stars for a Roof; This Man Can't Die. 1969: I Am Sartana, Your Angel of Death; Sabata. 1970: Sartana's Here... Trade Your Pistol for a Coffin. 1971: Heads I Kill You... Tails You're Dead! They Call Me Hallelujah; His Name Was King; Return of Sabata. 1972: Jesse & Lester: Two Brothers in a Place Called Trinity; Man of the East. 1973: Tequila; White Fang. 1974: Challenge to White Fang.

BATTAGLIA, RIK
[Caterino Bertaglia; 'Rick Battaglia']
(Corbola, Italy. 1927-)

After toiling in a variety of professions, Battaglia was spotted working in a bar by director Mario Soldati, who immediately cast him opposite Sophia Loren in the drama *The River Girl* (1954). Battaglia thereafter pursued an acting career and was soon a mainstay of *pepla* and westerns, where stardom eluded him but he was always a robust and reliable presence. Perhaps his most memorable moment comes at the end of the Karl May adaptation *Desperado Trail* when his bullet strikes and kills the noble chief Winnetou.
1964: Apaches' Last Battle; The Sheriff Was a Lady. 1965: Desperado Trail; Pyramid of the Sun God; The Treasure of the Aztecs. 1966: Legacy of the Incas; Thunder at the Border. 1968: Black Jack; Shoot, Gringo, Shoot; This Man Can't Die; Winnetou and Shatterhand in the Valley of Death. 1970: Chapagua's Gold. 1971: A Fistful of Dynamite; Hey Amigo! A Toast to Your Death. 1972: The Call of the Wild; The Deadly Trackers. 1973: White Fang. 1975: A Genius, Two Partners and a Dupe. 1977: A Man Called Blade. 1991: Buck at the Edge of Heaven.

BENUSSI, FEMI
[Eufemia Benussi; 'Femi Martin']
(Rovigno d'Istria, Italy. 1945-)
Actress. After entering theatre in 1964, she landed a role in Pasolini's *Hawks and Sparrows* (1966), but her career quickly followed the path of many other beautiful, shapely actresses. From fetching heroines in westerns she came to specialise in strumpets in erotic comedies, *Decameron* rip-offs and other such historical hokum, before giving up films in the early Eighties.

1967: Born to Kill; Death Walks in Laredo; Last of the Badmen; Rattler Kid. 1968: Requiem for a Gringo; Zorro the Fox. 1969: Quintana. 1971: Finders Killers. 1974: The Stranger and the Gunfighter. 1975: Seven Devils on Horseback.

BERGER, WILLIAM
[Wilhelm Berger]
(Innsbruck, Austria. 1928-1993)

Talismanic character actor who shone as morally dubious and/or treacherous second leads. The son of Austrian refugees who fled the Second World War and pitched up in America in the Forties, young Berger had no particular profession in mind until he drifted into acting, initially on stage. Broadway experience was followed by a small role in *Von Ryan's Express* (1965) while he was holidaying in Rome, and his connections quickly secured him the lead in a low-budget western, *Ringo's Big Night*, in which he displayed hints of the charismatic amorality that typified his later roles. He spent the rest of his career in a wide range of European productions, among which were many further westerns. He was a devious foil for Gianni Garko in *If You Meet Sartana, Pray for Your Death* and Lee Van Cleef in *Sabata*, and later matured into mellower, more sympathetic parts, as in *Keoma* and *California*. While living in Italy, he was imprisoned for a time in the late Sixties on drugs charges; his wife, who had also been jailed for a while, died while he was inside (Brett Halsey appropriated this tragedy for his novel-cum-memoir, *The Magnificent Strangers*) and the experience reputedly changed his outlook on everything. According to his daughter, actress/artist Debra Berger, his life became "a kind of rebellion against repression", while Garko says, "He was very free as a person… he was *bello e dannato* – beautiful and damned." Berger continued acting until his death. He has two other children in the acting profession, daughter Katy and son, Kasmir.

1966: El Cisco; Ringo's Big Night. 1967: Face to Face. 1968: If You Meet Sartana, Pray for Your Death; A Name That Cried Revenge; Today It's Me… Tomorrow You! 1969: No Room to Die; Sabata. 1970: Sartana in the Valley of Death. 1971: They Call Him Cemetery. 1973: A Colt in the Hand of the Devil; Fast-Hand Is Still My Name; God's Executioner; Kung Fu Brothers in the Wild West; On the Third Day Arrived the Crow; The Son of Zorro; Yankee Dudler. 1976: Keoma. 1977: California. 1985: Tex and the Lord of the Deep. 1987: Django Strikes Again. 1991: Buck at the Edge of Heaven.

BERGONZELLI, SERGIO
['Serge Bergon']
(Alba, Italy. 1924-2002)

Writer/director. Beginning in the early Fifties, he acted in small roles and assisted other directors. He was involved in westerns as early as 1964, but his entries are mostly middling affairs. He is also believed to have helmed a number of other titles, such as the Peter Lee Lawrence vehicle *Hands Up, Dead Man! You're Under Arrest* (1971), that were officially credited to Spanish directors for tax purposes. He later specialised in sleazy exploitation films.

1964: The Last Gun (d). 1965: A Stranger in Sacramento (w/p/d). 1966: El Cisco (w/d). 1967: A Colt in the Fist of the Devil (w/p/d). 1971: Hands Up, Dead Man! You're Under Arrest (w – and probably director).

BERTI, ALDO
(Florence, Italy. 1936-2010)

Rangy Italian supporting actor with leathery features, usually third gang member from the left, who made a decent fist of a relatively major role in *A Stranger in Sacramento* as an ambiguous, sardonic outlaw and in *The Dirty Outlaws* as a roving charlatan.

1965: A Stranger in Sacramento; Why Go On Killing? 1966: Go with God, Gringo; Ramon the Mexican. 1967: Born to Kill; The Dirty Outlaws; Fifteen Scaffolds for a Killer; For a Dollar in the Teeth. 1968: Once Upon a Time in the West. 1969: El Puro. 1970: Have a Nice Funeral, Sartana Will Pay; Sartana in the Valley of Death. 1971: Heads I Kill You… Tails You're Dead! They Call Me Hallelujah; Hey Amigo! A Toast to Your Death; My Name Is Mallory. 1972: Death Played the Flute; A Gunman Called Dakota; Gunmen and the Holy Ghost; Return of the Holy Ghost.

BIANCHINI, PAOLO
['Paul Maxwell']
(Rome, Italy. 1931-)

Director with only a handful of feature films to his credit, among them four westerns. He started his career as an assistant director in the Fifties and Sixties, studying under Luigi Zampa among others. Two of his westerns, *I Want Him Dead* and *Gatling Gun*, take audacious liberties with American history while weaving exciting tales of vengeance and intrigue. He later moved into advertising, but has recently returned to directing for TV, earning sufficient cachet in Italy to be appointed a UNICEF Goodwill Ambassador.

1968: Gatling Gun (w/d); God Forgive… His Life Is Mine; I Want Him Dead. 1971: Hey Amigo! A Toast to Your Death.

BIANCHI MONTERO, ROBERTO
['Robert M. White']
(Rome, Italy. 1907-1986)

Director/writer. An actor in his youth, Bianchi Montero turned director after the Second World War, toiling in all manner of genres without making any truly noteworthy films. His son is director Mario Bianchi.

1959: The Sheriff (d). 1964: The Last Tomahawk (w). 1965: The Man from Oklahoma (d). 1966: Seven Pistols for a Gringo (w). 1967: Two Faces of the Dollar (d). 1971: Durango Is Coming, Pay or Die (d). 1972: Django… Adios! (w); Thunder Over El Paso (d).

BILLA, SALVATORE
(Catania, Italy. 1943-2006)

Cruel-faced, bushy-haired, solidly built supporting actor who played his share of unwashed gunmen and *bandidos* in westerns such as *Beyond the Law*, *Adios, Sabata* and *Blindman*. He subsequently transferred to *polizieschi* and other exploitation films, and also found time to work for Fellini in two of the latter's autumnal features.

1968: Beyond the Law. 1970: Adios, Sabata; Chuck Mool; Django Against Sartana. 1971: Blindman; Return of Sabata; Vengeance Trail. 1972: Gunmen and the Holy Ghost; Return of the Holy Ghost. 1974: Court Martial. 1975: Red Coat.

BLANC, ERIKA
[Enrica Bianchi Colombatto; 'Diana Sullivan'; 'Erica White']
(Gargnano, Italy. 1942-)

Actress. Distinguished by her prominent cheekbones and a glacial complexion, she was educated in France, was briefly a fashion journalist and made her film debut in her early 20s. After a stint in *fotoromanzi* (photo storybooks) she hopped from one genre to another. Although she played her share of good girls – her usual function in westerns – she was most impressive as a temptress or villainess in horror films and *gialli* such as *The Vendetta of Lady Morgan* (1965), *The Night Evelyn Came Out of the Grave* and *The Devil's Nightmare* (both 1971). Eventually tiring of her sex-symbol status, she took to theatre in the Eighties and has also worked on television. Formerly married to producer/director Bruno Gaburro, she was also involved with actor Alberto Lionello.

1965: Colorado Charlie. 1966: Blood at Sundown; De Guello; Django Shoots First. 1967: The Greatest Robbery in the West. 1968: Shoot, Gringo, Shoot; Shotgun. 1970: Sartana's Here... Trade Your Pistol for a Coffin; Stagecoach of the Condemned. 1971: Durango Is Coming, Pay or Die; Lobo the Bastard. 1972: Thunder Over El Paso. 1974: The Stranger and the Gunfighter.

BLONDELL, SIMONE
[Simonetta Vitelli]

Doe-eyed actress daughter of Demofilo Fidani and Mila Vitelli. She usually appeared in their films as wench or victim, sometimes as a blonde, sometimes a faux-Mexican brunette.
1968: Say Your Prayers and Dig Your Grave; Stranger, Make the Sign of the Cross. 1969: Four Came to Kill Sartana; Shadow of Sartana... Shadow of Your Death! 1970: Dead Men Don't Make Shadows; Django and Sartana Are Coming... It's the End; One Damned Day at Dawn... Django Meets Sartana! 1971: A Barrel Full of Dollars; His Name Was Sam Wallash... But They Called Him Amen!; A Man Called Django. 1972: Zorro the Lawman. 1973: Anything for a Friend.

BÓDALO, JOSÉ
[José Bódalo Zúffoli]
(Córdoba, Argentina. 1916-1985)
This bullish character actor was the son of an actress mother and tenor father. Initially he studied medicine, but then worked in radio and was, for a while, a professional soccer player. Finally settling on acting, he appeared on stage, screen and television from the late Forties until his death, maintaining both critical acclaim and popular appeal. He was especially memorable as the two-faced Mexican 'revolutionaries' in Sergio Corbucci's Django and Compañeros.
1966: Django; $100,000 for Lassiter; Ringo's Big Night; Thompson 1880. 1967: Red Blood, Yellow Gold. 1968: One After the Other; A Train for Durango. 1969: Garringo. 1970: Compañeros. 1971: Captain Apache.

BOGART, WILLIAM
[Guglielmo Spoletini; 'William Spolt/Spoletin']
(Italy. 1932-2005)

Thickset supporting actor and occasional leading man whose dark looks proved suitable for Mexican parts in particular. His best role was a rare lead as a doomed social bandit in Tierra Brava, and he was later the focus of L'America a Roma (1998), Gianfranco Pannone's affecting documentary on Italian B-western stalwarts.
1965: Gold Train. 1966: Arizona Colt; Fort Yuma Gold; The Hills Run Red; Kill Johnny Ringo! 1967: Death Rides a Horse; Last of the Badmen; Rattler Kid. 1968: One Against One... No Mercy. 1969: Night of the Serpents; Tierra Brava. 1970: And Sartana Kills Them All. 1972: They Call Him Veritas. 1974: Carambola.

BOLOGNINI, MANOLO
(Pistoia. 1922-2001)
Influential producer (he was the main man behind BRC Produzione) with a long association with Franco Nero – he produced Django and was instrumental in getting Keoma off the ground. If Nero's memory serves him correctly, Bolognini was the one who christened both these iconic characters. His brother is director Mauro Bolognini.
1966: Django; Texas Adios. 1967: Rita of the West. 1969: The Forgotten Pistolero. 1974: Carambola. 1976: Keoma. 1977: California.

BOLZONI, ADRIANO
['Mark Salter']
(Cremona, Italy. 1919-)
Writer. A former journalist, he wrote stories and scripts in every genre, distinguishing himself with westerns. Some of these have a pronounced populist/political flavour, notably Viva Carrancho, Kill and Pray and A Professional Gun.
1964: Minnesota Clay. 1965: Viva Carrancho. 1966: My Name Is Pecos; Ringo and His Golden Pistol; Savage Gringo. 1967: Kill and Pray; Pecos Cleans Up. 1968: A Hole Between the Eyes; I Want Him Dead; A Professional Gun. 1971: Shoot the Living and Pray for the Dead; Thirteenth Is a Judas. 1972: Bandits; Hallelujah & Sartana Strike Again!; They Called Him Amen; Trinity and Sartana Are Coming. 1978: Silver Saddle.

BORGESE, SALVATORE
['Sal Borgese']
(Rome, Italy. 1937-)
Swarthy stuntman, master of arms and supporting actor. He worked in all the main Italian B-genres of the Sixties and Seventies and, as a consummate acrobat, he was a particular favourite of Gianfranco Parolini and Giuliano Carnimeo, bounding around in the 'Three Fantastic Supermen' franchise and the 'Sartana' and 'Sabata' series. His character's

method of dispatching enemies in Adios, Sabata – with lethal ballbearings propelled via his boot – is one of the most memorable in the genre.
1965: One Silver Dollar. 1966: Blood at Sundown; Massacre Time; My Name Is Pecos. 1967: Any Gun Can Play; The Greatest Robbery in the West. 1968: If You Meet Sartana, Pray for Your Death; Two Pistols and a Coward. 1969: I Am Sartana, Your Angel of Death; In the Name of the Father. 1970: Adios, Sabata; Gunman in Town. 1972: Can Be Done... Amigo; Man of the East. 1973: Karate, Fists and Beans; A Man Called Invincible; Three Supermen of the West. 1974: Patience Has a Limit, We Don't; Sons of White Fang.

BOSCH, JUAN
['John Wood']
(Valls, Spain. 1926-)
Prolific Spanish writer/director who arrived late on the western scene but made up for lost time with nine low-budget quickies in the Seventies, including a fairly faithful transposition of Dashiell Hammett's Red Harvest as La ciudad maldita.
1970: Stagecoach of the Condemned (d). 1971: And the Crows Will Dig Your Grave (w/d); Dig Your Grave Friend... Sabata's Coming (d). 1972: God in Heaven... Arizona on Earth (w/d); My Horse.. My Gun... Your Widow (w/d); Too Much Gold for One Gringo (w/d). 1975: Dallas (w/d). 1978: La ciudad maldita (w/d).

BOSIC, ANDREA
['Andrew Bosich']
(Gomilsko, Slovenia. 1919-)

Austere-looking supporting player with an air of haughtiness belying humble origins. He learnt his trade on stage in the Fifties and, in movies, was well suited for playing town burghers, corrupt politicians, army officers and so on.
1966: Arizona Colt; Fort Yuma Gold; Kill or Be Killed. 1967: Day of Anger; Days of Violence; Death Rides Along; Fifteen Scaffolds for a Killer; 32 Caliber Killer; Two Faces of the Dollar. 1968: I Want Him Dead; Two Pistols and a Coward. 1969: Tierra Brava. 1971: Heads I Kill You... Tails You're Dead! They Call Me Hallelujah.

Who's Who In Euro-Westerns

BÖTTCHER, MARTIN
(Berlin, Germany. 1927-)
Prolific German composer whose career stretches back 50 years. He is principally associated with the 'Winnetou' adaptations, his lush scores distilling the romanticism inherent in the films' plots, characterisations and settings.
1962: The Treasure of Silver Lake. 1963: Winnetou the Warrior. 1964: Among Vultures; Last of the Renegades. 1965: Desperado Trail; Flaming Frontier; Rampage at Apache Wells. 1966: Halfbreed. 1968: Winnetou and Shatterhand in the Valley of Death. 1998: Winnetou Returns.

BOYD, RICK
[Federico Boido]
(Novi Ligure, Italy. 1938 or 1940-)
Skinny, sneering character actor who habitually played cowardly criminals beset by tics, twitches and other stereotypical signs of deviancy and mental unrest. He has barely been seen on screen since the late Seventies, save for one or two television productions.
1964: Samson and the Treasure of the Incas. 1966: Djurado. 1967: The Bang Bang Kid; Cjamango; Django Kills Softly; Face to Face; The Greatest Robbery in the West; Seven Winchesters for a Massacre. 1968: Ace High; I Want Him Dead; Run, Man, Run; The Ruthless Four; A Sky Full of Stars for a Roof. 1969: I Am Sartana, Your Angel of Death. 1970: Adios, Sabata; Chapagua's Gold; Django Against Sartana; Have a Nice Funeral, Sartana Will Pay; Roy Colt and Winchester Jack; Sartana in the Valley of Death; Sartana's Here... Trade Your Pistol for a Coffin; Wind from the East. 1971: Acquasanta Joe; Doomsday; Heads I Kill You... Tails You're Dead! They Call Me Hallelujah; His Name Was King; Return of Sabata; They Call Him Cemetery; Vendetta at Dawn. 1972: His Name Was Holy Ghost; Jesse & Lester: Two Brothers in a Place Called Trinity; Shoot Joe, and Shoot Again; They Call Him Veritas; Where the Bullets Fly. 1973: Anything for a Friend; The Fighting Fists of Shanghai Joe; Halleluja to Vera Cruz; Here We Go Again, Eh Providence? 1976: Apache Woman.

BOYD, STEPHEN
(Glengormley, Northern Ireland. 1931-1977)
Actor. His career path took him from the stage (he began as a child actor) to the television screen before he began landing film roles. He scored an early success as Messala in *Ben-Hur* (1959) – a number of further epics followed – and was briefly considered to play James Bond in *Dr No* (1962). His post-Hollywood European career was hit and miss, although he gave genial, intelligent performances in a handful of westerns. He died of a heart attack while playing golf.
1968: Shalako. 1971: Hannie Caulder. 1973: The Man Called Noon; Those Dirty Dogs. 1976: Potato Fritz.

BRAÑA, FRANK
[Francisco Braña Pérez]
(Asturias, Spain. 1934-)
Intimidating Spanish character actor whose robust build and chiselled features were put to good use in around 50 Euro-westerns. In his teens he was a miner, and first entered cinema as a stuntman. He was a supporting villain in most of Leone's westerns, acquitted himself well as the lead heavy when the chance arose, and displayed excellent mobility in fight scenes. As with so many of his contemporaries, his filmography bristles with titles in the Sixties and Seventies, the peak co-production period, but thins out after that. More recently he has been active on television.
1964: Cavalry Charge; A Fistful of Dollars; The Fury of the Apaches; Massacre at Fort Grant; Ride and Kill; Tomb of the Pistolero; Two Violent Men. 1965: Adios Gringo; A Coffin for the Sheriff; For a Few Dollars More; The Last Tomahawk; Murieta; Outlaw of Red River; The Secret of Captain O'Hara; Sunscorched. 1966: The Bounty Killer; The Good, the Bad and the Ugly; Mestizo; Savage Gringo; Sugar Colt; A Taste for Killing; The Texican. 1967: The Big Gundown; Django, Kill!; Face to Face; Fifteen Scaffolds for a Killer; God Forgives… I Don't!; The Man Who Killed Billy the Kid; Rattler Kid. 1968: Ace High; Cowards Don't Pray; A Gun for a Hundred Graves; I Want Him Dead; Once Upon a Time in the West; One for All; Ringo the Lone Rider. 1969: Death on a High Hill; Garringo; The Price of Power. 1970: And Sartana Kills Them All; Clumsy Hands; Gunman in Town. 1971: And the Crows Will Dig Your Grave; Let's Go and Kill Sartana. 1972: The Boldest Job in the West; God in Heaven… Arizona on Earth; Kill the Poker Player; Prey of Vultures; Zorro the Lawman. 1973: Fast-Hand Is Still My Name; Three Supermen of the West; Yankee Dudler. 1975: In the Name of the Father, of the Son and of the Colt. 1976: If You Shoot… You Live! 1980: The Black Wolf; Revenge of the Black Wolf. 1984: Yellow Hair and the Fortress of Gold. 1985: Tex and the Lord of the Deep.

BRAVO, CHARLY
[Ramón Carlos Mirón-Muñoz Bravo]
(Casablanca, Morocco. 1943-)
Actor. The son of Spanish republican exiles, he was educated and studied acting in France. Virile and athletic, he slotted neatly into westerns and other popular genres as a second lead or supporting player.
1969: Cemetery Without Crosses; Land Raiders; 100 Rifles; The Price of Power; Vengeance Is Mine. 1970: And Sartana Kills Them All; El Condor. 1971: Captain Apache; The Hunting Party; A Town Called Bastard. 1972: The Boldest Job in the West; The Call of the Wild. 1973: The Man Called Noon; The Son of Zorro. 1975: Cipolla Colt. 1978: China 9, Liberty 37. 1981: Comin' at Ya! 1985: Tex and the Lord of the Deep. 1986: Scalps; White Apache.

BREGA, MARIO
['Richard Stuyvesant']
(Rome, Italy. 1923 or 1931-1994)
Another member of Leone's stock company, this heavyweight actor made an imposing villain. He was particularly nasty in the 'Dollars' movies, his Sergeant Wallace dispensing one of the genre's most vicious beatings to Eli Wallach in *The Good, the Bad and the Ugly*. According to Giulio Petroni, who directed him in *Death Rides a Horse*, Brega's off-screen personality was almost as unappealing: "He was a typical Roman bully… rough and rude and full of himself."
1964: Buffalo Bill, Hero of the Far West; A Fistful of Dollars; Two Gangsters in the Wild West. 1965: For a Few Dollars More. 1966: The Bounty Killer; The Good, the Bad and the Ugly. 1967: Death Rides a Horse; The Greatest Robbery in the West. 1968: The Great Silence; A Minute to Pray, a Second to Die; A Name That Cried Revenge. 1969: El Puro; No Room to Die. 1971: Finders Killers. 1973: My Name Is Nobody. 1975: A Genius, Two Partners and a Dupe; Seven Devils on Horseback.

above: **Rick Boyd** in **Return of Sabata** (*far left*).

above: **Stephen Boyd**, as seen in **The Man Called Noon**.

above: **Frank Braña**, as seen in **The Boldest Job in the West** (*left*).

above: **Charly Bravo**, as seen in **White Apache**.

above: **Mario Brega**, as seen in **The Great Silence**.

BRESCIA, ALFONSO
['Hal/Al Bradley']
(Rome, Italy. 1930-2001)
Director/writer. Son of producer Edoardo, he worked in various positions and was assistant to Mario Amendola and Mario Caiano in the early Sixties. He became a busy director in every fashionable genre and made a brace of westerns with Peter Lee Lawrence that are among the actor's best.
1959: The Sheriff (ad). 1963: The Sign of Zorro (ad). 1965: The Colt Is My Law (w/d); Gold Train (w). 1967: Days of Violence (d); 32 Caliber Killer (d); Turn... I'll Kill You! (d). 1968: Lynching (d). 1975: White Fang and the Gold Diggers (d); White Fang and the Hunter (d).

BRICE, PIERRE
[Pierre Louis de Bris]
(Brest, France. 1929-)

French actor with matinee looks forever associated with the role of Winnetou, the saintly Apache chief he played, on and off, for almost 40 years on film, television and in open-air festivals. In 1992, he passed the mantle to Gojko Mitic, the similarly iconic star of former East Germany's DEFA western series.
1962: The Treasure of Silver Lake. 1963: Samson and the Slave Queen; Winnetou the Warrior. 1964: Among Vultures; Apaches' Last Battle; Last of the Renegades. 1965: Desperado Trail; Flaming Frontier; A Place Called Glory; Rampage at Apache Wells. 1966: Halfbreed; Thunder at the Border. 1968: Winnetou and Shatterhand in the Valley of Death. 1972: You Are a Traitor and I'll Kill You. 1998: Winnetou Returns (act/w).

BROCHERO, EDUARDO MANZANOS
(Madrid, Spain. 1919 or 1924-1987)
Screenwriter/producer/director.
A former poet and playwright, he entered the film industry in the late Forties and was at his busiest during the co-production era. He wrote or co-wrote stories and scripts for more than 20 second-grade Italian-Spanish westerns, producing a number of these as well (he ran the production company Copercines), including oddities such as Cowards Don't Pray and Matalo!, as well as minor gems such as the Sartana vehicle Gunman in Town and Dead Men Ride. Outside the genre, he made a documentary on Franco in 1980 and was married to actress Maria Luz Galicia.
1964: Four Bullets for Joe (p); Heroes of Fort Worth (w/p); Man of the Cursed Valley (w). 1965: A Coffin for the Sheriff (p); For a Fist in the Eye (w/p); Outlaw of Red River (w/p). 1966: Kid Rodelo (w/p); Ringo the Mark of Vengeance (w); Ringo's Big Night (p). 1967: Kill the Wicked (p); Rattler Kid (w); Seven Pistols for a Massacre (w); Two Crosses at Danger Pass (w/p). 1968: Cowards Don't Pray (w); Dead Men Don't Count! (p); A Gun for a Hundred Graves (w); One Against One... No Mercy (w/p); One for All (w); Ringo the Lone Rider (w/p); A Stranger in Paso Bravo (w). 1969: Death on a High Hill (w); Tierra Brava (w/p). 1970: Gunman in Town (w/p); A Man Called Joe Clifford (w); Matalo! (w). 1971: El bandido malpelo (w); Dead Men Ride (w/p). 1973: Fast-Hand Is Still My Name (w). 1975: In the Name of the Father, of the Son and of the Colt (p).

BRONSON, CHARLES
[Charles Buchinski/Buchinsky]
(Ehrenfeld, USA. 1921-2003)

Born to Lithuanian immigrants (he was one of 15 children), Bronson's working life began in a coal mine. After military service in the Second World War, he discovered acting, firstly on stage, and eventually found himself in B-movies before hitting the big time courtesy of The Magnificent Seven (1960). One of Leone's original choices to play 'Joe' in A Fistful of Dollars (1964) and the Colonel in For a Few Dollars More (1965), Bronson finally worked with the maestro in Once Upon a Time in the West, creating one of the most enigmatic avengers in western history and making Bronson one of the biggest box-office draws in Europe. After a series of starring roles there, he transferred back to Hollywood and became an action-film icon.
1968: Guns for San Sebastian; Once Upon a Time in the West; Villa Rides. 1971: Red Sun. 1972: Chato's Land. 1973: The Valdez Horses.

BUCHS, JULIO
[Julio Buchs García]
(Madrid, Spain. 1926-1973)
Writer/director, the son of director José Buchs, whose brief career was highlighted by the exemplary Vengeance Is Mine, one of the few revenge westerns to get the balance between tragedy and machismo spot-on. He also made an entertaining, facts-be-damned contribution to the William Bonney legend with The Man Who Killed Billy the Kid, with Peter Lee Lawrence smoothing over the cracks in Bonney's character. He died from a heart attack.
1966: Mestizo (w/d). 1967: The Man Who Killed Billy the Kid (w/d). 1969: Vengeance Is Mine (w/d).

BURTON, LEE
[Guido Lollobrigida]
(Rome, Italy. 1928-)
Actor. Versatile, hollow-cheeked character actor who played shifty, surly or sympathetic roles with equal conviction in westerns and other popular films. A one-time racing driver, he is Gina Lollobrigida's cousin.

1965: $100,000 for Ringo. 1966: Django Shoots First; Kill Johnny Ringo!; The Sons of Ringo. 1967: Man, Pride and Vengeance; Viva Django. 1968: A Long Ride from Hell; Vengeance. 1969: Cemetery Without Crosses. 1970: And God Said to Cain; The Beast; Roy Colt and Winchester Jack. 1971: Doomsday; Red Sun; Vendetta at Dawn. 1973: The Blue Gang; Those Dirty Dogs.

BYRNES, EDD
[Edward Breitenberger]
(New York City, USA. 1933-)

Fresh-faced American actor who, like Clint Eastwood, exchanged a recurring role in a successful TV series (77 Sunset Strip) for appearances in a trio of Italian westerns. Again, like Eastwood, Byrnes wasn't the first actor his director had in mind – Enzo Castellari originally wanted Robert Redford for the lead in Seven Winchesters for a Massacre, but the producers felt that Byrnes represented better business. The similarity with Eastwood ends there, however: Byrnes's attempts at toughness and callousness were as unconvincing as his films were disappointing at the box office. He quickly returned to the States, where he has worked intermittently on television.
1967: Any Gun Can Play; Red Blood, Yellow Gold; Seven Winchesters for a Massacre.

CAIANO, MARIO
['Mike Perkins'; 'Allan Grunewald'; 'William Hawkins'; 'Edoardo Re']
(Naples, Italy. 1933-) Director. Son of producer/distributor Carlo Caiano, he apprenticed for many of the directors who worked for his father and rapidly blossomed into an all-purpose craftsman. He has several solid westerns to his credit, including the historically significant Bullets Don't Argue, made as part of a two-picture deal alongside A Fistful of Dollars; A Train for Durango, a spoof of sorts of political westerns; and the bloody The Fighting Fists of Shanghai Joe, by far the best of Italy's kung-fu crossovers.

1963: *The Magnificent Three* (w); *The Sign of the Coyote* (w/d); *The Sign of Zorro* (d). 1964: *Bullets Don't Argue* (d). 1965: *A Coffin for the Sheriff* (d). 1966: *Ringo the Mark of Vengeance* (w/p/d). 1967: *Seven Pistols for a Massacre* (w/d). 1968: *A Name That Cried Revenge* (w/d); *Ringo the Lone Rider* (w); *A Train for Durango* (w/d). 1973: *The Fighting Fists of Shanghai Joe* (w/d). 1974: *Return of Shanghai Joe* (w).

CALVO, JOSÉ or PEPE
[José Calvo Salgado]
(Madrid, Spain. 1916-1980) Actor. After studying medicine, Calvo turned to acting, beginning on the stage. The role of world-weary Silvanito in *A Fistful of Dollars* showed him in a sympathetic light, but he was comfortable in all kinds of parts and personalities – he was a stubbornly vengeful, murderous patriarch, for example, in *Why Go On Killing?*
1955: *The Coyote*. 1962: *Two Against All*. 1963: *Gunfight at Red Sands*. 1964: *A Fistful of Dollars*. 1965: *In a Colt's Shadow*; *The Man from Oklahoma*; *Why Go On Killing?* 1966: *Fort Yuma Gold*; *Legacy of the Incas*; *Renegade Gunfighter*. 1967: *Day of Anger*. 1968: *A Stranger in Paso Bravo*. 1969: *The Price of Power*; *Twice a Judas*. 1971: *Dead Men Ride*; *In the Dust of the Sun*.

CAMARDIEL, ROBERTO
[Roberto Camardiel Escudero]
(Alagón, Spain. 1917-1986) Robust, rotund character actor. His first experience was on stage (he was part of a popular troupe run by actor Ismael Merlo), after which he made more than 100 films. He was typically cast as either a foolish sidekick (*Arizona Colt* [1966]) or ebullient Mexican villain (*Django, Kill!* [1967]). Robert Woods says of Camardiel that, before he was consumed by co-productions, "He was the Jason Robards of Spain at one time."
1963: *The Jaguar*. 1965: *Adios Gringo*; *For a Few Dollars More*; *Johnny West*; *Murieta*; *The Relentless Four*; *Son of Jesse James*. 1966: *Arizona Colt*; *$100,000 for Lassiter*. 1967: *The Big Gundown*; *Django, Kill!*; *Seven Pistols for a Massacre*; *Up the MacGregors*. 1968: *Between God, the Devil and a Winchester*; *Gatling Gun*; *A Train for Durango*. 1969: *Quinto: Fighting Proud*. 1970: *Arizona*; *Challenge of the MacKennas*. 1971: *Heads I Kill You… Tails You're Dead!*; *They Call Me Hallelujah*; *Kill Django... Kill First*. 1972: *Ben and Charlie*; *Can Be Done… Amigo*; *God in Heaven… Arizona on Earth*; *The Return of Hallelujah*. 1973: *Tequila*. 1978: *La ciudad maldita*. 1980: *The Black Wolf*.

CAMASO, CLAUDIO
[Claudio Volonté]
(?-1977)
Actor-brother of Gian Maria Volonté who had a similarly intense style without demonstrating the same range – or ideological interests. Nor did he earn the same respect, mainly because he chose to remain in genre pieces while his brother left them behind. He was especially good as Manuel Vasquez, the incorrigible outlaw in *$10,000 Blood Money*, and Mendoza, the colourful criminal mastermind in *Vengeance*. Brought a troubled life to a premature end by committing suicide in prison, where he was serving time for the attempted murder of his girlfriend and/or the murder of a man – different stories have circulated. "He had a certain power, but not the talent of his brother," says Richard Harrison, Camaso's co-star in *Vengeance*. "He was just waiting to do damage."
1967: *For $100,000 Per Killing*; *John the Bastard*; *$10,000 Blood Money*. 1968: *Garter Colt*; *Vengeance*.

CAMERON, JEFF
[Giovanni/Nino Scarciofolo]
(?-1985)
Stuntman-turned-leading player in a string of low-budget Seventies westerns. Thick-lipped and burly, his no-nonsense 'heroes' were little more than vicious thugs who enjoyed dispensing beatings. He played a pseudo-Sartana in this vein on two occasions for Demofilo Fidani.
1966: *Arizona Colt*; *The Hills Run Red*; *Sugar Colt*. 1967: *The Greatest Robbery in the West*; *Up the MacGregors*. 1968: *And Now… Make Your Peace with God*; *Say Your Prayers and Dig Your Grave*; *Stranger, Make the Sign of the Cross*; *Today It's Me… Tomorrow You!* 1969: *Four Came to Kill Sartana*; *Shadow of Sartana… Shadow of Your Death!* 1971: *The Ballad of Django*; *A Barrel Full of Dollars*; *Django's Cut Price Corpses*; *A Fistful of Death*; *Paid in Blood*. 1972: *Beyond the Frontiers of Hate*; *A Bounty Killer for Trinity*; *God Is My Colt*.

CAMERON, ROD
[Nathan Cox]
(Calgary, Canada 1910-1983)
Actor. A stalwart of B-westerns (and, in the Republic serial *Secret Service in Darkest Africa* [1943], prototype Indiana Jones) who caused a scandal in Hollywood in 1960 when he divorced his wife to marry her mother. His patrician bearing in early Italian westerns such as *Bullets Don't Argue*, in which he plays Wyatt Earp, and *Bullets and the Flesh* underlines the films' debt to Hollywood stereotypes. Wound down his career doing TV spots and cheap American films.
1964: *Bullets and the Flesh*; *Bullets Don't Argue*. 1966: *Thunder at the Border*.

CAMINITO, AUGUSTO
(Naples, Italy. 1939-)
Screenwriter. Active in several genres, he wrote some impressive westerns, the best being *The Ruthless Four*, modelled on *The Treasure of the Sierra Madre*. He later formed a production company and became a director.
1967: *Death Rides Along*; *Django, the Last Killer*; *The Greatest Robbery in the West*; *Long Days of Vengeance*; *Pecos Cleans Up*; *Poker with Pistols*. 1968: *The Ruthless Four*. 1973: *The Blue Gang*.

above: **José Calvo** (*left*), as seen in **A Fistful of Dollars**.

above: **Roberto Camardiel** in **The Return of Hallelujah**.

above: **Claudio Camaso** on the cover of this soundtrack release for **$10,000 Blood Money**.

above: **Jeff Cameron**, as seen in **Today It's Me… Tomorrow You!**

above: **Rod Cameron**, as seen in **Bullets Don't Argue**.

CANALEJAS, JOSÉ
[José Alvarez Canalejas; 'Joe Camel/Kamel']
(Madrid, Spain. 1925-)

Actor, one of the legion of Spanish character players who flourished in westerns. For the first 15 years of his career he worked in theatre; later, when big-screen roles became scarce, he turned to television. His sister, Lina, was a popular actress in her own right.
1962: Torrejón City. 1963: The Sign of the Coyote. 1964: Billy the Kid; Bullets Don't Argue; A Fistful of Dollars; Man of the Cursed Valley; Minnesota Clay; Ride and Kill; Seven from Texas; Tomb of the Pistolero. 1965: For a Few Dollars More; The Relentless Four; The Secret of Captain O'Hara; Son of Jesse James. 1966: The Bounty Killer; Django; A Few Dollars for Django; Mutiny at Fort Sharp; Savage Gringo; Sugar Colt; A Taste for Killing. 1967: Fifteen Scaffolds for a Killer; God Forgives… I Don't!; The Hellbenders; A Man and a Colt; The Man Who Killed Billy the Kid. 1968: I Want Him Dead; A Minute to Pray, a Second to Die; One After the Other; A Professional Gun; A Stranger in Paso Bravo; A Train for Durango; Villa Rides; White Comanche. 1969: Cemetery Without Crosses; The Price of Power; Quinto: Fighting Proud. 1970: Compañeros; Reverend Colt; Viva Sabata! 1971: Hands Up, Dead Man! You're Under Arrest. 1972: What Am I Doing in the Middle of a Revolution? 1973: The Man Called Noon; The Three Musketeers of the West; Three Supermen of the West. 1974: Blood River. 1975: The Cry of the Wolf. 1976: If You Shoot… You Live! 1986: Scalps; White Apache.

CAPITANI, REMO
['Ray O'Connor']
(Rome, Italy. 1927-)

Another stocky stunt performer who also played supporting parts, typically Mexican bandits, in low-budget westerns. He sent up this persona in his biggest film, They Call Me Trinity.
1966: Kill or Be Killed. 1967: Death Rides a Horse; Face to Face; God Forgives… I Don't! 1968: Ace High; Saguaro; Tequila Joe; Today It's Me… Tomorrow You!; Vengeance for Vengeance. 1969: Django the Bastard. 1970: The Beast; They Call Me Trinity; The Twilight Avengers. 1971: Bastard, Go and Kill; A Man Called Django. 1972: Ben and Charlie; Death Played the Flute; The Grand Duel; Gunmen and the Holy Ghost; Panhandle Calibre 38; Return of the Holy Ghost. 1973: Bad Kids of the West. 1975: The Crazy Adventures of Len and Coby. 1979: Porno-Erotic western.

CARDINALE, CLAUDIA
(Tunis, Tunisia. 1938-)

A stunning brunette with large, shining eyes, Cardinale was voted the most beautiful girl of Italian origin in Tunis while still a teenager and won a trip to the Venice Film Festival. She took acting classes and was swiftly offered movie roles. She married producer Franco Cristaldi and her career took off with small but pivotal parts in major works such as 8½ and The Leopard (both. 1963). She mastered both serious and comedic roles and became established internationally in the mid-Sixties, giving gave a warm, affecting performance in Once Upon a Time in the West as Jill, the genre's most famous female character. After an indifferent Seventies, she re-emerged with critical favour in the Eighties and is today one of Italy's most admired actresses.
1968: Once Upon a Time in the West. 1971: The Legend of Frenchie King.

CARDONE, ALBERTO
['Albert Cardiff']
(Genoa, Italy. 1920-1977)
Writer/director of rough-and-ready revenge films. Like many others, he began as an assistant director and second-unit man and was very busy in the Forties and Fifties (Ben-Hur is among his credits). Two of his westerns in particular, Blood at Sundown and Seven Dollars to Kill, exemplify the hyper-emotionalism and domestic focus of second-tier Italian westerns. "Cardone was my favourite western director", says Brett Halsey. "I have always thought [he] should have had a much more important career."
1964: Massacre at Marble City (d - with Paul Martin). 1965: The Black Eagles of Santa Fe (d). 1966: Blood at Sundown (d); Seven Dollars to Kill (d). 1967: $20.000 on Number Seven (w/d). 1968: The Long Day of the Massacre (w/d); The Wrath of God (w/d). 1969: $20,000 Stained in Blood (w/d). 1970: El Condor (ad). 1973: Fast-Hand Is Still My Name (w).

CARNIMEO, GIULIANO
['Anthony Ascot(t)'; 'Jules Harrison']
(Bari, Italy. 1932-)
Prolific writer/director with a boundless imagination. He abandoned a law career for the cinema, collaborating on many comic films with Giorgio Simonelli in the Sixties. He made his directorial debut, in a limited sense, in 1962, helming the Italian version of the comedy Panic Button, an American co-production, but really got started in 1968 when he made his first westerns. He made 13 in all, taking over the 'Sartana' franchise from Gianfranco Parolini and later specialising in madcap comedies, starring first Gianni Garko and then George Hilton. His films manage to be both fast-paced and densely plotted, making up in inventiveness what they often lack in discipline.
1964: Two Gangsters in the Wild West (ad). 1965: Two Sergeants of General Custer (ad). 1966: The Sons of Ringo (with Giorgio Simonelli). 1967: Two Faces of the Dollar (ad). 1968: Find a Place to Die (w/d); The Moment to Kill (d). 1969: I Am Sartana, Your Angel of Death (d). 1970: Gunman in Town (d); Have a Nice Funeral, Sartana Will Pay (d); Sartana's Here… Trade Your Pistol for a Coffin (d). 1971: Heads I Kill You… Tails You're Dead! They Call Me Hallelujah (d); They Call Him Cemetery (d). 1972: His Name Was Holy Ghost (w/d); The Return of Hallelujah (d). 1973: A Man Called Invincible (d). 1974: The Crazy Bunch (w/d).

CARPI, TITO
(?-1998)
Writer.
A close friend and colleague of Enzo Castellari, he was a busy screenwriter with a taste for bizarre humour and eccentric characters. As well as Castellari, he has worked with directors of a similar stripe such as Giuliano Carnimeo, co-writing his 'Sartana', 'Holy Ghost' and 'Hallelujah' movies, and Antonio Margheriti.
1964: Badmen of the West. 1966: Django Shoots First; A Few Dollars for Django; Renegade Gunfighter. 1967: Any Gun Can Play; Rick and John, Conquerors of the West; Seven Winchesters for a Massacre; Son of Django. 1968: Between God, the Devil and a Winchester; Dead for a Dollar; Johnny Hamlet; Kill Them All and Come Back Alone; The Moment to Kill; A Name That Cried Revenge; One Against One… No Mercy; Shotgun.

above: **Remo Capitani** (smiling, third from right) takes on a typical Mexican bandit role in **They Call Me Trinity**.

1969: *I Am Sartana, Your Angel of Death.* 1970: *Gunman in Town; Reverend Colt; Sartana's Here... Trade Your Pistol for a Coffin.* 1971: *Heads I Kill You… Tails You're Dead! They Call Me Hallelujah.* 1972: *His Name Was Holy Ghost; The Return of Hallelujah; Tedeum.* 1973: *A Man Called Invincible; The Three Musketeers of the West.* 1974: *The Crazy Bunch.* 1991: *Buck at the Edge of Heaven.*

CASAS, ANTONIO
[Antonio Casas Barros]
(La Coruña, Spain. 1911-1982)

Seasoned character actor usually seen in sympathetic roles. He played professional soccer for a time and worked in diverse occupations before settling on acting, initially on stage. He was excellent as the dauntless Major in *A Pistol for Ringo* and tragic sheriff in the sequel.
1960: *Juanito.* 1964: *Minnesota Clay; Ride and Kill.* 1965: *A Pistol for Ringo; The Return of Ringo; Son of a Gunfighter.* 1966: *Four Dollars of Revenge; The Good, the Bad and the Ugly; The Texican.* 1967: *The Big Gundown; Face to Face; Fifteen Scaffolds for a Killer.* 1969: *Alive or Preferably Dead; The Price of Power; $20,000 Stained in Blood.* 1970: *Clumsy Hands.* 1972: *Pancho Villa.* 1973: *Three Supermen of the West.*

CASTEL, LOU
[Ulv Quarzell]
(Bogotá, Colombia. 1943-)

Baby-faced actor and political activist. Of Swedish-English parentage, he and his family pitched up in Italy in the early Sixties, and he was soon drawn to acting. He was electrifying in his first major film, *Fists in the Pocket* (1965), and went on to star in the leftist westerns *A Bullet for the General*, playing a Yankee mercenary, and *Kill and Pray*, as yet another of his rebellious characters. He was also the unlikely, boomerang-wielding protagonist of the psychedelic western *Matalo!*, and has acted in an array of disparate films over the years. Naming Che Guevara as his biggest inspiration, his political activities in the south of Italy saw him expelled from the country for two years in the early Seventies. He has also directed a number of experimental features.
1966: *A Bullet for the General.* 1967: *Kill and Pray.* 1970: *Matalo!* 1991: *Arizona Road.*

CASTELLARI, ENZO G.
[Enzo Girolami; 'EG Rowland']
(Rome, Italy. 1938-)

Arguably Italy's finest director of action films, Castellari (he adopted his mother's maiden name for professional purposes) is the most successful member of the Girolami filmmaking dynasty. He learnt the business alongside his father and apprenticed with other commercial directors such as Alberto De Martino. A pioneer of comedy westerns, Castellari moved on to urban thrillers in the Seventies before briefly reigniting the Euro-western flame with the lyrical *Keoma* in 1976. (He has occasionally alluded to the genre in other films, paying tribute directly in his post-apocalyptic adventure *The New Barbarians* [1983], channelling *A Fistful of Dollars* for its showdown finale.) He and the star, Franco Nero, tried again, without the same success, with *Jonathan of the Bears* in 1993, and have been planning another western for some time. "During the action scenes I never leave anything to chance," he says. "It is all thought out and the smallest detail is double-checked. The position of the camera is very important to exalt the action and to have the scene look realistic." His brother is actor Enio Girolami, whom he has often cast in his films.
1965: *$100,000 for Ringo* (ad). 1966: *Django Shoots First* (ad); *A Few Dollars for Django* (d/act); *Ringo's Big Night* (ad); *Ruthless Colt of the Gringo* (ad). 1967: *Any Gun Can Play* (w/d); *Seven Winchesters for a Massacre* (w/p/d). 1968: *Johnny Hamlet* (w/d); *Kill Them All and Come Back Alone* (w/d); *The Moment to Kill* (w); *One Dollar Too Many* (d). 1972: *Tedeum* (w/d). 1975: *Cipolla Colt* (d); *Keoma* (w/d). 1993: *Jonathan of the Bears* (w/d).

CATENACCI, LUCIANO
['Luciano Lorcas'; 'Max Lawrence'; 'Lewis Lawrence']
(Rome, Italy. 1933-1990)

Scowling, bullet-headed character actor. He was a production director in the Sixties until friends and colleagues, notably Mario Bava, convinced him to try acting. He typically portrayed violent, sometimes humorous heavies in westerns and crime films, but earned good notices for his performance as Mussolini in Damiano Damiani's historical drama *Girolimoni* (1972).
1967: *A Colt in the Fist of the Devil; Fury of Johnny Kid; The Greatest Robbery in the West.* 1971: *The Price of Death.* 1972: *Ben and Charlie; Can Be Done… Amigo.* 1973: *Here We Go Again, Eh Providence?* 1974: *Carambola.*

CECCARELLI, PIETRO
['Peter Barclay'; 'Peter Cester' etc]
(Rome, Italy. 1934-)

Bald, beefy stuntman who also took supporting roles. He played minor brutes and killers in numerous *pepla*, costume adventures and westerns, usually dying at the hero's hands. He made an unlikely appearance in the Fellini documentary *A Director's Notebook* (1969).
1963: *The Sign of Zorro.* 1964: *Badmen of the West.* 1966: *Arizona Colt; The Good, the Bad and the Ugly; The Hills Run Red.* 1967: *Ballad of a Gunman; The Handsome, the Ugly and the Stupid; Kill and Pray.* 1968: *Find a Place to Die; The Moment to Kill; The Nephews of Zorro; One Dollar Too Many; Three Silver Dollars; Two Pistols and a Coward.* 1970: *Chuck Mool.* 1971: *Acquasanta Joe; They Call Him Cemetery.* 1972: *His Name Was Holy Ghost; Pistol Packin' Preacher; They Call Him Veritas.* 1973: *A Man Called Invincible.* 1974: *The Crazy Bunch.* 1977: *El Macho.*

CERAMI, VINCENZO
(Rome, Italy. 1940-)

Screenwriter. Long before teaming up with Roberto Benigni (they wrote *Life Is Beautiful* together), the highly regarded Cerami helped devise some of the most unusual Italian westerns, including *The Forgotten Pistolero*, *Hate Is My God* and *Blindman*. A noted novelist, he was a protégé of Pier Paolo Pasolini.
1967: *The Dirty Outlaws.* 1968: *The Silent Stranger.* 1969: *The Forgotten Pistolero; Hate Is My God.* 1971: *Blindman.*

CICERO, NANDO
[Fernando Cicero]
(Asmara, Italy. 1931-1995)

Initially an actor and assistant to the likes of Rossellini, Visconti and Rosi, Cicero turned director in the mid-Sixties. Although he specialised in saucy comedies, he made three contrasting westerns, the best being *Last of the Badmen*, which features a compelling performance by Frank Wolff as a cruel, epileptic villain.
1967: *Last of the Badmen; Red Blood, Yellow Gold.* 1969: *Twice a Judas.*

CIPRIANI, STELVIO
(Rome, Italy. 1937-)

Composer. After studying at Rome's Santa Cecilia Conservatory, he veered towards pop and jazz, honing his skills in the US alongside Dave Brubeck, before composing his first film score for *The Bounty Killer*. The best known among his 200 or so soundtracks is probably *The Anonymous Venetian* (1970), while other notable western work includes a trio of Tony Anthony films, *Shoot First, Laugh Last*, *The Silent Stranger* and *Blindman*, in each of which he utilises

Morricone-esque motifs – amped-up guitar riffs, onomatopoeic effects, shrieking vocals – while adding further humorous touches of his own.
1966: The Bounty Killer. 1967: Shoot First, Laugh Last. 1968: The Silent Stranger. 1969: The Law of Violence. 1970: The Beast. 1971: Blindman; Finders Killers; Heads I Kill You… Tails You're Dead! They Call Me Hallelujah. 1972: The Boldest Job in the West; The Magnificent West; The Return of Hallelujah. 1974: Sons of White Fang. 1975: The Cry of the Wolf; Seven Devils on Horseback.

COBURN, JAMES
(Laurel, USA. 1928-2002)
Actor.

Having rejected the lead in *A Fistful of Dollars* (1964), Coburn – revered among western aficionados, especially at that time, for his ultra-laconic performance in *The Magnificent Seven* (1960) – later accepted Leone's invitation to play a world-weary insurgent in *A Fistful of Dynamite*. Stayed in Italy to portray another jaded protagonist in *A Reason to Live, a Reason to Die* for Leone acolyte Tonino Valerii.
1971: A Fistful of Dynamite. 1972: A Reason to Live, a Reason to Die.

COLIZZI, GIUSEPPE
(Rome, Italy. 1925-1978)
Director/writer. Colizzi learnt the ropes under the tutelage of his uncle, Luigi Zampa, and gained experience as assistant director, scriptwriter, production manager (on Fellini's *The Swindlers* [1954], for example) and producer before making his directorial debut with *God Forgives… I Don't*! This was the first of the Hill-Spencer westerns and was a massive hit – stylish, violent and slyly humorous. He made two sequels in the same subtly seriocomic vein, *Ace High* and *Boot Hill*, but just three further films after that, all contemporary comedies, before his premature death from heart disease. He also published two novels inspired by his travels around North and South America.
1967: God Forgives… I Don't! (w/d). 1968: Ace High (w/d). 1969: Boot Hill (w/p/d/).

CONVERSI, SPARTACO
['Sean/Spean/Spanny Convery'; 'Robert Anthony']
(Rome, Italy. 1916-1989)

Perpetually bearded bit-parter with craggy, lived-in features – memorably shot in the eye through the toe of Cheyenne's boot in *Once Upon a Time in the West*.
1965: Johnny West. 1966: A Bullet for the General; Seven Dollars to Kill; Seven Guns for Timothy; Three Bullets for Ringo. 1967: The Big Gundown; Death, at Owell Rock; Django Kills Softly; Kill and Pray; Seven Pistols for a Massacre; Turn… I'll Kill You!; $20.000 on Number Seven; Two Faces of the Dollar; Viva Django. 1968: Full House for the Devil; The Great Silence; I'll Sell My Skin Dearly; A Long Ride from Hell; Lynching; A Minute to Pray, a Second to Die; Once Upon a Time in the West; One for All. 1969: Quintana; Sabata; Zorro in the Court of England. 1970: Franco and Ciccio on the War-Path; Sartana's Here… Trade Your Pistol for a Coffin; Shango; The Twilight Avengers. 1972: Man of the East. 1973: Charity and the Strange Smell of Money; Halleluja to Vera Cruz.

CORAZZARI, BRUNO
(Castellarano, Italy. 1940-)

Actor. One of the great villainous faces of Italian westerns and *polizieschi*, not dissimilar in looks to Klaus Kinski. He was especially nasty as a cocky, cold-hearted bounty hunter in *The Great Silence*, chilling as a fascistic gang boss in *A Taste of Death* and a sociopathic rapist-killer in *Vendetta at Dawn*. In between playing lowlifes, he was cast against type to good effect in the Altaville sequence of *The Four of the Apocalypse*.
1967: Death Rides a Horse; For $100,000 Per Killing; The Greatest Robbery in the West. 1968: Ace High; The Belle Starr Story; The Great Silence; A Long Ride from Hell; Once Upon a Time in the West; A Professional Gun; A Taste of Death. 1970: Adios, Sabata; Gunman in Town; A Man Called Sledge; Roy Colt and Winchester Jack; Stagecoach of the Condemned. 1971: Doomsday; Vendetta at Dawn. 1975: The Four of the Apocalypse; Red Coat.

CORBUCCI, BRUNO
['Frank B. Corlish'; 'Billy Michaels']
(Rome, Italy. 1931-1996)
Writer/director brother of Sergio, with whom he often collaborated. Principally associated with comedies, Bruno began directing spy spoofs in the mid-Sixties and later had considerable success in Italy with the long-running Nico Giraldi series starring Tomas Milian. In a serious vein, he co-wrote some celebrated westerns, including his brother's *Django* and *The Great Silence*, and directed one of his own, the modest but proficient *Shoot, Gringo, Shoot*. The tiresome comedy *The Three Musketeers of the West* represents a black mark against him.

1961: The Magnificent Three (w). 1966: Django (w); For a Few Dollars Less (w); Four Dollars of Revenge (w); Rebels on the Loose (w/d). 1967: Hate for Hate (w). 1968: The Great Silence (w); Shoot, Gringo, Shoot (w/d); Three Silver Dollars (w). 1970: Franco and Ciccio on the War-Path (w). 1973: Bad Kids of the West (w); The Three Musketeers of the West (w/d).

CORBUCCI, SERGIO
['Stanley Corbett', 'Gordon Wilson Jr']
(Rome, Italy. 1927-1990)
Writer/director. One of the pillars of the genre along with Leone, Sollima and Tessari, Corbucci began as a critic and then wrote scripts, providing material for comedy giants such as Totò and Steno and collaborating on historical films. As a director, he churned out small-scale dramas, comedies and *pepla* efficiently for more than a decade before making his first westerns, in 1964: *Massacre at Grand Canyon* was heavily indebted to American traditions; his next film, *Minnesota Clay*, less so. The extraordinary *Django* is one of the genre's key works, a baroque, bloody masterpiece that continues to exert an influence, and Corbucci did much to popularise political themes in *A Professional Gun* and *Compañeros*. His mature films display a vivid visual style resembling comic strips, characterised by a restless camera, fast cutting, lurid colours, extreme violence and, usually, plenty of gags and pratfalls. Outside the western, he made mostly comedies for domestic consumption, often with great commercial success. He continued working right up until his death of a heart attack. "Corbucci always had this kind of cool, black humour, even in life", remembers Franco Nero. "I remember he used to say to the cameramen, 'Be sure to light those blue lakes of Franco Nero's' – meaning my eyes – 'they will make me a lot of money!' He always possessed that humour. [He] was an incredible character. I remember when he called Jack Palance for *The Mercenary* and said, 'Jack, you're going to play a homosexual in this movie.' He had such amazing charisma he could have convinced anybody to play anything."
1964: Massacre at Grand Canyon (w/d); Minnesota Clay (w/d). 1966: Django (w/p/d); For a Few Dollars Less (w); Navajo Joe (d); Ringo and His Golden Pistol (d). 1967: The Hellbenders (d). 1968: The Great Silence (d); Johnny Hamlet (w); A Professional Gun (w/d). 1969: The Specialists (w/d). 1970: Compañeros (w/d). 1972: Bandits (w/d); What Am I Doing in the Middle of a Revolution? (w/d). 1975: The White, the Yellow, and the Black (w/d).

COSTA, MARIO
['John W. Fordson']
(Rome, Italy. 1908-1995)
Director. A former editor and documentarist, Costa had been directing films since the late Thirties, mainly costume pieces, when he took charge of the mid-budget *Buffalo Bill, Hero of the Far West*, a lively, Hollywoodian adventure that was a considerable hit with home audiences. His last film, another western, was a tawdry Klaus Kinski vehicle, *The Beast*, which seems to have been an unhappy experience for both parties judging from Kinski's acerbic comments in his autobiography, in which

Kinski mistakenly (and rather smugly) asserts that Costa died shortly after completing the film. (According to Marco Giusti, Costa shot some material for another western, *El Rojo* [1966], before the film was taken over by Leopoldo Savona.)
1964: *Buffalo Bill, Hero of the Far West*. 1970: *The Beast* (w/d).

COTTEN, JOSEPH
(Petersburg, USA. 1905-1994)
Actor. The Mercury Player's illustrious career was in decline when he relocated to Italy in the mid-Sixties. He proceeded to give a series of increasingly eccentric performances in westerns (*The Tramplers*, *The Hellbenders*), crime and horror films (including the title role in Mario Bava's *Baron Blood* [1972]). In America he founded his own television production company, and wound down his career with character turns in international productions.
1965: *The Tramplers*. 1967: *The Hellbenders*. 1968: *White Comanche*.

CREA, GIANNI
(Siderno, Italy. 1938-)
Director/writer.
Although he started out as Roberto Rossellini's assistant, Crea's own directorial career was disappointing to say the least. He made only a handful of films, five of them cheap, rough, wretched westerns. The 'best' is probably *On The Third Day Arrived the Crow*, featuring a spirited turn from William Berger.
1969: *The Law of Violence* (w/d). 1971: *Finders Killers* (d); *The Magnificent West* (w/d). 1973: *On The Third Day Arrived the Crow* (d). 1975: *Seven Devils on Horseback* (w/d).

CRESSOY, PIERRE
['Peter Cross'; 'Peter Cabot']
(Vendôme, France. 1924-1980)
Actor. Having previously studied medicine, this suave Frenchman began a career on stage and screen in the Forties. After a brief sojourn in Hollywood (he had a small role in *The War of the Worlds* [1953]), he put his powerful build to profitable use in *pepla* and other Italian co-productions from the Fifties onwards. Moving inevitably on to westerns, he played smooth villains in Giuliano Gemma films and the doctor with a shady past in *Navajo Joe*.
1964: *Samson and the Treasure of the Incas*. 1965: *Adios Gringo*; *One Silver Dollar*. 1966: *Fort Yuma Gold*; *Navajo Joe*; *Seven Guns for the MacGregors*.

DALLAMANO, MASSIMO
['Jack Dalmas'; 'Max Dillman']
(Milan, Italy. 1917-1976)
Cinematographer. A documentary cameraman in the Forties, he made his breakthrough as a cinematographer on the first two 'Dollars' movies. His sharp lighting and strong colour contrasts were integral to the new western aesthetic, which he mastered in his first film as director, the superb *Bandidos*. He completed a few films in other genres before his untimely death in a car accident.
1963: *Gunfight at Red Sands*. 1964: *Buffalo Bill, Hero of the Far West*; *Bullets Don't Argue*; *A Fistful of Dollars*. 1965: *For a Few Dollars More*. 1967: *Bandidos* (d).

DAMIANI, DAMIANO
(Pasiano, Italy. 1922-)
Idiosyncratic writer/director who, rather like Carlo Lizzani, achieved his best results with popular political films. He studied painting before embracing cinema, where he began as an assistant director and scriptwriter. He made the first and arguably the best of the political westerns, *A Bullet for the General*, although he insists the 'western' tag is inappropriate for a story of the Mexican Revolution. Later directed *A Genius, Two Partners and a Dupe*, a rambling Terence Hill vehicle produced by Sergio Leone that proved, if nothing else, that Damiani is uncomfortable with comedy. Many of his films outside the genre have explored organised crime and institutional corruption.
1966: *A Bullet for the General* (w/d). 1975: *A Genius, Two Partners and a Dupe* (w/d).

DAMON, MARK
[Alan Harris]
(Chicago, USA. 1933-)
Actor/producer. The son of Romanian immigrants, Damon travelled to Italy after a low-key career in American movies. He played a self-seeking, smirking gunfighter in *Ringo and His Golden Pistol*, *Johnny Yuma* and several other westerns, but his most satisfying genre performance was as the sadistic southern tyrant in *Kill and Pray*. (We can add Damon's name to the still-growing list of American actors who claim to have been offered a role in *A Fistful of Dollars* by Sergio Leone – in his case, the part of Ramon. Damon also claims, in his recent biography, to have suggested Clint Eastwood to Leone for the lead. He also says that he co-wrote the original story of *Django* with Sergio Corbucci; Damon was to have played the title character in that film, but scheduling conflicts ruled him out.) His acting career petered out in the Seventies but he swiftly turned his attention to other areas of the industry. Putting a business degree acquired in his youth to good use, he flourished first in international sales and distribution before becoming one of Hollywood's most successful independent producers, his remit running from faux erotica (*9½ Weeks*) to critical hits, including the Oscar-winning *Monster* (2003).
1966: *Johnny Yuma*; *Ringo and His Golden Pistol*. 1967: *Death, at Owell Rock*; *Kill and Pray*. 1968: *Dead Men Don't Count!*; *One for All*; *A Train for Durango*. 1972: *The Great Treasure Hunt*; *Pistol Packin' Preacher*; *They Call Him Veritas*.

DAWSON, ANTHONY
(Edinburgh, Scotland. 1916-1992)
Tall, gaunt British actor whose looks pushed him towards villainous roles – he played 'Four Aces', one of John Philip Law's quarries in *Death Rides a Horse*, and the evil patriarch Samuel Pratt in *A Sky Full of Stars for a Roof*. Not to be confused with 'Anthony M. Dawson', aka director Antonio Margheriti.
1967: *Death Rides a Horse*. 1968: *A Sky Full of Stars for a Roof*. 1970: *Deadlock*. 1971: *Red Sun*.

DE ANGELIS, GUIDO (Rome, Italy. 1944-)
DE ANGELIS, MAURIZIO (Rome, Italy. 1947-)
Prolific composer brothers heavily influenced by movements in rock and pop music. Their best-known scores are the ballad-heavy *Keoma* and *A Man Called Blade*, both featuring vocal

above: **Joseph Cotten** (*centre, wearing hat*), as seen in **The Hellbenders**.

above: **Pierre Cressoy**.

above: **Mark Damon**, as seen in **Ringo and His Golden Pistol**.

above: **Anthony Dawson** in **Death Rides a Horse**.

commentaries sung in a hyperbolic fashion that owes a lot to the work of Bob Dylan and Leonard Cohen. They have also recorded as Juniper and The Oliver Onions.
1971: Trinity Is Still My Name. 1972: Man of the East; Tedeum. 1973: Karate, Fists and Beans; The Valdez Horses. 1975: Cipolla Colt; Trinity Plus the Clown and a Guitar; The White, the Yellow, and the Black; Zorro. 1976: Keoma. 1977: A Man Called Blade. 2009: Doc West (Maurizio).

DE GEMINI, FRANCO
(Ferrara, Italy. 1928-)
Musician. De Gemini is to the harmonica what Alessandro Alessandroni is to whistling. His playing can be heard on innumerable western soundtracks, pushing the range of this traditional cowboy instrument past all previous barriers. He personally instructed Charles Bronson on how to make his playing look realistic in *Once Upon a Time in the West* (1968). He later became general manager of Italy's Beat Records.

DE LA LOMA, JOSÉ ANTONIO
(Barcelona, Spain. 1924-2004)
Director/writer of mostly undistinguished mainstream fare. A former teacher (a film was made of his book chronicling his experiences), he penned a number of second-grade Spanish westerns in the mid-Sixties, had his own production company and worked many times with the Balcázars. *1964: $5,000 on the Ace (w). 1965: The Last Tomahawk (w); The Man Who Came to Kill (w); Sunscorched (w); Viva Carrancho (dialogue); Why Go On Killing? (w/d). 1966: Dynamite Jim (w); Five Giants from Texas (w); Seven Guns for Timothy (w); The Texican (w). 1967: Clint the Stranger (w); Red Blood, Yellow Gold (w). 1972: The Boldest Job in the West (w/d).*

DELL'ACQUA, ALBERTO
['Cole Kitosch'; 'Robert Widmark'; 'Albert Waterman']
(1938-)

Coltish blond actor and stuntman usually cast as a naive and/or callow youth, typified by his role as Franco Nero's half-brother in *Texas Adios*. In the comedy phase, he co-starred as 'Trinity' in *Trinity and Sartana are Coming* and 'Sartana' in *Hallelujah & Sartana Strike Again!* for Mario Siciliano. Brother of fellow actors/stuntmen Aldo, Ottavio and Roberto and of actress 'Fern Water'.

1966: Seven Guns for the MacGregors; Texas Adios. 1967: Man, Pride and Vengeance; 32 Caliber Killer; Up the MacGregors; Wanted. 1968: Kill Them All and Come Back Alone; A Minute to Pray, a Second to Die; A Name That Cried Revenge; A Sky Full of Stars for a Roof; This Man Can't Die; Vengeance. 1969: Boot Hill. 1970: They Call Me Trinity; The Twilight Avengers. 1972: Hallelujah & Sartana Strike Again!; Panhandle Calibre 38; Trinity and Sartana Are Coming. 1973: The Son of Zorro. 1977: California. 1991: Buck at the Edge of Heaven.

DELL'AQUILA, VINCENZO
['Vincent Eagle']
(Naples, Italy. 1935-)
Screenwriter/director. Co-author – frequently with Fernando Di Leo – of some entertaining Sixties westerns (*Seven Guns for the MacGregors, Red Blood, Yellow Gold, I Am Sartana, Your Angel of Death*, and he may also have pitched some ideas for *For a Few Dollars More*), he also directed *Tequila Joe*, worth seeing for a gritty performance by Anthony Ghidra.
1966: A Golden Sheriff (w); Seven Guns for the MacGregors (w). 1967: Red Blood, Yellow Gold (w); Up the MacGregors (w). 1968: Bury Them Deep (w); Tequila Joe (w/d). 1969: I Am Sartana, Your Angel of Death (w).

DELL'ORSO, EDDA
[Edda Sabatini]
(Genoa, Italy. 1935-)
Soprano whose soaring, wordless vocals contribute a sense of epic romanticism to Morricone's scores for Leone and many others. Her range is particularly impressive in the euphoric 'The Ecstasy of Gold' from *The Good, the Bad and the Ugly* (1966) and the incomparably beautiful 'Jill's Theme' from *Once Upon A Time in the West* (1968). She is married to composer Giacomo Dell'Orso.

DELLI COLLI, FRANCO
(Rome, Italy. 1929-2004)
Brother of Tonino and a talented cinematographer in his own right, evinced by his stunning work on *Django, Kill!*, his use of colour filters and high-contrast lighting making this one of the most visually arresting and hallucinatory of all Euro-westerns.
1967: Django, Kill! 1968: Dead Men Don't Count!; Shotgun; Zorro the Fox. 1973: The Son of Zorro.

DELLI COLLI, TONINO
(Rome, Italy. 1922 or 1923-2005)
Cinematographer. Entered cinema in his teens and was a fully fledged DP by the age of 21. He shot Italy's first colour film, *Totò a colori* ('Totò in colour'), in 1952, and worked many times with Pasolini, creating vivid urban locales as well as bringing historical worlds to bustling, vibrant life. Beginning with *The Good, the Bad and the Ugly*, he was Leone's third eye, mastering complex set-ups and difficult locations and conditions with wonderful results, reaching a pinnacle – in his estimation – with *Once Upon a Time in America* (1984). He also shot Fellini's final three films and *Life Is Beautiful* (1997), after which he retired. Received the International Achievement Award from the American Society of Cinematographers in 2005.
1966: The Good, the Bad and the Ugly. 1968: Once Upon a Time in the West. 1973: Deaf Smith & Johnny Ears.

DEL POZO, ANGEL
[Angel del Pozo Merino; 'Anthony Clark']
(Madrid, Spain. 1934-)

Actor/director. Making his film debut in 1960, he tended to play unworldly youths in his early career. In westerns, however, he often portrayed devious, cowardly or villainous characters, such as the rapist-killer in *The Big Gundown* and traitorous officer in *Fort Yuma Gold*. He also directed a handful of films in the Seventies, later moving into television production and public relations.
1964: Black Angel of the Mississippi. 1965: The Colt Is My Law; A Place Called Glory. 1966: Fort Yuma Gold; Savage Pampas. 1967: The Big Gundown; Face to Face. 1968: The Wrath of God. 1969: The Price of Power. 1970: El Condor. 1971: Catlow; In the Dust of the Sun. 1972: Now They Call Him Sacrament; Pancho Villa. 1973: The Man Called Noon.

DE LUCA, LORELLA
['Hally Hammond']
(Florence, Italy. 1940-)

Making her debut at 15 in Fellini's *The Swindlers* (1955), she became, for a few years in the late Fifties, a popular teen starlet of the fragile, naive, wholesome variety. She later married director Duccio Tessari and acted almost exclusively for him, notably as the uptight heroine of *A Pistol for Ringo* and anguished wife in the sequel.
1965: A Pistol for Ringo; The Return of Ringo.

DE MARTINO, ALBERTO
(Rome, Italy. 1929-)
Director/writer. After dabbling in documentaries, he worked as an assistant director and scriptwriter throughout the Fifties, turning director at the beginning of the next decade. A specialist in hastily assembled imitations of popular hits, he directed a few effective westerns, such as the money-spinning *$100,000 for Ringo* and the light-hearted *Django Shoots First*.
1962: Two Against All (credited to Antonio Momplet). 1964: Heroes of Fort Worth (w/d). 1965: $100,000 for Ringo (w/d). 1966: Django Shoots First (w/d). 1971: A Fistful of Dynamite (second unit). 1973: Here We Go Again, Eh Providence? (d).

DE MASI, FRANCESCO
['Frank Mason', 'Frank De Masi']
(Rome, Italy. 1930-2005)
Almost as prolific a composer as Morricone, De Masi worked tirelessly in B-movies. He scored dozens of westerns in a bold, heroic style, exemplified by his work for Enzo Castellari on *Any Gun Can Play, Seven Winchesters for a*

Massacre; Johnny Hamlet and Kill Them All and Come Back Alone. His father was once Italy's ambassador to Romania. De Masi succumbed to cancer in 2005.

1962: The Shadow of Zorro. 1963: The Magnificent Three; The Sign of the Coyote. 1964: Badmen of the West; Man of the Cursed Valley; Massacre at Marble City; Two Violent Men. 1965: A Coffin for the Sheriff; For a Fist in the Eye; The Last Tomahawk; The Man from Oklahoma. 1966: Arizona Colt; Ringo the Mark of Vengeance; Ruthless Colt of the Gringo; Seven Dollars to Kill. 1967: Any Gun Can Play; Fifteen Scaffolds for a Killer; The Magnificent Texan; Rattler Kid; Seven Pistols for a Massacre; Seven Winchesters for a Massacre; Two Crosses at Danger Pass. 1968: Blood for Blood; Johnny Hamlet; Kill Them All and Come Back Alone; The Moment to Kill; Ringo the Lone Rider; Sartana Does Not Forgive; A Taste of Death; Tequila Joe. 1970: Challenge of the MacKennas; Sartana's Here... Trade Your Pistol for a Coffin. 1971: Vendetta at Dawn; Zorro, Rider of Vengeance. 1976: Kid Vengeance. 1984: Man Hunt. 1991: Arizona Road.

DE MENDOZA, ALBERTO
[Alberto Manuel Rodríguez Gallego de Mendoza]
(Buenos Aires, Argentina. 1923-)

Character actor whose Latin features steered him towards suave or sleazy roles. In films from the Forties and theatre from the Fifties, firstly in Argentina and Mexico, he settled in Spain in the early Sixties and was a familiar face in the co-production period, equally believable as an untrustworthy sidekick or a villain.
1969: The Forgotten Pistolero; Vengeance Is Mine. 1970: Clumsy Hands.

DEMICHELI, TULIO
[Armando Bartolomé Demicheli]
(Buenos Aires, Argentina. 1914-1992)
Spain-based writer/director who dabbled in various genres, from horror and crime flicks to soft porn and westerns. His finest effort in the last-named field was the briskly paced Robert Hundar/Fernando Sancho film A Man and a Colt, a distant cousin of the revolutionary westerns.
1964: Gunmen of the Rio Grande (w/d). 1967: The Big Gundown (p); A Man and a Colt (w/p/d). 1970: Viva Sabata! (d). 1973: Tequila (d).

DE SANTIS, LUCIO
(Bologna, Italy. 1922-)

Actor. Chubby minor villain, usually prominently moustached, conspicuous as a whip-wielding Mexican at the beginning of Django and as one of the Santa Maria brothers in And God Said to Cain.
1965: A Coffin for the Sheriff. 1966: Django; The Hills Run Red; Ringo and His Golden Pistol; Texas Adios. 1967: Rattler Kid; Son of Django; Viva Django. 1968: Execution; One Against One... No Mercy; Two Pistols and a Coward; Vengeance. 1970: And God Said to Cain.

DI LEO, FERNANDO
(San Ferdinando di Puglia, Italy. 1932-2003)
First-rate screenwriter who worked (uncredited) on A Fistful of Dollars and For a Few Dollars More, as well as The Return of Ringo, Navajo Joe, Johnny Yuma and many other top-flight westerns. Later made his mark as a director with a string of hard-boiled, streetwise crime thrillers. (He also shot some scenes for Florestano Vancini's unjustly overlooked Giuliano Gemma vehicle, Long Days of Vengeance.).
1964: A Fistful of Dollars (w – uncredited). 1965: For a Few Dollars More (w – uncredited/ad); A Pistol for Ringo (w – uncredited); The Return of Ringo (w/ad). 1966: Django (w – uncredited); Johnny Yuma (w); Massacre Time (w); Navajo Joe (w); Seven Guns for the MacGregors (w); Sugar Colt (w). 1967: Death Rides Along (w); Hate for Hate (w); Long Days of Vengeance (w/ad); Pecos Cleans Up (w); Poker with Pistols (w); Up the MacGregors (w); Wanted (w). 1968: Beyond the Law (w); God Forgive... His Life Is Mine (w); The Ruthless Four (w); Tequila Joe (w).

DI STEFANO, FELICE
Little-known composer whose western scores were generally for lower-tier productions. His best work in the genre is the melodramatic/tragic accompaniment to Why Go On Killing? and the brassy, aggressive May God Forgive You – I Won't.
1965: The Sheriff Won't Shoot; A Stranger in Sacramento; Why Go On Killing? 1966: Go with God, Gringo; Ramon the Mexican. 1967: Born to Kill; Cjamango; Don't Wait, Django, Shoot! 1968: May God Forgive You – I Won't. 1969: Quintana. 1970: The Revenge of Ringo. 1971: Brother Outlaw; The Sheriff of Rocksprings.

DONATI, SERGIO
(Rome, Italy. 1933-)
Author/screenwriter. Donati wrote mystery stories in his early career before switching to the advertising industry, from where Sergio Leone sought his services. Initially reluctant to get involved in the western boom, Donati polished up the script to For a Few Dollars More and laboured long and hard to get The Good, the Bad and the Ugly into shape. "For [GBU] I worked eight to nine months on the whole edition of the movie. I rewrote dialogues and, with [the editor] Nino Baragli, we made a kind of miracle. Everybody had decided to cut 20-25 minutes of the movie, and so I was in the movieola with Baragli for two or three days and I adapted new dialogue in the scene with Van Cleef and the soldier without legs. The new dialogue was intended to cover all that was cut out of the movie." Donati went on to play a major part in the politicisation of the genre. His exemplary work with Sollima (The Big Gundown, Face to Face) is matched only by his contributions to Once Upon a Time in the West and A Fistful of Dynamite. We can therefore excuse him the rather less edifying Cipolla Colt.
1965: For a Few Dollars More. 1966: The Good, the Bad and the Ugly; $100,000 for Lassiter. 1967: The Big Gundown; Face to Face. 1968: Once Upon a Time in the West. 1971: A Fistful of Dynamite. 1972: Ben and Charlie. 1975: Cipolla Colt. 1981: Buddy Goes West. 1987: Renegade. 1996: North Star.

EASTMAN, GEORGE
[Luigi Montefiori/Montefiore; 'George Histman']
(Forte dei Marmi, Italy. 1942-)

Actor/writer/director. A giant of a man – he stands 6ft 9in – Eastman initially seemed set for a 'serious' acting career (he studied for a while at the Centro Sperimentale), but, like so many others of his generation (and his physique), he found himself immersed in genre films from the outset. "My height has been a setback throughout my career," he has said, only half jokingly. Employing his mighty frame and malicious smile to his advantage, he played unconventional leads and cruel villains, initially in westerns and later in horror films or whatever filone was flavour of the month. Has also written scripts, including the westerns Chuck Mool and Ben and Charlie, crafted the story outline of Keoma and directed a horror film.
1966: Django Shoots First; My Name Is Pecos. 1967: Django Kills Softly; Django, the Last Killer; Poker with Pistols; Viva Django. 1968: The Belle Starr Story; Hate Your Neighbour. 1969: Boot Hill. 1970: Chuck Mool (act/w). 1971: Bastard, Go and Kill; Vendetta at Dawn. 1972: Ben and Charlie (act/w); The Call of the Wild. 1973: The Three Musketeers of the West. 1975: Red Coat (w); The Tiger from the River Kwai. 1976: Keoma (w).

EASTWOOD, CLINT
[Clinton Eastwood Jr]
(San Francisco, USA. 1930-)
Actor/director/producer. The embodiment of the regenerative power of pastures new, Eastwood's frustration with his faltering Hollywood career led him to take a gamble on a role in a Japanese-inspired, European-produced western that paid off spectacularly.

above: **Eduardo Fajardo** (*centre*), in **Django**. Perpetual whipping-boy **Luciano Rossi** lurks in the background.
left: Minor matinee idol **Clint Eastwood** became a Euro-western icon after appearing in **A Fistful of Dollars**.

He and Leone redefined the concept of heroism in the 'Dollars' films, distilling the essence of the classical western hero – his poise, his understatement, his pistol skills – to an almost parodic degree, largely relieving him of his civic function to create a ruthlessly autonomous, parasitic killing machine whose relationship to society was defined strictly on his terms. Eastwood applied this approach to the mean streets of modern-day San Francisco in the 'Dirty Harry' series, while his finest westerns – *High Plains Drifter* (1973), *The Outlaw Josey Wales* (1976) and *Unforgiven* (1992) – found him wryly evaluating, and eventually moving beyond, his mysterious persona into mature pastures new.
1964: *A Fistful of Dollars*. 1965: *For a Few Dollars More*. 1966: *The Good, the Bad and the Ugly*. (In. 1967, opportunistic producers cut together two episodes of *Rawhide*, titled their illicit feature *The Magnificent Stranger* – *A Fistful of Dollars*' working title – and sold it as a continuation of the 'Dollars' series. Litigation ensued and it was swiftly withdrawn.)

FAGO, GIOVANNI
['Sidney Lean']
(Rome, Italy. 1933-)
Director/writer. Regularly employed as an assistant director in the early Sixties (he was involved with many Franco and Ciccio comedies), Fago's first three solo features were all fine westerns. *For $100,000 Per Killing* fleshes out a bounty hunter's tragic family background; *Full House for the Devil* pulls off the difficult trick of switching from a light-hearted tone to something more serious; and *The Magnificent Bandits* transposes the characters and concerns of the political western to rural Brazil. Has worked largely in television since then.
1966: *Massacre Time* (ad). 1967: *For $100,000 Per Killing*. 1968: *Full House for the Devil*. 1969: *The Magnificent Bandits* (w/d).

FAJARDO, EDUARDO
[Eduardo Martínez Fajardo; 'Robert Warner'; 'Edward Hamilton']
(Mosteiro, Spain. 1918-)
Actor. After early work as a dubber, he played secondary roles in Spanish productions and had a spell in Mexican films. During the western period, Fajardo was the ultimate unctuous villain, his portrayal of Major Jackson in *Django* setting a benchmark. Could be silkily devious or extravagantly brutal as the role demanded, and was a worthy adversary for Anthony Steffen in nine films. In later years he took up drama teaching, and there is a street named after him near his home in Almería.
1964: *Heroes of Fort Worth*. 1965: *A Coffin for the Sheriff*. 1966: *Django; Ringo the Mark of Vengeance; Ringo's Big Night*. 1967: *Gentleman Killer; Last of the Badmen, Seven Pistols for a Massacre*. 1968: *A Gun for a Hundred Graves; Killer Adios; One Against One... No Mercy; One for All; A Professional Gun; A Stranger in Paso Bravo*. 1969: *The Magnificent Bandits; Tierra Brava*. 1970: *Compañeros; A Man Called Joe Clifford; Shango; Viva Sabata!* 1971: *Bad Man's River; El bandido Malpelo; Dead Men Ride; Kill Django... Kill First; Long Live Your Death*. 1972: *Bandits; Tedeum; What Am I Doing in the Middle of a Revolution?* 1973: *Tequila; The Three Musketeers of the West; Yankee Dudler*. 1984: *Yellow Hair and the Fortress of Gold*.

FANTASIA, FRANCO
['Frank Farrell']
(Rome, Italy. 1924-2002)

Beginning in the early Fifties, Fantasia acted in small roles in various *filoni* and was also a respected stunt performer, master of arms and, in the Seventies, assistant director. He was routinely cast in westerns as a sheriff, businessman or official of some kind, but his major contributions were made behind the scenes in the staging of action and stunts.
1962: *Zorro at the Court of Spain*. 1963: *The Sword of Zorro; Zorro and the Three Musketeers*. 1964: *Buffalo Bill, Hero of the Far West*. 1965: *One Silver Dollar; The Three from Colorado*. 1966: *Blood at Sundown; Seven Dollars to Kill*. 1968: *Blood for Blood; Hate Your Neighbour; The Long Day of the Massacre; A Long Ride from Hell; The Nephews of Zorro; The Wrath of God*. 1969: *Zorro in the Court of England*. 1970: *Adios, Sabata; Twenty Thousand Dollars for Every Corpse*. 1971: *Return of Sabata*. 1972: *Ben and Charlie; The Grand Duel*. 1973: *The Son of Zorro*. 1974: *Carambola*. 1977: *California*. 1991: *Buck at the Edge of Heaven*.

FELLEGHY, TOM
[Tommaso Felleghi]
(Budapest, Hungary. 1921-)

With his nondescript looks and medium build, Felleghy was a casting director's dream. He turns up in a vast number of films as officials, villains, patriarchal types, doctors, ranchers etc, effortlessly adopting an authoritative or unassuming demeanour as the role demanded.

1959: The Sheriff. 1961: The Magnificent Three. 1965: The Man from Oklahoma. 1966: Arizona Colt; El Cisco; El Rojo; Go with God, Gringo; Massacre Time; Renegade Gunfighter; Ringo's Big Night. 1967: The Big Gundown; Born to Kill; The Greatest Robbery in the West; Killer Kid; Lola Colt; Two Faces of the Dollar. 1968: Gatling Gun; If You Want to Live... Then Shoot!; Two Pistols and a Coward. 1971: His Name Was King. 1972: Ben and Charlie; A Gunman Called Dakota; Gunmen and the Holy Ghost; Return of the Holy Ghost. 1973: Deaf Smith & Johnny Ears; Halleluja to Vera Cruz. 1974: Court Martial; Return of Shanghai Joe. 1977: California. 1981: Buddy Goes West.

FERRIO, GIANNI
(Vicenza, Italy. 1924-)
Composer whose western work predates even that of Morricone, although Ferrio's scores for the spoofs and Hollywood clones of the pre-Leone days were as predictable as the films themselves. His music kept pace with the genre's development, however, and he provided excellent accompaniment to films such as Fort Yuma Gold (a collaboration with Morricone), Death Sentence and, especially, Vengeance Is Mine.
1960: Un dollaro di fifa. 1961: The Magnificent Three. 1962: Two Against All. 1963: Heroes of the West. 1964: Massacre at Grand Canyon; Three Dollars of Lead; Twins from Texas. 1965: One Silver Dollar. 1966: Djurado; Fort Yuma Gold; Rebels on the Loose. 1967: Death Sentence; The Dirty Outlaws; The Man Who Killed Billy the Kid; Wanted. 1968: Find a Place to Die. 1969: Alive or Preferably Dead; Vengeance Is Mine. 1970: A Man Called Sledge; Reverend Colt; The Twilight Avengers. 1971: Long Live Your Death. 1972: Ben and Charlie. 1973: Fast-Hand Is Still My Name; They Still Call Me Amen. 1977: California. 1985: Tex and the Lord of the Deep.

FERRONI, GIORGIO
['Calvin/Kelvin Jackson Padget']
(Perugia, Italy. 1908-1981)
Writer/director. Already a veteran by the time of the western craze, Ferroni had come to cinema by way of the legal profession. An award-winning documentarist, he also directed one of the first Italian westerns, the light-hearted The Girl of the Golden West (1942), and later enjoyed commercial success with a handful of pepla and three lucrative vehicles for Giuliano Gemma: One Silver Dollar, Fort Yuma Gold and Wanted, which all bucked trends to an extent by displaying a more traditional bias than most Euro-westerns.
1965: One Silver Dollar (w/d). 1966: Fort Yuma Gold. 1967: Wanted. 1968: Two Pistols and a Coward (w/d).

FIDANI, DEMOFILO
['Miles Deem'; 'Slim Alone'; 'Lucky Dickinson'; 'Sean O'Neil'; 'Dick Spitfire' etc]
(Cagliari, Italy. 1914-1994)
Originally a set designer, Fidani wrote and directed 13 peculiarly naïve but genuinely distinctive low-budget westerns, working repeatedly with the same performers and technicians, including his wife, Mila Vitelli, who fulfilled various creative functions, and their daughter, Simonetta, who acted as 'Simone Blondell'. With their haphazard plotting, slack pacing and facile characterisations, not to mention recycled footage, his films test the patience even as they amuse and astound with their narrative conceits. He had his own stock company, a mixture of (relatively) famous faces such as Hunt Powers, Klaus Kinski, Gordon Mitchell, Dean Stratford and Jeff Cameron, and the more obscure likes of 'Dennis Colt' [Benito Pacifico], 'Custer Gail' [Amerigo Leoni], 'Lucky MacMurry' [Luciano Conti] and 'Chet Davis' [Victoriano Gazzara]. Fidani, who apparently counted Fred Astaire musicals among his favourite films, was also a noted medium, even writing books on the subject. "Demofilo really was an adventurous sort of man," remembered Hunt Powers. "He went out and found locations, got casts, shot scenes, wrote scripts, and did everything by sheer determination and his clever wits."
1967: Poker with Pistols (ad). 1968: And Now... Make Your Peace with God (w/p/d); Say Your Prayers and Dig Your Grave (p); Stranger, Make the Sign of the Cross (w/p/d). 1969: Four Came to Kill Sartana (w/d); Shadow of Sartana... Shadow of Your Death! (w/d). 1970: Dead Men Don't Make Shadows (w/d); Django and Sartana Are Coming... It's the End (w/p/d); One Damned Day at Dawn... Django Meets Sartana! (w/p/d). 1971: The Ballad of Django (w/p/d); A Barrel Full of Dollars (w/d); A Fistful of Death (w/d); His Name Was Sam Wallash... But They Called Him Amen! (w/p/d); Lobo the Bastard (d). 1972: Run, Men! Eldorado Is Coming to Trinity (p). 1973: Anything for a Friend (w/p/d).

FIDENCO, NICO
(Rome, Italy. 1933-)
Composer who began his musical career as a pop singer. He had a special affinity for exploitation subjects, exemplified by his slick, sleazy scores for the 'Black Emanuelle' films of the late Seventies. His punchy soundtrack for A Taste for Killing, on which he also sang, is one of his finest, and in John the Bastard he made intelligent use of Alessandroni's Cantori Moderni.
1965: In a Colt's Shadow. 1966: Dynamite Jim; A Taste for Killing; The Texican. 1967: The Bang Bang Kid; John the Bastard. 1968: Bury them Deep; Full House for the Devil; I Want Him Dead. 1971: Lobo the Bastard. 1973: Those Dirty Dogs.

FINOCCHI, AUGUSTO
Writer of some excellent mid-period westerns, including Sugar Colt, Fort Yuma Gold and the ultra-nihilistic Black Jack.
1966: Fort Yuma Gold; Sugar Colt. 1967: Django, the Last Killer; The Greatest Robbery in the West; Wanted. 1968: Black Jack; Lynching; One Dollar Too Many; Two Pistols and a Coward. 1969: In the Name of the Father. 1973: A Colt in the Hand of the Devil; Deaf Smith & Johnny Ears. 1975: Who's Afraid of Zorro? 1977: El Macho.

FONDA, HENRY
(Grand Island, USA. 1905-1982)
Actor. The Hollywood legend's role as Frank in Once Upon a Time in the West was an inspired piece of anti-typecasting. Whatever reservations he may have had about the enterprise were assuaged by a combination of Eli Wallach's reassurances and Leone's persistence and enthusiasm. (The director had been pursuing Fonda for years, ever since trying to sign him up for A Fistful of Dollars.)

According to writer Sergio Donati, Fonda was delighted to play such a despicable character. "The first thing he said was, 'I'm so happy to make this movie, because I have to shoot a kid – to do something really nasty; the nastiest thing I ever did before this was to hurt slightly James Stewart.'" (Fonda and Stewart had recently co-starred in the western Firecreek [1968], with Fonda as another villain, albeit a romanticised one). The actor famously arrived for shooting with brown contact lenses, only for Leone to insist that Fonda's familiar blue eyes were key to the shock effect he was seeking. Fonda's presence also adds significant symbolic weight to the recursive My Name Is Nobody, where he embodies nothing less than the entire 'noble' tradition of the American western. There was no better man for the job.
1968: Once Upon a Time in the West. 1973: My Name Is Nobody.

FRANCHI, FRANCO
[Francesco Benenato]
(Palermo, Italy. 1922 or 1928-1992)
Rubber-faced, gesticulating comic actor who formed a hugely popular double act on stage and film with fellow Sicilian Ciccio Ingrassia. They clowned their way through more than 100 films, including a handful of western spoofs – their earlier ones were particularly big box-office hits – that mocked both American and Italian genre conventions.

1964: Two Gangsters in the Wild West. 1965: For a Fist in the Eye; Two Sergeants of General Custer. 1966: The Sons of Ringo. 1967: The Handsome, the Ugly and the Stupid; Two R-R-Ringos from Texas. 1968: Ciccio Forgives, I Don't!; The Nephews of Zorro. 1970 Franco and Ciccio on the War-Path. 1972: The Two Sons of Trinity. 1975: The Dream of Zorro.

FRANK, HORST
(Lübeck, Germany. 1929-1999)

German actor and singer with an elegant manner and wavy blond hair who specialised in refined, vaguely camp villains. He was good value in a slew of westerns, *gialli* and spy films, attending a stunt school in America to hone the physical requirements of his roles, and maintained a high profile and a heavy workload in Germany well past the peak years for co-productions. As George Hilton has put it, Frank was "a kind of Klaus Kinski in minor tones". Jason Forrester in *The Moment to Kill* is classic Frank: typically suave, he's led into town at one point as the heroes' captive, cowing the townsfolk who joke at his predicament with a peal of manic, menacing laughter.
1963: *Pirates of the Mississippi*. 1964: *Bullets Don't Argue; Massacre at Marble City*. 1965: *The Black Eagles of Santa Fe*. 1967: *Viva Django*. 1968: *Hate Your Neighbour; Johnny Hamlet; The Moment to Kill*. 1971: *Carlos*. 1972: *The Grand Duel*. 1974: *Carambola*.

FULCI, LUCIO
(Rome, Italy. 1927-1996)
Director/writer. Although his filmography is skewed towards gruesome Gothic horror films, Fulci dabbled in most *filoni* during his career and directed three disparate westerns: the gritty and stylish *Massacre Time*, poetic *The Four of the Apocalypse* and sentimental *Silver Saddle*.
1966: *Massacre Time* (d). 1973: *White Fang* (d). 1974: *Challenge to White Fang* (w/d). 1975: *The Four of the Apocalypse* (w/d). 1978: *Silver Saddle* (d).

GADDI, CARLO
['Charles Gate']
(Montefiascone, Italy. 1940-)

Swarthy, shifty-eyed actor who played surly, humourless villains in several westerns and crime films. He stands out among the parade of eccentric bad guys in *Requiem for a Gringo* and sparred memorably with George Hilton in *Full House for the Devil*.

1967: *For $100,000 Per Killing; Pecos Cleans Up*. 1968: *Beyond the Law; Full House for the Devil; The Nephews of Zorro; Requiem for a Gringo; Say Your Prayers and Dig Your Grave*. 1969: *Django the Bastard*. 1970: *Sartana's Here... Trade Your Pistol for a Coffin*. 1972: *God in Heaven... Arizona on Earth; His Name Was Holy Ghost; Kill the Poker Player; My Horse... My Gun... Your Widow*.

GARCÍA, TITO
(Salamanca, Spain. 1931-2003)

Actor. Burly, bald, wide-eyed and often sporting a Zapata moustache, García was inevitably typecast as a Mexican heavy. Starting out as a bullfighter, he appeared in scores of films from the early Sixties onwards and later became a familiar figure on Spanish television.
1963: *Gunfight at Red Sands; The Jaguar*. 1964: *Black Angel of the Mississippi; Bullets Don't Argue; Cavalry Charge; Four Bullets for Joe; Tomb of the Pistolero; Twins from Texas*. 1965: *Finger on the Trigger; For a Fist in the Eye; In a Colt's Shadow; Shoot to Kill*. 1966: *The Bounty Killer; Seven Guns for Timothy*. 1967: *God Forgives... I Don't!; Up the MacGregors*. 1968: *One Against One... No Mercy; One Dollar Too Many; One for All; A Professional Gun; A Train for Durango*. 1969: *Garringo; Vengeance Is Mine*. 1970: *Compañeros; Viva Sabata!* 1971: *Bad Man's River; Blindman; Catlow; Long Live Your Death; A Town Called Bastard*. 1972: *The Fabulous Trinity; The Fat Brothers of Trinity; Vente a ligar al Oeste*. 1973: *The Fighting Fists of Shanghai Joe; Yankee Dudler*. 1975: *The White, the Yellow, and the Black; Zorro*. 1975: *Who's Afraid of Zorro?* 1984: *Al este del Oeste*. 1995: *Sons of Trinity*.

GARKO, GIANNI
['John Garko'; 'Gary Hudson']
(Zara, Italy. 1935-)

Compelling stage-trained dramatic actor who progressed from the volcanic villain of *Blood at Sundown*, modelled partly on Klaus Kinski and partly on Richard Widmark, to the sinister, sardonic Sartana – the *ne plus ultra* of genre anti-heroes. His early theatre work included performances for esteemed directors such as Visconti and Giorgio Strehler, and he has also been prolific on television throughout his career. After Sartana he slipped effortlessly into comic westerns, always underplaying when he was paired with histrionic co-stars. He remains one of the most popular leading men among genre enthusiasts.
1966: *Blood at Sundown*. 1967: *For $100,000 Per Killing; $10,000 Blood Money*. 1968: *Cowards Don't Pray; If You Meet Sartana, Pray for Your Death*. 1969: *I Am Sartana, Your Angel of Death*. 1970: *And Sartana Kills Them All; Gunman in Town; Have a Nice Funeral, Sartana Will Pay*. 1971: *Bad Man's River; The Price of Death; They Call Him Cemetery*. 1972: *His Name Was Holy Ghost*. 1973: *Those Dirty Dogs*.

GARRONE, RICCARDO
['Richard/Rick Garrett']
(Rome, Italy. 1923-)

Actor brother of Sergio (who directed him in two westerns), with sharp features, a keen sense of humour and an air of self-assurance. As well as appearing in a vast number of films, for such distinguished directors as Fellini and Dino Risi, he has worked on television, in theatre and in dubbing, and directed a pair of minor comedies in 1975.
1965: *Two Sergeants of General Custer*. 1966: *De Guello*. 1967: *The Bang Bang Kid*. 1968: *If You Want to Live... Then Shoot!* 1969: *No Room to Die*. 1970: *A Man Called Sledge*. 1972: *The Return of Hallelujah; Tedeum; What Am I Doing in the Middle of a Revolution?; Zorro the Lawman*. 1974: *The Crazy Bunch*.

GARRONE, SERGIO
['Willy S. Regan']
(Rome, Italy. 1926-)
Serviceable director/writer whose best films among the dozen or so he has made were westerns. He began working in the industry in the late Forties but was busiest in the Sixties, writing and producing westerns such as *De Guello* and *Killer Kid*. He took over from Leopoldo Savona to complete his first film as director, *If You Want to Live... Then Shoot!*, and came up trumps with the brisk bounty-hunter film *No Room to Die* and horror-inflected *Django the Bastard*, both starring Anthony Steffen. His final western, *Vendetta at Dawn*, which he reshaped after it was begun by scriptwriter/director Gino Mangini (Mangini returned the favour with *Bastard, Go and Kill*, which Garrone had started directing), was a topical story of cold-blooded killing and retribution, with little in the way of customary Italian western escapism.

1966: *De Guello* (w/p). 1967: *Killer Kid* (w). 1968: *If You Want to Live... Then Shoot!* (w/d); *No Graves on Boot Hill* (w/d). 1969: *Django the Bastard* (w/d); *No Room to Die* (w/d). 1971: *Bastard, Go and Kill* (w); *Kill Django... Kill First* (w/d); *Vendetta at Dawn* (w/d).

GASTALDI, ERNESTO
['Julian Berry']
(Graglia, Italy. 1934-)
Writer/director. One of Italy's busiest and most reliable writers of commercial subjects. While studying at Rome's Centro Sperimentale, he wrote science-fiction stories and later created many excellent horror tales, *gialli* and westerns, including big earners such as *Arizona Colt*, *Day of Anger* and *My Name Is Nobody*. With Vittorio Salerno he invented the original, villainous Sartana in *Blood at Sundown*, before other writers bestowed the name on an altogether different character. He also co-wrote a couple of films in the subsequent 'Sartana' series, infusing them with his sure grasp of the mystery format. Has also directed two thrillers in collaboration with Salerno.
1964: *Buffalo Bill, Hero of the Far West*. 1966: *Arizona Colt*; *Blood at Sundown*. 1967: *Day of Anger*; *For $100,000 Per Killing*; *$10,000 Blood Money*. 1968: *Cowards Don't Pray*; *Full House for the Devil*. 1969: *I Am Sartana, Your Angel of Death*; *The Price of Power*. 1970: *Arizona*; *Gunman in Town*. 1972: *Can Be Done… Amigo*; *The Grand Duel*; *A Reason to Live, a Reason to Die*. 1973: *My Name Is Nobody*. 1975: *A Genius, Two Partners and a Dupe*.

GEMMA, GIULIANO
['Montgomery Wood']
(Rome, Italy. 1938-)
One of the giants of the genre, hugely popular in Italy in his heyday, his quixotic persona contrasting with the cynicism of the majority of his peers. Most of his protagonists fight for justice in one way or another, although his role in *A Pistol for Ringo* is, on the surface at least, as cynical as they come, and he was a picture of emotional torment in the sequel. He wielded considerable power at his peak, to the extent that he persuaded producer Edmondo Amati to replace Alberto De Martino with Giorgio Ferroni as director of *Fort Yuma Gold*. (Amati placated De Martino with *Django Shoots First*.) Subsequently blossomed into an award-winning dramatic actor of critical cachet, even branching out into the occasional unsympathetic role – he was outstanding as a military martinet in *Desert of the Tartars* (1976), for example. He returned to the saddle in 1985 to play the wholesome hero of a long-running Italian western comic strip in *Tex and the Lord of the Deep*. Artistic in more than one sense, he is also an accomplished sculptor. His two daughters launched their own fashion line in 2007 inspired partly by their father's films and partly by the Euro-western in general. Reflecting on the genre as a whole, he says, "The principle qualities lie in the sense of escapism – they are spectacular and relaxing films. The defects, which in fact became another quality, were their cruelty and their violence, which were taken to such a level that they couldn't influence anyone – it was clear that they were just choreography, a joke, that we were deliberately exaggerating."

1965: *Adios Gringo*; *One Silver Dollar*; *A Pistol for Ringo*; *The Return of Ringo*. 1966: *Arizona Colt*; *Fort Yuma Gold*. 1967: *Day of Anger*; *Long Days of Vengeance*; *Wanted*. 1968: *A Sky Full of Stars for a Roof*. 1969: *Alive or Preferably Dead*; *The Price of Power*. 1972: *Ben and Charlie*. 1975: *The White, the Yellow, and the Black*. 1977: *California*. 1978: *Silver Saddle*. 1985: *Tex and the Lord of the Deep*.

GHIDRA, ANTHONY
[Dragomir 'Gidra' Bojanic]
(Kragujevac, Serbia. 1933-1993)
Lean, rugged and adaptable, Ghidra was one of the most popular and prolific performers in his homeland, where he worked solidly from the Fifties until his death. He broke briefly onto the international stage in the late Sixties in five minor Italian westerns, in which he played ageing, world-weary gunfighters and, in one case, a brutal villain, with skill and sensitivity.
1964: *Among Vultures*. 1967: *Ballad of a Gunman*; *Django, the Last Killer*. 1968: *A Hole Between the Eyes*; *May God Forgive You – I Won't*; *Tequila Joe*.

GHIGLIA, BENEDETTO
(Florence, Italy. 1921-)
Composer. Son of a famous classical guitarist, Ghiglia made a small but worthy contribution to the western. The melancholic music for Giuliano Gemma's *Adios Gringo*, with its haunting Fred Bongusto vocal, and the stripped-down score to *For a Dollar in the Teeth*, which matches the raw feel of the film itself, are especially effective. Outside the genre, Pasolini's *Pigsty* (1969) was arguably the highpoint of Ghiglia's career.
1965: *Adios Gringo*. 1966: *El Rojo*; *Four Dollars of Revenge*; *Starblack*. 1967: *For a Dollar in the Teeth*.

GIOMBINI, MARCELLO
(Rome, Italy. 1928-2003)
Composer. His most notable western scores demonstrate his (and the genre's) versatility: the tongue-in-cheek music for *Sabata*, with quirky themes defining each of the principal characters, and the more sombre, but no less melodic, electric-guitar driven *Garringo*.
1965: *The Relentless Four*. 1966: *For a Few Dollars Less*; *$100,000 for Lassiter*. 1967: *Ballad of a Gunman*; *Death Walks in Laredo*. 1968: *Dead Men Don't Count!*; *One for All*. 1969: *Garringo*; *Sabata*. 1970: *And Sartana Kills Them All*; *Viva Sabata!* 1971: *Acquasanta Joe*; *El bandido malpelo*; *Return of Sabata*. 1972: *Too Much Gold for One Gringo*. 1975: *Dallas*.

GIORDANO, DANIELA
(Palermo, Italy. 1947-)
Actress. A former Miss Italy who progressed to acting in the late Sixties without ever securing a truly testing or interesting role. Raven-haired and self-assured, she breezed through a large number of second-rate films in the Seventies as the love interest or a glamorous cipher. Her westerns of note include Carnimeo's *Find a Place to Die* and *Have a Nice Funeral, Sartana Will Pay*, where her cunning character holds her own against the wily protagonist.
1968: *Find a Place to Die*; *The Long Day of the Massacre*. 1969: *The Five Man Army*; *Four Came to Kill Sartana*. 1970: *Challenge of the MacKennas*; *Have a Nice Funeral, Sartana Will Pay*. 1971: *Four Pistols for Trinity*; *Lobo the Bastard*. 1972: *Run, Men! Eldorado Is Coming to Trinity*; *Trinity and Sartana Are Coming*.

above: **Giuliano Gemma** in **The Return of Ringo**.

above: **Anthony Ghidra** (*right*), as seen in **Django, the Last Killer**.

above: **Daniela Giordano**.

GIRALDI, FRANCO
['Frank Garfield/Grafield']
(Comeno, now Komen, Slovenia. 1931-)
Director/writer. After a period as a critic, he served as assistant director from the mid-Fifties and took charge of second units, notably on *A Fistful of Dollars*, before turning director with the light-hearted 'MacGregor' movies and *Sugar Colt*, an expert blend of irony and drama that introduced Hunt Powers to the Italian western. Renowned for his sure comic touch, Giraldi diversified with the angry, outcast-themed *A Minute to Pray, a Second to Die*. He has never achieved great commercial success, but continued to work in the industry into the 21st Century.
1964: A Fistful of Dollars (second unit); Massacre at Grand Canyon (second unit). *1966*: Seven Guns for the MacGregors (d); Sugar Colt (w/d). *1967*: Up the MacGregors (w/d). *1968*: A Minute to Pray, a Second to Die (d).

GIROLAMI, ENIO
['Thomas Moore']
(Rome, Italy. 1934 or 1935-)

Elder brother of Enzo Castellari and frequently a supporting player in his films, usually as a villain. He began acting as a teenager, working with esteemed directors such as Bolognini, Lattuada and Fellini, but after 1960 he performed almost exclusively for his father, Marino, and, later, his younger brother.
1964: Bullets and the Flesh. *1965*: The Black Eagles of Santa Fe. *1966*: A Few Dollars for Django. *1967*: The Hellbenders; Seven Winchesters for a Massacre; Two R-R-Ringos from Texas. *1968*: Between God, the Devil and a Winchester; Johnny Hamlet. *1970*: Reverend Colt. *1993*: Jonathan of the Bears.

GIROLAMI, MARINO
['Frank Martin'; 'Fred Wilson']
(Rome, Italy. 1914-1994)
The patriarch of the Girolami clan and a flexible producer/director of commercial films. Abandoning medical studies, he trained at the Centro Sperimentale and learnt the ropes under such luminaries as Mario Bonnard and Mario Soldati. Among his 80 or so directed titles were a number of successful comedies and a few indifferent westerns.
1964: Badmen of the West (w/d); Bullets and the Flesh (w/d). *1966*: A Few Dollars for Django (p). *1967*: Seven Winchesters for a Massacre (w); Two R-R-Ringos from Texas (w/d). *1968*: Between God, the Devil and a Winchester (w/p/d); One Against One... No Mercy (w). *1970*: Reverend Colt (p/d). *1972*: Jesse & Lester: Two Brothers in a Place Called Trinity (d).

GORI, CORIOLANO
['Lallo Gori']
(Ravenna, Italy. 1927-1982)
Composer. As well as scoring comedies, sex and spy films in the Sixties, Gori wrote some infectious music for (mostly) cut-price westerns, notably for a string of Demofilo Fidani efforts. Given Fidani's tendency to recycle footage from one film to another, it's no surprise that Gori's music was reused several times as well.
1966: Massacre Time; My Name Is Pecos. *1967*: Buckaroo; Death Rides Along; The Handsome, the Ugly and the Stupid; Pecos Cleans Up; Poker with Pistols. *1968*: Black Jack; Execution, Lynching. *1969*: Shadow of Sartana... Shadow of Your Death!; Zorro the Conqueror. *1970*: Dead Men Don't Make Shadows; Django and Sartana Are Coming... It's the End; One Damned Day at Dawn... Django Meets Sartana! *1971*: The Ballad of Django; A Barrel Full of Dollars; Durango Is Coming, Pay or Die; A Fistful of Death; His Name Was Sam Wallash... But They Called Him Amen! *1972*: Pistol Packin' Preacher; Zorro the Lawman. *1973*: Anything for a Friend; Tequila.

GOZLINO, PAOLO
['Paul Stevens']
(Senigallia, Italy. 1921-)

Actor. Although often employed as a villain (as in *Django the Bastard* and several comic westerns in the Seventies), this former dancer, choreographer and supporting player of various *filoni* could also display a sympathetic side, as in *Full House for the Devil*, where he impresses as a good-natured outlaw who teams up with George Hilton. He enjoyed a rare leading role in the fun superhero caper *Flashman* (1967).
1959: The Sheriff; The Terror of Oklahoma. *1967*: Clint the Stranger. *1968*: Full House for the Devil; One After the Other; Vengeance. *1969*: Django the Bastard. *1971*: Heads I Kill You... Tails You're Dead! They Call Me Hallelujah. *1972*: His Name Was Holy Ghost; Now They Call Him Sacramento; The Return of Hallelujah; Thunder Over El Paso.

GRADOLI, ANTONIO
['Anthony Gradwell']
(Rome, Italy. 1917-)

Versatile character actor in the mould of Andrea Bosic and Tom Felleghy, typically cast in westerns as a crooked banker/businessman who bites off more than he can chew. Ferguson, the unctuous saloon owner in *Sabata*, was a typical role.
1962: Zorro at the Court of Spain. *1963*: The Magnificent Three; The Sign of the Coyote; The Sword of Zorro. *1964*: Ride and Kill; The Road to Fort Alamo; Samson and the Treasure of the Incas. *1966*: Savage Gringo. *1967*: Face to Face. *1969*: Death on a High Hill; Sabata; Zorro in the Court of England; Zorro, Marquis of Navarra. *1970*: Adios, Sabata. *1971*: Judge Roy Bean. *1972*: Where the Bullets Fly; Zorro the Lawman. *1973*: The Blue Gang. *1975*: Trinity Plus the Clown and a Guitar.

GRANGER, STEWART
[James Stewart]
(London, England. 1913-1993)

Swashbuckling leading man who brought a welcome sense of self-parody to the role of Karl May's Old Surehand in three of the best 'Winnetou' films. He was once married to Jean Simmons.
1964: Among Vultures. *1965*: Flaming Frontier; Rampage at Apache Wells.

GRIMALDI, ALBERTO
(Naples, Italy. 1925-)
Producer. Grimaldi was a lawyer who moved into film distribution in the early Sixties, picking up Joaquín Romero Marchent's first westerns for screening in Italy. He went on to set up Produzioni Europee Associati (PEA), which reaped enormous profits from Leone's *For a Few Dollars More* and *The Good, the Bad and the Ugly* – the latter co-produced by United Artists, with which Grimaldi had struck up a financing and distribution deal – and later produced successful works by Sollima, Corbucci, Parolini, Barboni and, outside the genre, Pasolini, Bertolucci and Rosi. Writer Sergio Donati worked with Grimaldi on several occasions: "He never came on the set. He was more of a businesslike producer, but he loved the job. He used to be very discreetly behind the scenes." Grimaldi returned to the international limelight by co-producing Martin Scorsese's *Gangs of New York* (2002).
1962: The Shadow of Zorro. *1964*: Two Violent Men. *1965*: For a Few Dollars More. *1966*: The Good, the Bad and the Ugly; Legacy of the Incas; $100,000 for Lassiter. *1967*: The Big Gundown; Face to Face. *1968*: A Professional Gun. *1969*: Sabata. *1970*: Adios, Sabata. *1971*: Return of Sabata. *1972*: Man of the East. *1975*: Dallas. *1978*: La ciudad maldita.

GRIMALDI, GIOVANNI
(Catania, Italy. 1917-2001)
Writer/director who specialised in comedies. A former journalist and critic, he wrote parodies for the likes of Totò and Franco and Ciccio and, as a director, squeezed in a couple of straight westerns – *In a Colt's Shadow* and *Starblack* – among a string of undistinguished spoofs.

1961: *The Magnificent Three* (w). 1965: *In a Colt's Shadow* (w/d). 1966: *Four Dollars of Revenge* (w); *Starblack* (w/d). 1967: *The Handsome, the Ugly and the Stupid* (w/d). 1970: *Franco and Ciccio on the War-Path* (w).

GUERRIERI, ROMOLO
[Romolo Girolami; 'Rod Gilbert']
(Rome, Italy. 1931-)
Director. Brother of Marino Girolami, under whose tutelage he served for much of the Fifties. His first three directed films were westerns: the lightweight Sean Flynn vehicle *Seven Guns for Timothy* was followed by two near-classics – the violent *Johnny Yuma* and brooding *$10,000 Blood Money*, and he shot some footage for *Boot Hill* (1969) before being replaced by Giuseppe Colizzi. He also made stylish crime films and *gialli*, and has worked more recently in television. Signed most of his films under his mother's maiden name of Guerrieri.
1964: *$5,000 on the Ace* (ad); *Minnesota Clay* (ad). 1965: *The Man Who Came to Kill* (ad). 1966: *Johnny Yuma* (w/d); *Seven Guns for Timothy* (d). 1967: *Any Gun Can Play* (w); *$10,000 Blood Money* (d).

HALSEY, BRETT
[Charles Oliver Hand; 'Montgomery Ford']
(Santa Ana, USA. 1933-)
Actor. A one-time contract player for Universal (where he was repeatedly cast as juvenile delinquents) and 20th Century Fox, this handsome leading man went to Europe in the early Sixties to star in costume adventures and westerns. He made a strong impression as an avenger in *Today It's Me...Tomorrow You!* and *The Wrath of God*, dressed sombrely, his characters drained of any other purpose but revenge. He later wrote a salacious novel, *The Magnificent Strangers*, inspired by his experiences in Europe and populated by self-absorbed, self-destructive expat musclemen and aspiring actors (some of them not so loosely based on real people, although Halsey, perhaps wisely, won't be drawn on their identities); there is even a cameo by one 'Monty Ford' – Halsey's own alter ego. Other books have followed, as well as acting appearances on US television, roles in a string of cheap Italian horror flicks in the Eighties, and stints in production and teaching. He is the nephew of Admiral 'Bull' Halsey, commandeer of the US Third Fleet in the Second World War, and was once married to Italian actress Luciana Paluzzi.
1966: *Kill Johnny Ringo!* 1968: *Today It's Me... Tomorrow You!*; *The Wrath of God*. 1969: *$20,000 Stained in Blood*. 1970: *Roy Colt and Winchester Jack*.

HARDIN, TY
[Orson Whipple Hungerford Jr]
(New York City, USA. 1930-)
Actor. The clean-cut star of Warners' TV western *Bronco* (1958-62) and a few forgettable B-movies, he stayed in Europe for a decade or so after filming *Battle of the Bulge* (1965). In Italy, he starred or co-starred in a number of adventures and minor westerns, notably as the eccentric, heavily disguised gravedigger-gunfighter out for revenge in the patchwork production *Doomsday*. Hardin's personal story is far more interesting than any of his films: after returning to the States in the mid-Seventies he was linked with a radical, anti-government 'survivalist' group, the Arizona Patriots (some reports claim he was their leader), which fell foul of the authorities and was disbanded in the Eighties. He gave up acting to become a preacher.
1964: *Man of the Cursed Valley*. 1966: *Savage Pampas*. 1967: *Custer of the West*. 1971: *Acquasanta Joe*; *Doomsday*; *The Last Rebel*; *Vendetta at Dawn*. 1972: *You're Jinxed, Friend, You've Met Sacremento*.

HARGITAY, MICKEY
[Miklos Hargitay]
(Budapest, Hungary. 1926-2006)
Actor and bodybuilder who won the Mr Universe title in 1955 and joined the muscle-bound 'May West Revue' with the likes of Gordon Mitchell and Brad Harris. He married Jayne Mansfield in 1958 and they made a peplum together, *The Loves of Hercules* (1960), before Hargitay was drawn towards offbeat westerns (mostly very cheap ones) and exploitation films. He is best known for his histrionic performance as the 'Crimson Executioner' in Italian trash classic *Bloody Pit of Horror* (1965). Father of Golden Globe-winning actress Mariska Hargitay.
1965: *The Sheriff Won't Shoot*; *A Stranger in Sacramento*. 1966: *Three Bullets for Ringo*. 1967: *Cjamango*. 1970: *The Revenge of Ringo*.

HARRIS, BRAD
['Brad Euston'; 'Robin McDavid']
(St. Anthony, USA. 1933-)
Actor. Harris was inspired by Steve Reeves's example to take up bodybuilding, and subsequently followed his idol's lead into acting. He earned small roles in America and undertook stunt work in *Spartacus* (1960), before travelling to Europe. He profited from the peplum craze before starring in three picturesque German westerns and a few forgettable Italian efforts. Worked many times with Gianfranco Parolini and partnered Tony Kendall in the long-running 'Kommissar X' spy series, in which Harris displayed a self-deprecating side to complement his physical abilities.
1963: *Pirates of the Mississippi*. 1964: *Massacre at Marble City*. 1965: *The Black Eagles of Santa Fe*. 1967: *Rattler Kid*. 1970: *Wanted Sabata*. 1971: *Durango Is Coming, Pay or Die*. 1972: *Django...Adios!*

HARRISON, RICHARD
(Salt Lake City, USA. 1935-)
Another American beefcake actor who left an indifferent Hollywood career behind to make his mark in *pepla*, westerns and other action films. (Not that there was as much variety in his roles as he would have liked. As he told me, "The worst thing about Italy is that they put you in a slot and you can't get out of it. I wanted to do completely different types of films and they wouldn't let me.") He famously turned down the lead role in *A Fistful of Dollars* and claims to have put Clint Eastwood's name forward instead. Harrison's understated style was best exploited in *Vengeance*, where he plays a brooding half-breed at odds with the world. He later dabbled in direction (with Marino Girolami) with the slapstick western *Jesse & Lester: Two Brothers in a Place Called Trinity*, and wrote the story for Bruno Mattei's *Scalps*.

above: **Brett Halsey** on the cover of this soundtrack release for **The Wrath of God**.

above: **Ty Hardin**.

above: **Mickey Hargitay**.

above: **Brad Harris**.

above: **Richard Harrison**, as seen in **Dig Your Grave Friend... Sabata's Coming**.

above: **Gérard Herter**.

above: **Craig Hill**.

above: **Terence Hill**.

above: **George Hilton**.

above: **Cris Huerta** (right).

His son Sebastian starred in another late Mattei western, *White Apache* (1986). Today Harrison is ambivalent about Euro-westerns, despite the lift they gave his career: "They did very well, but I thought they were so exaggerated. I guess it was the beginning of camp movies."
1963: *Gunfight at High Noon*; *Gunfight at Red Sands*. 1965: *$100,000 for Ringo*. 1966: *El Rojo*. 1968: *Between God, the Devil and a Winchester*; *One After the Other*; *Vengeance*. 1970: *Reverend Colt*; *Stagecoach of the Condemned*. 1971: *Acquasanta Joe*; *Dig Your Grave Friend… Sabata's Coming*; *His Name Was King*; *The Sheriff of Rocksprings*. 1972: *The Deadly Trackers*; *The Fabulous Trinity*; *Jesse & Lester: Two Brothers in a Place Called Trinity* (act/co-d/p); *Shoot Joe, and Shoot Again*. 1986: *Scalps* (w).

HERTER, GÉRARD
(Hamburg, Germany. 1928-)
Distinguished-looking European actor with a devilish glint in his eyes who specialised in autocratic, eccentric villains. After attracting attention as an Austrian officer in Mario Monicelli's *The Great War* (1959), he went on to play similarly stereotypical martinets in *The Big Gundown* and *Adios, Sabata*. He gave one of his best performances as another army type, the disgraced, misanthropic Colonel Blackgrave, in the downbeat caper western *Two Faces of the Dollar*.
1964: *The Road to Fort Alamo*. 1967: *Any Gun Can Play*; *The Big Gundown*; *Red Blood, Yellow Gold*; *Two Faces of the Dollar*. 1968: *Full House for the Devil*; *Gatling Gun*. 1970: *Adios, Sabata*.

HILL, CRAIG
[Craighill Fowler]
(Los Angeles, USA. 1926 or 1931-)
Actor. A multi-purpose leading man with a likeable persona, Hill's beginnings in Hollywood found him working with some of its biggest names: directors William Wyler, Sam Fuller and John Ford, and stars Bette Davis, James Cagney and Kirk Douglas. Despite this, his early career was unfulfilling (although he was co-lead in the popular TV series *Whirlybirds*), and he joined the exodus to Europe where he settled snugly into westerns, playing both gritty and light-hearted roles. From above-average entries such as *A Taste for Killing* and *I Want Him Dead* he drifted into mediocre productions in the Seventies, by which time he was branching out into other genres. Settled in Spain in 1978 and married popular Spanish actress Teresa Gimpera in 1990.
1965: *Hands of a Gunfighter*. 1966: *A Taste for Killing*. 1967: *Fifteen Scaffolds for a Killer*; *Rick and John, Conquerors of the West*; *Seven Pistols for a Massacre*. 1968: *Bury Them Deep*; *I Want Him Dead*; *No Graves on Boot Hill*. 1971: *And the Crows Will Dig Your Grave*; *Doomsday*. 1972: *An Animal Called Man*; *My Horse.. My Gun… Your Widow*; *Return of the Holy Ghost*; *Run, Men! Eldorado Is Coming to Trinity*. 1974: *Court Martial*. 1975: *In the Name of the Father, of the Son and of the Colt*.

HILL, TERENCE
[Mario Girotti]
(Venice, Italy. 1939-)
Actor/producer/director. Lithe, blue-eyed leading man of Italian-German parentage who passed through distinct phases on the journey to success. Discovered for the cinema by director Dino Risi, he played teenagers in sentimental comedies in Italy in the Fifties, landed a small role in *The Leopard*, took romantic supporting parts in a number of German westerns, then returned to Italy as the laconic co-protagonist of Giuseppe Colizzi's successful 'Cat and Hutch' trilogy. He then struck gold as the genial, family-friendly superstar of the 'Trinity' films, *My Name Is Nobody* and others. His partnership with Bud Spencer is one of the best loved and most enduring in Italian cinema history. Long based in America, he has also produced and directed for the cinema and television and has two sons who work in the film business. A recent TV mini-series/feature film, *Doc West*, demonstrates his continuing love affair with the western.
1964: *Among Vultures*; *Last of the Renegades*. 1965: *Duel at Sundown*; *Flaming Frontier*; *Rampage at Apache Wells*. 1967: *God Forgives… I Don't!*; *Rita of the West*; *Viva Django*. 1968: *Ace High*. 1969: *Boot Hill*. 1970: *The Anger of the Wind*; *They Call Me Trinity*. 1971: *Trinity Is Still My Name*. 1972: *Man of the East*. 1973: *My Name Is Nobody*. 1975: *A Genius, Two Partners and a Dupe*. 1987: *Renegade* (act/w). 1991: *Lucky Luke* (act/d). 1994: *Troublemakers* (act/d). 2009: *Doc West* (act/d).

HILTON, GEORGE
[Jorge Hill]
(Montevideo, Uruguay. 1934-)
Actor. Swarthy leading man who worked in radio and theatre in Uruguay before breaking into Argentinian films in the late Fifties. He soon transferred to the buoyant Italian scene – quite by chance, he says, after boarding the first plane out of Argentina to escape a complicated love affair. His Latin good looks were exploited in *fotoromanzi* (photo storybooks) and made him a natural for leading roles in adventure films and, especially, westerns, where he leaned towards light-hearted roles. After making his breakthrough as a drunkard in *Massacre Time*, still his own favourite performance, he made 20 further westerns in a very busy ten-year spell, during which time he also became a recurring shady suspect in *gialli*. Has taken smaller character parts since his heyday, often in television productions.
1966: *Massacre Time*; *The Sons of Ringo*. 1967: *Any Gun Can Play*; *The Greatest Robbery in the West*; *Kitosch, the Man Who Came from the North*; *Last of the Badmen*; *Poker with Pistols*; *Red Blood, Yellow Gold*. 1968: *Dead for a Dollar*; *Full House for the Devil*; *The Moment to Kill*; *The Ruthless Four*. 1969: *Vengeance Is Mine*. 1970: *Sartana's Here… Trade Your Pistol for a Coffin*. 1971: *Heads I Kill You… Tails You're Dead! They Call Me Hallelujah*. 1972: *The Return of Hallelujah*. 1973: *A Man Called Invincible*. 1974: *The Crazy Bunch*. 1975: *Trinity Plus the Clown and a Guitar*. 1975: *Who's Afraid of Zorro?* 1977: *El Macho*.

HOSSEIN, ROBERT
[Robert Hosseinoff]
(Paris, France. 1927-)
Actor/director. Son of composer André Hossein, he first began acting and directing at the infamous Théâtre du Grand-Guignol. In films, he starred in and directed a number of *noir*-esque thrillers, as well as a downbeat story of South American revolutionaries, *The Taste of Violence*, but became truly popular in France as co-star with Michèle Mercier in the romantic

'Angelique' series. He later cast Mercier in his moody revenge western, *Cemetery Without Crosses*, in which he is excellent as a haunted gunfighter. A friend of Sergio Leone, Hossein was lined up for a role in *Once Upon a Time in the West* (1968) until other commitments intervened. (Rumours persist that Leone shot some footage for *Cemetery* while in Almería scouting locations for *Once Upon a Time*.).
1961: *The Taste of Violence* (act/w/d). 1969: *Cemetery Without Crosses* (act/w/d). 1971: *Judge Roy Bean* (act).

HUERTA, CRIS
[Crisanto Huerta Brieva; 'Chris Huerta'; 'Christopher Harton']
(Lisbon, Portugal. 1935-2004)
Actor. The son of Spanish parents, his chubby physique, malleable face and exuberant acting style were exploited in many *pepla* (his debut was in Leone's *The Colossus of Rhodes* [1962]) and westerns, in which he was cast almost invariably as either a Mexican *bandido* or the hero's comic foil. Huerta plays the role of hotel clerk in *Cemetery Without Crosses* that was supposedly earmarked for Sergio Leone, and for which the director has mistakenly been credited in the past.
1964: *Massacre at Fort Grant; Two Violent Men.* 1965: *The Last Tomahawk; The Relentless Four; Seven Hours of Gunfire.* 1966: *Navajo Joe; Seven Guns for the MacGregors.* 1967: *Bandidos; Two Crosses at Danger Pass.* 1968: *One Against One... No Mercy; A Sky Full of Stars for a Roof; White Comanche.* 1969: *Alive or Preferably Dead; Cemetery Without Crosses.* 1970: *And Sartana Kills Them All; Cannon for Cordoba; Reverend Colt; Viva Sabata!* 1971: *Captain Apache; Four Candles for My Colt; The Legend of Frenchie King; A Town Called Bastard.* 1972: *Ben and Charlie; The Fabulous Trinity; The Fat Brothers of Trinity; His Name Was Holy Ghost; My Horse.. My Gun... Your Widow.* 1973: *Karate, Fists and Beans; A Man Called Invincible; The Three Musketeers of the West; Three Supermen of the West.* 1974: *The Crazy Bunch.* 1975: *Valley of the Dancing Widows; The White, the Yellow, and the Black.* 1985: *Tex and the Lord of the Deep.*

HUNDAR, ROBERT
[Claudio Undari; 'Bob Hunter']
(Castelvetrano, Italy. 1935-2008)

Actor. Very tall, and blessed with a blood-chilling scowl, this physically imposing Sicilian was equally credible as an anti-hero or a towering heavy – it is hard to imagine he was once destined for a career in accountancy. He first caught the eye in the Spanish-Italian westerns of Joaquín Romero Marchent in the early Sixties and was proud of his place in film history: "In a way we were pioneers of cinema… before Leone made his films with Clint Eastwood, we'd already done four or five films." He worked solidly in the Sixties and Seventies, latterly in crime films. He regretted having been typecast as a villain, but he invariably made a good (clenched) fist of his roles.
1962: *The Shadow of Zorro.* 1963: *Gunfight at High Noon; The Magnificent Three.* 1964: *Ride and Kill; Seven from Texas.* 1965: *The Relentless Four; Son of Jesse James.* 1966: *$100,000 for Lassiter; Ramon the Mexican.* 1967: *Death Rides Along; A Man and a Colt.* 1968: *A Hole Between the Eyes; A Name That Cried Revenge.* 1969: *Sabata.* 1971: *Cut-Throats Nine.* 1973: *The Fighting Fists of Shanghai Joe.* 1975: *Dallas; Red Coat; White Fang and the Gold Diggers; White Fang and the Hunter.* 1977: *California.*

INDUNI, LUIS
[Luigi Induni Radici; 'Albert Lockwood']
(Romano, Italy. 1920-1979)

Actor. A former Italian soldier, he arrived in Spain in the Forties and quickly became a fixture in domestic productions; he was made a Spanish national in 1959. A well-built man, he often played paternal or overbearing characters. He worked continuously right up until his death.
1963: *Gunfight at High Noon.* 1964: *Billy the Kid; Ride and Kill; Seven from Texas; Tomb of the Pistolero; Two Violent Men.* 1965: *Adios Gringo; Hands of a Gunfighter; The Last of the Mohicans; $100,000 for Ringo; The Relentless Four; Shoot to Kill; Son of Jesse James; Sunscorched; Why Go On Killing?* 1966: *Djurado; A Fistful of Songs; Ringo's Big Night; Ruthless Colt of the Gringo; The Texican; A Woman for Ringo.* 1967: *Fury of Johnny Kid; The Magnificent Texan; The Man Who Killed Billy the Kid; Rattler Kid; Turn... I'll Kill You!* 1968: *Cowards Don't Pray; Dead Men Don't Count!; Fedra West; Killer Adios; Mestizo; One for All.* 1969: *Garringo.* 1970: *Adios Cjamango; And Sartana Kills Them All; Clumsy Hands; Gunman in Town; Have a Nice Funeral, Sartana Will Pay; Plomo sobre Dallas; Twenty Steps to Death; Twenty Thousand Dollars for Every Corpse; Viva Sabata!* 1971: *Captain Apache; Dig Your Grave Friend... Sabata's Coming; The Legend of Frenchie King.* 1972: *Ben and Charlie; God in Heaven... Arizona on Earth; My Horse.. My Gun... Your Widow; Prey of Vultures; The Return of Clint the Stranger; Too Much Gold for One Gringo; Zorro the Lawman.* 1973: *Karate, Fists and Beans.* 1974: *Blood River.* 1975: *The White, the Yellow, and the Black.*

INGRASSIA, CICCIO
[Francesco Ingrassia]
(Palermo, Italy. 1922-2003)

Actor. Gaunt, long-suffering straight man to Franco Franchi's squat buffoon. After the partnership dissolved he took serious roles, memorably as Uncle Teo in Fellini's *Amarcord* (1974) and as a self-flagellating politician in Elio Petri's enigmatic *Todo Modo* (1976).
1964: *Two Gangsters in the Wild West.* 1965: *For a Fist in the Eye; Two Sergeants of General Custer.* 1966: *The Sons of Ringo.* 1967: *The Handsome, the Ugly and the Stupid; Two R-R-Ringos from Texas.* 1968: *Ciccio Forgives, I Don't!; The Nephews of Zorro.* 1970: *Franco and Ciccio on the War-Path.* 1972: *The Two Sons of Trinity.*

IPPOLITI, SILVANO
(Cagli, Italy. 1923-)
Cinematographer. He didn't make many contributions to the western but is responsible for one of the most visually striking of all: Corbucci's *The Great Silence*, with its white open spaces, contrasting moody interiors and eerie nocturnal finale, an unconventional showdown flecked with gently falling snow.
1966: *De Guello; Navajo Joe.* 1968: *The Great Silence.* 1974: *Challenge to White Fang.*

IQUINO, IGNACIO F.
['Steve M(a)cCohy']
(Valls, Spain. 1910-1994)
Director/writer/producer. A journeyman who began directing in the Thirties, Iquino – son of a musician father and actress/singer mother – tried his hand at most popular genres, including a handful of mediocre westerns, usually under the auspices of his production company, IFISA. Well known for his penny-pinching ways, Iquino, like Alfonso Balcázar, later took advantage of the 'S' classification, under which softcore sex films flourished in Spain between 1977 and 1982, making a series of profitable ventures in this vein. He was married to screenwriter Juliana San José de la Fuente.
1965: *Joe Dexter* (w/p/d). 1966: *A Dollar of Fire* (w/p); *Five Dollars for Ringo* (w/p). 1967: *Seven Pistols for a Gringo* (w). 1969: *El Puro* (w). 1970: *Stagecoach of the Condemned* (w/p); *Twenty Steps to Death* (w/p – some sources also credit Iquino as co-director). 1971: *Dig Your Grave Friend... Sabata's Coming* (w/p); *Four Candles for My Colt* (w/p/d). 1972: *The Fabulous Trinity* (w/p/d); *The Fat Brothers of Trinity* (w/p).

IRELAND, JOHN
(Vancouver, Canada. 1914-1992)
Actor. Although nominated as Best Supporting Actor for *All the King's Men* (1949), Ireland was restricted to B-movie leads and the occasional supporting turn in Hollywood. He didn't begin his Italian adventures until the late Sixties, when he played with great

gusto in a string of westerns as co-lead, villain or sympathetic bandit, giving a particularly strong performance as a guilt-ridden father-turned-outlaw who teams up with his long-lost son in *A Taste of Death*. Back in America in the Seventies, he continued to give decent performances in forgettable films and TV series right up until his death.

1967: Hate for Hate. 1968: Dead for a Dollar; Gatling Gun; A Gun for a Hundred Graves; One for All; Run, Man, Run; A Taste of Death; Vengeance for Vengeance; Villa Rides. 1970: Challenge of the MacKennas. 1974: Blood River. 1980: Bordello.

ISRAEL, VICTOR
[José María Soler Vilanova]
(Barcelona, Spain. 1929-2009)

Actor. A cult figure among aficionados of Spanish genre cinema, this stout actor, with his protruding eyes, jutting jaw and jagged teeth, was condemned principally to villainous parts, especially in horror movies, although over the course of his career he also played comedic roles.

1965: A Place Called Glory; Shoot to Kill. 1966: Dynamite Jim; The Good, the Bad and the Ugly; Seven Guns for the MacGregors; Sugar Colt; The Texican; Yankee. 1967: Bandidos; Up the MacGregors. 1968: A Gun for a Hundred Graves; Killer Adios; One Dollar Too Many; A Sky Full of Stars for a Roof; White Comanche. 1969: Alive or Preferably Dead. 1970: Arizona Kid; Compañeros. 1971: Catlow; Long Live Your Death. 1972: Bandits; His Name Was Holy Ghost; What Am I Doing in the Middle of a Revolution? 1975: The White, the Yellow, and the Black. 1984: Al este del Oeste.

JASPE, JOSÉ
(La Coruña, Spain. 1906-1974)

A stage actor since childhood, Jaspe's film career didn't get under way until after the Spanish Civil War. He spent much of the Fifties and Sixties in Italian co-productions, doing the rounds of all the most profitable genres. With his weathered features and salt-and-pepper beard, he was something of a utility player, finding regular work in westerns as a despot or bandit, typified by his tongue-in-cheek portrayal of the eccentric General Monk, one of Sartana's adversaries in *Gunman in Town*.

1963: The Magnificent Three; The Sign of the Coyote. 1964: Two Violent Men. 1965: The Relentless Four; Son of Jesse James. 1966: El Rojo; Savage Pampas; Thompson 1880. 1968: Cowards Don't Pray; A Gun for a Hundred Graves; Killer Adios; One After the Other; Ringo the Lone Rider; A Stranger in Paso Bravo; White Comanche. 1969: Zorro the Conqueror. 1970: Gunman in Town; More Dollars for the McGregors. 1971: Long Live Your Death; Red Sun. 1972: Thunder Over El Paso. 1973: The Man Called Noon.

KENDALL, TONY
[Luciano Stella]
(Rome, Italy. 1936-2009)

Actor. After swapping *fotoromanzi* for feature films, dark-haired, chisel-cheeked Kendall (he adopted this stage name at the suggestion of Vittorio de Sica) became a mainstay of all the popular European genres from the early Sixties onwards. He was allegedly one of the candidates to play the lead in *A Fistful of Dollars*, rejecting the opportunity. He formed a durable double-act with Brad Harris, playing suave private eye Joe Walker in the jokey 'Kommissar X' adventures, and dabbled in westerns – the offbeat revenge film *Hate Is My God*, in which his character has a peculiarly intense bond with his pet dog, was his best.

1963: Pirates of the Mississippi. 1965: The Black Eagles of Santa Fe. 1969: Hate Is My God. 1970: Django Against Sartana; The Twilight Avengers. 1971: Brother Outlaw; Gunman of 100 Crosses. 1978: Zanna Bianca e il grande kid.

KINSKI, KLAUS
[Nikolaus Nakszynski]
(Danzig, now Sopot, Poland. 1926-1991)

Actor. Possessing one of the great movie faces and a notoriously irascible personality ("He was hated throughout the whole film world," says George Hilton), Kinksi first demonstrated his trademark intensity in fiery poetry recitals and stage performances. He played minor roles in forgettable German films before breaking onto the international scene in the mid-Sixties. He earned good notices for his cameo as an anarchist prisoner in *Dr Zhivago* (1965), but it was his performance in the same year in a very different sort of film, *For a Few Dollars More*, that steered him away from prestige productions

towards lucrative guest spots in genre films. "The life I live is very expensive," he once said. "The best movie in the world I wouldn't do without money… There was a time I didn't read scripts at all – I just counted my lines and how much they were going to pay me." This apparent indifference to his art was consistent with the arrogance and/or indolence that characterise many of his cameos and villainous turns in westerns (his disingenuous Loco in *The Great Silence* is a strong contender for best spaghetti western bad guy) and other potboilers, although he did accept more challenging work in the Seventies, most famously his five films with Werner Herzog, before returning to genre flicks the following decade. His co-stars have never been short of an opinion on him. "Klaus Kinski spent his whole life fighting," says Richard Harrison. "He loved to make people squirm." Hunt Powers was more blunt: "He was a son of a bitch of the highest order… He treated everyone as if they were slaves." Father of actress Nastassja Kinski.

1964: Last of the Renegades; The Last Ride to Santa Cruz. 1965: For a Few Dollars More. 1966: A Bullet for the General. 1967: Man, Pride and Vengeance. 1968: The Great Silence; If You Meet Sartana, Pray for Your Death; The Ruthless Four. 1969: I Am Sartana, Your Angel of Death; Twice a Judas. 1970: And God Said to Cain; The Beast. 1971: A Barrel Full of Dollars; Black Killer; A Fistful of Death; His Name Was King; The Price of Death; Shoot the Living and Pray for the Dead; Vengeance Trail. 1972: The Return of Clint the Stranger. 1973: The Fighting Fists of Shanghai Joe. 1974: Return of Shanghai Joe. 1975: A Genius, Two Partners and a Dupe.

KLIMOVSKY, LEÓN
[León Dulfano]
(Buenos Aires, Argentina. 1906-1996)

Director. A former dentist whose parents were from Kiev, he made his first film in 1947 and crossed all genres over the course of a long career. His westerns are mostly dull affairs (though some of them were apparently helmed by other directors, with Klimovsky only credited for quota purposes), but he made a more favourable impression on the horror film in the newly permissive Seventies.

1962: Torrejón City. 1964: Billy the Kid. 1966: Ballad of a Bounty Hunter. 1967: Rattler Kid. 1969: Quinto: Fighting Proud; Tierra Brava. 1970: Challenge of the MacKennas (w/d). 1971: Hands Up, Dead Man! You're Under Arrest.

Who's Who In Euro-Westerns

KNOX, MICKEY
[Abraham Knox]
(New York City, USA. 1921 or 1922-)
Actor / writer / dialogue adaptor / producer. Knox's Hollywood acting career came to an abrupt halt when he was blacklisted after refusing to testify before the HUAC. Seeking refuge in Italy, he acted in minor roles and adapted dialogue, devising quotable lines for the English versions of *The Good, the Bad and the Ugly* (1966) and *Once Upon a Time in the West* (1968) in particular. He was also executive producer of Duccio Tessari's *Long Live Your Death* (1971), a none-too-happy experience he recounts with great wit in his 2004 autobiography *The Good, the Bad and the Dolce Vita*.

KOCH, MARIANNE
['Marianne Cook']
(Munich, Germany. 1931-)

Actress. Koch's minimal but memorable role as Marisol in *A Fistful of Dollars* was an astute piece of casting. After a brief flirtation with Hollywood, she became one of the most popular actresses in Germany in the early Sixties and her presence in Leone's film helped secure the funding of Munich's Constantin Film. She gave up acting in the early Seventies and later re-entered the medical profession, her first vocation.
1964: *A Fistful of Dollars; The Last Ride to Santa Cruz*. 1965: *A Place Called Glory; Sunscorched*. 1966: *Who Killed Johnny Ringo?* 1967: *Clint the Stranger*.

KOLDITZ, GOTTFRIED
(Altenbach, Germany. 1922-1982)
Director/writer. One of East German studio DEFA's stable of directors, he joined the organisation in the mid-Fifties after working in theatre and later made a handful of popular *Indianerfilme* – co-writing two of them, the handsomely mounted *Apaches* and its sequel, *Ulzana*, with star Gojko Mitic.
1968: *Trail of the Falcon*. 1973: *Apaches* (w/d). 1974: *Ulzana* (w/d). 1982: *The Scout* (w).

LACERENZA, MICHELE
(Taranto, Italy. 1922-1989)
Trumpeter and composer. Lacerenza's trumpet solos are used to great dramatic effect in *A Fistful of Dollars*, ranging from heroic to ominous, and they are a hallmark of the four scores he composed for director Alberto Cardone.
(As composer): 1966: *Blood at Sundown*. 1968: *The Long Day of the Massacre; The Wrath of God*. 1969: *$20,000 Stained in Blood*.

LANFRANCHI, MARIO
(Parma, Italy. 1927-)
Director/actor. Known principally for his work in television and theatre (he staged a number of successful operas – his first wife was American-born soprano Anna Moffo), Lanfranchi wrote and directed the elliptical, stylish revenge western *Death Sentence*, coaxing fine performances from a small cast including Tomas Milian as an epileptic albino addicted to gold and blondes.
1965: *A Stranger in Sacramento* (act). 1966: *A Golden Sheriff* (act); *Navajo Joe* (act). 1967: *Death Sentence* (w/d).

LAVAGNINO, ANGELO FRANCESCO
(Genoa, Italy. 1909-1987)
Composer. Born into a musical family, he trained at Milan's Giuseppe Verdi Conservatory and spent many years as a teacher (counting Francesco De Masi among his students) before he began composing for cinema in the early Fifties. He wrote around 300 film scores over a 30-year career, and was Leone's first choice to score *A Fistful of Dollars*. Although he didn't get that assignment, among the westerns he did write for is Corbucci's *The Specialists*, in which his jaunty, upbeat music jars initially, but synchronises gradually with the film's transgressive tone.
1963: *Samson and the Slave Queen*. 1964: *$5,000 on the Ace; Gunmen of the Rio Grande; Samson and the Treasure of the Incas*. 1965: *Hands of a Gunfighter; Johnny West; The Last of the Mohicans; The Man Who Came to Kill; Seven Hours of Gunfire; Son of Jesse James; The Tramplers; Two Sergeants of General Custer; Viva Carrancho!* 1966: *Four Dollars of Revenge; Legacy of the Incas; Zorro the Rebel*. 1967: *Kill the Wicked; Kitosch, the Man Who Came from the North*. 1968: *Dead for a Dollar; A Gun for a Hundred Graves; Requiem for a Gringo; Saguaro; A Stranger in Paso Bravo; Today It's Me... Tomorrow You!; Vengeance for Vengeance*. 1969: *The Specialists; Zorro in the Court of England; Zorro, Marquis of Navarra*.

LAWRENCE, PETER LEE
[Karl Hirenbach; 'Arthur Grant']
(Lindau, Germany. 1945-1974)

Actor. Blond-haired, boyish German lead who made his first appearance (uncredited) as the ill-fated suitor of Lee Van Cleef's sister in *For a Few Dollars More*. Adopting an Audie Murphy-like persona, he starred or co-starred as affecting young avengers or sharp-witted, fresh-faced gunfighters in a string of westerns, with his role as a psychopathic avenger in *Garringo* being a welcome departure. Once married to Spanish actress Cristina Galbo, he committed suicide upon learning he had a brain tumour.
1965: *For a Few Dollars More*. 1967: *Days of Violence; Fury of Johnny Kid; The Man Who Killed Billy the Kid; 32 Caliber Killer*. 1968: *A Gun for a Hundred Graves; Killer Adios; One Against One... No Mercy*. 1969: *Death on a High Hill; Garringo*. 1970: *Clumsy Hands; More Dollars for the McGregors; Viva Sabata!* 1971: *Four Pistols for Trinity; Hands Up, Dead Man! You're Under Arrest*. 1972: *God in Heaven... Arizona on Earth; Prey of Vultures*.

LEONE, SERGIO
['Bob Robertson']
(Rome, Italy. 1929-1989)
Director/producer. The son of a director father and actress mother, Leone developed into one of the most influential filmmakers of all time. An assiduous assistant director in the Fifties, he combined the lessons learnt from his Italian and American mentors with his encyclopaedic knowledge of cinema to radically transform one of his favourite genres, the western, which he believed had stagnated and felt compelled to rescue. His 'Dollars' trilogy portrayed a fantastical frontier, ruled by violence and venality, which bore little resemblance to any depiction that had come before, inspiring a legion of lesser filmmakers, both European and American, in the process. *Once Upon a Time in the West* was a major progression, a romantic elegy for a lost age and a loving tribute to the western itself, while *A Fistful of Dynamite*, written with Sergio Donati, countered the optimistic outlook of most other films in the political sub-genre. The bittersweet comedy *My Name Is Nobody*, which he produced, is almost a Leone film by proxy, and his last work as director, the sprawling *Once Upon a Time in America* (1984), almost does for the gangster film what his 'Dollars' series had done for the western. Meticulously detailed, boldly stylised and frequently very funny, albeit in the blackest of shades, his body of work is as substantial as that of any other popular director of the 20th Century.
1964: *A Fistful of Dollars* (w/d). 1965: *For a Few Dollars More* (w/d). 1966: *The Good, the Bad and the Ugly* (w/d). 1968: *Once Upon a Time in the West* (w/d). 1971: *A Fistful of Dynamite* (w/d). 1973: *My Name Is Nobody* (p). 1975: *A Genius, Two Partners and a Dupe* (p).

LIBERATORE, UGO
(San Valentino, Italy. 1927-)
Writer/director. Wrote stories and scripts for many *pepla*, as well as for critically acclaimed directors such as Bolognini and Damiani. His westerns include *The Hellbenders* and *A Minute to Pray, a Second to Die*. As a director, he courted controversy with two 1968 films – *Il sesso degli angeli* and *Bora Bora* – both centred on troubled young protagonists and featuring copious amounts of drugs, sex and violence.
1965: *The Tramplers* (w). 1966: *Mutiny at Fort Sharp* (w). 1967: *The Hellbenders* (w). 1968: *A Minute to Pray, a Second to Die* (w).

LINÉ, HELGA
[Helga Lina Stern]
(Berlin, Germany. 1932-)

Actress. Her family left Germany for Portugal at the outset of the Second World War. A gymnast, dancer, circus performer and model, Liné got her break in films when she was spotted in a beauty contest. Tall and sultry, with an air of calculating intelligence, she found gainful employment in the Sixties and Seventies in a great many westerns, spy films, horror films etc, usually playing cruel, refined beauties.
1963: The Sign of Zorro. 1965: In a Colt's Shadow; Seven Hours of Gunfire. 1970: Have a Nice Funeral, Sartana Will Pay. 1971: Hands Up, Dead Man! You're Under Arrest. 1973: Those Dirty Dogs. 1978: China 9, Liberty 37.

LIZZANI, CARLO
['Lee W. Beaver']
(Rome, Italy. 1922-)

Writer/director/film historian. Lizzani was a journalist who collaborated on scripts with some of the leading figures in neorealism, including Giuseppe de Santis and Roberto Rossellini. His own directed works, particularly his early ones, have a similarly gritty flavour and focus on socio-political themes (he also made well-received documentaries), and he is responsible for a number of thought-provoking commercial movies in a number of genres. He followed the enjoyable revenge western *The Hills Run Red* with a minor classic, *Kill and Pray*, a quasi-mystical fable about an angelic avenger-cum-revolutionary who challenges a power-mad Southern aristocrat. Lizzani wrote a much-praised critical survey of Italian cinema in 1953 and had a spell in charge of the Venice Film Festival (1979-82).
1966: The Hills Run Red. 1967: Kill and Pray (p/d).

LORENZON, LIVIO
['Charles Lawrence']
(Trieste, Italy. 1921 or 1923-1971)

Actor. Bald, bulbous-nosed, robustly built and usually dubbed with a suitably gruff, gravelly voice, Lorenzon was good value as a villain or rogue in numerous costume adventures, *pepla* and westerns in the Fifties and Sixties, and was capable of more than one gear – see his oddly endearing turn as a despot's reluctant trigger-man in *Texas Adios*. He made more than 70 films in a relatively short career.
1959: The Sheriff; Terror of Oklahoma. 1962: Zorro at the Court of Spain. 1963: Zorro and the Three Musketeers. 1964: The Last Gun. 1965: Colorado Charlie; The Colt Is My Law. 1966: Go with God, Gringo; The Good, the Bad and the Ugly; Savage Gringo; Texas Adios. 1967: Buckaroo; Cjamango; Rita of the West; Two R-R-Ringos from Texas. 1968: Ace High; Chrysanthemums for a Bunch of Swine; Gun Shy Piluk; A Rope for a Bastard. 1969: God Will Forgive My Gun.

LOY, MINO
(Sassari, Italy. 1933-)

Producer of stylish westerns (*$10,000 Blood Money*, *For $100,000 Per Killing*) and slick *gialli* (*Sweet Body of Deborah*, *So Sweet, So Perverse*) in the Sixties, Loy, who also directed the occasional film, later had hits with cannibal horror films.
1967: For $100,000 Per Killing; $10,000 Blood Money. 1971: They Call Him Cemetery. 1974: The Crazy Bunch.

LUCIDI, MAURIZIO
(Florence, Italy. 1932-)

A former editor and assistant director (his most prestigious credit being Pasolini's *The Gospel According to St Matthew*), he became a dexterous director. He delivered the stark, violent *My Name Is Pecos*, although his speciality was comedic action films in the vein of *The Greatest Robbery in the West*, a boisterous caper western, and the Bud Spencer vehicle *Can Be Done… Amigo*.
1966: My Name Is Pecos. 1967: The Greatest Robbery in the West; Pecos Cleans Up. 1972: Can Be Done… Amigo.

LULLI, PIERO
['Peter Carter'; 'Peter Lull']
(Florence, Italy. 1923-1991)

Actor. From an artistic background (his father was a baritone, his elder brother Folco a respected screen actor), Lulli was one of the cruellest and most charismatic genre villains. His craggy face was usually creased into a scowl or cracked by a sinister smile, and he gave the impression of fully inhabiting his wicked roles. Standout performances include the treacherous Oaks in *Django, Kill!* and the white-suited slave driver in *The Fighting Fists of Shanghai Joe*.
1963: The Sign of the Coyote; The Sign of Zorro. 1964: Buffalo Bill, Hero of the Far West; Bullets and the Flesh. 1965: Hands of a Gunfighter. 1966: El Rojo; Savage Gringo; A Taste for Killing. 1967: Cjamango; The Dirty Outlaws; Django, Kill!; For $100,000 Per Killing; Fury of Johnny Kid; Kitosch, the Man Who Came from the North; Seven Pistols for a Massacre. 1968: Dead Men Don't Count!; Find a Place to Die; God Forgive… His Life Is Mine; A Gun for a Hundred Graves; Ringo the Lone Rider; Shotgun. 1969: The Forgotten Pistolero. 1970: Chapagua's Gold; Gunman in Town; Sartana's Here… Trade Your Pistol for a Coffin. 1972: The Boldest Job in the West; Zorro the Lawman. 1973: The Fighting Fists of Shanghai Joe; My Name Is Nobody. 1975: The Crazy Adventures of Len and Coby; Trinity Plus the Clown and a Guitar.

LUPO, MICHELE
(Corleone, Italy. 1932-1989)

Director. A consummate craftsman, Lupo made first-rate genre films that usually contained a humorous streak. He mastered action scenes in a handful of *pepla*, and later worked several times with Giuliano Gemma – they fashioned the impressive *Arizona Colt* and made a telling late contribution with *California*, which proved that Lupo could handle darker material as well as any of his contemporaries. He retired in the Eighties when he inherited a chain of supermarkets.
1965: For a Fist in the Eye. 1966: Arizona Colt (w/d). 1972: Ben and Charlie. 1977: California. 1981: Buddy Goes West.

MACHIAVELLI, NICOLETTA
(Modena, Italy. 1944-)

Raven-haired actress descended from the famous statesman and playwright. She made her debut opposite Ugo Tognazzi in Luigi Zampa's popular *A Question of Honour* (1965) but, despite critical praise for this and other early performances, she was soon playing decorative roles in westerns and other genre films. The bizarre *Garter Colt*, in which she plays the lead role, was a failed attempt to make her a star, and she was lost among the international cast of the comedy *Monte Carlo or Bust* (1969). She abandoned acting in the late Seventies and today resides in America, where she teaches Italian at Washington University in Seattle.
1966: The Hills Run Red; Navajo Joe. 1968: Garter Colt; Hate Your Neighbour; A Minute to Pray, a Second to Die. 1969: No Room to Die.

MADISON, GUY
[Robert Moseley]
(Pumpkin Center, California, USA. 1922-1996)

Sturdy, square-jawed TV western star, briefly touted as a matinee idol in the Forties, who found work in Europe when Hollywood lost interest. Flexed his acting muscles as the embittered, renegade Confederate colonel in *Seven Winchesters for a Massacre*, but mostly played stolid, Hollywood-style heroes. He shared the bemusement/frustration of American actors at Italian working methods: "Even if we could have shot live sound", he once told *Westerns all'Italiana* magazine, "the Italians couldn't stop shouting at each other long enough for a take." *1964: Apaches' Last Battle; Gunmen of the Rio Grande. 1966: Five Giants from Texas; Legacy of the Incas. 1967: The Bang Bang Kid; Seven Winchesters for a Massacre; Son of Django. 1968: This Man Can't Die. 1970: Reverend Colt.*

MALLORQUÍ, JOSÉ
[José Mallorquí Figuerola]
(Barcelona, Spain. 1913-1972)
Prolific Spanish novelist and screenwriter who created the Zorroesque El Coyote – brought to the screen in 1955 by Joaquín Romero Marchent – and collaborated on several pioneering Spanish westerns, including more by Romero Marchent. His son César later revived El Coyote for a 1998 sequel.
1955: The Coyote (characters); The Judgement of the Coyote (characters). 1962: The Shadow of Zorro; Zorro the Avenger. 1963: Heroes of the West; The Magnificent Three; The Sign of the Coyote. 1964: Four Bullets for Joe; Ride and Kill. 1967: The Man Who Killed Billy the Kid. 1968: Killer Adios. 1969: Death on a High Hill.

MANCINI, CLAUDIO
Producer/production manager. A key figure in Rafran, Sergio Leone's production company. He played the part of Harmonica's brother in the flashback scenes in *Once Upon a Time in the West*. *(As producer): 1973: My Name Is Nobody. 1975: A Genius, Two Partners and a Dupe.*

MANCORI, SANDRO
[Alessandro Mancori]
Cinematographer. As Gianfranco Parolini's DP of choice, Mancori shot some of the genre's most energetic and imaginative action scenes. In addition, he conjured up some delirious lighting and colour schemes – particularly impressive in *If You Meet Sartana, Pray for Your Death* and the Gothic opening of *Return of Sabata*.
1967: Kill and Pray; Killer Kid. 1968: If You Meet Sartana, Pray for Your Death; If You Want to Live... Then Shoot!; No Graves on Boot Hill; Two Pistols and a Coward. 1969: Sabata. 1970: Adios, Sabata; Sartana in the Valley of Death. 1971: Return of Sabata. 1973: Charity and the Strange Smell of Money. 1976: God's Gun. 1987: Django Strikes Again.

MANN, LEONARD
[Leonardo Manzella]
(Albion, USA. 1947-)

Brooding Italian-American actor who broke into the profession at an early age while on a prolonged European vacation – "I was all of 21 and scared to death, but plunged ahead." He portrayed tragic, traumatised youngsters in *The Forgotten Pistolero*, *Chuck Mool* and *Vengeance Trail*, and went on to play similarly intense or troubled characters in dramas and *polizieschi*. He never achieved the kind of stardom his looks and talent deserved, and gave up acting at the end of the Eighties. "At that point in my life I had had enough of cocky casting directors and agents who would never tell you the truth," he says. He switched careers and today is a practising psychotherapist in California.
1969: The Forgotten Pistolero. 1970: Chuck Mool. 1971: Vengeance Trail.

MANNI, ETTORE
['Red Carter']
(Rome, Italy. 1927-1979)

Actor. Square-jawed and serious-looking, Manni displayed his versatility as lead or supporting actor in a wide variety of comedies, dramas, costume films, westerns and other adventures. He accidentally shot and killed himself while filming Fellini's *City of Women* in 1979.
1966: Ringo and His Golden Pistol; Starblack. 1967: Shoot First, Laugh Last. 1968: And Now... Make Your Peace with God; Bury Them Deep; Stranger, Make the Sign of the Cross. 1969: I Am Sartana, Your Angel of Death. 1970: Dead Men Don't Make Shadows; Django and Sartana Are Coming... It's the End. 1973: Anything for a Friend; The Valdez Horses. 1978: Silver Saddle.

MARGHERITI, ANTONIO
['Anthony M. Dawson'; 'Anthony Daisies']
(Rome, Italy. 1930-2002)
Famously resourceful director and special-effects technician who crafted the excellent Gothic westerns *Vengeance* and *And God Said to Cain*, which share many traits with his well-regarded horror films of the early Sixties. Margheriti made his mark in just about every genre (he was one of the first Italian directors to tackle science fiction with any success), and defines the kind of cost-conscious craftsman who flourished when Italian commercial cinema was at its peak.
1967: Dynamite Joe (d). 1968: Vengeance (w/d). 1970: And God Said to Cain (w/d). 1974: The Stranger and the Gunfighter (w/d); Whisky and Ghosts (w/d). 1975: Take a Hard Ride (d).

MARÍN, FRANCISCO
(Barcelona, Spain. 1920-1983)
Cinematographer who shot several titles for the Balcázars (Tessari's 'Ringo' films, for example) and was responsible for the wonderful vistas and vivid, copper-toned visages in *Tepepa*.
1965: The Last Tomahawk; A Pistol for Ringo; The Return of Ringo; Sunscorched. 1966: The Texican. 1967: Gentleman Killer; Long Days of Vengeance; Red Blood, Yellow Gold. 1968: Gatling Gun; Tepepa. 1969: Twice a Judas.

MARK, ROBERT
[Roger Francke/'Rod(d) Dana']
(Utah, USA. 1934-)

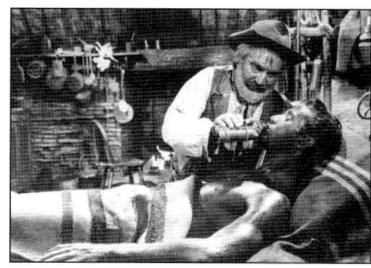

Actor, singer, voice artist and writer. Lead actor in two low-budget westerns by Tanio Boccia – in one of which, *Kill or Be Killed*, he supplemented his pistol rig with a violin – he was also one of the most sought-after voice artists in Rome during the Sixties. As a singer he preferred classical works, but did perform the theme song for Sergio Corbucci's *Massacre at Grand Canyon* (1964). Of the Italian approach to the western, he told me, "The thing I found so delightfully amusing was their almost naive and childlike approach to the genre. They were like unorganised children having an absolute ball trying to get all the other kids to play their game in their way. They just experimented following the American model of Ringo – Son of Ringo, the Ghost of Ringo, the Return of Ringo, etc, each hoping to luck out and create a Sergio Leone niche."
1966: Kill or Be Killed. 1967: Kill the Wicked.

MARTELL, PETER
[Pietro Martellanza]
(Bolzano, Italy. 1938-2010)

Actor. A former Mr Italy who segued into spaghetti westerns, Martell played both heroic leads and secondary villains, but subsequently 'dropped out' of society altogether. "He was kind of a 'wild child'. He was destined for a big career but his anger got in the way," remembers Leonard Mann, twice a co-star. A vigorous presence in his prime, Martell became something of a cult figure in Italy and was the subject of a documentary profile, *Starring Peter Martell*, in 1997.
1966: My Name Is Pecos. 1967: Death Rides Along; Fury of Johnny Kid; Lola Colt; Two Crosses at Danger Pass. 1968: God Forgive... His Life Is Mine; The Long Day of the Massacre; May God Forgive You – I Won't; Ringo the Lone Rider; This Man Can't Die. 1969: The Forgotten Pistolero. 1970: Chuck Mool; The Revenge of Ringo. 1971: His Name Was Sam Wallash... But They Called Him Amen!; Lobo the Bastard. 1974: Patience Has a Limit, We Don't.

above: **Daniel Martín** in **A Fistful of Dollars** (*left*).

above: **George Martin** in **Red Blood, Yellow Gold**.

above: **José Manuel Martín** in **God Forgives... I Don't!**

MARTÍN, DANIEL
[José Daniel Martínez Martínez]
(Cartagena, Spain. 1935-2009)
Actor. Beginning on the stage, he switched to the big screen in the early Sixties and played many supporting roles in westerns and other commercial films. He was Marisol's bullied husband in *A Fistful of Dollars*.
1963: Gunfight at Red Sands. 1964: A Fistful of Dollars. 1965: The Last of the Mohicans; The Last Tomahawk; The Man Called Gringo. 1966: Seven Guns for Timothy. 1968: A Minute to Pray, a Second to Die. 1971: Bad Man's River; Dead Men Ride; Let's Go and Kill Sartana. 1972: The Fat Brothers of Trinity; The Return of Clint the Stranger; Too Much Gold for One Gringo; Watch Out Gringo! Sabata Will Return. 1973: White Fang. 1974: Blood River. 1975: Cipolla Colt; Valley of the Dancing Widows. 1978: La ciudad maldita. 1984: Yellow Hair and the Fortress of Gold.

MARTÍN, EUGENIO
['Gene Martin']
(Granada, Spain. 1925-)
Director. Took his first steps in the industry as a documentarist, made short films and was assistant director on international co-productions shot in Spain such as *55 Days at Peking* and *The 7th Voyage of Sinbad*. While Martín's first western, *The Bounty Killer*, is a minor classic, his others – *Bad Man's River* and *Pancho Villa* – are marred by clumsy direction, excessive slapstick and camera-mugging performances by big-name casts. He fared much better with horror films when that craze took off in Spain in the early Seventies. (Some sources credit Martín as co-director of *Requiem for a Gringo* [1968].)
1966: The Bounty Killer (w/d). 1971: Bad Man's River (w/d). 1972: Pancho Villa (w/d).

MARTIN, GEORGE
[Francisco Martínez Celeiro]
(Barcelona, Spain. 1937-)
Beefy Spanish leading man with the perfect looks and physique for westerns. A prodigious sportsman in his youth, excelling at fencing, swimming and athletics, he became a stunt performer and subsequently an actor. In westerns, he made a greater impression as a villain (see *The Return of Ringo* and *A Taste for Killing*) than as a hero. He has also dabbled in production and direction.
1964: Billy the Kid; The Fury of the Apaches; Tomb of the Pistolero; Two Violent Men. 1965: Joe Dexter; A Pistol for Ringo; The Return of Ringo; The Three from Colorado. 1966: A Taste for Killing; Thompson 1880. 1967: Clint the Stranger; Fifteen Scaffolds for a Killer; Red Blood, Yellow Gold. 1969: Sartana Does Not Forgive. 1971: Let's Go and Kill Sartana. 1972: The Return of Clint the Stranger (credited as director on the Spanish version); Watch Out Gringo! Sabata Will Return. 1973: Three Supermen of the West (credited as director on the Spanish version).

MARTÍN, JOSÉ MANUEL
[José Manuel Martín Pérez]
(Casavieja, Spain. 1924-)
Haggard, hollow-cheeked Spanish character actor in films from the early Fifties. A philosophy student and poet, he learnt acting on stage and also worked in radio. He was known for villainous performances even before the advent of the Euro-western, and is especially memorable as Frank Wolff's ambitious but none-too-bright lieutenant in *God Forgives... I Don't!* and as the malevolent Jack Blood in *I Want Him Dead*.
1960: Juanito. 1962: The Savage Guns. 1963: Gunfight at High Noon. 1964: Bullets Don't Argue; Gunfighters of Casa Grande; Minnesota Clay. 1965: The Last of the Mohicans; A Pistol for Ringo; Viva Carrancho. 1966: Arizona Colt; A Bullet for the General; Django Shoots First; Five Giants from Texas; Four Dollars of Revenge; Seven Dollars to Kill; A Taste for Killing. 1967: Fifteen Scaffolds for a Killer; God Forgives... I Don't!; Man, Pride and Vengeance. 1968: I Want Him Dead; A Minute to Pray, a Second to Die; One After the Other; A Train for Durango. 1969: Alive or Preferably Dead; The Forgotten Pistolero; 100 Rifles; Vengeance Is Mine. 1970: The Anger of the Wind; Arizona. 1971: Bad Man's River; Bastard, Go and Kill; Cut-Throats Nine. 1972: Ben and Charlie. 1984: Al este del Oeste.

MARTINO, LUCIANO
(Italy. 1933-)
Writer/producer brother of Sergio Martino. He started out writing stories and screenplays and, from 1962, moved into production. Has also co-directed a handful of films with Mino Loy.
1964: Buffalo Bill, Hero of the Far West (w). 1966: Arizona Colt (w). 1967: For $100,000 Per Killing (p); $10,000 Blood Money (w/p). 1968: Full House for the Devil (w/p). 1970: Arizona (p); Gunman in Town (p); Stagecoach of the Condemned (w/p). 1971: And the Crows Will Dig Your Grave (p); Dig Your Grave Friend... Sabata's Coming (w). 1972: His Name Was Holy Ghost (p). 1973: A Man Called Invincible (p). 1974: The Crazy Bunch (p). 1975: Zorro (p).

MARTINO, SERGIO
['Martin Dolman']
(Rome, Italy. 1938-)
Director. Grandson of Gennaro Righelli, a pioneer of Italian silent films, Martino began in the Sixties as assistant director, writer and general organiser on many titles produced by his brother Luciano. As a director he has specialised in smartly executed imitations of popular films, including two westerns – *Arizona*, a sequel of sorts to *Arizona Colt* (1966), and *A Man Called Blade*, a Gothic revenge film inspired by *Keoma*. Now employed almost exclusively on television.
1967: For $100,000 Per Killing (w). 1970: Arizona. 1977: A Man Called Blade (w/d).

MASCIOCCHI, MARCELLO
Cinematographer. Shot the first two 'Stranger' films cheaply but attractively, undeterred by having only a handful of locations to work with (the 'skulking' camera style of the first film is particularly effective), while his close-up work is strikingly atmospheric in Giuseppe Colizzi's *Ace High* and *Boot Hill*.
1965: Gold Train. 1966: Kill Johnny Ringo! 1967: For a Dollar in the Teeth; Shoot First, Laugh Last. 1968: Ace High. 1969: Boot Hill. 1971: A Man Called Django; Zorro the Lawman.

MASSACCESI, ARISTIDE
['Joe D'Amato' etc]
(Rome, Italy. 1936-1999)
Cinematographer/director. The son of a film-studio technician, Massaccesi alternated schoolwork with odd jobs on film sets, eventually graduating from assistant cameraman to

director of photography. In this capacity he gave a bright, clean sheen to several Demofilo Fidani westerns, maximising the limited potential of cheap sets and unattractive locations. He directed one low-budget western himself, plus a romanticised Canadian Mountie adventure, before moving on to horror films and, with great success and under a plethora of pseudonyms, sexploitation flicks and hardcore porn.

As director of photography (unless otherwise stated): 1968: Stranger, Make the Sign of the Cross (ad). 1970: Dead Men Don't Make Shadows (ph); Django and Sartana Are Coming... It's the End (ph). 1971: A Barrel Full of Dollars (ph); A Fistful of Death (ph). 1972: Ben and Charlie (ph); A Bounty Killer for Trinity (w/ph/d); Run, Men! Eldorado Is Coming to Trinity (ph/d). 1974: Challenge to White Fang (second unit/ph). 1975: Red Coat (w/ph/d).

MASSI, STELVIO
['Max Steel']
(Civitanova Marche, Italy. 1929-2004)
Cinematographer. Massi's creativity with a camera was a crucial factor in realising Giuliano Carnimeo's ambitions, particularly in *A Moment to Kill* and the dynamic 'Sartana' series, while he shot Tonino Valerii's *The Price of Power* in evocation of the Leone/Delli Colli style. The one western to bear his name as director, *Halleluja to Vera Cruz*, was, according to Marco Giusti, actually the work of Bianco Manini. Massi later directed a series of successful crime thrillers.

1965: In a Colt's Shadow (ph); The Man Who Came to Kill (ph). 1966: A Taste for Killing (ph). 1967: Fifteen Scaffolds for a Killer (ph); Two Faces of the Dollar (ph). 1968: I'll Sell My Skin Dearly (ph); The Moment to Kill (ph). 1969: God Will Forgive My Gun (ph); The Price of Power (ph). 1970: Have a Nice Funeral, Sartana Will Pay (ph); Sartana's Here... Trade Your Pistol for a Coffin (ph). 1971: Heads I Kill You... Tails You're Dead! They Call Me Hallelujah (ph); They Call Him Cemetery (ph). 1972: The Return of Hallelujah (ph). 1973: Halleluja to Vera Cruz (credited as director); A Man Called Invincible (ph).

MAURI, ROBERTO
['Robert Johnson']
(Castelvetrano, Italy. 1924-)
A director of mostly uninspiring exploitation films, Mauri began as an actor in the Fifties. He subsequently made a handful of cheap westerns, including three 'Holy Ghost' titles unrelated to the better-known Giuliano Carnimeo-Gianni Garko collaboration.

1965: Colorado Charlie. 1968: Shotgun (w/d). 1970: Sartana in the Valley of Death (w/d); Wanted Sabata (w/d). 1971: He Was Called the Holy Ghost (w/d). 1972: An Animal Called Man (w/d); Django... Adios! (w/d); Gunmen and the Holy Ghost (w/d); Return of the Holy Ghost (w/d). 1974: Court Martial (w/d).

MENICONI, FURIO
['Men Fury']
(Rome, Italy. 1924-1981)

Actor. Tall and powerfully built, with a prominent nose, Meniconi played bullies and grizzled bad guys in many westerns and B-pictures, sometimes in bit parts but occasionally in featured roles. He is the nominal leader of the outlaws in the twisted, claustrophobic *Kill the Wicked*.

1966: Fort Yuma Gold; Kill or Be Killed. 1967: John the Bastard; Kill the Wicked; Wanted. 1968: Gatling Gun; I'll Sell My Skin Dearly; Kill Them All and Come Back Alone; Shoot, Gringo, Shoot; Tequila Joe; Two Pistols and a Coward. 1969: Django the Bastard. 1970: And God Said to Cain; Sartana's Here... Trade Your Pistol for a Coffin. 1971: Bastard, Go and Kill; A Fistful of Dynamite; Heads I Kill You... Tails You're Dead! They Call Me Hallelujah; Kill Django... Kill First; Long Live Your Death; A Man Called Django; They Call Him Cemetery; Trinity Is Still My Name. 1972: The Deadly Trackers; The Grand Duel; Hallelujah & Sartana Strike Again!; His Name Was Holy Ghost; Man of the East; They Called Him Amen. 1973: A Man Called Invincible; They Still Call Me Amen; Those Dirty Dogs. 1974: The Crazy Bunch. 1975: Dallas; A Genius, Two Partners and a Dupe.

MERINO, JOSÉ LUIS
(Madrid, Spain. 1927-)
Director / writer / production manager. Best known outside Spain for lurid horror films, Merino imported aspects of that genre into the overblown revenge western *Requiem for a Gringo*, which confounds expectations with its flashback structure, eccentric characterisations and frequently disorienting visual style.

1966: A Fistful of Songs (w/d). 1967: Kitosch, the Man Who Came from the North (w/d). 1968: Gatling Gun (w); Requiem for a Gringo (d). 1969: Zorro the Conqueror (w/d). 1970: More Dollars for the McGregors (w/d). 1971: Zorro, Rider of Vengeance (w/d); Zorro, the Mask of Vengeance (w/d). 1980: Siete cabalgan hacia la muerte (w/d).

MIGLIARDI, MARIO
(Alessandria, Italy. 1919-)
Composer. Migliardi's scores for *Matalo!* and *The Price of Death* blended western bombast with acid rock and atonal sound effects, creating suitably unsettling sonic backdrops for two particularly idiosyncratic films.

1970: Matalo! 1971: The Price of Death; Shoot the Living and Pray for the Dead.

MILIAN, TOMAS
[Tomás Quintin Rodriguez Milian]
(Havana, Cuba. 1933 or 1937-)
Actor. Born in troubled times, Milian's early years were scarred by tragedy. His father, a former army general, was traumatised by a period of political imprisonment and, in 1945, he committed suicide before his son's eyes. Milian strove to put this behind him and left Cuba for America in the Fifties. Having gained entry to the Actors' Studio, he was invited to perform at a theatre festival in Spoleto, and was such a success that producer Franco Cristaldi offered him a contract. He was repeatedly cast as serious young men in Italian art-house dramas before achieving stardom with westerns: after a Method-style performance as an outlaw in *The Bounty Killer*, Milian played tatterdemalion, underprivileged outcasts in three films for Sergio Sollima, and was the archetypal social bandit in *Tepepa*, *The Magnificent Bandits* and *Compañeros*. (From

time to time he supplemented his film work with pop music, and sung the title song in the Italian version of Sollima's *Run, Man, Run*.) He became even more firmly entrenched in Italian popular culture with his earthy portrayals of the Serpico-style cop Nico Giraldi and streetwise minor crook Monnezza in several rough-hewn crime films, finally returning to America in the early Eighties. Hugely talented, his taste for improvisation proved unpalatable for some of his directors, as Giulio Petroni remembers: "He was an extremely difficult actor to manage, always inventing something crazy. I had a hard time keeping him inside acceptable boundaries." He has never been out of work and, over the course of the past decade, has enjoyed a steady, if not exactly challenging, career as a supporting player in major Hollywood productions.

1966: The Bounty Killer. 1967: The Big Gundown; Death Sentence; Django, Kill!; Face to Face. 1968: Run, Man, Run; Tepepa. 1969: The Magnificent Bandits. 1970: Compañeros. 1972: Bandits; Sometimes Life Is Hard, Right, Providence? 1973: Here We Go Again, Eh Providence? 1975: The Four of the Apocalypse; The White, the Yellow and the Black.

MILLAND, GLORIA
[Mara Fiè]
(Cagliari, Italy. 1940-)

Actress. A favourite of Joaquín Romero Marchent, this refined and attractive leading lady was never given a truly testing or assertive role. She was wife, mother and wench in several comedies, *pepla* and westerns (her 'sons' in *Gunfight at High Noon* and *The Man Who Killed Billy the Kid* were played by actors around her age), her sensitivity in even these clichéd parts suggesting a talent that was never fully tapped. She gave up acting at the end of the Sixties, perhaps unsatisfied with the direction her career had taken.

1963: Gunfight at High Noon; The Sword of Zorro. 1964: Seven from Texas. 1965: Hands of a Gunfighter; The Man Who Came to Kill. Seven Hours of Gunfire. 1967: Hate for Hate; A Man and a Colt; The Man Who Killed Billy the Kid.

above: **Cameron Mitchell** stars in **Minnesota Clay**.

above: **Gordon Mitchell**.

above: **Gojko Mitic**.

MITCHELL, CAMERON
[Cameron Mitzell]
(Dallastown, USA. 1918-1994)
Actor. The son of a minister, Mitchell first came to prominence on Broadway. On screen, he toiled in minor American productions before switching to Europe in the early Sixties. Rugged and robust, he worked steadily in whatever genre was in vogue. He made two westerns, the Hollywood-esque *The Last Gun* and Sergio Corbucci's more expansive *Minnesota Clay*, in which he gave a clichéd role – that of an ailing, over-the-hill outlaw – a fresh coat of paint.
1964: *The Last Gun; Minnesota Clay*.

MITCHELL, GORDON
[Charles Pendleton; 'Mitchell Gordon']
(Denver, USA. 1923-2003)
Actor. Blessed with one of the all-time great film faces, not to mention an impressively muscular physique, Mitchell was a cult cinema legend. He made more than 130 movies including 20+ Euro-westerns, usually playing brutes and killers, and built his own western town virtually single-handedly at Cave, near Rome – it was the location for many low-budget productions, including a number by Demofilo Fidani.
1966: *Kill or Be Killed; Thompson 1880; Three Bullets for Ringo*. 1967: *Born to Kill; John the Bastard; Rita of the West*. 1968: *Beyond the Law; Dead for a Dollar; Lynching; Saguaro*. 1969: *I Am Sartana, Your Angel of Death*. 1970: *Arizona Kid; Dead Men Don't Make Shadows; Django and Sartana Are Coming... It's the End*. 1971: *The Ballad of Django; A Barrel Full of Dollars; Doomsday; Finders Killers; A Fistful of Death; His Name Was Sam Wallash... But They Called Him Amen!; Let's Go and Kill Sartana; Lobo the Bastard*. 1972: *A Gunman Called Dakota; The Magnificent West; Run, Men! Eldorado Is Coming to Trinity*. 1973: *Anything for a Friend; The Fighting Fists of Shanghai Joe; Once Upon a Time in the Wild, Wild West; They Called Him Trinity [Himself, His Colt, His Revenge]*. 1975: *Seven Devils on Horseback; The Tiger from the River Kwai*. 1978: *Zanna Bianca e il grande kid*. 1979: *Porno-Erotic western*.

MITIC, GOJKO
(Leskovac, former Yugoslavia. 1940-)
Actor. With his chiselled looks and athletic frame, Mitic embodied Native American physical perfection and resolve in a series of East German westerns that turned the western's ideological bias on its head. He made an impassioned hero in films that paid careful attention to tribal culture and opposed the tenets of Manifest Destiny. Until recently, Mitic performed the role of Winnetou in the nostalgic Karl May festivals staged in Germany, having taken it over from Pierre Brice, as well as playing the character on television.
1963: *Winnetou the Warrior*. 1964: *Among Vultures; Apaches' Last Battle; Last of the Renegades*. 1965: *Desperado Trail; The Sons of Great Bear*. 1967: *Chingachgook, the Great Snake*. 1968: *Trail of the Falcon*. 1969: *White Wolves*. 1970: *Fatal Error*. 1971: *Osceola*. 1972: *Tecumseh*. 1973: *Apaches (act/w)*. 1974: *Ulzana*. 1975: *Blood Brothers*. 1978: *Severino*. 1982: *Der lange Ritt zur Schule; The Scout*. 1998: *Präriejäger in Mexico: Geierschnabel/Benito Juarez*.

MOLINO ROJO, ANTONIO
['Red Mills']
(Venta de Baños, Spain. 1926-)
Actor/director. A sporting youth, Molino Rojo began his film career as an extra and then became stunt double for one of Spain's most popular stars, Fernando Fernán Gómez. It was during the western boom, however, that he did most of his work, proving indispensable – along with the likes of Sambrell, Braña, Robledo etc – in a variety of rugged character roles. In the early Eighties he tried directing, turning out a few minor erotic movies under the name 'Red Mills'.
1962: *Two Against All; Zorro the Avenger*. 1964: *Black Angel of the Mississippi; A Fistful of Dollars; $5,000 on the Ace; Two Violent Men*. 1965: *Finger on the Trigger; For a Few Dollars More; A Place Called Glory; Seven Hours of Gunfire; Viva Carrancho*. 1966: *Ballad of a Bounty Hunter; Five Giants from Texas; Fort Yuma Gold; Four Dollars of Revenge; The Good, the Bad and the Ugly; Seven Guns for the MacGregors; The Texican*. 1967: *The Big Gundown; Fifteen Scaffolds for a Killer; The Man Who Killed Billy the Kid*. 1968: *Ace High; Kill Them All and Come Back Alone; A Minute to Pray, a Second to Die; Once Upon a Time in the West*. 1969: *Garringo; Vengeance Is Mine*. 1970: *Clumsy Hands; Stagecoach of the Condemned; Twenty Steps to Death*. 1971: *And the Crows Will Dig Your Grave; Four Candles for My Colt*. 1972: *Death Played the Flute; Now They Call Him Sacramento; You Are a Traitor and I'll Kill You*. 1973: *My Name Is Nobody*. 1978: *La ciudad maldita*.

MORRICONE, ENNIO
['Dan Savio'; 'Leo Nichols']
(Rome, Italy. 1928-)
One of the world's most prolific and respected composers. The five-time Oscar nominee – who received an honorary Academy Award at the 2007 ceremony – has more than 300 film scores to his credit, but it was his innovative work with Sergio Leone – all unconventional instrumentation, insistent melodies and quirky vocal arrangements – that first brought him to international attention and introduced a new set of conventions for western film music. He also collaborated repeatedly with Sollima, Tessari, Petroni and Corbucci in the western field, and continues to move smoothly through all genres and styles.

above: **Antonio Molino Rojo**, as seen in **For a Few Dollars More** *(right)*.

(Composing credits): 1963: Gunfight at Red Sands. 1964: Bullets Don't Argue; A Fistful of Dollars. 1965: For a Few Dollars More; A Pistol for Ringo; The Return of Ringo. 1966: A Bullet for the General ('supervisor'); Fort Yuma Gold (with Gianni Ferrio); The Good, the Bad and the Ugly; The Hills Run Red; Navajo Joe; Seven Guns for the MacGregors. 1967: The Big Gundown; Death Rides a Horse; Face to Face; The Hellbenders; Up the MacGregors. 1968: The Great Silence; Guns for San Sebastian; Once Upon a Time in the West; A Professional Gun; A Sky Full of Stars for a Roof; Tepepa. 1969: The Five Man Army. 1970: Compañeros. 1971: Doomsday (uncredited); A Fistful of Dynamite. 1972: Bandits; The Return of Clint the Stranger; Sometimes Life Is Hard, Right, Providence?; What Am I Doing in the Middle of a Revolution? 1973: Here We Go Again, Eh Providence?; My Name Is Nobody. 1975: A Genius, Two Partners and a Dupe. 1981: Buddy Goes West. 1996: North Star.

MORSELLA, FULVIO
(Duronia, Italy. 1923-2002)
Producer/writer. Sergio Leone's brother-in-law and business adviser, he also contributed to the scripts of For a Few Dollars More, My Name Is Nobody and A Genius, Two Partners and a Dupe, as well as developing the treatment of A Fistful of Dynamite. 1965: For a Few Dollars More (w). 1968: Once Upon a Time in the West (p). 1971: A Fistful of Dynamite (p). 1973: My Name Is Nobody (w/p). 1975: A Genius, Two Partners and a Dupe (w/p).

MULARGIA, EDOARDO
['Edward G. Muller']
(Torpè, Italy. 1925-)
Director. After studying law and working as a journalist, he began making short films, commercials and co-writing scripts, and at one time was assistant director to Pietro Germi. As a director, he crafted a number of routine, medium-budget westerns, although Shango, with his favourite star, Anthony Steffen, and the downbeat Robert Woods vehicle El Puro both display greater flair and originality.
1965: Why Go On Killing? (w/d). 1966: Go with God, Gringo (w/d). 1967: Cjamango (d); Don't Wait, Django, Shoot! (d). 1968: Say Your Prayers and Dig Your Grave (w/d). 1969: El Puro (w/d). 1970: Challenge of the MacKennas (w); Shango (w/d). 1971: Brother Outlaw (w/d); A Man Called Django (d).

MULOCK, AL
[Alfred Mulloch]
(Toronto, Canada. 1925 or 1926-1968)

Actor. One of the most distinctive Euro-western character actors, Mulock's brief career began in Canadian theatre before he moved to England, where he tried to establish a London equivalent of New York's Actors' Studio in the Fifties. (He wrote an article about this in Films and Filming magazine.) He played supporting roles in several British productions before he found himself working in Spain. His gnarled, cadaverous face is prominent in two of the genre's best openings: the intimately detailed close-up that begins The Good, the Bad and the Ugly; and the celebrated pre-credits sequence of Once Upon a Time in the West, where he plays 'Knuckles'. It was while filming Once… that Mulock committed suicide, allegedly still wearing his costume and with one more close-up to perform, giving rise to a legend about Leone's lack of compassion. As Sergio Donati remembers, "Months later during the editing Sergio said, 'Couldn't [Mulock] wait another 24 hours before killing himself?'"
1966: The Good, the Bad and the Ugly. 1967: Day of Anger; The Hellbenders. 1968: Once Upon a Time in the West.

MUSOLINO, VINCENZO
['Glenn Vincent Davis']
(Reggio Calabria, Italy. 1930-1969)
Director / producer / writer / actor. A one-time fisherman, Musolino was discovered for the screen by Renato Castellano, who gave him one of the leads in Two Pennyworth of Hope. He was a busy actor throughout the Fifties, but failed to build on his early break. In the western era he turned his attentions to writing, producing and directing.
1965: Why Go On Killing? (w/p). 1966: Go with God, Gringo (w/p). 1967: Cjamango (w/p); Don't Wait, Django, Shoot! (w/p). 1968: May God Forgive You – I Won't (w/p/d). 1969: Quintana (w/p/d).

NAVARRO, NIEVES
[Nieves Navarro García; 'Susan Scott']
(Almería, Spain. 1938-)

Actress. A beguiling beauty, Navarro/Scott was a fashion model whose appearances in TV promotions led to the female lead in the comedy Totò of Arabia (1964). She found her niche in westerns and thrillers, her characters exuding a self-aware sensuality that elevates them above their nominally decorative function. She married producer/director Luciano Ercoli in the early Seventies and gradually turned towards soft-core erotica. She retired from the screen in the Eighties.
1965: A Pistol for Ringo; The Return of Ringo. 1966: El Rojo. 1967: The Big Gundown; Long Days of Vengeance. 1970: Adios, Sabata; Gunman in Town. 1972: Kill the Poker Player.

NERI, ROSALBA
['Sara Bay']
(Furli, Italy. 1939-)

Sultry actress with exotic features. A graduate of Rome's Centro Sperimentale, she dyed her dark locks blonde in her early career and was cast in dizzy roles in domestic comedies. As a brunette, however, she thrived in assertive parts, and often played loose women or femmes fatales in sleazy horror movies, gialli and more than a dozen westerns. Her best performance in the last-named genre was as the protagonist's devious, sexually provocative 'aunt' in Johnny Yuma.
1966: Arizona Colt; Dynamite Jim; Johnny Yuma. 1967: Days of Violence; Wanted Johnny Texas. 1968: Killer Adios; A Long Ride from Hell; Sartana Does Not Forgive; This Man Can't Die. 1969: El Puro. 1970: Arizona. 1971: Doomsday. 1972: The Great Treasure Hunt; Watch Out Gringo! Sabata Will Return. 1973: Charity and the Strange Smell of Money; A Man Called Invincible. 1974: Blood River.

NERO, FRANCO
[Francesco Sparanero; 'Frank Nero']
(Parma, Italy. 1941-)

Actor. Abandoned economics studies to train as an actor in Milan under famed theatre director Giorgio Strehler. A meeting with John Huston in Rome led to the role of Abel in The Bible (1966), and Huston's assistant, Albert Band, chose him to play clean-cut Charlie Garvey in The Tramplers. From there he secured the title role in Django, which resulted in several further westerns, most notably with Sergio Corbucci and Enzo Castellari. He broke onto the world stage in Camelot (1967) and attracted headlines with a well-publicised affair with Vanessa Redgrave. He has dextrously juggled international roles with prestige productions (Buñuel was one of his favourite directors) and small-scale genre pieces ever since. (One of his most significant later roles was that of earnest American journalist John Reed, chronicler of the Mexican Revolution, in Sergei Bondarchuk's Mexico in Flames. The character contrasts nicely with the conniving opportunists Nero played in Corbucci's 'Zapata' westerns.) He remains an enthusiastic ambassador for the Italian western and a veritable icon in his own right.
1965: The Tramplers. 1966: Django; Massacre Time; Texas Adios. 1967: Man, Pride and Vengeance. 1968: A Professional Gun. 1970: Compañeros. 1971: Long Live Your Death. 1973: Deaf Smith & Johnny Ears; White Fang. 1974: Challenge to White Fang. 1975: Cipolla Colt. 1976: Keoma. 1982: Mexico in Flames. 1987: Django Strikes Again. 1993: Jonathan of the Bears (act/w/p).

NICOLAI, BRUNO
['Paul Clemente']
(Rome, Italy. 1926-1991)

Composer/conductor. He trained at the Conservatory of Santa Cecilia where he met Ennio Morricone, who became a close friend and collaborator for many years. A masterful melodist, he scored many westerns, spy films and *gialli*, employing the same mixture as Morricone (his frequent collaborator) of pop, classical and avant-garde styles, producing many classic scores in the process. His music for *Have a Nice Funeral, Sartana Will Pay* (portions of which were used in a number of other westerns), *Gunman in Town* and *Adios, Sabata* is among the most powerful in the genre.

(Composing credits): 1965: $100,000 for Ringo. 1966: Django Shoots First; El Cisco. 1967: Days of Violence; Gentleman Killer. 1968: Run, Man, Run. 1969: Land Raiders. 1970: Adios, Sabata; Arizona; Gunman in Town; Have a Nice Funeral, Sartana Will Pay; A Man Called Joe Clifford. 1971: And the Crows Will Dig Your Grave; Dead Men Ride; They Call Him Cemetery. 1972: God in Heaven… Arizona on Earth; His Name Was Holy Ghost; My Horse… My Gun… Your Widow. 1973: The Fighting Fists of Shanghai Joe; The Hellhounds of Alaska; A Man Called Invincible.

NUSCIAK, LOREDANA
[Loredana Cappelletti]
(Rome, Italy. 1940 or 1942-)

Actress who came to westerns via *pepla*. In *Django* and *$10,000 Blood Money*, this attractive strawberry blonde epitomised the powerlessness of women out west, suffering all manner of depredations partly provoked by their desperate love for the hero. Far more satisfying, if no less stereotypical, is her performance as the grasping villainess in the comic-strip caper *Superargo Versus Diabolicus* (1967), where she enjoys making others suffer for a change. Busy throughout the Sixties, she made just four films in the Seventies.

1965: Viva Carrancho. 1966: Django; Seven Dollars to Kill. 1967: $10,000 Blood Money. 1968: Vengeance for Vengeance. 1969: God Will Forgive My Gun.

O'BRIEN, DONAL
['Donald O'Brien']
(Pau, France. 1930-2003)

Actor. Sturdy, reliable American supporting actor and occasional leading man who made a number of westerns without really imposing himself upon them. He later earned cult popularity for eccentric turns in horror and fantasy films. Continued to act late in life despite being severely injured in a car accident in the early Nineties.

1961: Dynamite Jack. 1968: Run, Man, Run. 1971: Finders Killers; Paid in Blood; The Sheriff of Rocksprings; Thirteenth Is a Judas. 1972: God Is My Colt; Jesse & Lester: Two Brothers in a Place Called Trinity. 1973: God's Executioner; Kung Fu Brothers in the Wild West; Six Bounty Killers for a Massacre. 1974: Challenge to White Fang. 1975: The Four of the Apocalypse; White Fang to the Rescue. 1976: Keoma. 1977: A Man Called Blade. 1978: Silver Saddle.

ORLANDI, NORA
['Joan Christian']
(Voghera, Italy. 1933-)

Composer/singer/musician. In the Fifties, Orlandi formed her own choral quartet, which achieved considerable success at festivals, on radio and television. In the Sixties she began composing for cinema, becoming the first woman to score for westerns: her sombre music for *$10,000 Blood Money* and *For $100,000 Per Killing* underlines the desperate, tragic mood of both films, and she provided haunting accompaniments for a number of *gialli* as well, sometimes singing on her own scores.

(Composing credits): 1966: A Golden Sheriff; Johnny Yuma. 1967: Clint the Stranger; Death, at Owell Rock; For $100,000 Per Killing; $10,000 Blood Money. 1972: Prey of Vultures. 1973: On the Third Day Arrived the Crow.

ORTOLANI, RIZ
(Pesaro, Italy. 1931-)

Composer. Born into a musical family, he came to prominence in 1962 with the massively popular music to *Mondo cane*, which spawned the hit single 'More'. In the intervening years he has scored around 200 movies, both Italian and international, covering all moods and styles, with a particular affinity for jazz. He composed some excellent western scores – from the blaring brass of *Day of Anger* to the more easygoing *Chuck Mool* – its main theme is a jaunty delight.

1963: Gunfight at High Noon. 1964: Apaches' Last Battle; Ride and Kill; Seven from Texas. 1967: Day of Anger; Kill and Pray. 1968: Beyond the Law. 1969: The Magnificent Bandits; Night of the Serpents. 1970: Chuck Mool. 1971: The Hunting Party. 1972: A Reason to Live, a Reason to Die; Where the Bullets Fly.

PACHECO, RAFAEL
(Madrid, Spain. 1921-)

Cinematographer. One of the first DPs to realise the potential of Almería, he gave most of Joaquín Romero Marchent's westerns their handsome sheen and painted the Spanish locations of Sollima's *Face to Face* using a warm, sun-burnished palette.

1962: The Shadow of Zorro; Zorro the Avenger. 1963: Gunfight at High Noon; The Magnificent Three. 1964: Seven from Texas. 1965: Seven Hours of Gunfire. 1966: Fort Yuma Gold; $100,000 for Lassiter. 1967: Face to Face. 1969: Four Rode Out. 1972: Kill the Poker Player. 1973: The Three Musketeers of the West.

PAJARITO
[Manuel Muniz/Murriz Brandariz]

This diminutive, quizzical-looking Spanish supporting actor provided light relief in the 'Ringo' films, as the hero's helper, and a handful of other westerns.

1965: A Pistol for Ringo; The Return of Ringo. 1966: Dynamite Jim; Sugar Colt. 1967: Long Days of Vengeance. 1971: Let's Go and Kill Sartana. 1972: The Return of Clint the Stranger; You Are a Traitor and I'll Kill You.

PALACIOS, RICARDO
[Ricardo López Nuño; 'Dick Castle'; 'Richard Palance']
(Santander, Spain. 1940-)

Actor/writer/director. Having studied acting and direction in Madrid, Palacios made his debut as a performer in 1964, switching between theatre and cinema. His considerable girth saw him cast in comedic or villainous supporting roles in many westerns, including that of an obnoxious, oversized sexual sadist in *Comin' at Ya*! There are more strings to his bow, however: he has written and directed popular films, including the successful comedy *Biba la banda* (produced by his frequent employer Jesús Franco) in 1987, and performed the same functions on television.

1965: For a Few Dollars More. 1966: The Bounty Killer; The Good, the Bad and the Ugly; Return of the Seven. 1967: Day of Anger; Dynamite Joe; Fifteen Scaffolds for a Killer; Kitosch, the Man Who Came from the North; The Treasure of Pancho Villa. 1968: Run, Man, Run. 1970: El Condor. 1971: Bad Man's River; Captain Apache; Doc; Red Sun. 1972: The Deadly Trackers; The Fabulous Trinity; The Fat Brothers of Trinity. 1973: The Man Called Noon. 1974: The Spikes Gang; The Stranger and the Gunfighter; Whisky and Ghosts. 1975: The Cry of the Wolf; Dallas; Take a Hard Ride. 1981: Comin' at Ya! 1985: Tex and the Lord of the Deep. 1998: Dollar for the Dead.

PALANCE, JACK
[Walter Jack/Vladimir Palahnuik]
(Lattimer Mines, Pennsylvania, USA. 1919-2006)

The son of a coal miner, Palance's boxing career was interrupted by the Second World War, during which he suffered facial burns and underwent plastic surgery, resulting in his famously gaunt appearance. After the war he began acting, excelling as the hired gun in *Shane* (1953), and spent many years in European productions. He gave a number of self-deprecating, over-the-top performances in westerns, notably Sergio Corbucci's *A Professional Gun* and *Compañeros* and Gianfranco Parolini's *God's Gun*.

1968: A Professional Gun. 1969: The Desperados. 1970: Compañeros. 1972: Can Be Done… Amigo; Chato's Land; Tedeum. 1973: The Blue Gang. 1975: The Cry of the Wolf. 1976: God's Gun.

PALLOTTINI, RICCARDO
(Italy. ?-1981)
Cinematographer. Working his way up from camera assistant, he turned DP in the early Fifties and commenced a career that spanned all manner of films. He became a close colleague of Antonio Margheriti, shooting the classic horror films *Castle of Blood* and *The Long Hair of Death* (both 1964) in menacing monochrome and using colour with ravishing results in *The Virgin of Nuremberg* (1963). His colour work is equally impressive in Margheriti's Gothic westerns *Vengeance* and the largely nocturnal *And God Said to Cain*. He died in a plane crash on the final day of shooting the same director's *Tiger Joe* (1981).

1966: Django Shoots First; Massacre Time; Ringo and His Golden Pistol. 1967: The Greatest Robbery in the West. 1968: Find a Place to Die; Vengeance. 1969: In the Name of the Father. 1970: And God Said to Cain; Chapagua's Gold. 1971: Blindman. 1972: They Called Him Amen. 1975: Take a Hard Ride.

PALMARA, MIMMO
[Domenico Palmara; 'Dick Palmer']
(Cagliari, Italy. 1928-)

Actor. Worked in his early career with directors of worldwide renown – he was in Visconti's *Senso* (1954) and King Vidor's *War and Peace* (1956) – but his stern countenance and robust build 'condemned' him to many roles in *pepla* and westerns. He was always convincingly tough and took the work seriously, no matter how frivolous the film. A close friend of Sergio Leone's, he apparently rejected the role of Ramon in *A Fistful of Dollars* in favour of what seemed like a safer bet, the more traditional *Bullets Don't Argue*.

1964: Bullets Don't Argue. 1965: Johnny West. 1966: Renegade Gunfighter; The Sons of Ringo. 1967: The Handsome, the Ugly and the Stupid; Poker with Pistols. 1968: Black Jack; Dead for a Dollar; Execution; A Long Ride from Hell; A Rope for a Bastard; Shotgun; Tequila Joe. 1970: The Deserter. 1971: Gunman of 100 Crosses; He Was Called the Holy Ghost. 1972: Gunmen and the Holy Ghost; Panhandle Calibre 38.

PAROLINI, GIANFRANCO
['Frank Kramer'; 'Frank/John Littlewords']
(Rome, Italy. 1930-)
Director/writer/actor. Eccentric and wildly imaginative, Parolini was a leading director of *pepla*, spy films, westerns and comedies in the Sixties and Seventies. He apprenticed under various directors, including Rossellini and Jean Negulesco, and fulfilled several functions – editor, production designer, writer – before making his first strides as a director during the vogue for ancient epics. In 1965 he made the first of the tongue-in-cheek 'Kommissar X' spy films, based on a popular German pulp hero, and continued creating *fumetti*-style franchises with his westerns. *If You Meet Sartana, Pray for Your Death* and *Sabata* featured black-clad, sinister tricksters knee-deep in corpses and conspiracies. *Sabata* also demonstrated Parolini's penchant for acrobatics (already revealed in his war film, *Five for Hell* [1969]), which gives many of his films a carnivalesque flavour. He often played cameos in his films as well, appearing as a gambler who challenges the title character in *Pray for Your Death*. From the end of the Seventies he shifted his attentions to distribution, but his far-out films retain a special place in fans' affections. One of his regular stars, Brad Harris, told me, "As you see in his pictures he always has lots of little gimmicks; he's like a kid, and he still has the same fantasies about these characters that he creates." In recent years Parolini announced far-fetched plans to return to cinema with a trilogy of historical epics, motivated by the success of Ridley Scott's *Gladiator* (2000). To date, nothing has come of these ambitions.

1963: Pirates of the Mississippi (second unit). 1965: Johnny West (w/d). 1968: If You Meet Sartana, Pray for Your Death (w/d/act). 1969: Sabata (w/d). 1970: Adios, Sabata (w/d). 1971: Return of Sabata (w/d). 1976: God's Gun (w/d).

PAZZAFINI, NELLO
[Giovanni Pazzafini; 'John Carey'; 'Red Carter'; 'Ted Carter']
(Rome, Italy. 1933-1997)
Hulking stuntman and supporting player who attended Italy's first school for stunt performers and went on to appear in more than 120 films. Pazzafini was always good value, regardless of the size of his roles. He was an excellent fighter – a hallmark of his sporting ability – and a thoroughly convincing villain, in which capacity he was often cast opposite Giuliano Gemma. Occasionally he was given the opportunity to display an appealingly deadpan comedic style, as in *Wanted*, for example.

1963: Samson and the Slave Queen. 1964: Badmen of the West. 1965: Adios Gringo; One Silver Dollar. 1966: Arizona Colt; Fort Yuma Gold; Zorro the Rebel. 1967: The Big Gundown; Days of Violence; Death, at Owell Rock; Face to Face; Seven Pistols for a Massacre; 32 Caliber Killer; Wanted. 1968: Find a Place to Die; Killer Adios; A Long Ride from Hell; Lynching; Run, Man, Run; Two Pistols and a Coward. 1969: Death on a High Hill. 1970: Sartana's Here… Trade Your Pistol for a Coffin. 1971: They Call Him Cemetery; Vendetta at Dawn. 1972: Ben and Charlie; Hallelujah & Sartana Strike Again!; His Name Was Holy Ghost; Panhandle Calibre 38; The Return of Hallelujah; Trinity and Sartana Are Coming. 1973: Here We Go Again, Eh Providence?; A Man Called Invincible. 1974: Carambola; The Crazy Bunch. 1975: The Crazy Adventures of Len and Coby; The Tiger from the River Kwai; White Fang and the Gold Diggers; White Fang and the Hunter. 1977: A Man Called Blade.

above: **Nello Pazzafini**, as seen in **Adios Gringo** (*left*).

PERNICE, GINO
[Luigi Pernice; 'Jimmy Douglas']
(Rome, Italy. 1927-1997)

Actor. His features often pinched into a sneer, Pernice shone in devious, slimy roles; he was a favourite of Sergio Corbucci, standing out as the sanctimonious Brother Jonathan in *Django* and the rabid Jeff in *The Hellbenders*.
1966: Django; Texas Adios. 1967: The Hellbenders; Rita of the West. 1969: The Specialists. 1970: Compañeros.

PESCE, FRANCO
['Frank Fisher']
(Naples, Italy. 1890-1975)

Actor. Son of Italian film pioneer Ettore Pesce, Franco began his film career as a cameraman during the silent period. He turned actor in the Forties and, in his twilight years, he played garrulous eccentrics in many westerns, notably as Gianni Garko's doddering sidekick in the 'Sartana' series.
1965: Why Go On Killing? 1966: Seven Guns for Timothy. 1967: Don't Wait, Django, Shoot!; Turn... I'll Kill You! 1968: If You Meet Sartana, Pray for Your Death; May God Forgive You – I Won't; A Gun for a Hundred Graves; This Man Can't Die. 1969: The Forgotten Pistolero; I Am Sartana, Your Angel of Death. 1970: Gunman in Town; Have a Nice Funeral, Sartana Will Pay; Roy Colt and Winchester Jack; Shango. 1971: Heads I Kill You... Tails You're Dead! They Call Me Hallelujah; Where the Bullets Fly. 1972: God in Heaven... Arizona on Earth; His Name Was Holy Ghost.

PETRONI, GIULIO
(Rome, Italy. 1920-2010)
Director/writer. A wartime partisan and one-time Communist, Petroni studied literature at university and later blossomed into an astute director of commercial subjects. After the war, he accepted an invitation to take charge of what was then Ceylon's film industry, from 1948-51, and, back in Italy, he made short films, co-wrote scripts and worked for RAI television for a time. Not the most prolific of directors (he stated that he preferred writing), his finest and most successful films by far were westerns, chiefly the muscular Lee Van Cleef vehicle *Death Rides a Horse* and two contrasting showcases for Tomas Milian, the political-themed *Tepepa* and anarchic comedy *Sometimes Life Is Hard, Right Providence?* His *noir*-inflected psychological western, *Night of the Serpents*, is also recommended.
1967: Death Rides a Horse. 1968: A Sky Full of Stars for a Roof; Tepepa (d). 1969: Night of the Serpents (w/d). 1972: Sometimes Life Is Hard, Right Providence? (w/d).

PETZOLD, KONRAD
(Dresden, Germany. 1930-1999)
Director/writer. Having worked his way up through the ranks (supporting actor, assistant director) in post-war productions made by the GDR's all-powerful DEFA studio, Petzold later made a clutch of westerns, describing them as "a counterweight to the western capitalist film industry". His films (in which he often played minor roles) included *Kit & Co*, a Jack London adaptation that was Dean Reed's first film in the Republic, and *The Scout*, the last of Gojko Mitic's revisionist *Indianerfilme*.
1969: White Wolves. 1970: Fatal Error (d/act). 1971: Osceola (d/act). 1974: Kit & Co. 1982: The Scout (w/d/act).

PIAGET, PAUL
[Paul Piaget Ducurroy]
(Jerez de la Frontera, Spain. 1934-1986)

This tall, broad-shouldered leading man/supporting player was a member of the Piaget watchmaking dynasty. He strode through a number of early Spanish westerns before disappearing from the screen. Although he never displayed a broad range in his roles, his considerable physical presence (reportedly, he doubled for Charlton Heston in *El Cid*, which was shot in Spain) was a notable asset to the films in which he appeared, and he was comfortable as both heroic and unsympathetic characters. Father of model Cristina Piaget.
1962: The Shadow of Zorro; Zorro the Avenger. 1963: The Magnificent Three. 1964: Black Angel of the Mississippi; Four Bullets for Joe; Heroes of Fort Worth; Seven from Texas.

PICCIONI, PIERO
[Giampiero Piccioni; 'Piero Morgan']
(Turin, Italy. 1921-2004)
Composer. Pianist and jazz musician who composed the first of his numerous film and TV scores in the early Fifties. He was able to combine highbrow work (he was a favourite of Francesco Rosi and worked with Godard and Visconti) with music for Alberto Sordi comedies and many exploitation films, among them several westerns. His jazzy, playful score for *If You Meet Sartana, Pray for Your Death* stands out for its subtly humorous qualities.
1964: Minnesota Clay. 1968: Fedra West; Gatling Gun; If You Meet Sartana, Pray for Your Death. 1970: The Deserter. 1972: Watch Out Gringo! Sabata Will Return. 1973: A Colt in the Hand of the Devil; God's Executioner; Six Bounty Killers for a Massacre. 1975: In the Name of the Father, of the Son and of the Colt.

PIGOZZI, LUCIANO
['Alan Collins']
(Novellara, Italy. 1927-)

Actor. Squat, bug-eyed character actor in the Peter Lorre mould who often played nervous, Lorre-esque ne'er-do-wells. He began his career in regional theatre before landing film roles with Vittorio de Sica and Alberto Lattuada, although it is B-movies that have sustained him. He has played everything from shifty, cowardly villains to more sympathetic characters, and was a particular favourite of Antonio Margheriti, in whose films he usually meets a violent end. "I worked many times with Margheriti and always ended up in a coffin," he once joked.
1967: Death, at Owell Rock. 1968: Cowards Don't Pray; Vengeance. 1969: Sabata. 1970: And God Said to Cain; Sartana in the Valley of Death. 1971: Dead Men Ride; His Name Was King; The Price of Death. 1972: Can Be Done... Amigo. 1978: La ciudad maldita. 1986: White Apache.

PISTILLI, LUIGI
(Grosseto, Italy. 1929-1996)

Who's Who In Euro-Westerns

Intense, flexible character actor who flitted between stage and screen throughout his career. Leone used him as both saint (Padre Ramirez in *The Good, the Bad and the Ugly*) and sinner (Groggy in *For a Few Dollars More*), he excelled in westerns by Sergio Corbucci and Giulio Petroni, and was a boon to several *gialli* and crime films. Apparently suffering from depression, exacerbated by the break-up of a relationship and negative reviews for his latest theatrical work, he committed suicide in 1996.
1965: For a Few Dollars More. 1966: The Good, the Bad and the Ugly; $100,000 for Lassiter; Texas Adios. 1967: Death Rides a Horse. 1968: The Great Silence. 1969: Night of the Serpents.

POWELL, DON
Singer/actor.
Little is known about Powell except that he was a black man who provided dramatic vocals for some of the genre's most memorable theme songs. Highlights include the melancholic *Texas Adios*, strident *Death Walks in Laredo*, 'Gambling Man' from *$5,000 on the Ace*, the quasi-spiritual *And God Said to Cain* and the rousing opener to *A Few Dollars for Django*.
1964: $5,000 on the Ace. 1966: A Few Dollars for Django; Texas Adios. 1967: Death Walks in Laredo. 1968: A Long Ride from Hell. 1970: And God Said to Cain.

POWERS, HUNT
[Jack Betts]
(Miami, USA)

Actor. Another American who exchanged an unpromising TV career for leading parts in European westerns, Powers suited tongue-in-cheek roles better than conventional tough guys. He excelled in his debut, *Sugar Colt*, in which his casting was assured by the approval of director Franco Giraldi's wife, but looked less convincing when called upon to play Django by Demofilo Fidani, who also cast him, absurdly, as a Mexican bandit in *A Barrel Full of Dollars*. Having sung in Broadway shows and in nightclubs earlier in his career, he contributed vocals to a song in *The Greatest Robbery in the West*. Back in America since the early Seventies, he has worked regularly on television and more recently in character parts on the big screen, notably as Boris Karloff in *Gods and Monsters* (1998).
1966: Sugar Colt. 1967: The Greatest Robbery in the West. 1970: Dead Men Don't Make Shadows; Django and Sartana are Coming... It's the End; One Damned Day at Dawn... Django Meets Sartana! 1971: The Ballad of Django; A Barrel Full of Dollars; A Fistful of Death; He Was Called the Holy Ghost. 1974: Court Martial.

PREGADIO, ROBERTO
['Bob Deramont']
(Catania, Italy. 1928-2010)
Composer. While most of his scores were as routine as the films they accompanied, Pregadio's music for *The Forgotten Pistolero* is among the most evocative in the genre. The main theme in particular – which arranges all the key ingredients of shuffling percussion, whistling, strings, brass and Spanish guitar into a wonderfully melodic whole – has been endlessly recycled by advertisers keen to convey a sense of the far west, irrespective of the Italian origins of the piece itself.
1967: Django, the Last Killer. 1968: Ciccio Forgives, I Don't; A Hole Between the Eyes. 1969: The Forgotten Pistolero. 1970: Franco and Ciccio on the War-Path. 1971: Four Pistols for Trinity; My Name Is Mallory. 1973: Three Supermen of the West.

PRESTON, WAYDE
[William Strange]
(Denver, USA. 1929-1992)

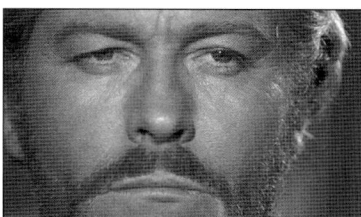

Burly actor in the Guy Madison mould. The star of the Warner Bros. TV series *Colt 45* for three years until 1960, he gravitated to Rome where, among other activities, he played leads and supporting roles in eight westerns, adequately interpreting both noble and ignoble roles. He died of cancer.
1968: A Long Ride from Hell; Today It's Me... Tomorrow You!; The Wrath of God. 1969: God Will Forgive My Gun; Tierra Brava. 1970: A Man Called Sledge; Sartana in the Valley of Death. 1971: Hey Amigo! A Toast to Your Death.

PUENTE, JESÚS
[Jesús Puente Alzaga; 'Joe Punter']
(Madrid, Spain. 1930-2000)

Actor. He studied to be a doctor but took up stage acting instead. He was also involved in the earliest Spanish television productions and dubbed foreign films in the early Sixties – he was the Spanish voice of James Stewart and Ray Milland, for example. A stout everyman sort, he was a regular in the films of Joaquín Romero Marchent (his most sympathetic part being that of the tragic heroine's husband in *Seven from Texas*), and returned to the stage in the Seventies with great success. He later became a popular TV personality.
1964: Behind the Mask of Zorro; The Fury of the Apaches; The Return of Clay Stone; Seven from Texas. 1965: Adios Gringo; For a Fist in the Eye; Hands of a Gunfighter; The Man from Oklahoma. 1966: $100,000 for Lassiter. 1967: Rattler Kid; Two Crosses at Danger Pass. 1968: Ringo the Lone Rider.

PUPPO, ROMANO
['Roman Barrett']
(Rome, Italy. 1937-1994)

With a physique like a brick wall, this stone-faced stunt performer (he regularly doubled for Lee Van Cleef) was often cast in Enzo Castellari movies, as well as westerns and other action films, as a minor villain or brutal henchman. He was killed in a road accident.
1965: The Tramplers. 1966: The Good, the Bad and the Ugly; Massacre Time. 1967: The Big Gundown; Day of Anger; Days of Violence; Death Rides a Horse; Rita of the West. 1968: Beyond the Law; Two Pistols and a Coward. 1969: Boot Hill; Death on a High Hill; Sabata. 1970: Chuck Mool. 1971: Dead Men Ride. 1972: Trinity and Sartana Are Coming. 1973: Deaf Smith & Johnny Ears; On the Third Day Arrived the Crow; Those Dirty Dogs. 1975: Cipolla Colt; The White, the Yellow and the Black. 1977: California. 1978: China 9, Liberty 37. 1981: Buddy Goes West.

QUESTI, GIULIO
(Bergamo, Italy. 1924-)
Director/writer. After completing his studies in literature, Questi became a journalist and author. He was a partisan in the Second World War, an award-winning documentarist in the Fifties and an occasional director of decidedly leftfield features from the mid-Sixties onwards. Few of his films have been seen outside of Italy (the last few were made for television), and his international reputation rests on two provocative variations on western and thriller themes: *Django, Kill!* and *A Curious Way to Love* (1968). Both were co-written and edited by the brilliant Franco Arcalli, and benefited from reasonably widespread distribution. The grotesque, hyper-violent *Django, Kill!* at once epitomises and criticises spaghetti western conventions.
1967: Django, Kill! (w/d).

RASSIMOV, IVAN
[Ivan Djerasimovic; 'Sean Todd']
(Trieste, Italy. 1938-2003)
Actor. Striking leading man/villain with sculptural features and a piercing gaze. Born to Croatian parents, he played in a few minor Italian productions in the early Sixties and was then cast in a small role in John Huston's *The Bible* (1966), although most of his scenes were cut. As 'Sean Todd', he made an amiable hero in a quartet of low-budget westerns, but was more effective in wicked parts – as a racist land baron in *Vengeance Trail*, for example, and killers and sociopaths in *gialli* and crime films. He also became a totemic figure in cannibal horror films and later became a director of *fotoromanzi*. His sister is actress Rada Rassimov – they appeared together in Edoardo Mulargia's *Don't Wait, Django, Shoot!* and in a subsequent TV movie.

above: **Ivan Rassimov** on a lobby card for **Cjamango**.

above: **Dean Reed**.

above: **Franco Ressel** (*left*) has a potentially explosive confrontation with **Lee Van Cleef** in **Sabata**.

above: **Fernando Rey** (*left*) in **The Price of Power**.

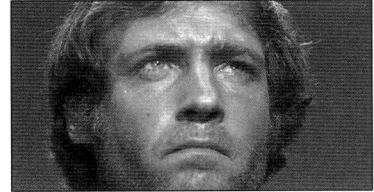

above: **John Richardson**.

1967: *Cjamango; Don't Wait, Django, Shoot!* 1968: *Cowards Don't Pray; If You Want to Live... Then Shoot!* 1971: *Vengeance Trail.*

REED, DEAN
(Denver, USA. 1938-1986)
Actor and singer with all-American looks but decidedly un-American political beliefs. A visit to Latin America early in his singing career transformed his outlook on life. "I was really awakened by the fascist dictatorships and the poverty," he said, explaining his adoption of socialism. His convictions alienated him from his homeland but endeared him to audiences in Latin America, Eastern Europe and the Soviet Union, where he played sell-out concerts singing rock'n'roll standards and his own protest songs, although his popularity waned in the Eighties. He made a handful of westerns in Italy and in the GDR, where he lived until his death from drowning. The official verdict of suicide continues to be disputed by conspiracy theorists.
1967: *Buckaroo.* 1968: *God Forgive... His Life Is Mine; The Nephews of Zorro.* 1970: *Adios, Sabata; Twenty Steps to Death.* 1971: *Damnation.* 1973: *Karate, Fists and Beans.* 1974: *Kit & Co.* 1975: *Blood Brothers* (act/w). 1981: *Sing, Cowboy, Sing* (act/w/d).

REINL, HARALD
(Bad-Ischl, now Austria. 1908-1986)
Once an assistant of Leni Riefenstahl, as a director Reinl is best known today for German *krimis* – atmospheric thrillers often derived from Edgar Wallace stories – and the Sixties 'Winnetou' films. He made five titles in the series, including the first, *The Treasure of Silver Lake*, and the last, *Winnetou and Shatterhand in the Valley of Death*. His 1970 documentary, *Chariots of the Gods*, was nominated for an Oscar. Married three times (once to the popular German actress Karin Dor), he was stabbed to death by his last wife.
1962: *The Treasure of Silver Lake.* 1963: *Winnetou the Warrior.* 1964: *Last of the Renegades.* 1965: *Desperado Trail; The Last Tomahawk.* 1968: *Winnetou and Shatterhand in the Valley of Death* (w/d). 1972: *Cry of the Black Wolves.* 1973: *The Hellhounds of Alaska.*

RESSEL, FRANCO
[Domenico Orobona; 'Ray Russel']
(Aversa, Italy. 1925-1985)
Actor. Beginning in the theatre, bug-eyed Ressel was a reliable and versatile character actor. He played in both comic and serious films without missing a beat, with his camp, supercilious villain in *Sabata* exemplifying his work in westerns.
1965: *In a Colt's Shadow.* 1966: *El Rojo; A Taste for Killing.* 1967: *Man, Pride and Vengeance.* 1968: *Dead for a Dollar; A Professional Gun.* 1969: *Sabata; Zorro in the Court of England.* 1970: *Have a Nice Funeral, Sartana Will Pay; Sartana in the Valley of Death.* 1971: *They Call Him Cemetery; Trinity Is Still My Name.* 1972: *The Two Sons of Trinity; Where the Bullets Fly.* 1973: *Bad Kids of the West.* 1977: *California.*

REY, FERNANDO
[Fernando Casado Arambillet]
(La Coruña, Spain. 1917-1994)
Actor. Elegant, dignified Spanish character actor, formerly an architect who fought on the republican side in the Civil War. He overcame the obstacles this presented under Franco's reign and began a long and distinguished acting career in both Spanish and international productions. Never one to shy away from genre fare, his notable western roles included a scheming aristocrat in *The Price of Power* and pacifist intellectual in *Compañeros*.
1962: *The Savage Guns.* 1965: *Son of a Gunfighter.* 1966: *Legacy of the Incas; Navajo Joe; Return of the Seven.* 1968: *Villa Rides.* 1969: *Guns of the Magnificent Seven; Land Raiders; The Price of Power.* 1970: *The Anger of the Wind; Compañeros.* 1971: *A Town Called Bastard.* 1973: *White Fang.* 1985: *Rustlers' Rhapsody.*

RICHARDSON, JOHN
(Worthing, England. 1934-)
Lean, handsome British leading man who spent the bulk of his career in Italy. As well as horror films, *gialli* and other popular forms, he made two ambitious westerns: *John the Bastard*, in which he gives an authoritative performance as the manipulative rake of the title; and *Execution*, where he plays twin brothers in a rambling revenge narrative. He retired from acting in the Nineties.
1967: *John the Bastard.* 1968: *Execution.*

RIGAUD, GEORGE
[Pedro Jorge Rigato Delissetche; Jorge Rigaud]
(Buenos Aires, Argentina. 1905-1984)
Actor. Born to a French mother and Argentinian father, Rigaud was a popular romantic lead in France during the Thirties and Forties. He moved to Spain and continued to perform in diverse roles, specialising in gentlemanly types, and was much in demand for westerns. He is fondly remembered as the patriarch of the MacGregor clan in Franco Giraldi's two comic westerns. He was killed in a traffic accident.
1964: *Ride and Kill.* 1965: *A Coffin for the Sheriff; Finger on the Trigger; A Place Called Glory.* 1966: *Ringo's Big Night; Savage Pampas; Seven Guns for the MacGregors; Sugar Colt; The Tall Women; The Texican; A Woman for Ringo.* 1967: *Up the MacGregors.* 1968: *Gatling Gun.* 1969: *Alive or Preferably Dead; Guns of the Magnificent Seven; Vengeance Is Mine.* 1971: *A Town Called Bastard.* 1972: *Ben and Charlie; His Name Was Holy Ghost.* 1974: *The Stranger and the Gunfighter; Whisky and Ghosts.* 1975: *Cipolla Colt; Valley of the Dancing Widows.*

RIZZO, GIANNI
[Giovanni Rizzo]
(Brindisi, Italy. 1924-1992)
Actor. With his haughty air and wry expression (he was a natural as Roman senators and emperors in *pepla*), Rizzo was a specialist in camp, corpulent fat cats, usually embroiled in criminal conspiracies (see *Face to Face*, the first 'Sartana' film and the 'Sabata' series). He wasn't given many opportunities to display his range, even outside the western genre, although he did work with a few lauded directors in the Seventies, including Pasolini, Germi and Rossellini.
1962: *Zorro at the Court of Spain.* 1963: *Zorro and the Three Musketeers.* 1967: *Face to Face.* 1968: *If You Meet Sartana, Pray for Your Death; Run, Man, Run.* 1969: *Sabata.* 1970: *Adios, Sabata.* 1971: *Return of Sabata.*

Who's Who In Euro-Westerns

ROBARDS, JASON
(Chicago, USA. 1922-2000)
Actor. After distinguished Naval service in the Second World War, Robards' acting career blossomed on Broadway. He broke into movies in the late Fifties and played a wide variety of character parts. He was in few westerns but – after apparently rejecting the lead in *A Fistful of Dollars* – he was outstanding as Cheyenne, the outdated outlaw in *Once Upon a Time in the West* (1968).

ROBLEDO, LORENZO
['Norman Preston']
(Spain. 1921-2006)
Actor. Squat, fair-haired character actor who appeared in more than two-dozen westerns. He usually played a gunman, villain or victim and had some memorably gruesome death scenes, notably at the hands of Gian Maria Volonté in *Face to Face* and Tomas Milian in *The Four of the Apocalypse*.
1962: *The Shadow of Zorro*. 1963: *The Magnificent Three*. 1964: *Billy the Kid*; *A Fistful of Dollars*; *$5,000 on the Ace*; *Relevo para un pistolero*; *Seven from Texas*; *Tomb of the Pistolero*. 1965: *The Black Eagles of Santa Fe*; *For a Few Dollars More*; *Hands of a Gunfighter*; *The Last of the Mohicans*; *The Relentless Four*; *Seven Hours of Gunfire*. 1966: *Fort Yuma Gold*; *The Good, the Bad and the Ugly*; *Navajo Joe*; *A Taste for Killing*. 1967: *The Big Gundown*; *Face to Face*. 1968: *Bury Them Deep*; *Cowards Don't Pray*; *A Minute to Pray, a Second to Die*; *Once Upon a Time in the West*; *One Against One... No Mercy*; *A Professional Gun*; *Three Silver Dollars*; *A Train for Durango*. 1969: *Cemetery Without Crosses*; *Garringo*; *The Price of Power*; *Vengeance Is Mine*. 1970: *Clumsy Hands*; *Compañeros*; *Viva Sabata!* 1971: *Cut-Throats Nine*; *Hands Up, Dead Man! You're Under Arrest*; *In the Dust of the Sun*; *Kill Django... Kill First*; *Long Live Your Death*. 1972: *Prey of Vultures*. 1973: *Fast-Hand Is Still My Name*. 1975: *The Four of the Apocalypse*; *The White, the Yellow, and the Black*.

ROLAND, GILBERT
[Luis Antonio Damaso de Alonso]
(Ciudad Juárez, Mexico. 1905-1994)
Actor. When his family moved to America during the Mexican Revolution, Roland abandoned plans to become a bullfighter, like his father, and took up acting instead. In films since the Twenties, he was given mostly clichéd Latin parts to play, reviving his flagging career in the Forties by playing the dashing Cisco Kid in 11 westerns. His work in Italy was no less stereotypical – he played bandits and other shady types – but even so he demonstrated abundant charm, charisma and humour. Once married to actress Constance Bennett.
1967: *Any Gun Can Play*. 1968: *Between God, the Devil and a Winchester*; *Johnny Hamlet*; *The Ruthless Four*. 1969: *Santana Does Not Forgive*.

ROMERO MARCHENT, CARLOS
(Madrid, Spain. 1944-)
The youngest of the Romero Marchent brothers began acting in his early teens, and during his adolescence he juggled performing with work outside the industry. He played supporting roles in several of his brothers' films, displaying plenty of youthful dash and vigour, if not natural ability. As his acting career petered out he dabbled in dubbing and distribution, and made an unsuccessful foray into directing in 1987.
1962: *The Shadow of Zorro*; *Zorro the Avenger*. 1963: *Gunfight at High Noon*. 1965: *Hands of a Gunfighter*; *Seven Hours of Gunfire*. 1966: *$100,000 for Lassiter*. 1968: *Dead Men Don't Count!*; *Fedra West*. 1969: *Garringo*. 1970: *And Sartana Kills Them All*; *Arizona*. 1971: *Cut-Throats Nine*. 1972: *Prey of Vultures*; *Zorro the Lawman*.

ROMERO MARCHENT, JOAQUÍN
[Joaquín Luis Romero Hernández Marchent; 'Joaquín Romero Hernández']
(Madrid, Spain. 1921-)
The most important Spanish director of westerns, predating even Leone as a maker of quality features. His father was a popular author, critic and film producer, but Romero Marchent climed the industry ladder of his own accord. He assisted other directors until the mid-Fifties, when he began directing himself. The influence of American westerns on his early films – including two adaptations of author José Mallorquí's El Coyote novels and a pair of sprightly Zorro adventures – was particularly pronounced in *The Magnificent Three* and *Gunfight at High Noon*, the latter especially confirming the director's ability to reinvigorate tired characters and themes. Although most of his westerns adhere to (pre-Sixties) Hollywood stereotypes, he did helm one of the most stridently nihilistic of all European genre films, the gruesome *Cut-Throats Nine*, which was, appropriately, his last word on the subject. (He remained active behind the scenes, however, as a screenwriter, and ran his own production company, Centauro Films.) Of his later work, his contribution to the popular Spanish TV series *Curro Jiménez* (1976-79), chronicling the adventures of a 19th Century Andalusian bandit, is the most noteworthy.
1955: *The Coyote*; *The Judgement of the Coyote*. 1962: *The Shadow of Zorro* (w/d); *Zorro the Avenger* (w/d). 1963: *Gunfight at High Noon* (w/p/d); *The Magnificent Three* (w/d). 1964: *Seven from Texas* (w/p/d). 1965: *Hands of a Gunfighter* (w); *Seven Hours of Gunfire* (w/p/d). 1966: *$100,000 for Lassiter* (w/p/d). 1967: *Fifteen Scaffolds for a Killer* (p). 1968: *Fedra West* (w/d); *I Want Him Dead* (p); *Kill Them All and Come Back Alone* (w/p). 1969: *Garringo* (w). 1970: *And Sartana Kills Them All* (w); *Arizona* (w); *Clumsy Hands* (w). 1971: *Cut-Throats Nine* (w/p/d). 1973: *The Son of Zorro* (w). 1980: *The Black Wolf* (w); *Revenge of the Black Wolf* (w).

ROMERO MARCHENT, RAFAEL
[Rafael Romero Hernández Marchent; 'Ralph R. Marchent']
(Madrid, Spain. 1926-)
Director/writer. Joaquín's younger brother learnt the trade under his sibling's tutelage before making his directorial debut with *Hands of a Gunfighter* in 1965, a sombre variation on the gunman-trying-to-go-straight theme. His later westerns are grittier and more ironic, the best of them (*Garringo*, *Clumsy Hands*) veering into dark, psychological territory.
1962: *The Shadow of Zorro* (ad). 1963: *Gunfight at High Noon* (w). 1964: *Seven from Texas* (ad). 1965: *Hands of a Gunfighter* (d). 1966: *A Woman for Ringo* (d). 1967: *Two Crosses at Danger Pass* (d). 1968: *Dead Men Don't Count!* (w/d); *One Against One... No Mercy* (d); *Ringo the Lone Rider* (d). 1969: *Garringo* (d); *The Magnificent Bandits* (w). 1970: *And Sartana Kills Them All* (w/d); *Clumsy Hands* (d). 1972: *Prey of Vultures* (w/d); *Zorro the Lawman* (w/d). 1980: *The Black Wolf* (w/d); *Revenge of the Black Wolf* (w/d).

above: **George Rigaud**.

above: **Gianni Rizzo**.

above: **Jason Robards**.

above: **Lorenzo Robledo** (*centre*) in trouble again, this time in **For a Few Dollars More**.

above: **Gilbert Roland**, as seen in **The Ruthless Four**.

above: **Carlos Romero Marchent** in **Cut-Throats Nine**.

ROSSETTI, FRANCO
['Fred Gardner']
(Siena, Italy. 1930-)
One of the genre's key scriptwriters, Rossetti studied law before attending the Centro Sperimentale. He wrote film reviews before entering the industry as an assistant director in the Fifties. He co-wrote *Django, Texas Adios* – two films connected by subplots involving popular uprisings – and the equally populist *Viva Django*, one of the most 'faithful' entries in that particular franchise. Directed one western of his own, the squalid, brutal Andrea Giordana vehicle *The Dirty Outlaws*.
1966: Django; Ringo and His Golden Pistol; Texas Adios. 1967: The Dirty Outlaws (w/p/d); Rita of the West; Viva Django. 1970: Chuck Mool.

ROSSI, LUCIANO
['Edwin/Edward (G) Ross'; 'L(o)u Kamante'; 'Karl Simon']
(Collepardo, Italy. 1934-2005)

Pale, physically slight character actor with an anxious, wild-eyed expression. His performances as sneering, petty psychopaths and demented villains rarely failed to make an impression, and he became a cult favourite for his appearances in all manner of genres. He steals *Django the Bastard* as the insecure, unhinged Luke Murdock, enjoyed himself as the increasingly exasperated lead villain in *Django Kills Softly* and displayed a more subdued side as a manipulated Mexican in *The Forgotten Pistolero*.
1966: Django; A Golden Sheriff; Ramon the Mexican. 1967: Death Sentence; Django Kills Softly; The Greatest Robbery in the West; Son of Django; Viva Django. 1968: Run, Man, Run. 1969: Boot Hill; Django the Bastard; The Forgotten Pistolero; Hate Is My God. 1970: Chuck Mool; A Man Called Sledge; Sartana's Here... Trade Your Pistol for a Coffin; They Call Me Trinity. 1971: Heads I Kill You... Tails You're Dead! They Call Me Hallelujah; Return of Sabata. 1972: Jesse & Lester: Two Brothers in a Place Called Trinity; Watch Out Gringo! Sabata Will Return. 1973: Deaf Smith & Johnny Ears. 1974: Sons of White Fang. 1975: White Fang to the Rescue.

ROSSI-STUART, GIACOMO
['Jack Stewart'; 'James R. Stuart']
(Todi, Italy. 1931-1994)

above: **Giacomo Rossi-Stuart** (*right*) on this lobby card for *Gunfight at Red Sands*.

Actor. Handsome in a bland sort of way, he was the lead or co-lead in a vast number of popular films from the Fifties onwards. His first western was *Gunfight at Red Sands*, where he played the first of many duplicitous characters. When called upon to carry a film in a more conventional role (as in *De Guello*) he was less impressive. Father of the actor Kim Rossi Stuart.
1963: Gunfight at Red Sands; Zorro and the Three Musketeers. 1964: Badmen of the West; $5,000 on the Ace; Massacre at Grand Canyon. 1965: Duel at Sundown. 1966: De Guello. 1968: Zorro the Fox. 1969: The Five Man Army. 1971: Kill Django... Kill First. 1972: Ben and Charlie; You're Jinxed, Friend, You've Met Sacremento. 1973: The Fighting Fists of Shanghai Joe. 1975: Zorro.

RUPP, SIEGHARDT
['Simon Rupp']
(Bregenz, Austria. 1931-)

Actor. With his dark, Latin features, Rupp was a perfect fit for sneering, villainous supporting roles in early westerns and crime films. His best-known part was that of the slow-witted, but dashing and cruel, Esteban Rojo in *A Fistful of Dollars*, who gleefully shoots down Consuela Baxter during the Rojos' fiery assault on their foes. He later turned to stage work.
1964: Among Vultures; A Fistful of Dollars; The Last Ride to Santa Cruz. 1965: The Man Called Gringo. 1966: Blood at Sundown; Who Killed Johnny Ringo?

RUSTICHELLI, CARLO
['Evirust'; 'Jim Murphy']
(Carpi, Italy. 1916-2004)
Composer. Studied at the Academia Filarmonica in Bologna and at Santa Cecilia in Rome. His reputation as a composer was forged with Pietro Germi, and over the years he worked on every conceivable type of film, including a handful of westerns. Introduced elements of circus music into his scores for Colizzi's *Ace High* and *Boot Hill*.
1964: Buffalo Bill, Hero of the Far West; Heroes of Fort Worth. 1966: Kill or Be Killed; Ringo's Big Night. 1967: God Forgives... I Don't!; A Man and a Colt; Man, Pride and Vengeance. 1968: Ace High; A Minute to Pray, a Second to Die; One Dollar Too Many; The Ruthless Four; Three Silver Dollars; A Train for Durango; Two Pistols and a Coward. 1969: Boot Hill. 1970: The Twilight Avengers. 1971: Bastard, Go and Kill. 1972: The Call of the Wild. 1973: The Three Musketeers of the West; White Fang. 1974: Challenge to White Fang. 1975: Red Coat; White Fang to the Rescue.

RUZZOLINI, GIUSEPPE
(Rome, Italy. 1930-)
Cinematographer. Best known for his work with Pasolini, following in the footsteps of the peerless Tonino Delli Colli, Ruzzolini succeeded the latter again when he became Leone's DP in the Seventies. A master of rendering natural landscapes and exotic locations (proved by his photography on Pasolini's *Oedipus Rex* [1967] and *Arabian Nights* [1974]), he shot vivid backdrops and sweeping vistas for *A Fistful of Dynamite*, in which he also helped Leone conjure the look of Goya's *The Third of May* for a nocturnal execution scene, and *A Genius, Two Partners and a Dupe*, and experimented with deep-focus in *My Name Is Nobody*.
1971: A Fistful of Dynamite. 1973: My Name Is Nobody. 1975: A Genius, Two Partners and a Dupe.

SABATO, ANTONIO
(Palermo, Italy. 1943-)

Actor. A busy B-movie leading man of the Seventies and early Eighties, Sabato started out with a series of westerns. In two of these he gave good-natured, vigorous performances opposite more seasoned actors – John Ireland in *Hate for Hate* and Lee Van Cleef in *Beyond the Law*. His son is also an actor and has starred in several American TV productions and action films.
1967: Hate for Hate. 1968: Beyond the Law; One Dollar Too Many. 1969: Twice a Judas. 1972: Thunder Over El Paso; Where the Bullets Fly.

SALERNO, ENRICO MARIA
(Milan, Italy. 1926-1994)

Actor/director. An award-winning actor of stage and screen, Salerno was adept at both leading and supporting roles, proving his worth in both genre films and prestige productions. His first major contribution to the western was made offscreen, when he gave Clint Eastwood a commanding tone in the Italian version of *A Fistful of Dollars* (1964), his voice being one of his prime assets as a performer, and he later gave a first-class performance as an ageing marksman in *Bandidos*. He died of lung cancer.
1967: Bandidos; Death Sentence; Death Walks in Laredo. 1968: A Train for Durango.

SALERNO, VITTORIO
(Milan, Italy. 1938-)
Writer/director. Brother of Enrico, Vittorio wrote stories and scripts for a number of impressive westerns, often in tandem with Ernesto Gastaldi, with whom he created the character of Sartana. They co-wrote and co-directed the tortuous thriller *Libido* in 1965 and the horror film *Notturno gon grida* in 1982.
1966: Blood at Sundown. 1968: Dead Men Don't Count!; A Gun for a Hundred Graves. 1969: $20,000 Stained in Blood. 1973: Fast-Hand Is Still My Name.

SAMBRELL, ALDO
[Alfredo Sanchez Brell; 'Aldo Sanbrell']
(Madrid, Spain. 1931 or 1937-2010)

Actor/director. He grew up in Mexico where he studied the dramatic arts. Back in Spain he played soccer before pursuing an acting career. Facially and physically perfect for westerns, he racked up an impressive number of appearances, specialising in Mexican or mixed-race heavies. Usually given little more than glowering cameos – he played a minor villain in all Leone's westerns – it has been said, by Sambrell at least, that Leone promised to cast him as Tuco in *The Good, the Bad and the Ugly* should Eli Wallach, who had already signed for the role, become unavailable. Although fate conspired against him there, his performance as the half-breed Duncan in *Navajo Joe* proved he could electrify the screen if given the chance. "I have died more than anyone else in the history of cinema," he boasted, "more than 150 times!" One of the genre's unsung heroes, he also ran a production company and directed several features. In. 2006 he produced and starred in a short film commemorating the western years called *Río seco*, directed by José Manuel Serrano Cueto, whose interview with Sambrell was published in book form in 2003.
1963: Gunfight at High Noon; Gunfight at Red Sands; The Magnificent Three. 1964: Billy the Kid; Cavalry Charge; A Fistful of Dollars; The Fury of the Apaches; Gunfighters of Casa Grande; Massacre at Fort Grant; Relevo para un pistolero; Tomb of the Pistolero; Two Violent Men. 1965: For a Few Dollars More; In a Colt's Shadow; A Place Called Glory; Son of a Gunfighter. 1966: A Bullet for the General; Dynamite Jim; The Good, the Bad and the Ugly; Navajo Joe; $100,000 for Lassiter; Savage Gringo; The Texican. 1967: Face to Face; Fifteen Scaffolds for a Killer; The Hellbenders. 1968: A Long Ride from Hell; A Minute to Pray, a Second to Die; Once Upon a Time in the West; Requiem for a Gringo; A Train for Durango; Villa Rides; White Comanche. 1969: 100 Rifles; Vengeance Is Mine. 1970: Arizona; Cannon for Cordoba; Clumsy Hands. 1971: Bad Man's River; A Fistful of Dynamite; Hands Up, Dead Man! You're Under Arrest; Hannie Caulder; Kill Django... Kill First; Rain for a Dusty Summer; A Town Called Bastard. 1972: Ben and Charlie; Charley One-Eye. 1973: The Man Called Noon; Tequila. 1978: Silver Saddle. 1981: Ahora mis pistolas hablan. 1983: Al oeste de Río Grande. 1984: Yellow Hair and the Fortress of Gold. 1985: Tex and the Lord of the Deep. 1996: Here Comes Condemor (the Sinner of the Plains). 1999: Outlaw Justice.

SANCHEZ, PEDRO
[Ignazio Spalla]
(Siena, Italy. 1924-1995)

Heavyset supporting actor, a low-rent Fernando Sancho, who provided light relief in a number of westerns, almost always interpreting an effusive, slovenly Mexican or money-grubbing lowlife. He was Lee Van Cleef's sidekick in the 'Sabata' series.
1964: Bullets and the Flesh; Two Gangsters in the Wild West. 1965: One Silver Dollar; Two Sergeants of General Custer; Why Go On Killing? 1966: Go with God, Gringo; The Sons of Ringo; Thompson 1880. 1967: Any Gun Can Play; Cjamango; Death, at Owell Rock; Don't Wait, Django, Shoot!; Pecos Cleans Up; Son of Django. 1968: Johnny Hamlet; May God Forgive You – I Won't; The Nephews of Zorro; Vengeance; Zorro the Fox. 1969: Quintana; Sabata; Tierra Brava. 1970: Adios, Sabata; Reverend Colt. 1971: Return of Sabata; Tara Poki. 1972: My Horse.. My Gun... Your Widow. 1973: Seven Nuns in Kansas City; Three Supermen of the West. 1974: Carambola. 1975: The Dream of Zorro; Trinity Plus the Clown and a Guitar; White Fang and the Gold Diggers; White Fang and the Hunter.

SANCHO, FERNANDO
[Fernando Sancho Les]
(Zaragoza, Spain. 1916-1990)

Brash, bullish character actor who became the definitive Mexican *bandido*, appearing in more than 50 westerns. He gained experience in regional theatre prior to the Spanish Civil War, during which he fought on the Nationalist side, and after the conflict he worked for Radio Barcelona. In films from 1941, he amassed one of the densest filmographies in Spanish cinema history over more than 40 years, aided in part by his prominent position in the powerful National Show Business Union. (He also worked as a dubber, providing the Spanish voice for Oliver Hardy.) Although he displayed versatility in a variety of character roles in the first phase of his acting career (during which he had small roles in *King of Kings, Lawrence of Arabia* and *55 Days of Peking*, all shot in Spain) and played his share of loveable, comedic sidekicks during the western period, it is his exuberant performances as gruff, blustering Mexican 'generals' and brigands that secured his popularity. Although his work rate declined considerably, he remained typecast as a bad guy in the Seventies and Eighties. "[He] was a really good guy", one of Sancho's co-stars, Robert Woods, told me. "I enjoyed [working with him], but keeping up with him and stopping him chewing the scenery was a different matter. It was easy to underplay with him – even if you were overplaying."
1962: Zorro the Avenger. 1963: Gunfight at High Noon; The Magnificent Three; The Sign of the Coyote. 1964: Black Angel of the Mississippi; $5,000 on the Ace; Gunmen of the Rio Grande; Minnesota Clay; Seven from Texas; Two Gangsters in the Wild West. 1965: The Man Who Came to Kill; $100,000 for Ringo; A Pistol for Ringo; The Return of Ringo; Shoot to Kill; Two Sergeants of General Custer; Viva Carrancho. 1966: Arizona Colt; Django Shoots First; Dynamite Jim; Seven Dollars to Kill; Seven Guns for the MacGregors; Seven Guns for Timothy; A Taste for Killing. 1967: The Big Gundown; Clint the Stranger; For $100,000 Per Killing; Hate for Hate; Killer Kid; A Man and a Colt; Rita of the West; $10,000 Blood Money; Turn... I'll Kill You!; Wanted Johnny Texas. 1968: Blood for Blood; Ciccio Forgives, I Don't; If You Meet Sartana, Pray for Your Death; Lynching; One for All; Requiem for a Gringo; The Wrath of God. 1969: $20,000 Stained in Blood. 1970: Stagecoach of the Condemned. 1971: And the Crows Will Dig Your Grave; Dig Your Grave Friend... Sabata's Coming. 1972: The Boldest Job in the West; The Fabulous Trinity; Too Much Gold for One Gringo; Watch Out Gringo! Sabata Will Return; Where the Bullets Fly; You Are a Traitor and I'll Kill You. 1973: Karate, Fists and Beans; The Son of Zorro; Three Supermen of the West. 1975: Dallas. 1980: The Black Wolf; Revenge of the Black Wolf. 1984: Al este del Oeste.

SAN MARTÍN, CONRADO
[Conrado San Martín Prieto]
(Avila, Spain. 1921-)

Actor. An amateur boxer in his youth, he was active in films from the Forties, playing leads and co-leads, and became a popular domestic star in the Fifties. His fortunes faded in the next decade when he was reduced to supporting status, often as grizzled characters in westerns, but he has continued to work solidly in Spanish films and television shows. *1965: In a Colt's Shadow. 1967: Long Days of Vengeance; Turn... I'll Kill You! 1968: Once Upon a Time in the West. 1971: A Fistful of Dynamite. 1984: Al este del Oeste.*

SANTINI, GINO

Cinematographer. A specialist in exploitation films, Santini showed considerable flair in his western assignments. Especially impressive is the dramatic shifting between light and darkness in *Blood at Sundown* and *Django the Bastard*, while the latter film and *Shango* show his dexterity with unusual and disorienting camera angles.

1966: Blood at Sundown. 1967: $20,000 on Number Seven (w/ph). 1968: Cowards Don't Pray; Garter Colt; A Stranger in Paso Bravo. 1969: Django the Bastard. 1970: Shango. 1972: Hallelujah & Sartana Strike Again!; Trinity and Sartana Are Coming. 1978: La ciudad maldita.

SANZ, PACO
[Francisco Sanz]

Actor. Beginning in the early Sixties, by which time he was in his middle years, this skinny, flexible, wild-eyed character actor became a stalwart of the genre, notching up 30 appearances in a variety of roles. He is best remembered as the devious, Bible-bashing Hagerman in *Django, Kill!*

1963: Gunfight at High Noon. 1964: $5,000 on the Ace; Relevo para un pistolero; Seven from Texas. 1965: Hands of a Gunfighter; $100,000 for Ringo; A Pistol for Ringo; The Relentless Four; Seven Hours of Gunfire; Shoot to Kill; Viva Carrancho. 1966: $100,000 for Lassiter; Savage Gringo; Yankee. 1967: Django, Kill!; Face to Face; God Forgives... I Don't!; The Man Who Killed Billy the Kid. 1968: A Minute to Pray, a Second to Die; One Against One... No Mercy; Tepepa. 1969: The Price of Power; $20,000 Stained in Blood. 1970: And Sartana Kills Them All; Gunman in Town. 1971: Dead Men Ride. 1972: Ben and Charlie; A Reason to Live, a Reason to Die. 1973: Fast-Hand Is Still My Name; The Fighting Fists of Shanghai Joe. 1975: In the Name of the Father, of the Son and of the Colt.

SAVINA, CARLO
(Turin, Italy. 1919-2002)

Composer/conductor. Trained at the Turin Conservatory. He worked chiefly in radio in the Fifties and was conductor of choice for Nino Rota, subsequently composing more than 140 film scores. He wrote for many Italian westerns, covering all its disparate moods; perhaps his best effort was also his last in the genre – his grandiose music for *Comin' at Ya!* imbues the film with a gravitas it scarcely deserves.

1962: Zorro at the Court of Spain. 1963: Zorro and the Three Musketeers. 1964: Bullets and the Flesh. 1965: Outlaw of Red River; The Three from Colorado. 1966: A Few Dollars for Django; Mutiny at Fort Sharp; Ringo and His Golden Pistol; The Tall Women. 1967: Dynamite Joe; Two R-R-Ringos from Texas. 1968: Between God, the Devil and a Winchester; Gun Shy Piluk; A Long Ride from Hell; Vengeance. 1969: Tails, You Lose...; Tierra Brava. 1970: And God Said to Cain; The Twilight Avengers. 1971: He Was Called the Holy Ghost; Hey Amigo! A Toast to Your Death; Thirteenth Is a Judas. 1972: An Animal Called Man; Gunmen and the Holy Ghost; Jesse & Lester: Two Brothers in a Place Called Trinity; Kill the Poker Player; Return of the Holy Ghost; Thunder Over El Paso; Trinity and Sartana Are Coming. 1974: The Stranger and the Gunfighter. 1981: Comin' at Ya!

SAVONA, LEOPOLDO
['Leo Coleman']
(Lenola, Italy. 1922-)

Director. An assistant to such luminaries as De Santis and Pasolini, Savona directed several polished commercial films. Among these were a number of modest westerns, the best being *Killer Kid*, an action-packed yet earnest addition to the political cycle.

1966: El Rojo (w/d). 1967: Killer Kid (w/d). 1969: God Will Forgive My Gun (w/d). 1970: A Man Called Joe Clifford (w/d). 1972: Pistol Packin' Preacher (w/d).

SAXSON, GLENN
[Roel Bos]
(The Hague, Netherlands. 1942-)

Actor. Fair-haired and handsome, Saxson segued from stage to screen in the mid-Sixties, enjoying a brief period as leading man without achieving top-rank stardom. His best-known roles were in *Django Shoots First*, where he played a typically amoral gunfighter with easygoing charm, and in two adaptations of the 'Kriminal' comic strip by Umberto Lenzi, He became a producer in the Seventies.

1966: Django Shoots First; Go with God, Gringo. 1967: The Magnificent Texan. 1968: The Long Day of the Massacre; Lynching.

SCAVOLINI, SAURO
(Pesaro, Italy. 1934-)

Writer. A graduate of the Centro Sperimentale in Rome, Sauro Scavolini began his cinema career as a script supervisor and assistant director. He went on contribute excellent screenplays for some of the finest westerns of the genre's golden age, including *Johnny Yuma* and *$10,000 Blood Money*, and later plundered the script of *A Man Called Blade*, which he worked on with Sergio Martino, one of his regular collaborators. His brother is exploitation filmmaker Romano Scavolini.

1966: Johnny Yuma. 1967: Any Gun Can Play; John the Bastard; $10,000 Blood Money. 1971: Dig Your Grave Friend... Sabata's Coming. 1972: My Horse... My Gun... Your Widow. 1977: A Man Called Blade.

SCOTTI, ANDREA
['Andrew Scott']
(Naples, Italy. 1931-)

Another of those hard-working, valuable actors who, like Tom Felleghy, had the kind of unassuming looks ideal for every type of supporting part. He moved smoothly, almost invisibly, through all the fashionable genres, occasionally catching the eye if a meatier role came his way.

1963: Gunfight at High Noon; Samson and the Slave Queen; The Sign of the Coyote. 1964: Apaches' Last Battle; Buffalo Bill, Hero of the Far West; Samson and the Treasure of the Incas; Two Violent Men. 1965: In a Colt's Shadow; One Silver Dollar. 1966: Starblack. 1967: The Dirty Outlaws; For $100,000 Per Killing; Lola Colt; Son of Django; Two Faces of the Dollar; Viva Django. 1968: Dead for a Dollar; I Want Him Dead; If You Meet Sartana, Pray for Your Death; A Gun for a Hundred Graves. 1970: Adios, Sabata; Shango. 1971: Durango Is Coming, Pay or Die; The Price of Death. 1972: The Two Sons of Trinity; Where the Bullets Fly. 1973: They Still Call Me Amen; Those Dirty Dogs.

above: **Andrea Scotti** can be seen on this lobby still for **In a Colt's Shadow** (right).

SECCHI, ANTONIO
['Toni Secchi'; 'Tony Dry']
(Genoa, Italy. 1924-)
Cinematographer/director. His luminous camerawork adds lustre to *A Bullet for the General* and he achieved some striking, stark tableaux in the almost expressionistic *Death Sentence*. Also directed the dire comedy western *Panhandle Calibre 38*.
1965: *One Silver Dollar*. 1966: *A Bullet for the General*; *The Hills Run Red*. 1967: *Death Sentence*; *Wanted*. 1972: *Panhandle Calibre 38 (w/d)*.

SICILIANO, MARIO
['Marlon Sirko'; 'Lee Castle']
(Rome, Italy. 1925-1987)
Producer / writer / director. His production company, Metheus, which specialised in action-adventure films, was founded in 1962. He formed a fruitful collaboration with director Alberto Cardone for a series of impassioned mid-Sixties westerns and directed the similar *Cowards Don't Pray* himself. Later made porn films as 'Lee Castle'.
1964: *Badmen of the West (p)*; *Massacre at Marble City (p)*. 1965: *The Black Eagles of Sante Fe (p)*. 1966: *Blood at Sundown (p)*; *Seven Dollars to Kill (p)*. 1968: *Cowards Don't Pray (w/p/d)*. 1972: *Hallelujah & Sartana Strike Again! (w/d)*; *Trinity and Sartana Are Coming (d)*.

SIMI, CARLO
['Charles Simons']
(Viareggio, Italy. 1924-2000)
Celebrated production designer. A former architect, he turned to set and costume design in the Fifties. He became one of Leone's key collaborators from *A Fistful of Dollars* onwards, worked with most of the major directors and designed the western town in Tabernas that is now the tourist attraction Mini Hollywood. He managed to marry gritty realism with stylish extravagance in a way that characterises the genre as a whole. He played the El Paso bank director in *For a Few Dollars More*, having designed the blockhouse structure himself – it still stands today. "He had a unique gift to perceive what could be effective in the new, revolutionary way we interpreted the art of making westerns," Sergio Sollima told Mario Marsili. "He was able to construct an environment *around* the camera, thus allowing for unimpeded, immediate and easy shooting. Carlo has earned an immortal position in the Italian western hall of fame."
(Credits as costume designer, art director, production manager or a combination thereof): 1964: *A Fistful of Dollars*; *Minnesota Clay*; *Two Gangsters in the Wild West*. 1965: *For a Few Dollars More (and actor)*. 1966: *Django*; *The Good, the Bad and the Ugly*; *$100,000 for Lassiter*; *Ringo and His Golden Pistol*; *A Taste for Killing*; *Texas Adios*; *A Woman for Ringo*. 1967: *The Big Gundown*; *Face to Face*. 1968: *Once Upon a Time in the West*. 1969: *Sabata*. 1975: *A Genius, Two Partners and a Dupe*. 1975: *The Crazy Adventures of Len and Coby*. 1976: *Keoma*. 1977: *California*. 1978: *Silver Saddle*. 1987: *Renegade*.

SIMONELLI, GIOVANNI
['Simon O'Neill']
(Rome, Italy. 1932-)
Writer who spent the Sixties and early Seventies churning out stories and scripts for *pepla*, spy films and westerns at a dizzyingly prolific rate. He also directed a couple of films, without much success.
1964: *Gunmen of the Rio Grande*. 1965: *Johnny West*; *The Last Tomahawk*; *The Man from Oklahoma*; *The Man Who Came to Kill*; *$100,000 for Ringo*. 1966: *Django Shoots First*; *Johnny Yuma*; *Seven Guns for Timothy*; *A Woman for Ringo*. 1967: *Any Gun Can Play*. 1968: *Fedra West*; *I'll Sell My Skin Dearly*; *One After the Other*. 1969: *Sartana Does Not Forgive*. 1970: *Have a Nice Funeral, Sartana Will Pay*. 1972: *Now They Call Him Sacramento*; *The Return of Clint the Stranger*; *The Return of Hallelujah*; *Tedeum*; *Watch Out Gringo! Sabata Will Return*. 1974: *The Stranger and the Gunfighter*; *Whisky and Ghosts*. 1975: *White Fang to the Rescue*.

SOLINAS, FRANCO
(Cagliari, Italy. 1927-1982)
Author/screenwriter. An ardent Communist, Solinas was a key figure in the development of popular political cinema in the Sixties and Seventies. Best known for his work with Rosi (*Salvatore Giuliano*) and Pontecorvo (*The Battle of Algiers*, for which the writer was nominated for an Oscar), Solinas's stories were also the basis for the strident westerns *The Big Gundown*, *A Professional Gun* and *Tepepa*, and he wrote dialogue for the trend-setting *A Bullet for the General*. One of his major themes is the relationship between First and Third World, symbolised by mercenaries and rebels/bandits respectively, and whether there can ever be a workable alliance between them in the furtherance of political and social reform. "I write scenarios which generally deal with political themes because in my opinion politics is a fundamental matter," he wrote in 1973. "Politics gets to the bottom of problems, doing it through real events."
1966: *A Bullet for the General*. 1967: *The Big Gundown*. 1968: *A Professional Gun*; *Tepepa*.

SOLLIMA, SERGIO
['Simon Sterling']
(Rome, Italy. 1921-)
Writer/director. Although he made only three westerns, Sollima is rightly regarded as one of the genre's key directors. Obsessed with films from an early age, he studied at the Centro Sperimentale and made documentaries during the Second World War before writing for the magazine *Cinema*. He tried his hand at second-unit work, scriptwriting (aided by his wife) and assisting other directors, principally on *pepla* and comedies. He directed a few spy films in the mid-Sixties without much enthusiasm but with above-average results, until Sergio Leone stepped in. As Sollima told Mario Marsili, "There was a group of people gravitating around producer Alberto Grimaldi, among them Sergio Leone. I was a very good friend of Leone. Rome is a village, and the few dozen people who count in the movie business knew each other. Leone had already made *For a Few Dollars More*, we are talking 1966. Leone, bless him, introduced me to Alberto Grimaldi. I owe Leone my becoming a successful Italowestern [sic] director." Sollima made an espionage adventure for Grimaldi before the latter invited him to make *The Big Gundown*. Merging rugged action with humour and strong characterisations, and not shying away from the political implications of Franco Solinas's original story, he and co-writer Sergio Donati created a classic, repeating the trick with *Face to Face*. *Run, Man, Run*, made without Donati but retaining Tomas Milian from the previous films, was somewhat less effective. Sollima moved on from westerns after this, making rewarding forays into the crime genre and a number of vigorous, populist period swashbucklers.
1967: *The Big Gundown (w/d)*; *Face to Face (w/d)*. 1968: *Run, Man, Run (w/d)*.

SOUTHWOOD, CHARLES
(Los Angeles, USA. 1937-)

Actor. A philosophy major, former dockworker and insurance executive, Southwood landed the lead in Demofilo Fidani's first western, *Stranger, Make the Sign of the Cross*, despite having practically no previous acting experience, getting by mainly on his chiselled looks and laid-back manner. He went on to star in *Three Silver Dollars*, a Leone-esque treasure-hunt film, and co-starred in Mario Bava's comedic *Roy Colt and Winchester Jack* with Brett Halsey. He followed this with finely judged performances in two further light-hearted westerns: Giuliano Carnimeo's *Sartana's Here... Trade Your Pistol for a Coffin* and *Heads I Kill You... Tails You're Dead! They Call Me Hallelujah*, stealing both films from co-star George Hilton. He retired from acting in the early Eighties.
1968: *Stranger, Make the Sign of the Cross*; *Three Silver Dollars*. 1970: *Roy Colt and Winchester Jack*; *Sartana's Here... Trade Your Pistol for a Coffin*. 1971: *Heads I Kill You... Tails You're Dead! They Call Me Hallelujah*.

SPENCER, BUD
[Carlo Pedersoli]
(Naples, Italy. 1929-)
Actor. A former swimming champion who competed in the Helsinki Olympics in 1952 and again in Melbourne four years later, the bearded, burly Spencer became one of Europe's best-loved comic actors. With Terence Hill he has starred in 18 films over 45 years, playing the long-suffering, gruff-tempered 'elder brother' – figuratively and, in the case of the 'Trinity' films, literally – to the other's romantic, trouble-prone scamp. Spencer's status as straight man in the partnership belies his shrewd comic timing, and he, like Hill, has proved on many occasions that he has the ability to carry a film on his own. "A cultured, gentle giant of a man" in the words of Brett Halsey, his co-star in *Today It's Me... Tomorrow You!*, Spencer unsuccessfully entered politics on behalf of Silvio Berlusconi's Forza Italia party in 2005.

above: **Bud Spencer** in **Buddy Goes West**.

above: **Lionel Stander** (*centre right, holding umbrella*) in **Beyond the Law**.

above: **Benito Stefanelli** (*second left, wearing sheriff's badge*) in **The Price of Power**.

above: **Antony Steffen**, as seen in **A Train for Durango**.

1967: God Forgives... I Don't! 1968: Ace High; Beyond the Law; Today It's Me... Tomorrow You! 1969: Boot Hill; The Five Man Army. 1970: They Call Me Trinity. 1971: Trinity Is Still My Name. 1972: Can Be Done... Amigo; A Reason to Live, a Reason to Die. 1981: Buddy Goes West. 1994: Troublemakers.

STANDER, LIONEL
(New York City, USA. 1908-1994)

Actor. Short, craggy-faced, gravel-voiced supporting player, a refugee from the McCarthyite blacklist who was never short of work in his European sojourn. He played roguish, comedic parts in several westerns, most famously as the gossipy barman who gazes lustily and longingly at Claudia Cardinale in *Once Upon a Time in the West*, and the sham medium in *Boot Hill*.

1968: Beyond the Law; Once Upon a Time in the West. 1969: Boot Hill. 1972: Tedeum; Where the Bullets Fly. 1973: Halleluja to Vera Cruz. 1975: Red Coat; Who's Afraid of Zorro?

STEFANELLI, BENITO
['Benny Reeves'; 'Ben Steffen']
(Rome, Italy. 1928-1999)

A skilful stunt co-ordinator or master of arms and hardy supporting actor, with ever-present bushy sideburns and beard, he introduced the idea of bodies spinning round when shot (as when Henry Fonda is outgunned in *Once Upon a Time in the West*) and designed the dramatic knife-versus-pistol duel at the end of *The Big Gundown*.

1959: The Sheriff (act); The Terror of Oklahoma (act/master of arms). 1963: Zorro and the Three Musketeers (act). 1964: A Fistful of Dollars (act/stunts); Massacre at Grand Canyon (act/master of arms). 1965: For a Few Dollars More (act); One Silver Dollar (act). 1966: Fort Yuma Gold (act/master of arms); The Good, the Bad and the Ugly (act); $100,000 for Lassiter (act). 1967: The Big Gundown (act/stunts); Day of Anger (act); Gentleman Killer (act); The Hellbenders (act); Kill the Wicked (act); Wanted (act/stunts). 1968: Once Upon a Time in the West (act/master of arms); A Sky Full of Stars for a Roof (act/master of arms); Two Pistols and a Coward (act). 1969: Cemetery Without Crosses (act); Night of the Serpents (act); The Price of Power (act/master of arms). 1971: A Fistful of Dynamite (stunts); A Man Called Django (act); Trinity Is Still My Name (act). 1972: A Reason to Live, a Reason to Die (act). 1973: My Name Is Nobody (act/master of arms). 1975: A Genius, Two Partners and a Dupe (act/master of arms); White Fang to the Rescue (act/stunts). 1977: El Macho (act).

STEFFEN, ANTHONY
[Antonio Luis de Teffè von Hoolholtz]
(Rome, Italy. 1929 or 1930-2004)

Actor/writer. Tall, lean, mournful-looking leading man with an elegant gait (not dissimilar to Henry Fonda's), whose stoical acting in more than two dozen westerns earned him equal parts iconic status and dismissive reviews. Of noble Brazilian parentage (his father was a Baron who went from being a Formula 1 driver to ambassador to Italy), Steffen's early exploits included fighting the Nazis as a teenage partisan. Following the war he gravitated towards the cinema, appearing in youth flicks and *pepla* before finding his métier in westerns. None of his films were international hits, but most are solidly crafted and sensibly centred on his aura of implacability and latent violence. From melodramatic revenge stories he drifted into light-hearted 'buddy' westerns without too much discomfort, and co-wrote two of his most effective vehicles, *Django the Bastard* and *Shango*. His success reportedly went to his head. Claudio Undari, his co-star in *A Name That Cried Revenge*, remembered: "In any scene where some minor amount of action was involved, he wanted a double. But not because it was technically necessary to have a double – it was not in most cases – but because getting a double upon request seemed, in his mind, to be distinctive of a star." In the early Eighties Steffen retired to Brazil, where he later died of cancer after a two-year illness.

1965: A Coffin for the Sheriff; The Last Tomahawk; Why Go On Killing? 1966: Blood at Sundown; A Few Dollars for Django; Ringo the Mark of Vengeance; Seven Dollars to Kill. 1967: Gentleman Killer; Killer Kid. 1968: Dead Men Don't Count!; A Name That Cried Revenge; A Stranger in Paso Bravo; A Train for Durango; Two Pistols and a Coward. 1969: Django the Bastard (act/w); Garringo; No Room to Die. 1970: Arizona; A Man Called Joe Clifford; Shango (act/w); Viva Sabata! 1971: Kill Django... Kill First; A Man Called Django. 1972: Too Much Gold for One Gringo. 1973: Tequila. 1975: Dallas.

STEGANI, GIORGIO
['George Finley']
(Milan, Italy. 1928-)

Director. Having learnt the trade under Giorgio Ferroni, Stegani made his mark with some money-spinning westerns, including the early, American-style Giuliano Gemma vehicle *Adios Gringo* – the sixth most popular film at the Italian box office in the 1965-66 season.

1965: Adios Gringo (w/d); One Silver Dollar (w). 1967: Gentleman Killer (d). 1968: Beyond the Law (w/d).

STEIGER, ROD
(Westhampton, New York, USA. 1925-2002)

Actor. An explosive screen presence in the Fifties and Sixties, Steiger's involvement in Sergio Leone's *A Fistful of Dynamite* proved no less combustible. Leone was exasperated by Steiger's reliance on the Method, and arguments between director and star were commonplace. But Steiger (who incorporated certain Leone mannerisms into his performance) struck a conciliatory tone in later years. "I'd much rather work with a person of talent and a pain in the ass, like he could be and I could be, than one who has no imagination." His colourful performance as Juan Miranda – a role intended at other times for Eli Wallach and Jason Robards – alternates between grandstanding and quiet, intuitive brilliance.
1971: A Fistful of Dynamite.

STEWART, EVELYN
[Ida Galli; 'Isli Oberon']
(Sestola, Italy. 1939-)

Actress. She made her debut in 1959 and was awarded a small role the next year in *La dolce vita*, followed shortly after by a turn in *The Leopard* (1963). From these heights she descended into supporting roles in a variety of popular genres. She projected a certain refinement, an emotional reserve that could represent either innocence (she was the love interest in several westerns) or arrogance, used to good effect in cold-hearted roles in *pepla* and *gialli*.
1965: Adios Gringo; One Silver Dollar; Why Go On Killing? 1966: Django Shoots First; Seven Guns for Timothy. 1968: Gatling Gun; A Name That Cried Revenge; No Graves on Boot Hill. 1970: Chuck Mool. 1971: Four Pistols for Trinity. 1973: A Man Called Invincible.

above: **Dean Stratford** (*right*), seen alonside Rick Boyd in **Don't Wait, Django, Shoot!**

STRATFORD, DEAN
[Dino Strano]
Actor. A onetime paratrooper turned peplum stuntman, his sturdy physique was well suited to villainous roles in westerns. Working mostly in cut-price productions for the likes of Gianni Crea and Demofilo Fidani (whom 'Stratford' credits with giving him his English pseudonym), he played grimacing, braying, teeth-gnashing bad guys to the hilt.
1964: Two Gangsters in the Wild West. 1966: Go with God, Gringo; The Sons of Ringo; Thompson 1880. 1967: Cjamango; Death, at Owell Rock; The Dirty Outlaws; Don't Wait, Django, Shoot! 1968: May God Forgive You – I Won't; Stranger, Make the Sign of the Cross. 1969: Boot Hill; Quintana; Shadow of Sartana... Shadow of Your Death! 1970: Chuck Mool; One Damned Day at Dawn... Django Meets Sartana! 1971: The Ballad of Django; Brother Outlaw; Finders Killers; His Name Was Sam Wallash... But They Called Him Amen!; Shoot the Living and Pray for the Dead; Thirteenth Is a Judas. 1973: On the Third Day Arrived the Crow; They Called Him Trinity [Himself, His Colt, His Revenge]. 1975: Seven Devils on Horseback.

STRODE, WOODY
[Woodrow Wilson Woolwine Strode]
(Los Angeles, USA. 1914-1994)
Actor. As he was a former athlete and American football star, Woody Strode's stony countenance and muscular 6ft 4in frame steered him naturally towards work in genre cinema. Although most of his roles were fairly negligible (barring such notable exceptions as *Sergeant Rutledge* [1960] and Valerio Zurlini's anti-colonialist parable *Black Jesus* [1968]), he was a dignified actor and a potent screen presence, something Leone exploited to the maximum in the opening sequence of *Once Upon a Time in the West*. Strode made further westerns and several other films in Italy, where the money was far better than he'd earned in America, commenting with characteristic modesty: "I am just a hard-working action actor and that's what the producers seem to like here."
1968: Once Upon a Time in the West; Shalako. 1969: Boot Hill. 1970: Chuck Mool; The Deserter. 1971: The Last Rebel. 1976: Keoma.

above: **Woody Strode** takes pride of place (*centre*) in a line-up including several genre stalwarts, in **Boot Hill**.

TATE, LINCOLN

Actor. Tall, lantern-jawed, sandy-haired American TV actor who broke into European films too late in the day to make an impact. After his debut in the spy thriller *The Fuller Report* (1967), he starred or co-starred in a handful of low-budget Seventies westerns, including *Acquasanta Joe* alongside fellow ex-pats Ty Hardin and Richard Harrison. After a hiatus in the mid-Seventies, he reappeared on American television in the Eighties.
1971: Acquasanta Joe; Bastard, Go and Kill; His Name Was Sam Wallash... But They Called Him Amen!; Lobo the Bastard. 1972: Gunmen and the Holy Ghost; The Return of Hallelujah. 1973: For a Book of Dollars; On the Third Day Arrived the Crow.

TERRÓN, JOSÉ
[José Terrón Peñaranda]
(Madrid, Spain. 1939-)

Stuntman and actor. Despite his distinctive features, Terrón has only recently been identified by film scholars as the shark-toothed outlaw Guy Calloway – granted a classic Sergio Leone close-up, followed by a bullet between the eyes, courtesy of Lee Van Cleef, at the beginning of *For a Few Dollars More* – and the scar-faced Ringo, dispatched by Franco Nero with such nonchalance in *Django*. Embodying the Leonean (and wider European) preoccupation with eye-catching countenances, he made only a handful of appearances in the mid-Sixties, all in westerns and all uncredited (reflecting his non-professional status), before disappearing off the radar.
1965: For a Few Dollars More. 1966: Arizona Colt; Django; The Good, the Bad and the Ugly; Navajo Joe. 1967: Death Rides a Horse; God Forgives... I Don't! 1968: I Want Him Dead; Shalako; White Comanche. 1969: The Forgotten Pistolero. 1970: The Deserter.

TESSARI, DUCCIO
(Genoa, Italy. 1926-1994)
Director/writer. Beginning as a documentarist, he went on to write or co-write many scripts for *pepla* and costume adventures. His first film as director, the well-judged peplum parody *Sons of Thunder* (1962), set the tone for his subsequent career, and he continued in this vein with *A Pistol for Ringo* and *Long Live Your Death*, the latter a freewheeling send-up of political westerns. The Homeric *The Return of Ringo* was his finest western, in which his trademark humour has a muted presence in a narrative tinged with tragedy. He also made excellent contributions to the *giallo*, crime and spy genres, eventually returning to westerns in the mid-Eighties with the disappointing *Tex and the Lord of the Deep*. Widely admired for his geniality (he would wear a red carnation in his lapel on the set), he was married to actress Lorella de Luca, who appeared in many of his films, and is the father of another actress, Fiorenza Tessari.
1964: A Fistful of Dollars (w). 1965: A Pistol for Ringo (w/d); The Return of Ringo (w/d). 1966: Seven Guns for the MacGregors (w). 1968: A Train for Durango (w). 1969: Alive or Preferably Dead (w/d). 1971: Long Live Your Death (w/d). 1975: Zorro (d). 1985: Tex and the Lord of the Deep (w/d).

TESTI, FABIO
['Stet Carson'; 'Martin Moore']
(Peschiera del Garda, Italy. 1941-)

Actor. A former model (he was the face of Coca Cola for a time) and stuntman, Testi's classic good looks and statuesque physique helped make him one of Italy's most profitable action stars in the Seventies. After making his debut in Demofilo Fidani's *Stranger, Make the Sign of the Cross*, he played a member of Frank's gang in *Once Upon a Time in the West* and, despite an appearance in Vittorio De Sica's *Garden of the Finzi-Continis* (1971), has remained in genre films for most of his career. He gave his most rounded performance in a western in the twilight tale *The Four of the Apocalypse*.
1968: And Now... Make Your Peace with God; Gun Shy Piluk; Once Upon a Time in the West; Stranger, Make the Sign of the Cross. 1970: One Damned Day at Dawn... Django Meets Sartana! 1971: Dead Men Ride; Zorro the Lawman. 1974: Blood River. 1975: The Four of the Apocalypse; Red Coat. 1978: China 9, Liberty 37.

TORRES, JOSÉ
(Valencia, Venezuela)

Bitten by the acting bug while still a child, Torres subsequently attended theatre school and was one of the first actors to make a name for himself on Venezuelan television. He arrived in Italy in 1959 and, as well as appearing on the stage, he was cast extensively in westerns and a few other genre pieces in the Sixties and Seventies. Gaunt and haggard in appearance, he was useful as a scrawny villain, though he also took on sympathetic roles, notably as a revolutionary in *Run, Man, Run* and as Judas to Tomas Milian's rebel martyr in *Tepepa*. In later years he returned to Venezuela, where he opened a restaurant and continues to appear on television.
1964: Two Gangsters in the Wild West. 1965: Gold Train; Why Go On Killing? 1966: De Guello; Ramon the Mexican. 1967: Any Gun Can Play; The Big Gundown; Death Rides a Horse; Face to Face; Poker with Pistols; Viva Django. 1968: One for All; Run, Man, Run; Tepepa. 1969: The Five Man Army; God Will Forgive My Gun; I Am Sartana, Your Angel of Death. 1970: Django Against Sartana. 1971: Durango Is Coming, Pay or Die; He Was Called the Holy Ghost. 1972: Django... Adios!; Return of the Holy Ghost; Shoot Joe, and Shoot Again. 1973: A Colt in the Hand of the Devil.

ULLOA, ALEJANDRO
(Madrid, Spain. 1926-)
Cinematographer. His background in Spanish films led him to assignments on *pepla* and other co-productions in the early Sixties, including almost two dozen westerns. He had a particularly sharp eye for landscape and his location work was exemplary, typified by Corbucci's Mexico-based films and *The Magnificent Bandits*, shot in Brazil. In *California*, meanwhile, he used desaturated colours to deepen the mood of gloom that permeates the plot.
1966: Seven Guns for the MacGregors; Sugar Colt. 1967: Hate for Hate; Up the MacGregors. 1968: Kill Them All and Come Back Alone; One Dollar Too Many; One for All; A Gun for a Hundred Graves; A Professional Gun. 1969: The Magnificent Bandits. 1970: Compañeros. 1971: Bad Man's River. 1972: Pancho Villa; A Reason to Live, a Reason to Die; What Am I Doing in the Middle of a Revolution? 1973: Here We Go Again, Eh Providence? 1974: The Stranger and the Gunfighter; Whisky and Ghosts. 1975: Cipolla Colt. 1977: California.

UMILIANI, PIERO
(Florence, Italy. 1926-2001)
Composer/arranger. As a jazz enthusiast, his trademark swinging sound accompanied mostly contemporary films (many espionage adventures, for instance), but, like most of his contemporaries, he couldn't completely avoid the western, although he didn't contribute any truly memorable scores. His most popular piece is arguably the insanely catchy 'Ma-Na-Mah-Na', composed for the sex film *Sweden Heaven and Hell* (1968) and later appropriated by the Muppets.

Who's Who In Euro-Westerns

1964: The Road to Fort Alamo. 1966: The Sons of Ringo. 1967: Last of the Badmen; Rick and John, Conquerors of the West; Son of Django. 1968: Chrysanthemums for a Bunch of Swine; The Nephews of Zorro. 1969: Quinto: Fighting Proud. 1970: Django Against Sartana; Reverend Colt; Roy Colt and Winchester Jack; The Twilight Avengers. 1971: A Man Called Django; Vengeance Trail. 1974: Blood River.

UNGER, GOFFREDO
[Goffredo Ungaro; 'John Silver'; 'Fred/Freddy/Fredi (H) Unger']
(Oslo, Norway. 1933-2009)

Bearded, beefy, balding bit-part actor and occasional assistant director who also worked as a stunt coordinator and master of arms on numerous titles from the early Sixties onwards. Richard Harrison, a friend of Unger's, remembers this scion of a circus family as bold, professional but occasionally reckless: "Freddy always did a good job, sometimes a little on the dangerous side. I had a fight with him one time and he was cut completely open on broken glass – he'd used real bottles."

1966: The Hills Run Red (act). 1967: Face to Face (act). 1968: Black Jack (act); Full House for the Devil (act); One After the Other (act); Run, Man, Run (act/master of arms); Vengeance (act). 1969: The Magnificent Bandits (ad/act). 1970: Chapagua's Gold (act). 1971: Dead Men Ride (act); Heads I Kill You... Tails You're Dead! They Call Me Hallelujah (act); His Name Was King (act); Shoot the Living and Pray for the Dead (act/stunts); They Call Him Cemetery (act). 1972: His Name Was Holy Ghost (act); Jesse & Lester: Two Brothers in a Place Called Trinity (act); The Return of Hallelujah (act/master of arms); Trinity and Sartana Are Coming (stunts); The Two Sons of Trinity (act). 1973: Deaf Smith & Johnny Ears (act); Here We Go Again, Eh Providence? (act); Karate, Fists and Beans (act); A Man Called Invincible (act); On the Third Day Arrived the Crow (master of arms). 1974: Challenge to White Fang (act/stunts); The Crazy Bunch (act). 1975: The Four of the Apocalypse (stunts). 1976: Apache Woman (ad/stunts). 1981: Comin' at Ya! (act).

VADIS, DAN
[Constantine Daniel Vafiadis]
(Shanghai, China. 1938-1987)

Actor. Born to a Greek father and Mongolian mother, Vadis moved to America in the Fifties where, through his interest in bodybuilding, he met and befriended Gordon Mitchell. He joined Mae West's stage show in Las Vegas with Mitchell's help and followed the latter to Italy at the height of the peplum boom. He landed a few leading roles and went on to play surly villains in westerns, notably the callous En Plein in *Shoot First, Laugh Last*. Back in America, he later appeared in several Clint Eastwood films. Reputedly a volatile man, he was found dead in his car in mysterious circumstances.

1963: Pirates of the Mississippi. 1966: De Guello; Fort Yuma Gold. 1967: Shoot First, Laugh Last. 1969: God Will Forgive My Gun.

VALERII, TONINO
(Montorio al Vomano, Italy. 1934-)

Director/writer. From being Leone's assistant director on the first two 'Dollars' films, Valerii made a series of proficient westerns of his own, all bearing the Leone stamp to some degree. The master's touch is most pronounced in the famous *My Name Is Nobody*, which Leone produced. Like most of Valerii's best films, this was co-written by Ernesto Gastaldi, who also worked on the highly successful *Day of Anger*, which teamed two of the genre's biggest stars, Lee Van Cleef and Giuliano Gemma, and *The Price of Power*, a riff on the JFK assassination starring Gemma again. (Gemma remembers pacifying one of his co-stars on the set of the latter film: "Van Johnson was a little worried because he knew the Kennedy family and said, 'I don't know about this film, what will they think about it when they see it?' To which I replied, 'I wouldn't worry if I were you.' 'Why not?' he asked me. 'Do you actually think the Kennedy family is ever going to see this film?'" I answered.)

1964: A Fistful of Dollars (ad); 1965: For a Few Dollars More (ad). 1966: A Taste for Killing (d). 1967: Day of Anger (w/d). 1969: The Price of Power (d). 1972: A Reason to Live, a Reason to Die (w/d). 1973: My Name Is Nobody (d).

VAN CLEEF, LEE
[Clarence Leroy Van Cleef Jr.]
(Somerville, USA. 1925-1989)

Actor. Tall and barrel-chested, with a hooked nose and hard, sharp features, Van Cleef was the archetypal Hollywood bit-part heavy. Of Dutch ancestry, he made his debut as one of the killers in *High Noon* (1952), dying at the hands of the hero and setting the pattern for the first phase of his career. His first opportunities to act, rather than merely glower, came when Leone rescued him from obscurity (he hadn't made a film for three years, acting only for television, and was a notoriously hard drinker) and took him to Italy. There, in the wake of *For a Few Dollars More* and *The Good, the Bad and the Ugly*, he became an unlikely superstar, switching between roles of ambiguous nobility (Mortimer, Jonathan Corbett, Ryan, in *Death Rides a Horse*, Sabata) and heartless villainy ('Angel Eyes', Frank Talby in *Day of Anger*). He never regained such stature after his European career had peaked in the early Seventies, but was regularly employed in leading and supporting roles on the Continent and in America until his death.

1965: For a Few Dollars More. 1966: The Good, the Bad and the Ugly. 1967: The Big Gundown; Day of Anger; Death Rides a Horse. 1968: Beyond the Law. 1969: Sabata. 1970: El Condor. 1971: Bad Man's River; Captain Apache; Return of Sabata. 1972: The Grand Duel. 1974: The Stranger and the Gunfighter. 1975: Take a Hard Ride. 1976: God's Gun; Kid Vengeance.

VAN HUSEN, DAN
(Gummersbach, Germany. 1945-)

Actor. Bit parts and supporting roles in Euro-westerns were Van Husen's staple diet in the first phase of an acting career that has encompassed film, theatre and television and seen him work with everyone from Sergio Corbucci to Werner Herzog and Federico Fellini. His sinister, cadaverous features were usually hidden behind shaggy facial hair in his western days, but more recently he has taken on more prominent parts, especially on German television, and played the heavy in recent American indie western *The Scarlet Worm*, opposite Brett Halsey.

1969: Alive or Preferably Dead; Vengeance Is Mine. 1970: Arizona; Arizona Kid; El Condor; Gunman in Town; More Dollars for the McGregors. 1971: Bad Man's River; Captain Apache; Catlow; Cut-Throats Nine; Doc; Long Live Your Death. 1972: Bandits; Cry of the Black Wolves; Hallelujah & Sartana Strike Again!; Pancho Villa. 1973: Yankee Dudler. 1975: Cipolla Colt; The White, the Yellow and the Black. 1976: Potato Fritz.

VANZI, LUIGI
['Vance Lewis']
(Rome, Italy. 1925-)
Director. A former assistant to Michelangelo Antonioni, Vanzi worked with Alessandro Blasetti on the successful pseudo-documentary *European Nights* (1958) and scored a hit with the follow-up, *World by Night* (1960), his first directed film. In the mid-Sixties he teamed up with Tony Anthony for the tongue-in-cheek 'Stranger' series. Despite minuscule budgets and scathing reviews, *For a Dollar in the Teeth* and *Shoot First, Laugh Last* made good money in both Italy and America, where they were distributed by MGM. The third and most ambitious in the series, *The Silent Stranger*, had a delayed release and few people saw it. He also directed Anthony in the humourless gangster film *Pete, Pearl and the Pole* (1973), but has done little since.
1967: For a Dollar in the Teeth; Shoot First, Laugh Last. 1968: The Silent Stranger.

VARI, GIUSEPPE
['Joseph Warren']
(Rome, Italy. 1924-1992)
Director. Beginning his career as an editor for the likes of Fellini and Damiani, he began directing in the early Fifties. Confined to genre pieces, he turned out a number of workmanlike westerns, the best being the Anthony Ghidra-Robert Hundar sparring match, *A Hole Between the Eyes*.
1966: De Guello (w/d). 1967: Death Rides Along (d); Django, the Last Killer (d); Poker with Pistols (d). 1968: A Hole Between the Eyes (d). 1971: Shoot the Living and Pray for the Dead (d); Thirteenth Is a Judas (d).

VASCO [Vassili/Vasili Kojucharov; Vasco Vassil Kojucharov] & [Elsio] MANCUSO
Composing team responsible for the bombastic scores to *Django the Bastard*, *No Room to Die* and *I Am Sartana, Your Angel of Death*, all notably lacking in generic mood music, among others. Mancuso also produced the occasional film.
1968: If You Want to Live... Then Shoot!; No Graves on Boot Hill; One Against One... No Mercy. 1969: Django the Bastard; God Will Forgive My Gun; I Am Sartana, Your Angel of Death; No Room to Die. 1970: Wanted Sabata (Kojucharov). 1971: Django's Cut Price Corpses (Kojucharov); Kill Django, Kill First (Mancuso); Paid in Blood (Mancuso). 1972: Beyond the Frontiers of Hate (Mancuso); A Bounty Killer for Trinity (Kojucharov); Django... Adios! (Kojucharov); God Is My Colt (Kojucharov); Shoot Joe, and Shoot Again; You are a Traitor and I'll Kill You (Kojucharov, with Daniele Patucchi).

VELÁZQUEZ, PILAR
[María del Pilar Velázquez Llorente]
(Madrid, Spain. 1946-)

Actress. Trained on the stage, this dark, sensuous Mediterranean beauty gave a fine dramatic performance as a grieving, vengeful daughter in *The Forgotten Pistolero* and a tragic Juliet figure in *Clumsy Hands*. She was also widely cast in comedies and horror films but never achieved the stardom she seemed destined for.
1969: The Forgotten Pistolero. 1970: Arizona Kid; Clumsy Hands. 1972: His Name Was Holy Ghost; Thunder Over El Paso.

VERAS, LINDA
[Sieglinde Veras]
(Bolzano, Italy. 1939-)

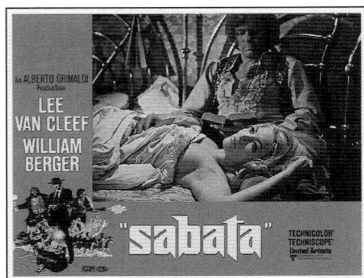

Little is known about this lithe, fiery blonde actress who played calculating gold-diggers in a handful of westerns – she made especially strong impressions in *Run, Man, Run*, *Sabata* and *Chapagua's Gold* – before disappearing from the screen.
1967: Face to Face. 1968: God Forgive... His Life Is Mine; Run, Man, Run. 1969: Sabata. 1970: Chapagua's Gold.

VILLA, FRANCO
(Italy. ?-2009)
Cinematographer. Employed on several B-grade westerns, usually filmed around Rome, he managed to make relatively confined locations such as quarries look grander than they were, boosting the scope of cheap productions like *My Name Is Pecos* and a number of Demofilo Fidani films. He also shot the murky urban environments for Fernando di Leo crime thrillers.
1961: The Magnificent Three. 1966: My Name Is Pecos; Thompson 1880. 1967: Pecos Cleans Up. 1968: And Now... Make Your Peace with God; Bury Them Deep; Say Your Prayers and Dig Your Grave; Stranger, Make the Sign of the Cross. 1969: No Room to Die; Shadow of Sartana... Shadow of Your Death! 1970: A Man Called Joe Clifford; One Damned Day at Dawn... Django Meets Sartana! 1971: Acquasanta Joe; The Ballad of Django; Black Killer; Gunman of 100 Crosses; His Name Was Sam Wallash... But They Called Him Amen!; The Price of Death; Shoot the Living and Pray for the Dead. 1973: On the Third Day Arrived the Crow. 1975: Who's Afraid of Zorro?

VINCENZONI, LUCIANO
(Treviso, Italy. 1926-)
Writer/script doctor. Vincenzoni would prefer to be remembered for his work with the likes of Germi, Petri and Monicelli (he co-wrote the famous black comedy *The Great War* [1959]), but his name became known because of his association with Sergio Leone. They met in the Fifties when both were taking their first steps in the industry, and went on to have what seems to have been a love-hate relationship. Vincenzoni made a strong contribution to the best Italian comedies, and claims credit for much of the humour in *For a Few Dollars More* and *The Good, the Bad and the Ugly*. He was also instrumental in securing the distribution deal with United Artists that took the 'Dollars' trilogy to America.
1965: For a Few Dollars More. 1966: The Good, the Bad and the Ugly. 1967: Death Rides a Horse. 1968: A Professional Gun. 1971: A Fistful of Dynamite. 1975: Cipolla Colt.

VOHRER, ALFRED
(Stuttgart, Germany. 1918-1986)
A proficient B-movie director, he made stylish and engaging instalments in two of Germany's most popular pulp series. His Edgar Wallace adaptations included the well-paced, atmospheric *Dark Eyes of London* (1961), while two of his three 'Winnetou' films, *Among Vultures* and *Flaming Frontier*, are among the best of the bunch.
1964: Among Vultures. 1965: Flaming Frontier. 1966: Thunder at the Border.

VOLONTÉ, GIAN MARIA
['John/Johnny Wells']
(Milan, Italy. 1933-1994)

Fiery, mesmerising actor who set a new benchmark for western villainy in the first two 'Dollars' movies. After graduating from Rome's National Academy of Dramatic Art in 1957, he honed his skills on stage and, on the small screen, starred in a well-received adaptation of *The Idiot*. His film career having stalled, he earned international exposure through working with Leone, although he later insisted he accepted the roles purely to get established. His left-wing political beliefs came to dictate his career choices – hence he appeared in the political westerns *A Bullet for the General* and *Face to Face* as a Mexican insurgent and proto-Fascist respectively, and worked repeatedly with like-minded directors such as Elio Petri and Francesco Rosi.
1964: A Fistful of Dollars. 1965: For a Few Dollars More. 1966: A Bullet for the General. 1967: Face to Face. 1970: Wind from the East.

WALLACH, ELI
(New York City, USA. 1915-)

Actor. A member of the Actors' Studio who transferred his skills from Broadway to the big screen, Wallach created one of the most fully realised of all genre characters: Tuco, the crafty, animalistic outlaw with combustible energy in *The Good, the Bad and the Ugly*. His parts in *Ace High* and *Long Live Your Death* are vivid variations on his most famous role.
1966: The Good, the Bad and the Ugly. 1968: Ace High. 1971: Long Live Your Death. 1975: The White, the Yellow and the Black.

WANG, GEORGE
[George Wang Jue]
(Peking, China. 1918-)

Actor. Called upon whenever a Chinese heavy (or sometimes an unconvincing 'Mexican') was required, Wang was cast exclusively in stereotypical roles. Most were forgettable, but he amuses as the sly boss of a gambling den who temporarily confounds the normally unflappable hero of *Have a Nice Funeral, Sartana Will Pay* with a surprise martial arts attack. Having worked in Italy throughout the Sixties, he transferred to Hong Kong action films in the mid-Seventies.
1966: El Cisco; A Taste for Killing. 1967: A Colt in the Fist of the Devil. 1968: Tepepa. 1970: Have a Nice Funeral, Sartana Will Pay. 1971: Kill Django... Kill First. 1972: The Deadly Trackers; Jesse & Lester: Two Brothers in a Place Called Trinity. 1973: A Colt in the Hand of the Devil; The Fighting Fists of Shanghai Joe; God's Executioner; Six Bounty Killers for a Massacre; The Son of Zorro.

WENDLANDT, HORST
(Berlin, Germany. 1922-2002)
Producer. After the Second World War (during which he spent time as a PoW), he joined Artur Brauner's CCC production house, moving to Rialto in 1961 where he was responsible for initiating the hugely popular Karl May adaptations. May's stock was low at the time and Wendlandt's investment was considered a risky venture, but the producer had the satisfaction of seeing the series become a phenomenon, eventually running to 11 entries. He produced nine, splitting the cost with companies from other countries, and the May films' success was an important spur for the new-wave Italian westerns.
1962: The Treasure of Silver Lake. 1963: Winnetou the Warrior. 1964: Among Vultures; Last of the Renegades. 1965: Desperado Trail; Flaming Frontier; Rampage at Apache Wells. 1966: Halfbreed; Thunder at the Border. 1981: Buddy Goes West.

WILSON, JERRY
[Roberto Miali]
(Trieste, Italy)
Actor. Willowy co-lead with a contrastingly intense acting style and piercing eyes. He played angry young men, victims of violence or circumstance, in four thematically linked Alberto Cardone/Mario Siciliano Westerns. Although anonymous as the lead in Cardone's *$20,000 on Number Seven*, he gave forceful performances as a tormented mute in *Blood at Sundown* and a surly, vengeful young gunman in *Seven Dollars to Kill*. He disappeared from the mainstream film scene in the late Sixties, but has evolved into quite the aesthete. An acclaimed, award-winning novelist, poet and playwright, he has written screenplays, produced films and directed for the stage and screen. One of his most recent ventures was a film version of his novel *Pepe nel latte*.
1966: Blood at Sundown; Seven Dollars to Kill. 1967: $20,000 on Number Seven (act/w). 1968: Cowards Don't Pray.

WOLFF, FRANK
[Walter Frank Hermann]
(San Francisco, USA. 1928-1971)

Actor. Considered following his parents' footsteps into the medical profession but was drawn to acting while still a student. He trod the boards in New York and pitched up in Italy at the beginning of the Sixties, where a critically praised performance in Rosi's *Salvatore Giuliano* (1962) seemed to herald an illustrious career. Instead, perhaps to his own disappointment but to the benefit of mass audiences, he became sidetracked in exploitation films. Arguably the most talented of the American ex-pats who worked regularly in Euro-westerns, Wolff's characters were unpredictable, paranoid and prone to sadistic outbursts, typified by his

above: **Jerry Wilson** (*far left*) appears on the sleeve of the title theme single for **Seven Dollars to Kill**.

egocentric Bill San Antonio in *God Forgives... I Don't!* and tightly wound, epileptic outlaw in *Last of the Badmen*. But he was also cast effectively against type, as with his bungling, well-meaning sheriff in *The Great Silence* and proud, though still obsessive, rancher in *Once Upon a Time in the West*. George Hilton recalls Wolff as a troubled man: "He was a walking bundle of problems – interior, psychological problems... he was under some kind of torture." Apparently despairing of his tangled love life, Wolff committed suicide in a hotel room, cutting off his penis in the process – not uncoincidentally, the same fate befalls one of the characters in Brett Halsey's controversial novel *The Magnificent Strangers*.
1966: *A Few Dollars for Django; Ringo the Mark of Vengeance*. 1967: *For a Dollar in the Teeth; God Forgives... I Don't!; Last of the Badmen*. 1968: *The Great Silence; Kill Them All and Come Back Alone; Once Upon a Time in the West; One Dollar Too Many; Villa Rides*. 1969: *I Am Sartana, Your Angel of Death*.

WOOD, KEN
[Giovanni Cianfriglia; 'Phil Karson'; 'John Richmond'; 'Jody Wanger']
(Rome, Italy. 1935-)

Actor. Dark-featured stuntman/actor built like an oak tree. He doubled for Steve Reeves in *Hercules* (1957) and other titles before putting his physique to good use in numerous westerns and adventure films, usually as a villain. Brother of actor Domenico Cianfriglia.
1965: *The Tramplers*. 1966: *Five Giants from Texas; Ringo and His Golden Pistol*. 1967: *Ballad of a Gunman; Killer Kid*. 1968: *Bury Them Deep; If You Want to Live... Then Shoot!; Kill Them All and Come Back Alone; No Graves on Boot Hill; Two Pistols and a Coward*. 1970: *Adios, Sabata; Challenge of the MacKennas; Chuck Mool; Wanted Sabata*. 1971: *Doomsday; Durango Is Coming, Pay or Die; A Man Called Django; Return of Sabata*. 1972: *Ben and Charlie; Django... Adios!; The Grand Duel; Gunmen and the Holy Ghost; Man of the East; Return of the Holy Ghost; Sometimes Life Is Hard, Right, Providence?; Thunder Over El Paso; You're Jinxed, Friend, You've Met Sacremento*. 1976: *Keoma*. 1981: *Buddy Goes West*.

WOODS, ROBERT
['Robert Wood']
(Denver, USA. 1936-)

Actor. Lanky American leading man in Europe from the early Sixties, where he worked in theatre, modelling and dubbing (he was the voice of Brad Harris for a time, when the latter was making his first films in Germany) before signing a contract with Alfonso Balcázar to star in westerns. He made very good ones (*Seven Dollars for the MacGregors, My Name Is Pecos, Gatling Gun, Black Jack*) and very bad ones (*Four Candles for My Colt, My Name Is Mallory*), and later sojourned in Jesús Franco movies before returning to the States. He was often billed erroneously as 'Wood': "I lost my 's' in Europe, man! On *Seven Guns...* they printed all the publicity with 'Wood' – I told them there's an 's' on my name but not they're going to redo all the titles for me. I just said, 'What the hell, take the money and run.'" He has appeared on television, written a historical novel (he began his career as a staff writer for Warner Bros television in the Fifties) and, in later years, taught acting.
1964: *$5,000 on the Ace*. 1965: *Viva Carrancho*. 1966: *Four Dollars of Revenge; My Name Is Pecos; Seven Guns for the MacGregors; Starblack*. 1967: *Pecos Cleans Up*. 1968: *The Belle Starr Story; Black Jack; Gatling Gun; Say Your Prayers and Dig Your Grave*. 1969: *El Puro*. 1970: *Challenge of the MacKennas*. 1971: *Four Candles for My Colt; His Name Was Sam Wallash... But They Called Him Amen!; My Name Is Mallory*. 1972: *Kill the Poker Player*. 1973: *A Colt in the Hand of the Devil; Six Bounty Killers for a Massacre*. 1975: *White Fang and the Gold Diggers; White Fang and the Hunter*.

ZAMPERLA, NAZZARENO
['Nick Anderson']
(Treviso, Italy. 1937-)
Prolific stunt performer and arranger born into a family of circus artists. Like many of his fellow stuntmen, he doubled as an enthusiastic supporting actor, his career encompassing *pepla*, westerns and other adventure films. He was prominent as one of the brothers in *Seven Guns for the MacGregors* and its sequel, and as Giuliano Gemma's sibling in *One Silver Dollar*.
1962: *Zorro at the Court of Spain* (act). 1963: *Samson and the Slave Queen* (act); *Zorro and the Three Musketeers* (act). 1965: *One Silver Dollar* (act); *A Pistol for Ringo* (act). 1966: *Seven Guns for the MacGregors* (act); *Sugar Colt* (act). 1967: *Seven Pistols for a Massacre* (act); *Up the MacGregors* (act). 1968: *Today It's Me... Tomorrow You!* (act). 1969: *Boot Hill* (act/stunts). 1975: *Cipolla Colt* (act); *The White, the Yellow, and the Black* (act/stunts). 1977: *California* (act/master of arms). 1978: *Silver Saddle* (ad/stunts). 1985: *Tex and the Lord of the Deep* (stunts).

ZINGARELLI, ITALO
(Lugo di Romagna, Italy. 1930-2000)
Writer/producer who achieved steady success in the Sixties with *pepla* and westerns before he and business partner Roberto Palaggi struck gold with the 'Trinity' films, which remain among the most financially successful Italian productions of all time. Zingarelli also dabbled in direction (one of his three films was, inevitably, a Hill/Spencer vehicle) before turning his attention to the wine business in the mid-Seventies.
1964: *Gunmen of the Rio Grande* (w/p). 1966: *Johnny Yuma* (p). 1967: *Hate for Hate* (p). 1968: *Ciccio Forgives, I Don't* (p). 1969: *The Five Man Army* (p/d – uncredited). 1970: *They Call Me Trinity* (p). 1971: *Trinity Is Still My Name* (p). 1995: *Sons of Trinity* (p).

above: **Nazzareno Zamperla,** (*second from the right in the front row*), *as seen in* **Seven Guns for the MacGregors**.

Appendix 2

Euro-Western Filmography

A Chronological Reference Guide

For the purposes of this book, the modern Euro-western era begins with Joaquín Romero Marchent's first entries in 1955, after which any feature film that can broadly be described as a 'western' is listed here provided it contains significant contributions from one or more of the four key nations – Italy, Spain, France and Germany – and/or was shot in European locations. For this reason, and with the exception of the important westerns made by DEFA studios in the former GDR, I have omitted titles from Eastern Europe, Scandinavia and other points of the continent.

Entries are organised by main English-language title, followed by original and alternative titles where known. Discrepancies abound where release dates are concerned, especially as we're talking largely about co-productions – films were often released in different years in different territories, frequently with reordered or, on occasion, substantially altered credits. I have arranged them according to year of first domestic release, where this can safely be established, and have deferred to individual countries' official sources wherever possible – Italy's ANICA (www.anica.it) and Spain's Ministry of Culture (www.mcu.es) both maintain excellent online databases, for example.

*Key: **D**: director; **P**: producer/production company; **W**: writer(s); **C**: cinematography; **M**: music; **AD**: assistant director(s); **S**: stars*

1955

Coyote, The (SP)
El Coyote
D: Joaquín Romero Marchent. **P:** Unión Films. **W:** José Mallorquí (characters), Jesús Franco. **C:** Ricardo Torres. **M:** Odón Alonso. **S:** Abel Salazar, Gloria Marín, Manuel Monroy, Rafael Bardem, Santiago Rivero, José Calvo.

Judgement of the Coyote, The (SP)
La justicia del Coyote
D: Joaquín Romero Marchent. **P:** Unión Films. **W:** José Mallorquí (characters), Jesús Franco, J. Maso, J. Chamorro. **C:** Ricardo Torres. **M:** Odón Alonso. **S:** Abel Salazar, Gloria Marín, Manuel Monroy, Rafael Bardem, Miguel Pastor, Ángel Álvarez.

1956

Fernand Cowboy (FR)
Fernand Cow-boy
D: Guy Lefranc. **P:** François Chavane. **W:** Yvan Audouard, Jean Redon. **C:** Maurice Barry. **M:** Louis Guglielmi. **S:** Fernand Raynaud, Dora Doll, Nadine Tallier, Noël Roquevert, Pierre Dudan.

1958

Serenade of Texas (FR)
Sérénade au Texas
D: Richard Pottier. **P:** Suzanne Goosens. **W:** Richard Pottier, Jean Ferry. **C:** Lucien Joulin. **M:** Francis Lopez. **S:** Luis Mariano, Bourvil, Germaine Damar, René Blancard, Robert Rocca.

Sheriff of Fractured Jaw, The (UK)
(shot in Spain)
D: Raoul Walsh. **P:** Daniel M. Angel.
W: Jacob Hay, Howard Dimsdale. **C:** Otto Heller. **M:** Robert Farnon. **S:** Kenneth More, Jayne Mansfield, Henry Hull, William Campbell, Bruce Cabot, Ronald Squire.

1959

Sheriff, The (IT)
La sceriffa
D: Roberto Bianchi Montero. **P:** Guido Paolucci. **W:** Mario Amendola. **C:** Sergio Pesce. **M:** C. Louvre. **AD:** Alfonso Brescia. **S:** Tina Pica, Ugo Tognazzi, Tina De Mola, Tom Felleghy, Livio Lorenzon, Paolo Gozlino, Benito Stefanelli.

Terror of Oklahoma, The (IT)
Il terrore dell'Oklahoma
D: Mario Amendola (as Irving Jacobs). **P:** Guido Paolucci. **W:** Mario Amendola. **C:** Adalberto Albertini. **M:** Manuel Parada, Carlo Innocenzi. **S:** Maurizio Arena, Delia Scala, Alberto Bonucci, Mario Carotenuto, Alberto Farnese, Livio Lorenzon, Paolo Gozlino, Benito Stefanelli.

1960

Dollaro di fifa, Un (IT)
D: Giorgio Simonelli. **P:** Emo Bistolfi, Renato Torrini. **W:** Mario Guerra, Giulio Scarnicci, Renzo Tarabusi. **C:** Tino Santoni. **M:** Gianni Ferrio. **S:** Ugo Tognazzi, Walter Chiari, Hélène Chanel, Dominique Boschero, Mario Carotenuto.

Juanito (SP-GER)
Unsere Heimat ist die ganze Welt
D: Fernando Palacios. **P:** Jesús Sainz Fernandez, Heinz Neubert. **W:** Hans Bertram, Wolf Neumeister. **C:** Ricardo Torres. **M:** Augusto Algueró. **S:** Pablito Calvo, Sabine Bethmann, Pilar Cansino, Hans von Borsody, Antonio Casas, Ángel Álvarez, José Manuel Martín.

1961

Call of the Wild Geese (AUS)
Ruf der Wildgänse
D: Hans Heinrich. **P:** Rudolf Stering. **W:** Martha Ostenso, Per Schwenzen. **C:** Walter Tuch. **M:** Rolf A. Wilhelm. **S:** Ewald Balser, Heidemarie Hatheyer, Marisa Mell, Gertraud Jesserer, Brigitte Horney.

Dynamite Jack (FR-IT)
Dinamite Jack – il terrore dell Texas
D: Jean Bastia. **P:** Jacques-Paul Bertrand. **W:** Jacques Ary, Jean Bastia, Jean Manse, Jacques Emmanuel. **C:** Roger Hubert. **M:** Pascal Bastia, Jean-Pierre Landreau. **S:** Fernandel, Eleonora Vargas, Adrienne Corri, Lucien Raimbourg, Jess Hahn, Donal O'Brien.

Magnificent Three, The (IT)
I magnifici tre
D: Giorgio Simonelli. **P:** Emo Bistolfi. **W:** Bruno Corbucci, Giovanni Grimaldi, Mario Guerra, Giulio Scarnicci, Renzo Tarabusi, Vittorio Vighi. **C:** Franco Villa. **M:** Gianni Ferrio. **S:** Ugo Tognazzi, Walter Chiari, Raimondo Vianello, Dominique Boschero, Anna Ranalli, Tom Felleghy.

Singer Not the Song, The (UK)
(shot in Spain)
D: Roy Ward Baker. **P:** Roy Ward Baker, Jack Hanbury, Earl St John. **W:** Audrey Erskine-Lindop (novel), Nigel Balchin. **C:** Otto Heller. **M:** Philip Green. **S:** Dirk Bogarde, John Mills, Mylene Demongeot, Laurence Naismith, John Bentley.

Taste of Violence, The (FR-IT-GER)
Le goût de la violence; Febbre di rivolta; Haut für Haut
D: Robert Hossein. **P:** Alain Podre, Ralph Baum. **W:** Claude St. Desailly, Robert Hossein, Louis Martin, Dany Jacquet, Hans Neubert, Jules Roy. **C:** Jacques Robin. **M:** André Hossein. **S:** Robert Hossein, Giovanna Ralli, Mario Adorf, Madeleine Robinson, Dany Jacquet.

1962

Savage Guns, The (UK-SP)
Tierra brutal
D: Michael Carreras. **P:** José Gutiérrez Maesso, Jimmy Sangster. **W:** Edmund Morris, José Gutiérrez Maesso, Jimmy Sangster. **C:** Alfredo Fraile. **M:** Antón García Abril. **S:** Richard Basehart, Paquita Rico, Don Taylor, Alex Nicol, José Nieto, Fernando Rey, José Manuel Martín.

Shadow of Zorro, The (SP-IT-FR)
Cabalgando hacia la muerte; L'ombra di Zorro; L'ombre de Zorro
D: Joaquín Romero Marchent. **P:** Copercines, PEA. **W:** José Mallorquí, Joaquín Romero Marchent. **C:** Rafael Pacheco (Italian version credits Enrico Betti Berutto). **M:** Manuel Parada (Italian version credits Francesco De Masi). **AD:** Rafael Romero Marchent. **S:** Frank Latimore, María Luz Galicia, Paul Piaget, Claudio Undari (as Robert Hundar), José Marco Davó, Raf Baldassarre, Lorenzo Robledo, Carlos Romero Marchent.

Torrejón City (SP)
D: León Klimovsky. **P:** Tyrys Films. **W:** Ramón Barreiro, Antonio de Lara, Rafael J. Salvia, Manuel Tamayo, José Antonio Verdugo. **C:** Manuel Hernández Sanjuán. **M:** Gregorio García Segura. **S:** Tony Leblanc, May Heatherly, Mara Laso, Mary Begoña, Antonio Garisa, José Canalejas.

Treasure of Silver Lake, The (GER-YUG-FR)
Der Schatz im Silbersee; Blago u srebrnom jezeru; Le trésor du lac d'argent
D: Harald Reinl. **P:** Horst Wendlandt. **W:** Karl May (novel), Harald G. Petersson. **C:** Ernst W. Kalinke. **M:** Martin Böttcher. **S:** Lex Barker, Pierre Brice, Götz George, Karin Dor, Ralf Wolter.

Two Against All (IT-SP)
Due contro tutti; El sheriff terrible
D: Alberto De Martino (Spanish version credits Antonio Momplet). **P:** Emo Bistolfi. **W:** Mario Guerra, Ruggero Maccari, Giulio Scarnicci, Ettore Scola, Vittorio Vighi, Renzo Tarabusi. **C:** Ricardo Torres, Dario Di Palma. **M:** Manuel Parada, Franco Pisano, Gianni Ferrio. **S:** Walter Chiari, Licia Calderón, María Silva, Raimondo Vianello, Aroldo Tieri, José Calvo, Antonio Molino Rojo.

Zorro at the Court of Spain (IT)
Zorro alla corte di Spagna; El Zorro al servicio de la reina
D: Luigi Capuano. **P:** Ferdinando Felicioni. **W:** Arpad De Riso, Nino Scolaro. **C:** Oberdan Troiani. **M:** Carlo Savina. **AD:** Gianfranco Baldanello. **S:** George Ardisson, Alberto Lupo, Nadia Marlowa, Franco Fantasia, Carlo Tamberlani, Antonio Gradoli, Livio Lorenzon, Gianni Rizzo, Nazzareno Zamperla.

Zorro the Avenger (SP-FR)
La venganza del Zorro; Zorro le vengeur; Shadow of Zorro; The Mark of Zorro
D: Joaquín Romero Marchent. **P:** Copercines, Eurociné. **W:** José Mallorquí, Jesús Franco, Joaquín Romero Marchent. **C:** Rafael Pacheco. **M:** Manuel Parada. **S:** Frank Latimore, María Luz Galicia, Howard Vernon, José Marco Davó, Jesús Tordesillas, Ángel Álvarez, Fernando Sancho, Antonio Molino Rojo, Carlos Romero Marchent, Paul Piaget.

1963

Gunfight at High Noon (SP-IT)
El sabor de la venganza; I tre spietati; Sons of Vengeance; Born to Kill
D: Joaquín Romero Marchent. **P:** Centauro Films, PEA. **W:** Joaquín Romero Marchent, Marcello Fondato (Spanish version credits Jesús Navarro, Rafael Romero Marchent). **C:** Rafael Pacheco. **M:** Riz Ortolani. **S:** Richard Harrison, Claudio Undari (as Robert Hundar), Gloria Milland, Miguel Palenzuela, Fernando Sancho, Luis Induni, José Manuel Martín, Carlos Romero Marchent, Aldo Sambrell, Paco Sanz, Andrea Scotti.

Gunfight at Red Sands (IT-SP)
Gringo; Duello nel Texas
D: Ricardo Blasco. **P:** Jolly Films, Tecisa. **W:** James Prindle, Albert Band, Ricardo Blasco. **C:** Massimo Dallamano (as Jack Dalmas). **M:** Ennio Morricone (as Dan Savio). **S:** Richard Harrison, Giacomo Rossi-Stuart, Mikaela Wood, Sara Lezana, Daniel Martín, Barta Barry, José Calvo, Tito García, Aldo Sambrell.

Heroes of the West (IT-SP)
Gli eroi del West; Los héroes del Oeste
D: Stefano Vanzina (as Steno). **P:** Emo Bistolfi. **W:** Sandro Continenza, Mario Guerra, José Mallorquí, Steno, Giulio Scarnicci, Renzo Tarabusi, Vittorio Vighi. **C:** Tino Santoni. **M:** Gianni Ferrio. **S:** Walter Chiari, Raimondo Vianello, Silvia Solar, María Andersen, Aurora Julia.

Jaguar, The (SP)
El llanero
D: Jesús Franco. **P:** Julian Esteban. **W:** Jesús Franco, Nicole Guettard. **C:** Emilio Foriscot. **M:** Daniel White. **S:** José Suárez, Sylvia Sorrente, Roberto Camardiel, Manuel Zarzo, Todd Martin, Tito García.

Magnificent Three, The (SP-IT)
Tres hombres buenos; I tre implacabili; The Implacable Three
D: Joaquín Romero Marchent. **P:** Copercines, PEA. **W:** José Mallorquí (novel), Mario Caiano, Joaquín Romero Marchent. **C:** Rafael Pacheco. **M:** Manuel Parada (Italian version credits Francesco De Masi). **S:** Geoffrey Horne, Paul Piaget, Claudio Undari (as Robert Hundar), Fernando Sancho, Charo del Río, Raf Baldassarre, Antonio Gradoli, José Jaspe, Aldo Sambrell, Lorenzo Robledo.

Pirates of the Mississippi (GER-IT-FR)
Die Flußpiraten vom Mississippi; Agguato sul grande fiume; Les pirates du Mississippi
D: Jürgen Roland (as John Roland). **P:** Wolf C. Hartwig. **W:** Friedrich Gerstäcker (novel), Johannes Kai, Werner P. Zibaso. **C:** Rolf Kästel. **M:** Willy Mattes. **S:** Brad Harris, Hansjörg Felmy, Horst Frank, Sabine Sinjen, Dorothee Parker, Luciano Stella (as Tony Kendall), Dan Vadis.

Samson and the Slave Queen (IT)
Zorro contro Maciste;
The Invincible Masked Rider
D: Umberto Lenzi. **P:** Fortunato Misiano. **W:** Guido Malatesta, Umberto Lenzi.
C: Augusto Tiezzi. **M:** Angelo Francesco Lavagnino. **S:** Pierre Brice, Sergio Ciani (as Alan Steel), Moira Orfei, Maria Grazia Spina, Andrea Aureli, Nello Pazzafini, Nazzareno Zamperla, Andrea Scotti.

Sign of the Coyote, The (IT-SP)
Il segno del Coyote; El vengador de California
D: Mario Caiano. **P:** PEA, Copercines. **W:** José Mallorquí, Mario Caiano. **C:** Aldo Greci. **M:** Manuel Parada, Francesco De Masi. **S:** Fernando Casanova, María Luz Galicia, Mario Feliciani, Arturo Dominici, Giulia Rubini, Raf Baldassarre, Fernando Sancho, José Canalejas, José Jaspe, Piero Lulli, Andrea Scotti, Antonio Gradoli, Fernando Sancho.

Sign of Zorro, The (IT-SP-FR)
Il segno di Zorro; El capitán intrépido; Le signe de Zorro; Duel at the Rio Grande
D: Mario Caiano. **P:** Benito Perojo, Harry Joe Brown. **W:** Guido Malatesta, Casey Robinson. **C:** Adalberto Albertini, Luigi Filippo Carta. **M:** Gregorio García Segura. **AD:** Alfonso Brescia. **S:** Sean Flynn, Folco Lulli, Helga Liné, Danielle de Metz, Mario Petri, Walter Barnes, Pietro Ceccarelli, Piero Lulli.

Sword of Zorro, The (IT-SP)
Le tre spade di Zorro; Las tres espadas del Zorro; The Three Swords of Zorro
D: Ricardo Blasco. **P:** Sergio Newman, Tulio Bruschi. **W:** Mario Amendola, José Gallardo, Luis Lucas, Daniel Ribera. **C:** Edmondo Affronti, Julio Ortas. **M:** José Pagán, Antonio Ramirez Angel. **S:** Guy Stockwell, Mikaela Wood, Gloria Milland, Antonio Prieto, Franco Fantasia, Antonio Gradoli.

Winnetou the Warrior (GER-YUG-FR-IT)
Winnetou I; Vinetu I; La révolte des indiens Apaches; La valle dei lunghi coltelli; Apache Gold
D: Harald Reinl. **P:** Horst Wendlandt. **W:** Karl May (novel), Harald G. Petersson. **C:** Ernst W. Kalinke. **M:** Martin Böttcher. **S:** Pierre Brice, Lex Barker, Mario Adorf, Marie Versini, Walter Barnes, Gojko Mitic.

Zorro and the Three Musketeers (IT)
Zorro e il tre moschettieri
D: Luigi Capuano. **P:** Jonia Film. **W:** Ferdinando Felicioni, Italo De Tuddo, Roberto Gianviti. **C:** Carlo Bellero. **M:** Carlo Savina. **AD:** Gianfranco Baldanello. **S:** Gordon Scott, José Greci, Maria Grazia Spina, Giacomo Rossi-Stuart, Franco Fantasia, Livio Lorenzon, Gianni Rizzo, Nazzareno Zamperla, Benito Stefanelli.

1964

Among Vultures (GER-FR-IT-YUG)
Unter Geiern; Parmi les vautours; La dove scende il sole; Medju jastrebovima; Frontier Hellcat
D: Alfred Vohrer. **P:** Horst Wendlandt. **W:** Karl May (stories), Eberhard Keindorff, Johanna Sibelius. **C:** Karl Löb. **M:** Martin Böttcher. **S:** Stewart Granger, Pierre Brice, Götz George, Elke Sommer, Walter Barnes, Anthony Ghidra, Terence Hill (as Mario Girotti), Gojko Mitic, Sieghardt Rupp.

Euro-Western Filmography

Apaches' Last Battle (GER-IT-FR-YUG)
Old Shatterhand; La battaglia di Fort Apache; Les cavaliers rouges
D: Hugo Fregonese. **P:** Artur Brauner. **W:** Karl May (characters), Ladislas Fodor, Robert A. Stemmle. **M:** Riz Ortolani. **S:** Lex Barker, Pierre Brice, Daliah Lavi, Guy Madison, Ralf Wolter, Rik Battaglia, Gojko Mitic, Andrea Scotti.

Badmen of the West (IT-FR-SP)
I magnifici Brutos del West; Los brutos en el Oeste; Les terreurs de l'Ouest
D: Marino Girolami (as Fred Wilson). **P:** Jacques-Paul Bertrand, Anna Maria Chretien, Alvaro Mancori, Emiliano Piedra, Mario Siciliano. **W:** Tito Carpi, Marino Girolami. **C:** Alvaro Mancori (as Al World). **M:** Francesco De Masi (as Frank Mason). **S:** Ettore Bruno, Nat Pioppi, Aldo Maccione, Gianni Zullo, Elio Piatti, Giacomo Rossi-Stuart, Pietro Ceccarelli, Nello Pazzafini.

Behind the Mask of Zorro (SP-IT)
El Zorro cabalga otra vez; Il giuramento di Zorro
D: Ricardo Blasco. **P:** Sergio Newman, Tulio Brushci. **W:** Luis Lucas, José Gallardo, Daniel Ribera, Mario Amendola. **C:** Julio Ortas. **M:** José Pagán, A. Ramirez Angel. **S:** Tony Russel, Maria José Alfonso, Roberto Paoletti, Jesús Puente, Mirella Maravidi.

Billy the Kid (SP)
Fuera de la ley
D: León Klimovsky. **P:** Carthago. **W:** Ángel del Castillo, S.G. Monner, Bob Sirens. **C:** Manuel Hernández Sanjuán. **M:** Daniel White. **S:** George Martin, Jack Taylor, Juny Brunell, Tomás Blanco, Luis Induni, José Canalejas, Lorenzo Robledo, Aldo Sambrell.

Black Angel of the Mississippi (SP-FR)
Bienvenido, Padre Murray; L'ange noir du Mississippi
D: Ramón Torrado. **P:** Copercines, Eurociné. **W:** Federico de Urrutia, Manuel Sebares. **C:** Ricardo Torres. **M:** Manuel Parada. **S:** René Muñoz, Paul Piaget, Howard Vernon, Rosa del Rio, Angel del Pozo, Tito García, Antonio Molino Rojo, Fernando Sancho.

Buffalo Bill, Hero of the Far West (IT-FR-GER) *Buffalo Bill, l'eroe del Far West; Buffalo Bill, le héro du Far West; Das war Buffalo Bill*
D: Mario Costa (as John W. Fordson). **P:** Massimo Massimi. **W:** Louis Agotay, Pierre Levy-Corti, Luciano Martino, Sigfrido Tomba, Nino Stresa, Ernesto Gastaldi (uncredited). **C:** Massimo Dallamano (as Jack Dalmas). **M:** Carlo Rustichelli. **AD:** Gianfranco Baldanello. **S:** Gordon Scott, Mario Brega (as Richard Stuyvesant), Jan Hendriks, Ingeborg Schöner, Hans von Borsody, Franco Fantasia, Piero Lulli, Andrea Scotti.

Bullets and the Flesh (IT-SP-FR)
Il piombo e la carne; El sendero del odio; Les sentiers de la haine
D: Marino Girolami (as Fred Wilson). **P:** Cines Europa, Hesperia Films, Marco Film. **W:** Gino De Sanctis. **C:** Mario Fioretti, Manuel Serra. **M:** Carlo Savina. **S:** Rod Cameron, Bruno Piergentili (as Dan Harrison), Patricia Viterbo, Manuel Zarzo, Enio Girolami, Piero Lulli, Ignazio Spalla.

Bullets Don't Argue (IT-SP-GER)
Le pistole non discutono; Las pistolas no discuten; Die letzten Zwei vom Rio Bravo; Pistols Don't Argue
D: Mario Caiano (as Mike Perkins). **P:** Jolly Films, Trio, Constantin. **W:** Franco Castellano, Giuseppe Moccia. **C:** Julio Ortas, Massimo Dallamano (uncredited), Enzo Barboni (uncredited). **M:** Ennio Morricone (as Dan Savio), Jaime Ortiz. **S:** Rod Cameron, Ángel Aranda, Horst Frank, Mimmo Palmara (as Dick Palmer), Hans Neilsen, José Canalejas, Tito García, José Manuel Martín.

Cavalry Charge (SP)
La carga de la policia montada
D: Ramón Torrado. **P:** Arturo González. **W:** Bautista Lacasa Nebot, Manuel Tamayo, Ramón Torrado. **C:** Ricardo Torres. **M:** Daniel White. **S:** Alan Scott, Frank Latimore, Diana Lorys, María Silva, Alfonso Rojas, Luís Barboo, Barta Barry, Frank Braña, Tito García, Aldo Sambrell.

Fistful of Dollars, A (IT-SP-GER)
Per un pugno di dollari; Por un puñado de dólares; Für eine Handvoll Dollar
D: Sergio Leone (as Bob Robertson). **P:** Arrigo Colombo, Giorgio Papi. **W:** Sergio Leone, Duccio Tessari, Fernando Di Leo, Víctor Andrés Catena (all uncredited; also credited by various sources: Jaime Comas Gil, A. Bonzzoni, G. Schock, Mark Lowell [English dialogue]). **C:** Massimo Dallamano (as Jack Dalmas), Federico G. Larraya. **M:** Ennio Morricone (as Dan Savio). **AD:** Tonino Valerii (uncredited). **S:** Clint Eastwood, Marianne Koch, Gian Maria Volonté (as Johnny Wels), José Calvo, Wolfgang Lukschy, Mario Brega (as Richard Stuyvesant), Sieghardt Rupp, Josef Egger, Antonio Prieto, Margarita Lozano, Daniel Martín, Luís Barboo, Antonio Molino Rojo, Benito Stefanelli (as Benny Reeves), Aldo Sambrell, Lorenzo Robledo, Frank Braña, José Canalejas, Raf Baldassarre, Nino Del Arco.

$5,000 on the Ace (SP-IT-GER)
Los pistoleros de Arizona; 5.000 dollari sull'asso; Die Gejagten der Sierra Nevada; El ranch de los implacables
D: Alfonso Balcázar. **P:** Fida, Balcázar. **W:** José Antonio de la Loma, Alfonso Balcázar. **C:** Carlo Carlini. **M:** Angelo Francesco Lavagnino. **AD:** Romolo Guerrieri. **S:** Robert Woods, Fernando Sancho, Maria Sebaldt, Giacomo Rossi-Stuart, Helmut Schmid, Antonio Molino Rojo, Lorenzo Robledo, Paco Sanz.

Four Bullets for Joe (SP-IT-FR)
Cuatro balazos; Il vendicatore di Kansas City; Quatre balles pour Joë; Shots Ring Out!
D: Agustín Navarro. **P:** Eduardo Manzanos Brochero, Emo Bistolfi, Marius Lesoeur. **W:** Fernando Galiana, Julio Porter, José Mallorquí, Vittorio Vighi, Mario Guerra. **C:** Ricardo Torres. **M:** Manuel Parada. **S:** Fernando Casanova (as Fred Canow), Paul Piaget, Barbara Nelli, Liz Poiter, Angela Cavo, Tito García.

Fury of the Apaches, The (SP-IT)
El hombre de la diligencia; La furia degli Apache
D: José Maria Elorrieta (as Joseph de Lacy). **P:** Tomás Cicuendez. **W:** Eduardo Guzmán (novel), José Maria Elorrieta, Howard Berk (as José Luis Navarro). **C:** Alfonso Nieva. **M:** Fernando Garcia Morcillo. **S:** Frank Latimore, Nuria Torray, Jesús Puente, Germán Cobos, Aldo Sambrell, Frank Braña, George Martin.

Gunfighters of Casa Grande (SP-US)
Los pistoleros de Casa Grande
D: Roy Rowland. **P:** Sam X. Abarbanel. **W:** Borden Chase, Patricia Chase, Clarke Reynolds. **C:** José F. Aguayo, Manuel Merino. **M:** Johnny Douglas. **S:** Alex Nicol, Jorge Mistral, Dick Bentley, Mercedes Alonso, Diana Lorys, José Manuel Martín, Aldo Sambrell.

Gunmen of the Rio Grande (SP-IT-FR)
Sfida a Rio Bravo; Desafio en Rio Bravo; Jennie Lee ha una nuova pistola; Duel at Rio Bravo
D: Tulio Demicheli. **P:** Italo Zingarelli. **W:** Italo Zingarelli, Tulio Demicheli, Gene Luotto, Chem Morrison, Giovanni Simonelli, Natividad Zaro. **C:** Mario Capriotti, Guglielmo Mancori. **M:** Angelo Francesco Lavagnino. **S:** Guy Madison, Madeleine Lebeau, Fernando Sancho, Carolyn Davys, Gérard Tichy.

Heroes of Fort Worth (SP-IT)
Gli eroi di Fort Worth; El séptimo de caballerà
D: Alberto De Martino (as Herbert Martin). **P:** Eduardo Manzanos Brochero, Arturo Marcos. **W:** Eduardo Manzanos Brochero, Emo Bistolfi (as Silver Bem). **C:** Eloy Mella. **M:** Manuel Parada, Carlo Rustichelli. **S:** Edmund Purdom, Paul Piaget, Priscilla Steele, Eduardo Fajardo, Mónica Randall, Luís Barboo.

Last Gun, The (IT)
Jim, il primo; Killer's Canyon
D: Sergio Bergonzelli (as Serge Bergon). **P:** Luigi Gianni. **W:** Dick Fulner, Ambrogio Molteni, James Wilde Jr. **C:** Romolo Garroni, Amerigo Gengarelli. **M:** Marcello Gigante. **S:** Cameron Mitchell, Carl Möhner, Célina Cély, Kitty Carver, Livio Lorenzon.

Last of the Renegades (GER-FR-IT-YUG)
Winnetou II; Le trésor des montagnes bleues; Giorni di fuoco; Vinetu II
D: Harald Reinl. **P:** Horst Wendlandt. **W:** Karl May (novel), Harald G. Petersson. **C:** Ernst W. Kalinke. **M:** Martin Böttcher. **S:** Pierre Brice, Lex Barker, Anthony Steel, Karin Dor, Klaus Kinski, Mario Girotti, Gojko Mitic.

Last Ride to Santa Cruz, The (GER-AUT)
Der letzte Ritt nach Santa Cruz; Ortiz le bandit
D: Rolf Olsen. **P:** Adolf Eder. **W:** Charles Sealsfield (story), Herbert Reinecker (as Alex Berg). **C:** Karl Löb. **M:** Erwin Halletz, Charly Niessen. **S:** Edmund Purdom, Mario Adorf, Marianne Koch, Klaus Kinski, Marisa Mell, Sieghardt Rupp.

Legend of a Gunfighter (GER-AUT)
Heiss weht der Wind; Mein freund Shorty; Le ranch de la vengeance
D: Rolf Olsen. **P:** Kurt Ulrich. **W:** Paul Clydeburn, Don Sharp. **C:** Hanns Matula. **M:** Erwin Halletz. **S:** Thomas Fritsch, Walter Giller, Gustav Knuth, Judith Dornys, Heidemarie Hatheyer.

Any Gun Can Play

Man of the Cursed Valley (IT-SP)
El hombre del valle maldito; L'uomo della valle maledetta
D: Siro Marcellini (as Omar Hopkins).
P: PEA, Fenix. **W:** Eduardo Manzanos Brochero, Eduardo De Lorenzo. **C:** Remo Grisanti, Alfredo Fraile. **M:** Francesco De Masi, Manuel Parada. **S:** Ty Hardin, Irán Eory, Piero Leri, José Canalejas, José Nieto, John Bartha.

Massacre at Fort Grant (SP)
Fuerte perdido
D: José Maria Elorrieta. **P:** José Maria Elorrieta. **W:** Howard Berk (as José Luis Navarro), José Maria Elorrieta. **C:** Pablo Ripoll. **M:** Fernando Garcia Morcillo. **S:** Germán Cobos, Marta May, Mariano Vidal Molina, Ethel Rojo, José Guardiola, Luís Barboo, Frank Braña, Cris Huerta, Aldo Sambrell.

Massacre at Grand Canyon (IT)
Massacro al Grande Canyon
D: Sergio Corbucci (as Stanley Corbett), Albert Band (uncredited). **P:** Albert Band. **W:** Edward C. Geltman, Albert Band, Sergio Corbucci. **C:** Enzo Barboni. **M:** Gianni Ferrio. **S:** James Mitchum, Milla Sannoner, George Ardisson, Giacomo Rossi-Stuart, Andrea Giordana, Benito Stefanelli.

Massacre at Marble City (GER-FR-IT)
Die Goldsucher von Arkansas; Alla conquista dell'Arkansas; Les chercheurs d'or de l'Arkansas
D: Paul Martin, Alberto Cardone (French version credited to Franz Joseph Gottlieb). **P:** Ludwig Spitaler. **W:** Friedrich Gerstäcker (novel), Hans Billian, Herbert Reinecker (as Alex Berg), Werner P. Zibaso. **C:** Jan Stallich. **M:** Heinz Gietz (Italian version credits Francesco De Masi). **S:** Brad Harris, Mario Adorf, Horst Frank, Dorothee Parker, Olga Schoberová, Serge Marquand.

Minnesota Clay (IT-FR-SP)
L'homme du Minnesota
D: Sergio Corbucci. **P:** Ultra, Jaguar, Franco London. **W:** Adriano Bolzoni, Sergio Corbucci. **C:** José F. Aguayo. **M:** Piero Piccioni. **AD:** Romolo Guerrieri. **S:** Cameron Mitchell, Georges Riviere, Ethel Rojo, Diana Martin, Fernando Sancho, Antonio Casas, José Canalejas (as Joe Kamel), José Manuel Martín.

Okay, Sheriff (IT)
Okay, sceriffo [compilation of Carosello TV spots]
D: Angio Zane. **P:** Angio Zane. **W:** Ignazio Colnaghi, Mike Douglas, Angio Zane. **C:** Diego Fiume. **M:** Juan Falenito, Paride Miglioli. **S:** Frank Senis, Bruno Salvador, Gilles Toothless, Dario Cipani.

Relevo para un pistolero (SP)
D: Ramón Torrado. **P:** José Luis Jerez Aloza, Arturo González. **W:** Antonio Gimenez Escribano, Luis Gaspar, Ramón Torrado. **C:** Ricardo Torres. **M:** Daniel Montorio. **S:** Alex Nicol, Luis Dávila, Silvia Solar, Laura Granados, Esperanza Roy, Lorenzo Robledo, Aldo Sambrell, Paco Sanz.

Return of Clay Stone, The (SP-IT-FR)
Las malditas pistolas de Dallas; Le maledette pistole di Dallas; Les pistolets maudits de Dallas; Damned Pistols of Dallas
D: José María Zabalza (as Joseph Trader; also credited to Pino Mercanti). **P:** Francesco Paolo Prestano. **W:** Luigi Emmanuele. **C:** Edmondo Affronti. **M:** Gioacchino Angelo. **S:** Fred Beir, Evi Marandi, Olivier Mathot, Roberto Messina, Ángel Álvarez, Jesús Puente.

Ride and Kill (IT-SP)
Cavalca e uccidi; Brandy
D: José Luis Borau. **P:** PEA, Rafael Merina. **W:** José Luis Borau, José Mallorquí. **C:** Manuel Merino, Mario Sbrenna. **M:** Riz Ortolani. **S:** Alex Nicol, Claudio Undari (as Robert Hundar), Renzo Palmer, Giuseppe Addobbati, Luis Induni, Frank Braña, José Canalejas, Antonio Casas, Antonio Gradoli, George Rigaud.

Road to Fort Alamo, The (IT-FR)
La strada per Fort Alamo; Arizona Bill
D: Mario Bava (as John Old). **P:** Pier Luigi Torri. **W:** Livia Contardi, Enzo Gicca Palli, Franco Prosperi. **C:** Ubaldo Terzano, Mario Bava (uncredited). **M:** Piero Umiliani. **S:** Ken Clark, Jany Clair, Michel Lemoine, Andreina Paul, Kirk Bert, Antonio Gradoli, Gérard Herter.

Samson and the Treasure of the Incas (IT-GER-FR)
Samson und der Schatz der Inkas; Sansone e il tesoro degli Incas; Samson et le trésor des Incas; Lost Treasure of the Aztecs
D: Piero Pierotti. **P:** Fortunato Misiano. **W:** Arpad De Riso, Piero Pierotti. **C:** Augusto Tiezzi. **M:** Angelo Francesco Lavagnino. **S:** Sergio Ciani (as Alan Steel), Toni Sailer, Mario Petri, Anna Maria Polani, Pierre Cressoy, Antonio Gradoli, Andrea Scotti, Federico Boido.

Seven from Texas (SP-IT)
Antes llega la muerte; I sette del Texas
D: Joaquín Romero Marchent. **P:** Manuel Castedo, Adriano Merkel. **W:** Pino Passalacqua, Marcello Fondato (Spanish sources credit Federico de Urrutia, Manuel Sebares, Joaquín Romero Marchent). **C:** Fausto Zuccoli (Spanish version credits Rafael Pacheco). **M:** Riz Ortolani. **AD:** Rafael Romero Marchent. **S:** Paul Piaget, Claudio Undari (as Robert Hundar), Fernando Sancho, Gloria Milland, Jesús Puente, Raf Baldassarre, John Bartha, José Canalejas, Luis Induni, Lorenzo Robledo, Paco Sanz.

Sheriff Was a Lady, The (GER-YUG)
Freddie und das Lied der Prarie; In the Wild West
D: Söbey Martin. **P:** Artur Brauner. **W:** Gustav Kampendonk. **C:** Siegfried Hold. **M:** Lothar Olias. **S:** Freddy Quinn, Mamie Van Doren, Rik Battaglia, Beba Loncar, Trude Herr.

Three Dollars of Lead (IT-SP)
Tre dollari di piombo; Tres dólares de plombo
D: Pino Mercanti (as Joseph Trader; Spanish version credited to José María Zabalza).
P: Coperfilm, Tellus Cinematografica, Paris International Productions. **W:** Silvio Siano, Mario Di Nardo (also sometimes credited: Pino Mercanti, Heriberto Santaballa Valdés, Nino Lillo). **C:** Manuel Hernández Sanjuán. **M:** Gioacchino Angelo, Gianni Ferrio. **S:** Fred Beir, Francisco Nieto, Evi Marandi, Richard St. Bris, Olivier Mathot, Ángel Álvarez.

Tomb of the Pistolero (SP)
La tumba del pistolero
D: Amando de Ossorio. **P:** Fenix Film, Eurociné. **W:** Amando de Ossorio, H.S. Valdés. **C:** Miguel Fernández Mila. **M:** Daniel White. **S:** George Martin, Mercedes Alonso, Jack Taylor, Silvia Solar, Luis Induni, Frank Braña, José Canalejas, Tito García, Lorenzo Robledo, Aldo Sambrell.

Twins from Texas (IT-SP)
I gemelli del Texas; Los gemelos de Texas
D: Stefano Vanzina (as Steno). **P:** Emo Bistolfi, Fenix Film. **W:** Santos Alcocer, Giulio Scarnicci, Renzo Tarabusi. **C:** Manuel Hernández Sanjuán. **M:** Gianni Ferrio. **S:** Walter Chiari, Raimondo Vianello, Diana Lorys, Alfonso Rojas, Miguel del Castillo, Tito García.

Two Gangsters in the Wild West (IT-SP)
Due mafiosi nel Far West; Dos pistoleros; Two Mafiamen in the Far West
D: Giorgio Simonelli. **P:** Edmondo Amati, Epoca Film. **W:** Marcello Ciorciolini, Giorgio Simonelli. **C:** Juan Julio Baena. **M:** Giorgio Fabor. **AD:** Giuliano Carnimeo. **S:** Franco Franchi, Ciccio Ingrassia, Fernando Sancho, Aroldo Tieri, Hélène Chanel, Mario Brega, José Torres, Dino Strano, Ignazio Spalla.

Two Violent Men (IT-SP)
I due violenti; Los rurales de Texas; Two Gunmen
D: Primo Zeglio (as Anthony Greepy; Spanish version credited to 'Omar Hopkins').
P: Norberto Soliño. **W:** Jesús Navarro, Marcello Fondato. **C:** Alfredo Fraile. **M:** Francesco De Masi. **S:** Alan Scott, George Martin, Susy Andersen, María Badmajev, Mike Brendel, Frank Braña, Cris Huerta, Luis Induni, José Jaspe, Aldo Sambrell, Antonio Molino Rojo, Andrea Scotti.

1965

Adios Gringo (IT-FR-SP)
Adiós gringo
D: Giorgio Stegani (as George Finley).
P: Bruno Turchetto. **W:** Harry Whittington (novel), José Luis Jerez, Michele Villerot, Giorgio Stegani. **C:** Francisco Sempere. **M:** Benedetto

Ghiglia. **S:** Giuliano Gemma, Ida Galli (as Evelyn Stewart), Roberto Camardiel, Pierre Cressoy (as Peter Cross), Jesús Puente, Nello Pazzafini, Frank Braña, Luis Induni.

Black Eagles of Santa Fe, The (GER-IT-FR)
Die Schwarzen Adler von Santa Fé; I gringos non perdonano; Les aigles noirs de Santa-Fe
D: Ernst Hofbauer, Alberto Cardone.
P: Gunther Raguse. **W:** Jack Lewis. **C:** Hans Jura.
M: Gert Wilden. **S:** Brad Harris, Joachim Hansen, Horst Frank, Werner Peters, Helga Sommerfeld, Enio Girolami, Lorenzo Robledo, Tony Kendall.

Carry On Cowboy (UK)
D: Gerald Thomas. **P:** Peter Rogers. **W:** Talbot Rothwell. **C:** Alan Hume. **M:** Eric Rogers.
S: Sid James, Kenneth Williams, Jim Dale, Charles Hawtrey, Joan Sims.

Coffin for the Sheriff, A (IT-SP)
Una bara per lo sceriffo; Una tumba para el Sheriff
D: Mario Caiano. **P:** Luigi Mondello.

W: David Moreno, Guido Malatesta.
C: Julio Ortas. **M:** Francesco De Masi.
S: Anthony Steffen, Eduardo Fajardo, George Rigaud, Luciana Gilli, Armando Calvo, Luís Barboo, Frank Braña, Lucio De Santis.

Colorado Charlie (IT)
D: Roberto Mauri (as Robert Johnson).
P: Francesco Paolo Prestano. **W:** Nino Stresa.
C: Edmondo Affronti. **M:** Gioacchino Angelo.
S: Jacques Berthier, Livio Lorenzon (as Charlie Lawrence), Brunella Bovo, Andrea Aureli, Luigi Ciavarro, Erika Blanc.

Colt Is My Law, The (IT-SP)
La colt è la mia legge; La ley del Colt; The Gun Is My Law
D: Alfonso Brescia (as Al Bradley).
P: UCI, Cine 3, Trebol Film, Procensa.
W: Alfonso Brescia, Franco Cobianchi, Ramón Comas, John Turner, Adriano Micantoni, Mario Musy. **C:** Eloy Mella. **M:** Carlos Castellanos Gómez. **S:** Angel del Pozo (as Anthony Clark), Luciana Gilli, Miguel de la Riva, Pietro Tordi, Aldo Cecconi, Livio Lorenzon.

Desperado Trail (GER-IT-YUG)
Winnetou III; Vinetu III
D: Harald Reinl. **P:** Horst Wendlandt.
W: Karl May (novel), Harald G. Petersson, J. Joachim Bartsch. **C:** Ernst W. Kalinke.
M: Martin Böttcher. **S:** Pierre Brice, Lex Barker, Rik Battaglia, Renato Baldini, Ralf Wolter, Gojko Mitic.

Duel at Sundown (GER-YUG-IT)
Duell von Sonnenuntergang; Sparate a vista su Killer Kid
D: Leopold Lahola. **P:** Leopold Lahola.
W: Marek Hlasko, Leopold Lahola, Anya Corvin.
C: Janez Kalisnik. **M:** Zvi Borodo. **S:** Peter van Eyck, Carole Gray, Wolfgang Kieling, Mario Girotti, Walter Barnes, Giacomo Rossi-Stuart.

Finger on the Trigger (SP-US)
El dedo en el gatillo; Blue Lightning
D: Sidney Pink. **P:** Sidney Pink. **W:** Sidney Pink, Luis de los Arcos. **C:** Antonio Macasoli, Miguel Barquero. **M:** José Solà. **S:** Rory Calhoun, James Philbrook, Silvia Solar, Leo Anchóriz, Todd Martin, Tito García, Antonio Molino Rojo, George Rigaud.

Flaming Frontier (GER-YUG)
Old Surehand; Lavirint smrti; Surehand - mano veloce
D: Alfred Vohrer. **P:** Wolfgang Kuhnlenz.
W: Karl May (novel), Eberhard Keindorff, Johanna Sibelius, Fred Denger. **C:** Karl Löb.
M: Martin Böttcher. **S:** Stewart Granger, Pierre Brice, Mario Girotti, Larry Pennell, Leticia Román, Milan Srdoc.

For a Few Dollars More (IT-SP-GER)
Per qualche dollaro in più; Für ein Paar Dollar Mehr; La muerte tenía un precio
D: Sergio Leone. **P:** Alberto Grimaldi.
W: Fulvio Morsella, Sergio Leone, Luciano Vincenzoni, Fernando Di Leo (uncredited), Sergio Donati (uncredited). **C:** Massimo Dallamano. **M:** Ennio Morricone. **AD:** Tonino Valerii, Fernando Di Leo (uncredited).
S: Clint Eastwood, Lee Van Cleef, Gian Maria Volonté, Mara Krup, Luigi Pistilli, Klaus Kinski, Mario Brega, Aldo Sambrell, Josef Egger, Panos Papadopoulos, Frank Braña, Roberto Camardiel, José Canalejas, Peter Lee Lawrence, Antonio Molino Rojo, Benito Stefanelli, Ricardo Palacios, Lorenzo Robledo, José Terrón, Carlo Simi.

For a Fist in the Eye (IT-SP)
Per un pugno nell'occhio; Dos caraduras en Texas
D: Michele Lupo. **P:** Ramo Film, Fenix Film.
W: Roberto Amoroso, Roberto Gianviti, Amedeo Sollazzo, Eduardo Manzanos Brochero. **C:** Alberto Fusi, Julio Ortas.
M: Francesco De Masi, Manuel Parada.
S: Franco Franchi, Ciccio Ingrassia, Francisco Morán, Lina Rosales, Mónica Randall, Jesús Puente, Tito García.

Gold Train (IT)
30 Winchester per El Diablo
D: Gianfranco Baldanello (as Frank G. Carroll).
P: Armando Novelli, Giovanni Vari. **W:** Giovanni Vari, Gianfranco Baldanello, Alfonso Brescia, Adriano Micantoni. **C:** Marcello Masciocchi.
M: Ghant. **S:** Carl Möhner, Alessandra Panaro,

Ivano Staccioli, José Torres, Mila Stanic, Guglielmo Spoletini (as William Bogart).

Graf Bobby, der Schrecken des Wilden Westens (AUT-YUG)
D: Paul Martin. **P:** Karl Schwetter, Mihajlo Rasic.
W: Kurt Nachmann, Robert Oxford. **C:** Sepp Ketterer. **M:** Heinz Gietz. **S:** Peter Alexander, Olga Schoberová, Gunther Philipp, Hanne Wieder, Elisabeth Markus.

Gunfight at Rio Grande (GER)
Die Banditen von Rio Grande; Bandits of the Rio Grande
D: Helmut M. Backhaus. **P:** Eva Rosskopf.
W: Helmut M. Backhaus, Gregor Trass.
C: Manfred Ensinger. **M:** Christian Bruhn.
S: Harald Leipnitz, Maria Perschy, Wolfgang Kieling, Ellen Schwiers, Gerlinde Locker.

Hands of a Gunfighter (SP-IT)
Ocaso de un pistolero; Il destino di un pistolero; Mani di pistolero; Gunman's Hands
D: Rafael Romero Marchent. **P:** PEA, Astro.
W: Joaquín Romero Marchent. **C:** Miguel Fernández Mila, Fausto Zuccoli. **M:** Angelo Francesco Lavagnino. **S:** Craig Hill, Gloria Milland, Carlos Romero Marchent, Conchita Nuñez, Piero Lulli, Jesús Puente, Raf Baldassarre, John Bartha, Luis Induni, Lorenzo Robledo, Paco Sanz.

In a Colt's Shadow (IT-SP)
All'ombra di una Colt; Plazo para morir
D: Giovanni Grimaldi (as Gianni Grimaldi).
P: Hercules Cinematografica, Hispamer Film.
W: Aldo Barni, Aldo Luxardo, Giovanni Grimaldi (Spanish sources also credit María del Carmen Martínez Román). **C:** Stelvio Massi, Julio Ortas.
M: Nico Fidenco. **S:** Stephen Forsyth, Conrado San Martín, Franco Ressel, Franco Lantieri, José Calvo, Tito García, Helga Liné, Aldo Sambrell, Andrea Scotti.

Joe Dexter (SP-IT)
Oeste Nevada Joe; La sfida degli implacabili; Guns of Nevada
D: Ignacio F. Iquino. **P:** IFI, Cineproduzioni Associate. **W:** Miguel María Astrain Bada, Alberto Colucci, Ignacio F. Iquino. **C:** Giuseppe La Torre, Julio Perez de Rozas. **M:** Enrique Escobar. **S:** George Martin, Adriana Ambesi, Katia Loritz, Giuseppe Addobbati, Miguel de la Riva.

Johnny West (IT-SP-FR)
Johnny West, il mancino; Johnny West; Les frères dynamite; Left-Handed Johnny West
D: Gianfranco Parolini (as Frank Kramer).
P: Giuseppe Fatigati. **W:** Jerez Aloza, Robert de Nesle, Gianfranco Parolini, Giovanni Simonelli.
C: Francesco Izzarelli. **M:** Angelo Francesco Lavagnino. **S:** Mimmo Palmara (as Dick Palmer), Adriano Micantoni, Dada Gallotti, Mara Cruz, Roberto Camardiel, Barta Barry, Spartaco Conversi.

Last of the Mohicans, The (SP-IT)
¡Uncas! El fin de una raza; L'ultimo dei Mohicani
D: Mateo Cano. **P:** Eguiluz Film, Italcaribe.
W: James Fenimore Cooper (novel), Alain Baudry, Vinicio Marinucci. **C:** Carlo Carlini.

Any Gun Can Play

M: Angelo Francesco Lavagnino. **S:** Jack Taylor, Sara Lezana, Daniel Martín, José Manuel Martín, Luis Induni, Lorenzo Robledo.

Last Tomahawk, The (GER-SP-IT)
Der Letzte Mohikaner; El ultimo Mohicano; La valle delle ombre rosse; Last of the Mohicans
D: Harald Reinl. **P:** International Germania Film, Procusa, Balcázar, Cineproduzioni Associate. **W:** James Fenimore Cooper (novel), J. Joachim Bartsch, Roberto Bianchi Montero, José Antonio de la Loma, Giovanni Simonelli. **C:** Ernst W. Kalinke (Italian version credits Giuseppe La Torre). **M:** Peter Thomas (Italian version credits Francesco De Masi). **S:** Daniel Martín, Anthony Steffen, Joachim Fuchsberger, Karin Dor, Carl Lange, Frank Braña, Cris Huerta.

Man Called Gringo, The (SP-GER-IT)
La ley del forastero; Sie Nahhten Ihn Gringo; Regresa un pistolero; Lo sceriffo non paga il sabato
D: Roy Rowland. **P:** Procusa, Hesperia, Germania Film. **W:** Francisco Gonzalvez, G. Schmidt, Clarke Reynolds. **C:** Manuel Merino. **M:** Heinz Gietz. **S:** Götz George, Daniel Martín, Alexandra Stewart, Helmut Schmid, Sieghardt Rupp.

Man from Oklahoma, The (SP-IT-GER)
Oklahoma John; Il ranch degli spietati; Der Sheriff von Rio Rojo; Ranch of the Ruthless
D: Jaime Jesús Balcázar (Italian version credited to Roberto Bianchi Montero). **P:** Balcázar, Cineproduzioni Associate, International Germania Film. **W:** Giuseppe Maggi, Helmut Harun, Alfonso Balcázar (Italian version credits Giovanni Simonelli, Roberto Bianchi Montero). **C:** Giuseppe La Torre. **M:** Francesco De Masi. **S:** Rick Horn, José Calvo, Sabine Bethmann, Giuseppe Addobbati, Jesús Puente, Tom Felleghy.

Man Who Came to Kill, The (SP-IT)
Doc, manos de plata; L'uomo dalla pistola d'oro; 10.000 dólares vivo o muerto
D: Alfonso Balcázar. **P:** Carlos Bove, Roberto Palaggi, Alfonso Balcázar. **W:** Miguel Cussó, Giovanni Simonelli, Alfonso Balcázar, José Antonio de la Loma. **C:** Mario Capriotti, Stelvio Massi, Victor Monreal. **M:** Angelo Francesco Lavagnino. **AD:** Romolo Guerrieri. **S:** Carl Möhner, Luis Dávila, Gloria Milland, Fernando Sancho, Umberto Raho.

Murieta (SP-US)
Joaquín Murrieta
D: George Sherman. **P:** Francisco Molero. **W:** James O'Hanlon. **C:** Miguel Fernández Mila. **M:** Antonio Pérez Olea. **S:** Jeffrey Hunter, Diana Lorys, Arthur Kennedy, Roberto Camardiel, Sara Lezana, Frank Braña.

$100,000 for Ringo (IT-SP)
100.000 dollari per Ringo; Sangre sobre Texas
D: Alberto De Martino. **P:** Edmondo Amati. **W:** Guido Zurli, Alberto De Martino, Alfonso Balcázar, Giovanni Simonelli, Vincenzo Flamini. **C:** Federico G. Larraya. **M:** Bruno Nicolai. **AD:** Enzo G. Castellari. **S:** Richard Harrison, Fernando Sancho, Massimo Serato, Gérard Tichy, Eleonora Bianchi, Guido Lollobrigida, Luis Induni, Paco Sanz.

One Silver Dollar (IT-FR)
Un dollaro bucato; Le dollar troué; Blood for a Silver Dollar
D: Giorgio Ferroni (as Kelvin Jackson Padget). **P:** Dorica Film, Explorer Film, Fono Roma, Films Concordia, Films Corona. **W:** Giorgio Stegani, Giorgio Ferroni. **C:** Antonio Secchi. **M:** Gianni Ferrio. **S:** Giuliano Gemma (as Montgomery Wood), Ida Galli (as Evelyn Stewart), Pierre Cressoy, Giuseppe Addobbati, Nello Pazzafini, Nazzareno Zamperla, Franco Fantasia, Salvatore Borgese, Benito Stefanelli, Ignazio Spalla (as Pedro Sanchez), Andrea Scotti.

Outlaw of Red River (SP)
El proscrito del Rio Colorado; Django the Condemned; Django the Honorable Killer
D: Maury Dexter. **P:** Eduardo Manzanos Brochero, Arturo Marcos. **W:** Eduardo Manzanos Brochero. **C:** Manuel Merino. **M:** Manuel Parada, Carlo Savina. **S:** George Montgomery, Elisa Montés, José Nieto, Jesús Tordesillas, Miguel del Castillo, Raf Baldassarre, Frank Braña.

Per un dollaro a Tucson si muore (IT)
D: Cesare Canevari (as D. Brownson). **P:** Cesare Canevari. **W:** Cesare Canevari. **C:** Adriano Bernacchi. **M:** Armando Sciascia. **S:** Ronny de Marc, Joco Turk, Gia Sandri, George Lycan, Maria Grazia Marescalchi.

Pistol for Ringo, A (IT-SP)
Una pistola per Ringo; Una pistola para Ringo
D: Duccio Tessari. **P:** Luciano Ercoli, Alberto Pugliese. **W:** Duccio Tessari, Fernando Di Leo (uncredited). **C:** Francisco Marín. **M:** Ennio Morricone. **S:** Giuliano Gemma (as Montgomery Wood), George Martin, Fernando Sancho, Nieves Navarro (as Susan Scott), Lorella De Luca (as Hally Hammond), Antonio Casas, José Manuel Martín, Pajarito, Paco Sanz, Nazzareno Zamperla.

Place Called Glory, A (GER-SP)
Die Hölle von Manitoba; Un lugar llamado Glory
D: Sheldon Reynolds. **P:** Bruce Balaban, Danilo Sabatini. **W:** Jerold Hayden Boyd, Eduardo De Lorenzo, Fernando Lamas. **C:** Federico G. Larraya. **M:** Angel Arteaga. **S:** Lex Barker, Pierre Brice, Marianne Koch, Gérard Tichy, Angel del Pozo, Luís Barboo, Victor Israel, Antonio Molino Rojo, George Rigaud, Aldo Sambrell, Wolfgang Lukschy.

Pyramid of the Sun God (GER-FR-IT)
Die Pyramide des Sonnengottes; Les mercenaires du Rio Grande; I violenti di Rio Bravo
D: Robert Siodmak. **P:** Artur Brauner, Willy Egger, Mihajlo Rasic. **W:** Karl May (novel), Ladislas Fodor, Robert A. Stemmle, Georg Marischka. **C:** Siegfried Hold. **M:** Erwin Halletz. **S:** Lex Barker, Gerard Barray, Rik Battaglia, Michèle Girardon, Ralf Wolter.

Rampage at Apache Wells (GER-YUG)
Der Ölprinz; Winnetou und der Ölprinz; Kralj petroleja
D: Harald Philipp. **P:** Horst Wendlandt. **W:** Karl May (novel), Fred Denger, Harald Philipp. **C:** Heinz Hölscher. **M:** Martin Böttcher. **S:** Stewart Granger, Pierre Brice, Walter Barnes, Harald Leipnitz, Milan Srdoc, Mario Girotti.

Relentless Four, The (IT-SP)
I quattro inesorabili; Los quatro implacables
D: Primo Zeglio. **P:** PEA, Aitor Film. **W:** Federico de Urrutia, Manuel Sebares de Caso, Marcello Fondato, Primo Zeglio. **C:** Miguel Fernández Mila. **M:** Marcello Giombini. **S:** Adam West, Claudio Undari (as Robert Hundar), Renato Rossini, Roberto Camardiel, Raf Baldassarre, Luis Induni, John Bartha, José Canalejas, Cris Huerta, José Jaspe, Lorenzo Robledo, Paco Sanz.

Return of Ringo, The (IT-SP)
Il ritorno di Ringo; El ritorno de Ringo
D: Duccio Tessari. **P:** Luciano Ercoli, Alberto Pugliese. **W:** Duccio Tessari, Fernando Di Leo. **C:** Francisco Marín. **M:** Ennio Morricone. **AD:** Fernando Di Leo. **S:** Giuliano Gemma, Fernando Sancho, George Martin, Lorella De Luca (as Hally Hammond), Nieves Navarro (as Susan Scott), Antonio Casas, Pajarito.

Secret of Captain O'Hara, The (SP)
El secreto del capitán O'Hara; I segreto di Ringo
D: Arturo Ruiz Castillo. **P:** Lacy Internacional. **W:** Luis García, Arturo Ruiz Castillo. **C:** Alfonso Nieva. **M:** Manuel Moreno Buendia. **S:** Germán Cobos, Marta Padovan, Mariano Vidal Molina, Frank Braña, José Canalejas.

Seven Hours of Gunfire (SP-IT-GER)
Aventuras del Oeste; Sette ore di fuoco; Die letzte Kugel traf den Besten
D: Joaquín Romero Marchent. **P:** Centauro Films, PEA, Constantin. **W:** Joaquín Romero Marchent. **C:** Rafael Pacheco. **M:** Angelo Francesco Lavagnino. **AD:** Rafael Romero Marchent. **S:** Rik Van Nutter (as Clyde Rogers), Adrian Hoven, Gloria Milland, Helga Sommerfeld, Raf Baldassarre, Paco Sanz, Cris Huerta, Helga Liné, Antonio Molino Rojo, Lorenzo Robledo, Carlos Romero Marchent.

Sheriff Won't Shoot, The (SP-IT)
El sheriff no dispara; Lo sceriffo che non spara
D: José Luis Monter, Renato Polselli. **P:** Accadia. **W:** Vincenzo Cascino, Guido Malatesta, María del Carmen Martínez Román, José Luis Monter, Renato Polselli, Reinat Rizlang. **C:** Aiace Parolin. **M:** Felice Di Stefano. **S:** Mickey Hargitay, Vincenzo Cascino, Dan Clark, Aïché Nana, Pilar Clemens.

Shoot to Kill (SP)
Los cuatreros; Se sparo... ti uccido; Texas Jim
D: Ramón Torrado. **P:** Arturo González. **W:** Gregorio Almendros, Fernando Butragueño, Antonio Jiménez Escribano, Ramón Torrado. **C:** Ricardo Torres. **M:** Daniel Montorio. **S:** Edmund Purdom, Frank Latimore, Fernando Sancho, María Silva, Silvia Solar, Tito García, Luis Induni, Victor Israel, Paco Sanz.

Son of a Gunfighter (US-SP)
El hijo del pistolero
D: Paul Landres. **P:** Lester Welch. **W:** Clarke Reynolds. **C:** Manuel Berenguer. **M:** Robert Mellin, Frank Barber. **S:** Russ Tamblyn, Kieron Moore, James Philbrook, Fernando Rey, María Granada, Antonio Casas, Aldo Sambrell, Barta Barry.

Son of Jesse James (SP-IT)
El hijo de Jesse James; Solo contro tutti; Man Alone
D: Antonio del Amo. **P:** PEA, Apolo Films. **W:** Pino Passalacqua, Marcello Fondato. **C:** Alfredo Fraile, Fausto Zuccoli. **M:** Angelo Francesco Lavagnino. **S:** Claudio Undari (as Robert Hundar), Mercedes Alonso, Raf Baldassarre, John Bartha, Roberto Camardiel, Luis Induni, José Canalejas, José Jaspe.

Sons of Great Bear, The (GDR)
Die Söhne der grossen Bärin
D: Josef Mach. **P:** DEFA. **W:** Liselotte Welskopf-Heinrich, Margot Beichler, Hans-Joachim Wallstein. **C:** Jaroslav Tuzar. **M:** Wilhelm Neef. **S:** Gojko Mitic, Jirì Vrstála, Rolf Römer, Hans Hardt-Hardtloff, Gerhard Rachold.

Stranger in Sacramento, A (IT)
Uno straniero a Sacramento; Un extranjero en Sacramento
D: Sergio Bergonzelli (as Serge Bergon). **P:** Films d'Equipe. **W:** J. Murphy (novel), Sergio Bergonzelli, Adalberto Albertini. **C:** Adalberto Albertini. **M:** Felice Di Stefano. **S:** Mickey Hargitay, Barbara Frey, Gabriella Giorgelli, Aldo Berti, Enrico Bomba (as Steve Saint-Clair), Mario Lanfranchi.

Sunscorched (SP-GER)
Tierra de fuego; Vergeltung in Catano; Jessy Does Not Forgive... He Kills!
D: Jaime Jesús Balcázar, Mark Stevens. **P:** Alfonso Balcázar. **W:** Alfonso Balcázar, José Antonio de la Loma, Mark Stevens, Irving Dennis. **C:** Francisco Marín. **M:** Michèle Auzépy, Silvestre Enzo. **S:** Mark Stevens, Mario Adorf, Marianne Koch, Vivien Dodds, Frank Oliveras, Frank Braña, Luis Induni.

Three from Colorado, The (SP-IT)
Rebeldes en Canada; I tre del Colorado
D: Amando de Ossorio. **P:** Coperfilm, PEA. **W:** Amando de Ossorio. **C:** Fausto Zuccoli. **M:** Carlo Savina. **S:** George Martin, Giulia Rubini, Diana Lorys, Santiago Rivero, Pamela Tudor, Raf Baldassarre, Franco Fantasia.

Tramplers, The (IT-FR)
Gli uomini dal passo pesante; Les forcenés
D: Albert Band (also credited to Mario Sequi). **P:** Anna Maria Chretien. **W:** Will Cook (novel), Albert Band, Ugo Liberatore. **C:** Alvaro Mancori. **M:** Agnelo Francesco Lavagnino. **S:** Gordon Scott, Joseph Cotten, James Mitchum, Franco Nero, Ilaria Occhini, Romano Puppo, Giovanni Cianfriglia (as Ken Wood).

Treasure of the Aztecs, The (GER-FR-IT)
Der Schatz der Azteken; Les mercenaires du Rio Grande; I violenti di Rio Bravo
D: Robert Siodmak. **P:** Artur Brauner, Götz Dieter Wulf. **W:** Karl May (novel), Ladislas Fodor, Robert A. Stemmle, Georg Marischka, Paul Jarrico. **C:** Siegfried Hold. **M:** Erwin Halletz. **S:** Lex Barker, Gerard Barray, Michèle Girardon, Ralf Wolter, Rik Battaglia.

Two Sergeants of General Custer (IT-SP)
I due sergenti del generale Custer; Dos vivales en Fuerte Alamo; Two Idiots at Fort Alamo
D: Giorgio Simonelli. **P:** Edmondo Amati, Alfonso Balcázar. **W:** Marcello Ciorciolini, Alfonso Balcázar, Giorgio Simonelli, Amedeo Sollazzo. **C:** Isidoro Goldberger. **M:** Angelo Francesco Lavagnino. **AD:** Giuliano Carnimeo. **S:** Franco Franchi, Ciccio Ingrassia, Margaret Lee, Moira Orfei, Fernando Sancho, Riccardo Garrone, Ignazio Spalla (as Pedro Sanchez).

Viva Carrancho (SP-IT)
L'uomo che viene da Canyon City
D: Alfonso Balcázar. **P:** Alfonso Balcázar, Adelphia Cinematografica. **W:** Attilio Riccio, José Antonio de la Loma, Adriano Bolzoni. **C:** Alfio Contini. **M:** Angelo Francesco Lavagnino. **S:** Fernando Sancho, Robert Woods, Luis Dávila, Loredana Nusciak, Gérard Tichy, José Manuel Martín, Antonio Molino Rojo, Paco Sanz.

Viva Maria! (FR-IT)
D: Louis Malle. **P:** Óscar Dancigers, Louis Malle, Vides. **W:** Louis Malle, Jean-Claude Carrière. **C:** Henri Decaë. **M:** Georges Delerue. **S:** Brigitte Bardot, Jeanne Moreau, George Hamilton, Paulette Dubost, Claudio Brook.

Why Go On Killing? (SP-IT)
Por que seguir matando?; Perché uccidi ancora; Stop the Slayings
D: José Antonio de la Loma, Edoardo Mulargia. **P:** Alfonso Balcázar, Vincenzo Musolino. **W:** Vincenzo Musolino, José Antonio de la

Loma, Edoardo Mulargia. **C:** Hans Burman, Vitaliano Natalucci. **M:** Felice Di Stefano. **S:** Anthony Steffen, Ida Galli (as Evelyn Stewart), Aldo Berti, Gemma Cuervo, José Calvo, Luis Induni, Franco Pesce, José Torres, Ignazio Spalla (as Pedro Sanchez).

1966

Arizona Colt (IT-FR)
The Man from Nowhere
D: Michele Lupo. **P:** Elio Scardamaglia. **W:** Ernesto Gastaldi, Luciano Martino. **C:** Guglielmo Mancori. **M:** Francesco De Masi. **S:** Giuliano Gemma, Fernando Sancho, Corinne Marchand, Nello Pazzafini, Roberto Camardiel, Andrea Bosic, Guglielmo Spoletini (as William Bogart), Giovanni Scarciofolo (as Jeff Cameron), Tom Felleghy, Pietro Ceccarelli, José Manuel Martín, Rosalba Neri, José Terrón.

Ballad of a Bounty Hunter (SP)
Dos mil dólares por Coyote; Django... cacciatore di taglie; Django, a Bullet for You; 2000 $ por Coyote
D: León Klimovsky. **P:** Sidney Pink, Salvadore Romero. **W:** Manuel Sebares, Federico de Urrutia, Sidney Pink. **C:** Pablo Ripoll. **M:** Fernando Garcìa Morcillo. **S:** James Philbrook, Nuria Torray, Perla Cristal, Mariano Vidal Molina, Alfonso Rojas, Antonio Molino Rojo.

Blood at Sundown (IT-GER)
1000 dollari sul nero; Sartana; One Thousand Dollars on the Black
D: Alberto Cardone (as Albert Cardiff). **P:** Metheus Film, Lisa Film. **W:** Ernesto Gastaldi, Vittorio Salerno. **C:** Gino Santini. **M:** Michele Lacerenza. **S:** Anthony Steffen, Gianni Garko (as John Garko), Erika Blanc, Carlo D'Angelo, Roberto Miali (as Jerry Wilson), Sieghardt Rupp, Salvatore Borgese, Franco Fantasia.

Bounty Killer, The (SP-IT)
El precio de un hombre; The Ugly Ones
D: Eugenio Martín. **P:** José Gutiérrez Maesso. **W:** Marvin H. Albert (novel), José Gutiérrez Maesso, Eugenio Martín, Don Prindle. **C:** Enzo Barboni. **M:** Stelvio Cipriani. **S:** Tomas Milian, Richard Wyler, Ella Karin, Hugo Blanco, Lola Gaos, Mario Brega, Luís Barboo, Frank Braña, José Canalejas, Tito García, Ricardo Palacios.

Bullet for the General, A (IT)
Quién sabe?
D: Damiano Damiani. **P:** Bianco Manini. **W:** Salvatore Laurani, Franco Solinas. **C:** Antonio Secchi. **M:** Luis Enríquez Bacalov. **S:** Gian Maria Volonté, Lou Castel, Klaus Kinski, Martine Beswick, Jaime Fernandez, Andrea Checchi, Spartaco Conversi, José Manuel Martín, Aldo Sambrell.

De Guello (IT)
Deguejo
D: Giuseppe Vari (as Joseph Warren). **P:** Sergio Garrone. **W:** Roberto Amaroso, Sergio Garrone, Giuseppe Vari. **C:** Silvano Ippoliti. **M:** Alessandro Derevitsky. **S:** Giacomo Rossi-Stuart (as Jack Stuart), Dan Vadis, Rosy Zichel, Riccardo Garrone, Dana Ghia, Erika Blanc, José Torres.

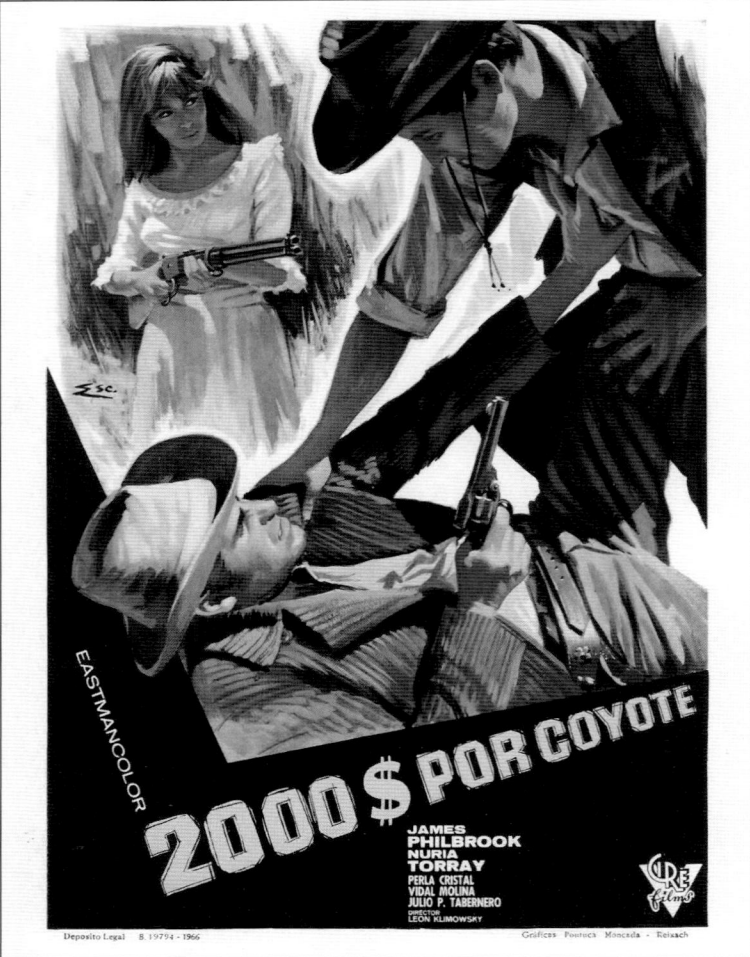

Django (IT-SP)
D: Sergio Corbucci. **P:** Manolo Bolognini, Sergio Corbucci. **W:** Sergio Corbucci, Bruno Corbucci, Franco Rossetti, Piero Vivarelli, José Gutierrez Maesso (uncredited), Fernando Di Leo (uncredited). **C:** Enzo Barboni. **M:** Luis Enríquez Bacalov. **S:** Franco Nero, José Bódalo, Loredana Nusciak, Ángel Álvarez, Eduardo Fajardo, Gino Pernice, José Canalejas, Luciano Rossi, José Terrón, Lucio De Santis.

Django Shoots First (IT)
Django spara per primo; He Who Shoots First
D: Alberto De Martino. **P:** Edmondo Amati. **W:** Massimo Cappriccioli, Tito Carpi, Sandro Continenza, Alberto De Martino, Vincenzo Flamini, Giovanni Simonelli. **C:** Riccardo Pallottini. **M:** Bruno Nicolai. **AD:** Enzo G. Castellari. **S:** Glenn Saxson, Fernando Sancho, Ida Galli (as Evelyn Stewart), Nando Gazzolo, Erika Blanc, Guido Lollobrigida (as Lee Burton), Alberto Lupo, Luigi Montefiori (as George Eastman), José Manuel Martín.

Djurado (IT-SP)
Jim Golden Poker
D: Gianni Narzisi. **P:** Studio T, Astro Film. **W:** William Azzella, Federico de Urrutia, Gianni Narzisi. **C:** Miguel Fernández Mila. **M:** Gianni Ferrio. **S:** Dante Posani (as Montgomery Clark), Scilla Gabel, Luis Induni, Margaret Lee, Federico Boido (as Rick Boyd).

Dollar of Fire, A (IT-SP)
Un dólar de fuego; Un dollaro di fuoco
D: Nick Nostro. **P:** Antonio Uzard, Ignacio F. Iquino. **W:** Mario Colucci, Ignacio F. Iquino, Astrain Bada. **C:** Victor Monreal, Julian Rosenthal. **M:** Enrique Escobar. **S:** Miguel de la Riva (as Michael Rivas), Dada Gallotti (as Diana Garson), Alberto Farnese, Gaspar 'Indio' González, Moises Rocha.

Dynamite Jim (SP-IT)
Dinamita Jim; Dinamite Jim
D: Alfonso Balcázar. **P:** Remo Odevaine, Antonio Liza. **W:** Alfonso Balcázar, José Antonio de la Loma, Mario Pasca, Alberto Liberati. **C:** Victor Monreal. **M:** Nico Fidenco. **S:** Luis Dávila, Fernando Sancho, Rosalba Neri, Aldo Sambrell, Maria Pia Conte, Victor Israel, Pajarito.

El Cisco (IT)
D: Sergio Bergonzelli (as Serge Bergon). **P:** Epoca Films. **W:** Sergio Bergonzelli, Paolo Lombardo. **C:** Aldo Greci. **M:** Bruno Nicolai.

S: William Berger, George Wang, Antonella Murgia, Lamberto Antinori, Tom Felleghy, John Bartha.

El Rojo (IT-SP)
Texas El Rojo
D: Leopoldo Savona (as Leo Colman; some sources credit Mario Costa as co-director). **P:** Roberto Amoroso, Luis Merino. **W:** Roberto Amoroso, Leopoldo Savona, Mario Casacci, Rate Furlan, Antonio Giambriccio, Roberto Gianviti, José-Maria Seone. **C:** Aldo Giordani. **AD:** Gianfranco Baldanello. **M:** Benedetto Ghiglia. **S:** Richard Harrison, Nieves Navarro (as Susan Scott), Piero Lulli, Mirko Ellis, José Jaspe, Raf Baldassarre, John Bartha, Tom Felleghy, José Jaspe, Franco Ressel.

Few Dollars for Django, A (SP-IT)
Alambradas de violencia; Pochi dollari per Django
D: Enzo G. Castellari (credited to León Klimovsky). **P:** Marino Girolami. **W:** Manuel Sebares, Tito Carpi. **C:** Aldo Pennelli. **M:** Carlo Savina. **S:** Anthony Steffen, Gloria Osuña, Frank Wolff, José Luis Lluch, José Canalejas (as Joe Kamel), Enio Girolami (as Thomas Moore), Enzo G. Castellari.

Fistful of Songs, A (IT-SP-LIECH)
Per un pugno di canzoni; Europa canta; Por un puñado de canciones
D: José Luis Merino. **P:** Theo M. Werner, Gustav Gavrin, José Luis Lorente, Carlo Infascelli. **W:** Carlo Infascelli, Mario Amendola, José Luis Merino, Carlo Veo, Franz-Otto Kruger, Sigrid Werner. **C:** Fulvio Testi. **M:** Enrico Polito. **S:** Vivi Bach, Gustavo Rojo, Renzo Palmer, Ermelinda De Felice, Nino Vingelli, Luis Induni.

Five Dollars for Ringo (SP-IT)
Cinco pistolas de Texas; Cinque pistole del Texas; 5 dollari per Ringo
D: Juan Xiol Marchal. **P:** Ignacio F. Iquino. **W:** Miguel Angel Astrain, Ignacio F. Iquino (Italian sources also credit Alberto Colucci). **C:** Victor Monreal, Giuseppe La Torre. **M:** Enrique Escobar. **S:** Julio Pérez Tabernero, Alberto Farnese, Maria Pia Conte, Gaspar 'Indio' González, Vicky Lagos.

Five Giants from Texas (IT-SP)
I cinque della vendetta; Los cinco de la venganza; The Last Showdown
D: Aldo Florio. **P:** Roberto Capitani, Aldo Ricci. **W:** Alfonso Balcázar, Aldo Florio, José Antonio de la Loma. **C:** Victor Monreal. **M:** Franco Salina. **S:** Guy Madison, Mónica Randall, Giovanni Cianfriglia, Mariano Vidal Molina, José Manuel Martín, Antonio Molino Rojo.

For a Few Dollars Less (IT)
Per qualche dollaro in meno
D: Mario Mattoli. **P:** Franco Palaggi. **W:** Bruno Corbucci, Mario Guerra, Vittorio Vighi, Sergio Corbucci. **C:** Giuseppe Aquari. **M:** Marcello Giombini. **S:** Lando Buzzanca, Elio Pandolfi, Gloria Paul, Raimondo Vianello, Lucia Modugno.

Fort Yuma Gold (IT-FR-SP)
Per pochi dollari ancora; Trois cavaliers pour fort Yuma; El hombre del Sur; The Rebel Lieutenant
D: Giorgio Ferroni (as Calvin Jackson Padget). **P:** Edmondo Amati. **W:** Massimiliano Capriccioli, Sandro Continenza, Remigio Del Grosso, Gilles Demoulin, Augusto Finocchi, Leonardo Martin. **C:** Rafael Pacheco. **M:** Gianni Ferrio, Ennio Morricone. **S:** Giuliano Gemma (as Montgomery Wood), Dan Vadis, Sophie Daumier, Jacques Sernas, Nello Pazzafini, Antonio Molino Rojo, Guglielmo Spoletini (as William Spoletin), Andrea Bosic, Benito Stefanelli, José Calvo, Pierre Cressoy, Angel del Pozo, Furio Meniconi (as Men Fury), Lorenzo Robledo.

Four Dollars of Revenge (SP-IT)
Cuatro dólares de venganza; Quattro dollari di vendetta; Four Dollars of Vengeance
D: Jaime Jesús Balcázar. **P:** Balcázar, Società Ambrosiana Cinematografica. **W:** Bruno Corbucci, Giovanni Grimaldi. **C:** Victor Monreal. **M:** Angelo Francesco Lavagnino. **S:** Robert Woods, Dana Ghia, Angelo Infanti, Antonio Casas, Gérard Tichy, José Manuel Martín, Antonio Molino Rojo.

Go with God, Gringo (IT)
Vayas con Dios, Gringo; Good Luck, Gringo; Vete con Dios, Gringo
D: Edoardo Mulargia (as Edward G. Muller). **P:** Vincenzo Musolino. **W:** Vincenzo Musolino, Edoardo Mulargia. **C:** Ugo Brunelli. **M:** Felice Di Stefano. **S:** Glenn Saxson, Lucretia Love, Ignazio Spalla (as Pedro Sanchez), Aldo Berti, Pasquale Simeoli, Tom Felleghy, Livio Lorenzon, Dino Strano.

Golden Sheriff, A (IT)
Uno sceriffo tutto d'oro; The Sheriff with the Gold
D: Osvaldo Civirani (as Richard Kean). **P:** Osvaldo Civirani. **W:** Roberto Gianviti, Vincenzo Dell'Aquila. **C:** Osvaldo Civirani. **M:** Nora Orlandi (as Joan/Jan Christian). **S:** Luigi Giuliani (as Louis McJulian), Jacques Berthier, Caterina Trentini, Roberto Messina, Nando Angelini, Mario Lanfranchi, Luciano Rossi.

Good, the Bad and the Ugly, The (IT)
Il buono, il brutto, il cattivo
D: Sergio Leone. **P:** Alberto Grimaldi. **W:** Luciano Vincenzoni, Sergio Leone, Agenore Incrocci, Furio Scarpelli, Sergio Donati (uncredited). **C:** Tonino Delli Colli. **M:** Ennio Morricone. **S:** Clint Eastwood, Lee Van Cleef, Eli Wallach, Aldo Giuffrè, Luigi Pistilli, Rada Rassimov, Mario Brega, Frank Braña, Antonio

Molino Rojo, John Bartha, Antonio Casas, Pietro Ceccarelli, Victor Israel, Livio Lorenzon, Al Mulock, Aldo Sambrell, Benito Stefanelli, Ricardo Palacios, Romano Puppo, Lorenzo Robledo, José Terrón.

Halfbreed (GER-YUG)
Winnetou und das Halbblut Apanatschi; Vinetu i Apanaci
D: Harald Philipp. **P:** Horst Wendlandt. **W:** Karl May (characters), Fred Denger. **C:** Heinz Hölscher. **M:** Martin Böttcher. **S:** Lex Barker, Pierre Brice, Götz George, Uschi Glas, Ralf Wolter, Walter Barnes.

Hills Run Red, The (IT)
Un fiume di dollari
D: Carlo Lizzani (as Lee W. Beaver). **P:** Luigi Carpentieri, Ermanno Donati. **W:** Piero Regnoli (as Dean Craig). **C:** Antonio Secchi. **M:** Ennio Morricone (as Leo Nichols). **S:** Thomas Hunter, Henry Silva, Dan Duryea, Nicoletta Machiavelli, Nando Gazzolo, Gianna Serra, Guglielmo Spoletini (as William Bogart), Pietro Ceccarelli, Lucio De Santis, Nino Scarciofolo (as Jeff Cameron), Goffredo Unger.

Johnny Yuma (IT)
D: Romolo Guerrieri. **P:** Italo Zingarelli. **W:** Fernando Di Leo, Romolo Guerrieri, Sauro Scavolini, Giovanni Simonelli. **C:** Mario Capriotti. **M:** Nora Orlandi. **S:** Mark Damon, Lawrence Dobkin, Rosalba Neri, Luigi Vannucchi, Fidel Gonzalez.

Kid Rodelo (US-SP)
Fugitivos de Yuma
D: Richard Carlson. **P:** Jack O. Lamont, Eduardo Manzanos Brochero. **W:** Eduardo Manzanos Brochero, Jack Natteford. **C:** Manuel Merino. **M:** Johnny Douglas, Manuel Parada. **S:** Don Murray, Janet Leigh, Broderick Crawford, Richard Carlson, José Nieto, Luís Barboo.

Kill Johnny Ringo! (IT)
Uccidete Johnny Ringo
D: Gianfranco Baldanello (as Frank G. Carroll). **P:** La Cine Associati. **W:** Arpad De Riso, Nino Scolaro. **C:** Marcello Masciocchi. **M:** Giuseppe Caruso. **S:** Brett Halsey, Greta Polyn, Nino Fuscagni, Barbara Loy, Guido Lollobrigida (as Lee Burton), Guglielmo Spoletini (as William Bogart).

Kill or Be Killed (IT)
Uccidi o muori; Kill or Die; Ringo Against Johnny Colt
D: Tanio Boccia (as Amerigo Anton). **P:** Luigi Rovere. **W:** Mario Amendola. **C:** Aldo Giordani. **M:** Carlo Rustichelli. **S:** Robert Mark, Elina De Witt, Fabrizio Moroni, Andrea Bosic, Alberto Farnese, Remo Capitani, Furio Meniconi, Gordon Mitchell.

Legacy of the Incas (BUL-IT-GER-SP)
Zavetut na Inkata; Viva Gringo; Das Vermächtnis des Inka; El ultimo rey de los Incas
D: Georg Marischka. **P:** Alberto Grimaldi, George Marischka, Franz Marischka. **W:** Karl May (novel), Winfried Groth, Georg Marischka, Franz Marischka. **C:** Siegfried Hold, Juan Marine. **M:** Angelo Francesco Lavagnino. **S:** Guy Madison, Rik Battaglia, Geula Nuni, Fernando Rey, William Rothlein, Raf Baldassarre, José Calvo.

Massacre Time (IT)
Le colt cantarono la morte e fu... tempo di massacro; Tempo di massacro; The Brute and the Beast; Colt Concert
D: Lucio Fulci. **P:** Colt, Mega Film. **W:** Fernando Di Leo. **C:** Riccardo Pallottini. **M:** Coriolano Gori. **AD:** Giovanni Fago. **S:** Franco Nero, George Hilton, Nino Castelnuovo, Giuseppe Addobbati (as John M. Douglas), Linda Sini (as Lynn Shayne), Tom Felleghy, Salvatore Borgese, John Bartha, Romano Puppo.

Mestizo (SP)
Django Does Not Forgive
D: Julio Buchs. **P:** José Frade, Luis Méndez. **W:** Julio Buchs, Ugo Guerra, Bautista Lacasa, José Luis Martínez Mollá. **C:** Francisco Sánchez Munoz, Francisco Sempere. **M:** Antonio Pérez Olea, Daniel White. **S:** Hugo Blanco, Susan Campos, Gustavo Rojo, Luis Prendes, Carlos Casaravilla, Frank Braña, Luis Induni.

Mutiny at Fort Sharp (IT-SP)
Per un dollaro di gloria; El escuadrón de la muerte
D: Fernando Cerchio. **P:** Terra Film, Filmes, Fenix Film. **W:** Jesús Navarro, Ugo Liberatore, Fernando Cerchio. **C:** Emilio Foriscot. **M:** Carlo Savina. **S:** Broderick Crawford, Elisa Montés, Mario Valdemarin, Umberto Ceriani, Hugo Arden, José Canalejas.

My Name Is Pecos (IT)
Due once di piombo
D: Maurizio Lucidi. **P:** Franco Palombi, Gabriele Silvestri. **W:** Adriano Bolzoni. **C:** Franco Villa. **M:** Coriolano Gori. **S:** Robert Woods, Pier Paolo Capponi (as Norman Clark), Lucia Modugno, Peter Carsten, Luigi Casellato, Salvatore Borgese, Luigi Montefiori (as George Eastman), Peter Martell.

Navajo Joe (IT-SP)
Un dollaro a testa; Joe, el implacable; A Dollar a Head
D: Sergio Corbucci. **P:** Luigi Carpentieri, Ermanno Donati. **W:** Ugo Pirro, Fernando Di Leo, Piero Regnoli. **C:** Silvano Ippoliti. **M:** Ennio Morricone (as Leo Nichols). **S:** Burt Reynolds, Aldo Sambrell, Nicoletta Machiavelli, Fernando Rey, Tanya Lopert, Franca Polesello, Lucia Modugno, Ángel Álvarez, Pierre Cressoy, Cris Huerta, Mario Lanfranchi, Lorenzo Robledo, José Terrón.

$100,000 for Lassiter (SP-IT)
La muerte cumple condena; 100.000 dollari per Lassiter; Dollars for a Fast Gun
D: Joaquín Romero Marchent. **P:** Centauro Films, PEA. **W:** Joaquín Romero Marchent, Sergio Donati. **C:** Rafael Pacheco (Italian version credits Fulvio Testi). **M:** Marcello Giombini. **S:** Claudio Undari (as Robert Hundar), Pamela Tudor, José Bódalo, Jesús Puente, Luigi Pistilli, Roberto Camardiel, Aldo Sambrell, Carlos Romero Marchent, Benito Stefanelli, Paco Sanz.

Ramon the Mexican (IT)
Ramon il Messicano
D: Maurizio Pradeaux. **P:** Marino Carpano. **W:** Maurizio Pradeaux. **C:** Oberdan Troiani. **M:** Felice Di Stefano. **S:** Claudio Undari (as Robert Hundar), Wilma Lindamar, Franco Gula, Renato Trottola, Aldo Berti, Luciano Rossi, José Torres.

Rebels on the Loose (IT-SP)
Ringo e Gringo contro tutti; Héroes a la fuerza
D: Bruno Corbucci. **P:** Emo Bistolfi. **W:** Mario Guerra, Giulio Scarnicci, Renzo Tarabusi, Vittorio Vighi, Bruno Corbucci. **C:** Sandro D'Eva, Alfonso Nieva. **M:** Gianni Ferrio. **S:** Lando Buzzanca, Raimondo Vianello, Maria Martinez, Mónica Randall, Alfonso Rojas.

Renegade Gunfighter (IT-SP)
Per mille dollari al giorno; Por mil dolares al dia; For One Thousand Dollars Per Day
D: Silvio Amadio. **P:** Tirso Film, Petruka Film. **W:** Silvio Amadio, Tito Carpi, Luciano Gregoretti. **C:** Mario Pacheco. **M:** Gino Peguri. **S:** Zachary Hatcher, Anna Maria Pierangeli, Mimmo Palmara (as Dick Palmer), José Calvo, Rubén Rojo, Tom Felleghy.

Return of the Seven (US-SP)
El regreso de los siete magníficos
D: Burt Kennedy. **P:** Ted Richmond. **W:** Larry Cohen. **C:** Paul Vogel. **M:** Elmer Bernstein. **S:** Yul Brynner, Robert Fuller, Julián Mateos, Warren Oates, Claude Akins, Fernando Rey, Ricardo Palacios.

Ringo and His Golden Pistol (IT)
Johnny Oro
D: Sergio Corbucci. **P:** Joseph Fryd. **W:** Adriano Bolzoni, Franco Rossetti. **C:** Riccardo Pallottini. **M:** Carlo Savina. **S:** Mark Damon, Valeria Fabrizi, Ettore Manni, Franco De Rosa, Andrea Aureli, Giovanni Cianfriglia (as Ken Wood), Lucio De Santis, John Bartha.

Ringo the Mark of Vengeance (SP-IT)
Los cuatro salvajes; Ringo, il volto della vendetta; Ringo: Face of Revenge
D: Mario Caiano. **P:** Mario Caiano. **W:** Eduardo Manzanos Brochero, Mario Caiano. **C:** Julio Ortas. **M:** Francesco De Masi. **S:** Anthony Steffen, Frank Wolff, Eduardo Fajardo, Armando Calvo, Alexandra Nilo.

Ringo's Big Night (IT-SP)
La grande notte di Ringo; Trampa para un forajido
D: Mario Maffei. **P:** Emo Bistolfi (as Silver Bem). **W:** Mario Maffei. **C:** Carlo Bellero, Emilio Foriscot. **M:** Carlo Rustichelli. **AD:** Enzo G. Castellari. **S:** William Berger, Eduardo Fajardo, Adriana Ambesi, Walter Maestosi, Tom Felleghy, José Bódalo, Luis Induni, George Rigaud.

Ruthless Colt of the Gringo (IT-SP)
La spietata colt del gringo; La venganza de Clark Harrison
D: José Luis Madrid. **P:** Zeljko Kunkera. **W:** Jesús Navarro, Mino Roli, Antonio Sant'Esteban. **C:** Marcello Gatti, Jaime Deu Casas. **M:** Enrique Escobar, Federico Martìnez Tudó, Francesco De Masi. **AD:** Enzo G. Castellari. **S:** Luigi Giuliani (as Jim Reed), Marta Padovan, Germana Monteverdi, Carlos Otero, Alberto Gadea, Luis Induni.

Savage Gringo (IT-SP)
Ringo del Nebraska; Ringo de Nebraska
D: Antonio Román (as Anthony Roman) and/or Mario Bava. **P:** Fulvio Lucisano. **W:** Jesús Navarro, Antonio Román, Adriano Bolzoni, Grazia Benedetti. **C:** Guglielmo Mancori. **M:** Nino Oliviero. **S:** Ken Clark, Yvonne Bastien,

Piero Lulli, Renato Rossini, Alfonso Rojas, Antonio Gradoli, Frank Braña, José Canalejas, Livio Lorenzon, Aldo Sambrell, Paco Sanz.

Savage Pampas (SP-ARG-US)
Pampa salvaje
D: Hugo Fregonese. **P:** Jaime Prades. **W:** Ulises Petit de Murat, Homero Manzi, Hugo Fregonese, John Melson. **C:** Manuel Berenguer. **M:** Waldo de los Rios. **S:** Robert Taylor, Ron Randell, Marc Lawrence, Ty Hardin, Rosenda Monteros, Angel del Pozo, Barta Barry, José Jaspe, George Rigaud.

Seven Dollars to Kill (IT-SP)
7 dollari sul rosso; Siete dólares al rojo
D: Alberto Cardone (as Albert Cardiff). **P:** Mario Siciliano. **W:** Alberto Cardone, Juan Cobos, Amedeo Mellone, Melchiade Coletti, Arnaldo Franciolini. **C:** José Aguayo. **M:** Francesco De Masi. **S:** Anthony Steffen, Fernando Sancho, Loredana Nusciak, Roberto Miali (as Jerry Wilson), Elisa Montés, Franco Fantasia (as Frank Farrell), Spartaco Conversi (as Spean Convery), José Manuel Martín.

Seven Guns for the MacGregors (IT-SP)
7 pistole per I MacGregor; Siete pistolas para los MacGregor
D: Franco Giraldi (as Frank Grafield). **P:** Dario Sabatello (as Tell O'Darsa). **W:** Fernando Di Leo (as Fernand Lion), Vincenzo Dell'Aquila (as Vincent Eagle), David Moreno, Duccio Tessari. **C:** Alejandro Ulloa. **M:** Ennio Morricone. **S:** Robert Woods, Manolo Zarzo, Fernando Sancho, Leo Anchóriz, Agata Flori, Pierre Cressoy, George Rigaud, Alberto Dell'Acqua (as Albert Waterman), Nazzareno Zamperla (as Nick Amderson), Cris Huerta, Antonio Molino Rojo, Victor Israel.

Seven Guns for Timothy (IT-SP)
Le sette magnifiche pistole; Siete pistolas para Timothy
D: Romolo Guerrieri (as Rod Gilbert). **P:** Alfonso Balcázar, MBS Cinematografica, Gia Societa Cinematografica. **W:** Giovanni Simonelli, José Antonio de la Loma, Alfonso Balcázar. **C:** Victor Monreal, Roberto Filippini. **M:** Gino Peguri. **S:** Sean Flynn, Fernando Sancho, Ida Galli (as Evelyn Stewart), Daniel Martín, Poldo Bendandi, Spartaco Conversi, Tito García, Franco Pesce.

Seven Pistols for a Gringo (SP-IT)
Río maldito; 7 pistole per El Gringo
D: Juan Xiol Marchal. **P:** Julio S. de la Fuente. **W:** Peter Kenn, Ignacio F. Iquino, Roberto Bianchi Montero. **C:** Julio Perez de Rozas. **M:** Enrique Escobar. **S:** Bruno Piergentili (as Dan Harrison), Gérard Landry, Fernando Rubio, Alberto Farnese, Patricia Loran.

Sons of Ringo, The (IT)
I due figli di Ringo
D: Giorgio Simonelli, Giuliano Carnimeo. **P:** Leo Cevenini, Vittorio Martino. **W:** Marcello Ciorciolini, Roberto Gianviti, Amedeo Sollazzo, Dino Verde. **C:** Tino Santoni. **M:** Piero Umiliani. **S:** Franco Franchi, Ciccio Ingrassia, George Hilton, Gloria Paul, Ignazio Spalla (as Pedro Sanchez), Guido Lollobrigida (as Lee Burton), Mimmo Palmara, Dino Strano.

Starblack (IT-GER)
Johnny Colt; Django - schwarzer Gott des Todes
D: Giovanni Grimaldi (as Gianni Grimaldi). **P:** Ambrosiana, Melodie Film. **W:** Giovanni Grimaldi. **C:** Guglielmo Mancori. **M:** Benedetto Ghiglia. **S:** Robert Woods, Elga Andersen, Franco Lantieri, Jane Tilden, Andrea Scotti.

Sugar Colt (IT-SP)
D: Franco Giraldi. **P:** Franco Cittadini, Stenio Fiorentini. **W:** Giuseppe Mangione, Franco Giraldi, Augusto Finocchi, Fernando Di Leo, Sandro Continenza. **C:** Alejandro Ulloa. **M:** Luis Enríquez Bacalov. **S:** Hunt Powers, Soledad Miranda, Giuliano Raffaelli, Gina Rovere, Erno Crisa, Luís Barboo, Frank Braña, José Canalejas, Victor Israel, George Rigaud, Nazzareno Zamperla, Pajarito.

Tall Women, The (IT-SP-AUT)
Las siete magníficas; Sette donne per una strage; Donne alla frontiera; Frauen, die durch die Hölle gehen
D: Sidney Pink. **P:** Sidney Pink. **W:** Mino Roli (as Mike Ashley), Jim Heneghan, Sidney Pink. **C:** Marcello Gatti. **M:** Gregorio García Segura. **S:** Anne Baxter, Maria Perschy, Gustavo Rojo, Perla Cristal, Adriana Ambesi, George Rigaud.

Taste for Killing, A (IT-SP)
Per il gusto di uccidere; Cazador de recompensas; Lanky Fellow
D: Tonino Valerii. **P:** Hercules Cinematografica, Montana Films. **W:** Victor Auz. **C:** Stelvio Massi. **M:** Nico Fidenco. **S:** Craig Hill, George Martin, Piero Lulli (as Peter Carter), Fernando Sancho, George Wang, Frank Braña, José Canalejas, José Manuel Martín, Franco Ressel, Lorenzo Robledo.

Texas Adios (IT-SP)
Texas, addio; Adiós, Texas; The Avenger
D: Ferdinando Baldi. **P:** Manolo Bolognini. **W:** Franco Rossetti, Ferdinando Baldi. **C:** Enzo Barboni. **M:** Antón García Abril. **S:** Franco Nero, José Suárez, Alberto Dell'Acqua (as Cole Kitosch), Elisa Montés, José Guardiola, Luigi Pistilli, Livio Lorenzon, Gino Pernice, Lucio De Santis.

Texican, The (US-SP)
Texas Kid; El Tejano
D: Lesley Selander. **P:** M.C.R. Productions, PC Balcázar. **W:** John C. Champion, José Antonio de la Loma, Jose Antonio de la Loma. **M:** Francisco Marín. **M:** Nico Fidenco. **S:** Audie Murphy, Broderick Crawford, Diana Lorys, Antonio Casas, Aldo Sambrell, Frank Braña, Luis Induni, Victor Israel, Antonio Molino Rojo, George Rigaud.

Thompson 1880 (IT-SP)
D: Guido Zurli. **P:** Franco Mannocchi. **W:** Jaime Jesús Balcázar, Enzo Gicca Palli. **C:** Victor Monreal. **M:** Marcello Gigante. **S:** George Martin, Gia Sandri, Paul Muller, José Bódalo, Gordon Mitchell, José Jaspe, Dino Strano, Ignazio Spalla (as Pedro Sanchez).

Three Bullets for Ringo (IT)
3 colpi di Winchester per Ringo; Three Graves for a Winchester
D: Emimmo Salvi. **P:** Franco Mannocchi. **W:** James Wilde Jr., Ambrogio Molteni, Emimmo Salvi. **C:** Mario Parapetti. **M:** Armando Sciascia. **S:** Gordon Mitchell, Mickey Hargitay, Milla Sannoner, Ivano Staccioli, Amedeo Trilli, Spartaco Conversi.

Thunder at the Border (GER-YUG)
Winnetou und sein Freund Old Firehand; Vinetu i njegov prijatelj Old Firehand
D: Alfred Vohrer. **P:** Horst Wendlandt. **W:** Karl May (characters), David DeReszke, C.B. Taylor, Harald G. Petersson. **C:** Karl Löb. **M:** Peter Thomas. **S:** Rod Cameron, Pierre Brice, Marie Versini, Nadia Gray, Todd Armstrong, Rik Battaglia.

Tumba para un forajido (SP)
Tomba per uno straniero
D: José Luis Madrid. **P:** Constelacion. **W:** Antonio G. Escribano, José Luis Madrid. **C:** Julio Pérez de Rozas. **M:** Federico Martinez Tudó. **S:** Luis Dávila, Miguel de la Riva, Patricia Loran, Marta Flores, Francisco Nieto.

Who Killed Johnny Ringo? (GER-SP)
Wer kennt Johnny R.?; La balada de Johnny Ringo
D: José Luis Madrid. **P:** Tilma Films, CCC. **W:** Ladislas Fodor, Paul Jarrico. **C:** Julio Pérez de Rozas, Marcello Gatti. **M:** Federico Martinez Tudó. **S:** Lex Barker, Joachim Fuchsberger, Marianne Koch, Ralf Wolter, Barbara Bold, Sieghardt Rupp.

Woman for Ringo, A (IT-SP)
Dos pistolas gemelas; Una donna per Ringo
D: Rafael Romero Marchent. **P:** Benito Perojo. **W:** Giovanni Simonelli, Manuel Sebares. **C:** Francesco Vitrotti. **M:** Gregorio García Segura. **S:** Sean Flynn, Pilar Bayona (as Pili), Emilia Bayona (as Mili), George Rigaud, Beni Deus, Luis Induni.

Yankee (IT-SP)
Yankee (L'americano); El Yankee
D: Tinto Brass. **P:** Antonio Lucatelli, Francesco Giorgi. **W:** Tinto Brass, Alberto Silvestri, Giancarlo Fusco, (Spanish version credits Alfonso Balcázar). **C:** Alfio Contini. **M:** Nini Rosso. **S:** Philippe Leroy, Adolfo Celi, Mirella Martin, Jacques Herlin, Tomas Torres, Victor Israel, Paco Sanz.

Zorro the Rebel (IT)
Zorro il ribelle
D: Piero Pierotti. **P:** Fortunato Misiano, Pascale Misiano. **W:** Piero Pierotti, Gianfranco Clerici, Giancarlo Olericitorio Marchi. **C:** Augusto Tiezzi. **M:** Angelo Francesco Lavagnino. **S:** Renato Rossini (as Howard Ross), Dina De Santis, Charles Borromel, Arturo Dominici, Gabriella Andreini, Nello Pazzafini.

1967

Any Gun Can Play (IT)
Vado... l'ammazzo e torno; Go Kill and Come Back; For a Few Bullets More
D: Enzo G. Castellari. **P:** Edmondo Amati. **W:** Sauro Scavolini, Romolo Guerrieri, Tito Carpi, Giovanni Simonelli, Enzo G. Castellari. **C:** Giovanni Bergamini. **M:** Francesco De Masi. **S:** Edd Byrnes, George Hilton, Gilbert Roland, Stefania Careddu, José Torres, Gérard Herter, Salvatore Borgese, Ignazio Spalla (as Pedro Sanchez).

Ballad of a Gunman (IT-GER)
Ballata per un pistolero; Rocco - der Einzelgänger von Alamo;The Pistoleros
D: Alfio Caltabiano. **P:** Alfredo Nicolai, Ernst R. von Theumer. **W:** Alfio Caltabiano, Ernst R. von Theumer. **C:** Guglielmo Mancori. **M:** Marcello Giombini. **S:** Anthony Ghidra, Angelo Infanti, Mario Novelli, Alfio Caltabiano, Dante Maggio, Pietro Ceccarelli, Giovanni Cianfriglia (as Ken Wood).

Bandidos (IT-SP)
Crepa tu... che vivo io!
D: Massimo Dallamano (as Max Dillman). **P:** Solly V. Bianco. **W:** Luis Laso, Juan Cobos, Romano Migliorini, Gianbattista Mussetto. **C:** Emilio Foriscot. **M:** Egisto Macchi. **S:** Enrico Maria Salerno, Terry Jenkins, Venantino Venantini, María Martín, Marco Guglielmi, Cris Huerta, Victor Israel.

Bang Bang Kid, The (IT-SP-US)
Il Bang Bang Kid; Bang Bang
D: Stanley Prager (Italian version credited to Luciano Lelli). **P:** Sidney Pink. **W:** José Luis Bayonas, Luciano Lelli, Howard Berk (as José Navarro). **C:** Antonio Macasoli. **M:** Nico Fidenco. **S:** Tom Bosley, Guy Madison, Sandra Milo, Riccardo Garrone, José María Caffarel, Federico Boido (as Rick Boyd).

Big Gundown, The (IT-SP)
La resa dei conti; El halcon y la presa
D: Sergio Sollima. **P:** Alberto Grimaldi. **W:** Franco Solinas, Fernando Morandi, Sergio Donati, Sergio Sollima. **C:** Carlo Carlini. **M:** Ennio Morricone. **S:** Lee Van Cleef, Tomas Milian, Walter Barnes, Gérard Herter, Nieves Navarro (as Susan Scott), Angel del Pozo, Fernando Sancho, Tom Felleghy, Nello Pazzafini, Luís Barboo, Roberto Camardiel, José Torres, Frank Braña, Benito Stefanelli, Antonio Molino Rojo, Antonio Casas, Romano Puppo, Barta Barry, Spartaco Conversi, Lorenzo Robledo.

Born to Kill (IT)
Nato per uccidere
D: Antonio Mollica (as Tony Mulligan). **P:** Antonio Mollica. **W:** Antonio Mollica. **C:** Oberdan Troiani. **M:** Felice Di Stefano. **S:** Gordon Mitchell, Femi Benussi, Aldo Berti, Tom Felleghy, Franco Gula.

Buckaroo (IT)
Buckaroo (Il Winchester che non perdona); The Winchester Does Not Forgive
D: Adelchi Bianchi. **P:** Magister Film. **W:** Antonio Romano, Leo Romano Scucciuglia. **C:** Oberdan Troiani. **M:** Coriolano Gori. **S:** Dean Reed, Monika Brugger, Livio Lorenzon, Ugo Sasso, Omero Gargano.

Chingachgook, the Great Snake (GDR)
Chingachgook, die Grosse Schlange
D: Richard Groschopp. **P:** DEFA. **W:** James Fenimore Cooper (novel), Wolfgang Ebeling, Richard Groschopp. **C:** Otto Hanisch. **M:** Wilhelm Neef. **S:** Gojko Mitic, Rolf Römer, Helmut Schreiber, Jürgen Frohriep, Lilo Grahn.

Christmas Kid, The (SP-US)
Joe Navidad
D: Sidney Pink. **P:** Sidney Pink. **W:** Jim Henaghan, Rodrigo Rivero. **C:** Manuel Hernández Sanjuán. **M:** Fernando Garcia Morcillo. **S:** Jeffrey Hunter, Louis Hayward, Gustavo Rojo, Perla Cristal, Luis Prendes.

Cjamango (IT)
D: Edoardo Mulargia (as Edward G. Muller). **P:** Cio Film. **W:** Vincenzo Musolino. **C:** Vitaliano Natalucci. **M:** Felice Di Stefano. **S:** Ivan Rassimov (as Sean Todd), Mickey Hargitay, Hélène Chanel, Livio Lorenzon, Ignazio Spalla (as Pedro Sanchez), Piero Lulli, Federico Boido (as Rick Boyd), Dino Strano, Giusva Fioravanti.

Clint the Stranger (SP-IT-GER)
Clint, el solitario; Clint il solitario; Tal der Hoffnung; Ein Mann Kommt zuruck; Clint the Nevada Loner
D: Alfonso Balcázar. **P:** Valentin Sallent, Alfonso Balcázar, Guido M. Gatti, Renato Gualino. **W:** José Antonio de la Loma, Alfonso Balcázar, Helmut Harun. **C:** Victor Monreal. **M:** Nora Orlandi. **S:** George Martin, Marianne Koch, Paolo Gozlino, Gerhard Riedman, Fernando Sancho, Walter Barnes, Luís Barboo.

Cold Killer, The (IT)
Uccideva a freddo
D: Guido Celano (as William First). **P:** Guido Celano (uncredited). **W:** W. Charlie Reed (story), George W. Ballor, Ambrogio Molteni, Amedeo Trilli. **C:** Angelo Baistrocchi. **M:** John Ireson, Weyman Parham. **S:** Bruno Piergentili (as Dan Harrison), Philippe March, Luigi Barbieri, Rita Ferrel, Lillian Faber.

Colt in the Fist of the Devil, A (IT)
Una colt in pugno al diavolo; The Devil Was an Angel
D: Sergio Bergonzelli (some sources also credit Graziano Fabiani). **P:** Sergio Bergonzelli. **W:** Sergio Bergonzelli, Ambrogio Molteni. **C:** Aldo Greci. **M:** Giampiero Reverberi. **S:** Bob Henry, Marisa Solinas, George Wang, Lucretia Love, Gerardo Rossi, Luciano Catenacci.

Custer of the West (US-SP)
La ùltima aventura del General Custer
D: Robert Siodmak. **P:** Philip Yordan, Louis Dolivet. **W:** Bernard Gordon, Julian Zimet. **C:** Cecilio Paniagua. **M:** Bernardo Segall. **S:** Robert Shaw, Mary Ure, Ty Hardin, Jeffrey Hunter, Lawrence Tierney, Barta Barry.

Day of Anger (IT-GER)
I giorni dell'ira; Der Tod ritt dienstags; Days of Wrath; Gunlaw
D: Tonino Valerii. **P:** Enrico Chroscicki, Alfonso Sansone. **W:** Ron Barker (novel), Ernesto Gastaldi, Renzo Genta, Tonino Valerii. **C:** Enzo Serafin. **M:** Riz Ortolani. **S:** Lee Van Cleef, Giuliano Gemma, Walter Rilla, Ennio Balbo, Andrea Bosic, Christa Linder, José Calvo, Benito Stefanelli, Al Mulock, Romano Puppo, Ricardo Palacios.

Days of Violence (IT)
I giorni della violenza; The Dirty Pistolero
D: Alfonso Brescia (as Al Bradley). **P:** Bruno Turchetto. **W:** Mario Amendola, Antonio Boccacci, Gian Luigi Buzzi, Paolo Lombardo. **C:** Fausto Rossi. **M:** Bruno Nicolai. **S:** Peter Lee Lawrence, Rosalba Neri, Beba Loncar, Luigi Vannucchi, Nello Pazzafini, Andrea Bosic, Romano Puppo.

Death, at Owell Rock (IT)
La morte non conta i dollars
D: Riccardo Freda (as George Lincoln). **P:** Enrico Cogliati Dezza (uncredited). **W:** Riccardo Freda, Giuseppe Masini. **C:** Gábor Pogány. **M:** Nora Orlandi, Robby Poitevin. **S:** Mark Damon, Stephen Forsyth, Luciano Pigozzi (as Alan Collins), Luciana Gilli, Pamela Tudor, Nello Pazzafini, Spartaco Conversi, Dino Strano, Ignazio Spalla (as Pedro Sanchez).

Death Rides a Horse (IT)
Da uomo a uomo
D: Giulio Petroni. **P:** Alfonso Sansone, Enrico Chroscicki. **W:** Luciano Vincenzoni. **C:** Carlo Carlini. **M:** Ennio Morricone. **S:** Lee Van Cleef, John Phillip Law, Luigi Pistilli, Mario Brega, Anthony Dawson, José Torres, Guglielmo Spoletini (as William Bogart), Bruno Corazzari, Romano Puppo, José Terrón, Remo Capitani.

Death Rides Along (IT)
Con lui cavalca la morte; Death Rides Alone
D: Giuseppe Vari (as Joseph Warren). **P:** Franco Palombi, Gabriele Silvestri, Enzo Bulgarelli. **W:** Fernando Di Leo, Adriano Baracco, Augusto Caminito. **C:** Amerigo Gengarelli. **M:** Coriolano Gori. **S:** Mike Marshall, Giuseppe Addobbati, Carole André, Andrea Bosic, Hélène Chanel, Claudio Undari (as Robert Hundar), Peter Martell.

Death Sentence (IT)
Sentenza di morte
D: Mario Lanfranchi. **P:** B.L. Vision. **W:** Mario Lanfranchi. **C:** Antonio Secchi. **M:** Gianni Ferrio. **S:** Robin Clarke, Tomas Milian, Richard Conte, Enrico Maria Salerno, Adolfo Celi, Luciano Rossi.

Death Walks in Laredo (IT-ALG)
Tre pistole contro Cesare; Trois pistolets contre César; Three Golden Boys
D: Enzo Peri. **P:** Dino De Laurentiis, Casbah. **W:** Carmine Bologna, Piero Regnoli, Enzo Peri. **C:** Otello Martelli. **M:** Marcello Giombini. **S:** Thomas Hunter, James Shigeta, Nadir Moretti, Enrico Maria Salerno, Delia Boccardo, Femi Benussi.

Dirty Outlaws, The (IT)
El desperado; The Big Rip-Off
D: Franco Rossetti. **P:** Ugo Guerra, Elio Scardamaglia. **W:** Ugo Guerra, Franco Rossetti, Vincenzo Cerami. **C:** Angelo Filippini. **M:** Gianni Ferrio. **S:** Andrea Giordana (as Chip Corman), Rosemarie Dexter, Franco Giornelli, Dana Ghia, Aldo Berti, John Bartha, Piero Lulli, Dino Strano, Andrea Scotti.

Django, Kill! (If You Live Shoot!) (IT-SP)
Se sei vivo spara; Oro maldito; Oro Hondo
D: Giulio Questi. **P:** G.I.A. Cinematografica, Hispamer Film. **W:** Franco Arcalli, Giulio Questi, María del Carmen Martínez Román (credited for co-production purposes). **C:** Franco Delli Colli. **M:** Ivan Vandor. **S:** Tomas Milian, Piero Lulli, Roberto Camardiel, Paco Sanz, Milo Quesada, Marilù Tolo, Ray Lovelock, Patrizia Valturri, Frank Braña.

Euro-Western Filmography

Django Kills Softly (IT-FR)
Bill il taciturno; Django, le taciturne; Django Kills Silently
D: Massimo Pupillo (as Max Hunter). **P:** Jacques Leitienne. **W:** Renato Polselli, Lina Caterini, Paul Farjon, Marcello Malvestito. **C:** Mario Parapetti. **M:** Berto Pisano. **S:** Luigi Montefiori (as George Eastman), Luciano Rossi (as Edwin G. Ross), Liana Orfei, Mimmo Maggio, Peter Hellmann, Federico Boido (as Rick Boyd), Spartaco Conversi.

Django, the Last Killer (IT)
L'ultimo killer
D: Giuseppe Vari (as Joseph Warren). **P:** Juppiter Generale, Garfilm, Rofilm, Castor Film. **W:** Victor Catena, Arthur Frank, Augusto Caminito, Augusto Finocchi. **C:** Angelo Filippini. **M:** Roberto Pregadio. **S:** Luigi Montefiori (as George Eastman), Anthony Ghidra, Dana Ghia, Mirko Ellis, Gianni Medici.

Don't Wait, Django, Shoot! (IT)
Non aspettare, Django, spara
D: Edoardo Mulargia (as Edward G. Muller). **P:** Vincenzo Musolino. **W:** Vincenzo Musolino. **C:** Vitaliano Natalucci. **M:** Felice Di Stefano. **S:** Ivan Rassimov (as Sean Todd), Ignazio Spalla (as Pedro Sanchez), Rada Rassimov, Gino Buzzanca, Marisa Traversi, Franco Pesce, Dino Strano.

Dynamite Joe (IT-SP)
Joe l'implacabile; Dinamita Joe
D: Antonio Margheriti (as Anthony Dawson). **P:** Cleto Fontini. **W:** Maria del Carmen Martínez Román. **C:** Manuel Merino. **M:** Carlo Savina. **S:** Rik Van Nutter, Halina Zalewska, Mercedes Castro, Renato Baldini, Santiago Rivero, Barta Barry, Ricardo Palacios.

Face to Face (IT-SP)
Faccia a faccia; Cara a cara
D: Sergio Sollima. **P:** Alberto Grimaldi. **W:** Sergio Sollima, Sergio Donati (Spanish version also credits Fernando Morandi, Tulio Demicheli). **C:** Emilio Foriscot, Rafael Pacheco. **M:** Ennio Morricone. **S:** Tomas Milian, Gian Maria Volonté, William Berger, Jolanda Modio, Gianni Rizzo, Angel del Pozo, Nello Pazzafini, Aldo Sambrell, Carole André, Linda Veras, Federico Boido (as Rick Boyd), Paco Sanz, Frank Braña, Antonio Casas, Lorenzo Robledo, José Torres, Antonio Gradoli, Goffredo Unger, Remo Capitani.

Fifteen Scaffolds for a Killer (IT-SP)
15 forche per un assassino; Quince horcas para un asesino; The Dirty Fifteen
D: Nunzio Malasomma. **P:** Luis Vazquez, Centauro Films. **W:** Mario Di Nardo, J. Luis Bayonas. **C:** Stelvio Massi. **M:** Francesco De Masi. **S:** Craig Hill, Susy Andersen, George Martin, Eleonora Brown, Renato Rossini, Frank Braña, Aldo Berti, Andrea Bosic, José Canalejas, Antonio Casas, José Manuel Martín, Antonio Molino Rojo, Ricardo Palacios, Aldo Sambrell.

For a Dollar in the Teeth (IT-US)
Un dollaro tra i denti; A Dollar Between the Teeth; A Stranger in Town
D: Luigi Vanzi (as Vance Lewis). **P:** Roberto Infascelli, Massimo Gualdi. **W:** Giuseppe Mangione (as Jone Mang), Warren Garfield. **C:** Marcello Masciocchi. **M:** Benedetto Ghiglia. **S:** Tony Anthony, Frank Wolff, Jolanda Modio, Gia Sandri, Aldo Berti, Raf Baldassarre.

For $100,000 Per Killing (IT)
Per 100.000 dollari t'ammazzo; Vengeance Is Mine; A Taste of Death; Django der Bastard
D: Giovanni Fago (as Sidney Lean). **P:** Mino Loy, Luciano Martino. **W:** Sergio Martino, Ernesto Gastaldi. **C:** Federico Zanni. **M:** Nora Orlandi. **S:** Gianni Garko, Claudio Camaso, Claudie Lange, Piero Lulli, Fernando Sancho, Bruno Corazzari, Carlo Gaddi, Andrea Scotti.

Fury of Johnny Kid (IT-SP)
Dove si spara di più; La furia de Johnny Kidd (sic); Ride for a Massacre
D: Gianni Puccini. **P:** Francesco Merli. **W:** María del Carmen Martínez Román, Bruno Baratti. **C:** Mario Montuori. **M:** Gino Peguri. **S:** Peter Lee Lawrence (as Arthur Grant), Cristina Galbo, Maria Cuadra, Andrés Mejuto, Piero Lulli, Peter Martell, Ángel Álvarez, Luciano Catenacci (as Lewis Lawrence), Luis Induni.

Gentleman Killer (IT-SP)
Gentleman Jo... uccidi; Gentleman Jo
D: Giorgio Stegani (as George Finley). **P:** Alvaro Mancori, Anna Maria Chretien. **W:** Jaime Jesús Balcázar, Melchiade Coletti. **C:** Francisco Marín. **M:** Bruno Nicolai. **S:** Anthony Steffen, Eduardo Fajardo, Silvia Solar, Mariano Vidal Molina, Anna Orso, Benito Stefanelli, Luís Barboo.

God Forgives... I Don't! (IT-SP)
Dio perdona... io no!; Dios perdona, yo no; Blood River
D: Giuseppe Colizzi. **P:** Enzo D'Ambrosio. **W:** Giuseppe Colizzi. **C:** Alfio Contini. **M:** Carlo Rustichelli (credited to Angel Oliver Pina). **S:** Terence Hill, Bud Spencer, Frank Wolff, Gina Rovere, José Manuel Martín, Frank Braña, Luís Barboo, José Canalejas, Tito García, Remo Capitani, Paco Sanz, José Terrón.

Greatest Robbery in the West, The (IT)
La più grande rapina nel West
D: Maurizio Lucidi. **P:** Franco Cittadini, Stenio Fiorentini. **W:** Augusto Finocchi, Augusto Caminito. **C:** Riccardo Pallottini. **M:** Luis Enríquez Bacalov. **S:** George Hilton, Hunt Powers, Walter Barnes, Erika Blanc, Mario Brega, Salvatore Borgese, Federico Boido (as Rick Boyd), Luciano Catenacci, Tom Felleghy, Luciano Rossi, Jeff Cameron, Bruno Corazzari.

Handsome, the Ugly and the Stupid, The (IT-GER)
Il bello, il brutto, il cretino
D: Giovanni Grimaldi. **P:** Gino Mordini. **W:** Giovanni Grimaldi. **C:** Aldo Giordani. **M:** Coriolano Gori. **S:** Franco Franchi, Ciccio Ingrassia, Mimmo Palmara (as Dick Palmer), Lothar Gunther, Brigitte Petry, Pietro Ceccarelli.

Hate for Hate (IT)
Odio per odio
D: Domenico Paolella (some sources also credit Pedro Luis Ramírez). **P:** Italo Zingarelli. **W:** Mario Amendola, Bruno Corbucci, Fernando Di Leo, Domenico Paolella. **C:** Giovanni Bergamini, Alejandro Ulloa. **M:** Willy Brezza. **S:** Antonio Sabato, John Ireland, Mirko Ellis, Nadia Marconi, Gloria Milland, Fernando Sancho.

Hellbenders, The (IT-SP)
I crudeli; Los despiadados
D: Sergio Corbucci. **P:** Albert Band. **W:** Virgil C. Gerlach, Ugo Liberatore, José Gutiérrez Maesso (uncredited), Albert Band, Louis Garfinkle. **C:** Enzo Barboni. **M:** Ennio Morricone (as Leo Nichols). **S:** Joseph Cotten, Norma Bengell, Julián Mateos, Al Mulock, Aldo Sambrell, Gino Pernice, Ángel Aranda, María Martín, José Canalejas, Enio Girolami, Benito Stefanelli.

John the Bastard (IT)
John il bastardo; His Name Was Johnny
D: Armando Crispino. **P:** Francesco and Vincenzo Genesi. **W:** Sauro Scavolini, Lucio Manlio Battistrada, Armando Crispino. **C:** Sante Achilli. **M:** Nico Fidenco. **S:** John Richardson, Claudio Camaso, Martine Beswick, Claudio Gora, Gordon Mitchell, Furio Meniconi, Glauco Onorato.

Kill and Pray (IT-GER)
Requiescant; Mögen sie in Frieden ruhen; Let Them Rest
D: Carlo Lizzani. **P:** Carlo Lizzani, Tefi Film Produzione, Produzione Mancori Chretien. **W:** Renato Izzo, Franco Bucceri, Adriano Bolzoni, Lucio Manlio Battistrada, Armando Crispino, Karl-Heinz Vogelmann. **C:** Sandro Mancori. **M:** Riz Ortolani. **S:** Lou Castel, Mark Damon, Pier Paolo Pasolini, Barbara Frey, Rossana Martini, Spartaco Conversi, Pietro Ceccarelli.

Kill the Wicked (IT-SP)
Dio non paga il Sabato; Il prezo del oro; God Does Not Pay on Saturday; Kill the Wickeds (sic)
D: Tanio Boccia (as Amerigo Anton). **P:** Danny Film, RK Cinematografica. **W:** Camillo Boccia, Mino Roli. **C:** Giuseppe Aquari. **M:** Angelo Francesco Lavagnino. **S:** Larry Ward, Robert Mark, Furio Meniconi, Massimo Righi, Vivi Gioi, Benito Stefanelli.

Killer Kid (IT)
D: Leopoldo Savona. **P:** GV Cinematografica. **W:** Sergio Garrone, Ottavio Poggi, Leopoldo Savona. **C:** Sandro Mancori. **M:** Berto Pisano. **S:** Anthony Steffen, Luisa Baratto (as Liz Barrett), Fernando Sancho, Giovanni Cianfriglia (as Ken Wood), Nelson Rubien, Tom Felleghy.

Kitosch, the Man Who Came from the North (SP-IT)
Frontera al Sur; Kitosch, l'uomo che veniva dal nord
D: José Luis Merino (as Joseph Marvin). **P:** Pacific, Atlantida. **W:** Fulvio Gicca Palli, José Luis Merino. **C:** Fausto Rossi. **M:** Joseph Kosma, Angelo Francesco Lavagnino. **S:** George Hilton, Krista Nell, Piero Lulli, Enrique Avila, Ricardo Palacios, Luís Barboo.

Last of the Badmen (IT)
Il tempo degli avvoltoi; Time of Vultures
D: Nando Cicero. **P:** Vico Pavoni. **W:** Fulvio Gicca Palli. **C:** Fausto Rossi. **M:** Piero Umiliani. **S:** George Hilton, Frank Wolff, Pamela Tudor, Eduardo Fajardo, Franco Balducci, Femi Benussi, John Bartha, Guglielmo Spoletini (as William Bogart).

Lola Colt (IT)
Lola Baby; Black Tigress
D: Siro Marcellini. **P:** Aldo Pace. **W:** Luigi Angelo, Lamberto Antonelli, Siro Marcellini. **C:** Giuseppe La Torre. **M:** Ubaldo Continiello. **S:** Lola Falana, Peter Martell, Erna Schürer, Dada Gallotti, Tom Felleghy, Andrea Scotti.

Long Days of Vengeance (IT-SP)
I lunghi giorni della vendetta (Faccia d'angelo); Los largos días de la venganza; The Deadliest Gunfight (Ted Barnett)
D: Florestano Vancini (as Stan Vance). **P:** PCM Produzione, PC Mingyar. **W:** Mahnahen Velasco, Augusto Caminito, Fernando Di Leo. **C:** Francisco Marín. **M:** Armando Trovajoli. **AD:** Fernando Di Leo. **S:** Giuliano Gemma, Francisco Rabal, Gabriella Giorgelli, Conrado San Martín, Franco Cobianchi, Nieves Navarro, Pajarito.

Magnificent Texan, The (IT-SP)
Il magnifico texano; Diez horcas para un pistolero
D: Luigi Capuano (as Lewis King). **P:** Ferdinando Felicioni. **W:** Arpad De Riso, Luigi Capuano, Manuel Martínez Remís. **C:** Oberdan Trojani (credited to Pablo Ripoll). **M:** Francesco De Masi. **S:** Glenn Saxson, Massimo Serato, Beni Deus, Barbara Loy, Gloria Osuña, Luis Induni.

Man and a Colt, A (SP-IT)
Un hombre y un Colt; Dakota Joe; Un uomo e una colt
D: Tulio Demicheli. **P:** Tulio Demicheli, PEA. **W:** Tulio Demicheli, Nino Stresa. **C:** Emilio Foriscot. **M:** Carlo Rustichelli (credited to Angel Oliver Pina). **S:** Claudio Undari (as Robert Hundar), Fernando Sancho, Mirko Ellis, Gloria Milland, Marta Reves, Raf Baldassarre, José Canalejas.

Man, Pride and Vengeance (IT-GER)
L'uomo, l'orgoglio, la vendetta; Mit Django kam der Tod
D: Luigi Bazzoni. **P:** Regal Film, Fono Roma, Constantin. **W:** Luigi Bazzoni, Suso Cecchi d'Amico. **C:** Camillo Bazzoni. **M:** Carlo Rustichelli. **S:** Franco Nero, Klaus Kinski, Tina Aumont, Guido Lollobrigida (as Lee Burton), Franco Ressel, José Manuel Martín, Alberto Dell'Acqua.

Man Who Killed Billy the Kid, The (SP-IT)
El hombre que mató a Billy el Niño; …E divenne il piu spietato bandito del sud; A Few Bullets More; L'homme qui a tué Billy the Kid
D: Julio Buchs. **P:** Aitor, Kinesis. **W:** Julio Buchs, José Mallorquí, Federico de Urrutia. **C:** Miguel Fernández Mila. **M:** Gianni Ferrio. **S:** Peter Lee Lawrence, Fausto Tozzi, Dyanik Zurakowska (as Diane Zura), Gloria Milland, Carlos Casaravilla, Frank Braña, Luis Induni, Luís Barboo, Antonio Molino Rojo, Paco Sanz, Barta Barry, José Canalejas.

Pecos Cleans Up (IT)
Pecos è qui: prega e muori
D: Maurizio Lucidi. **P:** Franco Palombi, Gabriele Silvestri. **W:** Fernando Di Leo, Adriano Bolzoni, Augusto Caminito. **C:** Franco Villa. **M:** Coriolano Gori. **S:** Robert Woods, Luciana Gilli, Erno Crisa, Ignazio Spalla (as Pedro Sanchez), Carlo Gaddi.

Poker with Pistols (IT)
Un poker di pistole
D: Giuseppe Vari (as Joseph Warren). **P:** Gabriele Silvestri, Franco Palombi. **W:** Augusto Caminito, Fernando Di Leo. **C:** Angelo Lotti. **M:** Coriolano Gori. **AD:** Demofilo Fidani. **S:** George Hilton, Luigi Montefiori (as George Eastman), Annabella Incontrera, Mimmo Palmara (as Dick Palmer), José Torres.

Rattler Kid (SP-IT)
Un hombre vino a matar; L'uomo venuto per uccidere
D: León Klimovsky. **P:** Luigi Mondello. **W:** Eduardo Manzanos Brochero, Odoardo Fiory, Luigi Mondello. **C:** Julio Ortas. **M:** Francesco De Masi. **S:** Richard Wyler, Brad Harris, Guglielmo Spoletini (as William Spolt), Femi Benussi, Jesús Puente, Luís Barboo, Frank Braña, Lucio De Santis, Luis Induni.

Red Blood, Yellow Gold (IT-SP)
Professionisti per un massacro; Los profesionales de la muerte
D: Nando Cicero. **P:** Oreste Coltellacci. **W:** Jaime Jesús Balcázar, José Antonio de la Loma, Vincenzo Dell'Aquila, Roberto Gianviti. **C:** Francisco Marín. **M:** Carlo Pes. **S:** George Hilton, Edd Byrnes, George Martin, Gérard Herter, Mónica Randall, José Bódalo.

Rick and John, Conquerors of the West (IT)
Ric e Gian alla conquista del West
D: Osvaldo Civirani. **P:** Osvaldo Civirani. **W:** Tito Carpi, Osvaldo Civirani, Alessandro Ferrau. **C:** Osvaldo Civirani. **M:** Piero Umiliani. **S:** Riccardo Miniggio, Gianfabio Bosco, Craig Hill, Francesco Mulé, Tiberio Murgia.

Rita of the West (IT)
Little Rita nel West; Crazy Westerners
D: Ferdinando Baldi. **P:** Manolo Bolognini. **W:** Ferdinando Baldi, Franco Rossetti. **C:** Enzo Barboni. **M:** Robby Poitevin. **S:** Rita Pavone, Terence Hill, Lucio Dalla, Ferrucio Ricordi, Gordon Mitchell, Livio Lorenzon, Gino Pernice, Fernando Sancho, Romano Puppo.

Euro-Western Filmography

Seven Pistols for a Massacre (IT-SP)
Sette pistole per un massacro; Adiós, hombre; Con el corazón en la garganta
D: Mario Caiano. **P:** United Pictures, Copercines. **W:** Eduardo Manzanos Brochero, Mario Caiano. **C:** Julio Ortas. **M:** Francesco De Masi. **S:** Craig Hill, Piero Lulli, Eduardo Fajardo, Giulia Rubini, Nello Pazzafini, Roberto Camardiel, Spartaco Conversi, Nazzareno Zamperla.

Seven Winchesters for a Massacre (IT)
Sette Winchester per un massacro; Payment in Blood; The Final Defeat; Blake's Marauders
D: Enzo G. Castellari (as E.G. Rowland). **P:** Circus, Fono Roma. **W:** Tito Carpi, Enzo G. Castellari. **C:** Aldo Pennelli. **M:** Francesco De Masi. **S:** Edd Byrnes, Guy Madison, Enio Girolami (as Thomas Moore), Luisa Baratto, Attilio Severini, Federico Boido (as Rick Boyd).

Shoot First, Laugh Last (IT-GER)
Un uomo, un cavallo, una pistola; Western Jack; The Stranger Returns
D: Luigi Vanzi (as Vance Lewis). **P:** Massimo Gualdi, Roberto Infascelli. **W:** Roberto Infascelli, Giuseppe Mangione, Tony Anthony (uncredited). **C:** Marcello Masciocchi. **M:** Stelvio Cipriani. **S:** Tony Anthony, Daniele Vargas, Marco Guglielmi, Jill Banner, Dan Vadis, Ettore Manni, Raf Baldassarre.

Son of Django (IT)
Il figlio di Django; Vengeance Is a Colt 45
D: Osvaldo Civirani. **P:** Osvaldo Civirani. **W:** Alessandro Ferraù, Tito Carpi, Osvaldo Civirani. **C:** Osvaldo Civirani. **M:** Piero Umiliani. **S:** Guy Madison, Gabriele Tinti, Ingrid Schoeller, Daniele Vargas, Ignazio Spalla (as Pedro Sanchez), John Bartha, Lucio De Santis, Luciano Rossi, Andrea Scotti.

$10,000 Blood Money (IT)
10.000 dollari per un massacro; $10,000 for a Massacre
D: Romolo Guerrieri. **P:** Mino Loy, Luciano Martino. **W:** Franco Fogagnolo, Ernesto Gastaldi, Luciano Martino, Sauro Scavolini. **C:** Federico Zanni. **M:** Nora Orlandi. **S:** Gianni Garko (as Gary Hudson), Loredana Nusciak, Claudio Camaso, Fernando Sancho, Adriana Ambesi.

32 Caliber Killer (IT)
Killer calibro 32
D: Alfonso Brescia (as Al Bradley). **P:** Explorer Film 58. **W:** Enzo Gicca. **C:** Fulvio Testi. **M:** Robby Poitevin. **S:** Peter Lee Lawrence, Agnès Spaak, Alberto Dell'Acqua (as Cole Kitosch), Lucy Scay, Nello Pazzafini (as Red Carter), John Bartha, Andrea Bosic (as Andrew Bosich).

Treasure of Pancho Villa (SP-US)
Los siete de Pancho Villa; Seven for Pancho Villa
D: José Maria Elorrieta. **P:** Cinemagic. **W:** Manuel Sebares. **C:** Alfonso Nieva. **M:** Federico Contreras. **S:** John Ericson, Nuria Torray, Gustavo Rojo, Mara Cruz, Ricardo Palacios.

Turn… I'll Kill You! (IT-SP)
Voltati… ti uccido; Winchester Bill; If One Is Born a Swine
D: Alfonso Brescia (as Al Bradley). **P:** Rhodes International, Hispamer Film. **W:** María del Carmen Martínez Román, Renato Polselli. **C:** Alfonso Nieva. **M:** Uncredited. **S:** Richard Wyler, Fernando Sancho, Eleonora Bianchi, Conrado San Martín, Ric Burton Jr., Spartaco Conversi, Luis Induni, Franco Pesce.

$20,000 on Number Seven (IT)
20.000 dollari sul 7
D: Alberto Cardone (as Albert Cardiff). **P:** JE Cinematografica. **W:** Roberto Miali, Gino Santini, Alberto Cardone. **C:** Gino Santini. **M:** Franco Reitano, Gianni Sanjust. **S:** Roberto Miali (as Jerry Wilson), Aurora Bautista, Adriano Micantoni, Spartaco Conversi, Teodoro Corrà.

Two Crosses at Danger Pass (SP-IT)
Dos cruces en Danger Pass; Due croci a Danger Pass
D: Rafael Romero Marchent. **P:** United Pictures, Copercines. **W:** Enzo Battaglia, Eduardo Manzanos Brochero. **C:** Sergio Martinelli. **M:** Francesco De Masi. **S:** Peter Martell, Mario Novelli, Nuccia Cardinali, Luis Gaspar, Armando Calvo, Cris Huerta, Jesús Puente.

Two Faces of the Dollar (IT-FR)
Le due facce del dollaro; Poker d'as pour Django; Two Sides of the Dollar
D: Roberto Bianchi Montero. **P:** Francesco Giorgi, Antonio Lucatelli. **W:** Alberto Silvestri, Franco Verucci. **C:** Stelvio Massi. **M:** Giosofat and Mario Capuano. **AD:** Giuliano Carnimeo. **S:** Maurice Poli (as Monty Greenwood), Jacques Herlin, Gabriella Giorgelli, Gérard Herter, Andrea Bosic, Spartaco Conversi, Tom Felleghy, Andrea Scotti.

Two R-R-Ringos from Texas (IT)
Due Rrringos nel Texas
D: Marino Girolami. **P:** Francesco Orefici. **W:** Amadeo Sollazzo, Roberto Gianviti, Marino Girolami. **C:** Mario Fioretti. **M:** Carlo Savina. **S:** Franco Franchi, Ciccio Ingrassia, Enio Girolami, Hélène Chanel, Gloria Paul, Livio Lorenzon.

Up the MacGregors (IT-SP)
7 donne per I MacGregor; Siete mujeres para los MacGregor; 7 Women for the MacGregors
D: Franco Giraldi. **P:** Dario Sabatello. **W:** Fernando Di Leo (as Fernand Lion), Enzo Dell'Aquila (as Vincent Eagle), Paolo Levi, José Maria Rodriguez, Franco Giraldi. **C:** Alejandro Ulloa. **M:** Ennio Morricone. **S:** David Bailey, Agata Flori, Leo Anchóriz, George Rigaud, Roberto Camardiel, Giovanni Scarciofolo (as Jeff Cameron), Alberto Dell'Acqua, Nazzareno Zamperla, Tito García, Victor Israel.

Villa's Guerillas (SP-MEX)
La guerrillera de Villa
D: Miguel Morayta. **P:** Césareo González Rodriguez, Oro Films. **W:** Fernando Galiana, Miguel Morayta. **C:** Alex Phillips. **M:** Manuel Esperón. **S:** Carmen Sevilla, Vicente Parra, Julio Alemán, José Elias Moreno, José 'Ferrusquilla' Espinosa.

Viva Django (IT)
Preparati la bara!; Get the Coffin Ready
D: Ferdinando Baldi. **P:** BRC Produzione. **W:** Franco Rossetti, Ferdinando Baldi. **C:** Enzo Barboni. **M:** Gianfranco Reverberi. **S:** Terence Hill, Horst Frank, Luigi Montefiori (as George Eastman), José Torres, Pinuccio Ardia, Guido Lollobrigida (as Lee Burton), Spartaco Conversi, Lucio De Santis, Luciano Rossi, Andrea Scotti.

Wanted (IT)
D: Giorgio Ferroni (as Calvin Jackson Padget). **P:** Gianni Hecht Lucari. **W:** Augusto Finocchi, Massimiliano Capriccioli, Fernando Di Leo, Remigio Del Grosso. **C:** Antonio Secchi. **M:** Gianni Ferrio. **S:** Giuliano Gemma, Teresa Gimpera, Serge Marquand, Germán Cobos, Daniele Vargas, Alberto Dell'Acqua, Nello Pazzafini, Benito Stefanelli, Furio Meniconi.

Wanted Johnny Texas (IT)
D: Emimmo Salvi. **P:** Film-Kontor Italiana. **W:** Emimmo Salvi. **C:** Emilio Variano. **M:** Marcello Gigante. **S:** Willy Colombini (as James Newman), Fernando Sancho, Monika Brugger, Renato Rossini (as Howard Ross), Isarco Ravaioli, Rosalba Neri.

1968

Ace High (IT)
I quattro dell'Ave Maria; Revenge in El Paso
D: Giuseppe Colizzi. **P:** Bino Cicogna, Giuseppe Colizzi. **W:** Giuseppe Colizzi. **C:** Marcello Masciocchi. **M:** Carlo Rustichelli. **S:** Eli Wallach, Terence Hill, Bud Spencer, Brock Peters, Kevin McCarthy, Livio Lorenzon, Steffen Zacharias, Federico Boido (as Rick Boyd), Frank Braña, Bruno Corazzari, Remo Capitani, Antonio Molino Rojo.

And Now… Make Your Peace with God (IT)
Ed ora… raccomanda l'anima a Dio!; And Now Make Peace with God
D: Demofilo Fidani (as Miles Deem). **P:** Demofilo Fidani, Corrado Patara. **W:** Demofilo Fidani, Mila Vitelli. **C:** Franco Villa. **M:** Vincenzo Tempera. **S:** Fardin, Giovanni Scarciofolo (as Jeff Cameron), Fabio Testi, Ettore Manni, Cristina Penz.

Belle Starr Story, The (IT)
Il mio corpo per un poker
D: Piero Cristofani, Lina Wertmüller (as Nathan Wich). **P:** Oscar Righini. **W:** Lina Wertmüller. **C:** Alessandro D'Eva. **M:** Charles Dumont. **S:** Elsa Martinelli, Robert Woods, Luigi Montefiori (as George Eastman), Francesca Righini, Bruno Piergentili (as Dan Harrison), Bruno Corazzari.

Between God, the Devil and a Winchester (IT-SP)
Anche nel West c'era una volta Dio; Entre Dios y el diablo
D: Marino Girolami (credited to Dario Silvestri). **P:** Circus Films, RM Films. **W:** Tito Carpi, Manuel Martínez Remís, Amedeo Sollazzo, Marino Girolami. **C:** Pablo Ripoll, Alberto Fusi. **M:** Carlo Savina. **S:** Gilbert Roland, Richard Harrison, Dominique Boschero, Enio Girolami, Folco Lulli, Roberto Camardiel, Raf Baldassarre, Luís Barboo.

Beyond the Law (IT-GER)
Al di là della legge; Die letzte Rechnung zahlst du selbst; The Good Die First
D: Giorgio Stegani. **P:** Alfonso Sansone, Enrico

Chroscicki. **W:** Lorenzo Sabatini (as Warren Kiefer), Fernando Di Leo, Mino Roli, Giorgio Stegani. **C:** Enzo Serafin. **M:** Riz Ortolani. **S:** Lee Van Cleef, Antonio Sabato, Bud Spencer, Gordon Mitchell, Lionel Stander, Salvatore Billa, Carlo Gaddi, Romano Puppo.

Black Jack (IT)
Black Joe
D: Gianfranco Baldanello. **P:** Fernando Franchi, Alexander Hakohen. **W:** Luigi Ambrosini, Gianfranco Baldanello, Augusto Finocchi, Mario Mattei. **C:** Mario Fioretti. **M:** Coriolano Gori. **S:** Robert Woods, Mimmo Palmara (as Dick Palmer), Rik Battaglia, Lucienne Bridou, Larry Dolgin, Goffredo Unger, Federico Chentrens.

Blood for Blood (IT)
Sangue chiama sangue; Blood Calls to Blood
D: Luigi Capuano. **P:** Felice Zappulla. **W:** Fulvio Pazziloro. **C:** Tino Santoni. **M:** Francesco De Masi. **S:** Germán Cobos, Fernando Sancho, Stephen Forsyth, Antonella Judica, Léa Nanni, Franco Fantasia.

Bury Them Deep (IT)
All'ultimo sangue
D: Paolo Moffa (as John Byrd). **P:** Ambrosiana. **W:** Vincenzo Dell'Aquila. **C:** Franco Villa. **M:** Nico Fidenco. **S:** Craig Hill, Ettore Manni, Giovanni Cianfriglia (as Ken Wood), José Greci, Francesco Santovetti, Lorenzo Robledo.

Chrysanthemums for a Bunch of Swine (IT)
Crisantemi per un branco di carogne
D: Sergio Pastore. **P:** SCAA. **W:** Gianni Manera, Sergio Pastore. **C:** Tino Santori. **M:** Piero Umiliani. **S:** Edmund Purdom, Gianni Manera, Marilena Possenti, Joseph Logan, Ivano Davoli, Livio Lorenzon.

Ciccio Forgives, I Don't! (IT)
Ciccio perdona... io no!
D: Marcello Ciorciolini. **P:** Italo Zingarelli. **W:** Marcello Ciorciolini, Amedeo Sollazzo. **C:** Alessandro D'Eva. **M:** Roberto Pregadio. **S:** Franco Franchi, Ciccio Ingrassia, Adriano Micantoni, Mario Maranzana, Rossella Bergamonti, Fernando Sancho.

Cowards Don't Pray (IT-SP)
I vigliacchi non pregano; El vengador del Sur; Taste of Vengeance
D: Mario Siciliano (as Marlon Sirko). **P:** Mario Siciliano. **W:** Eduardo Manzanos Brochero, Mario Siciliano, Dulio Chianetta, Ernesto Gastaldi. **C:** Gino Santini. **M:** Gianni Marchetti, Manuel Parada. **S:** Gianni Garko, Ivan Rassimov (as Sean Todd), Elisa Montés, Roberto Miali (as Jerry Wilson), Carla Calò, Luis Induni, Frank Braña, Luís Barboo, José Jaspe, Luciano Pigozzi, Lorenzo Robledo.

Dead for a Dollar (IT)
T'ammazzo!... Raccomandati a Dio; I'll Kill You, and Recommend You to God
D: Osvaldo Civirani. **P:** Osvaldo Civirani. **W:** Tito Carpi, Osvaldo Civirani, Luciano Gregoretti. **C:** Osvaldo Civirani. **M:** Angelo Francesco Lavagnino. **S:** George Hilton, Sandra Milo, John Ireland, Mimmo Palmara (as Dick Palmer), Gordon Mitchell, Franco Ressel, Andrea Scotti.

Dead Men Don't Count! (IT-SP)
I morti non si contano; ¿Quién grita venganza?; Cry for Revenge
D: Rafael Romero Marchent. **P:** Eduardo Manzanos Brochero. **W:** Marco Leto, Rafael Romero Marchent, Vittorio Salerno. **C:** Aldo Ricci, Franco Delli Colli. **M:** Marcello Giombini. **S:** Anthony Steffen, Mark Damon, Luis Induni, María Martín, Dianik Zurakowska, Raf Baldassarre, Luís Barboo, Barta Barry, Piero Lulli, Carlos Romero Marchent.

Execution (IT)
D: Domenico Paolella. **P:** Fernando Franchi. **W:** Domenico Paolella, Fernando Franchi, Giancarlo Zagni. **C:** Aldo Scavarda. **M:** Coriolano Gori. **S:** John Richardson, Mimmo Palmara (as Dick Palmer), Franco Giornelli, Piero Vida, Rita Klein, Lucio De Santis.

Fedra West (SP-IT)
Ballad of a Bounty Hunter; Io non perdono... uccido
D: Joaquín Romero Marchent. **P:** Trébol Films, United Pictures. **W:** Víctor Auz, José Luis Hernández Marcos, Joaquín Romero Marchent, Giovanni Simonelli, Bautista Lacasa. **C:** Fulvio Testi. **M:** Piero Piccioni. **S:** James Philbrook, Norma Bengell, Simón Andreu, María Silva, Emilio Gutiérrez Caba, Luis Induni, Carlos Romero Marchent.

Find a Place to Die (IT)
Joe! Cercati un posto per morire
D: Giuliano Carnimeo (as Anthony Ascot). **P:** Hugo Fregonese. **W:** Leonardo Benvenuti, Hugo Fregonese, Giuliano Carnimeo. **C:** Riccardo Pallottini. **M:** Gianni Ferrio. **S:** Jeffrey Hunter, Pascale Petit, Piero Lulli (as Peter Lull), Gianni Pallavicino, Adolfo Lastretti (as Peter Lastrett), Daniela Giordano, Nello Pazzafini, Pietro Ceccarelli.

Full House for the Devil (IT)
Uno di più all'inferno; One More to Hell
D: Giovanni Fago. **P:** Luciano Martino. **W:** Luciano Martino, Ernesto Gastaldi. **C:** Anton Giulio Borghesi. **M:** Nico Fidenco. **S:** George Hilton, Paolo Gozlino (as Paul Stevens), Claudie Lange, Gérard Herter, Paul Muller, Carlo Gaddi, Goffredo Unger, Spartaco Conversi (as Robert Anthony).

Garter Colt (IT)
Giarrettiera Colt
D: Gian Rocco. **P:** Columbus Cinematografica. **W:** Vittorio Pescatori, Gian Rocco, Giovanni Gigliozzi, Brunello Maffei. **C:** Gino Santini. **M:** Giovanni Fusco, Gianfranco Plenizio. **S:** Nicoletta Machiavelli, Claudio Camaso, Walter Barnes, Marisa Solinas, Yorgo Voyagis, Brandino Machiavelli.

Gatling Gun (IT-SP)
Quel caldo maledetto giorno di fuoco; Machine Gun Killers; La ametralladora
D: Paolo Bianchini. **P:** Fida Cinematografica. **W:** Paolo Bianchini, Claudio Failoni, Franco Calderoni, José Luis Merino. **C:** Francisco Marín. **M:** Piero Piccioni. **S:** Robert Woods, John Ireland, Ennio Balbo, Ida Galli (as Evelyn Stewart), Roberto Camardiel, Gérard Herter, George Rigaud, Tom Felleghy, Furio Meniconi, Rada Rassimov.

God Forgive... His Life Is Mine (IT)
Dio li crea... io li ammazzo!; God Made Them... I Kill Them
D: Paolo Bianchini. **P:** Gabriele Crisanti. **W:** Fernando Di Leo. **C:** Sergio D'Offizi. **M:** Marcello Gigante. **S:** Dean Reed, Peter Martell, Piero Lulli, Agnès Spaak, Linda Veras.

Great Silence, The (IT-FR)
Il grande silenzio; Le grand silence; The Big Silence
D: Sergio Corbucci. **P:** Adelphia. **W:** Sergio Corbucci, Vittoriano Petrilli, Mario Amendola, Bruno Corbucci. **C:** Silvano Ippoliti. **M:** Ennio Morricone. **S:** Jean-Louis Trintignant, Klaus Kinski, Vonetta McGee, Frank Wolff, Luigi Pistilli, Mario Brega, Marisa Merlini, Raf Baldassarre, Spartaco Conversi, Bruno Corazzari.

Gun for a Hundred Graves, A (IT-SP)
Una pistola per cento bare;; El sabor del odio; Una pistola para cien tumbas; A Pistol for 100 Coffins
D: Umberto Lenzi. **P:** Tritone, Cine España, Copercines. **W:** Eduardo Manzanos Brochero, Umberto Lenzi, Marco Leto, Vittorio Salerno. **C:** Alejandro Ulloa. **M:** Angelo Francesco Lavagnino. **S:** Peter Lee Lawrence, John Ireland, Piero Lulli, Eduardo Fajardo, Andrea Scotti, Franco Pesce, Raf Baldassarre, Frank Braña, Victor Israel, José Jaspe.

Gun Shy Piluk (IT)
Giurò... e li uccise ad uno ad uno
D: Guido Celano (as William First). **P:** Guido Celano. **W:** Guido Celano, Luigi Silori. **C:** Angelo Baistrocchi. **M:** Carlo Savina. **S:** Edmund Purdom, Peter Holden, Micaela Pignatelli, Luigi Barbieri, Bruno Piergentili (as Dan Harrison), Livio Lorenzon, Fabio Testi.

Guns for San Sebastian (FR-IT-MEX)
La bataille de San Sebastian; I cannoni di San Sebastian; Los cañones de San Sebastián
D: Henri Verneuil. **P:** Jacques Bar. **W:** William Barby Flaherty (novel), Serge Ganzi, Miguel Morayta, Ennio De Concini. **C:** Armand Thirard. **M:** Ennio Morricone. **S:** Anthony Quinn, Anjanette Comer, Charles Bronson, Sam Jaffe, Silvia Pinal.

Hate Your Neighbour (IT)
Odia il prossimo tuo; Hate Thy Neighbour
D: Ferdinando Baldi. **P:** Enrico Cogliati Dezza. **W:** Luigi Angelo, Ferdinando Baldi, Roberto Natale. **C:** Enzo Serafin. **M:** Robby Poitevin. **S:** Spiros Focás, Luigi Montefiori (as George Eastman), Nicoletta Machiavelli, Horst Frank, Roberto Risso, Franco Fantasia.

Hole Between the Eyes, A (IT)
Un buco in fronte; A Hole in the Forehead
D: Giuseppe Vari (as Joseph Warren). **P:** Francesco Giorgi, Antonio Lucatelli. **W:** Adriano Bolzoni. **C:** Amerigo Gengarelli. **M:** Roberto Pregadio. **S:** Anthony Ghidra, Rosy Zichel, Claudio Undari (as Robert Hundar), John Bryan, Giorgio Gargiullo.

I Want Him Dead (IT-SP)
Lo voglio morto; Lo quiero muerto
D: Paolo Bianchini. **P:** Enrico Vega, Corrado Ferlaino. **W:** Carlos Sarabia (Italian sources

also credit Adriano Bolzoni). **C:** Ricardo Andreu. **M:** Nico Fidenco. **S:** Craig Hill, Lea Massari, José Manuel Martín, Andrea Bosic, Licia Calderón, Federico Boido (as Rick Boyd), José Canalejas, Andrea Scotti, Frank Braña, José Terrón.

If You Meet Sartana, Pray for Your Death (IT-GER)
...Se incontri Sartana, prega per la tua morte; Sartana - Bete um Deinen Tod
D: Gianfranco Parolini (as Frank Kramer). **P:** Aldo Addobbati. **W:** Adolfo Cagnacci, Luigi De Santis, Gianfranco Parolini, Fabio Piccioni, Guido Zurli, Werner Hauff, Renato Izzo. **C:** Sandro Mancori. **M:** Piero Piccioni. **S:** Gianni Garko (as John Garko), Klaus Kinski, Fernando Sancho, William Berger, Sydney Chaplin, Gianni Rizzo, Andrea Scotti, Franco Pesce, Salvatore Borgese, Gianfranco Parolini.

If You Want to Live... Then Shoot! (IT)
Se vuoi vivere... spara!; The Outlaw Rider
D: Sergio Garrone (as Willy S. Regan). **P:** GV, Cinegar. **W:** Franco Cobianchi, Sergio Garrone. **C:** Sandro Mancori. **M:** Vassili Kojucharov, Elsio Mancuso. **S:** Ivan Rassimov (as Sean Todd), Giovanni Cianfriglia (as Ken Wood), Riccardo Garrone (as Rick Garrett), Isabella Savona, Tom Felleghy, John Bartha.

I'll Sell My Skin Dearly (IT)
Vendo cara la pelle; The Hangman's Tree
D: Ettore M. Fizzarotti. **P:** Carlo Valerio. **W:** Giovanni Simonelli, Ettore Maria Fizzarotti. **C:** Stelvio Massi. **M:** Enrico Ciacci, Marcello Marrocchi. **S:** Mike Marshall, Michèle Girardon, Valerio Bartoleschi, Dane Savours, Spartaco Conversi, Furio Meniconi.

Johnny Hamlet (IT)
Quella sporca storia nel West; The Wild and the Dirty
D: Enzo G. Castellari. **P:** Ugo Guerra, Elio Scardamaglia. **W:** Sergio Corbucci, Tito Carpi, Francesco Scardamaglia, Enzo G. Castellari. **C:** Angelo Filippini. **M:** Francesco De Masi. **S:** Andrea Giordana, Gilbert Roland, Horst Frank, Stefania Careddu, Françoise Prévost, Gabriella Grimaldi, Ignazio Spalla (as Pedro Sanchez), Enio Girolami, John Bartha.

Kill Them All and Come Back Alone (IT-SP)
Ammazzali tutti e torna solo; Mátalos y vuelve
D: Enzo G. Castellari. **P:** Edmondo Amati. **W:** Tito Carpi, Enzo G. Castellari, Joaquín Romero Marchent, Francesco Scardamaglia. **C:** Alejandro Ulloa. **M:** Francesco De Masi. **S:** Chuck Connors, Frank Wolff, Franco Citti, Leo Anchóriz, Giovanni Cianfriglia (as Ken Wood), Alberto Dell'Acqua, Antonio Molino Rojo, John Bartha, Furio Meniconi.

Killer Adios (IT-SP)
Killer, adios; Winchester, uno entre mil; Winchester Justice
D: Primo Zeglio. **P:** Concordfilm, Copercines. **W:** Mario Amendola, José Mallorquí, Primo Zeglio. **C:** Julio Ortas. **M:** Claudio Tallino. **S:** Peter Lee Lawrence, Marisa Solinas, Eduardo Fajardo, Armando Calvo, Rosalba Neri, Luís Barboo, Luis Induni, Nello Pazzafini, Victor Israel, José Jaspe.

Long Day of the Massacre, The (IT)
Il lungo giorno del massacro
D: Alberto Cardone (as Albert Cardiff). **P:** Armando Morandi. **W:** Alberto Cardone, Armando Morandi, Mario Gariazzo. **C:** Aldo Greci. **M:** Michele Lacerenza. **S:** Peter Martell, Glenn Saxson, Manuel Serrano, Luisa Baratto (as Liz Barrett), Daniela Giordano, Franco Fantasia.

Long Ride from Hell, A (IT)
Vivo per la tua morte; I Live for Your Death
D: Camillo Bazzoni (as Alex Burks). **P:** BRC Produzione. **W:** Gordon D. Shirreffs (novel), Roberto Natale, Steve Reeves. **C:** Enzo Barboni. **M:** Carlo Savina. **S:** Steve Reeves, Wayde Preston, Mimmo Palmara (as Dick Palmer), Silvana Venturelli, Nello Pazzafini (as Ted Carter), Guido Lollobrigida (as Lee Burton), Rosalba Neri, Spartaco Conversi, Bruno Corazzari, Aldo Sambrell, Franco Fantasia.

Lynching (IT)
Carogne si nasce; If One Is Born a Swine... Kill Him
D: Alfonso Brescia (as Al Bradley). **P:** Silpal, Pegaso Film. **W:** Augusto Finocchi, Aldo Lado. **C:** Fausto Rossi. **M:** Coriolano Gori. **S:** Glenn Saxson, Gordon Mitchell, Renato Baldini, Philippe Hersent, Fernando Sancho, Nello Pazzafini, John Bartha, Spartaco Conversi, Antonio Monselesan (as Tony Norton).

Man Called Amen, A (IT)
O tutto o niente
D: Guido Zurli. **P:** Aldo Ricci. **W:** Franco Bucceri, Renato Izzo, Guido Zurli. **C:** Guglielmo Mancori. **M:** Gino Peguri. **S:** George Ardisson, Isarco Ravaioli, Lorenza Guerrieri, Akim Tamiroff, Paolo Carlini.

May God Forgive You – I Won't (IT)
Chiedi perdono a Dio, non a me; May God Forgive You, Not Me
D: Vincenzo Musolino (as Glenn Vincent Davis). **P:** Vincenzo Musolino. **W:** Vincenzo Musolino. **C:** Mario Mancini. **M:** Felice Di Stefano. **S:** George Ardisson, Anthony Ghidra, Peter Martell, Tano Cimarosa, Ignazio Spalla (as Pedro Sanchez), Cristina Iosani, Franco Pesce, Dino Strano.

Minute to Pray, a Second to Die, A (IT)
Un minuto per pregare, un istante per morire; Dead or Alive; Outlaw Gun; Escondido
D: Franco Giraldi. **P:** Albert Band. **W:** Albert Band, Ugo Liberatore, Louis Garfinkle. **C:** Aiace Parolin. **M:** Carlo Rustichelli. **S:** Alex Cord, Arthur Kennedy, Robert Ryan, Nicoletta Machiavelli, Enzo Fiermonte, Mario Brega, John Bartha, José Canalejas, Spartaco Conversi, Aldo Sambrell, Alberto Dell'Acqua, Daniel Martín, José Manuel Martín, Antonio Molino Rojo, Lorenzo Robledo, Paco Sanz.

Moment to Kill, The (IT-GER)
Il momento di uccidere; Django - Ein Sarg voll Blut
D: Giuliano Carnimeo (as Anthony Ascott). **P:** Vico Pavoni. **W:** Tito Carpi, Enzo G. Castellari, Bruno Leder, Francesco Scardamaglia. **C:** Stelvio Massi. **M:** Francesco De Masi. **S:** George Hilton, Walter Barnes, Loni von Friedel, Horst Frank, Renato Romano, Arturo Dominici, Pietro Ceccarelli.

Name That Cried Revenge, A (IT)
Il suo nome gridava vendetta; The Man Who Cried for Revenge
D: Mario Caiano (as William Hawkins). **P:** Bianco Manini. **W:** Mario Caiano, Tito Carpi. **C:** Enzo Barboni. **M:** Robby Poitevin. **S:** Anthony Steffen, William Berger, Claudio Undari (as Robert Hundar), Ida Galli (as Evelyn Stewart), Raf Baldassarre, Mario Brega, Luís Barboo, Alberto Dell'Acqua.

Nephews of Zorro, The (IT)
I nipoti di Zorro
D: Marcello Ciorciolini. **P:** Flora Film, Variety Film. **W:** Marcello Ciorciolini, Roberto Gianviti, Vittorio Metz, Dino Verde. **C:** Tino Santoni. **M:** Piero Umiliani. **S:** Franco Franchi, Ciccio Ingrassia, Dean Reed, Agata Flori, Ignazio Spalla (as Pedro Sanchez), Carlo Gaddi, Pietro Ceccarelli, Franco Fantasia.

No Graves on Boot Hill (IT)
Tre croci per non morire
D: Sergio Garrone (as Willy S. Regan). **P:** Elsio Mancuso. **W:** Sergio Garrone, Franco Cobianchi. **C:** Sandro Mancori. **M:** Vassili Kojucharov, Elsio Mancuso. **S:** Craig Hill, Ida Galli (as Evelyn Stewart), Giovanni Cianfriglia (as Ken Wood), Franco Cobianchi, Ivan Scratuglia.

Once Upon a Time in the West (IT)
C'era una volta il West
D: Sergio Leone. **P:** Fulvio Morsella. **W:** Sergio Donati, Sergio Leone, Dario Argento, Bernardo Bertolucci. **C:** Tonino Delli Colli. **M:** Ennio Morricone. **S:** Henry Fonda, Claudia Cardinale, Charles Bronson, Jason Robards, Gabriele Ferzetti, Frank Wolff, Paolo Stoppa, Lionel Stander, Woody Strode, Al Mulock, Keenan Wynn, Aldo Berti, Frank Braña, Aldo Sambrell, Spartaco Conversi, Bruno Corazzari, Benito Stefanelli, Antonio Molino Rojo, Fabio Testi, Claudio Mancini, Lorenzo Robledo, Conrado San Martín.

One After the Other (IT-SP)
Uno dopo l'altro; Uno después de otro
D: Nick Nostro (as Nick Howard). **P:** Marco Vicario, Bino Cicogna. **W:** Mariano de Lope, Nick Nostro, Giovanni Simonelli, Carlos E. Rodriguez. **C:** Mario Pacheco. **M:** Fred Bongusto, Berto Pisano. **S:** Richard Harrison, Pamela Tudor, Paolo Gozlino, José Bódalo, Jolanda Modio, Luís Barboo, José Canalejas, José Jaspe, José Manuel Martín, Goffredo Unger.

One Against One... No Mercy (SP-IT)
Uno a uno, sin piedad; Ad uno a uno... spietatamente; One By One
D: Rafael Romero Marchent. **P:** Eduardo Manzanos Brochero, Luigi Mondello, Roberto Santini. **W:** Eduardo Manzanos Brochero, Odoardo Fiory, Marino Girolami, Tito Carpi. **C:** Emilio Foriscot. **M:** Vassili Kojucharov, Elsio Mancuso. **S:** Peter Lee Lawrence, Guglielmo Spoletini (as William Bogart), Sidney Chaplin, Dianik Zurakowska, Eduardo Fajardo, Lucio De Santis, Tito García, Paco Sanz, Cris Huerta, Lorenzo Robledo.

One Dollar Too Many (IT-SP)
I tre che sconvolsero il West, I (Vado, vedo e sparo); Llego, veo, disparo; I Came, I Saw, I Shot
D: Enzo G. Castellari. **P:** Dario Sabatello. **W:** Augusto Finocchi, Vittorio Metz, José Maria

Rodriguez, Enrique Llovet. **C:** Alejandro Ulloa. **M:** Carlo Rustichelli. **S:** Antonio Sabato, John Saxon, Frank Wolff, Agata Flori, Leo Anchóriz, Luís Barboo, Pietro Ceccarelli, Tito García, Victor Israel.

One for All (IT-SP)
Tutto per tutto; La hora del coraje; Go for Broke; Copperface; All Out
D: Umberto Lenzi. **P:** PEA, Estela Film. **W:** Eduardo Manzanos Brochero, Nino Stresa. **C:** Alejandro Ulloa. **M:** Luis Enríquez Bacalov, Marcello Giombini. **S:** Mark Damon, John Ireland, Fernando Sancho, Mónica Randall, Eduardo Fajardo, Raf Baldassarre, Luís Barboo, Frank Braña, Spartaco Conversi, José Torres, Tito García, Luis Induni.

Professional Gun, A (IT-SP)
Il mercenario; Salario para matar; El mercenario; The Mercenary
D: Sergio Corbucci. **P:** Alberto Grimaldi. **W:** Giorgio Arlorio, Franco Solinas, Adriano Bolzoni, Sergio Corbucci, Sergio Spina, Luciano Vincenzoni. **C:** Alejandro Ulloa. **M:** Ennio Morricone. **S:** Franco Nero, Jack Palance, Tony Musante, Giovanna Ralli, Eduardo Fajardo, Franco Giacobini, Franco Ressel, Raf Baldassarre, José Canalejas, Tito García, Ángel Álvarez, Bruno Corazzari, Lorenzo Robledo.

Requiem for a Gringo (SP-IT)
Réquiem para el gringo; Duel in the Eclipse; Requiem per un gringo
D: José Luis Merino (some sources also credit Eugenio Martín). **P:** Prodimex, Hispamer. **W:** Enrico Colombo, Giuliana Garavaglia, María del Carmen Martínez Román. **C:** Mario Pacheco. **M:** Angelo Francesco Lavagnino. **S:** Lang Jeffries, Fernando Sancho, Aldo Sambrell, Femi Benussi, Carlo Gaddi, Rubén Rojo, Ángel Álvarez.

Ringo the Lone Rider (SP-IT)
Dos hombres van a morir; Ringo, il cavaliere solitario
D: Rafael Romero Marchent. **P:** Copercines, Emmeci Cinematografica. **W:** Mario Caiano, Eduardo Manzanos Brochero. **C:** Emanuele Di Cola. **M:** Francesco De Masi. **S:** Peter Martell, Piero Lulli, Paolo Hertz, Armando Calvo, Dianik Zurakowska, Jesús Puente, Frank Braña, Luís Barboo, José Jaspe.

Rope for a Bastard, A (IT)
Una forca per un bastardo
D: Amasi Damiani. **P:** S.P.E.F.D. **W:** Amasi Damiani (unconfirmed). **C:** Giovanni Varriano. **M:** Unknown. **S:** Mimmo Palmara (as Dick Palmer), Livio Lorenzon, Monica Millesi, Barth Warren, Caterina Trentini.

Run, Man, Run (IT)
Corri uomo corri
D: Sergio Sollima. **P:** Alvaro Mancori, Anna Maria Chretien. **W:** Sergio Sollima, Pompeo De Angelis. **C:** Guglielmo Mancori. **M:** Bruno Nicolai. **S:** Tomas Milian, Donal O'Brien, Linda Veras, Marco Guglielmi, José Torres, John Ireland, Chelo Alonso, Gianni Rizzo, Nello Pazzafini, Luciano Rossi, Calisto Calisti, Federico Boido (as Rick Boyd), Ricardo Palacios, Goffredo Unger.

Ruthless Four, The (IT-GER)
Ognuno per sé; Sam Cooper's Gold; Das Gold von Sam Cooper

D: Giorgio Capitani. **P:** Luciano Ercoli, Alberto Pugliese. **W:** Fernando Di Leo, Augusto Caminito. **C:** Sergio D'Offizi. **M:** Carlo Rustichelli. **S:** Van Heflin, Gilbert Roland, George Hilton, Klaus Kinski, Sarah Ross, Federico Boido (as Rick Boyd).

Saguaro (IT)
Sapevano solo uccidere; I'll Die for Vengeance
D: Tanio Boccia (as Amerigo Anton). **P:** Danny Film, Italian Film. **W:** Mario Moroni, Tanio Boccia. **C:** Fausto Rossi. **M:** Angelo Francesco Lavagnino. **S:** Adriano Bellini (as Kirk Morris), Larry Ward, Sergio Ciani (as Alan Steel), Gordon Mitchell, Kim Arden, Remo Capitani.

Sartana Does Not Forgive (SP-IT)
Sonora; Sartana non perdona
D: Alfonso Balcázar. **P:** Alfonso Balcázar. **W:** Giovanni Simonelli, Jaime Jesús Balcázar. **C:** Jaime Deu Casas. **M:** Francesco De Masi. **S:** George Martin, Gilbert Roland, Jack Elam, Antonio Monselesan (as Tony Norton), Donatella Turri, Rosalba Neri.

Say Your Prayers and Dig Your Grave (IT)
Prega Dio... e scavati la fossa!; Pray to God and Dig Your Grave
D: Edoardo Mulargia (as Edward G. Muller). **P:** Demofilo Fidani. **W:** Corrado Patara, Nino Masson, Edoardo Mulargia. **C:** Franco Villa. **M:** Marcello Gigante. **S:** Robert Woods, Giovanni Scarciofolo (as Jeff Cameron), Cristina Penz, Anthony Stevens, William Reed, Simonetta Vitelli (as Simone Blondell), Carlo Gaddi.

Shalako (UK-SP-GER)
Man nennt mich Shalako
D: Edward Dmytryk. **P:** Euan Lloyd, Artur Brauner. **W:** Louis L'Amour (novel), J.J. Griffith, Hal Hopper, Scott Finch. **C:** Ted Moore. **M:** Robert Farnon. **S:** Sean Connery, Brigitte Bardot, Stephen Boyd, Jack Hawkins, Peter van Eyck, Honor Blackman, Woody Strode, Eric Sykes, José Terrón.

Shoot, Gringo, Shoot (IT)
Spara, gringo, spara (Rainbow); The Longest Hunt
D: Bruno Corbucci (as Frank B. Corlish). **P:** Cemofilm. **W:** Mario Amendola, Bruno Corbucci. **C:** Fausto Zuccoli. **M:** Sante Maria Romitelli. **S:** Brian Kelly, Fabrizio Moroni, Keenan Wynn, Erika Blanc, Rik Battaglia, Furio Meniconi.

Shotgun (IT)
La vendetta è il mio perdono
D: Roberto Mauri (as Robert Johnson). **P:** Gia Produzione Film. **W:** Roberto Mauri, Tito Carpi, Francesco Degli Espinosa, Roberto Natale, Luciana Ridet. **C:** Franco Delli Colli, Mario Mancini. **M:** Giancarlo Rizzi. **S:** Tab Hunter, Mimmo Palmara (as Dick Palmer), Erika Blanc, Piero Lulli, Daniele Vargas.

Silent Stranger, The (IT-JAP-US)
Lo straniero di silenzio; Stranger in Japan (released in 1975 in the US, 1977 in Italy)
D: Luigi Vanzi (as Vance Lewis; Vincenzo Cerami also reported to have directed footage). **P:** Tony Anthony, Roberto Infascelli, Allen Klein, Ronald Schneider. **W:** Tony Anthony, Vincenzo Cerami, Giancarlo Ferrando, Lloyd Battista. **C:** Mario Capriotti. **M:** Stelvio Cipriani. **S:** Tony Anthony, Lloyd Battista, Kim Omae, Kita Mura, Kanji Ohara, Raf Baldassarre.

Sky Full of Stars for a Roof, A (IT)
...E per tetto un cielo di stelle; And for a Roof a Sky Full of Stars; Billy Boy
D: Giulio Petroni. **P:** Gianni Hecht Lucari. **W:** Alberto Areal, Francesco Martino (some sources also credit Stefano Strucchi, Fausto Sacaceni, Bernardino Zapponi). **C:** Carlo Carlini. **M:** Ennio Morricone. **S:** Giuliano Gemma, Mario Adorf, Magda Konopka, Julie Menard, Anthony Dawson, John Bartha, Federico Boido (as Rick Boyd), Alberto Dell'Acqua, Benito Stefanelli, Cris Huerta, Victor Israel.

Stranger in Paso Bravo, A (IT-SP)
Uno straniero a Paso Bravo; Los pistoleros de Paso Bravo
D: Salvatore Rosso. **P:** Francesco Carnicelli, Arturo Marcos. **W:** Eduardo Manzanos Brochero, Federico de Urrutia, Lucio Manlio Battistrada, Fernando Morandi. **C:** Alfonso Nieva, Gino Santini. **M:** Angelo Francesco Lavagnino. **S:** Anthony Steffen, Eduardo Fajardo, Giulia Rubini, Adriana Ambesi, José Calvo, José Canalejas, José Jaspe.

Stranger, Make the Sign of the Cross (IT)
Straniero... fatti il segno della croce!; Stranger, Say your Prayers
D: Demofilo Fidani (as Miles Deem). **P:** Demofilo Fidani, Corrado Patara. **C:** Franco Villa. **M:** Marcello Gigante. **AD:** Aristide Massaccesi. **S:** Charles Southwood, Giovanni Scarciofolo (as Jeff Cameron), Ettore Manni, Cristina Penz, Fabio Testi, Dino Strano, Massimo Righi, Simonetta Vitelli (as Simone Blondell).

Taste of Death, A (IT-FR)
Quanto costa morire; Les colts brillent au soleil; The Cost of Dying
D: Sergio Merolle. **P:** Cine Azimut, Les Films Corona. **W:** Biagio Proietti. **C:** Benito Frattari. **M:** Francesco De Masi. **S:** Andrea Giordana, John Ireland, Bruno Corazzari, Raymond Pellegrin, Betsy Bell.

Tepepa (IT-SP)
Viva la revolucion; Blood and Guns
D: Giulio Petroni. **P:** Alfredo Cuomo, Nicolò Pomilia. **W:** Ivan Della Mea, Franco Solinas. **C:** Francisco Marín. **M:** Ennio Morricone. **S:** Tomas Milian, Orson Welles, John Steiner, Luciano Casamonica, Anna Maria Lanciaprima, José Torres, George Wang, Paco Sanz.

Tequila Joe (IT)
...E venne il tempo di uccidere; Time and Place for Killing
D: Vincenzo Dell'Aquila (as Vincent Eagle). **P:** Otello Cocchi, Renzo Renzi. **W:** Vincenzo Dell'Aquila, Fernando Di Leo, Rino Filippini. **M:** Francesco De Masi. **S:** Anthony Ghidra, Jean Sobieski, Mimmo Palmara (as Dick Palmer), Furio Meniconi, Eleonora Ruffo, Remo Capitani.

This Man Can't Die (IT) *I lunghi giorni dell'odio; Long Days of Hate*
D: Gianfranco Baldanello. **P:** Gino Rossi. **W:** Luigi Emmanuele, Gino Mangini, Gianfranco

Euro-Western Filmography

Baldanello. **C:** Claudio Cirillo. **M:** Amedeo Tommasi. **S:** Guy Madison, Lucienne Bridou, Rik Battaglia, Rosalba Neri, Steve Merrick, Peter Martell, Alberto Dell'Acqua, Franco Pesce, John Bartha.

Three Silver Dollars (IT)
...Dai nemici mi guardo io!
D: Mario Amendola (as Irving Jacobs). **P:** Luigi Rovere. **W:** Mario Amendola, Bruno Corbucci. **C:** Aldo Giordani. **M:** Carlo Rustichelli. **S:** Charles Southwood, Julián Mateos, Alida Chelli, Mirko Ellis, Ivan Staccioli, Pietro Ceccarelli, Lorenzo Robledo.

Today It's Me... Tomorrow You! (IT)
Oggi a me... domani a te!; Today We Kill... Tomorrow We Die!
D: Tonino Cervi. **P:** Splendid Film, PAC. **W:** Dario Argento, Tonino Cervi. **C:** Sergio D'Offizi. **M:** Angelo Francesco Lavagnino. **S:** Brett Halsey (as Montgomery Ford), Bud Spencer, William Berger, Wayde Preston, Tatsuya Nakadai, Giovanni Scarciofolo (as Jeff Cameron), Diana Madigan, Remo Capitani, Nazzareno Zamperla.

Trail of the Falcon (GDR-SOV)
Spur des Falken; Sled sokola
D: Gottfried Kolditz. **P:** DEFA, Gruzia-Film. **W:** Günter Karl. **C:** Otto Hanisch. **M:** Wolfgang Meyer, Karl-Ernst Sasse. **S:** Gojko Mitic, Hannjo Hasse, Barbara Brylska, Lali Meszhi, Rolf Hoppe.

Train for Durango, A (IT-SP)
Un treno per Durango; Un tren para Durango
D: Mario Caiano (as William Hawkins). **P:** Bianco Manini. **W:** Duccio Tessari, Mario Caiano (Spanish version also credits José Gutiérrez Maesso; some sources also credit Fernando Di Leo, Augusto Caminito). **C:** Enzo Barboni. **M:** Carlo Rustichelli. **S:** Anthony Steffen, Mark Damon, Enrico Maria Salerno, Dominique Boschero, Roberto Camardiel, José Bódalo, José Canalejas, Tito García, Aldo Sambrell, José Manuel Martín, Lorenzo Robledo.

Two Pistols and a Coward (IT)
Il pistolero segnato da Dio; Gunman Sent By God
D: Giorgio Ferroni (as Calvin Jackson Padget). **P:** Nino Battifferi. **W:** Remigio Del Grosso, Giorgio Ferroni, Augusto Finocchi. **C:** Sandro Mancori. **M:** Carlo Rustichelli. **S:** Anthony Steffen, Richard Wyler, Luisa Baratto, Giovanni Cianfriglia (as Ken Wood), Ennio Balbo, Salvatore Borgese, Andrea Bosic, Nello Pazzafini, Tom Felleghy, Benito Stefanelli, Pietro Ceccarelli, Lucio De Santis, Furio Meniconi, Romano Puppo.

Vengeance (IT-GER)
Joko, invoca Dio... e muori; 5 blutige Stricke
D: Antonio Margheriti (as Anthony Dawson). **P:** Alfredo Leone. **W:** Antonio Margheriti, Renato Savino. **C:** Riccardo Pallottini. **M:** Carlo Savina. **S:** Richard Harrison, Claudio Camaso, Sheyla Rosin, Werner Pochath, Paolo Gozlino (as Paul Lino), Guido Lollobrigida (as Lee Burton), Alberto Dell'Acqua, Luciano Pigozzi (as Alan Collins), Lucio De Santis (as Louis Santis), Ignazio Spalla (as Pedro Sanchez), Goffredo Unger (as Fredi Unger).

Vengeance for Vengeance (IT)
Vendetta per vendetta; Revenge for Revenge
D: Mario Colucci (as Ray Calloway). **P:** Natalino Gullo. **W:** Mario Colucci. **C:** Giuseppe Aquari. **M:** Angelo Francesco Lavagnino. **S:** John Ireland, Gianni Medici, Loredana Nusciak, Lemmy Carson, Giuseppe Lauricella, Remo Capitani.

Villa Rides (US)
(shot in Spain)
D: Buzz Kulik. **P:** Ted Richmond. **W:** Robert Towne, Sam Peckinpah, William Douglas Lansford. **C:** Jack Hildyard. **M:** Maurice Jarre. **S:** Yul Brynner, Robert Mitchum, Maria Grazia Buccella, Charles Bronson, Herbert Lom, John Ireland, Fernando Rey, Frank Wolff, José Canalejas, Aldo Sambrell.

White Comanche (SP)
Comanche blanco
D: José Briz Méndez (as Gilbert Lee Kay). **P:** Sam White. **W:** Frank Gruber, Robert Holt, José Briz Méndez, Manuel Gómez Rivera. **C:** Francisco Fraile. **M:** Jean Ledrut. **S:** Joseph Cotten, William Shatner, Rosanna Yanni, Perla Cristal, Mariano Vidal Molina, Aldo Sambrell, Barta Barry, José Canalejas, Cris Huerta, Victor Israel, José Jaspe, José Terrón.

Winnetou and Shatterhand in the Valley of Death (GER-IT-YUG)
Winnetou und Shatterhand im Tal der Toten; L'uomo dal lungo fucile; Vinetu u dolini smrti
D: Harald Reinl. **P:** Artur Brauner. **W:** Karl May (characters), Herbert Reinecker, Harald Reinl. **C:** Ernst W. Kalinke. **M:** Martin Böttcher. **S:** Lex Barker, Pierre Brice, Rik Battaglia, Ralf Wolter, Karin Dor.

Wrath of God, The (IT-SP)
L'ira di Dio; Hasta la última gota de sangre
D: Alberto Cardone (as Albert Cardiff). **P:** Ugo Guerra, Elio Scardamaglia. **W:** Alberto Cardone, Italo Gasperini, Ugo Guerra, José Luis Martínez Mollá. **C:** Mario Pacheco. **M:** Michele Lacerenza. **S:** Brett Halsey (as Montgomery Ford), Dana Ghia, Fernando Sancho, Wayde Preston, Renato Rossini (as Howard Ross), Angel del Pozo, Franco Fantasia.

Zorro the Fox (IT)
El Zorro (La volpe); La espada del Zorro
D: Guido Zurli. **P:** Magic Film. **W:** Guido Leoni, Ambrogio Molteni, Angelo Sangermano, Giuliano Simonetti, Guido Zurli. **C:** Franco Delli Colli. **M:** Gino Peguri. **S:** George Ardisson, Giacomo Rossi-Stuart, Femi Benussi, Ignazio Spalla (as Pedro Sanchez), Paolo Tedesco.

1969

Alive or Preferably Dead (IT-SP)
Vivi, o preferibilmente morti; Vivos o preferiblemente muertos; Sundance Cassidy and Butch the Kid; Sundance and the Kid
D: Duccio Tessari. **P:** Ultra, Hesperia. **W:** Duccio Tessari, Ennio Flaiano, Giorgio Salvioni. **C:** Cesare Allione, Manuel Rojas. **M:** Gianni Ferrio. **S:** Giuliano Gemma, Nino Benvenuti, Sydne Rome, Cris Huerta, Antonio Casas, Luís Barboo, Victor Israel, José Manuel Martín, George Rigaud, Dan van Husen.

Boot Hill (IT)
La collina degli stivali; Boots (sic) Hill
D: Giuseppe Colizzi (begun by Romolo Guerrieri). **P:** Enzo D'Ambrosio, Giuseppe Colizzi. **W:** Giuseppe Colizzi. **C:** Marcello Masciocchi. **M:** Carlo Rustichelli. **S:** Terence Hill, Bud Spencer, Woody Strode, Eduardo Ciannelli, Luigi (Luca) Montefiori, Lionel Stander, Alberto Dell'Acqua, Romano Puppo, Luciano Rossi, Nazzareno Zamperla, Dino Strano.

Cemetery Without Crosses (FR-IT)
Une corde, un colt; Cimitero senza croci; The Rope and the Colt
D: Robert Hossein. **P:** Fono Roma, Loisirs du Monde, Films Copernic. **W:** Dario Argento, Claude Desailly, Robert Hossein. **C:** Henri Persin. **M:** André Hossein. **S:** Robert Hossein, Michèle Mercier, Anne-Marie Balin, Daniele Vargas, Guido Lollobrigida (as Lee Burton), Ángel Álvarez, Benito Stefanelli, Charly Bravo, José Canalejas, Cris Huerta, Lorenzo Robledo.

Death on a High Hill (IT-SP)
La morte sull'alta collina; Death on High Mountain; Sin aliento
D: Alfredo Medori (as Fred Ringoold; sometimes credited to Fernando Cerchio). **P:** Bruno Turchetto, Ignacio Gurierrez. **W:** Enzo Gicca Palli, José Mallorquí, Eduardo Manzanos Brochero. **C:** Julio Ortas Plaza. **M:** Luis Enríquez Bacalov. **S:** Peter Lee Lawrence, Luis Dávila, Antonio Gradoli, Tano Cimarosa, Agnès Spaak, Frank Braña, Nello Pazzafini, Romano Puppo.

Desperados, The (US)
(shot in Spain)
D: Henry Levin. **P:** Irving Allen. **W:** Clarke Reynolds, Walter Brough. **C:** Sam Leavitt. **M:** David Whitaker. **S:** Vince Edwards, Jack Palance, George Maharis, Neville Brand, Sheila Burrell.

Django the Bastard (IT)
Django, il bastardo; Strangers Gundown
D: Sergio Garrone. **P:** Pino De Martino. **W:** Anthony Steffen, Sergio Garrone. **C:** Gino Santini. **M:** Vassili Kojucharov, Elsio Mancuso. **S:** Anthony Steffen, Rada Rassimov, Paolo Gozlino, Luciano Rossi (as Lu Kamante), Teodoro Corrà, Carlo Gaddi, Remo Capitani, Furio Meniconi.

El Puro (IT-SP)
La taglia è tua... l'uomo l'ammazzo io; El Puro se sienta, espera y dispara; The Reward's Yours, The Man's Mine
D: Edoardo Mulargia (as Edward G. Muller). **P:** Filmar, IFISA. **W:** Ignacio F. Iquino, Fabrizio Gianni, Edoardo Mulargia. **C:** Antonio L. Ballesteros. **M:** Alessandro Alessandroni. **S:** Robert Woods, Maurizio Bonuglia, Marco Fiorini (as Ashborn Hamilton Jr), Rosalba Neri, Mario Brega, Aldo Berti.

Five Man Army, The (IT)
Un esercito di 5 uomini
D: Don Taylor, Italo Zingarelli. **P:** Italo Zingarelli. **W:** Dario Argento, Marc Richards. **C:** Enzo Barboni. **M:** Ennio Morricone. **S:** Peter Graves, Bud Spencer, Nino Castelnuovo, James Daly, Tetsuro Tamba, Daniela Giordano, Giacomo Rossi-Stuart, José Torres.

Forgotten Pistolero, The (IT-SP)
Il pistolero dell'Ave Maria; Tierra de gigantes
D: Ferdinando Baldi. **P:** Manolo Bolognini. **W:** Piero Anchisi, Ferdinando Baldi, Vincenzo Cerami, Federico de Urrutia, Mario Di Nardo. **C:** Mario Montuori. **M:** Roberto Pregadio. **S:** Leonard Mann, Luciana Paluzzi, Peter Martell, Alberto de Mendoza, Pilar Velázquez, Piero Lulli, José Suárez, Luciano Rossi, José Manuel Martín, Franco Pesce, José Terrón.

Four Came to Kill Sartana (IT)
...E vennero in quattro per uccidere Sartana; Sartana the Invincible Gunman; They Came to Kill Sartana
D: Demofilo Fidani (as Miles Deem). **P:** Mila Vitelli. **W:** Demofilo Fidani, Mila Vitelli. **C:** Luciano Tovoli. **M:** Italo Fischetti. **S:** Giovanni Scarciofolo (as Jeff Cameron), Franco Ricci, Daniela Giordano, Celso Faria, Benito Pacifico (as Dennis Colt), Simone Blondell.

Four Rode Out (SP-US)
Cuatro cabalgaron
D: John Peyser. **P:** Richard Landau, Pedro Vidal. **W:** Don Balluck. **C:** Rafael Pacheco. **M:** Janis Ian. **S:** Sue Lyon, Pernell Roberts, Julián Mateos, Leslie Nielsen, María Martín.

Garringo (SP-IT)
D: Rafael Romero Marchent. **P:** Tritone, Profilms 21. **W:** Joaquín Romero Marchent, Giovanni Scolaro, Arpad De Riso. **C:** Aldo Ricci. **M:** Marcello Giombini. **S:** Anthony Steffen, Peter Lee Lawrence, Solvi Stubing, Raf Baldassarre, Frank Braña, Barta Barry, Luis Induni, Antonio Molino Rojo, José Bódalo, Tito García, Lorenzo Robledo, Carlos Romero Marchent.

God Will Forgive My Gun (IT)
Dio perdoni la mia pistola
(nb: filmed 1966)
D: Mario Gariazzo, Leopoldo Savona. **P:** Aldo Addobbati, Paolo Moffa. **W:** Mario Gariazzo, Leopoldo Savona. **C:** Stelvio Massi. **M:** Vassili Kojucharov, Elsio Mancuso. **S:** Wayde Preston, Loredana Nusciak, José Torres, Dan Vadis, Giuseppe Addobbati, Livio Lorenzon.

Guns of the Magnificent Seven (US-SP)
La furia de los siete magníficos
D: Paul Wendkos. **P:** Vincent M. Fennelly. **W:** Herman Hoffman. **C:** Antonio Macasoli. **M:** Elmer Bernstein. **S:** George Kennedy, James Whitmore, Monte Markham, Reni Santoni, Bernie Casey, Fernando Rey, George Rigaud.

Hate Is My God (IT-GER)
L'odio è il mio dio; Il Nero - Hass war sein Gebet
D: Claudio Gora. **P:** LB Film, Fono. **W:** Pietro Anchisi, Vincenzo Cerami, Claudio Gora (German version also credits Werner Hauff). **C:** Lucio Trasatti. **M:** Pippo Franco. **S:** Luciano Stella (as Tony Kendall), Claudio Giordana, Ella Karin, Herbert Fleischmann, Marina Berti, Luciano Rossi.

I Am Sartana, Your Angel of Death (IT)
Sono Sartana, il vostro becchino; Sartana the Gravedigger
D: Giuliano Carnimeo (as Anthony Ascott). **P:** Aldo Addobbati, Paolo Moffa. **W:** Tito Carpi, Vincenzo Dell'Aquila, Ernesto Gastaldi (uncredited). **C:** Giovanni Bergamini. **M:** Vassili Kojucharov, Elsio Mancuso. **S:** Gianni Garko, Frank Wolff, Klaus Kinski, Gordon Mitchell, Ettore Manni, Salvatore Borgese, Federico Boido (as Rick Boyd), José Torres, Franco Pesce, John Bartha.

In the Name of the Father (IT)
I quattro del Pater Noster
D: Ruggero Deodato. **P:** Franco Cittadini, Stenio Fiorentini. **W:** Augusto Finocchi, Luciano Ferri, Maurizio Costanzo. **C:** Riccardo Pallottini. **M:** Luis Enríquez Bacalov. **S:** Paolo Villaggio, Lino Toffolo, Enrico Montesano, Oreste Lionello, Rosemarie Dexter, Salvatore Borgese.

Land Raiders (US)
(shot in Spain)
D: Nathan H. Juran. **P:** Charles H. Schneer. **W:** Jesse Lasky Jr., Ken Pettus, Pat Silver. **C:** Wilkie Cooper. **M:** Bruno Nicolai. **S:** Telly Savalas, George Maharis, Arlene Dahl, Janet Landgard, Guy Rolfe, Charly Bravo, Fernando Rey.

Law of Violence, The (IT-SP)
Legge della violenza; Todos o ninguno
D: Gianni Crea. **P:** Meridionale Cinematografica, Alfonso Balcázar. **W:** Alfonso Balcázar, Gianni Crea, Piero Regnoli. **C:** Jaime Deu Casas, Oberdan Troiani. **M:** Stelvio Cipriani. **S:** Giorgio Cerioni (as George Greenwood), Igli Villani, Ángel Aranda, Miguel de la Riva, Ugo Adinolfi.

Magnificent Bandits, The (IT-SP)
O' Cangaçeiro; Viva cangaceiro
D: Giovanni Fago. **P:** Salvatore Alabiso. **W:** Giovanni Fago, José Luis Jerez Aloza, Rafael Romero Marchent, Antonio Troiso, Bernardino Zapponi. **C:** Alejandro Ulloa. **M:** Riz Ortolani. **AD:** Goffredo Unger. **S:** Tomas Milian, Ugo Pagliai, Eduardo Fajardo, Renato Rossini (as Howard Ross), Leo Anchóriz, Goffredo Unger.

Night of the Serpents (IT)
La notte dei serpenti; Ringo Kill
D: Giulio Petroni. **P:** Gianni Minervini, Franco Clementi. **W:** Fulvia Gicca Palli, Enzo Gicca Palli, Giulio Petroni. **C:** Mario Vulpiani, Silvio Fraschetti. **M:** Riz Ortolani. **S:** Luke Askew, Luigi Pistilli, Magda Konopka, Chelo Alonso, Guglielmo Spoletini (as William Bogart), Benito Stefanelli.

No Room to Die (IT)
Una lunga fila di croci; A Noose for Django
D: Sergio Garrone. **P:** Gabriele Crisanti. **W:** Sergio Garrone (uncredited). **C:** Franco Villa. **M:** Vassili Kojucharov, Elsio Mancuso. **S:** Anthony Steffen, William Berger, Riccardo Garrone, Mario Brega, Nicoletta Machiavelli.

100 Rifles (US)
(shot in Spain)
D: Tom Gries. **P:** Marvin Schwartz. **W:** Robert MacLeod, Clair Huffaker, Tom Gries. **C:** Cecilio Paniagua. **M:** Jerry Goldsmith. **S:** Jim Brown, Raquel Welch, Burt Reynolds, Fernando Lamas, Dan O'Herlihy, Charly Bravo, José Manuel Martín, Aldo Sambrell.

Price of Power, The (IT-SP)
Il prezzo del potere; La muerte de un presidente
D: Tonino Valerii. **P:** Bianco Manini. **W:** Massimo Patrizi, Ernesto Gastaldi (uncredited). **C:** Stelvio Massi. **M:** Luis Enríquez Bacalov. **S:** Giuliano Gemma, Van Johnson, Warren Vanders, Fernando Rey, Maria Cuadra, José Suárez, Ray Saunders, Antonio Casas, Benito Stefanelli, Frank Braña, Charly Bravo, José Calvo, Angel del Pozo, José Canalejas, Paco Sanz, Lorenzo Robledo, Ángel Álvarez, Norma Jordán.

Quintana: Dead or Alive (IT)
Quintana
D: Vincenzo Musolino (as Glenn Vincent Davis). **P:** Vincenzo Musolino. **W:** Vincenzo Musolino. **C:** Vitaliano Natalucci. **M:** Felice Di Stefano. **S:** Osvaldo Ruggeri (as George Stevenson), Femi Benussi, Ignazio Spalla (as Pedro Sanchez), Aldo Bufi Landi, Marina Traversi, Spartaco Conversi, Dino Strano.

Quinto: Fighting Proud (SP-IT)
El valor de un cobarde; Quinto: non ammazzare

D: León Klimovsky. **P:** Cines Europa, RM Films. **W:** Manuel Martínez Remís, Dino De Rugeriis. **C:** Giuseppe La Torre. **M:** Piero Umiliani. **S:** Giuseppe Cardillo (as Steven Tedd), Germán Cobos, Sarah Ross, Roberto Camardiel, Raf Baldassarre, José Canalejas (as Joe Kamel).

Sabata (IT)
Ehi amico... c'è Sabata, hai chiuso!
D: Gianfranco Parolini (as Frank Kramer). **P:** Alberto Grimaldi. **W:** Gianfranco Parolini, Renato Izzo. **C:** Sandro Mancori. **M:** Marcello Giombini. **S:** Lee Van Cleef, William Berger, Franco Ressel, Ignazio Spalla (as Pedro Sanchez), Claudio Undari (as Robert Hundar), Antonio Gradoli, Gianni Rizzo, Linda Veras, Aldo Canti (as Nick Jordan), Luciano Pigozzi, John Bartha, Spartaco Conversi (as Spanny Convery), Romano Puppo.

Shadow of Sartana… Shadow of Your Death! (IT)
Passa Sartana... è l'ombra della tua morte; Sartana and His Shadow of Death
D: Demofilo Fidani (as Sean O'Neil). **P:** Tarquinia

Euro-Western Filmography

Film. **W:** Demofilo Fidani. **C:** Franco Villa. **M:** Coriolano Gori. **S:** Giovanni Scarciofolo (as Jeff Cameron), Benito Pacifico (as Dennis Colt), Paolo Figlia, Dino Strano (as Dean Stratford), Simonetta Vitelli (as Simone Blondell).

Specialists, The (IT-FR-GER)
Gli specialisti; Le spécialiste; Die Spezialisten; Drop Them or I'll Shoot
D: Sergio Corbucci. **P:** Adelphia, Les Films Marceau, Neue Emelka. **W:** Sergio Corbucci, Sabatino Ciuffini. **C:** Dario Di Palma. **M:** Angelo Francesco Lavagnino. **S:** Johnny Hallyday, Gastone Moschin, Mario Adorf, Françoise Fabian, Sylvie Fennec, Gino Pernice.

Tails, You Lose... (IT)
Testa o croce; Heads or Tails
D: Piero Pierotti (as Peter E. Stanley). **P:** Tirrenia Studios, Golden Gate. **W:** Piero Pierotti (as Peter E. Stanley). **C:** Fausto Zuccoli. **M:** Carlo Savina. **S:** John Ericson, Sheyla Rosin, Franco Lantieri, Edwige Fenech, Daniela Surina.

Talent for Loving, A (US)
(shot in Spain)
Gun Crazy
D: Richard Quine. **P:** Dudley Birch Films. **W:** Richard Condon. **C:** John Coquillon. **M:** Ken Thorne. **S:** Richard Widmark, Cesar Romero, Caroline Munro, Topol, Fran Jeffries.

Tierra Brava (SP-IT)
Pagó cara su muerte; ...E intorno a lui fu morte; Death Knows No Time
D: León Klimovsky. **P:** Luigi Mondello, Eduardo Manzanos Brochero. **W:** Miguel Cussó, Odoardo Fiory, Eduardo Manzanos Brochero. **C:** Emilio Foriscot. **M:** Carlo Savina. **S:** Guglielmo Spoletini (as William Bogart), Wayde Preston, Agnès Spaak, Eduardo Fajardo, Sydney Chaplin, Andrea Bosic, Ignazio Spalla (as Pedro Sanchez).

$20,000 Stained in Blood (SP-IT)
Forajidos implacables; Kidnapping: paga o uccidiamo tuo figlio; 20.000 dollari sporchi di sangue
D: Alberto Cardone (as Albert Cardiff). **P:** Ugo Guerra, Elio Scardamaglia. **W:** Alberto Cardone, Ugo Guerra, Vittorio Salerno, Manuel Sebares. **C:** Mario Pacheco. **M:** Michele Lacerenza. **S:** Brett Halsey, Germano Longo, Teresa Gimpera, Fernando Sancho, Eugenio Battisti, Antonio Casas, Paco Sanz.

Twice a Judas (IT-SP)
Due volte Giuda; Dos veces Judas; They Called Him Graveyard; Shoot Twice
D: Nando Cicero. **P:** Colt, Medusa and PC Balcázar. **W:** Jaime Jesús Balcázar. **C:** Francisco Marín. **M:** Carlo Pes. **S:** Klaus Kinski, Antonio Sabato, Cristina Galbo, José Calvo, Damian Rabal.

Vengeance Is Mine (SP-IT)
Los desesperados; Quei disperati che puzzano di sudore e di morte; A Bullet for Sandoval
D: Julio Buchs. **P:** Elio Scardamaglia, Ugo Guerra. **W:** Julio Buchs, Federico de Urrutia, Ugo Guerra, José Luis Martínez Mollá. **C:** Francisco Sempere. **M:** Gianni Ferrio. **S:** George Hilton, Ernest Borgnine, Annabella Incontrera, Alberto de Mendoza, Leo Anchóriz, Antonio Pica, Gustavo Rojo, George Rigaud, Luís Barboo, Charly Bravo, José Manuel Martín, Antonio Molino Rojo, Aldo Sambrell, Dan van Husen, Lorenzo Robledo, Tito García.

White Wolves (GDR-YUG)
Weisse Wölfe; Bijeli vukovi
D: Konrad Petzold. **P:** DEFA, Bosna Film. **W:** Günter Karl, Hans-Joachim Wallstein, Josip Lesic. **C:** Eberhard Borkmann. **M:** Karl-Ernst Sasse. **S:** Gojko Mitic, Horst Schulze, Barbara Brylska, Holger Mahlich, Slobodan Dimitrijevic.

Zorro in the Court of England (IT)
Zorro alla corte d'Inghliterra
D: Francesco Montemurro. **P:** Fortunato Misiano. **W:** Arpad De Riso, Franco Montemurro. **C:** Augusto Tiezzi. **M:** Angelo Francesco Lavagnino. **S:** Spiros Focás, Carol Wells, Daniele Vargas, Dada Gallotti, Franco Fantasia, Spartaco Conversi, Antonio Gradoli, Franco Ressel.

Zorro, Marquis of Navarra (IT)
Zorro, marchese di Navarra
D: Francesco Montemurro. **P:** Fortunato Misiano. **W:** Francesco Montemurro, Piero Pierotti. **C:** Augusto Tiezzi. **M:** Angelo Francesco Lavagnino. **S:** Nadir Moretti, Malisa Longo, Daniele Vargas, Loris Gizzi, Gisella Arden, Antonio Gradoli.

Zorro the Conqueror (SP-IT)
La ultima aventura del Zorro; Zorro il dominatore
D: José Luis Merino. **P:** Duca, Hispamer Film. **W:** María del Carmen Martínez Román, José Luis Merino, Enzo Gicca Palli. **C:** Emanuele Di Cola. **M:** Coriolano Gori. **S:** Charles Quiney, Maria Pia Conte, José Jaspe, Aldo Bufi Landi, Marta Monterrey, José Jaspe.

1970

Adios Cjamango (SP-IT)
Los rebeldes de Arizona; The Rebels of Arizona
D: José María Zabalza (as Harry Freeman). **P:** Procensa, Cinemec. **W:** José María Zabalza. **C:** Leopoldo Villaseñor. **M:** Ana Satrova, Gianni Marchetti. **S:** Carlos Quiney, Miguel de la Riva, Claudia Gravy, José Truchado, Enrique Navarro, Luis Induni.

Adios, Sabata (IT)
Indio Black: sai che ti dico? Sei un gran figlio di...; The Bounty Hunters
D: Gianfranco Parolini (as Frank Kramer). **P:** Alberto Grimaldi. **W:** Renato Izzo, Gianfranco Parolini. **C:** Sandro Mancori. **M:** Bruno Nicolai. **S:** Yul Brynner, Dean Reed, Ignazio Spalla (as Pedro Sanchez), Nieves Navarro (as Susan Scott), Gérard Herter, Salvatore Borgese, Salvatore Billa, Gianni Rizzo, Federico Boido (as Rick Boyd), Bruno Corazzari, Franco Fantasia, Antonio Gradoli, Giovanni Cianfriglia (as Ken Wood), Andrea Scotti, Ángel Álvarez.

And God Said to Cain (IT-GER)
...E Dio disse a Caino...; Satan der Rache; Revenge at Sundown
D: Antonio Margheriti (as Anthony M. Dawson). **P:** Giovanni Addessi. **W:** Antonio Margheriti, Giovanni Addessi. **C:** Luciano Trasatti, Riccardo Pallottini. **M:** Carlo Savina. **S:** Klaus Kinski, Peter Carsten, Marcella Michelangeli, Guido Lollobrigida (as Lee Burton), Antonio Cantafora, Lucio De Santis, Luciano Pigozzi, Furio Meniconi.

And Sartana Kills Them All (SP-IT)
Un par de asesinos; Lo irritarono... e Santana fece piazza pulita; And Sabata Killed Them All
D: Rafael Romero Marchent. **P:** Tritone, DIA. **W:** Joaquín Romero Marchent, Santiago Moncada, Mario Alabiso. **C:** Guglielmo Mancori. **M:** Marcello Giombini. **S:** Gianni Garko, Guglielmo Spoletini (as William Bogart), María Silva, Cristina Iosani, Raf Baldassarre, Frank Braña, Charly Bravo, Cris Huerta, Luis Induni, Carlos Romero Marchent, Paco Sanz.

Anger of the Wind, The (SP-IT)
La cólera del viento; La collera del vento; Trinity Sees Red; Revenge of Trinity
D: Mario Camus. **P:** Mario Cecchi Gori, Marciano de la Fuente, Cesáreo Gonzalez. **W:** Manolo Marinero, Mario Camus, Mario Cecchi Gori, Alberto Silvestri, Miguel Rubio, Franco Verucci, José Vicente Puente, Valerio Zurlini (uncredited). **C:** Roberto Gerardi. **M:** Augusto Martelli. **S:** Terence Hill, Maria Grazia Buccella, Fernando Rey, Mario Prado, Angel Lombarte, José Manuel Martín.

Arizona (IT-SP)
Arizona si scatenò... e li fece fuori tutti!; Arizona vuelve; Arizona Colt Returns
D: Sergio Martino. **P:** Devon Film, Astro. **W:** Ernesto Gastaldi, Joaquín Romero Marchent. **C:** Miguel Fernández Mila. **M:** Bruno Nicolai. **S:** Anthony Steffen, Marcella Michelangeli, Rosalba Neri, Aldo Sambrell, Roberto Camardiel, Raf Baldassarre, Luís Barboo, José Manuel Martín, Carlos Romero Marchent, Dan van Husen.

Beast, The (IT)
La belva; Rough Justice
D: Mario Costa. **P:** Paolo Prestano. **W:** Mario Costa. **C:** Luciano Trasatti. **M:** Stelvio Cipriani. **S:** Klaus Kinski, Gabriella Giorgelli, Giuseppe Cardillo (as Steven Tedd), Luisa Alcini, Guido Lollobrigida (as Lee Burton), Remo Capitani.

Cannon for Cordoba (US)
(shot in Spain)
D: Paul Wendkos. **P:** Vincent M. Fennelly. **W:** Stephen Kandel. **C:** Antonio Macasoli. **M:** Elmer Bernstein. **S:** George Peppard, Giovanna Ralli, Raf Vallone, Pete Duel, Don Gordon, Luís Barboo, Barta Barry, Cris Huerta, Aldo Sambrell.

Challenge of the MacKennas (SP-IT)
Un dólar y una tumba; La sfida dei MacKenna; Badlands Drifter
D: León Klimovsky. **P:** Giuseppe Maggi, José Frade, Luis Méndez. **W:** Antonio Viader, Edoardo Mulargia, Pedro Gil Paradela, León Klimovsky. **C:** Francisco Sánchez Munoz. **M:** Francesco De Masi. **S:** John Ireland, Robert Woods, Annabella Incontrera, Daniela Giordano, Mariano Vidal Molina, Roberto Camardiel, Giovanni Cianfriglia (as Ken Wood).

Any Gun Can Play

Chapagua's Gold (IT-FR)
L'oro dei Bravados; L'or des bravados
D: Renato Savino (as Don Reynolds; also credited to Giancarlo Romitelli). **P:** Luigi Nannerini. **W:** Renato Savino. **C:** Riccardo Pallottini. **M:** Luis Enríquez Bacalov. **S:** George Ardisson, Linda Veras, Rik Battaglia, Marco Zuanelli, Piero Lulli, Bobby Lapointe, Federico Boido (as Rick Boyd), Goffredo Unger.

Chuck Mool (IT)
Ciakmull, l'uomo della vendetta; The Unholy Four
D: Enzo Barboni (as E.B. Clucher). **P:** BRC Produzione, PAC. **W:** Mario Di Nardo, Franco Rossetti, Luigi Montefiori (uncredited). **C:** Mario Montuori. **M:** Riz Ortolani. **S:** Leonard Mann, Woody Strode, Ida Galli (as Evelyn Stewart), Luigi (Luca) Montefiori, Peter Martell, Salvatore Billa, Romano Puppo, Pietro Ceccarelli, Luciano Rossi, Giovanni Cianfriglia (as Ken Wood), Dino Strano.

Clumsy Hands (SP-IT)
Manos torpes; Quando Satana impugnà la Colt; Awkward Hands
D: Rafael Romero Marchent (as Ralph R. Marchent). **P:** Ricardo Sanz. **W:** Santiago Moncada, Joaquín Romero Marchent. **C:** Miguel Fernández Mila. **M:** Antón García Abril. **S:** Peter Lee Lawrence, Alberto de Mendoza, Pilar Velázquez, Antonio Casas, Manuel de Blas, Frank Braña, Luis Induni, Antonio Molino Rojo, Aldo Sambrell, Lorenzo Robledo.

Compañeros (IT-SP-GER)
Vamos a matar, compañeros; Los compañeros; Zwei Companeros
D: Sergio Corbucci. **P:** Tritone, Atlantida, Terra. **W:** Sergio Corbucci, Massimo De Rita, Fritz Ebert, Dino Maiuri. **C:** Alejandro Ulloa. **M:** Ennio Morricone. **S:** Franco Nero, Tomas Milian, Fernando Rey, Iris Berben, Jack Palance, Eduardo Fajardo, José Bódalo, José Canalejas, Tito García, Victor Israel, Gino Pernice, Lorenzo Robledo.

Dead Men Don't Make Shadows (IT)
Inginocchiati straniero… I cadaveri non fanno ombra!; Stranger That Kneels Beside the Shadow of a Corpse
D: Demofilo Fidani (as Miles Deem). **P:** Demofilo Fidani. **W:** Francesco Mannocchi, Demofilo Fidani, Ambrogio Molteni. **C:** Aristide Massaccesi. **M:** Coriolano Gori. **S:** Hunt Powers, Franco Borelli (as Chet Davis), Simonetta Vitelli (as Simone Blondell), Gordon Mitchell, Ettore Manni, Benito Pacifico (as Dennis Colt).

Deadlock (GER)
D: Roland Klick. **P:** Roland Klick, Arthur Cohn. **W:** Roland Klick. **C:** Robert van Ackeren. **M:** Can. **S:** Mario Adorf, Anthony Dawson, Marquard Bohm, Mascha Rabben, Betty Segal.

Deserter, The (IT-US-YUG)
La spina dorsale del diavolo; Djavolja kicma
D: Burt Kennedy, Niksa Fulgozi. **P:** Dino De Laurentiis, Norman Baer, Ralph B. Serpe. **W:** Stuart J. Byrne, William H. James, Clair Huffaker, Massimo D'Avack. **C:** Aldo Tonti. **M:** Piero Piccioni. **S:** Bekim Fehmiu, John Huston, Richard Crenna, Chuck Connors, Ricardo Montalban, Mimmo Palmara, Woody Strode, José Terrón.

Django Against Sartana (IT)
Django sfida Sartana; Django Challenges Sartana
D: Pasquale Squitieri (as William Redford). **P:** PAC, BCR. **W:** Pasquale Squitieri. **C:** Eugenio Bentivoglio. **M:** Piero Umiliani. **S:** Luciano Stella (as Tony Kendall), George Ardisson, José Torres, Doro Corrà, John Alvar, Salvatore Billa, Federico Boido (as Rick Boyd).

Django and Sartana Are Coming… It's the End (IT)
Arrivano Django e Sartana… è la fine; Django and Sartana's Showdown in the West
D: Demofilo Fidani (as Dick Spitfire). **P:** Demofilo Fidani. **W:** Demofilo Fidani, Maria Vitelli Valenza. **C:** Aristide Massaccesi. **M:** Coriolano Gori. **S:** Hunt Powers, Gordon Mitchell, Franco Borelli (as Chet Davis), Simonetta Vitelli (as Simone Blondell), Ettore Manni.

El Condor (US)
(shot in Spain)
D: John Guillermin. **P:** André De Toth. **W:** Larry Cohen, Steven W. Carabatsos. **C:** Henri Persin. **M:** Maurice Jarre. **AD:** Alberto Cardone. **S:** Jim Brown, Lee Van Cleef, Patrick O'Neal, Marianna Hill, Iron Eyes Cody, Charly Bravo, Angel del Pozo, Ricardo Palacios, Dan van Husen.

Fatal Error (GDR-POL)
Tödlicher Irrtum
D: Konrad Petzold. **P:** DEFA, Polski-Film, Kinostudio Sofia. **W:** Hans-Joachim Wallstein, Günter Karl, Rolf Römer. **C:** Eberhard Borkmann. **M:** Wilhelm Neef. **S:** Gojko Mitic, Armin Mueller-Stahl, Annekathrin Bürger, Krystyna Mikolajewska, Kati Bus, Konrad Petzold.

Franco and Ciccio on the War-Path (IT)
Franco e Ciccio sul sentiero di Guerra
D: Aldo Grimaldi. **P:** Sergio Bonotti. **W:** Bruno Corbucci, Giovanni Grimaldi. **C:** Fausto Zuccoli. **M:** Roberto Pregadio. **S:** Franco Franchi, Ciccio Ingrassia, Stelvio Rosi, Renato Baldini, Adler Gray, Spartaco Conversi.

Gunman in Town (IT-SP)
Una nuvola di polvere… Un grido di morte… Arriva Sartana; Llega Sartana; Light the Fuse… Sartana Is Coming; Run, Man Run… Sartana's In Town
D: Giuliano Carnimeo (as Anthony Ascott). **P:** Luciano Martino. **W:** Eduardo Manzanos Brochero, Tito Carpi, Ernesto Gastaldi. **C:** Julio Ortas. **M:** Bruno Nicolai. **S:** Gianni Garko, Nieves Navarro (as Susan Scott), Piero Lulli, Bruno Corazzari, Salvatore Borgese, Frank Braña, Paco Sanz, Luis Induni, José Jaspe, Franco Pesce, Dan van Husen.

Have a Nice Funeral, Sartana Will Pay (IT-SP)
Buon funerale amigos!.. Paga Sartana; Buen funeral, amigos, paga Sartana
D: Giuliano Carnimeo (as Anthony Ascott). **P:** Flora, National, Hispamer. **W:** Roberto Gianviti, Giovanni Simonelli. **C:** Stelvio Massi. **M:** Bruno Nicolai. **S:** Gianni Garko, Daniela Giordano, Antonio Vilar, George Wang, Ivano Staccioli, Aldo Berti, Franco Ressel, Federico Boido (as Rick Boyd), Luis Induni, Helga Liné, Franco Pesce.

Man Called Joe Clifford, A (IT-SP)
Un uomo chiamato Apocalisse Joe; Apocalypse Joe; Apocalipsis Joe
D: Leopoldo Savona. **P:** Italian International Film, Transeuropa, Copercines. **W:** Eduardo Manzanos Brochero, Leopoldo Savona. **C:** Julio Ortas, Franco Villa. **M:** Bruno Nicolai. **S:** Anthony Steffen, Eduardo Fajardo, Maria Paz Pondal, Stelio Candelli, Fernando Cerulli.

Man Called Sledge, A (IT)
Sledge
D: Vic Morrow, Giorgio Gentili. **P:** Dino De Laurentiis, Harry Bloom. **W:** Massimo D'Avack (uncredited), Frank Kowalsky, Vic Morrow. **C:** Luigi Kuveiller. **M:** Gianni Ferrio. **S:** James Garner, Laura Antonelli, Dennis Weaver, Claude Akins, John Marley, Barta Barry, Bruno Corazzari, Riccardo Garrone, Wayde Preston, Luciano Rossi.

Matalo! (IT-SP)
¡Mátalo!
D: Cesare Canevari. **P:** Rofima, Copercines. **W:** Mino Roli, Nico Ducci, Eduardo Manzanos Brochero. **C:** Julio Ortas. **M:** Mario Migliardi. **S:** Lou Castel, Corrado Pani, Antonio Salines, Luis Dávila, Claudia Gravy.

More Dollars for the McGregors (SP-IT)
La muerte busca un hombre; Ancora dollari per i MacGregor
D: José Luis Merino. **P:** Prodimex, Hispamer Film. **W:** José Luis Merino, Enrico Colombo, María del Carmen Martínez Román (uncredited). **C:** Emanuele Di Cola. **M:** Augusto Martelli. **S:** Peter Lee Lawrence, Carlos Quiney, Malisa Longo, Renato Paracchi, José Jaspe, Dan van Husen.

One Damned Day at Dawn… Django Meets Sartana! (IT)
Quel maledetto giorno d'inverno… Django e Sartana all'ultimo sangue
D: Demofilo Fidani (as Miles Deem). **P:** Demofilo Fidani. **W:** Demofilo Fidani, Mila Vitelli Valenza. **C:** Franco Villa. **M:** Coriolano Gori. **S:** Hunt Powers, Fabio Testi (as Stet Carson), Dino Strano (as Dean Stratford), Benito Pacifico (as Dennis Colt), Simonetta Vitelli (as Simone Blondell).

Plomo sobre Dallas (SP-IT)
Prendi la Colt e prega il padre tuo
D: José María Zabalza (as Charles Thomas). **P:** Procensa, Prestige Film. **W:** José María Zabalza. **C:** Leopoldo Villaseñor. **M:** Ana Satrova. **S:** Carlos Quiney, Marie-Claude Perin, Claudia Gravy, Luis Induni, José Truchardo.

Revenge of Ringo, The (IT)
Giunse Ringo e… fu tempo di massacro; Ringo, It's Massacre Time; Wanted Ringo (begun 1966, released 1971)
D: Mario Pinzauti (as Peter Launders). **P:** A. La Volpe. **W:** Mario Pinzauti. **C:** Vitaliano Natalucci. **M:** Felice Di Stefano. **S:** Jean Louis, Lucia Bomez, Mickey Hargitay, Anna Cerreto, Omero Gargano, Peter Martell.

Reverend Colt (SP-IT)
Reverendo Colt
D: Marino Girolami (credited to León Klimovsky). **P:** Marino Girolami. **W:** Tito Carpi, Manuel Martínez Remís. **C:** Salvatore Caruso.

M: Gianni Ferrio, Piero Umiliani. **S:** Guy Madison, Richard Harrison, Enio Girolami, María Martín, Germán Cobos, José Canalejas, Ignazio Spalla (as Pedro Sanchez), Cris Huerta.

Roy Colt and Winchester Jack (IT)
D: Mario Bava. **P:** Luigi Alessi. **W:** Mario Di Nardo. **C:** Antonio Rinaldi, Mario Bava. **M:** Piero Umiliani. **S:** Brett Halsey, Charles Southwood, Marilù Tolo, Teodoro Corrà, Isa Miranda, Bruno Corazzari, Federico Boido (as Rick Boyd), Guido Lollobrigida (as Lee Burton), Franco Pesce.

Sartana in the Valley of Death (IT)
Sartana nella valle degli avvoltoi; Sartana in the Valley of the Vultures; The Ballad of Death Valley; Sartana en el valle del oro
D: Roberto Mauri. **P:** Enzo Boetani. **W:** Roberto Mauri. **C:** Sandro Mancori. **M:** Augusto Martelli. **S:** William Berger, Wayde Preston, Aldo Berti, Jolanda Modio, Franco Ressel, Federico Boido (as Rick Boyd), Luciano Pigozzi (as Alan Collins).

Sartana's Here... Trade Your Pistol for a Coffin (IT)
C'è Sartana... vendi la pistola e comprati la bara!; Fistful of Lead
D: Giuliano Carnimeo (as Anthony Ascott). **P:** Franco Palaggi. **W:** Tito Carpi. **C:** Stelvio Massi. **M:** Francesco De Masi. **S:** George Hilton, Charles Southwood, Erika Blanc, Piero Lulli, Linda Sini, John Bartha, Federico Boido (as Rick Boyd), Carlo Gaddi, Nello Pazzafini, Spartaco Conversi, Luciano Rossi (as Lou Kamante), Furio Meniconi.

Shango (IT)
Shango la pistola infallibile
D: Edoardo Mulargia (as Edward G. Muller). **P:** PAC, SEPAC. **W:** Anthony Steffen, Edoardo Mulargia. **C:** Gino Santini. **M:** Gianfranco Di Stefano. **S:** Anthony Steffen, Eduardo Fajardo, Maurice Poli, Barbara Nelli, Giusva Fioravanti, Spartaco Conversi, Franco Pesce, Andrea Scotti.

Stagecoach of the Condemned (SP-IT)
La diligencia de los condenados; Prima ti perdono... poi t'ammazzo
D: Juan Bosch (as John Wood). **P:** Ignacio F. Iquino, Luciano Martino. **W:** Lou Carrigan (novel), Ignacio F. Iquino, Luciano Martino, Juliana de la Fuente, Vinicio Marinucci. **C:** Luciano Trasatti. **M:** Enrique Escobar. **S:** Richard Harrison, Erika Blanc, Fernando Sancho, Bruno Corazzari, Gustavo Ré, Antonio Molino Rojo.

They Call Me Trinity (IT)
Lo chiamavano Trinità
D: Enzo Barboni (as E.B. Clucher). **P:** Italo Zingarelli. **W:** Enzo Barboni. **C:** Aldo Giordani. **M:** Franco Micalizzi. **S:** Terence Hill, Bud Spencer, Farley Granger, Steffen Zacharias, Gisela Hahn, Remo Capitani, Alberto Dell'Acqua, Luciano Rossi, Antonio Monselesan (as Tony Norton).

Twenty Steps to Death (SP-IT)
Viente pasos para la muerte; Saranda
D: Manuel Esteba, Antonio Mollica (as Tony Mulligan; some sources also credit Ignacio F. Iquino). **P:** Admiral International Film, Ignacio F. Iquino. **W:** Ignacio F. Iquino, Lou Carrigan, Guido Leoni, Giorgio Rosati, Juliana de la Fuente. **C:** Antonio L. Ballesteros, Luciano Trasatti. **M:** Enrique Escobar. **S:** Dean Reed, Patty Shepard, Alberto Farnese (as Albert Farley), Cesar Ojinaga, Gustavo Ré, Luis Induni, Antonio Molino Rojo.

Twenty Thousand Dollars for Every Corpse (SP)
20,000 dólares por un cadaver
D: José María Zabalza. **P:** Procensa, Cinemec. **W:** José María Zabalza. **C:** Leopoldo Villaseñor. **M:** Ana Satrova, Gianni Marchetti. **S:** Miguel de la Riva (as Michael Rivers), Dianik Zurakowska, José Truchado, Guillermo Mendez, Fernando Sanchez Polack, Franco Fantasia, Luis Induni.

Twilight Avengers, The (IT)
I vendicatori dell'Ave Maria; Fighters from Ave Maria
D: Adalberto Albertini (as Al Albert). **P:** Lucio Marcuzzo. **W:** Adalberto Albertini. **C:** Antonio Modica. **M:** Piero Umiliani (also credited to Gianni Ferrio, Carlo Rustichelli and Carlo Savina). **S:** Luciano Stella (as Tony Kendall), Pietro Torrisi, Alberto Dell'Acqua, Ida Meda, Spartaco Conversi, Remo Capitani.

Viva Sabata! (SP-IT)
Reza por tu alma… y muere!; Arriva Sabata!; Dollars to Die For; Sabata the Killer
D: Tulio Demicheli. **P:** Tritone, DIA. **W:** Nino Stresa, Florentino Soria. **C:** Aldo Ricci. **M:** Marcello Giombini. **S:** Anthony Steffen, Peter Lee Lawrence, Eduardo Fajardo, Alfredo Mayo, Rossana Rovere, José Canalejas, Tito García, Cris Huerta, Luis Induni, Lorenzo Robledo.

Wanted Sabata (IT)
D: Roberto Mauri. **P:** Walter Brandi, Brad Harris, Ralph Zucker. **W:** Roberto Mauri, Ambrogio Molteni. **C:** Mario Mancini. **M:** Vassili Kojucharov. **S:** Brad Harris, Vassili Karamesinis (as Vassili Karis), Elena Pedemonte, Paolo Magalotti, Gino Lavagetto, Giovanni Cianfriglia (as Ken Wood).

Wind from the East (FR-IT-GER)
Le vent d'est; Vento dell'est; Ostwind
D: Jean-Luc Godard, Jean-Pierre Gorin, Gérard Martin (as Groupe Dziga Vertov). **P:** Anouchka Film, Poli Film, Filmkuntz. **W:** Sergio Bazzini, Daniel Cohn-Bendit, Jean-Luc Godard, Jean-Pierre Gorin. **C:** Mario Vulpiani. **M:** None credited. **S:** Gian Maria Volonté, Anne Wiazemsky, Daniel Cohn-Bendit, Allen Midgette, José Valéra, Federico Boido (as Rick Boyd).

1971

Acquasanta Joe (IT)
Holy Water Joe
D: Mario Gariazzo. **P:** Daunia 70. **W:** Mario Gariazzo, Nando Poggi (some sources also credit Nello Rossati). **C:** Franco Villa. **M:** Marcello Giombini. **S:** Lincoln Tate, Ty Hardin, Richard Harrison, Pietro Ceccarelli, Silvia Monelli, Federico Boido (as Rick Boyd).

And the Crows Will Dig Your Grave (SP-IT)
Los buitres cavarán tu fosa; I corvi ti scaveranno la fossa
D: Juan Bosch (as John Wood). **P:** Luciano Martino, Miguel de Echarri. **W:** Lou Carrigan, Juan Bosch, Roberto Gianviti. **C:** Giancarlo Ferrando. **M:** Bruno Nicolai. **S:** Craig Hill, Ángel Aranda, Fernando Sancho, Maria Pia Conte, Frank Braña, Raf Baldassarre, Antonio Molino Rojo.

Arizona Kid (PHIL)
(shot in Spain)
D: Luciano B. Carlos. **P:** Cirio H. Santiago. **W:** Lino Brocka, Luciano B. Carlos. **C:** Felipe Sacdalan. **M:** Restie Umali. **S:** Augusto Pangan (as Chiquito), Mamie Van Doren, Gordon Mitchell, Mariela Branger, Bernard Bonnin, Pilar Velázquez, Victor Israel, Dan van Husen.

Bad Man's River (SP-IT-FR)
El hombre de Rio Malo; E continuavano a fregarsi il milione di dollari; Et ils continuaient a se voler l'un l'autre le million de dollars
D: Eugenio Martín (as Gene Martin). **P:** Bernard Gordon. **W:** Eugenio Martín, Philip Yordan. **C:** Alejandro Ulloa. **M:** Waldo de los Rios. **S:** Lee Van Cleef, James Mason, Gina Lollobrigida, Gianni Garko (as John Garko), Simón Andreu, Eduardo Fajardo, Barta Barry, Tito García, Daniel Martín, José Manuel Martín, Ricardo Palacios, Aldo Sambrell, Dan van Husen.

Ballad of Django, The (IT)
Giù le mani… carogna! (Django Story); Reach You Bastard
D: Demofilo Fidani (as Lucky Dickinson). **P:** Demofilo Fidani, Maria Vitelli. **W:** Demofilo Fidani. **C:** Franco Villa. **M:** Coriolano Gori. **S:** Hunt Powers, Gordon Mitchell, Dino Strano (as Dean Stratford), Giovanni Scarciofolo (as Jeff Cameron), Benito Pacifico (as Dennis Colt), Luciano Conti (as Lucky McMurray).

Bandido malpelo, El (IT-SP)
Il lungo giorno della violenza
D: Giuseppe Maria Scotese. **P:** Suprania Films, Copercines. **W:** Giuseppe Maria Scotese, Eduardo Manzanos Brochero. **C:** Giampaolo Santini. **M:** Marcello Giombini. **S:** Eduardo Fajardo, George Garvell, Charo López, José Nieto, Sergio Doria.

Barrel Full of Dollars, A (IT)
Per una bara piena di dollari; Showdown for a Badman; Nevada Kid
D: Demofilo Fidani (as Miles Deem). **P:** Elektra Film. **W:** Demofilo Fidani, Teodoro Ricci, Alfredo Medori. **C:** Aristide Massaccesi. **M:** Coriolano Gori. **S:** Hunt Powers, Gordon Mitchell, Ray Saunders, Klaus Kinski, Simonetta Vitelli (as Simone Blondell), Giovanni Scarciofolo (as Jeff Cameron).

Bastard, Go and Kill (IT)
Bastardo… vamos a matar; Chaco
D: Luigi Mangini (begun by Sergio Garrone). **P:** ICP, Sal Cinco. **W:** Sergio Garrone, Luigi Mangini. **C:** Giuseppe Gatti. **M:** Carlo Rustichelli. **S:** Luigi Montefiori (as George Eastman), Lincoln Tate, Franco Lantieri, Antonella Steni, Furio Meniconi, Remo Capitani, José Manuel Martín.

Black Killer (IT)
D: Carlo Croccolo (as Lucky Moore). **P:** Virginia. **W:** Carlo Veo, Luigi Angelo. **C:** Franco Villa. **M:** Daniele Patucchi. **S:** Klaus Kinski, Fred Robsahm, Antonio Cantafora, Marina Malfatti (as Marina Mulligan), Carlo Croccolo.

Blindman (IT-US)
D: Ferdinando Baldi. **P:** Saul Swimmer, Tony Anthony. **W:** Piero Anchisi, Tony Anthony, Vincenzo Cerami. **C:** Riccardo Pallottini. **M:** Stelvio Cipriani. **S:** Tony Anthony, Ringo Starr, Lloyd Battista, Magda Konopka, Raf Baldassarre, Salvatore Billa, Agneta Eckemyr, Tito García.

Brother Outlaw (IT)
Rimase uno solo e fu la morte per tutti!
D: Edoardo Mulargia (as Edward G. Muller). **P:** Trans World Films. **W:** Edoardo Mulargia, Alessandro Schirò. **C:** Antonio Modica. **M:** Felice Di Stefano, Gianfranco Di Stefano. **S:** Luciano Stella (as Tony Kendall), Jean Louis, Sophia Kammara, Omero Gargano, Dino Strano (as Dean Stratford).

Captain Apache (UK-SP)
The Gun of April Morning; Capitán Apache
D: Alexander Singer. **P:** Milton Sperling, Philip Yordan. **W:** S.E. Whitman (novel), Milton Sperling, Philip Yordan. **C:** John Cabrera. **M:** Dolores Claman. **S:** Lee Van Cleef, Caroll Baker, Stuart Whitman, Percy Herbert, Elisa Montés, José Bódalo, Charly Bravo, Cris Huerta, Luis Induni, Ricardo Palacios, Dan van Husen.

Carlos (GER)
D: Hans W. Geissendörfer. **P:** Karl Helmer. **W:** Friedrich Schiller (book), Bernd Fiedler, Hans W. Geissendörfer. **C:** Robby Müller. **M:** Ernst Brandner, Can. **S:** Bernhard Wicki, Anna Karina, Geraldine Chaplin, Gottfried John, Horst Frank.

Catlow (UK)
D: Sam Wanamaker. **P:** Euan Lloyd. **W:** Louis L'Amour (novel), Scott Finch, J.J. Griffith. **C:** Edward Scaife. **M:** Roy Budd. **S:** Yul Brynner, Richard Crenna, Leonard Nimoy, Daliah Lavi, Jo Ann Pflug, Angel del Pozo, Tito García, Victor Israel, Dan van Husen.

Cut-Throats Nine (SP)
Condenados a vivir; Bronson's Revenge
D: Joaquín Romero Marchent. **P:** Films Triunfo. **W:** Santiago Moncada, Joaquín Romero Marchent. **C:** Luis Cuadrado. **M:** Carmelo Alonso Bernaola. **S:** Claudio Undari (as Robert Hundar), Emma Cohen, Alberto Dalbés, Antonio Iranzo, Manuel Tejada, José Manuel Martín, Lorenzo Robledo, Carlos Romero Marchent, Dan van Husen.

Damnation (IT)
La stirpe di Caino
(nb: seems to have remained unreleased)
D: Lamberto Benvenuti. **P:** Gabriele Crisanti. **W:** Lamberto Benvenuti. **C:** Aiace Parolin. **M:** Unknown. **S:** Stefania Careddu, Dean Reed, Umberto Raho, Gino Lavagetto, Catherine Damiani.

Dead Men Ride (IT-SP)
Anda muchacho, spara!; El sol baja la tierra; Il sole sotto la terra
D: Aldo Florio. **P:** Alfredo Nicolai. **W:** Eduardo Manzanos Brochero, Bruno Di Geronimo, Aldo Florio. **C:** Emilio Foriscot. **M:** Bruno Nicolai. **S:** Fabio Testi, Charo López, José Calvo, Ben Carrà, Eduardo Fajardo, Daniel Martín, Luciano Pigozzi, Romano Puppo, Goffredo Unger, Paco Sanz.

Dig Your Grave Friend… Sabata's Coming (SP-IT)
¡Abre tu fosa, amigo, llega Sabata!; Sei già cadavere amigo… ti cerca Garringo
D: Juan Bosch (as John Wood). **P:** Ignacio F. Iquino, Devon Film. **W:** Ignacio F. Iquino, Luciano Martino, Sauro Scavolini, Juliana de la Fuente. **C:** Floriano Trenker. **M:** Enrique Escobar. **S:** Richard Harrison, Fernando Sancho, Raf Baldassarre, Tania Alvarado, Indio Gonzalez, Luis Induni.

Django's Cut Price Corpses (IT)
Anche per Django le carogne hanno un prezzo; Even Django Has His Price
D: Luigi Batzella (as Paolo Solvay). **P:** Constitution Films. **W:** Luigi Batzella, Mario DeRosa, Gaetano Dell'Era. **C:** Giorgio Montagnani. **M:** Vassili Kojucharov. **S:** Giovanni Scarciofolo (as Jeff Cameron), John Desmont, Esmeralda Barros, Gengher Gatti, Edilio Kim.

Euro-Western Filmography

Doc (US)
(shot in Spain)
D: Frank Perry. **P:** Frank Perry. **W:** Peter Hamill. **C:** Gerald Hirschfeld. **M:** Jimmy Webb. **S:** Stacy Keach, Faye Dunaway, Harris Yulin, Michael Witney, Denver John Collins, Luís Barboo, Ricardo Palacios, Dan van Husen.

Doomsday (IT)
Il giorno del giudizio; Drummer of Vengeance; An Eye for an Eye
D: Mario Gariazzo. **P:** Mario Gariazzo. **W:** Franco Daniele, Mario Gariazzo, Nello Rossati. **C:** Alvaro Lanzoni. **M:** General Music. **S:** Ty Hardin, Craig Hill, Gordon Mitchell, Rossano Brazzi, Edda Di Benedetto, Raf Baldassarre, Rosalba Neri, Federico Boido (as Rick Boyd), Guido Lollobrigida (as Lee Burton), Bruno Corazzari, Giovanni Cianfriglia (as Ken Wood), Antonio Monselesan (as Tony Norton).

Durango Is Coming, Pay or Die (IT)
Arriva Durango: paga o muori; Here's Django... Pay or Die!!
D: Roberto Bianchi Montero. **P:** Gisleno Procaccini. **W:** Mario Guerra, Vittoriano Vighi. **C:** Mario Mancini. **M:** Coriolano Gori. **S:** Brad Harris, José Torres, Gisela Hahn, Gino Lavagetto, Erika Blanc, Maretta Procaccini, Giovanni Cianfriglia (as Ken Wood), Andrea Scotti.

Finders Killers (IT)
Se t'incontro, t'ammazzo
D: Gianni Crea. **P:** Fernando Morbis. **W:** Fabio Piccioni. **C:** Vitaliano Natalucci, Giovanni Varriano. **M:** Stelvio Cipriani. **S:** Donal O'Brien, Gordon Mitchell, Pia Giancaro, Dino Strano (as Dean Stratford), Emilio Messina, Femi Benussi, Mario Brega.

Fistful of Death, A (IT)
Giù la testa, hombre!; The Strange Tale of Minnesota Stinky; Doppia taglia per Minnesota Stinky
D: Demofilo Fidani (as Miles Deem). **P:** Diego Spataro. **W:** Demofilo Fidani, Maria Vitelli, Alfredo Medori. **C:** Aristide Massaccesi. **M:** Coriolano Gori. **S:** Hunt Powers, Klaus Kinski, Gordon Mitchell, Giovanni Scarciofolo (as Jeff Cameron), Benito Pacifico (as Dennis Colt).

Fistful of Dynamite, A (IT)
Giù la testa; Duck You Sucker
D: Sergio Leone. **P:** Fulvio Morsella. **W:** Sergio Leone, Sergio Donati, Luciano Vincenzoni. **C:** Giuseppe Ruzzolini. **M:** Ennio Morricone. **S:** Rod Steiger, James Coburn, Romolo Valli, Jean Michel Antoine, David Warbeck, Rik Battaglia, Maria Monti, Franco Graziosi, Aldo Sambrell, Furio Meniconi, Conrado San Martín.

Four Candles for My Colt (SP-IT)
Un colt por cuatro cirios; La mia Colt ti cerca... 4 ceri ti aspettano
D: Ignacio F. Iquino (as Steve McCohy). **P:** IFISA. **W:** Lou Carrigan (novel), Antonio Ramirez, Juliana de la Fuente (as Jackie Kelly), Ignacio F. Iquino (as Steve McCohy). **C:** Antonio L. Ballesteros Jr. **M:** Enrique Escobar. **S:** Robert Woods, Olga Roman, Mariano Vidal Molina, Cris (Kriss) Huerta, María Martín, Luis Ciges, Antonio Molino Rojo.

Four Pistols for Trinity (IT)
I quattro pistoleri di Santa Trinità; Four Gunmen of the Holy Trinity
D: Giorgio Cristallini. **P:** Umberto Russo. **W:** Giorgio Cristallini. **C:** Alessandro D'Eva. **M:** Roberto Pregadio. **S:** Peter Lee Lawrence, Ida Galli (as Evelyn Stewart), Daniele Vargas, Daniela Giordano, Valeria Fabrizi, Raf Baldassarre.

Girl Is a Gun, A (FR)
Une aventure de Billy the Kid
D: Luc Moullet. **P:** Luc Moullet. **W:** Luc Moullet. **C:** Jean Flori, Jean Gonnet. **M:** Patrice Moullet. **S:** Jean-Pierre Léaud, Rachel Kesterber, Jean Valmont, Bruno Kresoja, Michel Minaud.

Gunman of 100 Crosses (IT)
Una pistola per cento croci
D: Carlo Croccolo (as Lucky Moore). **P:** Kamar. **W:** Carlo Croccolo, Fabrizio Diotallevi. **C:** Franco Villa. **M:** Marcello Minerbi. **S:** Luciano Stella (as Tony Kendall), Ray Saunders, Marina Malfatti (as Marina Mulligan), Mimmo Palmara (as Dick Palmer), Monica Miguel.

Hands Up, Dead Man! You're Under Arrest (SP-IT)
Un dolár para Sartana; Su le mani, cadavere! Sei in arresto
D: León Klimovsky (actually believed to have been Sergio Bergonzelli). **P:** Sergio Bergonzelli. **W:** Sergio Bergonzelli, Howard Berk (as José Luis Navarro), José Maria Elorrieta, Enrico Zuccarini. **C:** Tonino Maccoppi. **M:** Alessandro Alessandroni. **S:** Peter Lee Lawrence, Espartaco Santoni, Helga Liné, Franco Agostini, Aldo Sambrell, Luís Barboo, José Canalejas, Lorenzo Robledo.

Hannie Caulder (UK)
(shot in Spain)
D: Burt Kennedy. **P:** Patrick Curtis. **W:** Z.X. Jones (actually Peter Cooper, David Haft, Burt Kennedy). **C:** Edward Scaife. **M:** Ken Thorne. **S:** Raquel Welch, Robert Culp, Ernest Borgnine, Christopher Lee, Jack Elam, Luís Barboo, Aldo Sambrell, Stephen Boyd.

He Was Called the Holy Ghost (IT)
...E lo chiamarono Spirito Santo
D: Roberto Mauri. **P:** Cepa. **W:** Roberto Mauri. **C:** Mario Mancini. **M:** Carlo Savina. **S:** Vassili Karamesinis (as Vassili Karis), Mimmo Palmara (as Dick Palmer), Margaret Rose, Hunt Powers, José Torres.

Heads I Kill You... Tails You're Dead! They Call Me Hallelujah (IT)
Testa t'ammazzo, croce... sei morto! Mi chiamano Alleluja; They Call Me Hallelujah; Guns for Dollars
D: Giuliano Carnimeo (as Anthony Ascott). **P:** Dario Sabatello. **W:** Tito Carpi. **C:** Stelvio Massi. **M:** Stelvio Cipriani. **S:** George Hilton, Charles Southwood, Agata Flori, Roberto Camardiel, Federico Boido (as Rick Boyd), Aldo Berti, John Bartha, Andrea Bosic, Paolo Gozlino, Franco Pesce, Luciano Rossi, Furio Meniconi, Goffredo Unger.

Hey Amigo! A Toast to Your Death (IT)
Ehi amigo... Sei morto!
D: Paolo Bianchini (as Paul Maxwell). **P:** Renato Savino. **W:** Roberto Colangeli, Renato Savino. **C:** Sergio D'Offizi. **M:** Carlo Savina. **S:** Wayde Preston, Marco Zuanelli, Rik Battaglia, Aldo Berti, Raf Baldassarre.

His Name Was King (IT)
Lo chiamavano King...; The Last Bullet
D: Renato Savino or Giancarlo Romitelli (as Don Reynolds). **P:** Luigi Nannerini. **W:** Renato Savino. **C:** Guglielmo Mancori. **M:** Luis Enríquez Bacalov. **S:** Richard Harrison, Klaus Kinski, Anne Puskin, Marco Zuanelli, Luciano Pigozzi, Federico Boido (as Rick Boyd), John Bartha, Tom Felleghy, Goffredo Unger.

His Name Was Sam Wallash... But They Called Him Amen! (IT)
Era Sam Wallash! ...Lo chiamavano... E "Cosí Sia"; Savage Guns
D: Demofilo Fidani (as Miles Deem). **P:** Demofilo Fidani. **W:** Mila Vitelli, Demofilo Fidani. **C:** Franco Villa. **M:** Coriolano Gori. **S:** Robert Woods, Dino Strano (as Dean Stratford), Benito Pacifico (as Dennis Colt), Amerigo Leoni (as Custer Gail), Simonetta Vitelli (as Simone Blondell), Gordon Mitchell, Peter Martell, Lincoln Tate.

Hunting Party, The (UK)
(shot in Spain)
D: Don Medford. **P:** Arthur Gardner, Jules V. Levy, Lou Morheim. **W:** Gilbert Ralston, Lou Morheim, William W. Norton. **C:** Cecilio Paniagua. **M:** Riz Ortolani. **S:** Oliver Reed, Gene Hackman, Candice Bergen, Simon Oakland, Mitch Ryan, Charly Bravo.

In the Dust of the Sun (FR)
Dans la poussière du soleil
D: Richard Balducci. **P:** Univers Galaxie. **W:** Richard Balducci (uncredited). **C:** Tadasu G. Suzuki. **M:** Francis Lai. **S:** Bob Cunningham, Maria Schell, Daniel Beretta, José Calvo, Karin Meier, Angel del Pozo, Lorenzo Robledo.

Judge Roy Bean (IT-FR)
Le juge; All'ovest di Sacramento
D: Federico Chentrens, Jean Girault (credited to 'Richard Owens'). **P:** Comacico, Milvia Cinematografica. **W:** Morris and René Goscinny (characters), Jacques Villfrid, Luigi Angelo, Federico Chentrens, Oscar De Mans. **C:** Mario Fioretti. **M:** Pierre Perret. **S:** Pierre Perret, Robert Hossein, Silvia Monti, Xavier Gélin, Angelo Infanti, Antonio Gradoli.

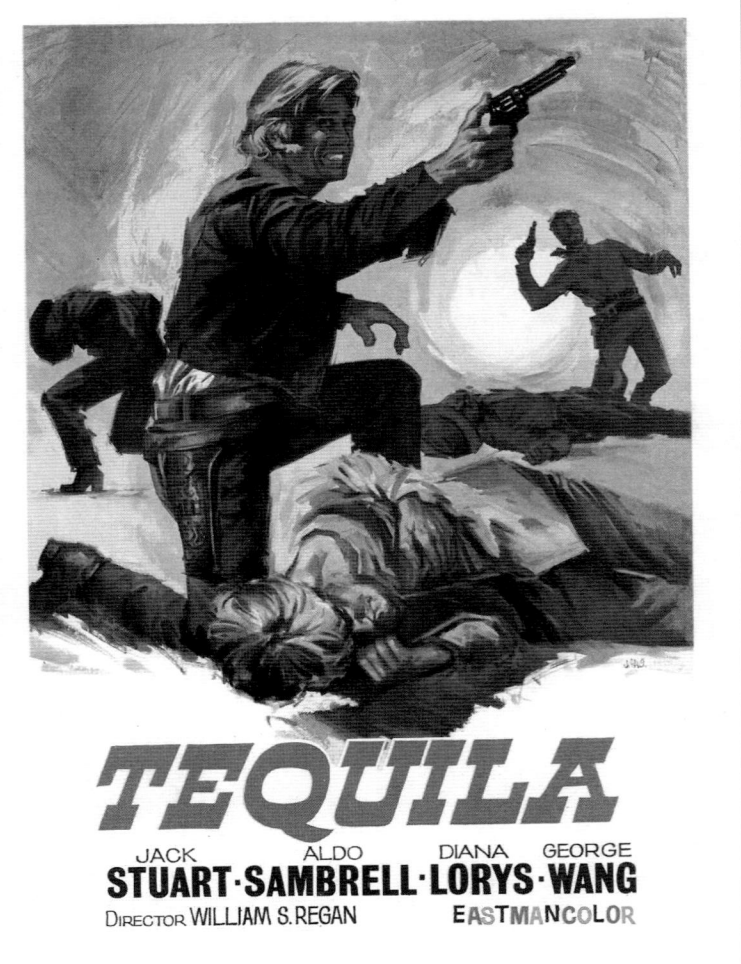

Kill Django... Kill First (IT-SP)
Uccidi Django... uccidi per primo!; Tequila
D: Sergio Garrone. **P:** Gianni Vari, Angel Alonso. **W:** Ambrogio Molteni, Víctor Andrés Catena (Italian sources also credit Sergio Garrone, Spanish sources also credit Jaime Comas Gil). **C:** Gaetano Valle. **M:** Elsio Mancuso. **S:** Giacomo Rossi-Stuart (as Jack Stuart), Aldo Sambrell, Diana Lorys, Krista Nell, George Wang, Roberto Camardiel, Silvio Bagolini, Eduardo Fajardo, Aldo Sambrell, Furio Meniconi, Lorenzo Robledo, Anthony Steffen.

Last Rebel, The (US)
Il suo nome è Qualcuno (shot in Italy)
D: Larry G. Spangler. **P:** Larry G. Spangler. **W:** Lorenzo Sabatini (as Warren Kiefer). **C:** Carlo Carlini. **M:** Tony Ashton, Jon Lord. **S:** Joe Namath, Jack Elam, Woody Strode, Ty Hardin, Victoria George.

Legend of Frenchie King, The (FR-IT-SP-UK)
Les petroleuses; Le pistolere; Las petroleras
D: Christian-Jaque (begun by Guy Casaril). **P:** Raymond Eger, Francis Cosne. **W:** Guy Casaril, Daniel Boulanger, Marie-Ange Aniès, Jean Nemours. **C:** Henri Persin. **M:** Francis Lai. **S:** Brigitte Bardot, Claudia Cardinale, Michael J. Pollard, Patty Shepard, Micheline Presle, Cris Huerta, Luis Induni.

Let's Go and Kill Sartana (IT)
Vamos a matar Sartana; Demasiados muertos para Tex
D: Mario Pinzauti (Spanish version credited to George Martin). **P:** Marco Claudio. **W:** Rafael Marina, Marco Masi. **C:** Jaime Deu Casas, Giovanni Raffaldi. **M:** José Espeita (also credited to Pat Bodio). **S:** George Martin, Gordon Mitchell, Isarco Ravaioli, Virginia Rodin, Monica Taber, Frank Braña, Daniel Martín, Pajarito.

Lobo the Bastard (IT)
Il suo nome era Pot... ma... lo chiamavano Allegria
D: Demofilo Fidani, Lucio Giachin (as Dennis Ford). **P:** Massimo Bernardi. **W:** Lucio Giachin, Diego Spataro. **C:** Mario Mancini. **M:** Nico Fidenco. **S:** Peter Martell, Lincoln Tate, Daniela Giordano, Gordon Mitchell, Xiro Papas, Erika Blanc, Carlos Romero Marchent.

Euro-Western Filmography

Long Live Your Death (IT-SP-GER)
Viva la muerte... tua!; Viva la muerte tuya; Zwei wilde Companeros; Don't Turn the Other Cheek
D: Duccio Tessari. **P:** Tritone, P.O.F., Terra. **W:** Lewis B. Patten (novel), Marcello Coscia, Massimo De Rita, Dino Maiuri, Duccio Tessari, Juan de Orduna y Fernandez, Gunter Eber. **C:** José F. Aguayo. **M:** Gianni Ferrio. **S:** Eli Wallach, Franco Nero, Lynn Redgrave, Eduardo Fajardo, Horst Janson, Tito García, Victor Israel, José Jaspe, Furio Meniconi, Lorenzo Robledo, Dan van Husen.

Long Ride to Eden, A (GER)
Ein langer Ritt nach Eden
D: Günter Hendel. **P:** Günter Hendel. **W:** Robert S. Gordon. **C:** Lutz Ziervogel. **M:** Stanley Fromm, Walter Geiger. **S:** Günter Hendel, Mike Run, Karin Heske, Ingrid Steeger, Achim Hammer.

Lucky Johnny: Born in America (MEX-IT)
Arde, baby, arde; Serpente a sonagli; Death Rattler; Dead Aim
D: José Antonio Bolaños. **P:** Juan Abusaid Ríos. **W:** Pedro F. Miret, José Antonio Balaños. **C:** Alex Phillips. **M:** Luchi De Jesús. **S:** Glen Lee, Virgil Frye, Venetia Vianello, James Westerfield, Jorge Russek.

Man Called Django, A (IT)
W Django!
D: Edoardo Mulargia (as Edward G. Muller). **P:** Pino De Martino. **W:** Nino Stresa. **C:** Marcello Masciocchi. **M:** Piero Umiliani. **S:** Anthony Steffen, Stelio Candelli, Chris Avram, Glauco Onorato, Esmeralda Barros, Simonetta Vitelli (as Simone Blondell), Remo Capitani, Furio Meniconi, Giovanni Cianfriglia (as Ken Wood), Benito Stefanelli.

Man in the Wilderness (US)
(shot in Spain)
D: Richard C. Sarafian. **P:** Sandy Howard. **W:** Jack DeWitt. **C:** Gerry Fisher. **M:** Johnny Harris. **S:** Richard Harris, John Huston, John Bindon, Prunella Ransome, Percy Herbert.

My Name Is Mallory (IT)
Il mio nome è Mallory, "M" come morte; Mallory Must Not Die
D: Mario Moroni. **P:** Cervo Film. **W:** Mario Moroni, Giuseppe Aquari. **M:** Roberto Pregadio. **S:** Robert Woods, Gabriella Giorgelli, Teodoro Corrà, Renato Baldini, Artemio Antonini, Aldo Berti.

Osceola (GDR-BUL-CUBA)
Osceola – Die rechte Hand der Vergeltung
D: Konrad Petzold. **P:** DEFA, Kino-Zentrum Sofia, ACAIC. **W:** Günter Karl, Walter Püschel, Hans-Joachim Wallstein. **M:** Wilhelm Neef. **S:** Gojko Mitic, Horst Schulze, Iurie Darie, Karin Ugowski, Kati Bus, Konrad Petzold.

Paid in Blood (IT)
Quelle sporche anime dannate
D: Luigi Batzella (as Paolo Solvay). **P:** Gino Turini. **W:** Aldo Barni. **C:** Giorgio Montagnani. **M:** Elsio Mancuso. **S:** Giovanni Scarciofolo (as Jeff Cameron), Donal O'Brien, Alfredo Rizzo, Krista Nell, Edilio Kim.

Price of Death, The (IT)
Il venditore di morte
D: Enzo Gicca Palli (as Vincent Thomas). **P:** Albano Ingrami. **W:** Enzo Gicca Palli. **C:** Franco Villa. **M:** Mario Migliardi. **S:** Gianni Garko, Klaus Kinski, Gely Genka, Franco Abbina, Luciano Catenacci (as Luciano Lorcas), Luciano Pigozzi (as Alan Collins), Andrea Scotti.

Rain for a Dusty Summer (US)
(shot in Spain)
Guns of the Revolution
D: Arthur Lubin. **P:** G.B. Buscemi. **W:** Franklin Lacey, G.B. Buscemi, Julius Evans. **C:** Manuel Berenguer. **M:** Wade Denning. **S:** Ernest Borgnine, Humberto Almazan, Sancho Gracia, Vicente Sangiovanni, Aldo Sambrell.

Red Sun (FR-IT-SP)
Soleil rouge; Sole rosso; Sol rojo
D: Terence Young. **P:** Ted Richmond. **W:** Laird Koenig, Denne Bart Petitclerc, William Roberts, Lawrence Roman. **C:** Henri Alekan. **M:** Maurice Jarre. **S:** Charles Bronson, Toshiro Mifune, Alain Delon, Ursula Andress, Capucine, Anthony Dawson, Guido Lollobrigida (as Lee Burton), Barta Barry, José Jaspe, Ricardo Palacios.

Return of Sabata (IT-FR-GER)
E' tornato Sabata... Hai chiuso un'altra volta; Le retour de Sabata; Sabata kehrt zurück
D: Gianfranco Parolini (as Frank Kramer). **P:** Alberto Grimaldi. **W:** Renato Izzo, Gianfranco Parolini. **C:** Sandro Mancori. **M:** Marcello Giombini. **S:** Lee Van Cleef, Reiner Schöne, Giampiero Albertini, Ignazio Spalla (as Pedro Sanchez), Annabella Incontrera, Salvatore Billa, Gianni Rizzo, John Bartha, Federico Boido (as Rick Boyd), Giovanni Cianfriglia (as Ken Wood), Franco Fantasia, Luciano Rossi.

Sheriff of Rocksprings, The (IT)
Lo sceriffo di Rockspring
D: Mario Sabatini. **P:** Ras Film. **W:** Elido Sorrentino, Gianni Luigi. **C:** Giovanni Raffaldi. **M:** Felice Di Stefano, Gianfranco Di Stefano. **S:** Richard Harrison, Cosetta Greco, Donal O'Brien, Maria Morgan, Joseph Logan.

Shoot the Living and Pray for the Dead (IT)
Prega il morto e ammazza il vivo; To Kill a Jackal
D: Giuseppe Vari (as Joseph Warren). **P:** Castor. **W:** Adriano Bolzoni (as Mark Salter). **C:** Franco Villa. **M:** Mario Migliardi. **S:** Klaus Kinski, Victoria Zinny, Paolo Casella (as Paul Sullivan), Dino Strano (as Dean Stratford), Patrizia Adiutori, Goffredo Unger.

Tara Pokì (IT)
D: Amasi Damiani. **P:** Pokì Cinematografica. **W:** Graziella Marsetti, Salvatore Siciliano, Stelio Tanzini. **C:** Giovanni Varriano. **M:** Mino, Domenico and Franco Reitano. **S:** Meno Reitano, Aliza Adar, Ignazio Spalla (as Pedro Sanchez), Fulvia Franco, Angelo Marano.

They Call Him Cemetery (IT)
Gli fumavano le Colt... lo chiamavano Camposanto; Bullet for a Stranger
D: Giuliano Carnimeo (as Anthony Ascott). **P:** Mino Loy. **W:** Enzo Barboni (as E.B. Clucher). **C:** Stelvio Massi. **M:** Bruno Nicolai. **S:** Gianni Garko, William Berger, Christopher Chittell, John Fordyce, Ugo Fangareggi, Federico Boido (as Rick Boyd), Franco Ressel, Pietro Ceccarelli, Furio Meniconi, Nello Pazzafini, Goffredo Unger.

Thirteenth Is a Judas (IT)
Il tredicesimo e' sempre Giuda; The Last Traitor
D: Giuseppe Vari (as Joseph Warren). **P:** Castor Film. **W:** Adriano Bolzoni. **C:** Angelo Lotti. **M:** Carlo Savina. **S:** Donal O'Brien, Maurice Poli, Dino Strano (as Dean Stratford), Maily Doria, Fortunato Arena.

Town Called Bastard, A (UK-SP)
A Town Called Hell; Una ciudad llamada Bastarda
D: Robert Parrish. **P:** S. Benjamin Fisz. **W:** Richard Aubrey. **C:** Manuel Berenguer. **M:** Waldo de los Rios. **S:** Robert Shaw, Telly Savalas, Stella Stevens, Fernando Rey, Martin Landau, Charly Bravo, Tito García, Cris Huerta, George Rigaud, Aldo Sambrell.

Trinity Is Still My Name (IT)
...Continuavano a chiamarlo Trinità
D: Enzo Barboni (as E.B. Clucher). **P:** Italo Zingarelli. **W:** Enzo Barboni. **C:** Aldo Giordani. **M:** Guido and Maurizio De Angelis. **S:** Terence Hill, Bud Spencer, Yanti Somer, Enzo Tarascio, Harry Carey Jr., Dana Ghia, Franco Ressel, Furio Meniconi, Benito Stefanelli, Antonio Monselesan (as Tony Norton).

Valdez Is Coming (US)
(shot in Spain)
D: Edwin Sherin. **P:** Roland Kibbee, Sam Manners, Ira Steiner. **W:** Elmore Leonard (novel), Roland Kibbee, David Rayfiel. **C:** Gábor Pogány. **M:** Charles Gross. **S:** Burt Lancaster, Susan Clark, Frank Silvera, Jon Cypher, Richard Jordan.

Vendetta at Dawn (IT)
Quel maledetto giorno della resa dei conti; The Last Day
D: Sergio Garrone (as Willy S. Regan; begun by Luigi Mangini). **P:** Felice Zappulla. **W:** Sergio Garrone, Luigi Mangini. **C:** Guglielmo Mancori. **M:** Francesco De Masi. **S:** Luigi Montefiori (as George Eastman), Ty Hardin, Bruno Corazzari, Costanza Spada, Dominic Barto, Federico Boido (as Rick Boyd), Guido Lollobrigida (as Lee Burton), Nello Pazzafini.

Vengeance Trail (IT)
La vendetta è un piatto che si serve freddo; Vengeance Is a Dish Served Cold
D: Pasquale Squitieri (as William Redford). **P:** Filmes. **W:** Monica Venturini, Pasquale Squitieri. **C:** Angelo Lotti. **M:** Piero Umiliani. **S:** Leonard Mann, Ivan Rassimov, Klaus Kinski, Elisabeth Eversfield, Steffen Zacharias, Salvatore Billa.

Whity (GER)
D: Rainer Werner Fassbinder. **P:** Peter Berling, Ulli Lommel, Peer Raben. **W:** Rainer Werner Fassbinder. **C:** Michael Ballhaus. **M:** Peer Raben. **S:** Ron Randell, Hanna Schygulla, Katrin Schaake, Harry Baer, Ulli Lommel.

Zorro, Rider of Vengeance (SP-IT)
El Zorro, caballero de la justicia; Zorro il cavaliere della vendetta
D: José Luis Merino. **P:** C.C. Carthago Film, Duca International. **W:** José Luis Merino (some

sources also credit María del Carmen Martínez Román). **C:** Emanuele Di Cola. **M:** Francesco De Masi. **S:** Carlos Quiney (as Charles Quiney), Malisa Longo, Fernando Hilbek, María Mahor, Pasquale Basile.

Zorro, the Mask of Vengeance (SP-IT)
El Zorro de Monterrey; Zorro, la maschera della vendetta
D: José Luis Merino. **P:** Hispamer Film, Filmar. **W:** Mario Damiani, Bautista Lacasa, María del Carmen Martínez Román, José Luis Merino (some Italian sources also credit Enzo Gicca Palli, Mario Damiani). **C:** Emanuele Di Cola, Antonio Modica. **M:** Alessandro Alessandroni. **S:** Carlos Quiney (as Charles Quiney), Léa Nanni, Mariano Vidal Molina, Pasquale Basile, Luis Marin.

1972

Animal Called Man, An (IT)
Un animale chiamato… uomo
D: Roberto Mauri. **P:** Romano Vincenzo. **W:** Roberto Mauri. **C:** Luigi Ciccarese. **M:** Carlo Savina. **S:** Vassili Karamesinis (as Vassili Karis), Omero Capanna, Gillian Bray, Craig Hill, Paolo Magalotti.

Bandits (IT-SP-GER)
La banda J & S.: cronaca criminale del Far West; Los hijos del dia y de la noche; Die Rote Sonne der Rache; J&S Gang; Bandera Bandits; Sonny & Jed
D: Sergio Corbucci. **P:** Roberto Loyola, Orfeo, Terra. **W:** Sergio Corbucci, Sabatino Ciuffini, Mario Amendola, Adriano Bolzoni, José Maria Forqué. **C:** Luis Cuadrado. **M:** Ennio Morricone. **S:** Tomas Milian, Susan George, Telly Savalas, Rosanna Yanni, Eduardo Fajardo, Victor Israel, Dan van Husen.

Ben and Charlie (IT)
Amico, stammi lontano almeno un palmo…; Humpty Dumpty Gang
D: Michele Lupo. **P:** Franco Committeri. **W:** Sergio Donati, Luigi Montefiori. **C:** Aristide Massaceesi. **M:** Gianni Ferrio. **S:** Giuliano Gemma, Luigi Montefiori (as George Eastman), Marisa Mell, Vittorio Congia, Giacomo Rossi-Stuart, Luciano Catenacci, Roberto Camardiel, Franco Fantasia, George Rigaud, Tom Felleghy, Remo Capitani, Nello Pazzafini, Cris Huerta, Aldo Sambrell, Luis Induni, José Manuel Martín, Giovanni Cianfriglia (as Ken Wood), Paco Sanz.

Beyond the Frontiers of Hate (IT)
Al di là dell'odio…
D: Alessandro Santini. **P:** Gaetano Ferri. **W:** Alessandro Santini, Bruno Vani. **C:** Gaetano Valle. **M:** Elsio Mancuso. **S:** Giovanni Scarciofolo (as Jeff Cameron), Stefania Nelli, George Cavendish, Cameron Steel, Laila Shed.

Boldest Job in the West, The (SP-IT-FR)
El mas fabuloso golpe del Far West; Nevada; Hold-up à Sun Valley
D: José Antonio de la Loma. **P:** José Maria Carcasona. **W:** José Antonio de la Loma. **C:** Hans Burman, Antonio Millan. **M:** Stelvio Cipriani. **S:** Mark Edwards, Fernando Sancho, Carmen Sevilla, Piero Lulli, Barbara Carroll, Frank Braña, Charly Bravo, Patty Shepard.

Bounty Killer for Trinity, A (IT)
Un bounty killer a Trinità
D: Aristide Massaccesi (as Oscar Faradine; also credited to Oscar Santaniello). **P:** Transglobe Italiana. **W:** Aristide Massaccesi, Romano Scandariato. **C:** Aristide Massaccesi. **M:** Vassili Kojucharov. **S:** Giovanni Scarciofolo (as Jeff Cameron), Enzo Pulcrano (as Paul MacCren), Marina Malfatti, Attilio Dottesio, Calogero Caruana (as Ted Jones).

Call of the Wild, The (UK-FR-GER-IT-SP)
L'appel de la forât; Ruf der Wildnis; Il richiamo della foresta; La selva blanca
D: Ken Annakin. **P:** Artur Brauner, Harry Allan Towers. **W:** Jack London (novel), Federico de Urrutia, Roberto De Leonardis, Hubert Frank, Tíbor Reves, Harry Alan Towers, Win Wells, Peter Yeldham. **C:** John Cabrera. **M:** Carlo Rustichelli. **S:** Charlton Heston, Michèle Mercier, Raimund Harmstorf, Luigi Montefiori (as George Eastman), Maria Rohm, Rik Battaglia, Luís Barboo, Charly Bravo.

Can Be Done… Amigo (IT-FR-SP)
Si può fare… amigo!; Amigo!… Mon colt a deux mots à te dire; En el Oeste se puede hacer… amigo; Bulldozer Is Back Amigo; The Big and the Bad
D: Maurizio Lucidi. **P:** Enrico Chroscicki, Alfonso Sansone. **W:** Ernesto Gastaldi, Rafael Azcona (some sources also credit Albert Kantoff). **C:** Aldo Tonti. **M:** Luis Enríquez Bacalov. **S:** Bud Spencer, Jack Palance, Renato Cestiè, Francisco Rabal, Dany Saval, Salvatore Borgese, Roberto Camardiel, Luciano Catenacci, Luciano Pigozzi.

Charley One-Eye (UK)
D: Don Chaffey. **P:** David Paradine, James Swann. **W:** Keith Leonard. **C:** Kenneth Talbot. **M:** John Cameron. **S:** Richard Roundtree, Roy Thinnes, Nigel Davenport, Jill Pearson, Aldo Sambrell.

Chato's Land (UK)
D: Michael Winner. **P:** Michael Winner. **W:** Gerald Wilson. **C:** Robert Paynter. **M:** Jerry Fielding. **S:** Charles Bronson, Jack Palance, Richard Basehart, James Whitmore, Simon Oakland.

Cry of the Black Wolves (GER)
Der Schrei der schwarzen Wölfe
D: Harald Reinl. **P:** Gunter Eulau. **W:** Jack London (novel), Kurt Nachmann, Rolf Olsen. **C:** Franz Xavier Lederle. **M:** Gerhard Heinz. **S:** Ron Ely, Raimund Harmstorf, Gila von Weitershausen, Arthur Brauss, Jean-Claude Hoffmann, Dan van Husen.

Deadly Trackers, The (IT)
La lunga cavalcata della vendetta
D: Tanio Boccia (as Amerigo Anton). **P:** Giovanni Vari. **W:** Tanio Boccia. **C:** Romolo Garroni. **M:** Carlo Esposito. **S:** Richard Harrison, Anita Ekberg, Dada Gallotti, Rik Battaglia, George Wang, Furio Meniconi, Ricardo Palacios.

Death Played the Flute (IT)
Lo ammazzò come un cane… ma lui rideva ancora; Requiem for a Bounty Hunter
D: Angelo Pannacció. **P:** Universalia Vision MP1. **W:** Craig Marina, Angelo Pannacció. **C:** Mauro Bergamini. **M:** Daniele Patucchi. **S:** Michael Forest, Franco Borelli (as Chet Davis), Giuseppe Cardillo (as Steven Tedd), Susana Levi, Giovanni Petti, Aldo Berti, Remo Capitani, Antonio Molino Rojo.

Django… Adios (IT)
Seminò morte… lo chiamavano castigo di Dio!; Death Is Sweet from the Soldier of God
D: Roberto Mauri (as Robert Johnson). **P:** Virginia Cinematografica. **W:** Roberto Mauri, Roberto Bianchi Montero. **C:** Mario Mancini. **M:** Vassili Kojucharov. **S:** Brad Harris, José Torres, Vassili Karamesinis (as Vassili Karis), Zara Cilli, Roberto Messina, Giovanni Cianfriglia (as Ken Wood).

Erotic Adventures of Zorro, The (US-GER-FR)
Zorro und seine lüsternen Mädchen; Les chevauchées amoureuses de Zorro
D: Colonel Robert Freeman, William Allen Castleman (uncredited). **P:** William Allen Castleman, David F. Friedman. **W:** Colonel Robert Freeman, Mona Lott, Joy Boxe, David F. Friedman. **C:** Ferd Sebastian. **M:** William Loose. **S:** Douglas Frey, Robyn Whitting, Penny Boran, John Alderman, Jude Farese.

Fabulous Trinity, The (SP-IT)
Los fabulosos de Trinidad; Alla larga amigos… oggi ho il grilletto facile; With Friends, Nothing Is Easy
D: Ignacio F. Iquino (as Steve McCohy; sometimes credited to Pedro L. Ramirez). **P:** IFI, Admiral International Film. **W:** Ignacio F. Iquino, Juliana de la Fuente. **C:** Antonio Ballesteros Jr. **M:** Enrique Escobar. **S:** Richard Harrison, Fernando Sancho, Fanny Grey, Cris Huerta, Ricardo Palacios, Tito García.

Fat Brothers of Trinity, The (SP)
Ninguno de los tres se llamaba Trinidad; None of the Three Were Called Trinity
D: Pedro L. Ramírez. **P:** Ignacio F. Iquino. **W:** Ignacio F. Iquino, Juliana de la Fuente. **C:** Antonio L. Ballesteros. **M:** Enrique Escobar. **S:** Daniel Martín, Tito García, Cris Huerta, Ricardo Palacios, Margit Kocsis.

God in Heaven… Arizona on Earth (SP-IT)
Una bala marcada; Dio in cielo… Arizona in terra
D: Juan Bosch (as John Wood). **P:** Lea Film, Astro. **W:** Juan Bosch, F. Daniele Ortosoli, Fabio Piccioni. **C:** Giancarlo Ferrando. **M:** Bruno Nicolai. **S:** Peter Lee Lawrence, Maria Pia Conte, Roberto Camardiel, Dada Gallotti, Carlo Gaddi, Frank Braña, Luis Induni, Franco Pesce.

God Is My Colt (IT-GER)
La colt era il suo Dio; Nur Gott war sein Colt
D: Luigi Batzella (as Dean Jones). **P:** Virginia Cinematografica, Regina Film. **W:** Arpad De Riso, Luigi Batzella. **C:** Giorgio Montagnani. **M:** Vassili Kojucharov. **S:** Giovanni Scarciofolo (as Jeff Cameron), Donal O'Brien, Krista Nell, Esmeralda Barros, Mark Davis.

Grand Duel, The (IT-FR-GER)
Il grande duello; Le grand duel; Drei Vaterunser für vier Halunken; The Big Showdown; Storm Rider
D: Giancarlo Santi. **P:** Mount Street, Corona, Societé Nouvelle de Cinématographic. **W:** Ernesto Gastaldi (some sources also credit Albert Kantoff). **C:** Mario Vulpiani. **M:** Luis Enriquéz Bacalov, Sergio Bardotti. **S:** Lee Van

Cleef, Horst Frank, Alberto Dentice (as Peter O'Brien), Marc Mazza, Jess Hahn, Franco Fantasia, Remo Capitani, Giovanni Cianfriglia, Furio Meniconi.

Great Treasure Hunt, The (IT-SP)
Monta in sella! Figlio di…; Repóker de bribones
D: Tonino Ricci. **P:** Continental Film, Industrial Producine, Roma. **W:** Tonino Ricci, Fabrizio Diotallevi, Giuseppe Pulieri (uncredited). **C:** Cecilio Paniagua. **M:** Luis Enríquez Bacalov. **S:** Mark Damon, Rosalba Neri, Stelvio Rosi, Alfredo Mayo, Giancarlo Badessi.

Gunman Called Dakota, A (IT)
Un uomo chiamato Dakota
D: Mario Sabatini. **P:** Pageant International Film. **W:** Mario Sabatini. **C:** Angelo Baistrocchi, Mario Capriotti. **M:** Carlo Esposito. **S:** Gordon Mitchell, Mario Novelli, Bill Vanders, Tamara Baroni, Fedele Gentile, Aldo Berti, Tom Felleghy.

Gunmen and the Holy Ghost (IT)
Spirito Santo e le 5 magnifiche canaglie
D: Roberto Mauri. **P:** Cepa. **W:** Roberto Mauri. **C:** Tonino Maccoppi. **M:** Carlo Savina. **S:** Vassili Karamesinis (as Vassili Karis), Remo Capitani, Daria Norman, Giovanni Cianfriglia (as Ken Wood), Lincoln Tate, Aldo Berti, Mimmo Palmara, Salvatore Billa, Tom Felleghy.

Hallelujah & Sartana Strike Again! (IT-GER)
Alleluja e Sartana figli di… Dio; Hundert Fäuste und ein Halleluja; 100 Fäuste und ein Vaterunser
D: Mario Siciliano. **P:** Metheus Film, Lisa Film. **W:** Adriano Bolzoni, Kurt Nachmann. **C:** Gino Santini. **M:** Elvio Monti, Franco Zauli (Italian sources credit Luis Enriqué Bacalov). **S:** Ron Ely, Alberto Dell'Acqua (as Robert Widmark), Uschi Glas, Ezio Marano (as Alan Abbott), Wanda Vismara, Stelio Candelli, Nello Pazzafini, Furio Meniconi, Dan van Husen.

His Name Was Holy Ghost (IT-SP)
Uomo avvisato, mezzo ammazzato… parola di Spirito Santo; Y le llamaban El Halcón; Blazing Guns
D: Giuliano Carnimeo (as Anthony Ascott). **P:** Lea Film, Astro. **W:** Tito Carpi, Federico de Urrutia, Giuliano Carnimeo. **C:** Miguel Fernández Mila. **M:** Bruno Nicolai. **S:** Gianni Garko, Pilar Velázquez, Cris Huerta, Paolo Gozlino, George Rigaud, Federico Boido (as Rick Boyd), Nello Pazzafini, Pietro Ceccarelli, Carlo Gaddi, Victor Israel, Goffredo Unger, Furio Meniconi, Franco Pesce.

Jesse & Lester: Two Brothers in a Place Called Trinity (IT)
Jesse & Lester: due fratelli in un posto chiamato Trinità
D: Richard Harrison, Marino Girolami (also credited to Renzo Genta, 'James London'). **P:** Richard Harrison, Fernando Piazza. **W:** Richard Harrison, Renzo Genta. **C:** Antonio Modica. **M:** Carlo Savina. **S:** Richard Harrison, Donal O'Brien, Gino Marturano, Anna Zinnemann, George Wang, Federico Boido (as Rick Boyd), Luciano Rossi, John Bartha, Goffredo Unger.

Kill the Poker Player (IT-SP)
Hai sbagliato… dovevi uccidermi subito!; La muerte llega arrastrándose; Creeping Death

D: Mario Bianchi. **P:** Silvio Battistini. **W:** Mario Bianchi, Paola Bianchi, Luis G. de Blain. **C:** Rafael Pacheco. **M:** Carlo Savina. **S:** Robert Woods, Nieves Navarro (as Susan Scott), Frank Braña, Ivano Staccioli, Ernesto Colli, Carlo Gaddi.

Magnificent West, The (IT)
Il magnifico West
D: Gianni Crea. **P:** Dinamica Film. **W:** Gianni Crea. **C:** Giovanni Raffaldi. **M:** Stelvio Cipriani. **S:** Vassili Karamesinis (as Vassili Karis), Dario Pino, Gordon Mitchell, Fiorella Mannoia, Lorenzo Fineschi.

Man of the East (IT-FR-YUG)
…E poi lo chiamarono il Magnifico; Et maintenant, on l'appelle El Magnifico
D: Enzo Barboni (as E.B. Clucher). **P:** Alberto Grimaldi. **W:** Enzo Barboni. **C:** Aldo Giordani. **M:** Guido and Maurizio De Angelis. **S:** Terence Hill, Gregory Walcott, Harry Carey Jr., Dominic Barto, Yanti Somer, John Bartha, Salvatore Borgese, Spartaco Conversi, Giovanni Cianfriglia (as Ken Wood), Antonio Monselesan (as Tony Norton), Furio Meniconi.

My Horse… My Gun… Your Widow (IT-SP)
Domani passo a salutare la tua vedova… parola di Epidemia; Tu fosa será la exacta… amigo
D: Juan Bosch (as John Wood). **P:** Lea Film, Astro. **W:** Juan Bosch, Sauro Scavolini. **C:** Giorgio Tonti. **M:** Bruno Nicolai. **S:** Craig Hill, Claudie Lange, Cris Huerta, Ignazio Spalla (as Pedro Sanchez), Carlo Gaddi, Luis Induni.

Now They Call Him Sacramento (SP-IT)
Hijos de pobres, pero deshonestos padres… le llamaban Calamidad; I bandoleros della dodicesima ora; Now They Call Him Amen
D: Alfonso Balcázar (as Al Bagran). **P:** Francsico Balcázar. **W:** Alfonso Balcázar, Giovanni Simonelli. **C:** Jaime Deu Casas. **M:** Willy Brezza. **S:** Michael Forest, Fernando Bilbao (as Fred Harrison), Malisa Longo, Luigi Bonos, Antonio Molino Rojo, Paolo Gozlino, Angel del Pozo.

Pancho Villa (SP)
El desafío de Pancho Villa
D: Eugenio Martín (as Gene Martin). **P:** Bernard Gordon. **W:** Julian Zimet (as Julian Halevy),

Eugenio Martín. **C:** Alejandro Ulloa. **M:** Antón García Abril. **S:** Telly Savalas, Clint Walker, Chuck Connors, Anne Francis, José María Pradia, Antonio Casas, Angel del Pozo, Barta Barry, Dan van Husen.

Panhandle Calibre 38 (IT)
…E alla fine lo chiamarono Jerusalem l'implacabile; Padella calibro 38
D: Toni Secchi. **P:** Cinegai. **W:** Mario Amendola, Massimo Franciosa, Luisa Montagnana, Toni Secchi. **C:** Giorgio Regis. **M:** Franco Micalizzi. **S:** Scott Holden, Delia Boccardo, Philippe Leroy, Keenan Wynn, Giorgio Trestini, Alberto Dell'Acqua, Mimmo Palmara, Nello Pazzafini, Remo Capitani.

Pistol Packin' Preacher (IT)
Posate le pistole, reverendo
D: Leopoldo Savona. **P:** Agata Film. **W:** Leopoldo Savona, Norbert Blake. **C:** Romano Scavolini. **M:** Coriolano Gori. **S:** Mark Damon, Rosario Borelli (as Richard Melville), Veronica Korosec, Giovanna Di Bernardo, Pietro Ceccarelli.

Prey of Vultures (SP-IT)
Un dólar de recompensa; La preda e l'avvoltoio; Revenge of the Resurrected
D: Rafael Romero Marchent. **P:** Devon Film, Copercines. **W:** Rafael Romero Marchent, Fernando Popoli, Howard Berk (as José Luis Navarro). **C:** Mario Capriotti. **M:** Nora Orlandi. **S:** Peter Lee Lawrence, Orchidea de Santis, Carlos Romero Marchent, Andrés Mejuto, Dada Gallotti, Raf Baldassarre, Frank Braña, Luis Induni, Lorenzo Robledo.

Reason to Live, a Reason to Die, A (IT-FR-SP-GER)
Una ragione per vivere e una per morire; La horde des salopards; Une raison pour vivre, une raison pour mourir; Una razón para vivir y una para morir; Sie verkaufen den Tod; Massacre at Fort Holman
D: Tonino Valerii. **P:** Arthur Steloff. **W:** Rafael Azcona, Ernesto Gastaldi, Tonino Valerii. **C:** Alejandro Ulloa. **M:** Riz Ortolani. **S:** James Coburn, Telly Savalas, Bud Spencer, José Suárez, Georges Géret, Benito Stefanelli, Ángel Álvarez, Paco Sanz.

Red Hot Zorro (FR-BEL)
Les aventures galantes de Zorro
D: Gilbert Roussel. **P:** Marius Lesoeur, Pierre Quérut. **W:** Henri Bral de Boitselier, Pierre Quérut. **C:** Johan Vincent. **M:** Gilbert Gardet. **S:** Jean-Michel Dhermay, Evelyne Scott, Alice Arno, Christine Chantel, Rose Kiekens.

Return of Clint the Stranger, The (IT-SP)
Il ritorno di Clint il solitario; El retorno de Clint el solitario; There's a Noose Waiting for You... Trinity!
D: Alfonso Balcázar (Spanish version also credited to George Martin; some sources also credit Pedro Luis Ramírez). **P:** Alfonso Balcázar, Enzo Doria, Pietro Sagliocco. **W:** Giovanni Simonelli, Enzo Passadore, Alfonso Balcázar (some sources also credit Enzo Doria). **C:** Jaime Deu Casas. **M:** Ennio Morricone (archive music). **S:** George Martin, Marina Malfatti, Klaus Kinski, Daniel Martín, Augusto Pesarini, Luis Induni, Pajarito.

Return of Hallelujah, The (IT-GER-FR)
Il West ti va stretto, amico… è arrivato Alleluja; Beichtet, Freunde, Halleluja kommt; Alléluia défie l'Ouest; The West Is Tough Amigo... Allelujah's Here
D: Giuliano Carnimeo (as Anthony Ascott). **P:** Colosseo Artistica, Hermes Film Syncron, Lyre. **W:** Tito Carpi, Ingo Hermes, Giovanni Simonelli. **C:** Stelvio Massi. **M:** Stelvio Cipriani. **S:** George Hilton, Lincoln Tate, Agata Flori, Raymond Bussieres, Umberto D'Orsi, Riccardo Garrone, Paolo Gozlino, Nello Pazzafini, Goffredo Unger, Roberto Camardiel.

Return of the Holy Ghost (IT)
Bada alla tua pelle, Spirito Santo!
D: Roberto Mauri. **P:** Cepa. **W:** Roberto Mauri. **C:** Giuseppe Pinori. **M:** Carlo Savina. **S:** Vassili Karamesinis (as Vassili Karis), Craig Hill, Remo Capitani, Giovanni Cianfriglia (as Ken Wood), José Torres, Aldo Berti, Salvatore Billa, Tom Felleghy.

Run, Men! Eldorado Is Coming to Trinity (IT)
Scansati… a Trinità arriva Eldorado; Pokerface
D: Aristide Massaccesi (also credited to 'Dick Spitfire', Demofilo Fidani, Diego Spataro, Romano Scandariato). **P:** Elektra Film. **W:** Romano Scandariato, Diego Spataro. **C:** Aristide Massaccesi. **M:** Giancarlo Chiaramello. **S:** Stelvio Rosi (as Stan Cooper), Craig Hill, Gordon Mitchell, Daniela Giordano, Enzo Pulcrano.

Shoot Joe, and Shoot Again (IT-SP)
Spara Joe… e così sia!; Dispara Joe... y asi sea; Joe Dakota
D: Emilio Miraglia (as Hal Brady). **P:** Benito Bertaccini. **W:** Jean Josipovici, Emilio Miraglia. **C:** Silvio Fraschetti. **M:** Vassili Kojucharov. **S:** Richard Harrison, José Torres, Franca Polesello, Gaspar 'Indio' González, Roberto Maldera, Federico Boido (as Rick Boyd).

Sometimes Life Is Hard, Right Providence? (IT-FR-GER)
La vita a volte è molto dura, vero Provvidenza?; On m'appelle Providence; Providenza - Mausefalle für zwei schräge Vögel
D: Giulio Petroni. **P:** Oceania Unidis, Le Rex, Terra. **W:** Giulio Petroni, Antonio Marino, Piero Regnoli (as Dean Craig), Franco Castellano, Giuseppe Moccia. **C:** Alessandro D'Eva. **M:** Ennio Morricone. **S:** Tomas Milian, Gregg Palmer, Janet Agren, Dieter Eppler, Stelio Candelli, Giovanni Cianfriglia (as Ken Wood).

Tecumseh (GDR-SOV-ROM)
D: Hans Kratzert. **P:** DEFA, Mosfilm, Bucaresti Film. **W:** Wolfgang Ebeling, Rolf Römer. **C:** Wolfgang Braumann. **M:** Günther Fischer. **S:** Gojko Mitic, Annekathrin Bürger, Rolf Römer, Leon Niemczyk, Milan Beli.

Tedeum (IT-SP)
Sting of the West; The Con Men; Father Jack-Leg
D: Enzo G. Castellari. **P:** Franco Palaggi, Virgilio De Blasi. **W:** Tito Carpi, Giovanni Simonelli, Enzo G. Castellari, José Gutiérrez Maesso. **C:** Manuel Rojas. **M:** Guido and Maurizio De Angelis. **S:** Jack Palance, Giancarlo Prete (as Timothy Brent), Lionel Stander, Francesca Romana Coluzzi, Eduardo Fajardo, Renzo Palmer, Riccardo Garrone, Ángel Álvarez.

They Call Him Veritas (IT)
Lo chiamavano Verità
D: Luigi Perelli. **P:** Giulio Scanni, Luigi Costanzo. **W:** Oreste Coltellacci. **C:** Mario Capriotti. **M:** Manuel De Sica. **S:** Mark Damon, Pat Nigro, Pietro Ceccarelli, Franco Garofalo, Maria D'Incoronato, Guglielmo Spoletini (as William Bogart), Federico Boido (as Rick Boyd).

They Called Him Amen (IT)
Così sia
D: Alfio Caltabiano. **P:** Laser Film. **W:** Adriano Bolzoni, Alfio Caltabiano (some sources also credit Dario Argento). **C:** Riccardo Pallottini. **M:** Daniele Patucchi. **S:** Luc Merenda, Alfio Caltabiano (as Alf Thunder), Tano Cimarosa, Mila Beran, Renato Cestiè, Pat Nigro, Furio Meniconi.

Thunder Over El Paso (IT-SP)
I senza Dio; Yo los mato, tà cobras la recompensa
D: Roberto Bianchi Montero. **P:** Luis Film, Dauro Film. **W:** Arpad De Riso, Maurizio Pradeaux, Antonio Fos. **C:** Alfonso Nieva. **M:** Carlo Savina. **S:** Antonio Sabato, Chris Avram, Erika Blanc, Paolo Gozlino, Pilar Velázquez, José Jaspe, Giovanni Cianfriglia (as Ken Wood).

Too Much Gold for One Gringo (SP-IT)
La caza del oro; Lo credevano uno stinco di santo
D: Juan Bosch. **P:** PEA, Cine XX. **W:** Juan Bosch, Renato Izzo, Fabio Piccioni. **C:** Julio Pérez de Rozas. **M:** Marcello Giombini. **S:** Anthony Steffen, Daniel Martín, Tania Alvarado, Fernando Sancho, Manuel Guitián, Luis Induni.

Trinity and Sartana Are Coming (IT)
Trinità e Sartana figli di…!; Trinity & Sartana... Those Dirty Sons o' B-S!
D: Mario Siciliano (as Marlon Sirko). **P:** Metheus Film. **W:** Adriano Bolzoni. **C:** Gino Santini. **M:** Carlo Savina. **S:** Alberto Dell'Acqua (as Robert Widmark), Harry Baird, Beatrice Pella, Daniela Giordano, Stelio Candelli, Nello Pazzafini, Romano Puppo.

Tschetan, Indian Boy (GER)
Tschetan, der Indianerjunge
D: Hark Bohm. **P:** Hark Bohm. **W:** Hark Bohm. **C:** Michael Ballhaus. **M:** Peer Raben. **S:** Marquard Bohm, Dschingis Bowakow, Willy Schultes, Erich Dolz, Edy Endorfer.

Two Sons of Trinity, The (IT)
I due figli dei Trinità
D: Osvaldo Civirani (as Richard Kean). **P:** Walter Civirani. **W:** Osvaldo Civirani. **C:** Walter Civirani. **M:** Sante Maria Romitelli. **S:** Franco Franchi, Ciccio Ingrassia, Lucretia Love, Franco Ressel, Fortunato Arena, Goffredo Unger, Andrea Scotti.

Vente a ligar al Oeste (SP)
D: Pedro Lazaga. **P:** ASPA, Filmayer Produccion. **W:** Vicente Escriva, Vicente Coello. **C:** Raul Pérez Cubero. **M:** Maximo Baratas. **S:** Alfredo Landa,

Euro-Western Filmography

Maria José Roman, Mary Carmen Duque, Saturno Serra, José Sacristán, Tito García.

Watch Out Gringo, Sabata Will Return (SP-IT)
Judas… toma tus monedas; Attento gringo, è tornato Sabata; Luck Morgan You Won't Get That Gold
D: Pedro Luis Ramírez (some sources also credit Alfonso Balcázar). **P:** Alfonso Balcázar. **W:** Alfonso Balcázar, José Ramon Larraz, Giovanni Simonelli. **C:** Jaime Deu Casas. **M:** Piero Piccioni. **S:** George Martin, Fernando Sancho, Vittorio Richelmy, Rosalba Neri, Daniel Martín, Luciano Rossi.

What Am I Doing in the Middle of a Revolution? (IT-SP)
Che c'entriamo noi con la rivoluzione?; ¡Qué nos importa la revolución!
D: Sergio Corbucci. **P:** Mario Cecchi Gori. **W:** Sergio Corbucci, Massimo Franciosa, Sabatino Ciuffini (Spanish sources also credit Miguel de Echarri). **C:** Alejandro Ulloa. **M:** Ennio Morricone. **S:** Vittorio Gassman, Paolo Villaggio, Riccardo Garrone, Eduardo Fajardo, Leo Anchóriz, José Canalejas, Victor Israel.

Where the Bullets Fly (IT-GER-SP)
Tutti fratelli nel West… per parte di padre; Fünf Klumpen Gold; Todos hermanos… en el Oeste; Miss Dynamite
D: Sergio Grieco. **P:** DC7, Terra, Copercines. **W:** Sergio Grieco, Romano Migliorini, Gianbattista Mussetto. **C:** Aldo De Robertis. **M:** Guycen. **S:** Antonio Sabato, Marisa Mell, Fernando Sancho, Lionel Stander, Peter Carsten, Federico Boido (as Rick Boyd), Franco Ressel, Antonio Gradoli, Franco Pesce, Andrea Scotti.

You Are a Traitor and I'll Kill You (SP-IT)
Una cuerda al amanecer; Sei una carogna… e t'ammazzo!; A Cry of Death
D: Manuel Esteba. **P:** Cire, Universalia Vision. **W:** Manuel Esteba. **C:** Girolamo La Rosa. **M:** Vassili Kojucharov, Daniele Patucchi. **S:** Pierre Brice, Giuseppe Cardillo (as Steven Tedd), Fernando Sancho, Mónica Randall, Marta Flores, Antonio Molino Rojo, Pajarito.

You're Jinxed, Friend, You've Met Sacramento (IT)
Sei jellato amico, hai incontrato Sacramento
D: Giorgio Cristallini. **P:** Canadian International Film. **W:** Giorgio Cristallini. **C:** Fausto Rossi. **M:** Franco Micalizzi. **S:** Ty Hardin, Christian Hay, Jenny Atkins, Giacomo Rossi-Stuart, Krista Nell, Dana Ghia, Giovanni Cianfriglia (as Ken Wood).

Zorro the Lawman (SP-IT)
El Zorro justiciero; …E continuavano a chiamarlo figlio di…
D: Rafael Romero Marchent. **P:** Copercines, Transeuropa Film, Italian International Film. **W:** Rafael Romero Marchent, Fernando Mateo, Fulvio Lucisano (Italian sources also credit Nino Stresa). **C:** Marcello Masciocchi. **M:** Coriolano Gori. **S:** Fabio Testi (as Martin Moore), Carlos Romero Marchent, Simonetta Vitelli (as Simone Blondell), Piero Lulli, Andrés Mejuto, Frank Braña, Riccardo Garrone, Antonio Gradoli, Luis Induni.

1973

Anything for a Friend (IT)
Amico mio… frega tu che frego io!; Everything for a Friend
D: Demofilo Fidani (as Miles Deem). **P:** Demofilo Fidani. **W:** Demofilo Fidani, Filippo Perrone, Mila Vitelli. **C:** Claudio Morabito. **M:** Coriolano Gori. **S:** Ettore Manni, Bud Randall, Sleepy Warren, Angela Portaluri, Federico Boido (as Rick Boyd), Simonetta Vitelli (as Simone Blondell), Gordon Mitchell.

Apaches (GDR-ROM-SOV)
Apachen
D: Gottfried Kolditz. **P:** Dorothea Hildebrandt. **W:** Gottfried Kolditz, Gojko Mitic. **C:** Helmut Bergmann. **M:** Hans-Dieter Hosalla. **S:** Gojko Mitic, Milan Beli, Colea Rautu, Gerry Wolff, Rolf Hoppe.

Bad Kids of the West (IT)
Kid, il monello del West
D: Tonino Ricci. **P:** Robert Amoroso. **W:** Mario Amendola, Bruno Corbucci, Roberto Amoroso. **C:** Silvio Fraschetti. **M:** Enrico Simonetti. **S:** Andrea Balestri, Cristiana, Mirko Ellis, Flavio Colombaioni, Franco Ressel, Remo Capitani.

Blue Gang, The (IT-FR)
Blu Gang (…E vissero per sempre felici e ammazzati); Blu gang - Et ils vecurent longtempte, heureux et…tues; The Short Happy Life of the Brothers Blue
D: Luigi Bazzoni (as Marc Meyer). **P:** Franco Rossellini. **W:** Augusto Caminito, Mario Fenelli. **C:** Vittorio Storaro. **M:** Tony Renis. **S:** Jack Palance, Antonio Falsi, Guido Mannari, Tina Aumont, Maurizio Bonuglia, Guido Lollobrigida (as Lee Burton), Antonio Gradoli.

Charity and the Strange Smell of Money (IT)
Sentivano… uno strano, eccitante, pericoloso puzzo di dollari; And They Smelled the Strange, Exciting, Dangerous Scent of Dollars
D: Italo Alfaro. **P:** Enzo Boetani, Giuseppe Collura. **W:** Pietro Regnoli. **C:** Sandro Mancori. **M:** Gianni Meccia, Bruno Zambrini. **S:** Robert Malcolm, Piero Vida, Rosalba Neri, Luigi Montini, Salvatore Puntillo, Spartaco Conversi.

Colt in the Hand of the Devil, A (IT)
Una colt in mano al diavolo; When the Devil Holds a Gun
D: Gianfranco Baldanello (as Frank G. Carroll). **P:** Giovanni Vari. **W:** Gianfranco Baldanello, Augusto Finocchi. **C:** Alvaro Lanzoni. **M:** Piero Piccioni. **S:** Robert Woods, William Berger, George Wang, Fiorella Mannoia, Nino Fuscagni, José Torres.

Deaf Smith & Johnny Ears (IT)
Los amigos
D: Paolo Cavara. **P:** Joseph Janni. **W:** Lucia Drudi Demby, Harry Essex, Augusto Finocchi, Oscar Saul, Paolo Cavara. **C:** Tonino Delli Colli. **M:** Daniele Patucchi. **S:** Franco Nero, Anthony Quinn, Pamela Tiffin, Franco Graziosi, Adolfo Lastretti, Tom Felleghy, Romano Puppo, Luciano Rossi, Goffredo Unger.

Fast-Hand Is Still My Name (IT-SP)
Mi chiamavano "Requiescat"… ma avevano sbagliato; Mano rápida
D: Mario Bianchi (as Frank Bronston). **P:** Silvio Battistini. **W:** Vittorio Salerno, Alberto Cardone, Eduardo Manzanos Brochero. **C:** Emilio Foriscot. **M:** Gianni Ferrio. **S:** Sergio Ciani (as Alan Steel), William Berger, Frank Braña, Fernando Bilbao, Gilberto Galimberti, Lorenzo Robledo, Paco Sanz.

Fighting Fists of Shanghai Joe, The (IT)
Il mio nome è Shangai Joe; To Kill or To Die; The Dragon Strikes Back
D: Mario Caiano. **P:** Renato Angiolini, Roberto Bessi. **W:** Fabrizio Trifone Trecca, Mario Caiano, Carlo Alberto Alfieri. **C:** Guglielmo Mancori. **M:** Bruno Nicolai. **S:** Chen Lee, Klaus Kinski, Carla Romanelli, Claudio Undari (as Robert Hundar), Gordon Mitchell, Giacomo Rossi-Stuart, Piero Lulli, Federico Boido (as Rick Boyd), George Wang, Tito García, Paco Sanz.

For a Book of Dollars (IT)
Più forte sorelle
D: Renzo Girolami (also credited as Renzo Spaziani, Mario Bianchi). **P:** New Film. **W:** Franco Vietri. **C:** Mario Parapetti. **M:** Nando De Luca. **S:** Lincoln Tate, Gabriella Farinon, Jean-Claude Jabès, Luigi Bonos, Clara Colosimo.

Any Gun Can Play

Girls of the Golden Saloon, The (FR-BEL)
Les filles du Golden Saloon
D: Pierre Chevalier. **P:** Marius Lesoeur, Daniel Lesoeur. **W:** H.B. de Boitsellier, H.L. Rastaine. **C:** Raymond Heil, Johan Vincent. **M:** Daniel White. **S:** Sandra Julien, Evelyne Scott, Roger Darton, Alice Arno, Allan Spencer.

God's Executioner (IT)
Il giustiziere di Dio
D: Franco Lattanzi. **P:** Giovanni Vari. **W:** Franco Lattanzi. **C:** Franco Appetito. **M:** Piero Piccioni. **S:** William Berger, Donal O'Brien, George Wang, Nuccia Cardinali, Attilio Dottesio.

Halleluja to Vera Cruz (IT)
Partirono preti, tornarono… curati
D: Bianco Manini (credited to Stelvio Massi). **P:** Bianco Manini. **W:** Ofelia Minaldi, Bianco Manini. **C:** Carlo Carlini. **M:** Luis Enríquez Bacalov. **S:** Lionel Stander, Riccardo Salvino, Jean Louis, Giampiero Albertini, Clara Hopf, Federico Boido (as Rick Boyd), Spartaco Conversi, Tom Felleghy.

Hellhounds of Alaska, The (GER-YUG)
Die Blutigen Geier von Alaska; Krvavi jastrebovi Aljaske; Fight for Gold
D: Harald Reinl. **P:** Günter Sturm. **W:** Johannes Weiss. **C:** Heinz Hölscher. **M:** Bruno Nicolai. **S:** Doug McClure, Harald Leipnitz, Heinze Reincke, Angelica Ott, Klaus Löwitz, Krista Nell.

Here We Go Again, Eh Providence? (IT-SP-FR)
Ci risiamo, vero Provvidenza?; Otra vez, verdad, Providencia; Nous en irons n'est ce pas Providence?
D: Alberto De Martino. **P:** Oceania, DIA, Les Films Corona. **W:** Franco Castellano, Giuseppe Moccia. **C:** Alejandro Ulloa. **M:** Ennio Morricone. **S:** Tomas Milian, Gregg Palmer, Carole André, Luciano Catenacci, Manuel Gallardo, Federico Boido (as Rick Boyd), Nello Pazzafini, Goffredo Unger.

Jack London Story, The (IT-YUG)
Jack London: la mia grande avventura
D: Angelo D'Alessandro. **P:** Transeuropa. **W:** Jack London (characters), Angelo D'Alessandro, Piero Pieroni, Antonio Saguera. **C:** Mario Sanga. **M:** Mario Pagano. **S:** Orso Maria Guerrini, Arnaldo Bellofiore, Andrea Checchi, Husein Cokic, Carlo Gasparri.

Karate, Fists and Beans (IT-SP)
Storia di karatè, pugni e fagioli; La ley del karate en el Oeste
D: Tonino Ricci. **P:** Sergio Borelli, Alfonso Balcázar. **W:** Alfonso Balcázar, Arpad De Riso, Ted Rusoff, Giovanni Scolaro. **C:** Jaime Deu Casas. **M:** Guido and Maurizio De Angelis (as Juniper). **S:** Dean Reed, Alfredo Mayo, Cris Huerta, Iwao Yoshioka, Salvatore Borgese, Luis Induni, Fernando Sancho, Goffredo Unger.

Kung Fu Brothers in the Wild West (IT-HK)
…altrimenti vi ammucchiamo; Kung fu nel pazzo West; I fratelli del kung fu; Laifoo ching sai; Master Killers; Golden City
D: Yeo Ban Yee (as George Bange). **P:** Yangtze Productions. **W:** Raymond Chow, Manuel Ruiz, Albert Young. **C:** Hsun Yang (as Albert Young). **M:** Franco Bracardi. **S:** William Berger, Jason Pai Piao, Donal O'Brien, Thompson Kao Kang, Winnie Pei Nie.

Man Called Invincible, A (IT)
Lo chiamavano Tresette… giocava sempre col morto; Once Upon a Time in the West There Was a Man Called Invincible
D: Giuliano Carnimeo (as Anthony Ascott). **P:** Lea Film. **W:** Tito Carpi. **C:** Stelvio Massi. **M:** Bruno Nicolai. **S:** George Hilton, Cris Huerta, Ida Galli (as Evelyn Stewart), Rosalba Neri, Umberto D'Orsi, Salvatore Borgese, Nello Pazzafini, Goffredo Unger, Pietro Ceccarelli, Furio Meniconi, Antonio Monselesan (as Tony Norton).

Man Called Noon, The (IT-SP-UK)
Un hombre llamado Noon; Lo chiamavano Mezzogiorno
D: Peter Collinson. **P:** Euan Lloyd. **W:** Louis L'Amour (novel), Scott Finch, Antonio Recoder. **C:** John Cabrera. **M:** Luis Enríquez Bacalov. **S:** Richard Crenna, Stephen Boyd, Rosanna Schiaffino, Farley Granger, Patty Shepard, Barta Barry, Charly Bravo, José Canalejas, Angel del Pozo, José Jaspe, Ricardo Palacios, Aldo Sambrell.

My Name Is Nobody (IT-FR-GER)
Il mio nome è Nessuno; Mon nom est personne; Mein Name ist Nobody
D: Tonino Valerii. **P:** Claudio Mancini. **W:** Fulvio Morsella, Ernesto Gastaldi. **C:** Giuseppe Ruzzolini, Armando Nannuzzi. **M:** Ennio Morricone. **S:** Terence Hill, Henry Fonda, Jean Martin, Leo Gordon, Neil Summers, R.G. Armstrong, Steve Kanaly, Geoffrey Lewis, Marc Mazza, Mario Brega, Piero Lulli, Antonio Molino Rojo, Benito Stefanelli.

On the Third Day Arrived the Crow (IT)
…E il terzo giorno arrivò il Corvo; A Fistful of Death
D: Gianni Crea (some sources also credit Mario Gariazzo and Perry Dell). **P:** Harlindel Film. **W:** Mino Roli. **C:** Giovanni Raffaldi, Franco Villa. **M:** Nora Orlandi. **S:** Lincoln Tate, William Berger, Dino Strano (as Dean Stratford), Fiorella Mannoia, Lorenzo Fineschi, Rosario Borelli (as Richard Melvill), Romano Puppo.

Once Upon a Time in the Wild, Wild West (IT)
C'era una volta questo pazzo, pazzo West
D: Vincenzo Matassi (also credited to Francesco Degli Espinosa). **P:** EMAT. **W:** Giuseppe Frontani, Vincenzo Matassi, Francesco Degli Espinosa. **C:** Ugo Brunelli. **M:** Francesco Santucci. **S:** Gordon Mitchell, Vincent Scott, Benito Pacifico (as Dennis Colt), Malisa Longo, Fiorella Magalotti.

Seven Nuns in Kansas City (IT)
Sette monache a Kansas City
D: Marcello Zeani. **P:** Lidia Puglia, Pietro Santini. **W:** Lidia Puglia, Marcello Cascapera. **C:** Mario Sbrenna. **M:** Gino Peguri. **S:** Ugo Fangareggi, Lea Gargano, Enzo Maggio, Enzo Pulcrano, Antonio Di Leo, Ignazio Spalla (as Pedro Sanchez).

Six Bounty Killers for a Massacre (IT)
Sei bounty killers per una strage
D: Franco Lattanzi. **P:** Ottavio Dolfi. **W:** Ottavio Dolfi, Ambrogio Molteni. **C:** Giovanni Varriano. **M:** Piero Piccioni. **S:** Robert Woods, Donal O'Brien, Attilio Dottesio, George Wang, Mauro Mannatrizio.

Son of Zorro, The (IT-SP)
Il figlio di Zorro; El hijo del Zorro
D: Gianfranco Baldanello (as Frank G. Carroll). **P:** International Films, Films Triunfo. **W:** Arpad De Riso, Guido Zurli, Gianfranco Baldanello. **C:** Franco Delli Colli. **M:** Marcello Gigante. **S:** Alberto Dell'Acqua (as Robert Widmark), William Berger, Fernando Sancho, Elisa Ramírez, George Wang, Charly Bravo, Franco Fantasia.

Tequila (SP-IT)
Uno, dos, tres… dispara otra vez; Shoshena
D: Tulio Demicheli. **P:** Norberto Soliño, Salvatore Alabiso. **W:** Enrique Iglesias, Miguel Josa, Nino Stresa. **C:** Guglielmo Mancori. **M:** Coriolano Gori. **S:** Anthony Steffen, Eduardo Fajardo, Roberto Camardiel, Maria Elena Arpon, Agata Lys, John Bartha, Aldo Sambrell.

They Called Him Trinity [Himself, His Colt, His Revenge] (IT)
Allegri becchini… arriva Trinità (filmed in 1971)
D: Ferdinando Merighi (as Fred Lyon Morris). **P:** Giulio Giuseppe Negri, Germano Longo. **W:** Ferdinando Merighi. **C:** Pasquale Fanetti, Giorgio Montagnani. **M:** Marcello Gigante. **S:** Dino Strano (as Dean Stratford), Gordon Mitchell, John Braun, Luciano Conti (as Lucky McMurray), Amerigo Leoni (as Custer Gail).

They Still Call Me Amen (IT)
Oremus, Alleluia e Così Sia; Mamma mia, e arrivato Così Sia; The Hallelujah Gang
D: Alfio Caltabiano. **P:** Fulvio Lucisano. **W:** Alfio Caltabiano, Sandro Continenza. **C:** Guglielmo Mancori. **M:** Gianni Ferrio. **S:** Luc Merenda, Alfio Caltabiano (as Alf Thunder), Tano Cimarosa, Katia Christine, Flavio Colombaioni, Furio Meniconi, Andrea Scotti.

Those Dirty Dogs (IT-SP)
Campa carogna… la taglia cresce; Charge!; Los cuatro de Fort Apache
D: Giuseppe Rosati (as Joseph Rosati). **P:** Horse Film, Plata Film. **W:** Carlo Veo, Enrique Llovet, Giuseppe Rosati. **C:** Godofredo Pacheco. **M:** Nico Fidenco. **S:** Gianni Garko (as John Garko), Stephen Boyd, Renato Rossini (as Howard Ross), Simón Andreu, Harry Baird, Guido Lollobrigida (as Lee Burton), Helga Liné, Furio Meniconi, Romano Puppo, Andrea Scotti.

Three Musketeers of the West, The (IT-SP-GER)
Tutti per uno… botte per tutti; Todos para uno, golpes para todos; Alle für einen - Prügel für alle
D: Bruno Corbucci. **P:** Edmondo Amati. **W:** Bruno Corbucci, Tito Carpi, Leonardo Martin, Peter Berling. **C:** Rafael Pacheco. **M:** Carlo Rustichelli. **S:** Luigi Montefiori (as George Eastman), Giancarlo Prete (as Timothy Brent), Eduardo Fajardo, Karin Schubert, Cris Huerta, Leo Anchóriz, José Canalejas.

Three Supermen of the West (IT-SP)
…E così divennero I tre supermen del West; Los tres superhombres en el Oeste
D: Italo Martinenghi (Spanish version credited to George Martin). **P:** Italo Martinenghi. **W:** Italo Martinenghi, Anthony Blond, George Martin. **C:** Jaime Deu Casas. **M:** Roberto

Pregadio (as Bob Deramont). **S:** George Martin, Salvatore Borgese, Frank Braña, Agata Lys, Gigi Bonos, Ignazio Spalla (as Pedro Sanchez), Fernando Sancho, Luís Barboo, Barta Barry, José Canalejas, Antonio Casas, Cris Huerta.

Valdez Horses, The (IT-SP-FR)
Valdez il mezzosangue; Caballos salvajes; Chino; Valdez the Halfbreed
D: Diulio Coletti, John Sturges. **P:** John Sturges, Diulio Coletti, Dino De Laurentiis. **W:** Lee Hoffman (novel), Massimo De Rita, Clair Huffaker, Dino Maiuri, Rafael J. Salvia. **C:** Armando Nannuzzi, Godofredo Pacheco. **M:** Guido and Maurizio De Angelis. **S:** Charles Bronson, Jill Ireland, Marcel Bozzuffi, Melissa Chimenti, Fausto Tozzi, Ettore Manni.

White Fang (IT-SP-FR)
Zanna Bianca; Colmillo blanco; Croc-blanc
D: Lucio Fulci. **P:** Harry Alan Towers. **W:** Jack London (novel), Guy Elmes, Roberto Gianviti, Thom Keyes, Piero Regnoli, Guillaume Roux, Harry Alan Towers. **C:** Pablo Ripoll. **M:** Carlo Rustichelli. **S:** Franco Nero, Virna Lisi, Fernando Rey, John Steiner, Carole André, Rik Battaglia, John Bartha, Daniel Martín.

Yankee Dudler (GER-SP)
Verflucht dies Amerika; La banda de Jaider
D: Volker Vogeler. **P:** Elías Querejeta. **W:** Bernardo Fernández, Ulf Miehe, Volker Vogeler. **C:** Luis Cuadrado. **M:** Luis de Pablo. **S:** Geraldine Chaplin, William Berger, Arthur Brauss, Francisco Algora, Sigi Graue, Eduardo Fajardo, Ángel Álvarez, Luís Barboo, Frank Braña, Tito García, Dan van Husen.

1974

Blood River (IT-SP)
Dieci bianchi uccisi da un piccolo indiano; Pasión salvaje
D: Gianfranco Baldanello. **P:** Gino Rossi, Giuseppe Maggi. **W:** Gianfranco Baldanello, Mario Damicelli, Juan Antonio Verdugo. **C:** Leopoldo Villaseñor. **M:** Piero Umiliani. **S:** Fabio Testi, John Ireland, Rosalba Neri, Luisa Rivelli, Miguel de la Riva, José Canalejas, Luis Induni, Daniel Martín.

Carambola (IT)
D: Ferdinando Baldi. **P:** Manolo Bolognini. **W:** Ferdinando Baldi, Nico Ducci, Mino Roli. **C:** Aiace Parolin. **M:** Franco Bixio, Vince Tempera. **S:** Paul L. Smith (as Paul Smith), Antonio Cantafora (as Michael Coby), Horst Frank, Guglielmo Spoletini (as William Bogart), Pino Ferrara, Luciano Catenacci, Franco Fantasia, Ignazio Spalla (as Pedro Sanchez), Nello Pazzafini.

Challenge to White Fang (IT-FR-GER)
Il ritorno di Zanna Bianca; Le retour de Croc Blanc; Die Teufelsschlucht der wilden Wölfe; The Return of White Fang
D: Lucio Fulci. **P:** Coralta, Corona, Terra. **W:** Roberto Gianviti, Alberto Silvestri, Lucio Fulci. **C:** Silvano Ippoliti, Aristide Massaccesi. **M:** Carlo Rustichelli. **S:** Franco Nero, Renato Cestiè, Virna Lisi, John Steiner, Harry Carey Jr., John Bartha, Donal O'Brien, Goffredo Unger.

Convoi de femmes (FR-IT)
Convoy of Women
D: Pierre Chevalier. **P:** Daniel Lesouer. **W:** A.L. Mariaux, Francesco Mazzei. **C:** Gérard Brisseau. **M:** Paul De Senneville, Olivier Toussaint. **S:** Anna Gladysek, Marianne Remont, Paul Muller, Olivier Mathot, Pierre Taylou.

Court Martial (IT)
Corte marziale
D: Roberto Mauri. **P:** Francesco Vitoli. **W:** Roberto Mauri. **C:** Luigi Ciccarese. **M:** Marcello Gigante. **S:** Vassili Karamesinis (as Vassili Karis), Craig Hill, Hunt Powers, Salvatore Billa, Margaret Rose Keil, Tom Felleghy.

Crazy Bunch, The (IT)
Di Tresette ce n'è uno, tutti gli altri son nessuno
D: Giuliano Carnimeo (as Anthony Ascott). **P:** Luciano Martino, Mino Loy. **W:** Tito Carpi. **C:** Federico Zanni. **M:** Alessandro Alessandroni. **S:** George Hilton, Cris Huerta, Antonio Monselesan (as Tony Norton), Memmo Carotenuto, Nello Pazzafini, Umberto D'Orsi, Riccardo Garrone, Goffredo Unger, Pietro Ceccarelli, Furio Meniconi.

Don't Touch the White Woman (FR-IT)
Touche pas à la femme blanche; Non toccare la donna bianca
D: Marco Ferreri. **P:** Jean-Pierre Rassam, Jean Yanne. **W:** Marco Ferreri, Rafael Azcona. **C:** Etienne Becker. **M:** Philippe Sarde. **S:** Marcello Mastroianni, Catherine Deneuve, Michel Piccoli, Philippe Noiret, Ugo Tognazzi.

Kit & Co. (GDR)
D: Konrad Petzold. **P:** Dorothea Hildebrandt. **W:** Jack London (novel), Günter Karl. **C:** Hans Heinrich. **M:** Karl-Ernst Sasse. **S:** Dean Reed, Rolf Hoppe, Renate Blume, Manfred Krug, Monika Woytowicz.

Patience Has a Limit, We Don't (IT-SP)
La pazienza ha un limite... noi no!; ¡Caray, qué palizas!
D: Franco Ciferri (as Frank Farrow). **P:** Panther Film, Ancla Century Film. **W:** Paolo Carboni, Amando de Ossorio, Armando Morandi. **C:** Alessandro Cariello, Miguel Fernández Mila. **M:** Leonerbert. **S:** Peter Martell, Salvatore Borgese, Rita Di Lernia, Pepe Ruiz, Marisa Medina, Luís Barboo.

Return of Shanghai Joe (IT-GER)
Che botte, ragazzi!; Il ritorno di Shanghai Joe; Zwei durch dick und dünn
D: Adalberto Albertini. **P:** CBA, KG Divina Film. **W:** Mario Caiano, Luigi Russo, Adalberto Albertini, Carlo Alberto Alfieri. **C:** Pier Luigi Santi. **M:** Mauro Chiari. **S:** Klaus Kinski, Ernest Van-Mohr (as Cheen Lie), Tommy Polgár, Karin Field, Tom Felleghy.

Sons of White Fang (IT)
I figli di Zanna Bianca
D: Maurizio Pradeaux. **P:** Egidio Gelso, Graziano Fabiani. **W:** Jack London (characters), Arpad De Riso, Maurizio Pradeaux, Giovanni Scolaro, Franco Salina. **C:** Gianni Antinori. **M:** Stelvio Cipriani. **S:** Salvatore Borgese, Ileana Rigano, Piero Fabiani, Danny Ribol, Antonio Maimone, Luciano Rossi.

Spikes Gang, The (US)
(shot in Spain)
D: Richard Fleischer. **P:** Richard Fleischer, Walter Mirisch, Irving Ravetch. **W:** Giles Tippette (novel), Irving Ravetch, Harriet Frank Jr. **C:** Brian West. **M:** Fred Karlin. **S:** Lee Marvin, Gary Grimes, Ron Howard, Charles Martin Smith, Arthur Hunnicutt, Ricardo Palacios.

Stranger and the Gunfighter, The (IT-SP-HK)
Là dove non batte il sole; El kárate, el Colt y el impostor; Long hu zou tian ya; Blood Money
D: Antonio Margheriti (as Anthony M. Dawson). **P:** Run Run Shaw, Carlo Ponti, Gustav Berne. **W:** Barth Jules Sussman, Giovanni Simonelli, Antonio Margheriti (Spanish version credits Miguel de Echarri). **C:** Alejandro Ulloa. **M:** Carlo Savina. **S:** Lee Van Cleef, Lo Lieh, Patty Shepard, Femi Benussi, Karen Yeh, Erika Blanc, George Rigaud, Barta Barry, Ricardo Palacios.

Ulzana (GDR)
D: Gottfried Kolditz. **P:** DEFA, Filmstudio Bucharest, Mosfilm. **W:** Gottfried Kolditz, Gojko Mitic, Hans-Joachim Wallstein. **C:** Helmut Bergmann. **M:** Karl-Ernst Sasse. **S:** Gojko Mitic, Renate Blume, Rolf Hoppe, Colea Rautu, Amza Pellea.

Whisky and Ghosts (IT-SP)
Whiskey e fantasmi; Fantasma en el Oeste
D: Antonio Margheriti (as Anthony M. Dawson). **P:** Champion, Cipi. **W:** Giovanni Simonelli, Antonio Margheriti, Miguel de Echarri. **C:** Alejandro Ulloa. **M:** Paolo Vasile. **S:** Alberto Terracina (as Tom Scott), Fernando Bilbao (as Fred Harris), Maribel Martín, Rafael Albaicin, Ricardo Palacios, Barta Barry, George Rigaud.

1975

Blood Brothers (GDR)
Blutsbrüder
D: Werner W. Wallroth. **P:** Gerrit List. **W:** Wolfgang Ebeling, Dean Reed, Hans-Joachim Wallstein. **C:** Hans Heinrich. **M:** Karl-Ernst Sasse. **S:** Dean Reed, Gojko Mitic, Gisela Freudenberg, Jörg Panknin, Cornel Ispas.

Cipolla Colt (IT-GER-SP)
Cry Onion; Spaghetti Western; Zwiebel-Jack räumt auf; Los locos del oro negro
D: Enzo G. Castellari. **P:** Carlo Ponti. **W:** Sergio Donati, Luciano Vincenzoni. **C:** Alejandro Ulloa. **M:** Guido and Maurizio De Angelis. **S:** Franco Nero, Sterling Hayden, Martin Balsam, Emma Cohen, Leo Anchóriz, Charly Bravo, Daniel Martín, George Rigaud, Romano Puppo, Nazzareno Zamperla, Dan van Husen.

Crazy Adventures of Len and Coby, The (IT)
Carambola filotto... tutti in buca; Carambola's Philosophy: In the Right Pocket
D: Ferdinando Baldi. **P:** Armando Todaro. **W:** Ferdinando Baldi, Nico Ducci, Mino Roli. **C:** Aiace Parolin. **M:** Franco Bixio, Vince Tempera. **S:** Paul L. Smith (as Paul Smith), Antonio Cantafora (as Michael Coby), Glauco Onorato, Gabriella Andreini, Enzo Monteduro, Piero Lulli, Nello Pazzafini, Remo Capitani.

Cry of the Wolf, The (IT-SP)
Il richiamo del lupo; La llamada del lobo; The Great Adventure
D: Gianfranco Baldanello. **P:** Dunamis, Estudios Cinematograficos Roma, Professionals Film. **W:** Jack London (story), Harry Alan Towers (as Peter Welbeck), Juan Lopez Garcia (uncredited), Jesús Rodriguez (uncredited). **C:** José Fernandez Aguayo Jr. **M:** Stelvio Cipriani. **S:** Jack Palance, Joan Collins, Manuel de Blas, Elisabetta Virgili, Fernando Romero, José Canalejas, Ricardo Palacios.

Dallas (SP-IT)
Il mio nome è Scopone e faccio sempre cappotto
(nb: filmed 1972 or 1973)
D: Juan Bosch. **P:** Alberto Grimaldi, Alberto De Stefanis. **W:** Juan Bosch, Renato Izzo. **C:** Giancarlo Ferrando, Julio Perez de Rozas. **M:** Marcello Giombini. **S:** Anthony Steffen, Fernando Sancho, Gillian Hills, Ricardo Palacios, Claudio Undari (as Robert Hundar), Furio Meniconi, Ricardo Palacios.

Dream of Zorro, The (IT)
Il sogno di Zorro; The Mark of Zorro
D: Mariano Laurenti. **P:** San Nicola Cinematografica. **W:** Mario Mariani, Francesco Milizia, Marino Onorati. **C:** Sergio Rubini. **M:** Ubaldo Continiello. **S:** Franco Franchi, Maurizio Arena, Gianni Musi, Ignazio Spalla (as Pedro Sanchez), Paola Tedesco.

Four of the Apocalypse, The (IT)
I quattro dell'Apocalisse
D: Lucio Fulci. **P:** Piero Donati. **W:** Bret Harte (stories), Ennio De Concini. **C:** Sergio Salvati. **M:** Franco Bixio, Fabio Frizzi, Vince Tempera. **S:** Fabio Testi, Tomas Milian, Lynne Frederick, Michael J. Pollard, Harry Baird, Bruno Corazzari, Donal O'Brien, Lorenzo Robledo.

Genius, Two Partners and a Dupe, A (IT-FR-GER)
Un genio, due compari, un pollo; Un genie, deux associes, une cloche; Nobody ist der Grosste; Nobody's the Greatest
D: Damiano Damiani (some footage directed by Sergio Leone). **P:** Fulvio Morsella, Claudio Mancini. **W:** Damiano Damiani, Fulvio Morsella, Ernesto Gastaldi. **C:** Giuseppe Ruzzolini. **M:** Ennio Morricone. **S:** Terence Hill, Miou-Miou, Robert Charlebois, Patrick McGoohan, Klaus Kinski, Rik Battaglia, Mario Brega, Benito Stefanelli, Furio Meniconi.

Get Mean (IT or US)
Vengeance of the Barbarians
D: Ferdinando Baldi. **P:** Tony Anthony. **W:** Tony Anthony (uncredited), Lloyd Battista, Wolf Lowenthal, Ferdinando Baldi. **C:** Mario Perino. **M:** Franco Bixio, Vince Tempera, Fabio Frizzi. **S:** Tony Anthony, Lloyd Battista, Raf Baldassarre, Diana Lorys, David Dreyer.

Hostage, The (IT)
L'ostaggio; Young Guns Go West
D: Luigi Valenzano. **P:** Roma Cinematografica. **W:** Luigi Valenzano, Enrico Bomba. **C:** Ugo Brunelli. **M:** Alessandro Blonksteiner. **S:** Aldo Ballanti, Tony Biccari, Marco Mirabella, Walter Battistelli, Annarita D'Orazio.

In the Name of the Father, of the Son and of the Colt (IT-SP)
In nome del padre, del figlio e della Colt; La máscara de cuero
(nb: filmed in 1971)
D: Mario Bianchi (as Frank Bronston; some sources also/alternatively credit Gino Mangini). **P:** Silvio Battistini, Eduardo Manzanos Brochero. **W:** Arpad De Riso, Mario Gariazzo. **C:** Emilio Foriscot. **M:** Piero Piccioni (some sources credit Gianni Ferrio). **S:** Craig Hill, Nuccia Cardinali, Gilberto Galimberti, Agata Lys, Lorenzo Piani, Frank Braña, Paco Sanz.

Red Coat (IT)
Giubbe rosse; Cormack of the Mounties
D: Aristide Massaccesi (as Joe D'Amato). **P:** Alfonso Donati. **W:** Aristide Massaccesi, Claudio Bernabei, Luigi Montefiori. **C:** Aristide Massaccesi. **M:** Carlo Rustichelli. **S:** Fabio Testi, Guido Mannari, Renato Cestiè, Lynne Frederick, Lionel Stander, Luigi Montefiori (as George Eastman), Salvatore Billa, Bruno Corazzari, Claudio Undari (as Robert Hundar).

Seven Devils on Horseback (IT)
I sette del gruppo selvaggio
(nb: filmed 1972)
D: Gianni Crea. **P:** Bleus Film. **W:** Gianni Crea. **C:** Silvio Fraschetti, Angelo Lotti. **M:** Stelvio Cipriani. **S:** Dino Strano (as Dean Stratford), Mario Brega, Femi Benussi, Gordon Mitchell, Giuseppe Mattei.

Take a Hard Ride (IT-US)
La parola di un fuorilegge... è legge
D: Antonio Margheriti (as Anthony M. Dawson). **P:** Harry Bernsen. **W:** Jerry Ludwig, Eric Bercovici. **C:** Riccardo Pallottini. **M:** Jerry Goldsmith. **S:** Lee Van Cleef, Jim Brown, Fred Williamson, Catherine Spaak, Jim Kelly, Dana Andrews, Barry Sullivan, Ricardo Palacios.

Tiger from the River Kwai, The (IT)
La tigre venuta dal fiume Kwai
D: Franco Lattanzi. **P:** Cine Fenix. **W:** Armando Visconti. **C:** Giovanni Visconti. **M:** Alberto Bembo. **S:** Luigi Montefiori (as George Eastman), Krung Srivilai, Gordon Mitchell, Kam Wong Long, Loredana Farnese, Nello Pazzafini.

Trinity Plus the Clown and a Guitar (IT-AUT)
Prima ti suono e poi ti sparo; Der kleine Schwarze mit dem roten Hut
D: Franz Antel. **P:** Franz Antel. **W:** Oreste Coltellacci, Michele Massimo Tarantini, Orthofer Heine. **C:** Mario Capriotti. **M:** Guido and Maurizio De Angelis. **S:** George Hilton, Rinaldo Talamonti, Piero Lulli, Herbert Fux, Hans Terofal, Antonio Gradoli, Ignazio Spalla (as Pedro Sanchez).

Valley of the Dancing Widows (GER-SP)
Das Tal der Tanzenden Witwen; El valle de las viudas
D: Volker Vogeler. **P:** Michael Fengler, Luis Megino. **W:** Volker Vogeler. **C:** Fernando Arribas. **M:** Carmelo Bernaola. **S:** Harry Baer, Leonie Thelen, Judith Stephen, Tilo Pruckner, Cris Huerta, Daniel Martín, George Rigaud.

White Fang and the Gold Diggers (IT)
La spacconata
D: Alfonso Brescia. **P:** Pleiade Film, Apotheosis Cinematografica. **W:** Piero Regnoli, Giuseppe Maggi. **C:** Silvio Fraschetti. **M:** Alessandro Alessandroni. **S:** Robert Woods, Ignazio Spalla (as Pedro Sanchez), Claudio Undari (as Robert Hundar), Franco Lantieri, Gabriella Lepori, Nello Pazzafini.

White Fang and the Hunter (IT)
Zanna Bianca e il cacciatore solitario; The Lone Hunter of the Wild North
D: Alfonso Brescia. **P:** Pleiade Film, Apotheosis Cinematografica. **W:** Giulio Berruti, Giuseppe Maggi, Franco Pietroletti, Odoardo Fiory. **C:** Silvio Fraschetti. **M:** Alessandro Alessandroni. **S:** Robert Woods, Ignazio Spalla (as Pedro Sanchez), Malisa Longo, Claudio Undari (as Robert Hundar), Franco Lantieri, Nello Pazzafini.

White Fang to the Rescue (IT)
Zanna Bianca alla riscossa
D: Tonino Ricci. **P:** Edmondo Amati. **W:** Sandro Continenza, Giovanni Simonelli. **C:** Giovanni Bergamini. **M:** Carlo Rustichelli. **S:** Henry Silva, Maurizio Merli, Renzo Palmer, Gisela Hahn, Donal O'Brien, Luciano Rossi, Benito Stefanelli.

White, the Yellow and the Black, The (IT-SP-FR)
Il bianco, il giallo il nero; El blanco, el amarillo y el negro; Le blanc, le jaune et le noir; Samurai
D: Sergio Corbucci. **P:** Tritone, Mundial, Filmel. **W:** Marcello Coscia, Antonio Troiso, Mario Amendola, Renee Asseo, Sergio Spina, Sergio Corbucci, Santiago Moncada. **C:** Luis Cuadrado. **M:** Guido and Maurizio De Angelis. **S:** Giuliano Gemma, Eli Wallach, Tomas Milian, Manuel de Blas, Jacques Berthier, Tito García, Cris Huerta, Luis Induni, Victor Israel, Romano Puppo, Lorenzo Robledo, Nazzareno Zamperla, Dan van Husen.

Who's Afraid of Zorro? (IT-SP)
Ah si? E io lo dico a ZZZorro!; Nuevas aventuras del Zorro; The Mark of Zorro
D: Franco Lo Cascio. **P:** Otello Finocchi, José María Cunillés. **W:** Augusto Finocchi, Francisco Lara Polop. **C:** Franco Villa, Juan Gelpi. **M:** Gianfranco Plenizio. **S:** George Hilton, Lionel Stander, Charo López, Antonio Pica, Tito García.

Zorro (IT-FR)
D: Duccio Tessari. **P:** Luciano Martino, Les Productions Artistes Associés. **W:** Giorgio Arlorio. **C:** Giulio Albonico. **M:** Guido and Maurizio De Angelis. **S:** Alain Delon, Ottavia Piccolo, Stanley Baker, Enzo Cerusico, Moustache, Giacomo Rossi-Stuart.

1976

Apache Woman (IT)
Una donna chiamata Apache
D: Giorgio Mariuzzo (as George McRoots). **P:** Zenith, National. **W:** Giorgio Mariuzzo, Antonio Racciopppi. **C:** Sergio Rubini. **M:** Roberto Donati, Fiamma Maglione (as Budy-Maglione). **AD:** Goffredo Unger. **S:** Al Cliver, Clara Hopf (as Yara Kewa), Corrado Olmi, Federico Boido (as Rick Boyd), Mario Maranzana.

Euro-Western Filmography

God's Gun (IT-ISR)
Diamante Lobo
D: Gianfranco Parolini (as Frank Kramer).
P: Menahem Golan. **W:** Sergio Colasanti (novel), John Fonseca, Gianfranco Parolini (as Frank Kramer). **C:** Sandro Mancori. **M:** Sante Maria Romitelli. **S:** Lee Van Cleef, Jack Palance, Richard Boone, Sybil Danning, Leif Garrett.

If You Shoot... You Live! (SP)
Si quieres vivir… dispara
D: José Maria Elorrieta. **P:** Enriqué Uvideo Herrera. **W:** Manuel Sebares, José Maria Elorrieta. **C:** Emilio Foriscot. **M:** Javier Elorrieta. **S:** James Philbrook, Frank Braña, Alejandro de Enciso, José Canalejas, Paula Pattier.

Keoma (IT)
The Violent Breed
D: Enzo G. Castellari. **P:** Uranos. **W:** Mino Roli, Nico Ducci, Luigi Montefiori, Enzo G. Castellari, Gianni Loffredo (uncredited). **C:** Aiace Parolin. **M:** Guido and Maurizio De Angelis. **S:** Franco Nero, Woody Strode, William Berger, Donal O'Brien, Olga Karlatos, Gabriella Giacobbe, Gianni Loffredo, Orso Maria Guerrini, Antonio Marsina, Giovanni Cianfriglia (as Ken Wood).

Kid Vengeance (IT-ISR-US)
L'uomo di Santa Cruz; Take Another Hard Ride
D: Joseph Manduke. **P:** Bob Burkhardt, Yoram Globus, Menahem Golan, Frank Johnson. **W:** Ken Globus, Bud Robbins, Jay Tefler. **C:** David Gurfinkel. **M:** Francesco De Masi. **S:** Lee Van Cleef, Jim Brown, Leif Garrett, John Marley, Glynnis O'Connor.

Potato Fritz (GER)
Zwei gegen Tod und Teufel; Montana Trap
D: Peter Schamoni. **P:** Peter Schamoni. **W:** Paul Hengge. **C:** Jost Vacano, Wolf Wirth. **M:** Anton Dvorak, Udo Jürgens. **S:** Hardy Krüger, Stephen Boyd, Anton Diffring, Friedrich von Ledebur, Arthur Brauss, Luís Barboo, Dan van Husen.

Trini (GDR)
Stirb für Zapata; Die Rache
D: Walter Beck. **P:** Alexander Losche. **W:** Ludwig von Renn (novel), Margot Beichler. **C:** Horst Hardt. **M:** Günther Fischer. **S:** Gunnar Helm, Giso Weißbach, Dimitrina Savova, Gunter Friedrich, Iwan Tomow.

1977

Another Man, Another Chance (FR-US)
Un autre homme, une autre chance
D: Claude Lelouch. **P:** Les Films 13. **W:** Claude Lelouch. **C:** Jacques Lefrançois, Stanley Cortez. **M:** Francis Lai. **S:** James Caan, Geneviève Bujold, Francis Huster, Jennifer Warren, Jacques Villeret.

California (IT-SP)
Lo chiamavano California; El Californiano
D: Michele Lupo. **P:** Uranos, José Frade Producciones. **W:** Franco Bucceri, Nico Ducci, Roberto Leoni, Mino Roli. **C:** Alejandro Ulloa. **M:** Gianni Ferrio. **S:** Giuliano Gemma, William Berger, Raimund Harmstorf, Miguel Bosè, Paola Bosè, Alberto Dell'Acqua, Franco Fantasia, Dana Ghia, Franco Ressel, Tom Felleghy, Romano Puppo, Nazzareno Zamperla, Robert Hundar.

El Macho (IT)
Macho Killers
D: Marcello Andrei. **P:** SB Produzione. **W:** Fabio Pittorru, Augusto Finocchi, Marcello Andrei. **C:** Luciano Trasatti. **M:** Marcello Ramoino. **S:** Carlos Monzón, George Hilton, Malisa Longo, Susanna Giménez, Benito Stefanelli, Pietro Ceccarelli.

Man Called Blade, A (IT)
Mannaja
D: Sergio Martino. **P:** Luciano Martino. **W:** Sergio Martino, Sauro Scavolini. **C:** Federico Zanni. **M:** Guido and Maurizio De Angelis. **S:** Maurizio Merli, John Steiner, Donal O'Brien, Sonja Jeannine, Philippe Leroy, Rik Battaglia, Nello Pazzafini.

1978

China 9, Liberty 37 (IT-SP)
Amore, piombo e furore; Clayton Drumm
D: Monte Hellman (Italian print credits Antonio Brandt). **P:** Gianni Bozzacchi, Valerio De Paolis, Monte Hellman. **W:** Ennio De Concini, Vicente Escrivá Soriano (credited on the American print to Jerry Harvey, Douglas Venturelli). **C:** Giuseppe Rotunno. **M:** Pino Donaggio. **S:** Fabio Testi, Warren Oates, Jenny Agutter, Sam Peckinpah, Isabel Mestres, Luís Barboo, Charly Bravo, Helga Liné, Romano Puppo.

Ciudad maldita, La (SP-IT)
La notte rossa del falco
D: Juan Bosch. **P:** José María Cunillés, Antonio Girasante, Luis Marin. **W:** Dashiell Hammett (novel), Juan Bosch, Alberto De Stefanis. **C:** Gino Santini. **M:** Franco Zulian. **S:** Chet Baken, Anna Vega (as Diana Lorys), Roberto Camardiel, Daniel Martín, Luciano Pigozzi (as Alan Collins), Antonio Molino Rojo.

Eagle's Wing (UK-SP)
Tu, pequeño hombre blanco
D: Anthony Harvey. **P:** Ben Arbeid. **W:** John Briley. **C:** Billy Williams. **M:** Marc Wilkinson. **S:** Martin Sheen, Sam Waterston, Harvey Keitel, Stephane Audran, José Carlos Ruiz.

Severino (GDR)
D: Claus Dobberke. **P:** Gerrit List. **W:** Edward Klein (novel), Inge Borde, Thea Richter. **C:** Hans Heinrich. **M:** Günther Fischer. **S:** Gojko Mitic, Violeta Andrei, Constantin Fugasin, Mircea Anghelescu, Leon Niemczyk.

Silver Saddle (IT)
Sella d'argento
D: Lucio Fulci. **P:** Rizzoli. **W:** Adriano Bolzoni. **C:** Sergio Salvati. **M:** Fabio Frizzi, Vince Tempera, Franco Bixio. **AD:** Nazzareno Zamperla. **S:** Giuliano Gemma, Sven Valsecchi, Ettore Manni, Donal O'Brien, Cinzia Monreale, Geoffrey Lewis, Aldo Sambrell.

Zanna Bianca e il grande kid (IT)
Zanna Bianca nel west
D: Vito Bruschini. **P:** International Film Constellation. **W:** Vito Bruschini. **C:** Federico Del Zoppo. **M:** Polizzi and Natali. **S:** Luciano Stella (as Tony Kendall), Fabrizio Mariani, Gordon Mitchell, Lea Lander, Dario Ghirardi.

1979

Blauvogel (GDR-ROM)
D: Ulrich Weiss. **P:** Hans-Erich Busch. **W:** Anna Jürgen, Ulrich Weiß, Gerd Gericke. **C:** Otto Hanisch. **M:** Peter Rabenalt. **S:** Robin Jaeger, Gabriel Marian Oseciuc, Jutta Hoffman, Kurt Böwe, Jan Spitzer.

Porno-Erotic Western (IT)
Porno erotico western
D: Angelo Pannacciò (as Gerard B. Lennox). **P:** Lux Internationale. **W:** Walter Femig. **C:** Maurizio Centini. **M:** Giuliano Sorgini. **S:** Karin Well, Remo Capitani, Rosemarie Lindt, Tomas Rudy, Gordon Mitchell.

1980

Black Wolf, The (SP-MEX)
El lobo Negro
D: Rafael Romero Marchent. **P:** Luis Méndez. **W:** Joaquín Romero Marchent, Rafael Romero Marchent. **C:** Jorge Herrero. **M:** Alfonso Agulló, E. Guerin, Carlos Villa. **S:** Fernando Allende, Esperanza Roy, Lola Forner, Carlos Ballesteros, Fernando Sancho, Frank Braña, Roberto Camardiel.

Bordello (SP-MEX)
La mujeres de Jeremías; Garden of Venus
D: Ramón Fernández. **P:** Carlos Vasallo. **W:** Alfredo Mañas, Sherry Frisch. **C:** Fernando Arribas. **M:** Renato Serio. **S:** Jorge Rivero, María José Cantudo, Andrés García, Ana de Sade, Chuck Connors, John Ireland.

Revenge of the Black Wolf (SP-MEX)
La venganza del lobo Negro; Duelo a muerte
D: Rafael Romero Marchent. **P:** Luis Méndez. **W:** Joaquín Romero Marchent, Rafael Romero Marchent. **C:** Jorge Herrero. **M:** Alfonso Agulló, E. Guerin, Carlos Villa. **S:** Fernando Allende, Alvaro de Luna, Carlos Ballesteros, Christian Bach, Esperanza Roy, Frank Braña, Fernando Sancho.

Siete cabalgan hacia la muerte (SP)
D: José Luis Merino. **P:** Golden Films Internacional. **W:** José Luis Merino. **C:** Manuel Hernández Sanjuán. **M:** Alfonso Linos, José Barranco, Ricardo Recuero. **S:** Luis Rosillo, Assumpta Serna, Tony Valento, Emilio Berrio, George Grandson.

1981

Ahora mis pistolas hablan (MEX-SP-COL)
(nb: some sources say released in 1986 or 1988)
D: Fernando Orozco, Aldo Sambrell. **P:** Asbrell Productions, Pedro Rivera. **W:** Fernando Orozco, Ulises Pérez Aguirre. **C:** Tote Trenas.

M: Luis Arcaraz. **S:** Felipe Arriaga, Beatriz Adriana, Aldo Sambrell, Emilio Fernández, Franco Portilla.

Buddy Goes West (IT)
Occhio alla penna; Eine Faust geht nach Westen
D: Michele Lupo. **P:** Horst Wendlandt. **W:** Sergio Donati. **C:** Franco Di Giacomo. **M:** Ennio Morricone. **S:** Bud Spencer, Amidou, Joe Bugner, Renato Scarpa, Piero Trombetta, Tom Felleghy, Romano Puppo, Giovanni Cianfriglia (as Ken Wood).

Chicano (SP)
D: José Truchado Reyes. **P:** César Gallego. **W:** César Gallego, Manuel Martínez Remís, José Truchado Reyes. **C:** José María Ochoa. **M:** Alfonso Linos. **S:** Guillermo Antón, Vicente Sanchez, José Luis Pacheco, Milagros Anton, Max Boulois.

Comin' at Ya! (IT-SP-US)
Pale Fighter; The Devil Rider; Yendo hacia ti
D: Ferdinando Baldi. **P:** Tony Anthony, Bruce Talbot, Stan Torchia. **W:** Tony Anthony, Lloyd Battista, Esteban Cuenca Sevilla, Wolf Lowenthal, Ramón Plana Castell, Gene Quintano. **C:** Fernando Arribas. **M:** Carlo Savina. **S:** Tony Anthony, Victoria Abril, Gene Quintano, Ricardo Palacios, Lewis Gordon, Luís Barboo, Charly Bravo, Goffredo Unger.

Sing, Cowboy, Sing (GDR)
D: Dean Reed. **P:** G.R. Johannishal. **W:** Dean Reed. **C:** Hans Heinrich. **M:** Karel Svoboda. **S:** Dean Reed, Václav Neckár, Kerstin Beyer, Violeta Andrei, Iurie Darie.

1982

Lange Ritt zur Schule, Der (GDR)
D: Rolf Losansky. **P:** DEFA. **W:** Gerhard Holtz-Baumert, Gisela Karau. **C:** Michael Göthe, Helmut Grewald. **M:** Karl-Ernst Sasse. **S:** Gojko Mitic, Klaus Piontek, Günter Schubert, Rolf Hoppe, Leon Niemczyk.

Mexico in Flames (MEX-SOV-IT)
Krasnye kolokola, film pervyy – Meksika v ogne; Campañas rojas; Messico in fiamme; Red Bells
D: Sergei Bondarchuk. **P:** Mosfilm, Vides International, Conacitez. **W:** John Reed (book), Sergei Bondarchuk, Valentin Ezhov, Ricardo Garibay, Carlos Ortiz Tejeda. **C:** Vadim Yusov. **M:** Jorge Eras. **S:** Franco Nero, Ursula Andress, Jorge Luke, Blanca Guerra, Heraclio Zepeda.

Scout, The (GDR-MONGOLIA)
Der Scout
D: Konrad Petzold. **P:** Filmtheater Prager Strasse, Kino-Studio Mongolkino. **W:** Konrad Petzold, Gottfried Kolditz. **C:** Otto Hanisch, Geserdshawijn Masch. **M:** Karl-Ernst Sasse. **S:** Gojko Mitic, Nazagdorshijn Bazezeg, Klaus Manchen, Milan Beli, Giso Weißbach, Konrad Petzold.

1983

Al oeste de Rio Grande (SP)
D: José María Zabalza. **P:** Uranzu Films. **W:** José María Zabalza. **C:** José de la Rica.

M: Ana Satrova. **S:** Miguel de la Riva, Cándida López, Remedios Hernandez, Joaquín Gómez Sáinz, Aldo Sambrell.

Triumphs of a Man Called Horse (SP-US-CAN)
El triumfo de un hombre llamado caballo
D: John Hough. **P:** Hesperia Films, Redwing, Transpacific Media Productions, Sandy Howard Productions. **W:** Dorothy M. Johnson, Jack DeWitt, Miriam DeWitt, Carlos Aured, Ken Blackwell. **C:** John Alcott, John Cabrera. **M:** Georges Garvarentz. **S:** Richard Harris, Michael Beck, Ana de Sade, Vaughn Armstrong, Anne Seymour.

1984

Al este del Oeste (SP)
D: Mariano Ozores Jr. **P:** José María Reyzabal, Salvador Ginés. **W:** Mariano Ozores Jr. **C:** Domingo Solano. **M:** Gregorio García Segura. **S:** Fernando Esteso, Antonio Ozores, Conrado San Martín, Adriana Vega, Fernando Sancho, Tito García, Victor Israel, José Manuel Martín.

Arrapaho (IT)
D: Ciro Ippolito. **P:** Ciro Ippolito. **W:** Silvano Ambrogi, Ciro Ippolito, Daniele Pace. **C:** Giuseppe Bernadini. **M:** Gaetano Savio. **S:** Alfredo Cerruti, Daniele Pace, Gaetano Savio, Giancarlo Bigazzi, Urs Althaus.

Louisiana (FR-IT)
Louisiane
D: Philippe de Broca, Jacques Demy, Etienne Perier. **P:** Gabriel Boustiani, Paulo De Oliveira, Denis Héroux, John Kemeny, Bashar Nasri. **W:** Maurice Denuzière (novels), Dominique Fabre, Etienne Perier, Charles E. Israel. **C:** Michel Brault. **M:** Claude Bolling. **S:** Margot Kidder, Ian Charleson, Andréa Ferréol, Lloyd Bochner, Victor Lanoux.

Man Hunt (IT)
Cane arrabbiato
D: Fabrizio De Angelis (as Larry Ludman). **P:** Fabrizio De Angelis. **W:** Fabrizio De Angelis, Dardano Sacchetti. **C:** Guglielmo Mancori. **M:** Francesco De Masi. **S:** Ethan Wayne, Raimund Harmstorf, Bo Svenson, Henry Silva, Ernest Borgnine.

Yellow Hair and the Fortress of Gold (US-SP)
Yellow Hair & Pecos Kid
D: Matt Cimber. **P:** Cinestar Productions, Continental Movie Productions. **W:** Matt Cimber, José Truchado. **C:** John Cabrera. **M:** Franco Piersanti. **S:** Laurene Landon, Ken Robertson, John Gaffari, Luis Lorenzo, Claudia Gravy, Frank Braña, Eduardo Fajardo, Daniel Martín, Aldo Sambrell.

1985

Atkins (GDR-ROM)
D: Helge Trimpert. **P:** Siegfried Kabitzke. **W:** Stefan Kolditz, Andreas Scheinert. **C:** Peter Brand. **M:** Jürgen Kehrt. **S:** Oleg Borisov, Peter Zimmermann, Colea Rautu, Barbara Dittus, Margit Bendokat.

Blood Church (IT)
D: Tom Vacca. **P:** Ferni Grabaldi, Tom Vacca. **W:** Ferni Grabaldi. **C:** Unknown. **M:** Buxx Banner. **S:** Gaithor Brownne, Carmella N. Hall, Buxx Banner, Woo Manchini, Mikel Short.

Rustlers' Rhapsody (US-SP)
Estos locos cuatereros
D: Hugh Wilson. **P:** David Giler, Michael Green, Hervé Hachuel, Walter Hill, José Antonio Sáinz de Vicuña. **W:** Hugh Wilson. **C:** José Luis Alcaine. **M:** Steve Dorff. **S:** Tom Berenger, G.W. Bailey, Marilu Henner, Andy Griffith, Fernando Rey.

Tex and the Lord of the Deep (IT)
Tex e il Signore degli abissi
D: Duccio Tessari. **P:** RAI, Cinecitta. **W:** Giovanni L. Bonelli (characters), Gianfranco Clerici, Marcello Coscia, Duccio Tessari, Giorgio Bonelli, Selma Dell'Ollio, Gianni Galassi. **C:** Pietro Morbidelli. **M:** Gianni Ferrio. **S:** Giuliano Gemma, William Berger, Carlo Mucari, Isabel Russinova, Peter Berling, Aldo Sambrell, Frank Braña, Charly Bravo, Cris Huerta, Ricardo Palacios.

1986

Scalps (IT-SP)
Scalps, venganza india
D: Bruno Mattei (as Vincent Dawn), Claudio Fragasso (US version credited to Werner Knox). **P:** Beatrice Fims, Multivideo. **W:** Italo Gasperini, Richard Harrison, Bruno Mattei, Roberto Di Girolamo. **C:** Julio Burgos, Luigi Ciccarese. **M:** Luigi Ceccarelli. **S:** Vassili Karamesinis (as Vassili Karis), Mapi Galàn, Alberto Farnese, Charly Bravo, Beni Cardoso, José Canalejas.

White Apache (IT-SP)
Bianco Apache; Apache Kid
D: Bruno Mattei (as Vincent Dawn), Claudio Fragasso (uncredited). **P:** José María Cunillés, Isabel Mula. **W:** Roberto Di Girolamo, José Maria Cunilles, Franco Prosperi. **C:** Lugi Ciccarese, Julio Burgos. **M:** Luigi Ceccarelli. **S:** Sebastian Harrison, Lola Forner, Alberto Farnese, Charly Bravo, José Canalejas, Luciano Pigozzi.

1987

Django Strikes Again (IT)
Django 2 – Il grande ritorno
D: Nello Rossati (as Ted Archer). **P:** Spartaco Pizzi. **W:** Franco Reggiani, Nello Rossati. **C:** Sandro Mancori. **M:** Gianfranco Plenizio. **S:** Franco Nero, Donald Pleasance, William Berger, Christopher Connelly, Licia Lee Lyon.

Renegade (IT)
Renegade (un osso troppo duro)
D: Enzo Barboni (as E.B. Clucher). **P:** Lucio Bompani. **W:** Marco Barboni, Sergio Donati, Terence Hill, Steven Siebert. **C:** Alfio Contini. **M:** Mauro Paoluzzi. **S:** Terence Hill, Robert Vaughn, Ross Hill, Norman Bowler, Donald Hodson.

Straight to Hell (UK)
D: Alex Cox. **P:** Cary Brokaw, Eric Fellner, Scott Millaney, Paul Raphael. **W:** Alex Cox,

Dick Rude. **C:** Tom Richmond. **M:** The Pogues, Pray for Rain. **S:** Dick Rude, Sy Richardson, Courtney Love, Joe Strummer, Biff Yeager.

1988

Bear, The (FR)
L'ours
D: Jean-Jacques Annaud. **P:** Claude Berri, Pierre Grunstein. **W:** James Oliver Curwood (novel), Gérard Brach. **C:** Philippe Rousselot. **M:** Philippe Sarde. **S:** Tcheky Karyo, Jack Wallace, André Lacombe.

It's Happening Tomorrow (IT)
Domani accadrà
D: Daniele Luchetti. **P:** Marco Alfieri, Angelo Barbagallo, Nanni Moretti, Cecilia Valmarana. **W:** Franco Bernini, Carlo Mazzacurati, Angelo Pasquini, Sandro Petraglia. **C:** Franco Di Giacomo. **M:** Nicola Piovani. **S:** Paolo Hendel, Giovanni Guidelli, Margherita Buy, Claudio Bigagli, Quinto Parmeggiani.

Präriejäger in Mexico: Geierschnabel/ Benito Juarez (GDR)
D: Hans Knötzsch. **P:** DEFA. **W:** Karl May (stories). **C:** Horst Hardt. **M:** Karl-Ernst Sasse. **S:** Gojko Mitic, Koljo Dontschev, Andreas Schmidt-Schaller, Djoko Rosic, Leon Niemczyk.

1991

Arizona Road (IT)
Fuga da Kayenta; Tortilla Road
D: Fabrizio De Angelis (as Larry Ludman). **P:** Ezio Palaggi, Marisa Palaggi. **W:** Vincenzo Mannino. **C:** Federico Del Zoppo. **M:** Francesco De Masi. **S:** Antonio Sabato Jr., Teresa Leopardi, Lou Castel, Franco Diogene, Donald Hodson.

Buck at the Edge of Heaven (IT)
Buck ai confini del cielo; Trustful Buck
D: Tonino Ricci (as Anthony Richmond). **P:** Gianluca Curti, Franco Di Nunzio. **W:** Tonino Ricci (as Anthony Richmond), Tito Carpi, Sheila Goldberg, Tonino Ricci. **C:** Giovanni Bergamini. **M:** David A. Hess. **S:** John Savage, David A. Hess, Jennifer Youngs, Jesse Alexander, Rik Battaglia, Alberto Dell'Acqua, Franco Fantasia, William Berger.

Jesuit Joe (FR-CAN)
D: Olivier Austen. **P:** Joe H. Jaizz. **W:** Olivier Austen, Ron Base, Hugo Pratt. **C:** Eric Dumage. **M:** Erik Armand. **S:** Peter Tarter, John Walsh, Laurence Treil, Geoffrey Carey, Chantal DesRoches.

Lucky Luke (IT)
D: Terence Hill. **P:** Lucio Bompani, Edoardo Margheriti. **W:** Morris and René Goscinny (characters), Lori Hill. **C:** Carlo Tafani, Gianfranco Transunto. **M:** David Grover, Aaron Schröder. **S:** Terence Hill, Nancy Morgan, Ron Carey, Fritz Sperberg, Dominic Barto.

1993

Jonathan of the Bears (IT-RUS)
Jonathan degli orsi; Dzhonatan - drug medvedey
D: Enzo G. Castellari. **P:** Franco Nero, Vittorio Noia, Alexandre Skodo. **W:** Franco Nero, Lorenzo De Luca, Enzo G. Castellari. **C:** Mikhail Agranovich. **M:** Clive Riche, Aleksandr Belyayev, Fabio Costantino, Knifewing Segura. **S:** Franco Nero, John Saxon, Floyd `Red Crow` Westerman, David Hess, Rodrigo Obregón, Enio Girolami, Melody Robertson.

Texas – Doc Snyder hält die Welt in Atem (GER)
D: Ralf Huettner, Helge Schneider. **P:** Hanno Huth. **W:** Helge Schneider, Schringo van den Berg. **C:** Diethard Prengel. **M:** Helge Schneider. **S:** Helge Schneider, Andreas Kunze, Peter Berling, Peter Thoms, Werner Abrolat.

1994

Fistful of Fingers, A (UK)
D: Edgar Wright. **P:** Daniel Figuero, Zygi Kamasa, Gareth Owen. **W:** Edgar Wright. **C:** Alvin Leong. **M:** François Evans. **S:** Graham Low, Oliver Evans, Nicola Stapleton, Martin Curtis, Jeremy Beadle.

Silent Tongue (FR-UK-NETH-US)
Le gardien des esprits
D: Sam Shepard. **P:** Ludi Boeken, Carolyn Pfeiffer. **W:** Sam Shepard. **C:** Jack Conroy. **M:** Patrick O'Hearn. **S:** Richard Harris, Sheila Tousey, Alan Bates, River Phoenix, Dermot Mulroney.

Troublemakers (IT-GER-US)
Botte di Natale; Die Troublemaker; The Fight Before Christmas
D: Terence Hill. **P:** Rialto Film. **W:** Jess Hill. **C:** Carlo Tafani. **M:** Pino Donaggio. **S:** Terence Hill, Bud Spencer, Neil Summers, Anne Kasprik, Eva Hassmann.

1995

Atolladero (SP)
D: Oscar Aibar. **P:** Arturo Duque. **W:** Oscar Aibar. **C:** Carlos Gusi. **M:** Javier Navarrete. **S:** Pere Ponce, Iggy Pop, Joaquín Hinojosa, Félix Rotaeta, Carlos Lucas.

Sons of Trinity (IT-SP-GER)
Trinità e Bambino… E adesso tocca a noi; Trinidad y Bambino: tal para cual; Trinity & Babyface - Vier Fäuste geh'n zum Teufel; Trinity and Babyface; Trinity & Bambino: The Legend Lives On
D: Enzo Barboni (as E.B. Clucher). **P:** Ezio Palaggi, Marisa Palaggi, Enrique Uviedo, Italo Zingarelli. **W:** Marco Barboni. **C:** Juan Amorós Andreu. **M:** Stefano Mainetti. **S:** Heath Kizzier, Keith Neubert, Yvonne De Bark, Fanny Cadeo, Renato Scarpa, Tito García.

1996

Here Comes Condemor (The Sinner of the Plains) (SP)
Aqui llega Condemor (el pecador de la pradera)
D: Alvaro Saenz de Heredia. **P:** A.S.H. Films. **W:** Alvaro Saenz de Heredia. **C:** Julio Bragado. **M:** Ramón Farran. **S:** Gregorio Sanchez (as Chiquito de la Calzada), Bigote Arrocet, Sol Abad, Naim Thomas, Julio Tejela, Aldo Sambrell.

North Star (FR-IT-NOR-UK)
Tashunga; Duello tra i ghiacci; Grand nord
D: Nils Gaup. **P:** Conchita Airoldi, Petter J. Borgli, Linda Chabert, Dino Di Dionisio, Anne François, Christopher Lambert, Luke Randolph, Jean-Pierre Rosenberg, Janice Shapiro. **W:** Will Henry (novel), Heck Allen, Gilles Behat, Marc Pecas, Lorenzo Donati, Sergio Donati, Paul Ohl, Philippe Schwartz. **C:** Bruno de Keyzer. **M:** Ennio Morricone, Bruce Rowland, John Scott. **S:** Christopher Lambert, James Caan, Catherine McCormack, Burt Young, Jacques François.

1997

Buck and the Magic Bracelet (IT)
Buck e il braccialetto magico
D: Tonino Ricci (as Anthony Richmond). **P:** Gianluca Curti. **W:** Fabio Carpi. **C:** Giovanni Bergamini. **M:** Stefano Curti, Mauro Ruvolo. **S:** Matt McCoy, Abby Dalton, Felton Perry, Béatrice Macola, Jane Alexander.

Any Gun Can Play

1998

Dollar for the Dead (US-SP)
Un dólar por los muertos
D: Gene Quintano. **P:** Tony Anthony, Enrique Cerezo. **W:** Gene Quintano, Imanol Uribe. **C:** Giovanni Fiore Coltellacci. **M:** George S. Clinton. **S:** Emilio Estevez, Howie Long, William Forsythe, Joaquim de Almeida, Jonathan Banks, Ricardo Palacios.

My West (IT)
Il mio West; Gunslinger's Revenge
D: Giovanni Veronesi. **P:** Vittorio Cecchi Gori, Mario Cotone, Rita Rusic. **W:** Vincenzo Pardini, Giovanni Veronesi, Leonardo Pieraccioni. **C:** José Luis Alcaine. **M:** Pino Donaggio. **S:** Leonardo Pieraccioni, Harvey Keitel, David Bowie, Sandrine Holt, Alessia Marcuzzi.

Return of El Coyote, The (SP)
La vuelta del Coyote
D: Mario Camus. **P:** Enrique Cerezo Producciones. **W:** Mario Camus, César Mallorquí. **C:** Jaume Peracaula. **M:** Sebastián Mariné. **S:** José Coronado, Nigel Davenport, Ramón Langa, Isabel Serrano, Ray Lovelock.

Winnetou Returns (GER)
Winnetous Rückkehr
D: Marijan David Vajda. **P:** Mariette Rissenbeek. **W:** Werner Waldhoff, Pierre Brice, Jean-Claude Deret. **C:** Eberhard Geick, Martin Stingl. **M:** Martin Böttcher. **S:** Pierre Brice, Candice Daly, Pierre Semmler, Tobias Hoesl, Christoph Moosbrugger.

1999

One Man's Hero (US-SP-MEX)
Héroes sin patria; El batallón de San Patricio
D: Lance Hool. **P:** Arturo Brito, Jaime Comas Gil, Julio Fernández, Conrad Hool, Lance Hool, Joseph Brad Kluge, William J. MacDonald, Bunnie Manchester, Paul L. Newman. **W:** Milton S. Gelman. **C:** João Fernandes. **M:** Ernest Troost. **S:** Tom Berenger, Joaquim de Almeida, Daniela Romo, Mark Moses, Stuart Graham.

Outlaw Justice (US-SP)
The Long Kill; La justicia de los forajidos
D: Bill Corcoran. **P:** Once Upon a Time Films, Enrique Cerezo Producciones. **W:** Gene Quintano, Imanol Uribe. **C:** Federico Ribes. **M:** Jay Gruska. **S:** Willie Nelson, Kris Kristofferson, Travis Tritt, Waylon Jennings, Danny Sullivan, Aldo Sambrell.

2000

At Full Gallop (SP)
A galope tendido
D: Julio Suárez Vega. **P:** Estirpe Producciones, Tesela Producciones. **W:** Julio Suárez Vega, Verónica Fernández, Carlos Morcillo. **C:** Juan Carlos Gómez. **M:** Pablo Vega. **S:** Aitor Merino, Ana Alvarez, Ramón Langa, Africa Gozalbes, Sancho Gracia.

Claim, The (UK-FR-CAN)
Rédemption; Le maître de Kingdom Come
D: Michael Winterbottom. **P:** Andrew Eaton. **W:** Thomas Hardy (novel), Frank Cottrell Boyce. **C:** Alwin H. Kuchler. **M:** Michael Nyman. **S:** Peter Mullan, Milla Jovovich, Wes Bentley, Nastassja Kinski, Sarah Polley.

2001

Dust (US-GER-IT-MAC)
Cenzias y polvora
D: Milcho Manchevski. **P:** Chris Auty, Vesna Jovanoska, Domenico Procacci. **W:** Milcho Manchevski. **C:** Barry Ackroyd. **M:** Kiril Dzajkovski. **S:** Joseph Fiennes, David Wenham, Adrian Lester, Anne Brochet, Nikolina Kujaca.

Manitou's Shoe (GER)
Der Schuh des Manitou
D: Michael Herbig. **P:** Michael Herbig, Michael Wolf. **W:** Michael Herbig, Alfons Biedermann, Rick Kavanian, Murmel Clausen. **C:** Eddie Schneidermeier, Stephan Schuh. **M:** Ralf Wengenmayr. **S:** Michael "Bully" Herbig, Christian Tramitz, Sky Dumont, Marie Bäumer, Rick Kavanian.

2002

800 Bullets (SP)
800 Balas
D: Alex de la Iglesia. **P:** Panico Films. **W:** Jorge Guerricaechevarria, Alex de la Iglesia. **C:** Flavio Martinez Labiano. **M:** Roque Baños. **S:** Sancho Gracia, Angel de Andrés Lopez, Carmen Maura, Luis Castro, Enrique Martinez.

2003

Raging Heart (IT)
Cuore scatenato
D: Gianluca Sodaro. **P:** Donatella Palermo. **W:** Andrea Pallanza, Gianluca Sodaro. **C:** Massimiliano Trevis. **M:** Almamegretta, Calexico. **S:** Antonio Reina, Rino Della Volpe, Gigio Alberti, Luigi Maria Burruano, Sebastiano Filocamo.

2004

Blueberry (FR-MEX-US)
Renegade
D: Jan Kounen. **P:** Thomas Langmann, Ariel Zeitoun. **W:** Jean-Michel Charlier and Jean Giraud (characters), Matt Alexander, Alexander Coquelle, Gérard Brach, Jan Kounen, Louis Mellis, David Scinto. **C:** Tetsuo Nagata. **M:** Jean-Jacques Hertz, François Roy. **S:** Vincent Cassel, Juliette Lewis, Michael Madsen, Temuera Morrison, Ernest Borgnine.

Daltons, The (FR-GER-SP)
Les Daltons; Los Dalton contra Lucky Luke; Die Daltons vs Lucky Luke
D: Philippe Haïm. **P:** Saïd Ben Saïd, Yves Marmion, Alfred Hurmer. **W:** Morris and René Goscinny (characters), Ramzy Bedia, Michel Hazanavicius, Eric Judor. **C:** David Carretero. **M:** Alexandre Azaria. **S:** Eric Judor, Ramzy Bedia, Til Schweiger, Said Serrari, Romain Berger.

2006

Bandidas (FR-MEX-US)
D: Joachim Roenning, Espen Sandberg. **P:** Luc Besson. **W:** Luc Besson, Robert Mark Kamen. **C:** Thierry Arbogast. **M:** Eric Serra. **S:** Penélope Cruz, Salma Hayek, Steve Zahn, Joseph D. Reitman, Sam Shepard.

2007

Big City (FR)
D: Djamel Bensalah. **P:** Farid Chaouche, Michael Frisley, Chad Oakes. **W:** Djamel Bensalah. **C:** Pascal Gennesseaux. **M:** Erwann Kermorvant. **S:** Vincent Valladon, Eddy Mitchell, Paolina Biguine, Jeremy Denistry, Samy Seghir.

2009

Doc West (IT)
D: Giulio Base, Terence Hill. **P:** Luca Ceccarelli, Alfonso Cometti, Guido De Angelis, Marco De Angelis, Nicola De Angelis, Anselmo Parrinello, Simone Tordi. **W:** Marco Barboni, Luca Biglione, Jess Hill, Marcello Olivieri. **C:** Massimiliano Trevis. **M:** Maurizio De Angelis. **S:** Terence Hill, Paul Sorvino, Ornella Muti, Boots Southerland, Adam Taylor.

Lucky Luke (FR-ARG)
D: James Huth. **P:** Saïd Ben Saïd, Oscar Kramer, Yves Marmion, Sonja Shillito. **W:** Morris and René Goscinny (characters), James Huth, Sonja Shillito. **C:** Stéphane Le Parc. **M:** Bruno Coulais. **S:** Jean Dujardin, Michaël Youn, Sylvie Testud, Daniel Prévost, Alexandra Lamy.

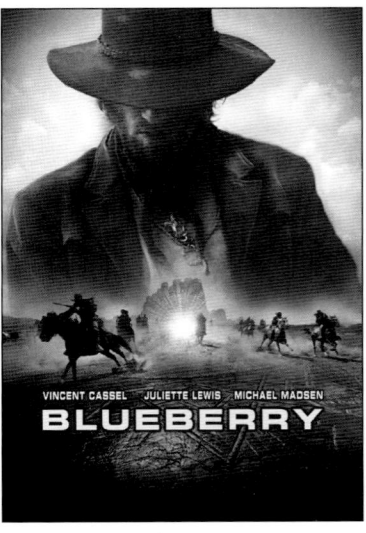

Appendix 3

Bibliography

References and Further Reading

Aguilar, Carlos – *Giuliano Gemma: El factor romano* (Diputacíon de Almería, Spain, 2003)
Aguilar, Carlos – *Joaquín Romero Marchent: La firmeza del profesional* (Diputacíon de Almería, Spain, 1999)
Aguilar, Carlos – *Ricardo Palacios: Actor, Director, Observador* (Ediciones Tantín, 2003)
Aguilar, Carlos – *Sergio Leone: El hombre, el rito, la muerte* (Diputacíon de Almería, Spain, 2000)
Atkins, Thomas R. (ed) – *Graphic Violence on the Screen* (Monarch Press, New York, 1976)
Badman, Keith – *The Beatles off the Record: The Dream Is Over* (Omnibus Press, London, 2001)
Balio, Tino – *United Artists: The Company That Changed the Film Industry* (University of Wisconsin Press, 1987)
Barzini, Luigi – *The Italians* (Hamish Hamilton, London, 1964)
Bazin, André – *What Is Cinema? Volume II* (University of California Press, Berkeley, 1971)
Beatrice, Luca – *Al cuore, Ramon, al cuore* (Tarab Edizioni, Florence, 1996)
Besas, Peter – *Behind the Spanish Lens: Spanish Cinema Under Fascism and Democracy* (Arden Press, Pennsylvania, 1985)
Betts, Tom (ed) – *Westerns all'italiana* (US fanzine, 1983-; westernsallitaliana.blogspot.com)
Bondanella, Peter – *Italian Cinema: From Neorealism to the Present* (Continuum, New York, 2001)
Bruckner, Ulrich P – *Für ein paar Leichen mehr* (Schwarzkopf and Schwarzkopf, Berlin, 2002)
Bruschini, Antonio – *Bizarre Sinema! Horror all'italiana 1957-1979* (Glittering Images, Florence, 1996)
Bruschini, Antonio and Tentori, Antonio – *Mondi incredibili: Il cinema fantastico-avventuroso italiano* (Granata Press, Bologna, 1994)
Bruschini, Antonio and Tentori, Antonio – *Western all'italiana: The Specialists* (Glittering Images, Florence, 1999)
Bruschini, Antonio and de Zigno, Federico – *Western all'italiana: The Wild, the Sadist and the Outsiders* (Glittering Images, Florence, 2001)
Bruschini, Antonio and de Zigno, Federico – *Western all'italiana: 100 More Must-See Movies* (Glittering Images, Florence, 2006)
Buscombe, Edward (ed) – *The BFI Companion to the Western* (Andre Deutsch, London, 1998)
Buscombe, Edward and Pearson, Roberta E. (eds) – *Back in the Saddle: New Essays on the Western* (BFI, London, 1998)
Camargo, Daniel, Vellozo, Fábio and Pereira, Rodrigo – *Anthony Steffen* (Matrix, 2007)
Cameron, Ian and Pye, Douglas (eds) – *The Movie Book of The Western* (Studio Vista, 1996)
Carr, Raymond and Fusi, Juan Fablo – *Spain: Dictatorship to Democracy* (George Allen and Unwin, 1981)
Castagna, Alberto and Graziosi, Maurizio Cesare – *Il Western all'italiana* (Federico Motta, Milan, 2005)
Cohen, Thomas V. – *Love and Death in Renaissance Italy* (University of Chicago Press, 2004)
Connolly, William (ed) – *Spaghetti Cinema* (US fanzine, 1984-; w.connolly.blogspot.com)
Cox, Alex – *10,000 Ways to Die* (Kamera Books, London, 2009)
Cumbow, Robert C. – *Once Upon a Time: The Films of Sergio Leone* (Scarecrow Press, London, 1987)
Curti, Roberto (ed) – *Il mio nome e Nessuno – Lo spaghetti Western secondo Tonino Valerii* (Un Mundo a Parte, Rome, 2008)
De Fornari, Oreste – *Sergio Leone: The Great Dream of Legendary America* (Gremese International, 1997)
De Gemini, Franco – *Così insegnai a Charles Bronson ad impugnare l'armonica* (Beat Records, Italy, 2010)
De Luca, Lorenzo – *C'era una volta il western Italiano* (Istituto Bibliografico Napoleone, Rome, 1987)
Dyer, Richard, and Vincendeau, Ginette – *Popular European Cinema* (Routledge, London and New York, 1992)
Fenin, George N. and Everson, William K. – *The Western: From Silents to the Seventies* (Penguin, Harmonsworth, 1978)
Frayling, Christopher – *Sergio Leone: Once Upon a Time in Italy* (Thames and Hudson, London, 2005)
Frayling, Christopher – *Something to Do with Death* (Faber and Faber, London, 2000)
Frayling, Christopher – *Spaghetti Westerns: Cowboys and Europeans from Karl May to Sergio Leone* (Routledge and Kegan Paul, London, 1981)
French, Philip – *Westerns: Aspects of a Movie Genre* (Carcanet Press, Manchester, 2005)
Fridlund, Bert – *Spaghetti Westerns: A Thematic Analysis* (McFarland Press, North Carolina, 2006)
García, Juan Gabriel – *Los Españoles del Western* (Editorial Círculo Rojo, Almería, 2010)
Ginsborg, Paul – *A History of Contemporary Italy* (Penguin, London, 1990)
Giré, Jean-François – *It était une fois... le western européen* (Dreamland Editeur, France, 2002)
González Ballesteros, Teodoro – *Aspectos jurídicos de la censura cinematoráfica en españa. Con especial referencia al periodo 1936-1977* (Editorial de la Universidad Complutense, Madrid, 1981)
Giusti, Marco – *Dizionario del western all'italiana* (Mondadori, Milan, 2007)
Gunst, Laurie – *Born Fi' Dead* (Payback Press, 1995)
Hardy, Phil (ed) – *The Aurum Film Encyclopedia: The Western* (Aurum Press, London 1983)
Harman Chris – *The Fire Last Time: 1968 and After* (Bookmarks, London, 1998)
Heredero García, Rafael – *La censura de guión en España* (Generalitat Valenciana, 2000)
Hillier, Jim (ed.) – *Cahiers du Cinema: The 1960s* (Harvard University Press, Massachusetts, 1986)
Hodgkiss, Clark (ed) – *Blood, Money and Vengeance* (UK fanzine, 1996)
Hohmann, Tobias – *Terence Hill–Bud Spencer Chronicles* (MPW Medien, Germany, 2010)
Hughes, Howard – *Once Upon a Time in the Italian West* (IB Tauris, London, 2004)
Janisse, Keir-La – *A Violent Professional: The Films of Luciano Rossi* (FAB Press, Surrey, 2007)
Kinski, Klaus – *Kinski Uncut* (Bloomsbury, London, 1996)
Kitses, Jim – *Horizons West* (Thames and Hudson Ltd, London, 1969/BFI, London, 2007)
Knight, Alan – *The Mexican Revolution* (Cambridge University Press, 1986)
Knox, Mickey – *The Good, the Bad and the Dolce Vita* (Nation Books, New York, 2004)
Kolker, Robert – *The Altering Eye* (Oxford University Press, 1983)
Landy, Marcia – *Italian Film* (Cambridge University Press, 2000)
Lázaro Reboll, Antonio and Willis, Andrew (eds.) – *Spanish Popular Cinema* (Manchester University Press, Manchester, 2004)
Leprohon, Pierre – *The Italian Cinema* (Secker and Warburg, London, 1972)
Lusted, David – *The Western* (Pearson, Harlow, 2003)
McGee, Patrick – *From Shane to Kill Bill: Rethinking the Western* (Blackwell, London, 2006)
McGilligan, Patrick, and Buhle, Paul – *Tender Comrades: A Backstory of the Hollywood Blacklist* (St. Martin's Griffin, New York, 1999)
McLynn, Frank – *Villa and Zapata: A Biography of the Mexican Revolution* (Pimlico, London, 2000)
Mitchell, Lee Clark – *Westerns* (University of Chicago Press, 1996)
Moscati, Massimo – *Western all'Italiana: Guida ai 407 film, ai registi, agli attori* (Pan, Milan, 1978)
Nowell-Smith, Geoffrey (ed.) – *The Companion to Italian Cinema* (BFI/Cassell, London, 1996)
Pines, Jim and Willemen, Paul – *Questions of Third Cinema* (BFI, London, 1989)
Prince, Stephen (ed.) – *Screening Violence* (Rutgers University Press, New Jersey, 2000)
Prince, Stephen – *The Warrior's Camera: The Cinema of Akira Kurosawa* (Princeton, New Jersey, 1991, 1999)
Rège, Phillippe – *Lee Van Cleef: Soledad y muerte* (Diputacíon de Almería, Spain, 2004)
Schickel, Richard – *Clint Eastwood* (Jonathan Cape, London, 1996)
Schreyer, Linda and Damon, Mark – *From Cowboy to Mogul to Monster: The Neverending Story of Film Pioneer Mark Damon* (AuthorHouse, Indiana, 2008)
Serrano Cueto, José Manuel – *Aldo Sambrell: La mirada más despiadada – Confesiones de uno de los malos del cine español* (Fancy, Valladolid, 2003)
Solvin, Pierre – *Italian National Cinema 1896-1996* (Routledge, London, 1996)
Staig, Laurence and Williams, Tony – *The Opera of Violence* (Lorrimer, London, 1975)
Trader Whitcombe, Rick – *Savage Cinema* (Lorrimer, London, 1975)
Tunau, Iván – *Crítica cinematográfica española: Bazin contra Arístarco, la gran controversia de los años sesenta* (University of Barcelona, 1984)
Vincendeau, Ginette (ed.) – *Encyclopedia of European Cinema* (Cassell/British Film Institute, 1995)
Wallach, Eli – *The Good, the Bad and Me* (Harcourt, San Diego, 2005)
Wayne, Mike – *Political Film* (Pluto Press, London, 2001)
Weisser, Thomas – *Spaghetti Westerns: The Good, the Bad and the Violent* (McFarland Press, North Carolina, 1992)
Whitney, Steven – *Charles Bronson: Superstar* (Coronet, London, 1975/1980)
Wright, Will – *Sixguns and Society* (University of California Press, Berkeley, 1975)

Any Gun Can Play

Index

Page references in **bold** refer exclusively to illustrations, though pages referenced as text entries may also feature relevant illustrations.

Abril, Victoria 336
Acción mutante 349
Ace High 22, 88, 93, **102**, **108**, 304, 447
Acquasanta Joe 456
Acque amare 54
Addobbati, Aldo 255
Addobbati, Giuseppi 144
Adios Cjamango 453
Adios Gringo 63, 65, 240, **417**, 436-437
Adios, Sabata 86, 93-94, **115**, **119**, 202, 248, 262-264, 266, 453
Adorf, Mario 59, 60, 303, **382**, 385
Agranovich, Mikhail 332
Aguilar, Carlos 8, 45, 50, 75
Agutter, Jenny 337
Ahora mis pistolas hablan 467-468
Aida 15
Al este del Oeste 348, 468
Al oeste de Rio Grande 468
Alabiso, Salvatore 220
Alamo, The 347
Albert, Marvin. H 75
Albertini, Bitto 320
Albertini, Giampiero 266
Aldrich, Robert 12, 69, 180
Alessandroni, Alessandro 8, 385
Alighiero, Carlo **218**
Alive or Preferably Dead 148, 261, 303, **304**, 338, 451
Allende, Fernando 348
Along Comes a Tiger 321
Alonso, Chelo 203
Álvarez, Ángel 385
Amati, Edmondo 386
Ambesi, Adriana **250**
Amendola, Mario 86, 386
Amityville 3-D 337
Ammann, Lukas **165**
Among Vultures 57-59, 434
Amori pericolosi 288
Anchisi, Piero 274
Anchóriz, Leo 85, 152, **175**, 215, 386
And God Said to Cain 94, 151, 152, 181-182, 250, **282**, 283, 284, 293-295, 453
And Now... Make Your Peace with God **393**, 447
And Sartana Kills Them All 453
And the Crows Will Dig Your Grave 456
Anderson, Broncho Billy 71, 235
Andrei, Marcello 338
Andreotti, Giulio 149
Andreu, Simón 173
Anger of the Wind, The 190, 196, 223, 224, 226, 227, 453
Animal Called Man, An 460
Annakin, Ken 333
Another Man, Another Chance 467
Anthony, Tony 23, 95, **111**, 134, 267-272, 274, 275, 316, 326, 336, 337, **364**, 376, 386
Antonelli, Laura 153
Antonio das Mortes 192, 193, 206, 223
Antonioni, Michelangelo 11, 14, 145, 191, 268, 291
Any Gun Can Play 9, 85, 92, **95**, **102**, 302, 342, 443
Anything for a Friend 463
Apache 29, 188
Apache Woman 330, 331, 466
Apaches 463
Apaches' Last Battle 56, 58, **371**, 435
Appaloosa 347
Aranda, Ángel 140
Arcalli, Franco 288, 290, 291
Ardisson, George 260, 276, 386
Argento, Dario 176, 218, 344, 386
Arizona 344, 453
Arizona Colt 94, 136, 148, 240, **241**, 344, 346, 440
Arizona Kid 456
Arizona Road 469
Arrapaho 468
Art of Getting Along, The 87
Askew, Luke 156, 157

At Full Gallop 470
Atkins 468
Atolladero 469
Autry, Gene 282
Bacalov, Luis Enríquez 246, 314, 386
Back to the Future Part III 349
Bad Company 327
Bad Day at Black Rock 314
Bad Kids of the West 463
Bad Man's River 135, **231**, 456
Badmen of the West 435
Bahía de Palma 226
Baird, Harry 306, 340
Bakon, Chet 287
Balcázar, Alfonso 61, 156, 237, 238, 386-387
Balcázar, Jaime Jesús 387
Baldanello, Gianfranco 168, 180, 337, 387
Baldassarre, Raf 46, **49**, 275, 387
Baldi, Ferdinando 16, 144, 145, 173, 174, 251, 253, 271, 272, 275, 302, 306, 326, 336, 337, 387
Balducci, Richard 172, 173
Ballad of a Bounty Hunter 440
Ballad of a Gunman 444
Ballad of Django, The 74, 249, 254, 456
Balsam, Martin 310
Band, Albert 53, 140, 141, 387
Bandidas 470
bandido malpelo, El 456
Bandidos 166-167, 316, **372**, 444
Bandits 134, 309, 460
Bandits in Milan 204
Banfield, Edward 131
Bang Bang Kid, The 444
Bankhead, Tallulah 267
Baños, Roque 349
Baragli, Nino 249, 387
Baratti, Bruno 173
Baratto, Luisa 215
Barboni, Enzo 21, 31, 44, 145, 146, 245, 249, 253, 277, 304-306, 309, 311, 313, 334, 348, 387
Barboo, Luis 29, **302**, 387-388
Bardot, Brigitte 138
Barker, Lex 55, **56**, 57-60, **371**, 388
Barnes, Walter 54, 59, 137, 200, 286, 388
Barrel Full of Dollars, A 456
Barreto, Lima 198, 223
Barry, Barta 388
Bartha, John 388
Barto, Dominic **309**
Barzini, Luigi 80, 130, 131, 142
Bastard, Go and Kill 456
Bastia, Jean 298
Bastien, Yvonne **38**
Bastos, Othon **193**
Battaglia, Rik 168, 388
Battista, Lloyd 95, 275
Battle of Algiers, The 186, 194, 198, 199
Bava, Mario 15, 245, 266, 282, 283, 293, 344
Baxter, Anne 24, 137
Bazzoni, Camillo 23
Bazzoni, Luigi 327
Bear, The 469
Beast, The 453
Beatrice, Luca 198
Beaudine, William 283
Behind the Mask of Zorro 435
Beir, Fred 43
Bell of Hell, The 297
Belle Starr Story, The 138, 447
Bellocchio, Marco 29, 186, 196
Bells of Death, The 321
Ben and Charlie 306, **307**, 460
Bengell, Norma 140, 173
Ben-Hur 12, 141
Benigni, Roberto 297
Benussi, Femi 388-389
Benvenuti, Nino 303, 338

Berben, Iris **211**, 212
Beretta, Daniel 172
Berger, William 24, 75, 93, **135**, 151, 153, 155, **180**, 204, 253, **256**, **257**, 258, 259, **261**, 265, 276, 277, 335, 342, 343, 347, **358**, **372**, 389
Bergman, Ingmar 342
Bergonzelli, Sergio 50, 389
Berlusconi, Silvio 328, 331
Bernaola, Carmelo Alonso 296
Berthier, Jacques 50, 135
Berti, Aldo 62, 389
Bertolucci, Bernardo 11, 32, 45, 139, 291
Beswick, Martine **136**, 147, 197
Between God, the Devil and a Winchester 156, **161**, 447
Beyond the Frontiers of Hate 460
Beyond the Law 156, 261, 303, **371**, **377**, **426**, 447-448
Bianchi Montero, Roberto 86, 286, 389
Bianchi, Mario 286
Bianchini, Paolo 176, 389
Bicycle Thieves 14
Biehn, Michael 236
Big City 470
Big Gundown, The 20, 21, 61, 89, 94, 95, **106**, **117**, 134, 153, 155, 189, 195, 199-204, 206, 209, 224, 229, 253, 264, 265, 328, **374**, 444
Billa, Salvatore 389
Billy the Kid 42, 435
Billy the Kid vs. Dracula 283
Bitter Love 179
Bitter Rice 14
Bixio, Franco 339
Black Angel of the Mississippi 435
Black Eagles of Santa Fe, The 60, 141, 437
Black God, White Devil 192, 193, 206, 223
Black Jack 87, 168, **372**, 448
Black Killer 456
Black Sabbath 181
Black Wolf, The 348, 467
Blanc, Erika 389-390
Blasco, Ricardo 132
Blasetti, Alessandro 268
Blauvogel 467
Blazing Saddles 325
Blindman 134, 270-272, 274-275, 316, 336, 338, **364**, 456
Blondell, Simone 390
Blood and Black Lace 15
Blood and Guns see Tepepa
Blood and Sand 32
Blood at Sundown 94, **133**, 134, 141-144, 174, 180, 255, 260, 284, 305, **370**, 440
Blood Brothers 465
Blood Church 468
Blood for Blood 448
Blood Money see Stranger and the Gunfighter, The
Blood River 337, 465
Blue Gang, The 327, 463
Blueberry 470
Boccaccio '70 15, 288
Bódalo, José 210, 244, **245**, 248, **362**, 390
Boetticher, Budd 30, 163
Bogart, William 390
Boldest Job in the West, The 87, **391**, 460
Bolognini, Manolo 243, 250, 341, 342, 346, 390
Bolzoni, Adriano 31, 53, 61, 62, 390
Bondanella, Peter 11, 18, 189, 190
Bonelli, Giovanni Luigi 235, 334
Bonnie and Clyde 33, 76, 309, 327
Boot Hill 88, **112**, 261, 304, **379**, **427**, 451
Borau, José Luis 156
Bordello 467
Borelli, Franco **180**
Borgese, Salvatore 259, 264, 390
Borgnine, Ernest 176
Born to Kill 444
Bosch, Juan 226, 287, 313, 390
Bosé, Lucia 338

472

Index

Bosé, Miguel 338, 346, 347
Bosé, Paola 347
Bosic, Andrea 178, 390
Böttcher, Martin 56, 391
Bottoms, Sam 346
Bounty Hunter, The 70
Bounty Killer, The (1965) 70-71
Bounty Killer, The (1966) **71**, 75, **112**, **122**, 141, 440
Bounty Killer for Trinity, A 21, 460
Bowie, David 348
Boxer, The 340
Boy Who Owned a Melephant, The 267
Boyd, Rick 29, 259, 391, **427**
Boyd, Stephen **137**, 391
Bragaglia, Carlo Ludovico 87
Braña, Frank 29, 348, 391
Brando, Marlon 166, **198**, 199, 214, 248
Brass, Tinto 22, 281
Braun, Zev 338
Bravados, The 88, 163
Bravo, Charly 391
Brazzi, Rossano 267
Brega, Mario 29, **79**, 391
Brent, Timothy 308
Brescia, Alfonso 392
Brice, Pierre 55, **56**, 57, **58**, 59, 60, 283, 347, **371**, 392
Bridge on the River Kwai, The 46
Brochero, Eduardo Manzanos 45, 392
Brokeback Mountain 347
Broken Arrow 39, 81, **188**, 331
Broken Lance 140
Bronson, Charles 23, 34, 85, 91, 179, 182, 248, 257, 318, **319**, **367**, 392
Bronston, Samuel 12
Brooks, Mel 248, 325
Brother Outlaw 456
Brown, Carroll 134, 142
Brown, Jim 329, 338
Brown, Johnny Mack 71
Brynner, Yul 24, 86, **94**, **115**, 262-264, **266**
Buccella, Maria Grazia 227
Buchs, Julio 175, 392
Buck and the Magic Bracelet 469
Buck at the Edge of Heaven 469
Buckaroo 444
Buddy Goes West 309, 311, 338, **426**, 468
Buffalo Bill, Hero of the Far West 41-42, 435
Bugner, Joe 338
Bulgarelli, Enzo 284
Bulldozer 338
Bullet for Sandoval, A see *Vengeance Is Mine*
Bullet for the General, A 18, 29, 61, 88, 90, **115**, **123**, 136, 155, 158, 185, 186, **187**, 189, 190, 195-199, 205, 206, 208, 209, 215, 226, 227, 440
Bullets and the Flesh 41, 435
Bullets Don't Argue 42-44, 53, **393**, 435
Buñuel, Luis 32, 139, 186, 227
Burn! 194, **198**, 214
Burr, Raymond 89
Burrowers, The 283
Burton, Lee 392
Burton, Richard 13
Bury Them Deep 448
Butch Cassidy and the Sundance Kid 327
Butkus, Dick 338
Buzzanca, Lando 298, 299
Byrnes, Edd 23, 85, 392
Cabiria 15, 16, 148
Caiano, Mario 12, 18, 61, 180, 281, 318, 319, 392-393
California 65, 133, 326, 328, 338, 339, 343, 345-347, 467
Call of the Wild, The 333, 460
Call of the Wild Geese 433
Calvino, Italo 268
Calvo, José **165**, 393
Calzada, Chiquito de la 348
Camardiel, Roberto 29, 288, **290**, 344, 348, 349, **377**, 393
Camaso, Claudio 74, 137, 143, 147, 181, 250, 284, 293, 393
Camerini, Mario 12
Cameron, Jeff 21, 217, 393
Cameron, Rod 43, 44, 55, 57, 393
Caminito, Augusto 87, 393
Camus, Mario 196, 217, 223, 224, 226, 227, 348
Can Be Done... Amigo 150, 309, 460
Canalejas, José 29, 394
Candy 275

Cannon for Cordoba 453
Cantafora, Antonio 294, 306
Canti, Aldo 264, **359**
canzone dell'amore, La 344
Capitani, Giorgio 87
Capitani, Remo 394
Capponi, Pier Paolo 168
Captain Apache 266, 456
Carambola 306, 465
Cardinale, Claudia **124**, 138, 139, **356**, 394
Cardone, Alberto 27, 141, 142, 156, 157, 255, 284, 394
Carlos 456
Carné, Marcel 14
Carnimeo, Giuliano 8, 11, 17, 18, 21, 35, 87, 95, 255, 259, 260, 266, 275-277, 286, 298, 300, 309, 312, 313, 394
Carpi, Tito 286, 312, 394-395
Carry On Cowboy 437
Carsten, Peter 294
Casas, Antonio 239, 242, 395
Cash, Johnny 60
Casomai 131
Castel, Lou 29, 155, 185, 193, 195, 196, **197**, 222, 230, **379**, 395
Castellani, Renato 14
Castellari, Enzo G. 7-9, 11, 32, 75, 85, 150, 159, 164, 172, 250, 259, 284, 286, 302, 308, 325, 328, 331-333, 341-345, 395
Castelnuovo, Nino 144, 145, 218, **378**
Castle of Blood 293
Castro, Luis 349
Cat Ballou 301
Catenacci, Luciano 395
Catlow 456
Cavalry Charge 41, 435
Cavani, Liliana 155
Cavara, Paolo 15
Ceccarelli, Pietro 158, 395
Cecchi Gori, Mario 226
Celentano, Adriano 236
Celi, Adolfo 268, 275
Cemetery Without Crosses 136, 176, **177**, 339, 451
Cerami, Vincenzo 174, 274, 395
Cervi, Tonino 163, 317
Cestiè, Renato 309
Chains 14
Challenge of the MacKennas 453
Challenge to White Fang 333, 465
Chan, Jackie 314, 320
Chanel, Hélène 301
Chang, Cheh 315
Chapagua's Gold 135, 454
Charity and the Strange Smell of Money 463
Charley One-Eye 460
Chato's Land 23, 460
Che! 191
Cheng, Chang-ho 314
Chentrens, Federico 168
Cheyenne Autumn 40
Chiari, Walter 298
Chicano 468
China 9, Liberty 37 326, 337, 467
Chingachgook, the Great Snake 444
Chretien, Anna Maria 203
Christmas Kid, The 444
Chrysanthemums for a Bunch of Swine 448
Chuck Mool 86, 144-146, 170, 174, 179, 305, 454
Ciccio Forgives, I Don't! 300, 448
Cicero, Nando 85, 254, 303, 395
Cinema Paradiso 149
Cipolla Colt 309, 310, 328, 334, 338, 465
Cipriani, Stelvio 275, 395-396
Circus World 12
Citti, Franco 85, 223
ciudad maldita, La 287, 467
Civirani, Osvaldo 170
Cjamango 132, **244**, **410**, **420**, 444
Claim, The 470
Clark, Ken 15
Clarke, Robin 167, 181
Cleopatra 12
Cliff, Jimmy 188, 249
Clint the Stranger 132, 133, 444
Closed Circuit 335
Clumsy Hands 50, 95, 284, 297, 316, **382**, 454
Coburn, James **4**, 24, 85, 88, 150, 228, **229**, 373, 396
Coffin for the Sheriff, A 61, 437
Cohen, Emma 296

Cohen, Ethan 347
Cohen, Joel 347
Cohen, Leonard 342
Cohn-Bendit, Daniel 194
Cold Eyes of Fear, The 259
Cold Killer, The 444
Colizzi, Giuseppe 11, 31, 35, 87, 88, 93, 303, 304, 396
Collinson, Peter 171
Colombo, Arrigo 43
Colorado Charlie 50, 62, 437
Colossus of the Stone Age 283
Colt in the Fist of the Devil, A 444
Colt in the Hand of the Devil, A 463
Colt Is My Law, The 437
Come scopersi l'America 158
Comencini, Luigi 14
Comin' at Ya! **118**, 152, 336-337, 468
Common Wealth 349
Compañeros **6**, **17**, 18, 80, 88, **107**, 150, 190, 195, 206, 209, 210, **211**, **212**, 213-216, 221, 227, 246, 248, 308, 328, **362**, 454
Con Men, The see *Tedeum*
Connelly, Christopher 253
Connors, Chuck 85, **120**, **369**
Conte, Richard 268
Contini, Alfio 88
Conversi, Spartaco 396
Convoi de femmes 465
Cooper, Gary 32, **40**, 69, 88, 250
Cooper, James Fenimore 60
Corazzari, Bruno 396
Corbucci, Bruno 244, 298, 309, 396
Corbucci, Sergio 7, 11, 16, 18, 31-33, 40, 45, 52-54, 76-78, 80, 82, 83, 92, 132, 140, 141, 150, 172, 185, 193-198, 206, 209, 210, 213, 215-217, 219-221, 228, 230, 235-237, 243-246, 248-251, 253, 283, 288, 298, 308, 309, 315, 328, 329, 351, 396
Cord, Alex 76, **77**
Corman, Roger 245, 250, 289
Corruption of Chris Miller, The 297
Costa, Mario 41, 42, 396-397
Costa-Gavras 186, 194, 199, 230
Costner, Kevin 331, 332, 347
Cottafavi, Vittorio 62
Cotten, Joseph 24, 62, 140, 222, 246, 397
Count of Monte Cristo, The 243
Court Martial 465
Covered Wagon, The 48
Cowards Don't Pray 94, 175, **383**, 448
Crazy Adventures of Len and Coby, The 306, 465
Crazy Bunch, The 95, 312, 465
Crea, Gianni 397
Crenna, Richard **170**
Cressoy, Pierre 397
Crime of Monsieur Lange, The 235
Crippled Avengers 315
Crispino, Armando 146, 147
Crist, Judith 33
Croccolo, Carlo 136
Crouching Tiger, Hidden Dragon 321
Crowther, Bosley 33
Cry of the Black Wolves 460
Cry of the Wolf, The 466
Cuadra, Maria 136, 173
Cuadrado, Luis 296
Culp, Robert **138**, 139
Cunningham, Bob 172
Curious Way to Love, A 290
Curse of the Golden Flower 321
Curse of the Undead 283
Custer of the West 444
Cut-Throats Nine 50, 296-297, **421**, 456
D'Alatri, Alessandro 131
Dallamano, Massimo 20, 40, 44, 129, 166, 397
Dallas 466
Daltons, The 470
Daly, James 218, **378**
Damiani, Damiano 165, 185, 187, 194-196, 198, 209, 217, 228, 230, 331, 351, 397
Damnation 456
Damon, Mark 23, 72, 73, 155, 168, **174**, 206, 222, 243, 246, 397
Dances with Wolves 331
Davoli, Ninetto 223
Dawson, Anthony 397
Day of Anger 24, 31, 33, 81-82, 87-89, **90**, **91**, 94, 95, **113**, **122**, 165, 170, 261, 264, 316, 321, 365, 444

Day of the Beast, The 349
Day of the Cobra 333
Days of Violence 444
De Angelis, Guido 328, 342, 344, 397-398
De Angelis, Maurizio 328, 342, 344, 397-398
De Angelis, Pompeo 203
De Concini, Ennio 339, 340
De Filippo, Eduardo 341
De Fornari, Oreste 72, 200
De Gemini, Franco 398
De Guello 440
De La Loma, José Antonio 398
De Laurentiis, Dino 12, 222
De Luca, Lorella 136, **237**, 239, 242, 398
De Martino, Alberto 236, 302, 306, 398
De Masi, Francesco 129, 259, 398-399
De Mendoza, Alberto 399
De Santis, Giuseppe 173, 221
De Santis, Lucio 399
De Sica, Vittorio 14, 15, 30, 288
Dead for a Dollar 448
Dead Men Don't Count! 72, 73, 448
Dead Men Don't Make Shadows 74, 454
Dead Men Ride 337, 456
Deadlock 454
Deadly Trackers, The 460
Deaf Smith & Johnny Ears **371**, 463
Death on a High Hill 451
Death Played the Flute 460
Death Rides a Horse 22, 88, 89, **90**, **108**, 157, 169-171, 175, 182, 189, 207, 261, 264, 287, 444
Death Rides Along 444
Death Sentence 19, 22, 94, 149, 166, 167, 181, 281, 444
Death Walks in Laredo 85, 166, 317, 444
Death, at Owell Rock 444
Deda, Massimo 333
Del Arco, Nino **130**
Del Balzo, Raimondo 333
del Pozo, Angel 398
Dell'Acqua, Alberto 306, 398
Dell'Aquila, Vincenzo 398
Dell'Orso, Edda 312, 398
Della Mea, Ivan 207-209
Delli Colli, Franco 290, 398
Delli Colli, Tonino 8, 20, 21, 129, 398
Delon, Alain 318
Demicheli, Tulio 86, 399
Demy, Jacques 145
Deneuve, Catherine 145
Deodato, Ruggero 333
Desailly, Claude 176
Deserter, The 454
Desperado Trail 55, 56, 59, 437
Desperados, The 451
Desperate Hours, The 237
Destry Rides Again 239
Devil's Commandment, The 15, 282
Devil's Doorway 188
Devils, The 152
Di Leo, Fernando 50, 82, 87, 237, 244, 399
Di Nardo, Mario 145
Di Stefano, Felice 399
Diabolik 15
Dig Your Grave Friend... Sabata's Coming **405**, 456, **457**
Dirty Dozen, The 85, 87, 218, 296
Dirty Outlaws, The 444
Divorce Italian Style 14, 149
Django **1**, 7, 20, 21, **34**, 54, 76, 80, 94, **110**, **121**, 140, 141, 148, 149, 153, 165, 188, 210, 222, 236, 243-246, **247**, 248-251, 258, 265, 283, 288, 289, 314, 321, 339, 341, 342, **357**, **400**, 440
Django Against Sartana 260, 276, 454
Django and Sartana Are Coming... It's the End 74, 249, 276, 454
Django Kills Softly 445
Django Shoots First 73, **74**, 94, **120**, 135, **279**, 302, **303**, 440
Django Strikes Again **121**, 155, 253-254, 326, 334, 468
Django the Bastard 153, 180-182, 249, 251, 257, 283, 291-293, **360**, 451
Django, Kill! 32, 80, 81, 148, 149, 158, 173, 224, **231**, 249, 251, 281, 283, 284, 288-291, 295, 349, 444
Django, the Last Killer 95, **399**, **403**, 445
Django… Adios! 460
Django's Cut Price Corpses 456
Djurado 440
Dobkin, Lawrence **174**

Doc 457
Doc West 334, 470
Dolce Vita, La 11, 13, 15, 149, 288
Dollar for the Dead 470
Dollar of Fire, A 149, 440
dollaro di fifa, Un 298, 433
Donati, Sergio 8, 30, 49, 69, 73, 84, 139, 185, 189, 198-201, 203, 204, 206, 219, 221, 228-230, 281, 306, 399
Don't Torture a Duckling 339
Don't Touch the White Woman 194, 465
Don't Wait, Django, Shoot! 250, **423**, **427**, 445
Doomsday 457
Dor, Karin 55, **57**
Douglas, Kirk 12, 13, 40, 59
Dream of Zorro, The 466
Drunken Master 320
Ducci, Nico 341
Duel at Diablo 75
Duel at Rio Bravo see *Gunmen of the Rio Grande*
Duel at Sundown 437
Dumas, Alexandre 137
Durán, Rafael 44
Durango Is Coming, Pay or Die 457
Durgnat, Raymond 84
Duryea, Dan 71, 221
Dust 470
Dying of Laughter 349
Dylan, Bob 338, 342
Dynamite Jack 298, 433
Dynamite Jim 440
Dynamite Joe 293, 445
Eagle's Wing 467
East Meets West 314, 317
Eastman, George 95, 138, **145**, 146, 175, 305, 306, **307**, 341, 399
Eastwood, Clint 14, 17, **20**, 21-23, **31**, **37**, 44, 51, 52, 63, **68**, 69, 73, 78, 82, **84**, **93**, 163, 164, 166, 180, 181, 244, 255, 258, 267, 269, 291, 299, 300, 302, 308, 321, 334, 346, 347, 349, **355**, **369**, 399-400
Easy Life, The 14
Easy Rider 76, 157, 191
Eckemyr, Agneta 134, 275
Edson, Barry 34
800 Bullets 348-349, 470
Ekberg, Anita 15
El Cid 12
El Cisco 440-441
El Condor 454
El Coyote 41, 45, 433
El Macho 338, 467
El Puro 157, 451
El Rojo 441
El Topo 290
Ellis, Mirko 152
Emergency Squad 151
Engagement Italiano 267
Ercoli, Luciano 239
Erice, Victor 224, 296
Ericson, John 82
Erotic Adventures of Zorro, The 460
Eroticist, The 339
Esteso, Fernando 348
European Nights 268
Everybody Go Home 14
Execution 448
Executioner, The 340
Exiled 351
Fabian, Françoise 135
Fabrizi, Aldo 149, 150
Fabulous Trinity, The 460
Face to Face 20, 29, 77, 88, 158, 190, 199-201, 204-206, 222, 340, 445
Fago, Giovanni 74, 143, 195, 202, 223, 224, 400
Fajardo, Eduardo 29, 214, 215, 223, 244, 246, 248, 286, 400
Falana, Lola 137
Falk, Lee 255
Fall of the Roman Empire, The 12
Fantasia, Franco 400
Fastest Guitar Alive, The 265
Fast-Hand Is Still My Name 463
Fat Brothers of Trinity, The 306, 460
Fatal Error 454
Father Jack-Leg see *Tedeum*
Fedra West 133, 173, 448
Felleghy, Tom 400-401
Fellini, Federico 11, 14, 15, 32, 45, 137, 223, 268, 288, 337

Felmy, Hansjörg 60
Feng, Yueh 321
Fernand Cowboy 298, 433
Fernandel 298
Fernandez, Jaime 195
Ferreri, Marco 194
Ferrio, Gianni 401
Ferroni, Giorgio 63, 240, 401
Ferzetti, Gabriel 229
Few Dollars for Django, A 3, **62**, 75, 235, 250, **380**, 441
Fidani, Demofilo 27, 74, 217, 249, 254, 276, 401
Fidenco, Nico 401
Fifteen Scaffolds for a Killer 21, 445
55 Days at Peking 12
Fighting Fists of Shanghai Joe, The 295, 318-319, 321, 463
Find a Place to Die 87, 149-150, 153, 276, 448
Finders Killers 457
Finger on the Trigger 437
Finocchi, Augusto 401
Fioravanti, Giusva **132**
Fiorini, Marco 157
Fistful of Death, A 457
Fistful of Dollars, A 7, 8, **10**, 11, 17, 20, 21, 23, 30, **31**, **37**, 39, 43-45, 48-53, 59, 61, 62, 65, 69, 94, 95, **130**, 131, 139, 148, 159, 166, 237, 242, 244-246, 248, 250, 255, 257, 258, 268, 269, 271, 300, 301, 314, 326, 344, **374**, **393**, **412**, **422**, 435
Fistful of Dynamite, A **4**, 88, **114**, 131, 150, 152, 158, **184**, 190, **196**, 197, 206, 209, 215, 217, 219, **220**, 221, 228-230, 328, **373**, 457
Fistful of Fingers, A 469
Fistful of Songs, A 236, 441
Fistful of Travellers' Cheques, A 351
Fists in the Pocket 29, 148, 196
Five Dollars for Ringo 441
Five for Hell 261
Five Giants from Texas 85, 441
Five Man Army, The 85, **116**, 190, 218, 317, **378**, 451
$5,000 on the Ace 52, 61, 238, **423**, **432**, 435
Flaming Frontier 58, 437
Flavia the Heretic 152
Fleming, Rhonda 139
Flori, Agata **301**
Florio, Aldo 337
Fonda, Henry 14, 24, 70, 71, 88, 90, 91, **94**, **125**, 183, 309, 311, 312, 326, 401
For $100,000 Per Killing 74-75, 94, 143, 153, 174, 224, 255, 445
For a Book of Dollars 463
For a Dollar in the Teeth 149, 151, 267, 268, 271, 445
For a Few Bullets More see *Any Gun Can Play*
For a Few Dollars Less 298-299, 441
For a Few Dollars More 20, 22, 23, 29, 39, 49, 61, 62, 65, **68**, 69-70, 72-74, 80, 84, 90-93, 95, 131, 152, 166, 169-171, 263, 276, 300, 301, 309, 321, **354**, **355**, **414**, **421**, 437
For a Fist in the Eye 299, 300, 437
Force of Impulse 267
Ford, Glenn 29, 70
Ford, John 30, 40, 164, 237, 314, 343, 348
Forgotten Pistolero, The 133, 134, 136, 146, 164, 168, 170, 171, 173, 176, 179, 339, 452
Fort of Death, The 321
Fort Yuma Gold **63**, 65, 346, 441
Forty Guns 39
Four Bullets for Joe 435
Four Came to Kill Sartana 452
Four Candles for My Colt 457
Four Dollars of Revenge 170, 172, 441
Four of the Apocalypse, The 81, **101**, 153, 296, 326, 328, 337, 339-342, 345, 347, 466
Four Pistols for Trinity 457
Four Rode Out 452
Fox, William Price 32
Fragasso, Claudio 331
Fraile, Alfredo 48
Franchi, Franco 62, 224, 299-301, 304, 305, 314, 348, 401-402
Francisci, Pietro 15
Franco and Ciccio on the War-Path 299, 454
Franco, Jesús 41
Frank, Horst 29, 44, 60, 172, 253, 402
Frayling, Sir Christopher 80, 130, 131, 178, 299, 351
Freda, Riccardo 15, 180, 282, 283, 293
Frederick, Lynne 339, 340
Fregonese, Hugo 56

Index

French, Philip 349
Frey, Barbara 222
Friedel, Loni von **286**
Frizzi, Fabio 339
From Dusk Till Dawn 3: The Hangman's Daughter 283
Fulci, Lucio 87, 133, 143, 295, 296, 327, 333, 334, 339-341, 345, 402
Full House for the Devil 152, 202, 224, 248, 265, 448
Fury of Hercules, The 27, 261
Fury of Johnny Kidd 136, 173, 283, 316, 445
Fury of the Apaches, The 41, 435
Gabriel, Teshome H. 191
Gaddi, Carlo 182, **291**, 402
Galbo, Cristina 173
Galimberti, Gilberto **261**
Galleppini, Aurelio 235, 334
Gallone, Carmine 15
García, Tito 402
Garden of Evil 276
Garfinkle, Louis 141
Garko, Gianni 8, 16, **22**, 27, 29, 74, 93, **135**, 142, 143, 153, 164, 191, 198, 236, 250, 251, 255, **256**, 258-261, 264, 276, 277, 284, 287, 308, 309, 312, 317, **373**, 402
Garner, James 153, 167
Garrett, Leif 334, **335**, 338
Garringo 50, 175, 452
Garrone, Riccardo **133**, **151**, 402
Garrone, Sergio 75, 175, 181, 250, 257, 291-294, 402-403
Garter Colt 137-138, 448
Gasparri, Rodolfo 192
Gassman, Vittorio 14, 151, 158, **210**, **214**, 215, 216, 301, 309
Gastaldi, Ernesto 8, 17, 31, 74, 89, 142, 240, 255, 260, 311, 344, 403
Gatling Gun 448
Gemma, Giuliano 8, 9, 16, 27, 29, 35, 40, 49, 62, 63, **64**, 65, 81, 89, **90**, **91**, **113**, **119**, 129, 133, 136, 148, 171, 178, 215, **237**, 238-240, 242, 243, 255, 261, 303, 307, 309, 325, 328, **329**, 334, 335, 338, 344-347, **365**, 403
Genius, Two Partners and a Dupe, A 309, 331, 466
Gentilomo, Giacomo 52, 283
Gentleman Killer 180, 445
George, Götz 59
George, Susan 3, 309
Gerima, Haile 191, 192, 207
Germany, Year Zero 221
Germi, Pietro 11, 14, 30, 297
Geronimo: An American Legend 332
Get Mean 95, 271, 336, 466
Getino, Octavio 191, 193
Gherardi, Piero 137
Ghidra, Anthony 86, 95, 153, 156, 403
Ghiglia, Benedetto 268, 403
Ghost Town 283
Ghost, The 181
Giacobbe, Gabriella 342
Giant of Metropolis, The 283
Giants of Rome, The 43
Gicca Palli, Enzo 82, 287
Giménez, Susana 338
Giombini, Marcello 403
Giordana, Andrea **125**, 172
Giordano, Daniela 403
Giraldi, Franco 11, 30, 31, 51, 53, 76, 129, 301, 306, 404
Girl Is a Gun, A 457
Girl Who Knew Too Much, The 15
Girls of the Golden Saloon, The 464
Girolami, Enio 172, 404
Girolami, Marino 41, 74, 156, 300, 345, 404
Girotti, Massimo 30
Giuliani, Luigi 135
Giusti, Marco 223, 337
Go with God, Gringo 441
gobbo, Il 223
God Forgive... His Life Is Mine 294, 448
God Forgives... I Don't! 9, 22, 87-88, **89**, **102**, **162**, 293, 294, 303, 304, 308, **381**, **394**, **412**, 445
God in Heaven... Arizona on Earth 319, **409**, 460
God Is My Colt 460
God Will Forgive My Gun 294, 452
Godard, Jean-Luc 186, 193, 194, 230
Gods and Generals 347
God's Executioner 155, 321, 464
God's Gun **128**, 133, 153, **154**, 155, 266, 326, 334, 335, 338, 467
Gold Train 437

Golden Sheriff, A 135, 441
Goldoni, Carlo 50
Goliath and the Vampires 52, 283
Good, the Bad and the Ugly, The 14, 18, 20, 21, 23, 73, 84-85, 88, 91-94, **129**, 131, 141, 152, 153, 206, 219, 220, 301, 302, 308, 346, 349, **369**, 441-442
Good, the bad, the Weird, The 347, 351
Gora, Claudio 147
Gori, Coriolano 404
Gorin, Jean-Pierre 193, 194
Goscinny, René 235, 305
Gosha, Hideo 321
Gospel According to St. Matthew, The 155, 215
Gottschalk, Thomas 59
Gozlino, Paolo **291**, 292, 404
Gracia, Sancho 349
Gradoli, Antonio **263**, 404
Graf Bobby, der Schrecken des Wilden Westens 437
Graf, Maurizio 238
Grand Duel, The 88, 89, **91**, **108**, **112**, 335, 460-461
Granger, Farley 311
Granger, Stewart 55, 57, 58, 199, 404
Graves, Peter 218, **378**
Great Silence, The 54, 76-78, **79**, 80, 95, 136, 148, 165, 170, 176, 189, 210, 321, **381**, 448
Great Treasure Hunt, The 86, 461
Great War, The 14, 202, 216
Greatest Robbery in the West, The 32, 145, 151, 303, 445
Greene, Lorne 236
Grey, Zane 45
Grimaldi, Alberto 45, 46, 49, 199, 203, 261, 404
Grimaldi, Gabriella 172
Grimaldi, Giovanni 404-405
Guareschi, Giovanni 150
Guerricaechevarria, Jorge 349
Guerrieri, Romolo 74, 250, 405
Guerrini, Orso Maria **98**, 342
Guglielmi, Marco 203, 269
Gun for a Hundred Graves, A 94, 146, **364**, 448
Gun Shy Piluk 448
Gunfight at High Noon 33, 42, 46-48, 132, 136, 170, 434
Gunfight at Red Sands 42, 43, 132, **422**, 434
Gunfight at Rio Grande 437
Gunfight at the O.K. Corral 29, 39, 139, 236
Gunfight, A 59
Gunfighter, The 39, 50, 157, 236
Gunfighters of Casa Grande 435
Gunman Called Dakota, A 457
Gunman in Town 95, 135, 256-260, 454
Gunman of 100 Crosses 136, 457
Gunmen and the Holy Ghost 158, 461
Gunmen of the Rio Grande 42, **43**, 435
Guns for San Sebastian 448
Guns of the Magnificent Seven 452
Gunst, Laurie 188
Hagmann, Stuart 191
Hakohen, Alexander 168
Halfbreed 57, 58, 442
Halleluja to Vera Cruz 464
Hallelujah & Sartana Strike Again! 150, 310, 461
Halliday Brand, The 140
Hallyday, Johnny 82, 210
Halsey, Brett 8, 24, 26, 27, 34, 62, 156, 157, 163, **165**, **166**, 179, 180, **285**, 317, **376**, 405
Hamman, Joë 235
Hammett, Dashiell 50, 287
Hands of a Gunfighter 49-50, 62, 437
Hands Up, Dead Man! You're Under Arrest 457
Handsome, the Ugly and the Stupid, The 300, 445
Hang 'Em High 163
Hannibal 87
Hannie Caulder **127**, 138-139, 457
Harakiri 182
Harder They Come, The 188, 249
Hardin, Ty 405
Hargitay, Mickey 62, 286, 405
Harmstorf, Raimund 346
Harris, Brad 8, 27, 42, 60, 261, 262, **382**, 405
Harris, Ed 347
Harrison, Richard 8, 16, 23, 24, 26, 27, 33, 42, 43, 47, **132**, 156, 157, 170, 172, 181, 293, **294**, 306, 405-406
Harte, Bret 21, 339
Hartwig, Wolf C. 60
Hate for Hate 54, 166, 171, 445
Hate Is My God 170, 281, 452
Hate Your Neighbour 175, 448
Hathaway, Henry 276

Have a Nice Funeral, Sartana Will Pay **22**, 255, **256**, 257, 258, 317, 319, **384**, 454
Hawks, Howard 30, 237, 242
Hayden, Sterling 95
He Was Called the Holy Ghost 457
Heads I Kill You... Tails You're Dead! They Call Me Hallelujah 86, 312, 458
Heaven's Gate 347
Heflin, Van 24, 87, **122**
Helen of Troy 12
Hellbenders, The 140-141, 210, 222, 246, **397**, 445
Hellhounds of Alaska, The 464
Hellman, Monte 337
Henzell, Perry 188
Herbig, Michael 59
Hercules 15-16
Hercules Against the Moon Men 283
Hercules and the Treasure of the Aztecs 283
Hercules Conquers Atlantis 283
Hercules in the Centre of the Earth 283
Hercules the Invincible 13
Hercules Unchained **16**
Hercules, Samson and Ulysses 48
Here Comes Condemor (The Sinner of the Plains) 348, 469
Here We Go Again, Eh Providence? 306, 320, 464
Hero 321, 351
Heroes of Fort Worth 41, 435
Heroes of the West 298, 434
Herter, Gérard 29, 94, 202, 248, 264, 265, 406
Heston, Charlton 13
Heusch, Paolo 186
Hey Amigo! A Toast to Your Death 458
High Crime 345
High Noon 29, 39, 81, 88, 242
High Plains Drifter 164, 181, 291
Hill, Craig 21, 23, **26**, 49, 50, 62, 73, 176, 406
Hill, Terence **20**, 23, 27, 29, 31, **57**, 59, 87, **88**, 90, 91, 93, **94**, **102**, **104**, **108**, **111**, **112**, **125**, 129, **153**, 196, **226**, 227, 236, 249, 251, 253, 261, 302-306, 309, **310**, 311-313, 325, 331, 334, 338, 345, 348, **361**, 406
Hill, Walter 332
Hills Run Red, The 54, 166, **220**, 221, 442
Hilton, George 8, 9, 27, 29, 85, 87, **104**, **122**, 129, 144, 145, 152, 175, 258-260, 286, 300-303, 309, 312, 313, 325, 338, **368**, **377**, 406
His Name Was Holy Ghost 86, 259, 312, 461
His Name Was King 458
His Name Was Sam Wallash... But They Called Him Amen! 458
History of the World Part 1 248
Holden, William 196
Hole Between the Eyes, A 86, 153, 448
Horne, Geoffrey 46
Hossein, Robert 176, **177**, 406-407
Hostage, The 466
Hoven, Adrian 48, **49**
How the West Was Won 40
Hu, King 315
Hudson, Rock 250
Huerta, Cris 29, 312, 320, **406**, 407
Hundar, Robert *see* Undari, Claudio
Hunter, Jeffrey 87
Hunter, Thomas 222
Hunting Party, The 458
Huston, John 140
I Am Sartana, Your Angel of Death 94, **121**, 153, 256, 258, 259, **260**, 452
I Want Him Dead 176, 178, 448-449
If You Meet Sartana, Pray for Your Death 93, 94, 255-262, 264, **372**, **373**, 449
If You Shoot... You Live! 467
If You Want to Live... Then Shoot! 132, **133**, **432**, 449
Iglesia, Alex de la 348, 349
Ikehiro, Kazuo 321
I'll Sell My Skin Dearly 132, 133, 172, 449
I'm for the Hippopotamus 338
Implacable Three, The see *Magnificent Three, The (1963)*
In a Colt's Shadow **126**, **423**, **424**, 437
In the Dust of the Sun 133, 172-173, 458
In the Name of the Father 452
In the Name of the Father, of the Son and of the Colt 286, 287, 466
In the Name of the Law 30
Incrocci, Agenore 14

Induni, Luis 170, 259, 407
Infascelli, Roberto 268
Inglourious Basterds 351
Ingrassia, Ciccio 62, 224, 299-301, 304, 305, 348, 407
Investigation of a Citizen Above Suspicion 204
Ippoliti, Silvano 407
Iquino, Ignacio F. 27, 313, 407
Irazoqui, Enrique 155, 215
Ireland, John 24, 171, 236, 407-408
Iseya, Yusuke 321
Israel, Victor 348, 408
Ito, Hideaki 321
It's Happening Tomorrow 348, 469
Izzo, Renato 260
Jack London Story, The 464
Jacopetti, Gualtiero 15, 268
Jacovitti, Benito 235, 305
Jagger, Mick 338
Jaguar, The 434
Jaspe, José 408
Jeffries, Lang 182, 283
Jenkins, Terry 166
Jerez Aloza, José Luis 223
Jesse & Lester: Two Brothers in a Place Called Trinity 306, 461
Jesse James Meets Frankenstein's Daughter 283
Jesuit Joe 469
Jodorowsky, Alejandro 290
Joe Dexter 437
John Carpenter's Vampires 283
John Paul Jones 12
John the Bastard 144, 146-147, 153, 174, 445
Johnny Guitar 39, 81, 82
Johnny Hamlet 86, **125**, 133, 148, **149**, 172, 174, 224, 250, 284, 341, 342, **368**, 449
Johnny West 262, 437
Johnny Yuma 134, 149, 168, 174, 442
Johnson, Lamont 59
Johnson, Van 178
Jonathan of the Bears 7, 326, 328, 331-333, 469
Jones, L.Q. 71
Jordán, Norma **125**
Juanito 433
Judge Roy Bean 458
justicia del Coyote, La 41, 433
Juzgado permanente 44
Kapò 198
Karate, Fists and Beans 320, 464
Karlatas, Olga 342
Katsu, Shintarō 272
Keitel, Harvey 348
Kelly, Jim 320, 329
Kendall, Tony 60, 261, 262, 276, 408
Kennedy, Arthur 164
Kennedy, Burt 138
Keoma 22, 32, 81, **98**, **99**, 144, 145, 148, 250, **324**, 325-328, 331, 339, 341-347, **353**, 467
Kewa, Yara 331
Kezich, Tullio 299
Kid Rodelo 442
Kid Vengeance 326, 336, 338, 467
Kill and Pray 62, 155, 158, 185, 190, 206, 215, 217, 221-223, 246, 284, **379**, 445
Kill Bill 314, 351
Kill Django... Kill First 458
Kill Johnny Ringo! 180, 442
Kill or Be Killed 442
Kill the Poker Player 286, 461
Kill the Wicked 87, 281, 445
Kill Them All and Come Back Alone 85, **120**, **369**, 449
Killer Adios 286, **287**, 449
Killer Kid **114**, **115**, 189, 195, 215, 217, 218, 445
King Boxer 314, 316, 319
King of Kings 12
King, Henry 163
Kinski, Klaus **28**, 29, 59, 76, **78**, 82, 87, **115**, **121**, **122**, 151, 155, **176**, 181, 182, 215, **227**, 255, 259, 293, 295, 319, 320, 330, **354**, 408
Kiss Kiss... Bang Bang 237
Kiss Kiss... Kill Kill 261
Kiss of Death 255
Kit & Co. 465
Kitano, Takeshi 274
Kitosch, the Man Who Came from the North 445
Kitses, Jim 30, 71, 94, 176, 349
Klein, Allen 270, 274
Klimovsky, León 86, 408

Knox, Mickey 220, 409
Kobayashi, Akira 314
Koch, Marianne 59, **130**, 409
Kojucharov, Vasco Vassil 430
Kolditz, Gottfried 409
Kolker, Robert 186, 194
Konopka, Magda 134, 275
Kramer, Stanley 88
Kristofferson, Kris 338
Ku Fu? Dalla Sicilia con furore 314
Kudo, Eiichi 321
Kung Fu Brothers in the Wild West 320, 464
Kurosawa, Akira 244, 245, 269, 270, 314, 315
Lacerenza, Michele 142, 409
Ladd, Alan 52, 133
Lam, Ringo 314
Lancaster, Burt 29, **40**, 62, 69
Land Raiders 452
Landy, Marcia 13, 91, 129, 131, 281, 298, 299
Lanfranchi, Mario 19, 167, 409
Lang, Fritz 164
Lange Ritt zur Schule, Der 468
Lantieri, Franco **62**
Last Day, The see *Vendetta at Dawn*
Last Days of Pompeii, The 52, 237
Last Feelings 333
Last Gun, The 50, 134, 435
Last of the Badmen 254, 293, 445
Last of the Mohicans, The 437-438
Last of the Renegades 57, 435
Last Rebel, The 458
Last Ride to Santa Cruz, The **385**, 435
Last Round, The 338
Last Snows of Spring, The 333
Last Tomahawk, The 60, 438
Lastretti, Adolfo 150, 153, 340
Latin Lovers 288
Lattanzi, Franco 320, 321
Lattimore, Frank 45
Lattuada, Alberto 221
Lavagnino, Angelo Francesco 409
Law and Jake Wade, The 75
Law of Violence, The 452
Law, John Phillip 89, **90**, **108**, 169, 175
Lawrence of Arabia 48
Lawrence, Peter Lee 9, 29, 50, 76, 95, 129, 171, 173, 286, 287, 330, 409
Leblanc, Tony 298
Lee, Ang 321, 347
Lee, Bruce 314, 319, 320
Lee, Chen 318-320
Lefranc, Guy 298
Left Handed Gun, The 39
Legacy of the Incas 442
Legend of a Gunfighter 435
Legend of Frenchie King, The 138, 458
Leipnitz, Harald 58
Lenzi, Umberto 146, 283
Leone, Sergio 7, 8, 11, 12, 15, 16, 18, 21, 24, 29-35, 39-41, 43-45, 48-52, 55, 59, 60, 62, 65, 69-72, 80, 84, 85, 87, 88, 90, 92-95, 129, 131, 132, 134, 139, 140, 152, 158, 159, 164, 170, 171, 176, 178-180, 193, 199, 200, 206, 210, 215, 217, 219, 221, 228-230, 235-237, 239, 242, 245, 249, 255, 257, 269, 270, 288, 291, 297-301, 304, 309, 311, 312, 315, 321, 330, 337, 342, 348, 349, 351, 409
Leopard, The 129, 130
Leroy, Philippe 175, 344
Let's Go and Kill Sartana 458
Let's Talk About Men 267
Levine, Joseph E. 16
Lewis, Geoffrey 334
Lewis, Herschell Gordon 290
Li, Jet 314
Liberatore, Ugo 141, 409
Life Is Beautiful 274, 297
Liné, Helga **62**, 410
Little Big Man 191, 249, 330
Lizard in a Woman's Skin, A 339
Lizzani, Carlo 18, 32, 185, 204, 217, 221-223, 230, 410
Lo, Lieh 314, 316, 319, 320
Lobo the Bastard 458
Loffredo, Gianni 342
Lola Colt 137, 446
Lollobrigida, Gina 135
Lom, Herbert 59
Loma, José Antonio de la 61
Lonely Are the Brave 40

Long Day of the Massacre, The 141, 449
Long Days of Vengeance **67**, 166, 243, 446
Long Hair of Death, The 181, 293, 294
Long Live Your Death **107**, 150, 190, 217, 219-221, 308, 320, 459
Long Ride from Hell, A 23, 166, 449
Long Ride to Eden, A 459
Longest Day, The 297
Lopez, Sylvia **16**
Loren, Sophia 14, 15
Lorenzon, Livio 62, 410
Louis, Jean 286
Louisiana 468
Lovelock, Ray 289
Loy, Mino 410
Lozano, Margarita **51**, 139
Luchetti, Daniele 348
Lucidi, Maurizio 32, 272, 303, 309, 410
Lucky Johnny: Born in America 459
Lucky Luke (1991) 331, 469
Lucky Luke (2009) 470
Lukschy, Wolfgang 59
Lulli, Piero 29, **38**, 174, 259, 288, 410
Lung, Ti 321
Lupo, Alberto **279**, **303**
Lupo, Michele 133, 240, 300, 306, 309, 326, 328, 338, 345-347, 410
Lynching 449
Ma, Wu 321
Macario, Erminio 14, 158
Maché, Eric 205
Machiavelli, Brandino 137
Machiavelli, Nicoletta **82**, 83, 137, 138, **165**, 410
Maciste alpino 16
Maciste in Hell 283
Madigan, Diana **166**
Madison, Guy 24, 42, 59, 74, 155, 156, 235, 410-411
Maesso, José Gutiérrez 141
Magic Blade, The 321
Magnificent Bandits, The 149, 190, 195, 197, 206, 217, 223-224, **225**, 452
Magnificent Seven, The 40, 187, 218, 264
Magnificent Texan, The 446
Magnificent Three, The (1961) 298, 433
Magnificent Three, The (1963) 45-46, 93, 170, 172, 434
Magnificent West, The 461
Malden, Karl 163, 248
Malfatti, Marina 136
Malle, Louis 138
Mallorquí, José 41, 45, 46, 348, 411
Man Alone, A 89
Man and a Colt, A 189, 195, 446
Man Called Amen, A 449
Man Called Blade, A 149, 170, 175, 250, 296, 326, 328, 339, 341, 342, 344-345, 467
Man Called Django, A 153, 170, 180, 459
Man Called Gringo, The 438
Man Called Invincible, A 95, 152, 158, 312-313, 464
Man Called Joe Clifford, A 180, 454
Man Called Noon, The 137, 170, 171, **391**, 464
Man Called Sledge, A 22, 87, 153, 167, 454
Man from Laramie, The 39, 43, 164
Man from Oklahoma, The 438
Man Hunt 348, 468
Man in the Wilderness 459
Man of the Cursed Valley 436
Man of the East 311, 461
Man Who Came to Kill, The 156, **158**, **159**, 438
Man Who Killed Billy the Kid, The 446
Man Who Shot Liberty Valance, The 40
Man, Pride and Vengeance 446
Mancini, Claudio **124**, 411
Mancori, Alvaro 203
Mancori, Sandro 21, 259, 266, 411
Mancuso, Elsio 430
Manduke, Joseph 336
Manfredi, Nino 267
Mangano, Silvano 14
Mangione, Giuseppe 269
Mangold, James 347
Manitou's Shoe 59, 470
Mann, Anthony 29, 30, 70, 74, 94, 164
Mann, Leonard 8, 14, 24, 29, **145**, 146, 174, 175, 179, 180, 236, 305, 330, 333, 411
Manni, Ettore 72, 153, 243, 411
Marano, Ezio 310
Marcellini, Siro 137

Index

Marchand, Corinne 136
Margheriti, Antonio 15, 43, 167, 181, 250, 293-295, 319, 320, 329, 344, 411
Marín, Francisco 411
Marín, Gloria 41
Marinero, Manolo 227
Mariuzzo, Giorgio 330
Mark, Robert 8, 24, 411
Marker, Chris 186
Marlowe 314
Marquand, Serge 60
Marquez, Evaristo **198**
Marshall, Mike 133
Marsina, Antonio 342
Martell, Peter 142, 146, 173-175, 303, 305, 411
Martín Fierro 192
Martín, Daniel 60, 412
Martin, Diana **53**, 54
Martín, Eugenio 75, 412
Martin, George 42, 73, **85**, **119**, 133, **237**, 239, 242, 412
Martin, Gérard 193
Martín, José Manuel 29, 178, 348, 412
Martín, María 73, 140
Martin, Strother 71
Martinelli, Elsa 138
Martínez Román, María del Carmen 173
Martino, Luciano 250, 344, 412
Martino, Sergio 296, 328, 344, 345, 412
Masciocchi, Marcello 412
Mask of Satan, The 282
Mason, James 135
Massaccesi, Aristide 337, 412-413
Massacre at Fort Grant 41, 436
Massacre at Grand Canyon 53, 165, 436
Massacre at Marble City 60, 141, **382**, 436
Massacre Time **7**, 87, **101**, 143-145, 174, 339, **367**, 442
Massi, Stelvio 21, 151, 286, 338, 413
Mastroianni, Marcello 14
Matalo! 22, 193, 281, 454
Matarazzo, Raffaello 14, 129
Mateos, Julián 140, **152**
Matrix, The 351
Mattei, Bruno 296, 330
Mattoli, Mario 298
Mauri, Roberto 50, 413
May God Forgive You - I Won't 73, 175, 449
May, Karl 39, 55-57, 59, 188
McCabe & Mrs. Miller 342
McCambridge, Mercedes 82
McCarthy, Kevin 88, 93
McCulley, Johnston 41
McGee, Vonetta 78, 136
McQueen, Steve 70, 163
Medium Cool 191
Mendoza, Alberto de 134, 174, **175**
Meniconi, Furio 413
Mercier, Michèle 136, 176
Merino, José Luis 75, 182, 283, 413
Merli, Maurizio 175, 333, 344, 345
Messalina 62
Mestizo 41, **278**, 442
Mexico in Flames 468
Michelangeli, Marcella 294
Mifune, Toshiro 200, 317, 318, **367**
Migliardi, Mario 287, 413
Miguel, Monica 136
Miike, Takashi 244, 314, 321, 351
Milian, Tomas **17**, 29, **71**, 74, 75, 89, 93-95, **106**, **107**, **117**, **122**, 134, 153, 167, 185, 195, 197, 199, 200, 203-205, 207-210, **211**, 213, 215, **216**, 221, 223, 224, **225**, 230, 249, 261, 288-291, **296**, 306, 308, 309, **310**, 328, 329, 340, 413
Milland, Gloria 46, **47**, 48, 49, 136, 413
Milland, Ray 89
Minnesota Clay 52-54, 141, 166, 206, 210, **414**, 436
Minute to Pray, a Second to Die, A 76, 77, 152, 189, **374**, 449
Mitchell, Cameron 50, 53, 54, 134, 414
Mitchell, Gordon 16, 24, **146**, 147, 302, 321, **371**, 414
Mitchum, Jim 53, 140
Mitchum, Robert 14, 53, 146
Mitic, Gojko 59, 348, 414
Modugno, Domenico 299
Möhner, Carl 156
Molino Rojo, Antonio 29, 59, 76, 414
Moment to Kill, The 21, 86, 87, **104**, 276, 286, 449
Moncada, Santiago 297

Mondo cane 15, 268
Monicelli, Mario 14, 15, 30, 216, 297
Monselesan, Antonio 309
Montaldo, Giuliano 288, 335
Montanari, Sergio 249
Monti, Maria 197, 209
Monzón, Carlos 338
Morandi, Fernando 199
Mordini, Stefano 131
More Dollars for the McGregors 22, 75-76, **109**, 454
Moreau, Jeanne 138
Moretti, Nanni 297, 348
Morricone, Ennio 12, 21, 32, 40, 44, 51, 70, 93, 129, 203, 218, 238, 242, 299, 300, 312, 414-415
Morris 235, 305
Morsella, Fulvio 415
Moschin, Gastone 77, 151
Muccino, Gabriele 131
Mulargia, Edoardo 61, 157, 217, 415
Mulock, Al **81**, 415
Murieta 438
Musante, Tony 93, **107**, **117**, 197, 210, **211**
Musolino, Vincenzo 415
Mutiny at Fort Sharp 41, 442
My Darling Clementine 29
My Horse... My Gun... Your Widow 461
My Name Is Mallory 459
My Name Is Nobody 22, 24, 31, 69, 89-91, 93, **94**, 95, **104**, **125**, 309, 311-312, 326, **328**, **361**, 464
My Name Is Pecos 168, 189, 272, 442
My West 348, 470
Nader, George 262
Nakadai, Tatsuya 317
Naked Spur, The 70, 73, 74
Name That Cried Revenge, A 170, 180, **357**, 449
Naples Connection, The 340
Naschy, Paul 283
Navajo Joe 82-83, **102**, 148, 149, 152, 165, 206, 210, 243, 328, **371**, 442
Navarro, Nieves 134-136, 203, 239, 242, **374**, 415
Near Dark 283
Ned Kelly 338
Negulesco, Jean 261
Nelson, Gary 70
Nelson, Ralph 331
Nelson, Turia **46**
Nephews of Zorro, The 449
Neri, Rosalba 134, 157, 415
Nero, Franco **1**, **6**, 7, 8, 11, 18, 22, 26, 27, 62, 93, **98**, **107**, **110**, **117**, **121**, **126**, 141, **143**, 144, **150**, 155, **160**, 170, 180, 188, **190**, 191, 195, 196, 206, 209, 210, **211**, **212**, 214, **216**, **219**, 220, 221, 236, 244, **245**, 246, **248**, 249-251, 253, 254, 258, 302, 304, 308, 309, 316, **324**, 325, 331-334, 339, 341-343, 345, **357**, 362, 415
Nevada Smith 163
Nicol, Alex 43, 156
Nicolai, Bruno 32, 203, 259, 319, 416
Night of the Doomed, The 181
Night of the Serpents 145, 155-157, 452
No Graves on Boot Hill 85, 156, 293, 449
No Room to Die 75, **76**, 151, 452
Nobody's Children 14
North Star 469
nostra vita, La 348
Now They Call Him Sacramento 461
Nudi per vivere 288
Nusciak, Loredana **34**, 245, 250, 416
O Cangaceiro 198, 223
Oates, Warren 337
O'Brian, Hugh 235
O'Brien, Donal 195, 201, 203, 306, **327**, 340, 342, 344, 416
O'Brien, Peter 89, **91**
Okamoto, Kihachi 314
Okay, Sheriff 436
Old Testament, The 27
On Her Majesty's Secret Service 147
On the Third Day Arrived the Crow 464
Once Upon a Time in America 229, 291
Once Upon a Time in China and America 314
Once Upon a Time in Mexico 351
Once Upon a Time in the Midlands 349
Once Upon a Time in the West 18, 20, 21, 23, 24, 34, 88, 91, 92, 94, **124**, 131, 139-140, 169, 171, 175, 178-179, 182, **183**, 220, 229, 230, 257, 311, 321, **356**, 449
Once Upon a Time in the Wild, Wild West 464

One After the Other 449
One Against One... No Mercy 449
One Damned Day at Dawn... Django Meets Sartana! 74, 249, 276, 454
One Dollar Too Many 150, 302, 449-450
One for All 450
100 Rifles 349, 452
$100,000 for Lassiter 48-49, 442
$100,000 for Ringo 236, 438
One Man's Hero 470
One Silver Dollar **62**, 63, 171, 240, 346, 438
One-Armed Swordsman, The 315
One-Eyed Jacks 166, 248
Ong-Bak 320
Onorato, Glauco 147
Open City 14, 149
Open Range 347
Orbison, Roy 265
Orlandi, Nora 75, 250, 416
Orso, Anna **81**
Ortas, Julio 44
Ortolani, Riz 46, 224, 416
Osceola 459
Outcry 223
Outlaw Josey Wales, The 163, 346
Outlaw Justice 470
Outlaw of Red River 438
Ozores, Mariano 348
Pacheco, Rafael 48, 416
Pacifico, Benito 276
Pagliai, Ugo 195, 223, 224
Pai Piao, Jason 320
Paid in Blood 459
Paiget, Paul 46, 48
Pajarito **237**, 242, 416
Palacios, Ricardo 336, 416-417
Palaggi, Roberto 304
Palance, Jack 24, 93, 153, 210, **213**, 214, 222, 308, 327, 417
Palenzuela, Miguel 47, 170
Pallottini, Riccardo 275, 293, 417
Palmara, Mimmo 168, 262, 300, 417
Palmer, Gregg 306
Palombi, Franco 272
Paluzzi, Luciana 134, 174, 179
Pancho Villa 461-462
Pandolfi, Elio 299
Panhandle Calibre 38 462
Papi, Giorgio 43
Parasite 337
Parolin, Aiace 342
Parolini, Gianfranco 8, 11, 16, 21, 27, 35, 93, 133, 255, 258-262, 264-266, 276, 326, 334, 417
Pasolini, Pier Paolo 11, 14, 32, 45, 155, 185, 186, 215, 222, 223, 249, 288
Passenger, The 291
Pat Garrett and Billy the Kid 76, 338, 342
Patience Has a Limit, We Don't 465
Patten, Lewis B. 220
Patton 349
Pavone, Rita 137, 302
Pazzafini, Nello 155, 203, 240, 286, 417
Peck, Gregory 50, 163, 236
Peckinpah, Sam 71, 192, 193, 337, 342, 344
Pecos Cleans Up **188**, 272, 446
Per un dollaro a Tucson si muore 438
Perdita Durango 349
Performance 204
Peri, Enzo 317
Pernice, Gino 140, 153, **246**, 248, 418
Pesce, Franco 255, 259, 418
Pete, Pearl and the Pole 268
Peters, Brock 93
Petri, Elio 11, 186, 204, 288
Petroni, Giulio 8, 11, 19, 32, 88, 129, 156, 157, 170, 207, 209, 303, 351, 418
Petzold, Konrad 59
Phantom Empire, The 282
Philbrook, James 43, 173
Philipp, Harald 56, 57
Piaget, Paul 418
Pica, Antonio **175**
Pica, Tina 298
Picazo, Miguel 224
Piccioni, Piero 53, 259, 418
Pieraccioni, Leonardo 348
Pierotti, Piero 82

Pigozzi, Luciano 153, **282**, 418
Pink, Sidney 137
Pinzauti, Mario 286
Pirates of the Mississippi 60, 261, 434
Pirro, Ugo 82
Pistilli, Luigi 29, 76, 176, 418-419
Pistol for Ringo, A 62, 148, **234**, 236-240, 242, 243, 298, 300, **403**, 438
Pistol Packin' Preacher 150, 158, 182, 462
Place Called Glory, A 59, 438
Planet of the Vampires 15
Plomo sobre Dallas 454
Poker with Pistols 446
Polgar, Tommy 320
Pollard, Michael J. **101**, 339
Pontecorvo, Gillo 186, 194, 198, 199, 223, 230
Ponti, Carlo 319, 320
Porno-Erotic Western 467
Potato Fritz 467
Powell, Don 419
Power, Tyrone 32
Powers, Hunt 23, 27, 74, 151, 236, 249, 276, 302, 303, 419
Prado, Mario **226**
Praise Marx and Pass the Ammunition 186
Präriejäger in Mexico: Geierschnabel/Benito Juarez 469
Pregadio, Roberto 419
Preston, Wayde **180**, 419
Prévost, Françoise 172
Prey of Vultures 171, 287, 462
Price of Death, The 82, 149, 287, 459
Price of Power, The **19**, 31, 94, **125**, 165, 176, 178, 189, 243, 261, **420**, **426**, 452
Professional Gun, A 18, 21, 62, 80, 88, 92-93, **107**, **117**, 150, 190, 197, 199, 206, 209, 210, **211**, 213-216, 222, 328, **368**, 450
Professionals, The 218
Prosperi, Franco 15, 340
Proud Ones, The 54
Psychic, The 339
Psycho 33
Puccini, Gianni 173, 283
Puente, Jesús 48, 419
Puppo, Romano 419
Purdom, Edmund 43
Pursued 146
Pyramid of the Sun God 438
Queimada! see Burn!
Quesada, Milo 288
Questi, Giulio 23, 81, 129, 250, 251, 288-291, 419
Quick and the Dead, The 60
Quiney, Carlos 75
Quintana: Dead or Alive 452
Quintano, Gene 336
Quinto: Fighting Proud 86, 452
Quo Vadis 12
Rabal, Francisco 150, 186
Raging Heart 470
Raimi, Sam 60
Rain for a Dusty Summer 459
Ralli, Giovanna 213
Ramon the Mexican 442
Rampage at Apache Wells 57, 58, 243, 438
Rancho Notorious 164
Rassimov, Ivan **132**, 330, 419-420
Rassimov, Rada 251, 292, 293
Rattler Kid 75, 446
Rauch, Siegfried 59
Raynaud, Fernand 298
Reason to Live, a Reason to Die, A 85, 150, 462
Rebel with a Cause 251
Rebels on the Loose 298-299, 442
Red Blood, Yellow Gold 85, 152, 303, **412**, 446
Red Coat 337, 340, 466
Red Hot Zorro 462
Red Sun 23, **270**, **316**, **318**, **319**, 320, 328, **367**, **397**, 459
Redgrave, Lynn 219
Reed, Dean 265, 320, 420
Reeves, Steve 15, **16**, 23, 52
Reggiani, Franco 253
Reinhardt, Django 248
Reinl, Harald 55, 56, 58, 60, 420
Relentless Four, The 438
Relevo para un pistolero 436
Remember Me, My Love 131
Renegade 348, 468
Renegade Gunfighter 442

Renoir, Jean 235
Requiem for a Gringo 173, 182, 283, 284, 450
Requiem for a Secret Agent 199
Requiescant see Kill and Pray
Reservoir Dogs 248
Ressel, Franco 94, **263**, 264, **310**, 311, 420
Return from the River Kwai 317
Return of Clay Stone, The 436
Return of Clint the Stranger, The 462
Return of El Coyote, The 348, 470
Return of Hallelujah, The 148, 312, **368**, **377**, **393**, 462
Return of Ringo, The **66**, **119**, **126**, 165, 168, 181, 235-238, **239**, 240, 242, 243, 245, 438
Return of Sabata **119**, 262-266, **364**, **391**, 459
Return of Shanghai Joe 320, 465
Return of the Holy Ghost 462
Return of the Seven 442
Revenge of Ringo, The 286, 454
Revenge of the Black Wolf 348, 467
Reverend Colt 74, 155, 454-455
Revolver 206
Rey, Fernando 139, 210, 227, 420
Reynolds, Burt 82, **83**, **103**, 168
Reynolds, Sheldon 59
Ricci, Tonino 86, 320, 345
Richards, Marc 218
Richardson, John 146, 147, 420
Rick and John, Conquerors of the West 446
Ride and Kill **43**, 156, 436
Ride in the Whirlwind 337
Ride Lonesome 163
Ride the High Country 40, 192
Riders of the Whistling Skull, The 283
Rififi 176
Rigaud, George 420, **421**
Righelli, Gennaro 344
Rigoletto 15
Rilla, Walter 89
Ringo and His Golden Pistol 72, 93, 243, **397**, 442
Ringo the Lone Rider 450
Ringo the Mark of Vengeance 442
Ringo's Big Night 442
Rio Bravo 39, 242, 243
Risi, Dino 14, 30, 87, 297
Rita of the West 137, 302, 446
Riviere, Georges 54
Rizzo, Gianni 208, **263**, 420, **421**
Road to Fort Alamo, The 15, **38**, **97**, 436
Robards, Jason 24, 152, 421
Robertson, Melody **332**
Robledo, Lorenzo 46, **205**, **296**, 340, 421
Rocco and His Brothers 11, 129, 297
Rocco, Gian Andrea 137, 138
Rocha, Glauber 192-195, 206, 223, 224
Rojo, Ruben 182
Roland, Gilbert 24, 85, 87, **122**, **125**, **133**, 156, 421
Roli, Mino 341
Rome Against Rome 283
Rome, Sydne 303
Romero Marchent, Carlos 47, 421
Romero Marchent, Joaquín 29, 32, 40-42, 44-51, 132, 136, 170, 173, 296, 297, 421
Romero Marchent, Rafael 44, 47, 49, 50, 171, 223, 284, 287, 297, 348, 421
Romulus and Remus 52, 237
Rope for a Bastard, A 450
Rosi, Francesco 11, 186, 189, 199, 230
Rosin, Sheyla 82
Rossati, Nello 253
Rossellini, Roberto 149, 155, 221, 261
Rossetti, Franco 146, 251, 253, 422
Rossi, Luciano 29, 203, **291**, 292, **400**, 422
Rossi-Stuart, Giacomo 422
Rosso, Salvatore 180
Roy Colt and Winchester Jack 15, 455
Rubio, Miguel 227
Run of the Arrow 188
Run, Man, Run 93-95, 135, 190, 195, 199-201, 203, 206, 210, 226, 450
Run, Men! Eldorado Is Coming to Trinity **26**, 462
Rupp, Sieghardt 422
Rustichelli, Carlo 93, 422
Rustlers' Rhapsody 468
Ruthless Colt of the Gringo 442
Ruthless Four, The **28**, **86**, 87, **109**, **122**, **421**, 450
Ruzzolini, Giuseppe 422
Ryan, Robert 71

Sabata **19**, 35, 93-94, 135, 153, 261, 263-266, **358**, **359**, **363**, **420**, **430**, 452
Sabato, Antonio 171, 422
Saguaro 450
Salazar, Abel 41
Salerno, Enrico Maria 166, 167, 422
Salerno, Vittorio 142, 255, 260, 423
Salvati, Sergio 339, 340
Salvatore Giuliano 186, 199
Sambrell, Aldo 8, 29, 46, 47, 59, 76, 83, 140, 141, 152, 182, 226, 344, **371**, 423
Samson 27, 261
Samson and the Slave Queen 283, 434
Samson and the Treasure of the Incas 436
Samurai Assassin 314
Samurai Wolf 321
San Martin, Conrado 423
Sanchez, Pedro 73, 172, **261**, **262**, 264, **265**, 266, 423
Sancho, Fernando 29, 46, **47**, 54, 61, 62, 142, 153, 168, 182, 203, 208, **238**, 239, 240, **257**, 259, **279**, **303**, 348, 423
Sander, Erol 59
Sandri, Gia 271
Santee 70
Santi, Giancarlo 88, 335
Santini, Gino 292, 424
Sanz, Paco **49**, 288, 424
Sartana Does Not Forgive 153, 450
Sartana in the Valley of Death 455
Sartana's Here... Trade Your Pistol for a Coffin 258, 259, 264, 455
Saunders, Ray **178**
Saura, Carlos 224
Savage Gringo 15, **38**, **97**, 442-443
Savage Guns, The 48, 434
Savage Pampas 443
Savina, Carlo 337, 424
Savona, Leopoldo 180, 182, 217, 218, 424
Saxon, John 332
Saxon, Glenn 73, **279**, **303**, 424
Say Your Prayers and Dig Your Grave 189, 217, 450
Scalps 296, 331, 468
Scarpelli, Furio 14
Scavolini, Sauro 424
sceriffa, La 298, 433
Schell, Maria 172
Schiaffino, Rosanna 137
Schneider, Tassilo 55
Schöne, Reiner **265**, 266
Scorsese, Martin 45
Scott, Gordon 42, 52, 62, 140
Scott, Randolph 43, 70, 163
Scotti, Andrea 424
Scout, The 468
Searchers, The 39, 164, 169
Secchi, Antonio 425
Secret of Captain O'Hara, The 41, 438
Seduced and Abandoned 14
Segura, Knifewing 331
Serenade of Texas 433
Sergeant Rutledge 342
Seven Commandments of Kung Fu, The 321
Seven Devils on Horseback 466
Seven Dollars to Kill 94, 141, 142, 168, 172, 174, 180, **366**, **431**, 443
Seven from Texas 48, 136, 296, 436
Seven Guns for the MacGregors 31, 76, 132, 301, **432**, 443
Seven Guns for Timothy 443
Seven Hours of Gunfire 42, 48, **49**, 438
Seven Nuns in Kansas City 464
Seven Pistols for a Gringo 443
Seven Pistols for a Massacre 447
Seven Samurai 200, 314
Seven Winchesters for a Massacre 246, 447
Seventh Seal, The 342
Seventh Sword, The 180
79 A.D. 27
Severino 467
Sex Can Be Difficult 199
Sexy proibito 15
Seydor, Paul 71
Shadow of Sartana... Shadow of Your Death! 452-453
Shadow of Zorro, The 45, 46, 434
Shalako 138, 450
Shane 39, 87, 132, 133, 243
Shanghai Noon 314

Index

Shango 246, 455
Sharif, Omar 191
Shaw, Robert 153
Shaw, Run Run 319, 320
Sheepman, The 29
Shepard, Patty 137
Sheriff and the Satellite Kid, The 338
Sheriff of Fractured Jaw, The 433
Sheriff of Rocksprings, The 459
Sheriff Was a Lady, The 436
Sheriff Won't Shoot, The 438
Shigeta, James 317
Shishido, Joe 314
Shoot 'Em Up 351
Shoot First, Laugh Last 111, 268, **269**, 271, **376**, 447
Shoot Joe, and Shoot Again 462
Shoot the Living and Pray for the Dead 459
Shoot to Kill 438, **439**
Shoot, Gringo, Shoot 450
Shooting, The 337
Shortest Day, The 297
Shotgun 450
Siciliano, Mario 142, 306, 425
Siete cabalgan hacia la muerte 467
Sign of the Coyote, The 434
Sign of Zorro, The 434
Silent Stranger, The 269-271, 316, 318, 450
Silent Tongue 469
Silva, Henry 221
Silver Saddle 133, 334, 341, 467
Silver, Alain 315
Silvestri, Gabriele 272
Simi, Carlo 19, 22, 40, 44, 53, 245, 249, 328, 342, 347, 425
Simonelli, Giorgio 276, 298, 300
Simonelli, Giovanni 425
Sing, Cowboy, Sing 468
Singer Not the Song, The 433
Sinjen, Sabine 60
Six Bounty Killers for a Massacre 464
Sky Full of Stars for a Roof, A 303, 306, 335, **375**, 450
Smalltown, Italy 131
Smith, Paul 306
So This Is God's Country? 268
Sodom and Gomorrah 12, 180
Solanas, Fernando 191, 193
Soldier Blue 82, 191, 330, 331
Soler, Fernando 45
Solinas, Franco 18, 30, 32, 185, 187, 194-196, 198, 199, 201, 206-209, 425
Sollima, Sergio 8, 11, 16, 30-32, 45, 70, 77, 94, 95, 185, 187, 198-201, 203-206, 209, 210, 217, 228, 230, 351, 425
Solo, Bobby 236
Sometimes Life Is Hard, Right Providence? 306, **310**, 462
Sommer, Elke 58, 226
Sommerfeld, Helga **49**
Son of a Gunfighter 438
Son of Django 156, 170, 175, 250, 447
Son of Jesse James 42, 170, 439
Son of Spartacus, The 52
Son of Zorro, The 464
Sons of Great Bear, The 439
Sons of Ringo, The 300, 301, 443
Sons of Thunder 62-63, 237, 238
Sons of Trinity 469
Sons of White Fang 333, 465
Sordi, Alberto 14, 87, 216, 301
Sorlin, Pierre 148, 149, 157, 158, 299
Southwood, Charles **152**, 260, 264, 425
Spartacus 342
Specialists, The 77, 82, 135, 210, 246, 453
Spencer, Bud 27, 31, 87, **89**, 93, **112**, **153**, **165**, **180**, 218, 261, 303-306, 309, **310**, 313, 334, 338, **360**, **377**, **378**, 425-426
Spielberg, Steven 335
Spikes Gang, The 465
Spirit of the Beehive, The 296
Spirits of the Dead 32
Squitieri, Pasquale 82, 276, 330
Srdoc, Milan 58
Srivilai, Krung 320, 321
Stagecoach 163, 236
Stagecoach of the Condemned 455
Stander, Lionel 24, 88, 220, 268, 426
Starblack 174, 272, **273**, 443
Starr, Ringo **134**, 275, 338
State of Siege 199
Steel, Alan 283

Steel, Anthony 57
Steele, Barbara 137, 293
Steele, Bob 71
Stefanelli, Benito 8, **62**, 94, 168, 426
Steffen, Anthony 9, 16, 21, 27, 50, 60-62, 73, 75, **76**, **114**, 142, 156, 168, 174, 180-182, 195, 215, 217, 236, 251, 255, 257, 291, 344, **357**, **360**, 426
Stegani, Giorgio 63, 240, 426
Steiger, Rod **4**, 24, 88, **114**, **131**, 152, 197, 209, **220**, 221, 228, **229**, **373**, 427
Steiner, John 175, 208, 344
Steno 298
Stewart, Evelyn 135, **303**, 427
Stewart, James 29, 70, 73, 164
Storaro, Vittorio 327
Story of a Cloistered Nun 152
Straight to Hell 349, 468-469
Stranger and the Gunfighter, The 149, **280**, 318-321, **323**, 465
Stranger in Paso Bravo, A 156, 168, 180, 450
Stranger in Sacramento, A 62, 439
Stranger in Town, A see *For a Dollar in the Teeth*
Stranger Returns, The see *Shoot First, Laugh Last*
Stranger, Make the Sign of the Cross 450
Stratford, Dean 427
Strawberry Statement, The 191
Stray Dog 314
Strode, Woody 24, 88, **145**, 146, 305, 327, 338, 343, 427
Sugar Colt 76, 301, 302, 443
Sugranes, Mónica **237**
Sukiyaki Western Django 244, 314, 321, 347, 351
Sunday Lunch 131
Sundown: The Vampire in Retreat 283
Sunscorched 439
Swimmer, Saul 267, 274
Sword of Doom, The 314
Sword of Zorro, The 434
Sydow, Max von 342
Tails, You Lose... 82, 149, 453
Take a Hard Ride 320, 326, 329, 336, 466
Talent for Loving, A 453
Tall Women, The **136**, 137, 443
Tamba, Tetsuro 218, 317, **378**
Tara Poki 459
Tarantino, Quentin 7, 314, 351
Taste for Killing, A 73, 93, **348**, 349, 443
Taste of Death, A 158, 450
Taste of Violence, The 176, 433
Tate, Lincoln 428
Taylor, Don 218
Taylor, Elizabeth 13
Tears of the Black Tiger 347, 351
Tecumseh 462
Tedeum **105**, 150, 308, 311, 462
Tell Them Willie Boy Is Here 191, 330
Tempera, Vince 339
$10,000 Blood Money 74-75, **109**, 250, 255, 339, **393**, **402**, 447
Tepepa 157, 190, 199, 206-209, 228, 230, 261, 450
Tequila **27**, 464
Tequila Joe 145, 156, 450
Terrón, José 428
Terror in a Texas Town 95
Terror of Oklahoma, The 433
Tessari, Duccio 7, 11, 16, 30, 31, 50, 52, 61-63, 129, 136, 210, 217, 219-221, 235-240, 242, 243, 245, 297, 298, 301-303, 308, 320, 325, 334, 335, 428
Testi, Fabio **101**, 276, 337, 339-341, 428
Tex and the Lord of the Deep 296, 334-335, 468
Texas - Doc Snyder hält die Welt in Atem 469
Texas Adios **126**, 144, 168, 170, 174, **398**, 443
Texican, The 443
Theorem 148
They Call Him Cemetery 276-277, 459
They Call Him Veritas 462
They Call Me Trinity **20**, 23, 77, **104**, 148, 227, 303-306, 309, **360**, **394**, 455
They Called Him Amen 462
They Called Him Trinity [Himself, His Colt, His Revenge] 464
They Still Call Me Amen 464
Thirteenth Is a Judas 459
32 Cailber Killer 287, 447
This Man Can't Die 111, 450-451
Thompson 1880 443
Those Dirty Dogs 259, 464
Three Bullets for Ringo 443

Three Crazy Jerks 59
Three Dollars of Lead 436
Three Fantastic Supermen, The 262
Three from Colorado 439
Three Musketeers of the West, The 309, 320, 464
Three Silver Dollars 86, 152, **425**, 451
Three Supermen of the West 464-465
3.10 to Yuma (1957) 87, 243
3:10 to Yuma (2007) 347
Three the Hard Way 329
Thunder at the Border 56, 59, 443
Thunder Over El Paso 462
Tierra Brava 453
Tiger from the River Kwai, The 320-321, 466
Tin Star, The 70, 71
To Live in Peace 87
To, Johnnie 351
Today It's Me... Tomorrow You! 85, 94, 163, **165**, 166, 168, 180, 317, **367**, 451
Todorov, Tzvetan 291
Tognazzi, Ugo 298
Tolo, Marilù 289
Tomb of the Pistolero 436
Tombstone 236
Too Much Gold for One Gringo 462
Torment 14
Torre Nilsson, Leopoldo 192
Torrejón City 298, 434
Torres, José 203, 207, 428
Torres, Ricardo 45
Toth, André de 70
Totò 14, 52
Totò of Arabia 297
Tough Ones, The **325**
Town Called Bastard, A 153, 459
Trail of the Falcon 451
Train for Durango, A 166, **426**, 451
Tramplers, The 62, 140, 141, 222, 439
Treasure of Pancho Villa 447
Treasure of Silver Lake, The 55-57, 434
Treasure of the Aztecs, The 439
Treasure of the Four Crowns 337
Treasure of the Sierra Madre, The 87
Trentini, Caterini 135
Trevor, Claire 163
Trini 467
Trinity and Sartana Are Coming 306, 462
Trinity Is Still My Name 153, 304, 306, **310**, 311, **360**, 459
Trinity Plus the Clown and a Guitar 466
Trintignant, Jean-Louis 70, 77, 78, **79**
Triumphs of a Man Called Horse 468
Troiso, Antonio 223
Troublemakers 334, 469
trovatore, Il 15
True Grit 347
Tschetan, Indian Boy 462
Tumba para un forajido 443
Turn... I'll Kill You! 75, 447
Twenty Steps to Death 455
Twenty Thousand Dollars for Every Corpse 455
$20,000 on Number Seven 141, 447
$20,000 Stained in Blood 142, 156, 284, 453
Twice a Judas 170, 174, 305, 453
Twilight Avengers, The 455
Twins from Texas 298, 436
Two Against All 298, 434
Two Crosses at Danger Pass 170, 175, 447
Two Faces of the Dollar 86, 447
Two Gangsters in the Wild West 62, 299, 300, 436
Two Marshals, The 215
Two Pennyworth of Hope 14
Two Pistols and a Coward 156, 451
Two R-R-Ringos from Texas 300, 447
Two Sergeants of General Custer 299, 439
Two Sons of Trinity, The 300, 301, 462
Two Violent Men 436
Ugly Ones, The see *Bounty Killer, The*
Ulloa, Alejandro 347, 428
Ulysses 12
Ulysses Against Hercules 48
Ulzana 465
Ulzana's Raid 191, 330
Umbrellas of Cherbourg, The 145
Umiliani, Piero 428-429
Undari, Claudio 8, 17, 27, 29, 35, **45**, 46-50, 170, 195, 296, 297, 319, 407
Unforgiven 347

Any Gun Can Play

Unger, Goffredo 168, 429
Up the MacGregors 302, 447
Vacation with a Gangster 87
Vadis, Dan **13**, 269, 429
Valdez Horses, The 23, 465
Valdez Is Coming 459
Valerii, Tonino 31, 73, 81, 85, 88, 90, 176, 311, 312, 429
Valley of the Dancing Widows 466
Valli, Romolo 228
Valsecchi, Sven 334
Valturri, Patrizia 288
Van Cleef, Lee 23, **24**, **25**, **68**, 69, 82, **84**, 88-90, **91**, **92**, 94, **112**, **113**, .**117**, **128**, **131**, 133-135, 153, **154**, 155, 156, 170, **189**, 195, 200, 201, **202**, **206**, 260-264, **265**, 266, 299, 302, 303, 309, 319-321, 326, 334-336, **358**, **359**, **364**, **365**, **377**, **420**, 429
Van Helsing 351
Van Husen, Dan 429
Van Nutter, Rik 48, **49**, 293
Vancini, Florestano 179
Vandor, Ivan 290
Van-Mohr, Ernest 320
Vannucchi, Luigi 168
Vanzi, Luigi 267, 268, 271, 316, 430
Vanzina, Carlo 131
Vari, Giuseppe 86, 430
Velázquez, Pilar 136, 174, 430
Venantini, Venantino 166
Vendetta at Dawn 175, 459
Vengeance 87, 94, 167, 172, 181, 250, 284, 293, 294, 344, 451
Vengeance for Vengeance 451
Vengeance Is Mine 152, 175-176, 453
Vengeance Trail 82, 170, 175, 179, 330, 331, 459
Vente a ligar al Oeste 462-463
Vera Cruz 29, 39, 40, 69, 187
Veras, Linda 135, 203, **358**, **363**, 430
Vergano, Aldo 223
Veronesi, Giovanni 348
Vianello, Raimondo 298, 299
Villa Rides 187, 248, 451
Villa, Franco 287, 430
Villaggio, Paolo 150, 158, **210**, 215, 309
Villa's Guerillas 447
Vincenzoni, Luciano 14, 32, 69, 84, 92, 93, 169, 229, 430
Violent City 206
Violent Naples 333
Violent Rome 345
Viridiana 139
Visconti, Luchino 11, 14, 15, 288, 297
Viva Carrancho 61-62, 439
Viva Django 94, **111**, 249, 251, **252**, 253, **378**, 447
Viva Maria! 138, 439
Viva Sabata! 86, 456
Vohrer, Alfred 56, 430

Volonté, Gian Maria 29, 44, **52**, 69, **92**, 143, **169**, 185, 186, 193-196, 200, 204, 205, 230, 268, 299, **355**, 430
Wagstaff, Christopher 61
Wakayama, Tomisaburo 321
Wallach, Eli 23, **84**, 88, **89**, 93, **102**, **107**, 129, **190**, 219-221, 304, 308, 328, **329**, 431
Walsh, Raoul 146
Walter e i suoi cugini 297, 298
Wang, George 317, 431
Wanted 155, 447
Wanted Johnny Texas 447
Wanted Sabata 456
Watch Out Gringo, Sabata Will Return 463
Wayne, John 7, 27, 32, 163, 164, 236
Wayne, John Ethan 348
Wayne, Mike 186
Weapons of Death 333
Welch, Raquel **127**, 138, 139, 349
Welcome Reverend 150
Welcome to the Jungle 351
Welles, Orson 24, 208
Wendlandt, Horst 55, 431
Wertmüller, Lina 138, 267
Westerman, Floyd Red Crow 331
Westward the Women 137, 275
Wexler, Haskell 191
What Am I Doing in the Middle of a Revolution? 150-151, 158, 190, 197, 210, **214**, 215-216, 309, 463
Where the Bullets Fly 463
Whip and the Body, The 344
Whisky and Ghosts 465
White Apache 296, 331, **391**, 468
White Comanche 451
White Fang **100**, 333, 345, 465
White Fang and the Gold Diggers 466
White Fang and the Hunter 466
White Fang to the Rescue 345, 466
White Wolves 453
White, the Yellow and the Black, The 215, 308, 320, 328, 329, 466
Whittington, Harry 65
Whity 459
Who Killed Johnny Ringo? 443
Who's Afraid of Zorro? 466
Why Go On Killing? 61, 180, 439-440
Wide Blue Road, The 198
Widmark, Richard 27, 255
Wild Bunch, The 33, 71, 76, 191, 196, 218
Wild in the Streets 191
Williamson, Fred 329, 338
Wilson, Jerry 141, 142, 174, 431
Winchester '73 29, 74, 164
Wind from the East 193-194, 456
Winnetou and Shatterhand in the Valley of Death 56, 451

Winnetou Returns 59, 347, 470
Winnetou the Warrior 58, 59, 434
With Fire and Sword **43**
Without Each Other 267
Wolff, Frank 24, 77, 85, 87, 150, **162**, **176**, 254, 268, 293, 431-432
Wolter, Ralf 58, 59
Woman for Ringo, A 443
Woo, John 314, 351
Wood, Ken 432
Woods, Robert 8, 14, 23, 26, 27, 61, 62, 157, 168, **188**, 189, 217, 236, 238, 272, **301**, 432
World By Night 268
Wrath of God, The 94, 142, 170, 172, 180, 284, **285**, **376**, **405**, 451
Wright, Will 81
Wyatt Earp 332, 347
Wyler, Richard **71**, 75
Wyler, William 12, 141, 237
Yankee 22, 281, 443
Yankee Dudler 465
Yellow Hair and the Fortress of Gold 468
Yeo, Ban Yee 320
Yojimbo **314**, **315**, 317
Yoshioka, Iwao 320
You Are a Traitor and I'll Kill You 463
You Only Live Twice 218, 317
Young, Terence 270, 316, 318
You're Jinxed, Friend, You've Met Sacramento 463
Yuen, Chor 321
Z 186
Zabriskie Point 76, 191, 291
Zachariah 338
Zampa, Luigi 87
Zamperla, Nazzareno **238**, 432
Zanna Bianca e il grande kid 467
Zanni, Federico 344
Zapponi, Bernardino 223
Zeffirelli, Franco 14
Zeglio, Primo 286
Zhang, Yimou 321, 351
Zingarelli, Italo 218, 219, 304, 305, 338, 432
Zorro 466
Zorro and the Three Musketeers 434
Zorro at the Court of Spain 434
Zorro in the Court of England 453
Zorro, Marquis of Navarra 453
Zorro, Rider of Vengeance 459-460
Zorro the Avenger 45, 434
Zorro the Conqueror 453
Zorro the Fox 451
Zorro the Lawman 463
Zorro, the Mask of Vengeance 460
Zorro the Rebel **277**, 443

www.fabpress.com

For news of our latest book releases and special events, or if you wish to order any of our stock and prefer to pay by credit card, you can do so by visiting our constantly updated website. At fabpress.com you can order books in confidence using our Secure Server Payment System. In addition to offering all current FAB Press titles at special discounted rates, you can browse our online store and choose from a hand-picked selection of the World's finest Cinema Books, T-shirts, Soundtrack CDs and DVDs.

Use any of these cards, or PayPal, to shop online at www.fabpress.com any time!

customer services tel/fax: 01483 527424 • email: info@fabpress.com • website: www.fabpress.com